DANTE

DANTE

JOHN TOOK

PRINCETON UNIVERSITY PRESS

Princeton and Oxford

PUBLISHED BY PRINCETON UNIVERSITY PRESS
41 William Street, Princeton, New Jersey 08540
6 Oxford Street, Woodstock, Oxfordshire OX20 1TR

press.princeton.edu

Library of Congress Control Number: 2019936642

ISBN: 978-0-691-1-5404-6

British Library Cataloging-in-Publication Data is available

Editorial: Ben Tate and Charlie Allen
Production Editorial: Ellen Foos
Text and Jacket Design: Chris Ferrante
Production: Merli Guerra
Publicity: Alyssa Sanford and Amy Stewart
Copy Editor: Cathryn Slovensky

Jacket and frontispiece illustration by Roland Sárkány

This book has been composed in Arno Pro

Printed on acid-free paper. ∞

PRINTED IN THE UNITED STATES OF AMERICA

1 3 5 7 9 10 8 6 4 2

TRISHA

'Wer ein holdes Weib errungen
Mische seinen Jubel ein!'

Friedrich Schiller, *An die Freude*

CONTENTS

Abbreviations   ix
Acknowledgements   xiii
Preface: In fondo, una serietà terribile   xix

PART I   Preliminary Considerations

Chapter 1   Historical Considerations   3
 • Florence between the Guelphs and Ghibellines (1215–79)   3
 • Florence between the Blacks and the Whites (1279–1302)   9
 • The Descent and Demise of Henry VII (1302–13)   21

Chapter 2   Biographical Considerations   27
 • Susceptibility and the Significant Encounter (1265–93)   27
 • Care, Conflict and Catastrophe (1293–1302)   46
 • Far-Wandering and the Agony of Exile (1302–21)   55

PART II   The Early Years: From Dante da Maiano to the *Vita nova*

Chapter 1   Preliminary Remarks: Love and Love-Intelligence   75

Chapter 2   Literary Hinterland: From Provençal to the *stilo de la loda*   82

Chapter 3   Literary Apprenticeship and a Coming of Age   114
 • Dante guittoniano   114
 • Dante cavalcantiano   121
 • Dante and the *Rose*: The *Fiore* and the *Detto d'amore*   133
 • Dante guinizzelliano   159

Chapter 4   The *Vita nova*   173
 • Preliminary Remarks: Antecedent Utterance and an
   Essay in Authoring   173
 • Love Seeking and Seeking Not Its Own   184
 • Conclusion: New Life and a *Commedia a minore*   201

PART III   The Middle Years: The Moral and Allegorical *Rime*, the *Convivio*, the *De vulgari eloquentia* and the Post-Exilic *Rime*

Chapter 1   Compassionate Lady of the Casement and a Woman of Stone: The Pre-Exilic *Rime*   209

Chapter 2   The *Convivio*   235
- Preliminary Remarks: Magnanimity, Possibility and Impossibility   235
- Course of the Argument   236
- Axes of Concern in the *Convivio*   264
- Language, Form and Function: An Essay in Beauty, Being and Becoming   277
- Conclusion: Being and Becoming as Yet in Waiting   285

Chapter 3   The *De vulgari eloquentia*: Language, Literature and the Ontologization of Art   287

Chapter 4   The Post-Exilic *Rime*   313

PART IV   The Final Years: The *Commedia*, the Political Letters and the *Monarchia*, the *Questio*, Cangrande and the *Eclogues*

Chapter 1   The *Commedia*   323
- Standing Alone in Respect of That Which Matters Alone: Dante, Cino and the Solitary Way   323
- The *Commedia à la lettre*   327
- An Anthropology and Ethic: Love and Love-Harvesting   377
- The Dialectics of Being: A Difficult Dimensionality   384
- A Phenomenology of Existence: The Mood as Mediator   414
- Dante and Significant Journeying   436
- Immanent Eschatology and the Triumph of the Image   459

Chapter 2   The *Monarchia* and the Political Letters   479

Chapter 3   The *Questio de situ aque et terre*, the Letter to Cangrande della Scala and the *Eclogues*   523

Afterword: A Coruscation of Delight   542
Select Bibliography   547
Index of Names   569

ABBREVIATIONS

AdI	*Annali d'Italianistica*
Aevum	*Aevum: Rassegna di scienze storiche, linguistiche e filologiche*
AIISS	*Annali dell'Istituto Italiano per gli studi storici*
AMAPSLA	*Atti e Memorie, Accademia patavina di Scienze, Lettere ed Arti*
ASI	*Archivio storico italiano*
AUSP	*Annali dell'Università per Stranieri di Perugia*
BIRCSLFL	*Bollettino di Italianistica: Rivista di critica, storia letteraria, filologia e linguistica*
BISIM	*Bullettino dell'Istituto Storico Italiano per il Medioevo*
BISIMAM	*Bullettino dell'Istituto Storico Italiano per il Medioevo e Archivio Muratoriano*
BSDI	*Bullettino della Società Dantesca Italiana*
CI	*Campi Immaginabili: Rivista semestrale di cultura*
CL	*Critica letteraria*
CN	*Cultura Neolatina*
Colombaria	*Atti e Memorie dell'Accademia Toscana di Scienze e Lettere, 'La Colombaria'*
Conv	*Convivium*
CP	*Cahiers Pédagogiques*
Cultura	*La Cultura: Rivista di Filosofia, Letteratura e Storia*
CS	*Cultura e scuola*
CT	*Critica del testo*
DDJ	*Deutsches Dante-Jahrbuch*
DRISDA	*Dante: Rivista internazionale di studi su Dante Alighieri*
DS	*Dante Studies*
DT	*Divus Thomas*
ED	*Enciclopedia dantesca*
EL	*Esperienze letterarie*
FC	*Filologia e Critica*
FI	*Foro interno: Anuario de teoría política*
FItal	*Forum Italicum: A Journal of Italian Studies*
FMLS	*Forum for Modern Language Studies*
FS	*Franciscan Studies*

FSt	Le Forme e la Storia
GD	Giornale dantesco
GIF	Giornale Italiano di Filologia
GSLI	Giornale storico della letteratura italiana
IQ	Italian Quarterly
ItSt	Italian Studies
JIRS	Journal of the Institute of Romance Studies
JHI	Journal of the History of Ideas
JMRS	Journal of Medieval and Renaissance Studies
L'Alighieri (RBD)	L'Alighieri: Rassegna bibliografica dantesca
L'Alighieri (RD)	L'Alighieri: Rassegna dantesca
LC	Letture classensi
LD	Lectura Dantis
LI	Lettere italiane
LIA	Letteratura italiana antica: Rivista annuale di testi e studi
LIt	La Lingua Italiana
LL	Linguistica e Letteratura
LM	Letterature moderne
LN	Lingua nostra
Logos	Logos: A Journal of Catholic Thought and Culture
LS	Lingua e stile
MC	Misure critiche
MD	Memorie domenicane
MDC	Motivi per la difesa della cultura
Med	Mediaevalia
MH	Medievalia et Humanistica
MLN	Modern Language Notes
MLR	Modern Language Review
MP	Modern Philology
MR	Medioevo Romanzo
MRom	Marche romane: Cahiers de l'Association des romanistes de l'Université de Liège
NRLI	Nuova Rivista di Letteratura Italiana
PL	Patrologia latina
PMLAA	Publications of the Modern Language Association of America
PRFC	La Panaria: Rivista Friulana di Cultura
PPM	Pensiero politico medievale
PT	La Parola del testo
QItal	Quaderni d'Italianistica
RCCM	Rivista di cultura classica e medioevale
REI	Revue des études italiennes

RELI	*Rassegna europea della letteratura italiana*
RFR	*Revista de Filologia Románica*
RIL	*Rendiconti dell'Istituto Lombardo, Accademia di Scienze e Lettere*
RLI	*Rivista di Letteratura Italiana*
RLIt	*Rassegna della letteratura italiana*
RMR	*Reti Medievali Rivista*
RMS	*Reading Medieval Studies*
RP	*Romance Philology*
RS	*Renaissance Studies*
RSANL	*Rendiconti delle Sedute dell'Accademia Nazionale dei Lincei*
RSD	*Rivista di Studi Danteschi*
RSI	*Rivista di studi italiani*
RSRN	*Rendiconti dell'Accademia di Archeologia, Lettere e Bella Arti della Società Reale di Napoli*
SC	*Strumenti critici*
SD	*Studi danteschi*
SFI	*Studi di filologia italiana*
SIR	*Stanford Italian Review*
SLI	*Studi Linguistici Italiani*
SLIt	*Studi di Lessicografia Italiana*
SM	*Studi medievali*
SMI	*Stilistica e Metrica Italiana*
SPCT	*Studi e problemi di critica testuale*
Spec	*Speculum*
SV	*Sotto il velame*
Tenzone	*Tenzone: Revista de la Asociación Complutense de Dantologia*
VR	*Vox Romanica*
YIS	*Yearbook of Italian Studies*

ACKNOWLEDGEMENTS

Indebted as I am to any number of people—friends, colleagues and students alike, who, as often as not by virtue of their simply being there, have encouraged me along the way—I must mention in particular Dr Francesca Knox of Heythrop College and Dr Alessandro Scafi of the Warburg Institute, each alike generous to a fault in reading over and commenting upon the text. I am grateful also to Ben Tate and Ellen Foos of Princeton University Press and to my copy editor Cathy Slovensky for their kindness and courtesy throughout. To the fore, however, among those to whom I owe most is my wife Trisha, to whom the book is affectionately dedicated.

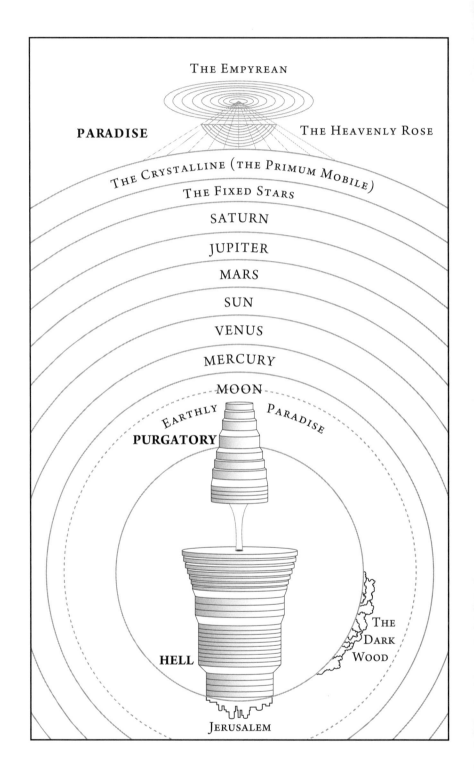

THE EMPYREAN

PARADISE

THE HEAVENLY ROSE

THE CRYSTALLINE (THE PRIMUM MOBILE)

THE FIXED STARS

SATURN

JUPITER

MARS

SUN

VENUS

MERCURY

MOON

EARTHLY PARADISE

PURGATORY

HELL

THE DARK WOOD

JERUSALEM

THE COSMOS

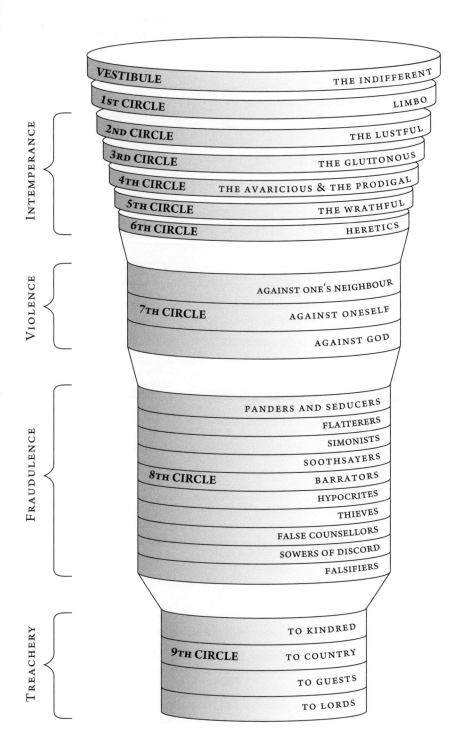

VESTIBULE — THE INDIFFERENT

1ST CIRCLE — LIMBO

2ND CIRCLE — THE LUSTFUL

3RD CIRCLE — THE GLUTTONOUS

4TH CIRCLE — THE AVARICIOUS & THE PRODIGAL

5TH CIRCLE — THE WRATHFUL

6TH CIRCLE — HERETICS

INTEMPERANCE

7TH CIRCLE
- AGAINST ONE'S NEIGHBOUR
- AGAINST ONESELF
- AGAINST GOD

VIOLENCE

8TH CIRCLE
- PANDERS AND SEDUCERS
- FLATTERERS
- SIMONISTS
- SOOTHSAYERS
- BARRATORS
- HYPOCRITES
- THIEVES
- FALSE COUNSELLORS
- SOWERS OF DISCORD
- FALSIFIERS

FRAUDULENCE

9TH CIRCLE
- TO KINDRED
- TO COUNTRY
- TO GUESTS
- TO LORDS

TREACHERY

HELL

THE EARTHLY PARADISE

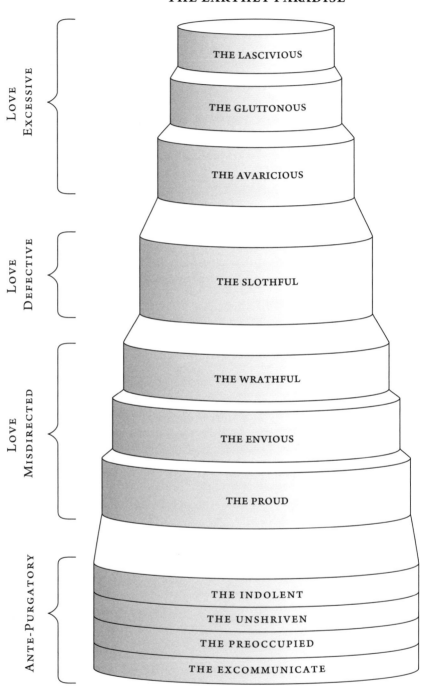

LOVE EXCESSIVE
- THE LASCIVIOUS
- THE GLUTTONOUS
- THE AVARICIOUS

LOVE DEFECTIVE
- THE SLOTHFUL

LOVE MISDIRECTED
- THE WRATHFUL
- THE ENVIOUS
- THE PROUD

ANTE-PURGATORY
- THE INDOLENT
- THE UNSHRIVEN
- THE PREOCCUPIED
- THE EXCOMMUNICATE

PURGATORY

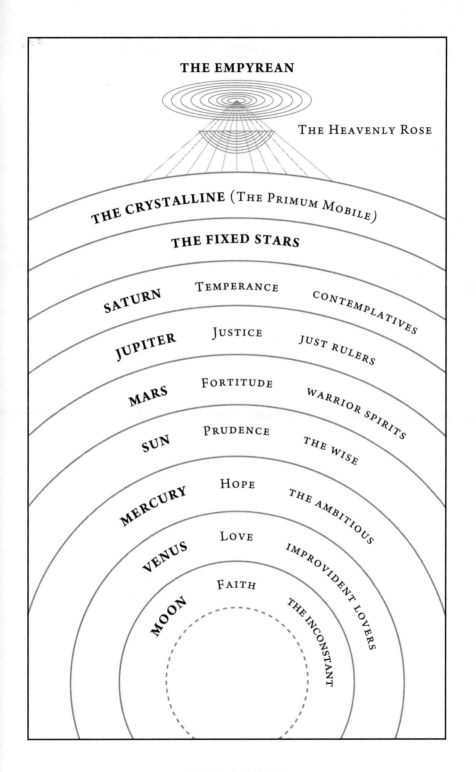

THE EMPYREAN

THE HEAVENLY ROSE

THE CRYSTALLINE (THE PRIMUM MOBILE)

THE FIXED STARS

SATURN — TEMPERANCE — CONTEMPLATIVES

JUPITER — JUSTICE — JUST RULERS

MARS — FORTITUDE — WARRIOR SPIRITS

SUN — PRUDENCE — THE WISE

MERCURY — HOPE — THE AMBITIOUS

VENUS — LOVE — IMPROVIDENT LOVERS

MOON — FAITH — THE INCONSTANT

PARADISE

PREFACE

In fondo, una serietà terribile

The greatest poetic expression of the Existentialist point
of view in the Middle Ages is Dante's *Divina Commedia*.
It remains, like the religious depth psychology of the
monastics, within the framework of the scholastic
ontology. But within these limits it enters the deepest
places of human self-destruction and despair as well as the
highest places of courage and salvation, and gives in poetic
symbols an all-embracing existential doctrine of man.

PAUL TILLICH[1]

When it came to great men and great books, T. S. Eliot was inclined in one and
the same moment to take away with one hand what he gave with the other; for
if indeed it is more satisfactory writing about greater as distinct from lesser men,
there being more scope for finding something useful to say about them, then
at the same time there is much to be said for leaving the great man in peace, he
himself being far and away his own best expositor. On the one hand, then, from
the twilight phase of his own meditation on the *Commedia*, Eliot writes:

> What I have written is, as I promised, not an 'introduction' to the study
> but a brief account of my own introduction to it. In extenuation, it may
> be observed that to write in this way of men like Dante or Shakespeare is
> really less presumptuous than to write of smaller men. The very vastness of
> the subject leaves a possibility that one may have something to say worth
> saying; whereas with smaller men, only minute and special study is likely
> to justify writing about them at all.[2]

---

1 Paul Tillich, *The Courage to Be* (Glasgow: Collins, 1980 [1952]), 128. For Gianfranco Contini on
the terrifying seriousness of it all, *Dante Alighieri: Rime* (Turin: Einaudi, 1965 [1946]), x: 'Mai in lui un
sospetto di scetticismo. Ci sono scherzi anche nella sua opera, ma remotissimi dai centri dell'ispirazione.
In fondo, una serietà terribile' (Never, in Dante, the least suspicion of scepticism. Moments of levity in
his work, yes, but far from the centre of inspiration. When all is said and done, a terrifying seriousness).
2 T. S. Eliot, *Dante* (London: Faber and Faber, 1945 [1929]), 63–64. For the 'effect of many books'

while from just a little earlier in the same essay we have these lines on starting with Dante himself, together with the books he himself read, as the best way forward:

> The effect of many books about Dante is to give the impression that it is more necessary to read about him than to read what he has written. But the next step after reading Dante again and again should be to read some of the books that he read, rather than modern books about his work and life and times, however good.

But that, alas, is not all, for already established fast by the time of his book on Dante is a sense on Eliot's part of interpretation—the main business, he suggests, of literary criticism—as a matter at best of dubious verifiability and at worst of mere posturing, herein lying its twofold bane and blessing, its lingering on somewhere between truth and untruth:

> There is a large part of critical writing which consists in 'interpreting' an author ... [But] it is difficult to confirm the 'interpretation' by external evidence. To anyone who is skilled in fact on this level there will be evidence enough. But who is to prove his own skill? And for every success in this type of writing there are thousands of impostures. Instead of insight you get fiction. Your test is to apply it again and again to the original, with your view of the original to guide you. But there is no one to guarantee your competence, and once again we find ourselves in a dilemma.

Now none of this makes easy reading for those of us busying ourselves in this sector, for those of us busying ourselves in this sector are busy, precisely, about introduction and interpretation, about forestalling the pristine encounter in all the 'terrifying seriousness' thereof. What possible justification, therefore, can there be for imposing yet again upon the reader and for indulging the will to interpretation?

The answer, I think, lies in our insisting, with as much good faith as we can muster, upon the notion that where Dante is concerned, *something* must be said, Dante himself going out of his way to engage the reader as party to the fundamental project, as there for the purposes not merely of discerning his meaning in the text but, by way of his or her role as reader, of helping to generate that meaning in the first place. In the context, then, of what in the case of the *Commedia* amounts to one of the most writerly of writerly texts in European literature, there can be no passing by on the other side.[3] On the contrary, the reader—Dante's ubiquitous

---

passage, page 62 of the same volume, while for the 'large part of critical writing' passage, 'The Function of Criticism', in *Selected Prose of T. S. Eliot*, ed. Frank Kermode (San Diego: Harcourt, 1975), 74–75.

3 Roland Barthes, *S/Z*, trans. Richard Miller (Oxford: Blackwell, 1992 [1974]), 4–5: 'Why is the

"lettore"—is at every point invited to step up to the mark and to speak on his or her own account to the matter in hand.

But with this we are as yet far from home, for having insisted that where Dante is concerned something has to be said, we have now to decide what that something might be, beginning, perhaps, with what actually matters about him. So what does actually matter about Dante? The depth and intensity of his meditation in any number of areas from theology to philosophy and from linguistics to literary aesthetics? Most certainly. His power and persuasiveness as a mythmaker, as one proceeding by way of a fiction which is, in truth, no fiction at all to confirm an ideal trajectory of the spirit? This too. His faith in the image, as distinct from the idea, as that whereby the human situation stands most completely to be contemplated? Absolutely. His fashioning from the as yet youthful Italian tongue a means of exploring the human situation in the at once sordid and sublime totality thereof? This to be sure. The resourcefulness and refinement both of the prose and of the metrical period as the hallmark of his consummate craftsmanship? No doubt. But over and beyond these things and serving the purpose of something greater than any of them is their commitment to the being and becoming of the otherwise anxious subject, of this or that individual or group of individuals concerned in respect of their properly human presence in the world as creatures of reasonable self-determination. This situation is everywhere discernible in the text and everywhere decisive for our reading and reception of it. It is discernible in the *Vita nova*, where it is a question of right understanding in love as that whereby the poet stands securely in his own presence as a maker of verses in the Italian vernacular, and it is discernible in the *Convivio*, where it is a question of how, in and through a more refined species of philosophical awareness, the 'many men and women in this language of ours burdened by domestic and civic care' might know themselves in their properly human happiness. It is discernible in the first book of the *De vulgari eloquentia*, where it is a question of how a certain group of people at a certain stage of their sociopolitical and cultural development might know themselves and in turn be known in their now recognizably Italian way of

---

writerly our value? Because the goal of literary work (of literature as work) is to make the reader no longer a consumer, but a producer of the text. Our literature is characterized by the pitiless divorce which the literary institution maintains between the producer of the text and its user, between its owner and its customer, between its author and its reader. This reader is thereby plunged into a kind of idleness—he is intransitive; ... instead of functioning himself, instead of gaining access to the magic of the signifier, to the pleasure of writing, he is left with no more than the poor freedom either to accept or reject the text: reading is nothing more than a referendum ... The writerly text is a perpetual present, upon which no consequent language (which would inevitably make it past) can be superimposed; the writerly text is ourselves writing, before the infinite play of the world (the world as function) is traversed, intersected, stopped, plasticized by some singular system (Ideology, Genus, Criticism) which reduces the plurality of entrances, the opening of networks, the infinity of languages.' Umberto Eco, *The Role of the Reader: Explorations in the Semiotics of Texts* (Bloomington: Indiana University Press, 1979).

being, and it is discernible in the second book of the *De vulgari eloquentia*, where it is a question of *poetic* form as but the *intelligible* form of a now—as Dante himself puts it—star-seeking humanity on the part of the one to whom the word is present as a discipline of the spirit. And it is discernible in the *Commedia*, where in the name and for the sake of a now consummate instance of specifically human being, it is a question of encountering self in its power to self-annihilation (*Hell*), of fashioning self afresh in point of properly human knowing and loving (*Purgatory*), and of rejoicing at last in the now properly speaking transcendent substance of it all (*Paradise*). Throughout, then, the pattern is the same, for throughout it is a question not simply of this or that high-level instance of cultural awareness, be it moral, social, political or linguistic, but of these things as making possible the emergence or coming about either of the individual or of the group of individuals in keeping with all they have it in themselves to be and to become.

Here, then, in what amounts to an honouring of the text by way of a reply in kind, of coming alongside the poet in respect of the leading idea, lies such justification as well as such consistency as this fresh exercise in interpretation possesses. Part 1, then, offers by way of contextualization an account of Florentine history from the early part of the thirteenth century through to the demise of Henry VII in 1313 and of Dante's life before and after his exile in 1302, while part 2 ('The Early Years') traces his activity as a lyric poet through to the *Vita nova* with its now secure sense of love as a principle of self-transcendence, of knowing self in the ecstatic substance of self. Part 3 ('The Middle Years') focuses on those works leading up to and culminating in the *Convivio* as an essay in the ways and means of properly human happiness and on the *De vulgari eloquentia* as a reflection upon language in general and poetic form in particular as a principle of collective identity and—in the case of the latter—of a now soaring spirituality, while part 4 ('The Final Years') gives an account (*a*) of the *Commedia* as, whatever else it is, an essay in significant journeying, (*b*) of the *Monarchia* as a meditation upon the deep reasons of imperial government and (*c*) of the *Questio de situ aque et terre*, the letter to Cangrande della Scala and the *Eclogues* as each in its way testifying to the strength of Dante's still scholastic and romance-vernacular allegiances. Finally, the afterword seeks to confirm yet again the deep seriousness of it all, a seriousness, however, 'inmantled' at last by a smile as but its outward aspect.[4]

What, then, of Eliot's misgiving relative to those daring to take up the pen yet again where Dante is concerned? Given that the text is indeed it own best interpreter then deep down we cannot but concur, misgiving at every point rising

---

4 *Paradiso* 20.13–15: 'O dolce amor che di riso t'ammanti, / quanto parevi ardente in que' flailli, / ch'avieno spirto sol di pensier santi!' (O sweet love that mantles yourself in a smile, how radiant your showing forth in those flutes filled only with the breath of sacred thoughts). Indebted as I am to the translations noted in the 'Select Bibliography' below, I have from time to time modified them in the interest of further precision and readability.

up Leviathan-like from the depths to call into question the entire project. But that, thankfully, is probably not how Dante himself would have seen it, for his, everywhere, is an invitation to the feast and, with it, to talk it all over one with another; for rather like those coming down from Jerusalem to Emmaus in the evening hour, we too have witnessed a strange and marvellous thing, talking it all over one with another serving merely to confirm its continuing presence to us as a means of significant self-interpretation.

JOHN TOOK
University College London

DANTE

PART I

PRELIMINARY CONSIDERATIONS

CHAPTER 1

Historical Considerations

Exemplary in respect of just about everything coming next on the banks of the Arno over the next few decades was the case of Buondelmonte de' Buondelmonti on the threshold of the thirteenth century. Buondelmonte, a knight as comely as any in his day, had promised himself in marriage to a young woman of the Amadei. Sporting his skills as a horseman, he was one day hailed by a certain Aldruda of the Donati, who, losing no time in confronting him with the mistake he was about to make by marrying into the Amadei, took the opportunity of showing off one of her own daughters, a young woman sufficiently beautiful to turn Buondelmonte's head and to dispel any thoughts of his looking elsewhere. Without ado, then, he took her to wife, whereupon the Amadei at once swore vengeance, duly redeeming their promise on the morning of the Feast of the Resurrection in 1215, when, espying Buondelmonte richly caparisoned on a white stallion, they confronted him at the foot of the statue of Mars on the city side of the Ponte Vecchio, unhorsed him, and ran him through. Here, then, were Florence's woes in a nutshell: the rise of any number of dominant and mutually antagonistic power blocs, partisanship in plenty, dynastic struggle, endless alignment and realignment, and a steady hovering on the brink of social and civic chaos—everything, in fact, serving within the context of a genuine gift for political creativity to betray that gift at a stroke.[1]

Taking, then, as our point of departure the episode of Buondelmonte in all its at once exemplary and prophetic substance we may begin by distinguishing the two main moments of Florentine history over Dante's lifetime, the first of them, through to about 1290, marked by the to-and-fro ascendancy of Guelph

---

1 Giovanni Villani, *Cronica* (hereafter Villani) 5.38; Dino Compagni, *Cronica* (hereafter Compagni) 1.2. Editions: *Croniche storiche di Giovanni, Matteo e Filippo Villani a miglior lezione ridotte coll'aiuto dei testi a penna*, ed. Michele Sartorio (Milan: Borroni e Scotti, 1848) and *Dino Compagni: La cronica*, ed. Isidoro del Lungo (Florence: Le Monnier, 1939). Translations and digests: *Dino Compagni's Chronicle of Florence*, trans. Daniel Bornstein (Philadelphia: University of Pennsylvania Press, 1986), and in Temple Classics, *The Chronicle of Dino Compagni*, trans. E.C.M. Benecke and A. G. Ferrers Howell (London: Dent, 1906). For Villani (and with special reference to Florence together with an indication of parallel texts in Dante), *Selections from the First Nine Books of the 'Croniche Fiorentine' of Giovanni Villani*, trans. Rose E. Selfe and ed. Philip H. Wicksteed (Westminster: Constable, 1896).

and Ghibelline power and the second of them by a now triumphant Guelphism busy about its own undoing.[2] With the death, then, of Frederick II of Hohenstaufen in December 1250, the Guelphs who had taken refuge in the upper Val d'Arno were recalled to Florence with a view to inaugurating alongside their erstwhile Ghibelline opponents a new era of peace and reconciliation, in honour of which a fresh set of governmental and administrative arrangements were put in place together with, for good measure, two officials appointed from outside: a Captain of the People to protect the interests of the middle and merchant classes over against those of a potentially and for much of the time actually unruly nobility and a *podestà* or senior magistrate to preside over both civil and criminal cases. Further provisions on the home front included the setting up of a peace-keeping force operative both within and beyond the city, together with a regulation height for any towers erected by the magnates for the purposes of retreat in troubled times, such masonry as was retrieved from their modification to be used for more properly civic projects. On the military front, a war carriage drawn by two oxen complete with insignia was commissioned for the purposes of bolstering a sense of public pride, and arrangements were made for a bell to be rung (the Martinella) warning the populace of imminent hostilities. Meanwhile, on the fiscal front, a twenty-four-carat gold florin was minted in 1252 with a lily on one side and an image of John the Baptist on the other, a gesture designed to confirm once and for all Florence's might as a trading presence not only at home but in and beyond Christendom as a whole. Free passage of goods to the sea was agreed with—or, nearer the mark, imposed upon—Pisa, which, again as a sign of the times, settled accordingly for a system of Florentine weights and measures. And on the foreign and diplomatic front, alliances were formed with Siena, Pistoia and

2   On the origin of Guelphism and Ghibellinism (the former, nominally at any rate, looking to the Church and the latter to the emperor as the guarantor of its rights, privileges and immunities), Villani 5.38, ult.: 'I maladetti nomi di parte guelfa e ghibellina si dice che·ssi criarono prima in Alamagna, per cagione che due grandi baroni di là aveano guerra insieme, e aveano ciascuno uno forte castello l'uno incontro all'altro, che l'uno avea nome Guelfo e l'altro Ghibellino, e durò tanto la guerra, che tutti gli Alamanni se ne partiro, e l'uno tenea l'una parte, e l'altro l'altra; e eziandio infino in corte di Roma ne venne la questione, e tutta la corte ne prese parte, e l'una parte si chiamava quella di Guelfo, e l'altra quella di Ghibellino: e così rimasero in Italia i detti nomi' (The accursed names of the Guelf and Ghibelline parties are said to have arisen first in Germany by reason that two great barons of that country were at war together, and each had a strong castle, the one over against the other, and the one had the name of Guelf and the other of Ghibelline, and the war lasted so long that all the Germans were divided, one holding to one side and the other to the other side; and the strife came even as far as the court of Rome, all the court taking part in it. And the one side was called Guelf and the other called Ghibelline, the said names thus continuing in Italy). John Kenneth Hyde, 'Contemporary Views on Faction and Civil Strife in Thirteenth- and Fourteenth-Century Italy', in *Violence and Civil Disorder in the Italian Cities, 1200–1500*, ed. Lauro Martines (Berkeley: University of California Press, 1962), 273–307; Sergio Raveggi, *Ghibellini, guelfi e popolo grasso: I detentori del potere politico a Firenze nella seconda metà del Dugento* (Florence: La Nuova Italia, 1978); Carol Lansing, *The Florentine Magnates: Lineage and Faction in a Medieval Commune* (Princeton: Princeton University Press, 1991).

Arezzo, with cities further afield—Volterra, for example—likewise being drawn into the ambit of Florentine influence. All in all, then, this was a period of vigorous social, political and juridical creativity. Rarely, it is true, was life in Florence untouched by the restiveness now of Guelph now of Ghibelline ambition, but the fear of losing out either to the Church or, more especially, to the Empire, each alike making for an undermining of the status quo, was enough to ensure for the time being a modicum of civic stability.

For all its courage and resourcefulness, however, the Guelph-Ghibelline reconciliation in the wake of Frederick's demise was a fragile affair, and with the ascendancy of Manfred, natural son to Frederick, as king of Sicily and Puglia in 1258, and with all this meant by way of a weakening of the Church as a foil to imperial ambition in the peninsula, the Florentine Ghibellines spotted their chance. When, then, secret talks between the Uberti as especially prominent among the Ghibelline families in the city and Manfred were uncovered by the Guelphs reprisals were as swift as they were severe, for not only were the offenders expelled (the greater part of them taking refuge in Siena), but their towers were razed to the ground, their property confiscated and pillaged, and the abbot of Vallombrosa, suspected of Ghibelline sympathies, tortured and beheaded. The *fuorusciti*, with Farinata degli Uberti at their head and armed with plenary powers of negotiation, at once made representation to Manfred, who by way of a preliminary gesture made available to them one hundred horse, subsequently upped to eight hundred, for the purpose of assisting their return to Florence, the same reaching Siena in July 1260. The Florentines for their part, having rung the Martinella for a month and mustered a huge force from home and abroad (a force including a good number of trusted Ghibellines from their own ranks), set off, *carroccio* and all, to do battle in August of that year, pitching camp five miles or so from Siena on the west bank of the river Arbia with the hills of Montaperti in the background. Signs and portents everywhere abounded and spirits were high, but disaster struck almost immediately. Expecting the gates of the city to be opened to them by Guelph dissidents and other malcontents within, the Florentine army was straightaway wrong-footed by a huge amassing of Sienese forces and their transalpine allies, a situation further aggravated by a nicely timed defection of the trusted Ghibellines to the other side. Battle commenced and the Florentine standard was felled by a Bocca degli Abati among the Ghibelline turncoats. The ensuing slaughter was monstrous, the waters of Arbia running red with the blood of the slain.[3] True, a large part of the Florentine infantry fled and sought

---

3 *Inferno* 10.82–87 (Dante to Farinata degli Uberti in the circle of the heretics): 'E se tu mai nel dolce mondo regge, / dimmi: perché quel popolo è sì empio / incontr' a' miei in ciascuna sua legge?' / Ond' io a lui: 'Lo strazio e 'l grande scempio / che fece l'Arbia colorata in rosso, / tal orazion fa far nel nostro tempio' ('Were, then, you to return to the sweet world above, tell me why, in all its legislating, those people are so pitiless with regard to me and mine'; whence I to him: 'The rout and the slaughter

refuge in the castle of Montaperti, but even so the death toll was colossal with 2,500 Florentine fatalities and a further 1,500 taken prisoner, many of them systematically humiliated. At a stroke, Florence was deprived of some of the best and most promising of her young men, even the *carroccio* and the Martinella falling to the enemy.

Quite as drastic as the event itself, however, was the aftermath of Montaperti. Predictably (for this was generally the way of it in defeat) there was a mass exodus of such Guelphs as were left in Florence, there being every possibility now of a reign of terror. Florence, it is true, was well walled, well provisioned and, on the face of it, equal to hostilities waged from without, but no one, either among the populace or the nobility, was about to take a chance, flight being the better option. As a result, the victorious forces—Sienese, German and their assorted supporters and allies—entered the city on 16 September 1260, a fortnight or so after the rout proper on the fourth of that month. Oaths of loyalty were sworn to Manfred, and there was a general annulment in Florence of all the institutions, magistracies and mechanisms of government set up by the Guelph regime. Guelph property was subject to confiscation and Guelph houses pulled down stone by stone, the settling of old scores being in this as in every other sense more than ordinarily thorough. Worse still, however, was to come, for it was not long before a council was convened at Empoli under the auspices of Count Guido Novello of Casentino to consider the apportioning of costs and liabilities in Florence and, as a final solution, the possibility of destroying the city altogether as a way of settling the Guelph issue once and for all. In the event—and now famously in consequence of what in the *Commedia* he himself has to say in his defence[4]— there was a dissenting voice, that of Farinata degli Uberti, who, at the risk of antagonising his Ghibelline confederates, succeeded in winning them over and staving off the city's final demise. But for the Guelphs the situation was nonethe-

---

that stained the Arbia blood-red are the cause of such devotions in our temple'). Villani on Montaperti, 6.79. Robert Davidsohn, *Montaperti: La battaglia del 1260 tra Firenze e Siena e il castello ritrovato* (Florence: Aska, 2005); Federico Canaccini, *Ghibellini e ghibellinismo in Toscana da Montaperti a Campaldino (1260–1289)* (Rome: Istituto Storico Italiano per il Medioevo, 2009). For Bocca degli Abati, Villani 6.79 and *Inferno* 32.73–111.

4 *Inferno* 10.91–93: 'Ma fu' io solo, là dove sofferto / fu per ciascun di tòrre via Fiorenza, / colui che la difesi a viso aperto' (but it was I alone, where it was agreed by everyone to destroy Florence, who defended her with open face). Villani 6.82: 'Veggendo ciò il conte Giordano, e l'uomo, e della autoritade ch'era messer Farinata, e il suo gran seguito, e come parte ghibellina se ne potea partire e avere discordia, sì·ssi rimase, e intesono ad altro; sicché per uno buono uomo cittadino scampò la nostra città di Firenze da tanta furia, distruggimento, ruina' (Count Giordano [among those at Empoli in favour of razing Florence to the ground] perceiving this, and what manner of man and of what authority was Messer Farinata, and his great following, and how the Ghibelline party might be broken up and come to discord, abandoned the idea and took other counsel, so that by one good man and citizen our city of Florence was saved from so great fury, destruction and ruin). John A. Scott, '*Inferno* X: Farinata *magnanimo*', in *Dante magnanimo: Studi sulla 'Commedia'* (Florence: Olschki, 1977), 9–45.

less dire, even Lucca, hitherto a safe haven for Florentine refugees, agreeing to their expulsion on pain of decapitation. What followed, then, in the early part of the 1260s in the wake of Montaperti was a species of Guelph diaspora, the dispossessed taking cover wherever they could, either this side of the Apennines or else beyond them in Bologna.

But diaspora has a way of concentrating the mind, and from this moment on there was a slow but discernible improvement in Guelph prospects in and beyond Tuscany. Those seeking and finding refuge in Bologna not only mounted a successful campaign against the Ghibellines of Parma but were encouraged first by Urban IV and then by Clement IV (both of them Frenchmen of Angevin inclination) to square up to Manfred and the imperial idea. True, a good number of cities remained faithful to him (Verona, Brescia, Cremona, Piacenza, Pavia), but others, including Milan, came down on the side of the pope, expressions of everlasting allegiance flowing full and free. Fresh conflict, then, was inevitable, culminating this time on the planes of Grandella near Benevento where, in 1266, and by way of a spectacular combination of treachery and military miscalculation, the Hohenstaufen cause was just about totally eclipsed, Manfred, according to Dante's account of it in the *Purgatorio*, surviving his wounds just long enough to make peace with his maker.[5] As far, then, as Florence was concerned the result was predictable, Benevento fermenting a fresh set of Guelph hopes and aspirations, a bringing home of the Guelphs to their former honours, offices and privileges. Yet again, therefore—for this, always, was the Florentine way—a further round of executive and judicial provisions was approved and implemented, with increased representation for the minor arts at the highest level, each having a magistrate of its own for the administration of local affairs, a banner of its own,

---

5 *Purgatorio* 3.118–29: 'Poscia ch'io ebbi rotta la persona / di due punte mortali, io mi rendei, / piangendo, a quei che volontier perdona. / Orribil furon li peccati miei; / ma la bontà infinita ha sì gran braccia, / che prende ciò che si rivolge a lei. / Se 'l pastor di Cosenza, che a la caccia / di me fu messo per Clemente allora, / avesse in Dio ben letta questa faccia, / l'ossa del corpo mio sarieno ancora / in co del ponte presso a Benevento, / sotto la guardia de la grave mora' (With my body broken by two mortal stabs, I rendered myself, weeping, to him who pardons willingly. My sins were horrible, but the infinite goodness has such wide arms that it takes whatever turns to it. If the pastor of Cosenza, who was set to hunt me down by Clement, had then rightly read this page in God, the bones of my body would still be at the head of the bridge near Benevento under the protection of the heavy cairn). Villani 7.9. Mark Balfour, 'Orribil furon li peccati miei: Manfred's Wounds in *Purgatorio III*', *ItSt* 48 (1993), 4–17 (and in *Dante: The Critical Complex*, vol. 7, ed. Richard Lansing [New York: Routledge, 2003], 264–77); John A. Scott, 'Manfred and Bonconte', in *Dante's Political Purgatory* (Philadelphia: University of Pennsylvania Press, 1996), 85–95; Costanza Geddes da Filicaia, '*Purgatorio* III.103–45: La battaglia di Benevento tra scrittura storica e riscrittura poetica', in *La letteratura e la storia. Atti del IX Congresso nazionale dell'Adi, Bologna and Rimini, 21–24 settembre 2005*, vol. 1 (Bologna: Gedit, 2007), 307–14; Orazio Antonio Bologna, 'Il luogo della battaglia e delle sepolture di Manfredi', in *Manfredi di Svevia: Impero e Papato nella concezione di Dante* (Rome: Libreria Ateneo Salesiano, 2013), 153–72. On the battle itself, Paolo Grillo, *L'aquila e il giglio: 1266, la battaglia di Benevento* (Rome: Salerno editrice, 2015).

and the right as and when to take up arms. But as ever the peace was precarious, few if any of these provisions in the area of lawmaking and enforcement touching upon, still less resolving, the underlying rhythm of tension and resentment. Compromise was all well and good, but everywhere stirring in the minds of Guelph and Ghibelline alike was the dream of total triumph, the triumph of the Guelphs under the auspices of the Church and the House of Anjou, and the triumph of the Ghibellines under the auspices of Conradin as the final flickering of Swabian power in the peninsula.

With Benevento, then, we are on the threshold of a fresh period of Guelph ascendancy. True, the customary gestures had been made, most obviously by way of a dual Guelph-Ghibelline appointment to the *podesteria* in 1266 of a pair of Bolognese Knights of the Order of St Mary, notable in the event, however, less for their efficiency than for their easy living and hypocrisy.[6] But what with the seizure and redistribution of Ghibelline assets in the city, and, more provocatively still, the installation of Charles of Anjou as imperial vicar of the province as a whole, the tide was flowing in a Guelph direction. The Ghibellines, therefore, were on edge, theirs from this point on being a commitment to reinforcing as far as may be the Ghibelline axis in Tuscany generally (Pisa, Siena, Arezzo, Pistoia and Prato), and, at home, to a steady programme of civic disruption. The Guelphs for their part replied by strengthening still further the democratic institutions in the city by way of a now endless multiplication of executive and consultative mechanisms, and, in a further expression if not of Angevin allegiance then of Angevin accommodation, of bestowing upon Charles a decade's worth of *merum et mixtum imperium,* a comprehensive blend of sovereign and civil authority. These things between them, especially when combined with a continuing programme of Guelph reparation within the city and with a sustained suppression of Ghibelline interest both within and beyond it (the best part of a thousand

---

6 *Inferno* 23.91–108: 'Poi disser me: "O Tosco, ch'al collegio / de l'ipocriti tristi se' venuto, / dir chi tu se' non avere in dispregio". / E io a loro: "I' fui nato e cresciuto / sovra 'l bel fiume d'Arno a la gran villa, / e son col corpo ch'i' ho sempre avuto. / Ma voi chi siete, a cui tanto distilla / quant' i' veggio dolor giù per le guance? / e che pena è in voi che sì sfavilla?" / E l'un rispuose a me: "Le cappe rance / son di piombo sì grosse, che li pesi / fan così cigolar le lor bilance. / Frati godenti fummo, e bolognesi; / io Catalano e questi Loderingo / nomati, e da tua terra insieme presi / come suole esser tolto un uom solingo, / per conservar sua pace; e fummo tali, / ch'ancor si pare intorno dal Gardingo"' ('Then they said to me: 'O Tuscan who are come to the college of forlorn hypocrites, disdain not to tell us who you are.' And I to them: 'I was born and grew up in that great city on the fair stream of Arno, and am with the body I have always had. But who are you down whose cheek, as I discern, stream tears distilled from pain, and what penalty is it that glistens so upon you?' And one of them answered me: 'These golden cloaks are of lead, and weighty such as to make creak any balance. Jovial Friars were we and Bolognese, I Catalano and he Loderingo by name, and we were chosen together by that city of yours where customarily but one is taken to keep the peace, and what we were may still be seen there hard by the Gardingo'). Villani 7.13. Catherine Keen, 'Father of Lies: (Mis)readings of Clerical and Civic Duty in *Inferno* XXIII', in *Dante and the Church: Literary and Historical Essays,* ed. Paolo Acquaviva and Jennifer Petrie (Dublin: Four Courts Press, 2007), 173–207.

Ghibellines were either slaughtered or taken prisoner in the castle of Sant'Ellero, including members of the Uberti family),[7] were enough, the Guelphs thought, to rule out the nightmare possibility of Ghibelline resurgence in Florence, the grim spectre of neo-Fredericianism.

FLORENCE BETWEEN THE BLACKS AND THE WHITES (1279–1302)

The next distinctive phase of Florentine history begins in or around the year 1290, for it is in this period that we begin to see the tensions at work within Guelphism making both for the collective catastrophe of Florence and, as far as Dante himself was concerned, for the personal catastrophe of exile. But that, for the moment, is on the horizon, the years 1270 to 1290 being notable above all for their various attempts—as flamboyant as they were ill-fated—to resolve the Guelph-Ghibelline issue left over from the Frederician and post-Frederician era. So, for example, as more than ordinarily colourful among them, there was Gregory X's decree in July 1273 to the effect that the warring factions should under pain of excommunication foregather by the Rubaconte bridge with a view to exchanging a kiss of peace, all this to coincide with the founding of yet another church (San Gregorio) to mark the dawning of a new age—all promising enough were it not for a threat on the part of the Guelph contingent forthwith to dismember any representatives of the Ghibelline cause should they not at once vacate the city.[8] Gesturing on a grand scale was again everywhere to the fore a little further down the line when in the course of 1279 Nicholas III despatched yet another peacemaker, his cardinal legate Latino di Malabranca, O.P. (a nephew of his on his sister's side) with three hundred horsemen to help quell dissension in the city. As ever, the pageantry was superb, all parties to the unrest (including on the Ghibelline side the Adimari, the Tosinghi, the Donati, the Pazzi, the Buondelmonti and the Uberti) yet again assembling for the purposes of offering a kiss of peace and of laying the first stone this time for the church of Santa Maria Novella.[9] It is, however, amid the theatricality of it all that we witness once more the paradox of Florentine civic life in these middle and later years of the thirteenth century, namely its capacity, pantomime notwithstanding, for genuine political creativity, for in view of the continuing antagonism of Guelph and Ghibelline despite the peace of 1280 thought was given to a fresh structure more properly equal to the complexities of an expanding and ever more sophisticated urban economy

7 Villani 7.19.
8 Villani 7.42.
9 Villani 7.56. Mario Sanfilippo, 'Guelfi e ghibellini a Firenze: La "pace" del Cardinale Latino (1280)', *Nuova rivista storica* 64.1 (1980), 1–24.

and demography. Mindful, therefore, of the need as far as may be to combine orderliness and freedom as the twin properties of civic maturity, the Guelph regime—or, more exactly, a committee consisting of half a dozen Guelph *popolani* of whom one was the chronicler Dino Compagni —set up in 1282 a new system of priors or civic officials with the aim of preserving both the representative character of the government and its impartiality.[10] In the first instance there were just three priors, Bartolo de' Bardi (a nobleman) for the Oltrarno, Rosso Bacherelli (from the guild of moneychangers) for the *sesto* of San Piero Schieraggio and Salvi del Chiaro Girolami (of the wool guild) for the *sesto* of San Brancazio, all of whom would live at the expense of the commune, enjoy a team of servants and messengers, and reside in a state of semi-seclusion in houses alongside the Badia. Their remit would be to oversee the complex mechanisms of government, not least by checking their now unruly multiplication. With the success of the first magistracy, the number of priors was raised from three to six (one for each *sesto*), with—provided only that they were men of good standing and that they had subscribed to one or other of the arts—both noblemen and guildsmen being eligible for election, election being by way of secret ballot in the church of San Piero Schieraggio. There was also to be a strict electoral procedure both for the *capitano del popolo* or official representative of the by now thriving merchant classes, and for the *podestà*, each to be proposed by the councils of the commune in the aggregate. All the arts were furnished with a militia for the purpose of keeping good order in their jurisdiction, and they each had their own *gonfalone* or banner. The smaller arts, less flushed and correspondingly less formidable, were taken under the wing of those with a higher social and professional profile, this too helping to ensure proper representation for the people as a whole and to manage the conflicting forces of entrepreneurialism and free creativity on the one hand and power, partisanship and oppression on the other. Here, then, in the context of a social and political restiveness never far beneath the surface, is the supreme instance in these years of Florentine political nous, of a refinement and resilience of spirit if not equal to the matter in hand then by the same token lacking neither in imagination nor in goodwill.

Goodwill and a sense of purpose within, however, was in the selfsame moment met by a nasty configuration of forces without, the capture and imprisonment of Charles II of Naples in 1284 by the Aragonese once again serving to fire up Ghibelline hopes and aspirations in Tuscany. Home to the Ghibellines in this period was Arezzo, where without difficulty they had overthrown a relatively neutral administration and were now looking belligerently towards Florence, whose response was immediately to rearm, Florentine conscription, envisaging

10   Villani 7.79; Compagni 1.4–5. Nicola Ottokar, 'L'istituzione del priorato a Firenze', *ASI* 82.1 (1924), 5–71.

as it did anyone and everyone between the ages of fifteen and seventy as eligible for military service, being reinforced from Lucca, Siena, Prato, Volterra, San Miniato and Colle Val d'Elsa. Given their potential for treachery, Ghibellines in the city were excluded, but were nonetheless expected to provide cavalry and the associated accoutrements of war. Following, then, upon a series of minor skirmishes near Campaldino in 1289 preparations for battle began in earnest, the Ghibellines assembling at Bibbiena with eight hundred horse and ten times that number of infantry both from this side of the Apennines and from the Marches, Spoleto and Romagna on the other side, and the Guelphs engineering a massive movement of their own and allied troops into the Casentino in anticipation of further assistance from Bologna. Massive, indeed, is the word, for on the Florentine side there were a hundred and fifty light cavalry with Vieri de' Cerchi of the White Guelphs in Florence as one of their captains, together with any number of shield bearers, bowmen and lancers under the command of Corso Donati of the Black Guelphs (though for the moment on secondment to Pistoia as *podestà*). Their strategy was clear. The Aretines would be encouraged to advance towards the main body of the Florentine army, whereupon the flanks would close in upon them by way of a pincer movement designed to cut off any room either for manoeuvre or for retreat. And that is what happened. The Aretine advance guard surged forward, with Corso Donati—contrary, it seems, to every order but entirely in character—coming in from either side to complete the operation. The battle was bloody beyond words, fatalities on both sides—not least among those scrambling beneath the horses to disembowel them—being huge. Aretine deaths numbered more than seventeen hundred, with another two thousand made captive with a view to being ransomed for a good profit. Unusually, and indeed inexplicably, the victors held back from entering Arezzo, the Florentines contenting themselves with the seizure of Bibbiena, with the devastation of the Aretine *contado*, and, as an insult to the Bishop of Arezzo laid low in the battle, the ritual slaughtering of mitred asses. At home, the Florentines, no expense spared (thirty-six thousand gold florins was the total bill), celebrated for the best part of three weeks, seeing to it, however, that the popular militia was up and running lest the victorious nobility, as was their way, got out of hand.[11]

Considerations of a more properly economic kind apart, it was largely the unruliness of the nobility in Florence that, around the turn of the 1280s and into the 1290s, saw a shift of power towards the people generally, for this is the moment of the Ordinances of Justice, of a set of measures not without precedent either in Florence or elsewhere both in and beyond Tuscany but proclaimed now more than ever energetically. It is the moment too in which the tension between

11   Villani 7.131; Compagni 1.10. Herbert L. Oerter, 'Campaldino', *Spec* 43.3 (1968), 429–50; Federico Canaccini, *Gli eroi di Campaldino: 11 giugno 1289* (Poppi: Scramasax, 2002).

Guelph and Ghibelline hitherto decisive for the course of Florentine history in the second part of the thirteenth century begins to give way as a cause for concern to tension within the Guelph order itself, between the White Guelphs as, for all their misgiving with regard to the empire, no less circumspect when it came to the Church and to all this might mean by way of a loss of independence, and the Black Guelphs as more willing to court the papacy as the guarantor of their power and privileges in the community. For as long, then, as the menace of Ghibellinism subsisted, so also, without as yet too much trouble, did these diverse strands of Guelph consciousness. With its passing, however, they began seriously to unravel, with, by the turn of the century, disastrous consequences for the city as a whole.

To take first, then, the Ordinances, we may begin by saying this, that with the eclipse of their ancient power and prestige, the Ghibelline aristocracy was confronted by a new challenge, by the rise of the mercantile classes and of a nouveau riche together with all this meant by way of their claim to the exercise of power in the city.[12] With the continuing and indeed increasing ferocity of Guelph resentment, the Ghibelline nobility itself grew steadily more restive and undisciplined in its conduct, the prehistory of the Ordinances thus being a sense on the part of the injured party—both of the Guelph bourgeoisie and of its dependents down the social scale—of incessant scandal, insolence and outrage at the expense of those powerless to do much about it. In 1293, therefore, a group of guildsmen and merchants headed by Giano della Bella (himself of noble stock) and by the priors taking office on 15 February that year met to review and to address the situation. Authorized as they were by the rights and privileges of office, they drew up a fresh set of legal provisions, doubling the penalty for any outrage committed by the nobility on the people and involving not merely the perpetrator but kith and kin in the redemption thereof. Just two witnesses would be enough for conviction, or, failing that, the sworn oath of the injured party. Moreover, there could be no proceeding by a member of the nobility against an ordinary citizen without the consent of the priors, no street presence of the nobility in times of disturbance, and no bearing of arms by the nobility on family occasions, not to mention any number of further provisions in the area of civil and electoral law touching on securities, acquisitions, transactions, civic status and eligibility for office. Fur-

---

12   On the Ordinances, Villani at 8.1 and Compagni at 1.11. For the text, *Ordinamenti di giustizia, 1293–1993*, (Florence: SP44, 1993), the text itself being a reprint of Francesco Bonaini, *Gli ordinamenti di giustizia del comune e popolo di Firenze compilati nel 1293*, ASI 1 (1855) and of Gaetano Salvemini, *Magnati e popolani in Firenze dal 1280 al 1295* (Florence: Carnesecchi, 1899); Teresa Pugh Rupp, 'If You Want Peace, Work for Justice: Dino Compagni's *Cronica* and the Ordinances of Justice', in *Florence and Beyond: Culture, Society and Politics in Renaissance Italy (Essays in Honour of John M. Najemy)*, ed. David S. Peterson with Daniel E. Bornstein (Toronto: Centre for Reformation and Renaissance Studies, 2008), 323–37.

ther adjustment too was made in the area of public order and peacekeeping. Henceforth, therefore, there was to be a *Gonfaloniere di giustizia* or chief civil magistrate electable every two months and furnished in turn by each of the *sesti* or six districts of the city, complete with insignia, a phalanx of armed enforcers (one thousand to begin with and then two thousand and four thousand) together with an army of labourers skilled in the work of demolition as the preferred means of bringing grandees to their senses. All this, moreover, was to apply both *intra* and *extra urbem*, the civic solution looking in this sense to be complete. And for a time, with business appearing to flourish and the city gates remaining unlocked even by night, it all seemed to be working. But among those most affected by all this the underlying mood was scarcely less than seething, particularly in light of what the nobility was inclined to see as the regular abuse of the law as an instrument of tyranny and the not entirely unambiguous character of Giano della Bella as tireless, to be sure, in his dedication to civic order but himself not wholly unmoved by partisanship and a spirit of reprisal.

In the event, Giano della Bella's fall was as spectacular as his rise. In fact, for all his strength of personality and his apparent grip on things, his situation in Florence was fragile, the problem for him being that there was no clear dividing line between the nobility and, at any rate in its more aspirational aspect, the now wealthy mercantile constituency, all of which meant that while for those entrepreneurial souls doing well for themselves Giano was indeed their man, for those lower down the social and economic scale, and especially for the more bullheaded of the people, he could quite as well be seen—and in the event was seen—as in league with the nobility. The term 'bullheaded' is, in fact, more than ordinarily appropriate here in that the leading fomenter of discontent among the people was Pecora the butcher, he, unlike the more socially ambitious stratum of the merchant and middle classes, having much to gain from a freewheeling aristocracy with plenty to spend. In the early part, then, of 1295, Giano della Bella, rarely in fact caught unawares or wrong-footed by the shifting sands of Florentine sentiment, was alerted by the prominent White Guelph chronicler Dino Compagni as to the now near impossibility of his situation, the whole thing coming to a head by way of an incident involving Corso Donati, who, arraigned in connection with the death of a commoner in the course of a scuffle, was abruptly acquitted. The people, suspecting collusion between him and the powers that be, including Giano della Bella, straightaway launched a frenzied attack on the *podestà* and his wife, she for her part taking refuge in the houses of the Cerchi and Corso himself making good his escape over the roof. In fact, the *podestà*, his office ravaged and his files in tatters, was duly paid off the next day and straightaway departed the city, but for Giano della Bella the situation was precarious, his friends and supporters, of whom there was still a good number, advising him and his family to be off at once, which they were on 5 March 1295. With this, he was formally banished and condemned in person and property, the sentence being intensified by Pope Boniface's extension of his excommunication to the whole city should anyone come to his aid. Not only that, but his friends and supporters were fined between five hundred and a thousand lire depending on the extent of their association with him. So it was that a genuinely significant moment of Florentine history came to an end, 'genuinely significant', if not in resolving then at least in confronting a set of issues wholly transcending in their complexity—in their crisscrossing the customary boundaries of socioeconomic and political concern—the relatively straightforward Guelph/Ghibelline antagonisms of yesteryear.[13]

If, then, with Giano della Bella the nightmare prospect of Ghibelline resurgence had in some degree been allayed, a fresh set of tensions—tensions long since simmering in the depths—surfaced to disturb the peace, the tension not now between Guelph and Ghibelline but between Guelph and Guelph, between the ancient and the aspirational, between old and new money. On the one hand, then, and taking first the latter, there were the nouveau riche and the parvenus, those who by dint of their entrepreneurialism at home and abroad had fashioned for themselves a conspicuous presence in a conspicuous city, a city everywhere renowned for its business acumen and indeed for its having established something of a commercial empire in and beyond the peninsula. Into this category fell the Cerchi as to the fore among the up and coming bourgeoisie, among those

---

13   Compagni 1.12–16 for an account of the entire episode with reference to the substance of, and the tensions generated by, the Ordinances, to the riots of 23 January 1295, and to Giano della Bella's departure from Florence. On Giano della Bella himself, Compagni 1.11: 'savio, valente e buono uomo . . . assai animoso e di buona stirpe' (a wise, good, and worthy man . . . of high spirit and good stock) and Villani 8.8: 'ch'egli era il più leale e diritto popolano e amatore del bene comune che uomo di Firenze, e quegli che mettea in Comune e non ne traeva. Era presuntuoso e volea le sue vendette fare, e fecene alcuna contra gli Abati suoi vicini col braccio del Comune, e forse per gli detti peccati fu, per le sue medesime leggi fatte, a torto e sanza colpa da' non giusti giudicato. E nota che questo è grande esempio a que' cittadini che sono a venire, di guardarsi di non volere essere signori di loro cittadini né troppo presuntuosi, ma istare contenti a la comune cittadinanza' (a most loyal and upright man of the people and lover of both the common good and of every man in Florence, and one who gave all to the commonwealth taking nothing for himself therefrom. He was, however, arrogant and eager to avenge his wrongs, causing him on occasion to proceed with the arm of the law against the Abati, his neighbours, for which misdemeanours he was perhaps, by dint of the very laws he himself had fashioned, judged by the unjust and wrongly condemned. Let this, then, be an example to those down the line desirous of lording it over their fellow countrymen or simply too ambitious, that they should settle instead for common citizenship). Likewise Dante in the *Paradiso* at 16.127–32: 'Ciascun che de la bella insegna porta / del gran barone il cui nome e 'l cui pregio / la festa di Tommaso riconforta, / da esso ebbe milizia e privilegio; / avvegna che con popol si rauni / oggi colui che la fascia col fregio' (Everyone bearing the noble arms of the great baron [Hugh, Marquis of Tuscany, d. 1001], whose name and praise the feast of Thomas renews, had from him knighthood and privilege, though he who decks it with a border [Giano della Bella] sides today with the people), and Leonardo Bruni in the *Historiarum Florentini populi libri XII* at 8.8: 'Ita civis bene meritus, a populo ipso cuius auctoritatem contra potentiores asseruerat, ingrate desertus, in exilio diem obiit' (So it was that this most worthy citizen, ungratefully abandoned by the very people whose rights he asserted over against the more powerful, died in exile).

who, in a society sufficiently fluid to blur the lines between the merchant and the magnate, sought to cut a figure in the city by way of their money, their manners, their household, their horse, their dress, their display and of every other material appurtenance, all this amounting to a statement of political intent. On the other hand, there were the older, longer established families, those tracing their ancestry to one or other of the feudal and ecclesiastical regimes predating the rise of the commune, and indeed themselves feudatory figures with their ample estates, their castles and their loyal retinue both within and beyond the city—with, in short, their birth and their breeding. Into this category fell the Donati, men of noble and warrior descent more or less vociferously impatient of the boorish and unrefined ways of the newly arrived by whom they felt challenged and as often as not outdone in terms of wealth, purchasing power and sheer social presence.[14] Guelphism, then, even in its triumph and indeed especially in its triumph under Giano della Bella, was by no means an undifferentiated phenomenon, the Ordinances, never in truth equal to the now complex sociology and shifting allegiances of Florentine society, tending to separate out and to polarise those of Guelph persuasion jealous in respect of their independence and room for manoeuvre as free citizens of a free republic (the White Guelphs under Vieri de' Cerchi) and those not averse to enlisting the help of whomsoever—Angevin or apostolic—when it came to asserting their ancient rights and privileges (the Black Guelphs spearheaded by Corso Donati).

Here, then, was a nothing if not complex pattern of alignment and realignment containing within itself the seeds of catastrophe, three episodes in particular

---

14 Exact in this sense Villani's account of the situation at 8.39: 'Della casa de' Cerchi era capo messer Vieri de' Cerchi, e egli e quegli di sua casa erano di grande affare, e possenti, e di grandi parentadi, ricchissimi mercatanti, che la loro compagnia era delle maggiori del mondo; uomini erano morbidi e innocenti, salvatichi e ingrati, siccome genti venuti di piccolo tempo in grande stato e podere. Della casa de' Donati era capo messer Corso Donati, e egli e quelli di sua casa erano gentili uomini e guerrieri, e di non soperchia ricchezza, ma per motto erano chiamati *Malefami*. Vicini erano in Firenze e in contado, e per la conversazione de la loro invidia colla bizzarra salvatichezza nacque il superbio isdegno tra loro' (The head of the Cerchi family was one M. Vieri de' Cerchi, he and his house generally being prominent in city affairs, powerful, close-knit and influential as a family, and wealthy merchants one and all, his company being one of the largest in the world. These were an indulgent, naive, raucous and unrefined race after the manner of folk who in a short space of time had come to great wealth and power. The head of the Donati family was M. Corso Donati, he and his house being gentlemen and warriors, not especially wealthy but dubbed the infamous. Neighbours were they all both in Florence and in the country, but what with one relating to the other by way of boorish ostentation and envy respectively, it was all a matter between them of supreme disdain). Cf. Compagni 1.20: 'Cominciò per questo l'odio a multiplicare. E messer Corso molto sparlava di messer Vieri, chiamandolo l'asino di Porta, perché era uomo bellissimo, ma di poca malizia, né di bel parlare; e però spesso dicea: "Ha raghiato oggi l'asino di Porta?"; e molto lo spregiava' (By reason of this, hatred between them increased, Messer Corso greatly slandering Messer Vieri by calling him the 'Ass of Porta' [i.e. of Porta san Piero as the *sesto* in which they all lived], because, though a very comely man, he, Vieri, was small of wit and rude of speech, wherefore Corso, so complete was his scorn, would often say: 'Has the Ass of Porta been braying today?'). Enrico Pispisa, 'Lotte sociali e concetto di nobiltà a Firenze nella seconda metà del Duecento', *SM* 38.1 (1997), 439–63.

heralding the storm to come. First, there was the May Day scuffle of 1300 when the Cerchi, out riding in the city, jostled and were in turn jostled by some of the Donati, the Pazzi and the Spini in Piazza Santa Trinità, one of the Cerchi having his nose sliced off during the affray.[15] Then there was the affair of the Frescobaldi funeral, notable for the involvement of Guido Cavalcanti, in his own way a spirit as theatrical as any in Florence. With the commoners seated on bales of straw at the feet of the nobility on their benches, one of the former gestured in such a way as to offend the nobles ranged opposite him, whereupon Cavalcanti, clashing in person with Corso Donati and in turn being stoned by his retinue, suffered an injury to the hand. And then finally there was the Neri Abati prison episode involving the harassment of members of the Cerchi family near Remole as they were returning to Florence across Donati territory. Conflict, complete with casualties, once again broke out, with representatives from each side being fined and imprisoned, four of the Cerchi, however, dying in custody. Upon interrogation, the prison superintendent, Neri Abati, claimed that he had been put up to it by Corso, a claim, however, as was generally the way with Corso, not somehow substantiated. Substantial or not, however, the situation engendering and in turn engendered by these and similar incidents was perilous in the extreme, the Blacks, adept as ever at playing the game, appealing to the pope as an antidote to what they saw as the crypto-Ghibellinism of the Whites, as in effect their treating with the enemy. Boniface, banking as he was with the Spini of Florence, duly obliged by sending in Cardinal Matthew of Acquasparta in June of that year (1300) as overseer and peacemaker, his attempt to calm the situation by adjusting the shape of the government, however, not only meeting with resistance from the Whites as by instinct opposed to clerical meddling in civic affairs but once again being overtaken by events on the ground—by, this time, the manhandling of senior members of the guilds on their way to church on the eve of the festival of St John, the Blacks taking the opportunity to remind both them and the people generally who it was who had brought home victory at Campaldino and who, in consequence, deserved more recognition in the corridors of power than they currently seemed to be enjoying.[16] Chaos ensued, in the course of which an attempt was

---

15 Compagni 1.22. For the Frescobaldi funeral, Compagni 1.20 and for the Neri Abati episode and the Remole incident, Villani 8.41.

16 Compagni 1.21. N.P.J. Gordon, 'Plotting in Florence 1300', RS 24.5 (2010), 621–37. For Matthew of Acquasparta, Compagni 1.21 and Villani 8.40. Paradiso 12.121–26 (Bonaventure on the fortunes of Francis and of Franciscan spirituality): 'Ben dico, chi cercasse a foglio a foglio / nostro volume, ancor troveria carta / u' leggerebbe "I' mi son quel ch'i' soglio"; / ma non fia da Casal né d'Acquasparta, / là onde vegnon tali a la scrittura, / ch'uno la fugge e altro la coarta' (I allow indeed that he, searching our volume leaf by leaf, would still find a page where he might read: 'I am what I always was', but it will not be from Casale or from Acquasparta, where such come to the rule that one flees it and the other constrains it). Ovidio Capitani, 'L'allusione dantesca a Matteo d'Acquasparta', in Da Dante a Bonifacio VIII (Rome: Istituto Storico Italiano per il Medio Evo, 2007), 45–59; Leonardo Cappelletti, 'Dante e Matteo

made upon the life of the cardinal legate, who, despite being handsomely compensated by the powers that be, upped and left the city, taking care as he did so to place it once again under an interdict. Meanwhile, the priors, discomfited now to a man, took it upon themselves to banish an equal number of Black and White Guelphs, among whom was Cavalcanti . Corso, however, ever one for playing by his own rules, at once broke the terms of his banishment and made either for Rome or for Anagni—the details are uncertain—with a view to encouraging Boniface in something more resolute in Florence's regard, an initiative for which he was once more condemned by the White administration both in person and in property. What with this, then, and with news both of an imminent assault on the city by Guido da Battifolle and of conflict brewing in Pistoia and Lucca, the situation in Florence was once again critical, the city looking fair to fall either way. Had Vieri de' Cerchi been a greater man than he was, maybe he and the Whites could have held it. But with a now invincible alliance of the Blacks, the papacy and the House of Anjou, their fortunes were on the wane, Florence's descent into something close to civil war, not to mention civil atrocity, looking now all but inevitable.

The Angevin element in all this is fundamental, for had it not been for that and for the pope's espousal of the Angevin cause as a remedy for any resurgence of old-style imperialism it may have been possible for the White Guelphs to hold the line in Florence. But as Corso Donati straightaway opined, the alliance was invincible, and it was at this point that the Whites began to panic, despatching in September 1301 an embassy to the pope from whom, sensitive as he was to his own interest in this matter, they got short shrift. Meanwhile, Charles of Valois, brother to Philip the Fair of France and in Italy to assist Charles II of Naples in his struggle for Sicily, made his way to Bologna, where he too received deputations from both the White and the Black Guelphs of Florence, the Blacks, however, prevailing in his affections. At home, the White Guelphs set about making the best of it. Anxious to preserve the civic proprieties, they convened a general council of the Guelph and guild leaders with a view to deciding the best way forward, the general view (that of the bakers apart, who saw in all this nothing but the imminent annihilation of Florence) being that, provided he neither arrogated full jurisdiction nor abrogated any existing office in the city, nor sought in any other way to modify her laws and customs, then the Angevin prince would be welcome there as peacemaker. Now, therefore, it was a matter merely of fixing a time for Charles's reception in Florence (preferably not, it was felt, All Saints Day with its ample winebibbing and potential for public scandal) and, as far as maybe, persuading the populace generally that it was all a good idea, whereupon

d'Acquasparta', SD 74 (2009), 149–78; Dabney G. Park, 'The Good, the Bad, and the Ugly: What Dante Says about Bonaventure, Matthew of Acquasparta and Ubertino da Casale', DS 132 (2014), 267–312.

Dino Compagni, the mild-mannered chronicler of these events and himself one of the city priors, summoned the people generally to a meeting in St John's urging upon them a spirit of peace and goodwill, oaths to this effect being duly sworn upon the good book. But the Black Guelphs knew themselves now to be in the ascendant and their agenda was firm. With Boniface on their side and Charles well satisfied both on the political and on the pecuniary front (an advance of seventy thousand gold florins had already been made by the Blacks to defray his military expenses), all they had to do was to sit back and wait for events to take their course. On 1 November 1301, then, Charles entered Florence with the best part of a thousand French cavalry together with another four hundred from Lucca, Siena and, farther afield, Perugia and Romagna. From the outset it was an uneasy manoeuvre, the royal retinue taking up lodgings in the houses of the Frescobaldi on the far side of the Arno out of harm's way. On *this* side of the Arno, however, barricades were going up and there was a general call to arms. The priors for their part were now manifestly desperate, everything conspiring to bring them down. Invited by Charles to dine with him, even this posed problems, for not only was theirs a commitment to a life of seclusion for the period of their office but even to step out meant risking life and limb at the hands of the now hopelessly divided citizenry. Instead, then, of obliging him, the Guelph administration convened yet a further gathering of the general populace, this time in Santa Maria Novella and in the presence of Charles himself, with a view to confirming his status as peacemaker and thus forestalling any further descent into the abyss. But the abyss was now yawning, and with the wounding of a commoner by a member of the Medici family (the first stirring in Florence of an illustrious name) and the aforesaid breaching of his banishment by Corso Donati, the descent began, Corso and company straightaway setting about the business of sacking and setting on fire the houses of the priors who had expelled him and opening up the prisons.[17] Charles, it is true, took into custody the leading offenders on both

---

17 Villani 8.49: 'ed egli [Corso Donati] veggendosi crescere forza e séguito, la prima cosa che fece, andòe a le carcere del Comune, ch'erano nelle case de' Bastari nella ruga del palagio, e quelle per forza aperse e diliberò i pregioni; e ciò fatto, il simile fece al palazzo de la podestà, e poi a' priori, faccendogli per paura lasciare la signoria e tornarsi a·lloro case. E con tutto questo stracciamento di cittade, messer Carlo di Valos né sua gente non mise consiglio né riparo, né atenne saramento o cosa promessa per lui. Per la qual cosa i tiranni e malfattori e isbanditi ch'erano nella cittade, presa baldanza, e essendo la città sciolta e sanza signoria, cominciarono a rubare i fondachi e botteghe, e le case a chi era di parte bianca, o chi avea poco podere, con molti micidii, e fedite faccendo ne le persone di più buoni uomini di parte bianca. E durò questa pestilenzia in città per V dì continui con grande ruina della terra. E poi seguì in contado, andando le gualdane rubando e ardendo le case per più di VIII dì, onde in grande numero di belle e ricche possessioni furono guaste e arse' (and he [Corso Donati], seeing the increase in his forces and followers, straightaway made off to the city prisons in the Bastari houses hard by the *podestà's* palace, forced them open and set the prisoners free, whereupon he did as much at the palace itself, and then on to the Priors, causing them to lay down the reins of government out of fear and make for home. And with all this havoc being wrought in the city, Charles of Valois and his retinue offered neither

sides, but whereas the Black contingent was at once allowed to go free, the Whites were unceremoniously detained overnight. The bell summoning the citizens to take up arms in the interests of public order was rung, but while some dutifully patrolled the streets the majority merely turned tail and fled. The free-for-all, with its characteristic blend of considered and unconsidered violence, had begun. The city malefactors, pouring out of prison, began their programme not merely of looting and burning but of wounding and slaughtering the White population ad libitum, the Blacks for their part refining their campaign of bullying, extortion and rapine, with many a young woman, as Compagni puts it, being wedded against her will. With Charles looking on much after the manner of a spectator and Corso and his companions busy about plundering every kind of White Guelph asset, the violence continued for more than a week, the installation of a Black priorate inaugurating a succession of arbitrary arrests, false and disingenuous accusations and sordid plea bargaining. Charles, it is true, eventually stirred himself for the purposes of curbing the worst excesses of Black frenzy, and even the pope's cardinal legate Matthew of Acquasparta turned up once more to see what could be done, but neither initiative amounted to much, the mortal wounding of Niccola de' Cerchi among the Whites and of Simone Donati (son of Corso) among the Blacks ensuring a further spilling of blood over the Christmas season.

But that was not the end of it, for even with the triumph of Corso and company and the expulsion of hundreds of White Guelphs from the city, over the next weeks and months there remained any number of issues—including not least the rift now opening up among the Blacks themselves and the continuing problematics of Corso Donati's own personality—yet to address and to resolve. As far as the second of these things is concerned—the problematics of Corso's own personality—the fact is that, for all his loud proclamation of the Black Guelph cause, Corso was not in truth a party man. He was far too ambitious for this, far too impulsive, unpredictable and self-seeking, all of which nourished a now steady

---

counsel nor assistance, nor kept to the sworn oath he had made. Wherefore the tyrants, malefactors and banished roaming the city took courage, and, the town being without either guards or government, they set about pillaging the shops and storehouses together with everything belonging to the Whites, and, as regards anyone not being in a position to resist, slaughtering and maiming the good men and true of their party. And much to the detriment of the city, this pestilence went on unabated for five days, and thereafter in the *contado*, the militia continuing their robbery and arson for a further eight days, as a result of which many beautiful and valuable goods were either devastated or incinerated). Likewise Compagni 2.18–19 and 21: 'Molti disonesti peccati si feciono: di femmine vergini; rubare i pupilli; e uomini impotenti, spogliati de' loro beni; e cacciavanli della loro città' (Many shameful things were done. Maidens were outraged, entire wards pillaged and helpless souls deprived of their property and driven out of the city), with, at 2.19, the 'wedded against their will' motif (maritavansi fanciulle a forza). On the Niccola and Simone episode, Villani 8.49 (and cf. Compagni 3.41). On the Angevin aspect of all this, Edouard Jordan, *Les Origines de la domination angevine en Italie* (Paris: Picard, 1909).

sense on his part of greater deserving in the corridors of power.[18] His overall effect, therefore, was to deepen still further the already deep instability of the city, so much so that at one point in 1304 help was requested from Lucca for the purposes of keeping order there, the Lucchesi, in fact, holding the reins for more than a fortnight. And that was not all, for with the death of Boniface VIII in consequence of the fiasco—for Dante, of the blasphemy[19]—of Anagni and the appointment in January 1304 of a fresh peacemaker in the form of Cardinal Niccolò da Prato with all power made over to him for a year, there was every prospect of the Whites exiled after the coup d'état of 1301 flooding back in their hundreds. Straightaway, in fact, the cardinal set about reorganizing the city militia and negotiating with the White Guelph outcasts, an initiative waylaid, however, by the Black Guelphs, who, well aware of the feelings this would stir up in the neighbouring communes, diverted his energies into a campaign against Pistoia. Once again, then, nothing came of nothing as, despairing of the whole situation, yet another papal emissary shook the dust of the city from his shoes, placing it as he did so under yet another interdict.[20] The Blacks meanwhile, fearful for their hard-won hegemony, were once more on the rampage, vast tracts of the city being devoured by a massive fire started on 10 June that year by Neri Abati (a relative of the Bocca degli Abati responsible for the treacherous felling of the Florentine

18   Compagni 2.20, with a nicely judged account of Corso's person and presence in Florence: 'Uno cavaliere della somiglianza di Catellina romano, ma più crudele di lui, gentile di sangue, bello del corpo, piacevole parlatore, addorno di belli costumi, sottile d'ingegno, con l'animo sempre intento a malfare, col quale molti masnadieri si raunavano e gran sèguito avea, molte arsioni e molte ruberie fece fare, e gran dannaggio a' Cerchi e a' loro amici; molto avere guadagnò, e in grande altezza salì. Costui fu messer Corso Donati, che per sua superbia fu chiamato il Barone; che quando passava per la terra, molti gridavano: "Viva il Barone!"; e parea la terra sua. La vanagloria il guidava, e molti servigi facea' (A knight after the manner of Catiline the Roman, but more pitiless than he, of noble blood and handsome person, pleasant of speech, comely in manner, a man of subtle wit but with a mind forever intent on evil doing, with a considerable retinue and many a follower, he caused many acts of arson and robbery to be committed, wreaking great damage upon the Cerchi and their friends. Much wealth did he gain and to great height did he rise. This, then, was Messer Corso Donati, who on account of his pride was called the baron. When he passed through the city, many would cry out 'Long live the baron!' almost as though the city belonged to him. Moved only by vainglory he rendered many his services).

19   Qualifying an otherwise steady rhythm of indictment (*Inferno* 15.110–14, 19.55–57, 27.85–111 and *Paradiso* 27.22–26), *Purgatorio* 20.82–90: 'O avarizia, che puoi tu più farne, / poscia c'ha' il mio sangue a te sì tratto, / che non si cura de la propria carne? / Perché men paia il mal futuro e 'l fatto, / veggio in Alagna intrar lo fiordaliso, / e nel vicario suo Cristo esser catto. / Veggiolo un'altra volta esser deriso; / veggio rinovellar l'aceto e 'l fiele, / e tra vivi ladroni esser anciso' (O avarice, what more can you do to us, for to yourself you have so drawn my blood that it has no care for its own flesh? That past and future ill may seem no less, I see the fleur-de-lis enter Anagni and, in his vicar, Christ himself made captive. I see him mocked a second time. I see renewed the vinegar and the gall and him slain between living thieves). George Holmes, 'Dante and the Popes', in *The World of Dante: Essays on Dante and His Times*, ed. Cecil Grayson (Oxford: Clarendon Press, 1980), 18–43; Jennifer Petrie, ' "O papa Bonifazio": Dante, Boniface VIII and Jacopone da Todi', in *Dante and the Church: Literary and Historical Essays*, ed. Paolo Acquaviva and Jennifer Petrie (Dublin: Four Courts Press, 2007), 39–59.

20   Compagni 3.1 and 4–7 and Villani 8.69.

standard at Montaperti) reaching all the way down from the Mercato Nuovo where the Cavalcanti had their houses to the Ponte Vecchio. Yet again, then, Florence was ablaze, houses, livelihoods, artworks and other treasures all falling victim to the wantonness of the moment. With the destruction of the best part of two thousand properties as but the surface manifestation of something infinitely more tragic, both the super- and the substructure of a great city appeared once more to be disintegrating. Florence, in short, was doing what Florence was so good at, namely delivering herself despite herself to her undoing.

The Descent and Demise of Henry VII (1302–13)

In the degree to which these things were not already under way—the ascendancy, that is to say, of the signorial over the communal in the area of civic concern, of the conciliar over the hierocratic in the area of ecclesiastical concern, and of the humanist over the high-scholastic in the area of literary and philological concern—we witness in these early years of the fourteenth century the dawn of a new era, a fresh way of seeing and understanding the human predicament both in its sociopolitical and in its cultural aspect. But just for the moment, and certainly as far as Florence was concerned, it was business as usual, two events in particular—namely the siege of Pistoia in 1305 and 1306 and the death of Corso Donati in 1308—bearing witness to a long since inveterate state of mind, to the tragic as distinct from the triumphant side of communal civilization.

Pistoia, if anything more lawless than Florence, had for some time been in the hands of White Guelphs and Ghibellines with close connections in Arezzo and Lucca. But the time had come, the Florentines thought, to put paid to this situation and to bring the city to heel, easier said than done in that Pistoia was particularly well fortified. With the arrival, then, in April 1305 of Robert Duke of Calabria, the firstborn son of Charles II of Anjou, together with a formidable array of Aragonese and Catalan cavalry, the siege—notable only for its ferocity—was set up. 'Ferocity', in fact, hardly covers it, for not only was the state of the besieged in Pistoia more than ordinarily appalling, but the vengeance visited on those who ventured out was barbaric in the extreme: feet were cut off and noses slit regardless of gender or age, men, women and children alike being subject to the most merciless kind of mutilation. Clement V, catching wind of this, despatched a messenger in September of that year with orders to halt the carnage at once under pain of excommunication, whereupon the duke opted out, leaving the Florentines to make good by way of a fresh round of taxation at home and, in the *contado*, a fresh call up to the army with penalties awaiting those who failed to present themselves within twenty days. Thus the agony of it all persisted until well into the following year when another cardinal legate arrived in Florence, this time

Cardinal Napoleone degli Orsini, with a fresh injunction to treat with Pistoia in the hope of its surrender. And this, indeed, was what happened, the Pistoians giving way on 10 April only to witness as a reward the pulling down of their walls and the putting in place of a power-sharing scheme between Florence and Lucca as the victors in all this (the Florentines, it was agreed, would provide the *podestà* and the Lucchesi the *capitano*). With this, it only remained for Florence to put down whatever remained of White Guelph and Ghibelline resistance in the Mugello and the Apennines and the job was done.[21]

No less violent, however, and thus no less transparent to the times, was the demise of Corso Donati as the embodiment both of the psychology and of the psychopathology of the communal era, of its twofold brilliance and brutality. Corso, then, ever anxious on his own behalf, was notably restive in these early years of the new century in respect of his power, prestige and presence in the city, of his reaping his reward as man of the moment. With his standing in Florence much enhanced by his marriage to the daughter of Uguccione della Faggiuola as prominent among the Tuscan Ghibellines, and—more to the point—sensitive to the fact that this might be his last throw of the dice, he set about campaigning for a watering down of the Ordinances going back to Giano della Bella's time but more recently strengthened by Cardinal Napoleone as part of his remit as peacemaker. In this, though, he overplayed his hand, for what with his high-risk marriage alliance (for the said Uguccione was in the event busy amassing an expeditionary force against Florence) and the general unrest he had caused at home, he was arraigned and declared a traitor to the republic, whereupon he barricaded himself in his houses in anticipation of Uguccione's imminent arrival. Once more, then, the city descended into chaos, bodies everywhere and buildings ablaze. But for Corso, still worse was to come, for Uguccione, under the impression that he (Corso) had fallen and been injured, had turned tail, whereupon Corso, abandoned now by the greater part of his supporters (one of whom, a member of the Adimari family, had had his hand cut off by way of a warning to his clan generally), made good his escape. Captured, however, in October 1308 by a band of Catalan soldiers who, having been bribed by him not to do so nonetheless deemed it worth their while taking him back to Florence, he threw himself from

---

21   Compagni, more than ordinarily eloquent in respect of the savagery of it all, at 3.14–15: 'Molta migliore condizione ebbe Soddoma e Gomorra, e l'altre terre, che profondarono in un punto e morirono gli uomini, che non ebbono i Pistolesi morendo in così aspre pene. Quanto gli assalì l'ira d'Iddio! Quanti e quali peccati poteano avere a così repente giudicio?' (Sodom and Gomorrah and every other city overwhelmed in an instant with the citizenry slain fared better than the Pistoians dying as they did amid such suffering. How did the wrath of God assail them! What sins, and how many could they have committed to merit such sudden judgement? [3.14]). Giancarlo Savino, *Lo strazio di Pistoia: L'assedio del 1305–1306* (Pistoia: [unspecified], 1989); Giampaolo Francesconi, '11 aprile 1306: Pistoia apre le porte a Firenze dopo un anno di assedio; Cronaca, costruzione e trasmissione di un evento', *RMR* 8 (2007), http://www.retimedievali.it.

his horse, whereupon one of his captors ran him through and left him for dead. In the event a number of brothers from San Salvi, coming across him, conveyed him to a monastery, where some said that he repented in extremis of his sins, others, however, that he remained obdurate to the end. Fashioned afresh or not, however, he was, it seems, disinterred some two or three years later with a view to a more honourable despatch closer to home.[22]

It takes a leap of imagination to recover and to appreciate the mood generated by the removal of the papacy to Avignon under Clement V and the implications of this for the shape and substance of European politics generally and of Italian and Tuscan politics in particular, for over and beyond the humiliation of it all there was uncertainty now as to the pope's actually making any difference any more either in or beyond the peninsula.[23] It was in these circumstances, then, that, sensitive to his status as captive to a nothing if not ambitious French monarch and to all this meant by way of a fundamental reconfiguration of power in Europe, Clement committed himself to the imperial idea, to the election of an imperial candidate, and thus of an imperial power, standing over against the House of Anjou and ushering in a new age of papal-imperial cooperation. Both politically and in principle the idea was a radiant one, for not only would it

---

22 Nicely equilibrated in respect of the bête noire of White Guelphism, Compagni 3.21: 'La gente cominciò a riposarsi, e molto si parlò della sua mala morte in varii modi, secondo l'amicizia e inimicizia: ma parlando il vero, la sua vita fu pericolosa, e la morte reprensibile. Fu cavaliere di grande animo e nome, gentile di sangue e di costumi, di corpo bellissimo fino alla sua vecchieza, di bella forma con dilicate fattezze, di pelo bianco; piacevole, savio e ornato parlatore, e a gran cose sempre attendea; pratico e dimestico di gran signori e di nobili uomini, e di grande amistà, e famoso per tutta Italia. Nimico fu de' popoli e de' popolani, amato da' masnadieri, pieno di maliziosi pensieri, reo e astuto' (People eventually found some calm and spoke of his grievous death in various ways according to their disposition—friendly or hostile—towards him. But truth to tell, his life was as turbulent as his death was reprehensible. He was a knight of great ambition and renown, an aristocrat by birth and behaviour and of very great personal beauty even into his old age. He had a fine figure, delicate features and a fair complexion. He was pleasing, clever and an accomplished speaker, forever busying himself about great matters, familiar and indeed intimate with the lords and noblemen of the land, in possession of powerful friends and renowned throughout all Italy. He was the enemy of democracy and of the *popolani*, but beloved by his retainers. Full of wicked designs, he was unprincipled and astute). Villani 8.96. In Dante, and on the lips of his brother Forese, *Purgatorio* 24.82–87: ' "Or va", diss' el, "che quei che più n'ha colpa, / vegg' ïo a coda d'una bestia tratto / inver' la valle ove mai non si scolpa. / La bestia ad ogne passo va più ratto, / crescendo sempre, fin ch'ella il percuote, / e lascia il corpo vilmente disfatto" ' ('Now rest assured', said he, 'that the one most to blame for it I see dragged at the tail of a beast towards the valley where there is no absolution. With each step that same beast goes ever faster and faster till it dashes him down, leaving his body vilely disfigured').

23 Guillaume Mollat, *The Popes at Avignon, 1305–1378* (London: T. Nelson, 1963); Yves Renouard, *The Avignon Papacy, 1305–1403* (London: Faber, 1970); Thomas Renna, *Conflict between the Papacy and the Holy Roman Empire during the Early Avignon Era* (Lewiston, NY: Edwin Mellen Press, 2013); Joelle Rollo-Koster, *Avignon and Its Papacy, 1309–1417: Popes, Institutions and Society* (Lanham, MD: Rowman and Littlefield, 2015). For Clement V in particular, Georges Lizerand, *Clément V et Philippe IV le Bel* (Paris: Hachette, 1910); Sophia Menache, *Clement V* (Cambridge: Cambridge University Press, 1998); Claude Mossé, *Clément V: Premier pape d'Avignon, 1265–1314* (Paris: Stock, 1998).

remedy a now manifestly unsatisfactory situation on the ground, but at an at once deeper and more sublime level of consciousness it would revitalize the old Gelasian ideal, a dual order of government with each party to it living out its own proper reasons and responsibilities. Such, at any rate, combining as it did an element both of piety and of practicality, was the vision fermenting in the mind of a Dino Compagni, a Giovanni Villani and a Dante. Feelings at home, however, and especially in Tuscany, were mixed; for if, say, Pisa was more than ever eager in its espousal of the project, putting up in advance sixty thousand golden florins with more to come upon delivery, Florence, already perturbed by the appearance in the city of an imperial envoy charged with bringing her round, was in two minds, her reluctance manifesting itself by way both of a refusal to send a goodwill delegation to Lausanne as a stopping-off point for the emperor-elect on his way to Italy and of the setting up of a Tuscan and Lombard league designed to frustrate the whole thing. Nothing deterred, however, Henry of Luxembourg, having been elected to the imperial throne in November 1308, crowned at Aix-la-Chapelle in January 1309 and blessed by the pope later that same year, crossed into Italy by way of Mont Cenis towards the end of September 1310, staying first in Asti and then in Milan, where on 6 January the following year he assumed the iron crown of Lombardy.[24] The occasion was nothing if not fulsome, Henry's mission, he said, being one of peace and plenty, an exercise in shared sovereignty and universal concord. Straightaway, however, the implausibility of it all—a matter of both the underfunded and the underequipped character of the whole enterprise, but, more than this, of a transalpine prince hopelessly inexperienced when it came to the niceties of Italian political consciousness—was discernible, a constantly shifting pattern of allegiance in the peninsula serving to destabilize the imperial project before it had hardly begun. But for all his innocence and naïveté, Henry's difficulties were real enough, for as always there was Florence with her commitment to seeing off the imperial initiative by every conceivable means—by strengthening her defences, by promoting and financing the same strategy in the Guelph league generally, and even by putting up roadblocks across the Apennine passes. Exemplary in this sense was her high-handed treatment of the imperial legates, or, more exactly, of the papal legates acting on behalf of the emperor, Bishop Nicholas of Butranto and Pandolfo Savelli. Having already been detained against their will in Bologna, their misery and sense of the futility of it all were doubled when, once in Florence, the Florentines, having yet again denounced in general council the German tyrant and everything he stood for, took

---

24   Compagni 3.23–36 on the election and descent of Henry VII of Luxembourg through to his coronation on 1 August 1312 at St John Lateran in Rome; Villani 9.7–53. William M. Bowsky, *Henry VII in Italy: The Conflict of Empire and City-State, 1310–1313* (Lincoln: University of Nebraska Press, 1960); Mauro Tosti-Croce (ed.), *Il viaggio di Enrico VII in Italia* (Città di Castello: Edimond, 1993).

it upon themselves to lay siege to them in their quarters and to strip them of everything save the clothes they stood up in, their humiliation being in this sense just about complete. Turning their backs, therefore, on this den of incivility, they made their way to Arezzo to curry support for the cause on pain of excommunication, the Florentines for their part, in a now well-nigh orgasmic fit of Guelph purism, tearing down any sign or symbol of the imperial idea in the city and inaugurating a purge of anyone in the least suspect when it came to straying from the party line.

Florence it was, then, that, if not quite then almost single-handedly saw off the imperial idea. Henry, exasperated by the intractability of the situation in Tuscany and—what is more to the point—frustrated by his lacking the wherewithal swiftly and efficiently to deal with it, decided for the moment to give Florence a miss and to set off instead for Rome and the imperial crown proper. With this, however, the situation only got worse, for a massive influx of Angevin troops under King Robert's brother John had taken over and occupied whole swathes of the city from the old forum right across to Trastevere. Unable, therefore, to get across to St Peter's for his coronation, Henry had to settle instead for John Lateran and for the good offices, not of the pope as master of ceremonies, but of a stand-in delegation of three cardinal legates, whereupon, more than ever anxious to make his mark as master of the civilized world, he took himself and his troops first of all to Tivoli and then on to Perugia and Cortona, making a point as he did so of laying waste just about everything in his way. True, there was a glimmer of light when a Florentine deputation turned up in Cortona with a view to treating with the emperor, but again nothing came of it, Henry being more than ever determined now to deal with Florence in the way she deserved. Further conquests were made at Montevarchi and Figline, but as he approached Florence the situation deteriorated, for not only had the city made an excellent job of barring the Appenine crossing but at home had mustered some four thousand horse plus infantry, Henry, then, having perforce to content himself with a programme of mere local despoliation. But there was, in fact, more to it than that, for it had been evident for some time not only that Henry's health was not all it might be, but that his troops, many of them far from home, were not entirely with him in spirit, a state of affairs not lost on the Florentines, whose gates remained brazenly unlocked by night and whose city remained open for business as usual. Neither, however, was it lost on the emperor, who, weighing up the pros and cons, decided to step back from the brink, withdrawing instead over the Arno, lingering for a while in one of the Bardi castles and retiring for two months to San Casciano. Scuffles, at times not insignificant, marked the rhythm of his now desultory campaign and of his surviving long enough to reach Pisa in March 1313, where once again he fulminated against all those daring to slow his imperial progress. True, everything was eventually battle-ready, but Henry in the meantime—down, it was rumoured, to poisoning—was growing weaker by the day and died on 14 June that year in Buonconvento, his final and official resting place being the Camposanto in Pisa.[25]

25 Villani 9.52 on the emperor's passing. Compagni 3.42 in anticipation (he hoped) of his ultimate triumph and on the well-nigh apocalyptic intensity of it all: 'O iniqui cittadini, che tutto il mondo avete corrotto e viziato di mali costumi e falsi guadagni! Voi siete quelli che nel mondo avete messo ogni malo uso. Ora vi si ricomincia il mondo a rivolgere addosso; lo Imperadore con le sue forze vi farà prendere e rubare per mare e per terra' (Oh unrighteous citizens, you who have corrupted and defiled all the world with your evil customs and false gains! You it is who have breathed every evil into the world. But the world now turns against you, and the emperor ever mighty will by land and sea lay hold of you and strip you of your every ill-gotten gain). Achille Tartaro, 'Delusione e moralismo del Compagni', in *Il manifesto di Guittone e altri studi fra Due e Quattrocento* (Rome: Bulzoni, 1974), 103–9. For Compagni as at once chronicler and commentator, Louis Green, 'Historical Interpretation in Fourteenth-Century Florentine Chronicles', *JHI* 28.2 (1967), 161–78; Andrea Zorzi, 'Rileggendo la *Cronica* di Dino Compagni: Comuni, signori, tiranni', in *Roma e il Papato nel Medioevo: Studi in onore di Massimo Miglio* (Rome: Edizioni di Storia e Letteratura, 2012), 37–48. On Dante and the chroniclers, Giovanni Aquilecchia, 'Dante and the Florentine Chroniclers', *Bulletin of the John Rylands Library* 48 (1965), 30–55; Charles T. Davis, 'Il Buon Tempo Antico', in *Dante's Italy and Other Essays* (Philadelphia: University of Pennsylavia Press, 1984), 71–93.

CHAPTER 2

Biographical Considerations

Susceptibility and the Significant Encounter (1265–93)

If, then, by the time of Henry 's death in 1313 we are beginning to witness the emergence of new forces both political and cultural in kind—in the Church of a new species of conciliarism, in the city the consolidation of signorial government, on the battlefield the spectacular rise of the *condottiere* or soldier of fortune, and in the *studium* that of humanism and of nominalism as paradigms of philological and philosophical consciousness—then by the same token, and certainly as far as Tuscany in general and Florence in particular were concerned, things went on much as before. Pisa, as a focus of Ghibelline and latterly of imperial enthusiasm, was quickly taken by Uguccione della Faggiuola, who, with the help of what was left of the imperial forces south of the Alps, inaugurated a reign of terror engulfing both Lucca and, with her catastrophic defeat by those same forces at Montecatini on 29 August 1315, Florence too.[1] The carnage was complete, fatalities including not only King Robert's brother and nephew but two thousand Florentine cavalry and infantry, among them some of the finest of the city's youth and promise for the future. And underlying, quickening and sustaining it all? Nothing but the long since familiar rhythm of civic strife, Guelph once more being divided against Guelph, the rift now being between Pino and Simone della Tosa as disposed respectively for and against Robert as the guarantor of Guelph rights, privileges and immunities. Simone's was in the event the stronger party, he himself consolidating his strength by way of a *bargello* or chief of police of unspeakable cruelty, a certain Lando d'Agobbio, who made it his business to mutilate and flay alive anyone in the least suspected of Ghibellinism or of Ghibelline sympathy. In the event he was seen off by Robert's vicar, the Count of Battifolle, who oversaw the institution of a fresh priorate, a revised tax regime and a timely restoration of the walls, the whole thing, however, epitomizing Florence's presence to itself by way only of a

---

1 Villani 9.70–72. Franco Cardini, *Uguccione della Faggiuola nelle vicende storiche fra Due e Trecento. Atti del convegno, Casteldelci, 6–7 settembre 1986* (San Leo: Società di studi storici per il Montefeltro, 1995); Eugenio Lenzi, *Uguccione della Faggiuola e Castruccio nel Trecento toscano* (Lucca: M. Paccini Fazzi, 2001). For the *bargello* or chief of police episode, Simone della Tosa and Battifolle, Villani 9.76 and 79.

will in one and the same moment both to affirmation and to annihilation, to the unspeakable splendour of the one and to the unspeakable sadness of the other.

It was, then, into this situation—into a Florence forever in the grip of its own tragic contradiction—that Dante, with his heightened sense of what it means to be both tragically and triumphantly, was born somewhere between 14 May and 13 June 1265.[2] Now when it comes to the reconstruction of his childhood and, more especially, of his childhood temperament we are in the realm of inference, but for all that there is enough in the text to be going on with. If only, then, by way of inference the text bears witness to a more than ordinarily acute responsiveness to the world roundabout, to the sights and sounds both of the city and of the countryside in all the busyness of the one and the bucolic calm of the other, to a prodigious memory for both people and places, and, above all, to a delight in mythmaking, in fashioning a narrative line transparent to the leading idea—a condition of everything coming next by way both of the youthful *Vita nova* and of the as yet far distant *Commedia* as each in this sense exemplary. Now maturity brings with it, to be sure, a setting aside of the childish as a way of seeing and understanding, but not of the childlike, the childlike—meaning by this, precisely, the indispensability of the image to an act of spiritual intelligence—subsisting in Dante to the end.[3]

Dante, when it comes to his family history, has little to say, even the Cacciaguida episode of *Paradiso* 17 bearing less on the genealogical than on the need in Florence for a fresh prophetic intervention, on the notion of the *Commedia* as, whatever else it was intended to be, a moral and social irritant (the 'let them scratch where it itches' moment of line 129):

> indi rispuose: 'Coscïenza fusca
> o de la propria o de l'altrui vergogna

2 Angelo Solerti (ed.), *Le vite di Dante, Petrarca e Boccaccio scritte fino al secolo decimosesto* (Milan: Vallardi, 1904); Michele Barbi, *Vita di Dante* (Florence: Sansoni, 1965 [1933]); Giorgio Petrocchi, *Vita di Dante* (Bari: Laterza, 1983); Enrico Malato, *Dante* (Rome: Salerno, 1999); and, in English, Stephen Bemrose, *A New Life of Dante* (Exeter: Exeter University Press, 2000; rev. ed. 2014); Paget Jackson Toynbee, *Dante Alighieri: His Life and Works*, intro. Robert Hollander (New York: Dover Publications, 2005 [1910]); Zygmunt G. Barański and Lino Pertile (eds.), *Dante: Life, Works and Reception* (Cambridge: Cambridge University Press, 2015). Dante's earliest lives by, among others, Boccaccio and Leonardo Bruni are available in English in James Robinson Smith, *The Earliest Lives of Dante* (New York: Henry Holt, 1901) and in Philip Wicksteed (trans.), *The Early Lives of Dante* (London: Alexander Moring, 1904); rev. ed. entitled *Life of Dante: Giovanni Boccaccio* (London: Oneworld Classics, 2009). Barbi's *Vita di Dante* may be read in a translation by Paul Ruggiers, *Life of Dante* (Berkeley: University of California Press, 1954).

3 Thomas E. Mussio, 'Towards the Innocence of a Child? The Cluster of Child Similes in *Paradiso*', *DS* 130 (2012), 215–33; James F. McMenamin, 'The Poet's Inner Child: Early Childhood and Spiritual Growth in Dante's *Commedia*', *Italica* 93.2 (2016), 225–50. Also, Emilio Pasquini, 'Le icone parentali nella *Commedia*', *LC* 25 (1996), 39–50. For Villani on Dante's 'new and beautiful figures, analogies and poetry' (belle e nuove figure, comparazioni e poetrie) in the *Commedia*, 9.136.

pur sentirà la tua parola brusca.
Ma nondimen, rimossa ogne menzogna,
tutta tua visïon fa manifesta;
e lascia pur grattar dov' è la rogna.
Ché se la voce tua sarà molesta
nel primo gusto, vital nodrimento
lascerà poi, quando sarà digesta.'[4]

Of Cacciaguida himself, Dante's great-great-grandfather and, with his two
brothers Moronto and Eliseo, hailing possibly from the illustrious Elisei family
of Florence, we know little beyond what Dante tells us. Born around 1090, he was
knighted for his part in the second crusade by Conrad III of Hohenstaufen by
whom that crusade was led, but died in battle in about 1147. His wife, Alighiera
degli Alighieri, from the Po Valley and possibly Ferrara, was of noble extraction,
and by her he had two sons mentioned in a legal instrument dating from November 1189, namely Alighiero and Preitenitto, both of them, it seems, established in
Florence, in the parish of San Martino al Vescovo, by the 1180s. This same Alighiero, mentioned by Cacciaguida as busy serving his time among the proud in
purgatory,[5] married a sister of the "good Gualdrada" mentioned at one point in

---

4 *Paradiso* 17.124–32: 'then it [the light of Cacciaguida] replied: "A conscience dark either with its
own or another's shame will indeed feel your speech to be harsh. But nonetheless all falsehood set
aside; make manifest what you have seen; and let them scratch where it itches. For if at first taste your
voice be grievous, yet shall it leave thereafter vital nourishment when digested." ' For Villani on Dante's
occasional intemperance in the *Commedia*, 9.136: 'Bene si dilettò in quella Commedia di garrire e
sclamare a guisa di poeta, forse in parte più che non si convenia; ma forse il suo esilio gliele fece . . .
Questo Dante per lo suo savere fue alquanto presuntuoso e schifo e isdegnoso, e quasi a guisa di filosofo
mal grazioso non bene sapea conversare co' laici; ma per l'altre sue virtudi e scienza e valore di tanto
cittadino ne pare che si convenga di dargli perpetua memoria in questa nostra cronica, con tutto che
per le sue nobili opere lasciateci in iscritture facciamo di lui vero testimonio e onorabile fama a la nostra
cittade' (True, it was his delight in the *Comedy* to bewail and to denounce after the manner of poets,
and perhaps here and there as was more than fitting, but maybe his exile was the cause of this . . . This
Dante, because of his knowledge, was somewhat haughty, reserved and disdainful, and, after the fashion
of a philosopher, careless of the graces and not easy in his converse with laymen. But because of the
lofty virtues, of the knowledge and of the worth of so great a citizen, it seems fitting in this our chronicle
to confer lasting memory upon him, though the noble works left to us by him in writing are indeed his
true testimony and that whereby he is of honourable report to our city). Charles T. Davis, 'Il Buon
Tempo Antico (The Good Old Time)', in *Dante's Italy and Other Essays*, 71–93; Claire E. Honess,
'Feminine Virtues and Florentine Vices: Citizenship and Morality in *Paradiso* XV–XVII', in *Dante and
Governance*, ed. John R. Woodhouse (Oxford: Clarendon, 1997), 102–20. More generally on Cacciaguida and the Cacciaguida cantos, André Pézard, 'Les trois langues de Cacciaguida', *REI* 13 (1967),
217–38; Lodovico Cardellino, *Canti del cavalier Cacciaguida (Par. XIV.67–XVIII.69)* (Bornato in Fran-
ciacorta: Sardini, 2015).
5 *Paradiso* 15.91–96: 'Poscia mi disse: "Quel da cui si dice / tua cognazione e che cent' anni e piùe /
girato ha 'l monte in la prima cornice, / mio figlio fu e tuo bisavol fue: / ben si convien che la lunga
fatica / tu li raccorci con l'opere tue"' (And then he said to me: 'He from whom your house has its
name, and who for a hundred years and more has been circling on the first terrace of the mountain,

the *Inferno*, the sister in question being one of the daughters of Messer Bellincione Berti dei Ravegnani, and from this marriage there were two sons, Bello and another Bellincione, the family line thus dividing into two at this point, with, if anything, Bello's rather than Bellincione's side of the family maintaining more successfully the pride and the appurtenances of the aristocratic way. Not that Bellincione, Dante's grandfather, was not well connected in the city, for caught up as he was in the Guelph-Ghibelline troubles of the middle part of the century, he was twice exiled, first in 1248 (returning in 1251) and then again after Montaperti in 1260 (returning in 1264). But his way of life, that preeminently of a businessman, a purveyor of goods and a moneylender, was commercial rather than courtly, this, therefore, perpetuated as it was into the next generation by Dante's father, Alighiero, possibly constituting in Dante's eyes a distinct coming down in the world, an aspect of his ancestry to be glossed over in favour of something more glorious. It was, then, into these reduced circumstances that Dante himself was born under the sign of Gemini in 1265. His mother, Bella, possibly of the Abati family in Florence, was Alighiero's first wife, but with her death and his father's remarriage in 1270 or 1271 to Lapa di Chiarissimo Cialuffi he was presented with two half-siblings, Francesco, very definitely a friend in need to Dante over the years and still alive in the 1340s, and Gaetana or Tana, still alive in 1320.[6]

The course of Dante's earliest education and indeed of his education as a whole is similarly problematic. Proceeding, then, for the moment by way of the merely probable, we may say this, that Giovanni Villani, speaking admittedly of a period a little later than our own, estimates that there were something between eight and ten thousand children in Florence receiving elementary education, with up to a quarter of these enrolled in the abacus schools (numeracy for commerce being the main concern here) and five or six hundred or so going on to study logic and Latin as preliminary to a career in law, medicine or the Church.[7] Elementary education was largely in the hands of the *doctores puerorum* of whom, according to a document from 1277, one by the name of Romano was active in the area of San Martino. Before coming on, then, to selected readings or episodes from the

---

was my son and your great-grandfather; it is indeed most fitting, then, that his long labour be shortened by your good offices'). For the good Gualdrada (for it is her nephew, Guido Guerra, rather than she who lives on among the unnatural sinners), *Inferno* 16.34–39.

6 Renato Piattoli (ed.), *Codice diplomatico dantesco*, 2nd ed. (Florence: Gonnelli, 1950), with supplements in *SD* 30 (1951), 203–6 and *ASI* 127 (1969), 5–81. For Gaetana in particular, Giuseppe Indizio, 'Tana Alighieri sorella di Dante', *SD* 65 (2000), 169–76 and in *Problemi di biografia dantesca* (Ravenna: Longo, 2014), 51–56. Suggestive in respect of the misfortunes of the Alighieri family is the Belluzzo of the Forese tezone, an evidently impoverished uncle of Dante's on his father's side: 'Ma ben ti lecerà il lavorare, / se Dio ti salvi la Tana e 'l Francesco, / che col Belluzzo tu non stia in brigata' (But God keep Tana and Francesco for you, this alone seeing to it that you escape Belluzzo's company).

7 Villani 11.94. Charles T. Davis, 'Education in Dante's Florence', in *Dante's Italy and Other Essays*, 137–65.

classical *auctores*, Dante would probably have concentrated on the more elementary and accessible Latin of, for example, the *Disticha Catonis*, the *Liber Esopi* and the *Elegia* of Arrigo Settimello as a point of departure. But as time went on it was the personal encounter that, in a spirit as susceptible as it was sensitive, took over as decisive for the shaping of his personality. To the fore, then—though again the precise *when*, *where* and *how* of it is uncertain—was the figure of Brunetto Latini, notary, diplomat, philosopher, encyclopaedist, rhetorician, moralist, political theorist and, by dint of this and doubtless more besides, shaper and civilizer of the Florentine soul. But by the same token he was among the most vulnerable to civic reprisal, and following the triumph of the Ghibellines at Montaperti in 1260 he was forced into exile, in the course of which he composed the *Livres dou Tresor* confirming his status, if not as an original or speculative thinker, then certainly as an accomplished communicator, an able purveyor of ideas in the areas of natural and moral philosophy and of rhetoric. With the fall of the Hohenstaufen in 1266 he returned to Florence, where, having revised the *Tresor* and produced an Italian version of the text entitled the *Tesoro*, having fashioned a brief allegory along the same lines entitled the *Tesoretto* and a meditation after the manner of Cicero on the virtue of companionship entitled *Il Favolello*, and having completed a translation of the *De inventione*, he died in 1294. It was, then, in respect of what in Brunetto amounts to his particular species of pre- or protohumanism and of his engagement with the romance-vernacular tradition of verse making, not least in its Gallic aspect (it was probably by way of Brunetto that Dante came to the *Roman de la rose* as indispensable to any account of his own handling and resolution of the affective issue both in the *Vita nova* and in the as yet far-off *Commedia*), that Brunetto most clearly left his mark on Dante, the latter's acknowledgement of what he came to represent for him being for this reason worth reading in full:

> 'Se fosse tutto pieno il mio dimando',
> rispuos' io lui, 'voi non sareste ancora
> de l'umana natura posto in bando;
>   ché 'n la mente m'è fitta, e or m'accora,
> la cara e buona imagine paterna
> di voi quando nel mondo ad ora ad ora
>   m'insegnavate come l'uom s'etterna:
> e quant' io l'abbia in grado, mentr' io vivo
> convien che ne la mia lingua si scerna'.

> (*Inferno* 15.79–87)[8]

8 ' "Were my every wish to be fulfilled", I replied, "you would not yet be banished from human nature, for in my memory is fixed, and serves now merely to sadden my heart, the righteous and much

No less decisive a presence, however, to Dante in these early years was that of Guido Cavalcanti, for if with Brunetto Latini it was a matter of cultural and civic consciousness in the now properly refined substance of these things, with Cavalcanti it was a question of his coming home as a poet and philosopher of love in the high style of romance-vernacular lyricism. It was, in other words, by way of the depth and complexity of his relationship with Cavalcanti—of a relationship, that is to say, turning in one and the same moment about both sameness and otherness as conditions of the spirit—that Dante confronted and sought to resolve both the affective-philosophical and the literary-aesthetic aspects of his activity as a lyric poet in the Siculo-Tuscan and stilnovistic tradition of verse making. On the one hand, then, there is Cavalcanti the technician, militant in his commitment to the transparency of form in all its aspects to the movement of

cherished fatherly image I have of you as, moment by moment in the world above you taught me how man might live on forever, my gratitude being such that, for as long as I live, it will properly be upon my lips." ' Villani 8.10: 'Nel detto anno 1294 morì in Firenze uno valente cittadino il quale ebbe nome ser Brunetto Latini, il quale fu gran filosofo, e fue sommo maestro in rettorica, tanto in bene sapere dire come in bene dittare. E fu quegli che spuose la Rettorica di Tullio, e fece il buono e utile libro detto Tesoro, e il Tesoretto, e la Chiave del Tesoro, e più altri libri in filosofia, e de' vizi e di virtù, e fu dittatore del nostro comune. Fu mondano uomo, ma di lui avemo fatta menzione peroch'egli fue cominciatore e maestro in digrossare i Fiorentini, e farli scorti in bene parlare, e in sapere guidare e reggere la nostra repubblica secondo la politica' (In the said year 1294 there died in Florence a worthy citizen whose name was M. Brunetto Latini, who was a great philosopher, and was a perfect master in rhetoric, understanding both how to speak well and how to write well. And he it was who commented upon the rhetoric of Tully, and made the good and useful book called *The Treasure*, and *The Little Treasure* and *The Key to the Treasure*, together with many other books in philosophy and concerning vices and virtues. And he was too secretary of our commonwealth. He was a worldly man, but we have made mention of him because it was he who was the beginner and master in refining the Florentines and in teaching them how to speak well, and how to guide and rule our republic according to proper policy). Helene Wieruszowski, 'Brunetto Latini als Lehrer Dantis und der Florentiner (Mitteilungen aus Cod. II.VIII.36 der Florentiner National Bibliothek)', *Archivio italiano per la storia della pietà* 2 (1959), 179–98; Helene Wieruszowski, 'Rhetoric and the Classics in Italian Education', *Studia Gratiana* 11 (1967), 169–208 (and in *Politics and Culture in Medieval Spain and Italy* [Rome: Edizioni di Storia e Letteratura, 1971], 589–627); Quentin Skinner, *The Foundations of Modern Political Thought* (Cambridge: Cambridge University Press, 1978), 36–48; Julia Bolton Holloway, *Brunetto Latini: An Analytical Bibliography* (London: Grant and Cutler, 1986); John M. Najemy, 'Brunetto Latini's "Politica"', *DS* 112 (1994), 31–51; James T. Chiampi, 'Ser Brunetto, "scriba" and "litterato"', *RSI* 18.1 (2000), 1–25; Clément Godbarge, 'Brunetto Latini y la reconstrucción del "ethos" republicano', *FI* 5 (2005), 85–111. For Brunetto and Dante, Peter Armour, 'Dante's Brunetto: The Paternal Paterine', *ItSt* 38 (1983), 1–38; Peter Armour, 'Brunetto, the Stoic Pessimist', *DS* 112 (1994), 1–18; Charles T. Davis, 'Brunetto Latini and Dante', in *Dante's Italy and Other Essays*, 166–97 (originally in *SM* 8.1 [1967], 421–50); Julia Bolton Holloway, ' "Chancery" and "Comedy": Brunetto Latini and Dante', in *Lectura Dantis* 3 (1988), 73–94; Julia Bolton Holloway, *Twice-Told Tales: Brunetto Latini and Dante* (New York: Peter Lang, 1993); Richard Kay, 'The Sin(s) of Brunetto Latini', *DS* 112 (1994), 19–31; Peter Schwertsik, ' "Quel ver c'ha faccia di menzogna" (Dante, *Inf.* XVI, 124): Der Eingang eines moralphilosophischen Aphorismus aus Brunetto Latinis *Trésor* in Dantes Poetik der Allegorie', in *Allegorie und Wissensordnung: Volkssprachliche enzyklopädische Literatur des Trecento. Akten der DAAD-Fachtagung, München 10 Oktober bis 12 Oktober 2012*, ed. Florian Mehltretter (Munich: Herbert Hutz Verlag, 2014), 139–60; Johannes Bartuschat, 'La filosofia di Brunetto Latini e il *Convivio*', in *Il Convivio di Dante. Atti del Convegno di Zurigo (21–22 Maggio 2012)*, ed. Johannes Bartuschat and Andrea Aldo Robiglio (Ravenna: Longo Editore, 2015), 33–52.

thought and feeling whereby it is justified from out of the depths, from deep within the recesses of self—at which point Dante's acquiescence in the Cavalcantian initiative is complete. On the other hand there is Cavalcanti the philosopher, Cavalcanti as spokesman-in-chief for love as the way not of ulterior becoming on the plane of seeing, understanding and desiring but of moral and ontological undoing, as captivity to a dark and destructive passion of the sensitive soul—at which point Dante's, both in the *Vita nova* and in the *Commedia*, is in the nature of a systematic superseding of Cavalcantianism in this, its most distinctive and dramatic aspect. Companionship certainly, therefore, as the hallmark of one of the most creative literary encounters in European letters, but companionship of a certain kind, companionship as that whereby those party to it are each alike confirmed in the unique substance and complexion of their presence in the world.

After the death of Beatrice in June 1290, Dante turned by way of consolation—but also, he says, for the purposes of studying further in order that he might speak more fully of her as but a showing forth in time and space of all grace and goodness[9]—to philosophy and the philosophical schools in Florence: to Santa Croce as by the 1290s a *studium generale* or intermediate seat of Franciscan piety and preaching; to Santa Maria Novella as since 1281 a *studium theologiae* or likewise intermediate seat of Dominican learning; and, on the far side of the river, to Santo Spirito, already a *studium generale* by 1287 and fully functional as a centre of Augustinian spirituality. The key passage here, registering as it does both the as yet dreaming substance of the *Vita nova* and the excitement generated by a now fresh set of intellectual possibilities, runs as follows:

E però, principiando ancora da capo, dico che, come per me fu perduto lo primo diletto de la mia anima, de la quale fatta è menzione di sopra, io rimasi di tanta tristizia punto, che conforto non mi valeva alcuno. Tuttavia, dopo alquanto tempo, la mia mente, che si argomentava di sanare, provide, poi che né 'l mio né l'altrui consolare valea, ritornare al modo che alcuno sconsolato avea tenuto a consolarsi; e misimi a leggere quello non conosciuto da molti libro di Boezio, nel quale, cattivo e discacciato, consolato s'avea. E udendo ancora che Tullio scritto avea un altro libro nel quale, trattando de l'Amistade, avea toccate parole de la consolazione di Lelio,

---

9 *Vita nova* 42.1–2: 'Appresso questo sonetto, apparve a me una mirabile visione, ne la quale io vidi cose che mi fecero proporre di non dire più di questa benedetta infino a tanto che io potesse più degnamente trattare di lei. E di venire a ciò io studio quanto posso, sì com'ella sae veracemente. Sì che, se piacere sarà di colui a cui tutte le cose vivono, che la mia vita duri per alquanti anni, io spero di dicer di lei quello che mai non fue detto d'alcuna' (After this sonnet a miraculous vision appeared to me in which I beheld things which made me determined never to speak of that blessed lady until I were able to do so more worthily. To which end I study as hard as I can as she herself knows full well. If, therefore, it pleases him through whom all things have life that my own life may continue for a few years, I hope to write of her in a way never before said of any woman).

uomo eccellentissimo, ne la morte di Scipione amico suo, misimi a leggere
quello. E avvegna che duro mi fosse ne la prima entrare ne la loro sentenza,
finalmente v'entrai tanto entro, quanto l'arte di gramatica ch'io avea e un
poco di mio ingegno potea fare; per lo quale ingegno molte cose, quasi
come sognando, già vedea, sì come ne la Vita Nuova si può vedere. E sì
come essere suole che l'uomo va cercando argento e fuori de la 'ntenzione
truova oro, lo quale occulta cagione presenta, non forse sanza divino im-
perio; io, che cercava di consolarme, trovai non solamente a le mie lagrime
rimedio, ma vocabuli d'autori e di scienze e di libri: li quali considerando,
giudicava bene che la filosofia, che era donna di questi autori, di queste
scienze e di questi libri, fosse somma cosa. E imaginava lei fatta come una
donna gentile, e non la poteva immaginare in atto alcuno, se non misericor-
dioso; per che sì volentieri lo senso di vero la mirava, che appena lo potea
volgere da quella. E da questo imaginare cominciai ad andare là dov'ella si
dimostrava veracemente, cioè ne le scuole de li religiosi e a le disputazioni
de li filosofanti; sì che in picciol tempo, forse di trenta mesi, cominciai tanto
a sentire de la sua dolcezza, che lo suo amore cacciava e distruggeva ogni
altro pensiero.

(*Convivio* 2.12.1–7)[10]

At Santa Croce he would have encountered both the main strands of Franciscan sensibility in his time, conventual and spiritual, the former represented principally by the Bonaventure of the *Hexaemeron*, the *Breviloquium* and the *Itinerar-*

10 'And so, beginning again from the first stanza, I say that when I lost my soul's first delight—she
of whom I made mention above—I was pierced by such sorrow that no comfort availed me. Yet, after
a while, bent as I was upon recovery but aware that neither self-consolation nor the consolation of
others was of any avail, I purposed in my mind to go about it the way espoused by another anguished
spirit similarly in search of comfort, whereupon I began to read an in truth little known book by Boethius in which, captive and in exile as he was, he himself had found strength. And hearing further of
another book—this time one of Cicero's—in the course of which, discussing the notion of friendship,
he had spoken of the consolation experienced by Laelius (a man of outstanding character) upon the
death of his friend Scipio, I set about reading that too. True, I found them in the first instance hard
going, but as far as my limited Latin and a certain application of my native intelligence allowed—the
very intelligence that had alerted me to much besides, albeit as in a dream, in my *New Life*—I managed
to grasp their meaning. And just as it often happens that, perhaps as result of divine willing or some
other hidden reason, a man looking for silver discovers despite himself gold, so I, who was seeking to
console myself, not only found a remedy for my tears but wise utterance in the form of such authors,
books and disciplines of the mind as I came across. Thinking over this, I was quickly of the opinion
that philosophy, as the mistress of these things, was of the very highest, and, casting her in the image
of a noble lady, I could not conceive of her by way of anything other than her compassionate bearing.
My mind, then, delighting in the truth, thus made itself over to her, and indeed so much so that I could
scarce avert my gaze. I therefore began to frequent the places where she was most truly to be found,
namely the schools of the religious and places of philosophical disputation, such that in a relatively
short space of time—thirty months or so maybe—I so sensed her sweetness that every other thought
was driven out and destroyed by my love for her.'

ium mentis in Deum, and the latter by Pietro di Giovanni Olivi and Ubertino da Casale, both for a time resident in Florence during his formative years.[11] His precise relationship with Bonaventure, along with Thomas prominent in the *Paradiso*, is not easy to determine, Bonaventure's commitment to the notion (*a*) of seminal reasons (*rationes seminales*) or of the inchoate presence of form to matter, (*b*) of the body and soul as each alike constituting a substance in its own right, and (*c*) of understanding as a matter of prior intellection having no counterpart in Dante, for whom form, both in its first instantiation and thereafter, is bestowed on matter from beyond, for whom the rational soul is the intelligible and operative principle of being in its totality, and for whom understanding is a matter of abstraction by way of the active intellect. In all these senses, Dante is closer to the Angelic than to the Seraphic Doctor, whose instinct in the areas both of ontology and of epistemology retains much of the Augustinian and the Neoplatonist. But in respect of the substance and psychology of the soul's journey into God as the beginning and end of every significant determination of the spirit, he and Bonaventure are all of a mind, the soul's journey into God being for each alike a matter of desiring, of the kind of love-intensity whereby the individual moves ever more deeply into communion with the first and final principle of all loving. Quite as important, however, for the mark it leaves on Dante's spirituality particularly in its reformist aspect is the more properly spiritual strain of Franciscanism, a strain present to him by way not only of the figure of Francis himself as conveyed by the hagiographic tradition culminating in the *Legenda maior* and *minor* of Bonaventure, but, again, of its living representatives Pietro di Giovanni Olivi and

---

11 For Santa Croce, Raoul Manselli, 'Firenze nel Trecento: Santa Croce e la cultura francescana', *Clio: Rivista trimestrale di studi storici* 9 (1973), 325–42 (and in *Scritti sul Medioevo* [Rome: Bulzoni], 351–70); Giuseppina Brunetti and Sonia Gentili, 'Una biblioteca nella Firenze di Dante: I manoscritti di Santa Croce', in Emilio Russo (ed.), *Testimoni del vero: Su alcuni libri in biblioteche d'autore* (Rome: Bulzani, 2000), 21–55. For Dante and the Franciscans: Agnello Baldi et al., *Dante e il francescanesimo: Lectura Dantis Metelliana* (Cava dei Tirreni: Avagliano, 1987); Nick Havely, *Dante and the Franciscans: Poverty and the Papacy in the 'Commedia'* (Cambridge: Cambridge University Press, 2004); Giuseppe Mazzotta, 'Dante's Franciscans', in Santa Casciani (ed.), *Dante and the Franciscans* (Leiden: Brill, 2006, 171–98); George Holmes, 'Dante and the Franciscans', in Paolo Acquaviva and Jennifer Petrie (eds.), *Dante and the Church: Literary and Historical Essays* (Dublin: Four Courts Press, 2007), 25–38. For Dante and Bonaventure, Ronald Herzman, 'Dante and Francis', *FS* 42 (1982), 96–114; Edward Hagman, 'Dante's Vision of God: The End of the *Itinerarium Mentis*', *DS* 106 (1988), 1–20. For Dante, Olivi and the spiritual Franciscans, Raoul Manselli, 'Dante e l'ecclesia spiritualis', in *Dante e Roma. Atti del Convegno di Studi, Roma, 8–10 aprile, 1965* (Florence: Le Monnier, 1965), 115–35; Raoul Manselli, 'Dante e gli spirituali francescani', *LC* 11 (1982), 47–61; David Burr and David Flood, 'Peter Olivi: On Poverty and Revenue', *FS* 40 (1980), 18–58 (with the text of the *Quaestio* at 34); V. Stanley Benfell, 'Dante, Peter John Olivi, and the Franciscan Apocalypse', in Santa Casciani (ed.), *Dante and the Franciscans* (Leiden: Brill, 2006, 9–50); Alberto Forni, 'Dialogo tra Dante e il suo maestro: La metamorfosi della *Lectura super Apocalipsim* di Pietro di Giovanni Olivi nella *Divina Commedia*', *BISIMAM* 108 (2006), 83–122; Davide Bolognesi, ' "Et miror si iam non est": L'*Arbor Vitae* di Ubertino Casale nella *Commedia*', *DS* 126 (2008), 57–88. More generally, David Burr, *The Spiritual Franciscans: From Protest to Persecution in the Century after Saint Francis* (Philadelphia: University of Pennsylvania Press, 2001).

Ubertino da Casale, the former notable especially for his sense of ecclesiastical wealth as the proper patrimony of the poor, and the latter for his vivid sense of Francis and Franciscanism as preparing the way for the final overthrow of the papal Antichrist. True, Ubertine as distinct from Olivian Franciscanism had about it, Dante came to believe, something of the extravagant and maybe even of the reckless,[12] but that notwithstanding their shared commitment to a fresh sense in the Church of its proper mission both nourished the restiveness of his own spirit in this respect and, in key passages, furnished the means of its articulation.

At Santa Maria Novella Dante would have encountered by way if not of their actual then at any rate of their virtual presence there, of their shaping and sub-stantiating Dominican consciousness in just about its every aspect, the figures of Albert the Great and Thomas Aquinas, these between them quickening his own meditation in the areas both of natural and of moral philosophy—Albert by way of the *De natura locorum*, the *De causis et proprietatibus elementorum*, the *De intellectu et intelligibili* and the *De meteoris*, and Thomas by way of the *Contra gentiles* and the *Commentary on the Ethics*.[13] But there is a difference, for while in the case

---

12 *Paradiso* 12.121–26 (upon the lips of Bonaventure): 'Ben dico, chi cercasse a foglio a foglio / nostro volume, ancor troveria carta / u' leggerebbe "I' mi son quel ch'i' soglio"; / ma non fia da Casal né d'Acquasparta, / là onde vegnon tali a la scrittura, / ch'uno la fugge e altro la coarta' (Truly I say that he who would search our volume leaf by leaf would still find one whereupon he might read 'I am as I always was'; but it will not be from Casale or from Acquasparta, where such come to the rule that one flees it and the other constrains it).

13 For Santa Maria Novella, Michèle M. Mulchahey, 'Education in Dante's Florence Revisited: Remigio de' Girolami and the Schools of Santa Maria Novella', in Ronald B. Begley and Joseph W. Koterski (eds.), *Medieval Education: Essays in Honor of Louis B. Pascoe S.J.* (New York: Fordham University Press, 2005), 143–81; Emilio Panella, O.P., 'Ne le scuole de li religiosi e a la disputazioni de li filosofanti (Dante Alighieri): Lectio, disputatio, predicatio', in *Dal convento alla città: Filosofia e teologia in Francesco da Prato O.P. Atti del Convegno internazionale di Storia della Filosofia Medievale, Prato, 18–19 maggio 2007*, ed. Fabrizio Amerini (Florence: Zella, 2008, 115–31). With reference to Dante's 'library', Charles T. Davis, 'The Florentine "Studia" and Dante's "Library"', in Giuseppe Di Scipio and Aldo Scaglione (eds.), *The Divine Comedy and the Encyclopedia of Arts and Sciences. Acta of the International Dante Symposium, 13–16 November 1983* (Amsterdam: Benjamins, 1988), 339–66; Luciano Gargan, 'Per la biblioteca di Dante', *GSLI* 186 (2009), 161–93; Raffaella Zanni, 'Una ricognizione per le biblioteca di Dante in margine ad alcuni contributi recenti', *CT* 17.2 (2014), 161–204. On Dante and Christian Peripateticism in general, Bruno Nardi, *Nel mondo di Dante* (Rome: Edizioni di Storia e Letteratura, 1944); Bruno Nardi, *Dal Convivio alla Commedia: Sei saggi danteschi* (Rome: Istituto Italiano per il Medio Evo, 1960); Bruno Nardi, *Studi di filosofia medievale* (Rome: Edizioni di Storia e Letteratura, 1960); Bruno Nardi, *Saggi di filosofia dantesca*, 2nd ed. (Florence: La Nuova Italia, 1967); Bruno Nardi, *Dante e la cultura medievale*, ed. Paolo Mazzantini (Rome: Laterza, 1983 [1942]); Bruno Nardi, '*Lecturae*' *e altro saggi danteschi*, ed. Rudy Abardo (Florence: Le Lettere, 1990); Bruno Nardi, *Saggi e note di critica dantesca* (Spoleto: Centro italiano di studi sull'alto medioevo, 2013; facsimile of the 1966 ed.); Étienne Gilson, *Dante and Philosophy*, trans. D. Moore (New York: Harper and Row, 1963; *Dante et la philosophie* [Paris: Vrin, 1939]). On Dante and Albert the Great (cited by Dante in the *Convivio* at 2.13.21, 3.5.12, 3.7.3 and 4.23.13), Cesare Vasoli, 'Dante, Alberto Magno e la scienza dei peripatetici', in Patrick Boyde and Vittorio Russo (eds.), *Dante e la scienza. Atti del Convegno Internazionale di Studi, Ravenna 28–30 maggio 1993* (Ravenna: Longo, 1995), 55–70 and 'Fonti albertiane nel Convivio di Dante', in J.F.M.

of Albert it is a question of *indebtedness* and of *discovery*, of his suggesting ways of seeing and setting up issues in the areas especially of cosmology, psychology and epistemology, in that of Thomas it is one of *emancipation* and *discipline*, of freeing Dante for the development and expression of his own ideas. This situation is everywhere discernible in the text, the Thomist as often as not helping to shape and to substantiate the Dantean utterance from out of the depths, from out of a long since affectionate companionship. Take, for example, these lines from the central cantos of the *Purgatorio* relative to the ideal triumph of free will over determinism as the way of properly human being and of properly human happiness. True, the stars have a part to play in the shaping of personality and preference but never in such a way as to abolish accountability as the hallmark of specifically human being:

> 'Lo mondo è ben così tutto diserto
> d'ogne virtute, come tu mi sone,
> e di malizia gravido e coverto;
>   ma priego che m'addite la cagione,
> sì ch'i' la veggia e ch'i' la mostri altrui;
> ché nel cielo uno, e un qua giù la pone'.
>   Alto sospir, che duolo strinse in 'uhi!',
> mise fuor prima; e poi cominciò: 'Frate,
> lo mondo è cieco, e tu vien ben da lui.
>   Voi che vivete ogne cagion recate
> pur suso al cielo, pur come se tutto
> movesse seco di necessitate.
>   Se così fosse, in voi fora distrutto
> libero arbitrio, e non fora giustizia

Hoenene and A. De Libera, eds., *Albertus Magnus und der Albertismus: Deutsche philosophische kultur des Mittelalters* (Leiden: Brill, 1995), 33–49; Gianfranco Fioravanti, 'Dante e Alberto Magno', in *Il pensiero filosofico e teologico di Dante Alighieri* (Milan: V&P Università, 2001), 93–102; Andreas Kablitz, 'Alberto è di Cologna': *Albertus ist es, aus Köln; Dantes 'Göttliche Komödie'und die Scholastik* (Cologne: Fritz-Thyssen-Stiftung, 2002). On Dante and Aquinas (cited by Dante in the *Convivio* at 2.14.14, 4.8.1, 15.12 and 30.3, and in the *Monarchia* at 2.4.1), Philip H. Wicksteed, *Dante and Aquinas* (London: Dutton, 1913), with a facsimile reprint (Honolulu: University Press of the Pacific, 2002); Kenelm Foster, O.P., including 'The Tact of St Thomas', in *God's Tree and Other Matters* (London: Blackfriars, 1957), 141–49; Kenelm Foster, O.P., 'St Thomas and Dante', *New Blackfriars* 55 (1974), 148–55 (reprinted in *The Two Dantes and Other Studies* [London: Darton, Longmann and Todd, 1977], 56–65); Kenelm Foster, O.P., 'Tommaso d'Aquino', in the *ED*, 6 vols. (Rome: Istituto dell'Enciclopedia Italiana, 1970–78), 273–94; Giovanni Fallani, 'Dante e S. Tommaso', in *L'esperienza teologica di Dante* (Lecce: Milella, 1976), 205–38; Antonio C. Mastrobuono, *Dante's Journey of Sanctification* (Washington, DC: Regnery Gateway, 1990); Simon Gilson, 'Dante and Christian Aristotelianism', in Claire E. Honess and Matthew Treherne (eds.), *Reviewing Dante's Theology*, vol. 1 (Bern: Peter Lang, 2013), 65–109; Christoper J. Ryan, *Dante and Aquinas: A Study of Nature and Grace in the 'Comedy'* (London: Ubiquity Press [UCL Arts and Humanities Publications], 2013).

per ben letizia, e per male aver lutto.
　　Lo cielo i vostri movimenti inizia;
non dico tutti, ma, posto ch'i' 'l dica,
lume v'è dato a bene e a malizia,
　　e libero voler; che, se fatica
ne le prime battaglie col ciel dura,
poi vince tutto, se ben si notrica.
　　A maggior forza e a miglior natura
liberi soggiacete; e quella cria
la mente in voi, che 'l ciel non ha in sua cura.
　　Però, se 'l mondo presente disvia,
in voi è la cagione, in voi sì cheggia'.

(*Purgatorio* 16.58–83)[14]

—a passage testifying not, certainly, to anything approaching discipleship (this, emphatically, being nowhere the case in Dante) but rather to the status of the *Contra gentiles* in particular as a cherished text and companion; so, for example, Thomas's 'frustra etiam adhiberentur poenae et praemia bonis aut malis, ex quo non est in nobis haec vel illa eligere' for Dante's 'non fora giustizia / per ben letizia, e per male aver lutto'; or Thomas's 'licet corpora caelestia non sint directe causa electionum nostrarum quasi directe in voluntates nostras imprimentia' for Dante's 'Lo cielo i vostri movimenti inizia; / non dico tutti . . .'; or Thomas's 'cum homo per rationem possit eis resistere vel obedire' for Dante's 'lume v'è dato a bene e a malizia, / libero voler':

> Frustra etiam darentur leges et praecepta vivendi, si homo suarum elec-
> tionum dominus non esset. Frustra etiam adhiberentur poenae et praemia
> bonis aut malis, ex quo non est in nobis haec vel illa eligere . . . Non igitur
> homo est sic secundum ordinem providentiae institutus ut electiones eius

14 ' "The world is indeed, as you are saying, utterly bereft of every virtue, pregnant and overspread with evil, but I beg you point out to me the cause, so that I myself might see it and show it unto others; for one man puts it down to the heavens and another to the world here below." Heaving first, then, a deep sigh, constrained by grief to an "Alas", he began: "Brother, the world—whence you yourself come—is blind. You and all the living alike refer every cause upward to the heavens alone, as if they of necessity moved all things with them. If this were so, free will would be destroyed in you, and there would be no justice in meting out happiness for good or grief for evil. The heavens indeed initiate your move-ments—I do not say all of them, but given for the moment that that is indeed what I am saying, a light is given you to discern good and evil, and free will, which, provided only that it weary not in its first battles with the heavens, will afterwards, provided only that it be well nourished, emerge triumphant. To a greater power and better nature are you subject, a power and a nature that fashions in you a mind not ruled by the stars. If, then, the present world is awry, in you is the cause and in you be it sought." '

ex motibus caelestium corporum proveniant... Sciendum tamen est quod, licet corpora caelestia non sint directe causa electionum nostrarum quasi directe in voluntates nostras imprimentia, indirecte tamen ex eis aliqua occasio nostris electionibus praestatur, secundum quod habent impressionem super corpora... Manifestum autem est, et experimento cognitum, quod tales occasiones, sive sint exteriores sive sint interiores, non sunt causa necessaria electionis: cum homo per rationem possit eis resistere vel obedire.

(Contra gentiles 3.85.12 and 21–22)[15]

And what applies in the central cantos of the *Purgatorio* applies throughout, Thomas, past master as he is in the art of argumentation, everywhere being on hand to comfort and encourage Dante in respect of the precise formula, of how the leading idea stands ideally to be expressed: so, for example, the 'oportet igitur ultimum finem universi esse bonum intellectus' of the *Contra gentiles* at 1.1.2 for the 'Noi siam venuti al loco ov' i' t'ho detto / che tu vedrai le genti dolorose / c'hanno perduto il ben de l'intelletto' of *Inferno* 3.16–18 at the heart of his ethic;[16] or the 'Et sic non sunt in nobis plures animae' of 2.58.10 for the 'questo è contra quello error che crede / ch'un'anima sovr' altra in noi s'accenda' of *Purgatorio* 4.5–6 at the heart of his anthropology;[17] or the 'si aliquis non videret solem et lunam et alia astra' of 2.92.9 for the 'amor che move il sole e l'altre stelle' of *Paradiso* 33.145 at the heart of his affective theology;[18] or the 'ut ex hoc ad divinum amorem inflammarentur' of 4.55.14 for the 'Questo decreto, frate, sta sepulto / a li occhi di ciascuno il cui ingegno / ne la fiamma d'amor non è adulto' of *Paradiso* 7.58–60

15 'There would, moreover, be no point promulgating rules and regulations were man not master of his own choices. Pointless, too, would be the meting out of punishment and reward for good or evil deeds had we in this or that particular case no choice one way or the other... It is, therefore, no part of the providential plan that the choices a man makes originate with the heavenly bodies and the movement thereof... We should, however, note that, though those bodies are not the immediate cause of our choices in the sense of impacting immediately upon our wills, they may from time to time occasion our choices by way of their influence upon the body... yet for all that, it is both self-evident and tried and tested in practice that, whatever their origin, internal or external, such things do not necessarily cause us to act in this way or that, since, reasonable as he is, man is able either to desist or to acquiesce.'

16 '[Now the end of each thing is that which is intended by its first author or mover. But the first author and mover of the universe is an intellect.] The ultimate end of the universe must therefore be the good of the intellect' (Thomas); 'We have come to the place where, as I have said to you, you will see those wretched souls who have lost the good of the intellect' (Dante).

17 'There is, therefore, in us no plurality of souls' (Thomas); 'this is contrary to the opinion of those who believe one soul to be kindled above another in us' (Dante).

18 '[In the same way a person who had not seen] the sun or the moon or the other stars [and had heard that they were incorruptible bodies might call them by the names of corruptible bodies]' (Thomas); '[but now, like a wheel evenly turned, my desire and my will were themselves turned by the] love which moves the sun and the other stars' (Dante).

at the heart of his soteriology.[19] Dante's, then, when it comes to Thomas and by extension to all his *auctores*, is a lively encounter, for it is a question here, not of his administering the archetypal or authoritative text but of his openness to it as the means of his own distinctive humanity. It is indeed, then, a question of companionship as but a breaking of bread along the way, of an *in-youing* and *in-meing* of the spirit in a moment of shared concern.[20]

Quite as important, however, as the luminaries of the Dominican way for the shaping of Dante's philosophical temperament in its immediately post-Beatrician phase were their local representatives, the many teachers and preachers at Santa Maria Novella he would have heard by way of their sermons and disputations— men such as Riccoldus of Montecroce, Nicholas Brunacci of Perugia, Conrad of Pistoia, Michael of Florence, John of Spoleto and Francis of Perugia, with, to the fore among them, the prolific Remigio de' Girolami, lector at Santa Maria Novella from (on and off) 1273 to 1319.[21] Not so much a speculative or systematic spirit as a mediator of Parisian scholasticism, Remigio was in every sense an impressive

19 '[It was not right for God to take flesh incapable of suffering and death ... and first because it was necessary for men to know the beneficence of the Incarnation] that they too might be inflamed by divine love' (Thomas); 'this decree, my brother, lies hidden from the eyes of those whose spirit is less than adult in the flame of love' (Dante).

20 *Paradiso* 9.80–81: 'Già non attendere' io tua dimanda, / s'io m'intuassi, come tu t'inmii' (Were I in you as you are in me, I would not be waiting upon your reply).

21 Charles T. Davis, 'Remigio de' Girolami O.P. (d. 1319) Lector of S. Maria Novella in Florence', in *Le Scuole degli Ordini Mendicanti (secoli XIII–XIV): XVII Convegno del Centro di Studi sulla Spiritualità Medievale, Todi, 11–14 ottobre 1976* (Todi: Accademia Tudertina, 1978), 281–304; Emilio Panella, O.P., *Per lo studio di fra Remigio dei Girolami (†1319): 'Contra falsos ecclesiae professores' cc. 5–37* (Pistoia: Tipografia Pistoiese, 1979; special volume of the *MD*, new series, 10); Marian Michèle Mulchahey, 'Education in Dante's Florence Revisited: Remigio de' Girolami and the Schools of Santa Maria Novella', in *Medieval Education: Essays in Honor of Louis B. Pascoe S.J.*, ed. Ronald B. Begley and Joseph W. Koterski (New York: Fordham University Press, 2005), 143–81 (and more generally, Marian Michèle Mulchahey, *'First the Bow Is Bent in Study...': Dominican Education before 1350* (Toronto: Pontifical Institute of Medieval Studies, 1998); Anton Gavric, *Une métaphysique à l'école de Thomas d'Aquin: Le 'De modis rerum' of Rémi de Florence* (Fribourg: Academic Press, 2006). More especially on the political aspects of Remigio's teaching and preaching, Lorenzo Minio Paluello, 'Remigio Girolami's *De bono communi*', *ItSt* 11 (1956), 56–71; Maria Consiglia De Matteis, *La teologia politica comunale di Remigio de' Girolami* (Bologna: Pàtron, 1977); Charles T. Davis, 'An Early Florentine Political Theorist: Fra' Remigio de' Girolami', in *Dante's Italy* (Philadelphia: University of Pennsylvania Press, 1984), 198–223 (1960); Charles T. Davis, 'Remigio de' Girolami and Dante: A Comparison of Their Conceptions of Peace', in *Dante: The Critical Complex*, vol. 5, ed. Richard Lansing (New York: Routledge, 2003), 243–74; Matthew S. Kempshall, *The Common Good in Late Medieval Political Thought* (New York: Oxford University Press, 1999). For Riccoldus of Montecroce (absent from Florence, however, from 1288 to ca. 1301 in the Orient), Jean Marie Mérigoux, 'L'ouvrage d'un frère prêcheur florentin en Orient à la fin du XIIIe siècle: Le *Contra legem Sarracenorum* de Riccoldo da Monte di Croce', *MD* 17 (1986), 1–142; Emilio Panella, O.P., 'Ricerche su Riccoldo da Montecroce', *Archivio fratrum praedicatorum* 58 (1988), 5–85; Thomas E. Burman, 'How an Italian Friar Read His Arabic Qur'an', *DS* 125 (2007), 93–109; Rita George-Tvrtkovic, *A Christian Pilgrim in Medieval Iraq: Riccoldo da Montecroce's Encounter with Islam* (Turnhout: Brepols, 2012). For the other names mentioned here (assistant lectors assigned to Santa Maria Novella before Dante's exile in 1302), Charles T. Davis, 'Education in Dante's Florence', in *Dante's Italy and Other Essays*, 156–57.

figure, a friar wedded to the notion of theology as but the most sublime of the human sciences and yet open to every kind of cultural encounter from Aristotle, Cicero, Ovid, Seneca and Livy among the ancients to Ambrose, Augustine, the Areopagite and Bernard (not to mention Avicenna and Averroes) among the moderns. But that, where Remigio is concerned, is not all, for his was a pursuit of the philosophical and theological enterprise within the context of a Florence forever on the brink of catastrophe, notions of the common good, therefore, and of the ways and means of peace being constantly to the fore in his mind. True, Dante's, when it came to it, was a political solution quite other than Remigio's, for where Remigio was ever inclined to proceed by way of the commune as at once a condition and a coefficient of man's proper happiness as man, Dante, by contrast, opts (a) for a species of political theology involving a twofold order of papal and imperial jurisdiction fashioned from beforehand in the divine mind (the *Monarchia*), and (b) for a drastic reconfiguration of self in the recesses of self as the basis of all moral and political renewal (the *Commedia*). But for all his theologization and internalization of the issue, Dante could not but acquiesce in the basic project, in what amounts in Remigio to an ever anxious interrogation of the substance and psychology of civic existence with a view to resolving its otherwise impossible tension, its tendency—certainly as far as Florence was concerned—both to doing and to undoing as a basic habit of mind.

Prominent as a third seat of learning in Florence was the Augustinian school of Santo Spirito, the rise and consolidation of Augustinian houses both in and beyond Italy being in part a reaction against Aristotle and Aristotelianism as a now powerful presence in philosophy and theology. Dante's own Augustinianism is a complicated affair, since for all his absence as an interlocutor in the *Commedia*, indeed for all the much attenuated nature of his presence in the text generally, Augustine is everywhere discernible as, along with Thomas, Dante's other main companion along the way; so, for example (and taking first the *Inferno*), on the inexplicability of it all, the 'Quid enim est quod volo dicere, domine, nisi quia nescio, unde venerim huc, in istam, dico vitam mortalem, an mortalem vitalem?' of *Confessions* 1 for the 'Io non so ben ridir com' i' v'intrai' of *Inferno* 1;[22] or, on the slumberousness of it all, the 'Ita sarcina saeculi, velut somno assolet, dulciter premebar; et cogitationes, quibus meditabar in te, similes erant conatibus expergisci volentium, qui tamen superati soporis altitudine remerguntur' of *Confessions* 8 for the 'tant' era pien di sonno a quel punto' again of *Inferno* 1;[23] or, on the spirit as beset by the savage forces of annihilation, the 'Et aliud est de silvestri cacumine

22 *Confessions* 1.6.7: 'For what would I say, O Lord my God, but that I know not whence I came into this—how shall I call it?—dying life or living death?'; for *Inferno* 1.10: 'I cannot say how I came to be there.'

23 *Confessions* 8.5.12: 'Thus with the baggage of this present world was I held down pleasantly, as in sleep: and the thoughts wherein I meditated on thee were like the efforts of such as would awake,

videre patriam pacis et iter ad eam non invenire et frustra conari per invia circum obsidentibus et insidiantibus fugitivis desertoribus cum principe suo leone et dracone' of *Confessions* 7 for the 'Ed ecco . . . una lonza leggiera e presta molto . . . la vista m'apparve d'un leone . . . Ed una lupa, che di tutte brame / sembiava carca ne la sua magrezza' of the same canto;[24] or, on willing and unwilling as a fundamental state of mind, the 'ego eram, qui volebam, ego, qui nolebam; ego eram. Nec plene volebam nec plene nolebam. Ideo mecum contendebam et dissipabar a me ipso' of *Confessions* 8 for the 'E qual è quei che disvuol ciò che volle' of *Inferno* 2.[25] And what applies to the *Inferno* also applies to the *Purgatorio* and the *Paradiso*; so, for example, on the tearfulness of it all, the 'ego sub quadam fici arbore stravi me nescio quomodo, et dimisi habenas lacrimis, et proruperunt flumina oculorum meorum, acceptabile sacrificium tuum' of *Confessions* 8 for the 'sì scoppia' io sottesso grave carco, / fuori sgorgando lagrime e sospiri' of *Purgatorio* 31;[26] or, on divine pleasure as but the beginning and end of all spiritual tranquillity, the 'In bona voluntate tua pax nobis est' of *Confessions* 13 for the 'E 'n la sua volontade è nostra pace' of *Paradiso* 3.[27] And so it goes on, passage after passage from the *Commedia* recalling the Augustinian formula as registering with perfect precision the substance of fundamental journeying.[28] Again, the *what*, *when* and *how* of his

---

who yet overcome with a heavy drowsiness sinks back into the depths of slumber'; for *Inferno* 1.10–12: '[I cannot say how I came to be there] so full of sleep was I in the moment I forsook the true way.'

24 *Confessions* 7.21.27: 'It is one thing to descry the land of peace from a wooded hilltop, and, unable to find the way to it, struggle on through trackless wastes where traitors and runaways, constrained by their prince, who is lion and serpent in one, lie in wait to attack'; for *Inferno* 1.31–32, 45 and 48–49: 'And behold, at the foot of the slope a leopard light and swift as could be . . . the sight of a lion appearing there before me . . . and a wolf by the look of it lean with its every craving.' So also, in Augustine, the 'Continete vos ab immani feritate superbiae, ab inerti voluptate luxuriae, et a fallaci nomine scientiae, ut sint bestiae mansuetae et pecora edomita et innoxii serpentes. Motus enim animae sunt isti in allegoria, sed fastus elationis et delectatio libidinis et venenum curiositatis motus sunt animae mortuae' of 13.21.30 (Shield yourselves—that the wild beasts may be tamed, the cattle broken to the yoke, the serpents made harmless—from the unruliness of pride, the sluggish voluptuousness of luxury and the empty etiquette of understanding; for these—namely the haughtiness of pride, the delight of lust and the poison of curiosity—are the motions of our mind under an allegory, the motions of a dead soul).

25 *Confessions* 8.10.22: 'I myself it was, I myself, who willed and I myself who unwilled'; for *Inferno* 2.37–42: 'And as one who unwills what he himself willed'.

26 *Confessions* 8.12.28: 'I cast myself down, I know not how, under a certain fig tree, giving full vent to my tears, and the floods of my eyes gushed out, an acceptable sacrifice to you'; for *Purgatorio* 31.19–20: 'thus I broke down beneath that heavy burden, pouring forth tears and sighs'.

27 *Confessions* 13.9.10: 'In your good will is our peace'; for *Paradiso* 3.85: 'In his will is our peace.'

28 *Convivio* 1.2.14: 'L'altra è quando, per ragionare di sé, grandissima utilitade ne segue altrui per via di dottrina; e questa ragione mosse Agustino ne le sue Confessioni a parlare di sé, ché per lo processo de la sua vita, lo quale fu di [non] buono in buono, e di buono in migliore, e di migliore in ottimo, ne diede essemplo e dottrina, la quale per sì vero testimonio ricevere non si potea' (and this reason moved Augustine to speak of himself in his *Confessions*, because by the progress of his life, which proceeded from bad to good, good to better, and better to best, he gave us example and instruction beyond that ever furnished by albeit as trusty a witness). For texts other than the *Confessions*, *Monarchia* 3.4.7 (*De civitate Dei*); *Monarchia* 3.4.8 (*De doctrina christiana*); *Epistole* 13.80 (*De quantitate anime*), with further general (i.e. textually unspecified) references in the *Convivio* at 1.4.9, 4.9.8, 4.21.14, *Monarchia* 3.3.13, *Epistole* 11.16, *Paradiso* 10.120 and 32.35. Shirley J. Paolini, *Confessions of Sin and Love in the*

frequenting the Augustinian *studium* and of his having sight of the Augustinian text remains an imponderable, but for all that, and for all his newfound and ever more eager Peripateticism, Augustine subsists as a structure of consciousness, as the in-and-through-which of self-knowledge at its most profound and, often enough, its most painful.

Dante's, then, though scarcely systematic and complemented in the way we have seen by the dominant presence (Brunetto Latini and Guido Cavalcanti), was a formation at once Franciscan, Dominican and Augustinian in kind, each of these strands serving in its way to shape his undertaking as a poet, philosopher and ultimately prophet, as one called upon to speak to the generations. Meanwhile, events both on the domestic and on the civic front moved on. Domestically, it was a question of the death of Alighiero's first wife—Bella, Dante's mother—somewhere between 1270 and 1275 and of his remarriage to Lapa di Chiarissimo Cialuffi, followed in 1281 or 1282 by the demise of Alighiero himself, at which point responsibility for the estate would have fallen principally on Dante himself, though on a Dante assisted by his brother Francesco as again a true friend in need. And then, going by a document of 1329 (the original *instrumentum dotis* is not extant), there was his betrothal on 9 January 1277 to Gemma Donati of the powerful Black Guelph family in Florence, to whom he was married in 1285 or thereabouts and by whom he had three or possibly four children, Giovanni as his firstborn (though here we are dependent on a legal document of 1308), Pietro, Jacopo and Antonia. By the time of the *Vita nova*, then, in the early years of the 1290s Dante was already one of those 'many men and women in this language of ours burdened by domestic responsibility' for whom in the wake of his exile in 1302 he was to offer a philosophical banquet—the *Convivio*—designed

---

Middle Ages: Dante's 'Commedia' and St. Augustine's' 'Confessions' (Lanham, MD: University Press of America, 1982); John Freccero, 'Dante's Prologue Scene', in *Dante: The Poetics of Conversion*, ed. Rachel Jacoff (Cambridge, MA: Harvard University Press, 1986), 1–28; Caron Ann Cioffi, *St. Augustine Revisited: On 'Conversion' in the 'Commedia'*, Lectura Dantis Virginiana 5 (1989), 68–80 (and in *Dante: The Critical Complex*, vol. 4, ed. Richard Lansing, 372–84); John Took, 'Dante and the *Confessions* of Augustine', *AdI* 8 (1990), 360–82 (and in *Dante: The Critical Complex*, vol. 6, ed. Richard Lansing, 170–92); John Took, 'Dante, Augustine and the Drama of Salvation', in *Word and Drama in Dante: Essays on the 'Divina Commedia'*, ed. John C. Barnes and Jennifer Petrie (Dublin: Irish Academic Press, Foundation for Italian Studies, 1993), 73–92; Peter S. Hawkins, 'Divide and Conquer: Augustine in the *Divine Comedy*', *PMLAA* 106.3 (1991), 471–82 (subsequently in *The 'City of God': A Collection of Critical Essays*, ed. Dorothy F. Donnelly [New York: Peter Lang, 1995], 213–31; in *Dante's Testaments: Essays in Scriptural Imagination* [Stanford, CA: Stanford University Press, 1999], 197–212; and in *Dante: The Critical Complex*, vol. 4, ed. Richard Lansing, 343–54); Selene Sarteschi, 'Sant'Agostino in Dante e nell'età di Dante', in *Per la 'Commedia' e non per essa soltanto* (Rome: Bulzoni, 2002), 171–94; Robert Hollander, *Dante's Reluctant Allegiance to St. Augustine in the 'Commedia'*, L'Alighieri (RD) 32 (2008), 5–16; Simone Marchesi, *Dante and Augustine: Linguistics, Poetics, Hermeneutics* (Toronto: University of Toronto Press, 2011); Ovidio Capitani, 'Breve considerazioni sul significato della presenza di Agostino in Dante', in *Scritti di storia medievale offerti a Maria Consiglia De Matteis*, ed. Bernardo Pio (Spoleto: Centro italiano di studi sull'alto medioevo, 2011), 121–36; Elena Lombardi, 'Augustine and Dante', in *Reviewing Dante's Theology*, vol. 1, ed. Claire E. Honess and Matthew Treherne (Bern: Peter Lang, 2013), 175–208.

to encourage them in the ways and means of properly human happiness here and now.[29] Civically, by contrast, it was a question of his participation in the military, modest enough to begin with, but by the time of Campaldino sufficient to inspire in the still impressionable spirit something between fear and elation. First, then, there was the siege in the latter part of 1285 and into 1286 of Poggio Santa Cecilia, a small town encouraged by Arezzo to rebel against the Sienese, Florence for her part despatching a small contingent in late November for the purposes of maintaining the status quo. More impressive, however, were the twin actions of Caprona and Campaldino towards the end of that decade, Caprona turning on the recovery in July and August 1289 of a fortress seized by Guido da Montefeltro on behalf of Pisa from the Guelph exile judge Nino Visconti, and Campaldino on Arezzo's obstruction of the trade route between Florence and Rome. Both events left their mark on Dante, Caprona as furnishing some of the soldierly imagery of the *Inferno* and—going by a letter no longer extant but seen by Leonardo Bruni in the 1430s—Campaldino as the moment of Dante's coming of age as a citizen and all this entailed by way of fortune and misfortune, power and penury. On the one hand, then, and with reference first to Caprona and to the fear generated in the hearts and minds of those dependent on nothing more than a promise of safe passage (Dante's situation, precisely, in the *bolgia* of the barrators), we have these lines from canto 21 of the *Inferno*:

> e i diavoli si fecer tutti avanti,
> sì ch'io temetti ch'ei tenesser patto;
> così vid' ïo già temer li fanti
> ch'uscivan patteggiati di Caprona,
> veggendo sé tra nemici cotanti.
>
> (*Inferno* 21.92–96)[30]

while on the other, and bearing now on the chaos and cacophony of Campaldino (second only to the uncouth conduct of his guides in the same *bolgia*), we have these from canto 22:

---

29 *Convivio* 1.1.4 and 1.9.5: 'La prima è la cura familiare e civile, [la quale convenevolmente a sé tiene de li uomini lo maggior numero, sì che in ozio di speculazione esser non possono ... e questi nobili sono principi, baroni, cavalieri, e molt'altra nobile gente], non solamente maschi ma femmine, [che sono molti e molte in questa lingua, volgari, e non litterati]' (The first is domestic and civic responsibility [which quite properly engages the greater part of men such that they have no time for speculation ... these noble people consisting of princes, barons, knights and many other worthy folk], men and women alike, [schooled not in Latin but in the vernacular]).

30 'and the devils all pressed forward, and this such that I feared they might not keep their part of the bargain. Thus I once saw soldiers coming forth from Caprona under treaty terrified at seeing themselves among so many enemies.'

> Io vidi già cavalier muover campo,
> e cominciare stormo e far lor mostra,
> e talvolta partir per loro scampo;
>   corridor vidi per la terra vostra,
> o Aretini, e vidi gir gualdane,
> fedir torneamenti e correr giostra;
>   quando con trombe, e quando con campane,
> con tamburi e con cenni di castella,
> e con cose nostrali e con istrane;
>   né già con sì diversa cennamella
> cavalier vidi muover né pedoni,
> né nave a segno di terra o di stella.
>   Noi andavam con li diece demoni.
> Ahi fiera compagnia! ma ne la chiesa
> coi santi, ed in taverna coi ghiottoni.

(*Inferno* 22.1–15)[31]

—lines to which we may add these from the Bruni letter touching not merely on Dante's by this stage familiarity with arms but on his sense both of preparedness and of unpreparedness for everything coming next by way of civic responsibility:

> Tutti li mali e tutti l'inconvenienti miei dalli infausti comizi del mio priorato ebbero cagione e principio; del quale priorato, benché per prudenza io non fussi degno, nientedimeno per fede e per età non ne era indegno, perocché dieci anni erano già passati dopo la battaglia di Campaldino, nella quale la parte ghibellina fu quasi al tutto morta e disfatta, dove mi trovai non fanciullo nell'armi, dove ebbi temenza molta, e nella fine grandissima allegrezza, per li vari casi di quella battaglia.[32]

31 'Before now I have seen horsemen moving camp, beginning an assault, and making muster and, occasionally, making quick their escape. I have seen coursers over your land, you Aretines, I have seen raiding parties, I have seen tournaments and the din thereof, and I have seen the chasing of jousts, now with trumpets and now with bells, with drums and signalling from the castle walls, some familiar and some foreign—yet never have I seen horsemen or footmen set off to so strange a bugle nor ship by a sign from shore or sky. We were off with the ten demons—savage company indeed! But in church with the pious and in the pub with the pickled.'

32 'All my woes and misfortunes had their origin and commencement in my unlucky election to the priorate; of which priorate, although I was not worthy in respect of worldly wisdom, yet in respect of loyalty and of years I was not unworthy of it inasmuch as ten years had passed since the battle of Campaldino where the Ghibelline party was almost entirely broken and brought to an end; on which occasion I was present, no novice in arms, and was in great fear, and afterwards greatly elated by reason of the varying fortunes of that battle.' Giorgio Petrocchi, 'L'attività militare il soggiorno a Bologna', in

The years leading up to the *Vita nova*, then, as the first sustained instance of what in Dante amounts to a periodic reconstruction and organized expression of his own humanity, were years both of susceptibility and of involvement: of *susceptibility* in respect of the significant encounter and of all this meant by way of a quickening of his own spirit, and of *involvement* in respect of the rights and responsibilities of citizenship, be they civic or soldierly. True, for the moment all was well, friends such as Forese Donati, family such as Francesco, and patrons such as Brunetto Latini and Guido Cavalcanti enabling him for the time being to delight in his circumstances and indeed to fashion from them a nothing if not exquisite love-resolution all of his own (that, precisely, of the *Vita nova*). But with the shading off of youth and the sweet intuitionism thereof into manhood and maturity ('virile' is Dante's expression for this on the threshold of the *Convivio*)[33] came a fresh set of challenges, challenges more properly social and political in kind, and to this extent bearing deep within them the possibility—admittedly the as yet distant possibility, but nonetheless the possibility—of personal catastrophe.

CARE, CONFLICT AND CATASTROPHE (1293–1302)

The year 1289, marking as it did the eclipse of Ghibelline fortunes on the killing fields of Campaldino, ushered in a fresh set of tensions in Florence, tension on the one hand between the *popolani* and the aristocracy, and, on the other, between the aristocracy and the pseudo-aristocracy, between such as the Donati as long since established in the city and the Cerchi as newly arrived, wealthier still and ostentatious with it. This, then, was the situation addressed by the Ordinances of Justice sanctioned in 1293 and designed not least to curb the excesses of upper-class wilfulness. Uncompromising in the first instance with respect to the participation of the nobility in government (a ban had been placed on the election of grandees to the priorate, and indeed on the members of any family having about it a wisp of aristocracy over the preceding twenty years), the rules were softened

---

Vita di Dante, 2nd ed. (Bari: Laterza, 1984), 21–33; Zygmunt G. Barański, '"E cominciare stormo": Notes on Dante's Sieges', in John J. Kinder and Diana Glenn (eds.), *Legato con amore: Essays in Honour of John Scott* (Florence: Olschki, 2013), 175–203.

33 *Convivio* 1.1.16: 'E se ne la presente opera, la quale è Convivio nominata e vo' che sia, più virilmente si trattasse che ne la Vita Nuova, non intendo però a quella in parte alcuna derogare, ma maggiormente giovare per questa quella; veggendo sì come ragionevolmente quella fervida e passionata, questa temperata e virile esser conviene' (And if in the present work—a work entitled by design *The Banquet*—the matter to hand is treated in a sturdier manner than the *New Life*, this in no way implies a wish on my part to detract from the latter. Rather, seeing that—quite understandably—the latter is by nature fervent and passionate and the former temperate and muscular, my aim here is to add yet further weight to it).

in 1295 thus making it possible for Dante as subsisting somewhere on the lower edge of high society to enrol as a guildsman and thus to qualify for office. At some point in the summer of that year, then, he enrolled on the basis of his interest in natural philosophy, and doubtless with the example of Brunetto Latini in mind, in the Guild of Apothecaries and Physicians, an extract of 1447 witnessing in the absence of the original document to his matriculation in 1297. By this time, however, he had already served as a member of the special council of the *capitano del popolo* looking into the question of elections to the priorate, a task laid upon him by the people of San Martino, or, more precisely, of the *sesto* to which San Martino belonged. More significantly—for it is at this point that we discern a tightening of allegiances on his part, a gradual succumbing to the forces of polarization and partisanship in the city—he was, from May until the end of September 1296, a member of the Council of One Hundred, in which capacity he spoke in favour of two hotly contested proposals, one having to do with the barring of Pistoian exiles both from the city and from the *contado*, and the other seeking to confer full powers on the *Gonfaloniere di giustizia* and the priors when it came to exacting retribution from the magnates for injuring or insulting a *popolano* in public office.[34] The 'tightening of allegiances' element in this way of putting it is important, for while the situation of the White Guelphs with whom he was associated was for the moment reasonably secure in Florence, positions were hardening, and this in such a way as, with time, to leave little room for manoeuvre.

With this, then, we come to the critical period of Dante's term of office as one of the city priors, 'critical' in that diminishing room for manoeuvre began now to give way to something closer to inevitability, to the prospect—plain in retrospect but doubtless present to him at the time as a matter of foreboding—of impending catastrophe. First, though, and if only for the record, there are two other items to mention, one on the domestic front relating to his financial circumstances following Alighiero's death, and one on the diplomatic front relating to Florence, San Gimignano and the captaincy of the Guelph league. As far, then, as the first of these is concerned, there are grounds for supposing that family finances in this period were straitened, Dante, with his half-brother Francesco, being involved in the repayment of loans contracted originally, it would seem, in the interests of basic liquidity. Thus on 11 April 1297 a receipt was issued by Andrea di Guido de' Ricci as a family creditor for the sum of 227 florins, while on 23 December in that same year Dante and Francesco raised a secured loan of 480 florins, guaranteed by Manetto Donati and Durante degli Abati, for the purposes possibly of paying

---

34 *Codice Diplomatico Dantesco*, ed. Renato Piattoli (Florence: Luigi Gonnelli, 1950), 62–64 (no. 56): 'In consilio centum virorum . . . Dante Alagherii consuluit secundum propositiones praedictas' (In the Council of One Hundred . . . Dante Alighieri spoke to the foregoing propositions'; document dated 5 June 1296).

off an earlier liability. Neither was that all, for on 14 March 1300 Dante undertook to make good a loan of 125 florins from his half-brother Francesco (together with another ninety the following June), with Francesco himself, in October 1299, redeeming a loan of 53 gold florins, debts bearing witness, if not to the insolvency, then at the very least to a tight family budget.[35] As far, by contrast, as the second of them is concerned, it is enough to note his role as emissary to the Sangimignesi in May 1300 as evidence of his by this time lively involvement in the diplomatic affairs of the city.[36] The point of the mission was to draw the people of San Gimignano into the affairs of the Guelph League by providing troops for it and by participating in the arrangements being made for the election of its captain, something they agreed to do not only nor perhaps even primarily on the basis of Dante's specially prepared peroration but under pressure from Rome and the papal curia. Down to Dante or not, however, the San Gimignano intervention was quickly followed by his election in June 1300 to the priorate for July and August of that year, an election serving to confirm him once and for all in a sense of the depth and intractability of the Guelph crisis, of a now dominant sense among the Blacks of White Guelphism as but a form of crypto-Ghibellinism. Nor was any of this helped by the ratification, very probably in Dante's time as prior, of a sentence passed in Florence, over against the wishes of the pope and despite his request for an annulment, upon three men accused and convicted of high treason (to wit, Noffo di Quintavalle, Simone Spini and Neri Cambio), Dante's,

35 For the Andrea di Guido de' Ricci episode, Michele Barbi, BSDI 8 (1892), 11. Leonardo Bruni, 'Della vita studi e costumi di Dante', in Le vite di Dante, ed. Giuseppe Lando Passerini (Florence: Sansoni, 1917), 10: 'Dante, innanzi la cacciata sua di Firenze, contuttoché di grandissima ricchezza non fusse, nientedimeno non fu povero, ma ebbe patrimonio mediocre, e sufficiente a vivere onoratamente' (Dante, until such time as he was expelled from Florence, though not overly wealthy, was by no means destitute, having as he did a patrimony modest enough but sufficient to live on with dignity).

36 Pietro Fraticelli, Storia della vita di Dante Alighieri (Florence: Barbèra, 1861), 138–39: '1299. Die viij maii. Convocato et adunato Consilio generali Communis et homini Sancti Geminiani, in palatio dictae Communis, ad sonum campanae, vocemque preconis, ut moris est, de mandato nobilis et potentis militis domini Mini de Tolomeis de Senis, honor. Potestatis Comm. et hom. terrae Sancti Geminiani praedictae ... proposuit et consilium postulavit per eum per nobilem virum Dantem de Alleghe-riis, ambaxiatorem Communis Florentiae, qui pro parte dicti Comm. in praesenti Consilio exposuit, et dixit quod ad praesens in certo loco parlamentum et ratiocinatio more solito per omnes Communi-tates Talliae Tusciie, et pro renovatione et confirmatione novi Capitanei fieri expedit propter quae ad expediendum praedicta convenit, quod Sindici et ambaxiatores solemnes praedictarum Communi-tatum simul conveniant se' (On 8 May 1299, with the general Council of the Commune and the people of San Gimignano duly convoked and assembled in the palace of the said Commune by—as was their wont—the sounding of a bell and the voice of a crier, at the bidding of the noble and most worthy knight Messer Mini de Tolomei of Siena [honourable podestà of the Commune and people of the aforesaid city of San Gimignano] ... proposed and sought the counsel of that noble man Dante Alighieri, ambassador of the Commune of Florence, who on behalf of that same Commune and in the presence of the Council explained how it was at this time fitting for all the cities of the Tuscan league to parley and reason one with another at some appointed place with a view to electing and confirming a new captain, and how, moreover, it was expedient that the syndics and ambassadors of the said cities should forgather one with another for the purposes of expediting this matter).

therefore, looking more and more like an attitude of defiance in Rome's regard. But however this may be, ideas were now quickly being overtaken by events, among them the aforesaid festival of the St John's incident on 23 June 1300 when a number of government notables on their way to church were set upon by a group of predominantly Black insurgents more than ordinarily intent on making trouble. Both personally and politically the outcome for Dante was devastating: personally, in that following on from the affray an equal number of Blacks and Whites were expelled from the city (the Blacks or Donateschi to Castel della Pieve and the Whites to Sarzana), with Cavalcanti—Dante's 'first friend' [37]—sickening while away and dying shortly after his return to Florence; and politically in that it was precisely at this point—sometime between 15 and 18 July of that year—that the pope's special emissary (Cardinal Matthew of Acquasparta) was subjected to an assassination attempt, whereupon, shaking off the dust of the city from his shoes, he anathematized it, administration and all, in the round.

Given what we have described as Dante's by this time lively involvement in the diplomatic affairs of the city, it may be worth pausing for a moment over the, in truth, unlikely character of it all; for Dante, solicitous as he was in respect both of the institutions and of the independence of the commune, was by temperament neither a man of the people nor a spokesman for the entrepreneurial way of life. On the contrary, his, typically, was if anything an attitude both of mistrust when it came to wealth as a principle of properly human happiness and of misgiving when it came to what he saw as the dilution of Florence's ancient Roman stock by the now mass movement of people in and out of the city; so, for example, as regards the first of these things, namely the fallacy of wealth and the accumulation thereof as a means of significant self-affirmation, we have these lines (69–73) from the post-exilic canzone *Doglia mi reca*:

> Corre l'avaro, ma più fugge pace:
> oh mente cieca, che non pò vedere

37 The 'primo amico' of *Vita nova* 25.10: 'E questo mio primo amico e io ne sapemo bene di quelli che così rìmano stoltamente' (Both my first friend and I are fully aware of those rhyming in this foolish manner), with, at 3.14: 'E questo fue quasi lo principio de l'amistà tra lui e me, quando elli seppe che io era quelli che li avea ciò mandato' (And this—when he discovered that it was I who had sent him ⌊this sonnet⌋—was the beginning of our mutual friendship). On Cavalcanti's exile, his sickening, and his presence in Florence as a philosopher and man of parts, Villani 8.42: 'E per levare ogni sospetto il popolo mandò i caporali dell'altra parte a' confini a Serrezzano … Ma questa parte vi stette meno a' confini, che furono revocati per lo 'nfermo luogo, e tornonne malato Guido Cavalcanti, onde morìo, e di lui fue grande dammaggio, perciò ch'era come filosofo, virtuoso uomo in più cose, se non ch'era troppo tenero e stizzoso' (And to still all anxiety the people sent the protagonists of the other party out of the city and placed them under bounds at Sarzana … though this party abode less time under bounds, forasmuch as they were recalled by reason of the insalubriousness of the place, Guido Cavalcanti in particular coming home sick and dying—a great loss, this, in that, albeit oversensitive and unpredictable, he was both a philosopher and a man of many parts).

lo suo folle volere
che 'l numero, ch'ognora a passar bada,
che 'nfinito vaneggia.[38]

with a parallel passage in the *Convivio* at 3.15.9:

e in questo errore cade l'avaro maladetto, e non s'accorge che desidera sé
sempre desiderare, andando dietro al numero impossibile a giungere[39]

while as touching on the second of them, namely the watering down of the Florentine by the Fiesolan, we have these (lines 61–66 and 73–78) from canto 15 of
the *Inferno* placed upon the lips of Brunetto Latini but transparent, doubtless, to
Dante's own sense of it:

Ma quello ingrato popolo maligno
che discese di Fiesole *ab* antico,
e tiene ancor del monte e del macigno,
    ti si farà, per tuo ben far, nimico;
ed è ragion, ché tra li lazzi sorbi
si disconvien fruttare al dolce fico.
        . . .
Faccian le bestie fiesolane strame
di lor medesme, e non tocchin la pianta,
s'alcuna surge ancora in lor letame,
    in cui riviva la sementa santa
di que' Roman che vi rimaser quando
fu fatto il nido di malizia tanta.[40]

with something similar in the Cacciaguida cantos of the *Paradiso*:

Oh fortunate! ciascuna era certa
de la sua sepultura, e ancor nulla

---

38 'The miser runs, only to be ever further from peace. O blind spirit, which for its insane desire
cannot see that the sum which every moment it strives to pass stretches on to infinity!'

39 'this being the error into which, not recognizing that striving after a number impossible to reach
he desires only to be forever desiring, the accursed miser falls'.

40 'But that thankless and malign people who came down of old from Fiesole, and still smack of
the mountain and the rock, will by reason of your good deeds make of themselves your enemy, and
with reason, for among the bitter sorbs it is not fitting that the sweet fig should fruit . . . Let the Fiesolan
beasts make fodder of themselves and touch not the plant (if any yet spring upon their dungheap) in
which survives the holy seed of those Romans left there when it became the nest of so much
wickedness.'

era per Francia nel letto diserta.

. . .

Ma la cittadinanza, ch'è or mista
di Campi, di Certaldo e di Fegghine,
pura vediesi ne l'ultimo artista.

. . .

Sempre la confusion de le persone
principio fu del mal de la cittade,
come del vostro il cibo che s'appone;
    e cieco toro più avaccio cade
che cieco agnello; e molte volte taglia
più e meglio una che le cinque spade.

(*Paradiso* 15.118–20, 16.49–51 and 16.67–72)[41]

In Dante's case, then, there can be no question of alignment in any simple sense of the term, of his delivering himself without ado to the cause, his, for all his commitment to the civic project ('would it not be worse for man', he has one of his interlocutors say in the *Paradiso*, 'were he not a citizen?'), being at the same time a steady misgiving with respect to just about every structure of bourgeois consciousness. This, then, is what it means to speak of the unlikely character of it all, of the coexistence in Dante both of insiderness and of outsiderness, both of identity and of isolation, as concomitant dispositions of the spirit.

However this may be, the situation of the White Guelphs in the final part of 1300 and into 1301—again doubtless aggravated in part by the properties of Dante's own temperament as a political player—was more than ever parlous. On 11 November 1300, a White delegation was despatched from Florence with a view to pacifying the pope in the wake of the Acquasparta episode, the pope, however, having none of it; for Boniface, looking to his various interests, had discerned another way forward, and by the end of the month had written to the French clergy inviting them to help finance Charles of Valois in his attempt to retake Sicily, Florence being a matter for resolution en route. Dante in the meantime was still busy about communal affairs, speaking in April of that year to further issues in the area of electoral policy as well as—a shade incongruously—being appointed on an unpaid basis to oversee a civil engineering project (work on the

41 'O favoured women! Each was sure of her burial place and was not yet deserted in her bed for France ... but the citizenry, which is now mixed with Campi, Certaldo and Figline, was there to behold in its purity down to the humblest artisan ... The confusion of peoples was ever the beginning of the city's ills, as food in excess is of the body's; for a blind bull falls more headlong than a blind lamb, and one sword often enough cuts more and better than five.'

Via di San Procolo).[42] But more decisive for the course of events generally were his interventions in council on 19 June and on 13, 20 and 28 September 1301, eloquence and a still further stiffening of the spirit combining now to seal his fate. On 19 June there were, in fact, two meetings of the Consiglio del Cento to consider a request from the pope by way of Cardinal Acquasparta relative to the possibility of his retaining a contingent of one hundred Florentine horse for the purposes of settling his dispute with Margherita Aldobrandeschi in the Maremma. In the event, the matter was carried by a margin of forty-nine to thirty-two votes, Dante himself, however, advising that in no way should the request be honoured.[43] Personally, then, as well as politically, the lines were drawn, Dante, for reasons doubtless as principled as they were pragmatic, setting his face resolutely against any obliging of the pope as but a renegade priest. But that was not all, for the September sessions also had their part to play in determining his destiny. This time he spoke on three occasions, twice (on the 13th and the 20th) in plenary sessions of the Consiglio del Cento and then again, in a more restricted session of the council, on the 28th. In the plenary sessions it was a question inter alia of a renewal and perpetuation of the Ordinances and of a request on the part of the Bolognese to transport grain from Pisa across Florentine territory, each of these things, but especially the former, having a political aspect. In the restricted session of 28 September there were eight motions on the agenda, the sixth of them bear-

42 *Codice Diplomatico Dantesco*, ed. Renato Piattoli (Florence: Luigi Gonnelli, 1950), 93–94 (no. 82): 'Dante Alagherii consuluit quod capitudines et sapientes cuiuslibet sextus nominent unum in dicto sextu' (Dante Alighieri advised that the captains and optimates of each *sesto* nominate one representative apiece; document dated 14 April 1301). For the Via di San Procolo project, designed to facilitate troop movement between the *contado* and the city in the interests of safety and security *intra urbem*, Guido Pampaloni (ed.), *Firenze al tempo di Dante: Documenti sull'urbanistica fiorentina* (Rome: Ministero dell'interno: Pubblicazioni degli Archivi di Stato, fonti e sussidi IV, 1973), 125 (citing the Archivio di Stato di Firenze, Diplomatico, 28 April 1301), and see too the *Codice Diplomatico Dantesco*, 87–92 (no. 80): 'quod via Sancti Procule, que protenditur versus Burgum de la Plagentina, que est multum utilis et necessaria hominibus et personis civitatis Florentie, maxime propter victualium copiam habendam et maxime eo quod populares comitatus absque strepitu et briga magnatum et potentum possunt secure venire per eandem ad dominos priores et vexilliferum iustitie cum expedit' (for the Via San Procolo, stretching out as it does to the Piagentina district of the city, is especially useful, indeed necessary, for the people and citizenry generally of Florence, above all in respect of the plentiful supply of foodstuff and of the ability of those serving on the city councils as and when to gain access to their lordships the priors of the city and to the vexillifer of justice without being noisily harassed by the rich and powerful).

43 *Codice Diplomatico Dantesco*, 94–95 (no. 83): 'Die xviiij mensis junii [1301]. In consilio ccntum virorum, generali, spetiali, et capitudinum xij maiorum Artium, proposuit d[ominus] capitaneus infrascripta, presentibus prioribus et vexillifero: primo, de servitio d[omino] pape faciendo de centum militibus, secundum formam literarum d[omini] Mathei cardinalis . . . Dante Alagherii consuluit, quod de servitio faciendo d[omino] pape nichil fiat' (19 June [1301]. In the Council of One Hundred, plenary and particular, and in the presence of the heads of the twelve major guilds, of the priors and of the standard-bearer, the captain raised the matter of the pope's request, as formally specified by his lordship Cardinal Matthew [of Acquasparta], for a contingent of one hundred infantrymen . . . Dante Alighieri for his part advising that by no means should the request be granted).

ing on an amnesty for one Neri Diodati whose father had served as a prior immediately before Dante and who had been condemned to death by Cante de' Gabrielli in his capacity as *podestà* in 1298 but who had fled the city. The motion was
carried and an amnesty granted, but Cante de' Gabrielli was not a man for sitting
lightly to reversals of this or any other kind, and upon his return to Florence on
9 November 1301 he had, therefore, a score to settle; for it was he who set his
signature to Dante's indictment after the Black coup d'état, with worse to come
should he not show up to give an account of himself.

Dante's part in what amounted to the frantic character of the Whites' appeal
to Rome in the period immediately preceding the coup is uncertain, the chroniclers and commentators being divided among themselves. Compagni's view of
the matter, shared by the author of the *Ottimo Commento* on the *Commedia* and
by Leonardo Bruni, was that Dante, along with two others (Maso Minerbetti and
Corazza da Signa), was part of a delegation to Rome hastily organized in response
to the now well-nigh impossible situation of the White Guelph administration in
Florence as about to be engulfed—annihilated would be nearer the mark—by
the combined forces of the Black Guelphs, of the Church and of the House of
Anjou as represented by Charles of Valois (already by this stage on Italian soil).
On this version of events, Dante, having been detained in Rome by the pope on
account of his being the most troublesome of the three, would not have been able
to return to Florence—if indeed he did return to Florence—until after the violent
events of early November and the official inauguration of a Black regime later that
month.[44] Either that or, to go by the version espoused by Giovanni Villani and
Boccaccio, Dante would have been part of an earlier delegation prompted by the
eve of St John debacle just about a year earlier, in November 1300, in which case,
having by then returned to Florence, he would have fled in anticipation of a reign
of terror. On the second version (given if not conceded that it is correct), he must
have fled by 27 January 1302, for it was on that date that, along with a number of
others, he was condemned in absentia by the said Cante de' Gabrielli for illicit
profiteering, extortion and fraudulence in public office. However that may be, he
was, along with his codefendants, fined five thousand florins, prohibited from
ever again holding public office in the city and banished from Florentine territory
for two years. If, moreover, he refused to appear in person within three days, his

44 Compagni 2.4 on the pope's high-handedness vis-à-vis the White Guelph embassy to Rome
and at any rate by the looks of it Dante's detention in the curia: 'Giunti li anbasciadori in Roma, il Papa
gli ebbe soli in camera, e disse loro in segreto: "Perché siete voi così ostinati? Umiliatevi a me: e io vi
dico in verità, che io non ho altra intenzione che di vostra pace. Tornate indietro due di voi; e abiano
la mia benedizione, se procurano che sia ubidita la mia volontà"' (When the ambassadors arrived in
Rome, the pope received them alone in his chamber and said to them secretly, 'Why this obstinacy in
my regard? Humble yourselves before me, and I tell you in all truth that my purpose is none other than
to promote peace among you. Let two of you return, and—provided only that they cause my will to
be obeyed—may they all have my blessing').

entire estate would be devastated with any remaining assets being taken into common ownership, a provision extended on 10 March to being burnt alive should he present himself in or around Florence, and, on 9 June, to confirm the expulsion of wives, sons and all descendants on the male side of the exiled population generally upon their reaching the age of fourteen. As for the Alighieri house, it was to be torn down 'funditus et radicatus', foundations and all.[45]

45 For the 27 January indictment, *Codice Diplomatico Dantesco*, ed. Renato Piattoli (Florence: Luigi Gonnelli, 1950), 103–7 (no. 90): 'In nomine Domini, amen. Hec sunt condempnationes sive condempnationum sententie facte, late et promulgate per nobilem et potentem militem d[ominum] Cantem de Gabriellibus de Eugubio, honorabilem potestatem civitatis Florentie, super infrascriptis excessibus et delictis contra infrascriptos homines et personas . . . d. Palmerium de Altovitis de sextu Burgi, Dante Alleghieri de sextu Sancti Petri Maioris, Lippum Becche de sextu Ultrarni, Orlanduccium Orlandi de sextu porte Domus, contra quos processum est per inquisitionem ex offitio nostro et curie nostre factam super eo et ex eo, quod ad aures nostras et curie nostre notitiam, fama publica referente, pervenit, quod predicti, dum ipsi vel aliquis eorum existentes essent in offitio prioratus vel non existentes vel ipso offitio prioratus deposito, temporibus in inquisitione contentis, commiserunt per se vel alium baractarias, lucra illicita, iniquas extorsiones in pecunia vel in rebus . . . Idcirco ipsos d. Palmerium, Dante, Orlanduccium et Lippum, et ipsorum quemlibet, ut sate messis iuxta qualitatem seminis fructum percipiant, et iuxta merita commissa per ipsos dignis meritorum retributionibus munerentur, propter ipsorum contumaciam habitos pro confessis, secundum formam iuris, statutorum comunis et populi civitatis Florentie, ordinamentorum iustitie, reformationum, et ex vigore nostri arbitrii, in libr. quinque milibus flor. par. pro quolibet . . . et quod restituant extorta inlicite probantibus illud legiptime; et quod, si non solverint condempnationem infra tertiam diem, a die sententie computandam, omnia bona talis non solventis publicentur, vastentur et destruantur, et vastata et destructa remaneant in comuni; et si solverint condempnationem predictam ipsi vel ipsorum aliquis, [talis solvens] nicchilominus stare debeat extra provinciam Tuscie ad confines duobus annis; et ut predictorum d. Palmerii, Dante, Lippi et Orlanduccii perpetua fiat memoria, eorum nomina scribantur in statutis populi; et tamquam falsarii et baracterii nullo tempore possint habere aliquod offitium vel benefitium pro comuni vel a comuni Florentie in civitate, comitatu vel districtu vel alibi, sive condempnationem solverint sive non; in hiis scriptis sententialiter condempnamus' (In the name of God, amen . . . Herewith the indictment and the official announcement thereof, fully set forth and promulgated by the noble and worthy knight, dominus Cante de' Gabrielli of Gubbio, the honourable *podestà* of the city of Florence, relative to the excesses and delicts set out in what follows and against the persons and individuals of whom hereafter we make mention . . . dominus Palmerius de Altovitis of the Borgo *sesto*, Dante Alighieri of *sesto* St Peter the Great, Lippus Becche of the Oltrarno *sesto*, Orlanduccius of *sesto* Porta Domus. Against the aforesaid proceeding have been inaugurated by our office and curia on the basis and in consequence of such public report as has reached our ears and authority to the effect that the aforesaid persons, either occupying or otherwise the office of prior (or else having thence stepped down), were guilty during the period in question, and either alone or in collusion with another, of fraudulence in public office, of illicit profiteering and of reprehensible extortion either in money or in chattels . . . Concerning, then, dominus Palmerius, Dante, Orlanduccius and Lippus and of any thereunto associated, in order that the harvest may be understood to be the proper fruit of the seed, and in order that they in respect of their deserts and continuing contumacy might properly be rewarded, then in accordance with the laws and statutes of the commune and the people of the city of Florence, of the ordinances of justice in their successive revision, and by our own will as duly empowered, upon each of them is laid a fine of five thousand florins . . . with the further provision that any illicit gains be restored to the rightful party, and that, should not the aforesaid imposition be redeemed within three days counting from its promulgation then every property pertaining to the malfeasant be confiscated, dismantled and laid waste, and, thus dismantled and destroyed, pertain even so to the Commune—the subject, thus absolved, nonetheless to reside for a period of two years beyond the province of Tuscany and on the far confines thereof. And in order that the aforesaid Palmerius, Dante, Lippus and Orlan-

Far-Wandering and the Agony of Exile (1302–21)

Exile, for Dante, meant fashioning afresh his presence in the world as a poet, pedagogue and ultimately prophet, a situation variously open to documentation from the text but nowhere more eloquently than in the 'Ahi, piaciuto fosse al dispensatore de l'universo' passage of *Convivio* 1.3.3–5 as turning upon the melancholy

---

duccius be of perpetual memory, their names are to be inscribed in the statutes of the people, and that, moreover, as falsifiers and barrators, they are never at any time to hold public office or to enjoy the benefits of citizenship either afforded by the city of Florence or exercised on her behalf, whether within or without or wheresoever, and this regardless of whether the terms of this indictment be observed or otherwise. This, herewith, is our sentence duly and formally pronounced). For the provision of 10 March, *Codice Diplomatico Dantesco*, 107–9 (no. 91): 'talis perveniens igne comburatur sic quod moriatur' (such as stray into these parts to suffer death at the stake), with, following the battle of Montecatini in August 1315 and Florence's humiliation at the hands of Uguccione della Faggiuola (*Codice*, 155–56, no. 115) the further threat of death by decapitation: 'Dantem Adhegherii et ff., contra quos omnes et singulos superius nominatos ... processimus per inquisitionem, quod ... tanquam ghibellinos et rebelles comunis et populi civitatis Florentie et status partis guelfe, spreverunt nostra banna et precepta ... etiam multa alia et diversa malleficia commiserunt et perpetraverunt contra bonum statum comunis Florentie et partis guelfe ... si quo tempore ipsi vel aliquis predictorum, ut dictum est, in nostram vel comunis Florentie fortiam devenerint ... ducantur ad locum iustitie, et ibi eisdem capud a spatulis amputetur ita quod penitus moriantur' (among others Dante Alighieri, against whom and all the aforementioned, both individually and in the round, we proceed by way of investigation, for ... as Ghibellines and rebels in respect of the commune and people of Florence and the Guelph confederation generally, they did pour scorn upon our ensign and upon our laws ... in addition to which they committed and perpetrated many other and various misdeeds against the commune of Florence and the Guelph alliance ... such that [as indeed has already been made plain], should, in this period, any of the aforesaid perchance stray into our city or territory, then let them be led to a place of justice there forthwith to die by way of a severing of their heads from their shoulders). Bernardino Barbadoro, 'La condanna di Dante e le fazioni politiche del suo tempo', *SD* 2 (1920), 5–74; Giovanni Cuboni, 'Le condanne di Dante', *Convivium* 11 (1939), 1–45; Maurizio Campanelli, 'Le sentenze contro i Bianchi fiorentini del 1302: Edizione critica', *BISIMAM* 108 (2006), 187–377 (with reference to Dante at 224–28 and 253–55); Emiliano Bertin, 'Briciole fiorentine di fortuna dantesca: II, Le condanne del 1302; Due attestazioni inedite (e una dimenticata)', *RSD* 9.1 (2009), 92–98; Peter Armour, 'Exile and Disgrace', in *Dante in Oxford*, ed. Martin McLaughlin et al. (Oxford: Legenda, 2011), 39–68; Giuliano Milani, 'Appunti per una riconsiderazione del bando di Dante', *BIRCSLFL* 8.2 (2011), 42–70; Giuliano Milani, 'An Ambiguous Sentence: Dante Confronting His Banishment', in *Images and Words in Exile: Avignon and Italy during the First Half of the 14th Century*, ed. Elisa Brilli et al. (Florence: Sismel Edizioni del Galluzzo, 2015), 139–51; Giuliano Milani, 'Esili difficili: I bandi politici dell'età di Dante', in *Dante e l'esilio*, ed. Johannes Bartuschat (Ravenna: Longo, 2015), 31–46. More generally on Italy and exile: Randolph Starn, *Contrary Commonwealth: The Theme of Exile in Medieval and Renaissance Italy* (Berkeley: University of California Press, 1982); George Ulysses (ed.), *L'exil et l'exclusion dans la culture italienne. Actes du colloque franco-italien; Centre Aixos de Recherches Italiennes, Aix-en-Provence 19–21 octobre 1989* (Aix-en-Provence: Publications de l'Université de Provence, 1991); Fabrizio Ricciardelli, 'Notes on the Causes and Consequences of Political Exclusion in Late Medieval Italy', *Italian History and Culture* 8 (2002), 35–50; Fabrizio Ricciardelli, 'Exile as Evidence of Civic Identity in Florence in the Time of Dante: Some Examples', *RMR* 5.1 (2004), 1–16 (online at http://www.rmojs.unina.it/index. php/rm) and *The Politics of Exclusion in Early Renaissance Florence* (Turnhout: Brepols, 2007). The *Libro del chiodo*, or register of official recrimination, running from 1302 to 1378, and confirming as far as Dante is concerned both the January and the March indictments of 1302, may be consulted in facsimile, ed. with apparatus by Francesca Klein (Florence: Polistampa, 2004).

of a now nomadic existence; in the 'Florentiam adeo diligamus' passage of *De vulgari eloquentia* 1.6.2–3 as registering the struggle to redefine the horizons of a now displaced spirit; in the canzone par excellence of exile, *Tre donne intorno al cor mi son venute*, as but an essay in the telescoping of private and of cosmic injustice; and in the Cacciaguida cantos of the *Paradiso* as testimony to Dante's settling at last upon his destiny as one called from beforehand to speak out to the generations. First, then, we have the *Convivio* passage with its sustained sense of Dante's status as but a wanderer on the face of the earth, a hapless victim of circumstance and present to those about him by way only of the ignominy of it all:

> Ahi, piaciuto fosse al dispensatore de l'universo che la cagione de la mia scusa mai non fosse stata! ché né altri contra me avria fallato, né io sofferto avria pena ingiustamente, pena, dico, d'essilio e di povertate. Poi che fu piacere de li cittadini de la bellissima e famosissima figlia di Roma, Fiorenza, di gittarmi fuori del suo dolce seno—nel quale nato e nutrito fui in fino al colmo de la vita mia, e nel quale, con buona pace di quella, desidero con tutto lo cuore di riposare l'animo stancato e terminare lo tempo che m'è dato—per le parti quasi tutte a le quali questa lingua si stende, peregrino, quasi mendicando, sono andato, mostrando contra mia voglia la piaga de la fortuna, che suole ingiustamente al piagato molte volte essere imputata. Veramente io sono stato legno sanza vela e sanza governo, portato a diversi porti e foci e liti dal vento secco che vapora la dolorosa povertade; e sono apparito a li occhi a molti che forseché per alcuna fama in altra forma m'aveano imaginato, nel conspetto de' quali non solamente mia persona invilio, ma di minor pregio si fece ogni opera, sì già fatta, come quella che fosse a fare.[46]

—lines to which we must add these from the more or less contemporary *De vulgari eloquentia* with their commitment to a now radical reperspectivization of self, spatial, to be sure, but spiritual too:

46 'Ah, would to God as the dispenser of all things that I had no cause for such apology, others not having sinned against me and I myself not having suffered the unjust punishment of exile and penury! But since it pleased the citizens of that most beautiful city and famous daughter of Rome, Florence, to cast me from her sweet bosom—the city wherein I was born and nurtured through to maturity, and where, with her goodwill, I yearn with all my heart to rest my weary mind and live out the time vouchsafed me—I have wandered much like a beggar through just about every place our language is spoken, displaying willy-nilly the wounds inflicted upon me by fate whereby those afflicted are often unreasonably held accountable. In truth, I have been a ship without sail or rudder, borne to various harbours, havens and shores by the dry wind of grievous poverty, and have been exposed to the gaze of many who, having perchance heard tell of me in this way or that, imagined me as other than I am, such that not only was I personally scorned, but all my works—those complete as well as those yet to come— held in low esteem.' Johannes Bartuschat, ' "Poi che fu piacere delli cittadini della bellissima e famosissima figlia di Roma, Fiorenza, di gittarmi fuori del suo dolce seno": Intorno alla rappresentazione dell'esilio nel *Convivio*', *LC* 44 (2015), 9–29.

Nam quicunque tam obscene rationis est ut locum sue nationis delitiosis-
simum credat esse sub sole, hic etiam pre cunctis proprium vulgare licetur,
idest maternam locutionem, et per consequens credit ipsum fuisse illud
quod fuit Ade. Nos autem, cui mundus est patria velut piscibus equor, quanquam Sarnum biberimus ante dentes et Florentiam adeo diligamus ut, quia
dileximus, exilium patiamur iniuste, rationi magis quam sensui spatulas
nostri iudicii podiamus. Et quamvis ad voluptatem nostram sive nostre sensualitatis quietem in terris amenior locus quam Florentia non existat, revolventes et poetarum et aliorum scriptorum volumina quibus mundus universaliter et membratim describitur, ratiocinantesque in nobis situationes
varias mundi locorum et eorum habitudinem ad utrunque polum et circulum equatorem, multas esse perpendimus firmiterque censemus et magis
nobiles et magis delitiosas et regiones et urbes quam Tusciam et Florentiam, unde sumus oriundus et civis, et plerasque nationes et gentes delectabiliori atque utiliori sermone uti quam Latinos.[47]

Then, and more than ever eloquent in registering the near-impossible complexity of the poet's state of mind as but one now far from home, comes the
canzone *Tre donne intorno al cor mi son venute*, a meditation, precisely, upon the
to-and-fro conflict of defiance and despair and of resolution and repentance as
the truth of his now tortured existence:

> E io, che ascolto nel parlar divino
> consolarsi e dolersi
> così alti dispersi,
> l'essilio che m'è dato, onor mi tegno:
> ché, se giudizio o forza di destino
> vuol pur che il mondo versi
> i bianchi fiori in persi,
> cader co' buoni è pur di lode degno.
> E se non che de gli occhi miei 'l bel segno

47 'For whoever is so misguided as to think that the place of his birth is the most pleasing under
the sun may also believe that his own language or mother-tongue is preeminent among all others, even
going so far as to think that that same language was Adam's own. To me, however, though I drank from
the Arno before cutting my teeth, and love Florence so much that, because I loved her, I suffer exile
unjustly, the whole world, like the sea to the fish, is my country and I will weight the balance of my
judgement more with reason than with sentiment. And although speaking for myself and my own
pleasure and satisfaction there is no more agreeable place on earth than Florence, yet when I peruse
the poets and other writers by whom the world is described both in the round and in respect of its
various parts, and when I think over all the different places in the world and their disposition in respect
of the distant poles and of the circling equator, I am persuaded, and firmly maintain, that there are
many regions and cities more exalted and more delightful still than the Tuscany and the Florence where
I was born and whereof I am a citizen, and many nations and peoples who speak a more refined and
useful language than do the Italians.'

per lontananza m'è tolto dal viso,
che m'àve in foco miso,
lieve mi conterei ciò che m'è grave.
ma questo foco m'àve
già consumato sì l'ossa e la polpa,
che Morte al petto m'ha posto la chiave.
Onde, s'io ebbi colpa,
più lune ha volto il sol poi che fu spenta,
se colpa muore perché l'uom si penta.

(*Tre donne intorno al cor mi son venute*, lines 73–90)[48]

And finally there are the Cacciaguida cantos of the *Paradiso*, no less diligent, to be sure, than the canzone in registering the still conflicted substance of the poet's predicament as an outcast, but tending at last to privilege the virtues of courage and commitment, the virtues, that is to say, pertaining to the prophet and to the prophetic utterance. On the one hand, then, there is the sadness of it all, a sense of bereftness, destitution, dependence and humiliation as but the stuff of a now anguished existence:

Qual si partio Ipolito d'Atene
per la spietata e perfida noverca,
tal di Fiorenza partir ti convene.
    Questo si vuole e questo già si cerca,
e tosto verrà fatto a chi ciò pensa
là dove Cristo tutto dì si merca.
    La colpa seguirà la parte offensa
in grido, come suol; ma la vendetta
fia testimonio al ver che la dispensa.
    Tu lascerai ogne cosa diletta

48 'And I who listen to such noble exiles taking comfort and telling of their grief in divine colloquy count as an honour the exile imposed upon me, for if judgement and the force of destiny does indeed wish that the world turn the white flowers into dark, it is praiseworthy even so to fall with the good. And were it not that the fair object of my eyes—for which I am all ablaze—is stolen away by distance from my sight I would count as light that which weighs upon me. But that fire has already so consumed my bones and flesh that death has put his key to my breast. If, then, guilt dies with repentance, the sun, even were I to blame, has now circled for many a moon since it was cancelled.' Guy P. Raffa, 'Dante's Poetics of Exile', *AdI* 20 (2002), 73–87; Maria Teresa Balbiano d'Aramengo, "*Tre donne intorno al cor*": *Saggio di psicologia dantesca* (Turin: Riccadonna, 2006); Juan Varela-Portas de Orduña (ed.), *Tre donne intorno al cor mi son venute* (Madrid: Asociación Complutense de Dantología, 2007 [various authors]); Catherine Keen, 'Florence and Faction in Dante's Lyric Poetry: Framing the Experience of Exile', in "*Se mai continga . . .*": *Exile, Politics and Theology in Dante*, ed. Claire E. Honess and Matthew Treherne (Ravenna: Longo, 2013), 63–83.

più caramente; e questo è quello strale
che l'arco de lo essilio pria saetta.
    Tu proverai sì come sa di sale
lo pane altrui, e come è duro calle
lo scendere e 'l salir per l'altrui scale.

(*Paradiso* 17.46–60)[49]

while on the other there is the strength of purpose always and everywhere required of the one who, come what may, counts himself as but a friend to the truth:

'Ben veggio, padre mio, sì come sprona
lo tempo verso me, per colpo darmi
tal, ch'è più grave a chi più s'abbandona;
    per che di provedenza è buon ch'io m'armi,
sì che, se loco m'è tolto più caro,
io non perdessi li altri per miei carmi.
    Giù per lo mondo sanza fine amaro,
e per lo monte del cui bel cacume
li occhi de la mia donna mi levaro,
    e poscia per lo ciel, di lume in lume,
ho io appreso quel che s'io ridico,
a molti fia sapor di forte agrume;
    e s'io al vero son timido amico,
temo di perder viver tra coloro
che questo tempo chiameranno antico.'
    La luce in che rideva il mio tesoro
ch'io trovai lì, si fé prima corusca,
quale a raggio di sole specchio d'oro;
    indi rispuose: 'Coscïenza fusca
o de la propria o de l'altrui vergogna
pur sentirà la tua parola brusca.
    Ma nondimen, rimossa ogne menzogna,
tutta tua visïon fa manifesta;

---

49 'As Hippolytus departed from Athens, by reason of his pitiless and perfidious stepmother, so you from Florence must depart. So it is willed, so it is already plotted, and so shall it soon be accomplished by him who thinks on it there where every day Christ is bought and sold. The blame, loudly proclaimed, will as always follow the injured party, but vengeance shall bear witness to the truth which dispenses it. You shall leave everything you cherish most, this being the first of the arrows shot forth by the bow of exile. You shall come to know how salt is the taste of another's bread, and how hard a way it is to be forever going up and down another's stairs.'

e lascia pur grattar dov' è la rogna.
Ché se la voce tua sarà molesta
nel primo gusto, vital nodrimento
lascerà poi, quando sarà digesta.
Questo tuo grido farà come vento,
che le più alte cime più percuote;
e ciò non fa d'onor poco argomento.'

(*Paradiso* 17.106–35)[50]

By the middle of January 1302 the tribunals inaugurated against the White by the Black Guelphs and conducted as much on the basis of partisanship, prejudice and hearsay as of anything else were complete, with opposition to the pope and fraudulence in public office being the main substance of the indictment and exclusion on a grand scale the main consequence. True, Vieri de' Cerchi as leader and figurehead for the Florentine Whites both within and now without was sufficiently solvent to weather the storm and indeed to finance the resistance, but this was the exception rather than the rule, the majority of the *fuorusciti* staring ruination in the face. White resistance, in this early phase, took the form (*a*) of a review of the political and military situation on the ground, Bologna in particular being sympathetic to the White cause and Pistoia being in the hands of the Bianchi (this being the main business of a preliminary meeting at Gargonza on the road from Siena to Arezzo possibly in February of that year); (*b*) of a convention on 18 June 1302 in the church of San Godenzo in Val di Sieve, with Vieri in particular eager for action (Dante himself being present on this occasion but urging caution in case of bad weather); and (*c*) of an alliance headed up by Alessandro da Romena as its captain with Dante himself among its advisers.[51] The mood

50 '"I see well, my father, how time spurs towards me for to deal me such a blow as falls most heavily upon the heedless, wherefore it is good that I arm myself with foresight, so that if the place I hold most dear be taken from me, I lose not all the rest by reason of my songs. Below, in the realm of endless woe, and upon the mountain whence whose fair summit my lady's eyes raised me up, and, thereafter, through the heavens from light to light, I have learned that which, should I repeat it, will for many savour of great bitterness, and if I am a timid friend to the truth, I fear for my very being among those who will call this time ancient." The light wherein smiled the treasure I had found there flashed like a golden mirror in the sun and then replied: "What you have to say will indeed seem harsh to a conscience darkened either by its own or by another's shame, but for all that, and setting aside all falsehood, declare all you have seen, and let them scratch where it itches. For if at first your voice grieve them, yet thereafter it shall afford vital nourishment when digested. This cry of yours will be like the wind which smites most severely the loftiest summits, and this will redound not a little to your honour." ' Riccardo Ambrosini, 'Sul messianismo di Dante: A proposito del canto XVII del *Paradiso*', *L'Alighieri* (RBD) 42, 18 (2001), 75–98 (and in *Lectura Dantis Turicensis: Paradiso*, ed. Georges Güntert and Michelangelo Picone [Florence: Cesati, 2002], 243–64, with the title 'Canto XVII').
51 Leonardo Bruni, 'Della vita studi e costumi di Dante', ed. Giuseppe Lando Passerini (Florence: Sansoni, 1917), 8: 'Sentito Dante la ruina sua, subito partì da Roma, dove era imbasciadore, e cammi-

overall was buoyant, Dante busying himself about compensation for the Ubaldini (Ghibelline to a man) in respect of losses incurred in the recent upheaval and, more especially, setting off to Forlì—putting up on his way at the monastery of San Benedetto in Alpe—to enlist the help of the Ghibelline chieftain Scarpetta degli Ordelaffi in the spring offensive. In this, as in a visit at more or less the same time to Bartolomeo della Scala in Verona, he was singularly successful, so much so that by March 1303 the exiles were able to field eight hundred cavalrymen and six thousand foot soldiers. In advance of the main offensive, there were encounters on the battlefield (at Piantrevigne, for example, and in the Valdarno and Serravalle) with—to go by Compagni[52]—the Whites worsted; but when it came to the real thing White expectation was definitively put paid to, the combined forces of the White Guelphs and their Ghibelline allies being routed by Fulcieri de' Calboli with the rump put to flight. For Dante, as in some degree architect of the project, this not only put an end to his activity as an insurgent, but, opening up as it did still further the rift between him and his fellow exiles, it served merely to confirm him in his status as a solitary spirit, a seeker out of the sun and the stars as his only real companions.

Even now, though, with nothing to look forward to but other people's stairs and salty bread, there were, all of a sudden, grounds for optimism, for entertaining the possibility of a fresh start in Florence. At odds, then, with his White Guelph colleagues and doubtless scapegoated by some of them for the failure of the spring offensive, Dante had withdrawn to Verona in May or June 1303, where until sometime in the spring of 1304 he was hosted by Bartolomeo della Scala as prominent among his comforters in exile.[53] By this time Boniface VIII, largely as a result of

---

nando con gran celerità ne venne a Siena; quivi intesa chiaramente la sua calamità, non vedendo alcun riparo, deliberò accozzarsi con gli altri usciti: e il primo accozzamento fu in una congregazione delli usciti, la quale si fe' a Gargonsa, dove, trattate molte cose, finalmente fermaro la sedia loro ad Arezzo, e quivi ferono campo grosso, e crearono loro capitano generale il conte Alessandro Da Romena, ferono dodici consiglieri, del numero de' quali fu Dante, e di speranza in speranza stettero per infino all'anno 1304' (When Dante heard of his ruin he immediately left Rome, where he was an ambassador, and, journeying with all speed, came to Siena. Hearing there more particulars of the disaster, and seeing no remedy, he decided to ally himself with the other refugees. His first approach to them was in a meeting thereof held at Gargonza, where they considered many schemes and finally fixed their headquarters at Arezzo, where they made a great camp and appointed Count Alessandro da Romena as their captain with twelve counsellors, among whom was Dante, and where, entertaining one hope after another, they remained until 1304).

52 Compagni 2.28–30, with an account of Folcieri da Calvoli's war crimes at 30, ult. (cf. *Purgatorio* 14.55–66). Villani 8.59. For Piantrevigne, Compagni 2.28 and Villani 8.53, both with reference to the Carlino mentioned by Dante in the *Inferno* at 32.69 among the treacherous to cause and country. For the 'sun and the stars' motif, and in addition to *Paradiso* 33.145, *Epistole* 12.4: 'quod si per nullam talem Florentia introitur, nunquam Florentia introibo. Quidni? Nonne solis astrorumque specula ubique conspiciam' (But if by no such path may Florence be entered, then will I ne'er enter Florence. What! Can I not anywhere gaze upon the face of the sun and the stars?).

53 Giorgio Petrocchi, 'La vicenda biografica di Dante nel Veneto', in *Itinerari danteschi* (Milan: Angeli, 1994), 88–103; Giuseppe Indizio, 'Le tappe venete dell'esilio di Dante', *Miscellanea Marciana* 19

his manhandling by the French in Anagni, had died, his successor, Benedict XI, taking a more equitable line with regard to Florence and in fact setting up a peace initiative designed to resolve her yet again deepening divisions—divisions this time, not between Black and White but between Black and Black, between Rosso della Tosa as ensconced in the corridors of power and Corso Donati as (or so it seemed to him) undeservedly marginalized. What, then, with the arrival in Florence of Cardinal Niccolò da Prato as peacemaker in March 1304 and with the invitation to Black and White Guelphs alike to join in the ensuing festivities, Dante, anticipating now a welcome homecoming, set off to Arezzo, where either upon his arrival or while still on the way he composed on behalf of the captain and of the Council of the White Guelph party a letter addressed to the good cardinal expressing the gratitude of the exiled constituency and their commitment to whatever needed to be done in the name and for the sake of a new age of peace and prosperity at home:

> Ceu filii non ingrati litteras igitur pie vestre Paternitatis aspeximus, que totius nostri desiderii personantes exordia, subito mentes nostras tanta letitia perfuderunt, quantam nemo valeret seu verbo seu cogitatione metiri. Nam quam, fere pre desiderio sompniantes, inhiabamus patrie sanitatem, vestrarum litterarum series plusquam semel sub paterna monitione polluxit. Et ad quid aliud in civile bellum corruimus, quid aliud candida nostra signa petebant, et ad quid aliud enses et tela nostra rubebant, nisi ut qui civilia iura temeraria voluptate truncaverant et iugo pie legis colla submitterent et ad pacem patrie cogerentur? Quippe nostre intentionis cuspis legiptima de nervo quem tendebamus prorumpens, quietem solam et libertatem populi fiorentini petebat, petit, atque petet in posterum. Quod si tam gratissimo nobis beneficio vigilatis, et adversarios nostros, prout sancta conamina vestra voluerint, ad sulcos bone civilitatis intenditis remeare, quis vobis dignas grates persolvere attentabit? Nec opis est nostre, pater, nec quicquid florentine gentis reperitur in terris. Sed si qua celo est pietas que talia remuneranda prospiciat, illa vobis premia digna ferat, qui tante urbis misericordiam induistis et ad sedanda civium profana litigia festinatis.
>
> (*Epistole* 1.2)[54]

(2004), 35–64 (and, in a revised form, in *Problemi di biografia dantesca* [Ravenna: Longo, 2014], 93–114).

54 'As not ungrateful sons, therefore, we examined the letter of your gracious paternity, which, in that it gives expression to the prelude of the whole matter of our desires, forthwith filled our minds with joy so exceedingly great that by none could it be measured either in word or in thought. For the healing of our country, for which we have yearned, longing for it as it were even in our dreams, in the course of your letter, under the guise of fatherly admonition, is more than once promised us. And for

In the event, however, the Black administration was more than equal to the cardinal's plans for a more inclusive constitution and soon enough saw him off by way of a nicely contrived diversion of spiritual energy—by packing him off to Prato (his native city) to put down a carefully orchestrated uprising of Black fervour with distinct implications for the peace, such as it was, of Florence herself. Giving up, then, on the whole project, he too departed the city on 4 June that year (1304), placing her as he did so under yet another interdict. With the failure, then, of an in truth scarcely viable initiative, Dante made his way back to Verona, there, according to the testimony of Leonardo Bruni, but doubtless in a spirit of deepening despair, to commend himself yet again to the Florentines within as a good man and true:

> Fallita dunque questa tanta speranza, non parendo a Dante più da perder tempo, partì d'Arezzo e andossene a Verona, dove, ricevuto molto cortesemente da' Signori della Scala, con loro fece dimora alcun tempo, e ridussesi tutto a umiltà, cercando con buone opere e con buoni portamenti racquistar la grazia di poter tornare in Firenze per ispontanea rivocazione di chi reggeva la terra; e sopra questa parte s'affaticò assai, e scrisse più volte, non solamente a' particulari cittadini del reggimento, ma ancora al popolo: e intra l'altre una Epistola assai lunga, che incomincia: Popule mee, quid feci tibi?[55]

Once again, then, it was a question of hope and hopelessness vying one with the other for mastery, the wretchedness of it all being compounded by patronage and dependence as a way of life. True, there was the occasional distraction, the odd administrative task, for example, at the behest of Alboino della Scala in

---

what else did we plunge into civil war? What else did our white standards seek? And for what else were our swords and our spears dyed with crimson? Save that they, who at their own mad will and pleasure have maimed the body of civil right, should submit their necks to the yoke of beneficent law, and should be brought by force to the observance of their country's peace! In sooth, the lawful shaft of our purpose, leaping from the bowstring we held stretched, sought solely the peace and liberty of the people of Florence—sought, and ever will seek. But if your vigilance is intent on a consummation so dear to us, and you are resolved, as the end of your holy endeavours, that our foes shall return to the furrows of good citizenship, who shall attempt to render adequate thanks to you? Not in our power is it, O father, nor in that of any of the Florentine race throughout the world. But if there exists any goodness in heaven which looks upon such deeds as worthy of recompense, may it grant meet reward to you, who have clothed yourself with compassion for so great a city, and are hastening to compose the unholy strife of her citizens!' Compagni 3.4 and Villani 8.59.

55 Leonardo Bruni, *Le vite di Dante*, ed. Giuseppe Lando Passerini (Florence: Sansoni, 1917), 8: 'With his hopes dashed and thinking not to waste any more time, he left Arezzo and made his way to Verona, where, graciously received by the lords of that city, the Della Scala, he remained for some time, seeking with all humility, good works and deeds to secure the goodwill of those governing the city with a view to his ready recall to Florence. And to this he devoted himself endlessly, writing repeatedly, not only to those of his compatriots in government but to the people generally, one such missive—a particularly long one—beginning "O my people, what have I done to you?"'

Verona (Bartolomeo, his brother, had died in 1304) or of Gherardo da Camino in Treviso or of Moroello Malaspina in the Lunigiana (on whose behalf Dante acted as procurator and special envoy to Bishop Luni in respect of holdings in the Val di Magra).[56] And then too there was the occasional cultural encounter of significance, possibly with Giotto on the occasion of the consecration of the Church of the Annunziata in Padua in March 1306, together with the hospitality afforded by the 'Gentucca' or as yet unwidowed noblewoman of Lucca mentioned in the *Purgatorio* at 24.37–48. But it was only with the prospect towards the end of the decade of a fresh imperial descent that his spirits were revived, for this at last was the moment of truth, the moment in which the prisoner would be released and the proud scattered in the imagination of their hearts:

'Ecce nunc tempus acceptabile', quo signa surgunt consolationis et pacis. Nam dies nova splendescit auroram demonstrans, que iam tenebras diu-

---

56 With reference, however, to the scarce nobility of Alboino, *Convivio* 4.16.6. For the 'buon Gherardo' of Treviso, by contrast, 'antonomastically a good man' (Benvenuto da Imola, *Comentum super Dantis Aldigherij Comoediam* [Florence: G. Barbèra, 1887]), *Purgatorio* 16.121–26, with, in the *Convivio*, the 'fia sempre la sua memoria' and the 'blessed memory' passage of 4.14.12–13. For Dante, the Lunigiana and the Malaspina (the key text here being *Purgatorio* 8.109–39), Livio Galanti, *Il soggiorno di Dante in Lunigiana* (Mulazzo: Centro Dantesco della Biblioteca Communale, 1985); Franco Quartieri, 'Il pregio della borsa e della spada: Dante e i Malaspina', in *Analisi e paradossi su 'Commedia' e dintorni* (Ravenna: Longo, 2006), 69–81; Francesco Mazzoni, 'Dante e la Lunigiana', in *Con Dante per Dante: Saggi di filologia ed ermeneutica dantesca: I. Approcci a Dante*, ed. Carlo Garfagnini et al. (Rome: Edizioni di Storia e Letteratura, 2014 [1984]), 149–59. On Dante and Giotto, John C. Barnes, 'Dante, Cimabue and Giotto', *Strathclyde Modern Language Studies* 6 (1985), 5–27; George Holmes, 'Realistic Visual Narrative', in *Florence, Rome and the Origins of the Renaissance* (New York: Oxford University Press, 1986), 205–32; Giovanni Fallani, 'Dante e le arti', in *Lectura Dantis Modenese: Dante e la cultura* (Modena: Banca Popolare dell'Emilia, 1988), 155–67; Umberto Maria Milizia, 'La pittura di Dante: La concezione delle arti figurative in Dante', *Quaderni di letteratura, storia e arte* 1 (1996), 7–44; Christopher Kleinhenz, 'On Dante and the Visual Arts', in *Dante for the New Millennium*, ed. Teodolinda Barolini (New York: Fordham University Press, 2003), 274–92; Bruna Bianchi, 'Dante e l'arte coeva', in *La scuola italiana di Middlebury (1996–2005): Passione, didattica, pratica*, ed. Antonio Vitti (Pesaro: Metauro, 2005), 103–23. For Dante himself on the drama and plasticity of contemporary art, on the triumph of Giotto and of the Giottoesque, and on cultural activity generally as a matter of constant renewal the 'One would have sworn' moment of *Purgatorio* 10.40–45 and the 'vain glory' moment of 11.91–96: 'Giurato si saria ch'el dicesse "Ave!"; / perché iv' era imaginata quella / ch'ad aprir l'alto amor volse la chiave e avea in atto impressa esta favella / "Ecce ancilla Deï", propriamente / come figura in cera si suggella ... Oh vana gloria de l'umane posse! / com' poco verde in su la cima dura, / se non è giunta da l'etati grosse! / Credette Cimabue ne la pittura / tener lo campo, e ora ha Giotto il grido, / sì che la fama di colui è scura' (One would have sworn he said 'Ave!', for there was imaged she who turned the key to open the supreme love, and in her bearing she had these words imprinted 'Ecce ancilla Deï' as clearly as a figure is stamped in wax ... Oh vain glory of human power, how briefly lasts the green upon its summit if not overtaken by a dark age. Cimabue, in painting, thought to hold the field but now the acclaim is all Giotto's such that the other's fame is dark). For the 'Gentucca' moment of *Purgatorio* 24 (an apparently kindly presence in Lucca), Giorgio Varanini, '"Femmina è nata": Nota sulla Gentucca dantesca (*Purg*. XXIV.37–51)', in *Scritti in onore di Caterina Vassalini*, ed. Luigi Barbesi (Verona: Fiorini, 1974), 507–16 (and in *L'acceso strale: Saggi e ricerche sulla 'Commedia'* [Naples: Federico e Ardia, 1984], 130–35, with the title '"Femmina è nata" (*Purgatorio* XXIV. 37–51)').

turne calamitatis attenuat; iamque aure orientales crebrescunt; rutilat celum in labiis suis, et auspitia gentium blanda serenitate confortat. Et nos gaudium expectatum videbimus, qui diu pernoctitavimus in deserto, quoniam Titan exorietur pacificus, et iustitia, sine sole quasi eliotropium hebetata, cum primum iubar ille vibraverit, revirescet. Saturabuntur omnes qui esuriunt et sitiunt iustitiam in lumine radiorum eius, et confundentur qui diligunt iniquitatem a facie coruscantis. Arrexit namque aures misericordes Leo fortis de tribu Iuda; atque ullulatum universalis captivitatis miserans, Moysen alium suscitavit qui de gravaminibus Egiptiorum populum suum eripiet, ad terram lacte ac melle manantem perducens. Letare iam nunc miseranda Ytalia etiam Saracenis, que statim invidiosa per orbem videberis, quia sponsus tuus, mundi solatium et gloria plebis tue, clementissimus Henricus, divus et Augustus et Cesar, ad nuptias properat. Exsicca lacrimas et meroris vestigia dele, pulcerrima, nam prope est qui liberabit te de carcere impiorum; qui percutiens malignantes in ore gladii perdet eos, et vineam suam aliis locabit agricolis qui fructum iustitie reddant in tempore messis.

(Epistole 5.1–2 [2–6])[57]

57 'Behold now is the accepted time, wherein arise the signs of consolation and peace. For a new day is beginning to break, revealing dawn in the east, which even now is dispersing in the darkness of our long tribulation. Already the Orient breeze is freshening, the face of the heavens grows rosy, and confirms the hopes of the people with an auspicious calm. And we too, who have kept vigil through the long night in the wilderness, shall behold the long-awaited joy. For the Sun of peace shall appear on high, and justice which, like the heliotrope, deprived of his light, had grown faint, so soon as he shall dart forth his rays, once more shall revive. All they that hunger and thirst shall be satisfied in the light of his radiance, and they that delight in iniquity shall be put to confusion before the face of his splendour. For the strong line of the tribe of Judah has lifted up his ears in compassion, and moved by the lamentations of the multitudes in captivity has raised up another Moses, who shall deliver his people from the oppression of the Egyptians, and shall lead them to a land flowing with milk and honey. Rejoice, therefore, O Italy, you that are now an object of pity even to the Saracens, for soon shall you be the envy of the whole world, seeing that your bridegroom, the comfort of the nations, and the glory of thy people, even the most clement Henry, elect of God and Augustus and Caesar, is hastening to the wedding. Dry your tears, and wipe away the stains of your weeping, most beauteous one, for he is at hand who shall bring you forth from the prison of the ungodly, and shall smite the workers of iniquity with the edge of the sword, and shall destroy them. And his vineyard shall he let out to other husbandmen, who shall render the fruit of justice in the time of harvest.' Achille Tartaro, 'Dante e l'"alto Arrigo"', in *Il viaggio di Enrico VII in Italia*, ed. Mauro Tosti Croce (Città di Castello: Edimond, 1993), 57–60; Alex Novikoff, 'Henry VII and the Universal Empire of Engelbert of Admont and Dante Alighieri', *PPM* 3–4 (2005–6), 143–65; Federico Gagliardi, 'L'"alto Arrigo" nelle epistole dantesche del 1310–11: Modelli biblici e classici', *Cultura* 45.1 (2007), 133–42; Florence Rùsso, 'Henry VII and Dante's Dream of a New Golden Age', *FItal* 44.2 (2010), 267–86; Claire E. Honess, ' "Ecce nunc tempus acceptabile": Henry VII and Dante's Ideal of Peace', *The Italianist* 33.3 (2013), 484–504; Giuseppe Petralia and Marco Santagata (eds.), *Enrico VII, Dante e Pisa a 700 anni dalla morte dell'imperatore e dalla Monarchia (1313–2013)* (Ravenna: Longo, 2016). More generally on the imperial descent and the imperial idea, William M. Bowsky, *Henry VII in Italy: The Conflict of Empire and City State, 1310–1313* (Lincoln: University of Nebraska Press, 1960); Francesco Cognasso, *Arrigo VII* (Milan: Dall'Oglio, 1973); Malte Heidemann, *Heinrich VII(1308–1313): Kaiseridee im Spannungsfeld*

If, then, to this—part of Dante's letter to the Italian people and princes belonging ideally to September or October 1310—we add the so-called Battifolle letters
belonging to the spring of 1311 (letters addressed to Empress Margaret in the name
of the Countess of Battifolle but composed by Dante in his capacity as guest of
and secretary to the court at the Castle of Poppi in the Casentino), then we have
testimony enough to his state of mind and to the exhilaration thereof during this
first phase of Henry 's descent into Italy. Nicely chancelloresque in manner, it is
precisely by way of their formality and refinement that these occasional pieces
confirm his sense of the sacred substance of it all, of the imperial descent as har-
binger of a new age and of better things to come; so, for example, from the first
of the Battifolle letters—a letter coinciding probably with Henry's setting out
from Milan on 19 April 1311 to see to Cremona in its truculence—we have the
following passage to the effect that grace, now more than ever abounding, might
succour the Roman prince and his empress as overseers of a new world order:

> Nunc ideo regni siderii iustis precibus atque piis aula pulsetur, et impetret
> supplicantis affectus quatenus mundi gubernator eternus condescensui
> tanto premia coequata retribuat, et ad auspitia Cesaris et Auguste dexteram
> gratie coadiutricis extendat; ut qui romani principatus imperio barbaras
> nationes et cives in mortalium tutamenta subegit, delirantis evi familiam
> sub triumphis et gloria sui Henrici reformet in melius.
>
> *(Epistole* 8.5)[58]

to which we may add this passage from the second of the Battifolle letters dating
from just a little later that same year and similarly fulsome in its expression of
obedience to the prince and his first lady as between them the ground and guarantee of all civility in the world here below:

> Spero equidem, de celesti provisione confidens quam nunquam falli vel
> prepediri posse non dubito et que humane civilitati de Principe singulari
> providit, quod exordia vestri regni felicia semper in melius prosperata proce-
> dent. Sic igitur in presentibus et futuris exultans, ad Auguste clementiam
> sine ulla hesitatione recurro, et suppliciter tempestiva deposco quatenus me

---

von staufischer Universalherrschaft und frühneuzeitlicher Partikularautonomie (Warendorf: Fahlbusch,
2008). Compagni 3.24–37 and Villani 8.101–9.52.

58 'Now, therefore, let the court of the starry realm be assailed with just and holy prayers, and may
the zeal of the suppliant obtain that the eternal ruler of the world may recompense so great a condescension with proportionate reward, and may stretch forth the right hand of his grace in furtherance
of the hopes of Caesar and of Augusta; to the end that he, who for the safeguard of mankind brought
under the empire of the Roman prince all peoples barbarian and civilized, may by the triumphs and
glory of his servant Henry regenerate the human family of this demented age.'

sub umbra tutissima vestri Culminis taliter collocare dignemini, ut cuiusque
sinistrationis ab estu sim semper et videar esse secura.

(*Epistole* 9.4–5)[59]

together with, as coinciding with Henry's success at Cremona in the middle part
of May of that year, these lines from the third letter, piety, prayer and a protes-
tation of loyalty giving way now to rejoicing as the dominant mood of the
despatch:

Cum pagina vestre Serenitatis apparuit ante scribentis et gratulantis aspec-
tum, experta est mea pura fidelitas quam in dominorum successibus animi
subditorum fidelium colletentur. Nam per ea que continebantur in ipsa,
cum tota cordis hilaritate concepi qualiter dextera summi Regis vota Cesa-
ris et Auguste feliciter adimplebat. Proinde gradum mee fidelitatis experta,
petentis audeo iam inire officium . . . Audiat, ex quo iubet, Romanorum pia
et serena Maiestas, quoniam tempore missionis presentium coniunx predi-
lectus et ego, Dei dono, vigebamus incolumes, liberorum sospitate
gaudentes, tanto solito letiores quanto signa resurgentis Imperii meliora
iam secula promittebant.

(*Epistole* 10.2 and 5)[60]

But even here—for this, typically, is the way of it in exile—one thing is offset
by another, one intimation by its polar counterpart, for there is always Florence
in the height and depth of her perversity. Has she no inkling, then—for this is the
burden of Dante's open letter of March 1311 to the 'wretched Florentines within'
(scelestissimis Florentinis intrinsecis)—of the prior and providential purpose-
fulness of it all? Has she never learned that there can be no alienation of imperial

---

59 'I indeed hope, confiding in the providence of heaven, which, as I firmly believe, can never be
deceived nor be hindered of its purpose, and which has provided for civilized mankind one sole prince,
that the happy inauguration of your reign may be confirmed by ever-increasing prosperity. Exulting,
therefore, in the present as in the future, without hesitation I commit myself to the clemency of Augusta, and humbly make early supplication that you may deign to place me in safekeeping beneath your
eminence's shadow, in such wise that I may ever be, and may be seen to be, sheltered from the fiery
heat of all and every untoward chance.'

60 'When the letter of your serenity came before the eyes of her who writes and sends this greeting,
my sincere devotion proved in what measure the hearts of devoted servants are made glad by the happy
fortunes of their lords. From the contents of your letter I gathered with the most complete rejoicing
of heart how the right hand of the most high king was auspiciously bringing about the accomplishment
of the wishes of Caesar and of Augusta . . . May it please the gracious and serene majesty of the Romans
to learn, since such is her command, that at the moment of the despatch of these present tidings my
beloved husband and myself, by the gift of God, were prospering in good health, rejoicing in the welfare
of our children, and more than usually joyful in that the omens of the reviving fortunes of the imperial
cause were already giving promise of more happy times to come.'

rights by way of prescription or of customary arrogation? Is she not aware that to resist this fresh manifestation of Rome and of Roman might is to consign oneself to the dungeon of captivity? Has she no sense, in short, of the Christic substance of it all, of Henry's stature as one who, having no regard for himself, 'hath borne our griefs and carried our sorrows'?

> O miserrima Fesulanorum propago, et iterum iam punita barbaries! An parum timoris prelibata incutiunt? Omnino vos tremere arbitror vigilantes, quanquam spem simuletis in facie verboque mendaci, atque in somniis expergisci plerunque, sive pavescentes infusa presagia, sive diurna consila recolentes. Verum si merito trepidantes insanisse penitet non dolentes, ut in amaritudinem penitentie metus dolorisque rivuli confluant, vestris animis infigenda supersunt, quod Romane rei baiulus hic divus et triumphator Henricus, non sua privata sed publica mundi commoda sitiens, ardua queque pro nobis aggressus est sua sponte penas nostras participans, tanquam ad ipsum, post Christum, digitum prophetie propheta direxerit Ysaias, cum, spiritu Dei revelante, predixit: 'Vere languores nostros ipse tulit et dolores nostros ipse portavit.'
>
> (*Epistole* 6.6 [24–25])[61]

—lines to which, as confirming once and for all the completeness of Dante's investment in the imperial project, we may add these from his letter to Henry himself, a letter as fervent in respect of the idea as it is anxious in respect of its realization. Praise be, then, but please God—or, more exactly, please Henry—there be no delay, no postponing of the paschal project:

> Verum quia sol noster, sive desiderii fervor hoc submoneat sive facies veritatis, aut morari iam creditur aut retrocedere supputatur, quasi Iosue denuo vel Amos filius imperaret, incertitudine dubitare compellimur et in vocem Precursoris irrompere sic: 'Tu es qui venturus es, an alium expectamus?' Et quamvis longa sitis in dubium que sunt certa propter esse propinqua, ut adsolet, furibunda deflectat, nichilominus in te credimus et speramus, as-

---

61 'O most wretched offshoot of Fiesole! O barbarians punished now a second time! Does the foretaste not suffice to terrify you? Of a truth I believe that, for all that you simulate hope in your looks and lying lips, yet you tremble in your waking hours and ever start from your dreams in terror at the portents which have visited you or as you go over yet again the counsels you have debated by day. But if, while alarmed with good reason, you repent of your madness, yet feel no remorse, then, that the streams of fear and sorrowing may unite in the bitter waters of repentance, bear this further in mind, that the guardian of the Roman Empire, the triumphant Henry, elect of God, thirsting not for his own but for the public good, has for our sakes undertaken his heavy task, sharing our pains of his own free will, as though to him, after Christ, the prophet Isaiah has pointed the finger of prophecy, when by the revelation of the Spirit of God he declared: "Surely he hath borne our griefs and carried our sorrows."'

severantes te Dei ministrum et Ecclesie filium et Romane glorie promo-
torem. Nam et ego qui scribo tam pro me quam pro aliis, velut decet im-
peratoriam maiestatem benignissimum vidi et clementissimum te audivi,
cum pedes tuos manus mee tractarunt et labia mea debitum persolverunt.
Tunc exultavit in te spiritus meus, cum tacitus dixi mecum: 'Ecce Agnus
Dei, ecce qui tollit peccata mundi.'

(*Epistole* 7.2 [7–10])[62]

It is, then, in this context that, for Dante personally, Henry's death in August
1313 stands to be contemplated, for with the failure of the imperial enterprise it
was once more a question of seeking out the reasons of his now more than ever
displaced humanity, self-interrogation, as always in Dante, constituting the condition of new life, of the individual's affirming self afresh in the fullness of his or
her proper humanity. His circumstances at this time remain, alas, uncertain,
though it appears that from 1312 to 1318 he was the guest of Cangrande della Scala
in Verona, a man whom he admired both as a warrior-lord and as one more than
ordinarily sensitive to the nature of true friendship. Thereafter, from 1319 until the
time of his death in September 1321, he was the guest of the still more kindly
Guido Novello da Polenta of Ravenna, 'still more kindly' in that here especially
he was welcomed and indeed celebrated both as a scholar and as a poet, benefiting
now from access to the cathedral library, from the company of congenial colleagues and from the presence of members of his family; so at any rate Boccaccio,
who, though a shade novelistic in his reconstruction of Dante's life, offers a persuasive account of his situation in these, his twilight years:

Era in que' tempi signore di Ravenna, famosa e antica città di Romagna,
uno nobile cavaliere, il cui nome era Guido Novel da Polenta; il quale, ne'
liberali studii ammaestrato, sommamente i valorosi uomini onorava, e
massimamente quegli che per iscienza gli altri avanzavano. Alle cui orec-
chie venuto Dante, fuori d'ogni speranza, essere in Romagna, avendo egli
lungo tempo avanti per fama conosciuto il suo valore, in tanta disperazi-
one, si dispose di riceverlo e d'onorarlo. Né aspettò di ciò da lui essere
richiesto, ma con liberale animo, considerata qual sia a' valorosi la vergogna

---

62 'But because our sun (whether it be the fervour of our longing, or the appearance of truth which
suggests it) is believed to be tarrying, or is suspected to be turning back, as though at the bidding once
again of Joshua or of the son of Amoz, we are constrained in our uncertainty to doubt, and to break
forth in the words of the forerunner: "Are you he that should come? Or should we look for another?"
And although the frenzy of prolonged desire has a tendency to fashion doubt from those which, being
close at hand, seem certain, nevertheless we believe and hope in you, declaring you to be the minister
of God, the son of the Church, and the guardian of Rome's glory. For I too, who write as well for myself
as for others, beheld you most gracious, and heard you most clement, as beseems imperial majesty,
when my hands touched your feet and my lips paid their tribute. Then my spirit rejoiced within me,
when I said secretly within myself: "Behold the lamb of God that takes away the sins of the world." '

del domandare, e con proferte, gli si fece davanti, richiedendo di spezial grazia a Dante quello ch'egli sapeva che Dante a lui dovea dimandare: cioè che seco li piacesse di dover essere. Concorrendo adunque i due voleri ad un medesimo fine, e del domandato e del domandatore, e piacendo sommamente a Dante la liberalità del nobile cavaliere, e d'altra parte il bisogno strignendolo, senza aspettare più inviti che 'l primo, se n'andò a Ravenna, dove onorevolmente dal signore di quella ricevuto, e con piacevoli conforti risuscitata la caduta speranza, copiosamente le cose opportune donandogli, in quella seco per più anni il tenne, anzi infino a l'ultimo della vita di lui.

(Boccaccio, *Trattatello in laude in Dante 5*)[63]

It was, therefore, in circumstances of a now more settled existence, but also of a now seasoned sense of life as but a hastening towards death (the 'viver ch'è un correre a la morte' of *Purgatorio* 33.54), that Dante felt able to confirm and indeed to celebrate his status as a poet and philosopher in the romance-vernacular and high-scholastic way of being these things. On the one hand, then, we have the *Commedia*, a project long since under way but, by dint now of further discussion with those most accredited in the scholarly circles of Ravenna as his final home, brought at last to its ecstatic conclusion; while on the other, and consequent now upon his dealings with the philosophical spirits of Mantua and Verona and with Giovanni del Virgilio as prominent among the new humanists of Bologna, we

---

63 'In those times the Lord of Ravenna (a famous and ancient city of Romagna) was a noble knight whose name was Guido Novello da Polenta; he was well skilled in the liberal arts and held worthy men in the highest honour, especially those who excelled others in knowledge. And when it came to his ears that Dante, beyond all expectation, was now in Romagna and in such desperate plight, he, who had long since known his worth by repute, resolved to receive him and do him honour. He did not wait to be requested by him to do this, but considering how worthy men ask favours with great shame, with an open mind and free offers he approached him, requesting of Dante as a special grace that which he knew Dante would have to ask him—that it might please him to live with him. The two wills, therefore, of him who received and him who made the request thus uniting in the same aim, Dante, being highly pleased by the liberality of the noble knight, and on the other side constrained by his necessities, did not wait for a second invitation, and went to Ravenna. The lord there honourably received him, and revived his fallen hope by kindly fosterings; and giving him abundantly such things as were fitting, he kept him with him there for many years—even to the last year of his life.' Catherine Mary Phillimore, *Dante at Ravenna: A Study* (London: E. Stock, 1898); Corrado Ricci, *L'ultimo rifugio di Dante*, 3rd ed. (Ravenna: Longo, 1965 [1891]), à propos of which Emilio Pasquini, 'Corrado Ricci e *L'ultima rifugio di Dante* (1891),' in *Ottocento letterario: Dall periferia al centro* (Rome: Carocci, 2001), 155–63; Felice Mazzeo, *Dante e Ravenna* (Bologna: Cappelli, 1987; rev. ed. [Ravenna: Capit, 2011]); Guido Di Pino (ed.), *Dante e le città dell'esilio. Atti del Convegno Internazionale di Studi, 11–13 settembre 1987* (Ravenna: Longo, 1989); Augusto Vasina, 'Dante e Ravenna', *Ravenna Studi e Ricerche* 1–2 (2005), 15–44. Also, for (among others) the physicians Guido Vacchetta and Fiduccio de' Milotti, Romano Pasi, *Dante, i medici e la medicina* (Ravenna: Essegi, 1996); Augusto Campana, 'Guido Vacchetta e Giovanni del Virgilio (e Dante)', in *Scritti: I. Ricerche medievali e umanistiche*, vol. 2, ed. Rino Avesani et al. (Rome: Edizioni di Storia e Letteratura, 2012 [1965]), 729–42.

have the *Questio de situ aque et terre* and the Latin eclogues designed once and for all to confirm his competence in the area of natural philosophy and—by way of what amounts to a brilliant excursus in the bucolic manner—his commitment to the quintessential vernacularity of his undertaking as a poet and prophet.[64] Now there is no seeing into a man's soul in the moment of his death, and it may be that, in that moment (for Dante 14 September 1321 or possibly the previous evening), anxieties dating all the way back to his election as prior in Florence rose up once more to trouble his spirit, or it may be that, having emerged now on a fresh plane of love-understanding, of 'maturity in the flame of love', these same anxieties were in part at least, and maybe in the round, put to rest. By the same token it may be that his far-offness from Florence survived still to sadden him, or it may be that, sensitive now to his status as but a pilgrim spirit able anywhere to gaze upon the face of the sun and the other stars, he was at last equal to that sadness and to its power to annihilation. Or it may be all these things or none of them. But in the *Paradiso* as the point of arrival in respect of Dante's meditation as a poet and prophet there is perhaps a hint of what needs to be said here, for with nothing of the problematics either of personality or of circumstance left behind, the agony of these things is by grace taken up in a state of rejoicing, in a smile very definitely equal to the seriousness of it all.

---

64 For Dante, Giovanni del Virgilio and Giovanni del Virgilio's epitaph to Dante, Philip H. Wicksteed and Edmund Garratt Gardner, *Dante and Giovanni del Virgilio* (Westminster: Archibald Constable, 1902; repr. New York: Books for Libraries Press, 1971). The epitaph itself runs as follows: 'Theologus Dantes, nullius dogmatis expers, / quod foveat claro philosophia sinu: / gloria musarum, vulgo gratissimus auctor, / hic iacet, et fama pulsat utrumque polum: / qui loca defunctis gladiis regnumque gemellis / distribuit, laicis rhetoricisque modis. / Pascua Pieriis demum resonabat avenis; / Atropos heu letum livida rupit opus. / Huic ingrata tulit tristem Florentia fructum, / exilium, vati patria cruda suo. / Quem pia Guidonis gremio Ravenna Novelli / gaudet honorati conti / ad sua septembris idibus astra redit' (Here lies the theologian Dante, a stranger to no teaching, cherished by philosophy in her illustrious bosom, glory of the Muses and author beloved of the unlearned, whose fame reaches from world's end to world's end. He it is who assigned the dead to their places and made plain the roles of the two swords [i.e. of the empire and of the papacy], and this both in common and cultivated style [i.e. both in the vernacular and in Latin]. At the last pastures he made to resound with his Pierian pipes, darkling Atropos, alas, cutting short his joyous task. For him, her bard, ungrateful Florence, a cruel fatherland, afforded the bitter fruit of exile, but Ravenna rejoices in her compassion to have received him into the bosom of her most illustrious lord Guido Novello. In the year of Our Lord one thousand three hundred and thrice seven, on the Ides of September, he did then return unto the stars). Paget Toynbee, *Dante Alighieri: His Life and Works*, intro. Robert Hollander (Mineola: Dover Publications, 2005 [1900]), especially (as regards the funerary aspects of the matter), 105–8.

PART II

THE EARLY YEARS

From Dante da Maiano
to the *Vita nova*

CHAPTER 1

Preliminary Remarks:
Love and Love-Intelligence

Central to the *Vita nova* as the terminus ad quem or point of arrival in respect of what we may regard as the first phase of Dante's activity as a lyric poet is the notion of love as a principle less of *acquisition* than of *disposition*, as that whereby, seeking out the beloved as but an object of praise, the soul knows itself in the most radical kind of self-surpassing on the planes of understanding and desiring. The key passage here, remarkable for its delicate dramatization of a difficult transition from one species of love-understanding to another, runs as follows:

> Con ciò sia cosa che per la vista mia molte persone avessero compreso lo secreto del mio cuore, certe donne, le quali adunate s'erano, dilettandosi l'una ne la compagnia de l'altra, sapeano bene lo mio cuore, però che ciascuna di loro era stata a molte mie sconfitte; ed io passando appresso di loro, sì come da la fortuna menato, fui chiamato da una di queste gentili donne. La donna che m'avea chiamato, era donna di molto leggiadro parlare; sì che quand'io fui giunto dinanzi da loro, e vidi bene che la mia gentilissima donna non era con esse, rassicurandomi le salutai, e domandai che piacesse loro. Le donne erano molte, tra le quali n'avea certe che si rideano tra loro. Altre v'erano che mi guardavano aspettando che io dovessi dire; altre v'erano che parlavano tra loro. De le quali una, volgendo li suoi occhi verso me e chiamandomi per nome, disse queste parole: 'A che fine ami tu questa tua donna, poi che tu non puoi sostenere la sua presenza? Dilloci, ché certo lo fine di cotale amore conviene che sia novissimo'. E poi che m'ebbe dette queste parole, non solamente ella, ma tutte l'altre cominciaro ad attendere in vista la mia risponsione. Allora dissi queste parole loro: 'Madonne, lo fine del mio amore fue già lo saluto di questa donna, forse di cui voi intendete, ed in quello dimorava la beatitudine, ché era fine di tutti li miei desiderii. Ma poi che le piacque di negarlo a me, lo mio segnore Amore, la sua merzede, ha posto tutta la mia beatitudine in quello che non mi puote venire meno'. Allora queste donne cominciaro a parlare tra loro; e sì come talora vedemo cadere l'acqua mischiata di bella neve, così mi parea udire le loro parole uscire mischiate di sospiri. E poi che alquanto ebbero parlato tra loro,

anche mi disse questa donna che m'avea prima parlato, queste parole: 'Noi
ti preghiamo che tu ne dichi ove sia questa tua beatitudine'. Ed io, rispondendo lei, dissi cotanto: 'In quelle parole che lodano la donna mia'. Allora
mi rispuose questa che mi parlava: 'Se tu ne dicessi vero, quelle parole che
tu n'hai dette in notificando la tua condizione, avrestù operate con altro
intendimento'. Onde io, pensando a queste parole, quasi vergognoso mi
partìo da loro, e venia dicendo fra me medesimo: 'Poi che è tanta beatitudine in quelle parole che lodano la mia donna, perché altro parlare è stato
lo mio?' E però propuosi di prendere per matera de lo mio parlare sempre
mai quello che fosse loda di questa gentilissima; e pensando molto a ciò,
pareami avere impresa troppo alta matera quanto a me, sì che non ardia di
cominciare; e così dimorai alquanti dì con disiderio di dire e con paura di
cominciare.

(*Vita nova* 18)[1]

The passage is indeed in every sense remarkable: remarkable for its espousal
of notions both classical and Christian relative to friendship as a matter of disinterested concern (Aristotle and Cicero among the ancients, Aelred of Rievaulx
and Peter of Blois among the moderns) for the purposes of resolving a romance-
vernacular *questione d'amore*;[2] remarkable for its fresh implementation of a Gospel

---

1 'Since many people had guessed the secret of my heart from my face, certain ladies, gathered
together in order to delight in each other's company, well knew my inner condition, since they were
each of them often there to witness my discomfort; and I, passing as if by fortune, was beckoned by
one of these noble ladies. She who beckoned me was a lady gracious of speech, so that drawing near
and perceiving that my most noble lady was not among them, I was sufficiently reassured to greet them
and ask their pleasure. The ladies were many, and of them some were laughing amongst themselves
while others were looking upon me and waiting to hear what I might say, while yet others were talking
among themselves. Of these, one, turning her eyes towards me and addressing me by name, spoke thus:
"What, given that you cannot endure her presence, is the object of your love for this lady? Do tell us,
since the point of such love must surely be most strange." And having thus spoken, not only she, but
all the others seemed by their looks to await my reply, whereupon I addressed her thus: "My lady, the
object of my love hitherto was that lady's greeting—she of whom you perhaps know—and therein was
the only blessedness I ever sought. But since she was pleased to deny me that greeting, my lord Love,
in his mercy, has placed my every happiness in that which I cannot lose." Those same ladies began then
to speak one with another, and as we sometimes see the rain, in falling, mixed with beautiful snowflakes,
so I seemed to hear their words interlaced with sighs. And when they had spoken a while among
themselves, the one who had first addressed me spoke further, saying: "Tell us, then, we beseech you,
wherein now lies your blessedness." And I, replying, said: "In those words praising my lady." Then she
who had spoken to me made answer: "If what you say were indeed the truth, all you have written by
way of explaining yourself must have been set down with some other purpose," whereupon I, thinking
over her words and beset by shame, took my leave, saying to myself all the while: "Since there is indeed
such blessedness in those words praising my lady, why have I spoken otherwise?" And so I decided to
take henceforth as the theme of my every utterance only the praise of that most noble one, though for
fear of having upon reflection taken too much upon myself, I dared not begin. Albeit anxious to write,
I dared not, indeed for several days, to start.'
2 Aristotle, *Nicomachean Ethics* 8.3.12 (1156b11), with Thomas, in his commentary: 'Secundo ibi,

motif very much to the point here (praise and the blessedness thereof as the better part which cannot be taken away); and remarkable for the sheer tact and economy of it all, for its proposal of an issue as profound as it is complex by way of a narrative instance as exquisite as anything either in or beyond Dante himself. But remarkable above all is the centrality of this episode to what in the *Vita nova* as a whole amounts to a preliminary essay in the arduous dialectic of hell, purgatory and paradise as a matter, precisely, of *self-confrontation, self-reconfiguration* and *self-transcendence* in the already terrifying seriousness of these things. First, then, comes the moment of delight and of devastation (*her* greeting, *his* bliss, *her* denial and *his* now total destitution), Dante's in this sense, and before ever we get to the *Commedia*, being an already secure account of the substance and phenomenology of self-losing as preliminary in respect of the bliss of self-finding, of knowing self in the blessed ulteriority of self:

> Appresso di questa soprascritta visione, avendo già dette le parole che Amore m'avea imposte a dire, mi cominciaro molti e diversi pensamenti a combattere ed a tentare, ciascuno quasi indefensibilemente; tra li quali pensamenti quattro mi parea che ingombrassero più lo riposo de la vita. L'uno de li quali era questo: buona è la signoria d'Amore, però che trae lo intendimento del suo fedele da tutte le vili cose. L'altro era questo: non buona è la signoria d'Amore, però che quanto lo suo fedele più fede li porta, tanto più

---

volentes autem bona etc., ex hoc concludit quod talis amicitia sit maxima. Semper enim illud quod est per se est potius eo quod est per accidens. Cum igitur haec amicitia sit per se, aliae autem per accidens, consequens est quod virtuosi qui volunt bona amicis propter eos et non propter aliquid quod sibi ex eis proveniat, sunt maxime amici' (When, then, in the second place he says 'those willing the good' etc., he concludes from this that friendship of this kind is best, for that which is essential is always better than that which is incidental. Since, then, this is friendship essentially, anything else being friendship incidentally, those who out of their own goodness wish good to their friends for their friends' sake and not for favours accruing are the best type of friends); Cicero, *De amictia* 27: 'Quapropter a natura mihi videtur potius quam ab indigentia orta amicitia, applicatione magis animi cum quodam sensu amandi quam cogitatione quantum illa res utilitatis esset habitura' (Wherefore it seems to me that friendship springs rather from nature than from need, and from an inclination of the soul joined with a feeling of love rather than from a weighing up of how much profit the friendship is likely to afford); Aelred of Rievaulx, *De spirituali amicitia* 1 (PL 195.666B): 'Amicitia enim spiritualis, quam veram dicimus, non utilitatis cuiusque mundialis intuitur, non qualibet extra nascente causa, sed ex propriae naturae dignitate, et humani pectoris sensu desideratur, ita ut fructus eius praemiumque, non sit aliud quam ipsa' (For spiritual friendship of the kind we call true friendship should be desired, not for consideration of any worldly advantage or for any extrinsic cause, but from the dignity of its own nature and the feelings of the human heart, so that its fruition and reward is nothing other than itself); Peter of Blois, *De amicitia christiana* 4 (PL 207.875C): 'Non enim amor ille nomine vel honore amicitiae dignus est, qui alicujus mundanae utilitatis obtentu contrahitur. Amicitia siquidem ipsa sui causa est, ipsa sibi merces' (By no means, then, is that love contracted on the basis of worldly interest worthy of the name of honour of friendship, for friendship is its own cause and its own reward). For the 'better part which cannot be taken away' motif, Luke 10:42: 'Porro unum est necessarium. Maria optimam partem elegit quae non auferetur ab ea.'

gravi e dolorosi punti li conviene passare. L'altro era questo: lo nome d'Amore è sì dolce a udire, che impossibile mi pare che la sua propria operazione sia ne le più cose altro che dolce, con ciò sia cosa che li nomi sèguitino le nominate cose, sì come è scritto: 'Nomina sunt consequentia rerum'. Lo quarto era questo: la donna per cui Amore ti stringe così, non è come l'altre donne, che leggeramente si muova dal suo cuore. E ciascuno mi combattea tanto, che mi facea stare quasi come colui che non sa per qual via pigli lo suo cammino, e che vuole andare e non sa onde se ne vada . . . Io dico che molte di queste donne, accorgendosi de la mia trasfigurazione, si cominciaro a maravigliare, e ragionando si gabbavano di me con questa gentilissima; onde lo ingannato amico di buona fede mi prese per la mano, e traendomi fuori de la veduta di queste donne, sì mi domandò che io avesse. Allora io riposato alquanto, e resurressiti li morti spiriti miei, e li discacciati rivenuti a le loro possessioni, dissi a questo mio amico queste parole: 'Io tenni li piedi in quella parte de la vita, di là da la quale non si puote ire più per intendimento di ritornare'.

(Vita nova 13.1–6 and 14.7–8)[3]

This, then, is the infernal moment of the text, the moment in which, possessed as he is by a sense of love as but a matter of ingratiation, the lover is mocked by his own experience, by his living on in a land from which there can be no return. But then comes its purgatorial moment, the moment in which, having settled upon a fresh sense of love as a matter not of possession but of praise and of all this implies by way again of the most complete kind of spiritual self-surpassing, the poet is called upon to test its adequacy (*a*) to bereavement in the form of Beatrice's premature demise, and (*b*) of a surrogate love, of the love, that is to say, represented in the text by the 'donna gentile' or noble lady of the casement. On

---

3 'After this vision, and having by now set down the words that Love had bid me write, many different thoughts began to strive mightily within me, each of them, as it were, invincible. Of these, four seemed in particular to disturb my peace of mind. One was this: Love's dominion is good in that he dissuades the faithful from willing evil. The next was this: Love's dominion is not good since the greater his servant's faith in him the more grievous and painful the sorrow he must endure. The third was this: so sweet is Love's name to the ear, that his doings, or so it seems to me, can themselves be no other than sweet, since, as has been recorded, names derive from the things named ("Nomina sunt consequentia rerum"). The fourth was this: the lady by way of whom Love so constrains you is not like other ladies whose hearts are easily swayed. And each of these thoughts so contended within me, that I was like one who knows not which road to take, who wishes to set out but knows not which way to go . . . many of those ladies, I say, were aware of my altered state, and, starting to marvel at it and speaking of it one with another, together with this most noble lady made sport of me, at which point my friend, innocent of this and in all good faith, took me by the hand and led me from the sight of those ladies, enquiring of me then what was amiss; whereupon I, rested awhile and with my mortal spirits revived and with those scattered by the occasion at last come home to their proper place, replied thus to my friend: "I have set foot in that region of life where there is no going with any intention of coming back." '

the one hand, then, we have these lines from chapter 23 of the *libello*, lines straightaway calling into question the equality of love even in its now revised substance and finality to death as a principle of foreclosure:

Appresso ciò per pochi dì avvenne che in alcuna parte de la mia persona mi giunse una dolorosa infermitade, onde io continuamente soffersi per nove dì amarissima pena; la quale mi condusse a tanta debolezza, che me convenia stare come coloro li quali non si possono muovere. Io dico che ne lo nono giorno, sentendome dolere quasi intollerabilmente, a me giunse uno pensero lo quale era de la mia donna. E quando ei pensato alquanto di lei, ed io ritornai pensando a la mia debilitata vita; e veggendo come leggero era lo suo durare, ancora che sana fosse, sì cominciai a piangere fra me stesso di tanta miseria. Onde, sospirando forte, dicea fra me medesimo: 'Di necessitade convene che la gentilissima Beatrice alcuna volta si muoia'. E però mi giunse uno sì forte smarrimento, che chiusi li occhi e cominciai a travagliare sì come farnetica persona ed a imaginare in questo modo; che ne lo incominciamento de lo errare che fece la mia fantasia, apparvero a me certi visi di donne scapigliate, che mi diceano: 'Tu pur morrai'; e poi, dopo queste donne, m'apparvero certi visi diversi e orribili a vedere, li quali mi diceano: 'Tu se' morto'.

(*Vita nova* 23.1–4)[4]

while on the other we have these lines turning upon the surrogate possibility, but surrogate in a more than ordinarily subtle sense; for to look upon the noble lady of the casement, Dante suggests, was to intuit not so much an alternative possibility as a way back to Beatrice in the flesh, love for the moment, therefore, living on as a matter withal of *presence*, of the *being there* of my lady as an object of seeing and celebrating:

Avvenne poi che là ovunque questa donna mi vedea, sì si facea d'una vista pietosa e d'un colore palido quasi come d'amore; onde molte fiate mi ricordava de la mia nobilissima donna, che di simile colore si mostrava tuttavia.

4 'It happened a few days after this that I fell prey to a distressing condition in some part of my body from which, for nine days, I suffered without respite grievous pain—pain which reduced me to such weakness that I was perforce like one unable to move. I say, then, that on the ninth day, feeling my suffering to be beyond all endurance, a thought came to me concerning my lady. And having pondered her for a while, my thoughts then turned back to my own feeble existence, at which point, seeing even in the moment of my well-being how transitory it was, I began inwardly to weep at the wretchedness of it all. Then, sighing deeply, I said within myself: "It must needs be that the most noble Beatrice must some day die," at which point, closing my eyes, I fell into a delirium, imagining as I did so certain dishevelled women approaching me and saying: "You too must surely die!"—whereupon other faces, as diverse as they were dreadful to behold, said: "You are indeed dead!" '

E certo molte volte non potendo lagrimare né disfogare la mia tristizia, io andava per vedere questa pietosa donna, la quale parea che tirasse le lagrime fuori de li miei occhi per la sua vista.

(*Vita nova* 36.1–2)[5]

This, then, is the purgatorial moment of the text, the moment in which the contents of understanding are tried and tested in the crucible of pain, this and this alone being the guarantee of their serviceability, of their adequacy to a significant act of self-interpretation and, with it, of self-implementation. And the dividend? Sublime as ever, for it is by way of the struggle thus understood that the pilgrim spirit is able at last to rejoice in its homecoming, in the ecstatic commingling of knowing and unknowing proper to the lover in the moment of his drawing nigh:

> Oltre la spera che più larga gira,
> passa 'l sospiro ch'esce del mio core;
> intelligenza nova, che l'Amore
> piangendo mette in lui, pur sù lo tira.
>   Quand'elli è giunto là dove disira,
> vede una donna che riceve onore,
> e luce sì, che per lo suo splendore
> lo peregrino spirito la mira.
>   Vedela tal, che quando 'l mi ridice,
> io no lo intendo, sì parla sottile
> al cor dolente che lo fa parlare.
>   So io che parla di quella gentile,
> però che spesso ricorda Beatrice,
> sì ch'io lo 'ntendo ben, donne mie care.

(*Vita nova* 41.10–13)[6]

---

5 'It so happened thereafter that whenever this lady saw me, she had about her a compassion and pallor as though of love, thus frequently reminding me of my own most noble lady, herself forever of similar complexion. Often indeed, then, being unable to weep or express my sadness, I went to see this compassionate lady, the sight of whom seemed to draw tears from my eyes.'

6 'Beyond the sphere that circles most widely passes the sigh that issues from my heart. Fresh understanding, instilled there by Love with weeping, draws it upwards. And when it reaches the place of its desiring, it sees a lady most highly honoured and radiant such that the pilgrim spirit gazes upon her in her splendour. Thus contemplating her, it speaks such that I understand not, so subtly does it address my sorrowing heart bidding it tell. But I know it is of that noble one it speaks, for its words summon afresh my memory of Beatrice—which is why, dear my ladies, I understand full well.'

This, then, is the paradisal moment of the text, the moment in which by dint of a species of love-understanding confirmed now in its equality to every twist and turn of fate, the soul enters upon its proper patrimony as but a matter of coming forth, of knowing self in the now revised dimensionality of self. True, much remains to be said and done, the whole project needing by Dante's own admission to be put to one side until such time as he is able to do it justice, to speak of Beatrice as no woman has been spoken of before (the 'spero di dicer di lei quello che mai non fue detto d'alcuna' of the twilight moment of the book). And true, this is celebration under its still youthful aspect, as, for all its typically Dantean courage and consistency, conditioned still by the τόποι of contemporary verse-making in the vernacular. But for all that, this is youthfulness very definitely on the way to maturity in the flame of love, youthfulness as attuned already to the arduous itinerary of specifically human being and becoming.

CHAPTER 2

Literary Hinterland:
From Provençal to the
stilo de la loda

When it comes to the tradition in which Dante stands as the poet par excellence of love as a principle of spiritual self-surpassing, it is he himself who, both in the *De vulgari eloquentia* and in the *Commedia*, confirms the still massive presence to that tradition of its earliest Provençal representatives, geographically and linguistically remote, to be sure, but decisive for every kind of formal and thematic emphasis to come. The substance and psychology of Provençal lyric art—an art represented in its preliminary moment by William Count of Poitiers, Cercamon and Marcabrun active towards the end of the eleventh century and into the twelfth, but in its high or classical moment by Bertran de Born, Arnaut Daniel and Giraut de Bornelh as to the fore among Dante's own Provençal poets[1]—are as complicated as its cultural circumstances, any number of Greek, Latin and Hispano-Arabic ideas and intuitions combining with a feudal sensibility in the area of politics and a Marian sensibility in the area of religion to encourage a highly stylized sense of what it means to love and to love well. Transparent, then,

---

1 Henry John Chaytor, *The Troubadours of Dante: Being Selections from the Works of the Provençal Poets Quoted by Dante* (Oxford: Clarendon Press, 1902); Alan George Ferrers Howell, 'Dante and the Troubadours', in *Dante: Essays in Commemoration, 1321–1921* (London: London University Press, 1921), 191–223; Alfred Jeanroy, 'Dante et les troubadours', in *Dante: Mélanges de critique et d'erudition françaises publiés à l'occasion du VIe centenaire de la mort du poète* (Paris: Union Intellectuelle Franco-Italienne, 1921), 11–21; Salvatore Santangelo, *Dante e i trovatori provenzali* (Catania: Giannotti, 1921; rev. ed. 1959); Gianfranco Folena, *Vulgares eloquentes: Vite e poesie dei trovatori di Dante* (Padua: Liviana, 1961); Silvio Pellegrini, 'Dante e la tradizione poetica volgare dai provenzali ai guittoniani', *CS* 4 (1965), 27–35; François Pirot, 'Dante et les troubadours', *MRom* 15 (1965), 213–19; Sandro Orlando, 'Dante e i suoi trovatori', *LC* 20–21 (1992), 141–56; Stefano Asperti, 'Dante, i trovatori, la poesia', in *Le culture di Dante: Studi in onore di Robert Hollander. Atti del quarto Seminario Dantesco Internazionale, University of Notre Dame (Ind.), USA, 25–27 settembre 2003*, ed. Michelangelo Picone et al. (Florence: Cesati, 2004), 61–92 (with, in the same volume at 93–103, Paolo Cherchi, 'Dante e i trovatori'). More generally, Leslie T. Topsfield, *Troubadours and Love* (Cambridge: Cambridge University Press, 1975); Maurice Valency, *In Praise of Love* (New York: Octagon Books, 1975); Flavio Catenazzi, *L'influsso dei provenzali sui temi e immagini della poesia siculo-toscana* (Brescia: Morcelliana, 1977); Peter Dronke, *The Medieval Lyric* (New York: Cambridge University Press, 1977); Linda Paterson, *Troubadours and Eloquence*, 2nd ed. (Oxford: Oxford University Press, 1982); Simon Gaunt and Sarah Kay (eds.), *The Troubadours: An Introduction* (Cambridge: Cambridge University Press, 1999).

to the social and political circumstances of its coming about, to, again, the feudal component of Provençal lyricism, it was a question as far as love was concerned of the delicate etiquette and fine feeling demanded of the lover as first of all aspiring to love (a *fegnedor*), then as a suppliant in love (a *precador*), then as a suitor in love (an *entededor*), and finally as a liegeman proper (a *drut*). But over and beyond the protocol of fine loving (*fin amors*), and indeed as the hallmark of the fine lover, was the intensity of it all, an intensity faithfully registered by way of style—of the carefully cultivated formalities of the 'open' and 'closed' style (*trobar leu* and *trobar clus*)—as the means of exploring and expressing love's twofold bane and blessing, its presence to the lover as the way of both life and death. On the one hand, then, and of particular significance when it came to the *stilnovisti* or sweet new stylists of Dante's generation, there was Giraut de Bornelh with his commitment—love's complexity notwithstanding—to style as a matter of accessibility:

> A penas sai comensar
> Un vers que volh far leuger,
> E si n'ai pensat des er
> Que.l fezes de tal razo
> Que l'entenda tota gens
> E qu'el fass'a leu chantar;
> Qu'eu.l fatz per pla deportar.
>
> Be.l saupra plus cobert far,
> Mas non a chans pretz enter
> Can tuch no.n son parsoner.
> Qui que.s n'azir, me sap bo,
> Can auch dire per contens
> Mo sonet rauquet e clar,
> E l'auch a la fon portar.
>
> Ja, pos volrai clus trobar,
> No cut aver man parer
> Ab so que ben ai mester
> A far una leu chanso;
> Qu'eu cut c'atretan grans sens
> Es, qui sap razo gardar,
> Co mes motz entrebeschar.

(*A penas sai comensar*, lines 1–21)[2]

2 'I hardly know how to begin a poem which I want to make light and easy, though I've been thinking about it since yesterday, how I might compose it on such lines that everyone may understand it and that

while on the other hand, and representative now of the more properly 'closed' or 'difficult' aspect of Provençal verse making, there was Arnaut Daniel with his commitment to every kind of metrical and expressive refinement from identically rhymed stanzas (*coblas unissonans*) to anaphora, synonym, assonance, consonance, irony and hyperbole on a truly grand scale, style here being but a way into the darkling substance of the spirit:

> Sol sui qui sai lo sobr'afan qu'm sortz
> Al cor, d'amor sofren per sobr'amar,
> Car mos volers es tant ferms et entiers
> C'anc non s'esduis de celliei ni s'estors
> Cui encubic al prim vezer s'e puois.
> C'ades ses lieis dic a lieis cochos motz;
> Puois qan la vei, non sai, tant l'ai, que dire.
> D'autras vezer sui secs, e d'auzir sortz,
> Q'en sola lieis vei e aug et esgar;
> E ges d'aisso no.ill sui fals plazentiers,
> Que mais la vol non ditz la boca.l cors.
> Q'ieu no vau tant chams, vauz ni plas ni puois,
> Q'en un sol cors trob aissi bons aips totz,
> Q'en lieis los volc Dieus trïar et assire.

(*Sols sui qui sai lo sobr'afan qu.m sortz*, lines 7–14)[3]

---

it may be easy to sing; for I'm composing it purely for pleasure. I could easily make it more obscure, but a song's merit is not complete when all are not partners to it. No matter who's irked by it, I'm glad when I hear my little song sung in contention, rough or smooth, and I hear it borne to the public fountain. Never, should I wish to write in the closed style, do I think I'd have much company—apart from the fact that I've need enough to compose an easy song; for I think that it's just as much good sense, if one can keep to the point, as to twist my words round each other.' *Sämtliche Lieder des Troubadors Giraut de Bornelh*, ed. Adolf Kolsen (Halle: M. Niemeyer, 1910–35); Alan R. Press (trans.), *Anthology of Troubadour Lyric Poetry* (Edinburgh: Edinburgh University Press, 1971), 128–31; Bruno Panvini, *Giraldo di Bornelh, trovatore del sec. XIII* (Catania: Università di Catania, Facoltà di lettere e filosofia, 1949); Michelangelo Picone, 'Giraut de Bornelh nella prospettiva di Dante', *VR* 39 (1980), 22–43.

3 'I am the only one who knows the over-anguish which wells in my heart, the suffering of love through over-loving, for my desire is so steadfast and entire that it never turned nor cut loose from her whom I longed for at first sight and ever after. And ever, far from her, I say to her burning words; then, when I see her, I know not what—I've so much—to say. To see other women I am blind, and to hear them, deaf, since by her alone do I see and hear and watch; and in that I am no false flatterer to her, for my heart wants her more than my lips declare. And for all that I travel through so many fields, valleys, plains and hills, I find not thus in one person alone all such qualities, for in her God chose to display and establish them fast.' Arnaut Daniel, *Canzoni*, ed. Gianluigi Toja (Florence: Sansoni, 1960); Alan R. Press (trans.), *Anthology of Troubadour Lyric Poetry* (Edinburgh: Edinburgh University Press, 1971), 186; James J. Wilhelm, *The Poetry of Arnaut Daniel* (New York: Garland, 1981); Pierre Bec (ed. and trans.), *Fin' amor et folie du verbe: Arnaut Daniel* (Gardonne: Fédérop, 2012). With respect to form, Frank M. Chambers, *An Introduction to Old Provençal Versification* (Philadelphia: American Philosophical Society, 1985).

To this, the Sicilians, as constituting in the early part of the thirteenth century the first properly Italian school of lyric poetry, brought a new kind of aristocratic sensibility, a highly centralized, imperial and notarial sensibility as distinct from the provincial and feudal sensibility of the Provençaux, a state of affairs making for an order of verse responsive to the occitanic model but at the same time both thematically and stylistically more consistent, more focused on the substance and psychology of love as a disposition of the spirit and, by and large, more properly 'open' in manner. Essential to any more detailed account of what in this sense amounts to the migration south of Provençal literary concerns, and indeed of Provençal itself as the language of choice in certain sectors of the Italian nobility, would be a review of the social, political and commercial ties linking the two communities and of the diaspora created by the Albigensian crusade soon after the turn of the twelfth century, these between them accounting both for the presence on Italian soil of several of the most prominent Provençal exponents of the art (Pierre Vidal, Aimeric de Pegulhan, Gaucelm Faidit, Uc de Saint-Circ) and for the flourishing of a number of specifically Italian poets writing in Provençal (Lanfranc Cigala, Bonifacio Calvi, Bartolomeo Zorzi and—especially important for the Dante of the *Purgatorio*—Sordello). But none of this, materially significant as it is, can be said single-handedly to explain either the extraordinary self-confidence, at once thematic and technical, of the earliest representatives of the Sicilian tradition of lyric poetry in Italy or their indispensability to what comes next by way of its Tuscan and stilnovistic inflexion. And neither can the fact that the greater part of the Sicilian heritage has come down by way of its Tuscanization detract from our sense of a literary civilization secure in its appropriation of the Provençal precedent and yet faithful to its own sense of the matter to hand; for the Sicilian initiative, content as it is to retreat into the commonplace and merely imitative, even so stands proud of that precedent, any number of its leading representatives from Giacomo da Lentini and Guido delle Colonne among the Sicilians proper to Rinaldo d'Aquino and Giacomino Pugliese among their continental cousins fashioning from it a discourse notable for its tendency to sidestep the contingencies of love in favour of an enquiry into its essential nature and of its status as a property of pure consciousness. So, for example, among the Sicilians proper, we have Judge Guido delle Colonne, happy to settle for the time-honoured programme of service to madonna as the poet's high calling but engaged above all at the point of awareness, of the twofold sensation and symptomatology of love:

> La mia gran pena e lo gravoso af[f]anno,
> c'ò lungiamente per amor patuto,
> madonna lo m'à 'n gioia ritornato;
> pensando l'avenente di mio danno,
> in sua merze[de] m'ave riceputo
> e lo sofrire mal m'à meritato:

ch'ella m'à dato—tanto bene avire,
che lo sofrire—molta malenanza
agi' ubriato, e vivo in allegranza.

(*La mia gran pena e lo gravoso af[f]anno*, lines 1–9)[4]

while prominent among the continental representatives of Sicilian verse making
is Rinaldo d'Aquino, words failing him, he says, when it comes to describing the
tyranny and turmoil of it all:

In amoroso pensare
ed in gran disïanza
per voi, bella, son miso,
sì ch'eo non posso posare,
tant'agio tempestanza.
Vostr'amor, che m'à priso
a lo core tanto coralemente,
mi distringe e distene
la voglia e la spene
e donami martiri,
sì ch'io non por[r]ia diri
come m'avete preso fortemente.

(*In amoroso pensare*, lines 1–12)[5]

4 'My lady has from the great pain and deep grief that I have long since suffered fashioned but joy;
pondering in her beauty that same suffering, she has in her mercy received me and rewarded the
wretchedness I have known; for she has made mine so much good that I, living on as I do in bliss, have
quite forgotten the evil I have suffered.' Gianfranco Contini (ed.), *Poeti del Duecento*, vol. 1 (Milan:
Riccardo Ricciardi, 1960), 97–98; also Bruno Panvini (ed.), *Le rime della scuola siciliana* (Florence:
Olschki, 1962–64). Vincenzo De Bartholomaeis, *Primordi della lirica d'arte in Italia* (Turin: Società
editrice internazionale, 1943); Salvatore Santangelo, *Le origini della lirica provenzaleggiante in Sicilia*
(Catania: Gianotta, 1949); Gianfranco Folena, 'Cultura e poesia dei Siciliani', in *Storia della letteratura
italiana*, ed. Emilio Cecchi and Natalino Sapegno (Milan: Garzanti, 1965), 271–347; Gianfranco Folena,
'La poesia dei siciliani e le origini della tradizione lirica italiana', in *Dizionario critico della letteratura
italiana*, ed. Vittore Branca (Turin: Unione tipografico-editrice torinese, 1974), 385–96 (2nd ed., 1986);
Emilio Pasquini and Antonio Enzo Quaglio, *Le origini e la scuola siciliana* (Bari: Laterza, 1971); Frede
Jensen (ed. and trans.), *The Poetry of the Sicilian School* (New York: Garland, 1986); Bruno Panvini,
Poeti della corte di Federigo II, rev. ed. (Naples: Liguori Editore, 1994); Karla Mallette, *The Kingdom of
Sicily, 1100–1250: A Literary History* (Philadelphia: University of Pennsylvania Press, 2005). On the
Italian troubadours, Giulio Bertoni, *I trovatori d'Italia: Biografie, testi, traduzioni, note* (Geneva: Slatkine
Reprints, 1974 [1915]); Francesco Ugolini, *La poesia e l'Italia: Scelta di testi con introduzione e note*
(Modena: Società tipografica modenese, 1939).
5 'To such thoughts of love, o beauteous lady, and to such great desiring have I been brought by
you, that, burdened by grief, I know no peace. Your love, which has so completely taken hold of my

True, the Sicilian poet has more strings than this to his bow, any number of distinctive emphases feeding into the Dantean *dolce stil novo* or sweet new style as under one at least of its aspects a systematic resolution of the Sicilian initiative; so, for example, the case of Giacomo da Lentini with his already developed sense of love as a matter of praise, a motif, it is true, closer for the moment to conceit than to confession but even so presaging things to come:

> Io m'ag[g]io posto in core a Dio servire,
> com'io potesse gire in paradiso,
> al santo loco, c'aggio audito dire,
> u' si mantien sollazzo, gioco e riso.
> Sanza mia donna non vi voria gire,
> quella c'à blonda testa e claro viso,
> che sanza lei non poteria gaudere,
> estando da la mia donna diviso.
> Ma no lo dico a tale intendimento,
> perch'io peccato ci volesse fare;
> se non veder lo suo bel portamento
> e lo bel viso e 'l morbido sguardare:
> ché lo mi teria in gran consolamento,
> veg[g]endo la mia donna in ghiora stare.[6]

And then too, and quite as indispensable to everything coming next, there is the scientific or love-philosophical component of Sicilian lyricism, at its most refined in the *tenzone* or poetic correspondence of Jacopo Mostacci, of the Pier delle Vigne of *Inferno* fame, and, again, of the Notaro Giacomo da Lentini, where it is a question of what love actually is. Is it a mere nothing, a mere passing inflexion of the spirit, a mood of the moment engendered by this or that occasional

---

heart, constrains and destroys my willing and my hoping such that, burdened by suffering, I find no words to explain how completely you have laid hold of me.'

6 'I am of a mind to serve God in order that I may go to heaven, to that sacred place where, as I have heard tell, there is endless peace, joy and laughter. But I would not wish to go there without my lady, her of the fair hair and radiant complexion, for were I to be separated from her there could be no rejoicing. I do not say this, however, with any sinful intent, only to see her gracious bearing, her beautiful face and gentle glance; for I would count it my greatest happiness to see my lady in glory.' *The Poetry of Giacomo da Lentino, Sicilian Poet of the Thirteenth Century*, ed. Ernest F. Langley (Cambridge, MA: Harvard University Press, 1915; repr. New York: Kraus, 1966); Ernest Hatch Wilkins, 'The Invention of the Sonnet', *MP* 13.8 (1915), 463–94 (and in a revised form in *The Invention of the Sonnet* [Rome: Edizioni di Storia e Letteratura, 1959], 11–39); Christopher Kleinhenz, *The Early Italian Sonnet: The First Century (1220–1321)* (Lecce: Milella, 1986); Roberto Antonelli, 'L'"invenzione" del sonetto', *CN* 47 (1987), 19–59; Roberto Antonelli, 'Giacomo da Lentini e l'"invenzione" della lirica italiana', *CT* 12.1 (2009), 1–24. For Giacomo da Lentini and Dante, Christopher Kleinhenz, 'Giacomo Lentini and Dante: The Early Italian Sonnet Tradition in Perspective', *JMRS* 8.2 (1978), 217–34.

encounter? Or are we in the presence here of something more substantial, of a force operative from out of the depths and thus making a bid for being in its entirety? Mostacci, evidently perplexed by the whole thing and unable to see in it anything other than a passing principle of pleasure, is for this reason happy to defer to those more properly in the know:

> Sollicitando un poco meo savire
> e con lui mi vogliendo delettare.
> un dubbio che mi misi ad avire,
> a vui lo mando per determinare.
> Onn'omo dice ch'amor ha podire
> e li coragi distringe ad amare,
> ma eo no lo voglio consentire,
> però ch'amore no parse né pare.
> Ben trova l'om una amorositate
> la quale par che nasca da placire,
> e zo vol dire om che sia amore.
> Eo no li sazzo altra qualitate;
> ma zo che è da vui voglio odire;
> per zo ve ne fazzo sentenzatore.[7]

Pier delle Vigne, by contrast, happy as he is to concur in point of love's invisibility, is nonetheless persuaded of its status as something rather than nothing, as—like a magnet—an innate and abiding principle of attraction all the more powerful for its elusiveness:

> Però ch'amore non si pò vedire
> e non si tratta corporalemente,
> manti ne son di sì folle sapire
> che credeno ch'amor sïa nïente.

---

7 'Taxing for a moment my own wit, and wishing thereby to derive some pleasure, I began to have some doubt, which I send on to you for settlement. Everyone says that love is possessed of power and constrains the heart to love, but I am not inclined to accept this because love never has and never does put in an appearance. A man, to be sure, discovers in himself an amorous disposition apparently engendered by pleasure, and that's what people wish to call love. For myself, that's all I can see to it, but I'd like to know what you make of it, which is why I call upon you to pronounce on the matter.' Michelangelo Picone, 'La tenzone "de amore" fra Iacopo Mostacci, Pier della Vigna e il Notaio', in *Il genere "tenzone" nelle letterature romanze delle origini. Atti del Convegno Internazionale, Losanna 13–15 novembre 1997*, ed. Matteo Pedroni (Ravenna: Longo, 1999), 13–31 (and in Michelangelo Picone, *Percorsi della lirica duecentesca: Dai Siciliani alla 'Vita Nova'* [Florence: Cadmo, 2003], 47–67). More generally, Salvatore Santangelo, *Le tenzoni poetiche nella letteratura italiana delle origini* (Geneva: Olschki, 1928); Simone Marcenaro, 'Polemiche letterarie nella lirica italiana del Duecento', *RFR* 27 (2010), 77–99.

> Ma po' ch'amore si face sentire
> dentro dal cor signoreggiar la gente,
> molto maggiore presio de' avire
> che se 'l vedessen visibelemente.
>   Per la vertute de la calamita
> como lo ferro attrai no se vede,
> ma sì lo tira signorivolmente;
>   e questa cosa a credere mi 'nvita
> ch'amore sia, e dàmme grande fede
> che tuttor fia creduto fra la gente.[8]

And then finally there is Giacomo da Lentini, who, taking up where his corre-spondents leave off, proceeds by way of the psychogenesis of love, of its coming about as a disposition of the spirit. Happy, therefore, to acquiesce in Pier delle Vigne's sense of the power of love fully and unequivocally to possess the lover, he opts for a species of intentionalism, of the heart, that is to say, as nourished by the phantasm or image of madonna as generated by the positive encounter, in the moment itself of seeing and sighing:

> Amor è un desio che ven da core
> per abbundanza de gran placimento;
> e gli ochi en prima generan l'amore
> e lo core li dà nutricamento.
>   Ben è alcuna fiata om amatore
> senza vedere so 'nnamoramento,
> ma quell'amor che stringe cum furore
> da la vista de li ochi à nascimento:
>   ché li ochi rapresentan a lo core
> d'onni cosa che veden bon' e ria,
> cum è formata naturalemente;
>   e lo cor, che di zo è concepitore,
> immagina, e [qual] place, quel desia:
> e questo amore regna fra la gente.[9]

8 'Because love cannot be seen or encountered in the flesh, there are many foolish enough to be-lieve that it does not exist. But because love makes itself felt from within the heart whence it rules those subject to it, it should be prized all the more than were it visible. How it is that a magnet attracts iron we cannot see, but it does, and powerfully, which is what inclines me to believe both that love actually exists and that that, henceforth, is how people will see it.'

9 'Love is a yearning proceeding from the heart by way of a surfeit of delight. The eyes, to begin with, generate love, which is then nourished by the heart. Sometimes, to be sure, a man loves other than by way of perception, but the love which lays hold of him most fervently is that born of the eyes and of seeing; for the eyes pass on to the heart every good and evil thing they see according to its proper

If, then, to this we add a characteristic delight in paradox, an able deployment of the naturalistic image and a refined implementation of just about all the main genres of vernacular lyric art, including the lament or *planctus* and the indictment or *improperium*, we have a literary phenomenon scarcely less than astonishing in point both of confidence and of sophistication, a lyric culture fully adult, so to speak, before its time. But with the eclipse of the Hohenstaufen dynasty at Benevento in 1266 and the shifting of the centre of poetic gravity northwards, it was the turn of the Tuscan or transitional school of lyric art under the auspices of Guittone d'Arezzo as its dominant presence. In fact, for the purposes of understanding the new school and its function within the Siculo-Tuscan and stilnovistic tradition of verse making generally, it is better to speak not so much of 'transitionalism' with all this suggests by way of mere administration as of an attempt to fashion from fine loving and from the exquisite psychologism thereof a discourse genuinely transparent to its new circumstances, genuinely expressive of communal as distinct from courtly civility. True, both substance and tone alike are for much of the time passive enough, some of its most prominent representatives persevering come what may in the ways and means of Sicilian versifying; so, for example, Dante's spokesman in the *Purgatorio* for the old Tuscan way, Bonagiunta da Lucca, from time to time as adventurous a spirit as Guittone himself but as often as not a mere purveyor of the Sicilian legacy and distinctly restive in respect of anything threatening its ascendancy. On the one hand, then, there is the sonnet *Tutto lo mondo si mantien per fiore*, recognizably Sicilian in substance and spirit but testifying in its mannerism to, somewhere in the recesses, the self-conscious longueur of it all:

> Tutto lo mondo si mantien per fiore:
> se fior non fosse, frutto non seria;
> [e] per lo fiore si mantene amore,
> gioie e alegrezze, ch'è gran signoria.
> E de la fior son fatto servidore
> sì di bon core che più non poria:
> in fiore ho messo tutto 'l meo valore;
> si fiore mi falisse, ben moria.
> Eo son fiorito e vado più fiorendo;
> in fiore ho posto tutto il mi' diporto;
> per fiore ag[g]io la vita certamente.
> Com' più fiorisco, più in fior m'intendo;

---

form, and the heart, as alert to this, fashions an image thereof and desires whatsoever pleases it. And this is the love that holds sway in the world.' Ulrich Mölk, 'Le sonnet *Amor è un desio* de Giacomo da Lentini et le problème de la genèse de l'amour', *Cahiers de Civilisation Médiévale* 14 (1971), 329–39.

se fior mi falla, ben serïa morto,
vostra mercé, madonna, fior aulente.[10]

while on the other hand, and registering explicitly the reactionary mood of Tuscan lyricism, its looking askance at the philosophical and psychological sophistication of the sweet new style now on the horizon (suspiciously Bolognese and bookish), there is the sonnet *Voi, ch'avete mutata la mainera* addressed to Guinizzelli and touching precisely upon, as Bonagiunta sees it, the betrayal of the old school by the new:

> Voi, ch'avete mutata la mainera
> de li piagenti ditti de l'amore
> de la forma dell'esser là dov'era,
> per avansare ogn'altro trovatore,
>   avete fatto como la lumera,
> ch'a le scure partite dà sprendore,
> ma non quine ove luce l'alta spera,
> la quale avansa e passa di chiarore.
>   Così passate voi di sottigliansa,
> e non si può trovar chi ben ispogna,
> cotant' è iscura vostra parlatura.
>   Ed è tenuta grave dissimigliansa,
> ancor che 'l senno vegna da Bologna,
> traier canson per forsa di scritura.[11]

But for all his no less eager commitment to the substance and psychology of Siculo-Tuscan lyricism in its now ageing aspect, it was Guittone rather than

---

10 'Everything that is, is thanks to the flower, for where there is no flower there can be no fruit; and love too, with all its joy and happiness, is thanks to the flower in its sovereignty. And of the flower I have become the most willing of servants, investing in it my every worth. Should it fail me, I would most certainly die. I am in flower and shall go on flourishing, for in the flower is my every delight and, for sure, my very life. The more I flower, the more I love the flower, which, should it fail will—thanks to you, my lady, flower most fragrant—most certainly be my death' (*Poeti del Duecento*, vol. 1, ed. Gianfranco Contini [Milan: Riccardo Ricciardi, 1960]), 271; see too *Bonagiunta Orbicciani da Lucca: Rime*, ed. Aldo Menichetti (Florence: Edizioni del Galluzzo per la Fondazione Ezio Franceschini, 2012); Elda Coffari, *Bonagiunta Orbicciani* (Palermo: Corselli, 1934); Decio Pierantozzi, 'Bonagiunta Orbicciani campione del "trobar leu"', *Conv* 2 (1948), 873–87; Nicola Nuzzi, *Bonagiunta Orbicciani da Lucca e la civiltà letteraria del Duecento: Studio storico, filologico, critico* (Rome: Aurelia, 1972).

11 'You who have changed the way of love's sweet sayings, nay their very form and substance as it once was, and this simply for the sake of outdoing every other versifier, you have indeed been like a light to lighten up dark places, but not here where shines the sovereign star surpassing all others in its brilliance. So completely do you outdo everyone with your subtlety that none can explain the obscurity of what you say. And although the sense of it is from Bologna, it is deemed mightily untoward to fashion canzoni from mere books.'

Bonagiunta who addressed most strenuously the real issue here, namely that of fashioning from his inheritance a poetic voice more properly faithful to the times, to the sturdy substance of bourgeois consciousness. True, a sense of the hopelessness of it all eventually won out with the result that halfway through this life of ours Guittone took the habit, or at any rate enrolled in the Order of the Knights of St Mary (an order subsisting somewhere on the frontiers of the religious and of the secular life), this, he says, freeing him at last for his authentic voice:

> Ora parrà s'eo saverò cantare
> e s'eo varrò quanto valer già soglio,
> poiché del tutto Amor fug[g]h' e disvoglio,
> e più che cosa mai forte mi spare;
>   ch'a om tenuto saggio audo contare
> che trovare—non sa né valer punto
> omo d'Amor non punto;
> ma' che digiunto—da vertà mi pare,
> se lo pensare—a lo parlare—sembra;
> ché 'n tutte parte ove distringe Amore,
> regge follore—in loco di savere.
> Donque como valere
> pò, né piacere—di guisa alcuna fiore,
> poi dal Fattore—d'ogni valor—disembra
> e al contrar d'ogne mainer' asembra?

> (*Ora parrà s'eo saverò cantare*, lines 1–15)[12]

12 'Now we shall see whether I can still sing, and this as well as I once did, since now, appearing to me as he does more than all else odious, I eschew and disown Love altogether. Since from one acclaimed for his wisdom I've heard tell that no one can make verses or be of any avail whatever unless bitten by Love; but thinking and speaking being of a piece, he seems to me wide of the mark, for wherever Love is in power, there reigns folly in place of wisdom. How, then, given that he is so far from the author of all goodness and indeed resembles in all his ways the very enemy thereof, can he commend himself or please in any way?' *Poeti del Duecento*, vol. 1, ed. Gianfranco Contini (Milan: Riccardo Ricciardi, 1960), 214–17; see too Francesco Egidi, *Le rime di Guittone d'Arezzo* (Bari: Laterza, 1940). Achille Pellizzari, *La vita e le opere di Guittone d'Arezzo* (Pisa: Fratelli Nistri, 1906; repr. Rome: Studio Bibliografico A. Polla, 1976); Mario Marti, 'Ritratto e fortuna di Guittone d'Arezzo', in *Realismo dantesco e altri studi* (Milan: Riccardo Ricciardi, 1961), 126–55; Claude Margueron, *Recherches sur Guittone d'Arezzo: Sa vie, son époque, sa culture* (Paris: Presses Universitaires de France, 1966); Agnello Baldi, *Guittone d'Arezzo fra impegno e poesia* (Salerno: Società Editrice Salernitana, 1975); Vincent Moleta, *The Early Poetry of Guittone d'Arezzo* (London: Modern Humanities Research Association, 1976); Francesco Bruni, 'Agonismo guittoniano: Risemantizzazione, polisemia e colori dell'ambiguità in una sequenza di sonetti', in *Guittone d'Arezzo nel settimo centenario della morte*, ed. Michelangelo Picone (Florence: Cesati, 1995), 89–123; Olivia Holmes, 'Guittone d'Arezzo', in Olivia Homes, *Assembling the Lyric Self: Authorship from Troubadour Song to Italian Poetry Book* (Minneapolis: University of Minne-

—lines to which, for the purposes of confirming the confessional intensity of it all, we may add these from one of his more properly ascetic canzoni, lines for all their leaden-footedness—or perhaps better *by way* of their leaden-footedness—testifying to a genuine capacity in Guittone for spiritual self-confrontation and thus for the significant statement:

> Ahi, quant'ho che vergogni e che doglia aggio,
> e quant'ho che sbaldisca e che gioire,
> se bene isguardo, col veder d'om saggio,
> u' so, u' fui, u' spero anche venire!
> Vergognar troppo e doler, lasso, deggio,
> poi fui dal mio principio a mezza etate
> in loco laido, desorrato e brutto,
> ove m'involsi tutto,
> e venni ingrotto, infermo, pover, nuto,
> cieco, sordo e muto,
> desviato, vanito, morto e peggio:
> ché tutto el detto mal m'avea savore;
> ché quanto al prenditore
> più mal piace, è peggiore.
> Ché pur nel mal, lo qual for grato offende,
> alcun remedio om prende,
> ma mal gradivo ben tutto roina,
> e non ha medicina,
> che solo la divina pietate.

(*Ahi, quant'ho che vergogni e che doglia aggio,* lines 1–19)[13]

---

sota Press, 2000), 47–70; Antonio Gagliardi, *Il filosofo e il poeta Guittone d'Arezzo* (Pisa: Edizioni ETS, 2015).

13 'Ah, what shame and sorrow is mine, and what gladness and rejoicing if carefully I look, and consider with the eyes of a wise man, where I am, where I have been and where I hope to be. I ought, alas, to be more than ashamed and more than anguished in that from the time of my birth to my middle years I languished in a filthy, disreputable and repulsive state, a state in which I wallowed, sickened, became enfeebled, impoverished, naked, blind, deaf, dumb, lost, empty, dead and worse besides. For all this evil I positively relished, for the more evil pleases its disciple, the more evil it is. For while the evil in which a man takes no delight may find a remedy, my own evil was to rejoice in my ruin, and for this there can be no salve but divine mercy.' For the 'love as *un*love' motif in the second Guittone, the same canzone at lines 26–31: 'Fra gli altri miei follor fo, ch'eo trovai / de disamor, ch'amai: / pregiai onta, e cantai dolze di pianto; / ed ingegnaime manto / in fare me ed altrui saccente e forte / 'n perder perdendo nostro Dio e amico' (Among my other follies I wrote of unlove, which I loved. I prized shame and sang sweetly of tears, and spared no pains in enlightening and strengthening both myself and others in the way of losing—of losing both our God and our friend).

But for all the misgiving of Fra Guittone with respect to love under its neo-courtly aspect (love under its neocourtly aspect amounting as far as he is concerned merely to *un*love or 'disamor', to a parody of the real thing in its power to distract and to waylay the spirit), it is, for our present purposes, the poetry of the as yet unbrothered Guittone that most matters, the Guittone struggling to fashion from his Sicilian heritage a means of self-understanding and self-actualization, something that in the event issues in one or other—or both—of two things: either (*a*) a poetic utterance indeed transparent to the problematics of his own troubled existence, or (*b*) a species of mannerism standing in for anything more substantial, a virtuosity sufficient unto itself. So, for example, as far as the first of these things is concerned, we have the sonnet *Lo dolor e la gioi' del meo coraggio*, a sonnet which, though on the face of it largely routine, gives expression to a characteristically Guittonian angst, to a species of self-inexplicability transcending the merely commonplace:

> Lo dolor e la gioi del meo coraggio
> non vo poria, bona donna, contare;
> ché dolor ò, che m'è d'onni altro maggio,
> che voi pur reo voletemi pensare;
> 　gioi ò di ciò, che mi' amore e mi' omaggio
> vi piace, al modo de lo meo parlare;
> ma non mi torna guaire inn-allegraggio,
> se voi per fin non mi posso aprovare.
> 　Però vo prego, per mercé, che agio
> e loco date me, du' pienamente
> demostrive s'eo son bon u malvagio;
> 　e, s'eo son bon, piaccia vo pienamente,
> e s'eo so reo, sofrir pena e mesagio
> voglio tutto, sì con voi serà gente.[14]

while as far as the second of them is concerned we have the sonnet *Già lungiamente sono stato punto*, a sonnet turning ostensibly on the need in art for a measure of dissimulation (this being the only way of holding prying eyes at bay), but victim in the event to technique pure and simple, form here—as alas it so often does in Guittone —straying in the direction of irresponsibility:

14 'The sorrows and the joy I bear within me, my good lady, I could not recount, for the sorrow I have, which I count greater than any other, is that you are inclined to think ill of me. The joy I have is that my love, my homage and my words are alike pleasing to you. But there will be no speedy return to happiness for me for as long as you withhold your acknowledgement of my goodness. I therefore beseech you of your mercy that you grant me ease and opportunity whence I might prove to you my worth or otherwise. And if I prove worthy, then may this please you above aught else; and if I prove unworthy then I shall embrace, as acceptable in your sight, every pain and suffering.'

Già lungiamente sono stato punto,
sì punto—m'ave la noiosa gente,
dicendo de saver uve mi punto;
sì tal punto—mi fa quasi piangente.
    Poi, se·mmi miro, non credone punto,
sì punto—so', 've 'n stando onor v'è gente,
poi mïo voler de gioi' ha punto,
che punto—è verso, sì face ha piagente.
    Ferò como lo bono arcero face:
face—fa de fedire in tale parte,
sparte—di ciò, u' non par badi, fede.
    A tutti amanti sì de' farse face:
sface—ciò de penser l'aversa parte,
parte—che vive in error de su' fede.[15]

Guittone's, then, was a struggle to make his own a legacy which, from the point of view of an earnest rather than of an elegant spirit, remained fundamentally alien to him, his espousal of fine loving as a means of self-elucidation making at the level of content only for a sense of the impossibility of it all and at the level of style for difficulty as the only solution. And what applies to Guittone as by common consent the leading light of Tuscan lyricism applies also to those of his acolytes and admirers who, if not indifferent to the forces making now for a renewal and, with it, for a purification both of substance and of style, remained even so wedded to the old way, to the stock-in-trade of occitanic and Sicilian verse making; so, for example, Onesto da Bologna, Rustico di Filippo and Chiaro Davanzati, with, as prominent among them, the very Guido Guinizzelli present to the Dante of the *Purgatorio* as father both to himself and to all those still more accomplished in the deployment of love's sweet rhymes.[16] Now Guinizzelli was a nothing if not

15 'For a while now I have been stung, so stung have I been by the noisome folk enquiring after where I was stung, a stinging that has made me well-nigh weep. But taking stock of myself, I believe not a word of it; so stung am I that only honour and nobility can come of it; for my will now has its every joy, and—so beautiful is she to behold—will never turn away. So I shall do as a good archer does, who, appearing to take aim and shoot in a direction other than he actually intends, distracts attention from his real target, appearing not to care about it. Every lover should thus dissimulate, diverting attention elsewhere and leaving others to mistake his true intention.'

16 *Purgatorio* 26.97–99 ('il padre / mio e de li altri miei miglior che mai / rime d'amore usar dolci e leggiadre'). Roberto Rea, 'Guinizzelli Praised and Explained (da "[O] caro padre meo" al XXVI del *Purgatorio*)', *The Italianist* 30.1 (2010), 1–17; Donato Pirovano, 'Il padre mio e degli altri miei miglior: Guido Guinizzelli', in *Il dolce stil novo* (Rome: Salerno, 2014), 266–80. More generally, Francesco Biondolillo, 'La poesia di Guido Guinizzelli', *Archivium Romanicum* 21 (1937), 327–35; Raffaele Spongano, 'La gloria del primo Guido', in *Dante e Bologna nei tempi di Dante* (Bologna: Commissione per i testi di lingua, 1967), 3–12; Guglielmo Gorni, 'Guido Guinizzelli e la nuova "mainera"', in *Per Guido Guinizzelli* (Padua: Antenore, 1980; vol. 40 in the series *Medioevo e umanesimo*), 37–52; Italo Bertelli, *La poesia di Guido Guinizzelli e la poetica del "Dolce Stil Novo"* (Florence: Le Monnier, 1983); Pietro Pelosi, *Guido*

able administrator of the tradition in which he stands in both its Sicilian and its Tuscan aspect, any number of his sonnets and canzoni reflecting the metrical, rhetorical and imaginative moeurs of, say, a Giacomo da Lentini or a Guido delle Colonne among the Sicilians or indeed of Guittone himself among the Tuscans. But for all that, his is a conscientious espousal of the stilnovistic idea both in its thematic and in its stylistic aspects, in respect, that is to say, both of love's power to new life and of all this implies by way of the transparency in the poem of form to substance, of the justification of form in its every lexical, syntactical and rhetorical aspect from out of the depths. Exemplary in this sense is the praise poem *Io voglio del ver la mia donna laudare*, a poem perfectly accountable to the tradition within which it stands but nonetheless qualitatively other both thematically and technically, more than ever attentive, that is to say, to the hidden dialectic of love on the one hand and to the gentle discursiveness of the line on the other:

> Io voglio del ver la mia donna laudare
> ed asembrarli la rosa e lo giglio;
> più che stella dïana splende e pare,
> e ciò ch'è lassù bello a lei somiglio.
> Verde river'a lei rasembro e l'âre,
> tutti color di fior', giano e vermiglio,
> oro ed azzurro e ricche gioi per dare;
> medesmo Amor per lei rafina meglio.
> Passa per via adorna, e sì gentile
> ch'abassa orgoglio a cui dona salute,
> e fa 'l de nostra fé se non la crede;
> e no·lle pò apressare om che sia vile;
> ancor ve dirò c'ha maggior vertute;
> null' om pò mal pensar fin che la vede.[17]

True, the Sicilian model is not very far away, the quatrains especially recalling the praise style of Giacomo da Lentini as apt to delight in the radiance of madon-

---

Guinizzelli: Stilnovo inquieto (Naples: Liguori, 2000); Paolo Borsa, *La nuova poesia di Guido Guinizzelli* (Florence: Cadmo, 2007).

17 'I wish in truth to praise my lady and liken her to the rose and to the lily; brighter than the morning star does she seem in her radiance, and I compare her to everything most beautiful there above. I liken her to a green bank and to the very air, to flowers of every colour, yellow, red, gold and blue and every rich jewel worthy of giving, for Love himself is perfected through her. So exquisite and so noble is she as she passes by, that pride is everywhere brought low in those whom she greets, and the unbeliever, if thus he be, confirmed in belief. There is no approaching her by the wretched, and again I say to you that she is replete in all goodness. No man, having once seen her, can think ill.' *Poeti del Duecento*, vol. 2, ed. Gianfranco Contini (Milan: Riccardo Ricciardi, 1960), 472; see too Edoardo Sanguineti, *Guido Guinizzelli: Rime* (Milan: Mondadori, 1986), and for Guinizzelli in translation, Robert Edwards, *The Poetry of Guido Guinizzelli* (New York: Garland, 1987).

na's presence in the world, its sheer outshining. But with the imaginative generosity of the quatrains behind us we come in the tercets to something if not absent
from the tradition so far then subject now to systematic statement, namely to a
sense of love as but a principle of being and becoming in the lover, as that whereby
he knows himself in the now more refined substance of self—a notion that brings
us to the first of the great manifesto pieces of the sweet new style, to the canzone
Al cor gentil rempaira sempre amore as a meditation upon the power of love to
spiritual transfiguration, to a species of new life. True, when it comes to the power
of love to spiritual renewal, we remain with Guinizzelli somewhere in the foothills
of the Dantean *stil novo*, for everywhere present in Guinizzelli, and not least in
this very canzone, are the safeguards, caveats, qualifications and misgivings of the
timid spirit. On the one hand, then, there is Guinizzelli's sense of *gentilezza* or
nobility not as a *product* but as a *principle* of love, as the prior and necessary condition of its coming home and of its in-abiding as a disposition of the spirit. Thus
on the very threshold of the text we have the following, an essay, precisely, on
nobility—meaning by this nobility of the spirit—as the *prius* of love properly
understood:

> Al cor gentil rempaira sempre amore
> come l'ausello in selva a la verdura;
>   né fe' amor anti che gentil core,
> né gentil core anti ch'amor, natura;
> ch'adesso con' fu 'l sole,
>   sì tosto lo splendore fu lucente,
> né fu davanti 'l sole;
> e prende amore in gentilezza loco
> così propïamente
> come calore in clarità di foco.
>   Foco d'amore in gentil cor s'aprende
> come vertute in petra prezïosa,
>   che da la stella valor no i discende
> anti che 'l sol la faccia gentil cosa;
>   poi che n'ha tratto fòre
> per sua forza lo sol ciò che li è vile,
> stella li dà valore;
> così lo cor ch'è fatto da natura
> asletto, pur, gentile,
> donna a guisa di stella lo 'nnamora.[18]

18 'Love repairs to the noble heart like a bird to the green wood; neither was love fashioned by
nature before the noble heart, nor the noble heart before love. For only in the moment of its making
did the light of the sun shine forth, that light in no wise preceding the sun. And love takes its proper

while on the other hand we have these lines from the end of the poem with their abrupt stopping short of anything approaching Dante's radical theologization of the matter, his sense of madonna as in very truth an epiphanous presence among us. It was simply, says Guinizzelli, that she *seemed* like an angel. What fault of mine that I loved her?

> Donna, Deo mi dirà: 'Che presomisti?',
> sïando l'alma mia a lui davanti.
>   'Lo ciel passasti e 'nfin a Me venisti
> e desti in vano amor Me per semblanti:
>   ch'a Me conven le laude
>   e a la reina del regname degno,
>   per cui cessa onne fraude'.
> Dir Li porò: 'Tenne d'angel sembianza
> che fosse del Tuo regno;
> non me fu fallo, s'in lei posi amanza'.

(*Al cor gentil rempaira sempre amore*, lines 51–60)[19]

But for all that, we are on new ground, for timidity aside it is a question now of the lover's standing obediently in the presence of his lady with a view, not merely to looking upon her in a spirit of adoration but to living out all that she is and all that she signifies by way of her surpassing excellence:

> Splende 'n la 'ntelligenzïa del cielo
> Deo crïator più che ['n] nostr'occhi 'l sole:
> ella intende suo fattor oltra 'l cielo,

---

place in the noble heart just as warmth does in the light of the fire. The fire of love cleaves to the noble heart as virtue to a precious stone, for that power enters not into it before the sun has fashioned from it something noble. As soon as the sun has purged it of all ignobility, the star lends it virtue. So it is with the heart, which, chosen by nature, pure and refined, is enamoured by my lady as the stone is empowered by the star.' Giovanni Federzoni, *La canzone di Guido Guinizzelli: "Al cor gentil ripara sempre amore"* (Bologna: Zanichelli, 1905); Ernest Hatch Wilkins, 'A Note on Guinizzelli's "Al cor gentil"', *MP* 12.6 (1914), 325–30; Francesco Torraca, 'La canzone "Al cor gentil ripara sempre amore"', *Atti della Reale Accademia di Archeologia, Lettere e Belle Arti* 13.1 (1935), 41–66; Mario Casella, 'Al cor gentil repara sempre amore', *Studi romanzi* 30 (1943), 5–53; Vincent Moleta, ' "Al cor gentil": Canzone pre-dantesca o post-guittoniana?', *SPCT* 13 (1976), 24–46; Stefano Asperti, 'Sull'incipit di Guinizzelli, "Al cor gentil . . ."', *NRLI* 7.1–2 (2004), 81–121.

19 ' "Woman", God will say to my soul when it stands before him, "What presumption is this? You bypassed heaven to enter into my presence and sought to compare me to a love more vain; for all honour is due to me and to the queen of this noble realm by whom every false profession of faith is ended." To him I shall be able to say: "She had about her the likeness of but an angel of your realm. If, then, I loved her, I did no wrong." '

e 'l ciel volgiando, a Lui obedir tole;
   e con' segue, al primero,
del giusto Deo beato compimento,
così dar dovria, al vero,
la bella donna, poi che ['n] gli occhi splende
del suo gentil, talento
che mai di lei obedir non si disprende.

(*Al cor gentil rempaira sempre amore*, lines 41–50)[20]

Guinizzelli's, then, for all his holding back when it comes as it does in Dante to a still more sublime proposal of the whole matter, to a now thoroughgoing sense of madonna's miraculous not to say messianic presence in the world, constitutes even so a response to the impasse of Guittonian lyricism, to—as far as Guittone was concerned—the impossibility of fashioning from the love-lyric hitherto a persuasive means of self-interpretation. And with this—this seeing and setting up of the affective issue in terms of living out at first hand the deep substance of the encounter—we come, almost, to Dante, almost but not quite; for no less decisive for his coming about as a sweet new stylist, though serving in the event both to facilitate and to complicate it, is the figure of Guido Cavalcanti as author, architect and spokesman-in-chief for the Florentine *stil novo*. The key text here is the studiously difficult canzone *Donna me prega perch'eo voglio dire*, studiously difficult in point (a) of its sense of love as but a principle of radical destabilization in human experience, and (b) of its marshalling every kind of expressive strategy—lexical, syntactical and metrical alike—for the purpose of affirming the well-nigh atrocious agony of this situation, the power of love, properly understood, as but an instrument of moral, intellectual and ontological undoing. First, then, and rejoicing from the outset in the relentlessness of its rhyme scheme, comes Cavalcanti's sense of love as a passion of the sensitive soul generated by the intentional presence of madonna to the possible intellect, by the idea or image of madonna as installed at the pinnacle of the mind and as subsisting there as an object of contemplation:

In quella parte—dove sta memora
prende suo stato,—sì formato,—come
diaffan da lume,—d'una scuritate

---

20 'God the Creator shines still more brightly in the Intelligence on high than even the sun in our eyes. That Intelligence intuits its maker beyond the heavens, and, setting them in motion, readies itself to obey him, thus straightaway giving blessed effect to his just purpose. So truly should the beautiful lady when she shines in the eyes of her noble lover inspire a yearning never to slacken in his obedience to her.'

la qual da Marte—viene, e fa demora;
elli è creato—ed ha sensato—nome,
d'alma costume—e di cor volontate.
Vèn da veduta forma che s'intende,
che prende—nel possibile intelletto,
come in subietto,—loco e dimoranza.
In quella parte mai non ha possanza
perché da qualitate non descende:
resplende—in sé perpetüal effetto;
non ha diletto—ma consideranza;
sì che non pote largir simiglianza.

(*Donna me prega perch'eo voglio dire*, lines 15–28)[21]

With what amounts, therefore, to an account of love as but a darkling passion—indeed as but a Martian or warrior passion—within the economy of the
whole, Cavalcanti turns to the pathology thereof, to the moral and psychological
dysfunctionality of those under its sway. Morally, he suggests, it is a question of
love as an impediment to the orderly process in man of seeing, understanding

---

21 'Love, brought about as it is by a darkness deriving from Mars in the same way as anything diaphanous is but an effect of the light, abides thus formed in that part of the soul wherein is memory.
Created, and so called by way of its sense perception, it constitutes both a disposition of the soul and
an appetition of the heart. Proceeding from form as perceived and installed intentionally in the possible
intellect, there, as in its proper subject, it has its whereabouts and its dwelling. Deriving as it does from
nothing determinate in the world, it has there no power of its own (and still less, therefore, that of
producing further phantasms), but rather shines forth in its perpetuity as an object, not of predilection,
but of contemplation.' *Poeti del Duecento*, vol. 2, ed. Gianfranco Contini (Milan: Riccardo Ricciardi,
1960), 522–29; *Guido Cavalcanti: Rime*, ed. Marcello Ciccuto, intro. Maria Corti (Milan: Rizzoli Editore, 1978); *Rime: Guido Cavalcanti*, ed. Domenico de Robertis (Turin: Einaudi, 1986); *Guido Cavalcanti: The Complete Poems*, trans. Marc Cirigliano (New York: Italica Press, 1992); *The Selected Poetry
of Guido Cavalcanti: A Critical English Edition*, ed. Simon West (Leicester: Troubador, 2009); *Complete
Poems: Guido Cavalcanti*, trans. Anthony Mortimer (London: Oneworld Classics, 2010). Also, *The
Sonnets and Ballate of Guido Cavalcanti*, trans. and intro. Ezra Pound (Westport, CT: Hyperion, 1983).
For the canzone *Donna me prega* in particular, Mario Casella, 'La canzone d'amore di Guido Cavalcanti',
SFI 7 (1942), 97–160; Bruno Nardi, 'Di un nuovo commento alla canzone del Cavalcanti sull'amore',
in *Dante e la cultura medievale*, 2nd ed. (Bari: Laterza, 1949), 130–52; James Eustace Shaw, *Guido Cav-
alcanti's Theory of Love: The Canzone d'amore and Other Related Problems* (Toronto: University of To-
ronto Press, 1949); Guido Favati, 'La canzone d'amore del Cavalcanti', *LM* 3 (1952), 422–53; Fernando
Pappalardo, 'Per una rilettura della canzone d'amore del Cavalcanti', *SPCT* 13 (1976), 47–76; Maria
Corti, *La felicità mentale: Nuove prospettive per Cavalcanti e Dante* (Turin: Enaudi, 1983, especially 1–37);
Enrico Fenzi, *La canzone d'amore di Guido Cavalcanti e i suoi antichi commenti* (Genoa: Il Melangolo,
1999); Antonio Gagliardi, *Guido Cavalcanti: Poesia e filosofia* (Alessandria: Edizioni dell'Orso, 2001);
*Guido Cavalcanti tra i suoi lettori. Proceedings of the International Symposium for the Seventh Centennial
of His Death, New York, 10–11 November 2000*, ed. Maria Luisa Ardizzone (Florence: Cadmo 2003) with,
at 131–47, Christopher Kleinhenz, 'Tradition and Innovation in the Poetry of Guido Cavalcanti'; Donato Pirovano, 'Guido Cavalcanti', in *Il dolce stil novo* (Rome: Salerno, 2014), 281–311.

and choosing, the lover being forever prey to the indiscipline and undiscerning of his passion. Indeed as one no longer having dominion over himself, he is forever at death's door, forever on the point of ceasing to be as a creature of reasonable determination:

> Non è vertute,—ma da quella vène
> ch'è perfezione—(ché si pone—tale),
> non razionale—ma che sente, dico;
>   for di salute—giudicar mantene,
> ché la 'ntenzione—per ragione—vale:
> discerne male—in cui è vizio amico.
>   Di sua potenza segue spesso morte,
> se forte—la vertù fosse impedita,
> la quale aita—la contraria via:
> non perché oppost' a naturale sia;
>   ma quanto che da buon perfetto tort'è
> per sorte,—non pò dire om ch'aggia vita,
> che stabilita—non ha segnoria.
> A simil pò valer quand' om l'oblia.

(*Donna me prega perch'eo voglio dire*, lines 29–42)[22]

Psychologically, by contrast, it is a question of the lover's knowing himself only in the volatility of self, in his forever hovering between laughter and tears, certainty and uncertainty, sighing and suffering. His, in short, is a crippled humanity, a humanity present to itself by way only of its unique combination of restlessness and inertia, of desiring and despairing:

> L'essere è quando—lo voler è tanto
> ch'oltra misura—di natura—torna,
> poi non s'adorna—di riposo mai.
>   Move, cangiando—color, riso in pianto,
> e la figura—con paura—storna;
> poco soggiorna;—ancor di lui vedrai

22 'Love itself is not a power of the soul, but rather flows from what is deemed to be the principle of perfection in man—not, that is to say, from the rational but from the sensitive part of his being. As such it waylays his moral judgement, wilfulness standing in for reason, with those in the grip of such vice having but little discernment. More often than not, then, death alone is the product of its power whenever those forces making for the contrary are obstructed. Not that love in itself is contrary to nature, but because whenever by chance a man is distracted from his highest good, he can no longer be said to be alive, for just like the one who has forgotten that good altogether, he has no dominion over himself.'

che 'n gente di valor lo più si trova.
La nova—qualità move sospiri,
e vol ch'om miri—'n non formato loco,
destandos' ira la qual manda foco
    (imaginar nol pote om che nol prova),
né mova—già però ch'a lui si tiri,
e non si giri—per trovarvi gioco.
né cert' ha mente gran saver né poco.

(*Donna me prega perch'eo voglio dire*, lines 43–56)[23]

—lines to which we need for the record to add these from the final part of the poem relative to reciprocity as a solution to love thus understood, reciprocity alone as a coming home of like to like on the plane of love-understanding being equal to its otherwise relentless affliction of the spirit. Herein alone, in other words, in the mutual countenancing of lovers similarly sensitive to the subtle psychology of it all, lies the palliative for love's pain:

De simil tragge—complessione sguardo
che fa parere—lo piacere—certo:
non pò coverto—star, quand' è sì giunto.
    Non già selvagge—le bieltà son dardo,
ché tal volere—per temere—è sperto:
consiegue merto—spirito ch'è punto.
    E non si pò conoscer per lo viso:
compriso—bianco in tale obietto cade;
e, chi ben aude,—forma non si vede:
dunqu' elli meno, che da lei procede.
    For di colore, d'essere diviso,
assiso—'n mezzo scuro, luce rade.
For d'ogne fraude—dico, degno in fede,
che solo di costui nasce mercede.

(*Donna me prega perch'eo voglio dire*, lines 57–70)[24]

23 'Love begins whenever desire grows such as to surpass nature's limits, from which point on it knows no peace. A forever shifting complexion, laughter and tears, this, together with a terrifying disfigurement of the lover's every outward aspect, is love's effect, its volatility, as you yourself will observe, being evident above all in those of a noble disposition. This novel state provokes endless sighing and causes a man to cast about angrily, nay feverishly, even for the as yet unsubstantial object of his desire—something of which there can be no conception short of experiencing it for oneself. Drawn on by his love, he is nonetheless frozen to the spot, unable to move in search of his proper pleasure, all wisdom, be it great or small, deserting him.'

24 'From one of like disposition love draws a glance which makes of pleasure a certainty; nor

It is, then, in this context—that of a 'natural dimostramento' (*Donna me prega,* line 8) or reasoned account of what love actually is—that we have now to consider the four moments of Cavalcantian lyricism in the round, namely its praise moment, its tragic moment, its ludic or bucolic moment and, as decisive for the stilnovistic initiative generally, its technical moment. Taking first, then, the first of these things, to wit, the praise moment of Cavalcanti's art, we have over against the tragic negativity of the canzone his capacity for looking even so in the opposite direction, for rejoicing by way of the positive encounter in a moment of pure awareness. Exemplary, therefore, in respect of Cavalcanti's praise style is the superlatively conceived and exquisitely crafted sonnet *Chi è questa che vèn, ch'ogn'om la mira,* an essay, precisely, in love under the aspect of rapt intuition:

> Chi è questa che vèn, ch'ogn'om la mira,
> che fa tremar di chiaritate l'âre
> e mena seco Amor, sì che parlare
> null' omo pote, ma ciascun sospira?
> 	O Deo, che sembra quando li occhi gira,
> dical' Amor, ch'i' nol savria contare;
> cotanto d'umiltà donna mi pare,
> ch'ogn'altra ver' di lei i' la chiam' ira.
> 	Non si poria contar la sua piagenza,
> ch'a le' s'inchin' ogni gentil vertute,
> e la beltate per sua dea la mostra.
> 	Non fu sì alta già la mente nostra
> e non si pose 'n noi tanta salute,
> che propiamente n'aviàn canoscenza.[25]

—lines to which, as confirming the unsayability of beauty in its beholding, and this as a topos of Cavalcantian discourse, we may add these from the canzone *Io non pensava che lo cor giammai:*

---

having reached this point can it remain hidden. Beauty is the arrow capable of wounding in love (though not the arrow of beauty unkempt, for then the lover's inclination is put to flight by fear), the one struck by this arrow therefore reaping his reward. But neither is there any seeing love, for like white in the object of perception it fades from view. Moreover—and mark my words—just as form itself cannot be seen, still less can the love proceeding from it. Colourless, knowing no substance of its own, and situated in a dark medium, its scorns all light. I say, then, in very truth and all good faith, only ever from love thus conceived can come any recompense.'

25 'Who is this who comes that all men gaze upon her, and who causes the very air to tremble, and who brings with her Love himself, so that no man can speak but rather sigh? Oh God, how she seems as hither and thither she glances let love declare, for I myself could not. So consummate she seems in her humility, that others by comparison I would call uncouth. There is no describing her beauty, for before her every noble virtue bows, and beauty in her divinity is by her made known. Never were our minds so exalted, nor ever was such bliss ours as to know her as she truly is.'

> Di questa donna non si può contare;
> ché di tante bellezze adorna vène,
> che mente di qua giù no la sostene
> sì che la veggia lo 'ntelletto nostro.[26]

or these from the nicely Sicilianizing ballad *Fresca rosa novella* with its sense of the impossibility of thinking, let alone saying, 'beyond nature', beyond the connatural paradigms of consciousness:

> Vostra cera gioiosa,
> poi che passa e avanza
> natura e costumanza,
> ben è mirabil cosa.
> Fra lor le donne dea
> vi chiaman, come sete;
> tanto adorna parete,
> ch'eo non saccio contare;
> e chi poria pensare—oltra natura?[27]

But it is at this point—in the moment of rapt intellection—that love as a disruptive passion of the sensitive soul intervenes to destabilize the whole experience, leaving the lover to contemplate the imminence, indeed the actuality, of his demise as a creature of reasonable self-possession. Exemplary once again, therefore, but in the sense now of the sorrowing spirituality of it all, is the no less exquisitely conceived and executed sonnet *Le mie' foll' occhi, che prima guardaro*, an essay this time, however, in death alone as the outcome of the lover's hapless existence:

> Li mie' foll' occhi, che prima guardaro
> vostra figura piena di valore,
> fuor quei che di voi, donna, m'acusaro
> nel fero loco ove ten corte Amore,
>   e mantinente avanti lui mostraro
> ch' io era fatto vostro servidore:
> per che sospiri e dolor mi pigliaro,

---

26 'There are no words whereby to describe this lady, for she comes by beauty so adorned that our mind here below, insufficient thereunto, sees her not in understanding' (lines 15–18).

27 'Your radiant countenance, passing and surpassing every natural and customary excellence, is indeed a wondrous thing. Among women you are deemed a deity, for that is what you are. So seems your beauty that I would not be able to give an account of it, for who can think beyond nature' (lines 23–31).

vedendo che temenza avea lo core.
Menârmi tosto, sanza riposanza,
in una parte là 'v' i' trovai gente
che ciascun si doleva d'Amor forte.
Quando mi vider, tutti con pietanza
dissermi: 'Fatto se' di tal servente,
che mai non déi sperare altro che morte.'[28]

This, then, is the tragic moment of the Cavalcantian lyric, a moment that, as yet lightly figured in *Li mie' foll' occhi*, enjoys more systematic expression in the sonnet *L'anima mia vilment' è sbigotita*, a poem with which we enter more completely into the war zone of the mind, into the theatre of conflict—where the notion of 'theatre' has the advantage of confirming the fundamentally spectatorly character of it all, the status of the lover as but an onlooker in respect of his own spiritual disintegration. Here, then, anxiety gives way to something closer to anguish, to an unfolding of the poet's experience in terms of invasion, captivity and diaspora, of forces making in the round for a dissolution of self beneath the weight of its unhappiness:

L'anima mia vilment' è sbigotita
de la battaglia ch'el[l]'ave dal core;
che s'ella sente pur un poco Amore
più presso a lui che non sòle, ella more.
Sta come quella che non ha valore,
ch'è per temenza da lo cor partita;
e chi vedesse com' ell' è fuggita
diria per certo: 'Questi non ha vita'.
Per li occhi venne la battaglia in pria,
che ruppe ogni valore immantenente,
sì che del colpo fu strutta la mente.
Qualunqu' è quei che più allegrezza sente,
se vedesse li spirti fuggir via,
di grande sua pietate piangeria.[29]

28 'My foolish eyes, which first glimpsed your worthy form, were those, my lady, which denounced me as yours in that fell place where Love holds court, and straightaway confirmed in his presence that I was made your liege man, for which reason, seeing how sighing and sorrowing had taken hold of me, fear gripped my heart. Without delay they at once led me away to a place where I found people one and all grieving profoundly over Love. Catching sight of me, they all of them cried pityingly: "You are enslaved by one from whom you can only hope for death."'

29 'My soul, wretchedly cast down as it is by the battle waged from my heart, should it sense Love a fraction closer than its wont, then it will die. Having fled the heart through fear, it is as one whose strength has ebbed, and anyone witness to its flight would for sure say: "Life is here no more." Battle

Now it is true that, in the case of a repertoire as complete, not to mention a humanity as ambiguous, as Cavalcanti's, there are poems setting off in another direction, in the direction, that is to say, of the more innocently Sicilian, of the neatly caricatural and of the nicely suggestive or 'bucolic'; so, for example, relative to the first of these things—to the more innocently Sicilian—there is the sonnet *Avete 'n vo' li fior' e la verdura*, a sonnet not entirely untouched by a hint of Cavalcantian foreboding (the 'chi d'amor si teme' of line 7) but settling all the same for the highways and byways of Siculo-Tuscan verse making:

> Avete 'n vo' li fior' e la verdura
> e ciò che luce od è bello a vedere;
> risplende più che sol vostra figura;
> chi vo' non vede, ma' non pò valere.
> In questo mondo non ha creatura
> sì piena di bieltà né di piacere;
> e chi d'amor si teme, lu' assicura
> vostro bel vis' a tanto 'n sé volere.
> Le donne che vi fanno compagnia
> assa' mi piaccion per lo vostro amore;
> ed i' le prego per lor cortesia
> che qual più può più vi faccia onore
> ed aggia cara vostra segnoria,
> perché di tutte siete la migliore.[30]

while relative to the second of them, to the caricatural Cavalcanti, we have the sonnet *Pegli occhi fere un spirito sottile* as, whatever else it is, an elegant instance of self-parody:

> Pegli occhi fere un spirito sottile,
> che fa 'n la mente spirito destare,
> dal qual si move spirito d'amare,
> ch'ogn'altro spiritel[lo] fa gentile.
> Sentir non pò di lu' spirito vile,

---

to begin with was waged through the eyes, at once breaking down all resistance and destroying the mind at a blow. Should there be any more a friend to happiness, were he to see my spirits thus put to flight, he would at once weep tears of pity.'

30 'In you are flowers, all things green and whatever shines and is fair to behold. More radiant than the sun is your countenance and none is worthy who looks not upon you. Beauty and comeliness so complete has no creature here below, and he who lives in fear of love is but confirmed in the height and depth of his desiring by the loveliness of your face. Loving you as I do, I rejoice in all those ladies party to your presence, and I beg them of their kindliness that those able most to honour you do so to the utmost and indeed hold dear your sovereignty, for you are the finest of them all.'

di cotanta vertù spirito appare;
quest' è lo spiritel che fa tremare,
lo spiritel che fa la donna umìle.
E poi da questo spirito si move
un altro dolce spirito soave,
che sieg[u]e un spiritello di mercede:
lo quale spiritel spiriti piove,
ché di ciascuno spirit' ha la chiave,
per forza d'uno spirito che 'l vede.[31]

and relative to the third of them, to the bucolic Cavalcanti, the ballad *In un boschetto trova' pasturella*, an essay this time in the sylvan sensuality of it all:

In un boschetto trova' pasturella
più che la stella—bella, al mi' parere.
Cavelli avea biondetti e ricciutelli,
e gli occhi pien' d'amor, cera rosata;
con sua verghetta pasturav' agnelli;
[di]scalza, di rugiada era bagnata;
cantava come fosse 'namorata:
er' adornata—di tutto piacere.
D'amor la saluta' imantenente
e domandai s'avesse compagnia;
ed ella mi rispose dolzemente
che sola sola per lo bosco gia,
e disse: 'Sacci, quando l'augel pia,
allor disïa—'l me' cor drudo avere'.
Po' che mi disse di sua condizione
e per lo bosco augelli audìo cantare,
fra me stesso diss' i': 'Or è stagione
di questa pasturella gio' pigliare'.
Merzé le chiesi sol che di basciare
ed abracciar,—se le fosse 'n volere.
Per man mi prese, d'amorosa voglia,
e disse che donato m'avea 'l core;

---

31 'A subtle spirit strikes by way of the eyes to awaken a spirit in the mind, whence it moves a spirit of love to ennoble every more particular spirit. Of this spirit, so powerful is it, no base spirit may sense anything whatever, for this is the spirit that both causes a man to tremble and confirms a woman in her humility. And then from this same spirit proceeds another sweet spirit, in turn engendering a spirit of compassion. This spirit then showers forth other spirits besides, for of every spirit it holds the key by virtue of the spirit that sees.'

menòmmi sott' una freschetta foglia,
là dov'i' vidi fior' d'ogni colore;
e tanto vi sentìo gioia e dolzore,
che 'l die d'amore—mi pàrea vedere.[32]

But for all the importance of these things—of the retrospective, the caricatu-ral, the ludic and (especially) the tragic—as each alike facets of his first friend's genius, it was above all Cavalcanti's sense of the accountability of form to sub-stance within the economy of the poetic utterance as a whole that left its deepest and most lasting mark upon Dante. Already, then, the issue had been raised by Guinizzelli, who, replying to Bonagiunta's sense of his having changed the whole nature of vernacular verse making by rarefying it out of all recognition (the 'Così passate voi di sottigliansa' of the sonnet *Voi, ch'avete mutata la mainera* at line 9),[33] had noted simply that, inasmuch as there are as many ways of doing poetry as there are poets, patience, goodwill and forbearance are all that matter. But Caval-canti, in this as in most other respects, was made of sterner stuff, and, with the Guittoniani in general and Guittone in particular in his sights, he moves straight onto the offensive, confirming as he does so the function—indeed the high call-ing—of form in the poem as that whereby the contents of understanding (such as they are in Guittone) are lifted above the threshold of consciousness. First, then, there is the sonnet *Da più a uno face un sollegismo* as but an indictment of Guittone's technique under both its ratiocinative and its rhetorical aspect, in-dictment going hand in hand with admonition lest by way of his—Guittone's—persistence he continue to make a fool of himself:

---

32 'In a wooded place I found a shepherdess, lovelier by far, I thought, than any star. Blond hair she had and curls, her eyes lit up by love and her complexion rosy. With a little staff she minded her flock, the dew bathing her naked feet. Bearing about her all beauty, she sang as one in love. Straightaway I greeted her in the name of love and enquired of her company, to which she replied sweetly that she was all alone on the woodland way, adding the while: "as the birds begin to chirrup so then you know my heart seeks out a friend." Telling me thus of her state, I heard the birds in that wooded place begin to sing, and said to myself: "Now is the time to take pleasure of this shepherdess." All I sought of her was a kiss and, if she wished, an embrace. But, all eager in love, she took me by the hand and swore her heart was mine, leading me then beneath the fresh foliage where I saw flowers of every colour. And such was the joy and sweetness I knew that the very god of love I seemed to see.'

33 'You, with all that subtlety of yours, outdo them all.' For the 'all that actually matters' moment of the argument (Guinizzelli to Bonagiunta), the sonnet *Omo ch'è saggio non corre leggero* at lines 12–14: 'Dëo natura e 'l mondo in grado mise, / e fe' despari senni e intendimenti; / perzò ciò ch'omo pensa non de' dire' (God ordained nature and the world with endless difference, and made provision for any number of ways of sensing and understanding, which is why whatever we think of it we should hold our tongue). Maria Picchio Simonelli, 'Bonagiunta da Lucca e la problematica dello stil novo (*Purg.* XXIV)', *DS* 66 (1968), 65–75; Guglielmo Gorni, *Il nodo della lingua e il verbo d'Amore: Studi su Dante e altri duecentisti* (Florence: Olschki, 1981); Claudio Giunta, *La poesia italiana nell'età di Dante: La linea Bonagiunta-Guinizzelli* (Bologna: Il mulino, 1998); Paolo Borsa, *La nuova poesia di Guido Guinizzelli* (Florence: Cadmo, 2007).

Da più a uno face un sollegismo;
in maggiore e in minor mezzo si pone,
che pruova necessario sanza rismo;
da ciò ti parti forse di ragione?
Nel profferer, che cade 'n barbarismo,
difetto di saver ti dà cagione;
e come far poteresti un sofismo
per silabate carte, fra Guittone?
Per te non fu giammai una figura;
non fòri ha' posto in tuo un argomento;
induri quanto più disci; e pon' cura,
ché 'ntes' ho che compon' d'insegnamento
volume; e fòr principio ha da natura.
Fa' ch'om non rida il tuo proponimento![34]

to which we must add the following sonnet addressed now to Guido Orlandi—another Guittonian spirit responsible for yet a further and in the event somewhat niggling account of stilnovistic abstruseness (the sonnet *Per troppa sottiglianza il fil si rompe*)—and confirming afresh the notion of style as but the form of love's own subtle magisterium. Just because you've read a bit of Ovid and can cobble together the odd tired image and false rhyme, says Cavalcanti, don't flatter yourself, for there is matter here well beyond your ken and competence:

Di vil matera mi conven parlare
[e] perder rime, silabe e sonetto,
sì ch'a me ste[sso] giuro ed imprometto
a tal voler per modo legge dare.
Perché sacciate balestra legare
e coglier con isquadra archile in tetto

---

34 'A syllogism proceeds from the one to the many, there being a major, a minor and a middle term producing a necessary conclusion without vesture of rhyme. Have you some reason for proceeding otherwise? In that your every utterance falls away into barbarism, lack of understanding can be the only cause. And how is it, Fra Guittone, that you essay sophistry in verse? Never have we had from you either a legitimate figure of speech or any useful argument to speak of, for the more you say, the more obtuse you are. So take care, for I have heard that you have it in mind to write a manual of instruction, and this in a manner bereft of first principles. Be sure not to make a laughingstock of yourself with this proposal.' Marcello Ciccuto, 'Il sonetto cavalcantiano: "Da più a uno face un sollegismo"', *CL* 6.2 (1978), 305–30 (and in *Il restauro de "L'Intelligenza" e altri studi dugesteschi* [Pisa: Giardini, 1986], 13–47); Nicolò Pasero, 'Contributi all'interpretazione del sonetto "Da più a uno face un sollegismo" di Guido Cavalcanti', *Medioevo Letterario d'Italia: Rivista internazionale di filologia, linguistica e letteratura* 6 (2009), 25–43; Noemi Ghetti, '"Da più a uno face un sollegismo": Amore, conoscenza e poesia', in *L'ombra di Cavalcanti e Dante* (Rome: L'Asino d'oro edizioni, 2010), 25–34. More generally, Guido Favati, *Inchiesta sul Dolce stil novo* (Florence: Le Monnier, 1975).

e certe fiate aggiate Ovidio letto
e trar quadrelli e false rime usare,
non pò venire per la vostra mente
là dove insegna Amor, sottile e piano,
di sua manera dire e di su' stato.
Già non è cosa che si porti in mano;
qual che voi siate, egli è d'un'altra gente;
sol al parlar si vede chi v'è stato.
Già non vi toccò lo sonetto primo;
Amore ha fabricato ciò ch'io limo.[35]

Here, then, alongside his commitment to the notion of love as but a principle of moral and intellectual undoing, is a further property of Cavalcanti's temperament as a poet, his, at every stage, being a sense of the intrinsic justification of form, of its across-the-board accountability to the innermost movement of the spirit. And it is this sense of the accountability of form to substance within the economy of the poem as a whole that allows us to speak of the sweet new style as a shared enterprise, as a literary phenomenon, that is to say, which, differentiated as it is in just about every other sense, united its various practitioners; so, for example—and taking Cavalcanti (the Cavalcanti, that is to say, of the exquisite *Chi è questa che vèn, ch'ogn'om la mira*) as read—there is a Guido Guinizzelli as likewise sensitive to the twofold beauty and persuasiveness of the now uncluttered line:

Gentil donzella, di pregio nomata,
degna di laude e di tutto onore,
ché par de voi non fu ancora nata
né sì compiuta de tutto valore,
      pare che 'n voi dimori onne fïata
la deïtà de l'alto deo d'amore;
de tutto compimento siete ornata
[e] d'adornezze e di tutto bellore;
      ché 'l vostro viso dà sì gran lumera
che non è donna ch'aggia in sé beltate
ch'a voi davante non s'ascuri in cera;

---

35 'Since I have now to speak of a less than worthy matter, and to waste rhyme, syllable and sonnet over it, I swear solemnly and undertake to be disciplined about it. Just because you can tension a crossbow and strike a nearby target foursquare, and though you have read Ovid on and off and know how to shoot darts and fashion false rhymes, you have no inkling of there where, subtly and softly, Love teaches us to speak of what and how it is with him (no matter, this, merely of display). As for you, then, whoever you might be, love belongs elsewhere, for to know whether or not a man has been there it is enough simply to hear him speak. My former sonnet touched you not, but Love itself fashioned what I now refine.'

per voi tutte bellezze so' afinate,
e ciascun fior fiorisce in sua manera
lo giorno quando vo vi dimostrate.[36]

or a Dante Alighieri as, in the interest of praise as a now secure disposition of the spirit, similarly inclined to rejoice in the purity of the poetic utterance, its sweet continuum of sound and sense alike:

Vede perfettamente onne salute
chi la mia donna tra le donne vede;
quelle che vanno con lei son tenute
di bella grazia a Dio render merzede.
E sua bieltate è di tanta vertute,
che nulla invidia a l'altre ne procede,
anzi le face andar seco vestute
di gentilezza d'amore e di fede.
La vista sua fa onne cosa umile;
e non fa sola sé parer piacente,
ma ciascuna per lei riceve onore.
Ed è ne li atti suoi tanto gentile,
che nessun la si può recare a mente,
che non sospiri in dolcezza d'amore.[37]

or a Cino da Pistoia, less committed, to be sure, at the theological level than at that of love's sweet occasionality but a past master even so when it comes to the cadencing of the line, to thought and form as all of a piece in their sweet consequentialism ('e se ... e fatt'han ... e quando ... quando ... e tanto ... sed e'):

Veduto han gli occhi miei sì bella cosa,
che dentro dal mio cor dipinta l'hanno,
e se per veder lei tuttor no stanno,

36 'Gracious damsel, renowned for your great goodness, worthy of all praise and honour, for none, it seems, was born your equal nor so replete in every virtue; for in you, it seems, abides the very godliness of the god of love on high. Yours by way of adornment is every perfection, every embellishment and every beauty, your countenance being so radiant that no woman, be she ever so beautiful, is darkling to behold. Through you every beauty is refined and, on the day you come forth, every flower flourishes after its manner.'

37 'He sees to perfection every goodness who sees among others my lady, her every companion being called upon to give thanks to God for this, her exquisite grace. So compelling is her loveliness that of envy there is, in other women, no trace; rather, themselves clothed in love, faith and the nobility thereof, they are by her prevailed upon to accompany her as she goes her way. The very sight of her humbles all things, whereby her beauty shines forth, but not this alone, for by her all women are honoured. And in her every gesture she is so noble that no one can call her to mind without sighing in the sweetness of love.'

infin che non la trovan non han posa,
e fatt'han l'alma mia sì amorosa,
che tutto corro in amoroso affanno,
e quando col suo sguardo scontro fanno,
toccan lo cor che sovra 'l ciel gir osa.
Fanno li occhi a lo mio core scorta,
fermandol ne la fé d'amor più forte,
quando risguardan lo su' novo viso;
e tanto passa in su' desiar fiso,
che 'l dolce imaginar li daria morte,
sed e' non fosse Amor che lo conforta.[38]

Throughout, then, the pattern is the same: a variously differentiated account of love in its essential nature and finality but a shared commitment to form and to the purification thereof as that whereby the poet stands securely in his own presence as a creature of seeing, understanding and willing. This at any rate, or something close to it, is Dante's meaning when, speaking now from out of the seasoned spirituality of the *Purgatorio*, he confirms over against the mannerism of his interlocutor (the Bonagiunta of *Voi, ch'avete mutata la mainera*) a sense of form in the sacredness thereof, as the ground and guarantee of understanding at the point of ultimate concern:

'O anima', diss' io, 'che par sì vaga
di parlar meco, fa sì ch'io t'intenda,
e te e me col tuo parlare appaga'.
'Femmina è nata, e non porta ancor benda',

38 'My eyes have seen so beautiful an object that they have painted it in my heart, and if for a moment they have no sight of her, then until such time as they find her afresh, they know no peace; they've made my soul so amorous that I am caught up in a flurry of amorous anxiety; and when at last they encounter her, they touch my heart that dares now reach out for heaven. My eyes accompany my heart, confirming all the more its faith in love whenever they gaze once more upon her miraculous countenance; and so complete is its desiring that sweet imagining would be the death of it were it not for Love as its comforter.' Domenico de Robertis, 'Cino da Pistoia', in *I Minori* (Milan: Marzorati, 1961), 285–306; Christopher Kleinhenz, 'Cino da Pistoia and the Italian Lyric Tradition', in *L'Imaginaire courtois et son double*, ed. Giovanna Angeli et al. (Naples: Edizioni Scientifiche Italiane, 1992), 147–63; Donato Pirovano, 'Cino da Pistoia', in *Il dolce stil novo* (Rome: Salerno, 2014), 312–21. On Dante and Cino, Vincenzo Pernicone, 'Dante e lo "stil novo" di Cino', *Studi danteschi e altri saggi*, ed. Matilde Dillon Wanke (Genoa: Università degli Studi di Genova, 1984), 1–6; Robert Hollander, 'Dante and Cino da Pistoia', *DS* 110 (1992), 201–31 (and in *FSt* 6 [1994], 125–57); Maria Pica, 'Dante e l'"amicus eius": Per una rilettura di Cino', *EL* 19.1 (1994), 67–93; John Took, 'The Still Centre of Concern and Communicability: Dante, Cino and Their Non-Correspondence', *JIRS* 6 (1998), 43–59; Michelangelo Picone, 'Dante e Cino: Una lunga amicizia; Prima parte i tempi della *Vita Nova*, *DRISDA* 1 (2004), 39–54; John Scott, 'Cino da Pistoia and Dante Alighieri', in *Flinders Dante Conferences: 2002 and 2004*, ed. Margaret Baker et al. (Adelaide: Lythurum Press, 2005), 26–37.

comincіò el, 'che ti farà piacere
la mia città, come ch'om la riprenda.

    Tu te n'andrai con questo antivedere:
se nel mio mormorar prendesti errore,
dichiareranti ancor le cose vere.

    Ma dì s'i' veggio qui colui che fore
trasse le nove rime, cominciando
"Donne ch'avete intelletto d'amore"'.

    E io a lui: 'I' mi son un che, quando
Amor mi spira, noto, e a quel modo
ch'e' ditta dentro vo significando'.
'O frate, issa vegg' io', diss' elli, 'il nodo
che 'l Notaro e Guittone e me ritenne
di qua dal dolce stil novo ch'i' odo!

    Io veggio ben come le vostre penne
di retro al dittator sen vanno strette,
che de le nostre certo non avvenne;

    e qual più a gradire oltre si mette,
non vede più da l'uno a l'altro stilo';
e, quasi contentato, si tacette.[39]

---

39 *Purgatorio* 24.40–63: ' "O soul", said I, "that seems so eager to speak with me, pray do so that I may hear you, and satisfy us both by what you have to say." "A woman is born who bears not yet the wimple", he began, "who, for all the blame heaped upon it, shall make my city pleasing to you. Go, then, thus alerted to what will be, and should my murmuring mislead you the event itself will make all plain. But tell me if I see here him who brought forth the new rhymes, beginning *Ladies who have understanding of love?*" And I to him: "I am one who, when Love inspires me, takes note and sets it forth after the fashion he dictates from within." "O brother", he said, "now I see the knot which kept the Notary and Guittone and me short of the sweet new style I hear; for it is clear to me now how—unlike ours, to be sure—your pens follow immediately the one who dictates, and anyone looking still more deeply into this will find no other difference between the one style and the other", with which, as if content, he fell silent.' Domenico de Robertis, 'Definizione dello "Stil novo" ', *L'Approdo* 3 (1954), 59–64; Emilio Bigi, 'Genesi di un concetto striografico: "Dolce stil novo" ', *GSLI* 32 (1955), 333–71; Guido Favati, 'Contributo alla determinazione del problema dello Stil nuovo', *Studi mediolatini e volgari* 4 (1956), 57–70; Aurelio Roncaglia, 'Precedenti e significato dello "Stil novo" dantesco', in *Dante e Bologna nei tempi di Dante* (Bologna: Commissione per i testi di lingua, 1967), 13–34; Antonio Enzo Quaglio, 'Analisi di un concetto storiografico', in *Lo stilnovo e la poesia religiosa*, 2nd ed. (Rome: Laterza, 1975), 9–17; Vittorio Russo, 'Il "nodo" del Dolce Stil Novo', *MR* 3 (1976), 236–64; Ronald L. Martinez, 'The Pilgrim's Answer to Bonagiunta and the Poetics of the Spirit', *SIR* 3 (1983), 37–63; Lino Pertile, 'Il nodo di Bonagiunta, le penne di Dante e il dolce stil novo', *LI* 46 (1994), 44–75.

CHAPTER 3

Literary Apprenticeship and a Coming of Age

DANTE GUITTONIANO

The *Vita nova* is by any standard an astonishing text, astonishing as a retrospective, as at once an anthology and a critique of Dante's activity so far as a lyric poet, and as a resolution of the affective issue at the very far limits of moral and ontological possibility, in terms, that is to say, of love as a principle of new life. But no less astonishing is the fact that, if as yet merely embryonically, just about everything leading up to it either contains or else anticipates the dialectic of the *libello*, the *Vita nova* constituting in this sense but a text in waiting, the terminus ad quem of a continuing meditation. Take, for example, as, in an ideal chronology of Dante's work, the earliest of his extant *rime*, a poetic correspondence with his namesake Dante da Maiano. Motives, to be sure, are on both sides well and truly mixed, Dante da Maiano for his part anxious to indulge his delight in sexual innuendo (the 'Così ridendo, molto la baciai, / del più non dico, ché mi fé giurare' moment of the sonnet *Provedi, saggio, ad esta visïone*),[1] and Alighieri, for his, busy about getting started as an apprentice poet by insinuating himself in the good graces of his correspondent (the 'ché già inver voi so non avria valore' moment of the sonnet *Per pruova di saper come vale o quanto*). But for all that, Alighieri opts for the genuinely worthwhile, for thoughtfulness proper in

---

1 'So, smiling as she was, I kissed and kissed her, but—for she made me swear to it—will say not what followed.' For the 'ché già inver voi so non avria valore' moment of the sonnet *Per pruova di saper come vale o quanto*: 'for I know full well that I am no match for you'. In addition to Kenelm Foster and Patrick Boyde (eds.), *Dante's Lyric Poetry* (Oxford: Clarendon Press, 1967) and Teodolinda Barolini (ed.), with notes by Manuele Gragnolati, *Dante Alighieri: Rime giovanili e della Vita Nuova* (Milan: Rizzoli, 2009), Raoul Blomme, 'Rime di corrispondenza con Dante da Maiano', in *Studi per una triplice esperienza* (Gent: Rijksuniversiteit, 1978), 32–85; Mario Marti, 'Per Dante da Maiano', in *Nuovi contributi dal certo al vero: Studi di filologia e storia* (Ravenna: Longo, 1980), 23–40; Teodolinda Barolini, 'The Poetic Exchanges between Dante Alighieri and his "amico" Dante da Maiano: A Young Man Takes His Place in the World', in *Legato con amore in un volume: Essays in Honour of John Scott*, ed. John J. Kinder and Diana Glenn (Florence: Olschki, 2013), 39–61. For Dante da Maiano's verse generally, *Rime*, ed. Rosanna Bettarini (Florence: Le Monnier, 1969).

the area of love and of love-understanding. On the one hand, then, with its sense of goodness and beauty as the final cause of all properly human desiring and of constancy on the part of madonna as its proper reward, there is the sonnet *Savete giudicar vostra ragione* as a preliminary meditation upon what it means to love and to love well:

> Savete giudicar vostra ragione,
> o om che pregio di saver portate
> per che, vitando aver con voi quistione,
> com so rispondo a le parole ornate.
>
> Disio verace, u' rado fin si pone,
> che mosse di valore o di bieltate,
> imagina l'amica oppinïone
> significasse il don che pria narrate.
>
> Lo vestimento, aggiate vera spene
> che fia, da lei cui desïate, amore;
> e 'n ciò provide vostro spirto bene;
> dico, pensando l'ovra sua d'allore.
> La figura che già morta sorvene
> è la fermezza ch'averà nel core.[2]

while on the other hand, there is the sonnet *Savere e cortesia, ingegno ed arte*, a poem offering over and against Da Maiano's ostentatious Ovidianism an account of the ways and means of love proper, of the kind of intelligence, courtesy and kindliness apt to win over its presiding deity:

> Savere e cortesia, ingegno ed arte,
> nobilitate, bellezza e riccore,
> fortezza e umiltate e largo core,
> prodezza ed eccellenza, giunte e sparte,
>
> este grazie e vertuti in onne parte
> con lo piacer di lor vincono Amore;
> una più ch'altra ben ha più valore
> inverso lui, ma ciascuna n'ha parte.

---

2 'Noted as you are for your wisdom, you are quite able to gloss your own argument, and so I will not enter into dispute with you, but only answer as best I can your elegantly phrased question. My view—speaking as a friend—is that the gift you first mention signified true desire, proceeding from merit or beauty, a desire seldom satisfied. As for the garment, rest assured that, as you yourself correctly opined, this—and I speak in view of what followed—will be the love you crave of her. The now deceased figure that then appeared is the constancy she'll bear in her heart.'

> Onde se voli, amico, che ti vaglia
> vertute naturale od accidente,
> con lealtà in piacer d'Amor l'adovra,
>   e non a contastar sua graziosa ovra;
> ché nulla cosa gli è incontro possente,
> volendo prender om con lui battaglia.[3]

Careful, then, to credit his correspondent's wisdom hereabouts and indeed his touching upon a significant issue (the need for perseverance in love), Dante nonetheless passes over the now antiquated rigmarole of suffering and service in favour of the more properly reflective, of the lover's knowing himself, if not yet as a new creation, then at least in the elementary integrity of his profession as such, seriousness thus taking over from strategy as the basic mood of the undertaking. True, there is as far as Dante and Dante da Maiano are concerned rather more to it than this, Dante's correspondence with his namesake testifying not only to a sense of the morally and intellectually worthwhile but to the irresistibility of the challenge, to the need as far as may be to outdo the opposition in point of technique; so, for example, from the 'duol d'amor' or 'love's greatest sorrow' moment of the exchange, there is the sonnet *Lasso, lo dol che più mi dole e serra* where exhaustion at the level of ideas issues in an essay less in elucidation than in equivocation, in taxing to the point of torturing the word in its power to signify:

> Lasso, lo dol che più mi dole e serra
> è ringraziar, ben non sapendo como;
> per me più saggio converriasi, como
> vostro saver, ched ogni quistion serra.
>   Del dol che manta gente dite s'erra
> è tal voler qual voi lor non ha como;
> el propio sì disio saver dol como,
> di ciò sovente, dico, essendo a serra.
>   Però pregh'eo ch'argomentiate, saggio,
> d'autorità mostrando ciò che porta
> di voi la 'mpresa, a ciò che sia più chiara;

---

3 'Understanding and courtesy, a lively intelligence and skills duly mastered, nobility, beauty, wealth, courage, gentleness and generosity, valour and distinction—these are the gifts and virtues which, together or severally, invariably win Love over with their power to please. One may influence him more than another but each has its part to play. If therefore, my friend, you wish either any natural or additional virtue to benefit you, set them to work, not to oppose Love's gracious activity but faithfully to do his will, for nothing avails against Love should one choose to do battle with him.'

e poi parrà, parlando di ciò, chiara,
e qual più chiarirem dol pena porta,
d'ello assegnando, amico, prov' e saggio.[4]

Even this, however, in its paroxysmal difficulty, its rejoicing in every kind of technical possibility from double entendre and composite rhyme (the 's'erra' of line 5) to consonantalism (at once dental and plosive) at its most insistent, enters into the mainstream of Dante's development as a poet, for it is by way of his confronting Guittone and the Guittoniani on their own ground that he settles at last on a fresh sense of form as but the outward aspect of love's inwardness, of, in a word, its sacramentality.

Similarly representative of the Guittonian phase of Dante's activity as a lyric poet, though of a Guittonianism marked now by a deepening of the moral and indeed of the salvific substance of love properly understood, are those poems clustered around the canzone *La dispietata mente, che pur mira* and represented in the *Vita nova* by the *improperium* or 'indictment of death' poem *Morte villana, di pietà nemica* and by the *planctus* or lament *Piangete, amanti, poi che piange Amore*. True, technique here is still retrospective (definitely archaic, for example, are the 'giudicio incontastabile gravoso' and the 'lo tuo fallar d'onni torto tortoso' moments of *Morte villana*, a 'sonetto rinterzato' or double sonnet to boot), but this is retrospection constrained by something more than itself, by an incipient sense of madonna as a special presence in the world, as apt to initiate those who look upon her in the ways and means of new life. On the one hand, then, there is the *improperium* with its sense of youth, gaiety and goodness as each alike liquidated by death—by the death in this case of the 'donna giovane e di gentile aspetto molto' of the eighth chapter of the *Vita nova*:

Dal secolo hai partita cortesia
e ciò ch'è in donna da pregiar vertute:
in gaia gioventute
distrutta hai l'amorosa leggiadria.
Più non voi discovrir qual donna sia
che per le propietà sue canosciute.

---

4 'Alas, the grief that grieves me most and holds me in its grip is that of thanking you but of not knowing how. It needs here someone wiser than I, someone with your ability to clinch each successive argument. As for the grief which, you say, afflicts so many, it is a question of their desiring in a way other than you yourself desire. And this, precisely—being myself, as I say, one frequently subject to it—is the grief I wish to understand. That is why, wise as you are, I pray you reason it through, citing your authorities, with a view to substantiating your thesis and confirming its lustre; at which point, discussing the matter in the full light of day, we shall be able to clarify which of love's pains is the most grievous, bringing to bear, my friend, both reason and experience.'

> Chi non merta salute
> non speri mai d'aver sua compagnia.

> (*Morte villana, di pietà nemica*, lines 13–20)[5]

while on the other there is the *planctus*, all of a piece with *Morte villana* in its arraignment of death as the ultimate spoiler, but coming round in the tercets to the notion of apotheosis and thus, in the moment of looking upon madonna, of a lifting of the spirit:

> Audite quanto Amor le fece orranza,
> ch'io 'l vidi lamentare in forma vera
> sovra la morta imagine avvenente;
> e riguardava ver lo ciel sovente,
> ove l'alma gentil già locata era,
> che donna fu di sì gaia sembianza.

> (*Piangete, amanti, poi che piange Amore*, lines 9–14)[6]

Already, then, there are inklings here of something greater to come, a sense of love and of the question of love as open to resolution on a higher plane, as conducive to an order of happiness transcending the provisionality, the ambiguity and, as here, the agony of the historical instant. And this precisely, or something very like it, is what needs to be said about the most impressive and most sustained of these early Guittonian *rime*, the canzone *La dispietata mente, che pur mira*, ostensibly a separation or distance poem (an *amor de lonh*) in, again, the old style, but here too entertaining amid its welter of commonplaces a fresh set of possibilities, a sense of my lady as having in her gift the power to new life, to an act of existence equal to everything both from within and from

---

5 'You have left the world bereft of graciousness and of everything deemed virtuous in womankind. Loving and lovely, you have destroyed each alike in the springtime of their youth. Who the lady was I will not disclose other than by way of those things for which she is known. Let those who merit not salvation ever hope to be of her company.' For the 'sonetto rinterzato' (a standard sonnet with settenari or seven-syllable lines intercalated along the way and, in this case, rhymed as follows: AaBBba—AaBBbA—CDdC—CDdC), Francesco d'Ovidio, *Versificazione italiana e arte poetica medioevale* (Milan: Hoepli, 1910); Theodor W. Elwert, *Versificazione italiana dalle origini ai giorni nostri* (Florence: Le Monnier, 1973); Mario Pazzaglia, *Teoria e analisi metrica* (Bologna: Pàtron, 1974); Giuseppe Sangirardi, *Breve guida alla metrica italiana* (Milan: Sansoni, 2002). For the the 'donna giovane e di gentile aspetto molto' motif of the *Vita nova*: 'a young woman of most noble bearing'.

6 'Hear how greatly Love honoured her! For I saw him in person lamenting her beauty even in death; and often he looked towards heaven, where the noble soul of one so radiantly present to us had already taken her place.'

beyond making for its attenuation. On the one hand, then, there is the predictability of it all, the rehearsal of a now antiquated set of courtly and neocourtly motifs:

> Piacciavi, donna mia, non venir meno
> a questo punto al cor che tanto v'ama,
> poi sol da voi lo suo soccorso attende:
>   ché buon signor già non ristringe freno
> per soccorrer lo servo quando 'l chiama,
> ché non pur lui, ma suo onor difende.
>   E certo la sua doglia più m'incende,
> quand'i mi penso ben, donna, che vui
> per man d'Amor là entro pinta sete:
>   così e voi dovete
> vie maggiormente aver cura di lui;
> ché Que' da cui convien che 'l ben s'appari,
> per l'imagine Sua ne tien più cari.

(*La dispietata mente, che pur mira*, lines 14–26)[7]

while on the other hand there is a now developed sense of madonna as the wellspring of hope, compassion and a fuller and more radiant humanity, with—as very definitely anticipatory as regards things to come—the 'salute' or greeting of line 53 as but the means of her power to spiritual renewal. True, the dialectic of service and suffering survives intact and to this extent the text remains captive to convention, but this nonetheless is service and suffering in the name and for the sake of something closer to *being* than to *having*, to a mode of existence transcending the substance and psychology of mere acquisition:

> E voi pur sete quella ch'io più amo,
> e che far mi potete maggior dono,
> e 'n cui la mia speranza più riposa;

---

7 'I beg you, my lady, do not fail in this critical moment the heart that so loves you, since from you alone does it await help. A good lord will not rein in when coming to the aid of the servant who calls upon him, for it is not only the latter he thus defends but his own honour too. And the pain I bear within me, my lady, is all the more intense for my recalling how you yourself stand depicted there by Love's own hand, which is why, given that he who is the measure of all goodness cherishes us the more for being made in his image, you too should have greater care of it.' Michelangelo Zaccarello, 'La dispietata mente che pur mira', in *Dante Alighieri: Le quindici canzoni. Lette da diversi*, vol. 2 (Lecce: Pensa Multimedia, 2012), 121–51; Valter Leonardo Puccetti, 'Lettura de "La dispietata mente"', in *Lectura Dantis Lupiensis*, vol. 1 (Ravenna: Longo, 2013), 89–113.

ché sol per voi servir la vita bramo,
e quelle cose che a voi onor sono
dimando e voglio; ogni altra m'è noiosa.
　　Dar mi potete ciò ch'altri non m'osa,
ché 'l sì e 'l no di me in vostra mano
ha posto Amore; ond'io grande mi tegno.
La fede ch'eo v'assegno
muove dal portamento vostro umano;
ché ciascun che vi mira, in veritate
di fuor conosce che dentro è pietate.
　　Dunque vostra salute omai si mova,
e vegna dentro al cor, che lei aspetta,
gentil madonna, come avete inteso.

(*La dispietata mente, che pur mira*, lines 40–55)[8]

Less anguished because less ambitious than *La dispietata mente* in its seeking to fashion something new from the old, in its seeking to pour new wine into an old skin, is the single-stanza canzone *Lo meo servente core*, another separation poem and another essay in service and supplication. But even here, if as yet but lightly figured, it is a question of seeing, understanding and, by implication at any rate, of self-surpassing, of rejoicing in the 'valore' of madonna as the final cause of the poet's every yearning. True, it is for the moment a question of patient self-recommendation as the encompassing, but somewhere in the recesses there is withal a stirring of the spirit, a desire to interrogate the routine utterance in the name and for the sake of something more sublime:

Lo meo servente core
vi raccomandi Amor, che vi l'ha dato,
e Merzé d'altro lato
di me vi rechi alcuna rimembranza;
　　ché, del vostro valore
avanti ch'io mi sia guari allungato,
mi tien già confortato

8 'And yet you are the one I most love, and you it is—you in whom my every hope rests—that can make me the greatest gift of all; for it is to serve you and you alone that I wish to live, and I ask and desire only that which brings you honour, all else being but wearisome. You are able to bestow upon me what no one else can, for into your hands—and in this I glory—Love has placed the power of life and death over me. From your kindly bearing derives the faith I place in you, for it is in truth from that bearing that all those who look upon you sense the compassion within. Now therefore, my lady, vouchsafe your greeting, that it may enter my—as you know full well—awaiting heart.'

di ritornar la mia dolce speranza.
Deo, quanto fie poca addimoranza,
secondo il mio parvente:
ché mi volge sovente
la mente per mirar vostra sembianza;
per che ne lo meo gire e addimorando,
gentil mia donna, a voi mi raccomando.[9]

DANTE CAVALCANTIANO

Restiveness in respect of the routine utterance—but restiveness as again veri-
fiable at the point both of literary-aesthetic and of philosophical concern—is
the hallmark too of the Cavalcantian phase of Dante's activity as a lyric poet,
Dante's, from this point on and indeed right up to the very end, being a constant
negotiation with his 'first friend' at the level both of substance and of style, both
of the *what* of human experience in the round and of the *how* of its honest
expression.

The myth of Cavalcanti as cultivated by the chroniclers Dino Compagni and
Giovanni Villani and by the *novelliere* and commentator upon Dante Giovanni
Boccaccio combines with what we know of him from his own work to suggest an
in every sense powerful presence in the lives of those around him, a presence as
colourful politically as it was adventurous philosophically.[10] When, how and in

---

9 'May Love—who made it yours—commend to you my loyal heart, and may Compassion for
her part remind you of me the while; for not as yet far off from your goodness already am I comforted
by the sweet hope of homecoming. Ah, how brief—or so it seems to me—will be my being away from
you, for ofttimes my mind is turned to gaze upon your likeness; and so, my gracious lady, both as
journeying and as sojourning, I commend myself to you.'

10 Compagni 1.20: 'Uno giovane gentile, figliuolo di messer Cavalcante Cavalcanti, nobile cavaliere, chiamato Guido, cortese e ardito ma sdegnoso e solitario e intento allo studio' (A young man
of noble birth named Guido, son of the noble knight M. Cavalcante Cavalcanti, elegant and bold but
disdainful, solitary and intent on study); Villani 8.42: 'era come filosofo, virtudioso uomo in più cose,
se non ch'era troppo tenero e stizzoso' (albeit oversensitive and unpredictable, he was both a philosopher and a man of many parts); Boccaccio, *Decameron* 6.9: 'Tralle quali brigate n'era una di messer
Betto Brunelleschi, nella quale messer Betto e' compagni s'eran molto ingegnati di tirare Guido di
messer Cavalcante de' Cavalcanti, e non senza cagione: per ciò che, oltre a quello che egli fu un de'
migliori loici che avesse il mondo e ottimo filosofo naturale (delle quali cose poco la brigata curava),
si fu egli leggiadrissimo e costumato e parlante uom molto e ogni cosa che far volle e a gentil uom
pertenente seppe meglio che altro uom fare; e con questo era ricchissimo, e a chiedere a lingua sapeva
onorare cui nell'animo gli capeva che il valesse. Ma a messer Betto non era mai potuto venir fatto
d'averlo, e credeva egli co' suoi compagni che ciò avvenisse per ciò che Guido alcuna volta speculando
molto abstratto dagli uomini divenia; e per ciò che egli alquanto tenea della oppinione degli epicuri,
si diceva tralla gente volgare che queste sue speculazioni erano solo in cercare se trovar si potesse che
Iddio non fosse' (Among which companies was one of which Messer Betto Brunelleschi was the
leading spirit, a company into which Messer Betto and his comrades had striven hard to bring Guido,

what order these things impinged upon Dante as he looked on is impossible to say, but the depth and decisiveness of his first friend's presence to him both in life and in death (Cavalcanti died in 1300) are each alike beyond question, the pre-liminary moments of that presence being documented in the *Vita nova* of 1293 or thereabouts; for it is in the *Vita nova* that, in the course of what amounts to a systematic response on Dante's part to Cavalcanti's sense of love as but a darkling and destructive property of the sensitive soul, he goes out of his way to register both the origin of his friendship with him and their shared sense of the ideal ac-countability of form to substance within the economy of the poetic utterance as a whole. On the one hand, then, we have these lines from chapter 3 of the *libello*, lines straightaway privileging Cavalcanti as to the fore among those decisive for everything coming next by way of Dante's own account of the nature and finality of love properly understood:

A questo sonetto fue risposto da molti e di diverse sentenzie; tra li quali fue rispnditore quelli cui io chiamo primo de li miei amici, e disse allora uno sonetto, lo quale comincia: *Vedeste, al mio parere, onne valore.* E questo fue quasi lo principio de l'amistà tra lui e me, quando elli seppe che io era quelli che li avea ciò mandato.[11]

son of Cavalcante de' Cavalcanti, and not without reason, inasmuch as, besides being one of the best logicians in the world and an excellent natural philosopher (qualities of which the company made no great account), he was without a peer for gallantry and courtesy and excellence of discourse and aptitude for all matters which he might set his mind to, and that belonged to a gentleman; and there-withal he was very rich, and, when he deemed any worthy of honour, knew how to bestow it to the uttermost. But, as Messer Betto had never been able to gain him over, he and his comrades supposed that 'twas because Guido, being addicted to speculation, was thereby estranged from men. And, for that he was somewhat inclined to the opinion of the Epicureans, the vulgar averred that these spec-ulations of his had no other scope than to prove that God did not exist). For Cavalcanti and Dante, Bruno Nardi, 'Dante e Guido Cavalcanti', in *Saggi e note di critica dantesca* (Milan: Ricciardi, 1966), 190–219; Gianfranco Contini, 'Cavalcanti in Dante', in *Un'idea di Dante* (Turin: Einaudi, 1976 [1968]), 143–57; Teodolinda Barolini, *Dante's Poets: Textuality and Truth in the 'Comedy'* (Princeton: Princeton University Press, 1984), 123–53; Teodolinda Barolini, 'Dante and Guido Cavalcanti (On Making Dis-tinctions in Matters of Love): *Inferno* 5 in Its Lyric and Autobiographical Context', DS 116 (1998), 31–63 (and in *Dante and the Origins of Italian Literary Culture* [New York: Fordham University Press, 2006], 70–101); Enrico Malato, *Dante e Guido Cavalcanti: Il dissidio per la 'Vita nuova' e il 'disdegno' di Guido* (Rome: Salerno, 1997; 2nd ed. 2004); *Guido Cavalcanti tra i suoi lettori. Proceedings of the International Symposium for the Seventh Centennial of His Death, New York 10–11 November 2000*, ed. Maria Luisa Ardizzone (Florence: Cadmo, 2003); Zygmunt G. Barański, 'Guido Cavalcanti and His First Readers', in *Guido Cavalcanti tra i suoi lettori* (Florence: Cadmo, 2003), 149–75; Maria Corti, *Scritti su Cavalcanti e Dante: La felicità mentale: Percorsi dell'invenzione e altri saggi* (Turin: Einaudi, 2003); Alberto Gessani, *Dante, Guido Cavalcanti, e l'"amoroso regno"* (Macerata: Quodlibet, 2004); Guglielmo Gorni, *Guido Cavalcanti: Dante e il suo "primo amico"* (Rome: Aracne, 2009); Noemi Ghetti, *L'ombra di Cavalcanti e Dante* (Rome: L'Asino d'oro edizioni, 2010); Francesco Fioretti, *Ethos e leggiadria: Lo stilnovo dialogico di Dante, Guido e Cino da Pistoia* (Rome: Aracne, 2012).

11 'Many were the replies I had to this sonnet, each with its own interpretation, and among those who responded was he whom I consider to be foremost among my friends and who at that point

while on the other we have these from chapter 25, where as part of a parenthesis designed to justify his use of personification when it comes to talking about love (for love, in the *Vita nova*, appears to live and laugh just like anybody else), Dante registers once and for all their common commitment to form as but the outshining of substance, registering thus understood straightaway shading off into rejoicing, into a sturdy affirmation of like-mindedness:

> E acciò che non ne pigli alcuna baldanza persona grossa, dico che né li poete parlavano così sanza ragione, né quelli che rìmano dèono parlare così, non avendo alcuno ragionamento in loro di quello che dicono; però che grande vergogna sarebbe a colui che rimasse cose sotto vesta di figura o di colore rettorico, e poscia, domandato, non sapesse denudare le sue parole da cotale vesta, in guisa che avessero verace intendimento. E questo mio primo amico e io ne sapemo bene di quelli che così rìmano stoltamente.[12]

—passages to which we must add the sonnet *I' vegno 'l giorno a te 'nfinite volte*, addressed by Cavalcanti to Dante possibly in the wake of Beatrice's death in 1290 and thus bearing witness to something approaching a now seasoned sense of companionship when it comes to making verses in the vernacular:

> I' vegno 'l giorno a te 'nfinite volte
> e trovoti pensar troppo vilmente;
> molto mi dòl della gentil tua mente
> e d'assai tue vertù che ti son tolte.
>
> Solevanti spiacer persone molte;
> tuttor fuggivi l'annoiosa gente;
> di me parlavi sì coralemente,
> che tutte le tue rime avie ricolte.
>
> Or non ardisco, per la vil tua vita,
> far mostramento che tu' dir mi piaccia,
> né 'n guisa vegno a te, che tu mi veggi.
>
> Se 'l presente sonetto spesso leggi,

---

wrote a sonnet beginning *Vedeste, al mio parere, onne valore*. And this it was—his learning that it was I who had sent him this sonnet—that saw the beginning, as it were, of our friendship one with the other.'

12 'And in case any ignorant person should assume too much, I will add that just as the poets did not themselves speak in this way without good reason, neither should those who, being unable to give a reasonable account of what they are saying, compose in rhyme; for it would be shameful in the extreme should anyone thus rhyming embellish the line by way of this or that figure of speech or a rhetorical flourish and be unable, upon being asked, to strip away that embellishment in favour of its true meaning—my best friend and I knowing only too well of those rhyming thus foolishly.'

> lo spirito noioso che ti caccia
> si partirà da l'anima invilita.[13]

But then, and more than ever eloquent as testimony to the twofold substance and complexity of Dante's relationship with Cavalcanti as author and architect of the new way, comes the *utinam* sonnet *Guido i' vorrei che tu e Lapo ed io* together with the correspondence to which it gave rise, eloquence here tending in one and the same moment both to confirm and to qualify a mutual in-abiding of the spirit. First, then, we have as in truth but a superlative confection the sonnet *Guido i' vorrei che tu e Lapo ed io*, superlative not least in its countenancing at a stroke both the *that it is* and the *would that it were* moment of an ideal companionship:

> Guido, i' vorrei che tu e Lapo ed io
> fossimo presi per incantamento,
> e messi in un vasel ch'ad ogni vento
> per mare andasse al voler vostro e mio,
>   sì che fortuna od altro tempo rio
> non ci potesse dare impedimento,
> anzi, vivendo sempre in un talento,
> di stare insieme crescesse 'l disio.
>   E monna Vanna e monna Lagia poi
> con quella ch'è sul numer de le trenta
> con noi ponesse il buono incantatore;
>   e quivi ragionar sempre d'amore,
> e ciascuna di lor fosse contenta,
> sì come i' credo che saremmo noi.[14]

---

13 'Every day I come to you times without number finding you lost to ever viler thoughts. I grieve for your noble mind and for the many virtues torn from you. Many hitherto were displeasing to you and you've always fled the boorish. Warm as you were in your appreciation of me, it is for this reason that I gathered up all your poems. But given the now wretched life you lead I dare not openly proclaim my delight in your work, nor in any way approach you or be seen by you. Ponder, then, my present sonnet, for perchance the base spirit haunting you may then abandon your wretched existence.' Luigi Pastine, 'Il sonetto di Guido', *GD* 34 (1931), 201–208; Antonino Pagliaro, 'Il disdegno di Guido', in *Saggi di critica semantica* (Messina: G. D'Anna, 1953), 355–79; Mario Marti, 'Sulla genesi del realismo dantesco', in *Realismo dantesco e altri studi* (Milan: Ricciardi, 1961), 1–32; Alberto Gessani, 'Guido a Dante: "I' vegno 'l giorno a te 'nfinite volte"', in *Dante, Guido Cavalcanti, e l'"amoroso regno"* (Macerata: Quodlibet, 2004), 155–203.

14 'Guido, I would that you, Lapo and I were taken up by magic and placed in a boat, that, whatever the wind, was carried over the sea at your behest and mine such that neither storm nor foul weather should hinder us, but rather that, forever all of a mind, our wish to be together should ever be the more. And with us the kindly enchanter would bring monna Vanna, monna Lagia, and she who numbers thirty, there forever to speak of love; and that they each of them would be content as so also, I believe, would we ourselves.' Guglielmo Gorni, 'Guido, i' vorrei che tu e Lippo ed io' (Sul canone del "Dolce Stil Novo")', *SFI* 36 (1978), 21–37; Antonio Lanza, 'Guido, i' vorrei che tu e Lapo (o Lippo?) ed io', in

but then—and wholly at the expense of countenancing thus understood—comes Cavalcanti's reply to the effect that he must perforce refuse, his, as a lover, being an order of experience quite other than Dante's, an existence not so much blessed as burdened by love and knowing to that extent neither hope nor resolution:

> S'io fosse quelli che d'amor fu degno,
> del qual non trovo sol che rimembranza,
> e la donna tenesse altra sembianza,
> assai mi piaceria siffatto legno.
> E tu, che se' de l'amoroso regno
> là onde di merzé nasce speranza,
> riguarda se 'l mi' spirito ha pesanza;
> ch'un prest' arcier di lui ha fatto segno
> e tragge l'arco, che li tese Amore,
> sì lietamente, che la sua persona
> par che di gioco porti signoria.
> Or odi maraviglia ch'el disia:
> lo spirito fedito li perdona,
> vedendo che li strugge il suo valore.[15]

—lines to which, as belonging ideally to the same moment, we must add the putatively but probably Dantean sonnet *Amore e monna Lagia e Guido ed io*, a poem which, while registering any number of fault lines within the stilnovistic project generally, confirms Cavalcanti's status as but an outsider to it (the 'che n'è del tutto fore' of line 12), as subsisting at a distance:

> Amore e monna Lagia e Guido ed io
> possiamo ringraziare un ser costui
> che 'nd'ha partiti, sapete da cui?

Dante oggi: Convegno di studi, Latina, 18 maggio 1991 (Anzio: De Rubeis, 1994), 47–54; Leonardo Sebastio, 'Da "Guido i' vorrei" alla *Commedia*. Un tema dantesco: L'amicizia', *CL* 23.1–2 (1995), 347–63; Alberto Gessani, '"Guido, i' vorrei" e la risposta di Cavalcanti', in *Dante, Guido Cavalcanti, e l'"amoroso regno"* (Macerata: Quodlibet, 2004), 23–44; Simon West, 'A Short-Lived Enchantment: Some Observations on the Sonnet Exchange between Dante and Cavalcanti', in *Flinders Dante Conferences 2002 and 2004*, ed. Margaret Baker et al. (Adelaide: Lythurum Press, 2005), 17–25; Noemi Ghetti, '"Guido, i' vorrei che tu e Lapo ed io": Nascita e crisi del sodalizio poetico', in *L'ombra di Cavalcanti e Dante* (Rome: L'Asino d'oro edizioni, 2010), 105–10.

15 'Were I to be found worthy of love (of which I know now only by recall), and were my lady's looks otherwise, then such a boat would please me greatly. But you who are of Love's realm, there where there is hope of compassion, see how my spirit is weighed down, for an eager archer has made it his target and shoots from the bow so cheerfully provided for him by Love that he appears exceedingly to rejoice. And witness now the strangeness of my spirit's desiring, for stricken and seeing itself undone by him, it forgives him!'

Nol vo' contar per averlo in oblio;
   poi questi tre più non v'hanno disio,
ch'eran serventi di tal guisa in lui,
che veramente più di lor non fui
imaginando ch'elli fosse iddio.
   Sia ringraziato Amor, che se n'accorse
primeramente; poi la donna saggia,
che 'n quello punto li ritolse il core;
   e Guido ancor, che n'è del tutto fore;
ed io ancor che 'n sua vertute caggia;
se poi mi piacque, nol si crede forse.[16]

But—and this now is the point—Dante's, for all his difficulty with Cavalcanti (and Cavalcanti's with him) in the area of love-understanding, was even so a continuing exploration of his own humanity and a continuing refinement of his skills as a technician under the aegis of his first friend. His, in other words, was at every point along the way a rejoicing in both the substance and the style of the Cavalcantian line while, as and when he saw fit, fashioning it afresh in his own image. Take, for example, the Dante of the Cavalcantian ballads, the Dante, that is to say, of *Per una ghirlandetta* and of *Deh Violetta che in ombra d'amore*, essays in the floral, the fragrant and the feminine as exquisite as anything in Cavalcanti but registering in relation to the archetypal text a freshly inflected spirituality, a spirituality less of discerning than of desiring, less of perceiving than of praising; on the one hand, then, there is the Cavalcanti of *Fresca rosa novella*, a moment, precisely, of pure consciousness, of rapt intellection:

Angelica sembranza
in voi, donna, riposa;
Dio, quanto aventurosa
fue la mia disïanza!

16 'Love, monna Lagia, Guido and I can thank a certain Messer So and So who (though for the sake of passing quickly over it I'll not enter into detail) has parted us from you know who; for these three, who were such good servants of his, no longer have any desire to be with him, even though I myself, imagining him to be something of a god, was no more a devoted servant of his than they. Thanks be to Love that he noticed it first; then the wise lady who in that very moment withdrew her heart from him; and then Guido who is quite out of it where love is concerned; and then I myself who am still under Love's sway. That then I should still rejoice in this takes, perhaps, some believing.' Allusive as it is, and to that extent uncertain in point of exact interpretation, the sonnet turns probably on the disintegration of the ideal company of *Guido, i' vorrei che tu e Lapo ed io* in consequence of Lapo Gianni's slighting of Amore in his canzone *Amor, nova ed antica vanitate* and Cavalcanti's disenchantment with love as a principle of anything approaching properly human happiness. Teodolinda Barolini, *Dante Alighieri: Rime giovanili e della Vita Nuova* (Milan: Rizzoli, 2009), 196–201.

Vostra cera gioiosa,
poi che passa e avanza
natura e costumanza,
ben è mirabil cosa.
 Fra lor le donne dea
vi chiaman, come sète;
tanto adorna parete,
ch'eo non saccio contare;
e chi poria pensare–oltra natura?

(*Fresca rosa novella*, lines 19–31)[17]

while on the other there is the Dante of the ballad *Per una ghirlandetta*, no less committed, to be sure, to seeing and understanding as preliminary in respect of each and every subsequent movement of the spirit, but attuned now less to the noetic than to the hymnic, desire in the intensity thereof and praise in the fullness thereof insinuating themselves in such a way as to refresh not merely the complexion but the substance of the text, what in truth it sets out to say:

Per una ghirlandetta
ch'io vidi, mi farà
sospirare ogni fiore.
 I' vidi a voi, donna, portare
ghirlandetta di fior gentile,
e sovr'a lei vidi volare
un angiolel d'amore umile;
e 'n suo cantar sottile
dicea: 'Chi mi vedrà
lauderà 'l mio signore'.
 Se io sarò là dove sia
Fioretta mia bella a sentire,
allor dirò la donna mia
che port'in testa i miei sospire.
Ma per crescer disire
mïa donna verrà

17 'There abides in you, my lady, the likeness of an angel. My God, how blessed was my desiring! Your radiant countenance, surpassing and excelling as it does nature and custom alike, is indeed a thing wonderful to behold. Women among themselves speak of you as a goddess, as indeed you are. So perfect you seem that I know not how to tell of it, for who can think beyond the limits of nature herself?'

coronata da Amore.

Le parolette mie novelle,
che di fiori fatto han ballata,
per leggiadria ci hanno tolt'elle
una vesta ch'altrui fu data:
però siate pregata,
qual uom la canterà,
che li facciate onore.[18]

—a poem to which we may add the aforesaid and no less exquisite ballad *Deh, Vïoletta, che in ombra d'Amore*, again nothing if not responsive to the epistemic moment of the Cavalcantian text but sensitive now, albeit in the midst of love's travail, to the salvific aspect of the encounter, to my lady's presence as a principle of both hope and healing:

Deh, Vïoletta, che in ombra d'Amore
ne gli occhi miei sì subito apparisti,
aggi pietà del cor che tu feristi,
che spera in te e disïando more.
Tu, Vïoletta, in forma più che umana,
foco mettesti dentro in la mia mente
col tuo piacer ch'io vidi;
poi con atto di spirito cocente
creasti speme, che in parte mi sana
là dove tu mi ridi.
Deh, non guardare perché a lei mi fidi,
ma drizza li occhi al gran disio che m'arde,
ché mille donne già per esser tarde
sentiron pena de l'altrui dolore.[19]

18 'For a garland I have seen, every flower will henceforth make me sigh. I saw you, my lady, wearing a garland of sweet flowers, and over it a little angel hovering, a gentle angel of love, who said in his delicate song: "Whosoever looks upon me will praise my Lord." Should I find myself where my fair Fioretta may hear me, I shall say that my lady wears my sighs around her head. But she, to increase my desire, will come crowned by Love. These brief words of mine, freshly fashioned and woven one with another to make a ballad of flowers, have taken to adorn themselves a garment made over to another; so I pray you, my lady, be gracious to whoever sings them.'

19 'Ah, Violetta, you who so suddenly appeared to my eyes in Love's shadow, pity the heart wounded by you, that puts its trust in you, and that is dying of desire. You, Violetta, in a more than human form, kindled by way of the beauty I glimpsed a fire in my mind, whereupon you quickened by means of a no less fiery spirit a hope that in part heals as you smile upon me. Ah, regard not my trusting to this hope, but consider rather the great desire burning within me; for in their slowness to respond countless ladies have themselves suffered on account of their lovers' anguish.'

But what applies in the ballads as but a gentle inflexion of the Cavalcantian utterance applies altogether more dramatically in the great canzoni of this early period, for here it is a question of Dante's affirming over and against the love-scepticism of his first friend a Beatrice full of grace and truth, a Beatrice, that is to say, as the bringer of blessing and of new life. True, the upward way, the path from one species of love-understanding to another, is more than ever fraught, the key texts here remaining fully transparent to the substance and psychology of *Donna me prega* as an essay in the agony of it all; so, for example, these lines from the beginning of the canzone *Lo doloroso amor che mi conduce*, lines turning after the manner of Cavalcanti upon a sense of love as but a matter of spiritual foreclosure, a drawing nigh unto death:

> Lo doloroso amor che mi conduce
> a fin di morte per piacer di quella
> che lo mio cor solea tener gioioso,
>   m'ha tolto e toglie ciascun dì la luce
> che avëan li occhi miei di tale stella
> che non credea di lei mai star doglioso;
>   e 'l colpo suo, c'ho portato nascoso,
> omai si scopre per soverchia pena,
> la qual nasce del foco
> che m'ha tratto di gioco,
> sì ch'altro mai che male io non aspetto;
> e 'l viver mio (omai esser de' poco)
> fin a la morte mia sospira e dice:
> 'Per quella moro c'ha nome Beatrice'.[20]

—lines to which we might add these from the canzone *E' m'incresce di me sì duramente* with its still more sustained account of love as but a principle of pain and of pitilessness:

> E' m'incresce di me sì duramente
> ch'altrettanto di doglia

---

20 'The grievous love which at the behest of she who was once my heart's every happiness but which now leads me on to death has denied the light—and daily denies it more—from a star once delightful to behold but now, in a way I could never have foretold, the cause of my distress. And the wound inflicted, hitherto hidden from sight, is now plain to see in all its surpassing pain, in all the agony which, born of the conflagration putting an end to my every happiness, means that nothing remains to me but despair. And my life (or what little remains of it), drawing nigh unto death, murmurs amid its sighing: "Through her I die whose name is Beatrice."' Aldo Menichetti, 'Lo doloroso amore che mi conduce', in *Dante Alighieri: Le quindici canzoni. Lette da diversi*, vol. 2 (Lecce: Pensa Multimedia, 2012), 287–304 (with Giuseppe Marani at 65–86 on *E' m'incresce di me sì duramente*).

mi reca la pietà quanto 'l martiro,
  lasso, però che dolorosamente
sento contro mia voglia
raccoglier l'aire del sezza' sospiro
  entro 'n quel cor che i belli occhi feriro
quando li aperse Amor con le sue mani
per conducermi al tempo che mi sface.
Oimè, quanto piani,
soavi e dolci ver' me si levaro,
quand'elli incominciaro
la morte mia, che tanto mi dispiace,
dicendo: 'Nostro lume porta pace'.

. . .

Io ho parlato a voi, giovani donne,
che avete li occhi di bellezze ornati
e la mente d'amor vinta e pensosa,
perché raccomandati
vi sian li detti miei ovunque sono;
e 'nnanzi a voi perdono
la morte mia a quella bella cosa
che me n'ha colpa e mai non fu pietosa.

(*E' m'incresce di me sì duramente*, lines 1–14 and 85–92)[21]

But—and this now is what matters—stirring in the depths of this situation are forces making for its transfiguration, for the transfiguration not, to be sure, of Cavalcanti himself but rather of the Cavalcantian moment of Dante's youthful experience as a lover, for stirring in the depths and making by way of a remarkable process of action and reaction for renewal on the plane of love-intelligence is a sense of that same love as the in-and-through-which of spiritual ascent, of blissful ulteriority. True, the agony of it all is as intense as ever, but this is the agony proper to a species of love-understanding as yet on the way, as attuned withal to a pres-

21 'I pity myself so intensely that my pity brings me no less pain than my suffering; for painfully, alas, and against my every inclination, I feel gathered there in my heart—in the heart smitten by those lovely eyes in the moment Love with his own hands opened them to bring me to the point of my undoing—the breath of my last sigh. Alas, how soft, sweet and gentle in the moment of their lifting upon me and of their precipitating—saying the while "Our light is your peace"—this my demise ... It is to you, young ladies, whose eyes have but beauty for their adornment but minds overcome and troubled by love, that I speak, commending my verses to you wherever they may go; and in your presence I pardon that fair one for my death, for she it is who, in her pitilessness, bears the blame for it.'

ence—that, precisely, of madonna—apt even so to out-paradise paradise in its splendour:

> Quel dolce nome, che mi fa il cor agro,
> tutte fïate ch'i' lo vedrò scritto
> mi farà nuovo ogni dolor ch'io sento;
>   e de la doglia diverrò sì magro
> de la persona e 'l viso tanto afflitto,
> che qual mi vederà n'avrà pavento.
>   E allor non trarrà sì poco vento
> che non mi meni, sì ch'io cadrò freddo;
> e per tal verrò morto,
> e 'l dolor sarà scorto
> con l'anima che sen girà sì trista;
> e sempre mai con lei starà ricolto,
> ricordando la gio' del dolce viso,
> a che nïente par lo paradiso.

(*Lo doloroso amor che mi conduce*, lines 15–28)[22]

And this too is the situation in the canzone *E' m'increse di me sì duramente* as, whatever else it is, an intimation of things to come, of the book of the *Vita nova* no less—here in *E' m'increse* the 'book of my mind'—with its reconstruction of a spiritual itinerary by way of love's endless paradoxes and the grief of bereavement. True, fear and trembling persist to tax the spirit, but this is fear and trembling functional in respect of something infinitely greater than themselves, of, in a word, Beatrice and the Beatrician as the way of emancipation:

> Lo giorno che costei nel mondo venne,
> secondo che si trova
> nel libro de la mente che vien meno,
>   la mia persona pargola sostenne
> una passïon nova,
> tal ch'io rimasi di paura pieno;

---

22 'The name, so sweet, that makes my heart so bitter, will refresh my every pain whensoever I see it written; and from sorrow I shall in my frame be so wasted and in my face so afflicted that just to see me will be fearful, whereupon the least breath of wind will sweep me along until I fall frozen to the ground. So shall I die, my sorrow accompanied by my soul on her sad departure and forever more at one with her as she recalls the joy of that sweet face to which paradise itself seems nothing by comparison.'

ch'a tutte mie virtù fu posto un freno
subitamente, sì ch'io caddi in terra,
per una luce che nel cuor percosse:
e se 'l libro non erra,
lo spirito maggior tremò sì forte,
che parve ben che morte
per lui in questo mondo giunta fosse:
ma or ne increse a quei che questo mosse.

Quando m'apparve poi la gran biltate
che sì mi fa dolere,
donne gentili a cu' i' ho parlato,
quella virtù che ha più nobilitate,
mirando nel piacere,
s'accorse ben che 'l suo male era nato;
e conobbe 'l disio ch'era creato
per lo mirare intento ch'ella fece;
sì che piangendo dissi a l'altre poi:
'Qui giugnerà, in vece
d'una ch'io vidi, la bella figura,
che già mi fa paura;
che sarà donna sopra tutte noi,
tosto che fia piacer de li occhi suoi'.

(E' m'incresce di me sì duramente, lines 57–84)[23]

---

23 'The day she came into the world—as I find it written in the book of my mind now but faintly present to me—my childlike being suffered so strange a passion that I was filled with fear; and suddenly my every faculty was checked such that I fell to the ground for a light which struck my heart. And, provided only the book err not, my spirit shook so violently that it seemed as though death had entered the world to take it. But now he himself who set it all in train grieves for it. And then, noble ladies whom I address, when that beauty beyond compare—though the cause of my suffering—appeared, that faculty which is above all, looking upon it, understood well that here, together with the desire engendered by its own rapt gaze, was the beginning of its pain; so that, weeping, it addressed the other faculties, saying: "Here, in the moment it pleases her eyes, will come, under the aspect of one I have seen, the wondrous form of she who, filling me already with fear, will rule as mistress over us all." ' Philippe Guiberteau, 'La poésie E' m'incresce di me sì duramente', Bulletin de la Société d'études dantesques 11 (1962), 67–77; Enrico Fenzi, 'E' m'incresce di me sì duramente', in Le Rime di Dante: Gargnano del Garda 25–27 settembre 2008, ed. Claudia Berra and Paolo Borsa (Milan: Cisalpino, 2010), 135–75. For the 'ideal spiritual itinerary' and 'book of the mind' moment of the argument, Teodolinda Barolini, 'A Cavalcantian Vita Nuova: Dante's Canzoni Lo doloroso amor che mi conduce and E' m'incresce di me sì duramente', in Dantean Dialogues: Engaging with the Legacy of Amilcare Iannucci, ed. Maggie Kilgour and Elena Lombardi (Toronto: University of Toronto Press, 2013), 41–65.

If, then, Dante remains for the moment in communion with Cavalcanti, and Cavalcanti with him, as party to a fresh experiment in point both of love-understanding and of love-expression, then here at least, in *Lo doloroso amor che mi conduce* and *E' m'incresce di me sì duramente*, is something quite other than anything envisaged by his first friend, a love-dialectic not merely indifferent but irreducible to the deep substance of *Donna me prega* as—then as now—a land-mark in the area of Siculo-Tuscan and stilnovistic lyricism. And it is this antici-pation in Dante—in the Dante of *Lo doloroso amor che mi conduce* and *E' m'incresce di me sì duramente*—of something other in the offing that invites us to look again at the whole question of his Cavalcantianism, since for all his susceptibility to Cavalcanti both as a philosopher of love and as a technician, and indeed for all his delight in Cavalcanti as a companion or fellow breaker of bread, his is but a pale reflection of the real thing, a living out of the Cavalcantian drama under the aspect less of its substance than of its symptomatology. Never, in other words, even in his bleakest moments, is it a question in Dante of love *in and for itself* as a principle of undoing on the plane of properly human being—of confusion, con-sternation and near-impossibility, to be sure, but never, in and for itself and prop-erly understood, of anything other than new life.

DANTE AND THE *ROSE*:
THE *FIORE* AND THE *DETTO D'AMORE*

With what amounts, then, in the canzone *E' m'incresce di me sì duramente* to a preliminary meditation upon the Beatrician moment of Dante's experience as a lyric poet, we are fast approaching the *Vita nova* as a point of arrival in respect of the first phase of his activity as a poet and philosopher of love, though not before spending time with the so-called *Fiore*, the editorial title for a series of 232 sonnets surviving in a sole manuscript in the University of Montpellier and of-fering a selective but faithful reading of the *Roman de la Rose*. In the years follow-ing its first publication in 1881,[24] the case for Dante's authorship of the *Fiore* rested

24 Ferdinand Castets, *Il fiore* (Paris: Maisonneuve, 1881). For the manuscript, textual tradition and bibliography, John Took, *Dante Alighieri: Il Fiore. Introduction, Text, Translation and Commen-tary* (Lewiston, NY: Edwin Mellen Press, 2004), 13–18. On the problem of the *Fiore* in general, in-cluding authorship and intepretation: Luigi Foscolo Benedetto, *Il Roman de la Rose e la letteratura italiana* (Halle a. S.: Niemeyer, 1910); Gianfranco Contini, 'La questione del *Fiore*', *CS* 13–14 (1965), 768–73; Gianfranco Contini, 'Un nodo della cultura medievale: La serie *Roman de la Rose—Fiore—Divina Commedia*, *LI* 25 (1973), 162–89; (also in *Un'idea di Dante: Saggi danteschi* [Turin: Einaudi, 1976 (1970)], 245–83 and in Luca Carlo Rossi's edition of the *Fiore* [Milan: Mondadori, 1996], 281–316); Mario Muner, 'Perché il *Fiore* non può essere di Dante (e a chi invece potrebbe attribuirsi)', *MDC* 7 (1968–69), 88–105; Michelangelo Picone, '*Il Fiore*: Struttura profonda e problemi attributivi',

on two things: on its 'internal signature', on the 'Durante' of 82.9 and 202.14 of which the name 'Dante' is but a hypocorism or domestic form, and on the possible identification of the *Fiore* and the 'pulzelletta' or young woman mentioned by Dante in a sonnet addressed to a certain Messer Brunetto (of, however, uncertain identity) and offering him, he says, a little food for thought, a riddle to be solved. Should, by chance, the text present any difficulty, he goes on, then let it be referred on to a certain Giano as possibly Jean de Meun himself as author of the second and weightier part of the *Roman*:

> Messer Brunetto, questa pulzelletta
> Con esso voi si ven la pasqua a fare:
> Non intendete pasqua di mangiare,
> Ch'ella non mangia, anzi vuol esser letta.
> La sua sentenzia non richiede fretta
> Né luogo di romor né da giullare;
> Anzi si vuol più volte lusingare
> Prima che 'n intelletto altrui si metta.
> Se voi non la intendete in questa guisa,
> In vostra gente ha molti frati Alberti
> Da intender ciò ch'è posto loro in mano.
> Con lor vi restringete sanza risa;

VR 33 (1974), 145–56; Luigi Vanossi, *Dante e il 'Roman de la Rose': Saggio sul 'Fiore'* (Florence: Olschki, 1979); Luigi Peirone, *Tra Dante e 'Il Fiore': Lingua e parola* (Genoa: Tilgher, 1982); Aldo Vallone, 'Il *Fiore* come opera di Dante', *SD* 56 (1984), 141–67; Aldo Vallone, 'Du Roman de la Rose au Fiore attribué à Dante', *Cahiers de littérature médiévale italienne* 1 (1992), 7–14; Remo Fasani, 'L'attribuzione del *Fiore*', *SPCT* 39 (1989), 5–40; Earl Jeffrey Richards, 'The *Fiore* and the *Roman de la Rose*', in Jeanette Beer (ed.), *Medieval Translators and Their Craft* (Kalamazoo: West Michigan University, 1989), 265–328; Leonardo Sebastio, *Strutture narrative e dinamiche culturali in Dante e nel 'Fiore'* (Florence: Olschki 1990); Leonardo Sebastio, 'Amore e verità nel Fiore', in *Il poeta e la storia: Una dinamica dantesca* (Florence: Olschki, 1994), 161–218; Leonardo Sebastio, ' "Ragion la Bella" nel Fiore: Preistoria o genesi dell'idea di cultura in Dante', in *Dante: Summa medievalis. Proceedings of the Symposium of the Centre for Italian Studies*, ed. Charles Franco and Leslie Morgan (Stony Brook: Forum Italicum, 1995), 52–86; Peter Armour, 'The *Roman de la Rose* and the *Fiore*: Aspects of a Literary Transplantation', *JIRS* 2 (1993), 63–81; Zygmunt G. Barański et al. (eds.), *Lettura del 'Fiore'*, *LC* 22 (Ravenna: Longo, 1993); Zygmunt G. Barański and Patrick Boyde (eds.), *The 'Fiore' in Context: Dante, France, Tuscany* (Notre Dame: University of Notre Dame Press, 1997). On questions of style and technique in the *Fiore*, Mary Dominic Ramacciotti, *The Syntax of 'Il Fiore' and of Dante's 'Inferno' as Evidence in the Question of the Authorship of 'Il Fiore'* (New York: AMS Press, 1969; 1936 thesis of the Catholic University of America); Aniello Fratta, 'La lingua del *Fiore* (e del *Detto d'amore*) e le opere di Francesco da Barberino', *MC* 14 (1984), 45–62; Jospeh A. Barber, 'Prospettive per un'analisi statistica del *Fiore*', *REI* 31 (1985), 5–24; Jospeh A. Barber, 'A Statistical Analysis of the *Fiore*', *LD* 6 (1990), 100–122; Letterio Cassata, 'Sul testo del *Fiore*', *SD* 58 (1986), 187–237; Arnaldo Moroldo, 'Emprunts et réseaux lexicaux dans le *Fiore*', *Revue des langues romanes* 92 (1988), 127–51.

E se li altri de' dubbî non son certi,
Ricorrete a la fine a messer Giano.[25]

Neither, in truth, was or is particularly persuasive, but since then the question of proprietorship has been taken up and developed by way of a more sustained analysis both of form and of substance, both of the *how* and of the *what* of the text;[26] so, for example, relative to the first of these things, to style as testimony to a distinctive set of preferences, we have the phonemic and acoustic patterning of the line from the *Fiore* to the canonical Dante:

Ragion sì parte, udendomi *parlare*	Amor mi mosse, che mi fa *parlare*
(*Fiore* 11.1)[27]	(*Inferno* 2.72)
di non far *grazia* al meo *domandamento*	tanto m'*aggrada* il tuo *comandamento*
(*Fiore* 14.4)	(*Inferno* 2.79)
allor si parte, ed *ivi* fece punto	*allor si* mosse, e *io* tenni dietro
(*Fiore* 140.12)	(*Inferno* 1.136)

25 'Messer Brunetto, this young maid comes to keep Easter with you; not, you understand, an eating Easter, for she doesn't eat but is meant, rather, to be read. Her meaning does not call for hasty reading or a place that is noisy. In fact, she will need to be coaxed more than once before entering a man's mind. And if you do not understand her thus, there are many brother Alberts in your company to make sense of whatever is put in their hands. Get together with them, but no laughing! And if none of them is clear about its difficulties then in the last resort go and ask Messer Giano.' Guglielmo Gorni, 'Una proposta per "messer Brunetto"', *SFI* 37 (1979), 19–32 (slightly revised in *Il nodo della lingua e il verbo d'amore: Studi su Dante e altri duecentisti* [Florence: Olschki, 1981], 49–69).

26 Gianfranco Contini, 'La questione del *Fiore*', *CS* 13–14 (1965), 772: 'non si tratta d'una somma d'indizi, come quella pure assai importante d'ordine esterno, ma di cosa ben più decisiva: l'incontro d'una memoria strettamente verbale, d'una memoria sinonimica, d'una memoria fonica in cui viene decrescendo l'eventuale coscienza riflessa e crescendo una ripresa istintiva e immediata. Tale morfologia non può riflettere che il rapporto d'una personalità con se stessa, non già con una "fonte", fosse pure profondamente penetrata nell'inconscio' (it is not a question here of references in the aggregate, important as this is as a matter of form, but of something much more decisive, namely the presence of a strictly verbal memory, synonymic, phonic, in which, with the waning of this or that passing presence to the mind of the right word as duly pondered there waxes instead an instinctive and instantaneous process of recall. Morphology thus understood, far from being a matter of 'sources' however deeply rooted in the subconscious, cannot be anything other than the encounter of self with self).

27 'Reason, hearing me speak, took her leave'; *Inferno* 2.72: 'Love it is that moves me and causes me to speak'; *Fiore* 14.4: '[you would do me wrong] were you not to grant my request'; *Inferno* 2.79: 'so pleasing to me is your command'; *Fiore* 140.12: 'Then, drawing to a close, she left'; *Inferno* 1.126: 'Whereupon he set off, I following on'.

while on a grander scale—phrasal now rather than phonemic—there is the mirroring and thus the mutual invocation of passages such as the following from the Fiore and, again, the *Inferno*:

Or m'à messo in *pensero e in dottanza*	E qual è quei che volontieri acquista,
di ciò ched i' credea aver per certano,	e giugne 'l tempo che perder lo face,
sì c[h]'or me ne par essere in bilanza.	che 'n *tutti suoi pensier piange e s'attrista*,
e tutto ciò m'à fatto quello strano.	tal mi fece la bestia sanza pace ...

(Fiore 7.9–12)²⁸   (Inferno 1.55–58)

'A te sì non *convien* far disfidaglia,	A te *convien* tenere altro vïaggio',
se·ttu vuo' ben civir di questa guerra;	rispuose, poi che lagrimar mi vide,
lasciala far a' gran' signor' di terra,	'se vuo' campar d'esto loco selvaggio;
che posson sof[f]erir oste e battaglia.	ché questa bestia, per la qual tu gride,
Mala-Bocca, che così ti travaglia,	non lascia altrui passar per la sua via,
è traditor ...	ma tanto lo 'mpedisce che l'uccide;
Se·ttu lo sfidi o batti, e' griderà,	e *ha natura sì malvagia e ria*,
chéd *egli è di natura di mastino*;	che mai non empie la bramosa voglia,
chi più 'l minaccia, più gli abaierà.	e dopo 'l pasto ha più fame che pria'.

(Fiore 69.1–6 and 9–11)²⁹   (Inferno 1.91–99)

From the point of view, by contrast, of substance, of the *what* as distinct from the *how* of the text, it is a question once again of Dante's toing-and-froing along the corridor of time with a view either to refining or to repudiating the leading idea or else to revising the mood—ironic or otherwise—of its proposal and recommendation; so, for example, as more than ever emphatic when it comes to confirming the quintessentially reasonable character of Dante's loving both before and after the death of Beatrice, its standing over against every darkling passion of the sensitive soul, we have these lines from the *Vita nova*:

28 'He has sown so much doubt and anxiety over what I believed beyond doubt to be mine that everything now seems to hang in the balance. That's what he's done to me, that savage!'; *Inferno* 1.55–58: 'And like one who at the point of winning is all eager, but, come the moment of his losing, is all tears and sadness in his mind, that's how that restive beast made me.'

29 'If it's victory in the war you're after you'd be better off not issuing challenges, matters of this kind being left to the great land barons who can sustain troops and warfare. Foul Mouth, who is giving you such a hard time, is a traitor ... and such is his mastiff nature that if you challenge or strike him he'll simply holler. The more you threaten him the more he barks'; *Inferno* 1.91–99: ' "If you would escape this wild place, then you must go by another way," he answered when he saw me weep, "for the beast causing you so much grief lets no man pass by, but rather obstructs to the point of obliterating him. She has a nature so savage and evil that never is her ravenous appetite satisfied, and, having fed, she's only ever hungrier than before." '

E avvegna che la sua imagine, la quale continuatamente meco stava, fosse
baldanza d'Amore a segnoreggiare me, tuttavia era di sì nobilissima vertù,
che nulla volta sofferse che Amore mi reggesse sanza lo fedele consiglio de
la ragione in quelle cose là ove cotale consiglio fosse utile a udire . . . Ed io,
accorgendomi del malvagio domandare che mi faceano, per la volontade
d'Amore, lo quale mi comandava secondo lo consiglio de la ragione, rispon-
dea loro che Amore era quelli che così m'avea governato . . . E anche si divide questa seconda parte in cinque, secondo cinque diverse narrazioni:
che ne la prima dico quello che Amore, consigliato da la ragione, mi dice
quando le sono presso . . . Contra questo avversario de la ragione si levoe
un die, quasi ne l'ora de la nona, una forte imaginazione in me, che mi parve
vedere questa gloriosa Beatrice con quelle vestimenta sanguigne co le quali
apparve prima a li occhi miei; e pareami giovane in simile etade in quale io
prima la vidi. Allora cominciai a pensare di lei; e ricordandomi di lei secondo l'ordine del tempo passato, lo mio cuore cominciò dolorosamente a
pentere de lo desiderio a cui sì vilmente s'avea lasciato possedere alquanti
die contra la costanzia de la ragione.

(*Vita nova* 2.9, 4.2, 15.8 and 39.1–2)[30]

—lines all the more significant for their recalling Amante's dismissal of Reason
not just once in the *Fiore* but at strategic moments throughout; so, for example,
as an essay in the peremptoriness of it all, this from near the beginning of the text:

L'Amante

> Udendo che Ragion mi gastigava
> perch'i' al Die d'Amor era 'nservito,
> di ched i' era forte impalidito,
> e sol perch' io a·llui troppo pensava,
>   i' le dissi: 'Ragion, e' no·mi grava
> su' mal, ch'i' ne sarò tosto guerito,

---

30 'And though her image, which was but the way of Love's holding sway over me, was always with
me, it was nonetheless so excellent to behold that never did it suffer Love to direct me without the
faithful guidance of reason wherever that guidance was useful to have . . . And I, aware of the ill will
underlying their questioning, replied as Love himself wished to the effect that it was he who, directing
me in accordance with reason, had brought me to this pass . . . The second part of the sonnet can itself
be divided into five parts in keeping with the five moments of the argument, for in the first I speak of
how Love, on the basis of reason, addresses me whenever I draw near to her . . . Over against this enemy
of reason, there one day arose within me, at about the ninth hour, a mighty vision in which I seemed
to behold Beatrice—clothed in the very crimson dress in which she had first appeared to my eyes and
seeming as young as when we first met—in glory. Then, as I looked back over the time that had now
passed and thought of her, I began deep within me gravely to repent of the desire which, contrary to
reason and the constancy thereof, had for a time so basely possessed it.'

ché questo mio signor lo m'à gradito',
e ch'era folle se più ne parlava;
  'chéd i' son fermo pur di far su' grado,
perciò ch'e' mi promise fermamente
ched e' mi mettereb[b]e in alto grado
  sed i' 'l servisse bene e lealmente':
per che di lei i' non pregiava un dado,
né su' consiglio i' non teneva a mente.

(*Fiore* 10)[31]

with this, as an essay now in disingenuousness, from just a little further down
the line:

L'Amante

Quando Ragion fu assà' dibattuta
e ch'ella fece capo al su' sermone,
i' sì·lle dissi: 'Donna, tua lezione
  sie certa ch'ella m'è poco valuta,
perciò ch'i' no·ll'ò punto ritenuta,
ché no·mi piace per nulla cagione;
ma, cui piacesse, tal amonizione
  sì gli sareb[b]e ben per me renduta.
  Chéd i' so la lezion tratutta a mente
pe·ripètall'a gente cu' piacesse,
ma già per me nonn-è savia nïente;
  ché fermo son, se morir ne dovesse,
d'amar il fior, e 'l me' cor vi s'asente,
o 'n altro danno ch'avenir potesse'.

(*Fiore* 46)[32]

31 '*The Lover*. Hearing Reason reproach me for having served the God of Love, as a result of which, solely because he'd been too much in my thoughts, I was white as a sheet and I said to her: "Reason, I set no store by the pain he has brought on me, for as my lord and master, he promised me I'd soon be cured of it", adding that it was foolish to speak further of this; "for provided I only remain a good and faithful servant", I went on, "Love swore to it that he'd see me right, which is why I'm firmly of a mind to do his bidding." As for Reason and her advice, I couldn't care less. In one ear and out of the other.'

32 '*The Lover*. When Reason had done ranting and called a halt to her preaching, I said to her: "Rest assured, ma'am, that this lecture of yours, which has benefited me not one bit, has done little for me, which is why I've retained not a word of it—though as a warning I'm quite happy to pass it on to

and this, as registering Reason's final exclusion from the roll of honour (hers, Amante says, being from beginning to end an exercise in obstruction), from the last but one sonnet of the cycle as a whole:

L'Amante

Al buono Amico e a Bellacoglienza
rendé' grazie mille e mille volte;

ma di Ragion non eb[b]i sovenenza,
che·lle mie gioie mi credette aver tolte.
Ma contra lei i' eb[b]i provedenza,
sì ch'i' l'ò tutte quante avute e colte.

(*Fiore* 231.9–14)[33]

And what by way of continuity—or perhaps better of complementarity—applies to the *Fiore* and to the still youthful *Vita nova* applies also to the *Fiore* and to the *Commedia* as the fruit of a now fully seasoned spirituality. Unmistakably Dantean, therefore, in their shaping from beforehand any number of emphases in the *Inferno* from the 'poco più è morte' moment of canto 1 via the 'Quivi sospiri, pianti e alti guai' moment of canto 3 to the 'folle volo' of canto 26 are these lines from the *Fiore* at 33 and 34, lines wanting for nothing in their account of the substance and psychology of self-alienation, of the desert-place of the soul in its obduracy:

L'Amante

Quand' i' vidi i marosi sì 'nforzare
per lo vento a Provenza che ventava,
c[h]'alberi e vele e ancole fiac[c]ava,
e nulla mi valea il ben governare,
     fra me medesmo comincia' a pensare
ch'era follia se più navicava,

---

anyone caring to lend an ear; for though I've learnt the whole thing off by heart and am ready to reel it off to anyone who might appreciate it, it is, as far as I'm concerned, entirely devoid of good sense, which is why I'm determined in my heart of hearts to love the flower come what may, even if I have to die for it."'

33 '*The Lover*. I thanked Friend, a good fellow, and Fair Welcoming more than a thousand times over, but spared not a thought for Reason who—or so she thought—had done me out of my pleasure. But I was wise to her and grabbed every bit of it.'

se quel maltempo prima non passava
che dal buon porto mi facé' alu[n]giare;
   sì ch'i allor m'ancolai a una piag[g]ia,
veg[g]endo ch'i' non potea entrar in porto;
la terra mi parea molto salvaggia.
   I' vi vernai co·molto disconforto.
Non sa che mal si sia chi non asaggia
di quel d'Amor, ond'i' fu' quasi morto.
   Pianto, sospiri, pensieri e afrizione
eb[b]i vernando in quel salvag[g]io loco,
ché pena de·ninferno è riso e gioco
   ver' quella ch'i' soffersi a la stagione
c[h]'Amor mi mise a tal distruzïone
ch'e' no·mi diè sog[g]iorno as[s]a' né poco.[34]

—lines to which, as likewise entering into the prehistory of the *Inferno* (the 'ch'io perdei la speranza de l'altezza' and the 'Quando vidi costui nel gran diserto' moment of canto 1, for example, or the 'amico mio, e non de la ventura' of canto 2), we may add these from 35 of the *Fiore*, here too attuned to 'dissimilitude' as the inevitable outcome of fine in the sense of foolish loving:

L'Amante e Ragione

Languendo lungiamente in tal manera,
e non sapea ove trovar socorso,
ché 'l tempo fortunal che m'era corso
m'avea gittato d'ogne bona spera,
   allor tornò a me, che lungi m'era,
Ragion la bella, e disse: 'Tu·sse' corso,

---

34 'The Lover. When I saw how the waves were being whipped up by the wind blowing from Provence, how masts, sails and anchors alike were all giving way, and how my efforts to steer a straight course were coming to nothing, I began thinking to myself that, until such time as the foul weather keeping me out of port passed over, it was madness pressing on. Seeing, then, that I was without safe haven, I dropped anchor on a beach. Everything about the place was desolate and I overwintered there most unhappily. He who has not tasted Love's pain—whence I nearly died—does not know what pain is. Tears, sighs, anxiety and grief, that was all I knew as I wintered on in that wild place, hell's torment being a joke compared with what I then had to put up with. So devastating was Love's assault on me that there was no respite, not even the slightest.' *Inferno* 1.7: 'but a little more, death itself'; 3.22: 'there nothing but sighs, weeping and loud wailing'; 26.125: 'my foolish flight'. Robert Pogue Harrison, 'The Bare Essential: The Landscape of the *Fiore*', in *Rethinking the Romance of the Rose: Text, Image, Reception*, ed. Kevin Bownlee and Sylvia Huot (Philadelphia: University of Pennsylvania Press, 1992), 289–303; Mark Davie, 'The *Fiore* Revisited in the *Inferno*', in *The 'Fiore' in Context: Dante, France, Tuscany*, ed. Zygmunt G. Barański and Patrick Boyde (Notre Dame: University of Notre Dame Press, 1997), 315–27 (with, at 273–313, Irene Maffia Scariati, '*Fiore Inferno in fieri*: Schede di lettura in parallelo').

> se·ttu non prendi i·me alcun ricorso,
> po' che Fortuna è 'nverso te sì fera'.[35]

If then, as far as authorship is concerned, this leaves us still a little way from home, then that notwithstanding we have *défaut di mieux*—in the absence, that is to say, of a sworn affidavit—something special in the *Fiore*, a text very definitely knocking on the door of canonicity; for everything here, technical and ideological alike, bears witness to the status of that text as a staging post in respect both of the *Vita nova* and of the *Commedia*, but, more than this, to the status of Dante himself as a more than ordinarily accomplished administrator of the *Rose* legacy.

With an exact sense, then, of what he is about in the *Fiore*, Dante loses no time in drawing up an agenda and marking the difference between the two kinds of love open to man as man, namely the love that seeks its own and the love that seeks not its own, Amore, or the God of Love, making it perfectly plain that it is a question of setting aside once and for all the evangelical in favour of fine loving as a profession of the spirit:

> *L'Amante e Amore*
>
> Con grande umilitate e pacïenza
> promisi a Amor a sofferir sua pena,
> e c[h]'ogne membro, ch'i' avea, e vena
> disposat' era a farli sua voglienza;
>   e solo a lui servir la mia credenza
> è ferma, né di ciò mai nonn-alena;
> 'insin ched i' avrò spirito o lena,
> i' non farò da·cciò giamà' partenza'.
>   E quelli allor mi disse: 'Amico meo,
> i' ò da·tte miglior pegno che carte;
> fa che m'adori, chéd i' son tu' deo;
>   ed ogn'altra credenza metti a parte,
> né non creder né Luca né Matteo
> né Marco né Giovanni'. Allor si parte.
>
> (*Fiore* 5)[36]

---

35 '*The Lover and Reason*. Not knowing where to find help, for the stormy weather I'd encountered had banished all hope of better things to come, I'd been in this forlorn state for quite some time when fair Reason, who'd been standing a way off, returned to me and said: "With Fortune so hostile towards you, you're riding for a fall if you don't accept my help." ' For *Inferno* 1.54: 'for I lost then every hope of the heights'; 1.64: 'when I espied him in that desert waste'; and 2.61: 'my friend but no friend of fortune'.

36 '*The Lover and Love*. I promised I'd bear Love's tribulations with great humility and patience,

With this, then, the narrative proper gets under way, Amante, as a now faithful disciple of Amore, duly embarking upon his pursuit of the rose in—as he himself puts it—the overwhelming fragrance thereof (the 'sì forte m'ulio' of 6.6). For all his cunning, calculation, fawning and flattery, however, Amante's looks straight-away to be a lost cause, one repulse—first by Disdain and then by Jealousy as between them engineering what amounts to his preliminary expulsion from the garden—following hard on the heels of another, Reason alone offering a kindly word of consolation:

> I' credo che·ttu à' troppo pensato
> a que' che·tti farà gittar in vano,
>   ciò è Amor, a cui dat'ài fidanza.
> Ma·sse m'avessi avuto al tu' consiglio,
> tu non saresti gito co·llui a danza;
>   ché, sie certano, a cu' e' dà di piglio,
> egli 'l tiene in tormento e malenanza,
> sì che su' viso nonn-è mai vermiglio.

(*Fiore* 9.7–14)[37]

Her advice, however—more, in truth, a comment to the effect that it was all a mistake in the first place—is rudely dismissed (the 'per che di lei i' non pregiava un dado, / né su' consiglio i' non teneva a mente' of 10.13–14),[38] whereupon the lover once more draws nigh unto the flower, crossing himself as he does so in pious anticipation of all he is about to receive:

> Nel giardin me n'andà' tutto 'n gonella,
> sanz'armadura, com'e' comandaro,
> e sì trovai quella col viso chiaro,
> Bellacoglienza; tosto a·ssé m'apella,

---

that I was ready in every fibre of my being to do his will, that my mind was set on serving him and him alone, and that in this it would never falter. "For as long as I have life and breath," I said, "never shall I go back on this." Whereupon he said to me: "The pledge I have from you is better than any document; be sure to worship me for I am your god. Set aside every other belief, and place no trust in either Luke or Matthew or Mark or John," at which point he took his leave.'

37 'It's my belief you've been thinking too much of the one to whom you've given your word— Love, that is to say—but with whom you'll dice in vain. Had you listened to my advice, you'd not have gone carolling with him, for you can be sure that such is the pain and suffering he imposes on those he lays hold of that nice red cheeks are a thing of the past.'

38 'As for Reason's advice I couldn't care less. In one ear and out of the other'; so also 73.5: 'Lo Schifo i' pregiava men ch'un fico' (As for Disdain, I couldn't have cared less).

E disse: 'Vien avanti e bascia'l fiore;
ma guarda di far cosa che mi spiaccia,
ché·ttu ne perderesti ogne mio amore'.
    Sì ch'i' alor feci croce de le braccia,
e sì 'l basciai con molto gran tremore.

(*Fiore* 20.5–13)[39]

But with Jealousy seeing to it that he is once again put forth from the garden
(the 'per ch'i' fu' del giardin rimesso in bando' of 21.8) and his bliss thus rudely
forestalled, his suffering—relative to which hell itself is but a joke—begins in
earnest:

L'Amante

Pianto, sospiri, pensieri e afrizione
eb[b]i vernando in quel salvag[g]io loco,
ché pena de·ninferno è riso e gioco
ver' quella ch'i' soffersi a la stagione
    c[h]'Amor mi mise a tal distruzione
che no·mi diè sog[g]iorno as[s]a' né poco.

(*Fiore* 34.1–6)[40]

With the comic, therefore, now shading off into the tragic, Reason returns, her
now more ample discourse taking the form of a meditation on the insecurity of
loving as a matter merely of acquiring, loving as a matter merely of acquiring
forever leaving the lover a hostage to fortune. By all means, therefore, let there

39 'Wearing just my tunic, therefore, as they bade me, and without weaponry, I made my way into
the garden, and there she was, Fair Welcoming, her face radiant as ever. Straightaway calling me over
she said: "Step forward and kiss the flower, but take care you do me no wrong, for one false move and
that's that as far as my love for you is concerned." So crossing my arms before me and full of trembling,
I kissed the flower.' For the moment of trembling, the *Vita nova* sonnet *Ciò che m'incontra, ne lo mente
more* at line 7: 'e per la ebrïetà del gran tremore', while for the kiss (again with trembling) the 'bocca
mi basciò tutto tremante' of *Inferno* 5.136.
40 '*The Lover.* Tears, sighs, anxiety and grief, that was all I knew as I overwintered in that wild
place, hell's torment being a joke compared with what I then had to put up with. So devastating was
Love's assault on me that there was no respite, not even the slightest.' With Guillaume de Lorris at
2275–76: 'Lors te vendront sospir e plaintes, / friçons e autres dolors maintes' (then you will sigh,
lament, tremble and suffer any number of other sorrows); for the overwintering motif, cf. the canzone
Io son venuto al punto de la rota at lines 57–58: 'e sarà mentre / che durerà del verno il grande assalto'
(and so it will be for as long as winter's great assault endures).

be love, but let love's proper pleasure be brought home to what actually and ultimately matters about it, to its suffering no impediment by way of mere eventuality:

Ragione

'Del dilettar non vo' chiti tua parte',
disse Ragion, 'né che sie sanz'amanza,
ma vo' che prendi me per tua 'ntendanza;
che'ttu non troverai i·nulla parte
    di me più bella (e n'ag[g]ie mille carte),
né che·tti doni più di dilettanza.
Degna sarei d'esser reina in Franza;
sì fa' follïa, s' tu mi getti a parte;
    ch'i' ti farò più ric[c]o che Ric[c]hez[z]a,
sanza pregiar mai rota di Fortuna,
ch'ella ti possa mettere in distrez[z]a.
    Se be·mi guardi, i·me nonn-à nes[s]una
faz[z]on che non sia fior d'ogne bellez[z]a:
più chiara son che nonn-è sol né luna'.

(*Fiore* 41)[41]

To be clear then, Reason goes on, it is a question here not of renunciation but rather of gathering in every proximate possibility on the plane of loving—be it that of drinking, lovemaking or anything else proper to specifically human being in the totality thereof—to man's proper finality as man, all else being a matter not of doing but of undoing and thus of knowing self in the destitution of self:

Ragione

'Ancor non vo' t'incresca d'ascoltarmi;
alquanti motti ch'i' voglio ancor dire
a ritenere intendi e a udire,
ché non potresti aprender miglior' salmi.

41 '*Reason.* "I wish you to give up neither your pleasure," said Reason, "nor your love, but to take me as the object of your affection, for—and read as many books as you like about it—you will nowhere find anyone more beautiful than I, nor anyone bringing you greater happiness. Worthy as I am to be queen of France, you'd be foolish to cast me aside, for without ever having to concern yourself with Fortune, her wheel, or her power to upset you, I'll make you richer than Wealth herself. Look carefully and you'll find nothing about me less than surpassingly beautiful, for I am more radiant than either the sun or the moon."'

Tu sì à' cominciato a biasimarmi
perch' i' l'Amor ti volea far fug[g]ire,
che fa le genti vivendo morire;
e tu 'l saprai ancor se no·lo spalmi!
    Sed i' difendo a ciaschedun l'ebrez[z]a,
non vo' che 'l ber per ciò nes[s]un disami,
se non se quello che la gente blez[z]a.
    I' non difendo a·tte che·ttu non ami,
ma non Amor che·tti tenga 'n distrez[z]a,
e nella fin dolente te ne chiami'.

(*Fiore* 45)[42]

Insisting as she does, then, on the ideal integration of one affective inflexion of the spirit with another, Reason looks on the face of it to be making good sense, the lover for his part being perfectly willing to pass it all on should the opportunity present itself. But for all that, it is advice at once seen off by his good friend Amico, who, committed as he is to reason as but a matter merely of calculation, straightaway puts it down to so much verbiage:

L'Amante e Amico

e disse: 'Guarda che n[on] sie ac[c]et[t]ato
il consiglio Ragion, ma da te il buglia,
ché ' fin' amanti tuttor gli tribuglia
con quel sermon di che·tt'à sermonato'.

(*Fiore* 49.5–8)[43]

And this—this passing by on the other side where Reason is concerned and, with it, the fashioning of an alternative way—is the deep substance of Friend's intervention, of his own nicely contrived discourse *de amicitia;* for love properly understood, he maintains, is all a matter of disguise and deception, of creating

42 '*Reason.* Bear with me, if you will for a little longer, for I've a few things still to say. Listen and mark them well, for there's no sweeter psalmody to learn than this. You're blaming me now for wanting you to abandon Love, who, as one of these days you'll know only too well if you don't rid yourself of him, visits death upon the living. But if I advise against drunkenness, I do not on that account wish people to renounce drinking except in so far as it damages them. My purpose, then, is not to stop you loving but to save you from the distress caused by Love as a result of which you are by your own acknowledgement made wretched.'

43 '*The Lover and Friend.* "Watch out", he said, "that you don't accept Reason's advice. On the contrary, have nothing to do with it, for she's forever distressing fine lovers with that sermon she preached you."'

and maintaining appearances: so, for example, the 'di pianger vo' che faccie gran semb[i]anti' of 53.7, or the 'sembianti fa che sie forte crucciato' of 55.7, or the 'non fa sembiante d'averla veduta' of 62.10, or the 'ma guarda non s'aveg[g]a che·tti'infinghe of 65.5[44]—fine loving this, he thinks, in a nutshell:

Amico

Il marinaio che tuttor navicando
va per lo mar, cercando terra istrana,
con tutto si guid' e' per tramontana,
sì va e' ben le sue vele cambiando
　e per fug[g]ire da terra e apressando,
in quella guisa c[h]'allor gli è più sana;
così governa mese e settimana
insin che 'l mar si va rabonacciando.
　Così dé far chi d'Amor vuol gioire
quand' e' truova la sua donna diversa;
un'or la dé cacciar, altra fug[g]ire.
　Allor sì·lla vedrà palida e persa,
ché sie certan che le parrà morire
insin che no·lli cade sotto inversa.

(*Fiore* 56)[45]

Neatly, the lover is scandalized. 'May God keep him', he says, from ever wishing harm to others or seeking to do them down (68.1–8). Needs must, though, and circumstance is sufficient to bring him to his senses, the reader for his or her part, however—for this is the high calling of readers of *Rose* literature—being left to ponder for themselves the tragicomic substance of it all.

Falsembiante's discourse (88–126) is but Amico's writ large, the dissimulation recommended by the latter constituting now a principle not simply of fine loving but of human activity generally, the substance and sine qua non of every social encounter. Happy, then, in response to the God of Love's invitation to offer an

44 'I want you to put on a good show of tears' (53.7); 'pretend to be mightily grieved' (55.7); 'appear not to have noticed her' (62.10); 'but watch out she doesn't catch on to your deceit' (65.5).
45 '*Friend.* A sailor endlessly roaming the seas in search of unknown land, though he sets his course by the pole star, nonetheless trims his sails either seaward or landward as seems best at the time, and in this way he sails for weeks and months at a stretch until the sea grows calm. This is what a man must do when, wishing to reap the benefits of love, he finds his lady hostile towards him; he must by turns come on and back off until she appears all drained and discoloured, at which point he can be sure that, until such time as she's flat on her back beneath him, she'll think herself at death's door.'

account of himself, of his going to and fro in the world and of his walking up and
down in it, he offers both a description and a critique of the hypocrisy he himself
embodies, thus confirming as he does so, and with an analytical calm truly wonderful to behold, the demonic nature of his presence there. Now here we need to
be careful, for it is indeed hypocrisy rather than any one group of its devotees that
stands centre stage here, this, therefore, being an essay not in antifraternalism in
and for itself but in false-seeming as a universal habit of mind, in disingenuousness as by and large the way of the world. That said, however, Falsembiante,
mythic to the point of monstrous in his self-recommendation, is the archetypal
instantiation of those who, putting on a religious face, have their reward:

Falsembiante

I' sì mi sto con que religïosi,
religïosi no, se non in vista,
che·ffan la ciera lor pensosa e trista
per parer a le genti più pietosi;
   e sì si mostran molto sofrettosi
e 'n tapinando ciaschedun a[c]quista;
sì che perciò mi piace lor amista,
c[h]'a barattar son tutti curïosi.

(*Fiore* 89.1–8)[46]

to which, as confirming his commitment to preaching and piety as but a cloak for
cunning, we may add these lines from the middle and final phase of his intervention, a hymn, precisely, to hypocrisy as a steady disposition of the spirit:

Falsembiante

I' sì vo per lo mondo predicando
e dimostrando di far vita onesta;
ogne mi' fatto sì vo' far a sesta,
e gli altrui penso andar aviluppando
   ...
Più amo il manto di papalardia

---

46 '*False Seeming*. I dwell with those religious souls—well, religious in appearance—who for the
sake of impressing the world with their piety, go about with long and sad faces. Showing off their in-
digence, they each of them make a pile begging, which is why, bent as they all are on deception, I'm
happy to cultivate their acquaintance.'

portar, perciò ch'egl[i] è mag[g]ior savere,
ché di lui cuopr' io mia gran rinaldia.

(*Fiore* 93.1–4 and 120.12–14)[47]

Here, then, in Falsembiante's intervention, we have both the fulcrum and the encompassing of the *Fiore* in its each and every inflexion as a meditation on the ways and means of fine loving, False Seeming himself, here as in the *Rose*, emerging as the Antichrist no less, as the archdeceiver forever ranged over against those for whom the word as but the form of intentionality—indeed of being itself under the aspect of intelligibility—is sacred:

Falsembiante

I' sì son de' valletti d'Antecristo,
di quel' ladron' che dice la Scrittura
che fanno molto santa portatura,
e ciaschedun di loro è ipocristo.
    Agnol pietoso par quand' uon l'à visto,
di fora sì fa dolze portatura;
ma egli è dentro lupo per natura,
che divora la gente Gesocristo.

(*Fiore* 123.1–8)[48]

But that is not all, for if the function of Falsembiante's discourse in the *Fiore* is to point up the insidiousness of Amante's conception of love as a matter merely of cunning, then that of the Vecchia—Durante's next interlocutor in the poem— is to confirm from the point of view of the victim of that love, of the one taken in by it, its twofold venality and vengefulness. Proceeding then, by way of her customary and now congenital rapaciousness, she step-by-step unfolds her own time-honoured art of loving as a matter of payment up front (the 'per che già femina non dee servire / insin ch'ella non è prima pagata' of 179.10–11) and of

---

47 '*False Seeming*. So I go about the world preaching and appearing to lead an honest life. Punctilious when it comes to the organization of my own affairs, my only thought is to confound other people's . . . My own, more astute preference is for the mantle of hypocrisy, the perfect disguise for my foxy ways.'

48 '*False Seeming*. I belong to those who serve the Antichrist. I am one of the thieves who, as Scripture proclaims, look for all the world like saints but who are hypocrites to a man. So sweet is their outward manner that to those who look on they seem pious lambs, but inwardly and by nature they are wolves that go about devouring Christ's people.'

hoisting the wretch with his own petard. True, she goes on, she herself is no longer in the first flush of youth, and having alas taken a while to cotton on, she missed many a fine entrepreneurial opportunity; never fear, however, for with the youthful Bellacoglienza under her wing as mentee and thus as the means of her now seasoned malevolence, her revenge will be complete:

La Vec[c]hia

> Non ne pos[s]' altrementi far vengianza
> se non per insegnarti mia dottrina,
> perciò che·llo me' cor sì m'indovina
> che·ttu darai lor ancor gran micianza,
>   a que' ribaldi che tanta viltanza
> me diceano da sera e da mattina;
> tutti gli met[t]erai anche a la china,
> se·ttu sa' ben tener la tua bilanza.
>   Ché sie certana, si'i' fosse dell'ag[g]io,
> figl[i]uola mia, che tu·sse' or presente,
> ch'i' gli pagherè' ben di lor oltrag[g]io,
>   sì che ciascuno farè' star dolente;
> già tanto non sareb[b]e pro' né sag[g]io
> ched i' non ne facesse pan-chiedente.

(Fiore 152)[49]

—lines to which, as registering the fundamental project (namely that of reducing the false lovers of this world to beggary while causing God to have a good giggle over it), we may add these from just a little further down the line:

La Vec[c]hia

> E quando sol' a sol con lui sarai,
> Sì fa che·ttu gli facci saramenti
> Che·ttu per suo danar non ti consenti,
> Ma sol per grande amor che·ttu in lui ài.

---

49 '*The Old Woman.* I cannot avenge myself for this other than by teaching you my doctrine, for deep within me I have an inkling that one day you will do them—those lechers who morning and evening heaped insults upon me—great mischief. Provided you can keep them only in suspense, then sooner or later you'll bring them all to ruin; for rest assured, my child, that, were I the age that you are now, I'd pay them back handsomely for their insolence, putting them one and all through the mill. There'd be no one, no matter how worthy or wise, but that I'd make him beg for his bread.'

Se fosser mille, a ciascun lo dirai,
E sì 'l te crederanno, que' dolenti;
E saccie far sì che ciascuno adenti
Insin c[h]'a povertà gli metterai.
    Che·ttu·sse' tutta loro, dé' giurare;
Se·tti spergiuri, non vi metter piato,
Ché Dio non se ne fa se non ghignare:
    Ché sie certana ch'e' non è peccato,
Chi si spergiura per voler pelare
Colui che fie di te così ingannato.

(*Fiore* 160)[50]

The picture, then, is clear: everyone—Amante, Amico, Falsembiante, the Vecchia and her whole clientele—joins the dance for reasons either of self-interest or, as in the case of the Vecchia as but another incarnation of the old *entremetteuse*, of vengeance and exploitation (the 'saccie far sì che ciascuno adenti / insin c[h]'a povertà gli metterai' of 160.7–8),[51] either way love's devaluation being complete. All that is needed now, therefore, is an appropriate denouement, in the event a masterpiece of decorum as each member of the cast acts out in turn the principles by which he or she is governed. First, then, Amante renews his oath to the God of Love, swearing solemnly upon the instruments of amorous assault:

Per far le saramenta sì aportaro,
en luogo di relique e di messale,
brandoni e archi e saette; sì giuraro
    di suso, e dis[s]er c[h]'altrettanto vale.
Color de l'oste ancor vi s'acordaro,
ché ciaschedun sapea le Dicretale.

(*Fiore* 219.9–14)[52]

50 'The Old Woman. And when you're all alone with him be sure to vow that you're his, not for his money, but for the great love you bear him. Just say the same thing over and over again and they, even if there are thousands of them, will believe you, the wretches. Practise sinking your teeth into them until they are reduced to penury. Be sure to swear that you're all theirs, and don't worry about perjuring yourself, for God will simply have a good snigger at it; for of this you can be certain, that perjuring yourself for the sake of skinning the one you're about to deceive is no sin.'
    51 'practise sinking your teeth into them until they are reduced each and every one to penury.'
    52 'To seal their oath they brought along, not relics and a missal, but torches, bows and arrows—just as good, they said—and swore on them. Expert to a man in the Decretals, the whole army agreed.'

whereupon Venus, declaring war on the sons and daughters of Reason, who have always sought to oppose her (the 'Ragione, / che sempre co' figl[i]uoi m'à guer[r] eg[g]iato' of 221.9–10),[53] takes the castle by fire and storm, at which point the lover, in what amounts to a now flagrant parody of a familiar text, sets out, staff and purse in hand, on his final pilgrimage (the 'e sì v'andai come buon pellegrino' of 228.5). Piety, then, in these closing moments of Amante's confession—his reverence for the veil, the sanctuary and relics—is all, the ineptitude of the rape being followed by a little *te deum* and by copious acknowledgement of all those who have made this possible, except, of course, Reason, whose mean-spiritedness in the end availed her naught:

> Al buono Amico e a Bellacoglienza
> rendé' grazïe mille e mille volte;
> ma di Ragion non eb[b]i sovenenza,
>   che·lle mie gioie mi credette aver tolte.
> Ma contra lei i' eb[b]i provedenza,
> sì ch'i' l'ò tutte quante avute e colte.

> (*Fiore* 231.9–14)[54]

What, then, are we to make of this? There are two main possibilities, the first of which involves seeing the *Fiore* as an exercise in bourgeois realism, urban, comic and, in its stripping away of the myths and illusions of fine loving, as fundamentally reductionist.[55] The problem with this view is that, sitting lightly as it

53 'Reason who, with those children of hers, has only ever waged war on me'; for 228.5: 'thus I set off like a good pilgrim'. For the 'staff and purse in hand' moment of the argument, Mark 6:8: 'Et praecepit eis ne quid tollerent in via nisi virgam tantum'; Luke 22:34–35: 'Et dixit eis: Quando misi vos sine saeculo et pera et calceamentis numquid aliquid defuit vobis?'

54 'I thanked Friend, a good fellow, and Fair Welcoming more than a thousand times over, but spared not a thought for Reason who—or so she thought—had done me out of my pleasure. But I was wise to her and grabbed every bit of it.'

55 Luigi Foscolo Benedetto, *Il 'Roman de la Rose' e la letteratura italiana* (Halle a. S.: Niemeyer, 1910), 106: 'Mi pare però che l'autore italiano superi quello francese nello scetticismo, nell'incredulità schernitrice e beffarda. Entrambi hanno un contegno irreverente verso le cose sacre ed i religiosi' (it seems to me, however, that the Italian outdoes the French author in point of scepticism, of scornful and mocking disbelief. They each of them look irreverently both upon things sacred and upon the religious themselves) through to, and beyond, Gianfranco Contini, 'Un nodo della cultura medievale: La serie *Roman de la rose*—*Fiore*—*Divina Commedia*', in *Un'idea di Dante* (Turin: Einaudi, 1976), 272: 'Se questo mosaico ha un qualche significato, a me sembra che la sola soluzione possibile sia che il *Fiore* provenga dalla mano di Dante, ma, di più, che rappresenti qualche cosa di organico nella sua carriera, che costituisca, insomma, una prima prova di adattamento della *Rose*, un primo conato, conato tuttavia, diciamo pure, massimalistico, in quanto riduzione a un realismo esclusivo, *Roman* portato alla mera affabulazione' (If this varied confection has any significance at all, the only possibility seems to me to be this, that the *Fiore* is indeed the work of Dante, but that, over and beyond this, it represents a properly developmental moment in his career, that it constitutes, in short, a first run at *Rose* adaptation, a

does both to the cultural hinterland of the poem and to the tension by which it is quickened and sustained from deep within it, it is itself reductionist. Taking first, then, the 'cultural hinterland' aspect of the text, there is its biblical component, any number of Pentateuchal, Gospel and Pauline motifs entering into it by way of a built-in mechanism of interpretation, a prior and paradigmatic order of awareness; so, for example, for the 'do not touch the flower' motif of 15.7 and 16.11 (ma non ched egli al fior sua mano ispanda . . . ma' che lungi dal fior le tue man tenghi), the 'praecepitque ei dicens: ex omni ligno paradisi comede; de ligno autem scientiae boni et mali ne comedas, in quocumque enim die comederis ex eo morte morieris' of Genesis 2.16–17;[56] or for the 'expulsion from the garden' motif of 21.8 (per ch'i' fu' del giardin rimesso in bando) the 'et emisit eum Dominus Deus de paradiso voluptatis' of Genesis 3:23;[57] or for the 'wolf in sheep's clothing' figure prominent in Falsembiante's discourse (the 'ched i' per lupo non sia conosciuto' of 97.10 or the 'ma egli è dentro lupo per natura' of 123.7) the 'ecce ego mitto vos sicut oves in medio luporum' of Matthew 10:16, Luke 10:3 and John 10:12;[58] or for the 'proud hypocrites' motif of 89.1–4 (I' sì mi sto con que' religiosi, / religiosi no, se non in vista) the 'nolite fieri sicut hypocritae tristes; exterminant enim facies suas ut appareant hominibus ieiunantes' of Matthew 6:16;[59] or for the nicely subversive 'I'd rather they served me than I them' motif of 117.12–14 (sì ch'i' vogl[i]'anzi c[h]'on mi sia ubidente, / come ch[ed] io a Cristo ne dispiaccia, / ched es[s]er in servag[g]io della gente) the 'nos autem servos vestros per Jesum' of 2 Corinthians 4:5 and Galatians 5:13[60]—these and any number of biblical texts serving as a call to attention, to a more than ordinarily careful reading of the text. And that is not all, for hard on the heels of Scripture as the means of integral intelligence hereabouts come Augustine, Boethius and the representatives, ancient and modern alike, of speculation de amicitia and de amicitia spir-

---

first albeit over-the-top attempt in its reduction of the whole thing to pure realism—a *Roman* produced to the point of mere storytelling). Emilio Pasquini, *La letteratura didattica e la poesia popolare del Duecento* (Bari: Laterza, 1971), 83; Luigi Vanossi, *La teologia poetica del 'Detto d'Amore' dantesco* (Florence: Olschki, 1974), 98.

56 'And the Lord God commanded the man: "You are free to eat from any tree in the garden, but you must not eat from the tree of the knowledge of good and evil, for in the moment you eat of it you will surely die." ' For the *Fiore*: 'provided only he does not reach out to touch the flower . . . only keep your hands well away from the flower'.

57 'So the Lord God banished him from the Garden of Eden.' For the *Fiore*: 'for which reason I was put out of the garden'.

58 'I am sending you out like sheep among wolves.' For the *Fiore*: 'that I be not recognized for the wolf I am . . . but within he is a wolf by nature'.

59 '[When you fast] do not look sombre after the manner of the hypocrites, for they disfigure their faces to show men they are fasting.' For the *Fiore*: 'I keep company with the religious, well, with the religious in appearance.'

60 '[For we do not preach ourselves, but Jesus Christ as Lord,] and ourselves as your servants for Jesus' sake.' For the *Fiore*: 'Anathema in the eyes of the Lord maybe, but for myself I'd rather other people serve me than I them.'

ituali. Thus to speak of love's proper fruition as Ragione does in 39 (the 'ma per trarne frutto' of line 7)[61] is at once to invoke the whole Augustinian problematic of use and enjoyment and of legitimate and illegitimate stewardship, while to speak of fortune as a shaping presence in human experience (the 'Se Fortuna m'à tolto or mia ventura, / ella torna la rota tuttavia, / e quell' è quel che molto m'asicura' on the lips of Amante at 38.12–14)[62] is straightaway to invoke the archetypal discourse of the *Consolatio philosophiae*. And what applies to Augustine and Boethius as, no less than Scripture itself, standing behind the narrative line of the *Fiore* applies also to Aristotle, Tully and, among the moderns, the likes of Aelred of Rievaulx and Peter of Blois as between them both quickening and in turn confirming just about everything Reason has to say in the area of friendship properly understood. In a word, then, the playing off of the text against the urtext in the name and for the sake of an ever livelier sense of the matter to hand—the point, precisely, of *Rose* literature in its scarcely less than scintillating substance.[63]

But there is more, for over and beyond the 'cultural hinterland' aspect of the argument is the internal dialectic of the *Fiore*, the way in which, playing as it does against its *auctores*, it plays steadily against itself, one set of emphases duly throwing into relief another. A glance at the *Rose* may be useful here, for whatever else it is this too is an oppositional text, a text at every point turning upon its own antitheses. True, the oppositionalism of the *Rose* is more complicated than that of the *Fiore*, for in the *Rose* it is a question not merely of Amant and Raison, but of Nature and Genius, presences making in their more or less insistent biologism for a reshaping of the affective issue. Not so, however, with the *Fiore*, for in recasting the *Rose* in the way it does it fashions from it a pure case of conscience, this, precisely, accounting for its dialectical energy, its proceeding by way of the sharpest possible species of consideration and counter-consideration. Following on, then, from Amore's preliminary account of love as in truth but an abdication of self in its power to orderly self-determination comes the first intimation of an alternative way, an invitation to love reasonably

---

61 '[I wish you to love her, not for carnal delight or pleasure,] but to draw fruit from it.'

62 'Fortune may have robbed me of my desire but for all that she still turns her wheel, which is why I am in good heart.'

63 Charles Dahlberg, 'Love and the *Roman de la Rose*', *Spec* 44 (1961), 568–84; Lionel J. Friedman, 'Jean de Meun and Ethelred of Rievaulx', *L'Esprit Créateur* 2 (1962), 135–41; Lionel J. Friedman, 'Gradus Amoris', *RP* 19 (1965), 167–77; D. W. Robertson, Jr, *A Preface to Chaucer: Studies in Medieval Perspectives* (Princeton: Princeton University Press, 1962, especially, with regard to the *Roman*, 195–203); Rosemond Tuve, *Allegorical Imagery: Some Mediaeval Books and Their Posterity* (Princeton: Princeton University Press, 1966); John V. Fleming, *The 'Roman de la Rose': A Study in Allegory and Iconography* (Princeton: Princeton University Press, 1969). See too, by way of reply to the 'Robertsonian' way in *Rose* criticism, William Matthews, 'A New Preface to Medieval Literature', *RP* 17 (1964), 634–42; Francis L. Utley, 'Robertsonianism Redevisus', *RP* 19 (1965), 250–60; and Jean Frappier, *Amour courtois et Table Ronde* (Geneva: Droz, 1973), 61–96.

rather than recklessly as the basis of a more stable act of existence (Ragione),
this in turn giving way (*a*) to a reduction of reason to mere calculation as but
the meanest of its manifestations (Amico); (*b*) to a scarcely short of terrifying
account of fine loving as but a matter of systematic lovelessness (Falsembiante);
and (*c*) to a case history designed to confirm the whole thing as but a further
instance of entrepreneurial nous (the Vecchia). It is at this point, then, that, for
all its appearing to subsist at a distance from the still centre of Dante's inspiration as a poet and philosopher of love in the deep seriousness thereof, the indispensability of the *Fiore* both to the *Vita nova* and to the as yet far-off *Commedia* moves into view—to the *Vita nova* in respect of its meditation on love as
the coefficient of new life, and of the *Commedia* as in its own right, but after its
own manner, an essay in rose-consciousness:

> E se l'infimo grado in sé raccoglie
> sì grande lume, quanta è la larghezza
> di questa rosa ne l'estreme foglie!
>
> . . .
>
> Nel giallo de la rosa sempiterna,
> che si digrada e dilata e redole
> odor di lode al sol che sempre verna,
>   qual è colui che tace e dicer vole,
> mi trasse Bëatrice, e disse: 'Mira
> quanto è 'l convento de le bianche stole!'
>
> . . .
>
> In forma dunque di candida rosa
> mi si mostrava la milizia santa
> che nel suo sangue Cristo fece sposa.

> (*Paradiso* 30.115–17, 124–26 and 31.1–3)[64]

64 'And if the lowest rank gathers unto itself so great a light, how spacious is this rose in its farthest
petals . . . In the yellow of the eternal rose which opens out, which rises rank by rank, and which gives
forth the fragrance of praise to the ever-burgeoning Sun, Beatrice, as one wishing to speak but holding
his peace, drew me, saying as she did so: "See how numberless this our assembly of white stoles!" . . .
In the form, then, of a white rose was displayed before me the sacred host espoused by Christ with his
own blood.' Roberto Durighetto, 'Il simbolo della rosa nella *Divina Commedia*', in *Atti della Dante
Alighieri a Treviso 1989–1996*, vol. 2, ed. Arnaldo Brunello (Mestre: Ediven, 1996), 129–33; Gisela
Seitschek, 'Von de profanen Rose zur Himmelsrose: Der Gedichtzyklus *Il Fiore* als Knotenpunkt
zwischen dem *Roman de la Rose* und Dantes *Divina Commedia*', in *Allegorie und Wissensordnung:
Volkssprachliche enzyklopädische Literatur des Trecento; Akten der DAAD-Fachtagung, München 10 Oktober bis 12 Oktober 2012*, ed. Florian Mehltretter (Munich: Herbert Hutz Verlag, 2014), 187–235; Enrico
Fenzi, 'Dante e il *Roman de la Rose*: Alcune note sulla "candida rosa" dei beati e sulla questione del
libero arbitrio', *CT* 19.1 (2016), 205–51.

Also belonging to the *Rose* moment of Dante's youth, and thus dating in an ideal chronology to the middle part of the 1280s, is the *Detto d'amore*, a further essay in *Rose* reading and reception. That this too belongs to Dante rests (*a*) on its accompanying the *Fiore* in the sole surviving manuscript of the text, and (*b*) on, as with the *Fiore*, its status as both notionally and expressively anticipatory of the canonical utterance. True, there are differences vis-à-vis the *Fiore* in point both of register and of technique, for not only does the *Detto* take its cue principally from the first part of the *Roman* in all its more patently stylized substance, but proceeding as it does by way of an uninterrupted flow of seven-syllable couplets each with its own equivocal rhyme it is also more recognizably Guittonian and Brunettian in spirit, more inclined than the *Fiore* to delight in its own difficulty. But that notwithstanding, each alike is busy about the same task, namely that of deconstructing and reconstructing the archetypal text, the mighty *Roman de la rose*, in favour of a more precisely conceived *questione d'amore*. First, then, and following on from a solemn statement of intent on the part of the lover as but Love's faithful liegeman, comes a further and fulsome expression of faith in Amore's good offices hereabouts, his tireless shepherding of the flock. True, the way is hard and never far beneath the surface lies despair as the lot of fine lovers, but not to worry, for Love is forever ready to honour those worthily professing his name, forever quick to raise them up and bring them home:

> Amor i·nulla part' è
> ch'e' non sia tutto presto
> a fine amante presto.
> Così sue cose livera
> a chi l'amor no·llivera
> e mette pene e 'ntenza
> in far sua penetenza
> tal chente Amor comanda
> a chi a·llu' s'acomanda;
> e chi la porta in grado,
> il mette in alto grado
> di ciò ched e' disia;
> per me cotal dì sia!
> Per ch'i' già non dispero,
> ma ciaschedun dì spero
> merzé, po' 'n su' travaglio
> i' son sanza travaglio,
> e sonvi sì legato
> ch'i' non vo' che legato

> giamai me ne prosciolga;
> se·nn'à d'altri pro', sciolga!

(*Detto d'amore*, lines 54–74)[65]

With this, Reason puts in an appearance, hers, here as in the *Fiore*, being an invitation to thoughtfulness, to a sense of fine loving as, left to itself, a matter of ceaseless anxiety and of impending doom, a situation once again explored in terms of the maritime and meteorological, of the soul as but a stormed-tossed victim of its own wayward spirituality:

> Lo dio dov' ài credenza
> non ti farà credenza
> se non come Fortuna.
> Tu·sse' in gran fortuna,
> se non prendi buon porto
> per quel ched i' t'ò porto,
> ed a me non t'aprendi
> e 'l mi' sermone aprendi.

(*Detto d'amore*, lines 111–18)[66]

And, as in the *Fiore*, the lover will have none of it, preferring instead to fall back on his particular brand of primitivism, his fundamentally unmeditated sense of Amore's beneficence and of the happiness in store for him provided only he remain true to his profession. It is at this point, however, that, by way of a 'head-to-toe' celebration of his lady's beauty amply open to documentation in the tradition,

---

65 'Love is never anything other than willing to assist fine lovers willing to serve him. Thus he bestows his bounty on all those who forsake not love and apply themselves come what may to the penitential way as imposed by Love on those putting their faith in him. And should any persevere gladly, Love exalts him on high with respect to all he seeks. Roll on, then, my own day! For this reason I despair not, but every day trust to his goodness such that, suffering on his account, I suffer not, and am indeed so bound to him that never should I wish by any cardinal legate to be unbound. Should others desire this boon, so be it. Not I!' Luigi Peirone, *Il 'Detto d'Amore' tra 'Il Fiore' e Dante* (Genoa: Tilgher, 1983); Luigi Vanossi, *La teologia poetica del 'Detto d'Amore'* (Florence: Olschki, 1974); Michelangelo Picone, 'Glosse al *Detto d'Amore*', *MR* 3 (1976), 394–409; Guglielmo Gorni, 'Il gemello del *Fiore*, ossia Il *Detto d'Amore*', in *Dante: Storia di un visionario* (Rome: Laterza, 2008), 69–74; Paolo Canettieri, 'Il *Fiore* e il *Detto d'Amore*', *CT* 14.1 (2011), 519–30. On the question of attribution, Mario Muner, 'La paternità brunettiana del *Fiore* e del *Detto d'Amore*', *MDC* 9 (1970–71), 274–320; Antonio Lanza, 'Il *Fiore* e il *Detto d'Amore*: Ser Durante, non Dante Alighieri; Storia di un miraggio', in *Primi secoli: Saggi di letteratura italiana antica* (Rome: Archivio Guido Izzi, 1991), 64–80.

66 'The god in whom you have put your faith will give you no guarantee other than that offered by fortune. You'll be forever storm-tossed if in keeping with what I've told you you don't seek out a safe haven—if you don't cling to me and learn from what I've said.'

we encounter something more properly innovative, namely a hint of the Guinizzellian—and indeed beyond that of the Dantean—praise style, something, in
short, more properly stilnovistic in kind. True, much of what the lover has to say
is predictable enough, but the tone and, with it, the substance of his discourse
bears witness, if not to a sea change exactly, then at least to a nicely conceived
nuancing of the old in favour of the new:

> Cape' d'oro battuto
> paion, che m'àn battuto,
> quelli che porta in capo,
> per ch'i' a·llor fo capo.
> La sua piacente ciera
> nonn-è sembiante a cera,
> anz' è sì fresca e bella
> che lo me' cor s'abella
> di non le mai affare,
> tant'à piacente affare.
> La sua fronte, e le ciglia,
> bieltà d'ogn' altr' eciglia;
> tanto son ben voltati
> che' mie' pensier' voltati
> ànno ver' lei, che gioia
> mi dà più c[h]'altra gioia
> in su' dolze riguardo.

(*Detto d'amore*, lines 167–83)[67]

But neither is that all, for just a little way down the line there is a hint of something still more radiant, namely a sense of the angelic, of the epiphanous even,
with—albeit as yet subliminally—an inkling of the power in madonna to new
life, of the shading off of the sensitive into the salvific:

> E quando va per via,
> ciascun di lei à 'nvia
> per l'andatura gente;
> e quando parla a gente,

---

67 'Her fine head of hair, all burnished gold it would appear, was what overcame me, so that's where
I'll begin. Her lovely face (no waxen complexion here) is so radiant and beautiful, that I delight in its
having no comparison, so lovely is it. Her forehead and eyebrows surpass in beauty those of every other
woman—so perfectly arched that they compel my every thought, the joy they afford me being above
all joy as in my direction she sweetly glances.'

> sì umilmente parla
> che boce d'agnol par là.

(Detto d'amore, lines 233–38)[68]

True, the intuition fades almost immediately, for almost immediately the possibilities opened up by this praise moment of the poem give way to the business and, with it, to the banality of fine loving—to fine loving as a matter mainly of its successive strategies:

> Cortese e franco e pro'
> convien che sie, e pro'
> salute e doni e rendi;
> se·ttu a·cciò ti rendi,
> d'Amor sarai in grazia,
> e sì ti farà grazia
> . . .
> Belle robe a podere,
> secondo il tu' podere,
> vesti, fresche e novelle,
> sì che n'oda novelle
> l'amor, cu' tu à' caro
> più che 'l Soldano il Caro.
> E s'elle son di lana,
> sì non ti paia l'ana
> a devisar li 'ntagli,
> se ttu à' chi gli 'ntagli.
> Nove scarpette e calze
> convien che tuttor calze;
> della persona conto
> ti tieni; e nul mal conto
> di tua boc[c]a non l'oda,
> ma ciascun pregia e loda.

(Detto d'amore, lines 403–8 and 427–42)[69]

---

68 'And as she passes by, everyone longs for her, so gracious is her bearing. And when with those around her she speaks, she speaks so sweetly that it seems but the voice of an angel.'

69 'You must be courteous, loyal and courageous, and must give and receive his greeting graciously, for if you do all this you will be in Love's good books and he will see you right . . . Within your means, sport the finest clothes you can, spruced up and brand new, so that your loved one—the one you hold

Ethics, in short, gives way to etiquette, the precious instant, with all it has to offer by way of a more spacious humanity, of a transfiguration of self on the planes of knowing and loving, somehow evaporating after the manner of the morning mist. But all is not lost, since for all their mesmeric obedience to the *Rose* (then as now a mesmerizing text) neither the *Fiore* nor the *Detto* live passively in its presence, each in its way furthering the process of love-interrogation everywhere decisive for Dante's imminent triumph hereabouts, for his restatement of the question of love in terms of something more properly sublime. For that, as Dante understood with perfect precision, is love's way. No interrogation, no sublimity. Simply an overwintering in the land of unlikeness.

DANTE GUINIZZELLIANO

The centrality of Guinizzelli to the initiative represented by Dante's 'praise style' or 'stilo de la loda' as a response to issues raised by contemporary verse making in the vernacular is acknowledged by him both at the time—in, so to speak, the heat of the moment—and in retrospect, as viewed across the now seasoned spirituality of the *Purgatorio*. Eloquent in respect of the first of these things, of his response at the time to issues in the area of contemporary verse making, is the sonnet *Amore e 'l cor gentil sono una cosa*, a sonnet fully and indeed explicitly transparent to the 'cor gentil' canzone of Guinizzelli (the 'sì come il saggio in suo dittare pone' of line 2) but looking now to proceed beyond the gentle equivalences, the imaginative generosity and the ultimately apologetic substance of the original utterance; for in what amounts to a wholly fresh inflexion of the argument, a quantum leap on the plane of love-understanding, it is a question now not of custom but of causality—not simply, that is to say, of love and the noble heart as in the ordinary way of it one and the same thing but of how the presence to the lover of his lady might be said to awaken love in the first place:

> Amore e 'l cor gentil sono una cosa,
> sì come il saggio in suo dittare pone,
> e così esser l'un sanza l'altro osa
> com'alma razional sanza ragione.
> Falli natura quand'è amorosa,
> Amor per sire e 'l cor per sua magione,

---

dearer than the Sultan does Cairo—gets to hear all about it (if they're made of wool it shouldn't be too difficult to think up decoration especially if you have someone fashion it for you). See to it that you always have new shoes and new breeches, and that you're always elegantly turned out. Let nothing disparaging pass your lips, but esteem and honour all men.'

dentro la qual dormendo si riposa
tal volta poca e tal lunga stagione.
    Bieltate appare in saggia donna pui,
che piace a gli occhi sì, che dentro al core
nasce un disio de la cosa piacente;
    e tanto dura talora in costui,
che fa svegliar lo spirito d'Amore.
E simil fàce in donna omo valente.[70]

No less eloquent, by contrast, in respect of the second of them, of Dante's looking back upon the Guinizzellian moment of his experience as a sweet new stylist, are these lines from the second canticle of the *Commedia*, lines as precise in their reconstruction of the lyric tradition as a whole as they are purgatorial in spirit, in their now exquisite sense of self-perspectivization on the part both of the one who says 'I' (Guinizzelli) and of the one standing humbly in his presence (Alighieri):

    'Farotti ben di me volere scemo:
son Guido Guinizzelli, e già mi purgo
per ben dolermi prima ch'a lo stremo'.
    Quali ne la tristizia di Ligurgo
si fer due figli a riveder la madre,
tal mi fec' io, ma non a tanto insurgo,
    quand' io odo nomar sé stesso il padre
mio e de li altri miei miglior che mai
rime d'amor usar dolci e leggiadre
    . . .
    E io a lui: 'Li dolci detti vostri,
che, quanto durerà l'uso moderno,
faranno cari ancora i loro incostri'.
    'O frate', disse, 'questi ch'io ti cerno

---

70 'Love and the noble heart are as the wise man states in his poem but one and the same, and the one can no more exist without the other than a rational soul without reason. Nature, whensoever disposed to love, fashions them, Love as lord and the heart as his dwelling, wherein sometimes a little and sometimes at length he lies sleeping. Then beauty appears in a woman so pleasing in her goodness to the eye that within the heart is born a desire for that same beautiful one, a desire from time to time lingering long enough to arouse the spirit of Love—the effect too of a worthy man upon a woman.' Vincent Moleta, *Guinizzelli in Dante* (Rome: Edizioni di Storia e Letteratura, 1980); Selene Sarteschi, 'Guinizzelli nella prospettiva dantesca', in *Intorno a Guido Guinizzelli. Atti della Giornata di Studio, Zurigo 16 giugno 2000*, ed. Luciano Rossi et al. (Alessandria: Edizioni dell'Orso, 2002), 137–53; Furio Brugnolo and Gianfelice Peron (eds.), *Da Guido Guinizzelli a Dante: Nuove prospettive sulla lirica del Duecento. Atti del Convegno di Studi, Padova-Monselice 10–12 maggio 2002* (Padua: Il Poligrafo, 2004).

col dito', e additò un spirto innanzi,
'fu miglior fabbro del parlar materno.
Versi d'amore e prose di romanzi
soverchiò tutti; e lascia dir li stolti
che quel di Lemosì credon ch'avanzi.
A voce più ch'al ver drizzan li volti,
e così ferman sua oppinïone
prima ch'arte o ragion per lor s'ascolti.
Così fer molti antichi di Guittone,
di grido in grido pur lui dando pregio,
fin che l'ha vinto il ver con più persone'.

(*Purgatorio* 26.91–99 and 112–26)[71]

But there is more, for testifying as it does to the status of Guinizzelli as father
to all those now seasoned in the ways and means of sweet versifying, this second
canticle of the *Commedia* testifies also to—as Dante now sees it and no doubt
saw it at the time—the taking up and perfecting of the Guinizzellian in the more
properly Dantean, in a now systematic commitment to the notion of love as a
matter of praise and of form as but the showing forth of its gentle interiority; so,
at any rate, these lines from canto 24 with their secure sense of the canzone *Donne
ch'avete intelletto d'amore* not simply as the point-*towards*-which of everything

71 ' "As for me I will indeed satisfy your wish. I am Guido Guinizzelli, and, having well and truly
sorrowed before my end, I am busy now about my purgation." As two sons became upon once more
seeing their mother in the moment of Lycurgus's grief, so also—though with greater restraint—became
I upon hearing from his own lips the name of both my own father and that of my every superior prac-
tised in the way of love's sweet lays ... And I to him: "Those sweet utterances of yours which, for as
long as this our new idiom endures, will ever cause us to cherish the very ink by which they are set
down." "O brother," he said, indicating a spirit a little way on, "he whom I point out to you, outdoing
them all as he did as a maker of both love lyrics and of romance tales, was the best of all craftsmen in
the mother tongue. Let those fools prattle on, then, who, extolling the excellence of him of Limoges,
give ear to tattle rather than to truth, coming down as they do so on this side or that before ever listening
either to art or reason, for that's just what many of our forbears did with regard to Guittone, one after
another proclaiming his merits until at last the truth has by common consent prevailed." ' Gianfranco
Folena, 'Il canto di Guido Guinizzelli', *GSLI* 94 (1977), 481–508 (and in *Textus testis: Lingua e culutra
poetica delle origini* [Turin: Bollati Boringhieri, 2002], 241–65); Mario Marti, 'Il XXVI del *Purgatorio*
come omaggio d'arte: Guinizzelli e Daniello nel cammino poetico di Dante', *L'Albero* 29 (1978), 5–26
(and then as 'Il canto XXVI del *Purgatorio*', in *Purgatorio: Letture degli anni 1976–79 nella Casa di Dante
in Roma*, ed. Silvio Zennaro [Rome: Bonacci, 1981], 601–25); Antonio Corsaro, 'The Language of Love:
Purgatorio XXVI', in *Word and Drama in Dante: Essays on the 'Divina Commedia'*, ed. John C. Barnes
and Jennifer Petrie (Dublin: Irish Academic Press, 1993), 123–42; Achille Tartaro, 'La riabilitazione di
Guinizzelli: *Purg.* XXVI', *Cultura* 46.1 (2008), 119–36 (and in *Cielo e terra: Saggi danteschi* [Rome:
Studium, 2008], 155–74); Roberto Rea, 'Guinizzelli "Praised and Explained" (da "[O] caro padre meo"
al XXVI del *Purgatorio*)', *The Italianist* 30.1 (2010), 1–17; Ignazio Baldelli, '*Purgatorio*, canto XXVI', *SD*
(Spoleto: Centro italiano di studi sull'alto medioevo, 2015), 315–34.

leading up to it (Guinizzelli's sweet rhymes included) but as the point-*about-which* of the entire stilnovistic enterprise:

> Ma dì s'i' veggio qui colui che fore
> trasse le nove rime, cominciando
> *Donne ch'avete intelletto d'amore.*
>   E io a lui: 'I' mi son un che, quando
> Amor mi spira, noto, e a quel modo
> ch'e' ditta dentro vo significando'.
>   'O frate, issa vegg' io', diss' elli, 'il nodo
> che 'l Notaro e Guittone e me ritenne
> di qua dal dolce stil novo ch'i' odo!
>   Io veggio ben come le vostre penne
> di retro al dittator sen vanno strette,
> che de le nostre certo non avvenne;
>   e qual più a gradire oltre si mette,
> non vede più da l'uno a l'altro stilo';
> e, quasi contentato, si tacette.

(*Purgatorio* 24.49–63)[72]

And it is indeed the canzone *Donne ch'avete intelletto d'amore* that, together with its retinue in the *Vita nova* (namely the sonnets *Amore e 'l cor gentil sono una cosa, Ne li occhi porta la mia donna Amore, Tanto gentile e tanto onesta pare* and *Vede perfettamente onne salute*), witnesses most completely (*a*) to what amounts now to a radical theologization of the matter to hand, to a taking up of the merely analogical substance of *Al cor gentil rempaira sempre Amore* ('she *seemed* like an angel which is why I could not but love her') in something approaching the fully ontological ('she *is*, in truth, a new creation, the hope of the blessed on high and a channel of grace here below'); and (*b*) to a now fully developed sense of *poetic* form as but the *intelligible* form of being itself at the point of emergence; so, for example, as far as the first of these things is concerned, namely Dante's now confident resolution of the anagogical in the actual,

---

72 ' "But tell me if I see here him who brought forth the new rhymes, beginning: *Ladies who have understanding of love?*" And I to him: "I am one who, when Love inspires me, takes note and sets it forth after the fashion he dictates within me." "O brother," he said, "now I see the knot which kept the Notary and Guittone and me short of the sweet new style I hear; for it is clear to me now how—unlike ours to be sure—your pens follow immediately the one who dictates, and anyone looking more deeply into this will find no other difference between the one style and the other," with which, as if content, he fell silent.'

we have the 'or voi di sua virtù farvi savere' moment of the canzone, a moment of ecstatic intimation:

> Madonna è disiata in sommo cielo;
> or voi di sua virtù farvi savere.
> Dico, qual vuol gentil donna parere
> vada con lei, che quando va per via,
>   gitta nei cor villani Amore un gelo,
> per che onne lor pensero agghiaccia e pere;
> e qual soffrisse di starla a vedere
> diverria nobil cosa, o si morria.
>   E quando trova alcun che degno sia
> di veder lei, quei prova sua vertute,
> ché li avvien, ciò che li dona, in salute,
> e sì l'umilia ch'ogni offesa oblia.
> Ancor l'ha Dio per maggior grazia dato
> che non pò mal finir chi l'ha parlato.

(*Donne ch'avete intelletto d'amore*, lines 29–42)[73]

while as far as the second of them is concerned, namely his commitment to *poetic* form as but the *intelligible* form of being at the point of emergence, we have the exquisite *Tanto gentile e tanto onesta pare*, exquisite in point both of its twofold musical and rhetorical complexion and of these things between them as productive of a hymn to Beatrice as succint as it is sublime. 'Musically', then—where by the term 'musical' we mean the overall structure and symmetry of the period as a whole[74]—we have a piece consisting of two equal *pedes* or feet (the two quatrains) and two equal *versus* (the tercets), these between them reflecting the da

---

73 'My lady is desired in the highest heaven, but now I wish to speak to you of her excellence. I say, then, that any woman wishing to show forth her nobility should walk with her, for when she passes on her way Love casts a chill upon the hearts of the wicked such that their every thought freezes and fades away; indeed, were any to linger and gaze upon her he would either be transfigured or perish completely. And whensoever she finds one worthy to look upon her, he proves for himself her power, for whatsoever he receives from her makes for his well-being, he, in his humility, overlooking every offence. And there is more, for such grace has God bestowed upon her, that none, speaking of her, can know an evil end.'

74 *De vulgari eloquentia* 2.4.2: 'Revisentes igitur ea que dicta sunt, recolimus nos eos qui vulgariter versificantur plerunque vocasse poetas: quod procul dubio rationabiliter eructare presumpsimus, quia prorsus poete sunt, si poesim recte consideremus; que nichil aliud est quam fictio rethorica musicaque poita' (Looking back, then, over what has just been said, we call to mind that on several occasions we have referred to those writing verses in the vernacular as poets, something which is perfectly reasonable; for taking the word 'poetry' in its true meaning—namely composition according to the rules of rhetoric and music—that is what they are, namely 'poets').

capo structure of the song or musical setting proper, while on the rhetorical side we have the *prolepsis* or inversion and *anaphora* or repetition of the first two lines ('Tanto gentile e tanto onesta pare / la donna mia'); the *synecdoche* of line 4 ('e li occhi no l'ardiscon di guardare'); the *conversiones* of lines 6 and 10 with their substantival promotion of the merely adjectival ('umiltà' for 'umile' and 'dolcezza' for 'dolce'); the *epanaphora* of lines 7 and 12 ('par che ... par che' as inaugurating successive periods in the text); the *capfinidas* of lines 8 and 9 (the 'mostrare ... Mostrasi' straddling the principal division in the poem, the giving way of the quatrains to the tercets); and the *emphasis* of the final line (the 'Sospira' of line 14 as gathering up and cadencing the at once speakable and unspeakable substance of the whole)—all this, however, by way not of decoration or of embellishment but of something closer to a species of self-presencing, to a knowing of self in the consistency of self by way of form in its own unique species of self-accountability:

I *pes*	Tanto gentile e tanto onesta pare	*prolepsis, anaphora*
	la donna mia, quand'ella altrui saluta,	
	ch'ogne lingua deven tremando muta,	
	e li occhi no l'ardiscon di guardare.	*synecdoche*
II *pes*	Ella si va, sentendosi laudare,	
	benignamente d'umiltà vestuta;	*conversio*
	e par che sia una cosa venuta	*epanaphora*
	da cielo in terra a miracol mostrare.	
I *versus*	Mostrasi sì piacente a chi la mira,	
	che dà per li occhi una dolcezza al core,	
	che 'ntender no la può chi non la prova;	
II *versus*	e par che de la sua labbia si mova	*epanaphora*
	un spirito soave pien d'amore,	
	che va dicendo a l'anima: Sospira.[75]	*emphasis*

And what applies to *Tanto gentile e tanto onesta pare* by way of form as but a showing forth of self in the otherwise shrouded substance thereof applies also to

---

75 'So noble and worthy appears my lady in greeting another that, trembling, every tongue falls silent and eyes dare not glance. Of her praise as sung she is aware, but graciously clothed as she is in humility, she goes her way, seeming as she does so to be a creature come down from heaven to earth to make known the miraculous. So beautiful she appears to those who gaze upon her that through the eyes she bestows upon the heart a sweetness such as none can understand but those who experience it; and from her lips seems to come forth a spirit, tender and full of love, a spirit addressing the soul and saying: "Sigh."' Gianfranco Contini, 'Esercizio d'interpretazione sopra un sonetto di Dante', *L'immagine* 5 (1947), 291–95 (and in *Un' idea di Dante: Saggi danteschi* [Turin: Einaudi, 1976], 21–31); Manuela Colombo, 'Il sonetto "Tanto gentile" e un passo apocalittico', in *Dai mistici a Dante: Il linguaggio dell'ineffabilità* (Florence: La Nuova Italia, 1987), 73–89.

its companion piece in the *Vita nova*, the sonnet *Vede perfettamente onne salute*, where again it is a question of the well-nigh sacred function of form as that whereby self stands securely—and indeed stands at all—in its own company; so, for example, as busy at the point both of introspection and of self-possession, the initial chiasmus ('Vede ... donna ... donne ... vede'), the ontic intensity of the *conversiones* ('bieltate ... virtute ... invidia ... gentilezza'), the gentle consequentialism of the text as step-by-step it unfolds its scarcely short of rapturous substance ('E ... che ... anzi ... ma ... Ed ... che ... che ...'), and the deep consistency of the whole as secured by way of its rich consonantalism ('Vede ... vede ... vanno ... vertute ... invidia ... vestute ... vista ... riceve'; 'onne ... donna ... donne ... vanno ... tenute ... render ... tanta ... nulla invidia ... anzi ... andar ... onne ... non ... onore ... tanto gentile ... nessun'; 'parer piacente ... per ... può'; 'd'amore ... di fede ... dolcezza d'amore')—all this combining within the delicately hyperbolic context of the whole to confirm the equality of the poetic instance to an experience as complex as it is otherwise elusive:

I *pes*	Vede perfettamente onne salute	*epanalepsis*
	chi la mia donna tra le donne vede;	*anaphora; chiasmus*
	quelle che vanno con lei son tenute	
	di bella grazia a Dio render merzede.	
II *pes*	E sua bieltate è di tanta vertute,	*conversio*
	che nulla invidia a l'altre ne procede,	*conversio*
	anzi le face andar seco vestute	*metaphor*
	di gentilezza d'amore e di fede.	*conversio*
I *versus*	La vista sua fa onne cosa umile;	
	e non fa sola sé parer piacente,	*anaphora*
	ma ciascuna per lei riceve onore.	
II *versus*	Ed è ne li atti suoi tanto gentile,	
	che nessun la si può recare a mente,	*alliteration*
	che non sospiri in dolcezza d'amore.[76]	*emphasis*

All in all, therefore, a twofold triumph: triumph on the plane of love-understanding, where it is a question of love as apt now not to enslave but to free the spirit for the kind of 'transhumanity' to which it is called from beforehand,

---

76 'He sees to perfection every goodness who sees among others my lady, her every companion being called upon to give thanks to God for this, her exquisite grace. So compelling is her loveliness that of envy there is, in other women, no trace; rather, themselves clothed in love, faith and the nobility thereof, they are by her prevailed upon to accompany her as she goes her way. The very sight of her humbles all things, whereby her beauty shines forth, but not this alone, for by her all women are honoured. And in her every gesture she is so noble that no one can call her to mind without sighing in the sweetness of love.'

and triumph on the plane of technique, where it is a question of form as but being itself in the now twofold integrity and intelligibility thereof. And this is a triumph perpetuated into all those poems associated in the *Vita nova* with Beatrice both in life and in death and in her ultimate apotheosis. Belonging, then, with the canzone *Donne ch'avete intelletto d'amore* and with the sonnets *Tanto gentile e tanto onesta pare* and *Vede perfettamente onne salute* as between them a celebration of Beatrice in life is the further sonnet *Ne li occhi porta la mia donna Amore*, a poem that, reaching out as it does to the Cavalcanti of *Chi è questa che ven, ch'ogn'om la mira* in its rapt spectatorliness, settles now for the notion of madonna as the *where*, the *when* and the *how* of new life, as that whereby every indisposition of the spirit is ousted in favour of humility and a quiet mind:

> Ne li occhi porta la mia donna Amore,
> per che si fa gentil ciò ch'ella mira;
> ov'ella passa, ogn'om ver lei si gira,
> e cui saluta fa tremar lo core,
>   sì che, bassando il viso, tutto smore,
> e d'ogni suo difetto allor sospira;
> fugge dinanzi a lei superbia ed ira.
> Aiutatemi, donne, farle onore.
>   Ogne dolcezza, ogne pensero umile
> nasce nel core a chi parlar la sente,
> ond'è laudato chi prima la vide.
>   Quel ch'ella par quando un poco sorride,
> non si pò dicer né tenere a mente,
> sì è novo miracolo e gentile.[77]

To the fore, by contrast, among the poems associated in the *Vita nova* with the death of Beatrice, and tending, along with *Donne ch'avete intelletto d'amore*, to dominate the landscape of the *libello*, is the canzone *Li occhi dolenti per pietà del core*, where, though it remains, to be sure, a question of praise, it is a question now of praise as making in circumstances of bereavement for a painful process of self-confrontation, of knowing self not merely in the grief but in the guilt of self. Such at any rate is the trajectory of this as, along perhaps with the post-exilic canzone *Tre donne intorno al cor mi son venute* to which we shall come presently, the most

---

77 'My lady bears Love in her eyes such that whatsoever she sees she ennobles. Wherever she goes, all turn towards her and whomsoever she greets she causes to tremble within, so that, lowering their gaze, they pale and sigh over their sins, pride and ill-humour fleeing before her. Help me, ladies, to do her honour. Every sweetness and every humble thought is born in the heart of those hearing her speak whence he who first sees her is himself praised. Of what she seems when she smiles a little there is no telling nor even thinking, for so special a thing is it and so noble.'

fraught instance of spiritual self-searching in Dante's canzoniere, the praise poems pure and simple not excepted. First, then, and in this sense taking up where *Donne ch'avete intelletto d'amore* left off, comes the iconic moment of the argument, Dante's sense of Beatrice as called into the presence of her maker and thus to an altogether nobler place—a moment, however, immeasurably complicated by a sense now of the chill, the emptiness and the ignominy of the place she has departed:

> Ita n'è Beatrice in l'alto cielo,
> nel reame ove li angeli hanno pace,
> e sta con loro, e voi, donne, ha lassate;
>   no la ci tolse qualità di gelo
> né di calore, come l'altre face,
> ma solo fue sua gran benignitate;
>   ché luce de la sua umilitate
> passò li cieli con tanta vertute,
> che fé maravigliar l'etterno sire,
> sì che dolce disire
> lo giunse di chiamar tanta salute;
> e fella di qua giù a sé venire,
> perché vedea ch'esta vita noiosa
> non era degna di sì gentil cosa.

(*Li occhi dolenti per pietà del core*, lines 15–29)[78]

But this, alas, is a chill, an emptiness and an ignominy in turn complicated by the inestimable suffering and indeed by the death-yearning of the one now knowing himself only in the guilt-ridden abjectness of his existence—the content, precisely, of the agonized fourth stanza of the poem:

> Dànnomi angoscia li sospiri forte,
> quando 'l pensero ne la mente grave
> mi reca quella che m'ha 'l cor diviso;
>   e spesse fiate pensando a la morte,
> venemene un disio tanto soave,

---

78 'Beatrice has departed to heaven on high, to that royal place where angels abide in peace; and dwelling as she herself does with them, she has left you, my ladies, bereft. Neither cold nor heat was it that, as with other things, took her from us, but only her great goodness; for the light of her lowliness so readily rose from sphere to sphere as to cause the forever sire to marvel and sweetly to conceive a desire to summon unto himself such perfection. Deeming, then, this grievous place of ours unfit for such a noble one as she, from here below he bade her come.'

che mi tramuta lo color nel viso.
    E quando 'l maginar mi ven ben fiso,
giugnemi tanta pena d'ogne parte,
ch'io mi riscuoto per dolor ch'i' sento;
e sì fatto divento,
che da le genti vergogna mi parte.
Poscia piangendo, sol nel mio lamento
chiamo Beatrice, e dico: 'Or se' tu morta?';
e mentre ch'io la chiamo, me conforta.

(*Li occhi dolenti per pietà del core*, lines 43–56)[79]

And this—the moment of inestimable suffering—is a state of mind perpetuated into the fifth stanza where Dante is beginning already to pace out the wasteland of hell. True, the dialectic of the *Inferno* in all the sustained substance and symptomatology thereof remains as yet over the horizon, but for all that, his, for the moment, is an order of existence present to itself by way only of the irretrievability of what once was and of the desolation of what now is:

Pianger di doglia e sospirar d'angoscia
mi strugge 'l core ovunque sol mi trovo,
sì che ne 'ncrescerebbe a chi m'audesse;
e quale è stata la mia vita, poscia
che la mia donna andò nel secol novo,
lingua non è che dicer lo sapesse;
    e però, donne mie, pur ch'io volesse,
non vi saprei io dir ben quel ch'io sono,
sì mi fa travagliar l'acerba vita;
la quale è sì 'nvilita,
che ogn'om par che mi dica: 'Io t'abbandono',
veggendo la mia labbia tramortita.
Ma qual ch'io sia, la mia donna il si vede,
ed io ne spero ancor da lei merzede.[80]

---

79 'Grievous is the pain of my sighing when thought reminds my burdened spirit of the death by which my heart is rent, and, thinking often of death, I yearn for it, my face all ashen. And in the moment of my mind's fixation such anguish lays hold of me on every side that I start up with the pain I feel, and for shame, having come to this, hide from all company. Then, alone and weeping, I call out to her in my distress, saying: "Are you indeed dead?," and, in calling upon her, find comfort.'

80 'With tears of sorrow and sighs of distress my heart is undone whenever I find myself alone, such that those hearing would not but pity me. And what my life has been since my lady left for a new world no tongue could express. And so, ladies, even were I to wish it, I could not fully tell how I fare,

And this—the well-nigh impossible commingling of grief and guilt in circumstances of bereavement—is a situation further explored in those poems associated in the *Vita nova* with *Li occhi dolenti* as the great canzone of love-sorrowing in Dante. On the one hand, then, and among those poems leading up to *Li occhi dolenti* in the *libello*, we have these lines from the canzone *Donna pietosa e di novella etate*, where, in anticipation of the event itself, it is a question of the hallucinatory, of Beatrice's demise as subject to exploration by way of the crucifixional and the apocalyptic, of a state of mind, that is to say, possessed only by a sense of all this implies by way of darkness and dereliction:

> Poi vidi cose dubitose molte,
> nel vano imaginare ov'io entrai;
> ed esser mi parea non so in qual loco,
>   e veder donne andar per via disciolte,
> qual lagrimando, e qual traendo guai,
> che di tristizia saettavan foco.
>   Poi mi parve vedere a poco a poco
> turbar lo sole ed apparir la stella,
> e pianger elli ed ella;
> cader li augelli volando per l'are,
> e la terra tremare;
> ed omo apparve scolorito e fioco,
> dicendomi: 'Che fai? non sai novella?
> Morta è la donna tua, ch'era sì bella'.

> (*Donna pietosa e di novella etate*, lines 43–56)[81]

while on the other hand, and as following on now from the canzone *Li occhi dolenti* as the key text hereabouts, there are poems such as the sonnet *Venite a 'ntender li sospiri miei* committed to the notion of Beatrice in glory but prey still to the agony of bereavement, to the notion of sighing as the poet's sole comfort amid the comfortlessness of it all:

---

so painful is this wretched existence of mine—an existence now so abject that all those seeing the deathly pallor of my lips seem to be saying: "You I leave to your lot." But howsoever I am, my lady sees it and my hope still is that she may have mercy.'

81 'Then, held fast by the vain imagining of my mind, I saw many fearful things. I seemed to be in a strange place—a place I know not where—and to see making their way dishevelled women, some weeping, some wailing, their words of woe as fiery arrows of sorrow. Then little by little the sun, it seemed, grew dark and the stars came out, both he and they alike weeping. The birds in full flight seemed likewise to fall to the ground and the earth shook, and, wan and weak, a man appeared saying to me: "What are you doing? Have you not heard? Your lady, once so beautiful, is dead."'

Venite a 'ntender li sospiri miei,
oi cor gentili, chè pietà 'l disia:
li quai disconsolati vanno via,
e s'e' non fosser, di dolor morrei;
     però che gli occhi mi sarebber rei,
molte fiate più ch'io non vorria,
lasso! di pianger sì la donna mia,
che sfogasser lo cor, piangendo lei.
     Voi udirete lor chiamar sovente
la mia donna gentil, che si n'è gita
al secol degno de la sua vertute;
     e dispregiar talora questa vita
in persona de l'anima dolente
abbandonata de la sua salute.[82]

or the canzone *Quantunque volte, lasso!, mi rimembra,* as, that same sense of Beatrice in glory notwithstanding, a canzone turning upon the notion of death as but the cause and now the ideal consummation of the poet's wretched existence, as uniquely adequate to his grief:

E' si raccoglie ne li miei sospiri
un sono di pietate,
che va chiamando Morte tuttavia;
     a lei si volser tutti i miei disiri,
quando la donna mia
fu giunta da la sua crudelitate;
     perché 'l piacere de la sua bieltate,
partendo sé da la nostra veduta,
divenne spirital bellezza grande,
che per lo cielo spande
luce d'amor, che li angeli saluta
e lo intelletto loro alto, sottile
face maravigliar, sì v'è gentile.

(*Quantunque volte, lasso!, mi rimembra,* lines 14–26)[83]

82 'Come, o noble hearts, and hearken unto my sighs, pity itself demanding no less, sighs taking their leave all disconsolate, which, were it not so, I should die of my sorrow; for then my eyes—and more often than I would wish it—would fail me, alas, in solacing a heart likewise lamenting my lady. You will hear them calling often enough for my noble lady, for one who has gone away for a place more worthy of her goodness, and, after the manner of a sorrowing soul bereft of its blessing, despising as they do so this life of ours.'
83 'And there amid my sighs is gathered a whisper of compassion calling endlessly upon Death, to

With what amounts, then, in *Li occhi dolenti* and her handmaidens to the poetry of praise by way of sorrowing, we come to the next and for the moment final pinnacle of Dante's 'stilo de la loda' as but obedience to the 'dittar dentro' or prompting of the spirit as seeing, understanding and celebrating—namely the sonnet *Oltre la spera che più larga gira*, an essay, precisely, in the twofold sayability and unsayability of the leading idea. On the one hand, then, we have the long since hallowed notion of Beatrice in glory, as brought home to the elect and thus as honoured on high, while on the other, and as the deep substance of this poem, we have the dialectic of knowing and of not knowing, of understanding and of not understanding, the sinuousness and subtlety of it all both stilling the spirit and yet in the selfsame moment drawing it ever onwards and upwards. This, then, is praise poetry of a more than ordinarily accomplished kind, praise by its very nature being—as Dante understood with perfect precision—a matter both of stasis and of ecstasis, of quietness and of quickening:

> Oltre la spera che più larga gira,
> passa 'l sospiro ch'esce del mio core;
> intelligenza nova, che l'Amore
> piangendo mette in lui, pur sù lo tira.
>
> Quand'elli è giunto là dove disira,
> vede una donna che riceve onore,
> e luce sì, che per lo suo splendore
> lo peregrino spirito la mira.
>
> Vedela tal, che quando 'l mi ridice,
> io no lo intendo, sì parla sottile
> al cor dolente che lo fa parlare.
>
> So io che parla di quella gentile,
> però che spesso ricorda Beatrice,
> sì ch'io lo 'ntendo ben, donne mie care.[84]

whom my every desire turned when by his cruelty my lady was taken from us; for her beauty and the loveliness thereof, departing our view, became a still greater spiritual beauty irradiating the heavens with the light of love, a beauty which, greeting the angels in their soaring but subtle intelligence, causes them to marvel, so gracious is it in that place.'

84 'Beyond the sphere that circles most widely passes the sigh that issues from my heart. Fresh understanding, instilled there by Love with weeping, draws it upwards. And when it reaches the place of its desiring it sees a lady most highly honoured and radiant such that the pilgrim spirit gazes upon her in her splendor. Thus contemplating her, it speaks such that I understand not, so subtly does it address my sorrowing heart bidding it tell. But I know it is of that noble one it speaks, for its words summon afresh my memory of Beatrice—which is why, dear my ladies, I understand full well.' Romano Guardini, 'L'ultimo sonetto della *Vita Nuova*', in *Studi su Dante*, ed. Maria Luisa Maraschini and Anna Sacchi Balestrieri (Brescia: Morcelliana, 1979), 207–19.

But for all his presence in the depths, and indeed for all his status as father to all those now rhyming sweetly in the *lingua di sì*, we have come a long way from the Guinizzelli of, say, the canzone *Al cor gentil rempaira sempre amore* or of the sonnet *Io voglio del ver la mia donna laudare*; for where in Guinizzelli it is a matter of elaborating a motif—to wit, the notion of love as but a matter of praise—already established fast as a property of the tradition in which he stands, in Dante it is a question of its espousal as a matter of fundamental self-interpretation, of restructuring and of confirming in its intelligibility the very course of his existence. Invested, in other words, with a seriousness at once unparalleled and unprecedented among his peers and predecessors, that same motif, pondered afresh and immeasurably deepened in respect of all it implies by way of self-transcendence on the planes both of knowing and of loving, furnishes a principle of ontic affirmation, of knowing self in the revised substance of self. Pondered afresh and immeasurably deepened in respect of all it implies by way of self-transcendence on the planes both of knowing and of loving, it functions, in short, as a principle of new life.

CHAPTER 4

The *Vita nova*

PRELIMINARY REMARKS: ANTECEDENT UTTERANCE AND AN ESSAY IN AUTHORING

To live with the *Vita nova* for any length of time is to be impressed by the need for its delicate handling, for this is a text apt with each successive reading to privilege now this, now that aspect of it.[1] On the one hand, then, there is its private and confessional aspect, the *Vita nova*, whatever else it is, being the product of a characteristic process in Dante of self-reconstruction, of shaping and substantiating his experience so far as a maker of rhymes in the *lingua di sì*. On the other hand there is its more specifically ideological aspect, where it is a question of confirming over against the notion of love as a property merely of the sensitive soul and thus as conducive to the most complete kind of moral and intellectual undoing its status as a principle of new life, as that whereby the seasoned lover knows himself at last in the fullness of his proper humanity. But as if that were not enough we have in the *Vita nova* something still more astonishing, namely a reaching out on Dante's part beyond the customary forms of high-scholastic disquisition—the *tractatus*, the *quaestio*, the *quodlibet*—in favour of something ap-

---

1 In addition to the general histories and biographies: James Eustace Shaw, *Essays on the Vita Nuova* (Princeton: Princeton University Press, 1929); Domenico de Robertis, *Il libro della Vita Nuova*, 2nd ed. (Florence: Sansoni, 1970); Margherita De Bonfils Templer, *Itinerario d'amore: Dialettica di amore e morte nella 'Vita nuova'* (Chapel Hill: University of North Carolina Department of Romance Languages and Literatures, 1973); Étienne Gilson, *Dante et Béatrice: Etudes dantesques* (Paris: Vrin, 1974); Michelangelo Picone, 'La *Vita Nuova* e la tradizione poetica', *DS* 95 (1977), 135–47; Michelangelo Picone, '*Vita nuova' e tradizione romanza* (Padua: Liviana, 1979); Michelangelo Picone (ed.), 'La *Vita Nuova* fra autobiografia e tipologia', *Dante e le forme dell'allegoresi* (Ravenna: Longo, 1987), 59–70; Charles S. Singleton, *An Essay on the Vita Nuova* (Baltimore: Johns Hopkins University Press, 1977 [1949]); Jerome Mazzaro, *The Figure of Dante: An Essay on the 'Vita nuova'* (Princeton: Princeton University Press, 1981); Giuseppe Mazzotta, 'The Language of Poetry in the *Vita nuova*', *RSI* 1 (1983), 3–14; Vittore Branca, 'Poetics of Renewal and Hagiographic Tradition in the *Vita Nuova*', in *Lectura Dantis Newberryiana*, ed. Paolo Cherchi and Antonio C. Mastrobuono (Evanston, IL: Northwestern University Press, 1988), 123–52; Guglielmo Gorni, '*Vita nuova di Dante Alighieri*', in *Letteratura italiana: Le opere*, vol. 1 (*Dalle origini al Cinquecento*), ed. Aberto Asor Rosa (Turin: Einaudi, 1992), 153–86; Vincent Moleta (ed.), '*La gloriosa donna de la mente': A Commentary on the 'Vita Nova'* (Florence: Olschki, 1994); John Scott, 'Dante's New Life: *Vita Nova*', in *Understanding Dante* (Notre Dame: University of Notre Dame Press, 2004), 1–31; Marco Santagata, 'La *Vita Nova*', in *L'io e il mondo: Un'interpretazione di Dante* (Bologna: Il Mulino, 2011), 113–224.

proaching the 'book' proper with all this implies by way of precise thematicization and authorial self-consciousness. Now here we have to be careful, since for all its novelty in this respect, the *Vita nova* deploys every discursive strategy from the scribal and scholiastic to the editorial, exegetical and glossatorial. First, then, there is its scribal aspect, its copying-out-from-the-book-of-memory aspect, the scribal, however, straightaway shading off into the editorial and the exegetical, into the proposing and disposing of events in the interests less of circumstance than of significance, of the meaning by which they are irradiated and commended as an object of contemplation:

> In quella parte del libro de la mia memoria, dinanzi a la quale poco si potrebbe leggere, si trova una rubrica la quale dice: *Incipit vita nova.* Sotto la quale rubrica io trovo scritte le parole le quali è mio intendimento d'asemplare in questo libello; e se non tutte, almeno la loro sentenzia.
>
> (*Vita nova* 1)[2]

And what applies to events in their candidacy or otherwise for inclusion in this ideal trajectory of the spirit applies also to those texts now ripe for commentary, some, by reason of their bearing albeit in a preliminary fashion upon the leading idea, ruling themselves in, and others, by dint either of their anti-Beatricianism or their generally plaintive complexion, ruling themselves out; so, for example, among the latter are the canzoni *Lo doloroso amor che mi conduce* and *E' m'incresce di me sì duramente* with their sense of Beatrice as a principle less of life than of death (the 'Per quella moro c'ha nome Beatrice' and 'alza li occhi micidiali' at lines 14 and 49 respectively), together with—for its privileging less of praise than of pain and pity as the dominant sensation—the sonnet *De gli occhi de la mia donna si move*:

> De gli occhi de la mia donna si move
> un lume sì gentil che, dove appare,
> si veggion cose ch'uom non pò ritrare
> per loro altezza e per lor esser nove;
> e de' suoi razzi sovra 'l meo cor piove

---

2 'In that part of my memory before which there is little to be read, there is a heading which says: *Here begins new life.* Beneath that heading I find written the words I propose to copy into this little book, or, if not all of them, then at least their meaning.' Domenico de Robertis, 'Incipit vita nova (V.N. 1): Poetica del (ri)cominciamento', in Vincent Moleta (ed.), "La gloriosa donna de la mente": A Commentary on the 'Vita Nuova' (Florence: Olschki, 1994), 11–20 (and in *Dal primo all'ultimo Dante* [Florence: Le Lettere, 2001], 103–10); Alberto Casadei, 'Incipit vita nova', NRLI 13.1–2 (2010), 11–18 and in DS 129 (2011), 179–86; Enrico Malato, 'L'"incipit" della *Vita Nuova*', RSD 10.1 (2010), 95–105.

tanta paura che mi fa tremare
e dicer: 'Qui non voglio mai tornare';
ma poscia perdo tutte le mie prove;
    e tornomi colà dov'io son vinto,
riconfortando gli occhi päurusi,
che sentiêr prima questo gran valore.
    Quando son giunto, lasso, ed e' son chiusi;
lo disio che li mena quivi è stinto;
però proveggia a lo mio stato Amore.[3]

And what applies in the case of *De gli occhi de la mia donna si move*, where it is a question of consigning the poem to the ranks of the *extravaganti* or far-wanderers on the basis of its as yet unsettled substance, applies also in the case of, say, *Onde venite voi così pensose?*, a sonnet that, while akin to some of those included in the *Vita nova* (to *Voi che portate la sembianza umile* and *Se' tu colui c'hai trattato sovente* as poems occasioned by the death of her father as registered in chapter 22 of the *libello*), has, in truth, less to do with Beatrice than with Dante himself in the turmoil of his spirit. Here too, then, is a candidate for deselection:

Onde venite voi così pensose?
Ditemel, s'a voi piace, in cortesia,
ch'i' ho dottanza che la donna mia
non vi faccia tornar così dogliose.
    Deh, gentil donne, non siate sdegnose,
né di ristare alquanto in questa via
e dire al doloroso che disia
udir de la sua donna alquante cose;
    avvegna che gravoso m'è l'udire:
sì m'ha in tutto Amor da sé scacciato
ch'ogni suo atto mi trae a ferire.
    Guardate bene s'i' son consumato,
ch'ogni mio spirto comincia a fuggire,
se da voi, donne, non son confortato.[4]

---

3 'From my lady's eyes there comes a light so noble that wherever it appears things are seen both sublime and wonderful beyond words. And from its rays such fear rains down on my heart as makes me tremble and say: "Here I wish never to return." But then, bereft of resolve, I return to the place of my overcoming, seeking as I do so to comfort the still fearful eyes which were the first to feel that great power. And when I reach that place, alas, they close, with the desire drawing them hither extinguished. Let Love, then, look to my state!' For the 'Per quella moro c'ha nome Beatrice' moment of *Lo doloroso amor che mi conduce*: 'I die for the one by the name of Beatrice', and for the 'alza li occhi micidiali' of *E' m'incresce di me sì duramente*: 'she raises those eyes swift to slay'.

4 'Whence come you sorrowing so? Tell me if you will, for courtesy's sake, for I have every fear

This, then, is what it means to speak of the editorial aspect of the *Vita nova*, each and every one of Dante's praise poems having to pass muster in respect of its precise distribution of emphases and overall accountability to the deep reasons of the book as a whole.

All of a piece, however, with the editorial aspect of the book is its exegetical aspect, where it is a question of Dante's eliciting from the poems chosen for inclusion an order of meaning either inchoate or inherent in them from the outset but fully discernible only in retrospect, from the point of view of one now at peace on the plane of love-understanding. Now here again the situation needs careful statement, for though it is indeed a matter in the *Vita nova* of Dante's fashioning from the *disjecta membra* of his experience so far as a poet and philosopher of love a spiritual journey open only now to contemplation in its totality, there can be no sitting lightly to the original utterance in its at once notional and expressive excellence. On the contrary, the original utterance stands always and everywhere to be honoured in respect of its equality to the matter in hand, of, even at the time, its power fully and freely to signify. But for all that, it *is*, in the *Vita nova*, a question of elucidation, of settling more than ever securely on the function of the urtext within the now consummate economy of the whole. True, this revisiting of the text for the purposes of its fresh explication is for much of the time a mild affair, a matter either of indicating the circumstances of its coming about and/or of confirming the leading idea, poetry and prose thus proceeding arm in arm. On occasion, however, the intervention is more complete, the former being immeasurably strengthened by the latter in respect of what it all means; so, for example, as the very first poem in the book, we have the sonnet *A ciascun'alma presa e gentil core*, an enigma sonnet possibly and indeed probably little more in the first instance than a means of social self-insinuation (for it was with this poem, Dante notes at 3.14, that his friendship with Cavalcanti was launched), but burdened now with every kind of prophetic responsibility, with registering in advance the substance of a drama at the time unimaginable in point either of substance or of intensity. On the one hand, then, there is the poem itself, enigmatic and fraught with possibility, to be sure, but just for the moment closer to the playful than to the prophetic:

> A ciascun'alma presa e gentil core,
> nel cui cospetto ven lo dir presente,
> in ciò che mi rescrivan suo parvente,

---

that it is my lady who causes you to return so sadly. Ah, most noble ladies, scorn not to stay a while along the way and to speak with one who, himself sorrowing, longs for news of his lady, painful as it may be to hear. For Love has so spurned me that his every act injures me. See how careworn I am. If from you I derive no comfort, my every spirit will take flight.'

salute in lor segnor, cioè Amore.
  Già eran quasi che atterzate l'ore
del tempo che onne stella n'è lucente,
quando m'apparve Amor subitamente,
cui essenza membrar mi dà orrore.
  Allegro mi sembrava Amor tenendo
meo core in mano, e ne le braccia avea
madonna involta in un drappo dormendo.
  Poi la svegliava, e d'esto core ardendo
lei paventosa umilmente pascea:
appresso gir lo ne vedea piangendo.[5]

while on the other hand there is the prose, duly seeing to it that the playful is indeed taken up in the prophetic, in a now dramatic sense of Love's sudden and solemn appearance—of his at once Pentateuchal and Psalmic turn of phrase, of his carrying in his arms a lady clothed in crimson in all the love-significance thereof, of his feeding her upon the heart now all aflame of the lover and of his bearing her away heavenward:

E pensando di lei, mi sopragiunse uno soave sonno, ne lo quale m'apparve una maravigliosa visione: che me parea vedere ne la mia camera una nebula di colore di fuoco, dentro a la quale io discernea una figura d'uno segnore di pauroso aspetto a chi la guardasse; e pareami con tanta letizia, quanto a sé, che mirabile cosa era; e ne le sue parole dicea molte cose, le quali io non intendea se non poche; tra le quali intendea queste: 'Ego dominus tuus'. Ne le sue braccia mi parea vedere una persona dormire nuda, salvo che involta mi parea in uno drappo sanguigno leggeramente; la quale io riguardando molto intentivamente, conobbi ch'era la donna de la salute, la quale m'avea lo giorno dinanzi degnato di salutare. E ne l'una de le mani mi parea che questi tenesse una cosa, la quale ardesse tutta, e pareami che mi dicesse queste parole: 'Vide cor tuum'. E quando elli era stato alquanto, pareami che disvegliasse questa che dormia; e tanto si sforzava per suo ingegno, che le

5 'To every captive soul and noble heart into whose sight this poem may come, that each, writing back, may say what he makes of it, a greeting in his lord, that is, Love. Already almost a third of the hours had passed of the time in which all the stars shine clear, when lo! Love appeared to me in a form that is terrifying to recall. Rejoicing, so it seemed, he held my heart in his hand, while in his arms lay my lady in a mantle wrapped and sleeping. Then he awoke her and, fearful as she was, he reverently fed her my heart all aflame, whereupon he made his way weeping.' Silvio Pellegrini, 'Intorno al primo sonetto della *Vita Nova*', in *Varietà romanze*, ed. Giuseppe Edoardo Sansone (Bari: Adriatica Editrice, 1977), 407–11; Justin Steinberg, 'Dante's First Dream between Reception and Allegory: The Response to Dante da Maiano in the *Vita nova*', in *Dante the Lyric and Ethical Poet: Dante lirico e etico*, ed. Zygmunt G. Barański and Martin McLaughlin (Oxford: Legenda, 2010), 92–118.

facea mangiare questa cosa che in mano li ardea, la quale ella mangiava
dubitosamente. Appresso ciò poco dimorava che la sua letizia si convertia
in amarissimo pianto; e così piangendo, si ricogliea questa donna ne le sue
braccia, e con essa mi parea che si ne gisse verso lo cielo; onde io sostenea
sì grande angoscia, che lo mio deboletto sonno non poteo sostenere, anzi
si ruppe e fui disvegliato.

(Vita nova 3.3–7)[6]

Here, then, for all its transparency to the text, is the first instance in the *Vita
nova* of exegesis in full flight, of systematic elaboration in respect of what Dante
understands now to be its innermost and abiding meaning, its proper gravitas.
And what applies to *A ciascun'alma presa e gentil core* applies also—and if anything
still more audaciously—to the sonnet *Ne li occhi porta la mia donna Amore* in
chapter 21 of the *Vita nova*, where an as yet gentle experimentation with the notion of Beatrice as a special presence among us (the 'novo miracolo' moment of
line 14) gives way in the prose to a fully-fledged account of her power, not only
to awaken love where it exists in potential, but to instil that potential in the first
place—to an essay, in short, in primary causality. On the one hand, then, there is
the poem, which, occupying as it does the space between *Donne ch'avete intelletto
d'amore* and *Tanto gentile e tanto onesta pare*, faithfully reflects the leading preoc-
cupations of both:

> Ne li occhi porta la mia donna Amore,
> per che si fa gentil ciò ch'ella mira;
> ov'ella passa, ogn'om ver lei si gira,
> e cui saluta fa tremar lo core,
>   sì che, bassando il viso, tutto smore,
> e d'ogni suo difetto allor sospira;
> fugge dinanzi a lei superbia ed ira.

6 'As I thought of her a gentle sleep fell upon me in which I saw a remarkable vision. I seemed to
see a flame-coloured cloud in my room, and in it I saw the figure of a lord, terrifying to behold. And
he seemed to have about him great rejoicing. And in speaking to me he said many things, of which I
understood but few, but among them this: "I am your lord." In his arms I saw a woman sleeping, naked
apart from a crimson cloth lightly wrapped around her. And, as I looked more closely, I recognized the
lady who had greeted me the day before, for it was she. In one of his hands he held something all aflame,
and he said: "Behold, your heart." Having lingered thus a while, he woke the sleeping woman and
obliged her to eat the glowing object in his hand, and she, with great misgiving, did so. And before a
moment had passed his joy turned to sorrow, and, thus lamenting, he gathered the lady in his arms and
with her made his way—or so it seemed—heavenward, whence my anguish was so great that, unable
to bear it, my fragile repose was broken and I awoke.' Cf. in addition to Exodus 20:2 ('Ego sum Dominus
Deus tuus') for the 'I am your lord' moment of the text, Psalm 18:46 ('et exaltetur Deus salutis meae'),
Psalm 50:14 ('Libera me de sanguinibus, Deus, Deus salutis meae') and Psalm 88:1 ('Domine Deus
salutis meae') for the 'donna de la salute' moment.

Aiutatemi, donne, farle onore.
Ogne dolcezza, ogne pensero umile
nasce nel core a chi parlar la sente,
ond'è laudato chi prima la vide.
Quel ch'ella par quando un poco sorride,
non si pò dicer né tenere a mente,
sì è novo miracolo e gentile.[7]

while on the other hand there is the prose, nothing if not courageous in its twofold Peripatecization and theologization of the whole thing, in its seeing in Beatrice not merely a catalyst but a cause of love, a bringer forth of something from nothing:

Poscia che trattai d'Amore ne la soprascritta rima, vennemi volontade di volere dire, anche in loda di questa gentilissima, parole per le quali io mostrasse come per lei si sveglia questo Amore, e come non solamente si sveglia là ove dorme, ma là ove non è in potenzia, ella, mirabilemente operando, lo fa venire ... La prima si divide in tre; che ne la prima parte dico sì come virtuosamente fae gentile tutto ciò che vede, e questo è tanto a dire quanto inducere Amore in potenzia là ove non è; ne la seconda dico come reduce in atto Amore ne li cuori di tutti coloro cui vede; ne la terza dico quello che poi virtuosamente adopera ne' loro cuori.

(*Vita nova* 21.1 and 6)[8]

But that is not all, for all of a piece with the editorial and the exegetical function of the text—meaning by this the prose part of the text—is its glossatorial and scholiastic function, 'glossatorial' in the sense of clarifying by way of a series of *razos* or *divisiones textus* the shape and structure of the poems in question, and 'scholiastic' in the sense of pausing from time to time to refine parenthetically the

7 'My lady bears love in her eyes such that she ennobles all those she looks upon. Wherever she goes all alike turn towards her, and she, greeting them, causes their heart to tremble, such that, lowering their gaze, they sigh, ashen, over their faults, pride and ill humour alike fleeing before her. Help me, ladies, to honour her. All gentleness and every humble thought is engendered in the heart of those who hear her speak such that he is blessed above all who first sees her. What she seems when discreetly she smiles is impossible to describe or even to hold fast in the mind, so rare a miracle is it and so noble.'
8 'After I had treated of Love in the above verse, the desire came over me to speak again in praise of this most graceful lady, words intended now to show how Love is awakened through her, and awakened not only where he is sleeping, but where he is not even in potential, she, working miraculously, causing him to come about ... The first part of the sonnet is itself divided into three parts, in the first of which I say how by way of the power properly hers she ennobles all she sees, which is as much as to say that she calls love into potentiality even where, as yet, he is not; in the second I say how she reduces love to actuality in the hearts of those whom she sees, while in the third I describe the effects she then has over their hearts by way, again, of her miraculous power.'

leading idea; so, for example, as far as the glossatorial moment of the book is concerned, we have these lines from the end of chapter 26, scrupulous to a fault in their dismantling of the text—in this case the sonnet *Vede perfettamente onne salute*—for the sake of confirming its substance and consistency on the plane of ideas:

> Questo sonetto ha tre parti: ne la prima dico tra che gente questa donna più mirabile parea; ne la seconda dico sì come era graziosa la sua compagnia; ne la terza dico di quelle cose che vertuosamente operava in altrui. La seconda parte comincia quivi: *quelle che vanno*; la terza quivi: *E sua bieltate.* Questa ultima parte si divide in tre: ne la prima dico quello che operava ne le donne, cioè per loro medesime; ne la seconda dico quello che operava in loro per altrui; ne la terza dico come non solamente ne le donne, ma in tutte le persone, e non solamente ne la sua presenzia, ma ricordandosi di lei, mirabilmente operava. La seconda comincia quivi: *La vista sua*; e la terza quivi: *Ed è ne li atti.*[9]

while as far as the scholiastic moment of the text is concerned we have these from early on in the book bearing upon the scarcely less than traumatic effect of Beatrice's 'saluto' or greeting upon the as yet apprentice lover:

> Dico che quando ella apparia da parte alcuna, per la speranza de la mirabile salute nullo nemico mi rimanea, anzi mi giugnea una fiamma di caritade, la quale mi facea perdonare a chiunque m'avesse offeso; e chi allora m'avesse domandato di cosa alcuna, la mia risponsione sarebbe stata solamente 'Amore', con viso vestito d'umilitade. E quando ella fosse alquanto propin-

---

9 'This sonnet has three parts. In the first part I speak of those to whom my lady most wondrously appeared, while in the second I speak of the gracious character of her presence to us, and in the third I speak of the things she miraculously accomplished in others. The second part begins with *her every companion* and the third with *So compelling is her loveliness.* This last part is further divided into three sections. In the first section I say what she accomplished in those women about her in respect of their own persons, while in the second section I speak of what she accomplished in them in the eyes of others, and in the third section I speak of her miraculous influence in respect not only of those women, but of everyone seeing her, and this not only in her immediate presence but as they think back upon her. The second section begins with: *The very sight of her*, and the third with *And in her every gesture*.' Vincenzo Crescini, 'Le "Razos" provenzali e le prose della *Vita Nuova*', *GSLI* 32 (1898), 463–64; John Henry Marshall, *The 'Razos de trobar' of Raimon Vidal and Associated Texts* (New York: Oxford University Press, 1972); Steven Botterill, 'Però che la divisione non si fa se non per aprire la sentenzia de la cosa divisa' (*V.N.* 14.13): The *Vita Nuova* as commentary', in *"La gloriosa donna de la mente": A Commentary on the 'Vita Nuova'*, ed. Vincent Moleta (Florence: Olschki, 1994), 61–76; Guglielmo Gorni, '"Divisioni" e formule introduttive delle poesie della *Vita Nova*', *Studi testuali* 4 (1996), 57–66; Jelena Todorović, 'Dante the Scribe and Dante the Commentator II: The Old Occitan Poetry Collections and the *Vita Nova*', in *Dante and the Dynamics of Textual Exchange: Authorship, Manuscript Culture, and the Making of the 'Vita Nova'* (New York: Fordham University Press, 2016), 102–34.

qua al salutare, uno spirito d'amore, distruggendo tutti li altri spiriti sensitivi, pingea fuori li deboletti spiriti del viso, e dicea loro: 'Andate a onorare
la donna vostra'; ed elli si rimanea nel luogo loro. E chi avesse voluto conoscere Amore, fare lo potea, mirando lo tremare de li occhi miei. E quando
questa gentilissima salute salutava, non che Amore fosse tal mezzo che
potesse obumbrare a me la intollerabile beatitudine, ma elli quasi per sover-
chio di dolcezza divenia tale, che lo mio corpo, lo quale era tutto allora sotto
lo suo reggimento, molte volte si movea come cosa grave inanimata. Sì che
appare manifestamente che ne le sue salute abitava la mia beatitudine, la
quale molte volte passava e redundava la mia capacitade.

(*Vita nova* 11)[10]

together with these from chapter 29 bearing upon the importance of the number
nine for any developed sense of Beatrice's properly speaking miraculous presence
in the world:

ma più sottilmente pensando, e secondo la infallibile veritade, questo numero fue ella medesima; per similitudine dico, e ciò intendo così. Lo numero del tre è la radice del nove, però che, sanza numero altro alcuno, per
sé medesimo fa nove, sì come vedemo manifestamente che tre via tre fa
nove. Dunque se lo tre è fattore per sè medesimo del nove, e lo fattore per
sé medesimo de li miracoli è tre, cioè Padre e Figlio e Spirito Santo, li quali
sono tre e uno, questa donna fue accompagnata da questo numero del nove
a dare ad intendere ch'ella era uno nove, cioè uno miracolo, la cui radice,
cioè del miracolo, è solamente la mirabile Trinitade. Forse ancora per più
sottile persona si vederebbe in ciò più sottile ragione; ma questa è quella
ch'io ne veggio, e che più mi piace.

(*Vita nova* 29.3–4)[11]

---

10 'I say this, then, that whenever and wherever she appeared, I felt, in anticipating her greeting,
that I no longer had an enemy in the world. In fact I positively glowed in the light of love, of a charity
which moved me to pardon any who had offended me; and if in that moment anyone put anything to
me my only reply—with a countenance clothed in humility—would have been: "Love." When she was
on the point of greeting me, a spirit of love, doing away with every other spirit of the senses, caused
the spirit of perception to flee in its frailty, saying to them: "Be off with you and pay homage to your
lady", Love alone remaining in their place. Anyone wanting then to behold Love could have done so
by seeing the trembling in my eyes. And when this most gracious one bestowed at last the saving power
of her greeting, it was not that Love, in coming between us, could cloud my unbearable bliss, but that
by way of its so to speak overpowering sweetness, my body—already by this time wholly under his
sway—stumbled forever heavy and inanimate from place to place. It is plain to see, therefore, that in
her greeting lay my every joy, a joy often enough exceeding and overflowing my every capacity.' Benvenuto Terracini, 'Il saluto di Beatrice', *RCCM* 7 (1965), 1068–74; Bernard S. Levy, 'Beatrice's Greeting
and Dante's "Sigh" in the *Vita nova*', *DS* 92 (1974), 53–62; Marco Santagata, 'Il saluto di Beatrice', *MR*
40.1 (2016), 160–68.
11 'But thinking it over again more carefully and looking now to truth in its infallibility, she

and—still on the scholiastic front—these from chapter 25 on the mutual accountability, and indeed on the mutual immanence, of form and substance in the poem
itself, the mutual immanence of form and substance in the poem itself serving in
Dante's view of it to confirm the emergence of the poet proper as distinct from
the mere 'rimatore' or rhymester in the vernacular:

> Potrebbe qui dubitare persona degna da dichiararle onne dubitazione, e
> dubitare potrebbe di ciò, che io dico d'Amore come se fosse una cosa per
> sé, e non solamente sustanzia intelligente, ma sì come fosse sustanzia cor-
> porale, la quale cosa, secondo la veritate, è falsa; ché Amore non è per sé
> sì come sustanzia, ma è uno accidente in sustanzia. E che io dica di lui come
> se fosse corpo, ancora sì come se fosse uomo, appare per tre cose che dico
> di lui. Dico che lo vidi venire; onde, con ciò sia cosa che venire dica moto
> locale, e localmente mobile per sé, secondo lo Filosofo, sia solamente
> corpo, appare che io ponga Amore essere corpo. Dico anche di lui che
> ridea, e anche che parlava; le quali cose paiono essere proprie de l'uomo,
> e spezialmente essere risibile; e però appare ch'io ponga lui essere uomo.
> A cotale cosa dichiarare, secondo che è buono a presente, prima è da in-
> tendere che anticamente non erano dicitori d'amore in lingua volgare, anzi
> erano dicitori d'amore certi poete in lingua latina; tra noi, dico avvegna
> forse che tra altra gente addivenisse, e addivegna ancora, sì come in Grecia,
> non volgari ma litterati poete queste cose trattavano. E non è molto numero
> d'anni passati, che apparìro prima questi poete volgari; ché dire per rima
> in volgare tanto è quanto dire per versi in latino, secondo alcuna propor-
> zione ... Onde, con ciò sia cosa che a li poete sia conceduta maggiore li-
> cenza di parlare che a li prosaici dittatori, e questi dicitori per rima non
> siano altro che poete volgari, degno e ragionevole è che a loro sia maggiore
> licenza largita di parlare che a li altri parlatori volgari; onde, se alcuna
> figura o colore rettorico è conceduto a li poete, conceduto è a li rimatori.
> Dunque, se noi vedemo che li poete hanno parlato a le cose inanimate, sì

---

herself—though I speak, as I shall explain, by way of likeness—*was* this number nine; for the number
three, independently of any other number, makes of itself for the number nine, which is what of course
we see when we say three threes are nine. If, then, three is the sole factor of nine, and the sole factor of
miracles is likewise three—that is, Father, Son and Holy Spirit who are themselves both three and
one—then the fact that this lady was accompanied by the number nine conveys that that indeed—a
nine—is what she was, that is, a miracle rooted like all miracles in nothing other than the most miraculous Trinity. A more subtle person, maybe, might see in this a more subtle reason, but that is what I
myself see in it, and that is what pleases me most.' John J. Guzzardo, 'Number Symbolism in the *Vita
Nuova*', *Canadian Journal of Italian Studies* 8.30 (1985), 12–31 (and in *Dante: Numerological Studies* [New
York: Peter Lang, 1987], 15–39); Carlo Vecce, '"Ella era uno nove, cioè uno miracolo" (*V.N.* XXIX.3):
Il numero di Beatrice', in *"La gloriosa donna de la mente": A Commentary on the 'Vita Nuova'*, ed. Vincent
Moleta (Florence: Olschki, 1994), 161–79; Bortolo Martinelli, 'L'ora di Beatrice: Genesi del simbolismo
numerico nella *Vita nova*', *CL* 23 (86–87): 1–2 (1995), 31–67.

come se avessero senso e ragione, e fattele parlare insieme; e non solamente cose vere, ma cose non vere, cioè che detto hanno, di cose le quali non sono, che parlano, e detto che molti accidenti parlano, sì come se fossero sustanzie ed uomini; degno è lo dicitore per rima di fare lo somigliante, ma non sanza ragione alcuna, ma con ragione, la quale poi sia possibile d'aprire per prosa ... E acciò che non ne pigli alcuna baldanza persona grossa, dico che né li poete parlavano così sanza ragione, né quelli che rìmano dèono parlare così, non avendo alcuno ragionamento in loro di quello che dicono; però che grande vergogna sarebbe a colui che rimasse cose sotto vesta di figura o di colore rettorico, e poscia, domandato, non sapesse denudare le sue parole da cotale vesta, in guisa che avessero verace intendimento. E questo mio primo amico e io ne sapemo bene di quelli che così rìmano stoltamente.

(Vita nova 25.1–4, 7–8 and 10)[12]

This, then, is what it means to speak of Dante's deploying in the *Vita nova* 'every discursive strategy from the scribal and the scholiastic to the editorial, exegetical and glossatorial', his account in the text both of the poems themselves and of the

---

12 'At this point someone worthy of airing such a doubt might be puzzled by the way I speak of Love as though it were a thing in itself, and not only a substance endowed with intelligence but a material substance, which is demonstrably false; for Love is not in itself a substance but, rather, an accident in a substance. That I speak of him as if he were a something bodily, and indeed as though he were a man, is apparent from three things I say of him, for I say first that I saw him coming, and since coming implies local movement, and local movement, according to the Philosopher, exists only in a body, it is plain that that is what I make Love out to be. I say of him too that he smiles and speaks, things which—especially smiling—properly belong to man, thus in this way too clearly making him out to be human. To clarify all this, and in a manner useful for our present purposes, we need first to under-stand that in ancient times there was no writing poetry about love in the vernacular, though there were poets in Latin writing on this topic. Amongst us, then—and doubtless, both now and then, among others such as the Greeks—only learned as distinct from vernacular poets would treat of this. But it is not so very long ago that the first of these vernacular poets appeared, and I say "poets" in that, relatively speaking, composing rhymes in the vernacular is not so very different from writing verse in Latin ... It follows, then, that since greater licence is granted to poets than to prose writers, and since those who speak in rhyme are nothing other than vernacular poets, it is right and proper that greater licence should be granted to them to speak than to others writing in the vernacular, such that any figure of speech or rhetorical flourish allowed to poets is likewise allowed to writers in rhyme. Thus if we see the poets of old speaking of inanimate things as if they had sense and reason, and making them talk to each other, and this not only with real but with imaginary things, making accidents speak as though they were substances and even real men, it is perfectly appropriate for those writing in rhyme to do the same, though not, certainly, without justification and open thereafter to prose commentary ... And should anyone ignorant of such matters take it upon himself to pronounce here, I will add that just as the poets did not write in this manner without good reason, neither should those who, composing in rhyme, cannot give a reasonable account of what they are saying; for it would be nothing less than disgraceful were someone composing in rhyme to avail himself of a figure of speech or rhetorical flourish without, upon request, being able to strip down his words with a view to saying what they actually mean. My best friend and I know a good number, in fact, who compose in precisely this foolish way.' Aldo Vallone, '*Vita Nuova* XXV e la cultura di Dante', in *Ricerche dantesche* (Lecce: Milella, 1967), 75–84.

circumstances of their coming about meeting in this sense every kind of com-
mentatorly expectation. But—and this now is what matters—to speak in this way
of an account both of the poems themselves and of the circumstances of their
coming about suggests something other and something more than mere commentary in all the more or less atrophied ways and means thereof. Rather, it suggests something closer to what once again we would and should call a 'book', a
confection, that is to say, fashioned from out of the depths and circling about its
own still centre of concern. Commentary, in other words, accountable as it is to
the antecedent utterance, gives way now to something other than itself, to a discourse transparent at every point along the way to its own leading idea.[13]

LOVE SEEKING AND SEEKING NOT ITS OWN

Busy, then, at the point both of clarification and of self-clarification, both of the
idea pure and simple and of this as a principle of new life in the one who says 'I',
the *Vita nova* is open to contemplation by way of its three moments: of a preliminary moment turning on the substance and psychology of love as a matter of
acquisition, a phase culminating in the mockery of the poet by his own aspirations
as a lover; of a further moment turning upon his redefinition of love in terms less
now of *acquisition* than of *disposition*, of praise as making by nature for a fresh
reaching out of the spirit, for the most radical kind of over-and-beyondness on
the planes of knowing and loving; and of a final moment represented by Beatrice's
death and by the episode of the 'donna gentile' as offering between them a challenge to Dante's new understanding of love and as resolved at last by way of a fresh
vision of the now 'glorious lady of my mind' and of a commitment to say no more
of her until such time as he feels more properly empowered to do so. First, then,
comes the preliminary encounter, an encounter explored, as far as Beatrice is
concerned, by way of the iconic and symbolic, and, as far as Dante is concerned,
by way of the psychological, of love's traumatic inception. On the one hand, then,
we have Beatrice, as yet in her ninth year, nobly attired in a delicate yet decorous
crimson but above all epiphanous, apparitional, made manifest:

> Nove fiate già appresso lo mio nascimento era tornato lo cielo de la luce quasi
> a uno medesimo punto, quanto a la sua propria girazione, quando a li miei

---

13 John Ahern, 'The New Life of the Book: The Implied Reader of the *Vita Nuova*', *DS* 110 (1992),
1–16 (and in *The Critical Complex*, vol. 1, ed. Richard Lansing [New York: Routledge, 2003], 157–72);
Toby Levers, 'The Image of Authorship in the Final Chapter of the *Vita Nuova*', *ItSt* 57 (2002), 5–19;
Jelena Todorović, 'Who Read the *Vita Nova* in the First Half of the Fourteenth Century?', *DS* 131 (2013),
197–217. More generally, Albert Russell Ascoli, *Dante and the Making of a Modern Author* (Cambridge:
Cambridge University Press, 2008). For the 'book of the *Vita Nuova*' motif, Domenico de Robertis, *Il
libro della 'Vita Nuova'*, 2nd ed. (Florence: Sansoni, 1970).

occhi apparve prima la gloriosa donna de la mia mente, la quale fu chiamata da molti Beatrice, li quali non sapeano che si chiamare. Ella era in questa vita già stata tanto, che ne lo suo tempo lo cielo stellato era mosso verso la parte d'oriente de le dodici parti l'una d'un grado, sì che quasi dal principio del suo anno nono apparve a me, ed io la vidi quasi da la fine del mio nono. Apparve vestita di nobilissimo colore, umile e onesto, sanguigno, cinta e ornata a la guisa che a la sua giovanissima etade si convenia.

(*Vita nova* 2.1–3)[14]

while on the other hand, there is the lover, who, standing now in the presence of one immeasurably more powerful than himself (to wit, Amore as the God of Love), knows himself only in the perturbation of his vital spirits: of the *life-spirit* dwelling in the heart and quickening by way of the arteries the various functions of the body, of the *animal spirit* dwelling in the brain and served by the various organs of sense perception, and of the *natural spirit* dwelling in the liver and responsible for nourishing the whole in its proper operation. This, then, is blessedness indeed, but blessedness conditioned withal by fear and trembling:

In quello punto dico veracemente che lo spirito de la vita, lo quale dimora ne la secretissima camera de lo cuore, cominciò a tremare sì fortemente che apparia ne li menimi polsi orribilmente; e tremando disse queste parole: 'Ecce deus fortior me, qui veniens dominabitur mihi'. In quello punto lo spirito animale, lo quale dimora ne l'alta camera ne la quale tutti li spiriti sensitivi portano le loro percezioni, si cominciò a maravigliare molto, e parlando spezialmente a li spiriti del viso, sì disse queste parole: 'Apparuit iam beatitudo vestra'. In quello punto lo spirito naturale, lo quale dimora in quella parte ove si ministra lo nutrimento nostro, cominciò a piangere, e piangendo, disse queste parole: 'Heu miser, quia frequenter impeditus ero deinceps!'.

(*Vita nova* 2.4–7)[15]

14 'Nine times since my birth the heaven of light had come back to just about the same point when the glorious lady of my mind—she whom many, little knowing what it meant to speak thus, called Beatrice—first appeared before my eyes. She had been in this life for just so long as it took the starry heaven to move eastwards by the twelfth part of one degree, so that she appeared to me just about at the beginning of her ninth year, I for my part seeing her towards the end of my own ninth year. She appeared dressed in noblest colour, a modest and discreet crimson, girded and adorned in a manner becoming her tender age.' Robert Hollander, '*Vita Nuova*: Dante's Perceptions of Beatrice', DS 92 (1974), 1–18 (also in *Studies in Dante* [Ravenna: Longo, 1980], 11–30).

15 'At that moment I say in all truth that the vital spirit which lives in the innermost chamber of the heart began to tremble so violently that I felt that trembling fearfully in the least of my pulses, uttering as it did so these words: "Behold a god more powerful than I, who, coming upon me, will rule over me." At that moment the animal spirit which lives in the uppermost chamber to which every sensitive spirit conveys its perception, began to wonder deeply, and, addressing in particular the spirit

With what amounts, then, to an encounter apt in one and the same moment both to tranquillize and to traumatize the spirit the narrative gets under way, Beatrice, for her part, deigning more than ever graciously to greet her lover, and Dante, for his, rejoicing in her power to light up the entire landscape of his existence:

> Poi che furono passati tanti die, che appunto erano compiuti li nove anni appresso l'apparimento soprascritto di questa gentilissima, ne l'ultimo di questi die avvenne che questa mirabile donna apparve a me vestita di colore bianchissimo, in mezzo a due gentili donne, le quali erano di più lunga etade; e passando per una via, volse li occhi verso quella parte ov'io era molto pauroso, e per la sua ineffabile cortesia, la quale è oggi meritata nel grande secolo, mi salutoe molto virtuosamente, tanto che me parve allora vedere tutti li termini de la beatitudine.
>
> (*Vita nova* 3.1)[16]

Inebriated, then, in the sense of drunken in the spirit (the 'come inebriato mi partio da le genti' of 3.2), the poet-lover retreats in keeping with a Gospel motif into the privacy of his own space (the 'in cubiculum tuum, et clauso ostio' of Matthew 6:5),[17] there to ponder afresh the rare substance of the encounter (the 'ricorsi a lo solingo luogo d'una camera, e puosimi a pensare di questa cortesissima' of the same chapter). Events, however, quickly take a turn for the worse, for catching wind of his preoccupation with a 'screen lady' or 'donna schermo' de-

---

of sight, said these words: "Behold now your blessedness displayed"; whereupon the natural spirit which lives in the part where we are nourished, began to weep, and, weeping, spoke thus: "Woe is me, for mine, henceforth, will be but impediment."' Cf. for the 'Ecce deus fortior me' moment of the text Matthew 3:11 ('qui autem post me venturus, fortior me est') and Luke 3:16 ('veniet autem fortior me'), and for the 'Apparuit iam beatitudo vestra' moment the 'Apparuit enim gratia Dei Salvatoris nostri omnibus hominibus' of the letter to Titus at 2:11 (with 'Apparuit autem illi Angelus' at Luke 1:11). Giovanni Barblan (ed.), *Dante e la Bibbia* [Florence: Olschki, 1988]); Giorgio Petrocchi, 'San Paolo in Dante', in *La selva del protonotario: Nuovi studi danteschi* (Naples: Morano, 1988), 65–82; Giuseppe di Scipio, *The Presence of Pauline Thought in the Works of Dante* (Lewiston, NY: Edwin Mellen Press, 1995).

16 'With the passing of time, of nine years, in fact, since the aforesaid appearance of this, the most noble of women, it happened that this most wondrous lady appeared to me once more, clothed in pure white and walking between two no less noble ladies but of greater age; and, as she passed by she turned her eyes to where in fear and trembling I myself was standing, whereupon, from out of her unspeakable goodness—a goodness now rewarded in heaven—she greeted me so graciously that, or so it seemed, my bliss knew no bounds.'

17 Matthew 6:5: 'Tu autem cum oraveris, intra in cubiculum tuum, et clauso ostio, ora patrem tuum in abscondito, et pater tuus qui videt in abscondito, reddet tibi' (But thou, when thou prayest, enter into thy closet, and when thou hast shut thy door, pray to thy Father which is in secret; and thy Father which seeth in secret shall reward thee openly; A.V.). For the 'come inebriato' moment of the argument: 'I withdrew from the company after the manner of one inebriated', and for the 'ricorsi a lo solingo luogo' moment: 'making straight for the privacy of my room I fell to thinking of this gracious lady.'

signed, Dante says, to conceal for the moment the true object of his love, Beatrice denies him her greeting, constraining him as she does so to a fundamental re-thinking of the whole affective issue, to a fresh account of love's essential nature and finality. First, then, we have the tortured psychology of it all, the pain and perplexity engendered by love's endless paradoxes, by its promising so much and delivering so little:

> Appresso di questa soprascritta visione, avendo già dette le parole che Amore m'avea imposte a dire, mi cominciaro molti e diversi pensamenti a combattere ed a tentare, ciascuno quasi indefensibilemente; tra li quali pensamenti quattro mi parea che ingombrassero più lo riposo de la vita. L'uno de li quali era questo: buona è la signoria d'Amore, però che trae lo intendimento del suo fedele da tutte le vili cose. L'altro era questo: non buona è la signoria d'Amore, però che quanto lo suo fedele più fede li porta, tanto più gravi e dolorosi punti li conviene passare. L'altro era questo: lo nome d'Amore è sì dolce a udire, che impossibile mi pare che la sua propria operazione sia ne le più cose altro che dolce, con ciò sia cosa che li nomi seguitino le nominate cose, sì come è scritto: "Nomina sunt consequentia rerum". Lo quarto era questo: la donna per cui Amore ti stringe così, non è come l'altre donne, che leggeramente si muova dal suo cuore. E ciascuno mi combattea tanto, che mi facea stare quasi come colui che non sa per qual via pigli lo suo cammino, e che vuole andare e non sa onde se ne vada; e se io pensava di volere cercare una comune via di costoro, cioè là ove tutti s'accordassero, questa era via molto inimica verso me, cioè di chiamare e di mettermi ne le braccia de la Pietà.
>
> (*Vita nova* 13.1–6)[18]

---

[18] 'It was after this vision that, having written after the manner Love had commanded, varied thoughts began to contend and strive one with another within me, each of them just about unanswerable. Four in particular of them seemed most to disturb my peace of mind. One of them was this: Love's lordship is a good thing because he deters the mind of those who follow him faithfully from all unworthiness. Another was this: Love's governance is not good because the more faithful his follower, the greater the pain and misery he must endure. The third was as follows: the name love is so sweet to hear that—or so it seems to me—it is impossible that its general effect can be anything other than sweet, since in keeping with the formula "Names follow upon things themselves" it is well known that the name of a thing derives from what that thing is. The fourth was this: the lady through whom Love constrains you so is not like other ladies whose hearts are easily swayed. Each of these thought so contended within me, that I was like one uncertain of which road to take, like one anxious to set out but not knowing where to start. And if I cast about to see how they might after all be reconciled, some way, that is to say, in which they all might be made to agree, the only way I could see—abhorrent to me as it was—was to call upon Pity and throw myself into her arms.' Domenico de Robertis, 'Cavalcanti ovvero la non-Beatrice', in *Il libro della 'Vita nuova'*, 2nd ed. (Florence: Sansoni, 1970), 71–85; Peter Hainsworth, 'Cavalcanti in the *Vita Nuova*', *MLR* 83.3 (1988), 586–90; Robert M. Durling, 'Guido Cavalcanti and the *Vita Nova*', in *Guido Cavalcanti tra i suoi lettori. Proceedings of the International Symposium for the Seventh Centennial of His Death, New York 10–11 November 2000*, ed. Maria Louisa

—lines to which, as marking the *non plus ultra* of Dante's grief, we may add these
from chapter 14, lines registering the humiliation of being mocked, not simply by
his lady but by the substance of his own love-understanding, a situation from
which short of a fundamental restructuring of self on the plane of that same love-
understanding there can be no hope of return:

> Io dico che molte di queste donne, accorgendosi de la mia trasfigurazione,
> si cominciaro a maravigliare, e ragionando si gabbavano di me con questa
> gentilissima; onde lo ingannato amico di buona fede mi prese per la mano,
> e traendomi fuori de la veduta di queste donne, sì mi domandò che io
> avesse. Allora io, riposato alquanto, e resurressiti li morti spiriti miei, e li
> discacciati rivenuti a le loro possessioni, dissi a questo mio amico queste
> parole: 'Io tenni li piedi in quella parte de la vita di là da la quale non si puote
> ire più per intendimento di ritornare'.
>
> (Vita nova 14.7–8)[19]

But then, in the wake of catastrophe, and indeed as born of that catastrophe,
comes just such a moment of self-restructuring, a moment of fresh love-
intelligence conducive as such moments always are to a sense of emancipation,
to a freeing of self for a now more spacious humanity. True, the signposting hereabouts, if by 'signposting' we mean Dante's announcement in chapter 17 to the
effect that, having spoken enough of himself, he has it in mind to speak of something altogether more noble, is peremptory enough; but this is peremptoriness
with a purpose, peremptoriness designed to mark the difference, to signal the
eclipse of the old by the new:

> Poi che dissi questi tre sonetti, ne li quali parlai a questa donna però che
> fuoro narratori di tutto quasi lo mio stato, credendomi tacere e non dire più
> però che mi parea di me assai avere manifestato, avvegna che sempre poi

---

Ardizzone (Fiesole: Cadmo, 2003), 177–85. For the 'Pity my enemy' motif, Cristina Zampese, 'Pietà
nemica (*Vita nova* 13 [6])', in *"Meminisse iuvat": Studi in memoria di Violetta de Angelis*, ed. Filippo
Bognini (Pisa: ETS, 2012), 723–40.

19 'A good number of those women present, seeing the change that had come over me, were
overcome with astonishment, and, discussing it among themselves, they, together with this most
gracious lady, began mocking me; whereupon my friend, who though in good faith had been unwise
enough to bring me along, took me by the hand and led me from the sight of those women, enquiring
of me what was wrong, I for my part, having recovered myself a little and—together with those that
had been expelled but returned now to their rightful estate—revived my lifeless spirits, replying
thus: "I have set foot in that part of life beyond which there is no going with any hope of returning."'
Giorgio Bàrberi Squarotti, 'Interpretazione del "gabbo"', in *L'artificio dell'eternità* (Verona: Florini,
1972), 107–30; Michelangelo Picone, 'Modelli e struttura della *Vita Nuova*: L'episodio del "gabbo"',
Pacific Coast Philology 13 (1978), 71–77; Diego Sbacchi, 'Sull'episodio del gabbo', *RLI* 34.3 (2016),
197–204.

tacesse di dire a lei, a me convenne ripigliare matera nuova e più nobile che la passata. E però che la cagione de la nuova matera è dilettevole a udire, la dicerò, quanto potrò più brievemente.[20]

What comes next, then, as the point-about-which of Dante's entire meditation in the *Vita nova* is a sort of *sacra rappresentazione* designed by way precisely of its inwardness or moving in the depths to communicate a sense of love as a matter not of *having* but—by way of the substance and psychology of praise as a disposition of the spirit—of *becoming*, of knowing self in the now and henceforth transfigured substance of self:

Le donne erano molte, tra le quali n'avea certe che si rideano tra loro; altre v'erano che mi guardavano aspettando che io dovessi dire; altre v'erano che parlavano tra loro. De le quali una, volgendo li suoi occhi verso me e chiamandomi per nome, disse queste parole: 'A che fine ami tu questa tua donna, poi che tu non puoi sostenere la sua presenza? Dilloci, ché certo lo fine di cotale amore conviene che sia novissimo'. E poi che m'ebbe dette queste parole, non solamente ella, ma tutte l'altre cominciaro ad attendere in vista la mia risponsione. Allora dissi queste parole loro: 'Madonne, lo fine del mio amore fue già lo saluto di questa donna, forse di cui voi intendete, e in quello dimorava la beatitudine, ché era fine di tutti li miei desiderii. Ma poi che le piacque di negarlo a me, lo mio segnore Amore, la sua merzede, ha posto tutta la mia beatitudine in quello che non mi puote venire meno'. Allora queste donne cominciaro a parlare tra loro; e sì come talora vedemo cadere l'acqua mischiata di bella neve, così mi parea udire le loro parole uscire mischiate di sospiri. E poi che alquanto ebbero parlato tra loro, anche mi disse questa donna che m'avea prima parlato,

---

20 'With the composition of these three sonnets—sonnets addressed to this lady and informing her of my condition in just about its entirety—I thought it right then to hold my peace and say no more, for it seemed to me that, even though this meant no longer addressing her further, I had spoken sufficiently of myself, and that it was time now to broach a new and nobler theme than hitherto. And since the occasion of my lighting on this new theme is agreeable to the ear, I shall speak of it as briefly as I am able.' *Roman de la rose*, 39–41: 'La matire est et bone e neuve, / or doint Dex qu'en gré le receve / cele por qui je l'ai empris' (The matter is good and new, and may God grant that she for whom I have undertaken it may receive it with grace) and 2058–64: 'Bien les devise cist romanz; / qui amer veut, or i entende, / que li romanz des or amende. / Des or le fet bon escouter, / s'il est qui le sache conter, / car la fin dou songe est mout bele / et la matire en est novele' (They [the commandments of the God of Love] are well set out in this romance, and anyone aspiring to love should pay attention, for the romance from now on gets better and better. For now on, should there be anyone to recite it, it will be well worth listening to, for the end of the dream is very beautiful and the matter of it is new). Domenico de Robertis, 'La Nuova Materia', in *Il libro della 'Vita nuova'*, 2nd ed. (Florence: Sansoni, 1970), 86–128; Francesco Tateo, 'La "nuova matera" e la svolta critica della *Vita nuova*', in *Questioni di poetica dantesca* (Bari: Adriatica 1972), 27–50.

queste parole: 'Noi ti preghiamo che tu ne dichi ove sta questa tua beatitudine'. Ed io, rispondendo lei, dissi cotanto: 'In quelle parole che lodano
la donna mia'.

(*Vita nova* 18.3–6)[21]

More than ever accomplished in its commingling of the dialectical and of the
dramatic, of the idea pure and simple and of the mise-en-scène as the means of
its contemplation, the passage testifies also to the most complete kind of cultural
appropriation, to an interweaving of any number of cherished emphases for the
purposes of producing a now seamless garment. Everything is there, from the
Psalmist on the new song to Luke on the better part which cannot be taken away
and to Paul on the new creation; from Aristotle to Cicero on friendship as a matter
of disinterested concern; from Bernard to Aelred on love as its own reward and
on the sweet perfection of friendship properly understood; and from Boethius
to Jean de Meun on self-posession as distinct from possession pure and simple as
the basis of properly human happiness.[22] And it is this honouring of its each and

21 'The ladies were many, some laughing among themselves, others looking at me waiting to hear
what I would say, and others again talking among themselves. Of these, one, turning her eyes towards
me and calling me by name, spoke thus: "What, since you are unable to endure her presence, can be
the object of your love for this, your lady? Do tell us, since the aim of such love must indeed be very
strange," whereupon, having spoken these words, not only she but all the others seemed from their
expression to await my reply. I, then, addressed her thus: "My lady, the aim of my love was once that
lady's greeting—the lady whereof you perhaps know—and in that greeting dwelt my every blessedness,
the object in turn of my every desiring. But since she saw fit to deny me her greeting, my lord Love, in
his mercy, has placed all my happiness in that which cannot fail me." At this, those ladies began to speak
among themselves: and as we sometimes see beautiful flakes of snow mixed in with the rain as it falls,
so I seemed to hear their words mingled with sighs. And when they had spoken a while among themselves, the lady who had addressed me first spoke to me saying: "Tell us, we beg you, wherein lies your
blessedness." And I, in reply, said: "In those words praising my lady." '

22 Psalm 33:3: 'Cantate ei canticum novum' (Sing to the Lord a new song); Luke 10:42: 'Porre
unum est necessarium. Maria optimam partem elegit quae non auferetur ab ea' (But one thing only is
necessary. Mary has chosen the better part which shall not be taken from her); Romans 12:2: 'Et nolite
conformari huic saecolo, sed reformamini in novitate sensus vestri' (Do not conform any longer to the
pattern of the world, but be transformed by the renewing of your mind) and 2 Corinthians 5:17: 'Si qua
ergo in Christo nova creatura, vetera transierunt: ecce facta sunt omnia nova' (Therefore if anyone is
in Christ he is a new creation. The old has gone and the new is come); Aristotle, *Ethics* 8.3 (1156b6–10):
'Bonorum autem amicitia similiumque virtute perfecta est amicitia. Hi namque mutuo sibi bona similiter volunt quo boni sunt. Boni vero sunt per seipsos' (Perfect friendship is the friendship of men who
are good, and alike in excellence; for these wish well to each other qua good, and they are good in
themselves); Cicero, *De amicitia* 9.31: 'sic amicitiam non spe mercedis adducti, sed quod omnis eius
fructus in ipso amore inest, expetendam putamus' (so we believe that friendship is desirable, not because we are influenced by hope of gain, but because its entire profit is in the love itself); Bernard of
Clairvaux, *De diligendo Deo* 7: 'Affectus est, non contractus; nec acquiritur pacto, nec acquirit. Sponte
afficit, et spontaneum facit. Verus amor seipso contentus est' (Love is an affection, not a contract; it is
not acquired by arrangement, nor indeed acquired at all. It is spontaneous in origin and impulse, true
love being its own blessing); Aelred of Rievaulx, *De spirituali amicitia* 1 (PL 195, 666B): 'In ipsa namque
vera amicitia itur proficiendo, et fructus capitur perfectionis illius dulcedinem sentiendo' (For true

every cultural instance that prepares the way and indeed authorizes and irradiates the great praise poems of the text in all the now hymnic substance thereof; so, for example, we have these lines from *Donne ch'avete intelletto d'amore*, as delicately interrogatory as they are rapt in their contemplation of the exemplary presence of madonna:

> Dice di lei Amor: 'Cosa mortale
> come esser pò sì adorna e sì pura?'
> Poi la reguarda, e fra se stesso giura
> che Dio ne 'ntenda di far cosa nova.
> Color di perle ha quasi in forma, quale
> convene a donna aver, non for misura;
> ella è quanto de ben pò far natura;
> per esemplo di lei bieltà si prova.
> De li occhi suoi, come ch'ella li mova,
> escono spirti d'amore inflammati,
> che feron li occhi a qual che allor la guati,
> e passan sì che 'l cor ciascun retrova:
> voi le vedete Amor pinto nel viso,
> là 've non pote alcun mirarla fiso.

(*Donne ch'avete intelletto d'amore*, lines 43–56)[23]

—lines to which, as preeminent among the handmaidens of *Donne ch'avete*, we may add the again incomparable sonnet *Tanto gentile e tanto onesta pare*, incomparable not least for its settling—though ne'er so exquisitely—upon fear and trembling as the mood of human affectivity at its most sublime:

---

friendship advances by perfecting itself, and the fruit thereof is derived from feeling the sweetness of that perfection); Boethius, *De consolatione philosophiae* 2, prologue: 'Et cara tibi est fortuna praesens nec manendi fida et cum discesserit adlatura maerorem?' (And is that present fortune dear unto you, of whose stay you are not sure and whose departure will furnish your grief?); Jean de Meun, *Roman de la rose*, lines 5301–6; 'touz les biens que dedanz toi senz / et que si bien les connois enz, / qui te demeurent sanza cessier / si qu'il ne te peuent lessier / por fere a autre autel servise: / cist bient sunt tien a droite guise' (Whatever of worth you have within you and which you recognize as truly your own, and which remains always with you, never taking leave of you to enter another's service, that is rightly and properly yours).

23 'Of her Love says: "Whence this beauty and purity in a mortal being?" Then, looking upon her, he avows within him that God intends here a miracle. Pearl in complexion is she, but discreetly so as becomes a woman. She is the sum of everything of which nature is capable, and, exemplary as she is, the measure of all beauty whatever. Forth from her eyes wherever her gaze she bends come spirits flaming with the power of love, striking as they do so those eyes in turn gazing upon her and making their way within until the heart they find. Look and you will see love depicted upon her face, there where no man dare linger with his gaze.'

> Tanto gentile e tanto onesta pare
> la donna mia, quand'ella altrui saluta,
>   ch'ogne lingua deven tremando muta,
>   e li occhi no l'ardiscon di guardare.
>   Ella si va, sentendosi laudare,
>   benignamente d'umiltà vestuta;
>   e par che sia una cosa venuta
>   da cielo in terra a miracol mostrare.
>   Mostrasi sì piacente a chi la mira,
>   che dà per li occhi una dolcezza al core,
>   che 'ntender no la può chi non la prova;
>   e par che de la sua labbia si mova
>   un spirito soave pien d'amore,
>   che va dicendo a l'anima: Sospira.[24]

But for all the incomparability of *Tanto gentile e tanto onesta pare* as an instance of Dante's praise style in its now pure form there is still more to come, for by dint of a further inflexion of the spirit the hymnic at once shades off into the Christic, into a sense of Beatrice as something approaching the messianic fulfilment of everything so far on the plane of verse making in the vernacular. The key text here, notable not least for its now definitive location of the Cavalcantian vis-à-vis the Dantean (Cavalcanti's Giovanna being to Dante's Beatrice as but one making straight the way of the Lord), runs as follows:

io vidi venire verso me una gentile donna, la quale era di famosa bieltade, e fue già molto donna di questo primo mio amico. E lo nome di questa donna era Giovanna, salvo che per la sua bieltade, secondo che altri crede, imposto l'era nome Primavera; e così era chiamata. E appresso lei, guardando, vidi venire la mirabile Beatrice. Queste donne andaro presso di me così l'una appresso l'altra, e parve che Amore mi parlasse nel cuore, e dicesse: 'Quella prima è nominata Primavera solo per questa venuta d'oggi; ché io mossi lo imponitore del nome a chiamarla così Primavera, cioè prima verrà lo die che Beatrice si mosterrà dopo la imaginazione del suo fedele. E se anche vogli considerare lo primo nome suo, tanto è quanto dire "prima

---

24 'So noble and worthy appears my lady in greeting another that, trembling, every tongue falls silent and eyes dare not glance. Of her praise as sung she is aware, but graciously clothed as she is in humility, she goes her way, seeming as she does so to be a creature come down from heaven to earth to make known the miraculous. So beautiful she appears to those who gaze upon her that through the eyes she bestows upon the heart a sweetness such as none can understand but those who experience it; and from her lips seems to come forth a spirit, tender and full of love, a spirit addressing the soul and saying: "Sigh."'

verrà", però che lo suo nome Giovanna è da quello Giovanni lo quale pre-
cedette la verace luce, dicendo: "Ego vox clamantis in deserto: parate viam
Domini" '.

(*Vita nova* 24.3–4)[25]

Now here we have as always to be careful, for in pursuit of a general interpretation of the *Vita nova* there can be no question of fashioning from it a work of
specifically Christian piety, for within the economy of the whole the Christic,
called upon as it is to confirm and strengthen both the substance and the intensity
of Dante's solutions in the book, nonetheless serves the purposes of the courtly,
of the issues, that is to say, proper to a specific tradition of vernacular verse making. But for all that, the analogy is there and is there insistently, for as Dante
himself is at pains to make clear it is a question where Beatrice is concerned, not
merely of her Christ-like *presence* (the 'da cielo in terra a miracol mostrare' of
Tanto gentile e tanto onesta pare), but of her Christ-like *operation* (the 'ella mirabilemente operando' of 21.1), these between them, for all their falling short of identity as distinct from mere resemblance as a structure of consciousness, witnessing
nonetheless to a moment of experimentation at the far limits of notional and
expressive possibility.

Structures of consciousness and the Christic moment of chapter 24 notwithstanding, however, the *Vita nova* as a study in the better part which cannot be
taken away awaits its final denouement, death and the agony thereof now moving
centre stage as a necessary condition of that denouement. And here again Dante's
handling of yet a further complex phase of the argument is consummate, death
and the agony thereof seeking out and finding a place within the now more than

25 'I saw coming towards me a noble lady, one famous for her beauty and who had long since been
beloved of my closest friend. Her name was Giovanna, but because of her beauty she had as some say
been given the name Primavera, and was known as such. And as I watched I saw coming after her the
miraculous Beatrice. These ladies passed close by me one after the other, at which point Love seemed
to say in my heart: "The lady you see first is called Primavera, the name which I, with this very proces-
sion in mind, inspired in the one who first called her thus; for she it is who, on the day of Beatrice's
self-revelation hard upon the vision of her faithful servant, will precede her. And if, moreover, you give
heed to her real name, Giovanna, that also means *she who comes first*, since Giovanna comes from
Giovanni, the one who preceded the true light saying: *I am the voice of one crying in the wilderness: prepare the way of the Lord*." John 1:23: 'Ait: "Ego vox clamantis in deserto. Dirigite viam Domini,
sicut dixit Isaias propheta" ' (He replied in the words of Isaiah the prophet [Isaiah 40:3]: 'I am the voice
of one calling in the desert. Make straight the way for the Lord') and Matthew 3:3: 'Hic est etiam,
qui dictus est per Isaiam prophetam dicentem: Vox clamantis in deserto: Parate viam Domini; rectas
facite semitas ejus' (This is he who was spoken of through the prophet Isaiah, a voice of one calling
in the desert: 'Prepare the way for the Lord, make straight the paths for him'). Lloyd Howard,
'Giovanna as John the Baptist and the "disdegno" of Guido', *QItal* 2.1 (1981), 63–70; Alberto Gessani,
'La "dedica" a Cavalcanti della *Vita nuova*: Giovanna e Beatrice', in *Dante, Guido Cavalcanti, e l'amoroso
regno* (Macerata: Quodlibet, 2004), 89–104; Enrico Malato, *Dante e Guido Cavalcanti: Il dissidio per la
'Vita nuova' e il "disdegno" di Guido*, 2nd ed. (Rome: Salerno, 2004).

ever adult economy of love-understanding. Already, then, before ever the praise
moment of the text reaches its apogee in the canzone *Donne ch'avete intelletto
d'amore* and its retinue in the *Vita nova* intimations of death intervene to secure
the notion of love as a disposition of the spirit equal to the contingencies thereof,
to every eventuality on the plane, so to speak, of the horizontal. First, then, comes
the death of Beatrice's father in chapter 22, an eventuality to be sure on the plane
of the horizontal but for all that fully functional within the thematic economy of
the whole:

> E con ciò sia cosa che, secondo l'usanza de la sopradetta cittade, donne con
> donne e uomini con uomini s'adunino a cotale tristizia, molte donne
> s'adunaro colà dove questa Beatrice piangea pietosamente; onde io veg-
> gendo ritornare alquante donne da lei, udio dicere loro parole di questa
> gentilissima, com'ella si lamentava; tra le quali parole udio che diceano:
> 'Certo ella piange sì, che quale la mirasse doverebbe morire di pietade'. Al-
> lora trapassaro queste donne; e io rimasi in tanta tristizia, che alcuna la-
> grima talora bagnava la mia faccia, onde io mi ricopria con porre le mani
> spesso a li miei occhi; e se non fosse ch'io attendea audire anche di lei, però
> ch'io era in luogo onde se ne giano la maggior parte di quelle donne che da
> lei si partiano, io mi sarei nascoso incontanente che le lagrime m'aveano
> assalito.
>
> (*Vita nova* 22.3–4)[26]

But then, and in consequence of an as yet mere insinuation of the idea, of its
subsisting somewhere on the edge of awareness, comes the death of Beatrice
herself, at which point the equality of love to the forces now ranged over and
against it is called definitively into question. And Dante's response to that question? First, and in advance of the event, a fevered sense of the inevitability of it
all, of death generally and thus of Beatrice's death in particular as but a parameter
both of living and of loving in the actuality thereof:

---

26 'Since it is the custom of the aforesaid city for women to foregather with women, and men with
men, on such sad occasions, a good number of women met together there where Beatrice was most
piteously weeping; whereupon I, seeing some of them making their way back, heard them talking
among themselves of how she mourned, and of what they were saying I was able to make out the following: "Such indeed is her weeping that simply to see her would be to die of compassion." With this,
they went their way, I for my part, however, being so overcome with sadness that tears flowed from my
eyes, whence I repeatedly covered them with my hands. And were it not that I awaited further news of
my lady (for most of the women, in taking their leave of her, would come my way) I would have hidden
myself away for the grief which had overtaken me.' Arshi Pipa, 'Personaggi della *Vita Nuova*: Dante,
Cavalcanti e la famiglia Portinari', *Italica* 62 (1985), 99–115; Louis Green, ' "Bono in alto grado" (*V.N.*
XXII, 2): Beatrice's Father, Nobility and the Nobility in Dante's Florence', in *"La gloriosa donna de la
mente": A Commentary on the 'Vita Nuova'*, ed. Vincent Moleta (Florence: Olschki, 1994), 97–117.

Appresso ciò per pochi dì, avvenne che in alcuna parte de la mia persona mi giunse una dolorosa infermitade, onde io continuamente soffersi per nove dì amarissima pena; la quale mi condusse a tanta debolezza, che me convenia stare come coloro li quali non si possono muovere. Io dico che ne lo nono giorno, sentendome dolere quasi intollerabilemente, a me giunse uno pensero, lo quale era de la mia donna. E quando ei pensato alquanto di lei, ed io ritornai pensando a la mia debilitata vita; e veggendo come leggero era lo suo durare, ancora che sana fosse, sì cominciai a piangere fra me stesso di tanta miseria. Onde, sospirando forte, dicea fra me medesimo: 'Di necessitade convene che la gentilissima Beatrice alcuna volta si muoia'.

(*Vita nova* 23.1–3)[27]

But then, and following on now from the event, a curious passing by on the other side, or rather—for this now is nearer the mark—three things: namely (*a*) a quotation from the book of Lamentations registering a state of universal or at any rate citywide suffering; (*b*) an oddly lapidary reference to Beatrice's death, Dante, he says, being at the time otherwise engaged; and (*c*) three reasons why it would not be appropriate for him to dwell further upon the circumstances of her passing, of which the first, bearing as it does on the fundamental nature of his undertaking in the *Vita nova*, is the weightiest. For as he himself says on the threshold of the book, Dante's, in the *Vita nova*, is an essay first and foremost in significance, the event itself figuring only to the extent that it speaks upon reflection of its own innermost meaning, of its indispensability to an itinerary of the spirit. This, then, inasmuch as it is a looking away or a passing by on the other side, is a looking away or passing by on the other side of a special kind, a diverting of attention to what actually matters about it all—to wit, the equality of love properly understood even to the greatest of its misfortunes:

---

27 'It happened a few days after this that I was in a certain part of my body sorely afflicted, my pain being such that for a good nine days I was drained of all energy and obliged to lie still like one unable to move. Then on the ninth day, suffering as I was intolerably, a thought came to me of my lady. And when I had reflected on her for a while, I fell to thinking again about my own enfeebled existence, and, pondering its ephemerality even in the best of circumstances, I began weeping at the wretchedness of it all; whence, sighing deeply, I said to myself: "One day, but of necessity, the noble Beatrice too will have to die."' Bortolo Martinelli, 'Il presagio della morte di Beatrice: "Donna pietosa e di novella etate"', in *Da Dante a Pascoli: Letture di testi esemplari della lirica italiana*, ed. Paola Paganuzzi (Brescia: Cooperativa Cattolico-Democratica di Cultura, 1994), 33–62; Stefano Carrai, 'I segni premonitori della morte di Beatrice nella *Vita Nova*', in *I sogni e la scienza nella letteratura italiana. Atti del Convegno di Siena, 16–18 novembre 2006*, ed. Natascia Tonelli (Pisa: Pacini, 2008), 49–58; Noemi Ghetti, ' "Ben converrà che la mia donna mora": La guarigione dalla malattia d'amore', in *L'ombra di Cavalcanti* (Rome: L'Asino d'oro edizioni, 2010), 121–30; Mira Mocan, 'Una morte "necessaria"', in *L'arca della mente: Riccardo di San Vittore nella 'Commedia'* (Florence: Olschki, 2012), 33–52.

Quomodo sedet sola civitas plena populo! facta est quasi vidua domina gentium. Io era nel proponimento ancora di questa canzone, e compiuta n'avea questa soprascritta stanzia, quando lo segnore de la giustizia chiamoe questa gentilissima a gloriare sotto la insegna di quella regina benedetta virgo Maria, lo cui nome fue in grandissima reverenzia ne le parole di questa Beatrice beata. E avvegna che forse piacerebbe a presente trattare alquanto de la sua partita da noi, non è lo mio intendimento di trattarne qui per tre ragioni: la prima è che ciò non è del presente proposito, se volemo guardare nel proemio che precede questo libello; la seconda si è che, posto che fosse del presente proposito, ancora non sarebbe sufficiente la mia lingua a trattare come si converrebbe di ciò; la terza si è che, posto che fosse l'uno e l'altro, non è convenevole a me trattare di ciò, per quello che, trattando, converrebbe essere me laudatore di me medesimo, la quale cosa è al postutto biasimevole a chi lo fae: e però lascio cotale trattato ad altro chiosatore.

(Vita nova 28.1–2)[28]

But the equality of love properly understood even to the greatest of its misfortunes does not rule out the difficulty of that love, the challenge represented in Dante's case by the alternative possibility, by, more exactly, the 'donna gentile' or gracious lady of the casement who looks piteously upon the lover in his loss. But here again we need to be careful, for this is by no means a matter of surrogate affection, of Dante's merely seeking out another woman to take Beatrice's place;

---

28 *'How doth the city sit solitary, that was full of people. How is she become a widow!* [Lamentations 1:1] I was busy composing this canzone and had just completed the above stanza, when the lord of all justice called this most gracious of women to glory under the insignia of that queen, the Blessed Virgin Mary, whose name was forever, and with the greatest reverence, upon the lips of the blessed Beatrice. And although it might perhaps be welcome were I at present to say something of her departure from us, it is not my intention here so to do, and this for three reasons: the first is that, for anyone caring to look back to the preface of this my little book, to speak thus of Beatrice's departure is no part of my present purpose; the second is this, that even if it were part of my present purpose, no words of mine would be adequate to do the matter proper justice; and the third is that, even if neither the one nor the other of these things were so, it would not be fitting for me to discuss this since it would of necessity be to heap praise upon myself, than which nothing is more reprehensible. I therefore leave this for another to comment on.' Salvatore Accardo, 'Morte di Beatrice e trasfigurazione: *Vita Nuova*, XVIII–XLII', in *Capitoli danteschi* (Rome: Bonacci, 1976), 21–38; Charles S. Singleton, 'La morte di Beatrice', in *La 'Vita Nuova': Il Paradiso Terrestre; Saggi e testi*, ed. Marziano Guglielminetti et al. (Turin: Il Segnalibro, 1992), 66–73; Roberto Antonelli, 'La morte di Beatrice e la struttura della storia', in *Beatrice nell'opera di Dante e nella memoria europea 1290–1990. Atti del convegno internazionale 10–14 dicembre 1990*, ed. Mario Picchio Simonelli (Florence: Cadmo, 1994), 35–56. Also, Mirko Tavoni, '"Converrebbe essere me laudatore di me medesimo" (*Vita Nuova* XXVIII 2)', in *Studi in onore di Pier Vincenzo Mengaldo per i suoi settant'anni*, vol. 1, edited by his students in Padua (Florence: Edizioni del Galluzzo, 2007), 253–61; Francesco Zambon, 'La terza "ragione" del silenzio di Dante sulla morte di Beatrice', in *Mimesis: L'eredità di Auerbach. Atti del XXV Convegno Interuniversitario, Bressanone/Innsbruck, 5–8 luglio 2007*, ed. Ivano Paccagnella et al. (Padua: Esedra, 2009), 177–84.

for it is clear from the text that this after all is a question not of replacement but of recovery, of Dante's discerning in the kindly countenance and fair complexion of the 'donna gentile' a way back to Beatrice, a means even now of sidestepping death as part and parcel of what it means to live and to love well. First, then, in what amounts within the economy of the *Vita nova* as a whole to a carefully structured critique of *seeing* as a necessary condition of *loving*—of the 'amor est passio quaedam innata procedens ex visione' formula woven so deeply into the fabric of occitanic and neo-occitanic verse making—comes the preliminary encounter, an encounter, however, apt by way of the compassion poured out upon him merely to deepen his sadness and to quicken his tears:

> Poi per alquanto tempo, con ciò fosse cosa che io fosse in parte ne la quale mi ricordava del passato tempo, molto stava pensoso, e con dolorosi pensamenti, tanto che mi faceano parere de fore una vista di terribile sbigottimento. Onde io, accorgendomi del mio travagliare, levai li occhi per vedere se altri mi vedesse. Allora vidi una gentile donna giovane e bella molto, la quale da una finestra mi riguardava sì pietosamente, quanto a la vista, che tutta la pietà parea in lei accolta. Onde, con ciò sia cosa che quando li miseri veggiono di loro compassione altrui, più tosto si muovono a lagrimare, quasi come di se stessi avendo pietade, io senti' allora cominciare li miei occhi a volere piangere; e però, temendo di non mostrare la mia vile vita, mi partio dinanzi da li occhi di questa gentile.
>
> (*Vita nova* 35.1–3)[29]

—but then, hard on the heels of that encounter, and no less exquisitely (for here again it is a question of the nicely calibrated psychology of it all), comes its func-

---

29 'Since but a little later I happened to be in a place calling to mind past times, I stood there lost in thought, my outward aspect, in consequence of my now grievous state of mind, being one of deep distress. Conscious of this my suffering, I looked around to see if anyone else was likewise aware of it, whereupon I saw a noble and very lovely young woman looking so compassionately upon me that she seemed to be compassion incarnate. And just as, sensing the sympathy of those round about them, the wretched (almost as though having compassion upon themselves) are all the more ready to weep, so I felt my eyes brimming with tears; and so, fearing lest I reveal anything more of my own wretchedness, I departed from her sight.' Giorgio Petrocchi, 'La donna gentile', in *L'ultima dea* (Rome: Bonacci, 1977), 97–104; Antonio D'Andrea, 'Dante interprete di se stesso: Le varianti ermeneutiche della *Vita Nuova* e la "donna gentile"', in *Miscellanea di studi in onore di Aurelio Ronacglia a cinquanta anni dalla sua laurea*, vol. 2, ed. Roberto Antonelli (Modena: Mucchi, 1989), 493–506; Christine Gosselin, 'The Shape of Things to Come: Dante and the "donne" of the *Vita Nuova*', *The Italianist* 15 (1995), 5–28; Gennaro Sasso, 'La "donna gentile" nella *Vita nuova* e nel *Convivio*', in *Le autobiografie di Dante* (Naples: Bibliopolis, 2008), 15–62 (with 'La polarità di Beatrice e della donna gentile' at 75–83); Friedrich Wolfzettel, ' "Io vidi venire verso me una gentile donna": Zur Dramaturgie des Sehens in der *Vita Nuova*', *DDJ* 89 (2014), 141–55; Nicolò Mineo, 'L'apparizione della "donna gentile"', in *Dante dalla "mirabile visione" a "l'altro viaggio": Tra 'Vita Nova' e 'Divina Commedia'* (Ravenna: Longo, 2016), 31–39.

tion as a means of gazing once more upon Beatrice in the flesh and thus, somewhere in the recesses, of spiritual retreat:

> Avvenne poi che là ovunque questa donna mi vedea, sì si facea d'una vista pietosa e d'un colore palido quasi come d'amore; onde molte fiate mi ricordava de la mia nobilissima donna, che di simile colore si mostrava tuttavia. E certo molte volte non potendo lagrimare né disfogare la mia tristizia, io andava per vedere questa pietosa donna, la quale parea che tirasse le lagrime fuori de li miei occhi per la sua vista.
>
> (*Vita nova* 36.1–2)[30]

But urged as it is upon the lover from out of the depths, yearning for what once was but is no longer now commends itself (for such yet again is the exquisitely calibrated psychology of it all) as a matter for misgiving, what follows, therefore, being a fulsome indictment of the eyes as but a principle of forgetfulness—of blessing, yes, but beyond that of betrayal:

> Io venni a tanto per la vista di questa donna, che li miei occhi si cominciaro a dilettare troppo di vederla; onde molte volte me ne crucciava nel mio cuore, ed aveamene per vile assai. Onde più volte bestemmiava la vanitate de li occhi miei, e dicea loro nel mio pensero: 'Or voi solavate fare piangere chi vedea la vostra dolorosa condizione, ed ora pare che vogliate dimenticarlo per questa donna che vi mira; che non mira voi, se non in quanto le pesa de la gloriosa donna di cui piangere solete; ma quanto potete fate, ché io la vi pur rimembrerò molto spesso, maladetti occhi, ché mai, se non dopo la morte, non dovrebbero le vostre lagrime avere restate'.
>
> (*Vita nova* 37.1–2)[31]

---

30 'And so it happened that whenever this lady saw me, her face grew pale and pitying as though from love, something which reminded me of my own most noble lady, who used to look at me in the same way. Not being able, then, to weep or express my grief, I would for this reason go to see this lady, simply to see the one who seemed capable of drawing tears from my eyes.'

31 'The sight of this lady began to have such an effect on me that my eyes began to delight too much in seeing her, whence, frequently taking myself to task within me, I held myself on this account to be the basest of men. Time and again I cursed the fickleness of my eyes, addressing them thus in conscience: "It was not long since you made those looking upon you weep for your sorrowful state, but now it seems that all you want is to put it out of your mind for this woman who gazes upon you, but this only insofar as she grieves for the now glorious lady for whom you yourself once wept. But have your own way, accursed eyes of mine, for I forever will remind you of her, your tears knowing of necessity no respite this side of death."' Corrado Calenda, 'L'amore e gli amori, la donna e le donne, "costanza de le la ragione" e "vanitate de li occhi": Significato e valore di un persorso non lineare', in *Ortodossia ed eterodossia in Dante Alighieri. Atti del convegno di Madrid, 5–7 novembre 2012*, ed. Carlota Cattermole et al. (Madrid: Ediciones de la Discreta, 2014), 489–505.

Here, then, following on in the wake of the infernal moment of the *Vita nova*, of the soul's knowing itself only in the agony of love under the aspect of acquisition, comes its purgatorial moment, the moment in which, clear-sightedness notwithstanding, the lover knows himself only in the difficulty of it all, in the endlessly embattled condition of the albeit willing spirit. But with what amounts in the episode of the 'donna gentile' to a fresh and more than ever ferocious instance of self-confrontation, of squaring up to self in the innermost parts of self, it only remains to put on record the paradisal moment of it all: to register the miraculous vision whereby he was at last rescued from the *waywardness* of his eyes; to confirm by way of the notion of pilgrimage that of human being in the round as but a matter of love-journeying; and to commit himself to a more adequate account of Beatrice and of the Beatrician as and when he feels more properly able to do so. With respect, then, to the first of these things we have the following lines from the beginning of chapter 39 on the poet's fresh vision of Beatrice in glory as that whereby he is at last confirmed in his equality to everything within him standing over and against right reason:

Contra questo avversario de la ragione si levoe un die, quasi ne l'ora de la nona, una forte imaginazione in me; che mi parve vedere questa gloriosa Beatrice con quelle vestimenta sanguigne co le quali apparve prima a li occhi miei; e pareami giovane in simile etade in quale io prima la vidi. Allora cominciai a pensare di lei; e ricordandomi di lei secondo l'ordine del tempo passato, lo mio cuore cominciò dolorosamente a pentere de lo desiderio a cui sì vilmente s'avea lasciato possedere alquanti die contra la costanzia de la ragione; e discacciato questo cotale malvagio desiderio, sì si rivolsero tutti li miei pensamenti a la loro gentilissima Beatrice. E dico che d'allora innanzi cominciai a pensare di lei sì con tutto lo vergognoso cuore, che li sospiri manifestavano ciò molte volte; però che tutti quasi diceano nel loro uscire quello che nel cuore si ragionava, cioè lo nome di quella gentilissima, e come si partìo da noi.[32]

---

32 'Over and against this adversary of reason, there arose within me one day, at about the ninth hour, a mighty vision in which, clothed in the crimson dress in which she had first appeared to me and seeming as young as young as when we first met, I beheld Beatrice in glory; whence I began thinking of her, and, recalling her thus in the order of time passing, I began in my heart, with much sorrowing, to repent of the desire to which, despite the steady insistence of reason, I had delivered it. But now, with the expulsion of this wretched desire, my every thought turned back upon this, my most gracious Beatrice. From that moment on, I say, I began to think on her with such shame in my heart that my every sigh spoke of it, just about every one of them bearing witness to its innermost utterance, to wit, the name of that most noble of women and the manner of her departure.' Donato Pirovano, ' "Contra questo avversario de la ragione": Dante, *Vita Nuova* XXXIX, e Guido Cavalcanti, *Rime* XV', in *"Per beneficio e concordia di studio": Studi danteschi offerti a Enrico Malato per i suoi ottant'anni*, ed. Andrea Mazzucchi (Cittadella [PD]: Bertoncello Artigrafiche, 2015), 755–67.

while, with respect to the second of them we have these from the following chapter confirming by way of the pilgrims passing through Florence on their way to Rome the notion of spiritual wayfaring as but the deep substance of the *Vita nova* in the round:

> Dopo questa tribulazione avvenne, in quello tempo che molta gente va per vedere quella imagine benedetta la quale Iesu Cristo lasciò a noi per esemplo de la sua bellissima figura, la quale vede la mia donna gloriosamente, che alquanti peregrini passavano per una via la quale è quasi mezzo de la cittade ove nacque e vivette e morìo la gentilissima donna. Li quali peregrini andavano, secondo che mi parve, molto pensosi; ond'io pensando a loro, dissi fra me medesimo: 'Questi peregrini mi paiono di lontana parte, e non credo che anche udissero parlare di questa donna, e non ne sanno neente; anzi li loro penseri sono d'altre cose che di queste qui, ché forse pensano de li loro amici lontani, li quali noi non conoscemo'. Poi dicea fra me medesimo: 'Io so che s'elli fossero di propinquo paese, in alcuna vista parrebbero turbati passando per lo mezzo de la dolorosa cittade'. Poi dicea fra me medesimo: 'Se io li potesse tenere alquanto, io li pur farei piangere anzi ch'elli uscissero di questa cittade, però che io direi parole le quali farebbero piangere chiunque le intendesse'.
>
> (*Vita nova* 40.1–4)[33]

and with respect to the third of them—the ascendancy of silence over saying as, for the moment at least, the better part—we have these from the very end of the book, with, in the final period, a doxology as finely tuned as any upon the lips of a neocourtly poet:

---

33 'It so happened that, in the wake of this sorrowing and at that time of the year when many make their way to see the blessed likeness which Christ Jesus left us as an instance of his beautiful countenance (the countenance upon which even now my lady gazes in glory), some of their pilgrim number were passing along the way running just about through the centre of the city wherein the noblest of women was born, lived and died. They made their way, or so it seemed to me, deep in thought, whereupon, thinking of them, I said to myself: "These, it seems, are pilgrims from a far-off place such that, as I believe, they cannot have heard of that lady. Knowing nothing of her, their thoughts must be of things other than those living here, thoughts, perhaps, of distant friends, friends of whom we here know nothing." Then again I said to myself: "I know that if they were indeed from somewhere nearby they too, as they made their way through the middle of this city in mourning, would likewise appear distressed," saying further to myself: "If then I could detain them but for a moment I would cause them likewise to weep before departing the city, for I would speak unto them words apt to cause any hearing them to weep."' Michelangelo Picone, '*Peregrinus Amoris*: La metafora finale', in *Vita nuova e tradizione romanza* (Padua: Liviana Editrice, 1979), 129–92; Bruno Basile, 'Il viaggio come archetipo: Note sul tema della "Peregrinatio" in Dante', *LC* 15 (1986), 9–26. More generally, Gerhart B. Ladner, '*Homo viator*: Medieval Ideas on Alienation and Order', *Spec* 42 (1967), 233–59; Frank Cook Gardiner, *The Pilgrimage of Desire: A Study of Theme and Genre in Medieval Literature* (Leiden: Brill, 1971).

Appresso questo sonetto, apparve a me una mirabile visione, ne la quale io vidi cose che mi fecero proporre di non dire più di questa benedetta, infino a tanto che io potesse più degnamente trattare di lei. E di venire a ciò io studio quanto posso, sì com'ella sae veracemente. Sì che, se piacere sarà di colui a cui tutte le cose vivono, che la mia vita duri per alquanti anni, io spero di dicer di lei quello che mai non fue detto d'alcuna. E poi piaccia a colui che è sire de la cortesia, che la mia anima se ne possa gire a vedere la gloria de la sua donna, cioè di quella benedetta Beatrice, la quale gloriosamente mira ne la faccia di colui *qui est per omnia secula benedictus.*

(*Vita nova* 42)[34]

In fact, by the time of the *Vita nova* as postdating Beatrice's death by perhaps three or four years, Dante had already been busy about redefining the shape and substance of his existence as a poet and philosopher, though along lines quite other now than Beatrice and the Beatrician, Beatrice and the Beatrician pertaining for a season at least less to the human than to the more-than-human (the 'più che umana' of *Convivio* 2.8.6).[35] For all that, though, a moment, in the *Vita nova*, of perfect self-possession, of knowing self, paradisally, in the perfect resolution of self.

CONCLUSION: NEW LIFE AND A *COMMEDIA A MINORE*

The *Vita nova*, encompassing as it does its leading concerns in a single pass of the mind and imagination, defies quick and easy interpretation, each of these con-

---

34 'After writing this sonnet a miraculous vision appeared to me, the contents of which made me determined to speak no further of this blessed lady until such time as I could do so more worthily. And as she herself well knows I am studying as hard as I can so that, should it please him by whom all things have life and breath that I myself live on a while, I hope to speak of her in a way no woman has ever been spoken of before. Whereafter, may it please him who is gracious above all, that my soul might behold the glory of its lady, that is, of that blessed Beatrice, who looks gloriously on the face of the One *who is throughout all ages blessed.*' Étienne Gilson, 'La Mirabil Visione', in *Dante e Béatrice* (Paris: Vrin, 1974), 103–17; Colin Hardie, 'Dante's "mirabile visione" (*Vita Nuova* xlii)', in *The World of Dante: Essays on Dante and His Times*, ed. Cecil Grayson (Oxford: Clarendon Press, 1980), 123–45; Alberto Casadei, 'La "mirabile visione" nel finale della *Vita nova*', *Italianistica* 44.2 (2015), 15–20; Nicolò Mineo, *Dante dalla "mirabile visione" a "l'altro viaggio": Tra 'Vita Nova' e 'Divina Commedia'* (Ravenna: Longo, 2016).

35 *Convivio* 2.8.7: 'Ma però che de la immortalità de l'anima è qui toccato, farò una digressione, ragionando di quella; perché, di quella ragionando, sarà bello terminare lo parlare di quella viva Beatrice beata, de la quale più parlare in questo libro non intendo per proponimento' (But since we have here touched upon immortality, I shall by way of parenthesis say a little more of it, this in turn furnishing a way of bringing to a fitting close my speaking here of the living and blessed Beatrice, of the one, that is to say, of whom I propose to say no more in this book).

cerns indwelling the other and in turn being indwelt by it. On the one hand, then, there is the affective-philosophical aspect of the book, love, once properly understood, constituting for the Dante of the *Vita nova* no less than for the Dante of the *Commedia* a principle—*the* principle—of properly human being and becoming, that whereby the individual attentive to the finality of his or her properly human presence in the world lays hold of that finality in all its ecstatic substance. On the other hand, there is the literary-aesthetic aspect of the book, its gathering in of the first fruits of Dante's activity so far as a poet and philosopher of love with a view to confirming the triumph of form—of the twofold musical and rhetorical complexion of the line—as that whereby the properties of selfhood are raised above the threshold of consciousness and proposed as an object of contemplation. True, the argument as it stands, especially in its Beatrician aspect, is as Dante himself acknowledges open-ended, susceptible to refinement by way of a still greater maturity in the flame of love; but for all its living on in anticipation of more to come the *Vita nova* wants for nothing in point either of clear-sightedness or of conviction, of equality to its own deep reasons.

But that is not all, for living on as it does in anticipation of more to come—and this in point both of the affective-philosophical and of the literary-aesthetic aspects of the text—we have here, at a still deeper level of awareness, a *Commedia avant la lettre*, a *Commedia a minore*, to be sure, but nonetheless a *Commedia* in everything but name. For all the particularity, in other words, of its cultural premises (Siculo-Tuscan and stilnovistic as variously nuanced by way of the Neo-Ciceronian and the Boethian), we have here a text that offers an account of the poet's presence in the world under the aspect of captivity, of emancipation and of emergence—of, precisely, the *infernal*, the *purgatorial* and the *paradisal*. First, then, comes its infernal moment, 'infernal' in its sense of the confused and darkling character of it all, of knowing self only in the impossibly conflicted character of self; so, for example, these lines from the embattled thirteenth chapter of the book, an essay, precisely, in pain, in perplexity and in knowing no longer which way to look:

> Appresso di questa soprascritta visione, avendo già dette le parole che Amore m'avea imposte a dire, mi cominciaro molti e diversi pensamenti a combattere ed a tentare, ciascuno quasi indefensibilemente; tra li quali pensamenti quattro mi parea che ingombrassero più lo riposo de la vita. L'uno de li quali era questo: buona è la signoria d'Amore, però che trae lo intendimento del suo fedele da tutte le vili cose. L'altro era questo: non buona è la signoria d'Amore, però che quanto lo suo fedele più fede li porta, tanto più gravi e dolorosi punti li conviene passare. L'altro era questo: lo nome d'Amore è sì dolce a udire, che impossibile mi pare che la sua propria operazione sia ne le più cose altro che dolce, con ciò sia cosa

che li nomi sèguitino le nominate cose, sì come è scritto: "Nomina sunt consequentia rerum". Lo quarto era questo: la donna per cui Amore ti stringe così, non è come l'altre donne, che leggermente si muova del suo cuore. E ciascuno mi combattea tanto, che mi facea stare quasi come colui che non sa per qual via pigli lo suo cammino, e che vuole andare e non sa onde se ne vada.

(Vita nova 13.1–6)³⁶

The situation is recognizably infernal in respect, not only of its phenomenology (of the moods, that is to say, of fear, confusion, inexplicability and despair generated, precisely, by this sense of the impossibility of it all), but of its deep structure; for here as in the *Inferno* on the as yet far horizon, it is a question of all this as referable to the centrality of self to its own universe, and, in consequence of this centrality, to its seeing the world under the aspect only of availability and ingratiation. True, it is hardly a question here in the *Vita nova* of the kind of self-centrality whereby, present to itself by way less of love than of lovelessness, the creature rises up against the creator, for here in the *Vita nova* it is a question merely of the 'saluto', of what accrues to the lover by way of madonna's graciousness towards him. But for all that, it *is*, in this early phase of the *libello*, a question of self-centrality, of love as seeking its own, and thus of the lover as knowing himself in the psychopathology thereof, in the near-nothingness of self as victim to love under the aspect of acquisition:

Appresso ciò che io dissi questo sonetto, mi mosse una volontade di dire anche parole, ne le quali io dicesse quattro cose ancora sopra lo mio stato, le quali non mi parea che fossero manifestate ancora per me. La prima de le quali si è che molte volte io mi dolea, quando a mia memoria movesse la fantasia ad imaginare quale Amore mi facea. La seconda si è che Amore spesse volte di subito m'assalia sì forte, che 'n me non rimanea altro di vita se non un pensero che parlava di questa donna. La terza si è che quando questa

36 'After this vision, and having by now set down the words that Love had bid me write, many different thoughts began to strive mightily within me, each of them, as it were, invincible. Of these, four seemed in particular to disturb my peace of mind. One was this: Love's dominion is good in that he dissuades the faithful from willing evil. The next was this: Love's dominion is not good since the greater his servant's faith in him the more grievous and painful the sorrow he must endure. The third was this: so sweet is Love's name to the ear, that his doings, or so it seems to me, can themselves be no other than sweet, since, as has been recorded, names derive from the things named ("Nomina sunt consequentia rerum"). The fourth was this: the lady by way of whom Love so constrains you is not like other ladies whose hearts are easily swayed. And each of these thoughts so contended within me, that I was like one who knows not which road to take, who wishes to set out but knows not which way to go.' Antonino Pagliaro, 'Nomina sunt consequentia rerum', in *Nuovi saggi di critica semantica* (Messina: G. d'Anna, 1956), 7–34.

battaglia d'Amore mi pugnava così, io mi movea quasi discolorito tutto per vedere questa donna, credendo che mi difendesse la sua veduta da questa battaglia, dimenticando quello che per appropinquare a tanta gentilezza m'addivenia. La quarta si è come cotale veduta non solamente non mi difendea, ma finalmente disconfiggea la mia poca vita.

(Vita nova 16.1–5)[37]

Here, however, as in the *Commedia* as but a still more sublime essay in the nature of human experience as a matter of spiritual journeying, homecoming is by way of the purgatoriality of it all, of the moment represented in the *Vita nova* by the life-and-death struggle of its protagonist to embrace and to live out a now revised understanding of love as but the in-and-through-which of the soul's proper coming forth—of its butterfly-emergence—on the plane of properly human being. Here, then, as upon the mountain, we witness the tears of one who finds himself by way only of the sorrowing of self:

Contra questo avversario de la ragione si levoe un die, quasi ne l'ora de la nona, una forte imaginazione in me, che mi parve vedere questa gloriosa Beatrice con quelle vestimenta sanguigne co le quali apparve prima a li occhi miei; e pareami giovane in simile etade in quale io prima la vidi. Allora cominciai a pensare di lei; e ricordandomi di lei secondo l'ordine del tempo passato, lo mio cuore cominciò dolorosamente a pentere de lo desiderio a cui sì vilmente s'avea lasciato possedere alquanti die contra la costanzia de la ragione; e discacciato questo cotale malvagio desiderio, sì si rivolsero tutti li miei pensamenti a la loro gentilissima Beatrice. E dico che d'allora innanzi cominciai a pensare di lei sì con tutto lo vergognoso cuore, che li sospiri manifestavano ciò molte volte; però che tutti quasi diceano nel loro uscire quello che nel cuore si ragionava, cioè lo nome di quella gentilissima, e come si partìo da noi . . . Per questo raccendimento de' sospiri si raccese lo sollenato lagrimare, in guisa che li miei occhi pareano due cose che desiderassero pur di piangere; e spesso avvenia che per lo lungo continuare del pianto, dintorno loro si facea uno colore purpureo, lo quale suole apparire

37 'No sooner had I finished writing this sonnet than the wish came over me to write yet another in which I would say four more things about my condition, things which it seemed to me I had not yet made clear. The first of these was that, whenever I called to mind and thought over afresh Love's treatment of me, I was sore distressed. The second was that Love so often and so savagely set about me that—other than those thoughts speaking of my lady—nothing within me was left alive. The third was that when Love thus assailed me, I, believing that to catch sight of her would ward off this attack, felt constrained even so—pallid as I was and oblivious to what always happened whenever I approached her in all her graciousness—to seek her out. The fourth is how that same glimpse of her not only failed to defend me but did away with what little life remained to me.'

per alcuno martirio che altri riceva. Onde appare che de la loro vanitade
fuoro degnamente guiderdonati.

(*Vita nova* 39.1–5)[38]

The pattern, then, is recognizably purgatorial, purgatory, in Dante's sense of it,
having everything to do with the kind of soul-sorrowing whereby each successive
inflexion of the spirit is brought home to the innermost reasons of its existence
as present if only hazily to the one who says 'I'. And just as in the major work
travail thus understood shades off into triumph as the pilgrim lays hold at last of
his being in the world as but a matter of its twofold self-possession and self-
overflowing, so here in the *libello* the trauma of the 'donna gentile' episode is resolved in an ascent of the spirit as rapturous as anything in Dante. Everything, in
short, necessary for his final exploration of the paradisal substance of human
experience in the height and depth of its rejoicing is here in this, his preliminary
meditation upon what in truth it means to be under way: the 'Ne la seconda dico
perché [lo mio pensero] va là suso, cioè chi lo fa così andare' of 41.4 for the 'tu 'l
sai, che col tuo lume mi levasti' of *Paradiso* 1.75;[39] the 'sì come peregrino lo quale
è fuori de la sua patria, vi stae' of 41.5 for the 'pur come pelegrin che tornar vuole'
of *Paradiso* 1.51;[40] the 'che io non lo posso intendere, cioè a dire che lo mio pensero
sale ne la qualitade di costei in grado che lo mio intelletto no lo puote compren-
dere' of 41.6 for the 'ch'io non lo 'ntesi, sì parlò profondo' of *Paradiso* 15.39;[41] the

---

38 'Against this adversary of reason there rose up, one day, about the ninth hour, a mighty vision,
such that I seemed to see the glorious Beatrice in the crimson garment in which she first appeared to
me, and seeming as young as when I first saw her. Then, thinking upon her and going back in my mind
over the sequence of events, I began in my heart deeply to repent of the desire by which—for several
days and contrary to all reason and good order—it had allowed itself so basely to be overtaken. Having
seen off, then, this wretched desire, I once again thought only of her, of the most noble Beatrice, and
confess that from that moment onwards I thought of her with such shame in my heart that my constant
sighs said it all, all of them, as they rose up, declaring what my heart within was saying—to wit, the
name of that most noble one and how she had left us . . . Through this rekindling of my sighs, my tears,
now assuaged, flowed forth once more, and this in such a way that my eyes, each of them alike, appeared
desirous only of weeping, and indeed through their much weeping were often, as with people in pain,
ringed in purple. Thus their inconstancy appeared to have its reward.' Anthony Presti Russell, 'Dante's
"forte immaginazione" and Beatrice's "occulta virtù": Lovesickness and the Supernatural in the *Vita
Nuova*', *Mediaevalia* 22.1 (1998), 1–33; Ernesto Livorni, 'Dream and Vision in Dante's *Vita Nova*', in
"Accessus ad auctores": Studies in Honor of Christopher Kleinhenz, ed. Fabian Alfie and Andrea Dini
(Tempe: Arizona Centre for Medieval and Renaissance Studies, 2011), 93–114; Ignazio Baldelli, 'Visione, immaginazione e fantasia nella *Vita Nuova*', *I sogni nel Medioevo. Seminario Internazionale, Rome
2–4 ottobre 1983*, ed. Tullio Gregory (Rome: Ed. dell'Ateneo 1985), 1–10 (and in *Studi danteschi*, ed. Luca
Seriani et al. [Spoleto: Centro italiano di studi sull'alto medioevo, 2015], 17–27). For the 'butterfly-
emergence' motif, *Purgatorio* 10.121–26.
39 'In the second part I speak of how it is that [my thought] rises up, of who it is, that is to say, who
causes it thus to do so'; 'you alone know who with your light raised me up'.
40 'there he stands like a pilgrim far from home'; 'as with a pilgrim anxious to return'.
41 'for I as yet am unable to understand, my thought entering so far into her essential nature that
my intellect cannot as yet make sense of it'; 'I understood her not, so profound were her words'.

'con ciò sia cosa che lo nostro intelletto s'abbia a quelle benedette anime sì come l'occhio debole a lo sole' of 41.6 for the 'e fissi li occhi al sole oltre nostr' uso' of *Paradiso* 1.54[42]—each of these passages and any number of others besides envisaging a coming home of self to self by way of an ever deeper and ever more secure sense of the love-substance and love-encompassing of every significant inflexion of the spirit. Now in the *Convivio*, the altogether 'more manly' *Convivio*, all this is put down to the fervour and indeed to the extravagance of youth, a fervour and extravagance duly honoured, to be sure, for what it once was and still is but nonetheless overtaken now by something more properly tempered:

> E se ne la presente opera, la quale è Convivio nominata e vo' che sia, più virilmente si trattasse che ne la Vita Nuova, non intendo però a quella in parte alcuna derogare, ma maggiormente giovare per questa quella; veggendo sì come ragionevolmente quella fervida e passionata, questa temperata e virile esser conviene. Ché altro si conviene e dire e operare ad una etade che ad altra; perché certi costumi sono idonei e laudabili ad una etade che sono sconci e biasimevoli ad altra, sì come di sotto, nel quarto trattato di questo libro, sarà propria ragione mostrata. E io in quella dinanzi, a l'entrata de la mia gioventute parlai, e in questa dipoi, quella già trapassata.
>
> (*Convivio* 1.1.16–17)[43]

But while indeed belonging to Dante's youth and thus to the first phase of his meditation as a poet and philosopher of love, there is, in truth, nothing especially youthful about the *Vita nova*; for in its adumbration of the infernal, of the purgatorial and of the paradisal in all the complex substance and psychology of these things, there is in the *libello* that which, for all the well-tempered character of the *Convivio* as the great expression of Dante's middle years, overarches that work and flows into the soaring spirituality of the *sacrato poema*.

42 'for inasmuch as our mind is to those blessed souls as a feeble eye is to the sun'; 'I gazed into the sun in a manner beyond our wont'.

43 'And if in this present work entitled Banquet (for that is what I wish it to be) matters are discussed more maturely than in the *Vita Nuova*, I do not intend in any way to detract from that book but, rather, to strengthen it still further, since it is right and proper for that work to be fervent and passionate and for this one to be mature and temperate. For it is fitting that we speak and act differently from one stage of our life to another, since—as I shall show later on, in the fourth book—what is becoming and appropriate at one stage is unbecoming and reprehensible at another. While, then, the earlier work I wrote on the threshold of my maturity, the other I wrote when well on into it.'

PART III

THE MIDDLE YEARS

The Moral and Allegorical *Rime,*
the *Convivio,* the *De vulgari eloquentia*
and the Post-Exilic *Rime*

CHAPTER 1

Compassionate Lady of the Casement and a Woman of Stone: The Pre-Exilic *Rime*

More than ordinarily eloquent in giving expression to what in Dante amounts to a certain anxiety in respect of how, if at all, one order of properly human concern stands to be reconciled with another within the economy of the whole is the sonnet *Due donne in cima de la mente mia*, a sonnet belonging ideally to the middle or latter part of the 1290s; for if on the one hand it is a question of beauty, elegance, charm and everything pertaining to 'bellezza' as an object of aspiration, then on the other it is a question of seeing, understanding, choosing and everything pertaining to 'onestade' as the way of properly human being and becoming. Are these things compatible, Dante wonders, as each alike setting up a claim in conscience? Amore, for his part, has no doubt; yes, he says, speaking as he does so from out of his status as the presiding genius hereabouts, each of these things properly commends itself to the attentive spirit, beauty for the sake of delight and virtue for the sake of righteousness:

> Due donne in cima de la mente mia
> venute sono a ragionar d'amore;
> l'una ha in sé cortesia e valore,
> prudenza e onestà in compagnia;
>   l'altra ha bellezza e vaga leggiadria,
> adorna gentilezza le fa onore;
> e io, merzé del dolce mio signore,
> mi sto a piè de la lor signoria.
>   Parlan Bellezza e Virtù a l'intelletto
> e fan quistion come un cor puote stare
> intra due donne con amor perfetto.
>   Risponde il fonte del gentil parlare

ch'amar si può bellezza per diletto
e puossi amar virtù per operare.[1]

Now this, indeed, is a more than ordinarily eloquent moment, a moment that, for all its seriousness, its turning upon the notion of beauty and/or goodness as a means of self-interpretation, proceeds by way of an imaginative confection as delicate as it is discriminating, as poised as it is persuasive. Rarely, however, are the tensions at work within the recesses of Dante's complex humanity as sweetly conceived and expressed as this, his commitment towards the end of the *Vita nova* to study as hard as he can in order that Beatrice might be spoken of in a way no woman had been spoken of before making just about immediately for a more fraught spirituality, for a spirituality, that is to say, divided against itself in point both of means and of ends. The key text here, scarcely less than traumatic in registering the eclipse of Beatrice and thus of the Beatrician moment of his experience as a poet and philosopher of love in the Siculo-Tuscan and stilnovistic tradition of verse making in favour of philosophy pure and simple—of, more exactly, philosophy as but the love of wisdom first and foremost in the mind of God—is the canzone *Voi che 'ntendendo il terzo ciel movete*, an essay, precisely, in the agony of a now conflicted existence. On the one hand, then, we have the putting to flight of the one by the other (the 'chi lo fa fuggire' of line 20) and, with it, the submission perforce of the spirit to a new seigneur (the 'signoreggiare me di tal virtute' of line 21):

Suol esser vita de lo cor dolente
un soave penser, che se ne gia
molte fiate a' pie' del nostro Sire,
    ove una donna gloriar vedia,
di cui parlava me sì dolcemente
che l'anima dicea: 'Io men vo' gire'.
    Or apparisce chi lo fa fuggire
e segnoreggia me di tal virtute,
che 'l cor ne trema che di fuori appare.
. . .
Trova contraro tal che lo distrugge

1 'Two women have come to the pinnacle of my mind to speak of love. One has about her graciousness and goodness, prudence, and decorum, while the other has comeliness and charm, fair nobility doing her honour. And I, thanks to my dear lord, kneel at their ladyships' feet. Beauty and Virtue, addressing thus my mind, debate between themselves how with perfect devotion the heart might serve two ladies. The source of every noble utterance replies that beauty may be loved for its delight and virtue for its good deeds.' Peter Dronke, 'Ethics and Aesthetics Are One', in *Dante's Second Love: The Originality and the Contexts of the 'Convivio'* (Leeds: Society for Italian Studies 1997), 51–71; Maria Rita Traina, ' "Due donne in cima della mente mia": Precedenti e sviluppi di una struttura', in *AlmaDante: Seminario dantesco 2013*, ed. Giuseppe Ledda et al. (Bologna: Aspasia, 2015), 33–51.

l'umil pensero, che parlar mi sole
d'un'angela che   'n cielo è coronata.
L'anima piange, sì ancor len dole,
e dice: 'Oh lassa a me, come si fugge
questo piatoso che m'ha consolata!'

(*Voi che 'ntendendo il terzo ciel movete*, lines 14–22 and 27–32)[2]

while on the other hand—and with respect to Dante's new love—there is a now overwhelming sense of grandeur, of a presence as exalted as it is self-effacing, as wise as it is wonderful, and apt as such to call forth from the poet-lover a fresh 'be it unto me according to thy word', an unqualified making over of self to the immeasurably greater than self:

'Tu non se' morta, ma se' ismarrita,
anima nostra, che sì ti lamenti,'
dice uno spiritel d'amor gentile;
'ché quella bella donna, che tu senti,
ha transmutata in tanto la tua vita,
che n'hai paura, sì se' fatta vile!
Mira quant' ell'è pietosa e umile,
saggia e cortese ne la sua grandezza,
e pensa di chiamarla donna, omai!
Ché se tu non t'inganni, tu vedrai
di sì alti miracoli adornezza,
che tu dirai: "Amor, segnor verace,
ecco l'ancella tua; fa che ti piace".'

(*Voi che 'ntendendo il terzo ciel movete*, lines 40–52)[3]

2 'The life of my sorrowing heart used to be a gentle thought which would often make its way to the feet of our Lord where it saw a lady in glory, of whom it would speak to me so sweetly that my soul would say: "I too wish to go there." But now there appears one who puts it to flight, and who lords it over me with such power that the trembling in my heart is plain for all to see . . . The quiet thought which would speak to me of an angel crowned in heaven now finds an adversary busy about destroying it. My sorrowing soul grieves still on that account, and says: "Alas, how it flees, that thought, my one consolation!"' Aldo M. Costantini, 'Battaglia di pensieri e nuovi amori nel dopo-Beatrice: "Voi che 'ntendendo" tra *Vita Nuova* e *Convivio*', in *"Vaghe stelle dell'Orsa . . .": L'"io" e il "tu" nella lirica italiana*, ed. Francesco Bruni (Venice: Marsilio, 2005), 107–18; Enrico Fenzi, 'Voi che 'ntendendo il terzo ciel movete', in *Dante Alighieri: Le quindici canzoni. Lette da diversi*, vol. 1 (Lecce: Pensa Multimedia, 2009), 29–69; Maria Luisa Ardizzone, 'Intelligere e muovere: "Voi che 'ntendendo il terzo ciel movete"', in *Dante: Il paradigma intellettuale. Un "inventio" degli anni fiorentini* (Florence: Olschki, 2011), 115–72; Natascia Tonelli (ed.), *Voi che 'ntendendo il terzo ciel movete* (Madrid: Asociación Complutense de Dantologia, 2011) (various authors).

3 '"You are not dead but merely bewildered, soul of ours which so laments," says a noble spirit of

That we are indeed dealing with philosophy pure and simple as the object of
Dante's affection in *Voi che 'ntendendo il terzo ciel movete* is confirmed by the text
both explicitly and implicitly—*explicitly* by what Dante has to say in the as yet
far-off *Convivio* relative to the comfort afforded him in his bereavement by, especially, the consolatory works of Boethius and Tully, and *implicitly* by a delicate
but nonetheless discernible modulation of the 'praise style' of the *Vita nova* as
subject now to fresh implementation; as far, then, as the first of these things is
concerned we have the following lines from the second book of the *Convivio*, lines
honouring, to be sure, the Beatrician moment of the *Vita nova* but nonetheless
secure in their sense of one order of concern making way now for another:

E però, principiando ancora da capo, dico che, come per me fu perduto lo
primo diletto de la mia anima, de la quale fatta è menzione di sopra, io
rimasi di tanta tristizia punto, che conforto non mi valeva alcuno. Tuttavia,
dopo alquanto tempo, la mia mente, che si argomentava di sanare, provide,
poi che né 'l mio né l'altrui consolare valea, ritornare al modo che alcuno
sconsolato avea tenuto a consolarsi; e misimi a leggere quello non conosciuto da molti libro di Boezio, nel quale, cattivo e discacciato, consolato
s'avea. E udendo ancora che Tullio scritto avea un altro libro nel quale,
trattando de l'Amistade, avea toccate parole de la consolazione di Lelio,
uomo eccellentissimo, ne la morte di Scipione amico suo, misimi a leggere
quello. E avvegna che duro mi fosse ne la prima entrare ne la loro sentenza,
finalmente v'entrai tanto entro, quanto l'arte di gramatica ch'io avea e un
poco di mio ingegno potea fare; per lo quale ingegno molte cose, quasi
come sognando, già vedea, sì come ne la Vita Nuova si può vedere. E sì
come essere suole che l'uomo va cercando argento e fuori de la 'ntenzione
truova oro, lo quale occulta cagione presenta, non forse sanza divino impe-
rio; io, che cercava di consolarme, trovai non solamente a le mie lagrime
rimedio, ma vocabuli d'autori e di scienze e di libri; li quali considerando,
giudicava bene che la filosofia, che era donna di questi autori, di queste
scienze e di questi libri, fosse somma cosa. E imaginava lei fatta come una
donna gentile, e non la poteva immaginare in atto alcuno, se non misericor-
dioso; per che sì volentieri lo senso di vero la mirava, che appena lo potea
volgere da quella.

(*Convivio* 2.12.1–6)[4]

---

love, "for that fair lady whom you sense speaking to you has so transformed your life that—so base
have you become—you go in fear. But see how merciful and modest she is, how wise and gracious amid
her grandeur. Be sure, then, to speak of her henceforth as your lady, for, provided only you misconstrue
her not, such beauty will you behold by way of the most wondrous miracles she works that you will
surely say: 'Love, my one true lord, behold your handmaid; be it unto me according to your
pleasure'."'

4 'And so, beginning all over again, I say that when I lost that first joy of my soul, of whom I made

—lines to which, as confirming that this after all was Dante's meaning when in
the *Vita nova* he spoke of the 'donna gentile' or gracious lady of the casement as
one looking compassionately upon him in his bereavement, we may add these
from earlier on in the same book:

Cominciando adunque, dico che la stella di Venere due fiate rivolta era in
quello suo cerchio che la fa parere serotina e matutina, secondo diversi
tempi, appresso lo trapassamento di quella Beatrice beata che vive in cielo
con li angeli e in terra con la mia anima, quando quella gentile donna, cui
feci menzione ne la fine de la Vita Nuova, parve primamente, accompag-

mention above, I was pierced by such sorrow that no comfort availed me. Yet, after a while, my mind,
intent on recovery but acknowledging that neither my own resources nor those made available to me
by others were such as to console me, settled on the possibility adopted by another disconsolate spirit
in search of comfort, and I began to read that little-known work of Boethius in which, imprisoned and
abandoned, he had found consolation. And hearing, moreover, of another book of Cicero's —his book
On Friendship—in the course of which he spoke of the consolation of Laelius (a man of the highest
merit) on the death of his friend Scipio, I set about reading that book too. And though at first I found
it hard to grasp their meaning, I eventually did so to the extent that such Latin as I had and my native
wit—which as can be seen in the *Vita nuova* had already enabled me if only in a dreamlike way to see
many things—allowed. And just as it often happens that someone looking for silver quite by chance
or some other hidden cause, perhaps even by divine providence, comes across gold, so I, in my search
for consolation, found not only a remedy for my tears but also authors, books and learning. And reflecting on these, I was firmly of the opinion that philosophy, who was the lady of these authors, of
these books and of this learning, was something superlative, whence, being unable to conceive of her
as anything other than compassionate, I imagined her in the form of a noble lady, with the result that
that part of my mind attuned to the truth so eagerly gazed upon her that I could scarce turn away.' For
Dante and Boethius, Rocco Murari, *Dante e Boezio (contributo allo studio delle fonti dantesche)* (Bologna:
Zanichelli, 1905); Walther Kranz, 'Dante und Boethius', *Romanische Forschungen* 63.1–2 (1951), 72–78;
Pierre Courcelle, *La Consolation de Philosophie dans la tradition littéraire: Antécédents et Postérité de
Boèce* (Paris: Études Augustiniennes, 1967); Edward Moore, *Studies in Dante: First Series (Scripture and
Classical Authors in Dante)* (Oxford: Clarendon Press, 1969 [1896]), 282–88 (Cicero at 258–73); Angelo
Gualtieri, 'Lady Philosophy in Boethius and Dante', *Comparative Literature* 23 (1971), 141–50; Peter
Dronke, 'Boethius, Alanus and Dante', in *The Medieval Poet and His World* (Rome: Edizioni di Storia
e Letteratura, 1984), 431–38; Miguel Lluch-Baixauli, 'De la félicité philosophique chez Boèce et chez
Dante', in *Actualité de la pensée médiévale*, ed. Jacques Follon and James McEvoy (Paris: Editions
Peeters, 1994), 202–15; Luca Lombardo, *Boezio in Dante: La 'Consolatio Philosophiae' nello scrittoio del
poeta* (Venice: Edizioni Ca' Foscari, 2014); Jelena Todorović, ' "Quello non conosciuto da molti libro
di Boezio": *De Consolatione Philosophiae* and Its Role in the Making of the *Vita Nova*', in Jelena Todorović, *Dante and the Dynamics of Textual Exchange: Authorship, Manuscript Culture, and the Making of
the 'Vita Nova'* (New York: Fordham University Press, 2016), 18–66. For Dante and Cicero, Alessandro Ronconi, 'Dante interprete di Cicerone', in *Interpretazioni letterarie nei classici* (Florence: Le Monnier, 1972), 189–210; Giulio Andreotti, 'Dante e Cicerone', *L'Alighieri (RBD)* 1–2 (1993), 101–11; Gabriele
Di Giammarino, 'Dante lettore di Cicerone', *Rivista del Centro di Studi Ciceroniani* 9 (1996), 121–32;
Simone Marchesi, 'La rilettura del *De officiis* e i due tempi della composizione del *Convivio*', *GSLI* 178
(2001), 84–107; Edoardo d'Angelo and Giovanni Polara (eds.), *Dante, Cicerone e i classici* (Naples: Il
Girasole, 2010). For Brunetto Latini as intermediary, Gian Carlo Alessio, 'Brunetto Latini e Cicerone
(e i dettatori)', *Italia Medioevale e Umanistica* 22 (1979), 123–69; Julia Bolton Holloway, *Twice-Told Tales:
Brunetto Latino and Dante Alighieri* (New York: Peter Lang, 1993); Johannes Bartuschat, 'La "filosofia"
di Brunetto Latini e il *Convivio*', in *Il 'Convivio' di Dante*, ed. Johannes Bartuschat and Andrea Aldo
Robiglio (Ravenna: Longo, 2015), 33–51.

nata d'Amore, a li occhi miei e prese luogo alcuno ne la mia mente. E sì
come è ragionato per me ne lo allegato libello, più da sua gentilezza che
da mia elezione venne ch'io ad essere suo consentisse; ché passionata di
tanta misericordia si dimostrava sopra la mia vedovata vita, che li spiriti
de li occhi miei a lei si fero massimamente amici. E così fatti, dentro [me]
lei poi fero tale, che lo mio beneplacito fu contento a disposarsi a quella
imagine.

(*Convivio* 2.2.1–2)[5]

As far, by contrast, as the *implicit* affirmation of the poem's content is concerned, its deployment of the 'stilo de la loda' for the purposes of hymning, not
now a woman in the flesh but philosophy as the love of wisdom coeval and consubstantial with the Godhead, we have its special tonality, its discrete modulation
in the interest of the more properly esoteric; so, once again, the 'Mira quant' ell'è
pietosa e umile' moment of the fourth stanza, where there is enough in the precise
lexical and syntactical configuration of the line—or more simply, perhaps, in the
solemn stillness of it all—to suggest a thematic shift, an alternative agenda:

> Mira quant' ell'è pietosa e umile,
> saggia e cortese ne la sua grandezza,
> e pensa di chiamarla donna, omai!
> Ché se tu non t'inganni, tu vedrai
> di sì alti miracoli adornezza,
> che tu dirai: 'Amor, segnor verace,
> ecco l'ancella tua; fa che ti piace'

(*Voi che 'ntendendo il terzo ciel movete*, lines 46–52)[6]

---

5 'I begin, then, by saying that after the passing away of the blessed Beatrice who lives in heaven
with the angels and on earth with my soul, Venus had completed two revolutions in that orbit of hers
which brings her into view either by evening or by morning according to the time of year, when the
noble lady of whom I made mention towards the end of the *Vita nuova* appeared for the first time accompanied by Love, making a certain place for herself in my mind. And, as I have said in that same
little book, I consented to be hers by way less of my choosing than of her nobility, for such compassion
she evidently had upon my widowed state that the spirits of my eyes were in the greatest degree enamoured of her. And thus enamoured, they then fashioned her image within me such that I put myself
willingly at its disposal.' Étienne Gilson, 'The Donna Gentile', in *Dante and Philosophy* (New York:
Harper and Row, 1963 [1939]; 2nd ed. 1953), 86–98; Kenelm Foster and Patrick Boyde, 'The Biographical Problems in "Voi che 'ntendendo"', in *Dante's Lyric Poetry*, vol. 2 (Oxford: Clarendon Press, 1967),
341–62; Peter Dronke, *Dante's Second Love: The Originality and the Contexts of the 'Convivio'* (Leeds:
Society for Italian Studies, 1997).

6 'But see how merciful and modest she is, how wise and gracious amid her grandeur. Be sure,
then, to speak of her henceforth as your lady, for, provided only you misconstrue her not, such beauty
will you behold by way of the most wondrous miracles she works that you will surely say: "Love, my
one true lord, behold your handmaid; be it unto me according to your pleasure."'

But if in *Voi che 'ntendendo il terzo ciel movete* rejoicing in the prospect, indeed in the reality, of a new love is tempered by the agony of transition, of setting aside the old in favour of the new, that same rejoicing surfaces in a now pure form in the canzone *Amor che ne la mente mi ragiona*, a high point in the area of Dante's post-stilnovistic lyricism. True, allegory persists as the in-and-through-which of his discourse hereabouts, the gracious lady of the casement standing in for the properly speaking sapiential object of his contemplation; but here again there is a difference, the at once rapt substance and tonality of the line confirming the poet's preoccupation with something qualitatively other and still more sublime:

> Non vede il sol, che tutto 'l mondo gira,
> cosa tanto gentil, quanto in quell'ora
> che luce ne la parte ove dimora
> la donna, di cui dire Amor mi face.
> Ogni Intelletto di là su la mira,
> e quella gente che qui s'innamora
> ne' lor pensieri la truovano ancora
> quando Amor fa sentir de la sua pace.
> Suo esser tanto a Quei che lel dà piace,
> che 'nfonde sempre in lei la sua vertute
> oltre 'l dimando di nostra natura.
> La sua anima pura,
> che riceve da Lui questa salute,
> lo manifesta in quel ch'ella conduce:
> ché   'n sue bellezze son cose vedute
> che li occhi di color dov'ella luce
> ne mandan messi al cor pien di desiri,
> che prendon aire e diventan sospiri.

(Amor che ne la mente mi ragiona, lines 19–36)[7]

7 'The sun that circles the whole world sees nothing so noble as when shining there where dwells the lady of whom Love bids me speak. Every Intelligence on high gazes at her, and those enamoured here below, whensoever Love imparts a sense of his peace, find her still in their thoughts. So far does her being please him who gives it her that he forever pours into her power beyond anything proper to our nature. In her presence to us she makes manifest the perfection her pure soul enjoys from him, for in the beauty thereof are seen such things that from the eyes of those lit up by that presence come messengers of yearning to the heart, messengers at once drawing breath and issuing forth in sighs.' Vittorio Russo, '"Voi che 'ntendendo" e "Amor che ne la mente": La diffrazione dei significati secondo l'auto-commento del *Convivio*', SD 61 (1989), 219–29 (and in *Saggi di filologia dantesca* [Naples: Bibliopolis, 2000], 71–80); Maurizio Fiorilla, '"Amor che ne la mente mi ragiona" tra ricezione antica e interpretazione moderna', RSD 5 (2005), 141–54; Domenico De Robertis, 'Amor che ne la mente mi

And what applies to this second stanza of the canzone by way of its fresh implementation of Dante's praise style as but an expression—indeed as but the intelligible form—of the lover's participation in the very life of the Godhead applies also to the third stanza with its sense of madonna as empowered from on high and to the fourth with its sense of her always and everywhere sovereign presence to the mortal mind; so, then, from this same third stanza, we have these lines with their sense of madonna's every word as but an intimation from above:

> In lei discende la virtù divina
> sì come face in angelo che 'l vede;
> e qual donna gentil questo non crede,
> vada con lei e miri li atti sui.
> Quivi dov'ella parla, si dichina
> un spirito da ciel, che reca fede
> come l'alto valor ch'ella possiede
> è oltre quel che si conviene a nui.

(*Amor che ne la mente mi ragiona*, lines 37–44)[8]

while from the fourth stanza we have these on her presence as a matter of grace and truth under the aspect of a smile:

> Cose appariscon ne lo suo aspetto,
> che mostran de' piacer di Paradiso,
> dico ne li occhi e nel suo dolce riso,
> che le vi reca Amor com'a suo loco.
> Elle soverchian lo nostro intelletto
> come raggio di sole un frale viso;
> e perch'io non le posso mirar fiso,
> mi convien contentar di dirne poco.

(*Amor che ne la mente mi ragiona*, lines 55–62)[9]

ragiona', in *Dante Alighieri: Le quindici canzoni. Lette da diversi*, vol. 1 (Lecce: Pensa Multimedia, 2009), 71–87; Noemi Ghetti, ' "Amor che ne la mente mi ragiona": Amore razionale e filosofia nel *Convivio*', in *L'ombra di Cavalcanti e Dante* (Rome: L'Asino d'oro edizioni, 2010), 149–58; Enrico Fenzi (ed.), *Amor che ne la mente mi ragiona* (Madrid: Asociación Complutense de Dantologia, 2013) (various authors); Paolo Borsa, ' "Amor che ne la mente mi ragiona" tra stilnovo, *Convivio* e *Purgatorio*', in *Il Convivio di Dante. Atti del Convegno di Zurigo (21–22 Maggio 2012)*, ed. Johannes Bartuschat and Andrea Aldo Robiglio (Ravenna: Longo Editore, 2015), 53–82.

8 'Divine goodness descends into her as into an angel looking upon it; and let any noble lady unable to believe this keep her company and contemplate her ways. Whenever she speaks a spirit descends from above to confirm how far her consummate perfection transcends our measure.'

9 'In her aspect—in her eyes, to wit, and her lovely smile—appear things that show forth the joys

Here too, then, it is a question of rapture, of—as is the way of it in Dante—a fresh apotheosis of the spirit, the only cloud upon the horizon being the difficulty of this new love, of philosophy's appearing to keep him at a distance and even to speak harshly to him. For the Dante of *Amor che ne la mente mi ragiona* it is indeed a question of *appearing*, for the fault, he maintains in the *congedo* or leave-taking stanza of the poem, lies not with philosophy herself but with the lover as but an apprentice hereabouts, as one as yet unpractised in the ways and means of philosophical disquisition (the 'Così, quand'ella la chiama orgogliosa, / non considera lei secondo il vero, / ma pur secondo quel ch'a lei parea' of lines 81–83).[10] But elsewhere the arduousness and indeed the intractability of it all moves into the ascendant, the ballata *Voi che savete ragionar d'Amore* and the sonnet *Parole mie che per lo mondo siete*, though belonging to the same constellation as *Amor che ne la mente mi ragiona*, nonetheless registering a sense of madonna's indifference and indeed disdain with respect to her devotees. Both, admittedly, are quickly enough subject to retraction (*Voi che savete ragionar d'Amore* in the *congedo* of *Amor che ne la mente mi ragiona* and *Parole mie che per lo mondo siete* in the sonnet *O dolci rime che parlando andate*), but both even so bear witness to the uneven course of Dante's affair with philosophy at least in its early stages. Philosophy, he suggests, for all her power to engender a yearning of the spirit, has in truth little time for the ardent admirer, her only concern being to contemplate narcissistically her own surpassing excellence (the 'quando si mira per volere onore' moment of *Voi che savete ragionar d'Amore* at lines 17–20),[11] which is why, Dante goes on in *Parole mie che per lo mondo siete*, honest lovers do well to look elsewhere:

---

of paradise, for it is there that Love leads them as to his proper domain. And they surpass our intellect as does a ray of sunlight a weak eye, which is why I, unable to look steadily at them, must be content thereof to say but little.'

10 'And so when the poem speaks of her as haughty, it does so by way not so much of truth as of appearance.'

11 'And I firmly believe that she thus withholds her eyes merely in order that, much as a good woman does when looking upon herself to seek there reason for honourable attention, she may look into them herself.' So also the canzone *Le dolci rime d'amor ch'i' solia* at lines 18–20 ('E, cominciando, / chiamo quel signore / ch'a la mia donna ne li occhi dimora, / per ch'ella di se stessa innamora' [And here on the threshold I invoke that lord dwelling in my lady's eyes and causing her thus to love her very self]), with, by way of commentary, the *Convivio* at 4.2.18: 'E dice: "Per ch'ella di sé stessa s'innamora", però che essa filosofia, che è, sì come detto è nel precedente trattato, amoroso uso di sapienza, sé medesima riguarda, quando apparisce la bellezza de li occhi suoi a lei; che altro non è a dire, se non che l'anima filosofante non solamente contempla essa veritade, ma ancora contempla lo suo contemplare medesimo e la bellezza di quello, rivolgendosi sovra sé stessa e di sé stessa innamorando per la bellezza del suo primo guardare' (It then says: 'And causes this lady to love herself', and this insofar as Philosophy—which, we said in the previous book, is but a loving familiarity with wisdom—rejoicing in the beauty of her own eyes, looks back upon herself, which is as much as to say that the philosophical soul, again by turning back upon itself and becoming enamoured thereof, contemplates not only the truth but also, in all the beauty thereof, its own contemplation).

Parole mie che per lo mondo siete,
voi che nasceste poi ch'io cominciai
a dir per quella donna in cui errai:
'Voi che 'ntendendo il terzo ciel movete',
    andatevene a lei, che la sapete,
chiamando sì ch'ell'oda i vostri guai;
ditele: 'Noi siam vostre, ed unquemai
più che noi siamo non ci vederete'.
    Con lei non state, ché non v'è Amore,
ma gite a torno in abito dolente
a guisa de le vostre antiche sore.
    Quando trovate donna di valore,
gittatelevi a' piedi umilemente,
dicendo: 'A voi dovem noi fare onore'.[12]

More sustained, however, in its account of the twofold exhilaration and anguish of his new love, are the two large-scale canzoni *Amor, che movi tua vertù da
cielo* and *Io sento sì d'Amor la gran possanza*, the second of them much prized by
Dante for its sweetness as a love song (the 'Canzon mia bella' and the 'dolce mia
amorosa' of lines 81 and 85) but each alike settling on the power of philosophy,
once espoused as mistress of the mind, both to delight and to disturb, to elate and
to lay waste. On the positive side, then, we have these lines (16–23) from *Amor,
che movi tua vertù da cielo*, lines as eager as anything in *Amor che ne la mente mi
ragiona* to acknowledge her presence as a matter of blessing:

Feremi ne lo cor sempre tua luce,
come raggio in la stella,
poi che l'anima mia fu fatta ancella

---

12 'Words of mine making their way in the world—you that were born when first I wrote for that
lady in whom I was deceived *Voi che 'ntendendo il terzo ciel movete*—go now to this lady known to you,
bidding her give ear to your grief and saying: "We are indeed yours, but others like unto us you will
never see." Abide not with her, for there Love himself abides not, but, like your elder sisters, go about
in grief apparelled. And when you meet one worthy of your love, cast yourself humbly at her feet saying:
"It is you we must honour."' Probably belonging to this same moment are the 'pargoletta' or 'young
woman' poems consisting of the two ballads *I' mi son pargoletta bella e nova* and *Perché ti vedi giovinetta
e bella* and of the sonnet *Chi guarderà già mai sanza paura*, likewise open to allegorical interpretation
and likewise registering the arduousness of the philosophical way. Angelo Jacomuzzi, 'La "pargoletta"
in *Purgatorio* (XXXI.58–60)', *LC* 8 (1979), 9–26 (and in *L'imago al cerchio* by Angelo Jacomuzzi [Milan:
Franco Angeli, 1995], 231–49); 'Sulle *Rime* di Dante: Dalle rime per la "pargoletta" alle "petrose"', *FSt*
6.1–2 (1994), 15–30; Maria Clotilde Camboni, 'La ballata *I' mi son pargoletta*', *REI* 56.1–2 (2010), 67–78;
Tristan Kay , 'Dante's Cavalcantian Relapse: The "pargoletta" Sequence and the *Commedia*', *DS* 131
(2013), 73–97; Furio Biondo, ' "... esta bella pargoletta": L'amore "giovane" nella lirica antica e in Dante',
DDJ 89 (2014), 55–82.

> de la tua podestà primeramente;
>   onde ha vita un disio che mi conduce
> con sua dolce favella
> in rimirar ciascuna cosa bella
> con più diletto quanto è più piacente.[13]

while on the negative side, we have these lines from the same poem (46–60), with, given love's endless to-and-froing between pain and pleasure, their plea for compassion, for a fresh intervention by Amore on behalf of the now suffering spirit:

> Dunque, segnor di sì gentil natura
> che questa nobiltate
> che avven qua giuso e tutt'altra bontate
> lieva principio de la tua altezza,
>   guarda la vita mia quanto ella è dura,
> e prendine pietate,
> ché lo tuo ardor per la costei bieltate
> mi fa nel core aver troppa gravezza.
>   Falle sentire, Amor, per tua dolcezza,
> il gran disio ch'i' ho di veder lei;
> non soffrir che costei
> per giovanezza mi conduca a morte;
> ché non s'accorge ancor com'ella piace,
> né quant'io l'amo forte,
> né che ne li occhi porta la mia pace.

> (*Amor, che movi tua vertù da cielo*, lines 46–60)[14]

---

13 'As the rays of the sun strike the stars, so also, from the moment my soul first became a servant beneath your sway, your light has ceaselessly struck me in my heart, whence is quickened a desire which, sweet of speech, leads me to gaze upon every object of beauty, the greater the beauty the greater my delight.'

14 'So then, lord, as you are of so noble a nature that whatever of excellence and indeed of every other goodness comes about here below has its origin in your majesty, see how hard my life is and have pity on it; for your fervour, born as it is of her beauty, weighs all too heavily upon my heart. Cause her to feel with your sweetness, O Love, the yearning I have to look upon her. Suffer not her youth to be my death, for yet she knows not how fair she is to me, nor how intensely I love her, nor that in her eyes she bears my peace.' Mario Pazzaglia, 'Due canzoni dantesche: "Amor, che movi tua vertù dal cielo" e "Io sento sì d'amor la gran possanza"', *LC* 26 (1997), 21–35; Selene Sarteschi, 'Notazioni intorno ad "Amor, che movi tua vertù dal cielo" e ad altre rime di Dante', in *Da Guido Guinizzelli a Dante: Nuove prospettive sulla lirica del Duecento. Atti del Convegno di Studi, Padova-Monselice 10–12 maggio 2002*, ed. Furio Brugnolo (Padua: Il Poligrafo, 2004), 305–32; Isabelle Battesti, 'La canzone "Amor che movi tua vertù dal cielo"', in *Maître et passeur: Per Marziano Guglielminetti dagli amici di Francia*, ed. Claudio

—lines to which we must add these from the canzone *Io sento sì d'Amor la gran possanza* relative to the shifting substance of it all, to the poet's living out in one and the same moment the twofold solace and sorrowing of his new love:

> Altri ch'Amor non mi potea far tale,
> ch'eo fosse degnamente
> cosa di quella che non s'innamora,
>   ma stassi come donna a cui non cale
>   de l'amorosa mente
>   che sanza lei non può passar un'ora.
>   Io non la vidi tante volte ancora
> ch'io non trovasse in lei nova bellezza;
> onde Amor cresce in me la sua grandezza
> tanto quanto il piacer novo s'aggiugne.
> Ond'elli avven che tanto fo dimora
> in uno stato e tanto Amor m'avvezza
> con un martiro e con una dolcezza,
> quanto è quel tempo che spesso mi pugne
> che dura da ch'io perdo la sua vista
> infino al tempo ch'ella si racquista.

(*Io sento sì d'Amor la gran possanza*, lines 65–80)[15]

Dante's, then, to begin with, was not an easy ride, the 'donna gentile' or gracious lady of the casement under her philosophical aspect being decidedly ambiguous in her attitude to him, at once kindly and cruel, loving and loveless. But there appeared upon reflection to be a solution, for if in the round philosophy

---

Sensi (Alessandria: Edizioni dell'Orso, 2008), 26–39; Carla Molinari, 'Amor che movi tua vertù dal cielo', in *Dante Alighieri: Le quindici canzoni. Lette da diversi*, vol. 1 (Lecce: Pensa Multimedia, 2009), 119–44; Carlos López Cortezo (ed.), *Amor che movi tua vertù dal cielo* (Madrid: Asociación Complutense di Dantologia, 2011) (various authors); Eduard Vilella, 'La giovane nella mente entrata: Immagine interiore e io lirico in "Amor che movi"', in *Ortodossia ed eterodossia in Dante Alighieri. Atti del convegno di Madrid 5–7 novembre 2012*, ed. Carlota Cattermole et al. (Madrid: Ediciones de la Discreta, 2014), 603–13; Eduard Vilella, '"Pintura" ed esperienza in "Amor che movi tua vertù dal cielo"', *Italianistica* 44.2 (2015), 53–67.

15 'Only Love could have made me worthy to belong to one who herself loves not, but who remains like a woman indifferent to the mind which does love and which cannot pass an hour other than in her company. Often as I have seen her, I still find in her fresh beauty, which is why Love is all the more powerfully present to me in proportion as her loveliness is itself all the more; and so it comes about that Love, for just as long as the agonizing moment lasts—the moment in which I lose sight of her until that in which I see her once more—holds me in one and the same unchanging state of suffering and sweetness.' Zygmunt G. Barański, 'Io sento sì la gran possanza', in *Dante Alighieri: Le quindici canzoni. Lette da diversi*, vol. 1 (Lecce: Pensa Multimedia, 2009), 145–211; Natascia Tonelli (ed.), *Io sento sì d'Amor la gran possanza* (Madrid: Asociación Complutense di Dantologia, 2015) (various authors).

turned out to be a false or at any rate fickle friend, then in certain respects at least—in the area of moral as distinct from natural philosophy—she might after all prove to be a more comfortable companion. That this indeed constitutes the direction of his thinking in these middle years of the 1290s is open to documentation both from the two canzoni generated at the time by this situation—namely *Le dolci rime d'amor ch'i' solia* and *Poscia ch'Amor del tutto m'ha lasciato*—and from the post-exilic *Convivio*, each alike explicit in respect of what in this sense amounts to a foreshortening on Dante's part of his philosophical perspective and thus to a settling of the spirit. On the one hand, then, we have on the threshold of *Le dolci rime* these lines with their sturdy indictment of My Lady Philosophy in her hardheartedness and their commitment by way less now of sweetness than of subtlety to matters of a more properly moral and social kind:

> Le dolci rime d'amor ch'i' solia
> cercar ne' miei pensieri,
> convien ch'io lasci; non perch'io non speri
> ad esse ritornare,
>   ma perché li atti disdegnosi e feri,
> che ne la donna mia
> sono appariti, m'han chiusa la via
> de l'usato parlare.
>   E poi che tempo mi par' d'aspettare,
> diporrò giù lo mio soave stile,
> ch'i' ho tenuto nel trattar d'amore;
> e dirò del valore,
> per lo qual veramente omo è gentile,
> con rima aspr' e sottile;
> riprovando 'l giudicio falso e vile
> di quei che voglion che di gentilezza
> sia principio ricchezza.

(*Le dolci rime d'amor ch'i' solia*, lines 1–17)[16]

—lines to which, as far as *Poscia ch'Amor del tutto m'ha lasciato* is concerned, we may add these—also from the beginning of the poem—likewise turning upon

16 'The sweet love poetry I was accustomed to seek out in my thoughts I must now forsake; not that I do not hope to return to it, but the bearing—at once disdainful and proud—that has become apparent in my lady has barred the path of my usual speech. And so, since it now seems a time for waiting, I will set aside that sweet style hitherto mine in writing of love, and I will speak instead in harsh and subtle rhymes concerning the quality by which man is truly noble, refuting as I do so the false and base opinion of those who hold that nobility depends on wealth.'

issues in the area of moral philosophy and upon this as a way of winning Love
round once more:

> Poscia ch'Amor del tutto m'ha lasciato,
> non per mio grato,
> ch, stato non avea tanto gioioso,
> ma però che pietoso
> fu tanto del meo core
> che non sofferse d'ascoltar suo pianto;
>   i' canterò così disamorato
> contra 'l peccato,
> ch'è nato in noi, di chiamare a ritroso
> tal ch'è vile e noioso
> con nome di valore,
> cioè di leggiadria, ch'è bella tanto
> che fa degno di manto
> imperial colui dov'ella regna:
> ell'è verace insegna
> la qual dimostra u' la vertù dimora
> per ch'io son certo, se ben la difendo
> nel dir com'io la 'ntendo,
> Ch'Amor di sé mi farà grazia ancora.

(*Poscia ch'Amor del tutto m'ha lasciato*, lines 1–19)[17]

while on the other hand we have the *Convivio* as recalling Philosophy's averting
her gaze when it came to the exquisitely speculative question of divine intentionality and Dante's therefore opting for ethics as his leading concern:

Per che, con ciò fosse cosa che questa mia donna un poco li suoi dolci
sembianti transmutasse a me, massimamente in quelle parti dove io mirava
e cercava se la prima materia de li elementi era da Dio intesa—per la qual
cosa un poco dal frequentare lo suo aspetto mi sostenni—quasi ne la sua
assenza dimorando, entrai a riguardare col pensiero lo difetto umano in-

---

17 'Since Love has completely abandoned me—not by my choice, for never had I been so happy,
but because he took such pity on my heart that he could not bear to listen to its weeping—I will direct
my song, thus devoid of love as I am, against the error which has arisen amongst us of misnaming
something which is base and boorish by giving it a name connoting goodness, that is, by calling it
charm—a thing so fair as to make him in whom it reigns fit for an emperor's mantle. It is a sure sign of
indwelling virtue; and so I am certain that if I defend it well by saying how I conceive it Love will look
kindly upon me once more.'

torno al detto errore. E per fuggire oziositade, che massimamente di questa donna è nemica, e per istinguere questo errore che tanti amici le toglie, proposi di gridare a la gente che per mal cammino andavano, acciò che per diritto calle si dirizzassero; e cominciai una canzone nel cui principio dissi: *Le dolci rime d'amor ch'i' solia.* Ne la quale io intendo riducer la gente in diritta via sopra la propia conoscenza de la verace nobilitade; sì come per la conoscenza del suo testo, a la esposizione del quale ora s'intende, vedere si potrà.

(*Convivio* 4.1.8–9)[18]

Hence, as predating the *Convivio* by the best part of a decade, the so-called moral *rime* belonging to the years leading up to Dante's exile in 1302, the first of which—*Le dolci rime d'amor ch'i' solia*—offers an account of *gentilezza* or nobility under its now communal as distinct from courtly aspect, as subject now, that is to say, to the most complete kind of moral and social transplantation. Now here, to be sure, Dante had a head start, Guinizzelli having already sought out and settled the notion in the canzone *Al cor gentil rempaira sempre amore.* But in consequence of his initiation in the ways and means of Peripatetic learning we breathe now a different air, Guinizzelli's garland of analogies (birds and forests, heat and light, stones and stars) giving way to reason, ratiocination and a sturdily civic statement of the matter to hand. First, then, comes the antithetical moment of the argument, that part of it turning on the idea of nobility as but a matter of wealth, genealogy and elegance, a notion at once set aside as pertaining to those of but shallow wit, indeed to those more dead than alive morally and intellectually:

> Tale imperò che gentilezza volse,
> secondo 'l suo parere,
> che fosse antica possession d'avere
> con reggimenti belli;
> e altri fu di più lieve savere,
> che tal detto rivolse,

18 'Since my lady's looks had lost something of their accustomed gentleness in my regard, especially in respect of my seeking to know whether the prime matter of elements was present intentionally to God, I refrained for a time from seeking out her gaze. So passing my time, as it were, other than in her company, I turned my attention to man's faulty understanding of this other matter [i.e. of the true nature of nobility]. And wishing to avoid idleness as offensive above all things to this lady, as well as anxious to do away with an error depriving her of so many friends, I proposed in a loud voice to address those on the wrong road with a view to bringing them back to the right way. I therefore began a canzone beginning *Le dolci rime d'amor ch'i' solia*, in which—as will be evident from the text upon which I am about to comment—I set about leading people back to the right path regarding an understanding of true nobility.'

e l'ultima particula ne tolse,
ché non l'avea fors'elli!
    Di retro da costui van tutti quelli
che fan gentile per ischiatta altrui
che lungiamente in gran ricchezza è stata;
ed è tanto durata
la così falsa oppinion tra nui,
che l'uom chiama colui
omo gentil che può dicere: 'Io fui
nepote, o figlio, di cotal valente'.
benché sia da niente.
Ma vilissimo sembra, a chi 'l ver guata,
cui è scorto 'l cammino e poscia l'erra,
e tocca a tal, ch'è morto e va per terra!

(*Le dolci rime d'amor ch'i' solia*, lines 21–40)[19]

Then, in what amounts to the *sed contra* and *responsio* moment of the argument (this, typically, being the high-scholastic way of going about it), comes the main contention of the text, namely the idea (*a*) that nobility, far from being something inherited or handed down, consists of the inclination in this or that individual to right doing; and (*b*) that nobility thus understood—as a steady inclination to right doing—is but a gift of grace, the 'seed of happiness implanted by God in the well-disposed soul':

Però nessun si vanti
dicendo: 'Per ischiatta io son con lei',
ch'elli son quasi dei
quei c'han tal grazia fuor di tutti rei;
ché solo Iddio a l'anima la dona
che vede in sua persona

---

19 'There was a ruler who maintained that in his view nobility was but a matter of ancient wealth and pleasing manners, while another, of shallower wit, looking over this saying, dispensed with the last detail—lacking it, perhaps, himself! In his wake come all those who count a man as noble for belonging to a family long since abounding in riches, and so persistent has this absurd opinion become among us that a man is deemed noble provided only he can say "I am the grandson or son of such and such a great man" even if he himself is next to worthless. But to anyone with an eye to the truth, he who, having been set on the right path, then goes astray, is doubly base, so much so, in fact, that he is but a dead man walking!' Roberto Leporatti, 'Le dolci rime d'amor ch'io solea', in *Dante Alighieri: Le quindici canzoni. Lette da diversi*, vol. 1 (Lecce: Pensa Multimedia, 2009), 89–117; Rosario Scrimieri (ed.), *Le dolci rime d'amor ch'io solea* (Madrid: Asociación Complutense di Dantologia, 2014) (various authors).

perfettamente star; sì ch'ad alquanti
ch'è 'l seme di felicità s'accosta,
messo da Dio ne l'anima ben posta.

(*Le dolci rime d'amor ch'i' solia*, lines 112–20)[20]

Notionally unexceptional as it is, then, in its transparency both to key emphases in the *Ethics* and to key strands of Guelph consciousness, the poem is in another sense anything but unexceptional; for here, in the wake of the *Vita nova* in all the at once thematic and stylistic particularity thereof, comes an opening out of the one—the thematic—on the predicament of all those perforce bowed down by domestic and civic care, and an opening out of the other—the stylistic—on every kind of argumentative and expressive possibility for the purposes of clinching the leading idea, all this offering further scope for the combative aspect of Dante's personality, for that part of him congenitally impatient with the ill-thought-out, the morally misconceived and the plain wrongheaded.

And what applies to *Le dolci rime d'amor ch'i' solia* by way of a now more ample notional and expressive programme applies also to *Poscia ch'Amor del tutto m'ha lasciato* as an exploration, not now of nobility in and for itself, but of the kind of graciousness proper to the genuinely refined spirit and everywhere distinguishable from its counterfeit among the boorish and indiscreet—of *leggiadria* as a matter of social and civic presencing. In fact, as is often enough the way of it in moments such as this, it is the counterfeit version of grace and graciousness that makes for the real interest of this poem, for what we have in *Poscia ch'Amor del tutto m'ha lasciato*, if only as the butt of Dante's criticism hereabouts, is a profiling of the aspirational classes in Florence, of the wealthy but socially untutored arrivistes. And the profile is indeed lively, Dante, by way of ushering in his more properly developed sense of *leggiadria*, turning his gaze mercilessly on the big spenders, the guzzlers, the lecherous and the in-crowd forever anxious to steal a march over their neighbour by way of their quick wit, snide innuendo, social affectation and particular brand of pseudocivility. He, therefore—Alighieri—has no intention of holding his peace hereabouts (the 'non tacerò di lei' of line 64), for there can be no doubt about the nature of *leggiadria*, once correctly understood, as but a showing forth of nobility under its moral aspect, as a property of the spirit. True, it is not the same as nobility, for subsisting as it does on the surface

---

20 'And therefore let no one boast saying, "I am noble by reason of birth"; for those who have this grace without any flaw are almost godlike, for it is God alone who gives it to a soul which he sees to be perfectly at one with the body. To some at least of us, then, nobility stands to be understood as the seed of happiness placed by God in a well-disposed soul.'

thereof it varies from individual to individual and from youth to maturity and seniority. But for all that, it *is* a matter of 'showing forth', of the kind of discerning, self-possession and congeniality irradiated by, and thus in turn testimony to, something more properly inward than itself—inwardness, Dante adds, being at a premium these days:

> Dona e riceve l'om cui questa vole,
> mai non sen dole;
> né 'l sole—per donar luce a le stelle,
> né per prender da elle
> nel suo effetto aiuto;
> ma l'uno e l'altro in ciò diletto tragge.
>   Già non s'induce a ira per parole,
> ma quelle sole
> ricole—che son bone, e sue novelle
> sono leggiadre e belle;
> per sé caro è tenuto
> e disïato da persone sagge,
>   ché de l'altre selvagge
> cotanto laude quanto biasmo prezza,
> per nessuna grandezza
> monta in orgoglio, ma quando gl'incontra
> che sua franchezza li conven mostrare,
> quivi si fa laudare.
> Color che vivon fanno tutti contra.

(*Poscia ch'Amor del tutto m'ha lasciato*, lines 115–33)[21]

---

21 'The man of true charm will both give and receive without misgiving, just like the sun in lighting up the stars and in enjoying their help in accomplishing its effects. For each alike this is but a pleasure. Never by words will he be roused to anger, for he pays heed only to those worthy of his attention, and his own are fine and forever gracious. His company is prized and sought after by persons of discernment, while as for the uncouth he values their praise no more than their blame. Never is he puffed up by honours heaped upon him, but when occasion requires and he shows forth his honesty and openness, then for that he is praised. Folk nowadays do just the opposite.' Fausto Montanari, 'La canzone della leggiadria: "Poscia ch'Amor del tutto m'ha lasciato"', *Lectura Dantis Romana, Casa di Dante in Roma* (Turin: Società Editrice Internazionale, 1961); Enrico Fenzi, '"Sollazzo" e "leggiadria": Un'interpretazione della canzone dantesca "Poscia ch'amor"', *SD* 63 (1997), 191–280; Claudio Giunta, 'Commento a "Poscia ch'Amor del tutto m'ha lasciato"', in *Le 'Rime' di Dante. Atti della giornata di studi (16 novembre 2007)*, ed. Paolo Grossi (Paris: Istituto Italiano di Cultura, 2008), 75–106; Guglielmo Barucci, '"Poscia ch'Amor del tutto m'ha lasciato": Gli "exempla" di comportamento', in *Le 'Rime' di Dante: Gargnano del Garda 25-27 settembre 2008*, ed. Claudia Berra and Paolo Borsa (Milan: Cisalpino, 2010), 251–77; Alessio Decaria, 'Poscia ch'Amor del tutto m'ha lasciato', in *Dante Alighieri: Le quindici canzoni. Lette da diversi*, vol. 2 (Lecce: Pensa Multimedia, 2012), 87–120.

This, then, is verse making very definitely other in kind from the sweet new rhymes of Dante's youth, its taut-to-the-point-of-tortured stanza structure, its rich intercalation of hepta- and pentasyllables and its considered *rimalmezzo* bearing witness (not, in the event, without a certain irony) to the neo-Guittonian component of his again complex personality. If, however, to the sweet new rhymes of Dante's youth *Poscia ch'Amor del tutto m'ha lasciato* and *Le dolci rime d'amor ch'i' solia* bring something both of the ratiocinative and of the vituperative, then within the economy of the whole they are nonetheless fellow travellers, each alike flowing at last into the *mare magnum* of the *Commedia* as party to the now prophetic undertaking.

With this, then, we come almost but not quite to the *Convivio* as the great work of Dante's middle years, as the developed expression of what amounts to the kind of philosophism awaiting in the fullness of time a still further resolution in the theologism of the *Commedia*, in a sense, that is to say, of the transparency of every high-level inflexion of the spirit to the theological as but the whereabouts of its proper contemplation. 'Almost but not quite' in that belonging in an ideal chronology to the middle years of the 1290s is a further set of poems—four in number—which we know as the *petrose*, together with which, as no less significant from the point of view of the scope and substance of the poetic utterance as now conceived by Dante, we may take the exchange of sonnets with Forese Donati belonging to much the same period. As regards, then, the *petrose*, these between them bear witness to yet a fresh moment of technical experimentation—to, more precisely, a now more than ever developed sense of the stanza in the precise structure thereof as a means of articulating a distinctive state of mind, and to a no less developed sense of the image, as distinct from the proposition pure and simple, as the means of moral and psychological elucidation. And it is here, with the moral and psychological situation they set out to explore, that we must begin when it comes to the *petrose*; for here in the *petrose*, and in a manner standing over and against the dominant emphases of Dante's lyric poetry so far, it is a question of love as a principle, not now of transcendence on the planes of knowing and desiring, but of the kind of obsession, frustration and irresolution making between them for a species of ontological catastrophe. Considered, in other words, from the point of view of their content, of the substance and psychology of love upon which they rest and which they in turn proclaim, the *petrose* enter with tremendous power and persuasiveness into what amounts to the dialectic of love in Dante, to a meditation countenancing at every point along the way its function as a principle both of being and of non-being, both of doing and of undoing, both of the divine and of the demonic; so, for example, we have these lines from—at any rate in our customary organization of these poems—the first canzone in the cycle, *Io son venuto al punto de la rota*, an essay already in the intractability of it all, in a passion as single-minded and obsessive as it is bereft of all hope:

Io son venuto al punto de la rota
che l'orizzonte, quando il sol si corca,
ci partorisce il geminato cielo,
    e la stella d'amor ci sta remota
per lo raggio lucente che la 'nforca
sì di traverso che le si fa velo;
    e quel pianeta che conforta il gelo
si mostra tutto a noi per lo grand'arco
nel qual ciascun di sette fa poca ombra;
    e però non disgombra
un sol penser d'amore, ond'io son carco,
la mente mia, ch'è più dura che petra
in tener forte imagine di petra.

(*Io son venuto al punto de la rota*, lines 1–13)[22]

—lines to which, as confirming the status of violence and vulnerability in love as the stuff of Dante's meditation hereabouts and thus of a moment present to itself under the aspect only of despair, we may add these from the final poem in the group, the canzone *Così nel mio parlar voglio esser aspro*:

Così nel mio parlar voglio esser aspro
com'è ne li atti questa bella petra,
la quale ognora impetra
maggior durezza e più natura cruda,

22 'I have come to that point on the wheel at which the horizon, once the sun goes down, presents us with the twin constellation, and the star of love stands at a distance by virtue of the shining beam at once bestriding it and drawing over it a veil. And that planet which so sharpens the cold stands fully revealed to us along the great arc where each of the seven casts a short shadow. Yet for all this my mind—harder than stone in holding fast to an image of stone—sets aside not a single thought of the love whence I am burdened.' Luigi Blasucci, 'L'esperienza delle "petrose" e il linguaggio della *Divina Commedia*', *Belfagor* 12 (1957), 403–31; Angelo Jacomuzzi, 'Invenzione e artificio nelle "petrose"', in *Il palinsisto della retorica* (Florence: Olschki, 1972), 7–42; Ignazio Baldelli, 'Lingua e stile dalle petrose a "Tre donne"', *RLIt* 82.1 (1978), 5–17; Bruce Comens, 'Stages of Love, Steps to Hell: Dante's "Rime petrose"', *MLN* 101.1 (1985), 57–88; Sara Sturm-Maddox, 'The "Rime petrose" and the Purgatorial Palinode', *Studies in Philology* 84.2 (1987), 119–33; Robert M. Durling and Ronald L. Martinez, *Time and the Crystal: Studies in Dante's "Rime petrose"* (Berkeley: University of California Press, 1990); Peter E. Bondanella, 'Arnaut Daniel and Dante's "Rime Petrose": A Re-examination', in *Dante: The Critical Complex*, ed. Richard Lansing, vol. 1 (New York: Routledge, 2003), 330–48; Johannes Bartuschat, 'Eléments pour una analyse stylistique et thématique des "Petrose"', in *Le 'Rime' di Dante. Atti della giornata di studi (16 novembre 2007)*, ed. Paolo Grossi (Paris: Istituto Italiano di Cultura, 2008), 27–52. For *Io son venuto al punto de la rota* in particular, Andrea Battistini, 'Lo stile della Medusa: I processi di pietri-ficazione in "Io son venuto al punto de la rota"', *LC* 26, ed. Emilio Pasquini (Ravenna: Longo, 1997), 93–110; Irene Maffia Scariati, 'Dante al "punto delle rota" e la stagione delle petrose (*Rime* [C], 5–7, 53–58)', *SD* 70 (2005), 155–92; Stefano Carrai, 'Io son venuto al punto della rota', in *Dante Alighieri: Le quindici canzoni. Lette da diversi*, vol. 2 (Lecce: Pensa Multimedia, 2012), 45–63.

> e veste sua persona d'un dïaspro
> tal che per lui, o perch'ella s'arretra,
> non esce di faretra
> saetta che già mai la colga ignuda;
>   ed ella ancide, e non val ch'om si chiuda
> né si dilunghi da' colpi mortali,
> che, com'avesser ali,
> giungono altrui e spezzan ciascun'arme:
> sì ch'io non so da lei né posso atarme.

(*Così nel mio parlar voglio esser aspro*, lines 1–13)[23]

And the solution, the way out of this predicament? Short of taking the object of that love by force, indeed by way of the most complete kind of orgasmic frenzy, there is none:

> S'io avessi le belle trecce prese,
> che fatte son per me scudiscio e ferza,
> pigliandole anzi terza,
> con esse passerei vespero e squille;
>   e non sarei pietoso né cortese,
> anzi farei com'orso quando scherza;
> e se Amor me ne sferza,
> io mi vendicherei di più di mille.
>   Ancor ne li occhi, ond'escon le faville
> che m'infiammano il cor, ch'io porto anciso,
> guarderei presso e fiso,
> per vendicar lo fuggir che mi face;
> e poi le renderei con amor pace.

(*Così nel mio parlar voglio esser aspro*, lines 66–78)[24]

---

23 'I want to be as harsh in my speech as this fair stone is in her manner, as she who, attired as she is in jasper such that either for this reason or by dint of her constant retreat she suffers no arrow from a quiver ever to catch her unprotected, becomes with every passing moment still harder and crueller by nature. But she herself is one who slays, for which reason there is no putting on armour or fleeing from her deadly blows—blows which seek out their target as if they were winged, shattering as they do so one's every weapon. For myself, then, I've neither the skill nor the strength to save myself from her.' Aldo Vallone, 'Lettura "interna" della canzone "Così nel mio parlar voglio esser aspro"', in *Letteratura e critica* 1 (1974–77), 235–69; Andrea Masini, 'Lettura linguistica di "Così nel mio parlar"', *DS* 62 (1990), 289–322; Luciano Rossi, '"Così nel mio parlar voglio esser aspro" (CIII)', *LC* 24, ed. Michelangelo Picone (Ravenna: Longo, 1995), 69–89; Giuliano Tanturli, '"Così nel mio parlar voglio esser aspro" (CIII)', in *Dante Alighieri: Le quindici canzoni. Lette da diversi*, vol. 1 (Lecce: Pensa Multimedia, 2009), 9–28.

24 'Having seized the fair tresses which have become my whip and my lash, seizing them before

But with what in this sense—and perhaps on the basis of a hapless encounter along the way—bears witness to a further stage in the working out of love's dialectic, of its power, that is to say, both to being and to non-being on the part of the one who says 'I' we are merely in the foothills where the *petrose* as by any reckoning the most sensational of Dante's initiatives as a lyric poet are concerned; for at issue here is not only a fresh sense of love in its power to ravish, nay to ravage the soul, but a fresh poetic, or, to be more exact, a poetic that, while affirming the ideal transparency in the poem itself of form to substance, ushers in a fresh set of expressive possibilities. First, then, there is the stanza as, properly speaking, the 'mansio capax', or fundamental unit of poetic discourse,[25] a unit already by virtue of its da capo structure a repetitive and to that extent an introspective entity, a situation immeasurably intensified in the *petrose* by its lexical complexion, by, especially, the insistence of one and the same set of terminal rhymes; so, for example, the canzone *Amor, tu vedi ben che questa donna* with its five rhyme words ('donna', 'tempo', 'luce', 'freddo' and 'petra'), arranged in such a way that the last rhyme of each successive stanza becomes the first in the next. And what applies in *Amor, tu vedi ben che questa donna* by way of its studied circularity applies all the more in the sestina *Al poco giorno e al gran cerchio d'ombra* as the *non plus ultra* in Dante of his own *trobar clus* or closed style of verse making, for here too it is a question of rhyme under the aspect of retrogradation (*retrogradatio*),[26] of art

---

terce I'd continue with them through vespers and the evening bell, and show no compassion or civility—nay I'd be like a bear at play. And though Love scourge me with them, I'd have revenge a thousandfold. More than this, to avenge myself for her fleeing from me I'd stare fixedly into those eyes whence come the sparks inflaming the heart slain within me, and then, with love, make our peace.' Ronald L. Martinez, 'Dante's Bear: A Note on "Così nel mio parlar voglio esser aspro"', *DS* 111 (1993), 213–22.

25 *De vulgari eloquentia* 2.9.2: 'Et circa hoc sciendum est quod hoc vocabulum [stantia] per solius artis respectum inventum est, videlicet ut in quo tota cantionis ars esset contenta, illud diceretur stantia, hoc est mansio capax sive receptaculum totius artis' (And what needs to be understood here is that this term [stanza] was coined in respect precisely of this art and this art alone, such that this should be the whereabouts of the whole art of the canzone, its spacious mansion or receptacle).

26 Under the aspect, more precisely, of a species of retrogradation whereby the last rhyme word of each successive stanza constitutes the first rhyme word for the next stanza, the rest of that stanza being a matter of taking a rhyme word alternately from the beginning and from the end of the one before, that is, 1 and 5 then 2 and 4, the remaining rhyme word being throughout the third of the previous stanza. The whole is followed up by a *congedo* consisting of three lines incorporating between them all six rhyme words, three in terminal position. Exact in this sense Gianfranco Contini's formula (*Dante Alighieri. Opere minori*, vol. 1, part 1 [Milan and Naples: Riccardo Ricciardi Editore, 1984], 438) to the effect that here in the *petrose* the line and indeed the canzone as a whole are delivered to the sovereignty of the rhyme-word in all the evocative power thereof: 'E da stanza a stanza il collegamento è alogico, appena tematico. Gravitando verso l'allucinazione della parola in rima, il verso può elaborare per solito solo un altro centro verbale di evocazione.' Leon Emile Kastner, *A History of French Versification* (Oxford: Clarendon Press, 1903; repr. Folcroft, PA: Folcroft Library Editions, 1973); F.J.A. Davidson, 'The Origin of the Sestina', *MLN* 25.1 (1910), 18–20; Mario Fubini, *Metrica e poesia: Lezioni sulle forme metriche italiane; I. Dal Duecento a Petrarca* (Milan: Feltrinelli, 1962); Aurelio Roncaglia, 'L'invenzione della sestina', in *Metrica* 2 (1981), 3–41; Dominique Billy, 'La Sextine à la lumière de sa préhistoire: Genèse d'une forme, genèse d'un genre', *MR* 18.2 (1993), 207–39 and 18.3 (1993), 371–402; Mikhail

under the aspect of algorithm. But neither is that all when it comes to what in truth amounts to the triumph of the *petrose* as a lyric utterance, for along with the stanza in all its inward-lookingness comes the image in all its suggestiveness as a means of exploring the pathology of obsession. Already, then, the *Vita nova* had insisted on the referability of form in its every manifestation to the plain sense of the text as the ground and guarantee of its authenticity; but with the *petrose* we have something more and indeed something other than this, namely a sense of the image, not now as the *product* but as the *prius* of understanding, as, by virtue of its unlimited power to signify, the first port of call when it comes to a consummate act of intellection. So, for example, we have these lines from the canzone *Amor, tu vedi ben che questa donna* with their commitment to disclosure, to a laying open of self in the devastation of self, by way of the chill of it all, this and this alone—chill in the stark simplicity and irreducibility thereof—being equal to the *what* and the *how* of being on the verge of non-being:

> Segnor, tu sai che per algente freddo
> l'acqua diventa cristallina petra
> là sotto tramontana ov'è il gran freddo,
> e l'aere sempre in elemento freddo
> vi si converte, sì che l'acqua è donna
> in quella parte per cagion del freddo;
> così dinanzi dal sembiante freddo
> mi ghiaccia sopra il sangue d'ogne tempo
> e quel pensiero che m'accorcia il tempo
> mi si converte tutto in corpo freddo,
> che m'esce poi per mezzo de la luce
> là ond'entrò la dispietata luce.

(*Amor, tu vedi ben che questa donna*, lines 25–36)[27]

Leonovich Gasparov, *A History of European Versification* (Oxford: Oxford University Press, 1996). For Dante, the sestina and *Al poco giorno e al gran cerchio d'ombra*, Maurice Bowra, 'Dante and Arnaut Daniel', *Spec* 27 (1952), 459–74; Salvatore Battaglia, *Le rime "petrose" e la sestina: Arnaldo Daniello, Dante, Petrarca* (Naples: Liguori, 1964); Maria Picchio Simonelli, 'La sestina dantesca fra Arnaut Daniel e il Petrarca', *DS* 91 (1973), 131–44; Andrea Pulega, 'Modelli trobadorici nella sestina dantesca: Esercizi di lettura', in *ACME: Annali della Facoltà di Lettere e Filosofia dell'Università di Milano* 31 (May–August 1978), 261–328; Rocco R. Vanasco, 'L'architettura della sestina dantesca', *SPCT* 18 (1979), 109–19; Piero Cudini, 'Il Dante della sestina', *Belfagor* 37 (1982), 184–98; Gabriella Frasca, 'Dante: "Al poco giorno e al gran cerchio d'ombra"', in *La furia della sintassi: La sestina in Italia* (Naples: Bibliopolis, 1992), 123–57; Michelangelo Picone, 'All'ombra della fanciulla in fiore: Lettura semantica della sestina dantesca', *LC* 24 (1995), 91–108; Luciano Formisano, 'Al poco giorno e al gran cerchio d'ombra', in *Dante Alighieri: Le quindici canzoni. Lette da diversi*, vol. 1 (Lecce: Pensa Multimedia, 2009), 213–39; Eduard Vilella (ed.), *Al poco giorno e al gran cerchio d'ombra* (Madrid: Asociación Complutense di Dantologia, 2016) (various authors).

27 'You know, my lord, that, there in the north where abides the mighty cold, water, with that same

—lines to which we may add these from the canzone *Io son venuto al punto de la rota* with their account of the *how it stands and how it fares* with the poet by way of the storm-swept substance of his forlorn existence, primordiality once again challenging the proposition as the means of self-elucidation:

> Levasi de la rena d'Etiopia
> lo vento peregrin che l'aere turba,
> per la spera del sol ch'ora la scalda;
>   e passa il mare, onde conduce copia
> di nebbia tal che, s'altro non la sturba,
> questo emisperio chiude tutto e salda;
>   e poi si solve, e cade in bianca falda
> di fredda neve ed in noiosa pioggia,
> onde l'aere s'attrista tutto e piagne:
> e Amor, che sue ragne
> ritira in alto pel vento che poggia,
> non m'abbandona, sì è bella donna
> questa crudel che m'è data per donna.

(Io son venuto al punto de la rota, lines 14–26)[28]

True, there is in all this a certain *letterarietà*, a certain negotiation with the Provençal hermeticists of the past and a certain flexing of the poetic muscles to see how it all might work. In short, the process of experimentation goes on apace. But this is experimentation in the name and for the sake of something more and of something other than this, for it is experimentation in the name and for the sake of eliciting the twofold *what it is* and *how it is* with self by way of the image as a matter not now of improper but of proper predication.

---

cold, becomes crystal stone; and there, into that same element of cold, does the air forever change, and so there water, because of that cold, is mistress. Just so, when I am in her icy presence my blood forever freezes and the thought which hastens my end becomes a frozen form that takes its leave of me by way of the very eyes whereby that pitiless light gained entrance.' Pietro Pelosi, *"La novità che per tua forma luce"*: Esegesi della canzone petrosa di Dante Alighieri *"Amor, tu vedi ben che questa donna"* (Naples: Federico e Ardia, 1992); Philippe Guérin, 'Une lecture de la canzone "Amor, tu vedi ben che questa donna"', *Chroniques Italiennes (Série Web)* 15.1 (2009), 1–21; Lucia Lazzerini, 'Amor, tu vedi ben che questa donna', in *Dante Alighieri: Le quindici canzoni. Lette da diversi*, vol. 2 (Lecce: Pensa Multimedia, 2012), 13–44; John Took, 'Style and Existence in Dante: An Essay in Cognitive Poetics', in *Language and Style in Dante: Seven Essays*, ed. John C. Barnes and Michelangelo Zaccarello (Dublin: Four Courts Press, 2013), 197–222.

28 'The pilgrim wind that darkens the air rises from the sands of Ethiopia, now heated by the sun's sphere; and crossing the sea, it brings up such quantity of cloud that, unless dispersed by another wind, the cloud-mass encloses and blocks up all our hemisphere; and then it dissolves and falls in white flakes of chill snow and dreary rain so that all the air grows sad and weeps. And yet Love, who draws his nets aloft with soaring wind, still does not leave me, so fair is this cruel lady who is given me as lady.'

Less drastically experimental but calling for consideration alongside the *petrose* for its extending still further the range of lexical possibility in the lyric poem is the sonnet exchange with Forese Donati, cousin to Dante's wife Gemma, an exchange belonging in an ideal chronology to much the same period. Under one of its aspects the Forese tenzone is but a further episode in the art of insolence with to the fore among its contemporary practitioners Rustico di Filippo and Cecco Angiolieri, and everywhere impressive at any rate on Dante's side of the correspondence is the sheer brilliance of it all, its expert trading of insults in the area of penury, pusillanimity, gluttony, thievery, beggary and illegitimacy, each successive thrust of the poetic lance nicely finessing its predecessor. But more significant as far as Dante himself is concerned are (*a*) the consummate artistry of his contribution to the exchange, and (*b*) the status of the exchange as again part of the prehistory of the *Commedia*, as entering by way of the as yet jocular into his reconstruction of what in the *Inferno* amounts to the now forlorn sociopsychology of being in its lostness (so, for example, the mutually vituperative episode of Adam of Brescia and Sinon of Troy among the counterfeiters and falsifiers). First, then, there is the sheer refinement of the exchange, Dante for his part fashioning over and against the rambling and inconsequential rigmarole of Forese's *L'altra notte mi venne una gran tosse* as a scarcely less than leaden-footed account of Dante's grim family fortunes the nicely turned *Chi udisse tossir la malfatata / moglie di Bicci vocato Forese*, as spirited an account of marital incompetence as one could possibly wish for:

> Chi udisse tossir la malfatata
> moglie di Bicci vocato Forese,
> potrebbe dir ch'ell'ha forse vernata
> ove si fa 'l cristallo, in quel paese.
>
> Di mezzo agosto la truovi infreddata;
> or sappi che de' far d'ogni altro mese!
> e non le val perché dorma calzata,
> merzé del copertoio c'ha cortonese.
>
> La tosse, 'l freddo e l'altra mala voglia
> no l'addovien per omor' ch'abbia vecchi,
> ma per difetto ch'ella sente al nido.
>
> Piange la madre, c'ha più d'una doglia,
> dicendo: 'Lassa, che per fichi secchi'
> messa l'avre' 'n casa del conte Guido.[29]

---

29 'Anyone hearing the coughing of the luckless wife of Bicci called Forese might say she'd passed the winter in the land where they make crystal. You'll find her frozen in mid-August, so guess how she gets on in any other month! And it's no use her keeping her stockings on, the bedclothes are too short. The coughing, cold and all her other woes derive, not from her ageing humours, but from the gap she

Here, then, we have yet another literary occasion, an occasion like every other in Dante bearing fruit both at the time and further down the line. But sweeter by far than its mere occasionality—and here we need look no further than the exquisite 'Quando fia ch'io ti riveggia?' (When shall I see you again?) placed by Dante upon the lips of Forese in *Purgatorio* 24—is its transparency less, withal, to contempt than to companionship as the encompassing.[30]

---

feels in the nest. Her mother, who has more than enough to worry about, weeps, saying: "Alas, for dried figs I could have married her off to one or other of the Counts Guidi!"' Fredi Chiappelli, 'Proposta d'interpretazione per la tenzone di Dante con Forese', in *Il legame musaico*, ed. Pier Massimo Forni (Rome: Edizioni di Storia e Letteratura [1984]), 41–70; Gennaro Savarese, *Una proposta per Forese e altri studi su Dante* (Rome: Bulzoni, 1992); Antonio Stäuble, 'La tenzone di Dante con Forese Donati', in *Le Rime di Dante*, LC 24 (1995), 151–70; Domenico De Robertis, 'Ancora per Dante e Forese Donati', in *Feconde venner le carte: Studi in onore di Ottavio Besomi*, vol. 1, ed. Tatiana Crivelli (Bellinzona: Casagrande, 1997), 35–48; Antonio Lanza, 'A norma di filologia: Ancora a proposito della cosiddetta "Tenzone tra Dante e Forese"', *L'Alighieri (RBD)* 10 (1997), 43–54; Antonio Enzo Quaglio, 'Intorno alla tenzone Dante-Forese', in *"Per correr miglior acque . . .": Bilanci e prospettive degli studi danteschi alle soglie del nuovo millennio. Atti del Convegno internazionale di Verona-Ravenna 25–29 ottobre 1999*, vol. 1 (Rome: Salerno, 2001), 247–80; Michelangelo Zaccarello, 'L'uovo o la gallina? *Purg.* XXIII e la tenzone di Dante e Forese Donati', in *L'Alighieri (RD)* 22 (2003), 5–26 (and, with the title 'The Chicken or the Egg? *Purgatorio* XXX and the "tenzone" with Forese', in *Language and Style in Dante*, ed. John C. Barnes and Michelangelo Zaccarello [Dublin: Four Courts Press, 2013], 133–60); Piero Boitani, 'Recognition and Poetry: Forese', in *Poetry of the Donati. The Barlow Lectures on Dante Delivered at University College London 17–18 March 2005* (Leeds: Maney, 2007) (and in *Dante e il suo futuro*, [Rome: Edizioni di Storia e Letteratura, 2013], 223–88); Claude Perrus, 'Modalités de l'expérience comique: La tenzone avec Forese', in *Le 'Rime' di Dante. Atti della giornata di studi (16 novembre 2007)*, ed. Paolo Grossi (Paris: Istituto Italiano di Cultura, 2008), 13–26; Fabian Alfie, *Dante's "tenzone" with Forese Donati: The Reprehension of Vice* (Toronto: University of Toronto Press, 2011). On the authenticity of the Forese tenzone, Ruggiero Stefanini, 'Tenzone sì e tenzone no', *LD* 18–19 (1996), 111–28; Mauro Cursietti, 'Nuovi contributi per l'apocrifia della cosiddetta "Tenzone di Dante con Forese Donati" ovvero "La tenzone del panìco"', in *Bibliologia e critica dantesca: Saggi dedicati a Enzo Esposito*, vol. 2, ed. Vincenzo De Gregorio (Ravenna: Longo, 1997), 53–72; 'Dante e Forese alla taverna del panìco: Le prove documentarie della falsità della "Tenzone"', in *L'Alighieri (RBD)* 16 (2000), 7–22; and 'A proposito di una nuova ipotesi sulla cosiddetta "Tenzone" di Dante con Forese', *PT* 8.1 (2004), 157–68; Menotti Stanghellini (ed.), *Rustico Filippi: I trenta sonetti realistici* (Monteriggioni: Edizioni Il Leccio, 2004) (with 'Il vero autore della "Tenzone fra Dante e Forese"' at 101–19). More generally on the genre (*vituperatio*), Paolo Orvieto and Lucia Brestolino, 'La poesia d'amore e il suo rovescio: I "vituperia" e le tenzoni poetiche', in *La poesia comico realistica: Dalle origini al Cinquecento* (Rome: Carocci, 2000), 13–44.

30 Stephen Bemrose, *A New Life of Dante* (Exeter: University of Exeter Press, 2000), 31–32: 'Dante accuses Forese of neglecting his wife (and perhaps also of impotence), of gluttony, theft and illegitimacy. Forese in turn scorns Dante's alleged humiliating and ridiculous poverty, obscurely insults his father, and accuses Dante of cowardice. Clearly the two were firm friends.'

CHAPTER 2

The *Convivio*

PRELIMINARY REMARKS: MAGNANIMITY, POSSIBILITY AND IMPOSSIBILITY

The *Convivio*, radiant as it is as an expression of all that most mattered to Dante in the early years of his exile, and fervent as it is in the pursuit of its successive emphases, is the great work of his middle period, a work as courageous in squaring up to the slings and arrows of outrageous fortune as it is generous in preparing a philosophical feast for the variously disenfranchised and disenchanted. On the one hand, then, there is its heroism, the energy with which it sets about fashioning in the wake of exile and of the catastrophe thereof both a significant presence and a significant purpose in the world; while on the other there is its openhandedness, the eagerness with which it seeks to address a certain set of people at a certain stage in their socioeconomic and political development with a view to confirming them in a sense of their proper humanity, of what it means to affirm self in the fullness of self. And then finally, as at once the efficient and the formal cause of these things, there is its affirmation of the vernacular as equal now to every high-level inflexion of the spirit, to every demand made upon it in the areas both of natural and of moral philosophy. In this, then, as in every other sense, this is in-deed a magnanimous or 'large-souled' text, the product of a spirit reaching in one and the same moment both downwards into the recesses of its author's own restive humanity, of a humanity, that is to say, forever engaged at the far limits of moral and ontological possibility, and outwards in addressing the predicament of those 'many noble folk in this language of ours, men and women alike, burdened by domestic and civic care' but in need even so of fresh feasting, of further nourishment for the soul.[1] But it is precisely at this point—at the point of its magnanimity or large-souledness—that the provisionality of the *Convivio*, and indeed its ultimate impossibility, as a treatise *de felicitate* moves into view; for it is at this point that a characteristically Dantean preoccupation with difference, with a qualitative separating out of the various species of happiness proper to man as man, and thus also of the means to that happiness, surfaces in all its power to

---

1 *Convivio* 1.9.5 and 1.1.13 : 'e molt'altra nobile gente, non solamente maschi ma femmine, che sono molti e molte in questa lingua ... [per cura] familiare o civile ne la umana fame rimaso'.

disrupt and ultimately to destroy the consistency of the whole. Courage, therefore, and generosity, to be sure, and indeed these things in abundance, but at the same time a text containing within itself, and not far beneath the surface, the seeds of its own superseding.

COURSE OF THE ARGUMENT

Few in the course of European letters have experienced in quite the same degree as Dante the intense loneliness of exile, the isolation consequent upon leaving behind everything most cherished by way of friends, family and Florence and upon 'making a party by and for oneself' (the 'sì ch'a te fia bello / averti fatta parte per te stesso' moment of *Paradiso* 17). But by the same token few have managed in quite the same degree to combine that loneliness and isolation with a will to reach out and to break bread with those round about (the "pane degli angeli" moment of *Convivio* 1.1). On the one hand, then, and duly registered on the threshold of the text, there is the catastrophe of exile in all the unspeakable sadness thereof, a catastrophe and sadness entailing and indeed demanding a fresh shaping and substantiation of his existence, this and this alone being the way of self-retrieval:

> Ahi, piaciuto fosse al dispensatore de l'universo che la cagione de la mia scusa mai non fosse stata! ché né altri contra me avria fallato, né io sofferto avria pena ingiustamente, pena, dico, d'essilio e di povertate. Poi che fu piacere de li cittadini de la bellissima e famosissima figlia di Roma, Fiorenza, di gittarmi fuori del suo dolce seno—nel quale nato e nutrito fui in fino al colmo de la vita mia, e nel quale, con buona pace di quella, desidero con tutto lo cuore di riposare l'animo stancato e terminare lo tempo che m'è dato—per le parti quasi tutte a le quali questa lingua si stende, peregrino, quasi mendicando, sono andato, mostrando contra mia voglia la piaga de la fortuna, che suole ingiustamente al piagato molte volte essere imputata. Veramente io sono stato legno sanza vela e sanza governo, portato a diversi porti e foci e liti dal vento secco che vapora la dolorosa povertade; e sono apparito a li occhi a molti che forseché per alcuna fama in altra forma m'aveano imaginato, nel conspetto de' quali non solamente mia persona invilio, ma di minor pregio si fece ogni opera, sì già fatta, come quella che fosse a fare.
>
> (*Convivio* 1.3.3–5)[2]

while on the other there is, again, the generosity of it all, the laying on of a feast for the benefit of those disadvantaged by circumstance with respect to their proper happiness as creatures of moral and intellectual determination, this, therefore, being where Dante begins in the *Convivio*. Least among the philosophers but loathe to pass by on the other side, he begins with the predicament of those of his fellow citizens who, bowed down as they are by domestic and civic care, have as yet but a hazy awareness of the *what might be* of their properly human presence in the world, this, therefore—the *Convivio*—being both in substance and in spirit a labour of love:

> Ma però che ciascuno uomo a ciascuno uomo naturalmente è amico, e ciascuno amico si duole del difetto di colui ch'elli ama, coloro che a così alta mensa sono cibati non sanza misericordia sono inver di quelli che in bestiale pastura veggiono erba e ghiande sen gire mangiando. E acciò che misericordia è madre di beneficio, sempre liberalmente coloro che sanno porgono de la loro buona ricchezza a li veri poveri, e sono quasi fonte vivo, de la cui acqua si refrigera la naturale sete che di sopra è nominata. E io adunque, che non seggio a la beata mensa, ma, fuggito de la pastura del vulgo, a' piedi di coloro che seggiono ricolgo di quello che da loro cade, e conosco la misera vita di quelli che dietro m'ho lasciati, per la dolcezza ch'io sento in quello che a poco a poco ricolgo, misericordievolmente mosso, non me dimenticando, per li miseri alcuna cosa ho riservata, la quale a li occhi loro, già è più tempo, ho dimostrata; e in ciò li ho fatti maggiormente vogliosi.
>
> (*Convivio* 1.1.8–10)³

I would have been spared my pain, the pain, that is to say, of exile and poverty. But since it pleased the citizens of Florence, the most beautiful and famous daughter of Rome, to cast me from her sweet bosom—where I was born and brought to maturity, and where, with her blessing, I wish with my whole heart to rest my weary mind and live out my allotted span—I have made my way much like a stranger and mendicant through just about every region covered by our language, displaying against my will the wounds inflicted upon me by fate, wounds for which the wounded man is often unjustly held accountable. Truly, I have been a ship without either sail or rudder, borne willy-nilly to harbours, estuaries and shores by the dry wind of grievous poverty; and I have been looked upon by many who, on the basis perhaps of reports heard, imagined me as other than I am, such that not only was my person held in low esteem, but that all my works, complete and yet to be completed, were cheapened.'

3 'But since every man is by nature a friend of every other man, and every man is grieved by any lack in the one he loves, those who are fed at such an exalted table are not without compassion towards those they see wandering in lowly pastures feeding on grass and acorns. And since compassion is the mother of action, those in possession of understanding always give generously from their bounty to those genuinely in need, for they are like a living fountain whose waters slake the natural thirst of which I spoke a moment ago. I, therefore, who do not myself sit at the blessed table, but rather, having fled the pasture of the commonalty, take my place at the feet of those who are so seated, gathering up as I do so whatever falls from it, acknowledge the wretched state of those I have left behind; and, sensitive to the sweetness of what little I have been able to save and moved by compassion, I have (albeit without

And it is this concern for the well-being of the next man as captive to circumstance that determines the main business of this first book of the *Convivio*, namely its opting for the vernacular rather than for Latin as best suited to the matter in hand. True, the choice requires some justification, Latin, from the point of view of its immunity to change over the generations, of its expressive power and of its sheer elegance being on the face of it the language of choice (the 'onde concedesi esser più bello, più virtuoso e più nobile' moment of 1.5.14). No sooner said, however, than rescinded, for by the time we reach chapter 10, a little way down the line, Dante has just about completely changed his mind; for if in respect of its incorruptibility Latin remains the nobler of the two languages, then in respect of its power fully and sufficiently to articulate the idea and of its gentle concatenation of sound and syntax the vernacular is quite the equal of 'grammar'. Neither expressively, then, nor aesthetically is there anything to choose between them, the competence and complexion of the vernacular line being matched only by its capacity to ravish the spirit:

> Ché per questo comento la gran bontade del volgare di sì [si vedrà]; però che si vedrà la sua vertù, sì com'è per esso altissimi e novissimi concetti convenevolmente, sufficientemente e acconciamente, quasi come per esso latino, manifestare; [la quale non si potea bene manifestare] ne le cose rimate, per le accidentali adornezze che quivi sono connesse, cioè la rima e lo ri[ti]mo e lo numero regolato; sì come non si può bene manifestare la

---

forgetting myself) set aside something for those poor folk—something for which, in that I placed it before them quite a while ago now, they are all the more eager.' Maria Picchio Simonelli, 'Pubblico e società nel *Convivio*', *Yearbook of Italian Studies* 4 (1980), 41–48; Richard H. Lansing, 'Dante's Intended Audience in the *Convivio*', *DS 110* (1992), 17–24 (and in *Dante: The Critical Complex*, vol. 3, ed. Richard Lansing [New York: Routledge, 2003], 27–34); Sonia Gentili, 'Il desiderio di conoscere e il dovere di divulgare: Il *Convivio* di Dante', in *L'uomo aristotelico alle origini della letteratura italiana* (Rome: Carocci, 2005), 127–65; Sonia Gentili, 'Bene comune e naturale socialità in Dante, Petrarca e nella cultura filosofica in lingua volgare (secc. XIII–XIV)', in *Il bene comune: Forme di governo e gerarchie sociali nel basso medioevo. Atti del XLVIII Convegno Storico Internazionale, Todi, 9–12 ottobre 2011* (Spoleto: Centro italiano di studi sull'alto medioevo [2012]), 371–90; Sonia Gentili, 'La vulgarisation de l'Éthique d'Aristote en Italie au XIIIe et XIVe siècles: Enjeux littéraires et philosophiques', *Médiévales: Langue, Textes, Histoire* 63 (2012), 47–58; Gianfranco Fioravanti, 'Il *Convivio* e il suo pubblico', *FSt* 7.2 (2014), 13–21; Gianfranco Fioravanti, 'La nobilità spiegata ai nobili: Una nuova funzione della filosofia', in *Il 'Convivio' di Dante*, ed. Johannes Bartuschat and Andrea Aldo Robiglio (Ravenna: Longo, 2015), 157–63; Franziska Meier, 'Educating the Reader: Dante's *Convivio*', *L'Alighieri (RD)* 45 (2015), 21–33; Nicolò Maldina, 'Raccogliendo briciole: Una metafora della formazione dantesca tra *Convivio* e *Commedia*', *SD* 81 (2016), 131–64. On Dante and friendship in the *Convivio*, Paolo Falzone, 'Il *Convivio* e l'amicizia secondo i filosofi', *AIISS* 17 (2000), 55–101; Filippa Modesto, 'Classical Friendship: Aristotle and Dante's *Convivio*', in *Dante's Idea of Friendship: The Transformation of a Classical Concept* (Toronto: Toronto University Press, 2015), 20–42. Also, and in addition to Julia Bolton Holloway, *Twice-Told Tales: Brunetto Latino and Dante Alighieri* (New York: Peter Lang, 1993), Concetto Marchesi, 'Le redazioni trecentistiche volgari del *De amicitia* secondo i codici fiorentini', in *Scritti minori di filologia e letteratura*, vol. 1 (Florence: Olschki, 1978 [1904]), 155–72.

bellezza d'una donna, quando li adornamenti de l'azzimare e de le vestimenta la fanno più ammirare che essa medesima. Onde chi vuole ben giudicare d'una donna, guardi quella quando solo sua naturale bellezza si sta con lei, da tutto accidentale adornamento discompagnata; sì come sarà questo comento, nel quale si vedrà l'agevolezza de le sue sillabe, le proprietadi de le sue co[stru]zioni e le soavi orazioni che di lui si fanno, le quali chi bene agguarderà, vedrà essere piene di dolcissima e d'amabilissima bellezza.

(Convivio 1.10.12–13)[4]

But that, where the vernacular is concerned, is not all, for the *Convivio* thus conceived, as a feast laid on for the benefit of those most in need of it, is a gift, and a gift is a gift only in the degree to which it is usefully given and usefully received, short of which it is merely a bequest or transaction. This, then, from the point of view of Dante's general undertaking in the *Convivio*, of his doing well by a spiritually undernourished lay intelligentsia, is the basis of his linguistic preference in the book; no vernacular, no generosity, simply an empty and thus meaningless gesture in respect of those both seeking and deserving better:

Tornando dunque al principale proposito, dico che manifestamente si può vedere come lo latino averebbe a pochi dato lo suo beneficio, ma lo volgare servirà veramente a molti. Ché la bontà de l'animo, la quale questo servigio attende, è in coloro che per malvagia disusanza del mondo hanno lasciata la litteratura a coloro che l'hanno fatta di donna meretrice; e questi nobili sono principi, baroni, cavalieri, e molt'altra nobile gente, non solamente

---

4 'By way, then, of this commentary, the great goodness of the Italian vernacular will become apparent; for in it will be seen the power it has to express the most sublime and novel ideas as fittingly, as fully and as elegantly as Latin itself—a power which cannot be shown forth so readily in verse on account of the incidental embellishment pertaining to it (namely rhyme and rhythm), any more, in fact, than can the beauty of a woman when the trappings of her finery and attire draw more attention than she herself (which is why whoever wishes properly to judge of a woman should irrespective of accidental adornment look upon her in her natural beauty). That, then, is how this commentary will appear, for everywhere apparent will be the gracious movement of its syllables, the elegance of its periods and the sweet discourse fashioned from it, which things, for those caring to look on attentively, will have about them both the sweetest and the loveliest beauty.' For the 'onde concedesi esser più bello, più virtuoso e più nobile' moment of 1.5.14: 'whence it will be allowed [that Latin] is the more beautiful, the more powerful and the nobler of the two'. Enrico Paradisi, 'La contraddizione che consente: Latino e volgare in Dante', in *Quaderni del Laboratorio di Linguistica* 4 (2003), 245–51; Mirko Tavoni, 'Volgare e latino nella storia di Dante', in *Dante's Plurilingualism: Authority, Knowledge, Subjectivity*, ed. Sara Fortuna et al. (Oxford: Legenda, 2010), 52–68; Mirko Tavoni (ed.), 'Che cosa erano il volgare e il latino per Dante', in *Dante e la lingua italiana*, LC 41 (Ravenna: Longo, 2013), 9–27; Gennaro Sasso, 'Il latino e il volgare fra *Convivio* e *De vulgari*', in *La lingua, la Bibbia, la storia: Su 'De vulgari eloquentia'* 1 (Rome: Viella, 2015), 13–38.

maschi ma femmine, che sono molti e molte in questa lingua, volgari, e non litterati.

(*Convivio* 1.9.4–5)[5]

In fact, however, the argument here runs a good deal deeper than this, for the greatest beneficiary of the vernacular has been, Dante thinks, he himself, at which point the love-intensity of the whole thing, not to say the deep vernacularity of his entire being and doing as a poet and philosopher, moves clearly into view. First, then, we have the moment of recognition, the moment in which, glancing away for an instant from his chosen clientele with a view to surveying his own situation, he testifies to the indispensability of the vernacular to his own coming about both in the flesh and in the spirit—in the flesh by way of the vernacular as the in-and-through-which of his parents' intercourse (the 'concorso a la mia generazione' moment of the argument), and in the spirit by way of that same vernacular as preliminary in respect of still greater things to come, of a Latin culture making not simply for his *being* but for his *being well* as a creature of moral and intellectual awareness:

Questo mio volgare fu congiugnitore de li miei generanti, che con esso parlavano, sì come 'l fuoco è disponitore del ferro al fabbro che fa lo coltello; per che manifesto è lui essere concorso a la mia generazione, e così essere alcuna cagione del mio essere. Ancora, questo mio volgare fu introduttore di me ne la via di scienza, che è ultima perfezione, in quanto con esso io entrai ne lo latino e con esso mi fu mostrato: lo quale latino poi mi fu via a più innanzi andare. E così è palese, e per me conosciuto, esso essere stato a me grandissimo benefattore.

(*Convivio* 1.13.4–5)[6]

But then, having confirmed the indispensability of the vernacular to his own coming about as a creature of seeing, understanding and choosing, comes the

5 'To return, then, to my main theme, it is, I maintain, perfectly plain to see how Latin would have benefited very few, whereas the vernacular will serve the interests of many; for excellence of mind is to be found only in those who, having alas neglected these things by reason of their busyness in the world, have abandoned letters only to those making a harlot of them—in those many worthy princes, barons, knights, including men and women alike, who, having the vernacular but no Latin, abound in this language of ours.'

6 'Just like the fire which readies the iron for the smith to make a knife, this vernacular of mine, being the language my parents spoke, brought them together, it being clear, therefore, that it was implicated in my coming about, among the causes of my being. Moreover, in that with its help I made a start in Latin and was helped in my understanding of it, this same vernacular set me on the road to knowledge as the greatest perfection, Latin being that whereby I was able to make further progress. It is clear, therefore—and this I gladly acknowledge—that this my vernacular has been my most wonderful benefactor.'

love-intensity moment of the argument, the moment in which, having confirmed the length, breadth, height and depth of his companionship with the vernacular, he commits himself yet again to its welfare, his meditation hereabouts culminating in something close to a giving and receiving of vows:

> Anche, è stato meco d'uno medesimo studio, e ciò posso così mostrare. Ciascuna cosa studia naturalmente a la sua conservazione; onde, se lo volgare per sé studiare potesse, studierebbe a quella; e quella sarebbe, acconciare sé a più stabilitade, e più stabilitade non potrebbe avere che in legar sé con numero e con rime. E questo medesimo studio è stato mio, sì come tanto è palese che non dimanda testimonianza. Per che uno medesimo studio è stato lo suo e 'l mio; per che di questa concordia l'amistà è confermata e accresciuta. Anche c'è stata la benivolenza de la consuetudine, ché dal principio de la mia vita ho avuta con esso benivolenza e conversazione, e usato quello diliberando, interpetrando e questionando. Per che, se l'amistà s'accresce per la consuetudine, sì come sensibilmente appare, manifesto è che essa in me massimamente è cresciuta, che sono con esso volgare tutto mio tempo usato. E così si vede essere a questa amistà concorse tutte le cagioni generative e accrescitive de l'amistade; per che si conchiude che non solamente amore, ma perfettissimo amore sia quello ch'io a lui debbo avere e ho.
>
> (*Convivio* 1.13.6–10)[7]

With this, then, and by way of what amounts now to the Gospel abundance of it all, it remains only to confirm his purpose in the book, namely a fresh feeding of the five thousand by means of a vernacular discourse designed to encourage them both severally and in the round in a fresh sense of their properly human being-in-the-world:

---

7 'Further, and as I shall now demonstrate, we have together sought out but one and the same goal; for everything naturally seeks to preserve its own being. If, then, the vernacular were itself able to seek out an end, that indeed is what it would seek—to wit, the still greater stability of rhythm and rhyme as that whereby it is properly bound up. This, as something requiring no further proof, is the very goal I have set myself. We both of us, then, have sought out the same thing, this common commitment of ours being by way of a firm and ever developing friendship. And then there has been the long-standing goodwill of it all, I, from my earliest days, having enjoyed with the vernacular a tender companionship, calling upon it for my every deliberation, my every judgement in point of meaning and my every enquiry after the truth. So if as most certainly seems to be the case friendship is deepened by familiarity, then this, manifestly and indeed supremely, has been true for me as having had a constant concern for this language of ours. Plainly, then, everything making for friendship whether by way of quickening or else of nurturing it has been at work here too, whence it follows that mine, for the vernacular, is a matter, not simply of love, but of the most perfect love, this being but what I owe and what I indeed profess.'

Così rivolgendo li occhi a dietro, e raccogliendo le ragioni prenotate, puotesi vedere questo pane, col quale si deono mangiare le infrascritte canzoni, essere sufficientemente purgato da le macule, e da l'essere di biado; per che tempo è d'intendere a ministrare le vivande. Questo sarà quello pane orzato del quale si satolleranno migliaia, e a me ne soperchieranno le sporte piene. Questo sarà luce nuova, sole nuovo, lo quale surgerà là dove l'usato tramonterà, e darà lume a coloro che sono in tenebre e in oscuritade, per lo usato sole che a loro non luce.

(*Convivio* 1.13.11–12)[8]

This, then, is by any standard a remarkable hors d'oeuvre, a truly astonishing starter, as astonishing in the depth and intensity of its confessionalism as it is in the completeness of its commitment to the vernacular as the means of philosophical disquisition. But that is not all, for the depth and intensity of Dante's confessionalism in the first book of the *Convivio* continue unabated into the second, where it is a question not now of language but of love, of his own enamouring of philosophy as but the love of wisdom first and foremost in God himself and tending in those surrendering to its sweet persuasiveness to fashion them afresh in the likeness of their maker. First, though, a procedural point, for if in the *Convivio*, as in the *Vita nova*, it is a question of Dante's commenting upon certain of his own poems, there is now a difference, for here in the *Convivio* it is a matter, not now of the plain text as, with a little assistance from the glossator, equal to the matter in hand, but of allegory, of the poem's saying one thing and meaning another. In fact, Dante's account hereabouts of his procedure in the *Convivio* is somewhat more complicated than this, his, here as in the letter to Cangrande as yet some way over the horizon, being a nod in the direction both of poets' and of theologians' allegory, both of the 'aut . . . aut . . . ' or *either/or* of the poets and rhetori-

---

8 'Looking back, then, over all that has been said, and gathering up the threads of the argument so far, it is clear that this bread, with which the following canzoni should be eaten, has been sufficiently purged of any blemish and excused for being but of barley. So now, then, it is time to think about serving the courses themselves, this commentary constituting the barley bread whereby—with many a basketful besides remaining to me—thousands will be satisfied. This will be a new light, a new sun rising where the old has set, a light to enlighten the overshadowed and darkling, the sun of old no longer shining upon them.' John 6:1–13, with, at verse 13, 'Collegerunt ergo, et impleverunt duodecim cophinos fragmentorum ex quinque panibus bordaceis, quae superfuerunt his, qui mandicaverant' (So they gathered them and filled twelve baskets with the pieces of the five barley loaves left over by those who had eaten), while for the 'luce nuova' motif, Esther 8:16, Isaiah 9:2, Matthew 4:16, Luke 1:76–79 etc. Carlo Curto, ' "Pane orzato", "luce nuova", "sole nuovo" nel *Convivio* di Dante', in *Studi di letteratura italiana da Dante a Pascoli* (Turin: Giappichelli, 1966 [1941]), 9–13; Mary Alexandra Watt, 'Take This Bread: Dante's Eucharistic Banquet', *QItal* 22.1 (2001), 17–35; Nicola De Blasi, ' "Quello pane orzato": La misericordia e il volgare', in *"Per beneficio e concordia di studio": Studi danteschi offerti a Enrico Malato per i suoi ottant'anni*, ed. Andrea Mazzucchi (Cittadella [PD]: Bertoncello Artigrafiche, 2015), 349–62.

cians (where it is a matter of saying one thing and meaning something else) and of the 'et ... et ...' or *both/and* of the theologians and biblical exegetes (where it is a question not so much of otherness as of sameness, of the mutual immanence of the literal, the allegorical, the moral and the anagogical within the overall economy of the text). That notwithstanding, however, Dante, he says, will settle for the 'way of the poets' (*lo modo de li poeti*), for an account first of the literal meaning of his poems and then of their allegorical or 'other' meaning, touching only as and when on their more esoteric substance:

> Io adunque, per queste ragioni, tuttavia sopra ciascuna canzone ragionerò prima la litterale sentenza, e appresso di quella ragionerò la sua allegoria, cioè la nascosa veritade; e talvolta de li altri sensi toccherò incidentemente, come a luogo e a tempo si converrà.
>
> (*Convivio* 2.1.15)[9]

With this, then, the way is open for an account of the first poem of the *Convivio*, namely the canzone *Voi che 'ntendendo il terzo ciel movete*, on the face of it a poem hovering somewhere between the *planctus* and the *psychomachia*, between the lamentation of the one and the conflictuality of the other. Here in other words, in a text addressed to the movers of the third heaven, is a fresh review of the

---

9 'I, then, for this reason, shall when it comes to each canzone consider first the literal meaning and thereafter its allegorical meaning, its hidden truth, touching thereafter only incidentally, as and when, on its other senses.' Philip Damon, 'The Two Modes of Allegory in Dante's *Convivio*,' *Philological Quarterly* 40 (1961), 144–49; Philip Damon, 'Allegory and Invention: Levels of Meaning in Ancient and Medieval Rhetoric', in *The Classics in the Middle Ages*, ed. Aldo S. Bernardo and Saul Levin (Binghamton, NY: Centre for Medieval & Renaissance Studies, 1990), 113–27; Marcia L. Colish, 'Medieval Allegory: A Historiographical Consideration', in *Clio: A Journal of Literature, History, and the Philosophy of History* 4.3 (1975), 341–55 (and in *Dante: The Critical Complex*, vol. 4, ed. Richard Lansing [New York: Routledge, 2003], 135–49); Manfred Lentzen, 'Zur Konzeption der Allegorie in Dantes *Convivio* und im *Brief an Cangrande della Scala*', in *Dante Alighieri 1985: In memoriam Hermann Gmelin*, ed. Richard Baum and Willi Hirdt (Tübingen: Stauffenburg, 1985), 169–90; Charles S. Singleton, 'Two Kinds of Allegory', in *Dante*, ed. Harold Bloom (New York: Chelsea House, 1986), 11–19 (and in *Dante Alighieri*, ed. Harold Bloom [Philadelphia: Chelsea House, 2004], 11–23); Antonio D'Andrea, 'L'"allegoria dei poeti": Nota a *Convivio* II. 1', in *Dante e le forme dell'allegoresi*, ed. Michelangelo Picone (Ravenna: Longo, 1987), 71–78; John A. Scott, '"Veramente li teologi questo senso prendono altrimenti che li poeti" (*Conv.* II i.5)', in *Sotto il segno di Dante: Scritti in onore di Francesco Mazzoni*, ed. Leonella Coglievina and Domenico De Robertis (Florence: Le Lettere, 1998), 299–309; Jean Pépin, 'La théorie dantesque de l'allégorie entre il *Convivio* et la *Lettera a Cangrande*', in *Dante: Mito e poesia. Atti del secondo Seminario Dantesco Internazionale, Monte Verità, Ascona, 23–27 giugno 1997*, ed. Michelangelo Picone and Tatiana Crivelli (Florence: Cesati, 1999), 51–64; Enrico Fenzi, 'L'esperienza di sé come esperienza dell'allegoria (a proposito di Dante, *Convivio* II i 2)', *SD* 67 (2002), 161–200; Gisela Seitschek , 'Dante und die "allegoria dei poeti" ', in *Schöne Lüge und verhüllte Wahrheit: Theologische uns poetische Allegorie in mittelalterlichen Dichtungen* (Berlin: Duncker & Humblot, 2009), 111–42; Francesco Bruni, 'Le due vie: Allegoria dei poeti e allegoria dei teologi (Ancora su *Convivio*, II 1)', in *"Per beneficio e concordia di studio": Studi danteschi offerti a Enrico Malato per i suoi ottant'anni*, ed. Andrea Mazzucchi (Cittadella [PD]: Bertoncello Artigrafiche, 2015), 221–37.

'donna gentile' or 'gracious lady of the casement' episode of the *Vita nova*, a review, however, registering not now her eclipse but her triumph within the economy of the whole, her winning through as the one whereby—albeit not without grave misgiving in conscience—Dante found comfort in his bereavement:

> Suol esser vita de lo cor dolente
> un soave penser, che se ne gia
> molte fiate a' pie' del nostro Sire,
>   ove una donna gloriar vedia,
> di cui parlava me sì dolcemente
> che l'anima dicea: 'Io men vo' gire.'
>   Or apparisce chi lo fa fuggire
> e segnoreggia me di tal virtute,
> che 'l cor ne trema che di fuori appare.
> Questi mi face una donna guardare,
> e dice: 'Chi veder vuol la salute,
> faccia che li occhi d'esta donna miri,
> sed e' non teme angoscia di sospiri.'

> (*Voi che 'ntendendo il terzo ciel movete*, lines 14–26)[10]

Who, then, as the recipients of Dante's anguished utterance, are these movers of the third heaven? Why simply the Intelligences, he explains, presiding over the complicated girations of Venus as (counting from the bottom) third in the heavenly hierarchy, and, in doing so, mediating her influence here below. First, then, comes a general cosmology, an account of the universe in, for Dante, the sublime concentricity of it all:

> Ed è l'ordine del sito questo, che lo primo che numerano è quello dove è la Luna; lo secondo è quello dov'è Mercurio; lo terzo è quello dov'è Venere;

---

10 'The life of my sorrowing heart used to be a gracious thought making its way often to the feet of our Lord, where, seeing a lady in glory of whom it would speak so sweetly my soul would declare: "I too wish to go there." But now there appears one putting it to flight, one who lords it over me with such power that the trembling of my heart is plain for all to see. This same one constrains me to look at a woman, saying the while: "Provided only that he shrink not from grievous sighing, let him who would know salvation gaze into the eyes of this lady." ' Bruno Nardi , 'Le figurazioni allegoriche e l'allegoria della "donna gentile" ', in *Nel mondo di Dante* (Rome: Edizioni di Storia e Letteratura, 1944), 21–40; Étienne Gilson, *Dante and Philosophy*, trans. David Moore (New York: Harper & Row, 1963 [1939]), especially 86–98; Peter Dronke, *Dante's Second Love: The Originality and the Contexts of the 'Convivio'* (Leeds: Society for Italian Studies, 1997); Gennaro Sasso, 'La "donna gentile" nella *Vita nuova* e nel *Convivio*', in *Le autobiografie di Dante* (Bibliopolis: Napoli, 2008), 15–62 (with 'La "polarità" di Beatrice e della donna gentile' at 75–83).

lo quarto è quello dove è lo Sole; lo quinto è quello di Marte; lo sesto è quello di Giove; lo settimo è quello di Saturno; l'ottavo è quello de le Stelle; lo nono è quello che non è sensibile se non per questo movimento che è detto di sopra, lo quale chiamano molti Cristallino, cioè diafano, o vero tutto trasparente. Veramente, fuori di tutti questi, li cattolici pongono lo cielo Empireo, che è a dire cielo di fiamma o vero luminoso; e pongono esso essere immobile per avere in sé, secondo ciascuna parte, ciò che la sua materia vuole. E questo è cagione al Primo Mobile per avere velocissimo movimento; ché per lo ferventissimo appetito ch'è in ciascuna parte di quello nono cielo, che è immediato a quello, d'essere congiunta con ciascuna parte di quello divinissimo ciel quieto, in quello si rivolve con tanto desiderio, che la sua velocitade è quasi incomprensibile. E quieto e pacifico è lo luogo di quella somma Deitade che sola [sé] compiutamente vede. Questo loco è di spiriti beati, secondo che la Santa Chiesa vuole, che non può dire menzogna; e Aristotile pare ciò sentire, a chi bene lo 'ntende, nel primo De Celo et Mundo. Questo è lo soprano edificio del mondo, nel quale tutto lo mondo s'inchiude, e di fuori dal quale nulla è; ed esso non è in luogo ma formato fu solo ne la prima Mente, la quale li Greci dicono Protonoè. Questa è quella magnificenza, de la quale parlò il Salmista, quando dice a Dio: "Levata è la magnificenza tua sopra li cieli". E così ricogliendo ciò che ragionato è, pare che diece cieli siano, de li quali quello di Venere sia lo terzo, del quale si fa menzione in quella parte che mostrare intendo.

(*Convivio* 2.3.7–12)[11]

11 'The heavens are arranged thus, the first of their number being that of the Moon; the second, Mercury; the third, Venus; the fourth, the Sun; the fifth, Mars; the sixth Jupiter; the seventh, Saturn; and the eighth, that of the fixed stars. The ninth which is not perceptible to the senses other than by way of the movement mentioned above, is called by many—diaphanous or totally transparent as it is—the Crystalline. Beyond these, however, Catholics locate the Empyrean, meaning the heaven of flame or, more exactly of light, which heaven, possessing as it does in its every part the perfection required by its matter, they hold to be motionless. That is why the primum mobile is so incredibly swift, for since in that ninth sphere there burns an ardent desire to be united in its every part with every part of that most divine heaven, it revolves within that heaven with a yearning so intense that its speed is beyond all understanding. Perfectly at peace, by contrast, is the dwelling place of the Godhead on high, of the One who alone fully sees himself. Indeed according to the Church, which bears no false witness, and with whom Aristotle, rightly understood, appears in the first book of the *De celo et mundo* to agree, this is the dwelling place of the blessed. It is the sovereign structure of the universe, by which the whole universe is contained and beyond which there is nothing at all. It is not itself in space, but rather was fashioned within the primal mind, within, as the Greeks call it, the *Protonoé*. It is the splendour of which the Psalmist spoke when, addressing God, he said: "Your splendour is exalted above the heavens." And so to sum up in respect of what we have said so far, it is clear that there are ten heavens, of which the heaven of Venus mentioned in that section of the *canzone* which I now intend to expound is the third.' Edward Moore, 'The Astronomy of Dante', in *Studies in Dante: Third Series* (Oxford: Clarendon Press, 1903), 1–108 (and as 'L'astronomia di Dante', in *Studi su Dante*, vol. 2, ed. Bruno Basile [Rome: Salerno, 2015], 696–800); Mary Acworth Orr, *Dante and the Early Astronomers* (London: Gall and Inglis, 1913); Patrick Boyde, *Dante Philomythes and Philosopher: Man in the Cosmos* (Cambridge:

together with, as far as the third heaven in particular is concerned, further precision as to its threefold motion and thus its threefold administration by the movers in question:

> E sono questi Troni, che al governo di questo cielo sono dispensati, in numero non grande, de lo quale per li filosofi e per gli astrologi diversamente è sentito, secondo che diversamente sentiro de le sue circulazioni; avvenga che tutti siano accordati in questo, che tanti sono quanti movimenti esso fae. Li quali, secondo che nel libro de l'Aggregazion[i] de le Stelle epilogato si truova da la migliore dimostrazione de li astrologi, sono tre: uno, secondo che la stella si muove verso lo suo epiciclo; l'altro, secondo che lo epiciclo si muove con tutto lo cielo igualmente con quello del Sole; lo terzo, secondo che tutto quello cielo si muove, seguendo lo movimento de la stellata spera, da occidente a oriente, in cento anni uno grado. Sì che a questi tre movimenti sono tre movitori . . . E questi movitori sono quelli a li quali s'intende di parlare, ed a cui io fo mia dimanda.
>
> (*Convivio* 2.5.15–18)[12]

—lines to which, as bearing on Dante's appeal to these same movers as, again, mediators of Venus's influence here below and thus as jointly responsible for his at once lamentable and elated state of mind, we may add these from the next chapter:

> Poi li ho chiamati ad udire quello ch'io voglio, assegno due ragioni per che io convenevolmente deggio loro parlare. L'una si è la novitade de la mia condizione, la quale, per non essere da li altri uomini esperta, non sarebbe

---

Cambridge University Press, 1981), 132–71; Paolo Pecoraro, 'La scienza ai tempi di Dante (con particolare riferimento alla astronomia e alla cosmologia)', in *Lectura Dantis Modenese*, ed. Società Dante Alighieri (Comitato di Modena) (Modena: Banca Popolare dell'Emilia, 1984), 41–58; Raffaele Barletti, 'La cosmologia medioevale con riferimento all'opera di Dante', *Giornale di Astronomia* 25.1 (1999), 19–26; Graziella Federici Vescovini, 'Dante e l'astronomia del suo tempo', *LIA* 3 (2002), 291–309; Cesare Vasoli, 'Dante e l'immagine del mondo nel *Convivio*', in *L'idea e l'immagine dell'universo nell'opera di Dante. Atti del Convegno Internazionale di Studi, Ravenna 12 novembre 2005* (Ravenna: Centro Dantesco dei Frati Minori Conventuali, 2008), 83–102; Attilio Ferrari and Donato Pirovano, *Dante e le stelle* (Rome: Salerno, 2015).

12 'And these Thrones, assigned as they have been to the governing of this heaven, are but few in number, philosophers and astronomers, differing as they do in their precise sense of Venus's revolutions, differing on this too, though all agree that there are as many movers as there movements in this heaven. According, then, to the summary account of this in [Alfragano's] *Aggregation of the Stars* as best set forth by the astronomers, there are three such movements: one according as the stars moves along its epicycle; a second as the epicycle moves with the entire heaven in keeping with the Sun; and a third inasmuch as the entire heaven moves from west to east in keeping with the firmament at the rate of one degree every hundred years. Thus to these three movements correspond three movers . . . These, then, are the movers to whom the poem sets out to speak and of which I make my request.'

così da loro intesa come da coloro che 'ntendono li loro effetti ne la loro operazione; e questa ragione tocco quando dico: *Ch'io nol so dire dire altrui, sì mi par novo.* L'altra ragione è: quand'uomo riceve beneficio, o vero ingiuria, prima de' quello retraere a chi liele fa, se può, che ad altri; acciò che se ello è beneficio, esso che lo riceve si mostri conoscente inver lo benefattore; e s'ella è ingiuria, induca lo fattore a buona misericordia con le dolci parole. E questa ragione tocco, quando dico: *El ciel che segue lo vostro valore, Gentili creature che voi sete, Mi tragge ne lo stato ov'io mi trovo.* Ciò è a dire: l'operazione vostra, cioè la vostra circulazione, è quella che m'ha tratto ne la presente condizione.

(*Convivio* 2.6.3–5)[13]

This, then, is the plain sense of *Voi che 'ntendendo* as the first of Dante's canzoni in the *Convivio*, a canzone turning upon the painful transition from one love to another. Hitherto, he says, his love for Beatrice was absolute, his only desire upon her premature passing being to rejoice with her in glory. But now, he goes on, his affection has been waylaid, a sequestering of the spirit, this, making only for a state of uncertainty and irresolution. Base, bewailing and bewildered, Dante has, in effect, taken his case to the top.

But—and this now is what matters—the canzone *Voi che 'ntendendo il terzo ciel movete* is allegorical, its literal sense being but a beautiful lie (the 'bella menzogna' of 2.1.3), a gracious mantle in respect of its true meaning. Properly understood, then, the poem has to do with Dante's preoccupation, not, in fact, with the compassionate lady of the casement but with 'the most beautiful and virtuous daughter of the Emperor of the Universe, known to Pythagoras as Philosophy' (the 'bellissima e onestissima figlia de lo imperadore de lo universo, a la quale Pittagora pose nome Filosofia' of 2.15.12), with the muse and mistress, that is to say, of those speculative spirits, ancient and modern alike, from whom he drew comfort in the moment of his bereavement. How so? By way, he explains, of the kind of analogy that may upon reflection be said to exist (*a*) between the stars

---

13 'After calling upon them to hear what I have to say, I give two reasons why it is they whom I may most appropriately address. One is the novelty of my condition, for inasmuch as other human beings lack any experience of it they—unlike those who, in understanding their own activity, understand also the effects flowing from it—would be unable to make sense of it. I touch on this reason when I say: "So novel is it that I know of no one else to whom I may speak of it." The second reason is this, that when someone receives either a benefit or an injury he should if possible bring it to the attention of the one responsible for it rather than to any other, so that, in the case of a benefit, the recipient may show himself grateful to his benefactor, and, in the case of an injury, he may by way of gentle persuasion move the one who caused it to kindly compassion. I touch on this reason when I say: "It is, moreover, noble creatures that you are, the heaven that responds to your power which draws me into my present state", meaning by this that it is your activity—namely the revolutions you cause—that accounts for my present condition.'

and the sciences in general (where by the term 'sciences' we mean the seven disciplines of the *trivium* and the *quadrivium*, the three Peripatetic sciences of physics, metaphysics and ethics, and the properly Christian science of theology), and (*b*) between this or that particular star and this or that particular science in—under a certain aspect at least—their comparability one with the other. As far, then, as the first of these things is concerned we may say this, that just as the stars in general move about a fixed point, ensuring as they do so the proper perfection of those things subject to their influence, so also do the sciences in general, each alike circling about its own still centre of concern and ensuring as it does so an orderly act of understanding. As far, by contrast, as the second of them is concerned we may say this, that everywhere discernible is a certain likeness between each of the heavens and each of the sciences; so, for example, the Moon and the science of grammar, each alike phased and changeable with the passage of time; or Mercury and the science of logic or dialectic, each alike as compact as it is subtle and sinuous; or Venus and rhetoric, each alike marvellous to behold in their twofold resplendence and sweetness; or the Sun and arithmetic, each alike a principle of elucidation; or Mars and music, each alike a matter of relativity (Mars being halfway up the heavenly hierarchy and music a matter of harmony and proportion); or Jupiter and geometry, the former a silvern star and the latter, in its suffering no uncertainty, a silvern science; or Saturn and astronomy, respectively the most elevated and stateliest of the stars and of the sciences. And what applies to those stars in, so to speak, our immediate vicinity applies also to the firmament or starry heaven still farther afield, as well as to the Crystalline or primum mobile and to the Empyrean as but the encompassing of it all. Thus the firmament, present to us as it is under the aspect both of the seen and of the unseen, resembles physics and metaphysics as turning respectively upon the empirical and upon the speculative encounter, while the Crystalline or primum mobile as the origin in the universe of all movement resembles ethics as the organizational science par excellence in human affairs, as that whereby our every initiative as creatures of free choice is properly regulated in respect of its orderly operation and outcome. And then finally there is the Empyrean, all of a piece with theology in its stillness and thus in its power to quieten the unquiet spirit. This then, Dante explains, is where we must look for his meaning in *Voi che 'ntendendo il terzo ciel movete*, the movers of the third heaven as but the heaven of rhetoric or of fine and persuasive speaking being none other than the likes of Boethius and Cicero, who, sought out by the poet in his bereavement, encouraged him by way precisely of the sweet utterance in a new order of love—in a love for the 'donna gentile' or compassionate lady of the casement as but My Lady Philosophy in all her power to detain and to delight the attentive spirit. So then, as perfectly at peace with itself on the exegetical front, indeed as scarcely less than self-congratulatory relative to a job well done, we have this

passage from the twilight moments of book 2 on the true meaning of the text
now before us:

> Per le ragionate similitudini si può vedere chi sono questi movitori a cu' io
> parlo. Ché sono di quello movitori, sì come Boezio e Tullio (li quali con la
> dolcezza di loro sermone inviarono me, come è detto di sopra, ne lo amore,
> cioè ne lo studio, di questa donna gentilissima Filosofia), con li raggi de la
> stella loro, la quale è la scrittura di quella: onde in ciascuna scienza la scrit-
> tura è stella piena di luce, la quale quella scienza dimostra. E, manifesto
> questo, vedere si può la vera sentenza del primo verso de la canzone
> proposta, per la esposizione fittizia e litterale.
>
> (*Convivio* 2.15.1–2)[14]

while as rejoicing now in the gracious aspect of philosophy as but Dante's new
love we have these lines from just a little further on in the same chapter, an essay,
precisely, in the sweet ineffability of it all, in an order of awareness apt straightaway to steal the spirit:

> Ove si vuole sapere che questa donna è la Filosofia; la quale veramente è
> donna piena di dolcezza, ornata d'onestade, mirabile di savere, gloriosa
> di libertade, sì come nel terzo trattato, dove la sua nobilitade si tratterà,
> fia manifesto. E là dove dice: *Chi veder vuol la salute, Faccia che li occhi
> d'esta donna miri*, li occhi di questa donna sono le sue demonstrazioni le
> quali, dritte ne li occhi de lo 'ntelletto, innamorano l'anima, liberata da le
> con[tra]dizioni. O dolcissimi e ineffabili sembianti, e rubatori subitani
> de la mente umana, che ne le mostrazioni de li occhi de la Filosofia appa-
> rite, quando essa con li suoi drudi ragiona! Veramente in voi è la salute,
> per la quale si fa beato chi vi guarda, e salvo da la morte de la ignoranza e
> da li vizii.
>
> (*Convivio* 2.15.3–4)[15]

14 'From the parallels now indicated, it may be seen who these movers are whom I address; for
they are the movers of that heaven—people such as Boethius and Cicero—who, through the sweetness
of their writings, set my steps on the path of love—which is to say my study—of this lady, the most
noble Philosophy. This they did by way of the rays emanating from their star, by way, that is, of those
works written about her. For in every branch of science the text is a star full of the light which that
science makes manifest. That said, the true meaning of the first stanza of the above canzone, duly
clarified in respect of its literal and fictitious form, may now be contemplated.'
15 'What we need to understand, then, is that the lady in question is Philosophy, in truth (and as
we shall make clear in the next part of the book focusing on her nobility), a woman tender beyond
words, graciously adorned, wondrous in her wisdom, and resplendent in her freedom. Thus where it
says "Who would see salvation, let him look into the eyes of this woman", her eyes are understood to
be her power to persuade—eyes which, once trained upon those of the mind, straightaway enamour
the soul in its freedom now from its every difficulty along the way. O glances most sweet and ineffable,

With what amounts, then, to a laying open of the true meaning of the text—of the canzone *Voi che 'ntendendo il terzo ciel movete*—as but a hymn to My Lady Philosophy, we come to book 3 of the *Convivio*, where it is a question not now of the guilt and misgiving of it all, of the agony implicit in forsaking the old in favour of the new, but rather of the 'love which discourses in my mind' and of this as the in-and-through-which of an again radical self-surpassing on the planes of seeing, understanding and desiring. This, then, is the burden of the third book of the *Convivio* in its now steady concern with philosophy as but the love of wisdom whereby the lover is made over again in the likeness of his or her maker, this fresh substantiation of self by way of the greater than self making for an ever more re-fined act of properly human being. But what, before going any further, *is* love, this well-nigh miraculous principle in man of ulterior becoming? At its most elemen-tary, Dante suggests, love is nothing other than a reaching out on the part of the lover for communion with the object of his delight, a reaching out variously con-ditioned, to be sure, by nature and circumstance but everywhere more or less pressing, more or less urgent, more or less 'athletic' in kind:

> Amore, veramente pigliando e sottilmente considerando, non è altro che unimento spirituale de l'anima e de la cosa amata; nel quale unimento di propia sua natura l'anima corre tosto e tardi, secondo che è libera o impedita.
>
> (*Convivio* 3.2.3)[16]

But that same love, Dante goes on, is, in man, a complex business, for man as man reaches out for the object of his affection, not merely morally and intellec-tually, but minerally, vegetatively and sensitively, after the manner, that is to say, not simply of the angels but of the stones beneath his feet, of the plants flourishing according to kind high up on the mountainside, deep in the shady valleys or along the seashore, and of the beasts of the field rejoicing one in the company of an-

---

which, in the moment you appear in madonna's eyes as she discourses with those she most cherishes, take possession of the human mind! Truly all blessedness is in you, those looking upon you knowing perfect bliss, nay salvation from the death of ignorance and error.' James Eustace Shaw, *The Lady "Phi-losophy" in the 'Convivio'* (Cambridge, MA: Dante Society of Cambridge, 1938). For the symmetry of stars and sciences, Helene Wieruszowski, 'An Early Anticipation of Dante's "Cieli e Scienze"', *MLN* 61.4 (1946), 217–28; Georg Rabuse, 'I corpi celesti, centri di ordinamento dell'immaginazione poetica di Dante', in *Gesammelte Aufsätze zu Dante*, ed. Erica Kanduth et al. (Stuttgart: Braumüller, 1976), 272–87. Also, Marie-Thérèse d'Alverny, 'La sagesse et ses sept filles: Recherches sur les allégories de la philosophie et des arts liberaux aux IX et au XII siècle', in *Mélanges dédiés à la mémoire de Felix Grat*, vol. 1 (Paris: Pecqueur-Grat, 1946), 245–78.

16 'Love, properly and carefully considered, is nothing other than the spiritual union of the soul and the object of its affection, which union the soul, in keeping with its proper nature, hastens on swiftly or slowly according to the degree or otherwise of its freedom.' Alberto di Giovanni, *La filosofia dell'amore nelle opere di Dante* (Rome: Abete, 1967).

other. True, the love most proper to man is the love of the rational soul whereby he reaches out for whatsoever things are pure, whatsoever things are lovely and whatsoever things are of good report, but for all that, he loves and loves legitimately in all these senses, man as man thus knowing himself by way only of his complex affectivity:

> Onde è da sapere che ciascuna cosa, come detto è di sopra, per la ragione di sopra mostrata ha 'l suo speziale amore. Come le corpora simplici hanno amore naturato in sé a lo luogo proprio, e però la terra sempre discende al centro; lo fuoco ha [amore a] la circunferenza di sopra, lungo lo cielo de la luna, e però sempre sale a quello. Le corpora composte prima, sì come sono le minere, hanno amore a lo luogo dove la loro generazione è ordinata, e in quello crescono e acquistano vigore e potenza; onde vedemo la calamita sempre da la parte de la sua generazione ricevere vertù. Le piante, che sono prima animate, hanno amore a certo luogo più manifestamente, secondo che la complessione richiede; e però vedemo certe piante lungo l'acque quasi c[ontent]arsi, e certe sopra li gioghi de le montagne, e certe ne le piagge e dappiè monti; le quali se si transmutano, o muoiono del tutto o vivono quasi triste, disgiunte dal loro amico. Li animali bruti hanno più manifesto amore non solamente a li luoghi, ma l'uno l'altro vedemo amare. Li uomini hanno loro proprio amore a le perfette e oneste cose. E però che l'uomo, avvegna che una sola sustanza sia, tuttavia [la] forma, per la sua nobilitade, ha in sé e la natura [d'ognuna di] queste cose, tutti questi amori puote avere e tutti li ha.
>
> (*Convivio* 3.3.2–5)[17]

Now, however, a discourse as yet preliminary in respect of the complex nature of properly human loving stands to be refined in terms of love's function as a principle of ulteriority, of being under the aspect of becoming; for to love, Dante thinks, or more exactly to love well, is not merely to be drawn into communion

---

17 'What, then, we need to understand is this, that, for the reason shown above, everything has its own proper love. Just as simple bodies have within them a natural love for their proper place, which is why earth is always drawn to the centre, and just as fire has a natural love for the sphere above us bordering that of the Moon, and so always rises towards it, so the primary compound bodies, the minerals, have a love for the place where they are created, and where they grow and whence they derive vigour and energy; thus we find that a magnet always acquires its power from the place whence it comes. Plants which are the primary form of animate being, have a clear preference for certain places, according to their needs; so some plants we see to be at their happiest alongside water, while others thrive on high peaks or else on slopes or in the foothills, all of which either perish or linger on sadly as uprooted and parted from their friends. Brute animals have an even more obvious love, not only for particular places, but for one another. Human beings too have their proper love, in this case for all things good and praiseworthy. And since man, though but one in substance, comprehends by way of the nobility of his form all these things, he can and does love in all these ways.'

with the object of that loving but to be made over again in the likeness thereof, all of which means that to love wisdom—which is what philosophy properly understood is all about (*philo-sophia*)—is to be made over again in the likeness of its origin, author and architect, of the Godhead itself as coeval and consubstantial with its every attribute. On the one hand, then, and taking first the coeval and consubstantial aspect of the argument, we have the notion of the Godhead, suffering as it does no addition, as all of a piece with philosophy as but the love of wisdom:

> Ché se a memoria si reduce ciò che detto è di sopra, filosofia è uno amoroso uso di sapienza, lo quale massimamente è in Dio, però che in lui è somma sapienza e sommo amore e sommo atto; che non può essere altrove, se non in quanto da esso procede. È adunque la divina filosofia de la divina essenza, però che in esso non può essere cosa a la sua essenzia aggiunta; ed è nobilissima, però che nobilissima è la essenzia divina; ed è in lui per modo perfetto e vero, quasi per etterno matrimonio.
>
> (*Convivio* 3.12.11–13)[18]

while on the other, and as Dante's point of arrival in this third book of the *Convivio*, there is the lover himself as forever drawn more deeply into the life of the One thus understood, there to rejoice in his status and subsistence as a creature in potential to the creator:

18 'For if we call to mind what was said above, philosophy is but a loving exercise of wisdom, something which—since in him are supreme wisdom, supreme love and supreme act—exists above all in God, and indeed is nowhere else to be found other than insofar as it proceeds from him. Given, then, that the divine essence admits of no addition, divine philosophy is of that essence, the surpassing nobility of the one being the surpassing nobility of the other. In him it subsists both perfectly and truly, by way, so to speak, of eternal wedlock.' Marie-Thérèse d'Alverny, 'Notes sur Dante et la Sagesse', *REI* 11 (1965), 5–24; Maria Corti, 'L'"amoroso uso di sapienza" nel *Convivio*', in *La felicità mentale: Nuove prospettive per Cavalcanto e Dante* (Turin: Einaudi, 1983), 72–155; Margherita De Bonfils Templer, 'Il dantesco "amoroso uso di sapienza": Sue radici platoniche', *SIR* 7.1–2 (1987), 5–27; Andreas Speer, ' "La bellezza de la sapienza": Philosophie und Weisheit bei Dante', *DDJ* 79–80 (2004–5), 15–43. On philosophy as the love of wisdom and on this as a matter not for self-congratulation on the part of the lover but for an ever more modest disposition of the spirit, see *Convivio* 3.11.5: 'Questo Pittagora, domandato se egli si riputava sapiente, negò a sé questo vocabulo e disse sé essere non sapiente, ma amatore di sapienza. E quinci nacque poi, ciascuno studioso in sapienza che fosse "amatore di sapienza" chiamato, cioè "filosofo"; ché tanto vale in greco "philos" com'è a dire "amore" in latino, e quindi dicemo noi: "philos" quasi amore, e "soph[os]" quasi sapien[te]. Per che vedere si può che questi due vocabuli fanno questo nome di 'filosofo' che tanto vale a dire quanto "amatore di sapienza": per che notare si puote che non d'arroganza, ma d'umilitade è vocabulo' (When Pythagoras was asked whether he considered himself a wise man, he refused to be designated by this term and declared himself to be not a wise man but a lover of wisdom. From this there arose the custom of calling anyone devoted to wisdom a 'lover of wisdom', that is a 'philosopher', for the Greek word 'philos' is the equivalent of 'love' in our language which is why we say 'philos' signifying love and 'sophia' signifying wisdom. It is clear, then, that these two words make up the one word 'philosopher', which is as much as to say a 'lover of wisdom'—from which one may note that it is a term indicative not of arrogance but of humility).

Onde in questo verso che seguentemente comincia: *In lei discende la virtù divina*, io intendo commendare l'amore, che è parte de la filosofia. Ove è da sapere che discender la virtude d'una cosa in altra non è altro che ridurre quella in sua similitudine, sì come ne li agenti naturali vedemo manifestamente; che, discendendo la loro virtù ne le pazienti cose, recano quelle a loro similitudine, tanto quanto possibili sono a venire ad essa. Onde vedemo lo sole che, discendendo lo raggio suo qua giù, reduce le cose a sua similitudine di lume, quanto esse per loro disposizione possono da la [sua] virtude lume ricevere.Così dico che Dio questo amore a sua similitudine reduce, quanto esso è possibile a lui assimigliarsi . . . E ciò si può fare manifesto massimamente in ciò, che sì come lo divino amore è tutto etterno, così conviene che sia etterno lo suo obietto di necessitate, sì che etterne cose siano quelle che esso ama. E così face questo amore amare; ché la sapienza, ne la quale questo amore fere, etterna è.

(*Convivio* 3.14.2–3 and 6)[19]

This, then—this sense of philosophy, properly understood, as but a participation in the light and life of the Godhead as all of a piece with its every attribute and its every activity—is the burden of this third book of the *Convivio*. For the author of this third book of the *Convivio*, to seek out, to lay hold of and to cherish the wisdom consubstantial with the Godhead is to know self in the now and henceforth transfigured substance of self, in the most radical kind of self-surpassing on the planes both of discerning and of desiring. Captive no longer to the contingencies of his existence—emancipation thus understood being the whole point of the *Convivio* (and indeed of Dante's undertaking in the round as a poet and philosopher)—the lover thus enamoured knows himself by way now only of the kind of 'transhumanity' proper to humanity as but the most immanent of its immanent possibilities, at which point his joy is complete.

With what amounts, then, to an account of philosophy as an assimilation of the created to the uncreated mind and of the unspeakable bliss thereof, we come to the first course proper of the banquet, where straightaway, however, we witness

19 'And so in the stanza immediately following—the one beginning "Divine power descends into her"—my purpose is to commend love as but part of philosophy. What, then, needs to be understood here is this, that to speak of the power of one thing descending into another is to speak of its fashioning that thing in its own likeness, for that, plainly, is the way things behave in the world; when their power descends into objects patient of this they draw those objects into their own likeness at any rate to the extent that those objects are capable thereof. So, for example, we see the sun's rays shed upon things here below and, to the extent, at least, that those things are fitted by nature for it, transforming them by way of the light falling upon them and duly received by them. What I am saying, then, is that insofar as its nature permits, God draws this love into a likeness of himself . . . and this is evident above all in that, just as divine love is itself all eternal, so of necessity is the object of that love, such that everything God loves is eternal. And so he causes this love to love, the wisdom upon which his love bears being itself eternal.'

a foreshortening of perspective, a preoccupation less with philosophy in the round than with an issue in the area of moral philosophy in particular—with what, given its now civic circumstances, it means to speak of 'gentilezza' or nobility as a property of this or that instance of specifically human being. True, there are various forces at work here, not least among them, Dante says, the difficulty he is having with philosophy in its more arcane reaches, in relation, more precisely, to the status of pure matter as an object of divine intentionality, all of which, he says, has had the effect of concentrating his mind upon lesser fare;[20] but this opting for lesser fare is in reality a matter not so much of difficulty as of discovery, of his settling at last upon his true genius as a philosopher, the genius less of a natural than of a moral philosopher, of one committed less to the idea pure and simple than to its espousal as a means of positive being and becoming. First, then, as far as 'gentilezza' is concerned, comes the antithesis, the idea of nobility as a matter of ancient wealth and custom, a notion endorsed, Dante says, both by the emperor Frederick II of Hohenstaufen and, as if that were not enough, by Aristotle—all of which means that, as a dissenting spirit, Dante must tread carefully.[21] And this indeed he does, taking care before all else to establish vis-à-vis both the one and the other the basis of his daring to disagree. As far, then, as the emperor is concerned, it is a question of his having qua emperor no right to pronounce here, imperial writ running absolutely only in matters of pure positive law, of those laws, that is to say, having about them no intrinsically moral component,[22] while

20 *Convivio* 4.1.8: 'Per che, con ciò fosse cosa che questa mia donna un poco li suoi dolci sembianti transmutasse a me, massimamente in quelle parti dove io mirava e cercava se la prima materia de li elementi era da Dio intesa—per la qual cosa un poco dal frequentare lo suo aspetto mi sostenni—quasi ne la sua assenzia dimorando, entrai a riguardare col pensiero lo difetto umano intorno al detto errore' (Since, therefore, it happened that, for a while, my lady chose to avert her sweet glance, particularly in respect of my seeking to understand God's own understanding of prime matter—for which reason I myself desisted for a time from seeing her—I gave my attention in, as it were, her absence to mankind's general misunderstanding hereabouts). Giovanni Busnelli, 'Un famoso dubbio di Dante intorno alla materia prima', *SD* 13 (1928), 47–60; Bruno Nardi , 'Se la prima materia de li elementi era da Dio intesa', in *Dante e la cultura medievale*, ed. Paolo Mazzantini (Rome: Laterza, 1983 [1942]), 197–206; Margherita de Bonfils Templer, 'La prima materia de li elementi', *SD* 58 (1986), 275–91.

21 For Aristotle, the 'ingenuitas enim est virtus et divitiae antiquae' of *Politics* 4.8; 1294a20–22 (thus nobility is but a matter of virtue and ancient wealth); cf. *Monarchia* 2.3.4: 'Est enim nobilitas virtus et divitie antique, iuxta Phylosophum in *Politicis*' (For as Aristotle says in the *Politics* 'nobility is virtue and ancient wealth'). For Frederick II, Klaus Ley, ' "Ultimo imperadore de li romani" (*Convivio* 4, 3): Friedrich II; als Exemplum Dantes', *DDJ* 68–69 (1993–94), 153–81; Fulvio Delle Donne, 'Una disputa sulla nobiltà alla corte di Federico II di Svevia', *MR* 23.1 (1999), 3–20; Adriana Diomedi, 'L'ideale dantesco della nobiltà: L'errore di Federico', in *Il principio di perfezione nel pensiero dantesco* (Leicester: Troubadour, 2005), 123–48. More generally, Cesare Segre, 'La figura di Federico II nella letteratura fino a Dante' in *Federico II e la civiltà communale nell'Italia del nord. Atti del convegno internazionale (Pavia-Rivellino, 13–15 ottobre, 1994)*, ed. Cosimo Damiano Fonseca et al. (Rome: De Luca, 2001), 417–26.

22 *Convivio* 4.9.14–15: 'Queste cose simigliantemente, che de l'altre arti sono ragionate, vedere si possono ne l'arte imperiale; ché regole sono in quella che sono pure arti, sì come sono le leggi de' matrimonii, de li servi, de le milizie, de li successori in dignitade, e di queste in tutto siamo a lo Imperadore subietti, sanza dubbio e sospetto alcuno. Altre leggi sono che sono quasi seguitatrici di natura,

as far as the Philosopher is concerned, it is a question not so much of his having endorsed the idea as of his simply having noted it as but one of the many misconceptions entertained by the commonality. Dante, then, is on safe ground, there being here no question of *lèse majesté*, of offending the powers that be. With this, therefore, he gets down to the main business of this fourth book of the *Convivio*, his first task being to demolish the notion of wealth in particular as a principle of nobility properly understood; for wealth, once in the ascendant as a means of happiness, makes less for pleasure than for pain, less for fulfilment than for fear and frustration. Knowing as it does no point of arrival and thus no proper perfection, its only effect is to engender dissatisfaction and indefinite desire, the key passage here, eloquent as ever in respect of the psychology and indeed of the pathology of avarice, running as follows:

> Promettono le false traditrici sempre, in certo numero adunate, rendere lo raunatore pieno d'ogni appagamento; e con questa promissione conducono l'umana volontade in vizio d'avarizia. E per questo le chiama Boezio, in quello De Consolatione, pericolose, dicendo: "Ohmè! chi fu quel primo che li pesi de l'oro coperto, e le pietre che si voleano ascondere, preziosi pericoli, cavoe?" Promettono le false traditrici, se bene si guarda, di torre ogni sete e ogni mancanza, e apportare ogni saziamento e bastanza; e questo fanno nel principio a ciascuno uomo, questa promissione in certa quantità di loro accrescimento affermando; e poi che quivi sono adunate, in loco di saziamento e di refrigerio danno e recano sete di casso febricante intollerabile; e in loco di bastanza recano nuovo termine, cioè maggiore quantitade a desiderio, e, con questa, paura grande e sollicitudine sopra l'acquisto. Sì che veramente non quietano, ma più danno cura, la qual prima sanza loro non si avea.
>
> (*Convivio* 4.12.4–5)[23]

---

sì come constituire l'uomo d'etade sofficiente a ministrare, e di queste non semo in tutto subietti' (What we have said relative to the other arts holds good too with respect to the art of imperial government, for there are here rules after the manner of pure arts, such as the laws governing matrimony, slavery, military service and the inheritance of titles, in all of which we are without any doubt at all subject to the emperor. But there are other laws following on, so to speak, from nature, such as deciding how old a man must be before assuming public office, and here we are not entirely subject to him). John Took, ' "Diligite iustitiam qui iudicatis terram": Justice and the Just Ruler in Dante', in *Dante and Governance*, ed. John R. Woodhouse (Oxford: Clarendon, 1997), 137–51.

23 'To those gathering them in sufficient quantity, these perfidious traitors forever promise satisfaction, a promise, however, conducive simply to the sin of avarice. That is why Boethius, in his *Consolation*, speaks of them as dangerous, saying: "Alas! Who was the first to unearth that mass of gold and gems, those precious perils, that sought to remain hidden?" These same traitors, should one study them closely, promise to do away with all desire and deficiency and to ensure complete satisfaction and sufficiency. That is what they do initially, guaranteeing the fulfilment of their promise once a certain amount has been reached. But once that amount *has* been reached, instead of sufficiency and spiritual

This sense in Dante of wealth as knowing no end and thus as constituting a principle merely of fear and frustration is worth pausing over; for if indeed human happiness is a matter of progression, then this, he thinks, is progression on the plane not of *having* but of *knowing*, progression, that is to say, in the sense not of accumulation but of a journeying of the spirit from one peak of perfection to another on the plane of understanding. In reply, then, to the perpetual caviller, to the one who sees no real difference between these things, he draws a distinction precisely to this effect:

A la questione rispondendo, dico che propriamente crescere lo desiderio de la scienza dire non si può, avvegna che, come detto è, per alcuno modo si dilati. Ché quello che propriamente cresce, sempre è uno; lo desiderio de la scienza non è sempre uno, ma è molti, e finito l'uno, viene l'altro; sì che, propriamente parlando, non è crescere lo suo dilatare, ma successione di picciola cosa in grande cosa. Che se io desidero di sapere li principii de le cose naturali, incontanente che io so questi, è compiuto e terminato questo desiderio. E se poi io desidero di sapere che cosa e com'è ciascuno di questi principii, questo è un altro desiderio nuovo, né per l'avvenimento di questo non mi si toglie la perfezione a la quale mi condusse l'altro; e questo cotale dilatare non è cagione d'imperfezione, ma di perfezione maggiore. Quello veramente de la ricchezza è propriamente crescere, ché è sempre pur uno, sì che nulla successione quivi si vede, e per nullo termine e per nulla perfezione.

(*Convivio* 4.13.1–2)[24]

---

refreshment, all they do is to create in the heart and mind of the individual nothing but an unbearably fevered thirst. Instead of satisfaction, they simply set up a new goal, a desire for still more, and, along with this, endless anxiety in respect of what has already been acquired. Theirs, rather than satisfaction, is simply suffering, an order of anxiety never there in the first place.' Boethius, *Consolatio* 2, m.5, 27–30: 'Heu, primus qui fuit ille / auri cui pondera tecti gemmasque latere volentes / pretiosa pericula fodit?' (Alas, who—oh wretched one!—was the first to unearth the storehouse of hidden gold, gems longing only to be undiscovered?). Patrick Boyde, 'Covetousness', in *Human Vices and Human Worth* (Cambridge: Cambridge University Press, 2000), 149–73; Mario Apollonio, 'Avarizia', in *Dante: Storia della 'Commedia'*, ed. Carlo Annoni et al. (Novara: Interlinea, 2013 [1951]), 177–84.

24 'I maintain, then, by way of response that the desire for knowledge cannot strictly be said to increase, although, as already noted, it expands in a certain way. For, strictly, whatever merely increases is always one, but the desire for knowledge is not always one, but, rather, many; for where one desire ends, another begins, so that, strictly speaking, its growth is a matter not of *increase* but rather of *progression*, of a movement from the lesser to the greater. For, if I wish to know the principles of natural things, as soon as I know them that wish is fulfilled and comes to an end. If I then seek to know the precise nature and modality of each one of these principles then that is a fresh and distinct desire. Nor by the advent of that new desire do I forfeit the satisfaction of my first desire, this development being a matter, not of imperfection, but of still greater perfection. In the case of riches, however, it is simply a matter of growth pure and simple, there being here, therefore, no discernible succession or end or perfection.'

—lines to which, as registering the same idea but in a spirit now of rejoicing, we may add these from the *Paradiso*, an essay in understanding as but a matter of its sublime periodicity, of its graduated ascent:

> 'O amanza del primo amante, o diva',
> diss' io appresso, 'il cui parlar m'inonda
> e scalda sì, che più e più m'avviva,
>
> non è l'affezion mia tanto profonda,
> che basti a render voi grazia per grazia;
> ma quei che vede e puote a ciò risponda.
>
> Io veggio ben che già mai non si sazia
> nostro intelletto, se 'l ver non lo illustra
> di fuor dal qual nessun vero si spazia.
>
> Posasi in esso, come fera in lustra,
> tosto che giunto l'ha; e giugner puollo:
> se non, ciascun disio sarebbe *frustra*.
>
> Nasce per quello, a guisa di rampollo,
> a piè del vero il dubbio; ed è natura
> ch'al sommo pinge noi di collo in collo'.

(*Paradiso* 4.118–32)[25]

So much, then, for wealth as a principle of nobility properly understood, but neither does genealogy or descent fair any better, for the purposes of confirming which Dante proposes a little scenario—the situation, to wit, of the one who, trusting only in himself, finds his way home over the snowy landscape and of the one who, treading in the footsteps of another, manages even so to lose his way, Dante for his part being here at his most peremptory:

---

25 ' "O beloved of the first lover, o divine one", said I then, "whose speech so floods and warms me such that I am ever more quickened, my affection for all its depth is scarce sufficient to render you grace for grace; but may he who sees and can indeed do so answer thereunto. Well do I see that never can our intellect be wholly satisfied unless there shine on it that truth beyond which no truth extends. Therein it rests, as a wild beast in his lair, so soon as it has reached it; and reach it it can, else every desire would be in vain. Our questioning thus springs up like a shoot at the foot of the truth, nature itself thus peak by peak urging us on to the summit." ' Kenelm Foster, O.P., 'The Mind in Love: Dante's Philosophy' (Aquinas Paper no. 25) (Oxford: Blackfriars, 1955); Kenelm Foster, O.P., 'Religion and Philosophy in Dante', in *The Mind of Dante*, ed. Uberto Limentani (Cambridge: Cambridge University Press, 1965), 47–78; Beatrice Arduini, 'Il desiderio naturale della conoscenza in "Le dolci rime d'amor ch'io solea" ', in *Le Rime di Dante. Gargano del Garda 25–27 settembre 2008*, ed. Claudia Berra and Paolo Borsa (Milan: Cisalpino, Istituto Editoriale Universitario, 2010), 231–49; Paolo Falzone, *Desiderio della scienza e desiderio di Dio nel 'Convivio' di Dante* (Bologna: Il Mulino, 2010; for the *Convivio*, 1–68).

Una pianura è con certi sentieri: campo con siepi, con fossati, con pietre, con legname, con tutti quasi impedimenti, fuori de li suoi stretti sentieri. Nevato è sì, che tutto cuopre la neve e rende una figura in ogni parte, sì che d'alcuno sentiero vestigio non si vede. Viene alcuno da l'una parte de la campagna e vuole andare a una magione che è da l'altra parte; e per sua industria, cioè per accorgimento, e per bontade d'ingegno, solo da sé guidato, per lo diritto cammino si va là dove intende, lasciando le vestigie de li suoi passi diretro da sé. Viene un altro appresso costui, e vuole a questa magione andare, e non li è mestiere se non seguire li vestigi lasciati; e, per suo difetto, lo cammino, che altri sanza scorta ha saputo tenere, questo scorto erra, e tortisce per li pruni e per le ruine, e a la parte dove dee non va. Quale di costoro si dee dicere valente? Rispondo: quegli che andò dinanzi. Questo altro come si chiamerà? Rispondo: vilissimo. Perché non si chiama non valente, cioè vile? Rispondo: perché non valente, cioè vile, sarebbe da chiamare colui che, non avendo alcuna scorta, non fosse ben camminato; ma però che questi l'ebbe, lo suo errore e lo suo difetto non può salire, e però è da dire non vile, ma vilissimo.

(*Convivio* 4.7.6–8)[26]

In neither respect, then, is there or can there be any hesitation, neither wealth nor lineage making for nobility in any sense approaching the real thing, at which point, therefore, Dante turns his attention less to what nobility is not than to what it is, namely—and on analogy with the sky as home to the stars—the locus or whereabouts of every refinement both spiritual and physical in man, of every comeliness both of mind and body. The key passage here, notable not least for its euphoria, for its sense of man as created not, in fact, a little lower but a little higher than the angels, reads as follows:

Dice dunque: *Sì com'è 'l cielo dovunqu'è la stella*, e non è questo vero *e converso*, cioè rivolto, che dovunque è cielo sia la stella, così è nobilitade dovun-

---

26 'Imagine, then, a plain crossed by any number of paths, a plain—with the exception of the narrow paths across it—covered with hedges, ditches, boulders, timber and, in short, every conceivable obstacle. Suppose, further, that there has been a heavy snowfall and that the snow covers everything, making the whole plain look alike, with no trace of a path in sight. Someone then comes along from the country on the one side wishing to make his way to a house that lies on the other side. Trusting to his own wit—his own observation, that is to say, and his native intelligence, with no one but himself as a guide—he reaches his destination by the direct route, leaving behind him, clearly enough, his footprints. Then someone else comes along making for the same house, someone who needs do no more than follow the marks already made. But through his own fault he strays from the path marked out by the one who knew how to keep to it without anyone to guide him, and, struggling to make his way through the thornbushes and the debris generally, he ends up in the wrong place. Which of these, then, is to be deemed a worthy soul? My reply: the one who went first. And when it comes to describing the other? Utterly base.'

que è vertude, e non vertude dovunque nobilitade; e con bello e convenevole essemplo, ché veramente è cielo ne lo quale molte e diverse stelle
rilucono. Riluce in essa le intellettuali e le morali virtudi; riluce in essa le
buone disposizioni da natura date, cioè pietade e religione, e le laudabili
passioni, cioè vergogna e misericordia e altre molte; riluce in essa le corpo-
rali bontadi, cioè bellezza, fortezza e quasi perpetua valitudine. E tante sono
le sue stelle, che del cielo risplendono, che certo non è da maravigliare se
molti e diversi frutti fanno ne la umana nobilitade; tante sono le nature e le
potenze di quella, in una sotto una semplice sustanza comprese e adunate,
ne le quali sì come in diversi rami fruttifica diversamente. Certo da dovvero
ardisco a dire che la nobilitade umana, quanto è da la parte di molti suoi
frutti, quella de l'angelo soperchia, tuttoché l'angelica in sua unitade sia più
divina.

(*Convivio* 4.19.5–6)[27]

But euphoria apart, it is possible to be more exact as to the nature and genesis
of man's proper nobility as man, for man's proper nobility as man, Dante explains,

---

27 'Next, then, the text says: *As wherever there is a star there is sky*—though not always the other
way round such that wherever there is sky there too is a star, for although there is always nobility where
there is virtue there is not always virtue where there is nobility. The analogy is as beautiful as it is fitting,
for nobility is truly a heaven in which any number of different stars shine. In it shine the intellectual
and moral virtues, just as in it shine those worthy dispositions of the soul bestowed by nature, namely
piety, religion and such praiseworthy feelings as modesty, mercy and much else besides, not to mention
beauty, strength and good health as pertaining in their excellence to the flesh. So numerous are the
stars scattered throughout the heavens, that it is no wonder that human nature in its nobility bears in
consequence so many and so diverse fruits, fruits endlessly varied in both kind and potentiality and
all of them gathered into and comprehended by a single substance, whence, as though on different
branches, they come to maturity. Indeed, I would go so far as to say that, though theirs, in the simplicity
of their being, is more divine, human nobility, in its manifold fruitfulness, is greater than that of the
angels themselves.' Maria Corti, 'Le fonti del *Fiore di virtù* e la teoria della "nobiltà" nel Duecento',
GSLI 136 (1959), 1–82; Mario Trovato, 'Dante's Stand against "l'errore de l'umana bontade": Bonum,
Nobility and Rational Soul in the Fourth Treatise of the *Convivio*', *DS* 108 (1990), 79–96; Cesare Vasoli,
'Dante maestro della nuova "nobiltà" ', in *Dante e la cultura del suo tempo: Dante e le culture dei confini.
Atti del Convegno Internazionale di Studi Danteschi, ottobre 1997* (Gorizia: Società Dante Alighieri, 1999),
147–62; Luigi Peirone, ' "Gentile" e "nobile" in Dante', *EL* 30.2 (2005), 37–47; Andrea A. Robiglio, 'The
Thinker as a Noble Man ("bene natus") and Preliminary Remarks on the Concept of Nobility', *Vivarium* 44.2–3 (2006), 206–47; Paolo Falzone, 'Desiderio di sapere e nobiltà dell'anima', in *Desiderio della
scienza e desiderio di Dio nel Convivio di Dante* (Bologna: Il Mulino, 2010), 1–68. More specifically sociopolitical, Carol Lansing, 'The Debate over True Nobility', in *The Florentine Magnates: Lineage and
Faction in a Medieval Commune* (Princeton: Princeton University Press, 1991), 212–28; Nicolai Rubinstein, 'Dante and Nobility', in *Studies in Italian History in the Middle Ages and Renaissance I: Political
Thought and the Language of Politics. Art and Politics*, ed. Giovanni Ciappelli (Rome: Edizioni di Storia
e Letteratura, 2004), 165–200; Marco Gallarino, 'Nobiltà e richezza nel quarto trattato del *Convivio*',
in *Identità cittadina e comportamenti socio-economici tra Medioevo età Moderna*, ed. Paolo Prodi et al.
(Bologna: Clueb, 2007), 231–40; Guido Castelnuovo, *Être noble dans la cité, Les noblesses italiennes en
quête d'identité (XIIIe-Xve s.)* (Paris: Classiques Garniers, 2014); Mario Alinei, *Dante rivoluzionario
borghese* (Velletri: PM, 2015).

is but the 'seed of happiness implanted by God in the well-disposed soul', a proposition open to development in terms of how that seed stands to be sown both
in good and in poor soil, both in the deserving and in the undeserving alike.
Taking first, then, the case of the seed as sown on good soil, it is a question here
of God's gracing still further those already graced by nature, gracing and gracing
again thus making *in casu*, in this or that individual man or woman, for something
close to another God incarnate:

> E però che la complessione del seme [i.e. of the male seed deposited in the
> matrix of the womb] puote essere migliore e men buona, e la disposizione
> del seminante puote essere migliore e men buona, e la disposizione del
> Cielo a questo effetto puote essere buona, migliore e ottima (la quale si
> varia per le constellazioni, che continuamente si transmutano); incontra
> che de l'umano seme e di queste vertudi più pura [e men pura] anima si
> produce; e, secondo la sua puritate, discende in essa la vertude intellettuale
> possibile che detta è ... E sono alcuni di tale oppinione che dicono, se tutte
> le precedenti vertudi s'accordassero sovra la produzione d'un'anima ne la
> loro ottima disposizione, che tanto discenderebbe in quella de la deitade,
> che quasi sarebbe un altro Iddio incarnato.
>
> (*Convivio* 4.21.7 and 10)[28]

28 'Since the seed may be variously constituted, some good and some less so, and since the disposition of the man generating the seed may likewise vary between the good and the less good, and
since, moreover, the configuration of the heavens effecting this can also differ from the good to the
better to the best (depending on the constellations as forever shifting), it comes about that the soul
brought into being by this seed and by way of these powers is itself of greater or lesser purity; and it
is in proportion to this purity that the power we speak of as the possible intellect descends in to it ...
And there are indeed some who go so far as to say that were all the aforementioned powers to be
optimally disposed in the moment of bringing forth a soul then such would be the in-breathing of
divinity that it would be another God incarnate.' Franco Ferrucci, 'Nobiltà della grazia', in *Le due
mani di Dio* (Rome: Fazi, 1999), 69–81; Paolo Falzone, 'Desiderio naturale, nobiltà dell'anima e grazia
divina nel IV trattato del *Convivio*', in *Dante the Lyric and Ethical Poet*, ed. Zygmunt G. Barański and
Martin McLaughlin (London: Modern Humanities Research Association, 2010), 24–55. More generally on Dantean embryology (with reference both to *Convivio* 4.21 and *Purgatorio* 25), Bruno Nardi,
'Sull'origine dell'anima umana', in *Dante e la cultura medievale*, ed. Paolo Mazzantini (Rome: Editori
Laterza, 1983 [1942]), 207–24; Stephen Bemrose, ' "Come d'animal divegna fante": The Animation of
the Human Embryo in Dante', in *The Human Embryo: Aristotle and the Arabic and European Traditions*,
ed. Gordon Reginald (Dunstan: University of Exeter Press, 1990), 123–35; Manuele Gragnolati, 'From
Plurality to (Near) Unicity of Forms: Embryology in *Purgatorio* 25', in *Dante for the New Millennium*,
ed. Teodolinda Barolini and Harry Wayne Storey (New York: Fordham University Press, 2003),
192–210; Manuele Gragnolati, 'Embryology and Aerial Bodies in Dante's *Comedy*', in *Experiencing the
Afterlife: Soul and Body in Dante and Medieval Culture* (Notre Dame, IN: University of Notre Dame
Press, 2005), 53–87; Jennifer Fraser, 'Dante/"Fante" ': Embriology in *Purgatory* and *Paradise*', in *Dante
and the Unorthodox: The Aesthetics of Transgression*, ed. James Mille (Waterloo [Ontario]: Wilfrid
Laurier University Press, 2005), 290–309; Joseph Ziegler, 'The Scientific Context of Dante's Embry-
ology', in *Dante and the Human Body: Eight Essays*, ed. John C. Barnes and Jennifer Petrie (Dublin:
Four Courts Press, 2007), 61–88; Giuliano Rossi, ' "Ma come d'animal divegna fante": Dante tra Al-

But even in circumstances of a seed's falling on good ground but thereafter poorly cultivated, or even of no seeds falling at all, the way is open either for grafting or for insemination, all of which means that never can there be any excuse in human experience for ignobility, one way or another all men being in a position to lay hold of their proper humanity and thus of their proper happiness as creatures of reasonable moral determination:

> E in questo . . . è nostra beatitudine e somma felicitade, sì come vedere si può; la quale è la dolcezza del sopra notato seme, sì come omai manifestamente appare, a la quale molte volte cotale seme non perviene per male essere coltivato, e per essere disviata la sua pullulazione. E similemente puote essere, per molta correzione e cultura, che là dove questo seme dal principio non cade, si puote inducere [n]el suo processo, sì che perviene a questo frutto; ed è uno modo quasi d'insetare l'altrui natura sopra diversa radice. E però nullo è che possa essere scusato; ché se da sua naturale radice uomo non ha questa sementa, ben la puote avere per via d'insetazione. Così fossero tanti quelli di fatto che s'insetassero, quanti sono quelli che da la buona radice si lasciano disviare!
>
> (*Convivio* 4.22.11–12)[29]

With what amounts, then, to a now more than ever elevated account of nobility in terms of its status (*a*) as the encompassing of every moral and intellectual excellence in man, and (*b*) as the proper patrimony of all men, it remains only to describe its manifestation or showing forth over the arc of life as a whole, over the four ages of man in his youth ('adolescenza'), in his early manhood ('gioventute'), in his seniority ('senettute') and in his senescence ('senio'). First, then, and lasting up to his twenty-fifth year, comes his youth, where it is a question of the decorum, deference and discretion conducive to a modest yet comely presence in the world, all this, Dante notes, making for a harmony at once delightful to behold and beyond words to describe.[30] Then, with his emergence into young

---

berto Magno e Tommaso', *CT* 13.2 (2010), 191–209; Nicola Fosca, 'Dante e l'origine dell'anima umana', *LIA* 16 (2015), 253–85.

29 'Herein, then, . . . in the sweetness of the aforesaid seed, lie as is plain to see our every blessing and joy. Often enough, it is true, that seed does not by reason of poor cultivation or disorderly growth come to proper fruition. But this may likewise be attained by careful cultivation, for even where the seed was not there from the outset it can be encouraged to grow and to bear fruit by way of the kind of grafting whereby a plant is raised from other rootstock. There can, then, be no excuse for anyone, for if a man lacks this seed by nature, it can even so be his by way of insemination. Nay would to God there were as many made good by insemination as there are astray in respect of the good stock properly theirs!'

30 *Convivio* 4.25.12: 'E quando elli è bene ordinato e disposto, allora è bello per tutto e per le parti; ché l'ordine debito de le nostre membra rende uno piacere non so di che armonia mirabile' (And when it is well ordered and disposed, then it is beautiful both severally and in the round, for due order among

manhood (lasting now from his twenty-fifth to his forty-fifth year), comes the
care and concern whereby he looks to the well-being both of self and of the other-
than-self, the courtesy whereby he engages civilly with his neighbours, and the
integrity whereby he both honours and delights in the law. Next, and more than
ever exquisite in its handling hereabouts in the *Convivio*, comes seniority as extending from a man's forty-fifth to his seventieth year, this being the moment in
which, like a rose in its maturity, personality opens up in all its now seasoned
substance to spread abroad its sweet fragrance, the fragrance of its now accumulated wisdom:

> Dunque appresso la propria perfezione, la quale s'acquista ne la gioventute,
> conviene venire quella che alluma non pur sé ma li altri; e conviensi aprire
> l'uomo quasi com'una rosa che più chiusa stare non puote, e l'odore che
> dentro generato è spandere.
>
> (*Convivio* 4.27.4)[31]

And then finally there is senescence or advanced age, where, having known at
first hand and lived out to the full the virtues of deference, decisiveness and generous counsel (the virtues, precisely, of adolescence, of maturity and of seniority
respectively), a man looks back, blesses the course of his existence so far and
prepares now to lower the sails of his barque with a view to slipping gently into
port, this, therefore, being the moment of anticipation, the moment in which the
attentive spirit sets aside every mortal preoccupation in favour of the qualitatively
other of what now is to come:

> Appresso de la ragionata particola è da procedere a l'ultima, cioè a quella
> che comincia: *Poi ne la quarta parte de la vita*; per la quale lo testo intende
> mostrare quello che fa la nobile anima ne l'ultima etade, cioè nel senio. E

---

our members is conducive to a delight—delight, precisely, in the wonderful harmony of it all—beyond
all telling).

31 'Following on, then, from the perfection of self as but the accomplishment of youth, it is proper
now that that perfection illumine not simply self but others too. It is proper that, like a rose content
no longer to stay closed, a man too opens up, spreading abroad as he does so the fragrance generated
within.' By the 'perfection of youth' Dante means those properties of personality laid down in one's
early years and apt in due course to benefit both self and everyone else (ibid., 3). Antonio Gagliardi,
'Scienza, felicità e perfezione', in *La tragedia intellettuale di Dante: Il 'Convivio'* (Catanzaro: Pullano,
1994), 41–85; Adriana Diomedi, *Il principio di perfezione nel pensiero dantesco* (Leicester: Troubadour,
2005); Giulio d'Onofrio, ' "Nobilissima perfezione": La "gioventute" di Dante e la dottrina della "per-
fectio" nel *Convivio*', in *Religione e politica: Da Dante alle prospettive teoriche contemporanee. Atti del
Convegno, Parma, 30 novembre–1 dicembre 2011*, ed. Beatrice Centi and Alberto Siclari (Rome: Edizioni
di Storia e Letteratura, 2013), 41–83. With reference to the 'arc of life' chapters as a whole, Bruno Nardi,
'L'arco della vita (nota illustrativa al *Convivio*)', in *Saggi di filosofia dantesca*, 2nd ed. (Florence: La
Nuova Italia, 1967), 110–38.

dice ch'ella fa due cose: l'una, che ella ritorna a Dio, sì come a quello porto onde ella si partio quando venne ad intrare nel mare di questa vita; l'altra si è, che ella benedice lo cammino che ha fatto, però che è stato diritto e buono, e sanza amaritudine di tempesta. E qui è da sapere, che, sì come dice Tullio in quello De Senectute, la naturale morte è quasi a noi porto di lunga navigazione e riposo. Ed è così: [ché], come lo buono marinaio, come esso appropinqua al porto, cala le sue vele, e soavemente, con debile conducimento, entra in quello; così noi dovemo calare le vele de le nostre mondane operazioni e tornare a Dio con tutto nostro intendimento e cuore, sì che a quello porto si vegna con tutta soavitade e con tutta pace.

(*Convivio* 4.28.1–3)[32]

Here at last, then, commitment, accountability, responsibility and the busyness generally of the active life give way to a gentle interiority, to the prospect of homecoming and of the welcome afforded the journeying spirit by those rejoicing already in the immediate presence of God (the again exquisite and indeed already perfectly paradisal 'a la nobile anima si fanno incontro, e deono fare, quelli cittadini de la etterna vita' of 4.28.5). With this, then, Dante's meditation on the substance and showing forth of nobility in its now recognizably civic aspect is complete; but—and this now is what matters—for all its elevated sense of 'gentilezza' as the seed of happiness implanted by God in the well-disposed soul, and for all its celebration thereof in terms of the tact, discretion, solicitude and gentle interiority of youth, maturity, seniority and senescence respectively, this is a meditation sustained from out of the depths by a blend of anger and sadness, now the one, now the other moving centre stage. On the one hand, then, there is the anger engendered by those merely playing at nobility, and playing at it, moreover, at the expense of the widow and the orphan:

---

32 'Having got this far in our account of the text we must turn now to its last part, the part beginning "And then in the final phase of a man's life", where its aim is to show how nobility expresses itself towards the end, in extreme old age. The soul, it says, does two things: it turns to God as to the port whence it departed when it first set out on the ocean of this life, and it blesses the journey now completed, a journey direct, wholesome and untroubled by storm and tempest. Indeed, it is good to remember here that, as Tully says in his book *On Old Age*, natural death is, as it were, a port or haven at the end of a long voyage, a place of rest. And that indeed is how it is, for just as a good sailor, on approaching a port, lowers his sails and slips more than ever gently into it, so ought we to lower the sails of our worldly affairs and turn to God with all our heart and mind, thus coming home with all sweetness and peace.' Cicero, *De Senectute* 19 (71): 'quae quidem mihi tam iucunda est, ut, quo propius ad mortem accedam, quasi terram videre videar aliquandoque in portum ex longa navigatione esse venturus' (To me [the thought of this ripeness for death] is so pleasant, that the nearer I approach death, the more I feel like one who is in sight of land at last and is about to anchor in his home port after a long voyage). For the 'a la nobile anima si fanno incontro' motif: 'whence the noble soul is greeted, as is right and proper, by those already citizens of the eternal life'.

Ahi malestrui e malnati, che disertate vedove e pupilli, che rapite a li men possenti, che furate e occupate l'altrui ragioni; e di quelle corredate conviti, donate cavalli e arme, robe e denari, portate le mirabili vestimenta, edificate li mirabili edifici, e credetevi larghezza fare! E che è questo altro a fare che levare lo drappo di su l'altare e coprire lo ladro la sua mensa? ... Udite, ostinati, che dice Tullio contro a voi nel libro de li Offici: 'Sono molti, certo desiderosi d'essere apparenti e gloriosi, che tolgono a li altri per dare a li altri, credendosi buoni essere tenuti, [se li] arricchiscono per qual ragione essere voglia. Ma ciò tanto è contrario a quello che far si conviene, che nulla è più.'

(*Convivio* 4.27.13–15)[33]

while on the other hand there is the sadness everywhere engendered by the spectacle of civilization lost to its civility, style hereabouts—meaning by this the *anaphora* and the *exclamatio* of a superbly constructed period—stepping up to confirm the twofold substance and intensity of Dante's discourse as a whole in the *Convivio*, a discourse turning, precisely, upon the social and civic *angst* of it all:

Oh misera, misera patria mia! quanta pietà mi stringe per te, qual volta leggo, qual volta scrivo cosa che a reggimento civile abbia rispetto!

(*Convivio* 4.27.11)[34]

AXES OF CONCERN IN THE *CONVIVIO*

Chronologically, but not only chronologically, the *Convivio* occupies a space somewhere between the *Vita nova* as Dante's preliminary essay in the at once infernal, purgatorial and paradisal journeying of the spirit by way of a revised understanding of love and the *Commedia* as his final meditation upon this same

33 'Alas, you ill-starred and ill-begotten, you who despoil widows and orphans, who plunder the most helpless, who steal and appropriate what belongs to others, with all of which you put on banquets, you bestow one upon another horses and weapons, goods and money, you sport splendid gowns and build magnificent palaces, all in the name of munificence. How does this differ from a thief's making off with the cloth from the altar and covering his table with it? ... Pay heed, you of obstinate spirit, to the harsh words Cicero has for you in his *On Offices* [*De officiis* 1.14.43]: "There are many people who, in their eagerness to cut a fine figure and gain renown, take from one to give to another, thinking they will be honoured no matter how they obtain the largesse they distribute; but there is nothing, but nothing, more completely opposed to what they should be doing."'

34 'O wretched, wretched country of mine! How overwhelmed I am with pity for you whenever I read or whenever I write aught to do with civil government!'

theme, upon the soul's descent into self and of its ascent across self as the condition of its ultimate and ultimately ecstatic homecoming. Needless to say, the differences between these texts as spanning a lifelong meditation are immense, the notional and expressive particularity of the former, not to mention its self-conscious provisionality, being taken up at last in the massive inclusivity of the latter and in its now consummate maturity in the flame of love. But for all their otherness in point both of the cultural premises upon which they rest and of the sheer scale of the undertaking, sameness prevails, for each in its way is but an essay in the substance and psychology of pilgrimage, in the never less than anguished experience of self-confrontation, the never less than arduous experience of self-reconfiguration, and the never less than rapturous experience of self-transcendence, of self as entering at last upon its proper inheritance. But if with the *Convivio* we have a text most certainly open to interpretation within the continuum of the whole, and indeed with a part to play in the fashioning of that continuum, then at the same time we have something qualitatively other, something closer to a proposal of human experience on the plane less, so to say, of the vertical than of the horizontal, by way of any number of proximate finalities and perfections along the way. Now here we have as always to be careful, for the vertical or ascensional aspect of the argument—that part of it turning upon man's participation in the very life of the Godhead—is as prominent as ever it was or will be in Dante, the *Convivio* no less than the *Vita nova* before it or the *Commedia* after it both knowing itself and rejoicing in its proper ecstasy. But in keeping with what in the *Convivio* amounts to a sense of matters to be resolved and structures of consciousness to be clarified before ever we reach this point—the point, that is to say, of rapt emergence—we have now a proposal of human experience in terms not only of the *height and depth* but of the *before and after* thereof, these things subsisting by way less of co-involvement than of contradistinction and indeed of mutual exclusion. And it is precisely this tension at the heart of the text that, for all its courage and magnanimity, accounts for its difficulty and indeed for its ultimate impossibility as a treatise on man's proper happiness as man, for, precisely as it stands, its inequality to the matter in hand.

Taking first, then, the vertical or ascensional aspect of the argument, that part of it turning upon the notion of the soul's movement into God (the 'indiarsi' of *Paradiso* 4.28) as the final cause of its every spiritual striving, this is a notion registered in the *Convivio* in three main ways: in terms (*a*) of the love-assimilation of the created to the uncreated mind; (*b*) of that same assimilation as that whereby this or that individual man or woman is, as Dante himself puts it, 'strengthened' in respect of his or her presence in the world as a creature of moral and intellectual determination; and (*c*) of the soul's return to God as the final cause of all significant journeying in human experience, as the ultimate appetible. As touching, then, on the first of these things, on the love-assimilation moment of the argument, we have these lines from book 3 with their sense of philosophy, properly understood, as but a bringing home of the creature to the creator on the plane of loving, man's, henceforth, being but a sharing in the primordial affectivity of his maker:

> Onde in questo verso che seguentemente comincia: *In lei discende la virtù divina*, io intendo commendare l'amore, che è parte de la filosofia. Ove è da sapere che discender la virtude d'una cosa in altra non è altro che ridurre quella in sua similitudine, sì come ne li agenti naturali vedemo manifestamente; che, discendendo la loro virtù ne le pazienti cose, recano quelle a loro similitudine, tanto quanto possibili sono a venire ad essa. Onde vedemo lo sole che, discendendo lo raggio suo qua giù, reduce le cose a sua similitudine di lume, quanto esse per loro disposizione possono da la [sua] virtude lume ricevere. Così dico che Dio questo amore a sua similitudine reduce, quanto esso è possibile a lui assimigliarsi.
>
> (*Convivio* 3.14.2–3)[35]

while as touching on the second of them, on the 'strengthening' moment of the argument, we have—again from book 3—these with their sense of man's participation in the life of the Godhead as, whatever else it is, a matter of ontic affirmation, of confirming the individual in the fullness and freedom of his or her proper humanity as a creature of ultimate accountability. Now here we need once again to tread carefully, for if like Thomas Dante too is inclined to refer essence to existence as the *prius* thereof (i.e. the *what it is* of a thing to the *that it is* as the condition of everything coming next by way of specificity) he is not in any sustained or systematic sense a philosopher of existence precisely as such. But for all that, existence as but the first and final cause of each and every subsequent inflexion of the spirit now moves centre stage as an object of concern:

> E però che naturalissimo è in Dio volere essere—però che, sì come ne lo allegato libro si legge, 'prima cosa è l'essere, e anzi a quello nulla è'—l'anima umana essere vuole naturalmente con tutto desiderio; e però che 'l suo

---

35 'So in the stanza coming next, the stanza beginning "The divine power descends into her", I set out to commend love as but part of philosophy. What we need to understand here is that to speak of the power of one thing entering into something else is to speak of its fashioning from that thing something after its own likeness. This we see clearly in the natural world, where any agent exercising its power to bear on things patient of that power, reduces it as far as may be to its own likeness. Thus we see the sun shedding its light on things here below and, in a manner proportionate to their capacity to receive that light, making them over again in its radiance. This, then, is what I am saying, that, as far as its nature allows, God draws this love into his likeness.'

essere dipende da Dio e per quello si conserva, naturalmente disia e vuole
essere a Dio unita per lo suo essere fortificare.

(*Convivio* 3.2.7)[36]

And then finally there is the 'God as the ultimate appetible' moment of the
argument, this, in truth, being but a restatement of everything so far under its
now journeying aspect, from the point of view, that is to say, of human experience

36 'And since the will to exist is proper above all to God—for as we read in the book cited above
[the *Book of Causes*, prop. 4] "existence comes first, there being nothing whatever prior to it"—the
human soul naturally desires above all things to exist; and since that existence depends on God and is
preserved by him, it naturally desires and wills to be at one with him for the purposes of strengthening
its own existence.' Similarly attuned to the notion of existence as but the encompassing the 'gloria primi
Motoris' moment of the letter to Cangrande (section 20): 'Dicit ergo quod "gloria primi Motoris", qui
Deus est, "in omnibus partibus universi resplendent", sed ita ut "in aliqua parte magis, et in aliqua
minus". Quod autem ubique resplendeat, ratio et auctoritas manifestat. Ratio sic: Omne quod est, aut
habet esse a se, aut ab alio: sed constat quod habere esse a se non convenit nisi uni, scilicet primo seu
principio, qui Deus est; cum habere esse non arguat per se necesse esse, et per se necesse esse non
competat nisi uni, scilicet primo seu principio, quod est causa omnium; ergo omnia que sunt, preter
unum ipsum, habent esse ab alio. Si ergo accipiatur ultimum in universo, non quodcunque, manifestum
est quod id habet esse ab aliquo; et illud a quo habet, a se vel ab aliquo habet. Si a se, sic est primum;
si ab aliquo, et illud similiter vel a se vel ab aliquo. Et esset sic procedere in infinitum in causis agentibus,
ut probatur in secundo Metaphysicorum, erit devenire ad primum, qui Deus est. Et sic, mediate vel
inmediate, omne quod habet esse habet esse ab eo; quia ex eo quod causa secunda recipit a prima,
influit super causatum ad modum recipientis et reddentis radium, propter quod causa prima est magis
causa. Et hoc dicitur in libro *De Causis* quod "omnis causa primaria plus influit super suum causatum
quam causa universalis secunda". Sed hoc quantum ad esse' (He says, then, that 'the glory of the First
Mover', which is God, 'shines forth in every part of the universe', but in such a way that it shines 'in one
part more and in another less'. That it shines in every part both reason and authority declare. We reason,
therefore, thus: everything which exists has its being either from itself or from some other thing. But
it is plain that being-from-itself can be the attribute of one being only, namely the primal or original
being, which is God, since to have being does not necessarily imply being-from-itself, being-from-itself
pertaining necessarily to one being only, namely the primal and original being, which is the cause of
all things; therefore everything which exists, except the One itself, has its being from some other thing.
If, then, we take, not any thing whatsoever, but that thing which is the most remote in the universe, it
is manifest that this has its being from something; and that from which it derives either has its being
from itself, or from something else. If from itself, then it is primal; if from something else, then that
again must either be being-from-itself, or derive from yet something else. But in this way we should go
on to infinity in the chain of effective causes, as is shown in the second book of the *Metaphysics*. So we
must come to a primal existence, which is God. Hence, mediately or immediately, everything that exists
has its being from Him, because, inasmuch as the second cause has its effect from the first, its influence
on what it acts upon is like that of a body which receives and reflects a ray; since the first cause is the
more effective cause. And this is stated in the book *On Causes*, namely that 'every primary cause has
influence in a greater degree on what it acts upon than any second cause. So much with regard to being).
Suggestive too the 'per lo gran mar de l'essere' passage of *Paradiso* 1.109–14 and the 'l'essere del mondo
e l'esser mio' sequence of *Paradiso* 26.55–66. Bortolo Martinelli, ' "Esse" ed "essentia" nell'*Epistola a
Cangrande* (capp. 20–23)', *CL* 12.4 (1984), 627–72. For Thomas, Étienne Gilson, *Le thomisme: Introduc-
tion à la philosophie de saint Thomas d'Aquin*, 5th ed. (Paris: Vrin, 1944); Étienne Gilson, *The Christian
Philosophy of St Thomas Aquinas* (New York: Random House, 1956); Frederick C. Copleston, S.J.,
Aquinas (Harmondsworth: Penguin, 1955; and reprints); and Denys Turner, *Thomas Aquinas: A Portrait*
(New Haven: Yale University Press, 2013).

as but a progression from one proximate possibility to another until at last the soul settles upon the object of its every sincere desire—upon communion with the One as the sure foundation of its existence:

> lo sommo desiderio di ciascuna cosa, e prima da la natura dato, è lo ritornare a lo suo principio. E però che Dio è principio de le nostre anime e fattore di quelle simili a sé (sì come è scritto: 'Facciamo l'uomo ad imagine e similitudine nostra'), essa anima massimamente desidera di tornare a quello. E sì come peregrino che va per una via per la quale mai non fue, che ogni casa che da lungi vede crede che sia l'albergo, e non trovando ciò essere, dirizza la credenza a l'altra, e così di casa in casa, tanto che a l'albergo viene; così l'anima nostra, incontanente che nel nuovo e mai non fatto cammino di questa vita entra, dirizza li occhi al termine del suo sommo bene, e però, qualunque cosa vede che paia in sé avere alcuno bene, crede che sia esso. E perché la sua conoscenza prima è imperfetta, per non essere esperta né dottrinata, piccioli beni le paiono grandi, e però da quelli comincia prima a desiderare. Onde vedemo li parvuli desiderare massimamente un pomo; e poi, più procedendo, desiderare uno augellino; e poi, più oltre, desiderare bel vestimento; e poi lo cavallo; e poi una donna; e poi ricchezza non grande, e poi grande, e poi più. E questo incontra perché in nulla di queste cose truova quella che va cercando, e credela trovare più oltre. Per che vedere si può che l'uno desiderabile sta dinanzi a l'altro a li occhi de la nostra anima per modo quasi piramidale, che 'l minimo li cuopre prima tutti, ed è quasi punta de l'ultimo desiderabile, che è Dio, quasi base di tutti.
>
> (*Convivio* 4.12.14–17)[37]

---

37 'What every being most desires as something implanted in it by nature is to return to its first cause, and, since God, who fashioned them after his own likeness (for it is written "Let us make man after our own image and likeness"), is the first cause of our souls, that soul seeks above all things to return to him. And just as a pilgrim travelling a road unfamiliar to him thinks every house he sees to be a hostel, and, finding that not to be the case, projects his belief onto the next house, and the next and the next, until such time as he does indeed discover it, so it is with this soul of ours; for no sooner has it started out on the new and unfamiliar road of this life, than it is forever on the lookout for its ultimate goal, its greatest good. And so whenever it sees anything having about it something of the good, it believes that to be its greatest good. As yet unschooled by experience or by instruction and insecure in its judgement, goods of little value seem to it to be goods of great value, these, therefore, constituting the first object of its desire. So we see small children wishing above all for an apple; then, when they are a bit older, a little bird; then, later still, fine clothes, then a horse, then a woman, then a little wealth, then great wealth, and then still more wealth—all because, finding what they are really seeking in none of these things, they think them to be somewhere further on. From this, then, we can see that, looking at it from the point of view of the soul, each desirable object, preceding as it does the next, relates to it after the manner, so to speak, of a pyramid, the smallest coming first and, like the apex of the pyramid, covering all the others until we come to God himself, at the base of the pyramid, as

This, then, is what it means to speak of the 'vertical' component of Dante's spirituality in the *Convivio*, of his proposal and exploration of the human project, that is to say, by way of a steady soaring of the spirit until at last it enters into communion with the One who *is* as of the essence, herein lying the condition, the sine qua non, both of its being and of its being well. But—and this now is the point—no less insistent in the *Convivio* is his proposal of that same project on the plane of the horizontal, of the *before and after* as distinct from the *height and depth* of each successive possibility along the way. And this too is a situation open to contemplation under its threefold aspect: in respect (a) of its settling, not upon metaphysics but (theology apart) upon ethics as supreme among the human sciences (book 2); (b) of its restriction of what we *wish* to know in this life to what we *can* know in this life (book 3); and (c) of its deferral of the properly pious moment of a man's life to its final, senescent phase, this being the moment in which, leaving behind his worldly cares, he turns his attention to the qualitative otherness of the life to come (book 4)—each of these things tending after its manner to interrupt the continuum of human experience in favour of the discrete instant, the sui generis moment of concern. To take, then, the first of them— namely the notion of ethics as (theology apart) supreme among the human sciences—we may say this, that where in the ordinary way of it we might have expected a privileging of metaphysics as paramount among them (for in metaphysics we have the science of being precisely as such), Dante opts instead for ethics as the architectonic or organizational science par excellence in human affairs, the science that governs, if not the substance, then the pursuit of all the others. True, metaphysics, as he confirms in the very first sentence of the *Convivio*, glories still in the etiquette of the 'first philosophy', but it is ethics that, as *our* science, the science we not only know but actually live out, reigns supreme. Were it not for ethics, Dante insists, as the science of orderly being and becoming in man then no amount of speculative learning, ancient or modern, could or would bring us home to our proper humanity:

> Lo Cielo cristallino, che per Primo Mobile dinanzi è contato, ha comparazione assai manifesta a la Morale Filosofia; ché Morale Filosofia, secondo che dice Tommaso sopra lo secondo de l'Etica, ordina noi a l'altre scienze. Che, sì come dice lo Filosofo nel quinto de l'Etica, "la giustizia legale ordina la scienze ad apprendere, e comanda, perché non siano abbandonate, quelle essere apprese e ammaestrate"; e così lo detto cielo ordina col suo movimento la cotidiana revoluzione di tutti li altri, per la quale ogni die tutti quelli ricevono [e mandano] qua giù la vertude di tutte le loro

---

the ultimate object of desiring.' Paolo Falzone, *Desiderio di scienza e desiderio di Dio nel 'Convivio' di Dante* (Bologna: Il Mulino, 2010).

parti. Che se la revoluzione di questo non ordinasse ciò, poco di loro
vertude qua giù verrebbe o di loro vista . . . E non altrimenti, cessando la
Morale Filosofia, l'altre scienze sarebbero celate alcuno tempo, e non
sarebbe generazione né vita di felicitade, e indarno sarebbero scritte e per
antico trovate.

(*Convivio* 2.14.14–16 and 18)[38]

And our master and mentor hereabouts? Why who but Aristotle, if not the
founder then most certainly the finisher of the whole discipline and thus by common consent guide to our proper well-being here below. On the one hand, then,
we have these lines from the middle part of 4.6 on the status of the Stagirite as, if
not uniquely, then maximally competent to pronounce hereabouts:

Che Aristotile sia dignissimo di fede e d'obedienza così provare si può. Intra
operarii e artefici di diverse arti e operazioni, ordinate a una operazione od
arte finale, l'artefice o vero operatore di quella massimamente dee essere
da tutti obedito e creduto, sì come colui che solo considera l'ultimo fine di
tutti li altri fini. Onde al cavaliere dee credere lo spadaio, lo frenaio, lo sel-
laio, lo scudaio, e tutti quelli mestieri che a l'arte di cavalleria sono ordinati.
E però che tutte l'umane operazioni domandano uno fine, cioè quello de
l'umana vita, al quale l'uomo è ordinato in quanto elli è uomo, lo maestro
e l'artefice che quello ne dimostra e considera, massimamente obedire e
credere si dee. Questi è Aristotile: dunque esso è dignissimo di fede e
d'obedienza.

(*Convivio* 4.6.6–7)[39]

---

38 'The Crystalline Heaven or, as we called it earlier, the Primum Mobile, is clearly like Moral
Philosophy, since Moral Philosophy, as Thomas says in his commentary on the second book of the
Ethics, directs us towards the other sciences. For, as Aristotle says in the fifth book of the *Ethics*, "justice
as enshrined in the law identifies the subjects to be studied, and, lest they be lost to sight, makes man-
datory their learning and teaching". In the same way, the aforesaid heaven governs the daily revolution
of the others, by means of which they each day receive and communicate here below the influence of
their every part; for were it not for the circling of this sphere, little of their influence would be felt here
below, not to mention our hardly seeing anything of them . . . Likewise, should Moral Philosophy cease
to be, the other sciences would for a period disappear, and, with the disappearance of everything that
had been discovered and set down by the ancients, all now pointless, there would be no lasting happiness or indeed any happiness at all.' For Thomas on the 'second of the *Ethics*', n. 245 in his commentary:
'Ratio ordinis est quia virtutes morales sunt magis notae et per eas disponimur ad intellectuales' (the
reason for this [i.e. for Aristotle's proceeding in quite the way he does hereabouts] is that the moral
virtues are more familiar, and through them we are prepared for a study of the intellectual virtues).
Étienne Gilson, *Dante and Philosophy*, trans. David Moore (New York: Harper and Row, 1963), 99–112
('The Primacy of Ethics').

39 'That Aristotle is entirely deserving of both trust and obedience can be shown thus: among
those labourers and artisans each busy in his own way but envisaging in the round an art or undertaking
having but one end, the artisan or operative overseeing that end ought by all to be trusted and obeyed,

while on the other we have these from later in the same chapter on Aristotle as, by virtue of his well-nigh divine intellect and of his having said the last word in the area of moral philosophy, a now and forever consummate guide to man's proper happiness as man:

Veramente Aristotile, che Stagirite ebbe sopranome, e Zenocrate Calcedonio, suo compagnone, [per lo studio loro], e per lo 'ngegno [eccellente] e quasi divino che la natura in Aristotile messo avea, questo fine conoscendo per lo modo socratico quasi e academico, limaro e a perfezione la filosofia morale redussero, e massimamente Aristotile. E però che Aristotile cominciò a disputare andando in qua e in lae, chiamati furono—lui, dico, e li suoi compagni—Peripatetici, che tanto vale quanto 'deambulatori'. E però che la perfezione di questa moralitade per Aristotile terminata fue, lo nome de li Academici si spense, e tutti quelli che a questa setta si

---

he and he alone looking to the end comprehending every intermediate end. So, for instance, the knight ought to be trusted by the swordsmith, by the bridle maker, by the saddle maker, by the shield maker and by everyone else whose craft is there to facilitate the knight in his own proper role as such. And since all human activities are necessarily directed to a single end, namely to human being precisely as such, to that by virtue of which a man is a man, then the master or expert in these things, the one who makes of this his special business, deserves above all to be trusted and obeyed. And that is Aristotle, of all men the most worthy of trust and obedience.' For Dante, Aristotle and Christian Aristotelianism, Edward Moore, 'Dante and Aristotle', in *Studies in Dante: First Series (Scripture and Classical Authors in Dante)* (Oxford: Clarendon Press, 1896 [1969]), 92–156; Martin Grabmann, *Mittelalterliches Geistesleben*, vol. 3 (Munich: Max Hueber, 1926 [1956]), 50–219; Bruno Nardi, *Nel mondo di Dante* (Rome: Edizioni di Storia e Letteratura, 1944 [2012]); Bruno Nardi, *Saggi e note di critica dantesca* (Milan: Riccardo Ricciardi, 1966; repr. Spoleto: Centro italiano di studi sull'alto medioevo, 2013); Bruno Nardi, *Saggi di filosofia dantesca*, 2nd ed. (Florence: La Nuova Italia, 1967); Bruno Nardi, *Dante e la cultura medievale*, ed. Paolo Mazzantini (Rome: Laterza, 1983 [1942]); and Bruno Nardi, *Dal Convivio alla Commedia* (Rome: Istituto Storico Italiano per il Medio Evo, 1992 [1960]). Lorenzo Minio Paluello, 'Dante's Reading of Aristotle', in *The World of Dante: Essays on Dante and His Times*, ed. Cecil Grayson (Oxford: Clarendon, 1980), 61–80; Maria Corti, 'La filosofia aristotelica e Dante', *LC* 13 (1984), 111–23; Robert D. Crouse, 'Dante as Philosopher: Christian Aristotelianism', in *Dionysius* 16 (1998), 141–56; Simon A. Gilson, 'Dante and Christian Aristotelianism', in *Reviewing Dante's Theology*, vol. 1, ed. Claire E. Honess and Matthew Treherne (Bern: Peter Lang, 2013), 65–109. For Dante's particular species of 'civic Aristotelianism', Gennaro Sasso, 'Aristotele nel *Convivio*', in *Dante, l'imperatore e Aristotele* (Rome: Istituto Storico Italiano per il Medio Evo, 2002), 57–92; Sonia Gentili, 'Il fondamento aristotelico del programma divulgativo dantesco (*Conv.* I)', in *Le culture di Dante: Studi in onore di Robert Hollander. Atti del quarto Seminario Dantesco Internazionale, University of Notre Dame (Ind.), USA, 25–27 settembre 2003*, ed. Michelangelo Picone, Theodore J. Cachey, Jr., and Margherita Mesirca (Florence: Cesati, 2004), 179–97; Sonia Gentili, *L'uomo aristotelico alle origini della letteratura italiana* (Rome: Carocci, 2005), especially 127–65 ('Il desiderio di conoscere e il dovere di divulgare: Il *Convivio* di Dante'). More generally on the late medieval recovery of Aristotle, Bernard G. Dod, 'Aristoteles latinus', in the *Cambridge History of Late Medieval Philosophy*, ed. Norman Kretzmann, Anthony Kenny, and Jan Pinborg (Cambridge: Cambridge University Press, 1982), 43–79; Luca Bianchi, *Il vescovo e i filosofi: La condanna parigina del 1277 e l'evoluzione dell'aristotelismo scolastico* (Bergamo: Lubrina, 1990); Luca Bianchi, 'La ricezione di Aristotele e gli 'aristotelismi' del XIII secolo', in *Ciencia y cultura en la Edad media: Actas VIII y X* (Canarias: Fundación Canaria Orotava de Historia de la Ciencia, 2003), 293–310.

presero Peripatetici sono chiamati; e tiene questa gente oggi lo reggimento del mondo in dottrina per tutte parti, e puotesi appellare quasi cattolica oppinione. Per che vedere si può, Aristotile essere additatore e conduttore de la gente a questo segno.

(*Convivio* 4.6.15–16)[40]

Already, then, a pattern is discernible, Dante, notwithstanding all he has to say about an ideal ascent of the mind by way of philosophy as but the love of wisdom first and foremost in God, proposing in just about the same breath—or perhaps, better, from out of another part of his being—an alternative order of activity and authority, this in turn setting up a similarly indisputable claim in conscience. But that, in truth, is only the beginning of it, for what follows in book 3 of the *Convivio* is nothing less than a systematic doing away with ascensionality altogether in favour of a now immanent as distinct from transcendent finality, of, more exactly, an order of desire proportionate to and delimited by the way man as man is as but an intellectual creature in the flesh. The key passage here comes towards the end of the book, Dante, before going any further, pausing for a moment to consider the case of the wretched caviller, of the one who, given (*a*) the notion of philosophy as but the love of wisdom all of a piece with the Godhead, and (*b*) the ideal readership of the *Convivio* (busy men and women one and all), finds himself wondering what use philosophy. Given, in other words, its fundamentally arcane substance, how, precisely, might philosophy thus understood be said to benefit the man in the street? To this Dante is ready with a reply. The truth of it, he says, is that we *wish* to know here and now only what we *can* know here and now, anything more or anything other than this on the plane of desiring being but an overshooting of the mark, an aberration of the spirit:

Veramente può qui alcuno forte dubitare come ciò sia, che la sapienza possa fare l'uomo beato, non potendo a lui perfettamente certe cose mostrare; con ciò sia cosa che 'l naturale desiderio sia a l'uomo di sapere, e sanza compiere lo desiderio beato essere non possa. A ciò si può chiaramente rispondere che lo desiderio naturale in ciascuna cosa è misurato secondo la possibilitade de la cosa desiderante; altrimenti andrebbe in contrario di sé medesimo, che impossibile è; e la Natura l'avrebbe fatto indarno, che è

40 'In truth, then, Aristotle, surnamed the Stagirite, and his companion Xenocrates of Chalcedon (but especially Aristotle), by way of their study and of the singular—one might almost say divine—intelligence bestowed by nature upon the former, exploring this goal by much the same methods as Socrates and the Academics, refined and perfected the science of moral philosophy. Since, then, moral philosophy was perfected by Aristotle, the name Academic faded from memory, everyone associated with his circle being called Peripatetics (so called because Aristotle began his deliberations walking up and down, this being the meaning of the word). Today, the teaching of this group holds sway everywhere, theirs, we might say, being the orthodox view. Clearly, then, Aristotle is the one who directs and guides mankind to the goal we have been discussing.'

anche impossibile. In contrario andrebbe, ché, desiderando la sua per-fezione, desiderrebbe la sua imperfezione; imperò che desiderrebbe sé sempre desiderare e non compiere mai suo desiderio (e in questo errore cade l'avaro maladetto, e non s'accorge che desidera sé sempre desiderare, andando dietro al numero impossibile a giungere). Avrebbelo anco la Natura fatto indarno, però che non sarebbe ad alcuno fine ordinato. E però l'umano desiderio è misurato in questa vita a quella scienza che qui avere si può, e quello punto non passa se non per errore, lo quale è di fuori di naturale intenzione. E così è misurato ne la natura angelica, e terminato, in quanto, in quella sapienza che la natura di ciascuno può apprendere. E questa è la ragione per che li Santi non hanno tra loro invidia, però che ciascuno aggiugne lo fine del suo desiderio, lo quale desiderio è con la bontà de la natura misurato. Onde, con ciò sia cosa che conoscere di Dio e di certe altre cose quello esse sono non sia possibile a la nostra natura, quello da noi naturalmente non è desiderato di sapere. E per questo è la dubitazione soluta.

(Convivio 3.15.7–10)[41]

—lines to which for good measure we may add these from book 4 as—with the help now of Averroes as uniformly doubtful in respect of our knowing anything of the suprasensible world in general and of the separate substances in particu-lar—confirming a now considered position in the *Convivio*:

Ben puote ancora calunniare l'avversario dicendo che, avvegna che molti desiderii si compiano ne lo acquisto de la scienza, mai non si viene a l'ultimo:

---

41 'There may in truth be some, however, who doubt whether wisdom can make a man happy if by it certain things cannot be made known to him, for man has a natural desire to know, which, unless satisfied, cannot make him happy. To this we may reply quite simply that natural desire in anything whatever is proportionate to the possibility of its fulfilment, for otherwise it would be forever going against its own nature, something not only impossible in itself, but which—no less impossibly—would entail nature's having made it in vain. It would be going against itself in that, while desiring perfection, it would in fact be desiring *im*perfection, since it would go on desiring and desiring without ever sat-isfying that desire (this being the mistake of the miser who, in his perversity, fails to understand that in seeking out an infinitely open-ended goal he desires only to desire). And nature would have created it in vain in that it would be directed to no specific end. Therefore human desire in this life is propor-tionate to the wisdom to be had here, and never is the limit overshot other than by way of something foreign to nature's intention. So it is with the angels, their desire being limited only by what they can see and understand. That too is why the saints are free from envy one of another, for each, in desiring in a manner consonant with their proper goodness, has reached the limit of his desiring. And that is why, since it is not within the reach of our nature to know either God in his essence or any number of similar things besides, we do not naturally desire to know these things. Thus the issue is resolved.' Gianfranco Fioravanti, 'A Natural Desire Can Be Fulfilled in a Purely Natural Manner', in *Dante and Heterodoxy: The Temptations of 13th Century Radical Thought*, ed. Maria Luisa Ardizzone (Newcastle upon Tyne: Cambridge Scholars, 2014), 35–46; Gianfranco Fioravanti, 'Desiderio e limite della cono-scenza in Dante', in *Forme e oggetti della conoscenza nel XIV secolo: Studi in ricordo di Maria Elena Reina*, ed. Luca Bianchi and Chiara Crisciani (Florence: Galluzzo, 2014), 7–20.

che è quasi simile a la 'mperfezione di quello che non si termina e che è pur uno. Ancora qui si risponde, che non è vero ciò che si oppone, cioè che mai non si viene a l'ultimo; ché li nostri desiderii naturali, sì come di sopra nel terzo trattato è mostrato, sono a certo termine discendenti; e quello de la scienza è naturale, sì che certo termine quello compie, avvegna che pochi per male camminare, compiano la giornata. E chi intende lo Commentatore nel terzo de l'Anima, questo intende da lui.

(*Convivio* 4.13.6–8)[42]

Now here quite possibly, and indeed quite probably, there is a subtext, namely a certain anxiety on Dante's part relative to the viability of the *Convivio* thus far as a vademecum for those caught up either by choice or by circumstance in the hurly-burly of the active life. Is there not in other words, Dante must have wondered, a sense in which the rapt spirituality of books 2 and 3 has got the better of him, the *Convivio*, as a feast laid on for the benefit of the socially and civically minded, having in this sense lost its way? Maybe. But for all that, there is something more fundamental going on here, since for all his rejoicing in the notion of man's forever being ahead of himself on the planes both of knowing and of loving, Dante's at every stage is a delight in the completeness of the noetic instance, noesis, for him, being but a progression from one pinnacle of perfection to the

---

42 'A further cavil on the part of those opposing this might take the following form: although the pursuit of knowledge sees the satisfaction of many desires, never is that desire wholly fulfilled; thus knowledge, all of a piece as it is and so lacking any point of arrival, has the same imperfection as anything else. My reply, however, is as before, for it is simply not true that, as my opponent claims, there is here no point of arrival, for as we demonstrated above, in the third treatise, our natural desire envisages a definite end. Our desire for knowledge, therefore, being just such a natural desire, has just such an accomplishable end, though few, it is true, taking as they do the wrong road, complete the day's journey. Anyone alert to the Commentator's meaning in the third book of the *De anima* will see this to be his view too.' Averroes, *Commentarium magnum in Aristotelis De anima libros III*, text 36, but also Aquinas, *Expositio super libros Boethii De Trinitate* (*Commentary on the* De Trinitate *of Boethius*), qu. 6, art. 4: 'Sed contra est quod Commentator dicit in III de anima quod ad hanc positionem sequitur vel quod scientiae speculativae nondum sint perfectae, cum illae scientiae nondum sint inventae, quibus possimus substantias separatas intelligere, et hoc, si contingat ex ignorantia aliquorum principiorum quod nondum substantias praedictas intelligamus; vel si contingat ex defectu naturae nostrae quod non possimus illas scientias speculativas invenire, quibus praedictae substantiae intelligantur, sequetur quod si aliqui nati sunt huiusmodi scientias invenire, quod nos et ipsi simus aequivoce homines; quorum primum est improbabile, secundum autem est impossibile. Ergo non potest hoc per aliquas speculativas scientias esse quod substantias praedictas intelligamus' (On the contrary, the Commentator says that there are two possible consequences of this position: *either* the speculative sciences are not yet perfect, because we have not discovered the sciences by which we can know the separate substances, and this owing to the fact we do not yet understand these substances because of our ignorance of some principles; *or* if it happens because of some defect in our nature that we cannot discover the speculative sciences by which these substances may be known, it follows that, if some men can discover these sciences, we and they are men only in an equivocal sense. The first of these is improbable; the second is impossible. So we cannot understand these substances through some speculative sciences).

next. Hence, in the way we have seen, the promotion of moral philosophy as but the structural science par excellence in human experience; hence too, and again in the way we have seen, the coronation of Aristotle as its presiding genius; and hence now, in the magnificent arc of life chapters of book 4, the postponing of piety proper—of everything required of the individual, that is to say, in preparation for life beyond the bar—until the last minute. On the one hand, then, the worldly and worldly-wise virtues of justice, prudence, temperance and fortitude as proper to man in his youth, maturity and seniority respectively, while on the other the courage of a quiet mind proper to the soul in its senescence:

Ed è così; [ché], come lo buono marinaio, come esso appropinqua al porto, cala le sue vele, e soavemente, con debile conducimento, entra in quello; così noi dovemo calare le vele de le nostre mondane operazioni e tornare a Dio con tutto nostro intendimento e cuore, sì che a quello porto si vegna con tutta soavitade e con tutta pace. E in ciò avemo da la nostra propria natura grande ammaestramento di soavitade, ché in essa cotale morte non è dolore né alcuna acerbitate, ma sì come uno pomo maturo leggiermente e sanza violenza si dispicca dal suo ramo, così la nostra anima sanza doglia si parte dal corpo ov'ella è stata. Onde Aristotile in quello De Iuventute et Senectute dice che 'sanza tristizia è la morte ch'è ne la vecchiezza'. E sì come a colui che viene di lungo cammino, anzi ch'entri ne la porta de la sua cittade, li si fanno incontro li cittadini di quella, così a la nobile anima si fanno incontro, e deono fare, quelli cittadini de la etterna vita; e così fanno per le sue buone operazioni e contemplazioni: ché, già essendo a Dio renduta e astrattasi da le mondane cose e cogitazioni, vedere le pare coloro che appresso di Dio crede che siano. Odi che dice Tullio, in persona di Catone vecchio: 'A me pare già vedere e levomi in grandissimo studio di vedere li vostri padri, che io amai, e non pur quelli [che io stesso conobbi], ma eziandio quelli di cui udi' parlare'.

(*Convivio* 4.28.3–6)[43]

43 'And that indeed is how it is, for just as a good sailor, on approaching a port, lowers his sails and slips more than ever gently into it, so ought we to lower the sails of our worldly affairs and turn to God with all our heart and mind, thus coming home with all sweetness and peace. And it is clearly our own nature which, magisterial in its gentleness, invites us so to do, for in death thus understood there is neither pain nor bitterness of any kind; rather, just as a ripe apple falls easily and of its own accord from the branch, so our soul leaves painlessly the body wherein it has dwelt, which is why, as Aristotle says in his *On Maturity and Age*, "without sadness is death in old age". Just as his fellow citizens, then, come out to greet a man completing a long journey before he passes through the gates of his city, so too, on account of its good works and reflective ways, those of the eternal city come forth to greet the noble soul; for having given itself to God and forsaken all worldly cares and concerns, it seems now to behold those it believes to be of his household. Hear, therefore, what Cicero has to say in the person of Cato the Elder: "I seem now to see, and indeed exalt all the more in my desire to do so, your much beloved fathers, and not only them but those others too of whom I have heard tell." ' On the range of Dante's

—lines to which, not least for their exquisite blend of tact and tenderness, we may add these from just a little later in the same chapter, an essay in their own right in *successionality* as distinct from *dimensionality* as, for the Dante of the *Convivio*, a fundamental structure of consciousness:

> E benedice anco la nobile anima in questa etade li tempi passati; e bene li può benedicere; però che, per quelli rivolvendo la sua memoria, essa si ri-membra de le sue diritte operazioni, sanza le quali al porto, ove s'appressa, venire non si potea con tanta ricchezza né con tanto guadagno. E fa come lo buono mercatante, che, quando viene presso al suo porto, essamina lo suo procaccio e dice: 'Se io non fosse per cotal cammino passato, questo tesoro non avre' io, e non avrei di ch'io godesse ne la mia cittade, a la quale io m'appresso'; e però benedice la via che ha fatta.
>
> (*Convivio* 4.28.11–12)[44]

This, then, is what it means to speak of axes of concern in the *Convivio*, a text at every point irradiated, to be sure, by its magnanimity but a text present to the attentive reader of Dante in the round, and doubtless upon reflexion to Dante himself, by way only of its as yet unresolved spirituality. This, in other words, is a text calling from deep within itself for a fresh meditation on the complex sub-stance and structure of human experience in the totality thereof, on the *how it is and how it fares* with man as a creature subsisting *in one and the same moment* upon the planes of the horizontal and of the vertical, both of the *before and after* and of the *height and depth* of the historical instant. Herein precisely, in a geometry of

---

auctores hereabouts in the *Convivio* (in addition to Aristotle, Cicero and Boethius among the philoso-phers, Virgil, Ovid, Lucan and Statius among the poets) and for the implications of this for Dante's particular brand of pre- or protohumanism, Giuseppe Toffanin, *Perché l'umanesimo comincia con Dante* (Bologna: Zanichelli, 1967); Roberto Weiss, 'Dante e l'umanesimo del suo tempo', *LC* 2 (1969), 11–27; Michelangelo Picone, 'Dante and the Classics', in *Dante: Contemporary Perspectives*, ed. Amilcare A. Iannucci (Toronto: University of Toronto Press, 1997), 51–73; Lucia Gualdo Rosa, 'Préhumanisme et humanisme en Italie: Aspects et problèmes', in *Cultures italiennes: XIIe–XVe siècles*, ed. Isabelle Heullant-Donat (Paris: Les Éditions du Cerf, 2000), 87–120; Alicja Raczyńska, 'Riflessioni sul preumanesimo dantesco alla luce del pensiero di Jacob Burckhardt', *Studia Litteraria* 4.1 (2009), 97–109; Luciano Gar-gan, *Dante, la sua biblioteca e lo studio di Bologna* (Rome: Antenore, 2014). More generally, Augustin Renaudet, *Dante humaniste* (Paris: Les Belles Lettres, 1952); Ernst Robert Curtius, *European Literature and the Latin Middle Ages*, trans. Willard R. Trusk (London: Routledge and Kegan Paul, 1953); Paul Renucci, *Dante, disciple et juge du monde gréco-latin* (Paris: Les Belles Lettres, 1954); Jacob Burckhardt, *The Civilization of the Renaissance in Italy* (London: Phaidon Press, 1960 [1860]); Giuseppe Billanovich, *Dal Medioevo all'umanesimo: La riscoperta dei classici*, ed. Paolo Pellegrini (Milan: C.U.S.L, 2001).

44 'And at this stage the noble soul blesses the years gone by, and this with good reason in that, pondering them afresh in memory, it calls to mind its every noble accomplishment in all the wealth and experience thereof as the condition of its homecoming. And just as the good merchant, as he approaches journey's end, looks over all he has acquired and acknowledges how, had he not come this way, he should neither possess such goods as he has nor yet know the pleasure of the place whereunto he draws nigh, so too that same noble soul blesses the way it has taken.'

human experience apt in one and the same moment to accommodate its alternative axes, lies the triumph of the *Commedia* as the fruit of Dante's coming home as a philosophical and theological spirit, everything for the moment, pulsating as it is with a characteristically Dantean energy, subsisting by way only of its provisionality.

LANGUAGE, FORM AND FUNCTION: AN ESSAY IN BEAUTY, BEING AND BECOMING

For all its transparency to a humanity as yet unresolved in respect of the tensions at work deep within it, and thus for all its entertaining sooner rather than later the prospect of its incompletability, the *Convivio*, in another sense, constitutes a resounding to the point of unqualified triumph; for it is here that his beloved *lingua di sì*—ever, for Dante, a friend in need—is vindicated in two respects: in respect of its 'bellezza' or connatural beauty ('connatural' in the sense of dispensing for the moment with rhyme, rhythm and prosody generally as but a matter of embellishment), and in respect of its 'virtù' or expressive power, of its equality to Latin as the long since accredited medium of high-cultural discourse. Taking first, then, the aesthetic aspect of the matter, things do not, alas, get off to a good start for the vernacular, Dante's preliminary remarks hereabouts turning upon a sense of its status as but the poor relation of Latin, as a matter less of art and artistry than of mere linguistic happenstance:

> Quella cosa dice l'uomo essere bella, cui le parti debitamente si rispondono, per che de la loro armonia resulta piacimento. Onde pare l'uomo essere bello, quando le sue membra debitamente si rispondono; e dicemo bello lo canto, quando le voci di quello, secondo debito de l'arte, sono intra sé rispondenti. Dunque quello sermone è più bello, ne lo quale più debitamente si rispondono [le parole; e più debitamente si rispondono] in latino che in volgare, però che lo volgare seguita uso, e lo latino arte.
>
> (*Convivio* 1.5.13–14)[45]

---

45 'A thing is said to be beautiful when its parts accord one with another, harmony being a source of delight. So a man is said to be beautiful when his members are properly proportionate, and a song when its sounds accord one with another in keeping with the art thereof. So language, then, is the more beautiful insofar as words properly countenance one another, which, Latin being a matter of art and the vernacular merely of usage, they do better in the former rather than in the latter.' Gioacchino Paparelli, 'Dante fra latino e volgare', in *Ideologia e poesia di Dante* (Florence: Olschki, 1975), 15–27; Fernando Salsano, 'Dante tra latino e volgare (*Conv.* I 5–13)', *MC* 7.23–24 (1977), 43–49 (and in *Pane quotidiano: Elzevìri* [Ravenna: Longo, 2007], 36–140); Massimo Arcangeli, 'La grammatica tra arte e scienza nella riflessione linguistica medievale e il confronto e volgare nella trattatistica italiana dei primi secoli', in *Lo scaffale bella biblioteca scientifica in volgare (secoli XIII–XVI). Atti del Convegno, Matera*

But it is not long before, warming as he does to his subject, Dante has a change of heart; for to contemplate the again unfussed beauty of the vernacular line—to wit, the gentle succession of its syllables, the integrity of its each and every construction and the sweet complexion of the expressive period as a whole—is at once to register its loveliness:

> Ché per questo comento la gran bontade del volgare di sì [si vedrà]; però che si vedrà la sua vertù, sì com'è per esso altissimi e novissimi concetti convenevolmente, sufficientemente e acconciamente, quasi come per esso latino, manifestare; [la quale non si potea bene manifestare] ne le cose rimate, per le accidentali adornezze che quivi sono connesse, cioè la rima e lo ri[ti]mo e lo numero regolato: sì come non si può bene manifestare la bellezza d'una donna, quando li adornamenti de l'azzimare e de le vestimenta la fanno più ammirare che essa medesima. Onde chi vuole ben giudicare d'una donna, guardi quella quando solo sua naturale bellezza si sta con lei, da tutto accidentale adornamento discompagnata; sì come sarà questo comento, nel quale si vedrà l'agevolezza de le sue sillabe, le proprietadi de le sue co[stru]zioni e le soavi orazioni che di lui si fanno; le quali chi bene agguarderà, vedrà essere piene di dolcissima e d'amabilissima bellezza.
>
> (*Convivio* 1.10.12–13)[46]

As far, then, as the first of these things is concerned, namely its gentle succession of syllables (the 'agevolezza de le sue sillabe' moment of the argument), it is a question, Dante explains, of the 'binding up' of the word by way of the vowel as—as he himself puts it—the soul of the word and thus the still centre and living principle of its beauty:

> È dunque da sapere che 'autoritade' non è altro che 'atto d'autore'. Questo vocabulo, cioè 'autore', sanza quella terza lettera C, può discendere da due

---

14–15 ottobre 2004, ed. Rita Librandi and Rosa Piro (Florence: Galluzzo, 2006), 439–52; Furio Brugnolo, 'Il plurilinguismo medievale e la coscienza distintiva degli idiomi romanzi', in *Comunicare nel Medioevo: La conoscenza e l'uso delle lingue nei secoli XII–XV. Atti del Convegno, Ascoli Piceno, 28–30 novembre 2013*, ed. Isa Lori Sanfilippo and Giuliano Pinto (Istituto Storico Italiano per il Medioevo, 2015), 13–32.

46 'For by means of this commentary the excellence of the *lingua di sì* will be made manifest, everyone seeing for himself its power to express fittingly, fully and gracefully, just as in Latin itself, the most lofty and original ideas. For just as the beauty of a woman is less properly manifest when the mere trappings of dress and finery command more attention than she herself does, so also there can be no showing forth of the excellence whereof we speak in verse, verse likewise having about it the accidental adornment of rhyme and rhythm. Whoever, then, wishes rightly to judge of a woman should look upon her natural, uncluttered beauty, which is how it will be with this commentary, the smooth succession of its syllables, the elegant construction and refinement of the period as a whole commending themselves such that those who look on attentively will find there, and find in abundance, sweetness and loveliness beyond compare.'

principii: l'uno si è d'uno verbo molto lasciato da l'uso in gramatica, che significa tanto quanto 'legare parole', cioè 'auieo'. E chi ben guarda lui, ne la sua prima voce apertamente vedrà che elli stesso lo dimostra, che solo di legame di parole è fatto, cioè di sole cinque vocali, che sono anima e legame d'ogni parole, e composto d'esse per modo volubile, a figurare imagine di legame. Ché, cominciando da l'A, ne l'U quindi si rivolve, e viene diritto per I ne l'E, quindi si rivolve e torna ne l'O; sì che veramente imagina questa figura: A, E, I,O, U, la quale è figura di legame. E in quanto 'autore' viene e discende da questo verbo, si prende solo per li poeti, che con l'arte musaica le loro parole hanno legate.

(*Convivio* 4.6.3–4)[47]

while as far as the integrity of its each and every construction is concerned (the 'proprietadi de le sue co[stru]zioni' moment of the argument) it is a question of its uniform equality to the matter in hand, of a period, that is to say, which, while faithful to the leading idea, honours even so its moment-by-moment articulation and/or its discreet nuancing within the economy of the whole; so, for example—and bearing in this case on the etiquette of public self-admonition—we have this passage from early on in the *Convivio* with by way of a neat disposition of causal and coordinate clause ('però che ... e ... onde ... e ... ') its gentle consequentialism:

Dispregiar sé medesimo è per sé biasimevole, *però che* a l'amico dee l'uomo lo suo difetto contare strettamente, *e* nullo è più amico che l'uomo a sé; *onde* ne la camera de' suoi pensieri se medesimo riprender dee e piangere li suoi difetti, *e* non palese.

(*Convivio* 1.2.5)[48]

47 'The first thing to say, then, is that "authority" is nothing other than the activity of an "author" as one who exercises that authority, and is a term which, lacking a C as its third letter, may derive from one or other of two sources. The first of these is a Latin verb (though one which has long since dropped out of use) meaning "to bind words together": "auieo". And anyone taking a close look at the word, and in particular at its first letter, will see for himself how this confirms its meaning, for it consists entirely of what ties words together, namely of the five vowels which, intertwining as they do after the manner of a knot, constitute between them the soul and ligament of all words whatever. Indeed the very word "auieo" suggests in its to-and-fro movement the notion of tying together; for beginning with the A that same knot reaches across to the U, then back to the E via the I, and then back across to the O, the resulting figure—AEIOU—being that, precisely, of a bow (though this understanding of the term "author" as deriving in point of provenance from the verb "aueio" is current only in poetic circles where it is a question, precisely, of binding up words by way of music and the discipline thereof).' Letterio Cassata, ' "Autore" e "auctore" nella *Commedia*', *SLI* 25.2 (1999), 271–74.
48 'Openly taking oneself to task is by nature reprehensible, since a man should confess his faults only to a friend, and no one is more of a friend than a man is to himself; thus it is only in the privacy of one's own thoughts that a man should admonish himself and lament his shortcomings, not publicly.' Giuseppe Lisio, *L'arte del periodo nelle opere volgari di Dante Alighieri e del secolo XIII* (Bologna: Zanichelli, 1902); Alfredo Schiaffini, *Tradizione e poesia nella prosa d'arte italiana dalla latinità medievale a*

together with, as similarly rich in its accumulation of subsidiary clauses ('Onde ... per che ... ma ... onde ...') all living on in anticipation of the main clause some way down the line ('conviemmi che con più alto stilo dea ...'), this passage from just a little further on in book 1 relative to gravitas as a way of restoring one's battered reputation:

> *Onde* con ciò sia cosa che, come detto è di sopra, io mi sia quasi a tutti li Italici appresentato, *per che* fatto mi sono più vile forse che 'l vero non vuole non solamente a quelli a li quali mia fama era già corsa, *ma* eziandio a li altri, *onde* le mie cose sanza dubbio meco sono alleviate; conviemmi che con più alto stilo dea, ne la presente opera, un poco di gravezza, per la quale paia di maggiore autoritade.
>
> (*Convivio* 1.4.13)[49]

or, by way now of a conscientious nesting of ancillary clauses within the main clause, this extract from Dante's discussion of the nature and extent of imperial jurisdiction in book 4:

> E queste tutte operazioni, avvegna che 'l considerare loro subiaccia a la nostra volontade, elle per loro a nostra volontade non subiacciono; *ché, perché* noi volessimo che le cose gravi salissero per natura suso, *e perché* noi volessimo che 'l silogismo con falsi principii conchiudesse veritade dimostrando, *e perché* noi volessimo che la casa sedesse così forte pendente come diritta, non sarebbe.
>
> (*Convivio* 4.9.6)[50]

G. *Boccaccio*, 2nd ed. (Rome: Edizioni di Storia e Letteratura, 1943); Cesare Segre, 'La sintassi del periodo nei primi prosatori italiani', *RSANL* 4 (1952), 41–193 (and in *Lingua, stile e società*, 2nd ed. [Milan: Feltrinelli, 1976], 81–270, especially 249); Cecil Grayson, 'Dante e la prosa volgare', *Il Verri* 8 (1963), 6–26; Tatiana Alisova, 'Studi di sintassi italiana', *SFI* 25 (1967), 223–313; Aldo Vallone, *La prosa del 'Convivio'* (Florence: Le Monnier, 1967); Letizia Leoncini, 'La "concinnitas" nella prosa di Dante: Da Cicerone ad Agostino, al di là (e al di qua) dell'"Ars dictaminis"', *Aevum* 81.2 (2007), 523–57. With respect to lexis, Franca Brambilla Ageno, 'Alcuni termini del latino medioevale nel volgare del *Convivio*', in *SPCT* 38 (1989), 5–10.

49 'Whence having, as I mentioned earlier, been exposed to just about everyone in Italy—which is why, perhaps, I am held in lower esteem than the truth warrants not only by those whom my reputation has reached but by others as well, for which reason everything of mine, including my own person, has beyond doubt been cheapened—it is only right by way of a loftier style I bestow upon the present work a certain gravity and air of greater authority.'

50 'Although, as far as these activities are concerned, it falls within our power to consider them, they, in themselves, are not subject to that power; for however much we might wish weighty things to move by nature upwards, and however much we would like a syllogism with false premises to yield a true conclusion, and however much we would wish a leaning structure to sit as securely as an upright structure, this would not happen.'

or finally, and as something of a tour de force in its accommodation of any number of coordinate and relative clauses before ever we reach the main verb, this passage from book 3 on the notion of philosophy as, in Dante's sense of it, an aid to faith:

E la nostra fede aiuta; *però che, con ciò sia cosa che* principalissimo fondamento de la fede nostra siano miracoli fatti per colui che fu crucifisso—*lo quale creò* la nostra ragione, *e* volle che fosse minore del suo potere—*e* fatti poi nel nome suo per li santi suoi; *e* molti siano sì ostinati che di quelli miracoli per alcuna nebbia siano dubbiosi, *e* non possano credere miracolo alcuno sanza visibilmente avere di ciò esperienza; *e* questa donna sia una cosa visibilmente miraculosa, *de la quale* li occhi de li uomini cotidianamente possono esperienza avere, *ed* a noi faccia possibili li altri; manifesto è che questa donna, col suo mirabile aspetto, la nostra fede aiuta.

(*Convivio* 3.7.16)[51]

But it is not, perhaps, in moments such as this, sophisticated as they are, that we delight in the 'soavi orazioni' or 'sweet orations' of the Dantean line but rather in what amounts to its delicate *specularitas*, its carefully cultivated introspection at the level of form; so, for example, these lines in honour of philosophy as the proper object of all desiring and as the repository of all peace, the period as a whole reaching out in its abundant anaphora and nicely contrived consonantalism ('desidera . . . desiderio . . . desiderata . . . desiderio'; 'dilettazione . . . dilettazione . . . diletto'; 'perfezione . . . perfezione . . . perfetta'; 'pensiero . . . pensieri') to caress the mind of the reader:

E a questo affermare, soggiungo quando dico: 'E quella gente che qui s'innamora'. Dove è da sapere che ciascuna cosa massimamente desidera la sua perfezione, e in quella si queta ogni suo desiderio, e per quella ogni cosa è desiderata. E questo è quello desiderio che sempre ne fa parere ogni dilettazione manca; ché nulla dilettazione è sì grande in questa vita che a l'anima nostra possa torre la sete, che sempre lo desiderio che detto è non rimagna nel pensiero. E però che questa è veramente quella perfezione, dico che quella gente che qua giù maggiore diletto riceve quando più hanno di pace,

---

51 'And she assists our faith in that since that faith rests above all on the miracles performed by him who died for us (by him who, fashioning our reason, willed even so its inequality to his power) and on those performed subsequently by the saints in his name; and since so many people, their minds somewhat clouded, are obstinate enough to doubt those miracles short of seeing them themselves; and since, further, this lady is a visibly miraculous presence, there for men daily to experience with their own eyes, confirming us as it does so in the possibility of all other miracles, then it is clear that, radiant as she is to behold, she assists our faith.'

allora rimane questa ne' loro pensieri, per questa, dico, tanto essere perfetta quanto sommamente essere puote l'umana essenzia.

(*Convivio* 3.6.7–8)[52]

Turning finally, then, to the 'expressive power' of the vernacular line (the 'sua vertù' moment of the argument), it is precisely this combination of form and functionality, of rhythm, refinement and resourcefulness that confirms the adequacy, indeed the ascendancy, of the vernacular as, for Dante, the lingua franca of high-cultural disquisition. Look no further then, he says, than the commentary now before you, for there for your delectation is a vernacular discourse perfectly empowered in respect of every inflexion of the spirit be it ne'er so arcane or so abstract:

Ché per questo comento la gran bontade del volgare di sì [si vedrà]; però che si vedrà la sua vertù, sì com'è per esso altissimi e novissimi concetti convenevolmente, sufficientemente e acconciamente, quasi come per esso latino, manifestare.

(*Convivio* 1.10.12)[53]

Throughout, then, the pattern is the same, for throughout it is a question of the *lingua di sì* as come of age, of a vernacular adequate both aesthetically and expressively to the matter in hand. If, then, for the purposes of anything approaching a satisfactory account of the stylistic complexion of the *Convivio*, we would have duly to acknowledge its transparency to the ways and means of the schoolmen (its 'dico dunque che', for example, for their 'dico igitur quod', its 'per che manifesto è' for their 'unde manifestum est quod', its 'onde è da sapere che' for their 'propter quod sciendum est', or its 'ancora ... ancora ...' for their 'item ... item ... '), then so be it, for this too is all part of the mix—but only part of it; for what in truth we have here is an instance less of *imitatio* than of *translatio*, less of emulation than of a making over of linguistic magisterium to a new and properly accredited keeper.

---

52 'And for the purpose of further confirming this I say: "And those here who are in love", where what needs to be understood is that all things desire above all their own perfection, in the accomplishment of which every desire is stilled and for the sake of which all else is sought out. This is that yearning which makes of every other desire something inadequate, for there is no desire so great in this life that it can satisfy the soul's innermost yearning or that can prevent that same yearning dominating the mind. And since this lady is indeed that perfection, it is my contention that those here below who rejoice in her and know the peace thereof, even for them she governs their every thought, which is why of her I say that she is the very greatest perfection of which man as man is capable.'

53 'For by means of this commentary the excellence of the *lingua di sì* will be made manifest, everyone seeing for himself its power to express fittingly, fully and gracefully, just as in Latin itself, the most lofty and original ideas.'

Impressive as this is, however, as an act of cultural accreditation, that is not the end of it, for the cultural, other than in the context of the ontological, is for Dante neither here nor there as a matter of concern. To speak, in other words, of the vernacular—in this case of the *lingua di sì*—as comparable to Latin in point of beauty and of expressive power, and indeed as successor to Latin in the area of high-cultural discourse, is in one and the same breath to speak of its status as the in-and-through-which of properly human being and becoming on the part of those befriended by it. It is, in other words, to speak of the function of the ver-nacular—in truth, of all language but supremely of the vernacular—as that whereby this or that individual or group of individuals affirm themselves in the twofold integrity and intelligibility of their properly human presence in the world. As far, then, as the individual is concerned—in this case Alighieri himself—we have the confessional moment of 1.13, a moment sensitive in the extreme to the function of that same vernacular as the principle both of his first and of his second perfection, both of his *being* and of his *being well*:

Dico, prima, ch'io per me ho da lei ricevuto dono di grandissimi benefici. E però è da sapere che intra tutti i benefici è maggiore quello che più è prezioso a chi riceve; e nulla cosa è tanto preziosa, quanto quella per la quale tutte l'altre si vogliono; e tutte l'altre cose si vogliono per la perfezione di colui che vuole. Onde con ciò sia cosa che due perfezioni abbia l'uomo, una prima e una seconda—la prima lo fa essere, la seconda lo fa essere buono— se la propria loquela m'è stata cagione e de l'una e de l'altra, grandissimo beneficio da lei ho ricevuto. E ch'ella sia stata a me d'essere [cagione, e an-cora di buono essere] se per me non stesse, brievemente si può mostrare. Non è [inconveniente] a una cosa esser più cagioni efficienti, avvegna che una sia massima de l'altre; onde lo fuoco e lo martello sono cagioni efficienti de lo coltello, avvegna che massimamente è il fabbro. Questo mio volgare fu congiugnitore de li miei generanti, che con esso parlavano, sì come 'l fuoco è disponitore del ferro al fabbro che fa lo coltello; per che manifesto è lui essere concorso a la mia generazione, e così essere alcuna cagione del mio essere. Ancora, questo mio volgare fu introduttore di me ne la via di scienza, che è ultima perfezione, in quanto con esso io entrai ne lo latino e con esso mi fu mostrato; lo quale latino poi mi fu via a più innanzi andare. E così è palese, e per me conosciuto, esso essere stato a me grandissimo benefattore.

(*Convivio* 1.13.2–5)[54]

54 'I say first of all, then, that I personally have benefited greatly from it, in relation to which we need first to understand that, of all benefits, there is none greater than that most prized by the recipient; and nothing is more prized than that for which all else is desired, all else being desired for the sake of

while as far as the community as a whole is concerned, we have the now familiar doxology of book 1 settling at last on the notion of language—of, more exactly, the now infinitely precious vernacular—as that whereby those who hitherto have walked in the darkness will see now a new light, a light to lighten the Gentiles and to bring them home to their proper humanity:

> Così rivolgendo li occhi a dietro, e raccogliendo le ragioni prenotate, puotesi vedere questo pane, col quale si deono mangiare le infrascritte canzoni, essere sufficientemente purgato da le macule, e da l'essere di biado; per che tempo è d'intendere a ministrare le vivande. Questo sarà quello pane orzato del quale si satolleranno migliaia, e a me ne soperchieranno le sporte piene. Questo sarà luce nuova, sole nuovo, lo quale surgerà là dove l'usato tramonterà, e darà lume a coloro che sono in tenebre e in oscuritade, per lo usato sole che a loro non luce.
>
> (*Convivio* 1.13.11–12)[55]

This, then, is what it means to speak in relation to Dante of language, and above all of the vernacular, as a matter of ontological concern, for his, everywhere, is a sense of that same vernacular as the in-and-through-which of emergence on the plane of existence. No vernacular, no emergence. Simply a standing of self over against the *what might be* of an otherwise stupendous presence in the world.

---

perfecting the one who desires it. Thus, since man has two perfections, a first and a second perfection—the former a matter of being and the latter of well-being—then if my native tongue has been the cause of them both, I shall have received from it the greatest of all benefits. That it has indeed been the cause of them both (any shortfall here being entirely down to me) may thus briefly be shown. Now it is quite possible for a thing to have several efficient causes, albeit one of them being to the fore; so, for instance, both fire and hammer are efficient causes of a knife, though only the smith is such in the fullest sense. This vernacular of mine, being the language spoken by my parents, in bringing them together functioned like the fire which readies the iron for the smith to fashion a knife. It is clear, then, that it was party to my birth, and indeed to that extent a cause of my being. But more than this, in assisting me at the outset with Latin and in helping me to understand it as the means of my making further progress, it set me on the road to knowledge as our greatest perfection. Plainly, then, and this is something I gladly acknowledge, my vernacular has been a wonderful benefactor to me.' Gianni Vattimo, 'Heidegger: Il linguaggio come evento dell'essere', in *Psicoanalisi e strutturalismo di fronte a Dante: Dalla letteratura profetica medievale agli odierni strumenti critici. Atti di mesi danteschi '69–'71*, vol. 1 (Florence: Olschki, 1972), 311–16.

55 'Looking back, then, over all that has been said, and gathering up the threads of the argument so far, it is clear that this bread, with which the following canzoni should be eaten, has been sufficiently purged of any blemish and excused for being but of barley. So now, then, it is time to think about serving the courses themselves, this commentary constituting the barley bread whereby—with many a basketful besides remaining to me—thousands will be satisfied. This will be a new light, a new sun rising where the old has set, a light to enlighten the overshadowed and darkling, the sun of old no longer shining upon them.' Antonio Pagliaro, 'La dottrina linguistica di Dante', *Quaderni di Roma* 1.6 (1947), 485–501.

CONCLUSION: BEING AND BECOMING AS YET IN WAITING

Looked at diachronically or from the point of view of Dante's own being and becoming as a poet and philosopher we have in the *Convivio* a work sensitive if not from the outset then very soon thereafter to its inadequacy as an account of human experience in the totality thereof, in respect, that is to say, of its complex dimensionality and finality. But no less important than the diachronic or *what comes next* when it comes to a proper appreciation either of this or of any other text along the way is its synchronic aspect or what it stood for at the time, and, where the *Convivio* is concerned, there can be no sitting lightly to this; for the *Convivio* is by any standard a text as courageous as it is magnanimous, as resolute in respect of Dante's personal predicament as perforce a wanderer upon the face of the earth as it is generous in respect of those 'many men and women in this language of ours' as yet adrift in point of their properly human happiness. On the one hand, then, there is the courage of the text, its squaring up to the agony of exile by way of a fresh implementation of self if not yet as a prophet then as a philosopher and teacher, this, for the moment, being the way of self-rationalization, of Dante's standing withal in his own presence. On the other hand there is its reaching out to nourish the distracted and the despairing, those who, conscious if only hazily of a good apt to assuage the spirit (the 'Ciascun confusamente un bene apprende / nel qual si queti l'animo' of *Purgatorio* 18), are nonetheless way-laid by the multiplicity of their loving, multiplicity on the plane of loving, left to itself, only ever making for the substance and sensation of loss, of knowing self in the far-offness of self. This, then, is what it means to speak of the courage and magnanimity of the *Convivio* in its synchronic aspect, in respect of what for Dante it meant at the time. For what for Dante it meant at the time was a strenuous interrogation of self in the innermost recesses of self, and, in consequence of this, a bringing on of the next man in the ways and means of a civic, certainly, but more than this of a properly civil humanity.

But for all its courage and magnanimity as a response to the catastrophe of exile, the *Convivio*—the boldly conceived and socially solicitous *Convivio*—remains a problematic text, problematic in respect of a tension discernible both on the surface and in the depths. On the surface, then, it is a question of the two axes of concern, of Dante's commitment, as the way of properly human happiness (*a*) to an ascent of the spirit by way of philosophy as but the love of wisdom coeval and consubstantial with the Godhead itself (the 'vertical' axis), and (*b*) to an order of understanding open to accomplishment here and now under the aegis of Aristotle (the 'horizontal' axis), these things relating one to the other by way less of complementarity than of contradistinction and indeed of mutual exclusiveness. In the depths, by contrast—where, however, the problem remains fundamentally the same—it is a question of the complex dimensionality of human experience in the round, of how within the economy of the whole it might be possible to reconcile the immanent and the transcendent, the temporal and the eternal, the philosophical and the theological as but the dominant structures of specifically human being in its moment-by-moment unfolding. In this sense the process of interrogation and of self-interrogation inaugurated by the catastrophe of exile has, with the *Convivio*, only just begun, the sheer power of Dante's reconstruction of the whole issue in the *Commedia*, the text whereby the *Convivio* is at once superseded, being registered from the word go. On the one hand, then, we have the 'As Aristotle says in the First Philosophy, all men naturally desire to know' formula on the threshold of the *Convivio*, a formula straightaway suggesting in respect both of substance and of spirit the nature of his undertaking hereabouts—philosophical, pedagogical and designed by way of reasonable demonstration to bring on both self and the other-than-self in the way of properly human happiness. On the other hand, we have the 'Midway through this life of ours I found myself in a dark wood' formula on the threshold of the *Commedia*, a formula suggesting in the way that only an image can a sense of radical self-losing and, with it, a commitment to the restructuring of the old in favour of the new. Now here, to be sure, there is no lack of continuity, any number of discrete emphases, and indeed the deep substance of the *Convivio*, feeding into the *Commedia* as an essential part of its prehistory. But for all that the *Convivio*—the magnanimous *Convivio*—calls once again from out of the depths for something both more and other than itself, for an account of the human situation more properly transparent to its unique complexity.[56]

---

56 Exact in this sense, Kenelm Foster, O.P., *The Two Dantes* (London: Darton, Longman and Todd, 1977), 246: 'Theologically speaking, this brilliant work [the *Convivio*] is immature. And if it is a sign of growing maturity that a man takes stock of tensions and contradictions latent in himself, then certainly the *Comedy* marks a great advance, in this respect, on the *Convivio*.' Bruno Nardi, *Dal 'Convivio' alla 'Commedia': Sei saggi danteschi* (Rome: Nella sede dell'Istituto, 1960); Antonio Gagliardi, *La tragedia intellettuale di Dante: Il 'Convivio'* (Catanzaro: Pullano, 1994); John A. Scott, 'The Unfinished *Convivio* as a Pathway to the *Comedy*', DS 113 (1995), 31–56 (and in *Dante: The Critical Complex*, vol. 3 [2003], 1–26); Robert Hollander, *Dante: A Life in Works* (New Haven: Yale University Press, 2001), especially 88–90; Ulrich Leo, 'The Unfinished *Convivio* and Dante's Rereading of the *Aeneid*', in *Dante: The Critical Complex*, vol. 2, ed. Richard Lansing (New York: Routledge, 2003), 189–212; Sabrina Ferrara, 'I trattati incompiuti: Il *Convivio* e il *De vulgari eloquentia*', in *La parola dell'esilio: Autore e lettori nelle opere di Dante in esilio* (Florence: Cesati, 2016), 59–100.

CHAPTER 3

The *De vulgari eloquentia*: Language, Literature and the Ontologization of Art

The seriousness of the text in Dante, and, with it, its power to commend itself to each successive generation as party to the ongoing discussion, lies in its preoccupation with the idea, not only nor even primarily as a pure determination of the mind, but as a principle of being and becoming on the part of those to whom it is present as an object of contemplation. This situation is everywhere discernible in his work. It is discernible in the *Vita nova* in its preoccupation with love-intelligence as that whereby the poet-lover knows himself as a new creation, as confirmed in a fresh order of seeing, understanding and desiring, and it is discernible in the *Convivio* in its laying on of a banquet designed to nourish the otherwise distracted spirit and, in nourishing it, to bring it home to its properly human happiness. And it is discernible in the *Commedia* in its proposal of the theological issue in terms of the agony and ecstasy of the one who says 'I', of Dante himself as protagonist in his own poem. And what applies to the *Vita nova*, to the *Convivio* and to the *Commedia* as the great utterances of Dante's youth, maturity and seniority respectively applies also to the infinitely precious moment of the *De vulgari eloquentia*, where again it is a question of being and becoming in the verifiability thereof—of, more precisely, the *vulgare illustre* as the means of self-affirmation and self-recognition on the part of a new Latin race generally (book 1) and of form as that whereby the poet in particular might know himself in the now and henceforth astripetal or star-seeking substance of his humanity (book 2). On the one hand, then, we have the "simple sign" passage of 1.16 with its sense of the *illustre* as that whereby a certain set of people at a certain time and a certain place might take their own measure and, in so doing, enter fully and unequivocally into their own presence:

> Quapropter in actionibus nostris, quantumcunque dividantur in species, hoc signum inveniri oportet quo et ipse mensurentur. Nam, in quantum simpliciter ut homines agimus, virtutem habemus (ut generaliter illam intelligamus); nam secundum ipsam bonum et malum hominem iudicamus;

in quantum ut homines cives agimus, habemus legem, secundum quam dicitur civis bonus et malus; in quantum ut homines latini agimus, quedam habemus simplicissima signa et morum et habituum et locutionis, quibus latine actiones ponderantur et mensurantur. Que quidem nobilissima sunt earum que Latinorum sunt actiones, hec nullius civitatis Ytalie propria sunt, et in omnibus comunia sunt; inter que nunc potest illud discerni vulgare quod superius venabamur, quod in qualibet redolet civitate nec cubat in ulla.

(*De vulgari eloquentia* 1.16.2–3)[1]

while on the other we have these lines from book 2—possibly among the most sublime of their kind in European letters—relative to the soaring substance of the poet's humanity and, provided only that he has tested the strength of his own shoulders and served his apprenticeship as a technician, his status as beloved of the gods:

Caveat ergo quilibet et discernat ea que dicimus; et quando pure hec tria cantare intendit, vel que ad ea directe ac pure secuntur, prius Elicone potatus, tensis fidibus ad supremum, secure plectrum tum movere incipiat. Sed cautionem atque discretionem hanc accipere, sicut decet, hic opus et labor est, quoniam nunquam sine strenuitate ingenii et artis assiduitate scientiarum-

---

1 'As regards our actions, therefore, various though they be in character, it behoves us to define a standard against which these too can be measured. Now, insofar as we act simply as human beings, we have (taking the term broadly for the moment) virtue, and it is up against this that we judge people to be good or bad. Insofar, by contrast, as we act as citizens, we have the law, this being the standard whereby we deem a citizen good or bad; insofar as we act as Italians, we have a certain manner, appearance and speech whereby our actions as such can be weighed and measured (though the noblest of specifically Italian actions are proper to no one Italian city but common to them all). Among these, therefore, is to be found the vernacular we have thus far been seeking out, a vernacular which has left its scent in every city but its lair in none.' Alfredo Schiaffini, *Interpretazione del 'De vulgari eloquentia' di Dante* (Rome: Ed. Ricerche, 1963); Pier Vincenzo Mengaldo, 'Introduzione al *De vulgari eloquentia*', in *Linguistica e retorica di Dante* (Pisa: Nistri-Lischi, 1978), 11–123; Marianne Shapiro, *De vulgari eloquentia: Dante's Book of Exile* (Lincoln: University of Nebraska Press, 1990); Saverio Bellomo, *De vulgari eloquentia*, in *Filologia e critica dantesca*, 2nd ed. (Brescia: La Scuola, 2012), 119–33. More especially on Dante's theory and philosophy of language, Francesco d'Ovidio, 'Dante e la filosofia del linguaggio', in *Opere di F. D'Ovidio*, vol. 2 (Naples: Guida, 1931), 291–325 (and Florence: Le Cariti, 2008); Alfred Ewert, 'Dante's Theory of Language', *MLR* 35 (1940), 355–66; Bruno Nardi, 'Il linguaggio', in *Dante e la cultura medievale*, 2nd ed. (Bari: Laterza, 1949), 148–75 (173–95 in the Mazzantini ed. of 1983); Gustavo Vinay, 'La teoria linguistica del *De vulgari eloquentia*', *CS* 2.5 (1962), 30–42; Ignazio Baldelli, 'Sulla teoria linguistica di Dante', *CS* 5.13–14 (1965), 705–13; Luigi Peirone, *Il 'De vulgari eloquentia' e la linguistica moderna* (Geneva: Tilgher, 1975); Ileana Pagani, *La teoria linguistica di Dante. De vulgari eloquentia: discussioni, scelte, proposte* (Naples: Liguori, 1982); Gian Carlo Alessio, 'Il *De vulgari Eloquentia* e la teoria linguistica del Medioevo', in *'Per correr miglior acque...' Bilanci e prospettive degli studi danteschi alle soglie del nuovo millennio. Atti del Convegno internazionale di Verona-Ravenna 25–29 ottobre 1999* (Rome: Salerno Editrice, 2001), 203–27.

que habitu fieri potest. Et hii sunt quos poeta Eneidorum sexto Dei dilectos et ab ardente virtute sublimatos ad ethera deorumque filios vocat, quanquam figurate loquatur. Et ideo confutetur illorum stultitia qui, arte scientiaque immunes, de solo ingenio confidentes, ad summa summe canenda prorumpunt; et a tanta presumptuositate desistant, et si anseres natura vel desidia sunt, nolint astripetam aquilam imitari.

(*De vulgari eloquentia* 2.4.9–11)[2]

The *De vulgari eloquentia*, then, ideally contemporary as it is with the *Convivio* and maybe even conceived and/or composed in the gap between books 1 and 2 thereof, is no exception, its too being a referral of the matter to hand—in this case of the linguistic and of the literary-aesthetic—to the existential as to what actually and ultimately matters about it.

First, then, turning now to the course of the argument, comes its sense of the superior nobility, not now of Latin in its immunity to change over the generations, but of the vernacular as a matter, to be sure, of childhood imitation but in truth of something closer to connatural linguisticity, every more learned language—to wit, Greek and Latin—merely coming next and acquired by way only of endless application:

Sed quia unamquanque doctrinam oportet non probare, sed suum aperire subiectum, ut sciatur quid sit super quod illa versatur, dicimus, celeriter actendentes, quod vulgarem locutionem appellamus eam qua infantes assuefiunt ab assistentibus cum primitus distinguere voces incipiunt; vel, quod brevius dici potest, vulgarem locutionem asserimus quam sine omni regola nutricem imitantes accipimus. Est et inde alia locutio secondaria

2 'Let everyone, then, take care to understand precisely what we are saying here; and, if still they propose to sing of these three themes or of any directly or indirectly flowing from them, let them first drink of Helicon and tune their strings to perfection, whereupon they will be able to take up the plectrum with confidence. But learning how to exercise caution and judgement, that is the hard part, for never can this be achieved without a strenuous application of the mind and endless endeavour in the ways of both art and science. Such are those whom the author of the *Aeneid* calls in the sixth book (though he is speaking figuratively) the beloved of God, raised up by their now ardent goodness and made sons of the gods. And thus is shown up and duly confounded the folly of those who, untouched either by art or by science and trusting solely in their own wit, rush in and presume to sing of the highest things in the highest style. Let them desist from their presumption, and if by nature or indolence they are but geese, let them not seek to imitate the star-seeking eagle.' For the 'tested the strength of his own shoulders' motif, *De vulgari eloquentia* 2.4.4: 'Ante omnia ergo dicimus unumquenque debere materie pondus propriis humeris coequare, ne forte humerorum nimio gravata virtute in cenum cespitare necesse sit: hoc est quod magister noster Oratius precipit, cum in principio Poetrie "Sumite materiam . . ." dicit' (First of all we declare that any writer must adjust the weight of his subject to his own shoulders, lest by overloading them and trying their strength too far he topple into the mud. That is what our master Horace teaches when at the beginning of his *Art of Poetry* [line 38] he says, 'Take upon yourself a subject . . .').

nobis, quam Romani gramaticam vocaverunt. Hanc quidem secundariam
Greci habent et alii, sed non omnes; ad habitum vero huius pauci perveni-
unt, quia non nisi per spatium temporis et studii assiduitatem regulamur et
doctrinamur in illa. Harum quoque duarum nobilior est vulgaris; tum quia
prima fuit humano generi usitata; tum quia totus orbis ipsa perfruitur, licet
in diversas prolationes et vocabula sit divisa; tum quia naturalis est nobis,
cum illa potius artificialis existat. Et de hac nobiliori nostra est intentio
pertractare.

(De vulgari eloquentia 1.1.2–4)[3]

This, then—the vernacular as the language most properly ours and, more especially, the 'illustrious vernacular' as that whereby the inhabitants of the Italian
peninsula might know themselves in their distinctiveness precisely as such—will
be Dante's theme in the first book of the *De vulgari eloquentia*, where, hard on the
heels of a truly rapturous account of man's first utterance in Eden, it will be a
question (*a*) of tracing the melancholy diaspora of language generally in the wake
of Babel; (*b*) of surveying the existing forms of the Italian language in particular
with a view to seeing which of them might best represent them in the round; and
(*c*) of, *défaut de mieux* (none of the possible candidates actually measuring up),
offering a more properly 'reasonable' or in-principle account of what this ideal
Italian eloquence might look like. The Edenic moment of the argument is worth
lingering over, for here as throughout in Dante it is a question of language as but
a matter of rejoicing, of—in this case by way of naming the name—knowing self
in the coming forth of self, in the status of self as but the first fruits of divine
intentionality:

Quid autem prius vox primi loquentis sonaverit, viro sane mentis in
promptu esse non titubo ipsum fuisse quod 'Deus' est, scilicet *El*, vel per

---

3 'But since as with any science what matters is not to prove it but to say what it is about, and this
in order that the basis upon which it rests may be clear, I shall without ado hasten on to define the
vernacular as that which children learn from those round about them when first they begin to make
out one word from another—or, more briefly, that which, without instruction, we acquire by way of
imitating our nurse. We have in addition a further secondary language which the Romans called "grammar". The Greeks too, as well as certain others have this secondary language but not all, and indeed
few get into the way of using it, for it is only with time and sustained effort that we are schooled and
become proficient in it. Of these two kinds of speech, the vernacular is the nobler; first, because it was
the kind originally adopted by the human race; second, because—though variously differentiated in
point of lexis and pronunciation—it is the kind used by all men everywhere; and third because it is
natural to us, the other, by contrast, being artificial. And it is this, the more noble kind of speech, that
we propose now to consider.' Cecil Grayson, ' "Nobilior est vulgaris": Latin and Vernacular in Dante's
Thought', *Centenary Essays on Dante by Members of the Oxford Dante Society*, with a preface by Colin
Hardie (Oxford: Clarendon Press, 1965), 54–76 (and, in translation, in *Cinque saggi su Dante* [Bologna:
Pàtron, 1972], 1–31); Alessandro Raffi, 'Latino, ebraico e volgare illustre: La questione della nobiltà
della lingua nel *De vulgari eloquentia*', *LI* 58.1 (2006), 88–112; Gennaro Sasso, 'Nobilior est vulgaris', in
La lingua, la Bibbia, la storia: Su 'De vulgari eloquentia I' (Rome: Viella, 2015), 39–58.

modum interrogationis vel per modum responsionis. Absurdum atque rationi videtur orrificum ante Deum ab homine quicquam nominatum fuisse, cum ab ipso et in ipsum factus fuisset homo. Nam sicut post prevaricationem humani generis quilibet exordium sue locutionis incipit ab 'heu', rationabile est quod ante qui fuit inciperet a gaudio; et cum nullum gaudium sit extra Deum, sed totum in Deo, et ipse Deus totus sit gaudium, consequens est quod primus loquens primo et ante omnia dixisset 'Deus'.

(*De vulgari eloquentia* 1.4.4)[4]

But the notion of language as but a matter of rejoicing, of knowing self in the coming forth of self, gives way just about immediately to something more forlorn; for if in the beginning language, like man himself, came fully formed,[5] then in consequence of Babel and the effrontery thereof it was a question of diaspora, of in effect, and indeed in very truth, of the most complete kind of linguistic forgetfulness:

Ecce, lector, quod vel oblitus homo vel vilipendens disciplinas priores, et avertens oculos a vibicibus que remanserant, tertio insurrexit ad verbera,

4 'Now I have no doubt that for anyone of sound mind the first thing the first speaker uttered, whether by way of question or answer, was the word meaning "God", namely the word *El*; for it is manifestly absurd, and indeed an offence against reason, to think that anything should have been named by man before God, man having been made both by him and for him. For since in the wake of man's first disobedience every attempt at speaking begins with the word "woe!", it is reasonable to suppose that he who was before that disobedience should have begun with an expression of joy; for since there is no joy other than in God, all joy being in him and indeed in him as of the essence, it follows that the first word of the first man, uttered before all else, would have been "God."' Aron Benvenuto Terracini, 'Natura ed origine del linguaggio umano nel *De vulgari eloquentia*', in *Pagine e appunti di linguistica storica* (Florence: Le Monnier, 1957), 237–46; Philip Damon, 'Adam on the Primal Language: *Paradiso* 26.124', *Italica* 38 (1961), 60–62; Glen C. Arbery, 'Adam's First Word and the Failure of Language in *Paradiso* XXXIII', in *Sign, Sentence, Discourse: Language in Medieval Thought and Literature*, ed. Julian N. Wasserman and Lois Roney (Syracuse: Syracuse University Press, 1989), 31–44; Ruedi Imbach, 'La langue d'Adam et la philosophie du langage de Dante', in *Dante, la philosophie et les laïcs: Initiation à la philosophie médiévale* (Fribourg: Editions universitaires and Paris: Editions du Cerf, 1996), 197–213; Massimiliano Corrado, 'Dante e la questione della lingua di Adamo (*De vulgari eloquentia* I.4–7; *Paradiso* XXVI.124–138)' (Rome: Salerno, 2010); Giacomo Gambale, 'Il "Primiloquium" di Adamo: La filosofia del linguaggio in *De vulg*. I.iv.4', *Rivista di Filosofia Neo-Scolastica* 102 (2010), 391–425 (and in *La lingua di foco: Dante e la filosofia del linguaggio* [Rome: Città Nuova, 2012], 229–67).

5 *De vulgari eloquentia* 1.6.4: 'Redeuntes igitur ad propositum, dicimus certam formam locutionis a Deo cum anima prima concreatam fuisse. Dico autem "formam" et quantum ad rerum vocabula et quantum ad vocabulorum constructionem et quantum ad constructionis prolationem; qua quidem forma omnis lingua loquentium uteretur, nisi culpa presumptionis humane dissipata fuisset, ut inferius ostendetur' (Returning, then, to the matter under discussion, what we are saying is that a particular form of speech was created by God with and for the first soul, where by 'form' I mean both the words we give to things and the construction of those words together with their pronunciation; and, as we shall demonstrate in what follows, this is the form which to this very day would be upon every tongue had it not been thrown to the wind by human arrogance). Riccardo Tesi, 'La lingua della grazia nel *De vulgari eloquentia*', in *La lingua della grazia: Indagini sul 'De vulgari eloquentia'* (Padua: Esedra, 2016), 17–67.

per superbam stultitiam presumendo. Presumpsit ergo in corde suo incurabilis homo, sub persuasione gigantis Nembroth, arte sua non solum superare naturam, sed etiam ipsum naturantem, qui Deus est, et cepit edificare turrim in Sennaar, que postea dicta est Babel, hoc est 'confusio', per quam celum sperabat ascendere, intendens inscius non equare, sed suum superare Factorem. O sine mensura clementia celestis imperii! Quis patrum tot sustineret insultus a filio? Sed exurgens non hostili scutica sed paterna et alias verberibus assueta, rebellantem filium pia correctione nec non memorabili castigavit. Siquidem pene totum humanum genus ad opus iniquitatis coierat: pars imperabant, pars architectabantur, pars muros moliebantur, pars amussibus regulabant, pars trullis linebant, pars scindere rupes, pars mari, pars terra vehere intendebant, partesque diverse diversis aliis operibus indulgebant; cum celitus tanta confusione percussi sunt ut, qui omnes una eademque loquela deserviebant ad opus, ab opere multis diversificati loquelis desinerent et nunquam ad idem commertium convenirent.

(De vulgari eloquentia 1.7.3–6)[6]

It is at this point, then, that, starting out from the diaspora consequent upon Babel, Dante embarks on an account of the geolinguistic patterning of the west

6 'See, then, reader, how man, either forgetting or despising the penalty formerly laid upon him, and averting his gaze from the stripes remaining from it, provoked in consequence of his foolish and presumptuous pride a lashing for the third time; for man, persuaded by the giant Nimrod and incorrigible as ever, presumed by his own skill to surpass not only nature but God himself as nature's very author. So, purposing in his ignorance not merely to equal but to outdo his maker, he set about building a tower in Sennaar latterly known as Babel (which is as much as to say "confusion") whereby he hoped to make it up to heaven. Oh boundless clemency of the heavenly kingdom! Who among fathers would suffer such insults from a son? So he arose and, with a scourge not so much hostile as paternal (a scourge which he had been accustomed in former times to wield) he chastised his rebellious son in a manner as merciful as it was memorable, for well-nigh the whole human race had come together to work this wickedness. Some were overseers, some were busy as architects, some were putting up walls, some were squaring off masonry with their levels, some were trowelling on the mortar, some were shaping stones, some were bringing them in by sea and some by land, while yet others were busy about these and other tasks when they were one and all struck by such confusion from above that, active as they were and united by one and the same language, they at once ceased their labours, and, estranged one from another by any number of different tongues, never again resumed the common task.' Maria Corti, 'Dante e la Torre di Babele: Una nuova allegoria in factis', in *Il viaggio testuale* (Turin: Einaudi, 1978), 243–56; Roger Dragonetti, 'Dante face à Nemrod: Babel mémoire et miroir de l'Éden?', *Critique* 387–88 (1979), 690–706; Irène Rosier-Catach and Ruedi Imbach, 'La tour de Babel dans la philosophie du langage de Dante', in Peter von Moos (ed.), *Zwischen Babel und Pfingsten (Entre Babel et Pentecôte)* (Berlin: Zürich: LIT, 2008), 183–204; Irène Rosier-Catach, 'Quelle langue après Babel? Réflexions sur les conceptions linguistiques de Dante', in Julia Kristeva (ed.), *Des expériences intérieures: Pour quelle modernité?* (Nantes: Editions nouvelles Cécile Defaut, 2012), 193–234; Gennaro Sasso, 'La Torre di Babele e la "confusio linguarum"', in *La lingua, la Bibblia, la storia: Su 'De vulgari eloquentia I'* (Rome: Viella, 2015), 115–26. More generally on the medieval sense of Babel and linguistic confusion, Arno Borst, *Der Turmbau von Babel: Geschichte der Meinungen über Ursprung und Vielfalt der Sprachen und Völker*, vol. 4 (Stuttgart: Hiersemann, 1957–63).

as ample in scope as it is bold in conception and articulation. First, therefore, come the macrolinguistic regions represented (*a*) by the peoples of northern Europe sharing as the sign of their common linguistic identity the affirmative particle *iò*; (*b*) by those inhabiting that part of the Greek-speaking world looking out upon Asia; and (*c*) by those living in the south and affirming themselves by way of the particles *oc, oïl* and *sì* as well as by a lexis of recognizably common provenance. Then come the microlinguistic regions such as—within the area encompassed by the *lingua di sì*—Spoleto, Tuscany and Genoa to the west of the Apennines and Ancona, Romagna, Lombardy, Treviso and Venice to the east, each of them host to any number of local speech patterns. But—and this now is what matters—by the time he reaches this stage of the argument the theological as a way of seeing and understanding the linguistic issue in human experience ('theological' in the sense of the 'confusio linguarum' visited upon man in consequence of Babel) has given way to something closer to the evolutionary, to a sense of the relativity of everything subject to man's *beneplacitum* under the conditions of time and space. Mature expression of what for this reason must have seemed to Dante a melancholy spectacle (man's every initiative being in this sense but a matter of its ephemerality) comes in the *Paradiso*, where, prompted by the pilgrim poet, Adam himself no less confirms the inherent changeability of whatever *is* as a product of specifically human determination:

> La lingua ch'io parlai fu tutta spenta
> innanzi che a l'ovra inconsummabile
> fosse la gente di Nembròt attenta:
>   ché nullo effetto mai razïonabile,
> per lo piacere uman che rinovella
> seguendo il cielo, sempre fu durabile.
>   Opera naturale è ch'uom favella;
> ma così o così, natura lascia
> poi fare a voi secondo che v'abbella.
>   Pria ch'i' scendessi a l'infernale ambascia,
> *I* s'appellava in terra il sommo bene
> onde vien la letizia che mi fascia;
>   e *El* si chiamò poi: e ciò convene,
> ché l'uso d'i mortali è come fronda
> in ramo, che sen va e altra vene.

> (*Paradiso* 26.124–38)[7]

---

7 'The language I spoke was all extinct before the people of Nimrod attempted their impossible task; for never, given the coming and going of preference with every shift of the stars above, did anything handed down by reason last indefinitely. That man should speak is down to nature, but

Confirmed as it is from on high, however, the basic idea is already there both in the *Convivio* and the *De vulgari eloquentia*, each alike fully alert to the transience of just about every reasonable provision of the spirit in man. On the one hand, then, we have this passage from the *Convivio* at 1.5.7–9 on the coming and going of lexis and on this as a principle of estrangement, as that whereby anyone travelling to and fro along the corridor of time would of necessity find himself a stranger in his own country:

> Per nobilità, perché lo latino è perpetuo e non corruttibile, e lo volgare è non stabile e corruttibile. Onde vedemo ne le scritture antiche de le comedie e tragedie latine, che non si possono transmutare, quello medesimo che oggi avemo; che non avviene del volgare, lo quale a piacimento artificiato si transmuta. Onde vedemo ne le cittadi d'Italia, se bene volemo agguardare, da cinquanta anni in qua molti vocabuli essere spenti e nati e variati; onde se 'l picciol tempo così transmuta, molto più transmuta lo maggiore. Sì ch'io dico, che se coloro che partiron d'esta vita già sono mille anni tornassero a le loro cittadi, crederebbero la loro cittade essere occupata da gente strana, per la lingua da loro discordante.[8]

while on the other we have this passage from the *De vulgari eloquentia* at 1.9.6 as a further essay on the shifting substance both of what man *does*—language in-

---

how, exactly, nature leaves it to you to decide. Before I tasted the deep sorrow of hell, the Supreme Good whence I know the joy by which I am enfolded was named *I* on earth, only later to be called *El*. And that, given the likeness of man's ways to leaves on a branch, one going and another coming, is how it must be.' Pier Vincenzo Mengaldo, 'Appunti sul canto XXVI del *Paradiso*', in *Linguistica e retorica di Dante* (Pisa: Nistri-Lischi, 1978), 223–46; Joseph Cremona, '*Paradiso* XXVI', in Kenelm Foster and Patrick Boyde (eds.), *Cambridge Readings in Dante's 'Comedy'* (Cambridge: Cambridge University Press, 1981), 174–90; Edoardo Ferrario, 'Il linguaggio nel XXVI canto del *Paradiso* (vv. 82–142)', *CN* 46.1–4 (1986), 109–29; Bruno Nardi, 'Il canto XXVI del *Paradiso*', in *'Lecturae' e altri studi danteschi*, ed. Rudy Abardo (Florence: Le Lettere, 1990), 185–92; Domenico Guerri, 'Il nome di Dio nella lingua di Adamo secondo il XXVI del *Paradiso* e il verso di Nembrotte nel XXXI dell'*Inferno*', in *Scritti danteschi e d'altra letteratura antica*, ed. Antonio Lanza (Rome: De Rubeis, 1990), 133–41; Angelo Mazzocco, ' "La lingua ch'io parlai fu tutta spenta": Dante's Reappraisal of the Adamic Language (*Paradiso* XXVI, 124–138)', in *Linguistic Theories in Dante and the Humanists: Studies of Language and Intellectual History in Late Medieval and Early Renaissance Italy* (Leiden: Brill, 1993), 159–79.

8 'As regards nobility, Latin is permanent and free from change, whereas the vernacular is unstable and shifting. Thus in the ancient Latin tragedies and comedies, immune as they are to change, we find the same Latin as we have now, which, fashioned as it is according to our pleasure, is not the case with the vernacular. So it is that we find upon inspection that many words in these Italian cities of ours have over the last fifty years become extinct, that many have been born, and that many have undergone a change in meaning—and if all this in fifty years, how much more over a longer period of time! Indeed it is my view that if people who departed this life a thousand years ago were to return to their native cities, they would think them occupied by foreigners, so much has today's language moved on from theirs.'

cluded—and of what man *is*, on forgetfulness as the hallmark of his presence in the world:

> Dicimus ergo quod nullus effectus superat suam causam, in quantum effectus est, quia nil potest efficere quod non est. Cum igitur omnis nostra loquela—preter illam homini primo concreatam a Deo—sit a nostro beneplacito reparata post confusionem illam que nil aliud fuit quam prioris oblivio, et homo sit instabilissimum atque variabilissimum animal, nec durabilis nec continua esse potest, sed sicut alia que nostra sunt, puta mores et habitus, per locorum temporumque distantias variari oportet.[9]

It is, then, in the context of what in Dante amounts to a developed sense of cultural relativity, indeed of man himself as but a creature of radical instability, that, encouraged by the example of the old grammarians in fashioning Latin as a response to the forces of generation and decay everywhere at work in this sector, he seeks now to identify a language proper to the Italian people as a whole, a language, that is to say, marking the difference in point of identity. None, however, rises to the occasion, each in its way—whether lexically, morphologically or phonologically—revealing its inadequacy to the task; so, for example, the untoward familiarity and eccentric vocalization of the *Messure, quinto dici?* of the Romans, just about as fetid, Dante notes, as their manners generally; the brusque accentuation of the Aquileians with their *Ces fas-tu?*; the inept Latinism of the Sardinians with their *dominus nova* and *domus novus*; the gross consonantalism of the Apulians with their *bòlzera* and *chiangesse* (for the immeasurably more refined *vorrei* and *piangesse* of Tuscany); the blandness of the Romagnoli with their *oclo meo* and *corada mea* (for the Tuscan *occhio mio* and *cuor mio*); the abrasiveness of the Genoese (totally lost linguistically, Dante says, short of the fricative *z*), and the 'rude asperity' (*rudis asperitas*) of the Brescians with their *mercò* and *bontè*, syncopated versions of the Latin *mercatus*, and *bonitas*; and the coarse regionalism of the Venetians (*plaghe* and *verras* for the again Tuscan *piaghe* and *verrai*). Not that the Tuscans themselves come off any better, for whatever of excellence has come about in Tuscany—and Dante has in mind the *stilnovisti* Guido Cavalcanti, Lapo Gianni, Cino da Pistoia and 'one other' (*unum alium*)—has come about as a result not of espousing but of eschewing the spoken language, Lucchese, Sienese,

---

9 'I say, therefore, that no effect exceeds its cause insofar as it is an effect, because nothing can bring about that which in itself it is not. Since, then, we at our own pleasure have made good our every language (other than that created by God along with the first man) in the wake of Babel and the confusion thereof as but a forgetting of everything leading up to it, and since man by nature is a most unstable and changeable creature, that language can be neither stable nor free from change, but must instead, like everything else of ours—custom and attire, for example—vary according to time and place in the extent of these things.'

Aretine, Pisan and even Florentine being in the ordinary way of it but a matter of mere municipalism (the 'non curialia sed municipalia tantum invenientur' of 1.13.1).[10]

Empirically, then, or by way of reviewing the existing possibilities, there is no way forward, none of them—not even Sicilian, Bolognese and Florentine as on the face of it more than ordinarily qualified in point of expressive refinement—wholly fitting the bill. Dante, therefore, giving up for the moment on the empirical, opts now for—as he himself puts it—a more properly 'reasonable' approach to the matter in hand, this perhaps, he says, being the way of cornering his quarry:

> Postquam venati saltus et pascua sumus Ytalie, nec pantheram quam sequimur adinvenimus, ut ipsam reperire possimus rationabilius investigemus de illa ut, solerti studio, redolentem ubique et necubi apparentem nostris penitus irretiamus tenticulis.
>
> *(De vulgari eloquentia* 1.16.1)[11]

Settling, then, upon the notion of the *illustre* as the 'simple sign' of the Italian vernacular generally, as the ideal everywhere discernible in its spoken forms but identifiable with none of them, he dwells for a moment upon its ideally fourfold complexion: on its *illustriousness* or resplendence, meaning by this its power to light up and indeed to glorify those party to it; on its status as *cardinal* or pivotal, as the hinge or point-about-which of linguistic form generally in the peninsula; on its *aulicity* or courtliness as but the common currency of—alas, were there such a thing—an Italian palatinate; and on its *curiality* as a sort of tribunal or court of appeal in respect of proper usage, these between them furnishing a vernacular nowhere discoverable in its pure form but everywhere normative vis-à-vis the local utterance:

> Itaque, adepti quod querebamus, dicimus illustre, cardinale, aulicum et curiale vulgare in Latio quod omnis latie civitatis est et nullius esse videtur, et

---

10 Paola Manni, 'Il quadro linguistico della Toscana secondo Dante: *De vulgari eloquentia* 1.13.2–3', in *La Lingua di Dante* (Bologna: Il Mulino, 2013), 157–64. For Lucca and the Lucchesi, Ornella Castellani Pollidori, 'Nuova proposta per il "lucchesismo" grassarra in *De vulgari eloquentia* I.xiii. 2', *SLI* 27.1 (2001), 3–12; and for Sardinia, Marinella Lorinczi, 'La casa del signore: La lingua sarda nel *De vulgari eloquentia*', *RFR* 17 (2000), 61–76. Also, Riccardo Tesi, 'Un termine-chiave della descrizione linguistica: "Vulgare semilatium" (*DVE* I.xix.1)', in *Lingua della grazia: Indagini sul 'De vulgari eloquentia'* (Padua: Esedra, 2016), 173–224.

11 'Having scoured the hills and pastures of Italy without as yet having found the panther we are seeking out, let us, in order that we may be able to find her, proceed by way more of reason, so that, by dint of our customary skills, we may entice and trap one whose fragrance is everywhere but who herself is nowhere to be seen.' Rossend Arqués, 'El rastro de la pantera perfumada (Dante en las poéticas catalanas de la modernidad)', *Tenzone* 1 (2000), 179–214; Daniele D'Urso, 'Il profumo della pantera: La metafora venatoria nel *De Vulgari Eloquentia*', *RCCM* 48.1 (2006), 137–55.

quo municipalia vulgaria omnia Latinorum mensurantur et ponderantur et comparantur.

(*De vulgari eloquentia* 1.16.6)[12]

It is, however, at this point that the element of sadness subsisting somewhere in the depths—the sadness contingent on the fact that, no less than Dante himself as an 'exul immeritus', this *illustre* of his is but a wanderer on the face of the earth—comes to the surface; for courtly and curial as it is, there is, alas, neither court nor curia to be found in Italy, and no place, therefore, for the *illustre* thus understood to lay its head. On the contrary, its destiny, at any rate for the moment, is to make its way from one humble abode to another, there to take refuge where and when it can:

Quia vero aulicum nominamus illud causa est quod, si aulam nos Ytali haberemus, palatinum foret. Nam si aula totius regni comunis est domus et omnium regni partium gubernatrix augusta, quicquid tale est ut omnibus sit comune nec proprium ulli, conveniens est ut in ea conversetur et habitet, nec aliquod aliud habitaculum tanto dignum est habitante; hoc nempe videtur esse id de quo loquimur vulgare. Et hinc est quod in regiis omnibus conversantes semper illustri vulgari locuntur; hinc etiam est quod nostrum illustre velut acola peregrinatur et in humilibus hospitatur asilis, cum aula vacemus.

(*De vulgari eloquentia* 1.18.2–3)[13]

12 'Having found, therefore, what we were looking for, we declare to be illustrious, cardinal, aulic and curial that vernacular belonging both to every city in Italy and—as seems evident—to none, and by which every local vernacular might be weighed, measured and compared.' Mario Casella, 'Il volgare illustre di Dante', *Giornale della Cultura Italiana* 1 (1925), 34–40; Angelo Mazzocco, 'Dante's Notion of the Illustrious Vernacular: A Reappraisal', in *Linguistic Theories in Dante and the Humanists: Studies of Language and Intellectual History in Late Medieval and Early Renaissance Italy* (Leiden: E. J. Brill, 1993), 108–58; Larissa G. Stepanova, 'On Dante's Linguistic Terminology: "Cardinale"', *Kulturologia: The Petersburg Journal of Cultural Studies* 1.1 (1993), 78–86; Simone Marchesi, 'Dante's Vertical Utopia: Aulicum and Curiale in the *De vulgari eloquentia*', in *Utopianism / Literary Utopias and National Cultural Identities: A Comparative Perspective*, ed. Paola Spinozzi (Bologna: Cotepra, 2001), 311–16; Stephen G. Nichols, 'Global Language or Universal Language? From Babel to Illustrious Vernacular', *Digital Philology: A Journal of Medieval Cultures* 1.1 (2012), 73–109; Claudio Marazzini, 'La teoria dantesca del volgare illustre', in *Da Dante alla lingua selvaggia: Sette secoli di dibattuti sull'italiano*, 2nd ed. (Rome: Carocci, 2013), 25–31; Gennaro Sasso, 'La ricerca del volgare illustre', in *La lingua, la Bibbia, la storia: Su "De vulgari eloquentia" I* (Rome: Viella, 2015), 157–65 (with 'Naturalità delle lingue e volgare illustre' at 127–34).

13 'Now the reason for calling this vernacular "aulic" is that if we Italians had a royal court this is where it would be spoken. For if the court is the common home of the entire realm and the august ruler of its every part, it is appropriate that everything common to all yet peculiar to none should frequent the court and live there, for no other place would be worthy of such a guest—and above all, it would seem, of the vernacular whereof we speak. This is why those who frequent any royal court

—lines to which, as registering yet again the sadness of it all, the sadness of an Italy no more, politically speaking, than the sum of its parts, we may add the following from just a little later in the same chapter, reason alone, Dante says, stepping in to make good:

> Sed dicere quod in excellentissima Ytalorum curia sit libratum, videtur nu-gatio, cum curia careamus. Ad quod facile respondetur. Nam licet curia, secundum quod unita accipitur, ut curia regis Alamannie, in Ytalia non sit, membra tamen eius non desunt; et sicut membra illius uno Principe uniun-tur, sic membra huius gratioso lumine rationis unita sunt. Quare falsum esset dicere curia carere Ytalos, quanquam Principe careamus, quoniam curiam habemus, licet corporaliter sit dispersa.
>
> (*De vulgari eloquentia* 1.18.5)[14]

But for all the melancholy of this situation, the melancholy attendant upon the fact that we have as yet no Italian court and curia for the *illustre* to call its own, all is not lost, for turning once again to the *illustre* in and for itself, there is the case of those who, having eschewed the *turpiloquium* of the times, have aspired to genuine eloquence in the vernacular:

> Sed quanquam fere omnes Tusci in suo turpiloquio sint obtusi, nonnullos vulgaris excellentiam cognovisse sentimus, scilicet Guidonem, Lapum et unum alium, Florentinos, et Cynum Pistoriensem, quem nunc indigne postponimus, non indigne coacti. Itaque si tuscanas examinemus loquelas, et pensemus qualiter viri prehonorati a propria diverterunt, non restat in dubio quin aliud sit vulgare quod querimus quam quod actingit populus Tuscanorum.
>
> (*De vulgari eloquentia* 1.13.4–5)[15]

---

always speak the illustrious vernacular, and why, given that we have no such thing, our own wanders up and down like a homeless stranger, finding hospitality only in the meanest abode.'

14 'Yet it seems trifling to say that it has been weighed in the balance of the most excellent tribunal in Italy, since we have no such thing. The answer to this is simple, for although it is true that here in Italy there is nothing comparable—at any rate in the sense of anything properly unified—to the royal court in Germany, yet its constituent parts are not lacking. And just as the elements of the German court are united under a single monarch, so too those of the Italian court are one by the gracious light of reason. It would not, therefore, be true to say that, even in the absence of a sole prince, the Italians are altogether bereft hereabouts, for though materially dispersed we do indeed have a curia.' Raffaella Zanni, 'Tra "curialitas" e cortesia nel pensiero dantesco: Una ricognizione e una proposta per *DVE* I.xviii.4–5', in *Ortodossia ed eterodossia in Dante Alighieri. Atti del convegno di Madrid, 5–7 novembre 2012*, ed. Carlota Cattermole et al. (Madrid: Ediciones de la Discreta, 2014), 233–49.

15 'However, though Tuscans to just about a man are steeped in their own hideous jargon, there are some, we feel, sensitive even so to the excellence of the vernacular, namely Guido, Lapo and one other, all from Florence, and Cino of Pistoia whom—unjustly as far as he is concerned but for good reason—I necessarily put last. Therefore, casting an eye over their dialects in the round, and bearing

—lines to which, as confirming the literary dimension of Dante's thinking in the *De vulgari eloquentia*, indeed a sense on his part of the literary as a way of seeing, of setting up and of resolving the linguistic issue, we may add these from the end of the first book relative to the status of the *illustre* as, thanks to its no less illustrious representatives from every part of the peninsula (poets one and all), fully up and running:

Hoc autem vulgare quod illustre, cardinale, aulicum et curiale ostensum est, dicimus esse illud quod vulgare latium appellatur. Nam sicut quoddam vulgare est invenire quod proprium est Cremone, sic quoddam est invenire quod proprium est Lombardie; et sicut est invenire aliquod quod sit proprium Lombardie, [*sic*] est invenire aliquod quod sit totius sinistre Ytalie proprium; et sicut omnia hec est invenire, sic et illud quod totius Ytalie est. Et sicut illud cremonense ac illud lombardum et tertium semilatium dicitur, sic istud, quod totius Ytalie est, latium vulgare vocatur. Hoc enim usi sunt doctores illustres qui lingua vulgari poetati sunt in Ytalia, ut Siculi, Apuli, Tusci, Romandioli, Lombardi et utriusque Marchie viri.

(*De vulgari eloquentia* 1.19.1)[16]

---

in mind how the aforementioned notables have made a point of eschewing their own, there can be no doubt that the vernacular we are after is something other than that entertained by the people generally of Tuscany.'

16 'This, then—the vernacular we have shown to be illustrious, cardinal, aulic and curial—is the vernacular we declare to be Italian. For, just as we come across one vernacular proper to Cremona, so also we come across another proper to Lombardy; and just as we discover one that belongs to Lombardy, so also do we discover another proper to the whole left-hand side of Italy; and just as we light in this way on all these, so also do we light on the vernacular proper to Italy as a whole. And just as we speak of the first as Cremonese, of the second as Lombard and of the third as "half-Italian", so also we speak of this last as proper to all Italy, as the Italian vernacular. This, then, is the language used by those illustrious authors who—from wherever they come (Sicily, Apulia, Tuscany, Romagna, Lombardy or either of the Marches)—have fashioned verses in the vernacular.' As regards Dante's sense, even in this first book of the *De vulgari eloquentia*, of the 'literary as a way of seeing, of setting up and of resolving the linguistic issue', and indeed of the exemplary status of the poetic with respect to the prose utterance, these lines from the beginning of book 2: 'Sollicitantes iterum celeritatem ingenii nostri et ad calamum frugi operis redeuntes, ante omnia confitemur latium vulgare illustre tam prosayce quam metrice decere proferri. Sed quia ipsum prosaycantes ab avientibus magis accipiunt et quia quod avietum est prosaycantibus permanere videtur exemplar, et non e converso—que quendam videntur prebere primatum—primo secundum quod metricum est ipsum carminemus' (Calling once more, then, upon my nimble intellect and taking up afresh the pen productive of my every fruitful labour, I declare first of all that the illustrious Italian vernacular is as fittingly employed for the writing of prose as for the writing of poetry. But, because writers of prose learn more from the writers of poetry rather than the other way round, and because what is written in poetry serves as a model for those who write prose rather than the other way about—something which would seem to confer upon the former a certain primacy—I shall first of all clarify the principles governing composition in verse).' Bruno Panvini, 'L'esperienza dei Siciliani e il volgare illustre di Dante', in *Atti del Convegno di studi su Dante e la Magna Curia (Palermo, Catania, Messina, 7–11 novembre 1965)* (Palermo: Centro di studi filologici e linguistici siciliani, 1967), 236–49; Roberto Antonelli, 'Quia regale solium erat Sicilia . . . sicilianum vocetur', *Siculorum Gymnasium: Rassegna della Facoltà di Lettere e Filosofia dell'Università di Catania* 53.1–2 (2000), 19–35.

With this, then, the time has come to consider, not so much now the *illustre* in and for itself, as the ways and means of specifically poetic discourse in the *illustre*, at which point, for all its once again sowing the seeds of its own supersession, we witness one of the pinnacles of Dante's reflection upon the art of verse making in the vernacular; for this, whatever else it is, is an essay not merely in the internalization of the poetic project but in its ontologization, its unfolding in relation to the being and becoming of the would-be poet in the high style. It is, in other words, a question now, not merely—indeed not at all—of the mutual countenancing of form and content in the poem itself, and still less of the kind of playfulness whereby one thing is transformed into another by way of a rhetorical sleight of hand, but rather of form as a principle of self-affirmation in the poet, as that whereby he knows himself in the soaring substance of his humanity. First, then, and preliminary in respect of everything coming next in this second book of the *De vulgari eloquentia*, comes the *who* of composition in the high style, the *who* of composition in the high style consisting, Dante thinks, of those most properly accredited in point of wit and wisdom, theirs and theirs alone being the privilege of discourse in the *illustre*, all else, he says, making merely for the preposterous and downright risible:

> Et cum loquela non aliter sit necessarium instrumentum nostre conceptionis quam equus militis, et optimis militibus optimi conveniant equi, ut dictum est, optimis conceptionibus optima loquela conveniet. Sed optime conceptiones non possunt esse nisi ubi scientia et ingenium est; ergo optima loquela non convenit nisi illis in quibus ingenium et scientia est . . . Quapropter, si non omnibus competit, non omnes ipsum debent uti, quia inconvenienter agere nullus debet. Et ubi dicitur, quod quilibet suos versus exornare debet in quantum potest, verum esse testamur; sed nec bovem epiphiatum nec balteatum suem dicemus ornatum, immo potius deturpatum ridemus illum; est enim exornatio alicuius convenientis additio.
>
> (*De vulgari eloquentia* 2.1.8–9)[17]

---

17 'And since language is as necessary a means to our thought as a horse is to a knight, and since as I have said the best horses are suited to the best knights, the best language is suited to the best thought. But there are no best thoughts other than where there is also knowledge and intelligence, and so the best language is suited only to those thus endowed . . . Insofar, then, as the best language is not appropriate to all, then not all should use it, inappropriateness everywhere to be eschewed. And as to my remarks to the effect that everyone should embellish the line as far as he can, that, I maintain, is true. But we would not speak of an ox as well turned out were it dressed up to look like a horse, or a swine were it sporting a baldric; rather, we would laugh at their wretched getup, for true adornment has to do with the addition of something suitable.' Francesco Di Capua, *Insegnamenti retorici medievali e dottrine estetiche moderne nel 'De vulgari eloquentia' di Dante* (Naples: L. Loffredo, 1945); August Buck, 'Gli studi sulla poetica e sulla retorica di Dante e del suo tempo', *Atti del Congresso Internazionale di*

But then, hard on the heels of the *who* of composition in the high style comes the *what* of that composition, Dante's account of the topics most appropriate for treatment in the *illustre*. Insofar, therefore, as man knows himself in terms of his threefold vegetative, sensitive and rational constitution—of the vegetative as a matter of elementary well-being, of the sensitive as a matter of reaching out for communion with the object of his delight, and of the rational as a matter of his living out his power to moral and intellectual determination—it is a question here of *salus*, *venus* and *virtus*, of prowess in arms, of ardour in love and of right willing as the leading candidates. True, prowess in arms, as far at any rate as Italian poets are concerned, comes some way down the list, Dante being unable for the moment to think of any examples, but given its prominence in the tradition generally of romance-vernacular verse making he has no hesitation about confirming its status as one of the three *magnalia*, as worthy, that is to say, of celebration in the *illustre*. Arms, then, affection and an upright spirit, these are the topics most fit for treatment in the high style:

> Sed disserendum est que maxima sint. Et primo in eo quod est utile, in quo, si callide consideremus intentum omnium querentium utilitatem, nil aliud quam salutem inveniemus. Secundo in eo quod est delectabile, in quo dicimus illud esse maxime delectabile quod per pretiosissimum obiectum appetitus delectat; hoc autem venus est. Tertio in eo quod est honestum, in quo nemo dubitat esse virtutem. Quare hec tria, salus videlicet, venus et virtus, apparent esse illa magnalia que sint maxime pertractanda, hoc est ea que maxime sunt ad ista, ut armorum probitas, amoris accensio et directio voluntatis.
>
> (*De vulgari eloquentia* 2.2.7)[18]

Studi Danteschi, vol. 1 (Florence: Sansoni, 1965), 249–78 (with, in vol. 2, Alfredo Schiaffini, 'Dante, Retorica, Medioevo', 155–86); Giovanni Nencioni, 'Dante e la retorica', in *Dante e Bologna nei tempi di Dante* (Bologna: Commissione per i testi di lingua, 1967), 91–112; Ignazio Baldelli, 'Il *De vulgari eloquentia* e la poesia di Dante', in *Nuove Letture Dantesche tenute nella Casa di Dante in Roma*, vol. 8 (Florence: Le Monnier, 1976), 241–58; Roger Dragonetti, 'La conception du langage poétique dans le *De vulgari eloquentia*', in *Dante: La langue et le poème*, ed. Christopher Lucken (Paris: Belin, 2006), 45–106.

18 'We must now discuss, however, what these greatest of all themes might be, beginning with those bearing on the useful, where, if we consider carefully the aim of all those seeking out what is useful, we shall find that this is nothing other than their security. Secondly, and in respect now of the pleasurable, here I say that what is pleasurable above all is what we prize most highly as the object of our desiring, namely love. And thirdly, there are those things bearing on the good, there being no doubt here that paramount among them is virtue. So these three things—security, love and virtue, together with those others most closely associated with them—would seem to be the loftiest themes and, in their loftiness, those most worthy to be treated in the lofty style: prowess in arms, ardour in love and right willing.' Michelangelo Picone, 'La poesia romanza della "salus" (Bertran de Born) nella *Vita Nuova*', *FItal* 15.1 (1981), 3–10 (and in *Scritti danteschi*, ed. Antonio Lanza [Ravenna: Longo, 2017], 413–18); Claire E. Honess, '*Salus, venus, virtus*: Poetry, Politics, and Ethics from the *De vulgari eloquentia*

And then finally, as leading up to the scarcely less than rapt content of chapter 4 as more than ever eloquent in its account of poetic form as but the intelligible form of this or that instance of specifically human being in its actuality, we have his account in chapter 3, not now of the *who* or of the *what*, but of the *how* of verse making in the high style, where it is a question of the canzone as uniquely appropriate in its twofold spaciousness and flexibility to discourse at the point of ultimate concern. True, the ballad and the sonnet offer themselves as candidates for consideration hereabouts, but only the canzone encompasses the art of vernacular versifying in its totality, which is why everything finding its way from the mind to the lips of great poets in the vernacular has flowed, and flows still, into the canzone form:

> Ad hoc, in artificiatis illud est nobilissimum quod totam comprehendit artem; cum igitur ea que cantantur artificiata existant, et in solis cantionibus ars tota comprehendatur, cantiones nobilissime sunt, et sic modus earum nobilissimus aliorum. Quod autem tota comprehendatur in cantionibus ars cantandi poetice, in hoc palatur, quod quicquid artis reperitur in omnibus aliis et in cantionibus reperitur; sed non convertitur hoc. Signum autem horum que dicimus promptum in conspectu habetur; nam quicquid de cacuminibus illustrium capitum poetantium profluxit ad labia, in solis cantionibus invenitur.
>
> (*De vulgari eloquentia* 2.3.8–9)[19]

But with this sense (*a*) of the poet in the high style as a man of wit and wisdom, (*b*) of *salus*, *venus* and *virtus* as uniquely worthy of treatment in the *illustre*, and (*c*) of the canzone as encompassing the entire art of vernacular verse making, we are as yet on the lower slopes of Dante's meditation hereabouts, for somewhat after the manner of tributaries feeding into a mighty river each of these things feeds into the ontological moment proper of his discourse, into the again scarcely less than rapt account in chapter 4 of what in truth it means to be a poet in the high style of vernacular verse making—a moment, Dante says, open to contem-

---

to the *Commedia*', *The Italianist* 27.2 (2007), 185–205; Rosario Scrimieri, ' "Salus", "Venus" e "Virtus" in *Doglia mi reca ne lo core ardire*', in *Doglia mi reca nel lo core ardire*, ed. Umberto Carpi (Madrid: Asociación Complutense di Dantologia, 2008), 41–63.

19 'Again, whatever is most noble in art is that which embraces the whole of that art. Since, then, song is a matter of art, and since the whole of that art is embraced by the canzone, the canzone is the noblest of poems and the canzone form the noblest of forms. That the entire art of poetry as song is indeed to be found in the canzone is evident from the fact that whatever we find by way of art elsewhere is found here too, though not the other way round, proof of which lies in the fact that, as is perfectly plain to see, whatever has flowed from the loftiest reaches of the mind down to the lips of illustrious poets is found only in the canzone.' Guglielmo Gorni, 'Le forme primarie del testo poetico', in *Metrica e analisi letteraria* (Bologna: Il Mulino, 1993), 15–134.

plation under the threefold aspect of self-interrogation, of commitment and of ultimate emergence. First, then, comes the moment of self-confrontation, the moment in which, looking deep into self there to discern the truth of self, the would-be poet in the high style weighs up his equality to the matter in hand, the slightest lack of discerning here making for a fall:

> Ante omnia ergo dicimus unumquenque debere materie pondus propriis humeris coequare, ne forte humerorum nimio gravata virtute in cenum cespitare necesse sit; hoc est quod Magister noster Oratius precipit, cum in principio Poetrie 'Sumite materiam' dicit.
>
> *(De vulgari eloquentia* 2.4.4)[20]

But then, following on from the moment of self-confrontation, comes that of commitment—of commitment in the sense (*a*) of drinking deeply the waters of Helicon, (*b*) of an apprenticeship in the ways and means of versifying, and (*c*) of vigilance in the deployment of technique, these between them constituting as Dante sees it the caveat of lyric art, its built-in invitation to beware:

> Caveat ergo quilibet et discernat ea que dicimus; et quando hec tria pure cantare intendit, vel que ad ea directe ac pure secuntur, prius Elicone potatus, tensis fidibus ad supremum, secure plectrum tum movere incipiat. Sed cautionem atque discretionem hanc accipere, sicut decet, hic opus et labor est, quoniam nunquam sine strenuitate ingenii et artis assiduitate scientiarumque habitu fieri potest.
>
> *(De vulgari eloquentia* 2.4.9–10)[21]

And the outcome? Nothing less than ecstatic, for having taken his measure and mastered his craft the would-be poet in the high style enters at last upon his proper patrimony as beloved of the gods. Let those, then, who are mere geese

---

20 'First of all I declare that everyone must adjust the weight of his material to his own shoulders, lest by overburdening them he perforce take a tumble in the mud—which is what our master Horace teaches at the beginning of his *Ars poetica* when he says "Choose carefully your subject matter."' *Ars poetica* 38–41: 'Sumite materiam uestris, qui scribitis, aequam / viribus et versate diu quid ferre / recusent, quid valeant umeri. Cui lecta potenter erit / res, nec facundia deseret hunc, nec lucidus ordo' (Take a subject, you who write, equal to your strength and ponder long what your shoulders refuse to bear and are able so to do; for whoever chooses well, neither eloquence nor lucid construction will fail him). Zygmunt G. Barański, 'Three Notes on Dante and Horace', *RMS* 27 (2001), 5–37.

21 'Let everyone, then, take care to understand precisely what it is we are saying, and, should they have it in mind to sing of these three themes either in themselves or in respect of matters flowing from them, let them first drink of Helicon and tune their strings to perfection, whereupon they will be able to take up the plectrum with confidence. But coming by the necessary tact and discerning, that is the really hard part, for never can this be achieved other than by way of a strenuous application of the mind, of ceaseless dedication to technique, and of cultivated intelligence.'

desist, for we are speaking now of a winged humanity, of a humanity as soaring as it is sublime:

> Et hii sunt quos poeta Eneidorum sexto Dei dilectos et ab ardente virtute sublimatos ad ethera deorumque filios vocat, quanquam figurate loquatur. Et ideo confutetur illorum stultitia qui, arte scientiaque immunes, de solo ingenio confidentes, ad summa summe canenda prorumpunt; et a tanta presumptuositate desistant, et si anseres natura vel desidia sunt, nolint astripetam aquilam imitari.
>
> (*De vulgari eloquentia* 2.4.11)[22]

This, then, is what it means to speak, not merely of the interiorization but of the ontologization of the literary-aesthetic question in book 2 of the *De vulgari eloquentia*. To speak not merely of the interiorization but of the ontologization of the literary-aesthetic question in this second book of the *De vulgari eloquentia* is to speak of Dante's long since but now fully-fledged sense of *poetic* form as but the *intelligible* form of being itself—of this or that instance of specifically human being—in all its *specularitas* or openness to contemplation. And specularity is indeed the order of the day here, for while on the face of it, and right up to the moment of its evaporating somewhat after the manner of the morning mist, Dante's, in the remaining part of the text, looks to be simply an exercise in prescription, in a laying down of the rules for composition, what in truth we have here—and on analogy with the notion of speculative grammar—is something close to a speculative poetic, a hymn to the canzone stanza as but a mirror held up to self in the now perfect resolution of self. True, Dante's account of the 'fasciare' or 'binding up' of the stanza does not begin until chapter 8, the intervening chapters having to do with the discrete components of the poetic line in preparation for that binding—with the metrics or syllabic structure of the line (chapter 5), with the construction and register of the syntactical period (chapter 6), and with lexis (chapter 7). But within the economy of the whole, it is, again, the bind-

---

22 'Those successful in this are those whom the author of the *Aeneid* in the sixth book (though proceeding figuratively) speaks of as beloved of the Most High, as raised up by their glowing goodness and made sons of the gods. Thus are refuted the foolish claims of those who, bereft of art and science alike and relying on ingenuity alone, take it upon themselves to sing of the noblest themes in the noblest style. Let them set aside their pride, and, if by nature or a sluggardly spirit they are but geese, let them not seek to imitate the star-seeking eagle.' Virgil, *Aeneid* 6.125–31: 'sate sanguine divum / Tros Anchisiade, facilis descensus Averno: / noctes atque dies patet atri ianua Ditis; / sed revocare gradum superasque evadere ad auras, / hoc opus, hic labor est. pauci, quos aequus amavit / Iuppiter aut ardens evexit ad aethera virtus, / dis geniti potuere' (O seed of blood divine, man of Troy, Anchises's son, the descent to Avernus is not hard, for every night and day black Pluto's door stands wide open. But to retrace steps and to escape once more to the upper air, therein lies the task and the toil. Some few—sons of gods for either that they were loved by Jupiter by way of fair favour or were exalted by their own radiant heroism above the world of men—have been thus empowered).

ing up of these things in the stanza as but self under the aspect of self-seeing that constitutes the still centre of Dante's meditation hereabouts in the *De vulgari eloquentia*, the point-about-which of its each successive emphasis.

As far, then, as these intervening chapters are concerned, the chapters preliminary in respect of the binding-up moment proper of the argument, we have first of all, in chapter 5, a celebration of the hendecasyllable or eleven-syllable line as the most excellent of them all, a line capable not merely of hosting the expressive period in its totality but of fashioning from its various parts something greater than the sum thereof:

> Quorum omnium endecasillabum videtur esse superbius, tam temporis occupatione quam capacitate sententie, constructionis et vocabulorum; quorum omnium specimen magis multiplicatur in illo, ut manifeste apparet; nam ubicunque ponderosa multiplicantur, [multiplicatur] et pondus.
>
> (*De vulgari eloquentia* 2.5.3)[23]

When, by contrast, it comes in chapter 6 to the question of construction, Dante has in mind not so much the spaciousness of the period as, by turns, its grammatical, syntactical and rhetorical complexion. First, then, and on the lowest rung of the ladder, comes the kind of rhetorically innocent utterance proper to the untutored spirit (the 'insipidus, qui est rudium' of 2.6.4), where it is a matter simply of subject, verb and object in that order: 'Petrus amat multum dominam Bertam', grammatically correct but stylistically unfussed. But then, and with a wisp now of the rhetorical, comes the 'sapidus' pure and simple, the modestly tasteful proper to scholars and teachers and notable for its rhythmic cadencing or *cursus* (in this case *planus* and *velox*) and for the artful disposition (*ordo artificialis*) of its various lexical and grammatical components; so, for example, with its placing of the main verb at the beginning of the period, its separating out of 'me' and its qualifier 'maiorem' and its postponing of the dependent verb 'revisunt'

---

23 'Of all these, clearly, the most splendid both for its ample measure and for its ease in accommodating ideas, constructions and lexis alike is the hendecasyllable; for here in the hendecasyllable, not only is each of these things, as is plain to see, immeasurably magnified in respect of their beauty, but, as is always the case when one good thing is put in the balance with another, their goodness in the round is correspondingly all the more.' Ugo Sesini, 'L'endecasillabo: struttura e peculiarità', *Conv* 11 (1939), 545–70; Pietro G. Beltrami, 'Cesura epica, lirica, italiana: Riflessioni sull'endecasillabo di Dante', *Metrica* 4 (1986), 67–107; Pietro G. Beltrami, 'Endecasillabo, décasyllabe, e altro', *RLI* 8.3 (1990), 465–513 (with, in 11.3 [1993], 'Quante sillabe ha un endecasillabo? Qualche problema intorno alla storia della metrica' at 393–410); Aldo Menichetti, 'Quelques considérations sur la structure et l'origine de l'"endecasillabo"', in *Mélanges de philologie et de littérature médiévales offerts à Michel Burger*, ed. Jacqueline Cerquiglini-Toulet (Geneva: Droz, 1994), 215–30 (and in *Saggi metrici*, ed. Paolo Gresti and Massimo Zenari [Florence: Galluzzo, 2006], 251–69); Remo Fasani, 'Intorno all'endecasillabo', in *L'infinito endecasillabo e tre saggi danteschi* (Ravenna: Longo, 2007), 25–43.

to the end of the period, the 'Piget me cunctis pietate maiorem, quicunque in exilio tabescentes patriam tantum sompniando revisunt' of 2.6.4 (I, assailed by compassion more than any other, grieve for all those who, languishing in exile, revisit their native lands only in their dreams). But there is more, for over and above the 'sapidus' pure and simple comes the 'sapidus et venustus', the at once tasteful and elegant, where it is a question not simply of artful organization and careful cadencing but of irony as the dominant mood of the period as a whole; so, for instance, as a nicely conceived commentary on the avarice of Azzo VIII of Este, the 'Laudabilis discretio marchionis Estensis, et sua magnificentia preparata, cunctis illum facit esse dilectum' of, again, 2.6.4 (The laudable discernment and open-handed munificence of the Marquis of Este makes him beloved of all). But neither is that all, for in what amounts to the acme of rhetorical possibility comes the 'sapidus et venustus etiam et excelsus', the 'tasteful, elegant and positively exalted', where all these things combine with metaphor, apostrophe, personifica-tion, *emphasis* and *abbreviatio* to fashion a period, Dante thinks, bordering now on the sublime: 'Eiecta maxima parte florum de sinu tuo, Florentia, nequicquam Trinacriam Totila secundus adivit' (With the greater part of its flowers cast from your bosom, O Florence, Totila II journeyed on in vain to Sicily—the Totila in question being that same Charles de Valois, who, having like the first Totila rav-aged Florence, attempted subsequently to wrest Sicily from the Angevins). Here, then, is but further confirmation of what in Dante amounts to a sense of the high calling and indeed of the sacredness of form as apt well-nigh single-handedly to inaugurate and sustain a moment of spiritual intelligence.[24]

And then finally—'finally', that is to say, before coming to the 'binding up' proper part of the argument—there is the question of lexis, of the kind of vo-cabulary properly to be employed in the high style of romance vernacular verse

---

24 Pier Vincenzo Mengaldo, 'Idee dantesche sulla *constructio*', in *Linguistica e retorica di Dante* (Pisa: Nistri-Lischi, 1978), 281–88; Mirko Tavoni and Emmanuele Chersoni, 'Ipotesi d'interpretazione della *supprema constructio* (*De vulgari eloquentia* 2.6)', *Studi di Grammatica Italiana* 31–32 (2012–13), 131–58. For Dante and the *cursus* in general—*planus* in the cases of *pietáte maiórem* and *sompniándo revísunt* (i.e. a paroxytone polysyllable followed by a paroxytone trisyllable) and *velox* in that of *exílio tabescéntes* (i.e. a proparoxytone polysyllable followed by a paroxytone tetrasyllable)—Pio Rajna, 'Per il "cursus" medievale e per Dante', *SFI* 3 (1932), 7–76; Francesco di Capua, 'Appunti sul "cursus" o ritmo prosaico nelle opere latine di Dante Alighieri', in *Scritti minori*, vol. 1, ed. Antonio Quacquarelli (Rome: Desclée, 1959), 564–85; Pier Vincenzo Mengaldo, 'Dante e il "cursus"', in *Linguistica e retorica di Dante*, 263–80. In relation to the *De vulgari eloquentia* in particular: Aristide Marigo, 'Il "cursus" nel *De Vulgari Eloquentia* di Dante', *AMAPSLA* 48 (1931–32), 85–112. More generally on the *cursus*, Albert Curtis Clark, *The Cursus in Medieval and Vulgar Latin* (Oxford: Clarendon Press, 1910); Mathieu G. Nicolau, *L'origine du "cursus" rhythmique et les débuts de l'accent d'intensité en latin* (Paris: Société d'éditions 'Les Belles Lettres', 1930); Aristide Marigo, 'Il "cursus" nella prosa latina dalle origini cris-tiane ai tempi di Dante', *AMAPSLA* 47 (1932), 321–56; Francesco di Capua, 'Per la storia del latino letterario medievale e del "cursus"', *GIF* 6 (1953), 19–34; Alfredo Schiaffini, *Tradizione e poesia nella prosa d'arte italiana dalla latinità medievale a G. Boccaccio*, 2nd ed. (Rome: Edizioni di Storia e Let-teratura, 1969).

making. Here there are two things to consider, cultural and acoustic, the former bearing on the register of the lexis under consideration and the latter on the aural configuration both of the word itself and of the period of which it forms part. Culturally, then, it is a question of excluding every kind of sylvan terminology (any mention of flocks, lyres and the like), every kind of childlike expression (*mamma, babbo, mate, pate*), anything smacking of the effeminate (*dolciada* or *placevole*, for example, with their particular kind of blandness), together with anything redolent not so much of the urbane than of the merely urban—words, for instance, like *corpo* with its coarse materiality and its guttural tonality; all of which, when taken together with the outlawing of any kind of ugly accentuation, consonantal asperity (double 'z's' for example) and other instances of extravagant gemination, leaves only those paroxytones commending themselves for their sweet cadencing, for, as Dante himself has it, their elegant 'grooming' (the *pexa* of 2.7.2): *amore, donna, disio, virtute, donare, letitia, salute, securtate, defesa*—terms which, once blended with the monosyllabic, the syncategorematic and the otherwise purely functional, make for a varied but consistent soundscape.[25]

Having, then, legislated for the component parts of the canzone stanza—namely the hendecasyllable as technically and expressively the most spacious of its lines, the various species of construction ranging from the insipid to the sublime, and lexis in the exclusiveness thereof—the time has come to assemble both the canzone in its totality and (more especially) the canzone stanza as the locus or whereabouts of all poetic artistry. As far, therefore, as the canzone in its totality is concerned it is enough to note, with Dante, that what we are speaking of here is simply 'an assembly of equal stanzas without refrain, in the tragic style, and all of a piece thematically' (the 'Dicimus ergo quod canto . . . est equalium stantiarum sine responsorio ad unam sententiam tragica coniugatio' of 2.8.8—lines to which, as confirming the ideal susceptibility of the canzone thus understood to a specifically musical setting, we should add these from just a little earlier in the same chapter: 'Et ideo cantio nichil aliud esse videtur quam actio completa dicentis verba modulationi armonizata').[26] But for all that, the *ars cantionis* or art

25 Luigi Peirone, 'Economia e ridondanza nella teoria dantesca dei "grandiosa vocabula" ', *LN* 33.4 (1972), 105–8.

26 *De vulgari eloquentia* 2.8.6: 'From all of which it is clear that a canzone is nothing other than a considered disposition of words with a view to their musical setting' (with, at 2.10.2, 'omnis stantia ad quandam odam recipiendam armonizata est' [every stanza is designed with a view to its musical setting]). Raffaello Monterosso, 'Musica e poesia nel *De vulgari eloquentia*', in *Atti della giornata internazionale di studio per il VII centenario (Ravenna, 6–7 marzo 1965)* (Faenza: Fratelli Lega, 1965), 82–100; Siegfried Heinimann, ' "Poesis" und "musica" in Dantes Schrift *De vulgari eloquentia*', in *Romanische Literatur*, ed. Rudolf Engler and Ricarda Liver (Wiesbaden: Reichert, 1987), 193–207; Mario Pazzaglia, 'Musica e metrica nel pensiero di Dante', in *La musica nel tempo di Dante*, ed. Luigi Pestalozza (Milan: Unicopli, 1988), 257–90; Maria Sofia Lannutti, 'Implicazioni musicali nella versificazione italiana del

of canzone in general comes down to the art of the canzone stanza in particular as the 'mansion' or receptacle of all artistic excellence (the 'mansio capax sive receptaculum totius artis' of 2.9.2) and indeed as the 'womb of the poet's entire art' (the 'sic stantia totam artem ingremiat' of the same chapter). There are, then, three things to be borne in mind when it comes to the shape and structure of the canzone stanza thus understood, namely the *cantus divisio* or partitioning of the stanza, the *partium habitudo* or relationship of its constituent parts, and the *numerus carminum et sillabarum* or its precise number of lines and their metrical organization. As far, then, as the first of these things is concerned, the *cantus divisio*, it is a question of the precise structure of the stanza, of its consisting, that is to say, of two parts—in effect, of a melody and a countermelody—either one of which (but usually the first) may at the discretion of the poet be further divided in such a way as to produce on either side of the *diesis* or principal division in the stanza two metrically identical measures. Where, then, there is no such further division we speak simply of a *frons* and *sirma* linked usually by a *rima chiave* or 'key rhyme' at the end of the one and the beginning of the other thus:

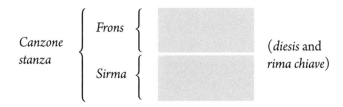

$$\text{Canzone stanza} \begin{cases} \text{Frons} \left\{ \quad \right. \\ \text{Sirma} \left\{ \quad \right. \end{cases} \quad (\textit{diesis} \text{ and } \textit{rima chiave})$$

Where, by contrast, either the first or the second part of the stanza is subject to further division, we speak of the 'feet' or *pedes* and of the 'verses' or *versus* thus:

Due-Trecento (con un *excursus* sulla rima interna da Guittone a Petrarca)', *SMI* 9 (2009), 21–53; Maria Sofia Lannutti, 'La canzone nel Medioevo: Contributo alla definizione del rapporto tra poesia e musica', *Semicerchio* 44.1 (2011), 55–67; Maria Clotilde Camboni, 'La stanza della canzone tra metrica e musica', *SMI* 12 (2012), 3–57. More generally on Dante's *ars cantionis* or art of the canzone, Francesco D'Ovidio, *Versificazione italiana e arte poetica medioevale* (Milan: Hoepli, 1910); W. Th. Marrocco, 'The Enigma of the Canzone', *Spec* 31 (1956), 704–13; Mario Pazzaglia, *Il verso e l'arte della canzone nel 'De vulgari eloquentia'* (Florence: La Nuova Italia, 1967); Dino Bigongiari, 'The Art of the Canzone', in *Dante in America: The First Two Centuries*, ed. A. Bartlett Giamatti (Binghamton: State University of New York, 1983), 228–43; Guglielmo Gorni, 'Ragioni metriche della canzone', in *Metrica e analisi letteraria* (Bologna: Il Mulino, 1993), 207–17; Lorenzo Somelli, 'Teoria e prassi della canzone dantesca: "Rithimorum relatio"', *RSD* 2.1 (2002), 3–32; Sergio Bozzola, 'Il modello ritmico della canzone', in *La metrica dei Fragmenta*, ed. Marco Praloran (Padua: Antenore, 2003), 191–248. More generally still, Ugo Sesini, *Le melodie trobadoriche nel Canzoniere provenzale della Biblioteca ambrosiana R.71 Sup.* (Turin: G. Chiantore, 1942); Roger Dragonetti, *La technique poétique des trouvères dans la chanson courtoise: Contribution à l'étude de la rhétorique médiévale* (Brugge: De Tempel, 1960); Clemente Terni, 'Musica e versificazione nelle lingue romanze', *SM* 16.1 (1975), 1–41; Klaus Kropfinger, 'Dante e l'arte dei trovatori', in *La musica nel tempo di Dante*, 130–74.

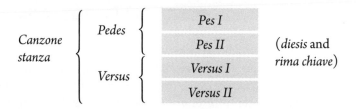

In practice, though, as Dante goes out of his way to confirm, any combination of these two models is permissible, be it a *frons* and two *versus* or, vice versa, two *pedes* and a single *versus*, tradition, provided only that good sense and proper accountability to the matter in hand prevail, authorizing them all:

> Vide igitur, lector, quanta licentia data sit cantiones poetantibus, et considera cuius rei causa tam largum arbitrium usus sibi asciverit; et si recto calle ratio te duxerit, videbis auctoritatis dignitate sola quod dicimus esse concessum.
>
> *(De vulgari eloquentia* 2.10.5)[27]

Coming now, then, to the 'disposition of parts within the whole' moment of the argument (the *partium habitudo*), discretion once again is all, the poet being free to proceed as he sees fit. True, there are, over and above the basic symmetry already noted, one or two further points to bear in mind, such as the ideal preponderance of the hendecasyllable as distinct from the hepta- and pentasyllable within the economy of the whole and the desirability of rounding off the stanza with a rhyming couplet, this invariably making for its sweet cadencing, for a gentle falling away of saying into silence (the 'pulcerrime tamen se habent ultimorum carminum desinentie si cum rithimo in silentium cadant' of 2.13.8). But for all that, prescribability shades off now into unprescribability, the necessary into the contingent. So, for example, when it comes to the relative size of, say, the *frons* and the *versus*, this, Dante suggests, will vary, for sometimes the *frons* will have more lines and syllables than the *versus* ('Nam quandoque frons versus excedit in sillabis et carminibus, vel excedere potest', 2.11.3), while at other times it will be the other way round, the *versus* having more lines and syllables than the *frons* ('Quandoque versus frontem superant sillabis et carminibus', 2.11.5). And sometimes the *frons* may exceed the *versus* with respect to the number of lines it has but contain fewer syllables ('Quandoque in carminibus excedere et in sillabis

---

27 'Behold then, reader, the licence granted to poets busy with canzoni, and consider why it is that usage has settled on such ample scope for discretion; and provided only that reason guides your steps, you will see for yourself that the freedom we have been discussing has been made possible only by the acknowledged excellence of all that has gone before.'

superari potest', 2.11.4), while at other times it will be the other way round, the *versus* having more lines than the *frons* but not so many syllables ('possent etenim versus frontem superare carminibus, et sillabis superari', 2.11.6). And what applies to the *partium habitudo* or relative size and shape of the main sections of the stanza applies too when it comes to the third of the aspects identified above, to the *numerus carminum et sillabarum* or precise distribution of the lines within the stanza; for provided only that, where they exist, the two *pedes* and the two *versus* remain symmetrical (anything other than this ruling out the possibility of a musical setting proper), then any number of lines and any admixture of lines— mostly, it is true, seven- and eleven-syllable lines—are possible within the stanza as a whole. In other words, it all depends. Provided only that the macrostructure of the stanza be secure, it is, for the rest, a matter of discerning, of the accountability of form in the otherwise endless flexibility thereof to the substance and spirit of what the poet has it in mind to say:

> Ex quo [duo] que sunt artis in cantione satis sufficienter tractavimus, nunc de tertio videtur esse tractandum, videlicet de numero carminum et silla- barum. Et primo secundum totam stantiam videre oportet aliquid; deinde secundum partes eius videbimus. Nostra igitur primo refert discretionem facere inter ea que canenda occurrunt, quia quedam stantie prolixitatem videntur appetere, quedam non. Nam cum ea que dicimus cuncta vel circa dextrum aliquid vel sinistrum canamus—ut quandoque persuasorie quan- doque dissuasorie, quandoque gratulanter quandoque yronice, quandoque laudabiliter quandoque contemptive canere contingit–, que circa sinistra sunt verba semper ad extremum festinent, et alia decenti prolixitate passim veniant ad extremum.
>
> (*De vulgari eloquentia* 2.14.1–2)[28]

And it is precisely the unprescribability of it all, the irreducibility of the art of verse making to any set or subset of regulations determining from beforehand its precise form, that presages and indeed renders inevitable the sudden demise of

---

28 'Having treated in sufficient depth two aspects of the art of the canzone, now, it seems, is the moment to move on to a third, namely the number of lines and syllables. First, then, we need a few remarks relative to the stanza as a whole, going on then to consider its parts. I begin, therefore, by distinguishing between the kinds of things suitable for treatment in the poem, some clearly requiring a certain spaciousness and others not. Given, then, that everything we touch upon in poetry we touch upon either positively or negatively—sometimes with a view to dissuasion and sometimes persuasion, sometimes with a view to endorsement and sometimes with a view to irony, sometimes to praise and sometimes to condemn—we need first of all, when it comes to matters appropriate for treatment in verse, to make a distinction between those requiring a stanza of some length and those not; for the things we say negatively ought to hasten quickly to an end and the things we say positively to proceed at a more leisurely pace.' Luigi Spagnolo, 'Sull'incompiutezza del *De vulgari eloquentia*', LIt 9 (2013), 37–56; Sabina Ferrara, 'I trattati incompiuti: Il *Convivio* e il *De vulgari eloquentia*', in *La parola dell'esilio: Autore e lettori nelle opere di Dante in esilio* (Florence: Cesati, 2016), 59–100.

this second book of the *De vulgari eloquentia,* a book surrendering at last to the insistent 'quandoque ... quandoque ... quandoque' (sometimes this ... sometimes that ... sometimes the other) as decisive for the shape and structure of the canzone stanza. Having, in other words, established the ground rules, at once musical and rhetorical in kind, the rest is down to the discerning—including the self-discerning—of the would-be poet in the high style, this and this alone serving to guarantee the significance, the seriousness and the sacredness of it all.

What, then, standing back for a moment, are we to make of this second book of the *De vulgari eloquentia?* An *Ars poetica* stranded at last on the sands of mere prescriptivism? More than likely. A text crippled in the round by its particular brand of exclusivity? Indeed. A discourse overtaken in the very moment of its conception by the more seasoned poetic of the now imminent *Commedia?* To be sure. All this and doubtless more besides. But—and this now is what matters—for all its variously problematic character what we have here is one of the most precious meditations upon the literary-aesthetic issue in the whole of European letters, a meditation that both lives and dies in the name and for the sake of the again unutterable seriousness of it all, of form as but the intelligible principle of this or that instance of specifically human being in act. No hint here, therefore, of the mere playfulness of, say, a Geoffrey of Vinsauf when it comes to art as a matter fundamentally of prestidigitation, of—in the name and for the sake of a momentary frisson of the spirit—changing the last into the first, the future into the present, the crooked into the straight, the far-off into the near-at-hand, the rustic into the urban, and the pitiful into the precious:

> [Ars] ludit quasi quaedam praestigiatrix
> et facit ut fiat res postera prima, futura
> praesens, transversa directa, remota propinqua;
> rustica sic fiunt urbana, vetusta novella,
> publica privata, nigra candida, vilia cara
> ...
> Quando venit tali sententia culta paratu,
> ille sonus vocum laetam dulcescit ad aurem,
> et fricat interius nova delectatio mentem.
>
> (*Poetria nova* 121–25 and 954–56)[29]

29 '[Art] plays much after the manner of a magician, ensuring as it does so that the last becomes the first, the future the present, the oblique direct, the remote near, and in such a way that the rustic is refined, the old made new, the public made private, black made white, and the vile made precious ... When the period appears thus decorated, it falls sweetly upon the delighted ear and inwardly excites the mind with fresh pleasure.' Ernest Gallo, *The 'Poetria Nova' and Its Sources in Early Rhetorical Doctrine* (The Hague: Mouton, 1971); Ernest Gallo, 'The *Poetria Nova* of Geoffrey of Vinsauf', in *Medieval Eloquence: Studies in the Theory and Practice of Medieval Rhetoric,* ed. James J. Murphy (Berkeley: University

Now Geoffrey of Vinsauf was an honourable man, a man no less anxious than Dante to confirm the accountability in art of form to content, of style to substance:

> Sit brevis aut longus, se semper sermo coloret
> intus et exterius, sed discernendo colorem
> ordine discreto. Verbi prius inspice mentem
> et demum faciem, cujus ne cerde colori;
> se nisi conformet color intimus exteriori,
> sordet ibi ratio . . .
>
> (*Poetria nova* 742–47)[30]

But for all that, his even so was a sense of the poetic undertaking as a matter preeminently of deftness and delight, of sweet persuasiveness. Not so, however, Alighieri, for whom art and artistry serve the purpose of the properly sublime, of, to wit, the soaring substance of historical selfhood. The slick, in short, gives way to the sacred, at which point the *De vulgari eloquentia*, foundering as it does upon its own equations, flows more than ever nobly into the *mare magnum* of the *Commedia*.

---

of California Press, 1978), 68–84. Also, Roberto Crespo, 'Brunetto Latini e la *Poetria Nova* di Geoffroi de Vinsauf', *LI* 24.1 (1972), 97–99. More generally, Charles Sears Baldwin, *Medieval Rhetoric and Poetic (to 1400): Interpreted from Representative Works* (New York: Macmillan, 1928); Douglas Kelly, *The Arts of Poetry and Prose* (Turnhout: Brepols, 1991); Rita Copeland and Ineke Sluiter, *Medieval Grammar and Rhetoric: Language, Arts and Literary Theory, AD 300–1475* (Oxford: Oxford University Press, 2009).

30 'Whether long or short, let the discourse always be decorated within and without, but choose among ornaments with care. First examine the soul of the word and then its face, whose outward show alone you should not trust, for only in the degree to which its inner conforms to its outer hue is there anything to be said for its deployment.'

CHAPTER 4

The Post-Exilic *Rime*

Never far beneath the surface of the *Convivio* and the *De vulgari eloquentia* is the agony of exile and its role in encouraging Dante in the purgatorial business of reshaping and resubstantiating his humanity, of defining afresh the deep reasons of his existence. As far, then, as the *Convivio* is concerned we have only to recall the 'Ahi, piaciuto fosse al dispensatore de l'universo' passage of 1.3.3–5 with its sense of exclusion, far-wandering and vilification, sensations decisive both for the coming about and for the overall interpretation of the text. As far, by contrast, as the *De vulgari eloquentia* is concerned, we have the 'et Florentiam adeo diligamus ut, quia dileximus, exilium patiamur iniuste' passage of 1.6.3, generous in its sense of there doubtless being places in the world more beautiful than Florence and idioms more congenial than Florentine, but, for all that, and somewhere in the depths, less than fully persuaded:

> Nos autem, cui mundus est patria velut piscibus equor, quanquam Sarnum biberimus ante dentes et Florentiam adeo diligamus ut, quia dileximus, exilium patiamur iniuste, rationi magis quam sensui spatulas nostri iudicii podiamus. Et quamvis ad voluptatem nostram sive nostre sensualitatis quietem in terris amenior locus quam Florentia non existat, revolventes et poetarum et aliorum scriptorum volumina quibus mundus universaliter et membratim describitur, ratiocinantesque in nobis situationes varias mundi locorum et eorum habitudinem ad utrunque polum et circulum equatorem, multas esse perpendimus firmiterque censemus et magis nobiles et magis delitiosas et regiones et urbes quam Tusciam et Florentiam, unde sumus oriundus et civis, et plerasque nationes et gentes delectabiliori atque utiliori sermone uti quam Latinos.[1]

1 'To me, however, though I drank from the Arno before cutting my teeth, and love Florence so much that, loving her as I did, I suffer exile unjustly, the whole world is my homeland just as the sea is to the fish, for which reason I shall weight the scales of my judgement less with sentiment than with reason. And although when it comes to my own pleasure and indeed to the indulging of my every sense, there is no more agreeable place on earth than Florence, yet when I turn the pages of those poets and other writers describing the world both as a whole and in its various parts, and when I reflect on the different regions of the world and their disposition with respect to the poles and the equator, I am convinced and firmly maintain that there are many places and cities at once more noble and more delightful than the Tuscany and Florence where I was born and of which I am a citizen, and that there

In neither case, then, is the text less than transparent to the trauma decisive for its inception, to the rhythm of sadness apt to inform even the most heroic gesture. Still more powerful, however, as an expression both of the substance and of the psychology of exile are the three great post-exilic canzoni, *Tre donne intorno al cor mi son venute, Doglia mi reca ne lo core ardire* and the so-called (after its *congedo*) 'montanina' canzone *Amor, da che convien pur ch'io mi doglia*, all, in an ideal chronology, belonging to the years 1302–6 and each in its way exploring the to-and-fro experience of despair and defiance in the mind of the far-wanderer, of the now nomadic spirit: in *Tre donne* by way of its deft interleaving of personal and universal catastrophe—of the catastrophe of self and of justice each alike in exile—and of its oscillation between pride and repentance as dispositions of the spirit; in *Doglia mi reca* by way of its scarcely less than seething indictment of greed and illiberality as but the way of the world; and in the 'montanina' by way of a yet fresh meditation upon those forces deep within him making less for being than for non-being, for the delivery of self despite self to the demonic. Difference, then, prevails and prevails absolutely in point both of substance and of style when it comes to these great canzoni of Dante's early exile, the solemnity and sadness of *Tre donne* contrasting absolutely with the wrath of *Doglia mi reca*, and these in turn with the self-inexplicability and near-despair of *Amor, da che convien*, the common denominator here, however, being precisely the restive substance and psychology of self as far from home.

The canzone *Tre donne intorno al cor mi son venute* is in every sense a special document, special not least for the mise-en-scène, indeed for the *sacra rappresentazione*, with which it begins and for the confessional intensity with which it ends, and, overall, for Dante's account of what it is to live somewhere between resolve and repentance as the now dominant moods of his existence. First, then, and by way of an *incipit* notable only for its imaginative, indeed iconic tact and economy, comes the moment of grief, the moment in which he has justice and her progeny (human law, perhaps, and the law of nations) stand at the door and knock, the object of their pilgrimage being but to drink once more from the wellspring of love—the lord, Dante says, of his heart—as the beginning and end of all righteousness. This indeed, then, is a congregation of the bereft, a forgathering of the displaced and dispossessed, the simplicity of the line, nota-

---

are many nations and peoples with a more agreeable and serviceable language than the Italians.' Vittorio Russo, 'Dante "exul inmeritus": Variazioni compositive sul/dal tema', in *L'exil et l'exclusion. Actes du colloque franco-italien; Aix-en-Provence, 19–20–21 octobre 1989*, ed. Georges Ulysses (Aix-en-Provence: Publications de l'Université de Provence, 1991), 13–23; Giuseppe De Marco, 'L'esperienza di Dante "exul immeritus" quale autobiografia universale', in *Le icone della lontananza: Carte di esilio e viaggi di carta* (Rome: Salerno, 2008), 15–54; Catherine Keen, 'Florence and Faction in Dante's Lyric Poetry: Framing the Experience of Exile', in *"Se mai continga . . .": Exile, Politics and Theology in Dante*, ed. Claire E. Honess and Matthew Treherne (Ravenna: Longo, 2013), 63–83.

ble above all for its gentle binomialism ('dolente e sbigottita . . . discacciata e stanca . . . vertute né beltà . . . discinta e scalza'), confirming the distraught substance of it all:

> Tre donne intorno al cor mi son venute,
> e seggonsi di fore;
> ché dentro siede Amore
> lo quale è in segnoria de la mia vita.
> Tanto son belle e di tanta vertute
> che 'l possente segnore,
> dico quel ch'è nel core,
> a pena del parlar di lor s'aita.
> Ciascuna par dolente e sbigottita,
> come persona discacciata e stanca,
> cui tutta gente manca
> e cui vertute né beltà non vale . . .
> Dolesi l'una con parole molto,
> e 'n su la man si posa
> come succisa rosa;
> il nudo braccio, di dolor colonna,
> sente l'oraggio che cade dal volto;
> l'altra man tiene ascosa
> la faccia lagrimosa;
> discinta e scalza, e sol di sé par donna.

(*Tre donne intorno al cor mi son venute*, lines 1–12 and 19–26)[2]

2 'Three women have come around my heart and sit without, for within sits Love, who holds sway over my life. So beautiful are they and of such nobility that the mighty lord—him, I mean, in my heart—can himself scarcely speak of them. Like those driven from home and weary, rejected by all, their goodness and beauty counting now for nothing, they are each of them sorrowful and full of sadness . . . One of them, resting her head on her hand like a clipped rose, begins bitterly to lament; her naked arm, a column for grief, feels the rain that falls from her eyes, her other hand hiding her tear-stained face. Ungirt and barefoot as she is, her bearing alone confirms her status as a lady.' Giosue Carducci, 'Delle rime di Dante' and 'La canzone di Dante, *Tre donne intorno al cor mi son venute*', in *Opere*, vol. 10 (Bologna: Zanichelli, 1936), 73–198 and 207–51; Michele Barbi, 'Per l'interpretazione della canzone *Tre donne*', SD 17 (1933), 97–103; Kenelm Foster, O.P., 'Dante's canzone *Tre donne*', ItSt 9 (1954), 56–68; Ignazio Baldelli, 'Lingua e stile dalle petrose a *Tre donne*', RLIt 82.1 (1978), 5–17; Gordon Poole, 'Dante's canzone *Tre donne intorno al cor*', DS 98 (1980), 123–44; Maria Teresa Balbiano d'Aramengo, *Tre donne intorno al cor: Saggio di psicologia dantesca* (Turin: Riccadonna, 2006 [1958]); Enrico Fenzi, '*Tre donne* 73–107: La colpa, il pentimento, il perdono', in *Tre donne intorno al cor mi son venute*, ed. Juan Varela-Portas de Orduña (Madrid: Asociación Complutense de Dantología, 2007), 91–124; Umberto Carpi, '*Tre donne intorno al cor mi son venute* . . .', in *Dante Alighieri: Le quindici canzoni. Lette da diversi*, vol. 2 (Lecce: Pensa Multimedia, 2012), 153–95; Marco Grimaldi, 'Come funziona una poesia allegorica: Una lettura di *Tre donne*', CT 15.1 (2012), 299–321.

But then, with the stupendous 'And I' of line 73, the spectacle of justice and of those dear to her as similarly excluded opens out to include the poet himself as party to one and the same misfortune, at which point any number of conflicting sensations—all of them sustained and intensified by the far-offness of Florence the fair—strive within him for mastery:

> E io, che ascolto nel parlar divino
> consolarsi e dolersi
> così alti dispersi,
> l'essilio che m'è dato, onor mi tegno;
>   ché, se giudizio o forza di destino
> vuol pur che il mondo versi
> i bianchi fiori in persi,
> cader co' buoni è pur di lode degno.
>   E se non che de gli occhi miei 'l bel segno
> per lontananza m'è tolto dal viso,
> che m'àve in foco miso,
> lieve mi conterei ciò che m'è grave.
> Ma questo foco m'àve
> già consumato sì l'ossa e la polpa,
> che Morte al petto m'ha posto la chiave.
> Onde, s'io ebbi colpa,
> più lune ha volto il sol poi che fu spenta,
> se colpa muore perché l'uom si penta.

(*Tre donne intorno al cor mi son venute*, lines 73–90)[3]

Here, then, in its telescoping of the public and the private, of justice in general and of self in particular as displaced, lies the greatness of this canzone, its status as one of the high peaks of Dante's activity as a lyric poet; for complementarity gives way here to something closer to mutual indwelling, such that what the private (the fate of one Dante Alighieri) gains by way of universalization the public (the fate of justice and her progeny) gains by way of intensification, the whole thus being immeasurably greater than the sum of its parts.

---

3 'And I, who listen to such noble exiles taking comfort and telling of their sorrow in divine collo-quy, deem an honour the exile imposed upon me, for if judgement and the force of destiny does indeed will that the world turn dark the white flowers, it is praiseworthy even so to fall with the good. And were not the fair object of my eyes stolen away by distance from my sight (for which I am all ablaze), I would count as light that which weighs upon me. But that fire has so consumed already my flesh and bones that death has put his key to my breast; whence if guilt dies with repentance, then with the passing now of many a moon, mine, were I indeed to blame, has long since expired.'

But *Tre donne*, immeasurably greater as it is than the sum of its parts, does not exhaust the psychology of exile, for always ready to interrupt the rhythm of Dante's anguish as a far-wanderer are other no less powerful inflexions of the spirit—anger, accusation and the stirring now of something more properly prophetic. This at any rate—this alternative way of coping with the agony of exile—is the substance of the ideally contemporary canzone *Doglia mi reca ne lo core ardire* as an essay in greed as a matter, not simply of self-seeking, but of self-forgetfulness, as a delivery of something to nothing, of possibility to impossibility, of reality to unreality and of truth to untruth, irony thus taking over from indictment as the dominant mood of the piece. So, for example, and indeed as constituting the nub of Dante's meditation hereabouts, we have these lines on the futility and, implicitly, the blasphemy of it all, on avarice as but a principle of self-wasting:

> Chi è servo è come quello ch'è seguace
> ratto a segnore, e non sa dove vada,
> per dolorosa strada;
> come l'avaro seguitando avere,
> ch'a tutti segnoreggia.
>
> Corre l'avaro, ma più fugge pace;
> oh mente cieca, che non pò vedere
> lo suo folle volere
> che 'l numero, ch'ognora a passar bada,
> che 'nfinito vaneggia.
>
> Ecco giunta colei che ne pareggia:
> dimmi, che hai tu fatto,
> cieco avaro disfatto?
> rispondimi, se puoi, altro che 'Nulla'.
> Maladetta tua culla,
> che lusingò cotanti sonni invano;
> maladetto lo tuo perduto pane,
> che non si perde al cane:
> ché da sera e da mane
> hai raunato e stretto ad ambo mano
> ciò che sì tosto si rifà lontano.

(*Doglia mi reca ne lo core ardire*, lines 64–84)[4]

---

4 'A man thus enslaved is like one following close upon his master along an anxious road knowing not where it leads, just like the miser chasing after his wealth as lord of all. The miser hastens on, but fleeing the while all peace of mind. Oh blind spirit, unable by way of its insane desire to see that the sum it seeks to surpass stretches on into all eternity! But behold now the great leveller. So tell me, oh miser, darkling and undone as you are, what *have* you done? Answer me if you can something other

Here, then, along with *Tre donne*, is a further step along the way to the *Commedia*, the peremptoriness of the text (unusually rich in *settenari*), together with its sense of the effrontery of it all, crying out for a more systematic statement of its substance, for a more sustained account—that, precisely, of the *Inferno*—of what it means for the individual to be lost to the reasons of his or her properly human presence in the world. But that, for the moment, is a little way off, *Doglia mi reca*, considered in itself, offering yet a further expression of the complicated psychology of exile, of an experience as variegated as it is irreducible to any one of its many components.

But for all the status both of *Tre donne* and of *Doglia mi reca* as each of them a further step along the way and as calling for a more developed and indeed for a more properly eschatological statement of the leading idea, there is as yet more to come by way of preparation for the major work, for it is a question now not simply of the world but of self as awry, as lost to the reasons of its proper humanity. Essential, in other words, to the coming about of the *Commedia* as, whatever else it is, an essay in ultimate journeying is a sense on the part of its author and architect of the mote in his own eye, this, precisely, being the function of the 'montanina' canzone as testimony to Dante's own engagement at the point of self-undoing. Having arrived then, he says (in a letter to Moroello Malaspina accompanying the poem and dating from 1308 or 1309), on the banks of the Arno in the Casentino, he was overtaken by yet a new love, by a passion serving not only to detain but to obsess and to waylay his very being. And this, basically, is the point of the poem, for recalling as it does any number of motifs and emphases both from the Cavalcantian and from the *petrose* phases of his activity as a lyric poet, this, fundamentally, is an account of the soul as busy about its own dismantling. Especially eloquent, therefore, is the second stanza of the poem with its setting aside of the contingencies of the case in favour of something wholly more disturbing, of a sense of self as both willing and unwilling, as guilty by way of the complicit:

> Io non posso fuggir ch'ella non vegna
> ne l'imagine mia,
> se non come il pensier che la vi mena.
> L'anima folle, che al suo mal s'ingegna,

---

than "nothing". Cursed be your cradle for all its flattering but futile dreams! Cursed be the bread you have wasted, bread wasted not even on dogs! Morning and evening alike you have gathered and hoarded with both hands things just as quickly slipping from your grasp.' Patrick Boyde, 'Style and Structure in Dante's canzone *Doglia mi reca*', ItSt 20 (1965), 26–41; Elena Artale, 'La liberalità in Dante', in *Studi per Umberto Carpi: Un saluto da allievi e colleghi pisani*, ed. Marco Santagata and Alfredo Stussi (Pisa: ETS, 2000), 69–97; Francesco Bausi, 'Doglia mi reca nello core ardire', in *Dante Alighieri: Le quindici canzoni. Lette da diversi*, vol. 2 (Lecce: Pensa Multimedia, 2012), 197–253.

com'ella è bella e ria,
così dipinge, e forma la sua pena;
  poi la riguarda, e quando ella è ben piena
del gran disio che de li occhi li tira,
incontro a sé s'adira,
c'ha fatto il foco ond'ella trista incende.
Quale argomento di ragion raffrena,
ove tanta tempesta in me si gira?
L'angoscia, che non cape dentro, spira
fuor de la bocca sì ch'ella s'intende,
e anche a li occhi lor merito rende.

(*Amor, da che convien pur ch'io mi doglia*, lines 16–30)[5]

—lines to which, by way of refining the terrifying and ultimately tragic substance of this situation, we may add these from the third stanza, 'terrifying' in their sense of the soul as dominated by those forces bearing upon it from beyond but 'tragic' in the sense of its even so seeking them out, of its delivering self despite self to its own demise:

---

5 'I cannot escape her coming into my imagination any more than I can prevent the thought bringing her there. My foolish soul, busy about its own undoing, depicts her in all her power to delight and to destroy, fashioning as it does so its own agony. Then, gazing at her until filled by the desire generated by her eyes, it reproaches itself for having kindled the fire whence it is wretchedly consumed. What by way of reason might be advanced to allay the tempest raging within me? My grief, which cannot be contained, issues audibly with my every breath, furnishing as it does tears for my eyes.' Colin Hardie, 'Dante's "Canzone Montanina" ', *MLR* 55 (1960), 359–70; Fausto Montanari, 'La canzone *Amor, da che convien pur ch'io mi doglia*', *LM* 12 (1962), 359–68; Francesco Maggini, 'La canzone "montanina" di Dante', in *Due letture dantesche inedite* (*Inf. XXIII and XXXII*) *e altri scritti poco noti* (Florence: Le Monnier, 1965 [1956]), 50–57; Giorgio Bàrberi Squarotti, 'La canzone "montanina" ', in *L'artificio dell'eternità* (Verona: Fiorini, 1972), 157–85; John C. Barnes and Zygmunt G. Barański, 'Dante's "Canzone Montanina" ', *MLR* 73.2 (1978), 297–307; Guglielmo Gorni, 'La canzone "Montanina" *Amor dacché convien pur ch'io mi doglia* (CXVI)', *LC* 24 (1995), 129–50; Emilio Pasquini, 'Un crocevia dell'esilio: La canzone "Montanina" e l'"Epistola" a Moroello', in *Studi dedicati a Gennaro Barbarisi*, ed. Claudia Berra and Michele Mari (Milan: CUEM, 2007), 13–29 (and in *Fra Due e Quattrocento: Cronotopi letterari in Italia* [Milan: Franco Angeli, 2012], 79–94); Umberto Carpi, 'Un congedo da Firenze?', in *Amor, da che convien pur ch'io mi doglia*, ed. Emilio Pasquini (Madrid: Asociación Complutense de Dantología, 2009), 21–30 (with Enrico Fenzi, 'La "montanina" e i suoi lettori' at 31–84); Natascia Tonelli, 'Amor, da che convien pur ch'io mi doglia', in *Dante Alighieri: Le quindici canzoni. Lette da diversi*, vol. 2 (Lecce: Pensa Multimedia, 2012), 255–83; Michelangelo Picone, 'Esilio e "peregrinatio": Dalla *Vita Nova* alla canzone montanina', in *Scritti danteschi*, ed. Antonio Lanza (Ravenna: Longo, 2017), 129–45 (with 'Sulla canzone "montanina" di Dante' at 89–95). Further on the circumstances of the 'montanina' and on Moroello Malaspina as its recipient, Francesco Mazzoni, 'Dante e la Lunigiana', *Rotary Club Firenze*, series 3.2 (1984), 99–105; Enrico Fenzi, 'Ancora sulla epistola a Moroello e sulla "montanina" di Dante', *Tenzone* 4 (2003), 43–84; John C. Barnes, 'Moroello "vapor": Metafora metiorica e visione dantesca del marchese di Giovagallo', *DS* 124 (2006), 35–56 (and ad voc. 'Moroello Malaspina', in Richard Lansing [ed.], *The Dante Encyclopedia* [New York: Garland], 628–29).

La nimica figura, che rimane
vittorïosa e fera
e signoreggia la vertù che vole,
vaga di sé medesma andar mi fane
colà dov'ella è vera,
come simile a simil correr sòle.
 Ben conosco che va la neve al sole,
ma più non posso; fo come colui
che, nel podere altrui,
va co' suoi piedi al loco ov'egli è morto.

(*Amor, da che convien pur ch'io mi doglia*, lines 31–40)[6]

Here, then, in these three great canzoni of Dante's early exile we have yet a further account of the substance and psychology thereof, of exile, that is to say, as a matter, not merely of 'going to and fro in the earth and of walking up and down in it', but of what it is to dwell for a season in the region of unlikeness. What, then, for those of us looking on from a distance? Grief, certainly, for Dante's—comprising as it does an endless pacing up and down the peninsula, a constant climbing up and down other people's stairs and a putting up perforce with the saltiness of other people's bread—is indeed suffering somewhere on the far limit thereof. But inasmuch as there is withal cause here for rejoicing it lies in the status of all this as but authorization in respect of something still greater, namely a fresh meditation upon the taking up of exile in existence as its point of arrival.

---

6 'Thus the hostile image, as merciless as it is triumphant, dominates my will, and, besotted as it is with itself, causes me much as like is attracted to like to seek it out where most truly it is to be found. Only too well am I aware that this is snow seeking out the sun, but other than this I cannot do. I am like one who, under the sway of another, steps out of his own accord to the place of his death.'

PART IV

THE FINAL YEARS

The *Commedia*, the Political Letters
and the *Monarchia*, the *Questio*,
Cangrande and the *Eclogues*

CHAPTER 1

The *Commedia*

In a more than ordinarily exquisite moment of the *Purgatorio* Dante registers the journeying character of his own humanity and, as he understands it, the journeying character of humanity as a whole. To journey—or, more exactly, to journey significantly—is to set sail in anticipation of all that might be, but also to look back tenderly upon all that once was and upon all those most dearly cherished. Hope, like grace, abounds, but built into the pilgrim way is in this sense an element of melancholy, the melancholy of the evening hour and of the dying day:

> Era già l'ora che volge il disio
> ai navicanti e 'ntenerisce il core
> lo dì c'han detto ai dolci amici addio;
>   e che lo novo peregrin d'amore
> punge, se ode squilla di lontano
> che paia il giorno pianger che si more;
>   quand' io incominciai a render vano
> l'udire e a mirare una de l'alme
> surta, che l'ascoltar chiedea con mano.
>   Ella giunse e levò ambo le palme,
> ficcando li occhi verso l'orïente,
> come dicesse a Dio: 'D'altro non calme'.
>   'Te lucis ante' sì devotamente
> le uscìo di bocca e con sì dolci note,
> che fece me a me uscir di mente;
>   e l'altre poi dolcemente e devote
> seguitar lei per tutto l'inno intero,
> avendo li occhi a le superne rote.

> (*Purgatorio* 8.1–18)[1]

---

1 'It was now the hour in which the seafarer, having that day bidden his friends farewell, looks back in longing and with a tender heart—that same hour which pierces with love the new pilgrim should

That Dante's was indeed a journeying humanity—a humanity jealous in re-spect of everything gathered up and taken to heart along the way but nonetheless a venturing humanity—is confirmed no less eloquently by a late exchange of sonnets with his colleague, admirer and, as far at any rate as poetry and poetics are concerned, his principal beneficiary, Cino da Pistoia, the Cynus Pistoriensis representative of the postglossatorial school of Roman law culminating a gener-ation or so later with Bartolus of Sassoferrato. As a *stilnovista*, Cino's was and is a remarkable case, for his, in one and the same instant, was both a confirmation and a liquidation of the sweet new style, an honouring of the principal emphases both of the Cavalcantian and of the Dantean *stil novo* and yet at the same time a fashioning from them something quite other in kind, something more properly sentimental, more attuned to the case history, to love under the aspect of its suc-cessive episodes and shifting sensations. Exemplary in this sense is the sonnet *Veduto han gli occhi miei sì bella cosa*, a sonnet nicely transparent to the substance and psychology of Dante's praise style but turning now on love's sweet imagining and gentle perturbation:

> Veduto han gli occhi miei sì bella cosa,
> che dentro dal mio cor dipinta l'hanno,
> e se per veder lei tuttor no stanno,
> infin che non la trovan non han posa,
>   e fatt'han l'alma mia sì amorosa,
> che tutto corro in amoroso affanno,
> e quando col suo sguardo scontro fanno,
> toccan lo cor che sovra 'l ciel gir osa.
>   Fanno li occhi a lo mio core scorta,
> fermandol ne la fé d'amor più forte,
> quando risguardan lo su' novo viso;
>   e tanto passa in su' desiar fiso,
> che 'l dolce imaginar li daria morte,
> sed e' non fosse Amor che lo conforta.[2]

he hear in the distance a bell seeming to mourn the dying day—when, catching but vaguely Sordello's words to me, I gazed upon one of those souls now risen up and signalling his wish to be heard. Putting his hands together and raising them up, he looked to the east as if saying to God, "For naught else I care." From his lips issued a *Te lucis ante* with such piety and notes so sweet that I perforce came forth from myself, the other souls then joining with him, no less sweetly and piously, for the rest of the hymn, their eyes fixed the while upon the celestial spheres.'

2 'My eyes have seen a thing so beautiful that they have inscribed it upon my heart such that, should for a moment they not behold her, then until such time as they fall upon her afresh they have no peace; and of her they have so enamoured my soul that I am forever caught up in a state of amorous anxiety such that whenever I encounter her gaze they touch a heart bold in its venturing beyond the skies. Constant companions to my heart, they forever—upon once more glimpsing her wondrous counte-

And it was the reiterative character, if not of Cino's verse exactly (for Dante was not unappreciative of his style as a maker of love poems),[3] then of his comportment generally as a lover, his fickleness in love, that accounts for the note of impatience that at last creeps into their correspondence and that colours the final stages of an otherwise genial and indeed generous relationship. Cino, then, anxious to justify as far as may be yet a further distribution of his affections, had solicited in his sonnet *Dante, quando per caso s'abbandona* Dante's view of this as a way of going on, Dante as himself a susceptible lover replying in the first instance sympathetically. I, he says, who have lived with love ever since I was nine years old, know only too well its ineluctability. Be prepared, therefore, to follow your instinct in this matter:

> Io sono stato con Amore insieme
> da la circulazion del sol mia nona,
> e so com'egli affrena e come sprona,
> e come sotto lui si ride e geme.
> Chi ragione o virtù contra gli sprieme,

nance—strengthen its faith in love, and so firm is its desiring that her sweet imagining would, were it not for the comfort afforded by Love, be the death of it.' Maria Corti, 'Il linguaggio poetico di Cino da Pistoia', *CN* 12.3 (1952), 185–223; Domenico De Robertis, 'Cino e le "imitazioni" dalle rime di Dante', *SD* 29 (1950), 103–77; Domenico De Robertis, 'Cino da Pistoia e la crisi del linguaggio poetico', *Conv* 1 (1952), 1–35; Domenico De Robertis, 'Cino e Cavalcanti o le due rive della poesia', *SM* 18 (1952), 55–107; Guido Favati, 'Cino de Sinibuldi da Pistoia poeta', in *Letteratura e critica: Studi in onore di Natalino Sapegno*, vol. 1, ed. Walter Binni et al. (Rome: Bulzoni, 1974–77), 149–78; Guglielmo Gorni, 'Cino "vil ladro": Parola data e parola rubata', in *Il nodo della lingua e il verbo d'amore: Studi su Dante e altri duecentisti* (Florence: Olschki, 1981), 125–39; Robert Hollander, 'Dante and Cino da Pistoia', *DS* 110 (1992), 201–31; Christopher Kleinhenz, 'Cino da Pistoia and the Italian Lyric Tradition', in *L'imaginaire courtois et son double*, ed. Giovanna Angeli and Luciano Formisano (Naples: Edizioni Scientifiche Italiane, 1992), 147–63; Catherine Keen, 'Images of Exile: Distance and Memory in the Poetry of Cino da Pistoia', *ItSt* 55 (2000), 21–36; Catherine Keen, 'Cino da Pistoia and the Otherness of Exile', *AdI* 20 (2002), 89–112; Leyla M. G. Livraghi, 'Dante (e Cino) 1302–1306', *Tenzone* 13 (2012), 55–98. On Dante and Cino as lawyer, Domenico Maffei, 'Il pensiero di Cino da Pistoia sulla donazione di Costantino: Le sue fonti e il dissenso finale da Dante', *LC* 16 (1987), 119–27; Lorenzo Valterza, 'Dante's Justinian, Cino's "Corpus": The Hermeneutics of Poetry and Law', *MH* 37 (2011), 89–110. Otherwise on Cino *legista*, Gennaro Maria Monti, *Cino da Pistoia giurista: Con bibliografia e tre appendici di documenti inediti* (Città di Castello: Il Solco, 1924); Luigi Chiappelli, *Cino da Pistoia giurista: Gli scritti del 1881 e del 1910–11* (Pistoia: Società pistoiese di storia patria, 1999); Domenico Maffei, 'Cino da Pistoia e il *Constitutum Constantini*', *Annali dell'Università di Macerata* 24 (1961), 95–115; Domenico Maffei, *La Lectura super Digesto Veteri di Cino da Pistoia: Studio sui MSS Savigny 22 e Urb. Lat. 172* (Milan: Giuffrè, 1963); Domenico Maffei, *La Donazione di Costantino nei giuristi medievali* (Milan: Giuffrè, 1964).

3 *De vulgari eloquentia* 2.2.8: 'Circa que sola, si bene recolimus, illustres viros invenimus vulgariter poetasse, scilicet Bertramum de Bornio arma, Arnaldum Danielem amorem, Gerardum de Bornello rectitudinem; Cynum Pistoriensem amorem, amicum eius rectitudinem' (Concerning which, we find, if I remember rightly, a number of illustrious men busy writing poetry in the vernacular: Bertran de Born on arms, Arnaut Daniel on love, Giraut de Bornelh on virtue, not to mention Cino da Pistoia on love and his friend on righteousness). Maria Pica, 'Dante e l'"amicus eius": Per una rilettura di Cino', *EL* 19.1 (1994), 67–93.

fa come que' che 'n la tempesta sona,
credendo far colà dove si tona
esser le guerre de' vapori sceme.
    Però nel cerchio de la sua palestra
liber arbitrio già mai non fu franco,
sì che consiglio invan vi si balestra.
    Ben può con nuovi spron' punger lo fianco,
e qual che sia 'l piacer ch'ora n'addestra,
seguitar si convien, se l'altro è stanco.[4]

But somewhere in all this there is a note of weariness, of paths well trodden and of ways of seeing and understanding slipping now into the past. This, at any rate, is the gist of the final sonnet in this, the final phase of Dante's by now ample correspondence with Cino as long since a fellow traveller, a sonnet that for all its honouring a companionship cemented by the misfortune of exile signals a fresh departure, a casting of the net on the other side:

Io mi credea del tutto esser partito
da queste nostre rime, messer Cino,
ché si conviene omai altro cammino
a la mia nave più lungi dal lito;
    ma perch'i' ho di voi più volte udito
che pigliar vi lasciate a ogni uncino,
piacemi di prestare un pocolino
a questa penna lo stancato dito.
    Chi s'innamora sì come voi fate,
or qua or là, e sé lega e dissolve,
mostra ch'Amor leggermente il saetti.
    Però, se leggier cor così vi volve,
priego che con vertù il correggiate,
sì che s'accordi i fatti a' dolci detti.[5]

---

4 'I, who have kept company with Love since my ninth revolution of the sun, know well how he both reins in and spurs on, and how under his sway one laughs and languishes. He who urges reason or virtue against him is like one who, thinking to make a difference where the warring vapours or rolling thunder are concerned, raises his voice in a storm. Thus within his circling bounds free will was never free, wise counsel only ever loosing its shafts in vain there. Love can well prick the flank with new spurs, and so, whatever the pleasure now stirring within us, follow we must should the old be weary.' Leyla M. G. Livraghi, 'Eros e dottrina nel sonetto dantesco *Io sono stato con amore insieme*', in *Alma Dante: Seminario Dantesco*, ed. Giuseppe Ledda and Filippo Zanini (Bolgona: Aspasia, 2015), 67–85.

5 'I truly thought, Messer Cino, to have left behind this poetry of ours, for now my ship, further as it is from the shore, must keep to a different course. But since I have heard that yet again you have

It is, then, by way of what amounts to a quantum leap of the spirit that, entirely without prejudice to his ancient allegiances (Cino among them), Dante sets about shaping and substantiating afresh his existence as a creature of ultimate accountability, embarking as he does so on the lonely way of self-encounter, self-reconfiguration and self-transcendence as the root meaning of hell, purgatory and paradise as structures of moral and ontological awareness. Nor is that all, for having by this stage tried, tested and made his own every expressive register available to him, he is in a position now to call upon form in the totality thereof as the in-and-through-which of elucidation at the point of ultimate concern. Companionship, then, to be sure, the *in-youing* and *in-meing* of self and the other-than-self subsisting still as an object of contemplation and a cause for rejoicing; but for all the blessing thereof it is, in truth, a question now of standing alone in respect of that which matters alone.

THE COMMEDIA À LA LETTRE

In the midst of his days, he says—the 'in dimidio dierum meorum' of Isaiah 38— Dante found himself lost to the reasons of his humanity, to the kind of settled purpose making for an orderly act of existence. Far-wandering and challenged by the forces of annihilation at work from deep within him (the lion, the leopard and the wolf of the first canto of the *Inferno*), he knows himself only in the nightmare sensation of disorientation, fear, inexplicability and, as the boundary condition of all these things and indeed of the psychopathology generally of hell, despair (the 'ch'io perdei la speranza de l'altezza' of line 54). Giving up, then, on the possibility of any escape to the sunlit uplands, he encounters in the depths of the dark wood the shadowy figure of the Roman poet Virgil, who, as himself a singer of significant voyaging, urges upon him as uniquely adequate to this situation a threefold journey down into the pit there to behold the completeness of man's degradation as a creature of moral and eschatological accountability, across the terraces of Mount Purgatory there to behold the struggle for a reshaping of self on the plane of properly human loving, and through the circling spheres of paradise there to behold the rejoicing of the elect in the immediate presence of their maker. Prey to begin with to every kind of doubt relative to the wisdom of it all but reassured by Virgil's account of Beatrice's concern for him

---

allowed yourself to be caught on hook after hook, I am willing albeit briefly to put my tired fingers to the pen. Anyone falling in love as you do, now here now there, binding and loosing himself as he does so, shows that Love strikes him but mildly. So if you are whirled about by a fickle heart, I beg you look to it in conscience so that your deeds match your sweet words.' John Took, 'The Still Centre of Concern and Communicability: Dante, Cino and Their Non-Correspondence', *JIRS* 6 (1998), 43–59; Raffaele Pinto, 'La poetica dell'esilio e la tenzone con Cino', *Tenzone* 10 (2009), 41–73.

in the high consistory of paradise, the pilgrim poet thus begins his descent, his first encounter, however, being not so much with the renegade spirits precisely as such as (*a*) with those who, being in a position to choose, chose not to, opting instead for a life of indifference and neutrality, and (*b*) with those who, living as they did either before or beyond the Christian dispensation, were not for that reason and in that sense in a position to choose at all. On the one hand, then, we have the *ignavi* or morally indolent, busy, certainly, but insignificantly so, and to that extent never fully alive:

> E io, che riguardai, vidi una 'nsegna
> che girando correva tanto ratta,
> che d'ogne posa mi parea indegna;
>   e dietro le venìa sì lunga tratta
> di gente, ch'i' non averei creduto
> che morte tanta n'avesse disfatta.
>   Poscia ch'io v'ebbi alcun riconosciuto,
> vidi e conobbi l'ombra di colui
> che fece per viltade il gran rifiuto.
>   Incontanente intesi e certo fui
> che questa era la setta d'i cattivi,
> a Dio spiacenti e a' nemici sui.
>   Questi sciaurati, che mai non fur vivi,
> erano ignudi e stimolati molto
> da mosconi e da vespe ch'eran ivi.
>   Elle rigavan lor di sangue il volto,
> che, mischiato di lagrime, a' lor piedi
> da fastidiosi vermi era ricolto.

> (*Inferno* 3.52–69)[6]

---

6 'And I, looking, saw a banner, which, whirling as it went, raced on so swiftly that it seemed to me impatient of any pause, and behind it came so long a train of folk that I would never have believed death had undone so many. After I had recognized some among them, I saw and knew the shade of him who through fear renounced his own high calling, whereupon I at once understood with perfect certainty that this was the evil crew displeasing both to God and to his enemies. Never really alive, these wretched spirits were stung in their nakedness by the hornets and wasps about them, the blood and tears from their faces flowing together to be gathered up by the loathsome worms at their feet.' Steno Vazzana, 'Chi sono gli ignavi?', *L'Alighieri (RBD)* 30.1 (1989), 3–14; Marcia L. Colish, ' "Sanza 'nfamia e sanza lodo": Moral Neutrality from Alan of Lille to Dante', in *Alain de Lille, le docteur universel: Philosophie, théologie et littérature au XIIe siècle. Actes du XIe Colloque international de la Société International pour l'Étude de la Philosophie Médiévale, Paris 23–25 octobre 2003*, ed. Jean-Luc Solère et al. (Turnhout: Brepols, 2005), 263–73; Roberto Mercuri, 'Pusillanimi e magnanimi alle soglie dell'*Inferno*', *LL* 33.1–2 (2008), 43–90.

while on the other hand, and subsisting in a state less of suffering than of sadness, we have the limbic spirits consisting (*a*) of unbaptized infants (the *limbus puerorum*); (*b*) and at any rate up until the Easter Saturday harrowing of hell, of the Old Testament prophets and patriarchs (the *limbus patrum*); and (*c*) of the virtuous pagans, of those who, having been born out of season and thus knowing not the Christ, live on by way only of an ever unfulfilled yearning:

> Lo buon maestro a me: 'Tu non dimandi
> che spiriti son questi che tu vedi?
> Or vo' che sappi, innanzi che più andi,
>   ch'ei non peccaro; e s'elli hanno mercedi,
> non basta, perché non ebber battesmo,
> ch'è porta de la fede che tu credi;
>   e s'e' furon dinanzi al cristianesmo,
> non adorar debitamente a Dio;
> e di questi cotai son io medesmo.
>   Per tai difetti, non per altro rio,
> semo perduti, e sol di tanto offesi
> che sanza speme vivemo in disio'.
>   Gran duol mi prese al cor quando lo 'ntesi,
> però che gente di molto valore
> conobbi che 'n quel limbo eran sospesi.

(*Inferno* 4.31–45)[7]

7 'And then my good master to me: "You ask not who these spirits are that you see? I would have you know before you go any further that these were not sinners, and that if aught they merit it is not enough, for they were without the baptism which for you is a gateway to the faith. And if they were before the Gospel, they did not worship God aright. Of such as these am I myself. For such defects and nothing worse we are lost and afflicted only insofar as, without hope, we live on in desire." Great sadness came upon me in hearing this, for I knew many of much worth to be suspended in that limbo.' Giorgio Padoan, 'Il limbo dantesco', *LI* 21 (1969), 369–88 (and in *Il pio Enea, l'impio Ulisse* [Ravenna: Longo, 1977], 103–24); Kenelm Foster, 'The Two Dantes (I). Limbo and Implicit Faith', in *The Two Dantes and Other Studies* (London: Darton, Longman and Todd, 1977), 156–89; Amilcare A. Iannucci, 'Limbo: The Emptiness of Time', *SD* 52 (1978), 69–128; Amilcare A. Iannucci, 'Dante's Limbo: At the Margins of Orthodoxy', in *Dante and the Unorthodox: The Aesthetics of Transgression*, ed. James Miller (Waterloo, Ontario: Wilfred Laurier University Press, 2005), 63–82 (and ad voc. in Richard Lansing [ed.], *The Dante Encyclopedia* [New York: Garland], 565–69); Giorgio Varanini, 'Il canto dei magnanimi (*Inferno* IV)', in *Lingua e letteratura italiana dei primi secoli*, vol. 2, ed. Luigi Banfi et al. (Pisa: Giardini, 1994), 347–62; Manlio Pastore Stocchi, 'Canto IV: A Melancholy Elysium', in *Lectura Dantis: 'Inferno'. A Canto-by-Canto Commentary*, ed. Allen Mandelbaum et al. (Berkeley: University of California Press, 1998), 50–62; Luigi Peirone, 'Il desiderio nel limbo dantesco', *LIA* 11 (2010), 339–43; John Marenbon, '*Inferno* IV: Virtuous Pagans, Hopeless Desire and Unjust Justice', in *Vertical Readings in Dante's Comedy*, ed. George Corbett and Heather Webb (Cambridge: Open Book, 2015), 77–95.

True, there is here in Limbo, and for the pilgrim poet personally, a moment of rejoicing, for it is here that Dante registers his status as sixth in succession to the poetic luminaries of antiquity, to Homer, Horace, Ovid, Lucan and Virgil himself as but members of one and the same family (the 'e più d'onore ancora assai mi fenno, / ch'e' sì mi fecer de la loro schiera, / sì ch'io fui sesto tra cotanto senno' of lines 100–102).[8] But for all its exhilaration there can be no softening either of the substance or of the sadness of this episode, of the former in respect of its implications for a general soteriology or theology of salvation and of the latter in respect of, as Dante understands it, the fate of those most decisive for his coming about both as a poet and as a philosopher. In both senses the pathos is intense.[9]

With what amounts, then, to an account of those in a position to choose but choosing not to (the greater part, it would seem, of mankind generally, for 'never would I have imagined that death had undone so many'), and of those through no fault of their own having no real choice, we come, if not as yet to malice aforethought, then to something closer to self-forgetfulness, to an inveterate making over of reason to desire (the 'peccator carnali, / che la ragion sommettono al talento' of 5.38–39)—in short, to intemperance as a condition of the spirit. First, then, in the second circle of hell, come the lustful and the adulterous, those who, having surrendered to the lusts of the flesh, are now and forever more borne upon the wings of the wind as but a figural fulfilment of their tempestuous existence,

---

8 'And, I, by them, was all the more honoured in that I was counted but one of them, sixth among such sapient spirits.' Luca Carlo Rossi, 'Canto IV: Autoincoronazione poetica nel limbo', in *Lectura Dantis Romana*, vol. 1, ed. Enrico Malato and Andrea Mazzucchi (Rome: Salerno, 2013), 131–61.

9 Francesco Ruffini, 'Dante e il problema della salvezza degli infedeli', *SD* 14 (1930), 79–92; Brunetto Quilici, *Il destino dell'infidele virtuoso nel pensiero di Dante* (Florence: Ariani, 1936); Raffaello Morghen, 'Dante tra l'"umano" e la storia della salvezza', in *L'Alighieri (RBD)* 21.1 (1980), 18–30; Nicolae Iliescu, 'Will Virgil Be Saved?', *Med* 12 (1986), 93–114 (and as 'Sarà salvo Virgilio?', in *Dante: Summa medievalis. Proceedings of the Symposium of the Center for Italian Studies, SUNY Stony Brook*, ed. Charles Franco and Leslie Morgan [Stony Brook, NY: Forum Italicum, 1995], 112–33); Mowbray Allan, 'Does Dante Hope for Vergil's Salvation?', *MLN* 104 (1989), 193–205; Cindy L. Vitto, 'The Virtuous Pagan in Legend and in Dante', in *The Virtuous Pagan in Middle English Literature* (Philadelphia: American Philosophical Society, 1989), 36–49; Teodolinda Barolini, 'Q: Does Dante Hope for Vergil's Salvation?', *MLN* 105.1 (1990), 138–44 and 147–49 (and in *Dante and the Origins of Italian Literary Culture* [New York: Fordham University Press, 2006], 151–57); Norberto Cacciaglia, ' "Per fede e per opere" (una lettura del tema della salvezza nella *Divina Commedia*)', *CL* 30.2–3 (2002), 265–74 (also *AUSP* 29 [2002], 123–31); Adriano Lanza, 'Giustizia divina e salvezza dei "senza fede"', in *Dante eterodosso: Una diversa lettura della 'Commedia'* (Bergamo: Moretti Honegger, 2004), 113–24; Christine O'Connell Baur, *Dante's Hermeneutics of Salvation: Passages to Freedom in the Divine Comedy* (Toronto: University of Toronto Press, 2007); Marcia L. Colish, 'The Virtuous Pagan: Dante and the Christian Tradition', in *The Fathers and Beyond: Church Fathers between Ancient and Medieval Thought* (Aldershot: Ashgate, 2008), 1–40. More generally on the soteriological issue in and beyond the High Middle Ages, Louis Capéran, *Le Problème du salut des infidèles*, 2 vols., rev. ed. (Toulouse: Grand Séminaire, 1934); Mario Frezza, *Il problema della salvezza dei pagani (da Abelardo al Seicento)* (Naples: Fiorentino, 1962); Ralph V. Turner, ' "Descendit ad Inferos": Medieval Views on Christ's Descent into Hell and the Salvation of the Ancient Just', *JHI* 27 (1966), 173–94; John Marenbon, *Pagans and Philosophers: The Problem of Paganism from Augustine to Leibniz* (Princeton: Princeton University Press, 2015).

these in turn being followed in the third circle by the gluttonous who, sodden beneath a darkling sky and cowered by the three-headed monster Cerberus, lie prostrate in the mire of their own making. In the fourth circle, by contrast, come the avaricious (a largely tonsured constituency) and the prodigal, each alike struggling Sisyphus-like to shift a well-nigh unshiftable boulder and intoning all the while their grim liturgy of indictment and counterindictment (the 'Perché tieni?' e 'Perché burli?' of 7.30).[10] And then finally as far as the intemperate are concerned, and immersed now in the slimy waters of the Styx, come the angry, where by anger we mean not so much, indeed not at all, the anger of the moment but rather that born of a biting back of self in the innermost recesses of self (the 'e 'l fiorentino spirito bizzarro / in sé medesmo si volvea co' denti' of 8.62–63),[11] at which point the fundamentally tragic substance of Dante's discourse hereabouts in the poem—the truth of *social* alienation as but the outward form of *self-alienation*—moves fully and unequivocally into view.

Descending still further into the pit we come next to the violent, to those moved less by self-forgetfulness and an indiscipline of the spirit than by malevolence, a group preceded in Dante's scheme of things by the heretics and heresiarchs represented here by the Epicureans, by those inclined to deny the immortality of the soul. In fact, it is a question here less of heresy stricto sensu (though it *is* that as well) than of obduracy, divisiveness and partisanship as the dominant mood of being, Farinata degli Uberti, Dante's spokesman-in-chief hereabouts, representing these things in their now pure form. His, then, is but a fiery tomb destined once and for all to be sealed on the day of judgement, the Epicureans, having thus sown the wind, reaping now the whirlwind.[12] With what amounts,

10 'What's with you hoarding?' and 'What's with you squandering?' Michele D'Andria, 'Dinamica della pena di avari e prodighi', in *Il volo cosmico di Dante e altri saggi per un nuovo commento della 'Divina Commedia'* (Rome: Edizioni dell'Ateneo, 1985), 169–90; Giovanni Bardazzi, 'Avari e prodighi, iracondi e accidiosi', *SD* 65 (2000), 1–39; Maria Luisa Doglio, 'Sul canto VII dell'*Inferno*: Avarizia e accidia; Vizi capitali e "gente" senza identità umana; Abruttimento e fango', in *Studi per Gian Paolo Marchi*, ed. Raffaella Bertazzoli et al. (Pisa: ETS, 2011), 339–51 (and in *"Più aperto intendi ancora": Tre letture dantesche* [Rome: Edizioni di Storia e Letteratura, 2015], 3–18); Roberto Rea, '*La paura della lupa e le forme dell'ira (lettura di 'Inferno' VII)*', *LL* 41.1–2 (2016), 79–110. For the gluttonous, Michele Rinaldi, 'Canto VI: "L'ombre che adona la greve pioggia": "Per la dannosa colpa de la gola"', in *Lectura Dantis Romana*, vol. 1, ed. Enrico Malato and Andrea Mazzucchi (Rome: Salerno, 2013), 206–38. For the 'never would I have imagined that death had undone so many' moment of the argument, the 'ch'i' non averei creduto / che morte tanta n'avesse disfatta' of *Inferno* 3.56–57.

11 'with which the frantic Florentine spirit turned his teeth upon himself'. Lodovico Cardellino, 'Ciacco e Filippo Argenti', in *Autocritica infernale* (Milan: Jaca Book, 1992), 207–21; Caron Ann Cioffi, 'Canto VIII: Fifth Circle; Wrathful and Sullen', in *Lectura Dantis: Inferno. A Canto-by-Canto Commentary*, ed. Allen Mandelbaum et al. (Berkeley: University of California Press, 1998), 111–21; Claudia Galfrè, 'Gli iracondi dell'*Inferno*', *CI* 30–31 (2004), 5–42.

12 Italo Borzi, 'Farinata degli Uberti: La tragedia degli odi civili nell'*Inferno* di Dante', *L'Alighieri (RBD)* 27.2 (1986), 23–46. On the Epicurean aspect of the canto, Giorgio Santangelo, 'Il canto degli epicurei', in *Dante e la Sicilia* (Palermo: S. F. Flaccovio, 1985), 73–101; Eric Brown, 'Epicurean Secularism in Dante and Boccaccio: Athenian Roots and Florentine Revival', in *Magister regis: Studies in Honor of*

then, to an essay in over-againstness as but a steady habit of mind, we come to the violent proper, to the violent against others (namely the variously despotic) as immersed in a river of blood according to the depth and depravity of their piti-lessness, to the violent against themselves and their inheritance (the suicidal and the profligate) as respectively bereft of the body they themselves forsook and torn limb from limb by the hellhounds forever snapping at their heels, and the violent against God, nature and art (the blasphemers, the sodomites and the usurers) as hostage to the abominable sand of sterility. Here as throughout, then, the pattern is the same, the surface equivalences of Dante's discourse, his careful coordination of the *what was* and of the *what now is* in the experience of the renegade spirit serving to confirm once and for all the continuity and indeed the identity of these things, the status of the latter as but the former under the aspect of ultimate affirmation.[13]

But there is, alas, more to come, for still on the downward way the pilgrim poet is confronted by something still more serious—more serious in the degree to which fraudulence is more serious than violence; for while violence is little more

---

Robert Earl Kaske, ed. Arthur Groos (New York: Fordham University Press, 1986), 179–93; Dino Bigongiari, 'The Florentine Epicureans: Farinata degli Uberti and Cavalcanti', in *Readings in the 'Divine Comedy'. A Series of Lectures* (Dover, DE: Griffon House, 2006), 72–84; George Corbett, *Dante and Epicurus: A Dualistic Vision of Secular and Spiritual Fulfilment* (London: Legenda, 2013).

13 In general on the circles of violence, Richard H. Lansing, 'Dante's Concept of Violence and the Chain of Being', DS 99 (1981), 67–87; Marcello Aurigemma, 'I gironi dei violenti: Pier della Vigna e Brunetto Latini', in *Lectura Modenese: 'Inferno'*, ed. Società Dante Alighieri (Modena: Banca Popolare dell'Emilia, 1984), 125–37; Giuseppe Giacalone, 'Dante personaggio e poeta nei gironi della violenza', in *Dante Alighieri: La Divina Commedia*, vol. 1, ed. Giuseppe Giacalone (Rome: Signorelli, 1988), 14–33; Mario Apollonio, 'Rapsodia dei violenti', in *Dante: Storia della 'Commedia'*, ed. Carlo Annoni and Corrado Viola (Novara: Interlinea, 2013), 49–66; Giuseppe Mazzotta, '*Inferno* 12–16', in *Reading Dante* (New Haven: Yale University Press, 2014), 66–77. More especially on the violent against others (the variously tyrannical), Vittorio Russo, 'Canto XII: The Violent against Their Neighbours', in *Lectura Dantis: Inferno. A Canto-by-Canto Commentary*, ed. Allen Mandelbaum et al. (Berkeley: University of California Press, 1998), 165–77. On the violent against self (the suicidal and the profligate), Rodney J. Payton, 'Canto XIII: Pier delle Vigne; The Sin of Despair', in *A Modern Reader's Guide to Dante's 'Inferno'* (New York: Peter Lang, 1992), 97–105; Alexander Murray, *Suicide in the Middle Ages: Volume I; The Violent against Themselves* (Oxford: Oxford University Press, 1998; with reprints); Giorgio Petrocchi, 'Canto XIII: The Violent against Themselves', *Lectura Dantis: Inferno. A Canto-by-Canto Commentary*, 178–84; Antonio Marzo, 'I violenti contro sé e le proprie cose. Lettura del canto XIII dell'*Inferno*', in *Lectura Dantis Lupiensis*, ed. Valerio Marucci et al. (Ravenna: Longo, 2013), 39–72. On the violent against nature, but touching upon the precise interpretation to be placed upon this and a number of other cantos in the *Commedia* bearing upon the homoerotic component of the text (notably *Purgatorio* 26), André Pézard, *Dante sous la pluie de feu* (Paris: Vrin, 1950); Peter Armour, 'Dante's Brunetto: The Paternal Paterine?', *ItSt* 38 (1983), 1–38; Joseph Pequigney, 'Sodomy in Dante's *Inferno* and *Purgatorio*', *Representations* 39 (1991), 22–42; John E. Boswell, 'Dante and the Sodomites', DS 112 (1994), 63–76; Richard Kay, 'The Sin(s) of Brunetto Latini', DS 112 (1994), 19–31; Deborah L. Contrada, 'Brunetto's Sin: Ten Years of Criticism (1977–1986)', in *Dante: Summa medievalis. Proceedings of the Symposium of the Center for Italian Studies, SUNY Stony Brook*, ed. Charles Franco and Leslie Morgan (Stony Brook, NY: Forum Italicum, 1995), 192–207; Adriano Lanza, 'Brunetto Latini e la sodomia (canto XV)', in *Dante all'inferno: I misteri eretici della 'Commedia'* (Rome: Tre Editori, 1999), 117–33.

than bestiality by another name, fraudulence, involving as it does an affront to the kind of reasonableness making for one man's standing creatively in the presence of another, is as Dante himself says a properly human pathology, a uniquely human condition (the 'frode è de l'uom proprio male' of 11.25). Bit by bit, then, and beginning with his descent into the depths on the back of Geryon as but the very embodiment of disingenuousness (a benign countenance and a scorpion's tail), the Dante figure is confirmed in a still more complete sense of human depravity, the image, as always, carrying all before, and, in carrying all before, finessing the plain statement in point of analytical power and precision. First, then, in the ten *malebolge* or circumambient ditches of the eighth circle containing the representatives of simple deception—of the kind of deception, that is to say, perpetrated on the innocent victim—come the panders and seducers, the scourge of the unsuspecting now themselves scourged for their particular kind of cruelty; the flatterers ever ready to coax and to cajole but immersed now in the ordure of their own making; the simonists or traders in ecclesiastical office stuffed topsy-turvy into a fissure of rock and tortured by a 'tongue like as of fire' playing, not now about their head but about their heels; the soothsayers, their heads twisted backwards in a grim parody of their profession; the barrators or traders in public office immersed to a man in the sticky pitch of their secrecy and collusion; the hypocrites, dazzlingly attired but in truth weighed down by the leaden substance of their stoles; the thieves who, indifferent to the mine and thine of collective consciousness, know themselves now by way only of the most atrocious kind of metamorphosis, of an endless making and unmaking of intelligible selfhood; the false counsellors, manipulators par excellence of the word as a means of honest exchange but captive now to the flame of their own rhetoric; the sowers of discord, mutilators of every kind of civilized relationship in human affairs but now, their tripes tumbling forth, themselves cruelly sundered; and the falsifiers and impersonators, their scabrous form and putrid presence in the stinking recesses of the last ditch testifying to a humanity in the final throes of decay. Whether any one of these things, in Dante's arrangement of them, is in truth worse than any other is neither here nor there, for at every stage it is a question of the lovelessness of it all, of a shattering of the 'vinco d'amor' or love-chain whereby one man is ideally bound to another in a spirit of mutual concern.[14] And it is the notion of

14 On the circles of fraud generally, Colin A. McCormick, 'The Ordering of Sins in the Eighth Circle of the *Inferno*', in *The Shared Horizon*, ed. Tom O'Neill (Dublin: Irish Academic Press, 1990), 1–12; James C. Nohrnberg, 'The Descent of Geryon: The Moral System of *Inferno* XVI–XXXI', *DS* 114 (1996), 129–87; James C. Nohrnberg, 'Canto XVIII: Introduction to Malebolge', *Lectura Dantis: Inferno. A Canto-by-Canto Commentary*, ed. Allen Mandelbaum et al. (Berkeley: University of California Press, 1998), 238–61; Michelangelo Picone, 'Attraverso le Malebolge dantesche', in *L'Inferno di Dante. Atti della giornata di studi (19 gennaio 2004)*, ed. Paolo Grossi (Paris: Istituto Italiano di Cultura, 2004), 65–94; Dino Bigongiari, 'Lower Hell: Malebolge', in *Readings in the 'Divine Comedy'. A Series of Lectures* (Dover, DE: Griffon House, 2006), 158–72; Mario Apollonio, 'La città della frode', in *Dante: Storia della*

lovelessness in the now unclouded truth thereof that dominates the final part of the canticle, for here, where fraudulence shades off into treachery, it is a question of the stilling of every creative and recreative impulse, of the tearing down and indeed of the liquidation of everything in human experience making for the unity of the Spirit in the bond of peace. True, the treacherous, like the fraudulent pure and simple, are various: traitors to their family in the region of Caina (after the biblical Cain who slew his brother), traitors to their country in the region of Antenora (after the Antenor who betrayed Troy to the Greeks), traitors to their guests in the region of Ptolomaea (after the Ptolemy who slew the high priest in the books of Maccabees), and traitors to their lords in the region of Judecca (after the Judas who betrayed God himself in the person of the Christ). But for all their otherness one in respect of another they are all of them captive now to the frozen wastes of the pit in its farthest reaches, the frozen wastes of the pit in its farthest reaches being in truth but the now petrified substance of their own humanity. With this, then, as preparatory to the pilgrim's embarking at last on the upward way, it remains only to gaze for a moment—mesmerically—upon the figure of Lucifer (erstwhile son of the morning and bearer of light) as he flays in his three-fold jaw Brutus, Cassius and Judas as the archtraitors of world history, an essay, to be sure, in defiance and despair, in impudence and impiety, in lovelessness and lifelessness, but over and above these things and as the encompassing hereabouts in the sheer banality of it all:

> Lo 'mperador del doloroso regno
> da mezzo 'l petto uscia fuor de la ghiaccia;
> e più con un gigante io mi convegno,
>   che i giganti non fan con le sue braccia:
> vedi oggimai quant' esser dee quel tutto
> ch'a così fatta parte si confaccia.
>   S'el fu sì bel com' elli è ora brutto,
> e contra 'l suo fattore alzò le ciglia,
> ben dee da lui procedere ogne lutto.
>   Oh quanto parve a me gran maraviglia
> quand' io vidi tre facce a la sua testa!
> L'una dinanzi, e quella era vermiglia;
>   l'altr' eran due, che s'aggiugnieno a questa
> sovresso 'l mezzo di ciascuna spalla,
> e sé giugnieno al loco de la cresta:

'Commedia', ed. Carlo Annoni and Corrado Viola (Novara: Interlinea, 2013), 67–76; Enrico Rebuffat, '"Luogo è in inferno detto Malebolge": Una ricerca di topografia dantesca', L'Alighieri (RD) 41 (2013), 32–62.

e la destra parea tra bianca e gialla;
la sinistra a vedere era tal, quali
vegnon di là onde 'l Nilo s'avvalla.

Sotto ciascuna uscivan due grand' ali,
quanto si convenia a tanto uccello:
vele di mar non vid' io mai cotali.

Non avean penne, ma di vispistrello
era lor modo; e quelle svolazzava,
sì che tre venti si movean da ello:

quindi Cocito tutto s'aggelava.
Con sei occhi piangëa, e per tre menti
gocciava 'l pianto e sanguinosa bava.

Da ogne bocca dirompea co' denti
un peccatore, a guisa di maciulla,
sì che tre ne facea così dolenti.

A quel dinanzi il mordere era nulla
verso 'l graffiar, che talvolta la schiena
rimanea de la pelle tutta brulla.

'Quell' anima là sù c'ha maggior pena',
disse 'l maestro, 'è Giuda Scarïotto,
che 'l capo ha dentro e fuor le gambe mena.

De li altri due c'hanno il capo di sotto,
quel che pende dal nero ceffo è Bruto:
vedi come si storce, e non fa motto!;

e l'altro è Cassio, che par sì membruto.
Ma la notte risurge, e oramai
è da partir, ché tutto avem veduto'.

(*Inferno* 34.28–69)[15]

---

15 'The emperor of the woeful realm from midbreast stood proud of the ice, and—for that you may see how the whole relates here to the part—I myself compare better with a giant than a giant with his arms. If, then, lifting his brow against his maker, he was once as fair as he is now foul then well may all sorrow proceed from him. Ah, how great my astonishment when I saw upon his head three faces, the one in front all ruddy, and the other two conjoined with it above the middle of each shoulder and at the crown. The one on the right seemed something between white and yellow and the one on the left complexioned after the manner of those where rises the Nile. Beneath each alike—and never sails at sea have I seen of the kind—issued two great wings befitting in size to such a bird, though bereft as they were of feathers more like those of a bat, and he was beating them such that the three winds coming forth from him kept frozen all Cocytus. With his six eyes he wept and over his three chins dripped tears and bloody saliva. In each mouth was a sinner crushed heckle-like with his teeth, all three thus preserved in their agony, though to him in front the biting was nothing relative to the clawing, his spine at times stripped of all skin. "The soul there above suffering the most", said my master, "is Judas Iscariot, his head within and his legs without. Of the other two, the one dangling from the black muzzle is Brutus

If, then, the *Inferno* is the canticle of captivity, of self as prisoner to the alternative project, the *Purgatorio*—the beautiful *Purgatorio*—is the canticle of emancipation, of the soul's freeing itself for the kind of transhumanity (the 'trasumanar' of *Paradiso* 1.70) present to it as the most radiant of its radiant possibilities. Thus liberty, the setting free of the soul for what actually matters about it, stands both at the beginning and at the end of Dante's discourse in this second part of the poem, shaping and substantiating as it does so his each and every successive emphasis along the way. On the one hand, then, and turning precisely on the notion of liberty as the final cause of all properly human striving, we have Virgil's words to Cato at the beginning of the canticle requesting permission to begin the ascent:

> Mostrata ho lui tutta la gente ria;
> e ora intendo mostrar quelli spirti
> che purgan sé sotto la tua balìa.
>   Com' io l'ho tratto, saria lungo a dirti;
> de l'alto scende virtù che m'aiuta
> conducerlo a vederti e a udirti.
>   Or ti piaccia gradir la sua venuta:
> libertà va cercando, ch'è sì cara,
> come sa chi per lei vita rifiuta.

(*Purgatorio* 1.64–72)[16]

while on the other we have these lines towards the end of the canticle confirming the pilgrim in a sense of his now perfect self-possession as a creature of reasonable willing, self-possession, Dante has Virgil say, at once kingly and clerical in kind:

(see how he writhes without a word), and the other, stalwart to behold, is Cassius. But night arises once more and it is time to go, for we have seen all." ' Anthony K. Cassell, 'The Tomb, the Tower and the Pit: Dante's Satan', *Italica* 56 (1979), 331–51; Dino Cervigni, 'Dante's Lucifer: The Denial of the World', *LD* 3 (1988), 51–62; Dino Cervigni, 'The Muted Self-Referentiality of Dante's Lucifer', *DS* 107 (1989), 45–74; Dino Bigongiari, 'Lucider/Satan, the Greatest Betrayer', in *Readings in the 'Divine Comedy'. A Series of Lectures*, ed. Anne Paolucci (Dover, DE: Griffon House, 2006), 199–209. More generally, Jeffrey Burton Russell, *Lucifer: The Devil in the Middle Ages* (Ithaca: Cornell University Press,1984); Annalisa Pirastu, 'Dante, il diavolo, i diavoli', in *Il diavolo nei primi secoli della letteratura italiana* (Cosenza: Pellegrini, 2004), 45–89; Laura Pasquini, 'La rappresentazione di Lucifero in Dante e nell'iconografia medievale', in *"Il mondo errante": Dante fra letteratura, eresia e storia. Atti del Convegno Internazionale di Studio Bertinoro, 13–16 settembre 2010*, ed. Marco Veglia et al. (Spoleto: Centro italiano di studi sull'alto medioevo, 2013), 267–88.

16 'I have shown him all the guilty and propose now to show him those spirits cleansing themselves under your charge. How I have brought him here would take too long to tell, the power whereby I lead him thus to see and to hear your words coming from on high. May it please you, then, to look graciously upon his being here, for he comes seeking liberty, the liberty which, as he who gives his life for it knows full well, is so very precious.' Giuseppe Godenzi, 'Libertà va cercando, ch'è sì cara', *Quaderni grigionitaliani* 56 (1987), 67–75; Andrea Maia, 'Libertà va cercando', *SV* 4 (2003), 183–93.

Tratto t'ho qui con ingegno e con arte;
lo tuo piacere omai prendi per duce;
fuor se' de l'erte vie, fuor se' de l'arte.
    Vedi lo sol che 'n fronte ti riluce;
vedi l'erbette, i fiori e li arbuscelli
che qui la terra sol da sé produce.
    Mentre che vegnan lieti li occhi belli
che, lagrimando, a te venir mi fenno,
seder ti puoi e puoi andar tra elli.
    Non aspettar mio dir più né mio cenno;
libero, dritto e sano è tuo arbitrio,
e fallo fora non fare a suo senno:
    per ch'io te sovra te corono e mitrio.

(*Purgatorio* 27.130–42)[17]

But liberty thus understood—as the freeing of self for its own highest possibility—is accomplished only at a price, that price being the most far-reaching kind of self-reconfiguration on the plane of loving, and, as the prior and necessary condition of these things, the most complete kind of self-recognition, a taking into self of the unglossed truth of self. This, then, is where Dante begins in this second canticle of the *Commedia*. He begins with an 'ante-purgatory' of his own invention designed, precisely, to stress the thoughtfulness of it all, the fresh and more than ever intense encounter of self with self as preliminary in respect of everything coming next by way of purgatory proper; so, for example, among the excommunicate, the late repentant, the unshriven and the indolent on the lower slopes of the mountain, we have the case of Manfred, more than ever eloquent in acknowledging in anticipation of the discipline proper of purgatory the depth of his guilt and the wideness of God's mercy:

Io mi volsi ver' lui e guardail fiso:
biondo era e bello e di gentile aspetto,
ma l'un de' cigli un colpo avea diviso.
    Quand' io mi fui umilmente disdetto

---

17 'Thus far, with skill and art, I have brought you, but take henceforth your own pleasure as your guide, for you are now come forth from the steep and narrow way. See there the sun shining upon your brow; see the grass, the flowers and the arbours which of itself the earth produces. Until those beautiful eyes come with gladness—the eyes which, weeping, made me first come to you—you may sit or else wander as you please among them. Expect neither word nor sign from me more, for free, upright and sound is your own will and other than to do its bidding would now be folly, wherefore I crown and mitre you over yourself.' Mira Mocan, 'Le ultime parole di Virgilio: Su *Purgatorio* XXVII.142', CT 13.2 (2010), 211–34; Mira Mocan, 'Il libero arbitrio "sovrano"', in *L'arca della mente: Riccardo di San Vittore nella 'Commedia' di Dante* (Florence: Olschki, 2012), 141–64.

d'averlo visto mai, el disse: 'Or vedi';
e mostrommi una piaga a sommo 'l petto.
   Poi sorridendo disse: 'Io son Manfredi,
nepote di Costanza imperadrice;
ond' io ti priego che, quando tu riedi,
   vadi a mia bella figlia, genitrice
de l'onor di Cicilia e d'Aragona,
e dichi 'l vero a lei, s'altro si dice.
   Poscia ch'io ebbi rotta la persona
di due punte mortali, io mi rendei,
piangendo, a quei che volontier perdona.
   Orribil furon li peccati miei;
ma la bontà infinita ha sì gran braccia,
che prende ciò che si rivolge a lei'.

(Purgatorio 3.106–23)[18]

With what amounts, then, to an encounter with self in the recesses of self, an encounter now mercifully free from every kind of self-evasion as the sole means of standing significantly (indeed of standing at all) in its own presence—the process proper of purgation gets under way, a process conceived by Dante as a matter of bringing home every contingent love-impulse of the spirit to the love given with the act itself of existence and thus making for communion with the One who *is* as of the essence. On each successive terrace of the mountain, then, the soul is constrained by a discipline quite as severe as anything in hell, but by a discipline positively embraced as the means to a consummate act of specifically human

---

18 'Turning towards him, I looked at him attentively, fair-haired, comely and of noble presence as he was, though with a gash upon one brow. When I had humbly foresworn ever seeing him, he said: "Look now!" and showed me a wound high upon his breast, whereupon smiling he continued: "I am Manfred, grandson of the Empress Constance; wherefore I pray you, when you return, that you seek out my beautiful daughter, mother of the pride of Sicily and of Aragon, and, if aught else be told, tell her the truth. My person doubly cleft by mortal blows, I surrendered weeping to him who pardons willingly. My sins were horrible, but such is the ample embrace of the infinite good that it takes willingly unto itself whosoever turns to it."' Franco Lanza, 'Nell'Antipurgatorio: Dai morti scomunicati ai morti per forza', in *Lectura Dantis Modenese: 'Purgatorio'* (Modena: Banco Popolare di Modena, 1985), 27–42; Maria Antonietta Morettini Bura, 'I temi elegiaci dell'antipurgatorio dantesco e il canto VIII della seconda cantica', *AUSP* 14 (1990), 113–51; Marc Cogan, 'The Antepurgatory', in *The Design in the Wax: The Structure of the 'Divine Comedy' and Its Meaning* (Notre Dame: University of Notre Dame Press, 1999), 299–303; Sandra Carapezza, 'Le anime in attesa dell'ascesa: Persistenze terrene e legge divina', in *La divina foresta: Studi danteschi*, ed. Francesco Spera (Naples: D'Auria, 2006), 141–99. For Manfred, Mark Balfour, '"Orribil furon li peccati miei": Manfred's Wounds in *Purgatorio* III', *ItSt* 48 (1993), 4–17; John Scott, 'Manfred and Bonconte', in *Dante's Political Purgatory* (Philadelphia: University of Pennsylvania Press, 1996), 85–95; Dino Bigongiari, 'The Meeting with Manfred', in *Readings in the 'Divine Comedy'. A Series of Lectures* (Dover, DE: Griffon House, 2006), 248–58.

being, to an act of existence, that is to say, transparent to the at once most profound and most sublime of its proper reasons. First, then, as representative of *love misdirected*, come the proud, the envious and the wrathful, the proud bent double beneath the rocky burden on their back (this, for them, being the way of thinking themselves through to a more sober estimate of self), the envious with their eyes cruelly sutured (this, for them, being the way of seeing more clearly when it comes to self, the other-than-self and the mutual countenancing thereof), and the wrathful enveloped by an acrid smoke (this, for them, being the way of a more tempered humanity). Next, as representative of *love deficient*, come the slothful or half-hearted with, in Dante's imagination of it, their headlong sprint around the cornice (this, for them, being the way of a fresh sense of urgency, of our not, in fact, having all the time in the world); and then finally, as representative of *love excessive*, come the avaricious, the gluttonous and the lustful, the avaricious as cleaving to the dust (this, for them, being the way of constraining the spirit to something more properly exalted), the gluttonous as emaciated in their hunger (this, for them, being the way of more orderly appetition) and the lustful as engulfed now by the flames of their own passion (this, for them, being the way of purging unreason on the plane of properly human loving). The discipline is in this sense intense, and all the more so for its being accompanied on each cornice by the whips and bridles of encouragement and admonition, by instances of Graeco-Roman and Judaeo-Christian vice and virtue designed by turns to encourage and to deter the resolute but still struggling spirit. But again, it is the inwardness of it all that matters, the formalities of purgatory proper—the precise *what* and *how* of the soul's suffering, the intimations of vice and virtue, the liturgical markers along the way (the *Paternoster* for the proud, the *Agnus Dei* for the wrathful, the *Labia mea, Domine* for the gluttonous)—not so much imposing upon the spirit as facilitating, encouraging and registering the drama of being and becoming, of, in short, ontic emancipation.[19]

And the outcome? For the clientele proper of purgatory the possibility of taking their place at last in the celestial rose and of knowing themselves in the kind of transhumanity constituting for Dante but humanity itself in act. For Dante

19 Edward Moore, 'Unity and Symmetry of Design in the *Purgatorio*', in *Studies in Dante: Second Series; Miscellaneous Essays* (Oxford: Clarendon Press, 1968 [1899]), 246–68; Anna Maria Chiavacci Leonardi, 'Le beatitudini e la struttura poetica del *Purgatorio*', *GSLI* 161 (1984), 1–29; Giorgio Petrocchi, '*Struttura e lingua del 'Purgatorio*', in *Lectura Dantis Modenese: 'Purgatorio'* (Modena: Banca Popolare dell'Emilia, 1985), 229–50; Simone Albonico, 'Un'interpretazione della struttura del *Purgatorio*', in *Letteratura e filologia tra Svizzera e Italia. Studi in onore di Guglielmo Gorni*, vol. 1, ed. Maria Antonietta Terzoli, Alberto Asor Rosa, and Giorgio Inglese (Rome: Edizioni di Storia e Letteratura, 2010), 213–37; Dante della Terza, 'I canti del disordinato amore: Osservazioni sulla struttura e lo stile del *Purgatorio*', in *Dante e noi: Scritti danteschi*, ed. Florinda Nardi (Rome: Edicampus, 2013 [1966]), 159–85; Rino Caputo, 'La struttura (e la poesia) del *Purgatorio*', in *Noi e Dante: Per una conoscenza della* Commedia *nella modernità*, ed. Carlo Santoli (Alessandria: Edizioni dell'Orso, 2015), 27–41.

himself, however, as but one passing through, it is a question of his own purgatorial moment, of a moment of confession urged upon him by Beatrice as awaiting him upon the summit of the mountain and turning upon his dereliction as a lover, of—in just about the moment of her demise—his having sought consolation in another, in the gracious lady of the casement, perhaps, or else in a 'pargoletta' or maiden of comparable beauty apt to detain his spirit:

> Mai non t'appresentò natura o arte
> piacer, quanto le belle membra in ch'io
> rinchiusa fui, e che so' 'n terra sparte;
>   e se 'l sommo piacer sì ti fallio
> per la mia morte, qual cosa mortale
> dovea poi trarre te nel suo disio?
>   Ben ti dovevi, per lo primo strale
> de le cose fallaci, levar suso
> di retro a me che non era più tale.
>   Non ti dovea gravar le penne in giuso,
> ad aspettar più colpo, o pargoletta
> o altra novità con sì breve uso.

(*Purgatorio* 31.49–60)[20]

—lines to which, as giving precision to the more properly ideological aspect of the matter, to (again in just about the moment of her demise) the eclipse of

---

20 'Never did nature or art set before you beauty such as the fair members wherein I was enclosed, now scattered abroad as dust. And if such beauty replete was thus lost to you by my death, then what mortal thing should have caught you up in desire? Truly you ought, at the first shaft of things illusory, to have risen up after me that was no more. No young maiden or other vanity of such brief value should have bent your wings downward there to await still fresh assaults.' Francesco Spera, 'La confessione di Dante', *LC* 8 (1979), 63–76; Pasquale Sabbatino, 'Dante lettore e critico di se stesso nel canto XXX del *Purgatorio*', in *Dante in lettura*, ed. Giuseppe De Matteis (Ravenna: Longo, 2005), 231–41; François Livi, 'De la purification au Paradis Terrestre: Regards sur le *Purgatoire* de Dante', in *De Florence à Venise. Études en l'honneur de Christian Bec*, ed. François Livi and Carlo Ossola (Paris: Presses de l'Université Paris-Sorbonne, 2006), 41–62; Nicola Fosca, 'Dante e Beatrice nell'Eden', *L'Alighieri (RD)* 33 (2009), 45–63; Nicolò Mineo, 'Il rimprovero di Beatrice', in *Dante dalla "mirabile visione" a "l'altro viaggio": Tra 'Vita Nova' e 'Commedia'* (Ravenna: Longo, 2016), 7–29. For the 'pargoletta' or 'fair young maiden' moment of the argument, a moment registered in those poems belonging possibly to the same moment as the 'donna gentile' poems of the *Vita nova* (the ballads *I' mi son pargoletta bella e nova* and *Perché ti vedi giovinetta e bella* and the sonnet *Chi guarderà già mai sanza paura*) and thus similarly open to a more properly allegorical interpretation, see, in addition to the commentaries, Angelo Jacomuzzi, 'Sulle *Rime* di Dante: Dalle rime per la "pargoletta" alle "petrose"', *FSt* 6.1–2 (1994), 15–30; Angelo Jacomuzzi, 'La "pargoletta" in *Purgatorio* (XXXI.58–60)', in *L'imago al cerchio e altri studi sulla 'Divina Commedia'* (Milan: Franco Angeli, 1995), 231–49; Maria Clotilde Camboni, 'La ballata *I' mi son pargoletta*', *REI* 56.1–2 (2010), 67–68; Tristan Kay, 'Dante's Cavalcantian Relapse: The "pargoletta" Sequence and the *Commedia*', *DS* 131 (2013), 73–97.

Beatrice and the Beatrician by a fresh set of cultural allegiances, we may add these from the last canto of the *Purgatorio* with their sense of there being more in heaven and earth, Alighieri, than was dreamt of in your philosophy:

> E io: 'Sì come cera da suggello,
> che la figura impressa non trasmuta,
> segnato è or da voi lo mio cervello.
>   Ma perché tanto sovra mia veduta
> vostra parola disïata vola,
> che più la perde quanto più s'aiuta?'
>   'Perché conoschi', disse, 'quella scuola
> c'hai seguitata, e veggi sua dottrina
> come può seguitar la mia parola;
>   e veggi vostra via da la divina
> distar cotanto, quanto si discorda
> da terra il ciel che più alto festina'.

(*Purgatorio* 33.79–90)[21]

But then, in the wake of confession—or, more exactly, as part and parcel of that confession—comes the liquidation if not of guilt itself then at the very least of the anguish of guilt by way of a flowing forth of tears, of, as Bernard of Clairvaux used to say, an 'assiduitas lacrymarum' making at last for a quietening of the troubled spirit:

> 'Guardaci ben! Ben son, ben son Beatrice.
> Come degnasti d'accedere al monte?
> non sapei tu che qui è l'uom felice?'
>   Li occhi mi cadder giù nel chiaro fonte;
> ma veggendomi in esso, i trassi a l'erba,
> tanta vergogna mi gravò la fronte.
>   Così la madre al figlio par superba,
> com' ella parve a me; perché d'amaro

---

21 'And I: "Even as the wax beneath a seal suffers no change in the imprint, so too my mind bears now your stamp; but why do your words so longed for soar so far beyond my sight, such that the more it strains after them the more it loses them?" "To the end that you may see clearly", she replied, "the school which you have followed and how remote its teaching from all I myself have taught you; indeed, to the end that you may see how far your way is from the divine way, as far as the swiftest heaven on high is from the earth."' John A. Scott, 'Beatrice's Reproaches in Eden: Which "School" Had Dante Followed?', *DS* 109 (1991), 1–23; Zygmunt G. Barański, '(Un)orthodox Dante', in *Reviewing Dante's Theology*, ed. Claire E. Honess and Matthew Treherne (Bern: Peter Lang, 2013), 251–330 (especially 251–65).

sente il sapor de la pietade acerba.

    Ella si tacque; e li angeli cantaro
di sùbito *'In te, Domine, speravi'*;
ma oltre *'pedes meos'* non passaro.

    Sì come neve tra le vive travi
per lo dosso d'Italia si congela,
soffiata e stretta da li venti schiavi,

    poi, liquefatta, in sé stessa trapela,
pur che la terra che perde ombra spiri,
sì che par foco fonder la candela;

    così fui sanza lagrime e sospiri
anzi 'l cantar di quei che notan sempre
dietro a le note de li etterni giri;

    ma poi che 'ntesi ne le dolci tempre
lor compatire a me, par che se detto
avesser: 'Donna, perché sì lo stempre?'

    lo gel che m'era intorno al cor ristretto,
spirito e acqua fessi, e con angoscia
de la bocca e de li occhi uscì del petto.

(*Purgatorio* 30.73–99)[22]

With this, then, the work of the *Purgatorio*—of the again beautiful *Purgatorio*—is done, Dante's account of what both in essence and in point of its positive

---

22 ' "Look well, for I in very truth am Beatrice. How dared you ever approach the mountain? Did you not know that here man is blessed?" My eyes lowered, they fell upon the clear fount, but, seeing myself therein, I looked afresh at the green bank. As to her son the mother seems severe, so seemed she to me, for bitter indeed is the taste of stern compassion. She, falling silent, the angels sang of a sudden: *In te Domine, speravi* but going no further than *pedes meos*. Even as the snow, among the living rafters upon the spine of Italy, is congealed, blown, and compacted by Sclavonian winds, and then, provided the land less overcast begins at last to breathe, trickles down—just like a candle melting in the flame—drop by drop, so also was I, before they who sing forever following the notes of the eternal spheres began their song, bereft of tears and sighs; but in the moment I perceived amid their sweet melodies their compassion for me—more, even, than if they had said: "Lady, why do you tax him so?"—the ice that was bound tight about my heart became breath and water, and, through my mouth and eyes, issued full of anguish from within me.' Giuseppe Clavorella, ' "Guardaci ben! Ben son, ben son Beatrice" (*Purgatorio* XXX)', in *PT* 14 (15).1–2 (2011), 25–48; Mario Alinei, 'Lo smarrimento di Dante alla luce dei rimproveri di Beatrice, del simbolismo della processione mistica, e della profezia del DVX', in *Dante rivoluzionario borghese: Per una lettura storica della 'Commedia'* (Velletri: PM edizioni, 2016), 201–56. For the 'assiduity of tears' (*assiduitas lacrymarum*) motif, Bernard of Clairvaux, *Sermones in octava paschae: Sermo* 1.7 (*Opera genuina juxta editionem monachorum Sancti Benedicti*, vol. 2) (Paris: Apud Gauthier Fratrem et Soc., 1835), 290: 'oculorum vero concupiscentiam superet studium compunctionis, et assiduitas lacrymarum' (steady misgiving and an abundance of tears triumphs over the concupiscence of the eyes); *In festo omnium sanct.* 1.10 (*PL* 183, 458A): 'Equum indomitum flagella domant; animam immitem contritio spiritus et assiduitas lacrymarum' (For just as a wild horse is tamed by the whip so also is the undisciplined spirit by sorrowing and an assiduity of tears).

living out it means to embark on the way of spiritual emancipation being complete. And it is the 'again beautiful' component of this formula that most matters about it, for nowhere in the *Commedia*, not even in the ecstatic phase thereof represented by the *Paradiso*, is the substance and psychology of journeying in all its commingling of travail and of tenderness quite as subtle in conception and quite as exquisitely nuanced in its exploration as here in the *Purgatorio*. Travail indeed—meaning by this the difficulty of the upward way—abounds, Dante going out of his way to comfort the reader with the thought that the agony of it all is in the event finite, nothing by way of man's proper suffering, he says, surviving the day of judgement (the 'pensa ch'al peggio / oltre la gran sentenza non può ire' of 10.110–11). But for all that, travail thus understood—as the difficulty of the upward way—is not what ultimately matters, the agony of the instant constituting for the Dante of this second canticle of his poem the means of spiritual 'regreening', of a repristination of the spirit in preparation for its final ascent to the stars:

> S'io avessi, lettor, più lungo spazio
> da scrivere, i' pur cantere' in parte
> lo dolce ber che mai non m'avria sazio;
>   ma perché piene son tutte le carte
> ordite a questa cantica seconda,
> non mi lascia più ir lo fren de l'arte.
>   Io ritornai da la santissima onda
> rifatto sì come piante novelle
> rinovellate di novella fronda,
>   puro e disposto a salire a le stelle.

(*Purgatorio* 33.136–45)[23]

Dante's, then, in the *Commedia*, is a journey into the divine mind as but the encompassing of everything that *is* in the universe in keeping with its proper reasons, the 'indiarsi' or movement of self into God constituting, he believes, the final cause of all spiritual striving. More exactly—and with this we come to the *Paradiso* as but the sublime canticle of the poem—it is a question of his winging his way ever more rapturously across the circling spheres of the universe, each sphere affording him the opportunity of exploring in the company of this or that group of the elect, not so much the idea pure and simple, the theological propo-

---

23 'Had I more space, reader, I would sing but in part of the sweet draught by which never would I be sated. But because all the leaves destined for this second canticle are full, I am constrained by my art. I came forth, then, from that sacred wave refreshed as a plant freshly foliated, pure and prepared to ascend to the stars.' For the 'regreening' moment of the argument, the 'che studio di ben far grazia rinverda' of *Purgatorio* 18.105 ('that striving for the good might regreen grace').

sition tout court, as that same idea, that same proposition, as but a principle of being—of this or that instance of specifically human being—in its now unqualified actuality. First, then, and as preliminary in respect of everything coming next by way of ascent, is Beatrice's account of how it is that everything that ever was, is and shall be in the universe according to kind both proceeds from and returns to the One as its first and final cause. On the one hand, then, and generated as far as the narrative is concerned by a strange sensation on the part of the pilgrim poet of his now soaring substance, of, in effect, the revised gravity of his existence, we have these lines from canto 1 turning on the movement of all things across the great ocean of existence until at last they come home to their proper port and their proper perfection:

> Ond' ella, appresso d'un pïo sospiro,
> li occhi drizzò ver' me con quel sembiante
> che madre fa sovra figlio deliro,
>   e cominciò: 'Le cose tutte quante
> hanno ordine tra loro, e questo è forma
> che l'universo a Dio fa simigliante.
>   Qui veggion l'alte creature l'orma
> de l'etterno valore, il qual è fine
> al quale è fatta la toccata norma.
>   Ne l'ordine ch'io dico sono accline
> tutte nature, per diverse sorti,
> più al principio loro e men vicine;
>   onde si muovono a diversi porti
> per lo gran mar de l'essere, e ciascuna
> con istinto a lei dato che la porti'.

(*Paradiso* 1.100–14)[24]

24 'Whereupon she, sighing compassionately and looking upon me as a mother might upon her wayward child, began: "All things whatsoever have order among themselves, this being the form whereby the universe is like unto God. Herein those creatures ranking most highly see the vestige of the eternal good as but the final cause of all such regularity. Within the order of which I speak, all beings, some nearer to and some further from their source, have their proper inclination, wherefore, each alike endowed as it is with its own instinct, they are one and all borne across the great ocean of being to their proper port."' For the 'indiarsi' moment of the argument, *Paradiso* 4.28–36: 'D'i Serafin colui che più s'india, / Moïsè, Samuel, e quel Giovanni / che prender vuoli, io dico, non Maria, / non hanno in altro cielo i loro scanni / che questi spirti che mo t'appariro, / né hanno a l'esser lor più o meno anni; / ma tutti fanno bello il primo giro, / e differentemente han dolce vita / per sentir più e men l'etterno spiro' (Neither of the Seraphim he that comes closest to God, nor Moses, Samuel or whichever John you will, none, not even Mary herself, have their seat in any other heaven than these spirits now appearing to you, nor, as regards their being, have more or fewer years; but all make fair the first circle and enjoy albeit in different measure the sweetness of existence as they feel more or less the eternal breath). Otello

while on the other hand, and by way of confirming how it is that everything present to us here below as an object of sensible perception proceeds from the One by way of a gradual process of materialization and individualization effected by the movers of the various heavens, we have these from canto 2, hymnic in their sense of the uninterupted rhythm of it all:

> Dentro dal ciel de la divina pace
> si gira un corpo ne la cui virtute
> l'esser di tutto suo contento giace.
> Lo ciel seguente, c'ha tante vedute,
> quell' esser parte per diverse essenze,
> da lui distratte e da lui contenute.
> Li altri giron per varie differenze
> le distinzion che dentro da sé hanno
> dispongono a lor fini e lor semenze.
> Questi organi del mondo così vanno,
> come tu vedi omai, di grado in grado,
> che di sù prendono e di sotto fanno.

$$(Paradiso\ 2.112-23)^{25}$$

But that, as far as man is concerned, cannot be all, for as far as man is concerned, this same flux and reflux of being from and to the One in whom it has its origin is a fully self-conscious affair, a matter of positive willing. Now here, when it comes to willing, we need for a moment to pause, for while for Dante man is man in respect precisely of his power fully and freely to will, this, within the now

---

Ciacci, *Concetto di ordine e struttura nella 'Divina Commedia'* (Perugia: Tip. Artigiana, 1989); Francesco Tateo, 'La forma che l'universo a Dio fa simigliante (fra *Paradiso* I e XXVIII)', in *Lectura Dantis (Potenza 1986-87)* (Galatina: Congedo, 1990), 9-30 (and in *Simmetrie dantesche* [Bari: Palomar, 2001], 215-38); Diego Sbacchi, '"Lo gran mar de l'essere" (*Paradiso* 1.113)', *L'Alighieri (RD)* 38 (2011), 143-49.

25 'Within the heaven of divine peace spins a body in the virtuality of which lies the being of everything it contains. The next heaven, with its many lights, distributes that being instance by instance, those instances being at once comprehended by and distinct from it. The remaining spheres, variously differentiated, order the now distinct forms they contain to their proper end and functionality. So it is that, as you can now see, these organs of the universe proceed step-by-step to receive from above and to fashion below.' Attilio Mellone, O.F.M., *La dottrina di Dante Alighieri sulla prima creazione* (Nocera: Convento di Santa Maria degli Angeli, 1950); Attilio Mellone, O.F.M., 'Emanatismo neoplatonico di Dante per le citazioni del *Liber de causis*', *DT* 54 (1951), 205-12; Attilio Mellone, O.F.M., 'Il concorso delle creature nella produzione delle cose secondo Dante', *DT* 56 (1953), 273-86; Bruno Nardi, 'La dottrina della macchie lunari nel secondo canto del *Paradiso*', in *Saggi di filosofia dantesca*, 2nd ed. (La Nuova Italia: Florence, 1967), 3-39; Christian Moevs, *The Metaphysics of Dante's 'Comedy'* (Oxford: Oxford University Press, 2005), especially 111-19; Bruno Basile, 'Canto II: La luna e l'ordine del cosmo', in *Lectura Dantis Romana: Cento canti per cento anni, III, Paradiso*, vol. 1, ed. Enrico Malato and Andrea Mazzucchi (Rome: Salerno, 2015), 61-84.

seasoned theological context of the *Paradiso*, is even so a matter of human willing as 'inwilled' by divine willing—a situation by no means abolishing the former in favour of the latter but, rather, confirming the coalescence of these things in the depths. On the one hand, then, there is the great free will passage on the threshold of canto 5 of the *Paradiso*, a passage more than ever eloquent in its sense of that same will as that whereby man most resembles his maker and is in turn most cherished by him:

> Sì cominciò Beatrice questo canto;
> e sì com' uom che suo parlar non spezza,
> continüò così 'l processo santo:
> 'Lo maggior don che Dio per sua larghezza
> fesse creando, e a la sua bontate
> più conformato, e quel ch'e' più apprezza,
>   fu de la volontà la libertate;
> di che le creature intelligenti,
> e tutte e sole, fuoro e son dotate.
>   Or ti parrà, se tu quinci argomenti,
> l'alto valor del voto, s'è sì fatto
> che Dio consenta quando tu consenti;
>   ché, nel fermar tra Dio e l'omo il patto,
> vittima fassi di questo tesoro,
> tal quale io dico; e fassi col suo atto'.

(*Paradiso* 5.16–30)[26]

while on the other hand there is the no less eloquent 'inwilling' or 'invogliare' passage of canto 3, a passage inaugurated by Dante's nicely serpentine question to Piccarda Donati to the effect that might she not be happier higher up in paradise and coming to rest in the no less nicely Augustinian formula to the effect that 'in his will is our peace', the whole thus constituting an essay in the co-presencing of man and God in the innermost parts of self:

26 'Thus Beatrice began this canto, and, like one reluctant to interrupt his flow, continued thus her sacred discourse: "The greatest gift which God of his bounty fashioned in creation, the most like unto his goodness and the one he deems the most precious, was freedom of the will, a freedom with which all creatures of understanding—they and they alone—were and are endowed. Reasoning thus, then, perfectly apparent to you will be the great value to be set upon the vow, for in the moment of your consenting so also does God consent; for in forging after the manner I describe a pact between man and God—a pact of its own making—that same treasure is forfeit."' Erminia Ardissino, ' "Lo maggior don . . . la libertate": Volontà e libero arbitrio', in *L'umana 'Commedia' di Dante* (Ravenna: Longo, 2016), 73–89.

'Ma dimmi: voi che siete qui felici,
disiderate voi più alto loco
per più vedere e per più farvi amici?'
    Con quelle altr' ombre pria sorrise un poco;
da indi mi rispuose tanto lieta,
ch'arder parea d'amor nel primo foco:
    'Frate, la nostra volontà quïeta
virtù di carità, che fa volerne
sol quel ch'avemo, e d'altro non ci asseta.
    Se disïassimo esser più superne,
foran discordi li nostri disiri
dal voler di colui che qui ne cerne;
    che vedrai non capere in questi giri,
s'essere in carità è qui *necesse*,
e se la sua natura ben rimiri.
    Anzi è formale ad esto beato *esse*
tenersi dentro a la divina voglia,
per ch'una fansi nostre voglie stesse;
    sì che, come noi sem di soglia in soglia
per questo regno, a tutto il regno piace
com' a lo re che 'n suo voler ne 'nvoglia.
    E 'n la sua volontade è nostra pace:
ell' è quel mare al qual tutto si move
ciò ch'ella crïa o che natura face'.

(*Paradiso* 3.64–87)[27]

With what amounts, then, in these first cantos of the *Paradiso* to an essay on how it is that man in particular enters into and plays his part in the sublime circularity of it all, in the *going out* and *coming in* of being generally as conceived from

---

27 ' "But tell me, you who are happy here, do you not wish for a higher place so as to see and to be cherished all the more?" With those other shades she first smiled a little, and then answered with such gladness that she seemed to glow in love's first flame: "Brother, the power of love composes our will and, engendering no other thirst, makes us wish only for what we have. Were we to wish for something more exalted, our desiring would be at odds with the will of the One who places us here—which as you can see is not possible in these circles where to be charitable (should you care to consider what charity actually is) is a condition of that being. Indeed, essential to this blessed existence is its constraining to God's will, whereby our wills are but one. Just, then, as our being thus from threshold to threshold throughout this realm is a joy to the realm as a whole, so also it is to the king who inwills us with his will. In his will is our peace. It is that sea into which all things, be they of God or of nature, flow." ' Alberto Chiari, 'Il canto di Piccarda e il preludio del *Paradiso*', *Aevum* 14 (1940), 348–66. For the 'in his will is our peace' motif, Augustine, *Confessions* 13.9 ('in bona voluntate tua pax nobis est').

beforehand in the recesses of the divine mind, we have in one and the same moment both a prelude and a context for everything coming next in this third and
final canticle of the *Commedia*; for everything coming next in this third and final
canticle of the *Commedia* is but an account of man's entering at last upon his
proper patrimony, of—by virtue of a commingling of the human and the divine
at the still centre of personality—his coming home to the *what might be* of self in
all the ecstatic substance thereof.

In the next heaven up—the heaven of Mercury—it is a question of this same
commingling of the human and the divine in the context now of the political, of
Rome as preordained to world governance, herein and herein alone lying the
ground and guarantee of world peace. Again the tone no less than the substance
of the argument is hymnic, the emperor Justinian offering in canto 6 of the *Paradiso* a solemn account of the inception, the progress and the triumph of Rome as
but an instrument of God's purposes for man, of Rome, in short, as soteriologi-
cally significant.[28] Rome it was, in other words, that not only oversaw the cruci-
fixion of the Christ under Tiberius, thus ensuring the universal efficacy and legitimacy thereof as but the way of man's long-awaited renewal (the burden of Dante's
argument in the second book of the *Monarchia*), but that under Titus visited upon
the Jews the consequences of their misdemeanour on Calvary. And it is at this
point—in the wake of his hymn to Rome as thus co-involved from the outset—
that Dante proceeds in canto 7 to one of the theological pinnacles of the poem,
to a theology of atonement faithful in one and the same moment both to an
Anselmian sense of God's doing for man what he could not do for himself and to
an authentically Dantean sense of God's work in Christ being one of moral co-
adequation, of making man equal in some degree to his own raising up. God then,
Dante maintains, in contemplating the depth of man's disobedience in Adam, had
just two choices, either to step in afresh or else to leave it for man to sort it out
for himself. In the event he chose both. Contemplating, in other words, the depth

28 Nancy Lenkeith, *Dante and the Legend of Rome: An Essay* (London: Warburg Institute, 1952);
Charles T. Davis, *Dante and the Idea of Rome* (Oxford: Clarendon Press, 1957); *Dante e Roma. Atti
del Convegno di studi; Rome, 8–9–10 aprile, 1965*, ed. Casa di Dante (Florence: Le Monnier, 1965);
Craig Kelly, 'Law, Justice and Providence in *Paradiso* VI', *Carte Italiane: A Journal of Italian Studies*
1 (1979–80), 1–8; Peter Armour, *Dante's Griffin and the History of the World* (Oxford: Oxford University Press, 1990); Paolo Brezzi, 'I buoni spirti che son stati attivi: Giustiniano', *L'Alighieri (RD)*
33.2 (1992), 23–41; Juan Carlos d'Amico, 'Dante et la "sainte Rome"', in *Le mythe impérial et l'allégorie
de Rome: Entre Saint-Empire, Papauté et Commune* (Caen: Presses Universitaires de Caen 2009),
103–22; Rachel Jacoff, 'Dante and Rome', *CT* 14.2 (2011), 43–66. For Justinian in particular, Silvia
Conte, 'Giustiniano e l'ispirazione divina dei *Digesta*', *L'Alighieri (RD)* 27 (2006), 25–40; Nino Borsellino, 'Giustiniano imperatore: La sovranità tra forza e diritto', *DRISDA* 5 (2008), 21–29 (and in *Il
poeta giudice: Dante e il tribunale della 'Commedia'* [Turin: Nino Aragno, 2011], 205–14); Lorenzo
Valterza, 'Dante's Justinian, Cino's "Corpus": The Hermeneutics of Poetry and Law', *MH* 37 (2011),
89–110; Steven Grossvogel, 'Justinian's "jus" and "justificatio" in *Paradiso* 6.10–27', *MLN* 127.2 (2012),
130–37.

of man's disobedience in Adam, but moved as ever by a massive and massively restorative movement of love, God chose in the person of Christ to suffer as man for man, thus in some sense and in some degree confirming man's adequacy to his own resurrection (the 'per far l'uom sufficiente a rilevarsi' of line 116), this precisely—this making equal of the beloved to its high calling—being what it means to love well and indeed in truth to love at all. On the one hand, then, we have the co-adequation moment of the argument, the refreshing of man's connatural power to new life by way of the Christ incarnate:

> Ficca mo l'occhio per entro l'abisso
> de l'etterno consiglio, quanto puoi
> al mio parlar distrettamente fisso.
>
>   Non potea l'uomo ne' termini suoi
> mai sodisfar, per non potere ir giuso
> con umiltate obedïendo poi,
>
>   quanto disobediendo intese ir suso;
> e questa è la cagion per che l'uom fue
> da poter sodisfar per sé dischiuso.
>
>   Dunque a Dio convenia con le vie sue
> riparar l'omo a sua intera vita,
> dico con l'una, o ver con amendue.
>
>   Ma perché l'ovra tanto è più gradita
> da l'operante, quanto più appresenta
> de la bontà del core ond' ell' è uscita,
>
>   la divina bontà che 'l mondo imprenta,
> di proceder per tutte le sue vie,
> a rilevarvi suso, fu contenta.
>
>   Né tra l'ultima notte e 'l primo die
> sì alto o sì magnifico processo,
> o per l'una o per l'altra, fu o fie;
>
>   ché più largo fu Dio a dar sé stesso
> per far l'uom sufficiente a rilevarsi,
> che s'elli avesse sol da sé dimesso;
>
>   e tutti li altri modi erano scarsi
> a la giustizia, se 'l Figliuol di Dio
> non fosse umilïato ad incarnarsi.

(*Paradiso* 7.94–120)[29]

---

29 'Look now, then, deep into the depths of the everlasting wisdom, following as closely as may be what I now say unto you. Man, through not being able to descend in humility by thereafter obeying

while on the other hand, and prefacing the whole thing, we have the affective moment of the argument, that part of it turning upon the notion of love as first and foremost a matter of facilitation, of 'letting a thing be', fully and freely, according to kind. Understand this, Dante has Beatrice say, and you have understood everything that needs to be understood when it comes to the precise nature and finality of love as but the encompassing:

> Questo decreto, frate, sta sepulto
> a li occhi di ciascuno il cui ingegno
> ne la fiamma d'amor non è adulto.

(Paradiso 7.58–60)[30]

By dint, then, of a turning back of the spirit upon the strangeness of it all, upon why God chose to act in the way he did, Dante manages to combine the necessities of Christian theological consciousness—a sense, that is to say, of the indispensability of the Christ event to a consummate act of properly human existence—with those of his own temperament as one always and everywhere inclined to start out, not, in fact, from man's first disobedience, but from the prior notion of God's having made it and of his having seen to it that it was good. True, the drastic character of that first disobedience required of him and requires of him still something more than he was and is capable of, Dante's too being in this sense (but how could it not be?) a theology of grace. But for all that, God's proceeding in the way he did—by way, that is to say, of Christ's contracting into the flesh—contains within it, he thinks, a continuing commitment to the human project in

---

so far as in his disobedience he had intended to ascend, could never within his own limits make satisfaction, which is why he was precluded from ever making good by himself. It was therefore necessary for God, by his own paths (by which I mean either this way or that, or else by both), to restore man to life in its fullness. But because the deed of the doer is so much the more prized the more it displays of the goodness of the heart whence it issues, the divine goodness which sets its impress upon the world was content to proceed by all its ways to raise you up. Nor between the last night and the first day has there ever been or will there ever be so lofty or magnificent a procedure be it by the one way or by the other; for God's generosity was all the greater for his having given himself in such a way as to make man equal to his own uplifting than had he only of himself pardoned him, every other way falling short of justice save that the Son of God should humble himself to take on the flesh.' Claudio Gigante, 'Canto VII: Teologia della creazione e della redenzione', in *Lectura Dantis Romana: Cento canti per cento anni, III Paradiso*, vol. 1, ed. Enrico Malato and Andrea Mazzucchi (Rome: Salerno, 2015), 200–27; Alessandro Ghisalberti, '*Paradiso*, canto VII: Dante risponde alla domanda perché un Dio uomo', in *Lectura Dantis Scaligera 2009–2015*, ed. Ennio Sandal (Rome: Antenore, 2016), 141–58.

30 'This decree, brother, lies buried from the eyes of everyone less than mature in the flame of love.' Gabriele Muresu, 'Le "vie" della redenzione (*Paradiso* VII)', *RLIt* 98.1–2 (1994), 5–19; Louis Marcello La Favia, *Soteriologia e poesia (Paradiso VII): Giustizia e amore* (Ravenna: Centro Dantesco dei Frati Minori Conventuali, 2011).

the proper viability thereof, to, withal, man's proper power to moral and ontological determination.[31]

Coming now to the heaven of Venus and thus to the erstwhile luxuriant in love, we witness a further aspect of what for Dante it means to be paradisally; for what, for Dante, it means to be paradisally is not so much—Lethe notwithstanding—a forgetting or obliteration of what once was but is no longer as its now smiling accommodation, its incorporation within the gracious economy of the whole. Nothing in short, is left behind, the erstwhile properties of personality living on not now to tax the individual in conscience but to confirm him or her in the again smiling serenity of all that he or she now is. This at any rate is Cunizza's meaning in canto 9 as—in a manner, she says, incomprehensible to the untutored spirit— she smiles upon her predicament, emphasizing as she does so the notion, not simply of pardoning but of self-pardoning as part and parcel of what it means to number among the elect:

> In quella parte de la terra prava
> italica che siede tra Rïalto
> e le fontane di Brenta e di Piava,
>   si leva un colle, e non surge molt' alto,
> là onde scese già una facella
> che fece a la contrada un grande assalto.
>   D'una radice nacqui e io ed ella;
> Cunizza fui chiamata, e qui refulgo
> perché mi vinse il lume d'esta stella;
>   ma lietamente a me medesma indulgo
> la cagion di mia sorte, e non mi noia;
> che parria forse forte al vostro vulgo.

(*Paradiso* 9.25–36)[32]

31 John Took, 'The Twin Peaks of Dante's Theology in the *Paradiso*', in *Conversations with Kenelm* (London: University College London Arts and Humanities Publications, 2013), 49–79.

32 'In that part of the depraved land of Italy lying between the Rialto and the springs of the Brenta and the Piave rises a hill of no great height from which there once came down a firebrand ravaging the countryside all around. Of one root were both he and I born. Cunizza was my name, and I shine forth in this place for that I was overcome by the light of this star. But gladly do I pardon in myself the reason of my ending up here, and nor—inexplicably, perhaps, to your coarse crowd—does this grieve me.' Riccardo Scrivano, 'Il "sermo" di Cunizza (*Par.* IX,25–63)', in *Medioevo e Rinascimento veneto: Con altri studi in onore di Lino Lazzarini*, vol. 1 (Padua: Antenore, 1979), 95–103; Adriano Lanza, 'Cunizza, Folchetto, Raab (Canto IX del *Paradiso*)', in *Dante eterodosso: Una diversa lettura della 'Commedia'* (Bergamo: Moretti Honegger, 2004), 180–90; Pamela Williams, 'Sexual Desire and the *Paradiso*', in *Through Human Love to God: Essays on Dante and Petrarch* (Leicester: Troubador, 2007), 35–59; Donato Pirovano, '"Mi vinse il lume d'esta stella": *Paradiso* IX', in *Dante e il vero amore: Tre letture dantesche* (Pisa:

—a notion taken up later in the same canto by the poet and priest Folco of Marseilles as likewise able to smile upon self in the former waywardness thereof, not, to be sure, complacently, but in the sense of knowing self as brought home now to its proper resolution and thus to its proper rejoicing. Again, then, nothing is left behind, the hitherto suffering subject knowing himself as but a product of the love-artistry whereby the properties of personality are both fashioned and brought to perfection by the One who orders all things from beforehand:

> Non però qui si pente, ma si ride,
> non de la colpa, ch'a mente non torna,
> ma del valor ch'ordinò e provide.
>   Qui si rimira ne l'arte ch'addorna
> cotanto affetto, e discernesi 'l bene
> per che 'l mondo di sù quel di giù torna.

(Paradiso 9.103–8)[33]

Here, then, is yet a further instance of Dante's coming of age as a theological spirit, further, that is to say, to the grace-co-adequation moment of *Paradiso* 7; for it is a question here, not of dreaming innocence or of a childlike oblivion to the problematics of personality, but rather of an accommodation of these things in what amounts to a now seasoned moment of awareness, to a standing *even so* in the now resolved presence of self.

With what amounts, therefore, to one of the most refined of Dante's grace-emphases in the *Commedia*—'refined' in its honouring the historicity of self as part and parcel of what it means now to 'rejoice forever in the Lord'[34]—we come

---

Fabrizio Serra, 2009), 71–89; Francesco Favaro, 'Cunizza da Romano: Dimenticarsi dell'amore, nell'amore', *RLIt* 116.1 (2012), 18–22.

33 'Yet here we repent not but rather smile, though not for any fault of ours (which returns not to mind), but rather for the power which ordained and foresaw. Here we gaze upon the art made beautiful by such love, and the good we see whereby the world above turns the world below.' Michelangelo Picone, 'Paradiso IX: Dante, Folchetto e la diaspora trobadorica', *MR* 8.1 (1981–83), 47–89 (and in *Scritti danteschi*, ed. Antonio Lanza [Ravenna: Longo, 2017], 581–613); Paolo Squillacioti, 'Folchetto di Marsiglia "trovatore di Dante": "Tant m'abellis l'amoros pessamens"', *RLI* 11.3 (1993), 583–607. More generally, Aldo S. Bernardo, 'Sex and Salvation in the Middle Ages: From the *Romance of the Rose* to the *Divine Comedy*', *Italica* 67 (1990), 305–18; James A. Brundage, *Law, Sex, and Christian Society in Medieval Europe* (Chicago: Chicago University Press, 1993); Hugh White, *Nature, Sex, and Goodness in a Medieval Literary Tradition* (Oxford: Oxford University Press, 2000).

34 Augustine in the *De civitate Dei* at 22.30: 'Erit ergo illius civitatis et una in omnibus et inseparabilis in singulis voluntas libera, ab omni malo liberata et impleta omni bono, fruens indeficienter aeternorum iucunditate gaudiorum, oblita culparum, oblita poenarum; nec ideo tamen suae liberationis oblita, ut liberatori suo non sit ingrata. Quantum ergo attinet ad scientiam rationalem, memor praeteritorum etiam malorum suorum; quantum autem ad experientis sensum, prorsus immemor . . . ita et obliviones malorum duae sunt. Aliter ea namque obliviscitur eruditus et doctus, aliter expertus

to the heaven of the sun, the heaven of the theologians, where by way of a species of pulpit exchange Thomas as spokesman-in-chief for the Dominican order offers an account of Francis as but one of Christ's poor, while Bonaventure as general to the Franciscan order celebrates Dominic as but a spiritual athlete (*santo atleta*) of the first rank. As far, then, as Bonaventure on Dominic is concerned, it is a question of drivenness (the *impeto suo* of 12.101), of a desire to root out heresy whenever and wherever it put in an appearance. 'Learned, zealous and duly authorized by the pope himself', says Bonaventure, contemplating as he does so the ferocity of it all, 'he went forth like a torrent, driven from a high spring, and on the heretic thickets struck with vigour wherever resistance was at its stoutest' (Poi, con dottrina e con volere insieme, / con l'officio appostolico si mosse / quasi torrente ch'alta vena preme; / e ne li sterpi eretici percosse / l'impeto suo, più vivamente quivi / dove le resistenze eran più grosse; lines 97–102).[35] But for all Dominic's tirelessness hereabouts, it is Francis and the Franciscan way as turning upon Christ's ministry to the poor that strikes a more resonant note, for Francis, in the course of what amounts on the lips of Thomas to an eminently careful redaction of his life history, emerges, if not as a *secundus Christus* exactly, then as second only to the Christ in his espousal of poverty as a way of being. Dispensing, then, with the more naive aspects of Franciscan hagiography, Thomas straight-

---

et passus; ille, si peritiam neglegat, iste, si miseria careat. Secundum hanc oblivionem, quam posteriore loco posui, non erunt memores sancti praeteritorum malorum; carebunt enim omnibus, ita ut penitus deleantur de sensibus eorum. Ea tamen potentia scientiae, quae magna in eis erit, non solum sua praeterita, sed etiam damnatorum eos sempiterna miseria non latebit. Alioquin si se fuisse miseros nescituri sunt, quomodo, sicut ait Psalmus: *Misericordias Domini in aeternum cantabunt*' (Thus the free will of that city will be one will present in all and inseparably fixed in each individual. It will be freed from every evil and filled with every good, enjoying incessantly the delight of eternal joys; it will forget past sins and punishments, but still will not for that reason forget its liberation and so be ungrateful to its liberator. As far as its rational knowledge is concerned, it also remembers its past evils, but as for actually feeling them they are completely forgotten . . . so also there are two kinds of forgetfulness of evils, for the well-educated and learned man forgets them in one way, and the man who has experienced and suffered them in another. The former forgets if he neglects his learning, the latter if he is free from distress. It is according to this second kind of forgetfulness that the saints will forget past evils, for they will be so unvexed by them that they will be completely erased from their senses. But by the faculty of knowledge which will be strong in them, they will know not only their own past but also the eternal misery of the damned. Otherwise if they do not know that they were once wretched, how will they, as the psalm says [89:1], 'rejoice forever in the Lord'?). Rachel Jacoff, 'The Post-Palinodic Smile: *Paradiso* VIII and IX', *DS* 98 (1980), 111–22.

35 Andrea Consoli, 'San Domenico quale fu nella realtà—quale è nella poesia di Dante', in *Dante ecumenico: Letture e postille* (Naples: Conte, 1973), 262–70; Giovanni di Giannatale, 'Dante e San Domenico: Per un'ipotesi di interpretazione di *Paradiso* XII,57', *MD* 13 (1982), 355–65; Giuseppe Ledda, 'Osservazioni sul panegirico di San Domenico (*Paradiso* XII.31–114)', *L'Alighieri* (*RD*) 27 (2006), 105–25; Giuseppe Ledda, 'S. Domenico e l'ordine dei predicatori nella *Commedia* di Dante', *MD* 39 (2008), 243–70; Inos Biffi, 'L'elogio di san Domenico', in *"De luce in luce": Teologia e bellezza nel 'Paradiso' di Dante* (Milan: Jaca Book, 2010), 79–86; Francesco Bausi, 'Canto XII: Il "santo atleta" della fede', in *Lectura Dantis Romana: Cento canti per cento anni III, Paradiso*, vol. 1, ed. Enrico Malato and Andrea Mazzucchi (Rome: Salerno, 2015), 351–81.

away comes to what in his view most matters about him, namely to the courage and commitment with which, in life as in death, he pursued his calling as, again, but one of Christ's poor. In life, therefore, naught but perseverance:

> Non era ancor molto lontan da l'orto,
> ch'el cominciò a far sentir la terra
> de la sua gran virtute alcun conforto;
>   ché per tal donna, giovinetto, in guerra
> del padre corse, a cui, come a la morte,
> la porta del piacer nessun diserra;
>   e dinanzi a la sua spirital corte
> *et coram patre* le si fece unito;
> poscia di dì in dì l'amò più forte.
>
> . . .
>
>   Né li gravò viltà di cuor le ciglia
> per esser fi' di Pietro Bernardone,
> né per parer dispetto a maraviglia;
>   ma regalmente sua dura intenzione
> ad Innocenzio aperse, e da lui ebbe
> primo sigillo a sua religïone.

(*Paradiso* 11.55–63 and 88–93)[36]

36 'Nor was he yet far from his rising before beginning to make the world sense a strengthening through his mighty influence; for while yet a youth he strove against his father for a lady to whom, as to death, none willingly unlocks the door, and before the spiritual court and in the presence of his father he was conjoined with her, thereafter loving her more and more every day . . . Neither was he abject in spirit nor brow-burdened for being son to Pietro Bernardone, nor yet for being so marvellously contemptible to behold, but regally laid before Innocent his stern purpose, from him obtaining the first seal upon his order.' In general on Dante, Francis and the Franciscans, Edmund Garratt Gardner, 'St Francis and Dante', in *St Francis of Assisi, 1226–1926: Essays in Commemoration*, ed. Walter Warren Seton (London: University of London Press, 1926), 65–93; Ronald Herzman, 'Dante and Francis', *FS* 42 (1982), 96–114; Raoul Manselli, 'Dante e gli spirituali francescani', *LC* 11 (1982), 47–61; Raoul Manselli, 'San Francesco e San Domenico nei canti del *Paradiso*', in *Da Gioacchino da Fiore a Cristoforo Colombo: Studi sul francescanesimo spirituale, sull'ecclesiologia e sull'escatologismo bassomedievali*, ed. Raoul Manselli (Rome: Istituto Storico per il Medioevo, 1997), 201–11; Vincent Moleta, *From St. Francis to Giotto: The Influence of St. Francis on Early Italian Art and Literature* (Chicago: Franciscan Herald Press, 1983); Attilio Mellone, O.F.M. (preface), *Dante e il francescanesimo, Lectura Dantis Metelliana* (Cava dei Tirreni: Avegliano Editore, 1987); Santa Casciani (ed.), *Dante and the Franciscans* (Leiden: Brill, 2006). On Dante, the Franciscans and poverty, Umberto Cosmo, 'Le mistiche nozze di Frate Francesco con Madonna Povertà', *GD* 6.2–3 (1898), 49–82 and 97–117; Giorgio Petrocchi, 'Dante and Thirteenth-Century Asceticism', in *From Time to Eternity: Essays on Dante's 'Divine Comedy'*, ed. Thomas G. Bergin (New Haven: Yale University Press, 1967), 39–64; Marguerite Chiarenza, 'Dante's Lady Poverty', *DS* 111 (1993), 153–75; Nick Havely, *Dante and the Franciscans: Poverty and the Papacy in the 'Commedia'* (Cambridge: Cambridge University Press, 2004). More generally on Franciscan poverty, Malcolm D. Lambert, *Franciscan Poverty: The Doctrine of the Absolute Poverty of Christ and the Apostles in the Franciscan Order, 1210–1323* (New York: Franciscan Institute, 1961; rev. ed., 1998); Charles

while in death naught but an earthen bier:

> Quando a colui ch'a tanto ben sortillo
> piacque di trarlo suso a la mercede
> ch'el meritò nel suo farsi pusillo,
>   a' frati suoi, sì com' a giuste rede,
> raccomandò la donna sua più cara,
> e comandò che l'amassero a fede;
>   e del suo grembo l'anima preclara
> mover si volle, tornando al suo regno,
> e al suo corpo non volle altra bara.

(*Paradiso* 11.108–17)[37]

But turning as they do upon a celebration of Francis and of Dominic as appointed from on high for the purpose of steering Peter's barque across the now stormy seas, these cantos are also the cantos of Thomas Aquinas, beloved of Dante as a matter not, certainly, of discipleship (for the differences here are as great as the similarities) but of admiration in respect of a superlative cast of mind, of consummate tact and attentiveness in the framing of philosophical and theological positions. Already, then, before ever we get to Francis and Dominic as each in his way a messianic presence, Thomas is busy already about doing what Thomas does, about drawing the distinctions always and everywhere indispensable to a precise act of understanding:

> Tu dubbi, e hai voler che si ricerna
> in sì aperta e 'n sì distesa lingua
> lo dicer mio, ch'al tuo sentir si sterna,
>   ove dinanzi dissi: 'U' ben s'impingua',
> e là u' dissi: 'Non nacque il secondo';
> e qui è uopo che ben si distingua.

(*Paradiso* 11.22–27)[38]

T. Davis, 'Ubertino da Casale and His Conception of *altissima paupertas*', *SM* 22.1 (1981), 1–56; David Burr, *Olivi and Franciscan Poverty: The Origins of the Usus Pauper Controversy* (Philadelphia: University of Pennsylvania Press, 1989); David Burr, *Petrus Iohannis Olivi, 'De Usu Paupere': The 'Quaestio' and the 'Tractatus'* (Florence: Olschki and University of Western Australia Press, 1992).

37 'When at last it pleased the One by whom he was destined to so much good to raise him up to the reward properly his by way of his self-humbling, to his brothers as to his rightful heirs he commended his most dear lady, bidding them love her faithfully; and from her bosom that glorious soul, returning to its proper realm, chose to set forth, nor for its body would have any other bier.'

38 'In respect of what I said earlier relative to there being "good fattening" and "there never arose

—lines to which for the sake of confirming what most mattered to Dante about the Angelic Doctor we may add these from a couple of cantos later, lines more than ever secure in their commitment to the kind of 'leaden-footedness' alone making for clarity and conciseness on the plane of understanding:

> Con questa distinzion prendi 'l mio detto;
> e così puote star con quel che credi
> del primo padre e del nostro Diletto.
> E questo ti sia sempre piombo a' piedi,
> per farti mover lento com' uom lasso
> e al sì e al no che tu non vedi;
> ché quelli è tra li stolti bene a basso,
> che sanza distinzione afferma e nega
> ne l'un così come ne l'altro passo;
> perch' elli 'ncontra che più volte piega
> l'oppinïon corrente in falsa parte,
> e poi l'affetto l'intelletto lega.

(Paradiso 13.109–20)[39]

Now, however, as marking the next phase of Dante's ascent, the radiant gives way to the roseate, the heaven of the sun to the heaven of Mars, where it is a question preeminently of the destitution of the times and of Dante's role as a

---

a second", you are perplexed and would have me speak more clearly, more amply and in a manner more accessible to you; and here we need to draw a clear distinction.' Kenelm Foster, O.P., 'The Tact of St Thomas', in *God's Tree: Essays on Dante and Other Matters* (London: Blackfriars Publications, 1957), 141–49; Bernard J. F. Lonergan, *Verbum: Word and Idea in Aquinas* (Toronto: Toronto University Press, 1996); Antonin Gilbert Sertillanges, *The Intellectual Life: Its Spirit, Conditions, Methods*, trans. Mary Ryan (Washington, DC: Catholic University of America Press, 1998). For Thomas himself on difference and distinction, the *Summa contra gentiles*, for example, at 1.14.2: 'Tanto enim unumquodque perfectius cognoscimus, quanto differentias eius ad alia plenius intuemur: habet enim res unaquaeque in seipsa esse proprium ab omnibus aliis rebus distinctum. Unde et in rebus quarum definitiones cognoscimus, primo eas in genere collocamus, per quod scimus in communi quid est; et postmodum differentias addimus, quibus a rebus aliis distinguatur; et sic perficitur substantiae rei completa notitia' (For we know a thing more perfectly the more fully we see its differences from other things; for each thing has within itself its own being, distinct from all other things. So, too, in the case of the things whose definitions we know. We locate them in a genus, through which we know in a general way what they are. Then we add differences to each thing, by which it may be distinguished from other things. In this way a complete knowledge of a subject is built up).

39 'Take, then, my words with this distinction, whereupon they may stand alongside all you believe relative to our first father and our most beloved. And let this always be lead upon your feet, that, in circumstances of seeing but uncertainly, you may be slow, like one weary, either to yes or to no; for he indeed ranks very low among the foolish who, either the one way or the other, affirms or denies without distinction, for frequently it is the case that hasty judgement errs on the wrong side, whereupon the mind is captive to mere sensation.'

prophet, as one called upon to speak out to the generations. First, then, comes the analytical phase of the argument, or, more exactly, its socioeconomic and demographic phase, where by way of a discourse placed upon the lips of his great-great-grandfather Cacciaguida and notable not least for its puritanical intensity Dante reconstructs over against the incivility of the nouveau riche the—as it now seems to him—golden age of Florentine history, sober, self-possessed and, on the distaff side, modestly arrayed and domestically attentive:

> Fiorenza dentro da la cerchia antica,
> ond' ella toglie ancora e terza e nona,
> si stava in pace, sobria e pudica.
> Non avea catenella, non corona,
> non gonne contigiate, non cintura
> che fosse a veder più che la persona.
> Non faceva, nascendo, ancor paura
> la figlia al padre, ché 'l tempo e la dote
> non fuggien quinci e quindi la misura.
> Non avea case di famiglia vòte;
> non v'era giunto ancor Sardanapalo
> a mostrar ciò che 'n camera si puote.
> . . .
> Oh fortunate! ciascuna era certa
> de la sua sepultura, e ancor nulla
> era per Francia nel letto diserta.
> L'una vegghiava a studio de la culla,
> e, consolando, usava l'idïoma
> che prima i padri e le madri trastulla;
> l'altra, traendo a la rocca la chioma,
> favoleggiava con la sua famiglia
> d'i Troiani, di Fiesole e di Roma.

(*Paradiso* 15.97–108 and 118–26)[40]

---

40 'Florence, within her ancient circle whence she still takes tierce and nones, abode in peace, sober and chaste. No bracelet had she, no tiara, no embroidered gown, no girdle more conspicuous than the one wearing it. Nor yet did a daughter at birth strike fear into the heart of her father, for neither marriageable age nor dowry eschewed proper measure either on this side or that. No houses had she stand empty of the family, nor yet had Sardanapalus appeared to show what could be done in the chamber . . . O women most favoured! Each was sure of her burial place and was as yet not deserted in her bed for France. One kept watch tending the cradle, and, soothing her child, would speak in the idiom that first delights fathers and mothers; another, drawing tresses from the distaff, would tell again, in the bosom of her family, tales of the Trojans, of Fiesole and of Rome.' Isidoro del Lungo, 'La gente nuova in Firenze ai tempi di Dante', in *Dante nei tempi di Dante* (Bologna: Zanichelli, 1888), 1–132;

But it is not long before the puritanical shades off into the prophetic, at which point we are once again in touch with the deep reasons of Dante's undertaking in the *Commedia*. For awaiting the poet, Cacciaguida says, and tending from this point on to determine the course of his entire existence, is nothing but the humiliation of exile and this as the context and crucible of the forthright utterance. On the one hand, then, we have the leave-taking and loneliness of it all, the burden of dependence and patronage, the scarcely bearable company of his fellow exiles and, in consequence of this, his 'making a party for himself':

> Tu lascerai ogne cosa diletta
> più caramente; e questo è quello strale
> che l'arco de lo essilio pria saetta.
> Tu proverai sì come sa di sale
> lo pane altrui, e come è duro calle
> lo scendere e 'l salir per l'altrui scale.
> E quel che più ti graverà le spalle,
> sarà la compagnia malvagia e scempia
> con la qual tu cadrai in questa valle;
> che tutta ingrata, tutta matta ed empia
> si farà contr' a te; ma, poco appresso,
> ella, non tu, n'avrà rossa la tempia.
> Di sua bestialitate il suo processo
> farà la prova; sì ch'a te fia bello
> averti fatta parte per te stesso.

> (*Paradiso* 17.55–69)[41]

Isidoro del Lungo, *La donna fiorentina del buon tempo antico* (Florence: Bemporad, 1906); Rafaello Ramat, *Il mito di Firenze e altri saggi danteschi* (Florence: G. D'Anna, 1976); Charles T. Davis, 'Il buon tempo antico (The Good Old Time)', in *Dante's Italy and Other Essays*, 71–93; Tobia R. Toscano, 'Memoria storia e progetto politico nei canti di Cacciaguida', *Lectura Dantis Octavianensis* (Ottaviano, Naples: Pisanti, 1987), 57–93; Claire E. Honess, 'Feminine Virtues and Florentine Vices: Citizenship and Morality in *Paradiso* XV–XVII', in *Dante and Governance*, ed. John R. Woodhouse (Oxford: Clarendon, 1997), 102–20; Elisa Brilli, 'Dalla "città partita" alla "civitas confusionis": Sulla tradizione e i modelli della Firenze dantesca', *BIRCSLFL* 3.1 (2006), 73–111; Elisa Brilli, 'Memorie degli antenati e invenzioni dei posteri: Cacciaguida tra Dante e Firenze', *LC* 44, ed. Johannes Bartuschat (Ravenna: Longo, 2015), 67–84; Kristina Olson, 'Shoes, Gowns and Turncoats: Reconsidering Cacciaguida's History of Florentine Fashion and Politics', *DS* 134 (2016), 26–47. More generally on the Cacciaguida cantos, Attilio Momigliano, 'La personalità di Dante e i canti di Cacciaguida', in *Dante, Manzoni, Verga* (Florence: G. D'Anna, 1944), 33–57; Fernando Figurelli, 'I canti di Cacciaguida', *CS* 4 (1965), 634–61; Angelo Jacomuzzi, 'Considerazioni sopra i canti di Cacciaguida', in *L'imago al cerchio: Invenzione e visione nella 'Divina Commedia'* (Milan: Silva, 1968), 155–91.

41 'You will leave everything you love most dearly, this being the shaft loosed first of all by the bow of exile. You will experience for yourself how salt is the taste of another man's bread and how hard the way up and down another man's stairs. But weighing most heavily upon your shoulders will be the

while on the other hand, and as constituting the point-towards-which of Dante's
entire discourse hereabouts, we have the commission, the first and final cause of
his journeying down into the pit and away across the circling spheres—that, precisely, of recalling all men, in every generation, to the journeying character of *their*
existence. His voice, to be sure, will grate, but this is grating in the interests of new
life, of freeing the spirit for all it has in itself to be and to become:

> Poi che, tacendo, si mostrò spedita
> l'anima santa di metter la trama
> in quella tela ch'io le porsi ordita,
> io cominciai, come colui che brama,
> dubitando, consiglio da persona
> che vede e vuol dirittamente e ama:
> 'Ben veggio, padre mio, sì come sprona
> lo tempo verso me, per colpo darmi
> tal, ch'è più grave a chi più s'abbandona;
> per che di provedenza è buon ch'io m'armi,
> sì che, se loco m'è tolto più caro,
> io non perdessi li altri per miei carmi.
> Giù per lo mondo sanza fine amaro,
> e per lo monte del cui bel cacume
> li occhi de la mia donna mi levaro,
> e poscia per lo ciel, di lume in lume,
> ho io appreso quel che s'io ridico,
> a molti fia sapor di forte agrume;
> e s'io al vero son timido amico,
> temo di perder viver tra coloro
> che questo tempo chiameranno antico'.
> La luce in che rideva il mio tesoro
> ch'io trovai lì, si fé prima corusca,
> quale a raggio di sole specchio d'oro;
> indi rispuose: 'Cosc ïenza fusca
> o de la propria o de l'altrui vergogna

wicked and senseless company of those with whom you fall into this valley, all of them, ungrateful,
witless and impious, turning against you—they, however, rather than you, being before long red-faced
for this. Their scheming will be proof enough of their bestiality, so much so that it will have been a fine
thing making a party but of yourself.' Jacques Goudet, 'La "parte per se stesso" e l'impegno politico di
Dante", in *Nuove Letture Dantesche tenute nella Casa di Dante in Roma VII* (Florence: Le Monnier, 1974),
289–316; Anne Paolucci, 'Exile among Exiles: Dante's Party of One', *Mosaic: A Journal for the Comparative Study of Literature and Ideas* 8 (1975), 117–25 (and in Anne Paolucci, *Dante Revisited* [New York:
Griffon House, 2008], 112–22).

pur sentirà la tua parola brusca.
Ma nondimen, rimossa ogne menzogna,
tutta tua visïon fa manifesta;
e lascia pur grattar dov' è la rogna.
Ché se la voce tua sarà molesta
nel primo gusto, vital nodrimento
lascerà poi, quando sarà digesta'.

(*Paradiso* 17.100–32)[42]

With what amounts, then, in the Cacciaguida cantos of the *Commedia* to a
profession both of the utopian and of the messianic substance of Dante's undertaking in the text—of the *utopian* by way of a hymn to Florence as she once was
and of the *messianic* by way of a fresh speaking out to the generations—we come
to the great justice cantos of the poem, to Dante's rethinking of the soteriological

42 'When by his silence that holy soul showed that he had finished putting the woof into the web
whereof I had set the warp, I began as one fearful and craving counsel of him who sees, wills and loves
aright: "I see well, my father, how time speeds towards me, dealing me a blow such as falls most heavily
upon the most unprepared. It is well, therefore, that I arm me with foresight such that if the place
dearest to me is snatched away I may not lose the others by my song. Down through the world of
endless bitterness and over the mountain from whose fair summit the eyes of my lady have lifted me,
and thereafter through the heavens from light to light, I have learnt that which, should I repeat it, will
for many taste most bitter, though should I be a timid friend to the truth I shall, I fear, be lost to those
speaking of this time as long gone." The light within which was smiling the treasure I had found there
first flamed like a mirror of gold in the sunlight and then replied: "A conscience dark with its own or
another's shame will indeed feel your words to be harsh, but set aside even so every fiction and make
manifest what you have seen, and let them scratch where it itches; for if upon first tasting it your voice
is harsh, it will, once digested, provide vital nourishment." ' For the prophetic moment of canto 17,
Piero Boitani, ' "Those who will call this time ancient": The Futures of Prophecy and Poetry', in *Medieval Futures: Attitudes to the Future in the Middle Ages*, ed. John Anthony Burrow and Ian P. Wei (Woodbridge: Boydell Press, 2000), 51–65 (and in *Dante e il suo futuro* [Rome: Edizioni di Storia e Letteratura,
2013], 289–304); Riccardo Ambrosini, 'Sul messianismo di Dante: A proposito del canto XVII del
Paradiso', *L'Alighieri* (RBD) 18 (2001), 75–98; Adriano Lanza, 'Stato del mondo e missione di Dante',
in *Dante eterodosso: Una diversa lettura della 'Commedia'* (Bergamo: Moretti Honegger, 2004), 86–101;
Elisa Brilli, 'Il profeta "sub specie Dantis" ', in *Firenze e il profeta: Dante tra teologia e politica* (Rome:
Carocci, 2012), 271–354; Marco Santagata, 'Tra (auto)biografia e profetismo utopico: Un viaggio nella
Commedia', in *Il manoscritto Egerton 943: II. Saggi e commenti*, ed. Marco Santagata (Rome: Istituto
della Enciclopedia Italiana, 2015), 1–39; Selene Sarteschi, 'Profezia e retorica: Lettura di *Paradiso* XVII',
LIA 18 (2017), 337–51. Further on Dante's exile and the psychology and phenomenology thereof, Cath-
erine Keen, 'The Language of Exile in Dante', *RMS* 27 (2001), 79–102; Yeo Wei Wei, 'Embodiment in
the *Commedia*: Dante's Exilic and Poetic Self-Consciousness', *DS* 121 (2003), 67–93; Giuseppe Ledda,
'Autobiografismo profetico e costruzione dell'identità: Una lettura di *Paradiso* XVII', *L'Alighieri* (RD)
36 (2010), 87–113; Juan Varela-Portas de Orduña, 'El exilio de Dante como costrucción ideológica
(*Paradiso* XVII)', *RFR* 7 (2011), 415–23; Elisa Brilli, ' "De exiliis Dantis": Raisons textuelles et culturelles
de l'harmonie entre exil politique et exil anagogique chez Dante', in *Écritures de l'exil dans l'Italie
médiévale*, ed. Anna Fontes Baratto and Marina Gagliana (Paris: Presses de la Sorbonne Nouvelle, 2013),
215–30; Karlheinz Stierle, 'Exil und Werk: Dantes Selbstbehauptung', *DDJ* 91 (2016), 5–22.

question as a whole, of the *who* and the *why* of God's choosing between one man and another. 'Rethinking' is indeed the right word, for already in the *Inferno* it is a question of the righteous of antiquity, graced as they are thus far in their righteousness, as living on in a twilight world of sorrowing and, beneath and beyond it all, of despair.[43] Now, however, in the heaven of Jupiter and in the presence of the eagle of justice as but an aquiline configuration of the elect on high, the issue is visited afresh, Dante, looking now to the love-substance of the faith he professes, fashioning from exclusivity a species of inclusivity, a bringing home of the hitherto estranged spirit. The question, then, is this: what are we to say about those good men and true who, through no fault of their own, know not the Gospel? Where oh where—the anaphora hereabouts being the pilgrim poet's own—can be the justice in condemning them?

> Assai t'è mo aperta la latebra
> che t'ascondeva la giustizia viva,
> di che facei question cotanto crebra;
>   ché tu dicevi: 'Un uom nasce a la riva
> de l'Indo, e quivi non è chi ragioni
> di Cristo né chi legga né chi scriva;
>   e tutti suoi voleri e atti buoni
> sono, quanto ragione umana vede,

---

43 *Inferno* 4.31–42: 'Lo buon maestro a me: "Tu non dimandi / che spiriti son questi che tu vedi? / Or vo' che sappi, innanzi che più andi, / ch'ei non peccaro; e s'elli hanno mercedi, / non basta, perché non ebber battesmo, / ch'è porta de la fede che tu credi; / e se' furon dinanzi al cristianesmo, / non adorar debitamente a Dio: / e di questi cotai son io medesmo. / Per tai difetti, non per altro rio, / semo perduti, e sol di tanto offesi / che sanza speme vivemo in disio"' (Then the good master to me: 'You ask not what spirits these are that you see. But before going any further I wish you to know that they sinned not, and though they have merit it suffices not, for they had not that baptism which is the portal of the faith that you believe; and seeing that they were before Christianity they worshipped not God aright, and of these I am myself. For such defects and for no other fault are we lost, and only insofar afflicted that without hope we live in desire'). Giovanni Busnelli, 'La colpa del "non fare" degli infedeli negativi', SD 23 (1938), 79–98; Giorgio Padoan, 'Il limbo dantesco', LI 21 (1969), 369–88 (and in *Il pio Enea, l'empio Ulisse* [Ravenna: Longo, 1977], 103–24); Kenelm Foster, O.P., 'The Two Dantes (I): Limbo and Implicit Faith', in the *The Two Dantes and Other Studies* (London: Darton, Longman and Todd, 1977), 156–89 (with, at 220–53, 'The Pagans and Grace'); Amilcare A. Iannucci, 'Limbo: The Emptiness of Time', SD 52 (1979–80), 69–128. Otherwise on Dante and the virtuous pagans, Gino Rizzo, 'Dante and the Virtuous Pagans', in *Dante Symposium in Commemoration of the 700th Anniversary of the Poet's Birth (1265–1965)*, ed. Gino Rizzo and William De Sua (Chapel Hill: University of North Carolina Press, 1965), 115–40; David Thompson, 'Dante's Virtuous Romans', DS 96 (1978), 145–62; H. A. Mason, 'A Journey through Hell: Dante's *Inferno* Revisited; Virtuous Pagans—"gente di molto valore". Canto IV', *Cambridge Quarterly* 16.3 (1987), 187–211; Cindy L. Vitto, 'The Virtuous Pagan in Legend and in Dante', in *The Virtuous Pagan in Middle English Literature* (Philadelphia: American Philosophical Society, 1989), 36–49; Marcia L. Colish, 'The Virtuous Pagan: Dante and the Christian Tradition', in *The Unbounded Community: Papers in Christian Ecumenism in Honor of Jaroslav Pelikan*, ed. William Caferro and Duncan G. Fisher (New York: Garland, 1996), 43–91 (and in *The Fathers and Beyond* [Aldershot: Ashgate, 2008], 1–40).

> sanza peccato in vita o in sermoni.
> Muore non battezzato e sanza fede:
> ov' è questa giustizia che 'l condanna?
> ov' è la colpa sua, se ei non crede?'

(Paradiso 19.67–78)[44]

Now the answer to this question comes in two parts, the first part being in truth no answer at all, merely a preliminary admonition. Let no one, Dante has the celestial eagle say in canto 19, take it upon himself to quibble with God when it comes to the *who*, the *when* and the *why* of his restoring those he loves to himself, his righteousness, here as throughout, pertaining to him as of the essence:

> Or tu chi se', che vuo' sedere a scranna,
> per giudicar di lungi mille miglia
> con la veduta corta d'una spanna?
> Certo a colui che meco s'assottiglia,
> se la Scrittura sovra voi non fosse,
> da dubitar sarebbe a maraviglia.
> Oh terreni animali! oh menti grosse!
> La prima volontà, ch'è da sé buona,
> da sé, ch'è sommo ben, mai non si mosse.
> Cotanto è giusto quanto a lei consuona:
> nullo creato bene a sé la tira,
> ma essa, radïando, lui cagiona.

(Paradiso 19.79–90)[45]

---

44 'The hidden depths keeping from your eyes the living justice after which you have so often enquired are now well enough open to you, for your question was this: "A man is born on the banks of the Indus where there is none to speak, read or write of the Christ, and, so far as human reason sees, he is, in point of all he does and of all he desires, a good man, without sin in word and deed. He dies unbaptized and without faith. Where, then, is the justice which condemns him? Where is his fault if he does not believe?"' Thomas O'H. Hahn, 'I "gentili" e "un uom nasce a la riva / de l'Indo" (*Paradiso* XIX, vv.70 sqq.)', *L'Alighieri (RBD)* 18.2 (1977), 3–8; Brenda Deen Schildgen, 'Dante and the Indus', *DS* 111 (1993), 177–93 (and, revised, in *Dante and the Orient* [Chicago: University of Illinois Press, 2002], 92–109 under the title 'Dante and the Indus: The Salvation of Pagans'); Brenda Deen Schildgen, 'Dante's Utopian Political Vision, the Roman Empire, and the Salvation of Pagans', *AdI* 19 (2001), 51–69.

45 'Now who are you who would sit upon the bench to judge a thousand miles away with the clipped vision of but a single span? Were it not for the Scriptures set over you, then to be sure there would be endless occasion to argue the matter through with me. O earthly creatures, gross minds to believe that the primal will could in its goodness be anything other than its own sublime substance! So much is just that accords to it, no created good drawing it to itself but that, shining forth, it is the cause of that good.'

But, then, from out of the stillness, comes the reply proper to Dante's question, a reply turning on a sense of the susceptibility, indeed of the vulnerability of the Godhead in respect of those living out in good faith the reasons of their existence, his vulnerability to each and every instance of warm affection and lively anticipation being the mark of his victory—at which point the twofold courage and refinement of Dante's temperament as a theological spirit once again moves fully and unequivocally into view:

> Regnum celorum vïolenza pate
> da caldo amore e da viva speranza,
> che vince la divina volontate;
>   non a guisa che l'omo a l'om sobranza,
> ma vince lei perché vuole esser vinta,
> e, vinta, vince con sua beninanza.

> (Paradiso 20.94–99)[46]

True, the pagan souls now party to the elect and rejoicing on high—the Virgilian Rhipeus and the Emperor Trajan—died not in fact as pagans but as Christians (Rhipeus as party avant la lettre to baptism in the Spirit and Trajan as raised up and brought home by prayer to a knowledge of the Christ), Dante thus hon-

---

46 'Regnum coelorum suffers violence from fervent love and from living hope which vanquishes the divine will; not in such wise as man overcomes man, but vanquishes it, because it wills to be vanquished, and, vanquished, vanquishes with its own goodness.' Michelangelo Picone, 'La "viva speranza" di Dante e il problema della salvezza dei pagani virtuosi: Una lettura di Paradiso 20', QItal 10.1–2 (1989), 251–68; Michelangelo Picone, 'Auctoritas classica e salvezza cristiana: Una lettura tipologica di Purgatorio XXII', Italianistica 21 (1992), 379–95; Giuseppe Cannavò (ed.), Regnum celorum vïolenza pate: Dante e la salvezza dell'umanità. Letture Dantesche Giubilari, Vicenza, ottobre 1999–giugno 2000 (Montella, Avellino: Accademia Vivarium Novum, 2002), with, at 193–203, Anna Maria Chiavacci Leonardi, 'La salvezza degli infedeli: Il canto XX del Paradiso' (subsequently in Le bianche stole: Saggi sul Paradiso di Dante [Florence: Sismel, 2009], 97–112). Also on the soteriological issue in Dante, Francesco Ruffini, 'Dante e il problema della salvezza degli infedeli', SD 14 (1930), 79–92; Brunetto Quilici, Il destino dell'infedele virtuoso nel pensiero di Dante (Florence: Ariani, 1936); Raffaello Morghen, 'Dante tra l' "umano" e la storia della salvezza', L'Alighieri (RBD) 21.1 (1980), 18–30; Gabriele Muresu, 'Le "vie" della redenzione (Paradiso VII)', RLIt 98.1–2 (1994), 5–19; Norberto Cacciaglia, ' "Per fede e per opere" (una lettura del tema della salvezza nella Divina Commedia)', CL 30.2–3 (2002), 265–74; Bortolo Martinelli, 'La fede in Cristo: Dante e il problema della salvezza (Paradiso XIX)', RLI 20.2 (2002), 11–39 (and in Dante: L'"altro viaggio" [Pisa: Giardini, 2007], 289–319); Giorgio Inglese, 'Il destino dei non credenti: Lettura di Paradiso XIX', Cultura 42.2 (2004), 315–29; Adriano Lanza, 'Giustizia divina e salvezza dei "senza fede" ', in Dante eterodosso (Bergamo: Moretti Honegger, 2004), 113–24; John Took, 'The Twin Peaks of Dante's Theology in the Paradiso', in Conversations with Kenelm (London: University College London Arts and Humanities Publications, 2013), 49–79. More generally, Louis Capéran, Le Problème du salut des infidèles, 2 vols. (Toulouse: Grand Séminaire, 1934); Mario Frezza, Il problema della salvezza dei pagani (da Abelardo al Seicento) (Naples: Fiorentino, 1962); Ralph V. Turner, ' "Descendit ad Inferos": Medieval Views on Christ's Descent into Hell and the Salvation of the Ancient Just', JHI 27 (1966), 173–94.

ouring the 'none ever rose to this kingdom who did not profess the Christ as before or after he was nailed to the tree' of scriptural provenance and duly registered at 19.103–5.[47] But for all that, there is here an inkling of something more besides, a sense of how it is that, given the twofold love-origin and love-encompassing of being in the round, then there is here an invitation—indeed an obligation—to rethink and somehow to redefine the boundaries of divine readiness. Here as throughout, in other words, the soteriological issue is on the brink of reconstruction in favour of something still more resplendent, more properly transparent to the love-susceptibility of the One upon whose will it all turns.

But with what amounts in canto 20 to a gracious meditation upon the theology of election and the mystery thereof (for not even the elect, Dante has the eagle of justice declare, are able to see into the recesses of the divine mind, this, however, being but part of their bliss),[48] we return to the destitution of the times, where by the expression 'destitution of the times' we mean the destitution of the ecclesiastical and monastic times. On the one hand, then, we have Peter Damian, scourge in his day of popes, prelates and the religious generally, and here in paradise as scathing as ever about the bloatedness of them all:

> Venne Cefàs e venne il gran vasello
> de lo Spirito Santo, magri e scalzi,

---

47 'A questo regno / non salì mai chi non credette 'n Cristo, / né pria né poi ch'el si chiavasse al legno' (John 14:6: 'Dicit ei Jesus: Ego sum via, et veritas, et vita; nemo venit ad Patrem nisi per me' [And Jesus said unto them: 'I am the way, the truth, and the life; no one comes to the Father but by me']). With respect to Rhipeus, Andrea Battestini, ' "Rifeo troiano" e la riscrittura della storia (*Paradiso* XX)', *LI* 42.1 (1990), 26–50 (and in *La retorica della salvezza: Studi danteschi* [Bologna: Il Mulino, 2016], 243–70); Edoardo Fumagalli, *Il giusto Enea e il pio Rifeo: Pagine dantesche* (Florence: Olschki, 2012); Luigi Peirone, 'Rifeo (*Paradiso* XX.68)', *LIA* 13 (2012), 177–80. For Trajan, Gordon Whatley, 'The Uses of Hagiography: The Legend of Pope Gregory and the Emperor Trajan in the Middle Ages', *Viator* 15 (1984), 25–63. As regards Virgil, Nicolae Iliescu, 'Will Virgil Be Saved?', *Med* 12 (1986), 93–114 (and as 'Sarà salvo Virgilio?' in *Dante: Summa medievalis. Proceedings of the Symposium of the Center for Italian Studies, SUNY Stony Brook*, ed. Charles Franco and Leslie Morgan [Stony Brook, NY: Forum Italicum, 1995], 112–33); Mowbray Allan, 'Does Dante Hope for Vergil's Salvation?', *MLN* 104 (1989), 193–205; Teodolinda Barolini, 'Q: Does Dante Hope for Vergil's Salvation?', *MLN* 105.1 (1990), 138–44 and 147–49 (and in *Dante and the Origins of Italian Literary Culture* [New York: Fordham University Press, 2006], 151–57).

48 *Paradiso* 20.130–38: 'O predestinazion, quanto remota / è la radice tua da quelli aspetti / che la prima cagion non veggion *tota*! / E voi, mortali, tenetevi stretti / a giudicar; ché noi, che Dio vedemo, / non conosciamo ancor tutti li eletti; / ed ènne dolce così fatto scemo, / perché il ben nostro in questo ben s'affina, / che quel che vole Iddio, e noi volemo' (O predestination, how far removed is your root from their gaze who see not the First Cause whole! And you mortals, set strict bounds upon your judging, for we who see God know not yet all the elect—a lack which, in that in this good our own good is perfected, is sweet to us, we too willing what God himself wills). Gabriele Muresu, 'Il tema della predestinazione in *Paradiso* XXI', *Bibliologia e critica dantesca: Saggi dedicati a Enzo Esposito*, vol. 2, ed. Vincenzo De Gregorio (Ravenna: Longo, 1997), 197–202; Nicola Fosca, 'Il canto XX del *Paradiso*: Giustizia e predestinazione', *SD* 79 (2014), 209–66; Pasquale Porro, ' "O predestinazion, quanto remota è la radice tua": Il canto XX del *Paradiso*', in *Lectura Dantis Lupiensis*, vol. 4 (Ravenna: Longo, 2016), 91–114.

prendendo il cibo da qualunque ostello.
   Or voglion quinci e quindi chi rincalzi
li moderni pastori e chi li meni,
tanto son gravi, e chi di rietro li alzi.
   Cuopron d'i manti loro i palafreni,
sì che due bestie van sott' una pelle;
oh pazïenza che tanto sostieni!

(*Paradiso* 21.127–35)[49]

while on the other hand we have Benedict, melancholy beyond words as he contemplates the little traffic nowadays upon Jacob's ladder, the neglect of his rule, the dereliction of his beloved mountain monastery and the monkish cowls now but sacks of rotting grain:

Infin là sù la vide il patriarca
Iacobbe porger la superna parte,
quando li apparve d'angeli sì carca.
   Ma, per salirla, mo nessun diparte
da terra i piedi, e la regola mia
rimasa è per danno de le carte.
   Le mura che solieno esser badia
fatte sono spelonche, e le cocolle
sacca son piene di farina ria.

(*Paradiso* 22.70–78)[50]

---

49 'Cephas came as did the great vessel of the Holy Spirit, lean and barefoot, taking their food from whatever quarter. Nowadays, by contrast, our shepherds need one on this side and one on that to prop them up, one to lead them on and—so portly are they—yet another to hoist them up. With one and the same mantle they cover both themselves and their palfrey such that two beasts go under one skin. O patience that suffers so much!' Alfredo Zini, 'San Pier Damiano in Dante', in *San Pier Damiano nel IX Centenario della morte (1072–1972)*, vol. 1 (Cesena: Centro Studi e Ricerche sulla antica Provincia ecclesiastica ravennate, 1972), 251–70; Giovanni Cattani, 'Il sacro zelo di San Pier Damiani a sostegno del sacro zelo di Dante nell'invettiva religiosa della *Commedia*', in *San Pier Damiani. Atti del Convegno di studi nel IX centenario della morte* (Florence: Società Torricelliana di Scienze e Lettere, 1973), 43–59; Febo Allevi, 'S. Pier Damiani nel "terzo sermo" di *Paradiso* XXI e la denuncia di una crisi ai suoi esordi', in *Atti e Memorie della Deputazione di Storia per le Marche* 88 (1983), 7–84; Giuseppe Ledda, 'San Pier Damiano nel cielo di Saturno (*Paradiso* XXI)', *L'Alighieri (RD)* 32 (2008), 49–72; Edoardo Fumagalli, 'Dante e Pier Damiani', in *Il giusto Enea e il pio Rifeo: Pagine dantesche* (Florence: Olschki, 2012), 147–57; Pantaleo Palmieri, 'Il "terzo sermo" di Pietro Damiano (*Paradiso* XXI,103–42)', *Bollettino Dantesco: Per il Settimo Centenario* 1 (2012), 111–26.
50 'Our patriarch Jacob witnessed there above its topmost soaring, heavy then, it seemed, with angels. But none now lifts a foot to climb it, my rule, to boot, being discarded as so much wastepaper. The walls that were once an abbey are now mere lairs and the cowls but sacks full of rotten meal.' Salvatore Accardo, 'S. Benedetto nel *Paradiso* di Dante', *Annuario dell'Accademia Etrusca di Cortona* 17

Here, then, in cantos 21 and 22 of the *Paradiso* is an account of clerical deca-dence, secular and regular alike, as pithy and painful as any in the *Commedia*, but in point neither of pith nor of pain does it bear comparison with what Peter himself has to say on the matter, his, in canto 27, being a discourse apt straightaway to reduce the entire company of heaven to silence. True, the canto gets off to a rapturous start as that same company offers up an ascription of praise making by way of its exquisite synaesthesia—of its status as a feast for ears and eyes alike—for a sweet intoxication of the senses:

> 'Al Padre, al Figlio, a lo Spirito Santo',
> cominciò, 'gloria!', tutto 'l paradiso,
> sì che m'inebrïava il dolce canto.
>   Ciò ch'io vedeva mi sembiava un riso
> de l'universo; per che mia ebbrezza
> intrava per l'udire e per lo viso.
>   Oh gioia! oh ineffabile allegrezza!
> oh vita intègra d'amore e di pace!
> oh sanza brama sicura ricchezza!
>
> (*Paradiso* 27.1–9)[51]

But in keeping with what at every point in the *Commedia* amounts to a sense of the historical instant as the whereabouts of moral and ontological doing and undoing and thus as a matter of concern even in paradise, ascription shades off into anger as Peter —the rock upon which the Church was founded—registers the vacancy of 'my place, my place, my place' (il luogo mio, il luogo mio, il luogo mio) in the sight of the Son of God, her desecration being in this sense complete:

> La provedenza, che quivi comparte
> vice e officio, nel beato coro
> silenzio posto avea da ogne parte,
>   quand' ïo udi': 'Se io mi trascoloro,

(1979), 3–21; Dante della Terza, 'L'incontro con S. Benedetto (*Paradiso* XX)', in *Dante e noi: Scritti danteschi*, 2013 (1989), 233–49; Alberto Chiari, 'San Benedetto cantato da Dante (*Paradiso* XXII,1–99)', in *Saggi danteschi e altri studi (1980–1990)* (Florence: Le Lettere, 1991), 89–101; Peter S. Hawkins, ' "By gradual scale sublimed": Dante's Benedict and Contemplative Ascent', in *Dante's Testaments* (Stanford, CA: Stanford University Press, 1999), 229–43.
   51 ' "Glory be to the Father and to the Son and to the Holy Ghost!" all paradise began such that with its sweet song my spirit reeled. What I saw seemed to be a smile of the universe, my inebriation being that at once of sight and sound. Oh joy beyond compare! Oh gladness unutterable! Oh life entire in love and peace! Oh wealth secure beyond all craving!'

non ti maravigliar, ché, dicend' io,
vedrai trascolorar tutti costoro.
    Quelli ch'usurpa in terra il luogo mio,
il luogo mio, il luogo mio, che vaca
ne la presenza del Figliuol di Dio,
    fatt' ha del cimitero mio cloaca
del sangue e de la puzza; onde 'l perverso
che cadde di qua sù, là giù si placa'.

(*Paradiso* 27.16–27)[52]

Never, he goes on, was 'gain of gold' (*acquisto d'oro*) part of the original plan, nor ever did this figure in the minds of his earliest successors, many of them, like himself, martyred spirits. Never part of the original plan was a partisan pope, a pope content to set one Christian soul over and against another, to tolerate the keys as emblazoned on a battle standard and to curry favour for cash. 'Where, O God', cries the prince of the apostles, 'are you in the midst of all this? Wherefore do you slumber? Do you not see the ravenous wolves here below in every pasture, the one conspiring with the other to drink our blood? And you, my son', he concludes, addressing Alighieri as but a voice crying out in the wilderness, 'be sure to make manifest there below my every word here above, suppressing as you do so not one iota of it':

In vesta di pastor lupi rapaci
si veggion di qua sù per tutti i paschi;
o difesa di Dio, perché pur giaci?
    Del sangue nostro Caorsini e Guaschi
s'apparecchian di bere; o buon principio,
a che vil fine convien che tu caschi!
    Ma l'alta provedenza, che con Scipio
difese a Roma la gloria del mondo,
soccorrà tosto, sì com' io concipio;
    e tu, figliuol, che per lo mortal pondo

---

52 'The providence which here determines proper order and office had in every part imposed silence upon the blessed choir, when I heard: "Marvel not should I change colour, for while I speak you will see all these do likewise. He who usurps on earth my place, my place, my place, which in the sight of the Son of God is vacant, has made of my tomb a sewer of blood and stench such that the perverse one who fell from this place has naught to do but rejoice."' Guido Favati, 'Paradiso XXVII: San Pietro in Dante', in *Psicoanalisi e strutturalismo di fronte a Dante: Dall letteratura profetica medievale agli odierni strumenti critici*, vol. 2 (Florence: Olschki, 1972), 327–54; Aldo Vallone, 'Paradiso XXVII', *DDJ* 71 (1996), 23–44; Sandra Carapezza, 'Il trascolorare di Pietro', in *Novella fronda: Studi danteschi*, ed. Francesco Spera (Naples: M. D'Auria, 2008), 199–214.

> ancor giù tornerai, apri la bocca,
> e non asconder quel ch'io non ascondo.
>
> (*Paradiso* 27.55–66)[53]

But with what amounts in these passages to Dante's last word on the violence visited latterly upon the Church as but the bride of Christ, upon Peter, and upon the earliest of those in apostolic succession to him, and indeed upon the very substance of the Gospel itself, we are getting ahead of ourselves, for between the Benedictine and the Petrine phases of the invective comes his matriculation as a pilgrim spirit. If, then, faith, properly understood is indeed but the substance of things hoped for and the evidence of things unseen, then what matters to Peter over and above the act pure and simple of understanding is whether or not Dante has the small change thereof in his purse. And if hope, again properly understood, is but the sure expectation of glory as a matter of grace and of antecedent merit, then what matters to James over and beyond the idea pure and simple is Dante's own standing as a pilgrim spirit, as one indeed nourished by the sure and certain expectation properly his in and through the Christ. On the one hand, then, we have Peter in canto 24 on a point now not of principle but of practice, not of consent but of coinage:

> Allora udi': 'Se quantunque s'acquista
> giù per dottrina, fosse così 'nteso,
> non lì avria loco ingegno di sofista'.
> Così spirò di quello amore acceso;
> indi soggiunse: 'Assai bene è trascorsa
> d'esta moneta già la lega e 'l peso;
>   ma dimmi se tu l'hai ne la tua borsa'.
> Ond' io: 'Sì ho, sì lucida e sì tonda,
> che nel suo conio nulla mi s'inforsa'.
>
> (*Paradiso* 24.79–87)[54]

---

53 'In shepherd's clothing, plain from here to see, ravening wolves roam every pasture. Oh strong arm of our God, wherefore do you rest? Cahorsines and Gascons alike prepare to drink our blood. Oh sweet beginning, to what wretched end you must needs come! But the high providence whereby Scipio preserved for Rome all worldly glory will, as I perceive, bring speedy succour. And you, my son, who bearing still about you your mortal burden will yet return below, open your lips, hiding not what I myself have not hidden.'

54 'Whereupon I heard: "If on earth everything thus taught were thus understood there would be no place for the sophist's wit." Thus breathed forth that enkindled love, to which it added: "Now that, indeed well enough, you have confirmed the weight and alloy of this coinage, tell me, do you have the

while on the other we have James in canto 25, likewise engaged at the point of possession, of the blossoming of hope in Dante's own spirit:

'Poi che per grazia vuol che tu t'affronti
lo nostro Imperadore, anzi la morte,
ne l'aula più secreta co' suoi conti,
    sì che, veduto il ver di questa corte,
la spene, che là giù bene innamora,
in te e in altrui di ciò conforte,
    di' quel ch'ell' è, di' come se ne 'nfiora
la mente tua, e dì onde a te venne'.
Così seguì 'l secondo lume ancora.

(*Paradiso* 25.40–48)[55]

And what applies in the case of faith and hope applies a fortiori in the case of love as but the greatest of these, Dante, answering now to the disciple whom Jesus

---

coin itself in your purse?" "Yes", I answered, "that I do, round and resplendent as it is, and of its coining I entertain no doubt."' Giovanni Getto, 'Il canto XXIV del *Paradiso*', *LC* 1 (1966), 83–108; Francesco Di Gregorio, 'Il canto XXIV del *Paradiso*: La fede tra "ansia" e letteratura', *L'Alighieri* (*RD*) 30.1 (1989), 15–44; Andrea Battistini, 'Fede e bellezza: Il tessuto metaforico del canto XXIV del *Paradiso*', *L'Alighieri* (*RD*) 24 (2004), 79–92; Gabriella Di Paola Dollorenzo, 'Dante e San Pietro, *Paradiso* XXIV', in *"Chi dite che io sia?" Dante e la fede. Atti del Convegno delle Scienze Umanistiche* (*Università LUMSA, Roma, 21 giugno 2013*), ed. Lia Fava Guzzetta and Paolo Martino (Florence: Cesati, 2014), 137–49; Gianfranco Ravasi, 'San Pietro e l'esame di teologia di Dante', in *Peccato, penitenza e santità nella Commedia*, ed. Marco Ballarini et al. (Rome: Bulzoni and Biblioteca Ambosiana, 2016), 3–9. For the 'substance of things hoped for and the evidence of things unseen' moment of the argument the 'Est autem fides sperandarum substantia rerum, argumentum non apparentium' of Hebrews 11:1, while for the 'sure expectation of glory as a matter of grace and of antecedent merit' moment the ' "Spene", diss' io, "è uno attender certo / de la gloria futura, il qual produce / grazia divina e precedente merto" ' of *Paradiso* 25.67–69, in relation to which, Christopher J. Ryan, 'Grace, Merit and "Buona Volontade" ', *ItSt* 35 (1980), 6–11; Christopher J. Ryan, 'Morality and Merit', in *Dante and Aquinas: A Study of Nature and Grace in the 'Comedy'* (London: UCL Arts and Humanities Publications, 2013), 5–37; Antonio C. Mastrobuono, 'Sanctifying Grace: Justification and Merit', in *Dante's Journey of Sanctification* (Washington, DC: Regnery Gateway, 1990), 1–129.

    55 'Since by grace it is willed that before your death you enter into the presence of our emperor, counts and all, in his most sacred hall, such that, having seen the truth of our court, the hope that is in you and others may be strengthened, tell me of what that hope consists, how in your own mind it has blossomed and whence it comes.' Davide Conrieri, 'San Giacomo e la speranza: Osservazioni su *Paradiso* XXV, vv. 13–99', *GSLI* 148 (1971), 309–15; Achille Tartaro, 'Certezze e speranza nel XXI del *Paradiso*', *L'Alighieri* (*RBD*) 24.1 (1983), 3–15; Emilio Pasquini, 'Il canto della speranza (*Paradiso* XXV)', in *Confini dell'Umanesimo letterario: Studi in onore di Francesco Tateo*, vol. 3, ed. Mauro di Nichilo et al. (Rome: Roma nel Rinascimento, 2003), 1039–47; Leonella Coglievina, 'Il canto XXV del *Paradiso*', in *Dante: Letture critiche e filologiche*, ed. Ruby Abardo (Rome: Edizioni di Storia e Letteratura, 2014), 105–31; Giuseppe Ledda, 'L'esilio, la speranza, la poesia: Modelli biblici e strutture autobiografiche nel canto XXV del *Paradiso*', *SPCT* 90.1 (2015), 255–77.

loved, offering a radiant account of the love-cords whereby he personally is bound and the love-teeth whereby he personally is bitten:

> E io udi': 'Per intelletto umano
> e per autoritadi a lui concorde
> d'i tuoi amori a Dio guarda il sovrano.
>   Ma dì ancor se tu senti altre corde
> tirarti verso lui, sì che tu suone
> con quanti denti questo amor ti morde'.
>   Non fu latente la santa intenzione
> de l'aguglia di Cristo, anzi m'accorsi
> dove volea menar mia professione.
>   Però ricominciai: 'Tutti quei morsi
> che posson far lo cor volgere a Dio,
> a la mia caritate son concorsi:
>   ché l'essere del mondo e l'esser mio,
> la morte ch'el sostenne perch' io viva,
> e quel che spera ogne fedel com' io,
>   con la predetta conoscenza viva,
> tratto m'hanno del mar de l'amor torto,
> e del diritto m'han posto a la riva.
>   Le fronde onde s'infronda tutto l'orto
> de l'ortolano etterno, am' io cotanto
> quanto da lui a lor di bene è porto'.
>   Sì com' io tacqui, un dolcissimo canto
> risonò per lo cielo, e la mia donna
> dicea con li altri: 'Santo, santo, santo!'

(*Paradiso* 26.46–69)[56]

---

56 'And I heard: "On the basis of human reason and of the authorities all of a piece with it, sovereign among your loves is your love for God; but so that you might name all the teeth whereby this love bites you, say further whether you sense within you other cords drawing you to him." The sacred intent of Christ's eagle was not lost upon me; nay, the direction he wished for my words was plain to see, wherefore I began again: "Each and every bite sufficient to turn the heart towards God has contrived one with another that I might love: the being of the world and my own being, the death he suffered that I might live, together with the hope proper to every faithful soul such as I, and the living assurance of which I made mention, have drawn me from the sea of perverse love to the shore of righteous loving. The leaves wherewith all the garden of the eternal gardener is enleaved I love in proportion to the good he has bestowed upon them." No sooner was I silent than the sweetest of sweet songs resounded through the heaven, my lady intoning with the rest: "Holy, holy, holy!"' Alberto Gessani, 'La "lezione" di Virgilio sull'amore e l'"esame" di San Giovanni sulla carità', in *Dante, Guido Cavalcanti e l'"amoroso" regno* (Macerata: Quodlibet, 2004), 247–71; Donato Pirovano, '"A la riva del diritto amore": *Paradiso* XXVI', in *Dante e il vero amore: Tre letture dantesche* (Rome: Fabrizio Serra, 2009), 91–126; Francesco

On the basis, then, of a profession of faith, hope and love as but the deep substance of his own being, the pilgrim poet prepares under the auspices of his third and final guide in the poem—of Bernard of Clairvaux as the theologian par excellence of loving in the specifically Christian way of loving—to enter into the presence of God as the One whose very being is but a matter of opening out in love. First, though, albeit in the company still of Beatrice as 'she who imparadises my mind', comes a preliminary glimpse of the as yet far-off shining of the Godhead—now not so much the encompassing as the point-about-which of the entire universe—as reflected in her eyes:

Poscia che 'ncontro a la vita presente
d'i miseri mortali aperse 'l vero
quella che 'mparadisa la mia mente,
  come in lo specchio fiamma di doppiero
vede colui che se n'alluma retro,
prima che l'abbia in vista o in pensiero,
  e sé rivolge per veder se 'l vetro
li dice il vero, e vede ch'el s'accorda
con esso come nota con suo metro;
  così la mia memoria si ricorda
ch'io feci riguardando ne' belli occhi
onde a pigliarmi fece Amor la corda.
  E com' io mi rivolsi e furon tocchi
li miei da ciò che pare in quel volume,
quandunque nel suo giro ben s'adocchi,
  un punto vidi che raggiava lume
acuto sì, che 'l viso ch'elli affoca
chiuder conviensi per lo forte acume.

(*Paradiso* 28.1–18)[57]

Zambon, 'Canti XXV–XXVI: La scrittura d'amore', in *Esperimenti danteschi: Paradiso 2010*, ed. Tommaso Montorfano (Genoa: Marietti, 2010), 247–68; Vincenzo Massimo Majuri, 'L'esame di carità', in *Nel mezzo del cammin de la mia vita* (Rome: Casa Editrice Leonardo da Vinci, 2015), 195–205, with 'L'esame sulla speranza' at 183–94. More generally on the confessional moment of the text, Giovanni Fallani, 'L'esame teologico', in *Dante teologo* (Milan: Marzorati, 1965), 274–87; Pierluigi Lia, 'La confessione di fede, speranza e carità', in *Poetica dell'amore e conversione: Considerazioni teologiche sulla lingua della 'Commedia' di Dante* (Florence: Olschki, 2015), 279–303; Giuseppe Frasso, '*Paradiso* XXIV–XXVI (appunti sulla santità apostolica)', in *Peccato, penitenza e santità nella 'Commedia'*, ed. Marco Ballarini et al. (Rome: Bulzoni and Biblioteca Ambrosiana, 2016), 47–62.

57 'When she who imparadises my mind had spoken out in truth against the mortal misery of life here and now, then, as in a mirror one beholds a fiery torch behind, and this before either it is glimpsed or even thought of as such, and, spinning round to see if the glass speaks truly, discovers that, as with a song and its melody, it does indeed, so, as I recall, did I as I looked into the eyes whereby Love fash-

But then, following on from the moment of seeing, comes that of supplication, the moment in which, in the course of a prayer consummate in point both of substance and of structure, of an interweaving of ascription and petition as but the phases of proper piety, Bernard intercedes with the Virgin on behalf of his charge, this, therefore, being the moment of grace-facilitation and spiritual strengthening:

> Vergine Madre, figlia del tuo figlio,
> umile e alta più che creatura,
> termine fisso d'etterno consiglio,
>   tu se' colei che l'umana natura
> nobilitasti sì, che 'l suo fattore
> non disdegnò di farsi sua fattura.
>   Nel ventre tuo si raccese l'amore,
> per lo cui caldo ne l'etterna pace
> così è germinato questo fiore.
>   Qui se' a noi meridïana face
> di caritate, e giuso, intra ' mortali,
> se' di speranza fontana vivace.
>   Donna, se' tanto grande e tanto vali,
> che qual vuol grazia e a te non ricorre,
> sua disïanza vuol volar sanz' ali.
>   La tua benignità non pur soccorre
> a chi domanda, ma molte fïate
> liberamente al dimandar precorre.
>   In te misericordia, in te pietate,
> in te magnificenza, in te s'aduna
> quantunque in creatura è di bontate.
>   Or questi, che da l'infima lacuna
> de l'universo infin qui ha vedute
> le vite spiritali ad una ad una,
>   supplica a te, per grazia, di virtute
> tanto, che possa con li occhi levarsi
> più alto verso l'ultima salute.
>   E io, che mai per mio veder non arsi
> più ch'i' fo per lo suo, tutti miei prieghi
> ti porgo, e priego che non sieno scarsi,

---

ioned the cord by which I am bound. And as I turned again, my eyes being met now by what appears in that volume to one gazing intently on its circling, I saw a point shining forth so keenly that the eye it kindles must perforce close for its else overwhelming intensity.'

perché tu ogne nube li disleghi
di sua mortalità co' prieghi tuoi,
sì che 'l sommo piacer li si dispieghi.

Ancor ti priego, regina, che puoi
ciò che tu vuoli, che conservi sani,
dopo tanto veder, li affetti suoi.

Vinca tua guardia i movimenti umani:
vedi Beatrice con quanti beati
per li miei prieghi ti chiudon le mani!

(*Paradiso* 33.1–27)[58]

58 'Virgin Mother, daughter of your own Son, all creation surpassing in your lowliness, fixed term of the eternal counsel, you it was who so ennobled human nature that its creator scorned not to become its creature. Within your womb was kindled afresh the love by whose warmth this flower has thus blossomed in eternal peace. You, here, are to us the noonday torch of charity, and below, to mortal man, the living fount of hope. You, my lady, great as you are and all-availing, are such that whoso would have grace but has not recourse to you would fain have desire fly without wings. Not only him who asks do you in your loving-kindness succour, but often enough that same loving-kindness anticipates the asking. Whatsoever in any creature there is of excellence—of mercy, compassion or munificence— is gathered in you. Here, therefore, is one who, having from the deepest abyss of the universe as far even as this place witnessed one by one those living on in the spirit, now begs you of your grace that you so strengthen him that he may raise his sight still further toward the ultimate salvation. And I, who never burned more for my own vision than I do for his, proffer you my every prayer—praying that it be not insufficient—that by your own prayer you so dispel his every cloud of mortality that he might see unveiled the sovereign joy. This too I beseech of you, oh Queen, equal as you are to your every desire, that, with all he sees here, you preserve intact his every affection, and, watching over him, his every passion constrain. Behold Beatrice among so many of the blessed, hands one and all clasped in furtherance of my prayer.' Celestino Cavedoni, 'L'orazione di San Bernardo alla beatissima Vergine nell'ultimo canto del *Paradiso* di Dante esposta co' riscontri di quel santo padre e d'altri', in *Raffronti tra gli autori biblici e sacri e la 'Divina Commedia'*, ed. Rocco Murari (Città di Castello: S. Lapi Tipografo-Editore, 1896), 137–64; Erich Auerbach, 'Dante's Prayer to the Virgin and Earlier Eulogies', *RP* 3 (1949–50), 1–26; Aldo Vallone, 'Le preghiera', in *Studi su Dante medievale* (Florence: Olschki, 1965), 83–109; Steven Botterill, 'Dante, Bernard and the Virgin Mary', in 'Bernard of Clairvaux in the *Commedia*', in *Dante and the Mystical Tradition: Bernard of Clairvaux in the 'Commedia'* (Cambridge: Cambridge University Press, 1994), 148–93; Pier Angelo Perotti, 'La preghiera alla Vergine (*Paradiso* XXXIII 1–39)', *L'Alighieri (RBD)* 6 (1995), 75–83; Giuseppe Ledda, ' "Vergine madre figlia del tuo figlio"; *Paradiso* XXXIII 1–57', in *Lectura Dantis Scaligera 2005–2007*, ed. Ennio Sandal (Rome and Padua: Antenore, 2008), 97–135; Elena Landoni, 'La preghiera di San Bernardo alla Vergine: Canto XXXIII del *Paradiso*', *Vita Consacrata* 45.6 (2009), 528–41; Edoardo Fumagalli, 'Sulla preghiera di San Bernardo alla Vergine madre', in *Il giusto Enea e il pio Rifeo: Pagine dantesche* (Florence: Olschki, 2012), 179–96; Bortolo Martinelli, 'Dante: La preghiera, la supplica e la visione finale (*Paradiso* XXXIII)', *LIA* 13 (2012), 209–317 (and in *Dante: Genesi della 'Commedia'* [Rome: Aracne, 2016], 285–434). On Dante and Bernard generally, Alexandre Masseron, *Dante et saint Bernard* (Paris: A. Michel, 1953); Steven Botterill, *Dante and the Mystical Tradition: Bernard of Clairvaux in the 'Commedia'*; Inos Biffi, 'San Bernardo nel cammino spirituale di Dante', in *La poesia e la grazia nella 'Commedia' di Dante* (Milan: Jaca Book,1999), 53–67; while on Bernard himself, Jean Leclercq, *Saint Bernard Mystique* (Bruges: Desclée de Brouwer, 1948); Étienne Gilson, *The Mystical Theology of Saint Bernard* (Kalamazoo: Cistercian Publications, 1990 [1932]).

From this point on, then, it is a question no longer of far-offness but of drawing nigh (the 'io ch'al fine di tutt' i disii / appropinquava' of 33.46–47) and of the soul's rejoicing at last in an act—in a state—of ultimate intellection, of its 'entering ever more completely into the light all of a piece with the truth of which it is but the outshining' (the 'e più e più intrava per lo raggio / dell'alta luce che da sé è vera' of lines 53 and 54). And the fruit of this drawing nigh? A sense, in short, of the love-conflation of it all, of the in-abiding of each and every substance, accident and modality in the universe by way of its now sublime singularity:

> Oh abbondante grazia ond' io presunsi
> ficcar lo viso per la luce etterna,
> tanto che la veduta vi consunsi!
> Nel suo profondo vidi che s'interna,
> legato con amore in un volume,
> ciò che per l'universo si squaderna:
> sustanze e accidenti e lor costume
> quasi conflati insieme, per tal modo
> che ciò ch'i' dico è un semplice lume.

(*Paradiso* 33.82–90)[59]

But that is not all, for the privilege of seeing into the simple light of divine being in the inclusiveness thereof, in its comprehending within itself all difference, gives way in a moment of still further empowering to something still more magnificent: to a discerning within the recesses of that light a triple circularity, a three-in-oneness and one-in-threeness somehow bearing inscribed upon it our likeness, 'la nostra effige'. First, then, comes the moment of *empowering*, the co-adequation of self to the other and infinitely greater than self:

> Omai sarà più corta mia favella,
> pur a quel ch'io ricordo, che d'un fante
> che bagni ancor la lingua a la mammella.
> Non perché più ch'un semplice sembiante

---

59 'Oh grace abounding whereby I presumed to fix my look on the eternal light such that I saw at the far limits of my seeing! I saw enclosed in its depths, bound up with love in one volume, everything unfolded leaf by leaf throughout the universe: substance and accidents and their modalities, fused, as it were, one with another such that what I speak of is but a simple light.' Gino Casagrande, 'Le teofanie di *Paradiso* XXXIII', SD 74 (2009), 199–224; Antonio Rossini, *Dante, il nodo e il volume: Una 'lectura' di 'Paradiso' 33* (Pisa: Fabrizio Serra, 2011); Pierluigi Lia, 'Io vidi che s'interna ciò che per l'universo si squaderna', in *Poetica dell'amore e conversione: Considerazioni teologiche sulla lingua della 'Commedia'* (Florence: Olschki, 2015), 37–52.

> fosse nel vivo lume ch'io mirava,
> che tal è sempre qual s'era davante;
> ma per la vista che s'avvalorava
> in me guardando, una sola parvenza,
> mutandom' io, a me si travagliava.

(Paradiso 33.106–114)[60]

—then that of *discerning,* of Dante's seeing in the depths of the simple light the smiling 'inseatedness' of the whole in its at once perfect multiplicity and perfect unity:

> Ne la profonda e chiara sussistenza
> de l'alto lume parvermi tre giri
> di tre colori e d'una contenenza;
> e l'un da l'altro come iri da iri
> parea reflesso, e 'l terzo parea foco
> che quinci e quindi igualmente si spiri.
> Oh quanto è corto il dire e come fioco
> al mio concetto! e questo, a quel ch'i' vidi,
> è tanto, che non basta a dicer 'poco'.
> O luce etterna che sola in te sidi,
> sola t'intendi, e da te intelletta
> e intendente te ami e arridi!

(Paradiso 33.115–26)[61]

---

60 'Now will my speech be shorter still in respect to what I remember than that of an infant who yet bathes his tongue at the breast. Not because the living light upon which I was gazing was of more than one simple substance, for that same light is forever what it always was, but because my seeing growing stronger as I looked on and I myself thus changing, that singular sight was itself transformed.'

61 'Within the deep and clear subsistence of the lofty light appeared to me three circles of three colours and of one dimension, the one seemingly reflected by the other, as iris by iris, and the third as fire breathed forth equally, both on this side and that, to each alike. Oh how scant is speech and feeble in respect of my conception, even this being less than "little" relative to what I saw. O Light Eternal that solely abides in yourself, solely knows yourself, and, by yourself alone understood and understanding, loves and smiles upon yourself!' For the—as one of the most exquisite Trinitarian utterances in European literature—'O luce etterna' moment of the text, Giovanni Busnelli, 'Dalla luce del cielo della luna alla trina luce dell'Empireo', *SD* 27 (1943), 95–116; Giovanni Fallani, *Dante poeta teologo* (Milan: Marzorati, 1965), 211–25; Giovanni Fallani, ad voc. 'Trinità', in the *ED*, vol. 5 (Rome: Istituto della Enciclopedia Italiana, 1970–78), 718–21; Giovanni Montanari, 'Terza parte: Saggio teologico. Una terzina da rivedere: *Par.* XXXIII.124–126 sulla Trinità?', in *Socrate, Cristo, Dante e la Bibbia: Saggi di filologia estetica e sull'ebraismo fondamento della cultura* (Ravenna: Girasole, 2002), 93–123. For the 'inseated' moment of the text (the 'che sola in te sidi' of line 124, the *circuminsessio* of the Latin and the 'peri-

—and finally, and as constituting yet a further pinnacle of Dante's theological genius, that of *inscription*, of the co-presencing of creature and creator alike at the very heart of the One from whom man proceeds, the genius of it all lying precisely in Dante's now more than ever secure sense of the centrality of the human project to the very life of the Godhead. The revelation, then, is complete, the rapture intense and the mind duly transfixed:

> Quella circulazion che sì concetta
> pareva in te come lume reflesso,
> da li occhi miei alquanto circunspetta,
>   dentro da sé, del suo colore stesso,
> mi parve pinta de la nostra effige;
> per che 'l mio viso in lei tutto era messo.

(*Paradiso* 33.127–32)[62]

Now Dante's is at every point a seeking out and a rejoicing in the intelligibility of the matter to hand, and neither here, therefore, can there be any looking the other way when it comes to making sense of it all, to—in this case—explaining how otherness might be inscribed on the face of sameness. Rising up, however, to resolve it—not, emphatically, to dismiss but to resolve this final transgressing of our every ordinary paradigm of consciousness—is a sense of the love-encompassing apt both to quieten and to quicken the pilgrim spirit, to allay its every uncertainty and—but ne'er so sweetly—to ensure an even circling of self about the still centre of its now blessed being-in-the-world:

> Qual è 'l geomètra che tutto s'affige
> per misurar lo cerchio, e non ritrova,
> pensando, quel principio ond' elli indige,
>   tal era io a quella vista nova;
> veder voleva come si convenne
> l'imago al cerchio e come vi s'indova;
>   ma non eran da ciò le proprie penne;

---

choresis' [περιχώρησις] of the Greek), August Deneffe, 'Perichoresis, circumincessio, circuminsessio,' in *Zeitschrift für katholische Theologie* 47 (1923), 497–532; Daniel F. Stramara, Jr, 'Gregory of Nyssa's Terminology for Trinitarian Perichoresis', *Vigiliae Christianae* 52.3 (1998), 257–63.

    62 'That circle, which, thus conceived, appeared in you to be but a reflected light, seemed as I dwelt upon it to bear depicted within itself, in one and the same hue, our likeness, wherefore my sight was wholly set upon it.' Bortolo Martinelli, ' "L'imago al cerchio, e come vi s'indova" (*Paradiso* XXXIII.138)', *PT* 14 (15), 1–2 (2011), 49–81 (and in *Dante: Genesi della 'Commedia'* [Rome: Aracne, 2016], 435–85); Piero Coda, 'L'effige dell'uomo nella luce di Dio Trinità: Rileggendo la *Divina Commedia* di Dante Alighieri', in *'Ambula per hominem et pervenies ad Deum': Studi in onore di S. E. mons. Ignazio Sanna*, ed. Antonio Sabetta (Rome: Studium, 2012), 363–77.

se non che la mia mente fu percossa
da un fulgore in che sua voglia venne.
A l'alta fantasia qui mancò possa;
ma già volgeva il mio disio e 'l velle,
sì come rota ch'igualmente è mossa,
l'amor che move il sole e l'altre stelle.

(Paradiso 33.133–45)[63]

AN ANTHROPOLOGY AND ETHIC:
LOVE AND LOVE-HARVESTING

To the fore among the miracles of the *Commedia*, for those, at any rate, who believe in miracles, is its countenancing in a single pass of the mind and imagination both the historical and the eschatological truth of this or that instance of specifically human being, the latter, within the economy of the whole, constituting but a definitive statement of the former in the innermost and abiding truth thereof. To the fore, more precisely, among the miracles of the *Commedia* is its fashioning from what, in Dante's imagining of it, constitutes the *what will be* of this or that instance of specifically human being under the aspect of eternity (where by 'eternity' we mean for the moment merely sempiternity or indefinite duration) an existential analytic of incomparable power and precision, an analytic open to contemplation in terms (*a*) of a *fundamental anthropology*, where it is a question of man's multiple affectivity; (*b*) of the *dialectics of being*, where it is a question of the complex dimensionality of his presence in the world as a creature of moral and ontological determination; (*c*) of a *phenomenology of existence*, where it is a question of the moods of being transparent upon reflection to the truth of being; and (*d*) of the *substance and structure of significant journeying*, where it is a question of the call in man to a scarcely less than traumatic process of self-encounter, of self-reconfiguration and of self-transcendence as the way of proper self-

---

63 'Like the geometer who wholly applies himself to measure the circle, and, for all his thinking, finds not the principle he needs, such was I at that strange sight. I wished to see how the image fitted the circle and was able there to find its place; but for this, were it not that my mind was smitten by a flash whence its wish was fulfilled, my wings were not sufficient. Yet my every power to image forth here failing me, desire and will alike, like a wheel evenly turned, were turned by the love which moves the sun and the other stars.' Philip McNair, 'Dante's Vision of God: An Exposition of *Paradiso* XXXIII', in *Essays in Honour of John Humphreys Whitfield*, ed. H. C. Davis et al. (London: St George's Press, 1975), 13–29; Kenelm Foster, O.P., 'Dante's Vision of God', in *The Two Dantes* (London: Darton, Longman and Todd, 1977), 66–85; Enzo Esposito, 'Il canto dell'ultima visione (*Paradiso* XXXIII)', *LC* 7 (1979), 13–26; Lino Pertile, '*Paradiso* XXXIII: L'estremo oltraggio', *FC* 6, 1981, 1–21 (and in a revised form in *Punta del disio: Semantica del desiderio nella 'Commedia'* [Fiesole: Cadmo, 2005], 247–63); Edward Hagman, 'Dante's Vision of God: The End of the *Itinerarium Mentis*', *DS* 106 (1988), 1–20.

affirmation. Now this, to be sure, does not exhaust the aforesaid miracle, for that same miracle is open to celebration by way of any set or subset of cultural categories, be they theological, philosophical, literary or linguistic, none of these things being far from the still centre of Dante's concern as the poet and philosopher par excellence in European letters of properly human being and becoming. But that precisely is the point, since for all the opening out of his spirit in ever fresh channels of concern, Dante's, at every stage, is a referral of the discrete emphasis to what actually and ultimately matters about it, namely its function as a coefficient of emergence, of the coming about of this or that individual or group of individuals in the fullness of his, her or their proper humanity.

Taking first, then, the anthropological aspect of the argument—though glancing back for a moment at its more properly theological context—we may say this, that both at the beginning and at the end of Dante's meditation upon the human situation stands the One who *is* as of the essence, the One who, comprehending as he does every difference and distinction in the universe knows himself only in the perfect simplicity of self; so, for example, on the Godhead as the uncircumscribed but all-circumscribing principle of everything that *is* in the world, we have these lines (1–6 and 28–30) from *Purgatorio* 11 and *Paradiso* 14:

> O Padre nostro, che ne' cieli stai,
> non circunscritto, ma per più amore
> ch'ai primi effetti di là sù tu hai,
>   laudato sia 'l tuo nome e 'l tuo valore
> da ogne creatura, com' è degno
> di render grazie al tuo dolce vapore
>   . . .
>   Quell' uno e due e tre che sempre vive
> e regna sempre in tre e 'n due e 'n uno,
> non circunscritto, e tutto circunscrive.[64]

while on the Godhead as containing without prejudice to that simplicity every kind of substantial and accidental form in the created order we have these (lines 85–90) from *Paradiso* 33:

> Nel suo profondo vidi che s'interna,
> legato con amore in un volume,
> ciò che per l'universo si squaderna:

64 'Our Father, who art in heaven, not circumscribed, but by reason of the surpassing love you bear your first works on high, hallowed be your name and your great goodness by every creature, it being meet and right to give thanks for your sweet exhalation . . . That one, two and three, which ever lives and ever reigns three, two and one, uncircumscribed and all-circumscribing.'

> sustanze e accidenti e lor costume
> quasi conflati insieme, per tal modo
> che ciò ch'i' dico è un semplice lume.[65]

But that is not all, for present as he is to himself in the perfect simplicity of self, God knows himself too by way of a continuing process of love-extrinsication, the key text here being the following from canto 29 of the *Paradiso*, an essay, precisely, in that same love-overflowing as all one with his very being:

> Non per aver a sé di bene acquisto,
> ch'esser non può, ma perché suo splendore
> potesse, risplendendo, dir 'Subsisto',
> in sua etternità di tempo fore,
> fuor d'ogne altro comprender, come i piacque,
> s'aperse in nuovi amor l'etterno amore.

> *(Paradiso* 29.13–18)[66]

Here, then, as throughout when it comes to the Godhead in Dante, it is a question of love-exponentiality, of a constant commitment to the kind of creativity whereby the first fruits of divine intentionality are brought forth and confirmed in point of their proper functionality. And nowhere is this love-exponentiality, this overflowing of divine concern, more evident than in the case of man, where it is a question of God's turning back in a spirit of rejoicing upon the handiwork of nature—upon the foetus as generated *ex materia*—with a view to fashioning from it a new creation, a being in potential by way of the possible intellect to every kind of intelligible form beneath the sun and circling as of the essence about the still centre of its own unique presence in the world. On the one hand, then, and before ever we reach the *Commedia*, we have this passage from the *Convivio* on the in-breathing of a rational soul in potential to a comprehensive act of understanding, indeed to seeing in some degree into the mind of its maker:

> E però dico che quando l'umano seme cade nel suo recettaculo, cioè ne la matrice, esso porta seco la vertù de l'anima generativa e la vertù del cielo e la vertù de li elementi legati, cioè la complessione; e matura e dispone la ma-

---

65 'In its depth I saw ingathered, bound by love in a single volume, the universe unfolded, substances, accidents and their relations fused as it were one with another, yet in my telling of it but a simple light.'

66 'Not for gain of good unto itself, which cannot be, but that his splendour might, in its resplendence, say "I AM", the eternal love, knowing neither time nor any other context, at its pleasure opened out in yet new loves.' Andrea Romano, '"S'aperse in nuovi amori l'etterno amore": Appunti sull'idea di Dio in Dante', *PRFC* 152 (2007), 55–58.

teria a la vertù formativa, la quale diede l'anima del generante; e la vertù
formativa prepara li organi a la vertù celestiale, che produce de la potenza del
seme l'anima in vita. La quale, incontanente produtta, riceve da la vertù del
motore del cielo lo intelletto possibile; lo quale potenzialmente in sé adduce
tutte le forme universali, secondo che sono nel suo produttore, e tanto meno
quanto più dilungato da la prima Intelligenza è.

(*Convivio* 4.21.4–5)[67]

while on the other we have this passage from the *Purgatorio* on the rejoicing of it
all, on God's forever delighting in man as—at any rate in his inception—a creature of grace and truth, of goodness and of self-attentiveness (the exquisite 'che
vive e sente e sé in sé rigira' of line 75):

> Apri a la verità che viene il petto;
> e sappi che, sì tosto come al feto
> l'articular del cerebro è perfetto,
>
> lo motor primo a lui si volge lieto
> sovra tant' arte di natura, e spira
> spirito novo, di vertù repleto,
>
> che ciò che trova attivo quivi, tira
> in sua sustanzia, e fassi un'alma sola,
> che vive e sente e sé in sé rigira.

(*Purgatorio* 25.67–75)[68]

---

67 'It is my contention, then, that when the human seed enters the womb, it bears with it a
threefold power: the power of the soul generating it, that of the heavens, and that of its elements as
bound up one with another within the economy of the whole. It ripens and readies matter to receive
the formative power deriving from the male parent, and this same formative power in turn prepares
the organs to receive that of the heavens which from the potentiality of the seed produces the living
soul. As soon as that soul is created, it receives from the mover of the heavens and the power thereof
the possible intellect, this in turn having the capacity to receive into itself (though in a manner
proportionate to its distance from the first mind) every kind of universal form as present to its
maker.'

68 'Open your heart now to the truth which follows, and be aware that no sooner is the fashioning
of the mind complete in the embryo than the first mover turns towards it and, rejoicing in the excellence of nature's handiwork, breathes into it a new spirit complete with its own power, this then
drawing into its substance every activity it finds there, making as it does so a single soul that lives,
feels and circles around its own centre.' Stephen Bemrose, ' "Come d'animal divegna fante": The Animation of the Human Embryo in Dante', in *The Human Embryo: Aristotle and the Arabic Traditions*,
ed. Gordon Reginald Dunstan (Exeter: Exeter University Press, 1990), 123–35; Jennifer Fraser, 'Dan-
te/"Fante": Embriology in Purgatory and Paradise', in *Dante and the Unorthodox: The Aesthetics of
Transgression*, ed. James Miller (Waterloo, Ontario: Wilfrid Laurier University Press, 2005), 290–309;
Giuliano Rossi, ' "Ma come d'animal divegna fante": Dante tra Alberto Magno e Tommaso', *CT* 13.2
(2010), 191–209.

This, then, is what it means to speak with Dante of God's forever opening out in fresh channels of love, of the love-abundance all of a piece with the God-head itself. But again there is more, for to be made in the likeness of God—and it is at this point that we pass from the theological to the anthropological and, with it, to the moral moment of the argument—is, for Dante, to share in that same affectivity, in that same knowing of self in the love-intensity thereof. But there is a difference, for while the Godhead, as at once coeval and consubstantial with that love-intensity, knows itself only in the, so to speak, undifferentiated love-abundance of its being, man, as an intellectual creature in the flesh, knows himself not so much in the unity as in the multiplicity of his loving, in the kind of love engendered by this or that positive encounter or occasional possibility along the way, and the kind of love given with the act itself of existence and bringing the soul at last into communion with God as the final cause of its every desiring. Preliminary, then, in respect of the multiplicity of human loving, of the many kinds of love proper to man in respect of his status as an intellectual creature in the flesh, we have these lines from early on in book 3 of the *Convivio*, eloquent indeed in their sense of man's loving after the manner of the stones beneath his feet, of the plants flourishing high up on the mountain slopes and in the shady valleys according to kind, of the beasts of the field delighting one in the company of another, and of those good men and true rejoicing as good men and true do in the prospect of whatsoever is pure, whatsoever is lovely and whatsoever is of good report—all part and parcel, Dante thinks, of man's proper patrimony as man, of his knowing himself in the endless variety of his affections:

> Onde è da sapere che ciascuna cosa, come detto è di sopra, per la ragione di sopra mostrata ha 'l suo speziale amore. Come le corpora simplici hanno amore naturato in sé a lo luogo proprio, e però la terra sempre discende al centro; lo fuoco ha [amore a] la circunferenza di sopra, lungo lo cielo de la luna, e però sempre sale a quello. Le corpora composte prima, sì come sono le minere, hanno amore a lo luogo dove la loro generazione è ordinata, e in quello crescono e acquistano vigore e potenza; onde vedemo la calamita sempre da la parte de la sua generazione ricevere vertù. Le piante, che sono prima animate, hanno amore a certo luogo più manifestamente, secondo che la complessione richiede; e però vedemo certe piante lungo l'acque quasi c[ontent]arsi, e certe sopra li gioghi de le montagne, e certe ne le piagge e dappiè monti; le quali se si transmutano, o muoiono del tutto o vivono quasi triste, disgiunte dal loro amico. Li animali bruti hanno più manifesto amore non solamente a li luoghi, ma l'uno l'altro vedemo amare. Li uomini hanno loro proprio amore a le perfette e oneste cose. E però che l'uomo, avvegna che una sola sustanza sia, tuttavia [la] forma, per la sua

nobilitade, ha in sé e la natura [d'ognuna di] queste cose, tutti questi amori puote avere e tutti li ha.

(*Convivio* 3.3.2–5)[69]

Here, however, we need to reinforce our distinction—Dante's distinction—between the two kinds of love proper to man as man, between (*a*) the kind of love engendered by this or that particular encounter and thus dependent for its actualization or enjoyment upon the moral moment proper of human experience (upon the aye or nay of the individual in question), and (*b*) the kind given—or so Dante is inclined to believe—with the act itself of existence and thus predating the moral moment proper of that experience, the aye or nay of the one who says 'I'. Admirable, then, for their precision in respect both of the basic idea here—for their distinction between 'amore d'animo' and 'amore naturale' respectively—and of the imperative engendered by this situation (namely the bringing home of the former to the latter within the economy of the whole) are these lines from canto 17 of the *Purgatorio*:

> 'Né creator né creatura mai',
> cominciò el, 'figliuol, fu sanza amore,
> o naturale o d'animo; e tu 'l sai.
>   Lo naturale è sempre sanza errore,
> ma l'altro puote errar per malo obietto
> o per troppo o per poco di vigore.
>   Mentre ch'elli è nel primo ben diretto,
> e ne' secondi sé stesso misura,
> esser non può cagion di mal diletto;

---

69 'What, then, we need to understand is this, that, for the reason shown above, everything has its own proper love. Just as simple bodies have within them a natural love for their proper place, which is why earth is always drawn to its centre, and just as fire has a natural love for the sphere above us bordering that of the Moon, and so always rises towards it, so the primary compound bodies, the minerals, have a love for the place where they are created, and where they grow and whence they derive vigour and energy; thus we find that a magnet always acquires its power from the place whence it comes. Plants which are the primary form of animate being, have a clear preference for certain places, according to their needs; so some plants we see to be at their happiest alongside water, while others thrive on high peaks or else on slopes or in the foothills, all of which either perish or else linger on sadly if up-rooted and parted from their friends. Brute animals have an even more obvious love, not only for particular places, but for one another. Human beings too have their proper love, in this case for all things good and praiseworthy. And since man, though but one in substance, comprehends by way of the nobility of his form all these things, he can and does love in all these ways.' Alberto Di Giovanni, *La filosofia dell'amore nelle opere di Dante* (Rome: Abete, 1967); Kenelm Foster, O.P., 'Dante and Eros', in *The Two Dantes* (London: Darton, Longman and Todd, 1977), 37–55; Gerald R. Midkiff, *Dante's Concept of Love*, Master's Thesis, University of Louisville, Kentucky, 1984; Dino Bigongiari, 'The Definition of Love: The Apprehensive and Appetitive Faculties', in *Readings in the 'Divine Comedy'. A Series of Lectures*, ed. Anne Paolucci (Dover, DE: Griffon House, 2006), 147–57.

ma quando al mal si torce, o con più cura
o con men che non dee corre nel bene,
contra 'l fattore adovra sua fattura'.

(*Purgatorio* 17.91–102)[70]

—lines to which, as bearing upon the notion of free will as that whereby this bringing home of the contingent to the connatural on the plane of properly human loving stands to be accomplished, we must add these from the next canto:

Or perché a questa ogn' altra si raccoglia,
innata v'è la virtù che consiglia,
e de l'assenso de' tener la soglia.
    Quest' è 'l principio là onde si piglia
ragion di meritare in voi, secondo
che buoni e rei amori accoglie e viglia.
    Color che ragionando andaro al fondo,
s'accorser d'esta innata libertate;
però moralità lasciaro al mondo.

(*Purgatorio* 18.61–69)[71]

To be, then, for Dante, is to know self not merely in the affectivity of self but in the multiplicity of one's loving. It is, more exactly, to know self both in the kind

70 'He began: "Neither Creator nor creature, my son, was—as well you know—ever without love, either natural or elective. Natural love can never err, but the other may in respect either of an unworthy object or else by way either of excess or defect. So long as it is directed on the highest good and as regards all others is properly proportionate, it cannot be the cause of doubtful pleasure. But bent upon evil or chasing the good with more or less zeal than it ought, against the creator works his creature."'

71 'Now in order that to this every other will may be brought home, innate in you and ideally presiding over the threshold of consent is the power to oversee, this, according as it garners and winnows out good and evil loves, being the origin and principle in you of deserving. Those looking most profoundly into this matter and intuiting as they did so this innate freedom of the will made over to men on this basis the entire science of ethics.' Christopher Ryan, 'Free Will in Theory and Practice: *Purgatorio* XVIII and Two Characters in the *Inferno*', in *Dante Soundings*, ed. David Nolan (Dublin and Totowa, NJ: Irish Academic Press / Rowman and Littlefield, 1981), 100–112; Giancarlo Rati, 'La soglia dell'assenso: Il canto XVIII del *Purgatorio*', *EL* 11.1 (1986), 3–19; Antonietta Bufano, 'Applicazione della dottrina del libero arbitrio nella *Commedia*', in *Miscellanea di studi danteschi in memoria di Silvio Pasquazi*, vol. 1, ed. Alfonso Paolella et al. (Naples: Federico e Ardia, 1993), 193–99; Cristiana Fordyce, 'Il problema di amore e libero arbitrio nella *Commedia* di Dante', *Romance Review* 4.1 (1994), 35–51; Enzo Noè Girardi, 'Al centro del *Purgatorio*: Il tema del libero arbitrio', in *Il pensiero filosofico e teologico di Dante Alighieri*, ed. Alessandro Ghisalberti (Milan: V&P Università, 2001), 21–38 (and in *Ultimi studi su Dante* [Milan: Vita e pensiero, 2016], 43–57); Pasquale Porro, 'Canto XVIII: Amore e libero arbitrio in Dante', in *Lectura Dantis Romana: Cento canti per cento anni, II Purgatorio*, vol. 2, ed. Enrico Malato and Andrea Mazzucchi (Rome: Salerno, 2014), 523–60.

of love all of a piece with existence itself ('amore naturale' or connatural love) and in the kind of love quickened and sustained by the positive encounter ('amore d'animo' or elective love). But that, in truth, is only the beginning of it, for everywhere operative from out of the depths is, again, the call to gather in the latter to the former, the occasional to the ontological on the plane of loving. Only in the degree to which the individual answers to this does he know himself in the blessed ulteriority of his presence in the world, as in potential to the kind of transhumanity as but humanity itself in act. Anything other than this and he knows himself only in the rising up of the creature against the creator (the 'contra 'l fattore adovra sua fattura' of *Purgatorio* 17.102) and thus in the effrontery of it all.

THE DIALECTICS OF BEING:
A DIFFICULT DIMENSIONALITY

But what in this sense amounts to a proposal of the existential issue by way of a bringing home of one kind of love to another as the way of properly human happiness stands now to be developed in terms of the dialectics of specifically human being, of the structures of consciousness which love thus understood is called upon to resolve. More precisely, it stands to be developed in terms of the bringing home of each successive parameter of consciousness to its polar counterpart on the plane of properly human being. Thus just as *time* as the before and after of human experience in its positive unfolding stands to be brought home to *eternity* as the immanent and abiding truth of self apt in its height and depth to transcend its every eventuality, so also *locality* as the whereabouts of this or that instance of specifically human being stands to be brought home to *universality* as a matter of its verifiability here, there and everywhere, as transcending, that is to say, the circumstances of its positive encounter. And just as *individuality* as but a circling of self about the still centre of its own being (the 'sé in sé rigira' of *Purgatorio* 25) stands to be brought home to *collectivity* as that whereby one man enters creatively into the presence of another, so also *freedom* as the power to self-determination stands to be brought home to *destiny* as the ground and guarantee of its significance. At every point, then, the imperative looms large, the triumph of time over eternity, of locality over universality, of individuality over collectivity and of freedom over destiny making only for despair as the dominant mood of existence. Now here we have to be careful, for never in Dante is it a question of liquidating one thing in favour of another—of time in favour of eternity, of locality in favour of universality, of individuality in favour of collectivity and of freedom in favour of destiny—his, typically, being an honouring of each and every parameter of awareness as in and for itself a proper object of concern. But that notwithstanding, man as man subsists, he thinks, by way of a difficult dimensionality, failure to address and, as far as may be, to resolve the tensions generated by this situation making only for the most complete kind of ontological catastrophe.

Time, in Dante's sense of it, is but a matter of the 'before and after of things under the aspect of number', and as such it is present to us first of all in respect of the before and after of intentionality, of the step-by-step character of properly human understanding; so, for example, with its sense of that same understanding as but a series of epistemic moments each qualitatively distinct in point both of substance and of proper perfection, we have this passage from the *Convivio* at 4.13.2:

> Che se io desidero di sapere li principii de le cose naturali, incontanente che io so questi, è compiuto e terminato questo desiderio. E se poi io desidero di sapere che cosa e com'è ciascuno di questi principii, questo è un altro desiderio nuovo, né per l'avvenimento di questo non mi si toglie la perfezione a la quale mi condusse l'altro; e questo cotale dilatare non è cagione d'imperfezione, ma di perfezione maggiore.[72]

while as confirming this situation by way of comparison with the uninterrupted character of angelic intelligence, of its proceeding by way less of recollection than of steady intellection, we have these lines from the *Paradiso* at 29.76–81:

> Queste sustanze, poi che fur gioconde
> de la faccia di Dio, non volser viso
> da essa, da cui nulla si nasconde:

---

72 'If, for instance, I wish to know the principles governing natural things, this wish is fulfilled and brought to completion as soon as I know what these principles are. If I then wish to know with respect to each of these principles how they are made up and wherein they have their origins this is another and distinct desire. Moreover, the occurrence of this new desire does not deprive me of the perfection enjoyed through the fulfilling of the first desire, for such opening out does not cause imperfection but, rather, greater perfection still.' For the 'time as the before and after of things under the aspect of number' moment of the argument, *Convivio* 4.2.6: 'Lo tempo, secondo che dice Aristotile nel quarto de la Fisica [4.11.219b1], è 'numero di movimento, secondo prima e poi'. Franco Masciandaro, *La problematica del tempo nella 'Commedia'* (Ravenna: Longo, 1976); Anne Higgins, 'Medieval Notions of the Structure of Time', *JMRS* 19.2 (1989), 227–50; Teodolinda Barolini, 'Problems in Paradise: The Mimesis of Time and the Paradox of *Più e Meno*', in *The Undivine Comedy: Detheologizing Dante* (Princeton: Princeton University Press, 1992), 166–93; Christian Moevs, 'The "Primum Mobile" as a Pot of Time: *Paradiso*, XXVII.115–20', *Romance Notes* 40 (2000), 247–57; Christian Moevs, *The Metaphysics of Dante's 'Comedy'* (Oxford: Oxford University Press, 2005), especially 134–40; Peter Armour, 'Time and Space in Dante's *Comedy*', *Studi d'Italianistica nell'Africa Australe* 2 (2001), 1–16. More generally, Pierre Duhem, *Le Système du monde: Histoire des doctrines cosmologiques de Platon à Copernic* (Paris: Hermann, 1913–17) and reprints, with a selection in *Medieval Cosmology: Theories of Infinity, Place, Time, Void, and the Plurality of the Worlds*, ed. and trans. Roger Ariew (Chicago: University of Chicago Press, 1985); Richard Sorabji, *Time, Creation and the Continuum: Theories in Antiquity and the Early Middle Ages* (Chicago: Chicago University Press, 2006 [1983]).

però non hanno vedere interciso
da novo obietto, e però non bisogna
rememorar per concetto diviso.[73]

Thus time enters into human experience in respect of one of the most fundamental aspects of man's activity as man, namely in respect of his intentional reconstruction both of self and of the world beyond self as the basis for everything
coming next by way of its proper conception and celebration. The intentional
reconstruction both of self and of the world beyond self, Dante thinks, is always
temporally conditioned. It is always a matter of its successive moments.

But over and beyond the epistemological, and indeed more fundamental than
the epistemological, there is the biographical aspect of the matter, time functioning in this sense as the means of self-perspectivization, of knowing self in the
variously modulated presence of self; so, for example, as far as Dante personally
is concerned, we have this passage from early on in the *Convivio* relative to the
otherness of his youthful and of his mature spirituality and to otherness thus
understood as but part of the natural rhythm of things:

> E se ne la presente opera, la quale è Convivio nominata, e vo' che sia, più
> virilmente si trattasse che ne la Vita Nuova, non intendo però a quella in
> parte alcuna derogare, ma maggiormente giovare per questa quella; veg-
> gendo sì come ragionevolmente quella fervida e passionata, questa temper-
> ata e virile esser conviene. Ché altro si conviene e dire e operare ad una
> etade che ad altra; perché certi costumi sono idonei e laudabili ad una etade,
> che sono sconci e biasimevoli ad altra.
>
> (*Convivio* 1.1.16–17)[74]

while in respect of otherness thus understood as a property of human experience
generally we have these lines from the 'arc of life' chapters towards the end of book

---

73 'These substances, since they were made glad with God's face from which nothing is hid, have
never turned their eyes from it, so that their sight is never intercepted by a new object and they have
no need to recall by way of discrete concepts.' Barbara Faes de Mottoni, 'Il linguaggio e la memoria
dell'angelo in Dante', in *Pour Dante: Dante et l'Apocalypse. Lectures humanistes de Dante (Travaux du
Centre d'études supérieures de la Renaissance autour de Dante, 1993–1998)*, directed by Bruno Pichard
(Paris: Champion, 2001), 237–53.

74 'And if in the present work, entitled *The Banquet*—which is what I wish it to be—the subject
matter is treated in a more mature fashion than in the *New Life*, this does not mean that I intend in any
way to disparage that early work. My intention is, rather, that this work give added weight to the former,
by making it clear how reasonable it is that the earlier work should be fervent and passionate and this
one temperate and mature. For what is required of us in our speaking and acting varies from one stage
of life to another, because certain ways of behaving that are appropriate and laudable at one stage are
demeaning and blameworthy at another.'

4, lines similarly attuned to the seasonality of it all, to the *as and when* of custom and comportment along the way:

> Dov'è da sapere che la nostra buona e diritta natura ragionevolmente procede in noi, sì come vedemo procedere la natura de le piante in quelle; e però altri costumi e altri portamenti sono ragionevoli ad una etade più che ad altra, ne li quali l'anima nobilitata ordinatamente procede per una semplice via, usando li suoi atti ne li loro tempi ed etadi sì come a l'ultimo frutto sono ordinati.
>
> (*Convivio* 4.24.8)[75]

Thus, to contemplate the course of one's existence is to register its periodicity, its phased implementation. One moment gives way to another as a matter both of development and of decorum, of a humanity gradually opening out after the manner of a rose in its maturity and able at last to rejoice in the path it has chosen:

> Dunque appresso la propria perfezione, la quale s'acquista ne la gioventute, conviene venire quella che alluma non pur sé ma li altri; e conviensi aprire l'uomo quasi com'una rosa che più chiusa stare non puote, e l'odore che dentro generato è spandere: e questo conviene essere in questa terza etade, che per mano corre . . . E dice ch'ella fa due cose: l'una, che ella ritorna a Dio, sì come a quello porto onde ella si partio quando venne ad intrare nel mare di questa vita; l'altra si è, che ella benedice lo cammino che ha fatto, però che è stato diritto e buono, e sanza amaritudine di tempesta.
>
> (*Convivio* 4.27.4 and 28.2)[76]

---

75 'It should be explained here that our nature when it is good and upright, develops in us in a fitting manner (just as we observe the nature of plants developing in them), and so different customs and different kinds of behaviour are fitting at one stage which are not so at another. In these the ennobled soul proceeds in an orderly way along a direct path, deploying its activities at the times and stages suited to producing its final fruit.' Bruno Nardi, 'L'arco della vita (nota illustrativa al *Convivio*)', in *Saggi di filosofia dantesca*, 2nd ed. (Florence: La Nuova Italia, 1967), 110–38; Elizabeth Sears, *The Ages of Man: Medieval Interpretations of the Life Cycle* (Princeton: Princeton University Press, 1986); Willi Hirdt, 'Les âges de la vie chez Dante', in *Les âges de la vie au Moyen Age. Actes du Colloque du Départment d'études médiévales de l'Université de Paris-Sorbonne et de l'Université Friedrick-Wilhelm de Bonn, 16–17 mars 1990*, ed. Henri du Bois and Michel Zink (Paris: Presses de l'Université de Paris-Sorbonne, 1992), 187–97.

76 'Therefore following upon our own perfection, which we acquire in the age of maturity, should come the perfection which illuminates not only ourselves but others; one should open out like a rose that can no longer remain closed, and spread abroad the fragrance which is produced within; and this should take place in the third age of life, which is our present concern . . . The text then says that the noble soul does two things: first, that it returns to God as to that port from which it departed when it

But there is more, and more, if anything, of still greater significance, for time is present to man in the sense that every proposal relative to the shaping and substantiation of self here and now is informed by death as the far limit of existentially significant activity. Thus time speaks in the imperative. It brooks no delay and urges the spirit to ever greater commitment; so, for example, on the lips of Beatrice and addressed in the final canto of the *Purgatorio* to the pilgrim poet, we have these lines, in all the stark economy thereof, on life as but a hastening towards death:

> Tu nota; e sì come da me son porte,
> così queste parole segna a' vivi
> del viver ch'è un correre a la morte.

(*Purgatorio* 33.52–54)[77]

—all of which means unremitting commitment, a giving of self wholly without qualification to the matter in hand; hence, as ever, Virgil on the need to press on lest time cheat the pilgrim poet of his proper patrimony:

> Più era già per noi del monte vòlto
> e del cammin del sole assai più speso
> che non stimava l'animo non sciolto,
>   quando colui che sempre innanzi atteso
> andava, cominciò: 'Drizza la testa;
> non è più tempo di gir sì sospeso.
>   Vedi colà un angel che s'appresta
> per venir verso noi; vedi che torna
> dal servigio del dì l'ancella sesta.
>   Di reverenza il viso e li atti addorna,
> sì che i diletti lo 'nvïarci in suso;
> pensa che questo dì mai non raggiorna!'
>   Io era ben del suo ammonir uso
> pur di non perder tempo, sì che 'n quella
> materia non potea parlarmi chiuso.

(*Purgatorio* 12.85–87)[78]

---

came to enter into the sea of this life; second, that it blesses the journey that it has made, because it has been straight and good and without bitterness of storm.'

77 'Note well what I say, and just as these words have been borne from me to you, do you bear them to those living the life which is a race towards death.' Thomas Werge, 'The Race to Death and the Race for Salvation in Dante's *Commedia*', DS 97 (1979), 1–21.

78 'Much farther now had we circled the mountain and much more the sun had covered of its track

Thus to understand the nature of the human predicament is to be committed to its swift resolution, time entering into human experience as a principle of delimitation, as defining the *thus far and no farther* of reasonable activity and forever inculcating as it does so a sense of the urgency of it all.

In each of these ways, then, time is present to the individual as a structure of awareness. As a structure of awareness in respect of *understanding*, it is present to him in the progressive character of human intellection, in the before and after of each successive determination of the mind. As a structure of awareness in respect of *being*, it is present to him in the periodicity of his presence in the world, in the forever fresh formulation of historical selfhood. And as a structure of awareness in respect of *willing*, it is present to him in the urgency of it all, in its suffering no delay. But—and this now is the point—time, like any other ontological parameter taken in isolation from its polar counterpart, is ambiguous; for if as a structure of awareness in respect of *understanding* it is present to him in the progressive character of human intellection, in the before and after of each successive determination of the mind, by the same token it engenders by way of the open-endedness of it all a perennial restiveness of the spirit. And if as a structure of awareness in respect of *being* it is present to him in the periodicity of his presence in the world, in the forever fresh formulation of historical selfhood, by the same token it engenders a sense of that same presence in the world as but a matter of its mere modality. And if as a structure of awareness in respect of *willing* it is present to him in the urgency of it all, by the same token it engenders anxiety in respect of death as but a matter of foreclosure. Time, therefore, is a double-edged sword, an element in the experience of the individual apt in one and the same moment both to facilitate an act of specifically human being and to rule out its definitive resolution, which is why man as man is summoned *even now* out of the restiveness of time into the stillness of eternity, eternity constituting a reply to the destructiveness of time as a dominant means of self-interpretation.

Dante, in thinking and speaking of eternity, thinks and speaks of it in different ways. Sometimes, as in the 'e io etterno duro' passage of *Inferno* 3.1–9, he thinks of it as a matter merely of everlastingness or indefinite temporality. Elsewhere, however, but especially in the *Paradiso*, he entertains the more recognizably Neoplatonic and Boethian sense of eternity as the kind of 'pointedness' or 'all-at-onceness' (*tota simul*) of time proper to the Godhead and present to the now transfigured spirit as a cause for rejoicing; so, for example, these lines from the

---

than I, my mind not being free, had reckoned when he, ever looking ahead as he went, began: "Look up! Time there is no more for going on thus absorbed. See there an angel hastening to meet us. See how the sixth handmaid returns from serving the day. Grace your aspect and bearing with reverence that it may please him to direct us upwards. Be mindful that this day will ne'er dawn again." I was well enough used to his admonitions not to lose time, so that in that regard nothing he said was for me obscure.' So also *Inferno* 24.46–60 and *Purgatorio* 3.73–78.

Cacciaguida moment of the *Paradiso*, rapt in their sense of the now gathered character of intellection among the elect:

> 'O cara piota mia che sì t'intusi,
> che, come veggion le terrene menti
> non capere in trïangol due ottusi,
>   così vedi le cose contingenti
> anzi che sieno in sé, mirando il punto
> a cui tutti li tempi son presenti'.

(Paradiso 17.13–18)[79]

—lines to which, as confirming the twofold aspatiality and atemporality of the Godhead together with this as again a cause for rejoicing among those privileged now to look on, we may add these from canto 29 as but a further essay in the adimensionality of the One who *is* as of the essence:

> Poi cominciò: 'Io dico, e non dimando,
> quel che tu vuoli udir, perch' io l'ho visto
> là 've s'appunta ogne *ubi* e ogne *quando*.'

(Paradiso 29.10–12)[80]

What, then, given the notion of time thus understood as the before and after of events on the plane of the horizontal and the notion of eternity thus under-

---

79 'O my dear seed-plot, who are raised so high that, even as earthly minds see that there cannot be two obtuse angles in a triangle, so you, gazing on the point to which all times are present, see contingent things before they are in themselves.' Marguerite Mills Chiarenza, 'Time and Eternity in the Myths of *Paradiso* XVII', in *Dante, Petrarch, Boccaccio: Studies in the Italian Trecento in Honor of C. S. Singleton*, ed. Aldo S. Bernardo and Anthony L. Pellegrini (Binghamton, NY: Center for Early Medieval and Renaissance Studies, 1983), 133–50; Giuseppe Giacalone, 'Tempo ed eternità nella *Divina Commedia*', in *Dante Alighieri: La Divina Commedia*, vol. 3, ed. Giuseppe Giacalone (Rome: Signorelli, 1988), 66–82 (subsequently in *Atti della Dante Alighieri a Treviso 1984–1989* [Treviso: Matteo, 1989], 170–81 and *Da Malebolge alla Senna: Studi letterari in onore di Giorgio Santangelo* [Palermo: Palumbo, 1993], 259–78); Italo Sciuto, 'Eternità e tempo in Dante', in *Tempus, aevum, aeternitas: La concettualizzazione del tempo nel pensiero tardomedievale. Atti del Colloquio Internazionale, Trieste, 4–6 marzo 1999*, ed. Guido Alliney and Luciano Cova (Florence: Olschki, 2000), 1–20; Remo Bodei, 'Tempo e eternità in Dante e in Petrarca', *LC* 32–34 (2005), 67–76. More generally, Richard C. Dales, 'Time and Eternity in the Thirteenth Century', *JHI* 49 (1988), 27–45; Richard C. Dales, *Medieval Discussions of Eternity* (Leiden: Brill, 1990). For the 'e io etterno duro' passage on the threshold of *Inferno* 3: 'and I endure eternally'.

80 'Then she began, "I tell, not ask, what you would hear; for I have seen it there where *every ubi* and every *quando* is centred."' Christian Moevs, *The Metaphysics of Dante's 'Comedy'* (Oxford: Oxford University Press, 2005), especially 151–60.

stood as the simultaneity of past, present and future in the One who *is* as of the essence, does it mean to speak with Dante of the call *even now* from time to eternity, from the restiveness of the one into the stillness of the other? In short, three things: in respect of *understanding* (where it is a question of intellection as but a series of proximate perfections), a sense of the transparency of every high-level or otherwise culturally conditioned inflexion of the spirit to the truth by which it is transcended; in respect of *being* (where it is a question of the ever fresh formulation of historical selfhood) a sense of the accountability of each successive implementation of self to the settled properties of personality; and in respect of *willing* (where it is a question of the immanence of death as the far limit of significant activity) a sense of standing even now in the ἔσχατος as the innermost and abiding substance of historical selfhood. At every point along the way, then, the call as but a call to emancipation is more than ever urgent, indifference here— meaning by this a more or less considered passing by on the other side—only ever making for the kind of despair always and everywhere generated by the triumph of time as a principle of self-interpretation.

Locality as a matter of situatedness, of the individual's having his being here rather than there in the world, is, like time, present to him first of all in point of understanding. It is present to him in point of understanding in that understanding in man turns upon the positive encounter, upon his abstracting from the phantasm or raw sensation of sense experience the *species intelligibilis* or intentional form of a thing thereafter established as an object of contemplation at the pinnacle of the mind, in the forum, that is to say, of pure consciousness. This, at any rate, is Virgil's point in the course of the great love cantos at the heart of the *Purgatorio*, love, as he understands it, being a matter, precisely, of perception, abstraction and positive inclination:

> L'animo, ch'è creato ad amar presto,
> ad ogne cosa è mobile che piace,
> tosto che dal piacere in atto è desto.
> Vostra apprensiva da esser verace
> tragge intenzione, e dentro a voi la spiega,
> sì che l'animo ad essa volger face;
> e se, rivolto, inver' di lei si piega,
> quel piegare è amor, quell'è natura
> che per piacer di novo in voi si lega.

> (*Purgatorio* 18.19–27)[81]

---

81 'The mind, created quick to love, is readily moved towards everything that pleases, as soon as by pleasure it is roused to action. Your perception takes from outward reality an impression and unfolds

Thus locality too enters into human experience in respect of one of the most fundamental aspects of man's activity as man, namely of his intentional reconstitution of the world as the basis for his every subsequent attempt to think and to speak significantly of it. This intentional reconstitution of the world, Dante thinks, is always spatially conditioned. It is always a matter of the individual's actually coming across what he seeks to understand.

But there is more, for locality as a matter of situatedness, of a man's having his being here rather than there in the world, is present to him in point of belonging. It is present to him in point of belonging in that his, typically, is both an acknowledgement of and an allegiance to the place of his coming about, the place of his coming about serving in just about every respect, and come what may, to determine the shape and substance of his presence in the world as a creature of seeing and of saying. Decisive, certainly, in Dante's own case, is the 'come what may' component of the argument, he himself, at every stage in the course of his exile, knowing himself by way of the anguished psychology of displacement, by way, that is to say, of the melancholy, the misgiving and the mirage of homecoming at every stage striving for mastery as the mood of his existence; so, for example, the 'famosissima figlia di Roma, Fiorenza' moment of the *Convivio*:

Poi che fu piacere de li cittadini de la bellissima e famosissima figlia di Roma, Fiorenza, di gittarmi fuori del suo dolce seno—nel quale nato e nutrito fui in fino al colmo de la vita mia, e nel quale, con buona pace di quella, desidero con tutto lo cuore di riposare l'animo stancato e terminare lo tempo che m'è dato—per le parti quasi tutte a le quali questa lingua si stende, peregrino, quasi mendicando, sono andato, mostrando contra mia voglia la piaga de la fortuna, che suole ingiustamente al piagato molte volte essere imputata.

(*Convivio* 1.3.4)[82]

---

it within you, so that it makes the mind turn to it; and if the mind, so turned, inclines to it, that inclination is love, that is nature as bound by pleasure in you afresh.' Stan Scott, 'Aspects of Dante's Epistemology', *Australian Journal of French Studies* 6.2–3 (1969), 440–46; Bruno Nardi, 'La conoscenza umana', in *Dante e la cultura medievale*, ed. Paolo Mazzantini (Rome: Editori Laterza, 1983), 135–72; Patrick Boyde, *Perception and Passion in Dante's 'Comedy'* (Cambridge: Cambridge University Press, 1993); Alfonso Maierù, 'Sull'epistemologia di Dante', in *Dante e la scienza*, ed. Patrick Boyde and Vittorio Russo (Ravenna: Longo, 1995), 157–72; Edward G. Miller, *Sense Perception in Dante's 'Commedia'* (Lewiston, NY: Edwin Mellen Press, 1996); Dino Bigongiari, 'The Definition of Love: The Apprehensive and Appetitive Faculties', in *Readings in the 'Divine Comedy'. A Series of Lectures*, ed. Anne Paolucci (Dover, DE: Griffon House, 2006), 147–57. More generally on medieval epistemology, Camille Berube, *La Connaissance de l'individuel au moyen âge* (Montreal: Presses de l'Université, 1964); John F. Boler, 'Intuitive and Abstractive Cognition', in *The Cambridge History of Later Medieval Philosophy*, ed. Norman Kretzman, Anthony Kenny, Jan Pinborg and Eleonore Stump (Cambridge: Cambridge University Press, 1982), 460–78; Marcia L. Colish, *The Mirror of Language: A Study in the Medieval Theory of Knowledge*, rev. ed. (Lincoln: University of Nebraska Press, 1983).

82 'But since it pleased the citizens of that most beautiful city and famous daughter of Rome, Florence, to cast me from her sweet bosom—the city wherein I was born and nurtured through to

or the 'per lontananza m'è tolto dal viso' moment of the canzone *Tre donne intorno al cor mi son venute*:

> E se non che de gli occhi miei 'l bel viso
> per lontananza m'è tolto dal viso,
> che m'have in foco miso,
> lieve mi conterei ciò che m'è grave.

> (*Tre donne intorno al cor mi son venute*, lines 81–84)

or the 'bello ovile ov' io dormi' agnello' moment of *Paradiso* 25:

> Se mai continga che 'l poema sacro
> al quale ha posto mano e cielo e terra,
> sì che m'ha fatto per molti anni macro,
>   vinca la crudeltà che fuor mi serra
> del bello ovile ov' io dormi' agnello,
> nimico ai lupi che li danno guerra;
>   con altra voce omai, con altro vello
> ritornerò poeta, e in sul fonte
> del mio battesmo prenderò 'l cappello.

> (*Paradiso* 25.1–9)[83]

where homecoming in all the depth and intensity thereof constitutes still the stuff of Dante's meditation, the final cause of his every yearning. And if then we add to these the 'loco' and 'luogo' moments of, say, the 'Poi che la carità del natio loco / mi strinse' of *Inferno* 14.1–2,[84] or the 'o pregio etterno del loco ond'io fui' of *Pur-*

---

maturity, and where, with her goodwill, I yearn with all my heart to rest my weary mind and live out the time vouchsafed me—I have wandered much like a beggar through just about every place our language is spoken, displaying willy-nilly the wounds inflicted upon me by fate whereby those afflicted are often unreasonably held accountable'. For the *Tre donne* passage, 'And were it not that the fair goal of my eyes has by distance been taken from me—this having set me ablaze—I would count as light that which weighs upon me'. Nicely nuanced in favour of a more ample sense of citizenship as but a matter of world-citizenship but eloquent withal in this respect is the 'Nos autem, cui mundus est patria velut piscibus equor, quanquam Sarnum biberimus ante dentes et Florentiam adeo diligamus ut, quia dileximus, exilium patiamur iniuste' of the *De vulgari eloquentia* at 1.6.3 ('But I, who have the whole world as my fatherland just as the fishes do the sea, and though I drank at the Arno before ever I cut my teeth, and love Florence so much that for her sake I suffered unjust exile').

83 'Should it ever come to pass that the sacred poem to which both heaven and earth have set their hand such that it has made me lean for many years should overcome the cruelty that bars me from the fair sheepfold where I slept as a lamb and an enemy to the wolves that make a war on it, with another voice now and another fleece shall I return a poet and at the font of my baptism take the laurel crown'.

84 'Since love of my native place constrained me'. For *Purgatorio* 7.18: 'O eternal honour of the place from which I come'; *Purgatorio* 13.105: 'tell me, either by place or by name, who you are'; *Purga-*

gatorio 7.18, or the 'fammiti conto o per luogo o per nome' of *Purgatorio* 13.105, or the 'però che 'l loco u' fui a viver posto' of *Purgatorio* 24.79, or the 'Li antichi miei e io nacqui nel loco' of *Paradiso* 16.40 or the 'In quel loco fu'io Pietro Damiano' of *Paradiso* 21.121, then here is evidence enough of the importance he attaches to place as a principle of self-recognition and thus of self-affirmation.

In both these ways, then, locality is present to man as a structure of awareness. As a structure of awareness in respect of *understanding*, it is present to him by way of the dependence of all knowing on the positive encounter, there being nothing in the mind which is not first in the senses; while as a structure of awareness in respect of *belonging* it is present to him by way of place as a principle of self-recognition and, by way of self-recognition, of self-affirmation. But—and this now is the point—locality, like any other ontological parameter taken in isolation from its polar counterpart, is ambiguous; for if as a structure of awareness in respect of *understanding* it is present to him by way of the dependence of knowing on the positive encounter, there being nothing in the mind which is not first in the senses, then by the same token it delivers that same act of understanding to the mere contingencies thereof, to the *what*, *when* and *where* of whatever the individual happens to come across. And if as a structure of awareness in respect of *belonging* it is present to him by way of place as the in-and-through-which of self-recognition and, by way of self-recognition, of self-affirmation, then it encourages also a sense of the over-againstness of it all (the 'Who were your ancestors?' moment of *Inferno* 10), of difference as a way of seeing and understanding the world. Locality too, therefore, is a double-edged sword, an element in the experience of the individual at once facilitating that experience and imposing adversely upon it, which is why man as man is summoned out of the exclusiveness of locality into the inclusiveness of universality, universality constituting a reply to the destructiveness of locality as a dominant means of self-interpretation.

Dante, in thinking and speaking of universality, thinks and speaks of it in two ways or, more exactly, under two aspects: in terms either of the *pointedness* or of the *encompassing* thereof, these things, however, as but models of understanding in respect of being precisely as such, relating the one to the other by way not so much of contradistinction as of mutual complementarity and indeed of mutual reducibility; so, for example, in respect of the first of them, of being under the aspect of pointedness, we have the familiar *when* and *where* passage of *Paradiso* 29.10–12, a passage perfectly attuned, however, to the status of that same being as but the encompassing, as comprehending its every discrete instantiation:

---

torio 24.79: 'for the place where I have been put to live'; for *Paradiso* 16.40: 'My ancestors and I were born at the place'; and for *Paradiso* 21.121: 'In that place I was Peter Damian.'

Poi cominciò: 'Io dico, e non dimando,
quel che tu vuoli udir, perch' io l'ho visto
là 've s'appunta ogne *ubi* e ogne *quando.*'[85]

while in respect of the second of them, of being as but the encompassing, we have
the again familiar 'forma universal' passage of *Paradiso* 33.82–93, a passage likewise
attuned, however, to the singularity of what *is* as of the essence:

Oh abbondante grazia ond' io presunsi
ficcar lo viso per la luce etterna,
tanto che la veduta vi consunsi!
Nel suo profondo vidi che s'interna,
legato con amore in un volume,
ciò che per l'universo si squaderna:
sustanze e accidenti e lor costume
quasi conflati insieme, per tal modo
che ciò ch'i' dico è un semplice lume.
La forma universal di questo nodo
credo ch'i' vidi, perché più di largo,
dicendo questo, mi sento ch'i' godo.[86]

Now here, to be sure, we are speaking of the being of the One who alone *is* as
of the essence, of the I AM at once preceding and comprehending all being what-

---

85 'Then she began, "I tell, not ask, what you would hear; for I have seen it there where every *ubi*
and every *quando* is centred."' For the 'opening out in ever fresh channels of love' motif, Andrea Romano, '"S'aperse in nuovi amori l'etterno amore": Appunti sull'idea di Dio in Dante', *PRFC* 152 (2007),
55–58.
86 'Oh grace abounding whereby I presumed to fix my look on the eternal light such that I saw at
the far limits of my seeing! I saw enclosed in its depths, bound up with love in one volume, everything
unfolded leaf by leaf throughout the universe: substance and accidents and their modalities, fused, as
it were, one with another such that what I speak of is but a simple light. I believe I then beheld the
universal form of this knot, for in speaking of it I sense my blessedness all the more.' So also, with respect
to the containing of everything that *is* in the world by the Protonoè or First Mind, the *Convivio* at 2.3.11:
'Questo [lo cielo Empireo] è lo soprano edificio del mondo, nel quale tutto lo mondo s'inchiude, e di
fuori dal quale nulla è; ed esso non è in luogo ma formato fu solo ne la prima Mente, la quale li Greci
dicono Protonoè' (This [the Empyrean] is the sovereign heaven of the universe, the heaven by which
that universe is contained and beyond which nothing exists. It is not itself in any place, but was fashioned by the divine mind—or as the Greeks call it, the Protonoè—alone), together with the *Paradiso*
at 22.61–67 (Benedict to Dante on the Empyrean as, in effect, coextensive with the divine mind): 'Ond'
elli: "Frate, il tuo alto disio / s'adempierà in su l'ultima spera, / ove s'adempion tutti li altri e 'l mio. /
Ivi è perfetta, matura e intera / ciascuna disïanza; in quella sola / è ogne parte là ove sempr' era, /
perché non è in loco e non s'impola"' (Whence he: 'Brother, this your most exalted desire will be
fulfilled there above in the last sphere wherein is the fulfilment of all others, my own included. There
all we long for is perfect, mature and entire. There and there alone all that is is where it ever was, for
there is neither space nor polarity'). See too the letter to Cangrande, *Epistole* 13.24.

ever and subsisting as the ground and guarantee both of its integrity and of its intelligibility. But (and this now is what matters) there is a sense, and indeed a sense apt to commend itself both logically and ontologically, in which the *being there* of a thing—of anything insofar as it actually *is* according to kind—may always and everywhere be said to transcend the whereabouts of its positive encounter, anything and everything, insofar as it actually *is* according to kind, thus having its being here, there and everywhere. What, then, from the point of view of the individual more or less anxious in respect of the twofold integrity and intelligibility of his or her discrete presence in the world as a creature of ultimate accountability does it mean to speak with Dante of the call *even now* from locality to universality, from the exclusiveness of the one to the inclusiveness of the other? In short, two things: as regards *understanding* (where it is a question of the positive encounter as the condition of significant intelligence), a now heightened sense of the epistemic instance as transparent to the ontological *prius* by which it is transcended and in the context of which it stands at last to be contemplated; and as regards *belonging* (where it is a question of place as a paradigm of ontic awareness), a now more ample sense of citizenship, of self as, withal, transcending the circumstances of its coming about. Here too, then, the call as but a call to emancipation is more than ever urgent, indifference here—meaning by this a more or less considered passing by on the other side—only ever making for the kind of despair always and everywhere generated by the triumph of locality as a principle of self-interpretation.

Individuality as a structure of consciousness everywhere looms large in Dante, his, typically, being a setting up both of the philosophical and of the theological issue in terms of the one who says 'I', of the individual seeking to affirm his or her discrete presence in the world as a creature of reasonable seeing, understanding and choosing. His, more precisely, is a proposal of that issue in terms (*a*) of a rejoicing in the notion of historical selfhood, in the at once unprecedented and unparalleled character of this or that instance of specifically human being and in the unique calling thereof, and (*b*) of the courage required of the individual when it comes to affirming self over against those forces operative out of the depths making at best for a neutralization and at worst for an obliteration of self. To take, first, then, the first of these things, namely Dante's commitment to the uniqueness of each and every instance of historical selfhood, this, everywhere implicit as it is in the text, is variously open to documentation. On the one hand, then, there are those passages—namely *Convivio* 4.21.4–5 and *Purgatorio* 25.67–75—confirming his sense of each individual as a new creation, as a fresh product of divine intentionality, the *Purgatorio* passage in particular confirming this as, again, a matter of divine rejoicing:

> Apri a la verità che viene il petto;
> e sappi che, sì tosto come al feto

l'articular del cerebro è perfetto,
  lo motor primo a lui si volge lieto
sovra tant' arte di natura, e spira
spirito novo, di vertù repleto,
  che ciò che trova attivo quivi, tira
in sua sustanzia, e fassi un'alma sola,
che vive e sente e sé in sé rigira.

(*Purgatorio* 25.67–75)[87]

while on the other hand there is, for example, the *Paradiso* 8.120–48 passage turning upon the notion of nature and providence combining to ensure the distinctiveness of self as that whereby the individual is made equal to his or her own
proper calling, this in turn, Dante thinks, serving to ensure the smooth operation
of the group to which they belong:

Ond' elli ancora: 'Or dì: sarebbe il peggio
per l'omo in terra, se non fosse cive?'
'Sì', rispuos' io; 'e qui ragion non cheggio'.
  'E puot' elli esser, se giù non si vive
diversamente per diversi offici?
Non, se 'l maestro vostro ben vi scrive'.

87 'Open your heart now to the truth which follows, and be aware that no sooner is the fashioning
of the mind complete in the embryo than the first mover turns towards it and, rejoicing in the excellence of nature's handiwork, breathes into it a new spirit complete with its own power, this then drawing
into its substance every activity it finds there, making as it does so a single soul that lives, feels and
circles around its own centre.' For the *Convivio* 4.21.4–5 passage: 'E però dico che quando l'umano seme
cade nel suo recettaculo, cioè ne la matrice, esso porta seco la vertù de l'anima generativa e la vertù del
cielo e la vertù de li elementi legati, cioè la complessione; e matura e dispone la materia a la vertù
formativa, la quale diede l'anima del generante; e la vertù formativa prepara li organi a la vertù celestiale,
che produce de la potenza del seme l'anima in vita. La quale, incontanente produtta, riceve da la vertù
del motore del cielo lo intelletto possibile; lo quale potenzialmente in sé adduce tutte le forme universali, secondo che sono nel suo produttore, e tanto meno quanto più dilungato da la prima Intelligenza
è' (It is my contention, then, that when the human seed enters the womb, it bears with it a threefold
power: the power of the soul generating it, that of the heavens, and that of its elements as bound up
one with another within the economy of the whole. It ripens and readies matter to receive the formative
power deriving from the male parent, and this same formative power in turn prepares the organs to
receive that of the heavens which from the potentiality of the seed produces the living soul. As soon
as that soul is created, it receives from the mover of the heavens and the power thereof the possible
intellect, this in turn having the capacity to receive into itself [though in a manner proportionate to its
distance from the first mind] every kind of universal form as present to its maker). Stephen Bemrose,
' "Come d'animal divegna fante": The Animation of the Human Embryo in Dante', in *The Human
Embryo: Aristotle and the Arabic Traditions*, ed. Gordon Reginald Dunstan (Exeter: Exeter University
Press, 1990), 123–35; Jennifer Fraser, 'Dante/"Fante": Embriology in Purgatory and Paradise', in *Dante
and the Unorthodox: The Aesthetics of Transgression*, ed. James Miller (Waterloo, Ontario: Wilfrid Lau-
rier University Press, 2005), 290–309; Giuliano Rossi, ' "Ma come d'animal divegna fante": Dante tra
Alberto Magno e Tommaso', *CT* 13.2 (2010), 191–209.

Sì venne deducendo infino a quici;
poscia conchiuse: 'Dunque esser diverse
convien di vostri effetti le radici:
   per ch'un nasce Solone e altro Serse,
altro Melchisedèch e altro quello
che, volando per l'aere, il figlio perse.
   La circular natura, ch'è suggello
a la cera mortal, fa ben sua arte,
ma non distingue l'un da l'altro ostello.
   Quinci addivien ch'Esaù si diparte
per seme da Iacòb; e vien Quirino
da sì vil padre, che si rende a Marte.
   Natura generata il suo cammino
simil farebbe sempre a' generanti,
se non vincesse il proveder divino.
   Or quel che t'era dietro t'è davanti:
ma perché sappi che di te mi giova,
un corollario voglio che t'ammanti.
   Sempre natura, se fortuna trova
discorde a sé, com' ogne altra semente
fuor di sua regïon, fa mala prova.
   E se 'l mondo là giù ponesse mente
al fondamento che natura pone,
seguendo lui, avria buona la gente.
   Ma voi torcete a la religïone
tal che fia nato a cignersi la spada,
e fate re di tal ch'è da sermone;
   onde la traccia vostra è fuor di strada'.

(*Paradiso* 8.115–48)[88]

---

88 'Whence he, taking up again: "Now tell me, would it or would it not be worse for man on earth were he not a citizen?" "Yes," I replied, "and here I seek no proof." "And can that be short of men living differently and performing different tasks? Not, certainly, if your master [Aristotle] writes well of this." Having, then, proceeded step-by-step thus far, he concluded: "That, then, is why the roots of your works must needs differ one from another; which is why one is born Solon, another Xerxes, another Melchisedech and another he who, flying through the air, lost thereby his son. Nature, which in its circling seals the mortal wax, performs its art well, but makes no distinction between one inn and another. So it comes about that an Esau differs in seed from a Jacob, and a Quirinus derives from so mean a father that he is ascribed to Mars. Should not divine foresight overcome this, nature as begotten would always follow the course of its begetters. Now that which was behind you is before you, but in order that you may know of the joy I have in you, I would that you cloak yourself with a corollary. Nature, should ever it find itself at odds with fortune, will, like every other displaced seed, come to no good. And if only the world there below would pay attention to the foundation she herself lays, it would,

But that is not all, for secure as he is in his sense of the status of the individual as a new creation and, to boot, as a new creation empowered from beforehand to his or her proper calling in the world, Dante's too is a sense of the courage *to be*, of the courage, that is to say, whereby that same individual confronts the forces of attenuation and indeed of annihilation operative from within. Again this is a situation everywhere open to documentation in the *Commedia* but nowhere more so than in the exquisitely Augustinian 'it was I who willed and I who nilled, I and I myself alone' episode of *Inferno* 3, where having set off with Virgil in high spirits, the pilgrim poet falls prey to every kind of doubt and misgiving, willing and counterwilling, courage and cowardice as between them striving for mastery:

> Io cominciai: 'Poeta che mi guidi,
> guarda la mia virtù s'ell' è possente,
> prima ch'a l'alto passo tu mi fidi.
>   Tu dici che di Silvïo il parente,
> corruttibile ancora, ad immortale
> secolo andò, e fu sensibilmente.
>   Però, se l'avversario d'ogne male
> cortese i fu, pensando l'alto effetto
> ch'uscir dovea di lui, e 'l chi e 'l quale
>   non pare indegno ad omo d'intelletto;
> ch'e' fu de l'alma Roma e di suo impero
> ne l'empireo ciel per padre eletto:
>   la quale e 'l quale, a voler dir lo vero,
> fu stabilita per lo loco santo
> u' siede il successor del maggior Piero.
>   Per quest' andata onde li dai tu vanto,
> intese cose che furon cagione
> di sua vittoria e del papale ammanto.
>   Andovvi poi lo Vas d'elezïone,
> per recarne conforto a quella fede
> ch'è principio a la via di salvazione.
>   Ma io, perché venirvi? o chi 'l concede?
> Io non Enëa, io non Paulo sono;
> me degno a ciò né io né altri 'l crede.
>   Per che, se del venire io m'abbandono,

---

taking account of that, have a people settled and content. But you wrest to religion one born to gird on the sword and you make a king of one fashioned for preaching, the path you follow being thus off the road." '

temo che la venuta non sia folle.
Se' savio; intendi me' ch'i' non ragiono'.
 E qual è quei che disvuol ciò che volle
e per novi pensier cangia proposta,
sì che dal cominciar tutto si tolle,
 tal mi fec' ïo 'n quella oscura costa,
perché, pensando, consumai la 'mpresa
che fu nel cominciar cotanto tosta.

(*Inferno* 2.10–42)[89]

—a situation open to resolution by way only of Virgil's stepping in at the behest of the Virgin Mary, Santa Lucia and Beatrice as guide and mentor for the pilgrim-poet and as that whereby he is freshly encouraged as a spiritual wayfarer:

'Dunque: che è? perché, perché restai,
perché tanta viltà nel core allette,
perché ardire e franchezza non hai,
 poscia che tai tre donne benedette
curan di te ne la corte del cielo,
e 'l mio parlar tanto ben ti promette?'
 Quali fioretti dal notturno gelo
chinati e chiusi, poi che 'l sol li 'mbianca,
si drizzan tutti aperti in loro stelo,
 tal mi fec' io di mia virtude stanca,

---

89 'I began: "You my poet and guide, consider my strength whether it be adequate before entrust-ing me to the deep pass. You tell me that Silvius's parent went while still corruptible to the immortal world and dwelt there in the flesh; and that, were the enemy of every evil truly thus kind to him, seems not unfitting to a man of intelligence, to one thinking over its noble outcome, over the *who* and the *what* of it; for in the heaven of the empyrean he was chosen for father of our revered Rome and of her empire, both of which, truth to tell, were ordained for the holy place where the successor of the great Peter has his seat. By dint of his journeying, of which you speak so impressively, he learned things which brought about both his own triumph and that of the papal mantle. Thereafter the chosen vessel went there to bring thence comfort to that faith which is the beginning of salvation. But I, why should I go there? Or who permits it? I am not Aeneas, I am not Paul. Neither I nor others think me worthy of this; wherefore if I thus consent, I fear it may be folly. You are a wise man and understand my meaning better than I myself speak of it." And just as one unwills what he willed, and by reason of new thoughts changes his mind and steps back from the project under way, such was my situation on that bleak strand.' Vittorio Russo, '"Timor", "audacia" e "fortitudo" nel canto II dell'*Inferno*', in *Sussidi di esegesi dantesca* (Naples: Liguori, 1975), 9–32; Giorgio Bàrberi Squarotti, 'II: "Io non Enëa, io non Paolo sono"', in *Tutto l'"Inferno': Lettura integrale della prima cantica del poema dantesco* (Milan: Franco Angeli, 2011), 34–37; Pierluigi Lia, 'Ma io perché venirvi? O chi 'l concede?', in *Poetica dell'amore e conversione: Considerazioni teologiche sulla lingua della 'Commedia'* (Florence: Olschki, 2015), 127–32. For Augustine, *Confessions* 8.10.22: 'ego eram qui volebam, ego qui nolebam'.

e tanto buono ardire al cor mi corse,
ch'i' cominciai come persona franca:
'Oh pietosa colei che mi soccorse!
e te cortese ch'ubidisti tosto
a le vere parole che ti porse!
    Tu m'hai con disiderio il cor disposto
sì al venir con le parole tue,
ch'i' son tornato nel primo proposto.
    Or va, ch'un sol volere è d'ambedue:
tu duca, tu segnore e tu maestro'.
Così li dissi; e poi che mosso fue,
    intrai per lo cammino alto e silvestro.

(*Inferno* 2.121–42)[90]

—lines to which, as confirming what amounts to a leitmotif of Dante's discourse in the *Commedia*, we may add the 'e io sol uno / m'apparecchiava a sostener la guerra / sì del cammino e sì de la pietate / che ritrarrà la mente che non erra' of *Inferno* 2.3–6,[91] or the 'Or sie forte e ardito. / Omai si scende per sì fatte scale' of 17.81–82, or the '"Ecco Dite", dicendo, "ed ecco il loco / ove convien che di fortezza t'armi"' of 34.20–21, or the 'Pon giù omai, pon giù ogni temenza; / volgiti in qua; vieni ed entra sicuro' of *Purgatorio* 27.31–32. Throughout, then, the pattern is the same, Dante's commitment to a first-person proposal of the theological project being matched only by his sense of the courage always and everywhere

---

90 '"What then? Why, why do you so delay? Why do you harbour such cowardice in your heart? Why are you not bold and free, when three such blessed ladies care for you in the court of heaven and my words promise you so much good?" As the flowerlets, bent and closed by the chill of night, once brightened by the sun stand tall and open on their stem, so became I with my flagging spirits, and, with courage oh so worthy coursing through my heart, I began like one set free: "O compassionate she who came thus to my aid, and o courteous you who did speedily obey the truth she spoke! You, with these words of yours, have so disposed my heart, now thus filled with the desire to be under way, that I am wedded again to my first intent. Now go, for ours is but one will: you, my leader, my lord and my master." Thus I addressed him, and, he moving on, I set foot upon that steep and savage path.' For the Beatrician moment of the argument, Rachel Jacoff, 'The Tears of Dante', *DS* 100 (1982), 1–12; Giorgio Brugnoli, 'Per "l'amico mio e non de la ventura" (Dante, *Inferno* 2,61)', *GIF* 54.2 (2002), 169–76; Dino Bigongiari, 'Beatrice's Descent into Hell', in *Readings in the 'Divine Comedy'. A Series of Lectures*, ed. Anne Paolucci (Dover, DE: Griffon House, 2006), 37–48; Carlos López Cortezo, 'Con angelica voce in sua favella', *Tenzone* 9 (2008), 11–43.

91 'And I alone was preparing myself for the anguish and pity of the way which my unerring memory shall retrace' (Dante on the threshold of his journey); for 17.81–82: 'Now be strong and courageous, for now by such stairs we must descend' (Dante borne by Geryon into nether hell); for 34.20–21: 'Behold Dis, the place where by courage you must be armed' (Dante in the presence of Lucifer); and for *Purgatorio* 27.31–32: 'Put away, put away all fear; turn hither and enter securely' (Dante entering the now purifying flames of the lustful).

required of the wayfaring spirit, of the one standing alone in respect of that which matters alone.

This, then, is individualism of a uniquely powerful kind, a species of individualism resting to be sure upon a sense of man's prior and continuing co-adequation by grace to the matter in hand but, for all that, looking to man himself—to this or that individual man or woman—as the key player hereabouts, as empowered both from beforehand and from out of the depths in respect of his or her emergence on the plane of properly human being. But—and this now is the point—for all his commitment to the intrinsic dignity of self in its power to self-actualization, Dante's even so is a call from individuality to collectivity, from the otherwise unspeakable loneliness of the one to the sweet communion of the other, indeed to the kind of co-immanence whereby the other-than-self is present to self as a structure of its very existence. Prominent already, then, in the *Convivio*—though as yet by way of an admittedly Peripatetic commonplace—is the notion of man as a sociable being, his proper well-being as man thus requiring of him, if only for the sake of elementary survival, something more than the sturdy properties of personality:

> E però dice lo Filosofo che l'uomo naturalmente è compagnevole animale. E sì come un uomo a sua sufficienza richiede compagnia dimestica di famiglia, così una casa a sua sufficienza richiede una vicinanza; altrimenti molti difetti sosterrebbe che sarebbero impedimento di felicitade. E però che una vicinanza non può sé in tutto satisfare, conviene a satisfacimento di quella essere la cittade. Ancora: la cittade richiede a le sue arti e a le sue difensioni vicenda avere e fratellanza con le circavicine cittadi; e però fu fatto lo regno.
>
> (*Convivio* 4.4.1–2)[92]

But by the time we reach the *Purgatorio* as a text bearing now on the innermost movement of the spirit the civic has given way to the choral, to a sense of self in all the *perseitas* of self as party to a shared spirituality, to a common utterance, to a single psalmic voice:

92 'Hence the Philosopher's dictum that man is by nature a social animal. And just as the individual for his fulfilment requires the domestic society of a family, so the household requires for its fulfilment to be part of a neighbourhood. It would otherwise be lacking in many ways, and thus be precluded from attaining happiness. Again, a single neighbourhood cannot satisfy all its own needs; for this a city is required. For the sake of trade and defence, the city in its turn needs to cooperate with, and have friendly relations with, surrounding cities, and so the kingdom was born.' Aristotle, *Pol.* 1.2 (1253a2), *Nic. eth.* 1.7 (1097b8–11) and so on. Allan H. Gilbert, 'Had Dante Read the *Politics* of Aristotle?', *PMLAA* 43.3 (1928), 602–13; Larry Peterman, 'Dante's *Monarchia* and Aristotle's Political Thought', *Studies in Medieval and Renaissance History* 10 (1973), 3–40; Lorenzo Minio Paluello, 'Dante's Reading of Aristotle', in *The World of Dante: Essays on Dante and His Times*, ed. Cecil Grayson (Oxford: Clarendon Press, 1980), 61–80.

Da poppa stava il celestial nocchiero,
tal che faria beato pur descripto;
e più di cento spirti entro sediero.
  'In exitu Israel de Aegypto'
cantavan tutti insieme ad una voce
con quanto di quel salmo è poscia scripto.

(*Purgatorio* 2.43–48)[93]

—a notion taken up and freshly substantiated both in the Justinian and in the Thomist cantos of the *Paradiso*, where it is a matter, precisely, of concelebration, of a co-presencing and complementarity of souls each alike rejoicing in the otherness of its neighbour as that whereby it stands more securely in its own presence. On the one hand, then, we have the 'diverse voci fanno dolci note' moment of the Justinian canto, choral to the point of fully symphonic in its exploration of the now soaring spirituality of the elect:

Questa picciola stella si correda
d'i buoni spirti che son stati attivi
perché onore e fama li succeda:
  e quando li disiri poggian quivi,
sì disvïando, pur convien che i raggi
del vero amore in sù poggin men vivi.
  Ma nel commensurar d'i nostri gaggi
col merto è parte di nostra letizia,
perché non li vedem minor né maggi.
  Quindi addolcisce la viva giustizia
in noi l'affetto sì, che non si puote
torcer già mai ad alcuna nequizia.
  Diverse voci fanno dolci note;
così diversi scanni in nostra vita
rendon dolce armonia tra queste rote.

(*Paradiso* 6.112–26)[94]

---

93 'On the poop stood the heavenly steersman, such that blessedness seemed written upon him, and more than a thousand spirits sat within. *In exitu Israel de Aegypto* they sang all together with one voice, with all that is written after of that psalm.' Helena Phillips-Robins, '"Cantavan tutti insieme ad una voce": Singing and Community in the *Commedia*', *ItSt* 71.1 (2016), 4–20.

94 'This little star is adorned with good spirits whose deeds were done for the honour and glory that should follow them; and when, there, desires rise up thus deviously then the rays of the true love must needs rise up with less life. But in the measuring of our rewards with our desert lies part of our

while on the other, and exemplary in respect of what it means for Dante to be paradisally, we have these lines from the Thomist cantos of the text with—by way of their careful countenancing of each of those party to the project—their settling definitively upon the exquisite sociology of being in its authenticity, upon the co-involvement of self and of the other-than-self within the ontic economy of the whole:

> Tu vuo' saper di quai piante s'infiora
> questa ghirlanda che 'ntorno vagheggia
> la bella donna ch'al ciel t'avvalora.
>   Io fui de li agni de la santa greggia
> che Domenico mena per cammino
> u' ben s'impingua se non si vaneggia.
>   Questi che m'è a destra più vicino,
> frate e maestro fummi, ed esso Alberto
> è di Cologna, e io Thomas d'Aquino.
>   Se sì di tutti li altri esser vuo' certo,
> di retro al mio parlar ten vien col viso
> girando su per lo beato serto.
>   Quell' altro fiammeggiare esce del riso
> di Grazïan, che l'uno e l'altro foro
> aiutò sì che piace in paradiso.
>   L'altro ch'appresso addorna il nostro coro,
> quel Pietro fu che con la poverella
> offerse a Santa Chiesa suo tesoro.
>   La quinta luce, ch'è tra noi più bella,
> spira di tale amor, che tutto 'l mondo
> là giù ne gola di saper novella:
>   entro v'è l'alta mente u' sì profondo
> saver fu messo, che, se 'l vero è vero,
> a veder tanto non surse il secondo.
>   Appresso vedi il lume di quel cero
> che giù in carne più a dentro vide
> l'angelica natura e 'l ministero.
>   Ne l'altra piccioletta luce ride
> quello avvocato de' tempi cristiani
> del cui latino Augustin si provide.

---

happiness, for we see them to be neither less nor more. Thus the living justice sweetens our affections so that never can they be constrained to any evil. Just as diverse voices make sweet music, so diverse ranks in our life render sweet harmony among these wheels.'

Or se tu l'occhio de la mente trani
di luce in luce dietro a le mie lode,
già de l'ottava con sete rimani.

Per vedere ogne ben dentro vi gode
l'anima santa che 'l mondo fallace
fa manifesto a chi di lei ben ode.

Lo corpo ond' ella fu cacciata giace
giuso in Cieldauro; ed essa da martiro
e da essilio venne a questa pace.

Vedi oltre fiammeggiar l'ardente spiro
d'Isidoro, di Beda e di Riccardo,
che a considerar fu più che viro.

Questi onde a me ritorna il tuo riguardo,
è 'l lume d'uno spirto che 'n pensieri
gravi a morir li parve venir tardo:

essa è la luce etterna di Sigieri,
che, leggendo nel Vico de li Strami,
silogizzò invidïosi veri.

(*Paradiso* 10.91–138)[95]

—lines to which, as bringing to a gentle conclusion a meditation as nicely analytical as it is elegant in conception and articulation we may add these from the very end of the canto, lines confirming in a single pass of the mind and imagination the rapt substance of the leading idea:

95 'You wish to know with what flowers this garland is decorated that encircles the fair lady who strengthens you for Heaven. I was of the lambs of the holy flock that Dominic leads on the path where there is good fattening provided only they stray not. He closest to me on my right was my master and my brother Albert of Cologne, and I, Thomas Aquinas. If of the rest you wish to know, then with your eyes follow my words around the blessed wreath. This next flamelet issues from Gratian's smile, he who served the one court and the other that well it pleased paradise. The next that adorns our choir was the Peter Lombard who, like the poor widow, offered up his treasure to holy Church. The fifth light, which is the most beautiful among us, breathes from such a love that all the world below hungers for news of it. Therein is the lofty mind of Solomon to which was granted wisdom so profound that if indeed truth be true never was there a second of such vision. Beside that, the light of that candle, Dionysius who below in the flesh saw farthest into the nature and ministry of the angels. In the next little light smiles that defender of Christian times—Orosius—of whose works Augustine made use. If now you proceed with your mind's eye from light to light following my eulogy, you are already eager for the eighth. Therein, pondering every righteousness, rejoices the sainted soul who made plain the deceitful world to those hearing him aright. The body from which he was driven lies there below in Cieldauro whence from exile and martyrdom he came to this peace. See then, glowing yonder, the breath of Isidore of Seville flaming forth, of Bede, and of Richard more than man in contemplation. The one from whom your look returns to me is the light of a spirit to whom, profound in thought, death seemed slow in coming. It is the eternal light of Siger who, lecturing in the Street of Straw, framed doubtful truths.'

> Indi, come orologio che ne chiami
> ne l'ora che la sposa di Dio surge
> a mattinar lo sposo perché l'ami,
>   che l'una parte e l'altra tira e urge,
> tin tin sonando con sì dolce nota,
> che 'l ben disposto spirto d'amor turge;
>   così vid' ïo la gloriosa rota
> muoversi e render voce a voce in tempra
> e in dolcezza ch'esser non pò nota
>   se non colà dove gioir s'insempra.

> (*Paradiso* 10.139–48)[96]

But even this is not quite all, for this, properly speaking, is co-involvement to the point of co-immanence, as pointing in the direction of, and as seeking out as its point of arrival, the mutual *in-abiding* of one man and another, the co-inherence of all those busy at the point of ultimate concern. Exquisite in this sense is the nicely neologistic but at the same time endlessly eloquent 'in-meing' and 'in-theeing' moment of canto 9 of the *Paradiso*, a moment here as throughout exemplary in respect of Dante's proceeding as a theological spirit by way less of the proposition (rarely, in truth, equal to the matter in hand) than of the minimal linguistic strategy, of form tout court as the in-and-through-which of spiritual intelligence:

> L'altra letizia, che m'era già nota
> per cara cosa, mi si fece in vista
> qual fin balasso in che lo sol percuota.
>   Per letiziar là sù fulgor s'acquista,
> sì come riso qui; ma giù s'abbuia
> l'ombra di fuor, come la mente è trista.
>   'Dio vede tutto, e tuo veder s'inluia',
> diss' io, 'beato spirto, sì che nulla
> voglia di sé a te puot' esser fuia.
>   Dunque la voce tua, che 'l ciel trastulla
> sempre col canto di quei fuochi pii
> che di sei ali facen la coculla,

---

96 'Then, just as a horologe calls at the hour when the bride of God rises to sing matins to her bridegroom that he may love her, in which the one part draws and urges the other, sounding a chime with notes so sweet that the well-disposed spirit swells with love, so I saw the glorious wheel move and render voice to voice with a harmony and sweetness which cannot be known save there where joy becomes eternal.'

perché non satisface a' miei disii?
Già non attendere' io tua dimanda,
s'io m'intuassi, come tu t'inmii'.

(*Paradiso* 9.67–81)[97]

Dante's, then, is a celebration of man's presence in the world under both its individual and its collective aspects, in terms, that is to say, both of his *being in self* (meaning by this his proper power to moral and ontological determination) and of his *being with another* (meaning by this the presence to him of the next man not merely as a companion or fellow breaker of bread but as a structure of his own existence, as a condition of his knowing self in the fullness of his own unique humanity). But for Dante *to be in self* and *to be with another* is to be these things not merely simultaneously but as part and parcel of one and the same inflexion of the spirit. To suppose otherwise—to pass by on the other side when it comes to what in this sense it means fully and unequivocally *to be* as man—is to risk, at best, the sadness and, at worst, the despair of solipsism, the former as but the mood of being in its far-offness and the latter as but the in-and-through-which of its denial and of its dismantling.

A fourth and for the moment final polarity of specifically human being in the positive living out thereof is that of freedom and destiny. By 'freedom' we mean the freedom always and everywhere proper to man as man to choose, to settle as far as may be without constraint on this or that existential possibility—a notion fundamental to Dante's general anthropology and ethic and decisive for the substance and structure of the *Commedia* in the round. But freedom, properly understood, is always freedom *for* or freedom *in respect of*, this, then, being what we mean by destiny. By 'destiny' we mean the *for* or *in respect of* whence freedom is redeemed from the merely free-floating as but a principle of unrecognizability on the plane of properly human being.

Freedom or 'libertà' is for Dante a matter of willing as unprejudiced by those forces operative both from within and from beyond making for its attenuation as a power of the rational soul. As such the notion is everywhere discernible and indeed everywhere commended in the text, but nowhere more systematically than in the *Purgatorio* as the canticle par excellence of emancipation, and this both on the threshold thereof and high up on the mountain. On the one hand, then, we have Virgil's plea to Cato in the first canto to the effect that Dante the pilgrim

97 'The other joy, already known to me as precious, became as I looked on such as a fine ruby upon which the sun is striking, for there above brightness follows on from joy just as there below the shade darkens outwardly as the mind is sad. "God sees all", I said, "and your seeing enters therein such that no desire can be hid from you. Why, then, does not your voice, which with those that have made their cowl of six wings, satisfy my yearning? I would not await your question were I in you as you are in me."'

poet be allowed to press on with his search for freedom as the final cause of his
treading now the upward way:

> Mostrata ho lui tutta la gente ria;
> e ora intendo mostrar quelli spirti
> che purgan sé sotto la tua balìa.
>   Com' io l'ho tratto, saria lungo a dirti;
> de l'alto scende virtù che m'aiuta
> conducerlo a vederti e a udirti.
>   Or ti piaccia gradir la sua venuta:
> libertà va cercando, ch'è sì cara,
> come sa chi per lei vita rifiuta.
>   Tu 'l sai, ché non ti fu per lei amara
> in Utica la morte, ove lasciasti
> la vesta ch'al gran dì sarà sì chiara.

$$(Purgatorio \ 1.64-75)^{98}$$

while on the other we have Virgil again, this time in canto 27—and by way of a
formula fraught now with every kind of theological, political and ecclesiological
implication—to the effect that, having made his way up the mountain, Dante the
pilgrim poet is from this point on a free spirit, king and bishop over himself:

> Tratto t'ho qui con ingegno e con arte;
> lo tuo piacere omai prendi per duce;
> fuor se' de l'erte vie, fuor se' de l'arte.
>   Vedi lo sol che 'n fronte ti riluce;
> vedi l'erbette, i fiori e li arbuscelli

---

98 'Every guilt-laden spirit have I shown him, my purpose now being to show him those cleansing themselves under your charge. How I have led him here would take too long to relate; from on high is the power enabling me to bring him here to see and to hear you, and so may it please you to welcome his coming; for his purpose is to seek out liberty, that same liberty which, as those know who give their lives for it—including you yourself, for whom death in Utica where you relinquished that vesture which on the great day will be so resplendent—is precious beyond words.' Andrea Maia, 'Libertà va cercando', SV 4 (2003), 183–93; Valter Boggione, 'La custodia, la vera libertà, la colpa, la pena: Ancora sul Catone dantesco', GSLI 139 (2012), 321–53. More generally and with reference to other passages in the text bearing on freedom and emancipation, Patrick Boyde, 'Aspects of Human Freedom', in Perception and Passion in Dante's 'Comedy' (Cambridge: Cambridge University Press, 1993), 93–214; Stephan Laqué, 'Führung und Freiheit in der Divina Commedia', DDJ 81 (2006), 71–93; Anna Cerbo, 'Espiazione e recupero totale della libertà dal peccato (Purgatorio XXI, vv. 58–78)', in Dante oltre il medioevo. Atti del convegno in ricordo di Silvio Pasquazi, Roma 16 e 30 november 2010, ed. Vincenzo Placella (Rome: Pioda Editore, 2012), 39–57; Raffaele Campanella, '"Tu m'hai tratta di servo a libertate" (Paradiso XXXI 85)', Tenzone 17 (2016), 211–25.

che qui la terra sol da sé produce.
Mentre che vegnan lieti li occhi belli
che, lagrimando, a te venir mi fenno,
seder ti puoi e puoi andar tra elli.
Non aspettar mio dir più né mio cenno;
libero, dritto e sano è tuo arbitrio,
e fallo fora non fare a suo senno:
per ch'io te sovra te corono e mitrio.

(*Purgatorio* 27.130–42)[99]

—lines to which, as confirming the nature of freedom as but the free passage from seeing and understanding to positively desiring, we may add these from the first book of the *Monarchia*:

Et ideo dico quod iudicium medium est apprehensionis et appetitus: nam primo res apprehenditur, deinde apprehensa bona vel mala iudicatur, et ultimo iudicans prosequitur sive fugit. Si ergo iudicium moveat omnino appetitum et nullo modo preveniatur ab eo, liberum est; si vero ab appetitu quocunque modo proveniente iudicium moveatur, liberum esse non potest, quia non a se, sed ab alio captivum trahitur. Et hinc est quod bruta iudicium liberum habere non possunt, quia eorum iudicia semper ab appetitu preveniuntur.

(*Monarchia* 1.12.3–5)[100]

---

99 'Thus far, with skill and art, I have brought you, but take henceforth your own pleasure as your guide, for you are now come forth from the steep and narrow way. See there the sun shining upon your brow; see the grass, the flowers and the arbours which of itself the earth produces. Until those beautiful eyes come with gladness—the eyes which, weeping, made me first come to you—you may sit or else wander as you please among them. Expect neither word nor sign from me more, for free, upright and sound is your own will and other than to do its bidding would now be folly, wherefore I crown and mitre you over yourself.' Gabriele Muresu, 'Virgilio, la corona, la mitria (*Purgatorio* XXVII)', *LIA* 8 (2007), 223–61; Mira Mocan, 'Le ultime parole di Virgilio: Su *Purgatorio* XXVII.142', *CT* 13.2 (2010), 211–34; Mira Mocan, 'Il libero arbitrio "sovrano"', in *L'arca della mente: Riccardo di San Vittore nella 'Commedia' di Dante* (Florence: Olschki, 2012), 141–64.

100 'And therefore I say that judgment is the link between perception and appetition; for first a thing is perceived, then it is judged to be good or evil, and finally the person who judges pursues it or shuns it. Now if judgment controls desire completely and is in no way preempted by it, it is free; but if judgment is in any way at all preempted and thus controlled by desire, it cannot be free, because it does not act under its own power, but is dragged along in the power of something else. And that is why the lower animals cannot have free will, because their judgments are always preempted by desire.' Paolo Falzone, 'Psicologia dell'atto umano in Dante', in *Filosofia in volgare nel medioevo. Atti del Convegno della Società Italiana per lo Studio del Pensiero Medievale, Lecce, 27–29 settembre 2002*, ed. Nadia Bray and Loris Sturlese (Louvain-La-Neuve: Fédération Internationale des Instituts d'Études Médiévales, 2003), 331–66.

But free as he is to choose, man even so knows himself as destined, or perhaps better (for this is the way Dante himself puts it) as desirous in respect both of the final and of the proximate cause of his properly human presence in the world, of the final cause in the sense of the desire he shares with all men to enjoy communion with his maker as the ground and guarantee of his very being, and of the proximate cause in the sense of that to which he is by temperament properly suited and properly equipped. So then, as regards the former—namely the calling of all men into communion with the One from whom they proceed and in whom alone lies their proper peace—we have the "stilling of every desire" moment of the *Convivio* at 4.12.14:

lo sommo desiderio di ciascuna cosa, e prima da la natura dato, è lo ritornare a lo suo principio. E però che Dio è principio de le nostre anime e fattore di quelle simili a sé (sì come è scritto: 'Facciamo l'uomo ad imagine e similitudine nostra'), essa anima massimamente desidera di tornare a quello.[101]

or, as part of the great love disquisition decisive for an overall interpretation of the *Commedia*, the 'good if but hazily perceived' moment of *Purgatorio* 17.127–29:

Ciascun confusamente un bene apprende
nel qual si queti l'animo, e disira;
per che di giugner lui ciascun contende.[102]

or, on the threshold of the final canticle, the 'concreate and perpetual thirst' moment of *Paradiso* at 2.19–21:

---

101 'The highest desire in every being, and the first implanted in it by nature, is the desire to return to its first cause.' Paolo Falzone, *Desiderio della scienza e desiderio di Dio nel 'Convivio' di Dante* (Bologna: Il Mulino, 2010); Paolo Falzone, 'Desiderio naturale, nobilità dell'anima e grazia divina nel IV trattato del *Convivio*', in *Dante the Lyric and Ethical Poet*, ed. Zygmunt G. Baranski and Martin McLaughlin (Oxford: Legenda, 2010), 24–55. More generally on the *Paradiso* as the canticle of desire, Lino Pertile, '*Paradiso*: A Drama of Desire', in *Word and Drama in Dante: Essays on the 'Divina Commedia'*, ed. John C. Barnes and Jennifer Petrie (Dublin: Irish Academic Press, 1993), 143–80; Lino Pertile, *La punta del disio: Semantica del desiderio nella 'Commedia'* (Florence: Cadmo, 2005); Anna Maria Chiavacci Leonardi, 'Il *Paradiso* di Dante: L'ardore del desiderio', in *Le bianche stole: Saggi sul 'Paradiso' di Dante* (Florence: Galluzzo, 2010), 27–38. More generally on Dante, desire and the *Commedia*, Giuliano Rossi, ' "Disio" nella *Commedia*', *PT* 9.1 (2005), 99–124; Pamela Williams, *Through Human Love to God: Essays on Dante and Petrarch* (Leicester: Troubadour, 2007); Manuele Gragnolati et al. (eds.), *Desire in Dante and the Middle Ages* (London: Modern Humanities Research Association, 2012); Tobias Leuker, 'Facetten des Verlangens: "Desiderium" in der christlichen Theologie vor 1300 und in Dantes *Commedia*', *DDJ* 85–86 (2010–11), 199–219; Christopher J. Ryan, 'Desire and Destiny', in *Dante and Aquinas: A Study of Nature and Grace in the 'Comedy'* (London: UCL Arts and Humanities Publications, 2013), 58–76.

102 'Every man, if but hazily, perceives a good in which the mind may rest, and desires that good, so that each strives to possess it.'

> La concreata e perpetüa sete
> del deïforme regno cen portava
> veloci quasi come 'l ciel vedete.[103]

or, just a little way down the line from this, the 'enamouring of the soul by the supreme beneficence' moment of 7.142–44:

> ma vostra vita sanza mezzo spira
> la somma beninanza, e la innamora
> di sé sì che poi sempre la disira.[104]

or, from the final phase of the poem, the 'approaching the object of my every longing' moment of 33.46–48:

> E io ch'al fine di tutt' i disii
> appropinquava, sì com' io dovea,
> l'ardor del desiderio in me finii.[105]

More properly sensitive, by contrast, to the notion of a man's seeking out the proximate finality of his presence in the world, of his projecting himself upon the calling given, so to speak, with the act of existence, are these now familiar lines from canto 8 of the *Paradiso*, lines nicely attuned to the notion of prior and proper responsibility, to—somewhere in the hinterland—the 'some he gave to be apostles; some, prophets; some, evangelists; some, pastors and teachers' moment of the urtext hereabouts:

> La circular natura, ch'è suggello
> a la cera mortal, fa ben sua arte,
> ma non distingue l'un da l'altro ostello.
> Quinci addivien ch'Esaù si diparte
> per seme da Iacòb; e vien Quirino
> da sì vil padre, che si rende a Marte.
> Natura generata il suo cammino

---

103 'The inborn and perpetual thirst for the divine realm bore us away, swift, well-nigh, as your glance towards heaven.' Maria Esposito Frank, ' "La concreata e perpetua sete" del *Paradiso*', EL 17 (1993), 41–56.

104 'But your life is in-breathed directly by the supreme beneficence which, enamouring that life as it does so of himself, causes it thereafter and ever more to yearn for him.'

105 'And I, drawing near as I was to the end of all my desiring, consummated perforce the ardour of my yearning.' Diego Fasolani, ' "E io ch'al fine di tutt'i desii appropinquava": Un'interpretazione teologica del "desiderium" nel XXXIII canto del *Paradiso*', FItal 37.2 (2003), 297–328.

> simil farebbe sempre a' generanti,
> se non vincesse il proveder divino.
>   Or quel che t'era dietro t'è davanti:
> ma perché sappi che di te mi giova,
> un corollario voglio che t'ammanti.
>   Sempre natura, se fortuna trova
> discorde a sé, com' ogne altra semente
> fuor di sua regïon, fa mala prova.
>   E se 'l mondo là giù ponesse mente
> al fondamento che natura pone,
> seguendo lui, avria buona la gente.
>   Ma voi torcete a la religïone
> tal che fia nato a cignersi la spada,
> e fate re di tal ch'è da sermone;
>   onde la traccia vostra è fuor di strada.

(*Paradiso* 8.127–48)[106]

—lines to which, as touching now upon Dante's own destiny as one called to speak truth to the generations, we may add these from the Cacciaguida cantos of the *Paradiso* turning upon the notion of that same calling as inscribed upon the very countenance of the One whence derives its now abiding authorization:

> 'La contingenza, che fuor del quaderno
> de la vostra matera non si stende,
> tutta è dipinta nel cospetto etterno;
>   necessità però quindi non prende
> se non come dal viso in che si specchia
> nave che per torrente giù discende.
>   Da indi, sì come viene ad orecchia
> dolce armonia da organo, mi viene

---

106 'Nature, which in its circling seals the mortal wax, performs its art well, but makes no distinction between one inn and another. So it comes about that an Esau differs in seed from a Jacob, and a Quirinus derives from so mean a father that he is ascribed to Mars. Should not divine foresight overcome this, nature as begotten would always follow the course of its begetters. Now that which was behind you is before you, but in order that you may know of the joy I have in you, I would that you cloak yourself with a corollary. Nature, should ever it find itself at odds with fortune, will, like every other displaced seed, come to no good. And if only the world there below would pay attention to the foundation she herself lays, it would, taking account of that, have a people settled and content. But you wrest to religion one born to gird on the sword and you make a king of one fashioned for preaching, the path you follow being thus off the road.' Ephesians 4:11: 'Et ipse dedit quosdam quidem Apostolos, quosdam autem Prophetas, alios vero Evangelistas, alios autem pastores et doctores.'

a vista il tempo che ti s'apparecchia.

. . .

   Tu lascerai ogne cosa diletta
più caramente; e questo è quello strale
che l'arco de lo essilio pria saetta.
   Tu proverai sì come sa di sale
lo pane altrui, e come è duro calle
lo scendere e 'l salir per l'altrui scale'.

. . .

   'Ben veggio, padre mio, sì come sprona
lo tempo verso me, per colpo darmi
tal, ch'è più grave a chi più s'abbandona;
   per che di provedenza è buon ch'io m'armi,
sì che, se loco m'è tolto più caro,
io non perdessi li altri per miei carmi.
   Giù per lo mondo sanza fine amaro,
e per lo monte del cui bel cacume
li occhi de la mia donna mi levaro,
   e poscia per lo ciel, di lume in lume,
ho io appreso quel che s'io ridico,
a molti fia sapor di forte agrume;
   e s'io al vero son timido amico,
temo di perder viver tra coloro
che questo tempo chiameranno antico'.

(*Paradiso* 17.37–45, 55–60 and 106–20)[107]

For Dante, then, man *is* under the aspect both of freedom and of destiny, both as determining and as determined. He *is* as determining in the sense of being free to structure and to resolve his existence as he himself sees fit. He *is* as determined

107 'Contingency, which does not extend beyond the volume of your material world, is all depicted in the eternal vision, yet does not thence derive necessity any more than does a ship that drops downstream from the eyes in which it is mirrored; from thence, as sweet harmony comes from an organ to the ear, comes to my sight the time that is in store for you . . . You shall leave everything loved most dearly and this is the shaft which the bow of exile shoots first. You will prove how salt is the taste of another man's bread and how hard is the way up and down another man's stairs' . . . 'I see well, my father, how time spurs towards me to deal me such a blow as falls most heavily on him that is most heedless; it is well, therefore, that I arm me with foresight, so that, if the dearest place is taken from me, I may not lose the others by my songs. Down through the world of endless bitterness and on the mountain from whose fair summit the eyes of my lady lifted me, and after, through the heavens from light to light, I have learned that which, if I tell again, will taste for many of bitter herbs; and if I am a timid friend to the truth I fear to lose my life among those who will call these times ancient.'

in the sense of possessing—or, more exactly, of being possessed by—a prior sense of calling, of a path perforce to be trodden. But to be as determining and to be as determined is to be these things *simultaneously*, with the result that in his every waking moment man as man is called upon to interpret the one in terms of the other: freedom in terms of the destiny whereby it is redeemed from the merely arbitrary and ultimately insignificant, and destiny in terms of the freedom whereby it is willingly and indeed lovingly espoused. Failure hereabouts, be it a matter either of wilfulness or merely of forgetfulness, is to risk despair, the despair either of hopelessness (destinyless freedom) and/or of helplessness (freedomless destiny), each alike an affront to the twofold substance and sacredness of man's proper presence in the world as man.

A Phenomenology of Existence: The Mood as Mediator

Somewhere, then, in the hinterland of the *Commedia* and decisive for an interpretation of the text as but a laying open of the human situation in its capacity both for annihilation and for affirmation—as 'entering into the deepest places of human self-destruction and despair as well as the highest places of courage and salvation'—are two things: on the one hand an anthropology and an ethic turning upon an ideal gathering in of those loves generated along the way to the love given with the act itself of existence, and on the other a dialectic of specifically human being turning upon a no less ideal bringing home of time to eternity, of locality to universality, of the individual to the collective, and of freedom to destiny, herein, in the countenancing of one thing by another, lying the seeds of man's proper well-being and thus of his proper happiness as man. But with this we are still far from home when it comes to the height and depth, the length and breadth of Dante's discourse in the *Commedia*, to the power and precision with which he sees into and proposes as an object of contemplation the *how it stands and how it fares* with man (Heidegger's 'wie einem ist und wird') in the moment of his self-losing and of his self-finding, of his being infernally and of his being paradisally; for over and beyond the anthropology, the ethics and the dialectics of that being comes its phenomenology, that part of Dante's Dasein analytic turning upon the mood of being in its moment-by-moment unfolding—upon, more precisely, the *mood* of being transparent in this or that instance thereof to the *truth* of being. In the degree, therefore, to which the individual comes home to self on the plane of loving and with respect to the successive polarities of his or her properly human presence in the world, then he or she knows self only in the kind of *pax* and *gaudium*—in the kind of self-possession and self-overflowing—proper to being in its authenticity. In the degree, by contrast, to which the individual delivers self despite self to this or that proximate possibility on the plane of loving or to this or that discrete polarity as a means of self-interpretation, he or she is present to self by way only of the kinds of fear, anger, restlessness and despair as between them the hallmark of being in its far-offness, as astray in the region of unlikeness. This, then, is what it means to speak of the phenomenological moment of Dante's meditation in the *Commedia*. To speak of the phenomenological moment of Dante's meditation in the *Commedia* is to speak of how it is that, by way of the mood as but the felt conditionality of being in the living-out thereof, the individual stands already in the truth of his or her existence as a creature of free moral determination, in the presence of the ἔσχατος as but the in-abiding of that truth.[108]

Taking first, then, the moods of being in its lostness to self, in its wandering despite self in a far-off region of dissimilitude, everywhere to the fore in Dante's mind is the kind of fear—the kind of ontological fear—generated by a sense of dividedness on the plane of willing, by a sense of knowing self in the prospect of ceasing *to be* as a free determinant. Now not all fear is ontological in kind, and Dante from time to time adverts to the 'expectation of evil' kind of fear described by Aristotle in the *Ethics*; so, for example, we have *Convivio* 4.13.11 on the kind of 'fearfulness and disquiet' (the 'paura grande e sollicitudine' of 4.12.5) engendered by the entrepreneurial search for material wealth: 'ben lo sanno li miseri mercatanti che per lo mondo vanno, che le foglie, che 'l vento fa menare, li fa tremare,

---

108 Among the moderns on mood as that whereby the individual is brought into the truth of his or her own presence in the world as a creature of free moral determination, Heidegger, *Being and Time*, trans. John Macquarrie and Edwin Robinson (Oxford: Blackwell, 1962), 1.5 (134): 'Both the undisturbed equanimity and the inhibited ill-humour of our everyday concern, the way we slip from one to the other, or slip off into bad moods, are by no means nothing ontologically, even if these phenomena are left unheeded as supposedly the most indifferent and fleeting in Dasein. The fact that moods can deteriorate and change means simply that in every case Dasein always has some mood. The pallid, evenly balanced lack of mood, which is often persistent and which is not to be taken for a bad mood, is far from nothing at all. Rather, it is in this that Dasein becomes satiated with itself. Being has become manifest as a burden. Why that should be, one does not *know*. And Dasein cannot know anything of the sort because the possibilities of disclosure which belong to cognition reach far too short a way compared with the primordial disclosure belonging to moods, in which Dasein is brought before its Being as "there". Furthermore, a mood of elation can alleviate the manifest burden of Being; that such a mood is possible also discloses the burdensome character of Dasein, even while it alleviates the burden. A mood makes manifest "how one is, and how one is faring". In this "how one is", having a mood brings Being to its "there".' John Macquarrie, in *An Existentialist Theology: A Comparison of Heidegger and Bultmann* (London: SCM Press, 1955), 67, glosses as follows: 'Mood has its own understanding, not in the sense of an explicit knowing, but in the sense that it discloses man to himself as "being-there."' See too Rollo May, 'The Therapist and the Journey into Hell', *Michigan Quarterley Review* 25 (1986), 629–41. For Dante, Marco Gallarino, 'L'immaginazione tra psicologia e poesia nella *Divina Commedia*', in *Immaginario e immaginazione nel Medioevo. Atti del Convegno della Società Italiana per lo Studio del Pensiero Medievale, Milan 25–27 settembre 2008*, ed. Maria Bettetini and Francesco Paparella (Louvain-La Neuve: Fédération Internationale des Instituts d'Études Médiévales, 2009), 339–51; John Alcorn, 'Suffering in Hell: The Psychology of Emotions in Dante's *Inferno*', *Pedagogy, Critical Approaches to Teaching Literature, Language, Composition and Culture* 13.1 (2013), 75–85; Stefano Milonia, '"Tu se' morto", Riflessioni sulle condizioni di esistenza dell'io nella *Commedia*', *SC* 31.3 (2016), 433–49.

quando seco ricchezze portano.'[109] But frequently lurking in the depths of contingent fear—of the kind of fear, that is to say, generated by circumstance or eventuality—is the ontological fear of non-being, of the individual's falling back into the void in consequence of the leading choice. Impressed in the very moment of its espousal by the fragility of the alternative project, the spirit fears progressively for its stability and self-intelligibility. Frustrated by the failure of every fresh initiative to affirm its well-being beyond the point of ambiguity, and sensing in all this something making less for distraction than for destruction, it edges ever closer to despair. This, at any rate, is where Dante's account of far-wandering on the plane of existence begins. It begins with the fear everywhere engendered by, and in turn everywhere engendering, the surrogate possibility, the self-consciously demonic enterprise:

> Nel mezzo del cammin di nostra vita
> mi ritrovai per una selva oscura,
> ché la diritta via era smarrita.
> Ahi quanto a dir qual era è cosa dura
> esta selva selvaggia e aspra e forte
> che nel pensier rinova la paura!
> Tant'è amara che poco è più morte;
> ma per trattar del ben ch'i' vi trovai,
> dirò de l'altre cose ch'i' v'ho scorte.
> Io non so ben ridir com'i' v'intrai,
> tant'era pien di sonno a quel punto
> che la verace via abbandonai.
> Ma poi ch'i' fui al piè d'un colle giunto,
> là dove terminava quella valle
> che m'avea di paura il cor compunto,
> guardai in alto, e vidi le sue spalle
> vestite già de' raggi del pianeta
> che mena dritto altrui per ogne calle.
> Allor fu la paura un poco queta,
> che nel lago del cor m'era durata
> la notte ch'i' passai con tanta pieta
>
> . . .

---

109 'This every wretched merchant wending his way in the world knows only too well, every rustling of a leaf in the wind causing him to tremble with fear for the wealth he has about him.' Aristotle, *Nicomachean Ethics* 3.6 (1115a7): 'Timemus autem scilicet terribilia; haec vero est simpliciter dicendum mala. Ideo et timorem diffiniunt, suspecionem mali' (We fear, that is to say, dire eventuality, the essence, in truth, of evil, fear for this reason being defined precisely as the expectation of evil).

Ed una lupa, che di tutte brame
sembiava carca ne la sua magrezza,
e molte genti fé già viver grame,
    questa mi porse tanto di gravezza
con la paura ch'uscia di sua vista,
ch'io perdei la speranza de l'altezza.

(*Inferno* 1.1–21 and 49–54)[110]

Already discernible here, in addition to fear as the primary phenomenon of being in its lostness, are several of its secondary phenomena, including the disorientation and self-inexplicability of the soul in its estrangement (the 'Io non so ben ridir com'i' v'intrai' of line 10), its fundamental self-forgetfulness (the 'tant' era pien di sonno a quel punto' of line 11), and the despair apt to inform and ultimately to drive every act of inauthentic willing (the 'ch'io perdei la speranza de l'altezza' of line 54). Each of these conditions is symptomatic of the soul as standing over against self in the forum of conscience, and each confirms it in a state of existential crisis. But each is reducible to the fear serving to remind the individual of his captivity to the proximate possibility and thus of his ceasing to be as a free determinant. And this, short of the contrition or brokenness whereby the guilt of dividedness is received into self as a first step towards its liquidation, is a self-perpetuating condition; for fear, in the absence of contrition as a matter of fundamental sorrowing, merely encourages the soul in its now inveterate choices, this in turn serving only to reinforce its anxiety.

110 'Midway in the journey of our life I found myself in a dark wood, for the straight way was lost. Try as I may, there is no telling how it was with that wood, so wild, rugged and harsh was it that even to think of it terrifies me afresh! So savage, in fact, that death itself is scarcely more. But for the sake of the good I found there, I'll tell of what else I saw. How I came to be there I cannot rightly say, so drowsy was I in the moment I forsook the true way, but when I had reached the foot of a hill at the far end of that valley, a valley which had so pierced my heart with fear, I looked up and saw its shoulders swathed already with the beams of that planet leading men aright on every path. Then was assuaged a little the fear which, for the night I had spent so grievously, had persisted in the lake of my heart . . . and a she-wolf that in her leanness seemed laden with every craving, a craving that had already brought so many to grief. Terrifying as it was to behold, I was so burdened in spirit that I lost all hope of scaling the heights.' Patrick Boyde, 'Fear', in *Perception and Passion in Dante's 'Comedy'* (Cambridge: Cambridge University Press, 1993), 217–44; Letterio Cassata, 'Tra paura e speranza (il canto I dell'*Inferno*)', LL 22 1–2 (1997), 11–54; Roberto Rea, 'Psicologia ed etica della "paura" nel primo canto dell'*Inferno*: La "compunctio timoris"', DS 130 (2012), 183–206; Andrea Battistini, 'Canto I: Dalla paura alla speranza', in *Lectura Dantis Romana*, vol. 1 (*Inferno* 1–17), ed. Enrico Malato and Andrea Mazzucchi (Rome: Salerno, 2013), 43–74; Luca Marcozzi, 'Dante, la paura e il dolore: Lettura di *Inferno* XVI', *L'Alighieri* (RD) 41 (2013), 83–113; Enrico Rebuffat, 'Effetti della paura sul sangue: *Inferno* I 19–21 e *Inferno* XXIV 82–84', DS 78 (2013), 15–44; Daniele Monticelli, 'Fear in Dante's *Inferno*: Phenomenology, Semiotics, Aesthetics', in *"I luoghi nostri": Dante's Natural and Cultural Spaces*, ed. Zygmunt G. Baranski et al. (Tallin: Tallin University Press, 2015), 106–28.

Likewise prominent among the phenomena of estrangement, of this or that instance of human being as lost to the prior and subsistent reasons of its properly human presence in the world, is anger, which both presupposes the sensation of fear and shares its basic structure. Called, then, *to be* in and through God as the beginning and end of being but hostage to the alternative project in all the self-conscious apostasy thereof, the individual knows himself only in the kind of frustration sooner or later flowing over into resentment both of self and of the world beyond self. Ranged over against himself in the innermost parts of his being, he knows himself only in the kind of indignation engendered by anything tending either from within or from beyond to impede or to oppose— or simply to point up the inadequacy of—his chosen form of self-affirmation. This situation is straightaway recognized by Dante in the *Inferno*, where both on the threshold of the text and throughout it is a question of habitual and indiscriminate rage, of every aspect of the soul's existence as but an object of reproach:

> Bestemmiavano Dio e lor parenti,
> l'umana spezie e 'l luogo e 'l tempo e 'l seme
> di lor semenza e di lor nascimenti.

> (*Inferno* 3.103–5)[111]

—lines to which, as attuned to the complex pathology of anger as a matter both of stridency and of sullenness, we may add these from *Inferno* 7:

> Lo buon maestro disse: 'Figlio, or vedi
> l'anime di color cui vinse l'ira;

111 'They blasphemed God, their parents and mankind as a whole, together with the place, time and the seed of their begetting and birth'; similarly, from the canto of the luxurious, the 'Quando giungon davanti a la ruina, / quivi le strida, il compianto, il lamento; / bestemmian quivi la virtù divina' of 5.34–36 (reaching then the rock face, nothing but cries, complaints and wailing there where the souls curse God). Fiorenzo Forti, 'Sul canto dell'ira nell'*Inferno* dantesco', *LC* 5 (1976), 101–22; Patrick Boyde, 'Anger', in *Perception and Passion in Dante's 'Comedy'* (Cambridge: Cambridge University Press, 1993), 245–74; Giovanni Bardazzi, 'Avari e prodighi, iracondi e accidiosi', *SD* 65 (2000), 1–39; Claudia Galfrè, 'Gli iracondi dell'*Inferno*', *CI* 30–31 (2004), 5–42; Roberta De Monticelli, 'L'ira e le ragioni del cuore: Dante, Tommaso e la fenomenologia delle passioni', *LC* 32–34 (2005), 169–88; Alfredo Cottignoli, '*Inferno* VIII: Il dramma dell'ira e della salvezza senza grazia', in *Lectura Dantis Bononiensis II*, ed. Emilio Pasquini and Carlo Galli (Bologna: Bononia University Press, 2012), 89–100; Mario Apollonio, 'Ira', in *Dante: Storia della 'Commedia'*, ed. Carlo Annoni and Corrado Viola (Novara: Interlinea, 2013), 165–71; Roberto Rea, 'La paura della lupa e le forme dell'ira (lettura di *Inferno* VII)', *LL* 41.1–2 (2016), 79–110. More generally, Carla Casagrande and Silvana Vecchio, *I sette vizi capitali: Storia dei peccati nel Medioevo* (Turin: Einaudi, 2000); Raymond Angelo Belliotti, 'The Seven Deadly Sins', in *Dante's Deadly Sins: Moral Philosophy in Hell* (Oxford: Wiley-Blackwell, 2011), 124–48.

e anche vo' che tu per certo credi
　che sotto l'acqua è gente che sospira,
e fanno pullular quest'acqua al summo,
　come l'occhio ti dice, u' che s'aggira.
　　Fitti nel limo, dicon: "Tristi fummo
ne l'aere dolce che dal sol s'allegra,
portando dentro accidïoso fummo:
　or ci attristiam ne la belletta negra".
Quest' inno si gorgoglian ne la strozza,
ché dir nol posson con parola integra'.

(*Inferno* 7.115–26)[112]

and, as sensitive to these things—stridency and sullenness alike—as making between them for an asphyxiation of the spirit, these from the next canticle:

Buio d'inferno e di notte privata
d'ogne pianeto, sotto pover cielo,
quant' esser può di nuvol tenebrata,
　non fece al viso mio sì grosso velo
come quel fummo ch'ivi ci coperse,
né a sentir di così aspro pelo,
　che l'occhio stare aperto non sofferse;
onde la scorta mia saputa e fida
mi s'accostò e l'omero m'offerse.
　Sì come cieco va dietro a sua guida
per non smarrirsi e per non dar di cozzo
in cosa che 'l molesti, o forse ancida,
　m'andava io per l'aere amaro e sozzo,

112 'My good master said then: "See now, my son, the souls of those overcome by anger. And I would have you be sure in the knowledge that beneath these waters there are souls a-sighing, their sighs, as well you can see all around, bubbling up to the surface. Captive to the slime, they were, they say, 'sullen in the sweet air made glad by the sun, bearing within but sulky smoke. Sullen are we now in the black sludge'. Unable any more plainly to speak, this woeful hymn they gurgle in their gullet."' Gino Casagrande, '"Accidïoso fummo" (*Inferno* VII 123)', *SD* 67 (2002), 55–71; John Thorp, 'Fuming accidie: The Sin of Dante's Gurglers', in *Dante and the Unorthodox: The Aesthetics of Transgression*, ed. James Miller (Waterloo, Ontario: Wilfrid Laurier University Press, 2005), 151–69; María Carla Iglesias Rondina, 'El "Accidïoso fummo" y la "belletta negra" en *Inferno* VII, vv. 100–24: Possibile influencia de la teoria de los humores', *Tenzone* 7 (2006), 51–69; Mario Apollonio, 'Accidia', in *Dante: Storia della 'Commedia'*, ed. Carlo Annoni and Corrado Viola (Novara: Interlinea, 2013), 173–76; Marco Dorigatti, 'The Acid Test of Faith: Dante and the Capital Sin of "accidia"', *RELI* 41 (2013), 11–30.

> ascoltando il mio duca che diceva
> pur: 'Guarda che da me tu non sia mozzo'.
>
> (*Purgatorio* 16.15)[113]

But that, alas, is not all, for in circumstances of far-wandering anger with the world is but a manifestation of anger with self, a deflection of the self-reproach everywhere engendered by dividedness on the plane of willing—a state of affairs reflected as far as the *Inferno* is concerned in its steady portrayal of wrath as reflexive, as forever turning back upon self as its true object of concern; so, for example, this from *Inferno* 7:

> Poi si rivolse a quella 'nfiata labbia,
> e disse: 'Taci, maladetto lupo!
> consuma dentro te con la tua rabbia'.
>
> (*Inferno* 7.7–9)[114]

or this from *Inferno* 8:

> Tutti gridavano: 'A Filippo Argenti!';
> e 'l fiorentino spirito bizzarro
> in sé medesmo si volvea co' denti.
>
> (*Inferno* 8.61–63)

or this from *Inferno* 9:

> Con l'unghie si fendea ciascuna il petto.
>
> (*Inferno* 9.49)

---

113 'Hell's gloom or a planetless night under a barren sky everywhere cloud overcast never spread over my sight a veil so heavy or stuff so coarse to the senses as the smoke that so engulfed us there that never for a moment could I keep open my eyes; whereupon my wise and trusted escort drew close and offered me his shoulder. Just as a blind man follows on behind his guide that he may not stray or stumble against something liable to injure him perhaps even fatally, so, attentive to my leader's every word to the effect that I should not for a moment be parted from him, I pressed on through that bitter air and foul.' Jeremy Tambling, 'Overcoming Anger', in *Dante in Purgatory: States of Affect* (Turnhout: Brepols, 2010), 127–44.

114 'Then he turned back on that bloated visage saying: "Silence, accursed wolf! Devour but yourself in your anger!"' For *Inferno* 8: 'Then cried they all: "at Filippo Argenti", whereupon the rabid Florentine spirit turned upon himself his own teeth'; *Inferno* 9: 'Each with her own nails tore at her chest'; *Inferno* 12: 'And seeing us, he turned his teeth upon himself like one by anger possessed'; and *Inferno* 18: 'that foul and dishevelled drab there scratching herself with her filthy nails'.

or this from *Inferno* 12:

> e quando vide noi, sé stesso morse,
> sì come quei cui l'ira dentro fiacca.

(*Inferno* 12.14–15)

or this from *Inferno* 18:

> quella sozza e scapigliata fante
> che là si graffia con l'unghie merdose

(*Inferno* 18.130–31)

Throughout, then, the pattern is the same, the chief victim of ontological anger being the angry spirit itself. Ontological anger, Dante suggests, is always destructive. It is destructive socially and it is destructive psychologically. It is destructive socially in that between the ontologically angry there can never be any communion, any accommodation of the next man as a coefficient of selfhood. And it is destructive psychologically in that, far from easing the soul's unhappiness, it compounds it intolerably. And this, short of the contrition whereby the guilt of dividedness is received into self as the first step towards its liquidation, is a self-perpetuating condition; for anger in the absence of contrition merely encourages the soul in its commitment to the surrogate scheme as a means of well-being, this in turn serving merely to strengthen its sense of self-abhorrence, and, as a way of coping with this, its abhorrence of the world.

Similarly conspicuous as a feature of human being in its estrangement is the inauthentic restlessness thereof, its knowing no settled purpose. The term 'inauthentic' is important here in that inauthentic restlessness, which in its turning upon the alternative project shares the same basic structure as inauthentic fear, has to be distinguished from the kind of authentic restlessness proper to the pilgrim spirit in time and space, the authentic restlessness to which Augustine refers in the 'our hearts find no peace until they rest in you' moment of the *Confessions*. Inauthentic restlessness, by contrast, is an indiscriminate and impulsive restlessness, a restlessness bereft both of discerning and of orderly progression; so, for example, in respect of restlessness as a mere hankering for more, we have this passage from the fourth book of the *Convivio* on the psychopathology of accumulation:

> Promettono le false traditrici, se bene si guarda, di torre ogni sete e ogni mancanza, e apportare ogni saziamento e bastanza; e questo fanno nel principio a ciascuno uomo, questa promissione in certa quantità di loro

accrescimento affermando; e poi che quivi sono adunate, in loco di sazia-
mento e di refrigerio danno e recano sete di casso febricante intollerabile;
e in loco di bastanza recano nuovo termine, cioè maggiore quantitade a
desiderio e, con questa, paura grande e sollicitudine sopra l'acquisto. Sì che
veramente non si quietano, ma più danno cura, la qual prima sanza loro non
si avea.

(Convivio 4.12.5)[115]

—lines to which, for their sense of—as Dante sees it—the heightened folly of
it all, we may add these from the post-exilic canzone Doglia mi reca ne lo core
ardire:

> Corre l'avaro, ma più fugge pace:
> oh mente cieca, che non pò vedere
> lo suo folle volere
> che 'l numero, ch'ognora a passar bada,
> che 'nfinito vaneggia.

(Doglia mi reca ne lo core ardire, lines 69–73)[116]

together with, from the Commedia, these passages from the cantos of the ignavi
or fundamentally indifferent and of the avari or indiscriminately acquisitive, each
alike turning upon the soul's preoccupation with one self-consciously inauthentic
project after another and upon this as a principle of enervation—this, Dante has
his pilgrim protagonist say, being more or less the way of the world generally (the
'I would never have believed death to have undone so many' moment of Inferno
3.56 and 57):

---

115 'Anyone looking at them closely can see how these false traitors promise to do away with
whatever thirst or lack one has and to bring complete satisfaction and fulfilment. This is what wealth
says to everyone at the outset, declaring that its promise will be made good as soon as it has reached a
certain amount. But once it is there, instead of cooling and calming the spirit it creates an unbearable
feverish thirst within. Far from satisfying the soul, it sets up a new goal, a desire for still more besides,
and, along with this, endless apprehension with respect to what has already been acquired. In truth,
then, rather than stilling the spirit, it generates an anxiety which was never there in the first place.' For
Augustine on authentic restlessness, Confessions 1.1: 'Tu excitas ut laudare te delectet, quia fecisti nos
ad te et inquietum est cor nostrum donec requiescat in te' (you so quicken him that he delights in your
praise, for you have created us for yourself, and our hearts find no peace until they rest in you). Patrick
Boyde, 'Covetousness', in Human Vices and Human Worth in Dante's 'Comedy' (Cambridge: Cambridge
University Press, 2000), 149–73.
116 'The miser runs, only to be ever further from peace. O blind spirit, which for its insane desire
cannot see that the sum which every moment it strives to pass stretches on to infinity!' Enrico Fenzi,
'Tra etica del dono e accumulazione: Note di lettura alla canzone Doglia mi reca', in Doglia mi reca ne
lo core ardire, ed. Umberto Carpi (Madrid: Asociación Complutense de Dantología, 2008), 147–211.

E io: 'Maestro, che è tanto greve
a lor che lamentar li fa sì forte?'.
Rispuose: 'Dicerolti molto breve.

Questi non hanno speranza di morte,
e la lor cieca vita è tanto bassa,
che 'nvidïosi son d'ogne altra sorte.

Fama di loro il mondo esser non lassa;
misericordia e giustizia li sdegna:
non ragioniam di lor, ma guarda e passa'.

E io, che riguardai, vidi una 'nsegna
che girando correva tanto ratta,
che d'ogne posa mi parea indegna;

e dietro le venìa sì lunga tratta
di gente, ch'i' non averei creduto
che morte tanta n'avesse disfatta.

. . .

'Or puoi, figliuol, veder la corta buffa
d'i ben che son commessi a la fortuna,
per che l'umana gente si rabuffa;

ché tutto l'oro ch'è sotto la luna
e che già fu, di quest' anime stanche
non poterebbe farne posare una.'

(*Inferno* 3.43–57 and 7.61–66)[117]

---

117 'And I: "Master, what is it that grieves them so, that they lament thus aloud?", whereupon he replied: "This I shall tell you in but a few words. These have no hope of death, and so abject is their blind existence that they envy every other lot. Of them, despised as they are by pity and justice alike, the world leaves no living trace. Let us not talk of them. Simply look and pass by." And, looking on, I saw as though impatient of any pause a whirling banner speed by, with, following on, so long a train of people that I should never have believed death had undone so many ... "Now, my son, you can see the fleeting mockery of those goods entrusted to mere fortune, for which men everywhere wrangle one with another; for all the gold that is or ever was beneath the moon could not calm any one of these weary souls."' On *ignavia* or sloth, indolence or indifference as a renunciatory condition of the spirit: Stefano Vazzana, 'Chi sono gli ignavi?', *L'Alighieri (RBD)* 30.1 (1989), 3–14; Adriano Lanza, 'Ignavi e angeli neutrali', in *Dante all'inferno: I misteri eretici della 'Commedia'* (Rome: Tre Editori, 1999), 57–67; Marcia L. Colish, '"Sanza 'nfamia e sanza lodo": Moral Neutrality from Alan of Lille to Dante', in *The Fathers and Beyond: Church Fathers between Ancient and Medieval Thought* (Aldershot: Ashgate, 2008), 263–73; Aleksandr N. Veselovskij, 'Sospesi, irresoluti e ignavi nell'inferno dantesco', *PT* 21.1–2 (2017; originally 1888), 117–40. On avarice, Florence Russo, '"Iustitia" and "avaritia" in Dante's *Comedy*', *IQ* 175–76 (2008), 5–25; Jeremy Tambling, 'On Avarice', in *Dante in Purgatory: States of Affect* (Turnhout: Brepols, 2010), 175–95; Mario Apollonio, 'Avarizia', in *Dante: Storia della 'Commedia'*, ed. Carlo Annoni and Corrado Viola (Novara: Interlinea, 2013), 177–84; John Scott, 'Avarice in Dante and His Age', *DS* 132 (2014), 1–33.

Hard upon the heels of fear, then, as to the fore among the moods of being in its estrangement come anger and restlessness, each alike testifying to a state of radical dividedness on the plane of willing, to the soul's standing over against itself in respect of the call to transcendence given with the act itself of existence. Wedded to the alternative project, but at the same time sensitive both to its inadequacy to the task in hand and to the guilt engendered by it, the soul either reacts angrily to whatever in the world appears to stand in its way or to call it into question, or else lurches more or less frantically from one surrogate possibility to another, each alike, as strategies of the spirit in its unhappiness, serving merely to compound that unhappiness.

But with anger and restlessness we are as yet only in the foothills of Dante's phenomenology of being in its far-offness, for in addition to anger and restlessness as but the most dramatic of its manifestations, being in its far-offness is present to itself by way also (a) of one or other (or both) of its more properly passive conditions, namely inertia and indecision, and (b) of one or other (or both) of its more properly neurotic conditions, namely obsession and paranoia. Taking first, then, the case of ontological inertia, this, like ontological fear, has its roots in the sensation of self as divided against self, as standing over against the reasons of its proper humanity, except that here the sensation of dividedness, far from reinforcing commitment to the alternative project as a means of self-affirmation, issues in a form of psychological paralysis, in what Augustine, in a passage anticipating a recognizably Dantean emphasis, describes as slumberousness of the spirit ('altitudo soporis . . . torpor in membris'):

Ita sarcina saeculi, velut somno assolet, dulciter premebar; et cogitationes, quibus meditabar in te, similes erant conatibus expergisci volentium, qui tamen superati soporis altitudine remerguntur. Et sicut nemo est, qui dormire semper velit, omniumque sano iudicio vigilare praestat, differt tamen plerumque homo somnum excutere, cum gravis torpor in membris est, eumque iam displicentem carpit libentius, quamvis surgendi tempus advenerit.

(*Confessions* 8.5.12)[118]

—this too being Dante's meaning on the threshold of the *Inferno* as he has his protagonist confess to a species of spiritual somnambulance and to this as the beginning of his far-wandering:

118 'In fact, I bore the burden of the world as contentedly as sometimes one bears a heavy load of sleep. My thoughts, as I meditated on you, were like the efforts of a man who tries to wake but cannot and sinks back into the depths of slumber. No one wants to sleep forever, for everyone rightly agrees that it is better to be awake. Yet a man often staves off the effort to rouse himself when his body is leaden with inertia. He is glad to settle down once more, although it is against his better judgement, and it is already time he were up and about.'

> Io non so ben ridir com'i' v'intrai,
> tant' era pien di sonno a quel punto
> che la verace via abbandonai.
>
> (*Inferno* 1.10–12)[119]

In circumstances of dividedness, Dante suggests, consciousness of self is an attenuated consciousness, a kind of half-waking half-sleeping impression that all is not well in the depths. Aware of being astray, the spirit is nonetheless at a loss to make sense of itself, of its own fundamentally distracted existence. In fact, not all inertia is ontological. The sort of inertia engendered by, for example, the pressure of events or by the weight of responsibility need not be existentially significant. And neither is all inertia of the slumberous variety, for prominent too—and thus duly acknowledged by Dante—is the 'superfluity of reflection' kind, the kind associated with the potential and often enough actual issuelessness of pure thought (the 'perché, pensando, consumai la 'mpresa / che fu nel cominciar cotanto tosta' clause of *Inferno* 2.41–42 and the 'ché sempre l'omo in cui pensier rampolla / sovra pensier, da sé dilunga il segno' clause of *Purgatorio* 5.16–17).[120] But the kind of inertia suggested by the 'tant' era pien di sonno' tercet of *Inferno* 1 is different, for this again is the inertia of self-inexplicability, of—again after the manner of Augustine (the 'factus eram ipse mihi magna quaestio' of the *Confessions* at 4.4)—self as present to self by way merely of the enigmatic and undiscoverable.

No less prominent, however, as a condition of being in its dividedness, in its seeing the best but clinging to the worst, is ontological indecision, meaning by this faintheartedness in respect of the leading idea, an inclination whenever possible to look the other way. True, not all indecision is ontological in kind, for not all indecision reaches down into the depths; and not all indecision is destructive, for not all indecision threatens the substance and structure of selfhood in its totality. But insofar as it *does* reach down into the depths, and, reaching down into the depths, threatens the stability and intelligibility of existence itself, it is always destructive, for here decisiveness is of the essence. Augustine, as, after Paul, the great analyst of willing and not willing, had observed this situation at first hand, for central to his account in the *Confessions* of his own emergence from lesser into greater being is, again, an acknowledgement both of his wishing and of his not wishing at the same time, and this is a situation reproduced by Dante in the

---

119 'How I came to be there I cannot rightly say, so drowsy was I in the moment I forsook the true way.' Roberto Pacifico, 'Io non so ben ridir com'io v'entrai', in *La "fera alla gaetta pelle": La corda e la frode della seduzione (studi sull'"Inferno' dantesco)* (Milan: ExCogita Editore, 2010), 21–27.

120 'For which reason, endlessly thinking it over, I extinguished an enterprise so ready in its inception . . . which is why the man piling thought upon thought only ever finds himself further from his goal.'

Commedia, where, especially in the early part of the poem, indecision thus understood repeatedly threatens the process of significant becoming; so, for example, this passage from canto 2 of the *Inferno* on—as, at any rate, the pilgrim poet sees it—discretion as the better part of valour:

> 'Ma io, perché venirvi? o chi 'l concede?
> Io non Enëa, io non Paulo sono;
> me degno a ciò né io né altri 'l crede.
>
> Per che, se del venire io m'abbandono,
> temo che la venuta non sia folle.
> Se' savio; intendi me' ch'i' non ragiono'.
>
> E qual è quei che disvuol ciò che volle
> e per novi pensier cangia proposta,
> sì che dal cominciar tutto si tolle,
>
> tal mi fec' ïo 'n quella oscura costa,
> perché, pensando, consumai la 'mpresa
> che fu nel cominciar cotanto tosta.
>
> 'S'i' ho ben la parola tua intesa',
> rispuose del magnanimo quell' ombra,
> 'l'anima tua è da viltade offesa;
>
> la qual molte fïate l'omo ingombra
> sì che d'onrata impresa lo rivolve,
> come falso veder bestia quand' ombra'.

(Inferno 2.31–48)[121]

---

[121] ' "But why should I go there, and upon what authority? I am no Aeneas and no Paul. Neither I nor any man thinks me fit for this, so that should I thus commit myself my going might, I fear, be foolish. You are a wise man, and understand better than I can explain." As one who unwills what he has willed and, thinking it through afresh, changes his mind and goes back on what he had begun, such I myself became on that dark slope; for by thinking it through afresh I brought to naught an undertaking so ready in its inception. "If I have rightly understood what you say", replied the shade of the great soul, "your spirit is smitten with cowardice, which many a time so oppresses a man that, as when—mistakenly—he sees an animal shying, he turns back from his own noble enterprise." ' Antonino Pagliaro, 'Io non Enea, io non Paolo sono', *Il Veltro* 1.1 (1957), 7–14; Rachel Jacoff and William A. Stephany, 'The Poet as Aeneas and Paul', in *Lectura Dantis Americana: 'Inferno II'* (Philadelphia: University of Pennsylvania Press, 1989), 57–72; Giorgio Bàrberi Squarotti, 'II: "Io non Enëa, io non Paulo sono" ', in *Tutto l'"Inferno": Lettura integrale della prima cantica del poema dantesco* (Milan: Franco Angeli, 2011), 34–37. For Augustine on willing and unwilling, *Confessions* 8.10.22: 'ego eram qui volebam, ego qui nolebam', while for Dante and Paul, Francesco D'Ovidio, 'Dante e San Paolo', *Nuova Antologia* 151 (1897), 214–38; Jospeh Anthony Mazzeo, 'Dante and the Pauline Modes of Vision', in *Structure and Thought in the 'Paradiso'* (Cornell: Cornell University Press, 1958), 84–110; Giuseppe di Scipio, *The Presence of Pauline Thought in the Works of Dante* (Lewiston, NY: Edwin Mellen Press, 1995).

—lines to which, as in this respect at one with canto 2, we may add these from canto 8 on, again, the triumph of reluctance over resolution as a disposition of the spirit, as the soul's preliminary response to the arduousness of it all:

> 'O caro duca mio, che più di sette
> volte m'hai sicurtà renduta e tratto
> d'alto periglio che 'ncontra mi stette,
>   non mi lasciar', diss' io, 'così disfatto;
> e se 'l passar più oltre ci è negato,
> ritroviam l'orme nostre insieme ratto'.
>   E quel segnor che lì m'avea menato,
> mi disse: 'Non temer; ché 'l nostro passo
> non ci può tòrre alcun; da tal n'è dato.
>   Ma qui m'attendi, e lo spirito lasso
> conforta e ciba di speranza buona,
> ch'i' non ti lascerò nel mondo basso'.
>   Così sen va, e quivi m'abbandona
> lo dolce padre, e io rimagno in forse,
> che sì e no nel capo mi tenciona.[122]

Committed, then, in one part of his being to the authentic project, the pilgrim poet is nonetheless caught up in the kind of yes/no conflict of willing and unwilling invariably engendered by the critical instant, by the more or less terrifying sensation of being as entailing something close to non-being—to a losing of self for the purposes of a finding of self—as the condition of its ultimate affirmation.

But that is not all, for being in its dividedness is an obsessive order of being, an order of being having no alternative but to commit itself to the inauthentic project. Wedded, in other words, to the surrogate scheme but at the same time sensitive to the inadequacy of it all, the soul in its contritionlessness has no choice but to deliver itself yet again—and again and again—to its own undoing, to the 'great refusal' at the centre of its existence. This situation is everywhere discernible in the *Inferno*, Francesca in canto 5, Farinata in canto 10, Ulysses in canto 26 and Ugolino in canto 33 all meeting the guilt of dividedness by affirming still more

---

122 ' "O dear leader of mine, who seven times and more have restored my confidence and saved me from the great peril confronting me, leave me not", I said, "undone so; and if going further be denied us, let us quickly retrace our steps together". And my lord, the same who had brought me here, made answer: "Fear not, for none can hinder our passage, for by such a One is it granted us; but await me here and comfort your weary spirit, feeding it upon good hope; for I'll not abandon you in the nether world", with which he went his way, my sweet father, leaving me there, I, amid my doubts, yes and no contending one with the other in my head.'

boldly the alternative project. Thus Francesca meets the guilt of her carnality, not by taking that guilt into self as the first step towards its resolution, but by setting it aside in favour of a fresh living-out of the critical moment, of the climactic moment of self-delivery:

> E quella a me: 'Nessun maggior dolore
> che ricordarsi del tempo felice
> ne la miseria; e ciò sa 'l tuo dottore.
>
> Ma s'a conoscer la prima radice
> del nostro amor tu hai cotanto affetto,
> dirò come colui che piange e dice.
>
> Noi leggiavamo un giorno per diletto
> di Lancialotto come amor lo strinse;
> soli eravamo e sanza alcun sospetto.
>
> Per più fïate li occhi ci sospinse
> quella lettura, e scolorocci il viso;
> ma solo un punto fu quel che ci vinse.
>
> Quando leggemmo il disïato riso
> esser basciato da cotanto amante,
> questi, che mai da me non fia diviso,
> la bocca mi basciò tutto tremante.
> Galeotto fu 'l libro e chi lo scrisse:
> quel giorno più non vi leggemmo avante'.

> (*Inferno* 5.121–38)[123]

123 'And she to me: "There is as your teacher knows full well no greater sorrow than that of recalling in circumstances of wretchedness good times past. But in that you have so great a desire to know of our love's first coming about, I shall speak of it as one who weeps in the very telling of it. One day, for pleasure pure and simple, we read of Lancelot and how he was constrained by love. We were alone and without misgiving. Often and enough as we read our eyes met and our faces blanched, but one moment alone was it that overcame us. Reading as we did how the longed-for smile was kissed by so great a lover, he who shall never be parted from me kissed my lips all atrembling. A Galeotto was the book and he who wrote it, and that day we read no farther in it."' D'Arco Silvio Avalle, *Analyse du récit de Paolo et Francesca: Dante Alighieri, Enfer V* (Krefeld: Scherpe Verlag, 1975); Fabio Cossutta, 'Francesca tra ragione e talento', *L'Alighieri (RBD)* 16.1–2 (1975), 102–14; Gioacchino Paparelli, 'Ethos e pathos nell'episodio di Francesca da Rimini', in *Ideologia e poesia di Dante* (Florence: Olschki, 1975), 171–200; Francesco De Sanctis, 'Francesca da Rimini', in *Saggi critici*, vol. 3, ed. Luigi Russo (Bari: Laterza, 1979), 275–93; Enrico Malato, 'Dottrina e poesia nel canto di Francesca', *FC* 11.2 (1986), 161–210; Guglielmo Gorni, 'Francesca, o la cognizione del dolore: Riscritture nel quinto dell'*Inferno*', *Anticomoderno* 3 (1997), 245–52; Franco Salerno, 'Ossessione e sdoppiamento nel V Canto dell'*Inferno*', *Nuova secondaria* 15.5 (1998), 70–71; Ignazio Baldelli, *Dante e Francesca* (Florence: Olschki, 1999); Stefano Carrai, 'Il lamento di Francesca, il silenzio di Paolo', *NRLI* 9.1 (2006), 9–26; Gennaro Sasso, 'Francesca da Rimini', in *Dante, Guido e Francesca* (Rome: Viella, 2008), 173–96 (with 'Le idee di Francesca' at 19–42); Robert Hollander, '*Inferno* V, 138: Francesca's Confession', *L'Alighieri (RD)* 40 (2012), 115–19; Elena Lombardi, *The Wings of the Doves: Love and Desire in Dante and Medieval Culture* (Montreal: McGill Queens

while Farinata, among the heretics, meets the guilt of his factionalism, not by lamenting that factionalism, but by trumpeting it all the more loudly:

> Subitamente questo suono uscìo
> d'una de l'arche; però m'accostai,
> temendo, un poco più al duca mio.
> Ed el mi disse: 'Volgiti! Che fai?
> Vedi là Farinata che s'è dritto;
> da la cintola in sù tutto 'l vedrai'.
> Io avea già il mio viso nel suo fitto;
> ed el s'ergea col petto e con la fronte
> com' avesse l'inferno a gran dispitto.
> E l'animose man del duca e pronte
> mi pinser tra le sepulture a lui,
> dicendo: 'Le parole tue sien conte'.
> Com' io al piè de la sua tomba fui,
> guardommi un poco, e poi, quasi sdegnoso,
> mi dimandò: 'Chi fuor li maggior tui?'

(Inferno 10.28–42)[124]

And what applies in the cases of Francesca and Farinata applies too in those of Ulysses and Ugolino as similarly relentless in pursuit of the self-consciously catastrophic project. Thus Ulysses, sensitive as he is to the folly of his undertaking in the southern seas (the 'folle volo' of 26.125), rejoices in it still as the way of self-affirmation:

> né dolcezza di figlio, né la pieta
> del vecchio padre, né 'l debito amore

University Press, 2012); Elena Lombardi, 'Francesca lettrice di romanzi e il "punto" di *Inferno* V', *L'Alighieri (RD)* 43 (2014), 19–39; Claudia Fernández, 'El beso de Francesca: Una lectura del Canto V del *Infierno*', *Tenzone* 16 (2015), 119–34.

124 'This sound, all of a sudden, came forth from one of the vaults, whereupon, fearful, I drew close to my leader. And he to me: "Come come, what are you about? See there Farinata, risen up erect. Behold from the waist up his full stature." Already were my eyes fixed upon his, he himself rising up breast and brow as though holding all hell in naught but scorn. With ready hands and bold, then, and a "Let your words be well chosen", my guide urged me towards him among the tombs, where, standing as I was at the foot of his sepulchre, he glanced briefly at me, demanding as he did so, all but contemptuously: "Who were your ancestors?"' John A. Scott, '*Inferno* X: Farinata "magnanimo"', in *Dante magnanimo* (Florence: Olschki, 1977), 9–45; Francesco De Sanctis, 'Il Farinata di Dante', *Saggi critici*, vol. 2, ed. Luigi Russo (Bari: Laterza, 1979), 320–48; Italo Borzi, 'Farinata degli Uberti: La tragedia degli odi civili nell'*Inferno* di Dante', *L'Alighieri (RBD)* 27.2 (1986), 23–46; Johannes Bartuschat, 'Farinata magnanime', *CP* 1 (2003), 5–14.

lo qual dovea Penelopè far lieta,
vincer potero dentro a me l'ardore
ch'i' ebbi a divenir del mondo esperto
e de li vizi umani e del valore;
ma misi me per l'alto mare aperto
sol con un legno e con quella compagna
picciola da la qual non fui diserto.

(*Inferno* 26.94–102)[125]

while Ugolino among the treacherous deep down in the pit, having contemplated and indeed lived out at first hand the dire consequences of it all—yet another slaughter of the innocents—returns more than ever ravenously to the sectarianism by which he was, is and ever will be driven:

Quand' ebbe detto ciò, con li occhi torti
riprese 'l teschio misero co' denti,
che furo a l'osso, come d'un can, forti.

(*Inferno* 33.76–78)[126]

125 'nor fondness for a son, nor feeling for an aged father, nor the love due to Penelope, which should have made her glad, could overcome in me my passion to know the world, the virtues, the vices and the worth of mankind; and so, with but one ship and with that little band of men by which I was never forsaken I put forth on the open sea'. Giorgio Padoan, *Il pio Enea, l'empio Ulisse: Tradizione classica e intendimento medievale in Dante* (Ravenna: Longo, 1977); John A. Scott, 'L'Ulisse dantesco', in *Dante magnanimo: Studi sulla 'Commedia'* (Florence: Olschki, 1977), 117–93; Guido Di Pino, 'Il canto di Ulisse', *Italianistica* 10.1 (1981), 5–20; Bruno Nardi, 'La tragedia di Ulisse', in *Dante e la cultura medievale*, ed. Paolo Mazzantini (Rome: Laterza, 1983), 125–34; D'Arco Silvio Avalle, 'L'ultimo viaggio di Ulisse', in *Dal mito alla letteratura e ritorno* (Milan: Il Saggiatore, 1990), 209–33; Antonio Gagliardi, 'Ulisse', in *Ulisse e Sigieri di Brabante: Ricerche su Dante* (Catanzaro: Pullano, 1992), 9–77; Antonio Gagliardi, 'Ogni altro Ulisse', in *La tragedia intellettuale di Dante: Il 'Convivio'* (Catanzaro: Pullano, 1994); Piero Boitani, *The Shadow of Ulysses: Figures of a Myth* (Oxford: Clarendon, 1994) (from the Italian, *L'ombra di Ulisse: Figure di un mito* [Bologna: Il Mulino, 1992]); Piero Boitani, *Sulle orme di Ulisse* (Bologna: Il Mulino, 1998); Piero Boitani, 'L'Ulysse de Dante et la modernité', *CT* 13.1 (2010), 41–58; Ignazio Baldelli, 'Dante e Ulisse', *LI* 50.3 (1998), 358–73 (and in *Studi danteschi*, ed. Luca Serianni et al. [Spoleto: Centro italiano di studi sull'alto medioevo, 2015], 263–77); Patrick Boyde, 'The Worth and Vices of Ulysses: A Case-Study', in *Human Vices and Human Worth in Dante's 'Comedy'* (Cambridge: Cambridge University Press, 2000), 231–72; Carlo Ossola, 'Il problema della conoscenza in Dante: Ulisse e il "quia"', in *Dante poeta cristiano* (Florence: Edizioni Polistampa, 2001), 41–53; Lino Pertile, 'Le penne e il volo', in *La punta del disio: Semantica del desiderio nella 'Commedia'* (Florence: Cadmo, 2005), 115–35; Paola Basile, *I folli voli di Ulisse* (Pesaro: Metauro, 2006); Aroldo Barbieri, 'Ulisse: Un eroe della conoscenza e una palinodia di Dante?', *DRISDA* 8 (2011), 43–67; Massimo Cacciari, 'Il "peccato" di Ulisse', *RSD* 13.1 (2013), 24–42; Jean-Louis Poirier, *Ne plus ultra: Dante et le dernier voyage d'Ulysse* (Paris: Les Belles Lettres, 2016).
126 'That said, he tore once again, his eyes askance and with teeth as strong on the bone as a dog's, into the wretched skull'. Giorgio Bàrberi Squarotti, 'L'orazione del conte Ugolino', in *L'artificio dell'eter-*

None of these spirits, in delivering itself yet again to the alternative project, has, in truth, any choice in the matter, for *not* to deliver oneself to the alternative project in circumstances of contritionlessness means to preside over the disintegration of self under the dead weight of guilt; hence the obsessive character of it all, obsession, in circumstances of contritionlessness, alone making for a measure of self-consistency, for a way of coping with self in the now infinite sadness of self. And it is at this point—at the point of obsession as the only way of coping in circumstances of estrangement with the sadness of it all—that obsession shades off into despair as at once the deep substance and the point of arrival of everything so far, of the fear, anger, restlessness, indifference, inertia and indecision everywhere besetting the soul in its hardness of heart. Now despair, in the sense of giving up on hope as a matter of sure expectation—or, as they themselves were inclined to put it, a sin in the area of the irascible[127]—figures prominently among the old theologians, but in Dante it is both this and more besides. For despair, in the *Inferno*, is a matter of the demonic—of the demonic in the sense not merely of giving up on hope as a matter of sure expectation but of systematic delivery to the ways and means of ontic annihilation, of standing foursquare over against the primordial *let it be*; so, for example, Francesca, who, burdened by a sense of the wretchedness of it all (the 'Nessun maggior dolore / che ricordarsi del tempo felice / ne la miseria' of 5.121–23), nonetheless delivers herself afresh to the old dance, to a reenactment and a reliving of the now abiding catastrophe of her existence (the 'bocca mi basciò tutto tremante' of 5.136), her gracious recitative in

---

nità (Verona: Fiorini, 1972), 283–332; Pier Angelo Perotti, 'Il conte Ugolino', *L'Alighieri (RBD)* 31.1 (1990), 45–51; Lodovico Cardellino, 'Ugolino', in *Autocritica infernale* (Milan: Jaca Book, 1992), 337–57; Dino Bigongiari, 'The Evil Counselors: Ulysses; The Story of Ugolino', in *Readings in the 'Divine Comedy'. A Series of Lectures*, ed. Anne Paolucci (Dover, DE: Griffon House, 2006), 173–85; Piero Boitani, 'Canti XXXIII–XXXIV: La Tragedia di Ugolino', in *Esperimenti danteschi: 'Inferno' 2008*, ed. Simone Invernizzi (Genoa: Marietti, 2009), 253–86; Peter Hawkins, 'Bottom of the Universe: Dante and Evil', in *Dante in Oxford: The Paget Toynbee Lectures*, ed. Martin McLaughlin et al. (Oxford: Legenda, 2011), 147–59; Enrico Malato, 'Canto 33: La "morte" della pietà', in *Lectura Dantis Romana: Cento canti per cento anni, I Inferno*, vol. 2, ed. Enrico Malato and Andrea Mazzucchi (Rome: Salerno, 2013), 1026–90.

127 So, for example, Thomas in the *Summa theologiae* at 1a 2ae.23.2: 'objectum irascibilis est sensibile bonum vel malum, non quidem absolute, sed sub ratione difficultatis vel arduitatis . . . Bonum autem arduum, sive difficile, habet rationem ut in ipsum tendatur inquantum est bonum quod pertinet ad passionem spei; et ut an ipso recedatur, inquantum est arduum et difficile, quod pertinet ad passionem desperationis' (the object of the irascible faculty is sensible good or evil, considered not absolutely but under the aspect of difficulty or arduousness . . . Now the good which is difficult or arduous, considered as good, is of such a nature as to produce in us a tendency to it, which tendency pertains to the passion of hope; whereas, considered as arduous or difficult, it makes us turn from it, and this pertains to the passion of despair). Ronald L. Martinez, 'Dante between Hope and Despair: The Traditions of *Lamentations* in the *Divine Comedy*', *Logos* 5.3 (2002), 45–76; Thomas Miles, 'Dante: Tours of Hell. Mapping the Landscape of Sin and Despair', in *Kierkegaard and the Patristic and Medieval Traditions*, ed. Jon Stewart (Aldershot: Ashgate, 2007), 223–35; Ryan Johnson, 'Kierkegaard and the Dialectic of Demonic Despair', *Postgraduate Journal of Aesthetics* 9.3 (2012), 29–41 (Dante at 33–37).

this sense containing a gesture of defiance no less absolute than that, say, of a Vanni Fucci or of a Capaneus; so too Farinata, who, for all his misgiving in conscience (the 'a la qual forse fui troppo molesto' of 10.27), rejoices still in his particular brand of sectarianism (the 'Chi fuor li maggior tui' of 10.42); and so too Ulysses, who, troubled somewhere in the depths by a sense of the recklessness of it all (the 'folle volo' of 26.125), sets sail again—intentionally at least—in search of world-expertise in the southern seas (the 'ch'i' ebbi a divenir del mondo esperto' of 26.98). Throughout, then, the pattern is the same, despair, for Dante, constituting not merely a giving in to the general unnegotiability of things but— in all the inner agony of this (for everywhere at work in the recesses is an albeit hazy perception of the *what might be* of self in respect of its properly human presence in the world)—a positive commitment to the work of ontological undoing, to tearing down as distinct from building up as the first and final cause of historical selfhood. This, then, is despair under the aspect not now of renunciation but of reiteration, not now of difficulty but of deliberation, of, in short, blasphemy in its now pure form.

In none of these cases, then, is the mood nothing. On the contrary, it is by way of the mood of being in its far-offness—of the fear, the anger, the inertia, the indecision, the obsession and, as the encompassing of these things, the despair everywhere clouding the existence of the alienated spirit—that the individual more or less anxious in respect of his or her properly human being knows self in the truth of self, in the *how it stands and how it fares* with self in the innermost parts thereof. And what applies in the case of the soul's far-offness applies also in that of its drawing nigh, for in consequence now of the courage whereby the guilt of dividedness is taken into self as the first step towards its liquidation the soul knows itself both in the peace of self-possession and in the joy of self-surpassing, both in the quietness of the one and in the quickening of the other. Now peace as the mood of being in the moment of emergence is everywhere there among the old theologians. When, for example, Augustine says in the *De vera religione* that 'every corporeal object has peace in consequence of its having form' he is speaking, precisely, of the peace proper to a thing at the point of emergence, of being and doing in keeping with what it actually is,[128] and when on the threshold of the *Confessions* he says that there can be no rest for the soul until such time as 'it rests in you' he is speaking of the peace present to man as but the final cause of

---

128 *De vera religione* 11.21: 'Habet corpus quandam pacem suae formae, sine qua prorsus nihil esset', while for the *Confessions*, 1.1: '[quia fecisti nos ad te et inquietum est cor nostrum,] donec requiescat in te'. For Richard of St Victor, *Benjamin minor* 38: 'Haec est illa vere beata terra, mentis videlicet stabilitas tranquilla, quando mens in seipsa tota colligitur, et in uno aeternitatis desiderio immobiliter figitur', while for Thomas, *Summa theologiae* 2a 2ae.29.3 respectively: 'Respondeo dicendum quod duplex unio est de ratione pacis . . . Quarum una est secundum ordinationem propriorum appetituum in unum' (I reply by saying that peace implies as of the essence a twofold union . . . the first of which lies in the ordering of one's appetites to a single end).

his every intellectual and moral striving. And when Richard of St Victor speaks in the *Benjamin minor* of the 'tranquil stability of the mind totally gathered within itself and unalterably fixed on the longing for eternity' he is speaking of the peace proper to self in its at once perfect possession and perfect projectedness, in its turning steadily but purposefully about its own still centre; and when, finally, Thomas speaks in the *Summa theologiae* of peace as but the 'direction of one's appetite to a single end' he is speaking of the peace always and everywhere contingent upon the orderly implementation of self on the plane of willing. But all this and more besides is in Dante as the celebrant par excellence in European letters of peace as the mood of homecoming, of the soul's laying hold at last of its proper patrimony; so, for example, in respect of the soul's knowing itself at last in the perfect peace of paradise, we have these lines (100–102) from *Paradiso* 30:

> Lume è là sù che visibile face
> lo creatore a quella creatura
> che solo in lui vedere ha la sua pace.[129]

while in respect of the peace of ultimate emergence and of a now integral act of properly human being we have this from the *Convivio* at 3.6.7:

> Dove è da sapere che ciascuna cosa massimamente desidera la sua perfezione, e in quella si queta ogni suo desiderio . . . [130]

or this from the *Purgatorio* at 26.53–54:

> O anime sicure
> d'aver, quando che sia, di pace stato[131]

or this from the *Paradiso* at 27.8:

> oh vita intègra d'amore e di pace![132]

---

129 'A light there is above which makes the creator visible to every creature that has in seeing him its only peace.'

130 'What, then, needs to be understood is that everything according to kind seeks out above all its proper perfection, wherein is sated its every desire.' Giuliana Carugati, 'Quando amor fa sentir de la sua pace', in *Dante for the New Millennium*, ed. Teodolinda Barolini and Harry Wayne Storey (New York: Fordham University Press, 2003), 211–27; Piero Boitani, 'Peace and the Mind in Love: Piccarda', in *Dante's Poetry of the Donati. The Barlow Lectures in Dante Delivered at University College London 17–18 March 2005* (Leeds: Maney, 2007; and in *Dante e il suo futuro* [Rome: Edizioni di Storia e Letteratura, 2013], 223–88); Vittorio Montemaggi, '"E 'n la sua volontade è nostra pace": Peace, Justice and the Trinity in the *Commedia*', in *War and Peace in Dante: Essays Literary, Historical and Theological*, ed. John Barnes and Daragh O'Connell (Dublin: Four Courts Press, 2015), 195–226.

131 'O souls confident of enjoying whensoever a state of peace.'

132 'Oh blessed existence, harmonious in love and tranquillity!'

as well as, in respect now of peace as the final cause of the soul's every sincere desire, the 'Vegna ver' noi la pace del tuo regno' moment of the *Purgatorio* at 11.7 and, from the same canticle, the 'pregar per pace' moment of 16.16–18:

> Io sentia voci, e ciascuna pareva
> pregar per pace e per misericordia
> l'Agnel di Dio che le peccata leva.[133]

In each of these cases, peace is the peace of love-harvesting, the peace always and everywhere contingent on the bringing home of the proximate to the ultimate on the plane of seeing, understanding and desiring. Peace, then, is the mood of properly human being in its stillness. It is, in short, the *static* mood of being in its authenticity.

Joy, as but being under the aspect of exhilaration, of its sheer overflowingness, is likewise everywhere present to the old theologians as a matter both of contemplation and of celebration. When, for example, Augustine says in the *Confessions* that 'true happiness is to rejoice in the truth, for to rejoice in the truth is to rejoice in you, my God, who are the truth' he registers the joy of being in God as the beginning and end of all being;[134] and when in the *Benjamin major* Richard of St Victor speaks of the 'joy of exultation whereby the mind is alienated from itself' he confirms the rapturous mood of being in its now proper self-losing, in its losing self, that is to say, for the sake of finding self. And when in his Lenten sermons *de psalmo Qui habitat* Bernard exclaims 'What is joy but a leaping out of self?' he gives expression to the peculiarly animated character of ontological bliss. But again all this and more besides is in Dante as the celebrant par excellence in European letters of joy as the mood of homecoming, of the soul's at last standing fully and freely in its own presence; so, for example, in respect of the joy of being in God as the beginning and end of all being we have these now familiar lines from *Paradiso* 27:

> Oh gioia! oh ineffabile allegrezza!
> oh vita intègra d'amore e di pace!
> oh sanza brama sicura ricchezza!

> (*Paradiso* 27.7–9)[135]

133 'I heard voices, all of them seeking in prayer from the Lamb of God who takes away the sins of the world peace and compassion.' For the petitionary moment of *Purgatorio* 11: 'Grant unto us the peace of your kingdom.'

134 *Confession* 10.23: 'Beata quippe vita est gaudium de veritate. Hoc est enim gaudium de te, qui veritas es.' For Richard of St Victor, *Benjamin major* 5.5: 'Magnitudine jocunditatis, et exsultationis mens hominis a seipsa alienatur', while for Bernard, *De psalmo Qui habitat* 7.5: 'Quid enim aliud exsultare, quam ex se ipso saltare est?'

135 'O joy! O gladness unspeakable! O life fulfilled with love and peace! O wealth secure with no

while in respect of the joy of radical self-surpassing, these from *Paradiso* 16:

> Io cominciai: 'Voi siete il padre mio;
> voi mi date a parlar tutta baldezza;
> voi mi levate sì, ch'i' son più ch'io.
>   Per tanti rivi s'empie d'allegrezza
> la mente mia, che di sé fa letizia
> perché può sostener che non si spezza'.

(*Paradiso* 16.16–21)[136]

or these from *Paradiso* 33:

> Da quinci innanzi il mio veder fu maggio
> che 'l parlar mostra, ch'a tal vista cede,
> e cede la memoria a tanto oltraggio.
>   Qual è colüi che sognando vede,
> che dopo 'l sogno la passione impressa
> rimane, e l'altro a la mente non riede,
>   cotal son io, ché quasi tutta cessa
> mia visïone, e ancor mi distilla
> nel core il dolce che nacque da essa.

(*Paradiso* 33.55–63)[137]

as well as, in respect now of the joy of coming home at last on the plane of properly human being, these from *Paradiso* 22:

> 'Tu se' sì presso a l'ultima salute',
> cominciò Beatrice, 'che tu dei

---

craving!' Stephen Bemrose, '*Gaudium et pax*: What Being in Heaven Means for Dante', *FMLS* 41.1 (2005), 71–89; Vittorio Bartoli, 'Su godere e gustare nel *Paradiso* dantesco', *Divinitas: Rivista internazionale di ricerca e di critica teologica* 51 (2008), 329–36; Marc Föcking, ' "Qui habitat in caelis irridebit eos": Paradiesisches und irdisches Lachen in Dantes *Divina Commedia*', in *Paradies: Topografien der Sehnsucht*, ed. Claudia Benthien et al. (Cologne: Böhlau, 2010), 77–96; Tamara Pollack, 'Light, Love and Joy in Dante's Doctrine of Beatitude', in *Reviewing Dante's Theology*, vol. 1, ed. Claire Honess and Matthew Treherne (Bern: Peter Lang, 2013), 263–319.

136 'I began: "You are my father, you give me all boldness to speak, you uplift me so that I am more than myself; by so many streams my mind is filled with happiness that it rejoices in itself withstanding even so the surge thereof." '

137 'From that moment my vision was greater than our speech, which fails at such a sight, and memory too fails at such excess. Like him that sees in a dream and after the dream the passion wrought by it remains and the rest returns not to his mind, such am I; for my vision almost wholly fades and still there drops within my heart the sweetness that was born of it.'

aver le luci tue chiare e acute;
   e però, prima che tu più t'inlei,
rimira in giù, e vedi quanto mondo
sotto li piedi già esser ti fei;
   sì che 'l tuo cor, quantunque può, giocondo
s'appresenti a la turba trïunfante
che lieta vien per questo etera tondo'.

(*Paradiso* 22.124–32)[138]

In each of these cases, joy is the joy of ultimate affirmation, the joy always and everywhere contingent on the soul's acting out the contents of understanding and of its affirming itself in the fullness of its proper presence in the world as a free existent. Joy, then, is the mood of properly human being, not now in its stillness (for the mood of properly human being in its stillness is peace), but in its coming forth from the stillness. It is, in short, the *ecstatic* mood of being in its authenticity.

DANTE AND SIGNIFICANT JOURNEYING

But if indeed the miracle of the *Commedia* lies—wherever else it lies—in its proposal of an existential analysis of unprecedented power and persuasiveness, then not least among its many parts is its exemplary aspect, its account by way of the one who in the poem says 'I' of what it means to be a pilgrim spirit, a 'homo viator'. Given, in other words, the notion (*a*) of the individual as sensitive from beforehand to the *what might be* of his or her presence in the world as a creature of moral and ontological accountability, and (*b*) of his or her awareness even so of wandering as yet in a region of unlikeness, then what exactly does it mean for him or her to be on the way, to embark here and now on the journey of properly human being and becoming?

To speak with Dante of spiritual journeying as the proper destiny of man under the conditions of time and space means three things: first, a descent into self there to behold the will everywhere at work in human nature less to being than to nonbeing, this, therefore, constituting the infernal phase of man's proper itinerary as man, the moment of *self-confrontation*; next, and as presupposing now a coales-

---

138 '"You are so near to the final blessedness", Beatrice began, "that you must have your eyes clear and keen; and therefore, before you go further into it, look down and see how much of the universe I have already put beneath your feet, so that with all fullness of joy your heart may present itself to the triumphal host that comes rejoicing through this rounded ether." '

cence of human and divine willing in the depths, the struggle to affirm self over
self on the plane of loving, this, therefore, constituting the purgatorial phase of
man's proper itinerary as man, the moment of *self-reconfiguration*; and finally, the
opening out of self upon the fullness of its proper humanity, this, therefore, constituting the paradisal phase of man's proper itinerary as man, the moment of
self-transcendence. Again, then, the miracle is complete, a massive act of moral and
ontological disclosure containing within itself, and indeed taking the form of, a
pilgrim's progress attuned as of the essence to the being and becoming of reader
and writer alike as party to one and the same undertaking.[139]

Hell, on the face of it, is indeed a matter of comeuppance, any number of
passages in the text bearing witness both to the anger and to the artistry—to the
divine anger and artistry—of it all; so, for example, on the first of these things, on
the depth and intensity of divine anger, we have these lines from canto 3 relative
to those who, dying in the wrath of God, hasten now—paradoxically—to embrace their lot:

'Figliuol mio', disse 'l maestro cortese,
'quelli che muoion ne l'ira di Dio
tutti convegnon qui d'ogne paese;
    e pronti sono a trapassar lo rio,
ché la divina giustizia li sprona,
sì che la tema si volve in disio.
    Quinci non passa mai anima buona;
e però, se Caron di te si lagna,
ben puoi sapere omai che 'l suo dir suona'.

(*Inferno* 3.121–29)[140]

139 Lawrence Baldassaro, 'Dante the Pilgrim: Everyman as Sinner', *DS* 92 (1974), 63–74; James T.
Chiampi, 'Dante's Pilgrim and Reader in the "Region of Want"', *SIR* 3.2 (1983), 163–82; Fernando
Salsano, 'Dante-pellegrino: *Inferno*' and 'Dante-pellegrino: *Purgatorio*', in *Personaggi della 'Divina Com-
media'* (Cassino: Sangermano, 1984), 13–44 and 147–70; Bruno Basile, 'Il viaggio come archetipo: Note
sul tema della "peregrinatio" in Dante', *LC* 15 (1986), 9–26; John Freccero, 'Pilgrim in a Gyre', in *Dante:
The Poetics of Conversion* (Cambridge, MA: Harvard University Press, 1986), 70–92 (and in *Dante: The
Critical Complex*, vol. 3, ed. Richard Lansing [New York: Routledge, 2003], 250–63); James Finn Cotter,
'Dante and Christ: The Pilgrim as "Beatus Vir"', *IQ* 107 (1987), 5–19; Peter Armour, 'Dante's *Purgatory*:
The Pilgrim's Progress', in *One Man's Canon: Five Essays on Medieval Poetry for Stephen Reckert*, ed. Alan
Deyermond (London: Department of Hispanic Studies, Queen Mary and Westfield College, 1998),
11–23; Antonio C. Mastrobuono, 'Poeta e pellegrino nella *Divina Commedia*', in *Letteratura e impegno:
Il pensiero critico di Rocco Montano*, ed. Francesco Bruni and Paolo Cherchi (Florence: Olschki, 2003),
37–43.
140 '"Those, my son", said my gracious master, "dying in the wrath of God foregather here from
every clime, and, for that divine justice so spurs them on that fear turns to desire, they are eager to cross
the river. By this way no good spirit ever passes, and if therefore Charon raises his voice against you,
then well you may understand the burden of what he says."'

to which for good measure we might add these from canto 11 on the precise loca-tion in hell of those who by way of their intemperance have likewise incurred his displeasure:

> Ma dimmi: quei de la palude pingue,
> che mena il vento, e che batte la pioggia,
> e che s'incontran con sì aspre lingue,
>   perché non dentro da la città roggia
> sono ei puniti, se Dio li ha in ira?
> e se non li ha, perché sono a tal foggia?

> (*Inferno* 11.70–75)[141]

while on the second of them, on the sheer artistry of it all, we have these lines from canto 14 on the inexhaustibility of God's imagination hereabouts:

> Indi venimmo al fine ove si parte
> lo secondo giron dal terzo, e dove
> si vede di giustizia orribil arte.

> (*Inferno* 14.4–6)[142]

This, then, whatever else it is, is retributive justice on a grand scale, justice as ample and intense as it is varied in its administration. But—and this now is what matters—even for those beyond the bar, and a fortiori for those still *in via*, hell is something both more and other than pain inflicted *ab extra* and brought only subsequently to bear; for over and beyond the specifically divine anger and art-istry of it all, and indeed preceding and accounting for that anger and artistry, it is a question here of the soul's entering into the recesses of its own existence there to live out the already abiding agony of it all, the agony of an existence long since

---

141 'But tell me, those of the slimy marsh, those driven by the tempest, those battered by the rain and those upon meeting so ferocious in expression, why, if God's wrath be upon them, are they not punished within the fiery city? And, if it be not, why are they put to such suffering?'

142 'Thus we came to the boundary of the second and the beginning of the third circle, there to behold the terrifying handiwork of justice.' Anthony K. Cassell, *Dante's Fearful Art of Justice* (Toronto: University of Toronto Press, 1984); James Dauphiné, '*Divine Comédie*: Divine Justice', in *La Justice au moyen âge: Sanction ou impunité* (Aix-en-Provence: Publications du CUERMA [Centre Universitaire d'Études et de Recherches Médiévales], 1986), 139–45; Marc Cogan, 'Delight, Punishment and the Justice of God in the *Divina Commedia*', DS 111 (1993), 27–52 (and in *Dante: The Critical Complex*, vol. 3, ed. Richard Lansing [New York: Routledge, 2003], 117–42); Gherardo Colombo, 'Il diritto: ". . . di Giustizia orribil arte" (*Inferno* 14.6) ovvero dalla retribuzione alla reconciliazione', in *Nostro Dante quotidiano* (Brescia: L'obliquo, 2008), 99–110; Francesco Tateo, ' "La divina giustizia": Divagazioni su un percorso della *Commedia*', *L'Alighieri* (RD) 32 (2008), 17–26.

divided on the plane of willing—a situation decisive for the interpretation of some of the very greatest episodes in the *Inferno*. Take again, then, the case of Francesca, a textbook case of the soul as tortured, not, in truth, from beyond but from within, from out of the recesses of a now impossible instance of specifically human being. Nicely, then—for here as elsewhere it is a question of the agony of it all subsisting just for the moment beneath the surface of things—the episode begins more than ever graciously, the more than ever gracious but in truth more than ever biddable Francesca going out of her way to accommodate the pilgrim poet in his desire to know more of her:

> I' cominciai: 'Poeta, volontieri
> parlerei a quei due che 'nsieme vanno,
> e paion sì al vento esser leggeri'.
>   Ed elli a me: 'Vedrai quando saranno
> più presso a noi; e tu allor li priega
> per quello amor che i mena, ed ei verranno'.
>   Sì tosto come il vento a noi li piega,
> mossi la voce: 'O anime affannate,
> venite a noi parlar, s'altri nol niega!'
>   Quali colombe dal disio chiamate
> con l'ali alzate e ferme al dolce nido
> vegnon per l'aere, dal voler portate;
>   cotali uscir de la schiera ov' è Dido,
> a noi venendo per l'aere maligno,
> sì forte fu l'affettüoso grido.
>   'O animal grazïoso e benigno
> che visitando vai per l'aere perso
> noi che tignemmo il mondo di sanguigno,
>   se fosse amico il re de l'universo,
> noi pregheremmo lui de la tua pace,
> poi c'hai pietà del nostro mal perverso.
>   Di quel che udire e che parlar vi piace,
> noi udiremo e parleremo a voi,
> mentre che 'l vento, come fa, ci tace'.

(*Inferno* 5.73–96)[143]

---

143 ' "Poet, willingly would I speak with those two who, bound one with another, come and go so lightly, it seems, upon the wind." And he to me: "Note well when they approach us, and do you then pray them in the name of that love by which they are led, and they will come." So soon as the wind swayed them toward us, I lifted my voice: "O weary spirits, come and, provided only no other deny it, speak with us." As doves, called by desire, with wings open and steady, come through the air borne by

Already, therefore, before ever we get to the nub of the issue, we are treated to a masterpiece of psychoanalytical precision, every detail of the passage from its borne-on-the-wings-of-the-wind imagery down to the insistent passivity of its syntax (the 'dal disio chiamate' of line 82, the 'dal voler portate' of line 84, and the 'Queste parole da lor ci fuor porte' of line 108) tending straightaway to confirm a distinctive state of mind, a readiness again gracious beyond words but containing somewhere deep within it the seeds of catastrophe. But with this we are still in the foothills of the episode, more—much more—waiting to come by way of that same psychoanalytical precision; for what comes next is the redistribution-of-guilt moment of the argument, the at all costs need of the unrepentant spirit to look the other way, to quieten in the name and for the sake of self-consistency the still small voice of conscience:

> 'Siede la terra dove nata fui
> su la marina dove 'l Po discende
> per aver pace co' seguaci sui.
>   Amor, ch'al cor gentil ratto s'apprende,
> prese costui de la bella persona
> che mi fu tolta; e 'l modo ancor m'offende.
>   Amor, ch'a nullo amato amar perdona,
> mi prese del costui piacer sì forte,
> che, come vedi, ancor non m'abbandona.
>   Amor condusse noi ad una morte.
> Caina attende chi a vita ci spense'.
> Queste parole da lor ci fuor porte.

(*Inferno* 5.97–108)[144]

---

their will to their sweet nest, these issued from the troop wherein dwells Dido, coming to us—so strong was my love-cry—through the malign air. "O creature gracious and benign who, cleaving the dark air, visit us who stained blood-red the world, were the king of the universe a friend we would pray for peace upon you, pitying as you do our perverse ill. Of whatsoever it be your pleasure to hear or to speak of, we will indeed, while the wind, as now, is hushed for us, both hear and speak of with you."' Paola Marconi, '"Per quello amor che i mena": *Inferno* V, 78 e il *Roman de Tristan* di Béroul', *L'Alighieri (RD)* 20 (2002), 77–93; Sergio Givone, '". . . li priega / per quello amor che i mena": Eros e colpa nel canto V dell'*Inferno*', *LC* 32–34 (2005), 39–49. For the 'colombe' motif, Lawrence V. Ryan, 'Stornei, gru, colombe: The Bird Images in *Inferno* V', *DS* 94 (1976), 25–45; Mariangela Semola, 'Le colombe e i lussuriosi: Una proposta di intertestualità dantesca', *LL* 35 (2010), 213–27; Giuseppe Ledda, '"Quali colombe dal disio chiamate": A Bestiary of Desire in Dante's *Commedia*', in *Desire in Dante and the Middle Ages*, ed. Manuele Gragnolati et al. (London: Maney, 2012), 58–70. For the 'sanguigno' motif, Christophe Libaude, '"Sanguigno": Lecture du chant de Francesca', in *Dante la pierre et le sang* (Paris: Kimé, 2014), 155–63, and for the 'mal perverso' motif, Kurt Ringger, 'Il dantesco "mal perverso" (*Inferno* V. 93)', *SC* 46.3 (1981), 435–41 (and in *Vom Mittelalter zur Moderne: Beiträge zur französischen und italienischen Literatur*, ed. Erich Loos [Tübingen: G. Narr Verlag, 1991], 126–30).

144 '"The place of my birth lies upon that shore where the Po comes down at last to enjoy peace

But it is at this point—at the point of Francesca's confirming her status as one
more sinned against than sinning—that Dante the author and architect of his
poem has Dante the pilgrim poet and protagonist ask the key question, the devastating 'Ma dimmi', at which point, with every mechanism of self-preservation
straightaway called into question, Francesca has nowhere to look other than into
the depths of her own existence, there to ponder yet again the completeness of
her self-betrayal and now, alas, the unnegotiable sadness of it all. First, then,
comes the question, the 'but tell me, Francesca' of line 118 as on the face of it quite
as courteous as anything upon the lips of Francesca herself but again devastating
in its at-a-stroke liquidation of every strategy of self-preservation, every disavowal
of responsibility:

> Poi mi rivolsi a loro e parla' io,
> e cominciai: 'Francesca, i tuoi martìri
> a lagrimar mi fanno tristo e pio.
> Ma dimmi: al tempo d'i dolci sospiri,
> a che e come concedette amore
> che conosceste i dubbiosi disiri?'

$$(Inferno\ 5.115-20)^{145}$$

and then comes the reply, generous as ever in its unfolding but, shorn now as it
is of every strategy of the spirit, of every sidestepping of guilt as but the abiding
substance of her existence, transparent to the inner and endless grief thereof, to
the now interminable agony of being under the aspect of dividedness:

> E quella a me: 'Nessun maggior dolore
> che ricordarsi del tempo felice
> ne la miseria; e ciò sa 'l tuo dottore.
> Ma s'a conoscer la prima radice
> del nostro amor tu hai cotanto affetto,

---

with its tributaries. Love, which quickly lays hold of the noble heart, seized this one by way of the fair
form that was taken from me, the manner thereof hurting me still. Love, which absolves no one loved
from loving, seized me by way of the charm properly his, and this so strongly that, as you see, it does
not even now abandon me. Love brought us to one death, Cain awaiting him who quenched our life."
These words were borne to us from them.' Saverio Fineo, 'Amor, che a cor gentil ratto s'apprende', in
Studi danteschi (Rome: Manzella, 1973), 120–35; Pier Angelo Perotti, 'Caina attende', *L'Alighieri (RBD)*
34.1–2 (1993), 129–34.
  145 'Then, turning to them once more to speak, I began: "Francesca, your suffering fills me with
sadness and compassion to the point of weeping. But tell me how, in the moment of your sweet sighing,
and by what means did love grant you understanding of these, your as yet uncertain desires?"' Lucia
Battaglia Ricci, 'I "dubbiosi disiri" di Francesca', *NRLI* 13.1–2 (2010), 151–64.

dirò come colui che piange e dice.
Noi leggiavamo un giorno per diletto
di Lancialotto come amor lo strinse;
soli eravamo e sanza alcun sospetto.
Per più fïate li occhi ci sospinse
quella lettura, e scolorocci il viso;
ma solo un punto fu quel che ci vinse.
Quando leggemmo il disïato riso
esser basciato da cotanto amante,
questi, che mai da me non fia diviso,
  la bocca mi basciò tutto tremante.
Galeotto fu 'l libro e chi lo scrisse;
quel giorno più non vi leggemmo avante'.
Mentre che l'uno spirto questo disse,
l'altro piangëa; sì che di pietade
io venni men così com' io morisse.
E caddi come corpo morto cade.

(*Inferno* 5.121–42)[146]

146 'And she to me: "There is as your teacher knows full well no greater sorrow than that of re-calling in circumstances of wretchedness good times past. But in that you have so great a desire to know of our love's first coming about, I shall speak of it as one who weeps in the very telling of it. One day, for pleasure pure and simple, we read of Lancelot and how he was constrained by love. We were alone and without misgiving. Often and enough as we read our eyes met and our faces blanched, but one moment alone was it that overcame us. Reading as we did how the longed-for smile was kissed by so great a lover, he who shall never be parted from me kissed my lips all atrembling. A Galeotto was the book and he who wrote it, and that day we read no farther in it." While thus one spirit spoke, the other wept such that for pity I myself, as if in death, swooned and fell as a dead body falls.' For the intertextual aspect of the passage, Daniela Delcorno Branca, 'Dante and the *Roman de Lancelot*', in *Text and Intertext in Medieval Arthurian Literature*, ed. Norris J. Lacy (New York: Garland, 1996), 133–45; Thomas Klinkert, 'Zum Status von Intertextualität im Mittelalter: Tristan, Lancelot, Francesca da Rimini', *DDJ* 81 (2006), 27–69; Leonardo Cecchini, ' "Galeotto fu il libro e chi lo scrisse": Some Remarks about Intertextuality in *Inferno* V', in *Dante: A Critical Reappraisal*, ed. Unn Falkeid (Oslo: Unipub [Oslo Academic Press]), 2008, 111–20; Valeria Bertolucci Pizzorusso, 'Strategie dantesche: Francesca e il *Roman de Lancelot*', *NRLI* 13.1–2 (2010), 135–50; Carlos López Cortezo, ' "Le Roman" de Francesca', *Tenzone* 12 (2011), 83–103; Michelangelo Picone, 'Dante e la tradizione arturiana', in *Scritti danteschi*, ed. Antonio Lanza (Ravenna: Longo, 2017 [1982]), 357–70. For the 'power of the book' and the psychology of reading aspect of the argument, Albert Classen (ed.), *The Book and the Magic of Reading in the Middle Ages* (New York: Garland, 1998), 61–97; Michele Dell'Aquila, ' "Versi d'amore e prose di romanzi": La reponsabilità della letteratura', *Italianistica* 32.2 (2003), 193–204; Katharina Műnchberg, 'Die Potentialität der Dichtung', in *Dante: Die Möglichkeit der Kunst* (Heidelberg: Winter, 2005), 169–226; Cristoph Irmscher, 'Reading for Our Delight', *DS* 128 (2010), 44–64; Elena Lombardi, 'Reading', in *The Wings of the Dove: Love and Desire in Dante and Medieval Culture* (Montreal: McGill-Queen's University Press, 2012), 212–47. For the kiss, Martino Marazzi, 'La bocca mi baciò tutto tremante', *Belfagor* 63.5 (2008), 590–96; Elena Lombardi, 'The Kiss', in *The Wings of the Dove*, 175–211. For the final line, the moment of swooning, Carmelo Ciccia, 'Lo svenimento di Dante

Hardly, then, are we into the pit before the notion of hell as a matter of simple retribution or comeuppance has been overtaken by something still more terrifying—by a sense of hell as a matter of ultimate self-presencing, of standing in the unclouded truth of self as a creature of free moral determination. And what applies in the case of Francesca by way of affliction as a matter of *self*-affliction, of living on in the agony of her own leading choice, applies also in that of Pier delle Vigne in the dark wood of the suicides, where, every strategy of self-preservation having evaporated after the manner of the morning mist, it is again a question of the protagonist's settling at last upon the stark truth of his existence, on the contradiction now crystallized at its centre. First, then, and in a passage once again exemplary in its trusting to the image as the means of elucidation, comes Dante's preliminary account of the psychology of despair, of, more precisely, the fear generated by a sense of the world as present to self by way only of its hostility:

> Non era ancor di là Nesso arrivato,
> quando noi ci mettemmo per un bosco
> che da neun sentiero era segnato.
> Non fronda verde, ma di color fosco;
> non rami schietti, ma nodosi e 'nvolti;
> non pomi v'eran, ma stecchi con tòsco.

> (*Inferno* 13.1–6)[147]

—a fear that, as Virgil bids his charge break off a twig for the purpose of verifying the strangest of strange metamorphoses, duly calls forth from the captive spirit a flood of imprecation:

davanti a Paolo e Francesca (*Inferno* V)', in *Allegorie e simboli nel 'Purgatorio' e altri studi su Dante* (Cosenza: Pellegrini, 2002), 97–101.

147 'Nessus had not yet reached the far side when we entered a wood unmarked by any path. No green leaves here, but all alike darkling; no smooth boughs but gnarled and twisted; no fruit but poisoned prickles.' John C. Barnes, '*Inferno* XIII', in *Dante Soundings: Eight Literary and Historical Essays*, ed. David Nolan (Dublin: Irish Academic Press, 1981), 28–58; Patrick Boyde, '*Inferno* XIII', in *Cambridge Readings in Dante's 'Comedy'*, ed. Kenelm Foster and Patrick Boyde (Cambridge: Cambridge University Press, 1981), 1–21; Gabriele Muresu, 'La selva dei disperati (*Inferno* XIII)', *RLIt* 99.1–2 (1995), 5–45 (and in *Il richiamo dell'antica strega* [Rome: Bulzoni, 1997], 11–71); Pier Vincenzo Mengaldo, 'Dante Alighieri: Pier della Vigna (*Inferno* XIII.1–78)', in *Attraverso la poesia italiana: Analisi di testi esemplari* (Rome: Carocci, 2008), 35–43; Sonia Gentili, 'La selva, gli alberi e il suicidio nell'*Inferno* di Dante: Fonti e interpretazione', in *Letteratura e filologia tra Svizzera e Italia: Studi in onore di Guglielmo Gorni*, vol. 1, ed. Maria Antonietta Terzoli, Alberto Asor Rosa and Giorgio Inglese (Rome: Edizioni di Storia e Letteratura, 2010), 149–63; Giorgio Bàrberi Squarotti, 'XIII: "Uomini fummo, e or siam fatti sterpi"', in *Tutto l'"Inferno": Lettura integrale della prima cantica del poema dantesco* (Milan: Franco Angeli, 2011), 93–99.

Allor porsi la mano un poco avante
e colsi un ramicel da un gran pruno;
e 'l tronco suo gridò: 'Perché mi schiante?'
     Da che fatto fu poi di sangue bruno,
ricominciò a dir: 'Perché mi scerpi?
non hai tu spirto di pietade alcuno?
     Uomini fummo, e or siam fatti sterpi:
ben dovrebb' esser la tua man più pia,
se state fossimo anime di serpi'.

(*Inferno* 13.31–39)[148]

The psychology, then, is familiar, as familiar as it is deeply woven into the fabric of the *Inferno* as but an account of being under the aspect of estrangement, for in circumstances of estrangement—of the soul's living on at a distance from its own intimate reasons—the next man, inasmuch as he is present to self at all, is present to him under the aspect only of menace, as a breaker-off of branches. And, as no less deeply woven into the fabric of the text, the guilt of it all at once issues in a further bout of self-exoneration, a strategy, however, serving as strategy always does in the *Inferno* merely to concentrate the mind, to focus the spirit more than ever completely upon the depth of its self-betrayal and upon the guilt thereof:

La meretrice che mai da l'ospizio
di Cesare non torse li occhi putti,
morte comune e de le corti vizio,
     infiammò contra me li animi tutti;
e li 'nfiammati infiammar sì Augusto,
che ' lieti onor tornaro in tristi lutti.
     L'animo mio, per disdegnoso gusto,
credendo col morir fuggir disdegno,
ingiusto fece me contra me giusto.

(*Inferno* 13.64–72)[149]

148 'Reaching out a little, then, and plucking from a large thornbush but a small twig, the trunk thereof cried out: "Why thus do you tear me?", straightaway taking up again, stained dark now with its own blood, "Why thus do you mangle me? Have you no hint of compassion. Turned now to stocks, we were ourselves once men. Were we but the souls of serpents your hand might well have been more kindly."' Andrea Celli, ' "Perché mi scerpi?": Il canto di Pier delle Vigne tra Hegel e De Sanctis', *LI* 62.2 (2010), 257–75.
149 'The harlot that never turned her whorish eyes from Caesar's household—everywhere the death and undoing of courts—inflamed everyone's minds against me, and they, thus inflamed, did so inflame Augustus that the honour in which I delighted gave way to the bitterest of griefs. My mind,

With this, then—this settling just for a moment on the drastic truth of self in all the no less drastic finality and unnegotiability thereof—the forlorn spirit embarks on a fresh round of self-exoneration as uniquely adequate to its ever standing in its own presence, Pier delle Vigne straightaway swearing to it that 'by the roots of this bush never did I break faith with my lord'.[150] But by this time self-exoneration thus understood is to no avail, for by this time the encounter—the encounter with self in the recesses of self and all this implies by way of the impossibility of it all—is as complete as it is completely devastating, there being, in truth, no survival at this level. On the contrary, all that can be done is yet again to busy oneself at the point of special pleading, herein lying the sole means of coping with self in the destitution of self.

And then, as a further and for the moment final example in the *Inferno* of hell as a matter less of affliction than of self-affliction, of guilt as forever mocking from out of the depths every high-level strategy of the spirit designed as far as may be to mitigate it, there is the case of Guido da Montefeltro in canto 27. Here too the drama is intense, for it is clear from the outset that in Guido da Montefeltro we have a covert creature, a man who functions from out of the shadows and to whom reason is present as but a matter of calculation, of weighing up the odds. His, then, by his own admission, was a foxy as distinct from a leonine humanity (the 'opere mie / non furon leonine, ma di volpe' of lines 74 and 75), and indeed still is, for there can, he says, be no question of his speaking with the pilgrim poet until such time as he has done the sums, weighed up the possibility, that is to say, of any of this ever getting out:

> 'S'i' credesse che mia risposta fosse
> a persona che mai tornasse al mondo,
> questa fiamma staria sanza più scosse;
> ma però che già mai di questo fondo
> non tornò vivo alcun, s'i' odo il vero,
> sanza tema d'infamia ti rispondo'.

(*Inferno* 27.61–66)[151]

scornfully disposed and thinking by death to escape scorn, made me unjust to my just self.' Steno Vazzana, 'Il "disdegnoso gusto" di Pier de le Vigne', *L'Alighieri (RD)* 11 (1998), 91–94. For the rhetorical component of the passage, Leo Spitzer, 'Speech and Language in *Inferno* XIII', *Italica* 19.3 (1942), 81–104; Ettore Paratore, 'Analisi "retorica" del canto di Pier della Vigna', *SD* 42 (1965), 281–338; David Sheehan, 'The Control of Feeling: A Rhetorical Analysis of *Inferno* XIII', *Italica* 51.2 (1974), 193–206.

150 *Inferno* 13.73–75: 'Per le nove radici d'esto legno / vi giuro che già mai non ruppi fede / al mio segnor, che fu d'onor sì degno' (By the new roots of this tree I swear to you, never did I break faith with my lord, who was so worthy of honour).

151 'If I thought my reply was to one who would ever return to the world, this flame would tremble no more. But since—to judge by what I've heard—no one from these depths ever came out alive, I

With this, then, the confession proper gets under way, the confession, insofar as that is what it is, beginning once again with the ritual indictment of the next man as the cause of every personal misfortune. Here too, however, ritualism is gradually overtaken by recognition as willy-nilly—for neither here is there any real room for manoeuvre—the soul settles upon the truth of its own existence, the truth lurking Leviathan-like in the depths and rising up despite every essay in suppression to tax the spirit with the contradiction at the heart of its being. As dramatic as it is devastating and as theatrical as it is terrifying, the episode deserves reading in its totality:

> Quando mi vidi giunto in quella parte
> di mia etade ove ciascun dovrebbe
> calar le vele e raccoglier le sarte,
>   ciò che pria mi piacëa, allor m'increbbe,
> e pentuto e confesso mi rendei;
> ahi miser lasso! e giovato sarebbe.
>   Lo principe d'i novi Farisei,
> avendo guerra presso a Laterano,
> e non con Saracin né con Giudei,
>   ché ciascun suo nimico era cristiano,
> e nessun era stato a vincer Acri
> né mercatante in terra di Soldano,
>   né sommo officio né ordini sacri
> guardò in sé, né in me quel capestro
> che solea fare i suoi cinti più macri.
>   Ma come Costantin chiese Silvestro
> d'entro Siratti a guerir de la lebbre,
> così mi chiese questi per maestro
>   a guerir de la sua superba febbre;
> domandommi consiglio, e io tacetti
> perché le sue parole parver ebbre.

answer without fear of infamy.' Antonietta Bufano, 'I peccati del nobilissimo Guido Montefeltrano', CL 49.4 (1985), 627–43; Agnello Baldi, 'Un francescano all'Inferno (Guido da Montefeltro)', in Dante e il francescanesimo (Cava dei Tirreni: Avagliano, 1987), 125–48; Giorgio Bàrberi Squarotti, 'La voce di Guido da Montefeltro', FItal 21.2 (1987), 165–96; Gabriele Muresu, 'La "rancura" di Guido da Montefeltro (Inferno XXVII)', SD 70 (2005), 47–86; Alfonso D'Agostino, 'I consiglieri frodolenti', in Leggere e rileggere la 'Commedia' dantesca, ed. Barbara Peroni (Milan: Unicopli, 2009), 255–73; Francesco Spera, 'Il malo ingegno di Guido da Montefeltro' (Florence: Cesati, 2010), 193–207; Mirko Tavoni, 'Guido da Montefeltro dal Convivio all'Inferno', NRLI 13.1–2 (2010), 165–96. More generally, Gabriella I. Baika, ' "Lingua dolosa", "the guileful tongue": Speaking Under the Sign of Fraud', in The Rose and Geryon: The Poetics of Fraud and Violence in Jean de Meun and Dante (Washington, DC: Catholic University of America Press, 2014), 110–204.

E' poi ridisse: 'Tuo cuor non sospetti;
finor t'assolvo, e tu m'insegna fare
sì come Penestrino in terra getti.

Lo ciel poss' io serrare e diserrare,
come tu sai; però son due le chiavi
che 'l mio antecessor non ebbe care'.

Allor mi pinser li argomenti gravi
là 've 'l tacer mi fu avviso 'l peggio,
e dissi: 'Padre, da che tu mi lavi

di quel peccato ov' io mo cader deggio,
lunga promessa con l'attender corto
ti farà trïunfar ne l'alto seggio'.

Francesco venne poi, com' io fu' morto,
per me; ma un d'i neri cherubini
li disse: 'Non portar: non mi far torto.

Venir se ne dee giù tra ' miei meschini
perché diede 'l consiglio frodolente,
dal quale in qua stato li sono a' crini;

ch'assolver non si può chi non si pente,
né pentere e volere insieme puossi
per la contradizion che nol consente'.

Oh me dolente! come mi riscossi
quando mi prese dicendomi: 'Forse
tu non pensavi ch'io löico fossi!'

(*Inferno* 27.79–123)[152]

152 'When, as I opined, I had reached that stage of life when men should consider lowering their sails and hauling in the ropes, then that which, hitherto, had pleased me then grieved me, and, sorrowing and confessing, I turned friar, and—woe is me!—it would have paid off. The prince of the new pharisees being at war hard by the Lateran (and not with Saracens or Jews, for every one of his enemies was Christian, with none of them at the taking of Acre or trading in the land of the Sultan), had regard neither for the supreme office and holy orders properly his own nor for that cord of mine apt erstwhile to make lean those wearing it; but, as Constantine sought out Sylvester in Soracte to cure his leprosy, so this man sought me out as a physician to cure the fever of his pride. He asked counsel of me, and, for that his words seemed drunken, I fell silent, whereupon he spoke again: "Have no fear in your heart, for but teach me how to bring Palestrina to the ground and I absolve you henceforth; for by way of the two keys cherished not by my predecessor it lies with me, as well you know, both to lock and to unlock heaven." Thus was I urged on by his weighty words to the point where silence seemed the greater offence, whereupon I said: "Since, Father, you cleanse me from the sin into which I must now fall, the promise you make—ample but scant in its observance—will to be sure cause you to triumph upon your lofty throne." No sooner, then, was I dead than Francis came for me, one of the dark cherubim, however, saying to him: "Bear him not away, neither do me out of him, for having given fraudulent counsel (from which moment I have had him by his locks), he must come down among my minions; for short of repentance there can be no absolution, and neither, for the contradiction that rules it out,

This, then, is what it means to speak of the infernal phase of properly human journeying as a matter of *self-confrontation*. What it means to speak of the infernal phase of properly human journeying as a matter of self-confrontation is to speak of how it is that, before ever embarking on the upward way, and indeed as a necessary condition of that embarking, the individual is called upon to enter into the deepest places of self there to dwell for a season in the antechamber of self-recognition and of self-sorrowing. Short of this—of this entering into the depths of self there to behold the truth of self—the adult in man is forever in thrall to the adolescent, to the as yet immature in the flame of love.

Whatever else it is, purgatory, both in its classic formulation and in Dante's sense of it, is a matter of satisfaction—of 'satisfaction' in the sense of making good the debts incurred by sin as repented and absolved but as yet less than fully redeemed or paid off. The notion needs careful statement, for as the old theologians were fully aware there can be no coming home of self to self other than by way (*a*) of the cross as that whereby the burden of sin is lifted, and (*b*) of contrition as that whereby the stain of sin is washed away. But that notwithstanding there needs to be some kind of restitution, a final and formal squaring of the account; so, for example, Thomas —or, more exactly, Thomas's continuator—to precisely this effect in the *Summa theologiae*:

> Respondeo dicendum quod ex illis quae supra determinata sunt, satis potest constare purgatorium esse post hanc vitam. Si enim, per contritionem deleta culpa, non tollitur ex reatus poenae, nec etiam se, per venialis, dimissis mortalibus tolluntur, et iustitia Dei hoc exigit et peccatum per poenam debitam ordinetur, oportet quod illi qui post contritionem de peccato decedit et absolutionem, ante satisfactionem debitam quod post hanc vitam puniatur. Et ideo illi qui purgatorium negant, contra divinam iustitiam loquuntur. Et propter hoc erroneum est, et a fide alienum. Unde Gregorius Nyssenus post praedicta verba subiungit: *Hoc praedicamus dogma veritatis servantes et ita credimus.* Hoc enim universalis Ecclesia tenet, *pro defunctis exorans ut a peccatis solvantur*; quod non potest nisi de illis qui sunt

---

can there be repentance and willing in one and the same instant." Oh woe, woe was I, and how I shuddered when, laying hold of me, he said: "Perhaps you reckoned not on my too being a logician!"' Leto Morvidi, 'Guido da Montefeltro e Bonifazio VIII (canto XXVII)', in *Figure infernali dantesche*, 2nd ed. (Viterbo: Eurograph, 1977), 343–55; Italo Borzi, 'Guido e Bonifacio (*Inferno* XXVII)', in *Verso l'ultima salute: Saggi danteschi* (Milan: Rusconi, 1985), 99–137; Massimo Seriacopi, '*Inferno* XXVII: Guido da Montefeltro e Bonifacio VIII; La limitazione dell'intelletto e il sovvertimento delle regole', *SD* 76 (2011), 1–25 (and in *L'Ulisse di Dante Alighieri e altri studi sulla 'Commedia'* [Rome: Aracne, 2016], 77–103); Selene Sarteschi, 'Canto di Guido da Montefeltro o di Bonifacio VIII? Lettura di *Inferno* XXVII', *L'Alighieri (RD)* 39 (2012), 91–108. For the 'dark angel' and 'consummate logician' moment of Guido's discourse, Gennaro Sasso, 'Guido e Buonconte da Montefeltro, il nero cherubino e il principio di non contraddizione', *Cultura* 48.2 (2010), 167–219.

in purgatorio intelligi. Ecclesiae autem auctoritati quicumque resistit haeresim incurrit.

(*Summa theologiae* 3a, app. 1 [*Quaestio de Purgatorio*], art. 1, resp.)[153]

And this too is Dante's understanding of it, passages such as the following from cantos 10 and 11 of the *Purgatorio* turning precisely upon the terminology of payment, of settling and signing off the account:

> Non vo' però, lettor, che tu ti smaghi
> di buon proponimento per udire
> come Dio vuol che 'l debito si paghi.
>
> . . .
>
> 'Io sono Omberto; e non pur a me danno
> superbia fa, ché tutti miei consorti
> ha ella tratti seco nel malanno.
> E qui convien ch'io questo peso porti
> per lei, tanto che a Dio si sodisfaccia,
> poi ch'io nol fe' tra ' vivi, qui tra ' morti'.
>
> . . .
>
> 'Quelli è', rispuose, 'Provenzan Salvani;
> ed è qui perché fu presuntüoso
> a recar Siena tutta a le sue mani.

153 'I answer thus, that from the conclusions we have drawn above it is sufficiently clear that there is a Purgatory after this life. For if the debt of punishment is not paid in full after the stain of sin has been washed away by contrition, nor again are venial sins always removed when mortal sins are remitted, and if justice demands that sin be set in order by due punishment, it follows that one who after contrition for his fault and after being absolved, dies before making due satisfaction, is punished after this life. Wherefore those who deny Purgatory speak against the justice of God, for which reason such a statement is erroneous and contrary to faith. Hence Gregory of Nyssa, after the words quoted above, adds: "This we preach, holding to the teaching of truth, and this is our belief; this the universal Church holds, by praying for the dead that they may be loosed from sins." This cannot be understood except as referring to Purgatory, and whosoever resists the authority of the Church incurs the note of heresy.' Robert Ombres, O.P., *Theology of Purgatory* (Dublin: Mercier Press, 1978); Robert Ombres, O.P., 'The Doctrine of Purgatory according to St Thomas Aquinas', *Downside Review* 99 (1981), 279–87; Joseph Ratzinger, *Eschatology: Death and Eternal Life*, trans. Michael Waldstein, 2nd ed. (Washington, DC: Catholic University of America, 1988), 218–33. More generally, Jacques Le Goff, *The Birth of Purgatory* (Chicago: Chicago University Press, 1984; *La Naissance du Purgatoire* [Paris: Gallimard, 1981]); Takami Matsuda, *Death and Purgatory in Middle English Didactic Poetry* (Cambridge: D. S. Brewer), 1997. On Dante and purgatory, Philip H. Wicksteed, *Dante and Aquinas* (London: J. M. Dent / New York: E. P. Dutton), 1913, 213–48; Francis Fergusson, *Dante's Drama of the Mind: A Modern Reading of the 'Purgatorio'* (Princeton: Princeton University Press, 1953; repr. 1968); Peter Armour, *The Door of Purgatory: A Study of Multiple Symbolism in Dante's 'Purgatorio'* (Oxford: Clarendon Press, 1983); Jeffrey T. Schnapp, 'Introduction to *Purgatorio*', in *The Cambridge Companion to Dante*, ed. Rachel Jacoff (Cambridge: Cambridge University Press, 1993), 192–207.

> Ito è così e va, sanza riposo,
> poi che morì; cotal moneta rende
> a sodisfar chi è di là troppo oso'.

(Purgatorio 10.106–8, 11.67–72 and 11.121–26)[154]

True, both the substance and the tone of this aspect of the *Purgatorio* are gentler than the 'monetary' or transactional way of putting it would suggest, for no less prominent in Dante's mind is the piety and affectivity of it all, the piety whereby the penitent spirit commits itself to the outstretched arms of the One anxious to bring it home (the 'bontà infinita ha sì gran braccia' of 3.122), and the affectivity whereby God for his part will waste no time in doing so (the 'ché cima di giudicio non s'avvalla / perché foco d'amor compia in un punto / ciò che de' sodisfar chi qui s'astalla' of 6.37–39). But for all that, the transactional aspect of the argument, its sense of purgatory as a making good in respect of liabilities incurred and a paying off of the 'debt of punishment', is there and there explicitly in the text, this, therefore, entering quite properly into its overall interpretation.

But the transactional aspect of the *Purgatorio*, entering as it does into its overall interpretation, comes nowhere near exhausting the implications of this canticle for the journeying spirit, for the universal 'I-self' represented and exemplified by the Dante character as himself but a spiritual wayfarer; for at issue here is something morally, psychologically and theologically wholly more substantial than a mere squaring of the account, namely a sense of how it is that a man comes home to God by coming home to self in the innermost parts thereof, at which point the transactional gives way to the transformative as the main thrust of Dante's discourse hereabouts. This situation is open to contemplation under two aspects, namely (*a*) the substance and psychology of repentance as the condition of everything coming next by way of new life, and (*b*) the discipline of the spiritual life making for a freeing of self for its proper humanity, at which point the purgatorial idea comes fully and unequivocally into its own as a parameter of being—of this or that instance of specifically human being—as under way. As far, then, as the first of these things is concerned, namely the substance and psychology of repentance as preliminary in respect of everything coming next by way of new life, it is a question, not simply of waiting, but of waiting upon self in, so to speak,

---

154 'I would not, indeed, reader, that, hearing how God wishes the debt to be paid, you be turned aside from your good purpose . . . "I am Omberto, and am not alone among my kinsfolk as a victim of pride, for they all of them have been dragged down by it. Here then, among the dead—since I did it not among the living—must I bear this burden for it, until such time as God be satisfied". . . "That", he answered, "is Provenzan Salvani, and he is here because he presumed to hold all Siena in his hands. Thus he has gone, and goes still, without respite from the day of his death, such being the coin everyone too bold there below pays by way of making good." '

the dawning light of self-understanding and of gentle self-sorrowing. Exquisite in this sense, therefore, is the Manfred episode of *Purgatorio* 3, an essay, precisely, in the deep thoughtfulness of it all, in the taking into self of every aberration of the spirit (the 'orribil furon li peccati miei' moment of line 121) but in the smiling expectation even so of an embrace equal to every iniquity (the 'poi sorridendo disse' moment of line 112):

> E un di loro incominciò: 'Chiunque
> tu se', così andando, volgi 'l viso:
> pon mente se di là mi vedesti unque'.
>   Io mi volsi ver' lui e guardail fiso:
> biondo era e bello e di gentile aspetto,
> ma l'un de' cigli un colpo avea diviso.
>   Quand' io mi fui umilmente disdetto
> d'averlo visto mai, el disse: 'Or vedi';
> e mostrommi una piaga a sommo 'l petto.
>   Poi sorridendo disse: 'Io son Manfredi,
> nepote di Costanza imperadrice;
> ond' io ti priego che, quando tu riedi,
>   vadi a mia bella figlia, genitrice
> de l'onor di Cicilia e d'Aragona,
> e dichi 'l vero a lei, s'altro si dice.
>   Poscia ch'io ebbi rotta la persona
> di due punte mortali, io mi rendei,
> piangendo, a quei che volontier perdona.
>   Orribil furon li peccati miei;
> ma la bontà infinita ha sì gran braccia,
> che prende ciò che si rivolge a lei'.

(*Purgatorio* 3.103–23)[155]

155 'And one of them began: "Whoever you are, look a moment upon me as you pass by and think, did you ever see me yonder?" I turned to him and looked closely. Comely, fair and of noble aspect as he was, one brow bore upon it a gash. When, humbly, I disclaimed ever having seen him, "Look here", he said, and showed me a wound high up on his chest, and then, smiling, "I am Manfred, grandson of the Empress Constance, which is why I beg you that, upon your return, you seek out my fair daughter, mother of the pride of Sicily and of Aragon, putting her right if aught else be told of me. With my body broken by a double blow I gave myself up with tears to Him who freely pardons. My sins were dire, but such are the ample arms of the infinite goodness that it takes unto itself whomsoever turns towards it."' Gilles Gerard Meersseman, O.P., 'Penitenza e penitenti nella vita e nelle opere di Dante', in *"Ordo Fraternitatis": Confraternite e pietà dei laici nel Medioevo*, vol. 1 (Rome: Herder, 1977), 513–34; Hans Urs von Balthasar, 'Purgatorio, penitenza e ispirazione', in *Scrittori e idee in Italia: Antologia della critica (Dalle Origini al Trecento)*, ed. Paolo Pullega (Bologna: Zanichelli, 1982), 200–209; Luigi Blasucci, 'Tempo e penitenza nel *Purgatorio*', in *Letture e saggi danteschi* (Pisa: Edizioni della Normale, 2014),

—lines to which, as registering the notion of self-recognition as the condition of spiritual ascent, we may note these from the final phase of the *Purgatorio* bearing upon Dante's own predicament as a penitent spirit, as, for the moment, one standing painfully in his own presence:

> Li occhi mi cadder giù nel chiaro fonte;
> ma veggendomi in esso, i trassi a l'erba,
> tanta vergogna mi gravò la fronte.
>
> . . .
>
> Quali fanciulli, vergognando, muti
> con li occhi a terra stannosi, ascoltando
> e sé riconoscendo e ripentuti,
>   tal mi stav'io
>
> . . .
>
> Tanta riconoscenza il cor mi morse,
> ch'io caddi vinto; e quale allora femmi,
> salsi colei che la cagion mi porse.

(*Purgatorio* 30.76–78, 31.64–67 and 88–90)[156]

59–74; Marianna Villa, 'Lo sguardo dell'"altro" e l'autoriconoscimento di Dante: Un percorso nel *Purgatorio*', *Tenzone* 13 (2012), 187–225; Marco Ballarini et al. (eds.), *Peccato, penitenza e santità nella 'Commedia'* (Milan: Bulzoni, 2016). More especially on the Manfred episode, Bruno Nardi, 'Il canto di Manfredi (*Purgatorio* III)', in *'Lecturae' e altri studi danteschi*, ed. Ruby Abardo (Florence: Le Lettere, 1990), 91–103; Mark Balfour, ' "Orribil furon li peccati miei": Manfred's Wounds in *Purgatorio* III', *ItSt* 48 (1993), 4–17 (and in *Dante: The Critical Complex*, vol. 7, ed. Richard Lansing [New York: Routledge, 2003], 264–77); John A. Scott, 'Manfred and Bonconte', in *Dante's Political Purgatory* (Philadelphia: University of Pennsylvania Press, 1996), 85–95; Dino Bigongiari, 'The Meeting with Manfred', in *Readings in the 'Divine Comedy'. A Series of Lectures*, ed. Anne Paolucci (Dover, DE: Griffon House, 2006), 248–58.

156 'Lowering my gaze to the clear fount, but seeing myself in it, I looked up again—such was the shame burdening my brow—to the green sward . . . As children, silent in shame, with their eyes cast down, stand listening, knowing themselves and repentant, so also stood I . . . So gnawed was I by such awareness that, overcome, I fell, what I then became she alone knowing who furnished the cause'— with, at an earlier stage of the canticle, the 'Là ne venimmo; e lo scaglion primaio / bianco marmo era sì pulito e terso, / ch'io mi specchiai in esso qual io paio' of 9.94–96 (Thence we came to the first great stair, a stair of white marble so polished and smooth that, as if in a mirror, I saw myself in it as I appear). Pasquale Sabbatino, 'Dante lettore e critico di se stesso nel canto XXX del *Purgatorio*', in *Dante in lettura* (Ravenna: Longo, 2005), 231–4; Erminia Ardissino, 'La storia dell'etterno e il rinnovamento battesimale del poeta', in *Tempo liturgico e tempo storico nella 'Commedia' di Dante* (Città del Vaticano: Libreria Editrice Vaticana, 2009), 89–108; Mario Alinei, 'Lo smarrimento di Dante alla luce dei rimproveri di Beatrice, del simbolismo della processione mistica, e della profezia del DVX', in *Dante rivoluzionario borghese: Per una lettura storica della 'Commedia'* (Velletri: PM edizioni, 2015), 201–56. More generally on Dantean confessionalism and autobiography, Giovanni Fallani, *Dante autobiografico* (Naples: Società Editrice Napoletana, 1975); Marziano Guglielminetti, *Memoria e scrittura: L'autobiografia da Dante a Cellini* (Turin: Einaudi, 1977; revised in *La Vita Nuova: Il Paradiso Terrestre*, ed. Marziano Guglielminetti and Eleonora Vincenti [Turin: Il Segnalibro, 1992]); Giuseppe Giacalone, 'Motivi autobiografici

But then, in consequence of the moment of watching and waiting, comes the struggle proper, the arduous business of affirming self over self on the plane of properly human loving. The pain, to be sure, is prolific, but it is the pain now, not simply of self-recognition nor even of self-sorrowing, but of laying hold of self in the revised substance of self and of this as a matter both of suffering and of solace, of, all in good time, knowing self withal in the resolution of self; so, for example, in respect of the 'pain as prolific' moment of the argument, we have these lines from the pride cantos of the poem, an essay, precisely, in the well-nigh intolerable burden of it all:

> Come per sostentar solaio o tetto,
> per mensola talvolta una figura
> si vede giugner le ginocchia al petto,
>> la qual fa del non ver vera rancura
> nascere 'n chi la vede; così fatti
> vid' io color, quando puosi ben cura.
>> Vero è che più e meno eran contratti
> secondo ch'avien più e meno a dosso;
> e qual più pazïenza avea ne li atti,
>> piangendo parea dicer: 'Più non posso'.

> (*Purgatorio* 10.130–39)[157]

while in respect of the 'suffering as solace' moment of the argument we have these from the cantos of the gluttonous, the gluttonous, Dante suggests, embracing the agony of it all no less gladly than Christ the agony of the cross:

> 'Tutta esta gente che piangendo canta
> per seguitar la gola oltra misura,
> in fame e 'n sete qui si rifà santa.
>> Di bere e di mangiar n'accende cura
> l'odor ch'esce del pomo e de lo sprazzo
> che si distende su per sua verdura.

---

e spirituali nella *Commedia* e nel *Paradiso*', in *Dante Alighieri: La 'Divina Commedia'*, vol. 3 (Rome: Signorelli, 1988), 41–53; Achille Tartaro, 'Momenti autobiografici e definizioni della *Commedia*', *EL* 32.2 (2007), 3–19 (and in *Cielo e terra: Saggi danteschi* [Rome: Studium, 2008], 17–34).

157 'As from time to time we see for the purposes of supporting a ceiling or a roof a figure with its knees drawn up to its chest, a figure engendering in its unreality a real sense of distress in those looking on, that is how, I myself looking on attentively, saw those now before me. Bent double they were indeed according to the greater or lesser weight on their back, those showing forth the greatest forbearance seeming amid their tears to say "Alas, I can no more."'

E non pur una volta, questo spazzo
girando, si rinfresca nostra pena;
io dico pena, e dovria dir sollazzo,
    ché quella voglia a li alberi ci mena
che menò Cristo lieto a dire *"Elì"*,
quando ne liberò con la sua vena'.

(*Purgatorio* 23.64–75)[158]

This, then, is what it means to speak of the purgatorial phase of properly human journeying as a matter of *self-reconfiguration*. What it means to speak of the purgatorial phase of properly human journeying as a matter of self-reconfiguration is to speak (*a*) of the watching and waiting whereby in an attitude of stillness, reflection and thoughtfulness the soul prepares for the imminent agony of purgation proper, and (*b*) of the struggle whereby the proximate is brought home to the ultimate in point of loving and the wayfarer freed for his or her proper destiny as party to the very life of the Godhead. Nothing, to be sure, is easy here, but by virtue of the grace operative both from within and from beyond self—by way, more exactly, of the co-inherence of human and divine willing at the centre of personality (the 'per ch'una fansi nostre voglie stesse' of *Paradiso* 3)—everything, Dante thinks, is possible.[159]

Having, then, confronted the truth of self in the innermost parts of self (the infernal phase of the journey), and having struggled to affirm self over self on the plane of properly human loving (the purgatorial phase of the journey), the pilgrim spirit knows itself, if not as yet in the fully transfigured substance thereof, then, by grace, as on the way with regard to its ultimately ecstatic finality. And by the term 'grace' here we mean—whatever else we mean—the kind of elevating grace

158 'All these who weep as they sing, having followed their appetite beyond measure, regain here, in hunger and thirst, their righteousness. The fragrance emanating from the fruit and from the spray and dispersed over its verdure kindles in us a craving to eat and to drink, and not once only is our pain renewed as we circle this space. I say pain but ought to say solace, for to the tree we are led by that will which led Christ gladly to say *"Elì"* when with his own veins he freed us.' Giulia Gaimari, 'La letizia di Cristo nel *Purgatorio*: Un'ipotesi di lettura', *SD* 81 (2016), 165–81; Romano Manescalchi, 'Il "Cristo lieto" (*Purgatorio* XXIII.74) a confronto con analoghe rappresentazioni', *PT* 20.1–2 (2016), 23–40.

159 For the *Paradiso* 3 passage: 'such that our wills are made but one'. Antonio C. Mastrobuono, 'Sanctifying Grace: Justification and Merit', in *Dante's Journey of Sanctification* (Washington, DC: Regnery Gateway, 1990), 1–129; Inos Biffi, *La poesia e la grazia nella Commedia di Dante* (Milan: Jaca Book, 1999; especially 29–35: 'Un viaggio che parte dalla grazia'); James T. Chiampi, 'The Role of Freely Bestowed Grace in Dante's Journey of Legitimation', in *RSI* 17.1 (1999), 89–111; Paolo Cherchi, 'Da me stesso non vegno (*Inferno* X, 61)', *RELI* 18 (2001), 103–6; John Took, 'Dante and the Modalities of Grace', in *Conversations with Kenelm: Essays on the Theology of the 'Commedia'* (London: UCL Arts and Humanities Publications, 2013), 81–104.

or *gratia elevans* whereby, in a manner exceeding his every proper power to seeing and understanding, man is raised from one peak of knowing and loving to the next; so, for example, as a hymn to grace in precisely this sense, we have these lines from *Paradiso* 10, an ascription of praise and thanksgiving to God tending just for an instant to eclipse even Beatrice as, for Dante, the in-and-through-which of its showing forth:

> E Bëatrice cominciò: 'Ringrazia,
> ringrazia il Sol de li angeli, ch'a questo
> sensibil t'ha levato per sua grazia'.
>   Cor di mortal non fu mai sì digesto
> a divozione e a rendersi a Dio
> con tutto 'l suo gradir cotanto presto,
>   come a quelle parole mi fec' io;
> e sì tutto 'l mio amore in lui si mise,
> che Bëatrice eclissò ne l'oblio.

> (*Paradiso* 10.52–60)[160]

or these from canto 14, no less fervent in their expression of gratitude in consequence of a more than ever rapturous 'translation' of the spirit, the poet's entire being, he says, constituting but a thank-offering for grace thus spread abroad:

> Quindi ripreser li occhi miei virtute
> a rilevarsi; e vidimi translato
> sol con mia donna in più alta salute.
>   Ben m'accors' io ch'io era più levato,
> per l'affocato riso de la stella,
> che mi parea più roggio che l'usato.
>   Con tutto 'l core e con quella favella

---

160 'And Beatrice began: "Give thanks, give thanks to the Sun of the angels who by grace has lifted you to such beholding." Never was mortal heart so intent upon devotion and so swift, as its every delight, to make itself over to God as I upon hearing those words. Indeed, so completely was my love set upon him that Beatrice herself was by its forgetfulness eclipsed.' For Dante and grace, both *sanans* and *elevans*, Kenelm Foster, O.P., *The Two Dantes and Other Studies* (London: Darton, Longman and Todd, 1977; but especially 'The Two Dantes' II and III, 190–253). For Thomas, Bernard J. F. Lonergan, *Grace and Freedom: Operative Grace in the Thought of St. Thomas Aquinas*, ed. J. Patout Burns (London: Darton, Longman and Todd, 1971); Cornelius Ernst, O.P., *The Gospel of Grace (1a2ae.106–14)*, vol. 30 of the English translation of the *Summa theologiae*, ed. Thomas Gilby, O.P. (Cambridge: Blackfriars, 1972); Joseph P. Wawrykow, *God's Grace and Human Action. Merit in the Theology of Thomas Aquinas* (Notre Dame: University of Notre Dame Press, 1995).

> ch'è una in tutti, a Dio feci olocausto,
> qual conveniesi a la grazia novella.

> (*Paradiso* 14.82–90)[161]

or these from canto 33, part of Bernard's plea to the Virgin to the end that, by grace, the one now in his charge may be vouchsafed his final well-being and happiness, his coming home at last to his proper blessedness as a spiritual voyager:

> Or questi, che da l'infima lacuna
> de l'universo infin qui ha vedute
> le vite spiritali ad una ad una,
>   supplica a te, per grazia, di virtute
> tanto, che possa con li occhi levarsi
> più alto verso l'ultima salute.

> (*Paradiso* 33.22–27)[162]

Grace, then, abounds as that whereby the pilgrim poet presumes to fix his gaze upon the light eternal, there to rejoice in an act of perfect intellection, a reading line by line, word by word and syllable by syllable in the book of being bound by love:

> Oh abbondante grazia ond' io presunsi
> ficcar lo viso per la luce etterna,
> tanto che la veduta vi consunsi!
>   Nel suo profondo vidi che s'interna,
> legato con amore in un volume,
> ciò che per l'universo si squaderna:
>   sustanze e accidenti e lor costume
> quasi conflati insieme, per tal modo
> che ciò ch'i' dico è un semplice lume.
>   La forma universal di questo nodo

---

161 'From this my eyes recovered strength enough to look up once more, and, alone with my lady, I beheld myself translated to still greater bliss. Well assured was I of my ascent by the enkindled smile of the star, fiery it seemed to me, beyond its wont, whereupon with all my heart and in the language thereof common to one and all I made unto God a holocaust such as befitted this further grace.'

162 'Now this man, who from the nethermost part of the pit to this height has witnessed severally the condition of all souls, begs you of your grace to vouchsafe such power that with his eyes he may rise still further towards our ultimate salvation.'

credo ch'i' vidi, perché più di largo,
dicendo questo, mi sento ch'i' godo.

(*Paradiso* 33.82–93)[163]

But—and this, now, is what matters—grace, for Dante, functions not only nor perhaps even primarily as an extrinsic principle of elevation but as an intrinsic principle of actualization, as, more exactly, that whereby man's power to deiformity is confirmed in its proper operation, its proper equality to the business in hand. Grace, in other words, for all its incomingness, is never less, for Dante, than a matter of honouring what already *is* by way of man's proper power to ulteriority. And this too, no less than the notion of grace as by definition grace from beyond, is a position open to documentation from the text; so, for example, with their more than ever fervent sense of grace as, so to speak, delighting in the athleticism of the intellect, of its leaping every hurdle along the way, we have these lines from early on in the canticle:

'O amanza del primo amante, o diva',
diss' io appresso, 'il cui parlar m'inonda
e scalda sì, che più e più m'avviva,
     non è l'affezion mia tanto profonda,
che basti a render voi grazia per grazia;
ma quei che vede e puote a ciò risponda.
     Io veggio ben che già mai non si sazia
nostro intelletto, se 'l ver non lo illustra
di fuor dal qual nessun vero si spazia.
     Posasi in esso, come fera in lustra,
tosto che giunto l'ha; e giugner puollo:
se non, ciascun disio sarebbe *frustra*.
     Nasce per quello, a guisa di rampollo,

163 'Oh grace abounding whereby I presumed to fix my look on the eternal light such that I saw at the far limits of my seeing! I saw enclosed in its depths, bound up with love in one volume, everything unfolded leaf by leaf throughout the universe: substance and accidents and their modalities, fused, as it were, one with another such that what I speak of is but a simple light. And of this singularity I believe I saw then the universal form, for in the very telling of it I feel the increase of my joy.' Marco Ariani, 'La forma universal di questo nodo: *Paradiso*, XXXIII 58–105', in *Lectura Dantis Scaligera 2005–2007*, ed. Ennio Sandal (Rome: Antenore, 2008), 137–81; Gino Casagrande, 'Le teofanie di *Paradiso* XXXIII', *SD* 74 (2009), 199–224. For the 'legato con amore in un volume' motif, John Ahern, 'Binding the Book: Hermeneutics and Manuscript Production in *Paradiso* 33', *PMLAA* 5 (1982), 800–809; Gioia Paradisi, 'Icone nella parola: Il "volume" "legato con amore" (*Paradiso* 33,86)', *CT* 14.2 (2011), 249–87; Pierluigi Lia, 'Io vidi che s'interna ciò che per l'universo si squaderna', in *Poetica dell'amore e conversione: Considerazioni teologiche sulla lingua della 'Commedia'* (Florence: Olschki, 2015), 37–52.

a piè del vero il dubbio; ed è natura
ch'al sommo pinge noi di collo in collo'.

(Paradiso 4.118–32)[164]

while from the other end of the canticle we have these bearing on grace as a principle, certainly, of *strengthening* in respect of man's proper power to understanding, but more than this, and by way of a characteristically Dantean nuancing of
the argument, of something approaching its *self-strengthening*, its rising *of itself* to
the occasion:

Non perché più ch'un semplice sembiante
fosse nel vivo lume ch'io mirava,
che tal è sempre qual s'era davante;
ma per la vista che s'avvalorava
in me guardando, una sola parvenza,
mutandom' io, a me si travagliava.

(Paradiso 33.109–113)[165]

—to which, as rejoicing now in the vocabulary of exponentiality, we may add
these lines from canto 23 with their sense of the mind's ever dilating ('dilatarsi'),
ever expanding ('fatta più grande') and ever issuing forth ('di sé stessa uscìo') in
the presence of the ever-epiphanous Beatrice:

Oh Bëatrice, dolce guida e cara!
Ella mi disse: 'Quel che ti sobranza
è virtù da cui nulla si ripara.
Quivi è la sapïenza e la possanza
ch'aprì le strade tra 'l cielo e la terra,
onde fu già sì lunga disïanza'.

164 ' "O beloved of the first lover, o divine one", said I then, "whose speech so floods and warms
me such that I am ever more quickened, my affection for all its depth is scarce sufficient to render you
grace for grace; but may he who sees and can indeed do so answer thereunto. Well do I see that never
can our intellect be wholly satisfied unless there shine on it that truth beyond which no truth extends.
Therein it rests, as a wild beast in his lair, so soon as it has reached it; and reach it it can, else every
desire would be in vain. Our questioning thus springs up like a shoot at the foot of the truth, nature
itself thus peak by peak urging us on to the summit." '

165 'Not that the living light upon which I gazed had more than a single aspect, for ever it remained
as it was before; but by my sight gaining strength as I looked on, an as yet undifferentiated appearance—I myself changing—was for me transformed.' For the 'self-strengthening' moment of the argument see too, and especially, the 'ché più largo fu Dio a dar se stesso / per far l'uom sufficiente a rilevarsi'
of *Paradiso* 7.115–16 (for all the greater was God's generosity in giving himself that man might be made
equal to his own raising up).

Come foco di nube si diserra
per dilatarsi sì che non vi cape,
e fuor di sua natura in giù s'atterra,
    la mente mia così, tra quelle dape
fatta più grande, di sé stessa uscìo,
e che si fesse rimembrar non sape.

(*Paradiso* 23.34–45)[166]

This, then, is what it means to speak of the paradisal phase of properly human journeying as a matter of *self-transcendence*. What it means to speak of the paradisal phase of properly human journeying as a matter of self-transcendence is to speak of paradise, properly understood, as a matter not, certainly in any simple sense of the term, of gratuitousness, and still less of reward, recompense or remuneration, but rather, and by way of grace as a principle less of strangeness than of sufficiency, of an opening out of self upon its proper ulteriority. Grace, then, abounds, and, with it, thanksgiving in abundance; but all this by way of commitment—or, more exactly, by way of commitment on the part now of a Dante more than ever adult in the flame of love—to the, by grace, equality of man to his own high calling.

IMMANENT ESCHATOLOGY AND THE TRIUMPH OF THE IMAGE

Dante's, in the *Commedia*, looks on the face of it to be an ultimate eschatology, an eschatology, that is to say, turning upon what comes next on the plane of the horizontal; first, then, this life then the next, the latter constituting but a crystallization of the former, a living out of the truth thereof in a now pure form. But to speak in this way of the crystallization of what *is* now in the *what will be* of what comes next, and of the living out in perpetuity of the truth thereof is to underline the status of the ἔσχατος as but the *innermost* as distinct from the *aftermost* truth of this or that instance of specifically human being, as subsisting on the plane not in fact of the horizontal but of the vertical. And it is into this situation that form— meaning by this language under the aspect of its precise lexical, syntactical, metrical and rhetorical complexion—enters as that whereby the truth of what is in the recesses of self is raised to the surface and proposed as an object of contemplation. Here, then, in what amounts to the sacramental and indeed to the sacred

166 'O Beatrice, sweet guide and dear! Thus she spoke: "Overcoming you is that power from which there is no defence. Here before you is the wisdom and the might which opened the ways between heaven and earth and for which of old there was such lengthy yearning." As fire breaks from a cloud swelling beyond every possibility of its containing, so my mind, grown greater at that feast, was transported beyond itself, having no remembrance of what then it became.'

status of form as the in-and-through-which of an immanent eschatology, lies the triumph of the *Commedia* as a theological utterance, form thus understood constituting a principle not merely of disquisition but of disclosure, of a species of ontic intelligence apt by turns to terrify and to tranquillize the attentive spirit.

Taking first, then, lexis as straightaway a matter of startling inclusivity, it is a question

(*a*) of the terminology, on the social and political side, of law and lawmaking, business and entrepreneurialism, warfare and navigation and, on the more properly scientific side, of astronomy, anatomy, embryology, pathology, mathematics, geometry, perspective and optics ('cittadinanza', 'civili', 'leggi', 'officio', 'provedimenti'; 'merca', 'mercatante', 'moneta'; 'cavalier', 'cennamella', 'corridor', 'stormo'; 'barca', 'marin', 'nave', 'navicella', 'navigio', 'nocchier', 'poppa', 'prora', 'remo'; 'cenìt', 'orizzonte', 'plenilunii', 'zona', 'emisperio'; 'ascelle', 'mascelle', 'moncherin', 'pancia', 'pilosa pelle', 'strozza', 'trangugia', 'trulla'; 'generante', 'natural vasello', 'organar', 'sangue perfetto', 'virtute attiva', 'virtute informativa'; 'arsura', 'epa', 'idropico', 'leppo', 'schianze'; 'arco declivo', 'arco superno', 'cerchio', 'circumcinto', 'circunferenza', 'geomètra', 'orbita'; 'apprensiva', 'spirto visivo');[167]

(*b*) of Latinism either in its pure form (classical, ecclesial and scholastic) or else as subject to vernacularization (*esse, quia, necesse*; 'ferace', 'fertile', 'fleto', 'laude', 'mesti', 'molesto'; 'perizoma'; 'umbriferi prefazi'; 'concipio', 'intenza', 'intenzione', 'quiditate', 'sustanza', 'silogismo', 'silogizzar'), together with those moments of the text (now more properly phrasal in kind) transparent to the Latin archetype (the 'casso / lo lume era' of *Inferno* 26 for the 'cassus lumine' of the *Aeneid* at 2.85, or the 'Con piangere e con lutto' of *Inferno* 8 for the 'cum fletu et luctu' of Baruch 4, or the 'così mi circunfulse luce viva' of *Paradiso* 30 for the 'subito de cœlo circumfulsit me lux copiosa' of the *Acts of the Apostles* at 22:6);[168]

(*c*) of Gallicism and Provençalism at the level both of lexis and of morphology ('beninanza', 'disïanza', 'possanza', 'sobranza'; 'argento', 'giuggia', 'inveggia', 'pennelleggia');[169]

---

167 Nicola Zingarelli, 'Appunti lessicali danteschi', *GSLI* 18 (1906), 368–80; Eric R. Vincent, 'Dante's Choice of Words', *ItSt* 10 (1955), 1–18; Piero A. Di Pretoro, 'Innovazioni lessicali nella *Commedia*', *RSANL* 25 (1970), 263–97.

168 Hermann Gmelin, 'I latinismi del *Paradiso*', in *Critica dantesca: Antologia di studi e letture nel Novecento*, ed. Giorgio Bàrberi Squarotti and Angelo Jacomuzzi (Turin: Società Editrice Internazionale, 1970), 423–32.

169 Reto R. Bezzola, *Abbozzo di una storia dei gallicismi italiani nei primi secoli (750–1300): Saggio*

(d) of the colloquial and municipal ('donno', 'issa', 'sipa');[170]

(e) of the still much cherished formulae of the Siculo-Tuscan and stilno-vistic tradition of vernacular verse making ('angelica voce', 'beata e bella', 'li occhi lucenti', 'li occhi rilucenti', 'sì dolcemente / che la dolcezza ancor dentro mi suona', 'sì dolcemente udissi', 'soave e piana', 'sorrise e riguardommi');[171]

(f) of neologism, preeminently but by no means exclusively parasynthetic and/or reflexive in kind ('m'intuassi', ''mparadisa', 's'indova', 's'inluia', 's'insempra', 's'interna', 's'inurba', 's'invera', 't'inmii'; transitive, by contrast, the 'imparadisare' of *Paradiso* 28.3);[172]

and

(g) of affixation, mostly suffixal in kind but both diminutive ('augelletti', 'erbette', 'fioretti', 'fiumicello', 'isoletta'; 'serocchia', 'una donna soletta', 'villanello', 'vedovella') and—though less frequently—augmentative ('girone', 'petrone').[173]

---

storico linguistico) (Zurich: Seldwyla, 1924; repr. Bologna: Forni, 1984); Bruno Migliorini, ad voc. 'Gallicismi', *ED*, vol. 3 (Rome: Istituto della Enciclopedia Italiana, 1970–78), 90–91; Riccardo Viel, *I gallicismi della 'Divina Commedia'* (Rome: Aracne, 2014). More generally, Roberta Cella, *I gallicismi nei testi dell'italiano antico: Dalle origini alla fine del sec. 14* (Florence: Accademia della Crusca, 2003); Maria Sofia Lannutti, 'Ancora sulle rime francesi e sui gallicismi nella poesia italiana delle origini', *SLIt* 22 (2005), 5–28.

170 Alfredo Schiaffini, 'Note sul colorito dialettale della *Divina Commedia*', *SD* 13 (1928), 31–45; Heinrich Kuen, 'Sprachen und Dialekte in der Göttliche Kömodie', *DDJ* 34–35 (1957), 63–95; Bruno Migliorini, ad voc. 'Idiotismi', *ED*, vol. 3 (Rome: Istituto della Enciclopedia Italiana, 1970–78), 355–56; Raffaello Caverni, *Voci e modi nella 'Divina Commedia' dell'uso popolare toscano: Dizionarietto* (Florence: Pagnini, 1987; an anastatic reproduction of the Giusti ed. [Florence, 1877]).

171 Selene Sarteschi, '*Purgatorio*, XXIV 49–53: Dante e il "dolce stil novo": Verifica di una continuità ideologica', *FC* 20.2–3 (1995), 242–77.

172 Brenda Deen Schildgen, 'Dante's Neologisms in the *Paradiso* and the Latin Rhetorical Tradition', *DS* 107 (1989), 101–19; Vincenzo Jacomuzzi, 'Dire l'indicibile: Il neologismo nel *Paradiso* dantesco', in *Homenaxe ó profesor Constantino Garcia*, vol. 1, ed. Mercedes Brea et al. (Santiago de Compostela: Universidade de Santiago de Compostela, 1991), 215–22; Joan Ferrante, 'A Poetics of Chaos and Harmony', in *The Cambridge Companion to Dante*, ed. Rachel Jacoff (Cambridge: Cambridge University Press, 1993), 153–71 (especially 161–62); Joseph Luzzi, ' "As a leaf on a branch . . . ": Dante's Neologisms', *PMLAA* 125.2 (2010), 322–36.

173 Ignazio Baldelli, 'Suffissi alterativi', *ED*, vol. 6 (*Appendice*) (Rome: Istituto della Enciclopedia Italiana, 1970–78), 480–85; Paola Ureni, 'Parasinteti verbali con prefisso "-in" e conoscenza intellettuale nel *Paradiso*', *Tenzone* 16 (2015), 143–65. More generally, Maria Corti, 'I suffissi dell'astratto "-or" e "-ura" nella lingua poetica delle origini', *RSANL* 8 (1953), 294–312; Smiljka Malinar, 'Formazione delle parole nelle opere di Guittone d'Arezzo. Parte prima: Derivazione con suffissi', *Studia Romanica et Anglica Zagrabiensia* 39 (1975), 107–59; D'Arco Silvio Avalle, 'Il prefisso "per-" nella lingua letteraria del Duecento (con un'appendice sul prefisso "pro-")', *SLIt* 1 (1979), 263–87.

Syntactically, by contrast, it is a question of the now perfect accountability of the period in point both of sound and of structure to the leading emphases thereof, of its organization by way:

(a) of anastrophe or simple inversion (the 'Poeta fui, e cantai di quel giusto / figliuol d'Anchise' of *Inferno* 1.73–4, or the 'biondo era e bello e di gentile aspetto' of *Purgatorio* 3.107, or the 'beata sono in la spera più tarda' of *Paradiso* 3.51);[174]

(b) of hypotaxis or clausular conjunction (the 'D'ogne malizia, ch'odio in cielo acquista, / ingiuria è 'l fine, *ed* ogne fin cotale / o con forza o con frode altrui contrista. / *Ma perché* frode è de l'uom proprio male, / più spiace a Dio; e *però* stan di sotto / li frodolenti, *e* più dolor li assale' of *Inferno* 11.22–27);[175]

or else

(c) of parataxis or clausular juxtaposition (the 'Di sùbito drizzato gridò: "Come? / dicesti 'elli ebbe'? non viv' elli ancora? / non fiere li occhi suoi lo dolce lume?"' of *Inferno* 10.67–69).[176]

—all these things combining with any number of rhetorical strategies (alliteration, anaphora, epanalexis, *exclamatio*, polysyndeton and—though less frequently—asyndeton) each alike functional as a principle not now of decoration but of determination, of fixing the precise meaning and/or expressive intensity of the line.

174 For *Inferno* 1.73–74: 'A poet was I, and I sang of that righteous son of Anchises'; for *Purgatorio* 3.107: 'blond he was and beautiful and of noble aspect'; and for *Paradiso* 3.51: 'blessed are they in the slowest of the spheres'. Giuseppe Lisio, *L'arte del periodo nelle opere volgari di Dante Alighieri e del secolo XIII: Saggio di critica e di storia letteraria* (Bologna: Zanichelli 1902), 150–69. Also, Maria Corti, 'Studi sulla sintassi della lingua poetica avanti lo stilnovo', *Colombaria* 4 (1953), 263–365.

175 'Of every evil intent that earns hatred in heaven injury is the object, and every such end afflicts another either by force or by fraud; but because fraud is a sin peculiar to man it is more offensive to God, and for that reason the fraudulent have their place lower down and more pain assails them." Mario Medici, ad voc. 'Congiunzioni', *ED*, vol. 6 (*Appendice*) (Rome: Istituto della Enciclopedia Italiana, 1970–78), 334–44.

176 'All of a sudden, erect, he screamed: "What? Did you say 'he had'? Is he not still alive? Strikes not the sweet light his eyes?"' For parahypotaxis of the kind represented by, say, the 'S'io dissi falso, e tu falsasti il conio' of *Inferno* 30.115 (If I spoke falsely, you it was who falsified the coin)—that is, a proleptic dependent clause with a main clause preceded by a coordinator—Franca Brambilla Ageno, ad voc. 'paraipotassi', *ED*, vol. 6 (*Appendice*) (Rome: Istituto della Enciclopedia Italiana, 1970–78), 441–42; Ghino Ghinassi, 'Casi di "paraipotassi relativa" in italiano antico', *LL* 3.1 (1978), 9–39; Marco Mazzoleni, 'Paraipotassi e strutture correlative', in *Grammatica dell'italiano antico*, vol. 2, ed. Giampaolo Salvi and Lorenzo Renzi (Bologna: Il Mulino, 2010), 763–90.

As far, by contrast, as prosody is concerned, and taking first the case of the tercet as the fundamental metrical unit of the text, it is a question both of form and of freedom, both of the integration of the metrical and the syntactical period and, as occasions demands, of its loosening in response to the narrative and/or notional substance thereof. On the one hand, then, and as an instance of their mutual countenancing, we have these lines from the very beginning of the text, syntax and prosody proceeding pari passu:

metrical

Nel mezzo del cammin di nostra vita
mi ritrovai per una selva oscura,
ché la diritta via era smarrita.

Ahi quanto a dir qual era è cosa dura
esta selva selvaggia e aspra e forte
che nel pensier rinova la paura!

Tant' è amara che poco è più morte;
ma per trattar del ben ch'i' vi trovai,
dirò de l'altre cose ch'i' v'ho scorte.

Io non so ben ridir com' i' v'intrai,
tant' era pien di sonno a quel punto
che la verace via abbandonai.

syntactical

(*Inferno* 1.1–12)[177]

while on the other, and as bearing witness now to the flexibility of it all, to the readiness of tercet and hendecasyllable alike to host by way of the richest kind of enjambment a more ample period, we have these lines from the next canto:

---

177 'Midway in the journey of our life I found myself in a dark wood, for the straight way was lost. Try as I may, there is no telling how it was with that wood, so wild, rugged and harsh was it that even to think of it terrifies me afresh! So savage was it, in fact, that death itself is scarcely more. But for the sake of the good I found there, I'll tell of what else I saw. How I came to be there I cannot rightly say, so drowsy was I in the moment I forsook the true way.' Tommaso Casini, 'Per la genesi della terzina e della *Commedia* dantesca', in *Miscellanea di studi storici in onore di Giovanni Sforza* (Lucca: Baroni, 1920), 689–97; Tibor Wlassics, 'Le caratteristiche strutturali della terzina', in *Interpretazioni di prosodia dantesca* (Rome: Signorelli, 1972), 9–23; Pietro G. Beltrami, 'Per una tipologia della terzina', in *Metrica, poetica, metrical dantesca* (Pisa: Pacini, 1981), 103–27; Guglielmo Gorni, 'Coscienza metrica di Dante: Terzina e altre misure', in *Il nodo della lingua e il verbo d'amore: Studi su Dante e altri duecentisti* (Florence: Olschki, 1981), 187–215; John Freccero, 'The Significance of Terza Rima', in *Dante, Petrarch, Boccaccio: Studies in the Italian Trecento in Honor of Charles S. Singleton*, ed. Aldo S. Bernardo and Anthony L. Pellegrini (Binghampton, NY: Centre for Medieval and Early Renaissance Studies, 1983), 3–17; Franco Gavazzeni, 'Approssimazioni metriche sulla terza rima', *SD* 56 (1984), 1–82; Michael D. Hurley, 'Interpreting Dante's "terza rima"', *FMLS* 41.3 (2005), 320–31; Paola Vecchi Galli, 'La fabbrica della terzina', in *Dante e la fabbrica della 'Commedia'. Atti del Convegno Internazionale di Studi, Ravenna, 14–16 settembre 2006*, ed. Alfredo Cottignoli et al. (Ravenna: Longo, 2008), 43–64.

$$\text{metrical} \left\{ \begin{array}{l} \text{Lo giorno se n'andava, e l'aere bruno} \\ \text{toglieva li animai che sono in terra} \\ \text{da le fatiche loro; e io sol uno} \\ \text{m'apparecchiava a sostener la guerra} \\ \text{sì del cammino e sì de la pietate,} \\ \text{che ritrarrà la mente che non erra.} \end{array} \right\} \text{syntactical}$$

(*Inferno* 2.1–6)[178]

or, still by way of enjambement but as rejoicing in a now rich amalgamation of assonance, alliteration and equivocation, these from canto 8:

caesura (*bis*)
metrical

$$\left\{ \begin{array}{l} \text{E io: 'Maestro, già le sue meschite} \\ \text{là \textit{entro certe} ne la valle \textit{cerno},} \\ \text{vermiglie come se di \textit{foco} uscite} \\ \text{fossero'. Ed ei mi disse: 'Il \textit{foco} etterno} \\ \text{ch'entro l'\textit{affoca} le dimostra rosse,} \\ \text{come tu vedi in questo basso inferno'.} \\ \text{Noi pur giugnemmo dentro a l'alte \textit{fosse}} \\ \text{che vallan quella terra sconsolata:} \\ \text{le mura mi parean che \textit{ferro fosse}.} \end{array} \right.$$

assonance

alliteration
syntactical

alliteration
rima equivoca

(*Inferno* 8.70–78)[179]

And what applies by way of its flexibility and resourcefulness to the tercet applies also to the hendecasyllable as, in respect of its at once technical and expressive spaciousness, the 'superbissimum carmen' or most exalted of the variously exalted lines—the heptasyllable, the pentasyllable and the trisyllable—available to poets in the area of Italian vernacular verse making.[180] As far, then, as

178 'Day was departing and the darkling air freeing every creature here below from its labours while I alone was readying myself for the arduousness and agony of the way now to be rehearsed by my unerring spirit.'

179 'And I: "Already, Master, I can make out the minarets there within the valley, red as if straight out of the fire", whereupon he made reply: "As you yourself can see in this nether hell, the fire blazing eternally within them makes them appear red." We then reached the very depths of that ditch surrounding that desolate place with its—or so it seemed—walls of iron.' For alliteration and assonance, Gian Luigi Beccaria, 'Alliterazioni dantesche', *Archivio Glottologico Italiano* 54 (1969), 240–47; James Wheelock, 'Alliterative Functions in the *Divina Commedia*', LS 13 (1978), 373–404; David Robey, 'Alliteration and Assonance', in *Sound and Structure in the 'Divina Commedia'* (Oxford: Oxford University Press, 2000), 18–58. More generally, Robert Longley Taylor, *Alliteration in Italian* (New Haven: Tuttle, Morehouse and Taylor, 1900); Paolo Valesio, *Strutture dell'alliterazione* (Bologna: Zanichelli, 1967).

180 *De vulgari eloquentia* 2.5.1–3: 'De gravitate sententiarum vel satis dixisse videmur vel saltim totum quod operis est nostri: quapropter ad superbiam carminum festinemus. Circa quod sciendum quod predecessores nostri diversis carminibus usi sunt in cantionibus suis, quod et moderni faciunt:

the hendecasyllable in particular is concerned, we have what eventually came to be regarded as the twofold canonical structure of the line: on the one hand the hendecasyllable *a maiore* with its stress on the sixth and tenth syllables, and on the other the hendecasyllable *a minore* with its stress either on the fourth, eighth and tenth (*a minore* pure and simple) or else on the fourth, seventh and tenth (*a minore di settima*); so, as representative of the first of these things, of the hendecasyllable *a maiore*, we have this line from, again, the very beginning of the text:

Nel | mè | zzo | del | ca | m̀min | di | no | stra | v̀i | ta   [(2)–6–10]

while as representative of the second of them, of the hendecasyllable *a minore* and *a minore di settima*, we have these from the same tercet:

mi | ri | tro | vài | per | u | na | sèl | va o | scu | ra   [4–8–10]
E | co | me | quèi | che | con | lè | na a | ffa | nà | ta   [4–7–10]

Within this pattern, however, there are any number of variations, alternative and/or additional accentuation serving to point up this or that inflexion of the line, be it dramatic or dialectical; so, for example, the 'disse: "Tu guardi sì, padre! che hai?"' of *Inferno* 33.51 with, in addition to its stress on the fourth, sixth and tenth, further stress, of varying intensity, on the first, third, seventh and ninth;[181]

---

sed nullum adhuc invenimus in carmen sillabicando endecadem transcendisse, nec a trisillabo descendisse. Et licet trisillabo carmine atque endecasillabo et omnibus intermediis cantores latii usi sint, pentasillabum et eptasillabum et endecasillabum in usu frequentiori habentur, et post hec trisillabum ante alia. Quorum omnium endecasillabum videtur esse superbius, tam temporis occupatione quam capacitate sentencie, construccionis et vocabulorum' (Now that enough has been said—or so it seems to me—as to the weight of the subject matter, or at least as much as is relevant for the purpose of my work, I shall move quickly onto the magnificence of the line, in respect of which we need first to acknowledge that our predecessors used lines of varying lengths in their canzoni, as do our contemporaries; but I have not yet found any case in which the number of syllables in a single line exceeds eleven or falls short of three. And although Italian poets have used trisyllabic lines, and hendecasyllables, and every type of line in between, the most popular have been the lines of five, seven and eleven syllables, with the trisyllable most favoured among those that remain. Of all these lines the most splendid is clearly the hendecasyllable, both for its measured movement and for the scope it offers for subject matter, constructions and vocabulary). Ugo Sesini, 'L'endecasillabo: Struttura e peculiarità', *Conv* 11 (1939), 545–70; D'Arco Silvio Avalle, *Preistoria dell'endecasillabo* (Milan: Ricciardi, 1963); Remo Fasani, 'Intorno all'endecasillabo', *SPCT* 50 (1995), 63–84 (and in *L'infinito endecasillabo e tre saggi danteschi* [Ravenna: Longo, 2007], 25–43); Marco Praloran, 'Alcune osservazioni sulla storia dell'endecasillabo', in *Testi e linguaggi per Paolo Zolli*, ed. Dipartimento di Italianistica dell'Università di Udine (Modena: Mucchi, 2001), 19–39; Aldo Menichetti, 'Quelques considérations sur la structure et l'origine de l'"endecasillabo"', in *Saggi metrici*, ed. Paolo Gresti et al. (Florence: Galluzzo, 2006), 251–69; and relative to caesura in particular, Pietro G. Beltrami, 'Cesura, epica, lirica, italiana: Riflessioni sull'endecasillabo di Dante', *Metrica* 4 (1986), 67–107; Remo Fasani, 'Endecasillabo e cesura', *SPCT* 36 (1988), 5–21 (and, in a revised form, in *La metrica della 'Divina Commedia' e altri saggi di metrica italiana* [Ravenna: Longo, 1992], 69–90).

181 ' "You stare so, father", he said, "but what can be wrong?" '

or the 'Oh', diss'io lui, 'or se' tu ancor morto?' of the same canto at line 121 with, again in addition to its stress on the fourth, sixth and tenth, its leaning heavily on the first, third, fifth, seventh and ninth;[182] or the 'Deh, bella donna, che a' raggi d'amore' of *Purgatorio* 28.43, where along with the customary fourth, seventh and tenth, the first and second syllables too carry a strong stress together with a robust caesura after the fifth.[183] But that is not all, for notable too is the role in this or that set of circumstances of the ninth syllable, by and large a Cinderella syllable relative to the tenth but powerful enough when it comes to strengthening the substance of the line in its twilight moments; so, for example, in the *Inferno*, the 'dicono e odono e poi son *giù* volte' of 5.15 while in the *Purgatorio* the 'o gente umana, per volar *sù* nata' of 12.95, essays precisely in the downward and upward way of the spirit in its respectively tragic and triumphant moments.[184] And what amounts in these and similar passages to a privileging of the ninth is accompanied elsewhere by a privileging of the first, where it is a question now of inaugurating by way of a tonic stress the weighty utterance, of determining the tone and indeed the substance of everything coming next in the period as a whole; so, for example, the 'Godi Fiorenza, poi che se' sì grande' of *Inferno* 26.1 with its heady mixture of irony and indictment, or the 'Vegna ver' noi la pace del tuo regno' of *Purgatorio* 11.7 with its seeking out of the peace apt to surpass all understanding—lines to which, as more than ordinarily accomplished in this sense we may add the 'Vergine Madre, figlia del tuo figlio, / umile e alta più che creatura, / termine fisso d'etterno consiglio' of the very last canto of the poem, spectacular not least for its implementation of this same scheme across a series of *sdruccioli* or proparoxytones at the beginning of each line.[185] Throughout, then, the pattern is the same, for throughout it is a question of the hendecasyllable as equal to the burden laid upon it.

With this we are approaching the more properly rhetorical—as distinct from metrical—component of the *Commedia*, but not quite, for we need first a word on rhyme as, no less than meter, a fully functional feature of the poem. Acknowledged already in the *De vulgari eloquentia* as part and parcel of the poetic undertaking, but for the moment in respect mainly of its precise disposition within the

---

182 ' "Oh", said I to him, "then are you dead already?" '

183 ' "Pray, fair lady, warming yourself in the rays of love [if at least I am to credit the looks customarily bearing witness to the heart", said I to her, "may it please you approach this stream that I may hear of what you sing"]'.

184 'O race of men born to ascend'. For the *Inferno* 5 passage: 'They speak, they hear, and then are despatched below'.

185 *Paradiso* 33.1–3: 'Virgin mother, daughter of your son, lowly and exalted more than any creature, fixed goal of the eternal counsel, [you are she who did so ennoble human nature that its maker disdained not himself to be made]'. For the *Inferno* 26 passage: 'Rejoice, Florence, for so great are you [that over land and sea you beat your wings and throughout hell your name is spread abroad!]'; and for the *Purgatorio* 11 passage: 'Come unto us the peace of your kingdom'.

stanza as the primary object of Dante's meditation in the Latin treatise, rhyme, there, is in truth a matter merely of passing concern, something for consideration further down the line.[186] Here in the *Commedia*, by contrast, it is top of the agenda, for here in the *Commedia* it is a question of rhyme as a matter both of structure and of significance, as tending in one and the same moment both to confirm the shape, symmetry and self-possession of the poetic utterance and to intensify at a stroke its notional substance. And the result? A courageous commitment both to the inclusive and to the virtuoso, to—over against the exclusivity hereabouts of the *De vulgari eloquentia*—an acknowledgement of every linguistic register in the now deep legitimacy thereof, and to endless experimentation in the area of complex and rare rhyme; so, for example, in respect of the first of these things, of the inclusivity of it all, we have the scatological moment of the *Inferno*, the flatterers of the second *bolgia* knowing themselves, and in turn being known, by way only of the shit ('sterco' in rhyme with 'cerco' and, especially, 'cherco'), making it difficult to tell layman and cleric apart:

> Quivi venimmo; e quindi giù nel fosso
> vidi gente attuffata in uno *sterco*
> che da li uman privadi parea mosso.
> E mentre ch'io là giù con l'occhio *cerco*,
> vidi un col capo sì di merda lordo,
> che non parëa s'era laico o *cherco*.

(Inferno 18.112–17)[187]

---

186 *De vulgari eloquentia* 2.13.1 and 13: 'Rithimorum quoque relationi vacemus, nichil de rithimo secundum se modo tractantes; proprium enim eorum tractatum in posterum prorogamus, cum de mediocri poemate intendemus . . . Et hec de arte, prout habitudinem respicit, tanta sufficient' (Let us turn now, not so much to rhyme in and for itself (our purpose being to take up this matter again in the context of poetry in the middle style), but to the relationship of rhymes [within the canzone stanza] . . . This, as far as their precise disposition is concerned, being enough for now). Alfonso de Salvio, *The Rhyme Words in the 'Divina Commedia'* (Paris: Champion, 1929); Dante Bianchi, 'Rima e verso nella *Divina Commedia*', *RIL* 95 (1961), 127–40; Allan H. Gilbert, 'Dante's Rimario', *Italica* 44.4 (1967), 409–24; Ignazio Baldelli, 'Rima', *ED*, vol. 4 (Rome: Istituto dell'Enciclopedia Italiana, 1970–78), 930–49; Gerhard Rohlfs, 'La lingua di Dante nelle rime della *Divina Commedia*' and *Studi e ricerche su lingua e dialetti d'Italia* (Florence: Sansoni, 1972), 132–38; Ernesto Giacomo Parodi, 'La rima nella *Commedia*', in *Scrittori e idee in Italia: Antologia della critica*, ed. Paolo Pullega (Bologna: Zanichelli, 1982 [1896]), 186–91; Gian Luigi Beccaria, 'Il linguaggio di Dante, la rima e altro (662° Annuale della morte di Dante)', *LC* 14 (1985), 9–19; Arianna Punzi, 'Appunti sulle rime della *Commedia*' (Rome: Bagatto Libri, 1995), together with 'Le rime della *Commedia* di Dante Alighieri', in *La costruzione del testo poetico: Metrica e testo* (Rome: Aracne, 2004), 269–310 (and, for the rhymes generally of the *Commedia*, *Rimario della 'Commedia' di Dante* [Rome: Bagatto Libri, 2001]); David Robey, 'Rhyme', in *Sound and Structure in the 'Divine Comedy'* (Oxford: Oxford University Press, 2000), 59–90.

187 'There we made our way, whence, in the ditch below us, I saw folk plunged in an excremental filth having all the appearance of tumbling forth from a human privy; and, casting about with my eyes there below, I saw one so befouled in ordure that, whether layman or cleric, who could tell?' Zygmunt

while at the other end of the spectrum we have the refined complexion of the 'shadowy prefaces' moment of the *Paradiso* with its sense of everything encountered along the pilgrim way as but a preliminary intuition of the truth by which it is transcended:

> Anche soggiunse: 'Il fiume e li *topazi*
> ch'entrano ed escono e 'l rider de l'erbe
> son di lor vero umbriferi *prefazi*'.

> (*Paradiso* 30.76–78)[188]

As regards, by contrast, the virtuosity of it all, Dante's sheer expertise as a rhymester, we have a programme of activity open to contemplation in terms:

(*a*) of *rima composta* or rhyme involving two lexemes: the 'urli ... *pur lì* ... burli' of *Inferno* 7.25–30 (howl ... at that point ... squander); or the 'oncia ... sconcia ... *non ci ha*' of 30.82–87 (inch ... crooked ... its not having); or the 'ventre ... Almen tre ... entre' of *Purgatorio* 19.31–36 (belly ... at least three ... you enter); or the 'piacerli ... *per li* ... merli' of 20.1–6 (to please him ... along the [way] ... battlements); or the '*dì, dì* ... annidi ... ridi' of *Paradiso* 5.121–26 (speak, speak ... you nest ... you smile);

(*b*) of *rima sdrucciola* or rhyme involving a stress on the antepenultimate syllable and thus productive of a hypermetric or twelve-syllable line: the 'màrgini ... àrgini' of *Inferno* 15.1–3 (margins ... banks); or the 'Cattòlica ... Maiòloca ... argòlica' of 28.76–84 (La Cattolica ... Majorca ... Grecian); or the 'razïonàbile ... duràbile' of *Paradiso* 26.124–29 (reasonable ... durable); or the 'gìrano ... ammìrano ... tìrano' of 28.124–29 (wheel around ... gaze ... draw [towards God]);[189]

(*c*) of *rima tronca* or rhyme involving stress on the ultimate as distinct from the penultimate syllable of the now hypometric or ten-syllable line: the 'Noè ... rè ... fè' of *Inferno* 4.55–60 (Noah ... king ... did); or the 'non

---

G. Barański, 'Scatology and Obscenity in Dante', in *Dante for the New Millennium*, ed. Teodolinda Barolini and Harry Wayne Storey (New York: Fordham University Press, 2003), 259–73. More generally, Pierre Bec, *Burlesque et obscenité chez les troubadours* (Paris: Stock, 1984) and Emma Dillon, 'Representing Obscene Sound', in *Medieval Obscenities*, ed. Nicola McDonald (Woodbridge, Suffolk: York Medieval Press, 2006), 55–84.

188 'The river and the topazes entering and coming forth from it, together with the rejoicing of every blossom, are but the shadowy prefacing of the truth properly theirs.'

189 Sandra Dieckmann and Oliver Huck, 'Versi sdruccioli e versi tronchi nella poesia e nella musica del Due- e Trecento', *SMI* 7 (2007), 3–31.

pò ... mette cò ... Pò' of 20.73–78 (cannot ... begins ... Po); or the 'Siòn ...
orizzòn ... Fetòn' of *Purgatorio* 4.67–75 (Zion ... horizon ... Phaeton); or
the 'Elì ... dì ... qui' of 23.73–78 (Eli ... day ... now); or the 's'udì ...
schiarì ... dì' of *Paradiso* 25.97–102 (was heard ... shone forth ... day);

(*d*) of *rima ricca* or rhyme words admitting a phoneme prior to the tonic
stress: the 'punto ... *compunto*' of *Inferno* 1.10–15 (moment ... pierced); or
the 'risposta ... posta' of 10.70–75 (replied ... request); or the 'rimorso ...
morso' of *Purgatorio* 3.7–9 (remorse ... sting); or the 's'accosta ... costa' of
Paradiso 20.43–48 (comes close ... costs);

(*e*) of derivative rhyme as a species of rich rhyme but sharing a common
lexeme: the 'donna ... s'indonna' of *Paradiso* 7.10–15 (my lady ... masters);
the 'ringrazia ... grazia' of 10.52–54 (give thanks ... grace); the 's'in-
fiamma ... *oria*fiamma ... fiamma' of 31.124–29 (is afflame ... oriflamme ...
flame);

(*f*) of *rima equivoca* or homonymic rhyme (identical spelling and/or pronunciation but alternative meaning): the 'al volto ... più volte volto' of *Inferno* 1.31–36 (face ... turned); or the 'io etterno duro ... m'è duro' of 3.7–12
(subsist ... intimidating); or the 'Verde ... verde' of *Purgatorio* 3.130–35
(Verde [the Garigliano perhaps] ... green); or the 'si parte ... la calda parte'
of 4.76–84 (as far distant ... torrid regions); or the 'spirto ... vocale spirto'
of 11.82–90 (soul ... spirit of song); or the 'voto ... voto' of *Paradiso* 3.25–30
(vacancy ... vow); or the 'Vinci ... vinci' of 14.124–29 (Conquer ... chain);
and

(*g*) of identical rhyme, as in the case of 'Cristo ... Cristo' (*Paradiso* 12.70–
73, 14.103–8, 19.100–108, 32.82–87), but also the 'ammenda ... ammenda'
(made good ... made good) of *Purgatorio* 20.65–69 and the 'vidi ... vidi ...
vidi' of *Paradiso* 30.91–99 (I saw ... I saw ... I saw).

If, then, this indeed is virtuosity at the far limit thereof it is even so a matter
here of saying under the aspect of seriousness, of rhyme too as called upon for
the purposes less now of embellishment than of elucidation, as, after its manner,
pointing up the leading idea.

And so at last we come to rhetoric as similarly authorized from out of the
depths. Prominent, then, among the 'easier' figures deployed by Dante in the
Commedia are the *anaphora* of, say, *Inferno* 30.136–37 ('Qual è colui che suo dannaggio *sogna*, / che *sognando* desidera *sognare*') or of *Purgatorio* 30.49–51 ('Ma
Virgilio n'avea lasciati scemi / di sé, *Virgilio* dolcissimo padre, / *Virgilio* a cui per

mia salute die'mi' with just a little later in the same canto the 'Dante, perché Virgilio se ne vada, / non *pianger* anco, non *piangere* ancora; / ché *pianger* ti conven per altra spada' of lines 55–57);[190] the *epanaphora* of *Inferno* 3.1–3 ('*Per me si va* ne la città dolente, / *per me si va* ne l'etterno dolore, / *per me si va* tra la perduta gente'), or of *Inferno* 5.100–108 ('*Amor*, ch'al cor gentil ratto s'apprende . . . *Amor*, ch'a nullo amato amar perdona . . . *Amor* condusse noi ad una morte'), or of *Purgatorio* 12.25–36 ('*Vedea* colui che fu nobil creato . . . *Vedëa* Brïareo fitto dal telo . . . *Vedea* Timbreo, *vedea* Pallade e Marte . . . *Vedea* Nembròt a piè del gran lavoro'), or of *Paradiso* 16.22–27 ('*Ditemi* dunque, cara mia primizia . . . *ditemi* dell'ovil di San Giovanni');[191] the *exclamatio* of *Inferno* 2.133 ('Oh pietosa colei che mi soccorse!'), or of *Purgatorio* 1.26–27 ('oh settentrïonal vedovo sito, / poi che privato se' di mirar quelle!'), or of *Paradiso* 33.82–84 ('Oh abbondante grazia ond' io presunsi / ficcar lo viso per la luce etterna, / tanto che la veduta vi consunsi!');[192] the *polysyndeton* of *Inferno* 1.5 ('esta selva selvaggia e aspra e forte'), or of 30.103–5 ('Bestemmiavano Dio *e* lor parenti, / l'umana spezie *e* 'l loco *e* 'l tempo *e* 'l seme / di lor semenza *e* di lor nascimenti'), or of *Purgatorio* 2.115–17 ('Lo mio maestro *e* io *e* quella gente / ch'eran con lui parevan sì contenti, / come a nessun toccasse altro la mente');[193] and the *asyndeton* of *Inferno* 3.25–27 ('Diverse lingue, orribili favelle, parole di dolore, accenti d'ira, / voci alte e fioche, e suon di man con elle') or of 5.35 ('quivi le strida, il compianto, il lamento')[194]—at which point the figure

---

190 'Like one who dreams of injury suffered, and who dreaming, wishes it were indeed a dream'; for *Purgatorio* 30.49–51: 'But Virgil had left us bereft of himself, Virgil sweetest father, Virgil to whom I entrusted my salvation', and for 30.55–57: 'Dante, because Virgil has departed weep not, weep not yet, for it behoves you weep for another sword.' Ernst Robert Curtius, 'Periphrase, Annominatio, Anaphora', in *Gesammelte Aufsätze zur romanischen Philologie* (Bern: Francke, 1960), 305–45; Francesco Tateo, ad voc. 'Anafora', *ED*, vol. 1 (Rome: Istituto dell'Enciclopedia Italiana, 1970–78), 243–46; Nicola Longo, 'L'arte della ripetizione nella *Divina Commedia*', *Atti e Memorie dell'Arcadia* 2 (2013), 23–38.

191 'Through me the way into the sorrowing city, through me the way to eternal suffering, through me the way among the lost'; for *Inferno* 5.100–107: 'Love quick to seize the noble heart . . . Love which absolves none beloved from loving . . . Love brought us to but one death'; for *Purgatorio* 12.25–36: 'I saw the one nobly created . . . I saw Briareus pierced by the heavenly shaft . . . I saw Thymbraeus, I saw Pallas and Mars . . . I saw Nimrod at the foot of his mighty work'; and for *Paradiso* 16.22–27: 'Tell me, then, dear stock of mine . . . tell me of the sheepfold of St John.' Lorenzo Renzi, 'L'anafora più famosa della letteratura mondiale', in *Le conseguenze di un bacio: L'episodio di Francesca nella 'Commedia'* (Bologna: Il Mulino, 2007), 53–84.

192 'Oh merciful she who came to my aid'; for *Purgatorio* 1.26–27: 'Oh widowed northern site, bereft as you are of gazing upon those!'; and for the *Paradiso* 33 passage: 'Oh grace abounding whereby I presumed to gaze upon the eternal light, so much so that my sight upon it was spent!' Mario Medici, ad voc. 'Interiezioni-esclamazioni', *ED*, vol. 6 (*Appendice*) (Rome: Istituto della Enciclopedia Italiana, 1970–78), 356–68.

193 'This wild wood, savage and dense'. For *Inferno* 30.103–105: 'They cursed God, their parents, the human race, the place and the time and the seed of their begetting and of their birth', and for *Purgatorio* 2.115–17: 'My master and the folk foregathered with him seemed content as though nothing else impinged upon their mind.' For this and for asyndeton in Dante, Mario Medici, ad voc. 'Asindeto e polisindeto', *ED*, vol. 6 (*Appendice*) (Rome: Istituto della Enciclopedia Italiana, 1970–78), 444–47.

194 'Strange tongues, fearsome language, words of pain, accents of anger, voices loud and hoarse and, with them, slapping of hands'.

of thought is on hand not merely, indeed not at all, to impress the reader but to confirm him or her in something close to a sense of insiderness when it comes to seeing, understanding and making sense of it all. And what applies to the various species of easy ornamentation in the *Commedia* applies also to the more difficult species of ornamentation represented by synecdoche, metonymy, simile and metaphor, each of these things serving once again to privilege the *writerliness* of the text over its *readerliness*, the co-involvement of the reader as party to the generation of meaning. As far, then, as synecdoche is concerned we have the 'Poi si rivolse a quella 'nfiata *labbia*' of *Inferno* 7.7 or the '*faccia tua*, ch'io lagrimai già morta' of *Purgatorio* 23.55 or the 'alta vittoria / che s'acquistò con *l'una e l'altra palma*' of *Paradiso* 9.122–23;[195] while as far as metonymy is concerned we have the 'tanto ch'i' ne perde' *li sonni e ' polsi*' of *Inferno* 13.63 or the 'ed è giunta la *spada / col pasturale*' of *Purgatorio* 16.109–10 or the 'di sùbito parve *giorno a giorno* / essere aggiunto' of *Paradiso* 1.61–62, the part or the property, as is the way with synecdoche and metonymy, duly standing in for the whole.[196]

But it is with simile and metaphor that *exornatio* and all that this implies—or at any rate *had* implied—by way of mere embellishment gives way to something more fundamental as a way of pursuing the poetic enterprise, namely the status of the image, not so much now as following on from the plain sense of the text, as constituting the *prius* thereof, the first port of call in respect of a significant act of understanding. True, simile, relying as it does on a 'così come ...' or a 'just as ...' as its linguistic means, constitutes the junior partner here, but, for all that, it figures both prominently and powerfully in the text as a means of confirming the reader in a sense of the familiarity of it all, of being there on the spot; so, for example, in respect of the stand-alone simile or *similitudo per brevitatem* we have the 'caddi come corpo morto cade' of *Inferno* 5.142 or the 'si dileguò come da corda cocca' of *Inferno* 17.136, while in respect of the extended simile or *similitudo per collationem there is* the 'come quei che con lena affannata' moment of *Inferno* 1:

> E come quei che con lena affannata,
> uscito fuor del pelago a la riva,
> si volge a l'acqua perigliosa e guata,

195 'Then he turned to that bloated lip'; for *Purgatorio* 23: 'this your face for which I wept in its dying' and for *Paradiso* 9: 'the victory of victories secured with the one palm and the other'.

196 'Such that I lost sleep and steady pulse'; for *Purgatorio* 16: 'and thus are conjoined the sword and the crook' and for *Paradiso* 1: 'it seemed as though, suddenly, day was added to day'. Holly Wallace Boucher, 'Metonymy in Typology and Allegory with a Consideration of Dante's *Comedy*', in *Allegory, Myth and Symbol*, ed. Morton W. Bloomfield (Cambridge, MA: Harvard University Press, 1981), 129–45; Harry Berger, Jr, 'Metaphor and Metonymy in the Middle Ages: Aquinas and Dante', in *Figures of a Changing World: Metaphor and the Emergence of Modern Culture* (Fordham: Fordham University Press, 2015), 82–93.

così l'animo mio, ch'ancor fuggiva,
si volse a retro a rimirar lo passo
che non lasciò già mai persona viva.

(*Inferno* 1.22–27)[197]

But it is with metaphor as paramount among the figures of speech that Dante's triumph as a rhetorician, indeed as architect and spokesman-in-chief for a now revised art of predication, moves centre stage, for it is at this point that the image as distinct from the idea again commends itself as the *prius* or antecedent condition of moral, intellectual and psychological awareness. Here too, then, it is a question both of the abbreviated and of the extended instance, of *translatio per brevitatem* and *per collationem*; so, for example, in respect of the first of these things, of metaphor 'in brief', we have the 'Allor fu la paura un poco queta / che nel *lago* del cor m'era durata / la notte ch'i' passai con tanta pieta' of *Inferno* 1.19– 21,[198] or the 'bel pianeto che d'amar conforta / *faceva tutto rider* l'orïente' of *Pur-*

197   'And like one who, with labouring breath, has escaped from the deep to the shore and, looking back over the perilous waters, gazes thereupon, so my mind, still in flight, turned back to contemplate again the strait never yet allowing anyone to pass alive.' For the *Inferno* 5 passage: 'and I fell as a dead body falls' and for the *Inferno* 17 passage: '[Geryon] vanished like an arrow from a string.' Luigi Venturi, *Le similitudini dantesche, ordinate, illustrate e confrontate* (Florence: Sansoni, 1874) with an anastatic edition (Rome: Salerno, 2008); James Applewhite, 'Dante's Use of Extended Simile in the *Inferno*', *Italica* 41.3 (1954), 294–309; Steno Vazzana, 'Le similitudini nella *Divina Commedia*', *Ausonia* 13 (1958), 3–10; Clive Staples Lewis, 'Dante's Similes', in *Studies in Medieval and Renaissance Literature*, ed. Walter Hopper (Cambridge: Cambridge University Press, 1966), 64–77; Oreste Allavena, *Stile e poesia nelle similitudini della 'Divina Commedia'* (Savona: Priamar, 1970); Richard H. Lansing, *From Image to Idea: A Study of the Simile in Dante's 'Commedia'* (Ravenna: Longo, 1977); Madison U. Sowell, 'A Bibliography of the Dantean Simile to 1981', *DS* 101 (1983), 167–80; Juan Varela-Portas de Orduña, 'La lógica productiva del símil dantesco', in *Introdución a la semántica de la 'Divina Commedia'* (Alpedrete, Madrid: Ediciones de La Discreta, 2002), 159–210. For a prehistory, Wilhelm Theodor Elwert, 'La dittologia sinonimica nella poesia lirica delle origini e nella scuola poetica siciliana', *Bollettino del Centro di studi filologici e linguistici* 2 (1954), 152–77.
198   'Then the fear persisting in the *lake* of my heart during the night I had passed so piteously was quieted a little'; for the *Purgatorio* 1 passage: 'The fair planet urging love upon us made *laugh* the eastern sky', and for the *Paradiso* 1 passage: 'The unwonted sound and the great light *kindled* in me a desire never so strongly felt to know their cause.' Friedrich Beck, *Die Metapher bei Dante, ihr System, ihre Quellen* (Neuburg: Griessmayer, 1895–86); Herbert Douglas Austin, *Di alcune metafore controverse nell'opera di Dante* (Florence: Olschki, 1932); Herbert Douglas Austin, 'Multiple Meanings and Their Bearing on the Understanding of Dante's Metaphors', *MP* 30 (1932), 129–40; Irma Brandeis, 'Metaphor in the *Divine Comedy*', *Hudson Review* 8.4 (1956), 557–85; Rudolf Palgen, 'Due particolarità dello stile epico di Dante: La nomenclatura pseudoclassica e le metafore allusive', *Conv* 31 (1963), 10–18; Fiorenzo Forti, 'La transumptio nei Dettatori bolognesi e in Dante', in *Dante e Bologna nei tempi di Dante* (Bologna: Commissione per i testi di lingua, 1967), 127–49 (and in his *"Magnanimitade": Studi su un tema dantesca* [Rome: Carocci, 2006 (1977)]), 103–35; Ezio Raimondi, *Metafora e storia: Studi su Dante e Petrarca* (Turin: Einaudi, 1970); Ezio Raimondi, 'Ontologia della metafora dantesca', *LC* 15 (1986), 99–109; Francesco Tateo, ad voc. 'metafora', *ED*, vol. 3 (Rome: Istituto della Enciclopedia Italiana, 1970–78), 926–32; Giuseppe Ledda, '"Tópoi" dell'indicibilità e metaforismi nella *Commedia*', *SC* 12.1 (1997), 117–40; Emilio Pasquini, 'Il dominio metaforico', in

gatorio 1.19–20, or the 'novità del suono e 'l grande lume / di lor cagion *m'accesero* un disio / mai non sentito di cotanto acume' of *Paradiso* 1.82–84; while in respect of the latter, of metaphor in its more ample form, we have this passage from *Paradiso* 4 with its celebration of Beatrice's generosity as a guide and comforter by way of the now accumulated terminology of fountains and floods, of a rippling forth of wisdom apt in one and the same moment to satisfy every desire and to call forth an expression of gratitude:

> Cotal fu l'*ondeggiar* del santo *rio*
> ch'*uscì del fonte* ond' ogne ver deriva;
> tal puose in pace uno e altro disio.
>   'O amanza del primo amante, o diva',
> diss' io appresso, 'il cui parlar m'*inonda*
> e scalda sì, che più e più m'avviva,
>   non è l'affezion mia tanto profonda,
> che basti a render voi grazia per grazia;
> ma quei che vede e puote a ciò risponda'.

(*Paradiso* 4.115–23)[199]

or this passage from Paradiso 23 with its celebration of the heavenly host in general and of Mary in particular by way of the flowers of King Jesus's garden:

> 'Perché la faccia mia sì t'innamora,
> che tu non ti rivolgi al bel *giardino*
> che sotto i raggi di Cristo *s'infiora*?
>   Quivi è la *rosa* in che 'l verbo divino
> carne si fece; quivi son li *gigli*
> al cui *odor* si prese il buon cammino'.

Dante e le figure del vero: La fabbrica della 'Commedia' (Milan: Mondadori, 2001); David Gibbons, *Metaphor in Dante* (Oxford: Legenda, 2002); Marco Ariani (ed.), *La metafora in Dante* (Florence: Olschki, 2009); Silvia Finazzi, 'La metafora nella tradizione antica fino a Dante', in *La metafora nella tradizione testuale ed esegetica della 'Commedia' di Dante* (Florence: Cesati, 2013), 31–94; Gaia Tomazzoli, 'La metafora in Dante: Temi e tendenze della critica', *L'Alighieri* (RD) 46.2 (2015), 41–60. More generally, Janet Martin Soskice, *Metaphor and Religious Language* (Oxford: Clarendon Press, 1985); William Purcell, '*Transumptio*: A Rhetorical Doctrine of the Thirteenth Century', *Rhetorica* 5.4 (1987), 371–410; Umberto Eco (ed.), *La metafora nel Medioevo* (Milan: CUEM, 2004); Elisa Brilli, 'La metafora nel Medioevo: Stato dell'arte e qualche domanda', *BIRCSLFL* 7.2 (2010), 195–213.

199 'Such was the rippling of the holy stream coming forth from the fount whence springs every truth that it set at rest both the one and the other desire. "O beloved of the first lover, o divine one", said I then, "whose speech floods and warms me such that I am ever more and more quickened, not all of depth of my affection is such as to render you grace for grace, but may he who sees all, and is able, make recompense."'

Così Beatrice; e io, che a' suoi consigli
tutto era pronto, ancora mi rendei
a la battaglia de' debili cigli.

(*Paradiso* 23.70–78)[200]

Here too, then, in relation to metaphor as but a matter of transference in the name and for the sake of a 'vivid mental picture', we have a perfect blend of competence and courage, a further instance of sheer technical assurance.[201] With this, then, we come for the final time to the leading idea hereabouts, to what in Dante amounts to a sense of the image in all its forms as a matter not now of subsequent deliberation but of analytical inevitability, as uniquely adequate to the *what* and to the *how* it is with the individual in the otherwise hidden recesses of self and, beyond this, to the shared intentionality or *in-youing* and *in-meing* of writer and reader as co-involved one with the other at the point of ultimate concern; so, for example, the very first lines of the poem where the entire burden of Dante's discourse hereabouts—namely the psychopathology of being in its alienation, in its captivity to the structures of destruction operative from out of the depths—is without ado entrusted to the image as, again, uniquely adequate to the matter in hand:

Nel mezzo del cammin di nostra vita
mi ritrovai per una selva oscura,
ché la diritta via era smarrita.
Ahi quanto a dir qual era è cosa dura
esta selva selvaggia e aspra e forte
che nel pensier rinova la paura!

(*Inferno* 1.1–12)[202]

200 ' "Why by my face are you so enamoured that you turn not to the fair garden flowering beneath the rays of the Christ? Behold the rose in which the divine word became flesh and there the lilies by whose fragrance the right path was chosen." Thus Beatrice, and I, ever eager for her counsel, delivered myself afresh to the battle of my feeble eyelids.'

201 [Cicero], *Ad Herennium* 4.34: 'Translatio est cum verbum in quandam rem transferetur ex alia re, quod propter similitudinem recte videbitur posse transferri. Ea sumitur rei ante oculos pondendae causa' (Metaphor occurs when a word applying to one thing is transferred to another, the similarity seeming to justify this transference. Metaphor is used for the sake of creating a vivid mental picture).

202 'Midway in the journey of our life I found myself in a dark wood, for the straight way was lost. Try as I may, there is no telling how it was with that wood, so wild, rugged and harsh was it that even to think of it terrifies me afresh!' On metaphor as a principle of intellection, Eva Feder Kittay, *Metaphor: Its Cognitive Force and Linguistic Structure* (Oxford: Oxford University Press, 1987); Andrew Ortony (ed.), *Metaphor and Thought*, 2nd ed. (Cambridge: Cambridge University Press, 1993); Zdravko Radman (ed.), *From a Metaphorical Point of View: A Multidisciplinary Approach to the Cognitive Content of*

And what applies on the threshold of the *Inferno* applies too on the threshold both of the *Purgatorio* and of the *Paradiso* as each in its way an essay in the resolution of self in the hitherto inveterate difficulty of self. On the one hand, then, we have the *Purgatorio* with its proposal of a now sustained meditation upon the notion of emancipation, of self as freed for the kind of transhumanity as but humanity itself in act, by way of the image—of an at once soaring and smiling skyscape—as its point of departure:

Dolce color d'orïental zaffiro,
che s'accoglieva nel sereno aspetto
del mezzo, puro infino al primo giro,
 a li occhi miei ricominciò diletto,
tosto ch'io usci' fuor de l'aura morta
che m'avea contristati li occhi e 'l petto.
 Lo bel pianeto che d'amar conforta
faceva tutto rider l'orïente,
velando i Pesci ch'erano in sua scorta.
 I' mi volsi a man destra, e puosi mente
a l'altro polo, e vidi quattro stelle
non viste mai fuor ch'a la prima gente.
 Goder pareva 'l ciel di lor fiammelle:
oh settentrïonal vedovo sito,
poi che privato se' di mirar quelle!

(*Purgatorio* 1.13–27)[203]

while on the other we have the *Paradiso* with its again preliminary statement of the matter to hand—namely the now ecstatic ascent of the spirit—by way of the light-exponentiality of it all, of day added to day and sun added to sun:

Metaphor (Berlin: W. de Gruyter, 1995); and with reference to Dante and the Middle Ages in particular, Alessandro Catellari, 'La metafora come strumento di conoscenza', in *Come si legge un testo: Da Dante a Montale* (1989), 27–76; Umberto Eco, 'Metafora e conoscenza nel Medioevo', in *Scritti sul pensiero medievale* (Milan: Bompiani, 2012), 824–934. On form generally as a principle of intellection in the *Convivio*, Massimo Donà, *Dante: 'Convivio'. Sulla fondazione dantesca dell'arte come forma eminente di intellezione del vero; Itinerario filosofico* (Paese, Treviso: Pegasus, 1992).

203 'The sweet hue of oriental sapphire gathering in the serene face of the heavens as far as the farthest horizon began again to gladden my sight as I came forth from the dark air weighing so heavily upon my eyes and upon my heart. The fair planet comforting us in our loves lit up with laughter the eastern sky veiling as it did so the fishes in her wake, and I, turning to my right and settling my mind upon the other pole, saw there four stars never glimpsed but by the first people. The whole sky, it seemed, rejoiced with them in their kindling. O widowed heavens of the north, bereft as you are of gazing upon them!'

> Io nol soffersi molto, né sì poco,
> ch'io nol vedessi sfavillar dintorno,
> com' ferro che bogliente esce del foco;
>   e di sùbito parve giorno a giorno
> essere aggiunto, come quei che puote
> avesse il ciel d'un altro sole addorno.
>   Beatrice tutta ne l'etterne rote
> fissa con li occhi stava; e io in lei
> le luci fissi, di là sù rimote.

(Paradiso 1.58–66)[204]

And so it goes on, the image at every stage serving the interests of the idea but again at every stage finessing it in point of power and precision. Again, then, as far as the *Inferno* is concerned we have the starling-borne-on-the-wings-of-the-wind imagery of canto 5 as confirming without ado a sense of the free-floatingness of it all under the aspect of *lussuria*:

> E come li stornei ne portan l'ali
> nel freddo tempo, a schiera larga e piena,
> così quel fiato li spiriti mali
>   di qua, di là, di giù, di sù li mena;
> nulla speranza li conforta mai,
> non che di posa, ma di minor pena.

(Inferno 5.40–45)[205]

or the wild wood of the suicides in canto 13 as likewise confirming the notion of oppression, paranoia and despair as between them a boundary condition of the spirit:

> Non era ancor di là Nesso arrivato,
> quando noi ci mettemmo per un bosco
> che da neun sentiero era segnato.

---

204 'I had not borne it long, nor yet so briefly as not to see it sparkling like iron that comes boiling from the fire; and suddenly it seemed that day was added to day, as if he that is able had decked the sky with a second sun. Beatrice stood with her eyes fixed only on the eternal wheels, and upon her I fixed my own, withdrawn from above.'

205 'And as in the winter chill starlings on the wing are borne on in their ample and teeming flock, so by that same gust the spirits thus guilty are borne this way and that, up and down, they—never mind of respite but even of lesser pain—having no hope to comfort them.'

Non fronda verde, ma di color fosco;
non rami schietti, ma nodosi e 'nvolti;
non pomi v'eran, ma stecchi con tòsco.

(*Inferno* 13.1–6)[206]

while as far as the *Purgatorio* is concerned we have the imagery of asphyxiation
as confirming at a stroke both the *what it is* and the *how it is*, both the *quid est* and
the *qualis est*, of anger as, albeit in the now penitent spirit, a dominant mood of
being:

Buio d'inferno e di notte privata
d'ogne pianeto, sotto pover cielo,
quant' esser può di nuvol tenebrata,
non fece al viso mio sì grosso velo
come quel fummo ch'ivi ci coperse,
né a sentir di così aspro pelo,
che l'occhio stare aperto non sofferse.

(*Purgatorio* 16.1–6)[207]

and as far as the *Paradiso* is concerned we have the imagery of the dance and of
the song, the sublime choreography of the one and the sweet chorality of the
other as confirming without ado—and in a manner transcending absolutely the
power of the proposition as a means of ontic awareness—the substance of properly human being at the point of emergence:

Sì tosto come l'ultima parola
la benedetta fiamma per dir tolse,
a rotar cominciò la santa mola;
e nel suo giro tutta non si volse
prima ch'un'altra di cerchio la chiuse,
e moto a moto e canto a canto colse.

(*Paradiso* 12.1–6)[208]

206 'Not yet has Nessus reached the other side when we set off through a wood unmarked by any
path. No green leaves, but of dusky hue; no smooth boughs, but knotted and warped; no fruit there,
just poisonous prickles.'
207 'Hellish gloom or night bereft of every planet under a barren sky as overcast as may be by cloud
never veiled my sight with matter so heavy or so harsh to the senses as the smoke there smothering us
and suffering us not even to open our eyes.'
208 'As soon as the blessed flame sounded thus the final word, so began to turn the holy millstone,

This, then, is what it means to speak in Dante and with Dante of a revised art of predication, of a final bringing home of rhetoric in general and of the metaphor in particular to the theological enterprise in the height and depth thereof. For though a Thomas Aquinas had been prepared to countenance and, in countenancing, to honour the metaphor as a means of expressing the inexpressible,[209] with Dante we have, in truth, something other and indeed something more than this, namely a privileging of the image as the way of ontic intelligence, of knowing self in the deep substance of self. In short, no image, no intelligence. Simply a lingering on the plane of reason, ratiocination and high-cultural consciousness.

---

and so before it ever it made a full circle it was enclosed by another matching motion for motion and song for song.'

209 *Summa theologiae* 1a.1.9, ad primum: 'poeta utitur metaphoris propter repraesentationem, repraesentatio enim naturaliter homini delectabilis est. Sed sacra doctrina utitur metaphoris propter necessitatem et utilitatem, ut dictum est' (Poetry makes use of metaphor for the sake of representation, for representation is naturally a source of pleasure for man. But sacred doctrine makes use of metaphors as both necessary and useful). Ralph M. McInerny, 'Metaphor and Analogy', in *Inquiries into Medieval Philosophy: A Collection in Honor of Francis P. Clarke*, ed. James F. Ross (Westport, CT: Greenwood, 1971), 75–96; Cornelius Ernst, O.P., 'Metaphor and Ontology in "Sacra Doctrina"', *The Thomist* 38 (1974), 403–25; Edmund Ryden, 'Aquinas on the Metaphorical Expression of Theological Truth', *Heythrop Journal* 27 (1986), 409–19; A. J. Doherty, 'Aquinas on Scriptural Metaphor and Allegory', *Proceedings of the American Catholic Philosophical Association* 76 (2002), 183–92.

CHAPTER 2

The *Monarchia* and the Political Letters

The political moment of Dante's thought is open to contemplation by way both of its systematic and of its pragmatic aspect, both of his meditation on the deep reasons of imperial government and his engagement with the practicalities of it all. On the systematic side the key text is the *Monarchia* dating ideally from the middle part of the second decade of the fourteenth century and offering an account (a) of the empire as the ideal form of human government, (b) of Rome, now as then, as called from beforehand to world domination, and (c) of the proper relationship between papal and imperial jurisdiction, between what is due to Peter and what is due to Caesar as each alike a holder of divine office.[1] On the practical side, by contrast, there are the four great addresses to the princes and peoples of Italy, to the 'wretched Florentines within', to the emperor Henry VII and to the cardinals in conclave following the death of Clement V in April 1314, the first three urging upon their recipients a fresh implementation of the imperial idea and the fourth lamenting the Babylonish captivity of the church in Avignon. But that is not all, for to the *Monarchia* as again the most complete statement of Dante's political thought and to the letters as the product of the moment we must add the many references in the *Commedia*—references running at times to entire episodes—turning upon the indifference, the perversity and the downright apostasy of priestly and princely power in the world, the political in this sense shading off into the prophetic in point of substance and spirit; so, for example, from the *Inferno*—Dante is addressing Pope Nicholas III as topsy-

---

1 For the chronology of the *Monarchia*, Gustavo Vinay, 'La cronologia del trattato', in *Dante Alighieri. Monarchia: Testo, introduzione, traduzione e commento*, ed. Gustavo Vinay (Florence: Sansoni, 1950), xxix–xxxviii; Pier Giorgio Ricci, 'L'ultima fase del pensiero politico di Dante e Cangrande vicario imperiale', in *Dante e la cultura veneta. Atti del Convegno di Studi 30 marzo–5 aprile 1967* (Florence: Olschki, 1966), 367–71; Emilia Mongiello, 'Sulla datazione del *Monarchia* di Dante', *Le Parole e le idee* 11 (1969), 290–324; Enrico Fenzi, 'È la *Monarchia* l'ultima opera di Dante? (A proposito di una recente edizione)', *SD* 72 (2007), 215–38 (in relation to which, Carlo Dolcini, 'Per la cronologia del trattato dantesco: Risposta a Enrico Fenzi', *PPM* 5 [2007], 145–50); Enrico Fenzi, 'Ancora sulla data della *Monarchia*', in *'Per beneficio e concordia di studio': Studi danteschi offerti a Enrico Malato per i suoi ottant'anni (2015)*, ed. Andrea Mazzucchi (Cittadella: Bertoncello Artigrafiche, 2015), 377–410; Ovidio Capitani, 'La questione della datazione della *Monarchia*', *SM* 51.2 (2010), 921–53.

turvy in a fissure of rock among the simonists or traders in ecclesiastical office—
we have these lines on the venality of it all:

> Io non so s'i' mi fui qui troppo folle,
> ch'i' pur rispuosi lui a questo metro:
> 'Deh, or mi dì: quanto tesoro volle
>
> Nostro Segnore in prima da san Pietro
> ch'ei ponesse le chiavi in sua balìa?
> Certo non chiese se non "Viemmi retro".
>
> Né Pier né li altri tolsero a Matia
> oro od argento, quando fu sortito
> al loco che perdé l'anima ria.
>
> Però ti sta, ché tu se' ben punito;
> e guarda ben la mal tolta moneta
> ch'esser ti fece contra Carlo ardito.
>
> E se non fosse ch'ancor lo mi vieta
> la reverenza de le somme chiavi
> che tu tenesti ne la vita lieta,
>
> io userei parole ancor più gravi;
> ché la vostra avarizia il mondo attrista,
> calcando i buoni e sollevando i pravi.
>
> . . .
>
> Fatto v'avete dio d'oro e d'argento;
> e che altro è da voi a l'idolatre,
> se non ch'elli uno, e voi ne orate cento?'

(*Inferno* 19.88–105 and 112–14)[2]

while from the *Purgatorio*, where in a truly apocalyptic moment of the text, the
pilgrim poet is witness to the cavorting of the princely and the priestly aboard the
chariot of the Church, we have these lines on the depravity of it all:

> Sicura, quasi rocca in alto monte,
> seder sovresso una puttana sciolta

---

2 'I do not know if here I was too bold in answering him in this strain: "Pray now tell me how much
treasure did our Lord require of Saint Peter before he put the keys into his keeping? Surely he asked
nothing save 'Follow me.' Nor did Peter or the others take gold or silver of Matthias when he was chosen
for the office which the guilty soul had lost. Therefore stay right here, for you are justly punished, and
guard well the ill-gotten gains that made you bold against Charles. And were it not for that reverence
for the supreme keys which you held in the joyful life above forbids me still, I would use yet harder
words, for your avarice afflicts the world, trampling down the good and exalting the bad . . . You have
made you a god of gold and silver, and wherein do you differ from the idolaters, save that they worship
one, and you a hundred?"'

m'apparve con le ciglia intorno pronte;
e come perché non li fosse tolta,
vidi di costa a lei dritto un gigante;
e basciavansi insieme alcuna volta.
Ma perché l'occhio cupido e vagante
a me rivolse, quel feroce drudo
la flagellò dal capo infin le piante;
poi, di sospetto pieno e d'ira crudo,
disciolse il mostro, e trassel per la selva,
tanto che sol di lei mi fece scudo
a la puttana e a la nova belva.

(*Purgatorio* 32.148–160)[3]

and from the *Paradiso* we have these on the usurpation of Peter's place by—for
Dante—the at once partisan and unprincipled Boniface VIII and thus on the
stench of it all:

La provedenza, che quivi comparte
vice e officio, nel beato coro
silenzio posto avea da ogne parte,
quand' ïo udi': 'Se io mi trascoloro,
non ti maravigliar, ché, dicend' io,
vedrai trascolorar tutti costoro.
Quelli ch'usurpa in terra il luogo mio,
il luogo mio, il luogo mio, che vaca
ne la presenza del Figliuol di Dio,

---

3 'Secure, like a fortress on a high mountain, there appeared to me an ungirt harlot sitting upon it,
with eyes quick to rove around; and, as if in order that she should not be taken from him, I saw standing
at her side a giant, and they kissed each other again and again. But because she turned on me her wanton
and wandering eye, that savage lover beat her from head to foot. Then, full of jealousy and fierce with
rage, he loosed the monster and dragged it through the wood so far that of that alone he fashioned a
screen to hide me from the harlot and from the strange beast.' Lino Pertile, *La puttana e il gigante: Dal
Cantico dei Cantici al Paradiso Terrestre di Dante* (Ravenna: Longo, 1998; especially chapter 9, 'La
puttana e il gigante', 202–25); also, in a revised form, in *Scrolls of Love: Ruth and the Song of Songs*, ed.
Peter Hawkins and Lesleigh Cushing Stahlberg (New York: Fordham University Press, 2006), 268–80
with the title 'The Harlot and the Giant: Dante and the *Song of Songs*'); Filippo Bognini, 'Gli occhi di
Ooliba: Una proposta per *Purgatorio* XXXII 148–60 and XXXIII 44–45', *RSD* 7.1 (2007), 73–103; An-
tonio Alessandro Bisceglia, 'Due nuove proposte esegetiche per *Purgatorio* XXXII', *SPCT* 77 (2008),
115–24. More generally on the apocalyptic moment of the *Purgatorio*, Robert Kaske, 'Dante's *Purgatorio*
XXXII and XXXIII: A Survey of Christian History', *University of Toronto Quarterly* 43 (1974), 193–214;
Nino Borsellino, 'Visione e profezia nel canto XXXII del *Purgatorio*', *FC* 12.1 (1987), 3–16; Peter Armour,
*Dante's Griffin and the History of the World: A Study of the Earthly Paradise ('Purgatorio', cantos xxix-
xxxiii)* (Oxford: Clarendon Press, 1989); Robert Wilson, *Prophecies and Prophecy in Dante's 'Commedia'*
(Florence: Olschki, 2008).

>fatt' ha del cimitero mio cloaca
>del sangue e de la puzza; onde 'l perverso
>che cadde di qua sù, là giù si placa'.

>(*Paradiso* 27.16–27)[4]

But neither is that all, for to the aforementioned letters to the princes and
peoples of Italy, to the 'wretched Florentines within', to the emperor Henry VII
and to the cardinals in conclave following the death of Clement V in April 1314
we need to add a number of satellite texts, slighter, to be sure, than the four great
set pieces but registering no less eloquently Dante's state of mind as regards Florence in particular and the imperial enterprise in general. First, then, there is the
letter of 1304 addressed possibly from Arezzo to Cardinal Niccolò da Prato, a letter
elegant in its plea for healing—and perhaps somewhere beneath the surface for
homecoming—in consequence of the good cardinal's appointment by Pope Benedict as 'pacifier' or peacemaker in Florence.[5] And then, dating probably from
just a little later than the Niccolò da Prato letter there is the putatively Dantean
letter to the Counts Oberto and Guido da Romena consoling them on the death
of their uncle Alessandro da Romena but eloquent above all in respect of the
agony of exile, of Dante's living on, as he himself puts it, in *durance vile*: 'Hec

4 'The providence which here determines proper order and office had in every part imposed silence upon the blessed choir, when I heard: "Marvel not should I change colour, for while I speak you
will see all alike do likewise. He who usurps on earth my place, my place, my place, which in the sight
of the Son of God is vacant, has made of my tomb a sewer of blood and stench such that the perverse
one who fell from this place has naught to do but rejoice."' Adriano Comollo, 'Il topos della corruzione
della Chiesa nella *Commedia* e negli autori cattolici del tempo', in *Il dissenso religioso in Dante* (Florence:
Olschki, 1990), 79–104; Riccardo Scrivano, 'Agostinismo e profetismo in *Paradiso* XXVII', *Italianistica*
32.3 (2003), 357–65; Nancy Enright, 'Dante and the Scandal of a Beloved Church', *Logos* 7.4 (2004),
17–36; Bortolo Martinelli, 'Tra San Pietro e Beatrice: La missione di Dante (*Paradiso* XXVII)', in *Dante:
L'altro viaggio* (Pisa: Giardini, 2007), 321–41; Giuseppe Frasso, 'Canto XXVII: Invettiva e profezia', in
Lectura Dantis Romana: Cento canti per cento anni, III, Paradiso, vol. 2, ed. Enrico Malato and Andrea
Mazzucchi (Rome: Salerno, 2015), 787–811; Massimo Seriacopi, 'Il canto XXVII del *Paradiso*: La condanna della corruzione e la necessità di una "via alternativa"', *SD* 80 (2015), 49–77.
5 *Epistole* 1.2: 'Nam quam, fere pre desiderio sompniantes, inhiabamus patrie sanitatem, vestrarum
litterarum series plusquam semel sub paterna monitione polluxit. Et ad quid aliud in civile bellum
corruimus, quid aliud candida nostra signa petebant, et ad quid aliud enses et tela nostra rubebant, nisi
ut qui civilia iura temeraria voluptate truncaverant et iugo pie legis colla submitterent et ad pacem
patrie cogerentur?' (For the healing of our country, for which we have yearned, longing for it as it were
even in our dreams, in the course of your letter, under the guise of fatherly admonition, is more than
once promised us. And for what else did we plunge into civil war? What else did our white standards
seek? And for what else were our swords and our spears dyed with crimson? Save that they, who at
their own mad will and pleasure have maimed the body of civil right, should submit their necks to the
yoke of beneficent law, and should be brought by force to the observance of their country's peace!).
Vincenzo Biagi, 'Dante e il cardinale Niccolò da Prato', in *Dante e Prato* (Prato: Archivio storico pratese
[supplemento 1], 1922), 75–98; Anna Benvenuti, 'Niccolò da Prato e la legazione fiorentina del 1304',
MD 44 (2013), 75–83.

etenim, velut effera persecutrix, equis armisque vacantem iam sue captivitatis me detrusit in antrum, et nitentem cunctis exsurgere viribus, hucusque prevalens, impia retinere molitur.'[6] Nicely chancelloresque by contrast—for it is a question now of Dante's exercising his epistolary skills on behalf of his host in the Casentino—are the three letters addressed in the name of the Countess of Battifolle to Empress Margaret (consort to Henry) rejoicing in the imperial progress and continuing to wish it well, these, therefore, belonging ideally to the spring of 1311. Again, the undertaking is secretarial and the tone, at the countess's behest, suitably discreet, loyal and ingratiating; but this even so is epistolography to the point, for there is in these letters neither a sentiment nor a turn of phrase indifferent to Dante's own commitment hereabouts, less than fully expressive of his own yearning in this early phase of the imperial descent:

> Nunc ideo regni siderii iustis precibus atque piis aula pulsetur, et impetret supplicantis affectus quatenus mundi gubernator eternus condescensui tanto premia coequata retribuat, et ad auspitia Cesaris et Auguste dexteram gratie coadiutricis extendat; ut qui romani principatus imperio barbaras nationes et cives in mortalium tutamenta subegit, delirantis evi familiam sub triumphis et gloria sui Henrici reformet in melius.
>
> (*Epistole* 8.5)[7]

But for all the bearing of these 'satellite' texts on Dante's state of mind as a political thinker in the wake first of his exile in 1302 and then of the imperial descent in 1310, it is the great set pieces that as far as his correspondence goes (or at any rate such correspondence as has come down to us) dominate the landscape. First, then, and dating probably from September or October 1310—shortly, that

---

6 *Epistole* 2.3: 'Poverty, a vindictive fury, has thrust me, deprived as I am of both horse and arms, into her prison den, where relentlessly she has set herself to keep me in durance; and though I struggle with all my strength to escape, she hitherto has prevailed against me.' Gian Paolo Marchi, ' "Equis armisque vacantem": Postille interpretative a un passo dell'epistola di Dante a Oberto e Guido da Romena', *Testo* 32 (2011), 239–52.

7 'Now therefore let the court of the starry realm be assailed with just and holy prayers, and may the zeal of the suppliant obtain that the Eternal Ruler of the world may recompense so great a condescension with proportionate reward, and may stretch forth the right hand of his grace in furtherance of the hopes of Caesar and of Augusta; to the end that he, who for the safeguard of mankind brought under the Empire of the Roman Prince all peoples barbarian and civilized, may by the triumphs and glory of his servant Henry regenerate the human family of this demented age.' Paget Toynbee, 'The Battifolle Letters Attributed to Dante', *MLR* 12.3 (1917), 302–9; Fredi Chiappelli, 'Osservazioni sulle tre epistole dantesche a Margherita imperatrice', *GSLI* 140 (1963), 558–65. For the chancelloresque, Armando Petrucci, 'Modello notarile e testualità', in *Il notariato nella civiltà toscana* (Rome: Consiglio nazionale del notariato, 1985), 123–45; Armando Petrucci, *Scrivere lettere: Una storia plurimillenaria* (Rome: Laterza, 2008); Attilio Bartoli Langeli, 'Cancellierato e produzione epistolare', in *Le forme della propaganda politica nel Due e Trecento. Atti del Convegno internazionale (Trieste, 2–5 marzo 1993)* (Rome: Publications de l'École française de Rome, 1994), 251–61.

is, before Henry's coming south across the Alps and not long after Pope Clement's encyclical of 1 September that year (*Exultet in gloria*) urging all good men and true to afford him a warm welcome—comes the letter to the princes and peoples of Italy, an essay in eager anticipation; for not only is this the providential moment, the kairotic instant, the new dawn putting an end to the darkness of our tribulation, but Henry, comforter of all nations and of all men, hastens to the wedding feast, there to set free every prisoner of the ungodly, to smite the workers of iniquity and to let out the vineyard of the empire to fresh husbandmen. Dire in point of retribution, his mercy will nonetheless be upon those who fear him, Dante's discourse at this point rising to ever fresh soteriological heights, at once Psalmic, Gospel and Pauline:

> Preoccupetis faciem eius in confessione subiectionis, et in psalterio penitentie iubiletis, considerantes quia 'potestati resistens Dei ordinationi resistit'; et qui divine ordinationi repugnat, voluntati omnipotentie coequali recalcitrat; et 'durum est contra stimulum calcitrare' . . . 'Non igitur ambuletis sicut et gentes ambulant in vanitate sensus' tenebris obscurati; sed aperite oculos mentis vestre, ac videte quoniam regem nobis celi ac terre Dominus ordinavit. Hic est quem Petrus, Dei vicarius, honorificare nos monet; quem Clemens, nunc Petri successor, luce Apostolice benedictionis illuminat; ut ubi radius spiritualis non sufficit, ibi splendor minoris luminaris illustret.
>
> (*Epistole* 5.4 and 10)[8]

8 'Come before his presence with confession, submitting yourselves unto him, and sing a psalm of repentance unto him with joy, remembering that "whosoever resists the power, resists the ordinance of God"; and that whoso fights against the divine ordinance, kicks against a will which is as the will of the Almighty; and "it is hard to kick against the pricks" . . . "Walk not therefore as the Gentiles walk, in the vanity of their senses, shrouded in darkness; but open the eyes of your mind and behold how the Lord of heaven and of earth has appointed us a king." This is he whom Peter, the Vicar of God, exhorts us to honour, and whom Clement, now successor to Peter, illumines with the light of Apostolic benediction; that where the spiritual ray suffices not, there the splendour of the lesser luminary may lend its light.' Paola Rigo, 'Tempo liturgico nell'Epistola ai Principi e popoli d'Italia', *LI* 32 (1980), 222–31 (and in *Memoria classica e memoria biblica in Dante* [Florence: Olschki, 1994], 33–44); Anna Fontes Baratto, 'Linguaggio biblico e missione imperiale nell'"Epistola" V di Dante', in *Enrico VII, Dante e Pisa a 700 anni dalla morte dell'imperatore e dalla 'Monarchia' (1313–2013)*, ed. Giuseppe Petralia and Marco Santagata (Ravenna: Longo, 2016), 223–42. Generally on the political epistles, Francesco di Capua, 'Tre note sull'Epistola di Dante ai Fiorentini', *GD* 39 (1938), 241–56; Francesco Mazzoni, 'Le epistole di Dante', in *Conferenze aretine 1965* (Arezzo: Zilli, 1966), 47–100; Angelo Jacomuzzi, *Dante: Le epistole politiche* (Turin: Giappichelli, 1974); August Buck, 'Die Funktion der antiken Autoren in Dantes politischen "Epistole" und in seiner *Monarchia*', in *Tradition und Wertung: Festschrift für Franz Brunhölzl zum 65. Geburtstag, herausgegeben von G. Bernt* et al. (Thorbecke: Sigmaringen, 1989), 267–76; Raffaele Lampugnani, 'Giustizia, libertà e vaticinio: Tre tappe del pensiero di Dante nelle "Epistole" politiche', in *Riflessi e riflessioni: Italian reflections* (Adelaide: Flinders University of South Australia, 1992), 29–43; Giuseppe Di Scipio, 'St Paul in Dante's "Political Epistles"', in *The Presence of Pauline Thought in the Works of Dante* (Lewiston, NY: Edwin Mellen Press, 1995), 143–84; Elisa Brilli, 'Reminiscenze scrit-

When by contrast it comes to the letter of March the following year (1311) to the 'wretched Florentines within' (a letter born explicitly of the agony of exile, of the 'exul immeritus' or unworthily outcast) it is a question of indictment, of summoning the rebellious before the bar of conscience there to confront the senselessness, the perversity and indeed the blasphemy of it all. Coming, then, to the strategies of Florentine recalcitrance but straightaway dismissing them on the basis of public right as everywhere finessing private prescription, Dante straightaway taxes the Florentines with the kind of lunatic presumption making not for freedom but merely for slavery and for the destitution thereof as the lot of his countrymen; so, for example, these lines from the middle part of the letter, lines more than ever adamant in their sense of reason as delivered now to unreason, albeit to unreason—and herein lies the dreadful paradox of it all—as busy about liberty:

> Non equidem spes, quam frustra sine more fovetis, reluctantia ista iuvabitur, sed hac obice iusti regis adventus inflammabitur amplius, ac, indignata, misericordia semper concomitans eius exercitum avolabit; et quo false libertatis trabeam tueri existimatis, eo vere servitutis in ergastula concidetis.
>
> (*Epistole* 6.3)[9]

And it is this sense of Florence as but a den of iniquity, arrogance and outrage that prompts the letter of April of that same year to the emperor himself, a letter urging him to get as quickly as possible to the heart of the matter and to root out once and for all this viper's nest of evil intent:

> Vere matrem viperea feritate dilaniare contendit, dum contra Romam cornua rebellionis exacuit, que ad ymaginem suam atque similitudinem fecit

---

turali (e non) nelle epistole politiche dantesche', *Cultura* 45 (2007), 439–55; Elisa Brilli, 'The Interplay between Political and Prophetic Discourse: A Reflection on Dante's Authorship in Epistles V–VII', in Elisa Brilli, Laura Fenelli and Gerhard Wolf (eds.), *Images and Words in Exile: Avignon and Italy during the First Half of the 14th Century* (Florence: Galluzzo, 2015), 153–69; Claire E. Honess, *Dante Alighieri: Four Political Letters* (London: Modern Humanities Research Association, 2007); Giuseppe Ledda, 'Modelli biblici e identità profetica nelle "Epistole" di Dante', *LI* 60 (2008), 18–42; Francesca Fontanella, 'Le "Epistole"', in *L'impero e la storia di Roma in Dante* (Bologna: Il Mulino, 2016), 171–210.

9 'The hopes which you vainly cherish in your unreason will not be furthered by your rebellion, but by this resistance the just wrath of the king at his coming will be but the more inflamed against you, and mercy, which ever accompanies his army, shall fly away indignant; and where you think to defend the threshold of false liberty, there in truth shall you fall into the dungeon of slavery.' On public right as everywhere finessing private prescription, 6.2: 'An ignoratis, amentes et discoli, publica iura cum sola temporis terminatione finiri, et nullius prescriptionis calculo fore obnoxia' (Are you unaware, senseless and perverse as you are, that public right can be subject to no reckoning by prescription but must endure as long as time itself?).

illam. Vere fumos, evaporante sanie, vitiantes exhalat, et inde vicine pecudes et inscie contabescunt, dum falsis illiciendo blanditiis et figmentis aggregat sibi finitimos et infatuat aggregatos. Vere in paternos ardet ipsa concubitus, dum improba procacitate conatur summi Pontificis, qui pater est patrum, adversum te violare assensum.

(*Epistole* 7.7)[10]

But for all this, it is its sense of the properly speaking messianic substance of the imperial undertaking that confirms the status and significance of the letter as but an expression of Dante's particular brand of political piety, of—if only for the moment—his living on in the hope and expectation of delivery from on high. For too long, he says, we have sorrowed beside the waters of Babylon, Henry's reluctance to make haste constraining us to a moment of doubt ('Are you the One or should we look for another?').[11] But no, he goes on, for just to have touched Henry's feet and to have offered in his presence an expression of unfailing obedience is to know that here indeed is the Lamb of God, the one who will take away the sins of the world. 'Up, then!', Dante concludes in a moment of unutterable urgency, 'and let there be an end to all delay'. Let Caesar hearken afresh to the voice of Curio and let Henry as the new scion of Jesse make haste to put down once and for all the Goliath of Florence, bringing home as he does so those who weep still in a far-off place:

> Eia itaque, rumpe moras, proles altera Isai, sume tibi fiduciam de oculis Domini Dei Sabaoth coram quo agis, et Goliam hunc in funda sapientie tue atque in lapide virium tuarum prosterne; quoniam in eius occasu nox et umbra timoris castra Philistinorum operiet: fugient Philistei et liberabitur Israel. Tunc hereditas nostra, quam sine intermissione deflemus ablatam, nobis erit in integrum restituta; ac quemadmodum, sacrosancte Ierusalem

---

10 'Verily with the ferocity of a viper she strives to rend her mother, when she sharpens the horns of rebellion against Rome, which made her in her own image and after her own likeness. Verily she exhales pestilential fumes from the reek of corruption, whence the neighbouring flocks all unknowing waste away, when by the lure of lying blandishments and deceit she wins over to herself those on her borders, and, having won them, deprives them of their senses.' Theodore Silverstein, ' "Rex iustus et pius": Henry's Throne and Dante's Christian Prince', in *Literate Laughter: Critical Essays in Medieval Narrative*, ed. John C. Jacobs (Bern: Peter Lang, 2002), 99–114; Alex Novikoff, 'Henry VII and the Universal Empire of Engelbert of Admont and Dante Alighieri', *PPM* 3–4 (2005–6), 143–65; Federico Gagliardi, 'L'"alto Arrigo" nelle epistole dantesche del 1310–11: Modelli biblici e classici', *Cultura* 45.1 (2007), 133–42; Florence Russo, 'Henry VII and Dante's Dream of a New Golden Age', *FItal*, 44.2 (2010), 267–86; Claire E. Honess, ' "Ecce nunc tempus acceptabile": Henry VII and Dante's Ideal of Peace', *The Italianist* 33.3 (2013), 484–504.

11 *Epistole* 7.2: 'Tu es qui venturus es, an alium expectamus' (Mattthew 11:3; Luke 7:19).

memores, exules in Babilone gemiscimus, ita tunc cives et respirantes in
pace, confusionis miserias in gaudio recolemus.

(*Epistole* 7.8)[12]

And this too—deliverance—is the keynote of the letter of May or June 1314
to the Italian cardinals in conclave following the death of Clement V in April of
that year, where it is a question now, however, not so much of mankind in general
as—tragically bereft as she is of both pope and emperor—of Rome in particular.
In the event, Dante's hopes for the bringing home of the Church from its captivity
abroad came to nothing, the conclave set up at Carpentras for the purposes of
appointing a new holy father being violently interrupted by the French faction in
the college of cardinals and followed by an interregnum of two years before the
election of the Cahorsine pope John XXII as yet another leech upon the lifeblood
of Christ's people (the 'del sangue nostro Caorsini e Guaschi / s'apparechian di
bere' of *Paradiso* 27.58–59).[13] But what matters most about a letter superlatively
well informed as to every aspect of the issue, even down to the Teverine and
Transteverine headquarters of its leading factions, is its sheer prophetic power,
its speaking out of the poet's situation as but least among the sheep of the pasture
to indict once again the greatest in the land, to tax the ecclesiastical powers that
be in respect not merely of their greed but of their lovelessness and forgetfulness
as between them an offence against the Spirit:

Non itaque videor quemquam exacerbasse ad iurgia; quin potius confusionis ruborem et in vobis et aliis, nomine solo archimandritis, per orbem
dumtaxat pudor eradicatus non sit totaliter, accendisse; cum de tot pastoris
officium usurpantibus, de tot ovibus, et si non ablatis, neglectis tamen et
incustoditis in pascuis, una sola vox, sola pia, et hec privata, in matris

12 'Up then! Make an end of delay, new scion of Jesse, and take confidence from the eyes of the
Lord God of Hosts, in whose sight you strive. Overthrow this Goliath with the sling of your wisdom
and with the stone of your strength; for at his fall night and the shadow of fear shall cover the camp of
the Philistines and they shall flee and Israel be delivered. Then our heritage which was taken away, and
for which we lament without ceasing, shall be made ours again in its entirety. But even as now, remembering the most holy Jerusalem, we mourn as exiles in Babylon, so then as citizens, and breathing in
peace, we shall think with joy on the wretchedness of our confusion.'
13 'The Cahorsines and Gascons prepare to drink our blood.' For Cahors, the Cahorsines and usury,
Inferno 11.48–51, while for Clement V and simony or trafficking in ecclesiastical office, 19.82–87; as
hostage—whore even—to the French monarchy, *Purgatorio* 32.151–60; and as traitor to Henry VII,
Paradiso 17.82–84. For the Gascons as striving in conclave to 'usurp for themselves the glory of the
Italians' (Latinorum gloriam sibi usurpare contendunt), Clement having set up court in Avignon in
1309, *Epistolae* 11.11, ult. Eugenio Dupré Theseider, *I papi di Avignone e la questione romana* (Florence:
Felice le Monnier, 1939); Guillaume Mollat, *The Popes at Avignon, 1305–1378*, trans. Janet Love (London:
Nelson, 1963).

Ecclesie quasi funere audiatur. Quidni? Cupiditatem unusquisque sibi duxit uxorem, quemadmodum et vos, que nunquam pietatis et equitatis, ut caritas, sed semper impietatis et iniquitatis est genitrix. A, mater piissima, sponsa Christi, que in aqua et Spiritu generas tibi filios ad ruborem! Non caritas, non Astrea, sed filie sanguisuge facte sunt tibi nurus; que quales pariant tibi fetus, preter Lunensem pontificem omnes alii contestantur. Iacet Gregorius tuus in telis aranearum; iacet Ambrosius in neglectis clericorum latibulis; iacet Augustinus abiectus, Dionysius, Damascenus et Beda; et nescio quod 'Speculum', Innocentium, et Ostiensem declamant. Cur non? Illi Deum querebant, ut finem et optimum; isti census et beneficia consecuntur.

(*Epistole* 11.6–7)[14]

If, then, to these large-scale political pieces born of the Henrician moment of Dante's time in exile and testifying to the again unspeakable intensity of that moment we add the aforesaid Battifolle letters despatched in the name of the good countess, we have evidence enough not simply of his ideological but of his expressive high-mindedness, the latter being but the outward aspect of the for-

---

14 'It seems then that I have provoked no one to railing; but rather that—provided only that shame has not altogether been eradicated in the world—I have kindled the blush of confusion in you and in others, chief priests in name only; for among so many who usurp the office of shepherd, among so many sheep who, if not driven away, at least are neglected and left untended in the pastures, one voice alone, one alone of filial piety, and that of a private individual, is heard at the obsequies as it were of Mother Church. And what wonder? Each one has taken avarice to wife, even as you yourselves have done; avarice, the mother never of piety and righteousness, but ever of impiety and unrighteousness. Ah! most loving Mother, Spouse of Christ, that by water and the spirit bear sons unto thy shame! Not charity, not Astraea, but the daughters of the horseleech have become your daughters-in-law. And what offspring they bear you all save the Bishop of Luni bear witness. Your Gregory lies among the cobwebs; Ambrose lies forgotten in the cupboards of the clergy, and Augustine along with him; and Dionysius, Damascenus and Bede; and they cry up instead I know not what *Speculum*, and Innocent, and him of Ostia. And why not? Those sought after God as their end and highest good; these get for themselves riches and benefices.' Cf. for the 'textual preferences' moment of the argument, the 'son derelitti' sequence of *Paradiso* 9.133–38: 'Per questo l'Evangelio e i dottor magni / son derelitti, e solo ai Decretali / si studia, sì che pare a' lor vivagni. / A questo intende il papa e ' cardinali; / non vanno i lor pensieri a Nazarette, / là dove Gabrïello aperse l'ali' (For this reason the great doctors and the Gospel itself are passed over, the Decretals alone—as may be seen by their margins—being studied. To this and this alone attend popes and cardinals, with never a thought for Nazareth where Gabriel spread his angel wings). Francesco di Capua, *Note all'epistola di Dante ai cardinali italiani* (Castellammare: Canzanella, 1919); Raffaello Morghen, 'Il conclave di Perugia del 1305 e la lettera di Dante ai Cardinali Italiani', in *L'Umbria nella storia, nella letteratura, nell'arte* (Bologna: Zanichelli, 1954), 103–24; Raffaello Morghen, 'La lettera di Dante ai Cardinali italiani', *BISIM* 68 (1956), 1–31 (and, as 'La lettera di Dante ai Cardinali Italiani e la coscienza della sua missione religiosa', in *Dante profeta: Tra la storia e l'eterno* [Milan: Jaca Book, 1983], 109–38); Raffaello Morghen 'Ancora sulla lettera di Dante ai Cardinali', *BISIM* 70 (1958), 513–19; Gustavo Vinay, 'A proposito della lettera di Dante ai Cardinali', *GSLI* 135 (1958), 71–80; Arsenio Frugoni, 'Dante tra due conclavi: La lettera ai Cardinali Italiani', in Arsenio Frugoni, *Incontri nel Medioevo* (Bologna: Il Mulino, 1979), 349–67.

mer. On the one hand, then, there is the idea, messianic in both substance and intensity, while on the other there is form in its now twofold notarial and rhetorical aspect—notarial in its scrupulous deployment of the *cursus* or system of terminal accentuation long since cherished as part and parcel of the *ars dictaminis* by civic and clerical functionaries alike,[15] and rhetorical in its rejoicing in just about every strategy (anaphora, hyperbole, synecdoche, simile and above all metaphor) known to the poet, the prophet or the plain public speaker. If, then, to this we add Dante's now ready familiarity with each and every one of his *auctores* from the Aristotle of the *Metaphysics* and *Ethics* to the Virgil of the *Eclogues* and the *Aeneid* and from the poets and prophets of the Old Testament to the evangelists and epistolographers of the New, then we have an impressive harvesting of his every cultural resource in the name and for the sake of the leading idea.

With what amounts, then, to the exalted substance of the political letters proper and of the Battifolle papers living on in their shadow we come, almost, to the *Monarchia* as Dante's most sustained meditation upon the imperial idea. 'Almost', because we need to pause for a moment over the 'Neither shall bread fail me' letter of 1315 to a friend in Florence as along with the canzone *Tre donne intorno al cor mi son venute* the most eloquent expression in Dante of the *how it stands* with the soul far from home. It appears, then, that in the course of 1315 Florence—or so his friend must have reported—had offered him an amnesty, his rehabilitation being by way of the usual species of ritual humiliation required of the penitent spirit, namely a sponsored trailing through the streets of Florence to the baptistery there to make amends in the presence of the Almighty, of John the Baptist and (especially) the great and good of the commune as a basis for absolution. Dante, predictably, was scandalized, defiance and yearning, here as in *Tre donne*, once again striving for mastery in the depths. But for all the continuing agony of it all there is here a fresh inflexion, a sense of citizenship as apt withal to transcend the merely civic as a structure of consciousness:

---

15 In Dante the *cursus planus* (a paroxytone polysyllable followed by a paroxytone trisyllable as in 'melióris / effúlsit' or 'affectuóse / depósco'), the *cursus tardus* (a paroxytone polysyllable followed by a proparoxytone as in 'véstra praepónderet') and the *cursus velox* (a proparoxytone polysyllable followed by a paroxytone tetrasyllable as in 'tálibus / continébant' or 'laetítia / perfundérunt'). Lorenzo Mascetta-Caracci, 'Il "cursus" ritmico, la critica dei testi medievali e l'*Epistolario* di Dante Alighieri', *La Biblioteca degli Studiosi* 2.8–9 (1910), 177–88 and 219–23; Ernesto Giacomo Parodi, 'Intorno al testo delle Epistole di Dante e al "cursus"', *BSDI* 19 (1912), 249–75 and 22 (1915), 137–44 (and in *Lingua e letteratura: Studi di teoria linguistica e di storia dell'italiano antico*, ed. Gianfranco Folena, vol. 2 [Venice: Neri Pozza, 1957], 399–442); Paget Toynbee, 'Dante and the *Cursus*', in *Dantis Alagherii Epistolae: The Letters of Dante*, 2nd ed. with a bibliographical appendix by Colin G. Hardie (Oxford: Clarendon Press, 1966 [1920]), 224–47. More generally on the 'cursus', Albert Curtis Clark, *The Cursus in Mediaeval and Vulgar Latin* (Oxford: Clarendon Press, 1910).

Estne ista revocatio gratiosa qua Dantes Alagherii revocatur ad patriam, per trilustrium fere perpessus exilium? Hocne meruit innocentia manifesta quibuslibet? hoc sudor et labor continuatus in studio? Absit a viro phylosophie domestico temeraria tantum cordis humilitas, ut more cuiusdam Cioli et aliorum infamium quasi vinctus ipse se patiatur offerri! Absit a viro predicante iustitiam ut perpessus iniurias, iniuriam inferentibus, velut benemerentibus, pecuniam suam solvat! Non est hec via redeundi ad patriam, pater mi; sed si alia per vos ante aut deinde per alios invenitur que fame Dantisque honori non deroget, illam non lentis passibus acceptabo; quod si per nullam talem Florentia introitur, nunquam Florentiam introibo. Quidni? nonne solis astrorumque specula ubique conspiciam? nonne dulcissimas veritates potero speculari ubique sub celo, ni prius inglorium ymo ignominiosum populo Florentino, civitati me reddam? Quippe nec panis deficiet.

(Epistole 12.3–4)[16]

---

16 'This, then, is the gracious recall of Dante Alighieri to his native city, after the miseries of well-nigh fifteen years of exile! This is the reward of innocence manifest to all the world, and of the sweat and toil of unremitting study! Far be from a familiar of philosophy such a senseless act of abasement as to submit himself to be presented at the oblation, like a felon in bonds, as one Ciolo and other infamous wretches have done! Far be it from the preacher of justice, after suffering wrong, to pay of his money to those that wronged him, as though they had deserved well of him! No, my father; not by this path will I return to my native city. If some other can be found, in the first place by yourself and thereafter by others, which does not derogate from the fame and honour of Dante, that will I tread with no lagging steps. But if by no such path Florence may be entered, then will I enter Florence never. What! Can I not anywhere gaze upon the face of the sun and the stars? Can I not under any sky contemplate the most precious truths, without I first return to Florence, disgraced, nay dishonoured, in the eyes of my fellow citizens? Assuredly bread will not fail me!' Arnaldo Della Torre, 'L'epistola di Dante all'"amico fiorentino"', <i>BSDI</i> 12 (1905), 121–74; Michele Barbi, 'Per un passo dell'epistola di Dante all'amico fiorentino e per la parentela di Dante', <i>SD</i> 2 (1920), 115–48 (and in <i>Problemi di critica dantesca: Seconda serie</i> [Florence: Sansoni, 1965], 305–28). Similarly eloquent already in respect of the Florence/not Florence dialectic everywhere uppermost in the mind of the displaced spirit, of reposing <i>in</i> and disposing <i>of</i> Florence as an object of yearning, is the 'cities more exalted and more delightful' moment of the <i>De vulgari eloquentia</i> at 1.6.3: 'Et quamvis ad voluptatem nostram sive nostre sensualitatis quietem in terris amenior locus quam Florentia non existat, revolventes et poetarum et aliorum scriptorum volumina quibus mundus universaliter et membratim describitur, ratiocinantesque in nobis situationes varias mundi locorum et eorum habitudinem ad utrunque polum et circulum equatorem, multas esse perpendimus firmiterque censemus et magis nobiles et magis delitiosas et regiones et urbes quam Tusciam et Florentiam, unde sumus oriundi et civis, et plerasque nationes et gentes delectabiliori atque utiliori sermone uti quam Latinos' (And although speaking for myself and my own pleasure and satisfaction, there is no more agreeable place on earth than Florence, yet when I peruse the poets and other writers by whom the world is described both in the round and in respect of its various parts, and when I think over all the different places in the world and their disposition in respect of the distant poles and of the circling equator, I am persuaded, and firmly maintain, that there are many regions and cities more exalted and more delightful still than the Tuscany and the Florence where I was born and whereof I am a citizen, and many nations and peoples who speak a more refined and useful language than do the Italians).

Coming, then, to the *Monarchia* as, again, dating ideally from the middle part of the second decade of the fourteenth century, this in every sense is an impressive work. Complete in three books, it is impressive for its conception and for its construction alike, for its conception as a hymn to the imperial idea as fashioned from beforehand in the depths of the divine mind, and for its construction as a tripartite meditation on monarchy as the way of man's proper well-being as man (book 1), on Rome as the properly appointed agent of universal government (book 2), and on the relationship between papal and imperial authority as each alike flowing immediately from God and as subsisting, therefore, not so much hierarchically as in parallel (book 3). Remarkable as it is, then, for its account of empire generally and of the Roman Empire in particular as a matter of divine intentionality, the *Monarchia* is no less impressive for its now consummate mastery of the ways and means of high-scholastic disquisition and for the courage and consistency of its reply to the tradition of political literature which it presupposes—to the still flourishing tradition of hierocratic and anti-hierocratic literature engendered in its most recent phase by the bull *Unam sanctam* of 1302. Impressive as it is, however, for these and any number of emphases along the way (quite superb, for example, is Dante's account in book 1 of imperial authority as but the ground and guarantee of properly human freedom, and, in book 3, of the Church, properly understood, as but the continuing life of Christ on earth), the *Monarchia* is not without its difficulties; for setting out as it does to distinguish between two orders of political jurisdiction, papal and imperial, it rests its case, at any rate in the final analysis, upon the most far-reaching kind of spiritual dualism. Of the essence, in other words, when it comes to the separating out of papal and imperial power precisely as such is a separating out of the two kinds of happiness proper to man as man, namely (*a*) of the kind proper to a living out of the moral and intellectual virtues as defined by the philosopher and overseen by the emperor, and (*b*) of the kind proper to a living out of the theological virtues of faith, hope and love as commended by Scripture and by the inspired teaching of the Church and as overseen by the pope as bridge-builder-in-chief to the next life. The key passage here, as clear-cut and symmetrical on the surface as it is responsive to one of the deepest exigencies of Dante's temperament as a philosophical and theological spirit, runs as follows:

> Duos igitur fines providentia illa inenarrabilis homini proposuit intendendos: beatitudinem scilicet huius vite, que in operatione proprie virtutis consistit et per terrestrem paradisum figuratur; et beatitudinem vite ecterne, que consistit in fruitione divini aspectus ad quam propria virtus ascendere non potest, nisi lumine divino adiuta, que per paradisum celestem intelligi datur. Ad has quidem beatitudines, velut ad diversas conclusiones, per diversa media venire oportet. Nam ad primam per phylo-

sophica documenta venimus, dummodo illa sequamur secundum virtutes morales et intellectuales operando; ad secundam vero per documenta spiritualia que humanam rationem transcendunt, dummodo illa
sequamur secundum virtutes theologicas operando, fidem spem scilicet
et karitatem.

(Monarchia 3.15.7–8)[17]

With this, then, we come to what in retrospect most matters about the *Monarchia*; for setting aside for the moment its specifically political content, its commitment over against the by this stage atrophied forms and formularies of late
medieval papal hierocracy to an unqualified species of political dualism, what in
retrospect most matters about the *Monarchia* is its witnessing yet again to the
self-consciously problematic character of Dante's own humanity, to a built-in
tendency to distinguish both formally and finally between one order of spiritual
activity and another. Gone, in other words, is any sense of the co-presencing of
reason and revelation, of nature and grace, and of philosophy and theology in the
depths of the historical instant, co-presencing thus understood giving way in the
interests of a high-level solution in the area of political philosophy to otherness
as a dominant structure of consciousness. Now Dante, it is true, offers in just
about the same breath a qualification, for all this, he says, 'should not be taken so
strictly as to preclude all observance of the priest by the prince, for after a certain
fashion our earthly happiness is subordinate to our heavenly happiness' (the 'Que
quidem veritas ultime questionis non sic stricte recipienda est, ut romanus Princeps in aliquo romano Pontifici non subiaceat, cum mortalis ista felicitas quodammodo ad inmortalem felicitatem ordinetur' of 3.15.17); but as regards what in
retrospect most matters about the *Monarchia*, this, as a caveat designed as far as
may be to soften a specifically political solution, goes in truth but part of the way,
the 'quodammodo' or 'after a certain fashion' moment of the argument guaranteeing as it does a measure of respect on the part of the prince for the pope,
nonetheless leaving the 'duos igitur fines' or 'two ends' moment free to go about
its business—about the dismantling of personality in the never less than complex
dimensionality thereof. By the time, in other words, we reach the 'quodammodo'

---

17 'Ineffable providence has thus set before us two goals: happiness in this life, which consists in
the exercise of our own proper powers and is figured in the earthly paradise, and happiness in the
eternal life, which consists in the enjoyment of the divine countenance itself, something to which our
own powers cannot raise us other than with the help of divine light and which is typified by the heavenly paradise. Now just as one reaches different conclusions by different means, so also with these two
kinds of happiness, for we arrive at the first by way of philosophical teaching and a faithful implementation of the moral and intellectual virtues, whereas we arrive at the second by way of the kind of
spiritual teaching which transcends human reason, implementing now the theological virtues of faith,
hope and charity.'

moment of the argument the die has been cast, there being now no real room for manoeuvre.[18]

With this, however—with what from a philosophical if not from a political point of view amounts to the problematic character of the *Monarchia*—we are getting ahead of ourselves, for first on the agenda when it comes to the political question proper is the notion of *government by one* as the sole guarantee of man's proper perfection as man. What then, Dante begins by asking, can be the final cause or point of arrival in respect of the activity, not now of this or that individual man or woman, but of mankind as a whole? The answer, he thinks, lies in the total actualization of the possible intellect in making known everything there is to be known. Now here we, or rather Alighieri, need and needed to tread carefully, for as the earliest and most ferocious of Dante's critics pointed out this, at first glance, looks awfully much like monopsychism, like the notion of every man's merely sharing pro tempore, for the time being, in a single intellectual principle. The critic in question was the Dominican Guido Vernani, who in his learned but often vitriolic treatise *De reprobatione Monarchiae* dating from about 1327 accuses Dante in precisely this sense of Averroism and of the pestilence thereof, of toying with the notion of a single subsistent intellect merely shared by man for the duration of his mortal life and by the same token ruling out anything else to follow. No, he says, this cannot be. The possible intellect is, and must always be thought of, as proper to the individual, anything short of this amounting to error in both natural and moral philosophy:

18 Hence the—here at least more than ordinarily equilibrated—response (ca. 1327) of a Guido Vernani as among the earliest of Dante's critics hereabouts to the 'duo ultima' moment of the *Monarchia*, a response turning, precisely, on an ideal taking up of the 'temporal' in the 'spiritual', the active in the contemplative and the philosophical in a quiet pondering of things eternal as the sole ground and guarantee of man's proper happiness: 'Dicit etiam, quod *homo ad istos duos fines ordinatos a Deo*. Ad hoc dico quod ad beatitudinem temporalem non ordinatur homo a Deo tanquam ad finem ultimum, quia talis beatitudo nunquam terminare et satiare potuit hominis appetitum; sed operatio talium virtutum, etiam philosophice loquendo, ordinatur ad felicitatem contemplativam, ut scilicet per virtutes, sedatis passionibus, homo per sapientiam possit aeterna quietius et liberius contemplari . . . Ordinatur ergo homo ad felicitatem aeternam, tanquam ad finem ultimum, propter quem consequendum omnia sua bona naturalia, moralia et gratuita debet dirigere et referre' (He says, moreover, that man is ordered to these two ends by God. To this I reply that a man is not directed by God to temporal happiness as to his last end, since never has happiness of this kind been enough to still and to satisfy his desire; on the contrary, even philosophically speaking, the exercise of these virtues is ordered to a contemplative happiness, such that, having allayed all other passions, he may the more freely and peacefully contemplate, in wisdom, the things of eternity . . . Man, therefore, is ordered to eternal happiness as to his last end, to the pursuit of which all goods, natural, moral and gratuitous alike, should be referred and directed) (Guido Vernani, *De reprobatione Monarchiae*, ed. and trans. G. Piccini [Florence: Bemporad, 1906, 42–44])—à propos of which Étienne Gilson, 'Philosophy in the *Monarchy*', in *Dante and Philosophy*, trans. David Moore (New York: Harper and Row, 1963), 162–224 at 201: 'There is not one original word in this criticism of Dante, but that is the very reason why it interests us. Guido Vernani's firm opposition to Dante is nothing but the opposition of the Thomist universe to one of the gravest dangers that have ever threatened it.'

Tertius error est pessimus. Dicit enim in eodem capitulo, et sequenti, quod intellectus possibilis, non potest actuari, idest perfici, nisi per totum genus humanum, sicut potentia materiae primae non potest totaliter reduci ad actum, et perfectionem nisi per multitudinem rerum naturalium. Et ad hoc adducit auctoritatem Averoys, qui hoc dicit in *Commemoratio* super 3. lib. *de anima*; et hunc dicit, esse finem, et perfectionem non unius singularis hominis, sed totius humani generis simul sumpti; sic autem dicendo, sequitur manifeste quod in omnibus hominibus est unus solus intellectus, quod quidem dicere et sentire est error pessimus, cujus auctor et inventor fuit ille Averoys quem allegat. Est enim error, primo quidem quantum ad philosophiam naturalem, quae dicit in 2. *de an.* quod, *anima est id qua vivimus, sentimus, et intelligimus*. Ergo oportet, quod anima nostra sit intellectiva, idest quod habeat potentiam per quam intelligimus. Et uti habetur in 3. *de anima* intellectus quo anima sapit et intelligit est pars animae, idest una de potentiis animae. Non est ergo intellectus possibilis substantia separata, nec est unus in omnibus hominibus. Est etiam contra philosophiam moralem, quae dicit in 6. *Etich.* scientiam, sapientiam et intellectum et prudentiam et artem esse virtutes hominis, quod non esset si intellectus esset quaedam substantia separata quia istae virtutes sunt in intellectu sicut in subjecto.

(*De reprobatione Monarchiae*, ed. Piccini, 8–10)[19]

19 'The third error is the worst of all, for he says in the same chapter, as well as in what follows, that, just as the potentiality of prime matter cannot in its totality be reduced to actuality and the perfection thereof other than by way of a multiplicity of natural phenomena, so also there can be no actualization or perfection of the possible intellect other than by way of the human race as a whole. And to this end he invokes the authority of Averroes, who, in his commentary on the third book of the *De anima* says just this, that man's proper end and perfection is a matter, not of this or that individual, but of the entire race taken together, from which it clearly follows that in all men there is but one single intellect, which even to think, let alone to say, is the very worst kind of error, an error authored and invented by the very Averroes he invokes. It is, first of all, an error in natural philosophy, which in the second book of the *De anima* specifies that "the soul is that whereby we live, perceive and understand", whence it follows that our soul is rational in kind, consisting, that is to say, of the power whereby we understand. And we have it on record in the third book of the *De anima* that the intellect is that part of the soul, indeed one of the powers of the soul, whereby it knows and understands, for which reason the possible intellect is quite other than a separate substance or one and the same in all men. But it is also an affront to moral philosophy, which, in the sixth book of the *Ethics* has it that knowledge, wisdom, understanding, prudence and art are all alike human virtues, which, were the intellect a separate substance, would not be the case, all these things pertaining to the intellect as but part of the subject.' Bruno Nardi, 'Di un'aspra critica di Fra Guido Vernani a Dante', in *Saggi e note di critica dantesca* (Milan: Ricciardi, 1966), 377–85; Anthony K. Cassell, 'Logic and Spleen: A Post-Mortem Dialogue between Dante and Guido Vernani (the *Monarchia* and the *Reprobatio Monarchiae*, Book III)', *L'Alighieri (RD)* 24 (2004), 5–24; Anthony K. Cassell, *The 'Monarchia' Controversy: An Historical Study with Accompanying Translations of Dante Alighieri's 'Monarchia', Guido Vernani's Refutation of the 'Monarchia' Composed by Dante, and Pope John XXII's Bull 'Si Fratrum'* (Washington, DC: Catholic University of America Press, 2004); Roberto Lambertini, 'Guido Vernani contro Dante: La questione dell'universalismo politico', in *"Il mondo errante": Dante fra letteratura, eresia e storia. Atti del Convegno Internazionale di Studio Bertinoro, 13–16 settembre 2010*, ed. Marco

Now Dante, in citing Averroes to the effect that there can be no perfection of
the possible intellect other than by way of the human race as a whole (the 'huic
sententie concordat Averrois in comento super hiis que *De anima*' of 1.3.9),[20] was
indeed playing with fire, its heady mixture of imperialism and impiety making
the banning and burning of the *Monarchia* in 1329 a near-foregone conclusion.
But given his sense both in the *Convivio* and in the *Commedia* of the direct inspiration of the rational soul in man and, in the *Commedia*, of Averroes having gone
seriously astray at this point (the 'quest' è tal punto, / che più savio di te fé già
errante, / sì che per sua dottrina fé disgiunto / da l'anima il possibile intelletto, /
perché da lui non vide organo assunto' of *Purgatorio* 25.62–66),[21] it is unlikely that
Dante should commit himself to that same error, to the kind of monopsychism
that he had formerly denounced both implicitly and explicitly. Rather, it is a question here, as so often it is in Dante, of his invoking his sources with a view to
fashioning them afresh after his own image, to his settling in this case upon the
notion of society *in the aggregate* as the means of consummate intellection:

Patet igitur quod ultimum de potentia ipsius humanitatis est potentia sive
virtus intellectiva. Et quia potentia ista per unum hominem seu per aliquam
particularium comunitatum superius distinctarum tota simul in actum re-

---

Veglia et al. (Spoleto: Centro italiano di studi sull'alto medioevo, 2013), 359–69. More generally, Bruno
Nardi, 'Fortuna della *Monarchia* nei secoli XIV and XV', in *Nel mondo di Dante* (Rome: Edizioni di
Storia e Letteratura, 1944), 91–106; Francis Cheneval, 'Dante's *Monarchia*: Aspects of Its History of
Reception in the 14th Century', in *Moral and Political Philosophies in the Middle Ages. Proceeding of
the Ninth International Congress of Medieval Philosophy, Ottawa, 17–22 August 1992*, ed. Carlos B. Bazán
et al. (New York: Legas, 1995), 1474–85; Leonella Coglievina, 'Primi momenti della "fortuna" della
Monarchia di Dante', in *Dante: Letture critiche e filologiche*, ed. Ruby Abardo (Rome: Edizioni di Storia
e Letteratura, 2014), 141–59.

20 'And Averroes is in agreement with this opinion in his commentary on the *De anima*.'

21 'This is the point which once caused one wiser than you to err such that, in what he taught,
and not seeing an organ appropriated by it, he made the possible intellect separate from the soul.' In
addition to Bruno Nardi (especially 'Dante e la filosofia', in *Nel mondo di Dante* [Rome: Edizioni di
Storia e Letteratura, 1944], 207–45 and *Dal Convivio alla Commedia (sei saggi danteschi)* [Rome: Istituto storico italiano per il Medio Evo, 1992]) and Étienne Gilson, *Dante and Philosophy*, trans. David
Moore (New York: Harper Row, 1963), Raffaello Morghen, 'Dante e Averroè', in *Tradizione religiosa
nella civiltà dell'Occidente cristiano: Saggi di storia e di storiografia* (Rome: Istituto storico italiano per
il Medio Evo, 1979), 49–62; Maria Corti, 'Tre versioni dell'aristotelismo radicale nella *Commedia*', in
Dante a un nuovo crocevia (Florence: Sansoni, 1981), 77–101; John Marenbon, 'Dante's Averroism', in
Poetry and Philosophy in the Middle Ages: A Festschrift for Peter Dronke, ed. John Marenbon (Leiden:
Brill, 2001), 349–74; Antonio Gagliardi, 'Dante fra Sigieri e Tommaso', in *Tommaso d'Aquino e Averroè:
La visione di Dio* (Soveria Mannelli, Catanzaro: Rubbettino Editore, 2002), 273–94; Italo Sciuto, 'Il
problema dell'intelletto in Dante e nell'averroismo', in *Echi letterari della cultura araba nella lirica provenzale e nella Commedia di Dante. Atti del Convegno Internazionale, Università di Udine, 15–16 aprile 2005*,
ed. Claudio Gabrio Antoni (Udine: Campanotto, 2006), 27–40; Márk Berényl, 'Influssi averroistici
nell'opera dantesca', in *Atti del Convegno Internazionale Commentare Dante oggi*, ed. János Keleman et
al. (Budapest: Eötvös University Press, 2015), 217–34; Luca Bianchi, 'L'averroismo di Dante: Qualche
osservazione critica', *Le Tre Corone: Rivista di Studi si Dante, Petrarca, Boccaccio* 2 (2015),
71–109.

duci non potest, necesse est multitudinem esse in humano genere, per quam quidem tota potentia hec actuetur; sicut necesse est multitudinem rerum generabilium ut potentia tota materie prime semper sub actu sit; aliter esset dare potentiam separatam, quod est inpossibile. Et huic sententie concordat Averrois in comento super hiis que *De anima*.

(*Monarchia* 1.3.7–9)[22]

But however that may be, it is on this basis—the basis of a now collective enterprise—that he goes on to describe the role of the emperor in all this; for there can, he thinks, be no collective enterprise without peace as the ground and guarantee of its success, man as man be it severally or in the round only ever coming home to his proper humanity by way of his proper tranquillity. Where, in short, there is no peace there can be no perfection, this therefore—the notion of universal peace as the condition of man's proper coming about as man—constituting the *principium directivum* of everything coming next in this first book of the *Monarchia*, its proper point of departure and guiding principle:

Satis igitur declaratum est quod proprium opus humani generis totaliter accepti est actuare semper totam potentiam intellectus possibilis, per prius ad speculandum et secundario propter hoc ad operandum per suam extensionem. Et quia quemadmodum est in parte sic est in toto, et in homine particulari contingit quod sedendo et quiescendo prudentia et sapientia ipse perficitur, patet quod genus humanum in quiete sive tranquillitate pacis ad proprium suum opus, quod fere divinum est iuxta illud 'Minuisti eum paulominus ab angelis', liberrime atque facillime se habet. Unde manifestum est quod pax universalis est optimum eorum que ad nostram beatitudinem ordinantur. Hinc est quod pastoribus de sursum sonuit non divitie, non voluptates, non honores, non longitudo vite, non sanitas, non robur, non pulcritudo, sed pax; inquit enim celestis militia: 'Gloria in altissimis Deo, et in terra pax hominibus bone voluntatis'. Hinc etiam 'Pax vobis' Salus hominum salutabat; decebat enim summum Salvatorem summam salutationem exprimere; quem quidem morem servare voluerunt discipuli eius et Paulus in salutationibus suis, ut omnibus manifestum esse potest. Ex hiis ergo que declarata sunt patet per quod melius, ymo per quod optime genus humanum pertingit ad opus proprium; et per consequens visum est pro-

---

22 'From this it is clear that man's greatest potentiality as man is an intellectual power or potentiality. And since that potentiality cannot be actualized all at once in any one individual or in any one of the particular social groupings enumerated above, mankind must of necessity consist of a multitude whereby this potentiality may in the round be actualized, just as there must of necessity be a multitude of things which can be generated from prime matter in order that the entire potentiality of that matter be reduced to act, the alternative being to make room for potentiality to exist separately, which is impossible—a view, this, with which Averroes in his commentary on the *De anima* is in agreement.'

pinquissimum medium per quod itur in illud ad quod, velut in ultimum finem, omnia nostra opera ordinantur, quia est pax universalis, que pro principio rationum subsequentium supponatur.

(Monarchia 1.4.1–5)[23]

With this, then, Dante sets about making the case for universal monarchy, a case resting on various kinds of argument, natural and moral-philosophical alike, but including most conspicuously (*a*) those turning upon the unity, stability and efficiency of monarchy or government by one; (*b*) those turning upon the priority of unity as distinct from multiplicity in the order of being generally; and (*c*) those turning upon the freedom of the individual in circumstances of an absolute ruler—emphases to which, as the encompassing of all these things, we must add his sense of monarchy as the pattern of God's own government in the world and as sanctioned in Scripture both by Christ himself and by the apostle Paul . Taking first, then, the first of these things—namely the argument from unity, stability and efficiency—we have these lines from 1.5 on the notion of empire as that whereby society as a whole is protected from those forces deep within it making otherwise for decay, disintegration and desolation:

Si denique unum regnum particulare, cuius finis est is qui civitatis cum maiori fiducia sue tranquillitatis, oportet esse regem unum qui regat atque

---

23 'It is, then, sufficiently clear that the activity proper to mankind considered as a whole is constantly to actualize the full potential of the possible intellect, primarily by way of speculation and secondarily by way of action as but a function and extension of this. And since what applies to the part applies also to the whole, and since this or that individual man "is perfected in judgment and wisdom by sitting at rest", so it is that mankind is most fully and freely prepared for this task—a task we learn from the scriptural "Thou hast made him a little lower than the angels" virtually divine in character—in the calm or quietness of peace. Hence it is clear that universal peace is the most excellent of those things making for our human happiness. That is why the message which rang out from on high to the shepherds was not one of wealth, of pleasure, of esteem, nor of long life, of health, of strength, or of beauty, but of peace, for which reason the heavenly host proclaimed: "Glory to God on high, and on earth peace to men of goodwill." And that is why the saviour of mankind used the greeting "Peace be with you", for it was fitting that the supreme saviour should utter the supreme salutation, a custom, as everyone knows, preserved both by his disciples and by Paul in their own greetings. From all this, then, it is clear what the better and indeed the best way of enabling mankind to accomplish his proper function is, and what also, in consequence, we see to be the most direct means of reaching the goal to which all our actions are directed as to their final end. That means is universal peace, which henceforth will constitute the first principle of our argument.' Charles T. Davis, 'Remigio de' Girolami and Dante: A Comparison of Their Conception of Peace', *SD* 36 (1969), 105–36 (and in *Dante: The Critical Complex*, ed. Richard Lansing, vol. 5 [New York: Routledge, 2003], 243–74); John Scott, 'Dante's Vision of World Empire and Peace: *Monarchia*', in *Understanding Dante* (Notre Dame: University of Notre Dame Press, 2004), 143–66; Matthew S. Kempshall, 'The Utility of Peace in *Monarchia*', in *War and Peace in Dante: Essays Literary, Historical and Theological*, ed. John C. Barnes and Daragh O'Connell (Dublin: Four Courts Press, 2015), 141–72; Takashi Shogimen, 'John of Paris and the Idea of Peace in the Late Thirteenth and Early Fourteenth Centuries', in *John of Paris*, ed. Chris Jones (Turnhout: Brepols, 2015), 239–61.

gubernet; aliter non modo existentes in regno finem non assecuntur, sed etiam regnum in interitum labitur, iuxta illud infallibilis Veritatis: 'Omne regnum in se divisum desolabitur'. Si ergo sic se habet in hiis et in singulis que ad unum aliquod ordinantur, verum est quod assummitur supra; nunc constat quod totum humanum genus ordinatur ad unum, ut iam preostensum fuit; ergo unum oportet esse regulans sive regens, et hoc 'Monarcha' sive 'Imperator' dici debet.

(*Monarchia* 1.5.8–9)[24]

while as far as the second of them is concerned, namely the priority of unity with respect to plurality in the order of being generally, we have these from 1.15, explicit in their sense of the many not simply as making for evil but as the very ground thereof, the political implications of this—of the indispensability of the emperor as the sole guarantor of unity on the plane of willing—speaking, Dante thinks, for themselves:

Item dico quod ens et unum et bonum gradatim se habent secundum quintum modum dicendi 'prius'. Ens enim natura precedit unum, unum vero bonum: maxime enim ens maxime est unum, et maxime unum maxime bonum; et quanto aliquid a maxime ente elongatur, tanto et ab esse unum et per consequens ab esse bonum. Propter quod in omni genere rerum illud est optimum quod est maxime unum, ut Phylosopho placet in hiis que *De simpliciter ente*. Unde fit quod unum esse videtur esse radix eius quod est esse bonum, et multa esse eius quod est esse malum; qua re Pictagoras in correlationibus suis ex parte boni ponebat unum, ex parte vero mali plurale, ut patet in primo eorum que *De simpliciter ente* ... Hiis premissis propter declarationem assummende propositionis ad propositum, sic arguatur: omnis concordia dependet ab unitate que est in voluntatibus; genus humanum optime se habens est quedam concordia; nam, sicut unus homo optime se habens et quantum ad animam et quantum ad corpus est concordia quedam, et similiter domus, civitas et regnum, sic totum genus humanum; ergo genus humanum optime se habens ab unitate que est in voluntatibus dependet. Sed hoc esse non potest nisi sit voluntas

---

24 'If, finally, we take this or that individual kingdom (kingdoms having the same aim as cities but more secure in their anticipation of peace), there must of necessity be one king to rule over and govern it, for not only would there then be no achieving of their aims by the citizens, but in keeping with the infallible Word to the effect that "every kingdom divided against itself faces only disaster", the kingdom itself will inevitably come to rack and ruin. If, then, it is indeed true that both communities and the individuals who make them up are destined to their proper end, then all we have been saying so far holds true; for if as we have agreed and indeed shown to be the case that mankind as a whole has but one end, then there must needs be just one person to preside as governor over it—the one, precisely, to whom we must accord the title "monarch" or "emperor." '

una, domina et regulatrix omnium aliarum in unum, cum mortalium voluntates propter blandas adolescentie delectationes indigeant directivo, ut
in ultimis *ad Nicomacum* docet Phylosophus. Nec ista una potest esse, nisi
sit princeps unus omnium, cuius voluntas domina et regulatrix aliarum
omnium esse possit.

(*Monarchia* 1.15.1–2 and 8–9)[25]

In both these senses, then, it is a question of the ascendancy of the one over
the many as in just about every conceivable sense—moral, political and aesthetic
alike—ideal, multiplicity, all very well in its way, standing at last to be taken up in
unity as the hallmark of being and thus of goodness in their actuality.

Now, however, and as constituting perhaps the most impressive phase of
Dante's meditation in this first book of the *Monarchia*, comes the notion of imperial government as the guarantee, not merely of peace, but of the freedom flowing from peace, of, in effect, the freedom *to be* in the light of conscience. First,
then, and as preliminary to what in this sense amounts to an essay in emancipation, comes the idea of justice as but a matter of rectitude in the sense of rectilin-
earity, of a line admitting of no deviation on either side. True, the line will in
practice waver a little, but rather like white, say, in respect to every other colour,
justice, precisely as such, is an absolute value, an entity suffering neither more nor
less: 'iustitia, de se et in propria natura considerata, est quedam rectitudo sive
regula obliquum hinc inde abiciens; et sic non recipit magis et minus, quemadmodum albedo in suo abstracto considerata.'[26] But from this sense of justice as
an unnegotiable principle of being and doing flow three things, each of them

25 'Again, I say that, according to the fifth sense of the term, priority is assigned to being, unity
and goodness in that order. For being naturally comes before unity, and unity before goodness. Perfect
being, moreover, is perfect unity, and perfect unity is perfect goodness, and the further removed a thing
is from perfect being, the further it is from being one and thus from being good. Within any kind of
thing, therefore, the best, as Aristotle says in the *Metaphysics*, is that which is most one. Hence unity,
it seems, is the ground of goodness, and plurality the ground of evil, which is why Pythagoras in his
Correlations placed unity on the side of goodness and plurality on the side of evil, as is clear from the
first book of the *Metaphysics* . . . This said, then, by way of clarifying the proposition we are adopting
for the purpose of pursuing our argument, we may proceed by saying (*a*) that concord generally is a
matter of unity in point of willing; (*b*) that mankind is at its best in just such a state of concord; and
(*c*) that just as man is at his best when at one with himself in body and soul, so the same is true of a
house, of a kingdom, and of mankind as a whole. For mankind to be at its best, that is to say, it must
be one in point of willing, something quite impossible unless there be one will regulating and directing
every other will, thus ensuring their overall unity; for as the Philosopher maintains towards the end of
the *Ethics*, the willing of mortal men, swayed as it is by the seductive pleasures of youth, is forever in
need of a director. Short, then, of their being but one prince overseeing all men, unity in point of willing
is simply impossible.'

26 *Monarchia* 1.11.3: 'justice, in itself and in respect of its proper nature, is a kind of rectitude or
rule permitting of no deviation and thus—just like whiteness considered in the abstract—insusceptible
either of more or of less'. Allan H. Gilbert, *Dante's Conception of Justice* (Durham, NC: Duke University
Press, 1925).

decisive for what comes next. First, then, there is the notion that justice thus understood will be at its strongest in the emperor as by definition wanting for nothing. Wanting for nothing, Dante thinks—for his jurisdiction by definition stretches from shore to shore—the emperor will be the very embodiment of justice, justice incarnate:

> Sed Monarcha non habet quod possit optare; sua nanque iurisdictio termi-natur Occeano solum, quod non contingit principibus aliis, quorum prin-cipatus ad alios terminantur, ut puta regis Castelle ad illum qui regis Ara-gonum. Ex quo sequitur quod Monarcha sincerissimum inter mortales iustitie possit esse subiectum.
>
> (*Monarchia* 1.11.12)²⁷

Second, there is the notion that, wanting for nothing, the emperor will be the embodiment, not simply of justice, but of the love of which justice is but the outshining, his only object, therefore, being the good of those committed to his care:

> Preterea, quemadmodum cupiditas habitualem iustitiam quodammodo, quantumcunque pauca, obnubilat, sic karitas seu recta dilectio illam acuit atque dilucidat. Cui ergo maxime recta dilectio inesse potest, potissimum locum in illo potest habere iustitia; huiusmodi est Monarcha; ergo, eo ex-istente, iustitia potissima est vel esse potest. Quod autem recta dilectio fa-ciat quod dictum est, hinc haberi potest: cupiditas nanque, perseitate ho-minum spreta, querit alia; karitas vero, spretis aliis omnibus, querit Deum et hominem, et per consequens bonum hominis. Cumque inter alia bona hominis potissimum sit in pace vivere—ut supra dicebatur—et hoc opere-tur maxime atque potissime iustitia, karitas maxime iustitiam vigorabit et potior potius.
>
> (*Monarchia* 1.11.13–14)²⁸

---

27 'But nothing remains for the monarch to covet, for—unlike other rulers, whose sovereignty extends only as far as the neighbouring kingdom, as is the case, for instance, with the kings of Castile and of Aragon—his jurisdiction is bounded only by the ocean. From this it follows that of all men the monarch can be the purest embodiment of justice.' József Nagy, 'L'ideale dell'impero universale nella *Monarchia* e nella *Commedia*', in *Ortodossia ed eterodossia in Dante Alighieri. Atti del convegno di Madrid, 5–7 novembre 2012*, ed. Carlota Cattermole et al. (Madrid: Ediciones de la Discreta 2014), 153–64.

28 'Moreover, just as greed, however slight, tarnishes the habit of justice, so charity or rightly or-dered love refines and irradiates it, so that justice finds its securest abode there where rightly ordered love is at its most intense. Such, then, is the monarch, he and he alone, in principle at least, being the whereabouts of supreme justice. That rightly ordered love does indeed all this follows from the fact that while greed, scorning the very nature of man, seeks out any number of other things besides, love, dismissing them all at a stroke, seeks out only God, man and man's proper good. Since, then, as we saw earlier, to live in peace is of all things the good most prized by man, and since justice is the most pow-

And third, there is the notion that herein—in this rapt sense of the emperor as but the embodiment of justice and thus of the love of which justice is but the outshining—lies the ground and guarantee of man's proper freedom as man, of his proper power to moral and ontological self-determination. For what, in truth, is freedom? Freedom, Dante thinks, is nothing other than the unhindered passage in the individual from *apprehension* to *appetition* via *judgement* as that whereby the whole process stands to be regulated and, by way of its regulation, to be confirmed in its status as a matter of properly human being. Only in the degree, therefore, to which judgement thus understood—as the middle term between seeing and desiring—is and remains unconstrained by those forces both from within and from beyond making for its enslavement can the individual be said to be free, a situation, Dante thinks, obtaining only in circumstances of government by one, by a ruler himself fully free, fully functional and fully focused. On the one hand, then, we have the psychological moment of the argument, that part of it turning upon the structures of seeing, understanding and desiring and upon the nature of freedom as the free passage from discerning to deciding:

> Et ideo dico quod iudicium medium est apprehensionis et appetitus; nam primo res apprehenditur, deinde apprehensa bona vel mala iudicatur, et ultimo iudicans prosequitur sive fugit. Si ergo iudicium moveat omnino appetitum et nullo modo preveniatur ab eo, liberum est; si vero ab appetitu quocunque modo proveniente iudicium moveatur, liberum esse non potest, quia non a se, sed ab alio captivum trahitur.
>
> (*Monarchia* 1.12.3–4)[29]

while on the other hand we have its hymnic moment, its celebration of monarchy as that whereby the evil of oligarchy, tyranny and, as but the perverted form of polity, democracy is held at bay, as that whereby the law and the legislator exist for the people rather than the other way round, as that whereby the good man and the good citizen are identical, and as that whereby the emperor functions— more or less Christically—as a *servus servorum*, a dedicated curator of souls:

> Propter quod sciendum quod illud est liberum quod 'sui met et non alterius gratia est', ut Phylosopho placet in hiis que *De simpliciter ente*. Nam illud

---

erful means to this end, then the greater the love as that whereby justice is quickened, the greater the justice.'

29 'Judgment, therefore, I maintain, is the link between perception and appetition, for first of all a thing is perceived, then it is judged to be good or bad, and finally the one doing the judging either pursues or rejects it. Now if judgment remains in complete control of desire and is in no way preempted by it, then it is free; but if judgment is at all preempted and thus controlled by desire, it cannot be free, for it does not now act of its own accord, but is dragged along captive to another.'

quod est alterius gratia necessitatur ab illo cuius gratia est, sicut via necessitatur a termino. Genus humanum solum imperante Monarcha sui et non
alterius gratia est; tunc enim solum politie diriguntur oblique—democratie
scilicet, oligarchie atque tyrampnides—que in servitutem cogunt genus
humanum, ut patet discurrenti per omnes, et politizant reges, aristocratici
quos optimates vocant, et populi libertatis zelatores; quia cum Monarcha
maxime diligat homines, ut iam tactum est, vult omnes homines bonos
fieri: quod esse non potest apud oblique politizantes. Unde Phylosophus
in suis *Politicis* ait quod in politia obliqua bonus homo est malus civis, in
recta vero bonus homo et civis bonus convertuntur. Et huiusmodi politie
recte libertatem intendunt, scilicet ut homines propter se sint. Non enim
cives propter consules nec gens propter regem, sed e converso consules
propter cives et rex propter gentem; quia quemadmodum non politia ad
leges, quinymo leges ad politiam ponuntur, sic secundum legem viventes
non ad legislatorem ordinantur, sed magis ille ad hos, ut etiam Phylosopho
placet in hiis que de presenti materia nobis ab eo relicta sunt. Hinc etiam
patet quod, quamvis consul sive rex respectu vie sint domini aliorum, respectu autem termini aliorum ministri sunt, et maxime Monarcha, qui minister omnium proculdubio habendus est.Hinc etiam patet quod, quamvis
consul sive rex respectu vie sint domini aliorum, respectu autem termini
aliorum ministri sunt, et maxime Monarcha, qui minister omnium proculdubio habendus est.

(*Monarchia* 1.12.8–12)[30]

Before, however, surrendering to the exhilaration of it all, to Dante's sense of
the emperor as the overseer and to that extent the agent of man's proper happiness

---

30 'What needs to be understood here is that a thing is free insofar as, as Aristotle says in the
Metaphysics, it exists "for its own sake rather than for that of something else." For a thing which exists
for the sake of something else is necessarily determined by it just as a route is determined by its point
of arrival. Now man as man exists for his own sake only when he is under the rule of a monarch, for as
will be only too clear to anyone looking closely at the matter, only then are perverted forms of government—such as democracies, oligarchies and tyrannies—forcing men into slavery put to rights. Only
then is the government of the people by kings, aristocrats and optimates generally, together with those
others zealous for their freedom, good government, and that because, as we have already demonstrated,
the monarch, in his great love for them, wishes upon them all their proper righteousness. This, under
perverted forms of government, is not possible—which is why the Philosopher in the *Politics* has it
that under bad government the good man is a bad citizen while under good government the good man
and the good citizen are one and the same thing. And these just forms of government aim at freedom—
freedom in the sense of making it possible for men to exist for their own sakes; for the citizens exist
not for the sake of the consuls, nor the people for the sake of the king, but rather the consuls for the
sake of the citizens and the king for the people. Indeed just as the body politic is made not for the sake
of the law, but, rather, the law for the sake of the body politic, likewise those living under the law exist
not for the sake of the legislator but, rather (as Aristotle says in such writings as he has left to us on this
matter), he for them. Thus it is apparent that, although consuls or kings preside over the rest with respect to means, with respect to ends they are but their servants, something especially true of the
monarch, who must beyond all doubt be thought of as the servant of all.'

as man here and now, we need to pause for a moment over the precise nature and extent of imperial authority as he himself understands it; for given his role as the guarantor of man's proper freedom as man, of the free passage, that is to say, from discerning to deciding among those subject to him, the emperor, for Dante, is not himself a moral authority. And neither, for that matter, does he or can he arrogate to himself sole responsibility for positive lawmaking within his jurisdiction. As far, then, as the first of these things is concerned, the key passage comes not, in fact, in the *Monarchia* but in the fourth book of the *Convivio*, in the course of Dante's vindicating his right to dissent from the emperor in matters of specifically moral interest. The passage in question, nicely attuned as it is to the notion of imperial writ running only in the case of pure positive law—of the kind of law, that is to say, accountable to the moral proposition but not in itself moral in kind—runs as follows:

> Queste cose simigliantemente, che de l'altre arti sono ragionate, vedere si possono ne l'arte imperiale; ché regole sono in quella che sono pure arti, sì come sono le leggi de' matrimonii, de li servi, de le milizie, de li successori in dignitade, e di queste in tutto siamo a lo Imperadore subietti, sanza dubbio e sospetto alcuno. Altre leggi sono che sono quasi seguita-trici di natura, sì come constituire l'uomo d'etade sofficiente a ministrare, e di queste non semo in tutto subietti. Altre molte sono, che paiono avere alcuna parentela con l'arte imperiale—e qui fu ingannato ed è chi crede che la sentenza imperiale sia in questa parte autentica—: sì come [diffin-ire] giovinezza e gentilezza, sovra le quali nullo imperiale giudicio è da consentire, in quanto elli è imperadore; però, quello che è di Dio sia ren-duto a Dio.
>
> (*Convivio* 4.9.14–15)[31]

while as far as the second of them is concerned—the notion, that is to say, that not all lawmaking pertains as of right to the emperor—we have this from book 1 of the *Monarchia* on the Scythians and the Garamantes as exemplary in this re-spect, Dante's, in fact, being a developed sense of the territoriality of it all and thus

---

31 'What applies to the other arts applies also to the imperial art, for in this case too there are rules and regulations falling under the heading of pure arts, such as the laws pertaining to marriage, condi-tions of service, the military or titular inheritance, where without any doubt or question we are wholly subject to the emperor. There are too other provisions which follow, as it were, those of nature itself, such as the age at which one is capable of administering one's own affairs, and here we are not wholly subject to him. Then again there are many other cases in which, for all their appearing to be a matter of imperial concern, it would be quite mistaken to believe that the emperor, as such, is within his rights to pronounce; so, for example, the definition of youth or nobility, where there can be no question of consenting necessarily to the emperor *qua* emperor. On the contrary, let what is God's be rendered unto God.' John Took, ' "Diligite iustitiam qui iudicatis terram": Justice and the Just Ruler in Dante', in *Dante and Governance*, ed. John R. Woodhouse (Oxford: Clarendon Press, 1997), 137–51.

of imperial law as but the encompassing, as the whereabouts, so to speak, of the
categorical imperative:

> Propter quod advertendum sane quod cum dicitur 'humanum genus
> potest regi per unum suppremum principem', non sic intelligendum est,
> ut minima iudicia cuiuscunque municipii ab illo uno immediate prodire
> possint; cum etiam leges municipales quandoque deficiant et opus
> habeant directivo, ut patet per Phylosophum in quinto *ad Nicomacum* ep-
> yikiam commendantem. Habent nanque nationes, regna et civitates intra
> se proprietates, quas legibus differentibus regulari oportet; est enim lex
> regula directiva vite. Aliter quippe regulari oportet Scithas qui, extra sept-
> imum clima viventes et magnam dierum et noctium inequalitatem pati-
> entes, intolerabili quasi algore frigoris premuntur, et aliter Garamantes
> qui, sub equinoctiali habitantes et coequatam semper lucem diurnam
> noctis tenebris habentes, ob estus acris nimietatem vestimentis operiri
> non possunt. Sed sic intelligendum est ut humanum genus secundum sua
> comunia, que omnibus competunt, ab eo regatur et comuni regula guber-
> netur ad pacem.
>
> (*Monarchia* 1.14.4–7)[32]

But this notwithstanding, the emperor, for Dante, enters even so into the soteriological scheme of things as fashioned from beforehand in the recesses of the
divine mind; for it was in the time of Caesar Augustus, from whom a decree went
out that all the world should be taxed, that God set about reconciling the world
to himself in the person of the Christ, 'nothing, therefore, ministering to our
happiness wanting for its minister':

> Nam si a lapsu primorum parentum, qui diverticulum fuit totius nostre
> deviationis, dispositiones hominum et tempora recolamus, non inveniemus
> nisi sub divo Augusto monarcha, existente Monarchia perfecta, mundum

32 'It is in this respect to be noted that when we say "mankind can be ruled by one supreme ruler",
this should not be taken to mean that—the occasional deficiency of local laws notwithstanding, and
thus (as is clear from what Aristotle says in the fifth book of the *Ethics* when it comes to commending
the principle of equity) the need for guidance in implementing them—each and every judgement in
each and every locality should come directly from him; for nations, kingdoms and cities are sufficiently
different one from another to require government by different laws, law, precisely, being a principle of
practical organization. Thus the Scythians, who live beyond the seventh zone and suffer nights and
days of the most unequal length, and who perforce endure a well-nigh unbearable cold, need to have
one set of laws, while the Garamantes, who live in the equatorial zone with days and nights of equal
length and with heat sufficiently intense to make clothes and the wearing thereof intolerable, another.
Rather, it is to be understood in the sense that mankind is to be ruled by him in those matters common
to all alike and touching all alike, such that by way of a common provision all men are steered in the
direction of peace.'

undique fuisse quietum. Et quod tunc humanum genus fuerit felix in pacis universalis tranquillitate hoc ystoriographi omnes, hoc poete illustres, hoc etiam scriba mansuetudinis Cristi testari dignatus est; et denique Paulus 'plenitudinem temporis' statum illum felicissimum appellavit. Vere tempus et temporalia queque plena fuerunt, quia nullum nostre felicitatis ministerium ministro vacavit.

(Monarchia 1.16.1–2)[33]

It is, therefore, to Rome in respect of her function in the world-historical scheme of things, as the means of God's reconciling the world to himself in its now longtime sickness both of mind and of heart (the 'intellectu egrotas utroque, similiter et affectu' of 1.16.5),[34] that Dante turns in the second book of the *Monarchia*, an essay precisely on Rome as but an instrument of divine intentionality. And the evidence for this? None needed, for everything about Rome in respect of her role in world history is self-evident. So, for example, in the very moment of her coming about, we have the figure of Aeneas combining as he did by way of character, ancestry and consanguinity the nobility of the entire ancient world, Asian, African and European alike. Who, then, Dante insists, can fail to discern here the force of destiny, the hand of God at work in the affairs of men? None, he goes on, for that way lies impiety, effrontery of the first order. And then there are Rome's many miracles, a truth everywhere registered by the *auctores* and everywhere testifying to the sublimity of it all: Livy and Lucan, for instance, on the shield that fell from heaven in the time of Numa Pompilius, Virgil on the goose summoning the Romans to defend the Capitol against the Gauls, and Orosius on the sudden hailstorm saving Rome from Hannibal and on Cloelia's otherwise incredible breaking of the siege of Porsenna by swimming across the Tiber—the miraculous as but a short-circuiting of secondary by primary causality constituting in this sense part and parcel of Roman history as well as the incontrovertible means of her accreditation. All this, then, in the first four chapters of book 2, a book that means to go on as it began, chapters 5 and 6 offering a celebration of Rome's steady commitment to the common good, the 'bonum rei publice', as the final cause of her every undertaking. One need only recall the cases, for example, of Cincinnatus, Fabritius, Camillus, Brutus, Mutius, Cato and Publius Decius,

---

33 'For if we review the times and temperament of men from the fall of our first parents as the whereabouts of our every self-losing, at no time do we light on universal peace other than under the immortal Augustus and his consummate monarchy. That mankind was at that time indeed resting happily in universal peace and in the tranquillity thereof is attested by every historian and poet of note. Even the chronicler of Christ's gentleness deigned to bear witness to it as, finally, did Paul in speaking of that happy state as but "the fullness of time". The times and all things temporal were indeed full, nothing ministering to our happiness wanting for its minister.'

34 'In mind you are doubly sick [i.e. both speculatively and in practice] as in affection.'

each of whom distinguished himself as a paragon of civic selflessness, and each
of whom, in so doing, confirmed the status of Rome as but the benefactor of
mankind as a whole, as begotten in the womb of piety:

> Patet igitur quod quicunque bonum rei publice intendit finem iuris inten-
> dit. Si ergo Romani bonum rei publice intenderunt, verum erit dicere
> finem iuris intendisse. Quod autem romanus populus bonum prefatum
> intenderit subiciendo sibi orbem terrarum, gesta sua declarant, in quibus,
> omni cupiditate summota que rei publice semper adversa est, et universali
> pace cum libertate dilecta, populus ille sanctus pius et gloriosus propria
> commoda neglexisse videtur, ut publica pro salute humani generis procu-
> raret. Unde recte illud scriptum est: 'Romanum imperium de Fonte nasci-
> tur pietatis'.
>
> (*Monarchia* 2.5.4–5)[35]

—at which point Dante appeals to the further notion of some being born to rule
and others to be ruled, a matter, however, not of might but of right, of the at once
prior and proper order of things:

> Propter quod videmus quod quidam non solum singulares homines, quine-
> tiam populi, apti nati sunt ad principari, quidam alii ad subici atque minis-
> trare, ut Phylosophus astruit in hiis que *De Politicis*; et talibus, ut ipse dicit,
> non solum regi est expediens, sed etiam iustum, etiamsi ad hoc cogantur.
> Que si ita se habent, non dubium est quin natura locum et gentem dispos-
> uerit in mundo ad universaliter principandum; aliter sibi defecisset, quod

---

35 'Thus it is clear that whoever looks to the good of the community looks to this as the object of
all lawmaking. If, therefore, the Romans too looked to the good of the community, then this in truth,
we have to say, was the object of *their* lawmaking. That the Roman people in conquering the world did
indeed have that good as their aim is shown by their deeds, for, having wholly suppressed the avarice
everywhere harmful to the community and cherishing instead universal peace and freedom, that holy,
pious and glorious people clearly sacrificed all personal advantage for the sake of the general well-being
of mankind. With good reason, therefore, it was written: "The Roman empire is born of the fountainhead of piety."' For the 'good of the community' moment of the passage, Giorgio Padoan, '"Alia utilia
rei publice": La composizione della *Monarchia* di Dante', *LC* 28 (1999), 7–27 (and in *Ultimi studi di
filologia dantesca e boccacciana*, ed. Aldo Maria Costantini [Ravenna: Longo, 2002], 41–57). For the
'fountainhead of piety' moment, Joseph Balogh, 'Romanum Imperium de Fonte nascitur pietatis', *DDJ*
10 (1928), 202–5; Theodore Silverstein, 'On the Genesis of *De Monarchia* II.v', *Spec* 13.3 (1938), 326–49;
Francesco Di Capua, 'La concezione mistica dell'Impero Romano in Dante ("Romanum Imperium
de fonte nasciture pietatis", *Monarchia* II.5.5)', *RSRN* 21 (1941), 27–52. More generally, Eugenio Dupré
Theseider, *L'idea imperiale di Roma nella tradizione del medioevo* (Milan: Istituto per gli studi di politica
internazionale, 1942); David Thompson, ed., *The Idea of Rome from Antiquity to the Renaissance* (Albu-
querque: University of New Mexico Press, 1971); Nancy Lenkeith, *Dante and the Legend of Rome* (London: Warburg Institute, 1972); Arturo Graf, *Roma nella memoria e nelle immaginazioni del Medio Evo*
(Sala Bolognese: Arnaldo Forni, 1987 [1882]).

est inpossibile. Quis autem fuerit locus et que gens, per dicta superius et per dicenda inferius satis est manifestum quod fuerit Roma, et cives eius sive populus.

(Monarchia 2.6.7–8)[36]

Nothing, then, not even the kind of counterconsideration relative to the brutality of Rome as recorded by Augustine and the monstrosity of Caesar as registered by Lucan, is sufficient to disturb either the depth or the serenity of Dante's conviction hereabouts, his sense of Rome as in one and the same moment but the means and the manifestation of God's good purposes. If, then, violence and victory were all part of it then so be it, for—certainly where Rome is concerned—wherever two or three are gathered together for the sake of doing battle there God will be in their midst:

Hoc autem fit cum de libero assensu partium, non odio, non amore, sed solo zelo iustitie, per virium tam animi quam corporis mutuam collisionem divinum iudicium postulator . . . Quod si formalia duelli servata sunt, aliter enim duellum non esset, iustitie necessitate de comuni assensu congregati propter zelum iustitie nonne in nomine Dei congregati sunt? Et si sic, nonne Deus in medio illorum est, cum ipse in evangelio nobis hoc promictat?

(Monarchia 2.9.2 and 5–6)[37]

With what amounts, then, to a scarcely less than exhaustive account of Rome as but a miracle in her own right, Dante comes once again to the soteriological aspect of the matter, to, more exactly, the fact of Christ's living and dying when he did; for Christ's living and dying when he did merely serves yet again to con-

---

36 'Thus we see that not just certain individuals, but certain peoples are as Aristotle affirms in the *Politics* born to rule while others are born to be ruled and to serve, for which reason, and again as Aristotle says, it is not only expedient but just that, even if force has to be used to bring this about, such people should be ruled. This being so, there is no doubt that nature ordained both a place and a people to exercise universal rule in the world, for otherwise she would in this respect have fallen short, which is impossible. What that place and what that people were will, from what was said above and from what follows, be clear enough: Rome was the place and her citizens the people.' Carlo Filosa, 'La "virtù" dei Romani nel giudizio di S. Agostino e di Dante', in *Dante e Roma. Atti del Convegno di studi, Roma 8–10 aprile*, ed. Casa di Dante sotto gli auspici del Comune di Roma (Florence: Le Monnier, 1965), 195–210; David Thompson, 'Dante's Virtuous Romans', DS 96 (1978), 145–62; Charles T. Davis, 'Ptolemy of Lucca and the Roman Republic', in *Dante's Italy and Other Essays*, 254–89.

37 'A duel takes place when, with the free assent of both sides, neither through hatred nor through love but solely out of concern for the right and in the context of a struggle involving both body and soul, God's judgement is sought . . . provided only, then, that these, as the proper conditions of trial by combat, have been respected (for short of this it would not be trial by combat), is it not true that those who, compelled by justice and out of concern for justice, have by common consent come together have done so in the name of God? And if so, is not he, as he promised us in the Gospel, in their midst?'

firm the legitimacy and indeed the righteousness of the regime into which he was
born and thus to set the seal upon Rome's status as but part of the grand design.
On the one hand, then, we have Christ's birth and registration under Caesar
Augustus as ruler of the world, evidence were evidence required of her indispensability to the salvific scheme of things:

> Sed Cristus, ut scriba eius Lucas testatur, sub edicto romane auctoritatis
> nasci voluit de Virgine Matre, ut in illa singulari generis humani descrip-
> tione filius Dei, homo factus, homo conscriberetur: quod fuit illud
> prosequi.
>
> (*Monarchia* 2.10.6)[38]

while on the other hand we have the efficacy of the cross as guaranteed by its
Roman administration, anything less than this—any imposition hereabouts by a
lesser authority—serving straightaway to compromise its twofold legality and
universality:

> Si ergo sub ordinario iudice Cristus passus non fuisset, illa pena punitio non
> fuisset. Et iudex ordinarius esse non poterat nisi supra totum humanum
> genus iurisdictionem habens, cum totum humanum genus in carne illa Cristi
> portantis dolores nostros, ut ait Propheta, puniretur.
>
> (*Monarchia* 2.11.5)[39]

Now here the aforesaid Guido Vernani (never, in truth, well disposed towards
Dante) was once more up in arms, his point being that Christ's death on Calvary
was a matter solely and exclusively of obedience to the will of the Father, this
being the way of his making good the first *dis*obedience of man, all else—to wit,
the precise circumstances of it all—being neither here nor there:

> Quis enim unquam tam turpiter erravit, ut diceret quod poena debita pro
> peccato originali potestati alicujus terreni iudicis subjaceret? . . . Peccatum

38 'But Christ, as Luke in writing of him relates, chose to be born of a virgin mother under an edict
of Roman authority, so that the Son of God, in becoming man, might be enrolled as a man in that
unique register of the human race—all of which amounts to an acknowledgement of that edict.' William
Henry Vincent Reade, 'Dante's Vision of History', *Proceedings of the British Academy* 25 (1939), 187–215;
Charles T. Davis, *Dante and the Idea of Rome* (Oxford: Clarendon Press, 1957); Charles T. Davis,
'Dante's Vision of History', in *Dante's Italy and Other Essays*, 23–41; Antonio C. Mastrobuono, *Essays
on Dante's Philosophy of History* (Florence: Olschki, 1979); Marjorie Reeves, 'Dante and the Prophetic
View of History', in *The World of Dante*, ed. Cecil Grayson (Oxford: Clarendon Press, 1980), 44–60;
August Buck, 'Dante und die Geschichte', *DDJ* 68–69 (1993–94), 15–30.

39 'If Christ, therefore, had not suffered under the appropriate judge that penalty would not have
been a punishment; for no judge could be accounted appropriate unless he had jurisdiction over the
whole of mankind, since it was the whole of mankind that was to be punished in the flesh of Christ,
who, as the Prophet says [Isaiah 53:4], "bore our sorrows."'

autem Adae, prout est in humane genere, nihil est aliud quam peccatum orig-
inale. Nec unquam aliquis homo legislator in suis legibus de hoc aliquid ordi-
navit, nec gentiles istud peccatum cognoverunt, nec Pilatus propter hoc indi-
cavit Christum; sed ad hoc, quod pro illo peccato, Deo esset pro toto humano
genere plenarie satisfactum, sufficiebat quod Christus verus Deus et verus
homo pro conservatione justitiae, esset 'obediens Deo Patri usque ad mortem,
mortem autem crucis'.

(*De reprobatione Monarchiae*, ed. Piccini, 28)[40]

For Dante, however, there neither is nor can be any separating out of these
things, the coincidence of substance and circumstance hereabouts serving merely,
he thinks, to confirm Rome's centrality to the soteriological scheme as a whole.
Things could not, in other words, have been other than they were, Rome no less
than Jerusalem having its part to play—its essentially sacred part to play—within
the economy of the whole.

The third book of the *Monarchia* looks on the face of it to signal a shift from
the prophetic to the publicistic, a now more immediate engagement with the
polemical literature of the time—with, for example, the *De ecclesiastica potestate*
of Aegidius Romanus, the *De regimine christiano* of James of Viterbo or the *De
regimine principum* of Tholemy of Lucca all belonging to the early years of the
fourteenth century. Straightaway, then, Dante identifies the opposition—namely
those who on the basis either of a papal-hierocratic view of the relationship between the spiritual and secular powers in Christendom or else of political self-
interest pure and simple will have nothing to do with the imperial idea as he
understands it. There are, more precisely, three groups to consider here, namely
(*a*) those pastors of the flock, who, proceeding more or less in good faith, are
nonetheless led astray by their zeal for the keys; (*b*) the kings and princes of
Christendom anxious for whatever reason to keep the emperor at arm's length;
and (*c*) the massed ranks of decretalists and canonists as in the main dyed-in-the-
wool advocates of the papal project, Dante for his part choosing to address the
first of them, the zealous but misguided keepers of the keys. Jealous as he is,
though, in respect of the proprieties, of the reverence properly due to those in
high office, his tone hereabouts is nonetheless very definitely combative rather
than conciliatory, his, he says, being a descent into the arena there to cast out the
wicked and the mendacious. Clad as he is with the breastplate of faith and com-

---

40 'Whoever, in fact, in maintaining that the penalty incurred by original sin fell within the power
of any earthly judge, unleashed so gross an error? . . . The sin, then, of Adam, as pertaining to mankind
as a whole, is nothing other than original sin. No human legislator, in framing the law, touched upon
sin of this kind, neither did any Gentile countenance it, and neither did Pilate condemn Christ on
these grounds; but rather, for that sin to be expiated for all mankind and for justice to be done, it was
enough that Christ, true God and true man, was "obedient to God unto death, even the death of the
cross."'

forted by the prophets, by the psalmist and by the one who by his blood led us
out of the darkness into the light, his, in short, is a gladiatorial undertaking, a task
laid upon him from on high and forever redounding to his credit:

assumpta fiducia de verbis Danielis premissis, in quibus divina potentia
clipeus defensorum veritatis astruitur, iuxta monitionem Pauli fidei loricam
induens, in calore carbonis illius quem unus de Seraphin accepit de altari
celesti et tetigit labia Ysaie, gignasium presens ingrediar, et in brachio Illius
qui nos de potestate tenebrarum liberavit in sanguine suo impium atque
mendacem de palestra, spectante mundo, eiciam. Quid timeam, cum Spiritus Patri et Filio coecternus aiat per os David: 'In memoria ecterna erit
iustus, ab auditione mala non timebit'?

(*Monarchia* 3.1.3–4)[41]

It is, then, in the spirit of hand-to-hand combat that Dante sets about dismantling the hierocratic case, a process consisting for the main part of pointing out
the nonsense of arguing on a syllogistic basis from this or that allusion in Scripture to the state of contemporary power politics; so, for example, by way of de-
molishing the notion that, just as the moon has no light other than what it receives
from the sun, so too the temporal power has no authority other than what it receives from the spiritual power, we have these lines from the fourth chapter with

41 'Having taken heart from the words of Daniel cited above to the effect that defenders of the
truth are shielded by a power from on high, and putting on "the breastplate of faith" as exhorted by
Paul, all-aflame with that burning coal taken by one of the seraphim from the heavenly altar to touch
Isaiah's lips, I shall now enter the arena, and, by the arm of the one who freed us from the power of
darkness with his blood and before the eyes of the whole world, I shall cast out the wicked and mendacious. For what have I to fear, when the Spirit coeternal with the Father and with the Son promised
upon the lips of David that "the righteous shall be in everlasting remembrance and shall not be afraid
of ill report"?' Jean Rivière, *Le Problème de l'église et de l'état au temps de Philippe le Bel* (Louvain: Spici-
legium sacrum lovaniensis, 1926); Walter Ullmann, *Medieval Papalism: The Political Theories of the
Medieval Canonists* (London: Methuen, 1949); Michele Maccarrone, *Vicarius Christi: Storia del titolo
papale* (Rome: Facultas Theologica Pontificii Athenaei Lateranensis, 1952); Brian Tierney, *The Crisis
of Church and State, 1050–1300* (Englewood Cliffs, NJ: Prentice-Hall, 1964); John A. Watt, 'The Theory
of Papal Monarchy in the Thirteenth Century', *Traditio* 20 (1964), 179–314 (and [London: Burns &
Oates, 1965]); Michael J. Wilks, *The Problem of Sovereignty in the Later Middle Ages* (Cambridge: Cambridge University Press, 1970); Colin Morris, *The Papal Monarchy: The Western Church from 1050–1250*
(Oxford: Oxford University Press, 1989). For the more immediate circumstances of the *Monarchia*,
Richard Scholz, *Die Publizistik zur Zeit Philipps des Schönen und Bonifaz VIII* (Stuttgart: F. Enke, 1903);
William M. Bowsky, 'Clement V and the Emperor-Elect', *MH* 12 (1958), 52–69; Charles Wood, *Philip
the Fair and Boniface VIII: State vs Papacy*, 2nd ed. (Huntingdon, NY: R. E. Krieger, 1976); Aldo Vallone,
Antidantismo politico e dantismo letterario (Rome: Bonacci, 1988); Sophia Menache, *Clement V* (Cambridge: Cambridge University Press, 1998). For *Monarchia* 3 in particular, Michele Maccarrone, 'Il terzo
libro della *Monarchia*, *SD* 23 (1955), 5–142; Bruno Nardi, 'Intorno ad una nuova interpretazione del
terzo libro della *Monarchia* dantesca', in *Dal Convivio alla Commedia* (Rome: Nella sede dell'Istituto,
1960), 151–313; Giuliana Angiolillo, 'Il *Manifesto* di Manfredi ai Romani e il III libro della *Monarchia* di
Dante', *Studi Romani* 21 (1973), 38–60.

their sense of an argument at once invalidated by a shift in meaning—from light
to authority—as the syllogism goes on:

> Et ideo argumentum peccabat in forma, quia predicatum in conclusione non
> est extremitas maioris, ut patet; procedit enim sic: luna recipit lucem a sole
> qui est regimen spirituale; regimen temporale est luna; ergo regimen tem-
> porale recipit auctoritatem a regimine spirituali. Nam in extremitate maioris
> ponunt 'lucem', in predicato vero conclusionis 'auctoritatem': que sunt res
> diverse subiecto et ratione, ut visum est.
>
> (*Monarchia* 3.4.21–22)[42]

And what applies in the case of the sun and the moon applies also in the case
of Levi and Judah as the fruit of the loins of Jacob, the fact that Levi was the firstborn of his father by no means entailing the priority of priestly with respect to
princely power, the terms 'birth' and 'authority' differing absolutely in point of
both 'subject and signification' (the 'nam aliud est auctoritas et nativitas subiecto
et ratione' of 3.5.3). But neither is that all, for even where there *are* grounds for
inferring one thing from another, the process must at every point be carefully
regulated; so, for example, there is the case of Samuel's deposition of Saul in the
Old Testament and that of the Magi's offering of gold and frankincense to the
Christ child in the New Testament, both of which, it is said, point to the ordering
of temporal to spiritual power on earth, of the emperor to the pope. But here,
Dante insists, we need a distinction, for in the case of Samuel, he, Samuel, was
neither a vicar nor a plenipotentiary in respect of the Most High but a mere messenger or functionary, while in the case of the Magi, it was the Christ who was
being honoured—not his vicar, his successor, his surrogate or his representative
but the Christ and the Christ alone. And what applies here by way of proper

---

42 'And thus the argument contained a formal error, for the predicate in the conclusion is clearly
not the same as the predicate in the major premiss; for it runs like this: the moon receives its light from
the sun, which is the spiritual power; the temporal power is the moon; therefore the temporal power
receives its authority from the spiritual power. Thus for the predicate in the major premiss they put
"light", while for in the predicate in the conclusion they put "authority", these, however, as we have
seen, both being different things and meaning different things.' Anthony K. Cassell, ' "Luna est Ecclesia": Dante and the "Two Great Lights" ', *DS* 119 (2001), 1–26; Anthony K. Cassell, *The 'Monarchia'
Controversy* (Washington, DC: Catholic University of America Press, 2004), 86–93; Diego Quaglioni,
' "Quanta est differentia inter solem et lunam": Tolomeo e la dottrina canonista del "Duo luminaria" ',
Micrologus: Natura, Scienze e Società Medievali 12 (2004), 395–406; Gabriele Carletti, 'Dante e la teoria
dei "Duo magna luminaria" ', in *Prima di Machiavelli*, ed. Gabriele Carletti (Pescara: Edizioni scienti-
fiche abruzzesi, 2007), 55–72. For the syllogistic aspect of the argument, Elizabeth Mozzillo-Howell,
'Dante's Art of Reason: A Study of Medieval Logic and Semantics in the *Monarchy*', Harvard University
Dissertation (1998); Elizabeth Mozzillo-Howell, 'Dante between Scholasticism and Humanism: Aspects of the *Monarchy*', in *Forms of the "Medieval" in the "Renaissance"*, ed. George Hugo Tucker (Char-
lottesville, VA: Rookwood Press, 2000), 29–48; Flavio Silvestrini, *Gli "invidiosi veri" della politica: Il
"Monarchia" dantesco e la scienza del sillogismo* (Rome: La Sapienza, 2012).

distinction applies too when it comes to the cornerstone of the hierocratic case, to the Matthean commission whereby Peter was empowered to the binding and loosing of all things on earth and in heaven, a commission to be understood, Dante says, in terms not of the unqualified administration of things here below but of the properly priestly prerogative of locking and unlocking the gates of heaven—that and no more:

> Cum ergo ita sit, manifestum est quod non absolute summenda est illa distributio, sed respective ad aliquid. Quod autem illa respiciat satis est evidens considerato illo quod sibi conceditur, circa quod illa distributio subiungitur. Dicit enim Cristus Petro: 'Tibi dabo claves regni celorum', hoc est 'Faciam te hostiarium regni celorum'. Deinde subdit 'et quodcunque', quod est 'omne quod', id est 'et omne quod ad istud offitium spectabit solvere poteris et ligare'. Et sic signum universale quod includitur in 'quodcunque' contrahitur in sua distributione ab offitio clavium regni celorum; et sic assummendo, vera est illa propositio; absolute vero non, ut patet. Et ideo dico quod etsi successor Petri, secundum exigentiam offitii commissi Petro, possit solvere et ligare, non tamen propter hoc sequitur quod possit solvere seu ligare decreta Imperii sive leges ut ipsi dicebant, nisi ulterius probaretur hoc spectare ad offitium clavium.
>
> (*Monarchia* 3.8.8–11)[43]

The reply is impressive, impressive for its honouring both in the letter and in the spirit Augustine's famous misgiving with regard to the presence of mystical meaning in holy writ, Dante for his part, just a few pages earlier, echoing the great bishop's sense of the need for caution hereabouts.[44] But that is not all, for what

43 'It is plain, then, that, in respect of terminology and its precise coverage, it is a question here, not of the absolute but of the relative, all of which becomes clear when, still from the point of view of coverage, we consider the nature and circumstances of the commission. For what Christ says to Peter is this: "To you I give the keys of the kingdom of heaven", that is: "I shall make you custodian of the kingdom of heaven". He then adds "and whatsoever"—in other words "everything" in the sense of everything pertaining to this office being in his power to loose and bind. Thus the universal content of the term "whatsoever" is in fact delimited by way of its reference to the office of the keys to the kingdom of heaven. Thus far, then, the proposition is true, but, as is now plain, not absolutely. And so I say that, although Peter's successor can in consequence of the office committed to him loose and bind, nonetheless it does not follow from this that, short of their proving that this does indeed pertain to that office, he can, as they [i.e. "those motivated by zealous concern for Mother Church", 3.3.18] insisted, loose or bind the decrees or the laws of the empire.'
44 *Monarchia* 3.4.7–8: 'Propter primum dicit Augustinus in Civitate Dei: "Non omnia que gesta narrantur etiam significare aliquid putanda sunt, sed propter illa que aliquid significant etiam ea que nichil significant actexuntur". . . Propter secundum idem ait in Doctrina Cristiana, loquens de illo aliud in Scripturis sentire quam ille qui scripsit eas dicit, quod "ita fallitur ac si quisquam deserens viam eo tamen per girum pergeret quo via illa perducit"; et subdit: "Demonstrandum est ut consuetudine deviandi etiam in transversum aut perversum ire cogatur"' (With respect to the first of these things,

in this third book of the *Monarchia* amounts to the deconstructive phase of the argument, that part of the book living on in anticipation of its positive resolution, stands to be rounded off by the dismantling of three further aspects of the hierocratic case in its customary formulation, namely the argument from allegory (chapter 9), the argument from history (chapter 10) and the argument from reason (chapter 11), none of them, Dante thinks, bearing scrutiny. As far, then, as the argument from allegory is concerned, it is a question of denying yet again the notion that everything in Scripture has an alternative meaning, a deeper and more abiding sense there for the benefit of those such as the papal hierocrats busy about their own agenda. When, for example, Peter, in Luke 22:38, speaks of his having two swords, he does not mean to imply that all power on earth, spiritual and secular alike, was his, for this was but another instance of our archimandrite's saying the first thing that came into his head (the 'tum quia Petrus de more subito respondebat ad rerum superficiem tantum' of 3.9.2),[45] allegory as but a steady desire to see something other in the text than what it actually says tending by and large less to elucidate than to injure it. As far, by contrast, as the argument from history is concerned, an argument resting primarily on the so-called Donation of Constantine as that whereby the emperor was said to make over the ancient seat of the empire to the papacy in perpetuity, it is a question of denying both the right of the Church to receive such a gift (there being no question here of possession beyond an administration of the goods of this world for the benefit of the poor) and the right of the emperor to make such a gift (there being no question here of an officeholder alienating the substance of the office to which he has succeeded).

Augustine, in his *City of God* [16.2.3] says: 'Not every happening that is recorded need be taken as significant, for those which are not significant may well be included for the sake of those which are'. . . while as far as the second are concerned, the same teacher, in his *On Christian Doctrine* [1.36.41], says of the one who seeks to give Scripture a sense other than that intended by the writer that 'he makes the same mistake as a person who leaves the main road and then only after a long detour makes it to the place to which the road was leading, which is why (he adds) he is to be corrected and shown that it is more useful not to leave the road, lest getting into the habit of straying forces him to go off at a tangent and take a wrong turning'). Roland J. Teske, 'Criteria for Figurative Interpretation in St Augustine', in *De doctrina christiana: A Classic of Western Culture*, ed. Duane W. H. Arnold and Pamela Bright (Notre Dame: University of Notre Dame Press, 1995), 109–22; Simone Marchesi, *Dante and Augustine: Linguistics, Poetics, Hermeneutics* (Toronto: University of Toronto Press, 2011).

45 'and then because it was Peter's habit to seize quickly on the superficial meaning of things', with, from a little later on in the same chapter: 'The fact that Peter usually seized upon the superficial meaning of his [Christ's] words is proved by the sudden and thoughtless way he would straightaway jump in; for he was moved, I believe, not only by the sincerity of his faith but also by his natural simplicity and purity' (Et quod Petrus de more ad superficiem loqueretur, probat eius festina et inpremeditata presumptio, ad quam non solum fidei sinceritas impellebat, sed, ut credo, puritas et simplicitas naturalis). John A. Watt, 'Spiritual and Temporal Powers', in *The Cambridge History of Medieval Political Thought*, c. 350–c. 1450, ed. J. H. Burns (Cambridge: Cambridge University Press, 1988), 367–90. For Dante, Paola Nasti, 'Dante and Ecclesiology', in *Reviewing Dante's Theology*, vol. 2, ed. Claire E. Honess and Matthew Treherne (Bern: Peter Lang, 2013), 43–88.

On neither side, then, the least hint of legitimacy, simply a demonstrable lack of self-understanding:

Adhuc, cum conferens habeat se per modum agentis et cui confertur per modum patientis, ut placet Phylosopho in quarto *ad Nicomacum*, non solum ad collationem esse licitam requiritur dispositio conferentis, sed etiam eius cui confertur . . . Sed Ecclesia omnino indisposita erat ad temporalia recipienda per preceptum prohibitivum expressum, ut habemus per Matheum sic: 'Nolite possidere aurum, neque argentum, neque pecuniam in zonis vestris, non peram in via' etc. Nam etsi per Lucam habemus relaxationem precepti quantum ad quedam, ad possessionem tamen auri et argenti licentiatam Ecclesiam post prohibitionem illam invenire non potui. Qua re, si Ecclesia recipere non poterat, dato quod Constantinus hoc facere potuisset de se, actio tamen illa non erat possibilis propter patientis indispositionem. Patet igitur quod nec Ecclesia recipere per modum possessionis, nec ille conferre per modum alienationis poterat. Poterat tamen Imperator in patrocinium Ecclesie Patrimonium et alia deputare, inmoto semper superiori dominio, cuius unitas divisionem non patitur. Poterat et vicarius Dei recipere non tanquam possessor, sed tanquam fructuum pro Ecclesia pro Cristi pauperibus dispensator, quod apostolos fecisse non ignoratur.

(*Monarchia* 3.10.13–17)[46]

46 'Again, since—as Aristotle says in the fourth book of the *Ethics*—the person granting a thing is related to the person receiving it as agent to patient, the validity of the gift requires a proper disposition on the part not simply of the one who gives but of the one who receives it . . . But on the basis of the express prohibition recorded by Matthew ("Possess neither gold nor silver, nor brass in your purses, nor scrip for your journey"), the Church was in no sense properly disposed to receive things temporal. And although in Luke we find a slight easing of this precept in certain respects, yet I have been unable to discover the granting of any subsequent permission to possess gold and silver. Thus even assuming that Constantine was in a position to make this donation, the act was impossible on account of the unsuitability of the patient, of the Church's inability to receive it. It is clear, in short, that the Church was no more able to take possession of it than the emperor was to make of it an unconditional gift. He could, to be sure, and provided only that it was without prejudice to his proper proprietorial rights (these permitting no alienation), grant the Church custody of this or that element of his patrimony, but, as the apostles are known to have done, only as administrator of the fruits of that patrimony for the benefit of the Church and of Christ's poor.' On the merely concessionary and leasehold status of temporal assets by the Church, Attilio Mellone, O.F.M., 'Il S. Francesco di Dante e il S. Francesco della storia', in *Dante e il Francescanesimo* (Cava dei Tirreni: Avagliano Editore, 1987), 11–73; Charles T. Davis, 'Dante and Ecclesiastical Property', in *Law in Medieval Life and Thought*, ed. Edward B. King et al. (Sewanee, TN: Press of the University of the South, 1990), 244–57. For Dante and the Donation, Bruno Nardi, 'La "Donatio Constantini" e Dante', in *Nel mondo di Dante* (Rome: Edizioni di Storia e Letteratura, 1944), 109–59; Otello Ciacci, 'La donazione di Costantino', in *Studi danteschi* (Perugia: Augusta Perusia, 1992), 1–49; Domenico Maffei, 'Il pensiero di Cino da Pistoia sulla donazione di Costantino: Le sue fonti e il dissenso finale di Dante', in *Studi di storia delle Università e della letteratura giuridica* (Goldbach: Keip, 1995), 103–13; Dabney G. Park, 'Dante and the Donation of Con-

And then finally there is the argument from reason, where it is a question of distinguishing—subtly, to be sure, but significantly—between the kinds of office exercised by the emperor on the one hand and by the pope on the other, imperial office being a matter of power (the emperor relating to his subjects by way of domination) and papal office being a matter of paternity (the pope relating to his people by way of fatherhood), neither one of these things being reducible to the other but to God alone as their author and architect:

Si ergo Papatus et Imperiatus, cum sint relationes superpositionis, habeant reduci ad respectum superpositionis, a quo respectu cum suis differential-ibus descendunt, Papa et Imperator, cum sint relativa, reduci habebunt ad aliquod unum in quo reperiatur ipse respectus superpositionis absque dif-ferentialibus aliis. Et hoc erit vel ipse Deus, in quo respectus omnis univer-saliter unitur, vel aliqua substantia Deo inferiori in qua respectus superpo-sitionis per differentiam superpositionis a simplici respectu descendens particuletur. Et sic patet quod Papa et Imperator, in quantum homines, habent reduci ad unum; in quantum vero Papa et Imperator, ad aliud; et per hoc patet ad rationem.

(Monarchia 3.11.10–12)[47]

All that remains, therefore, before proceeding to the constructive phase of the argument—to a separating out of papal and imperial authority by way of the 'duo ultima' or 'two last ends' of human activity under the conditions of time and eternity—is to administer the final coup de grâce, a final laying to rest of priestly pretension. Looking, then, at the hierocratic case in the round, there are, Dante thinks, three root objections to it, namely (*a*) the historical priority of the empire vis-à-vis the Church and this as ruling out any in-principle dependence of the former upon the latter; (*b*) the lack of any justification for the clerical position either in natural or in divine law; and (*c*) the essential nature of the Church as but the continuing life of Christ on earth. As far, then, as the first of these things

---

stantine', *DS* 130 (2012), 67–161. More generally, Domenico Maffei, *La Donazione di Costantino nei giuristi medievali* (Milan: Giuffrè, 1964); Jürgen Miethke, 'La Donazione di Costantino e la controversia pubblicistica tra papa e imperatore nel XIV secolo', in *Costantino il Grande tra medioevo e età moderna. Atti del Convegno, Trento 22–24 aprile 2004,* ed. Giorgio Bonamente et al. (Bologna: Il Mulino, 2008), 51–79.

47 'If, then, papacy and empire, being relations of authority, are to be referred to a single principle of authority whence they derive together with everything that distinguishes them one from the other, then pope and emperor (likewise a matter of relationship) must derive from an entity comprehending that relationship in an undifferentiated manner. And this will either be God himself, in whose unity every difference is resolved, or in some lesser entity which, proceeding as it does from God, realizes that same unity after its own manner. Clearly, then, pope and emperor *as men* are referable to one thing, but *as pope* and *emperor* to something else, this being our reply to the argument from reason.'

is concerned, namely the priority of empire vis-à-vis Church in the order of time, we have this passage from chapter 12 with its sense of the empire's coming about long before the Church was ever thought of:

> Quod autem auctoritas Ecclesie non sit causa imperialis auctoritatis proba-
> tur sic: illud, quo non existente aut quo non virtuante, aliud habet totam
> suam virtutem, non est causa illius virtutis; sed, Ecclesia non existente aut
> non virtuante, Imperium habuit totam suam virtutem; ergo Ecclesia non
> est causa virtutis Imperii et per consequens nec auctoritatis, cum idem sit
> virtus et auctoritas eius.
>
> (*Monarchia* 3.12.3)[48]

while as far as the second of them is concerned, namely the legality of the papal position, we have this from chapter 13 with its sense of, if anything, its positive exclusion under both the old and the new dispensation:

> Sed non per naturalem, quia natura non imponit legem nisi suis effectibus,
> cum Deus insufficiens esse non possit ubi sine secundis agentibus aliquid
> in esse producit. Unde, cum Ecclesia non sit effectus nature, sed Dei dicen-
> tis 'Super hanc petram hedificabo Ecclesiam meam', et alibi 'Opus consum-
> mavi quod dedisti michi ut faciam', manifestum est quod ei natura legem
> non dedit. Sed nec per divinam: omnis nanque divina lex duorum Testa-
> mentorum gremio continetur; in quo quidem gremio reperire non possum
> temporalium sollicitudinem sive curam sacerdotio primo vel novissimo
> commendatam fuisse. Quinymo invenio sacerdotes primos ab illa de pre-
> cepto remotos, ut patet per ea que Deus ad Moysen; et sacerdotes novissi-
> mos, per ea que Cristus ad discipulos.
>
> (*Monarchia* 3.13.3–5)[49]

---

48 'That the authority of the Church is not the cause of imperial authority is proved thus: one thing cannot be the cause of another thing in all its proper functionality unless it first exists itself in all its own proper power; but the empire, fully empowered as it was, came into being long before the Church either existed or had any influence whatever, for which reason the Church is the cause neither of the empire's power nor of its authority, these being one and the same thing.'

49 'But it did not come about as a matter of natural law because nature, in imposing its laws, does so only in respect of those things subject to it, God's perfection lying precisely in his ability to operate independently of nature. Since, therefore, the Church is not an effect of nature, but rather of God, who said of it: "Upon this rock I will build my Church" as well as elsewhere: "I have finished the work you gave me to do", it is evident that the Church is by no means a matter of nature and of nature's laws. But it did not come about by divine law either, for the whole of divine law is enshrined in the Old and New Testaments, I for my part being unable to find any recommendation in either of these places to the effect that priests either of the old or of the new dispensation busy themselves about things temporal. On the contrary, I find that priests of the old order were clearly excluded from them by God's words to Moses as were priests of the new order by Christ's words to his disciples.'

and as far as the third of them is concerned, namely the nature of the Church as but the continuing life of Christ on earth, we have this passage from chapter 14 with its sense of an ecclesiology ideally accountable to the otherness of Christ's kingdom properly understood, to, in a word, discipleship rather than domination as its proper substance:

Forma autem Ecclesie nichil aliud est quam vita Cristi, tam in dictis quam in factis comprehensa; vita enim ipsius ydea fuit et exemplar militantis Ecclesie, presertim pastorum, maxime summi, cuius est pascere agnos et oves. Unde ipse in *Iohanne* formam sue vite relinquens 'Exemplum' inquit 'dedi vobis, ut quemadmodum ego feci vobis, ita et vos faciatis'; et spetialiter ad Petrum, postquam pastoris offitium sibi commisit, ut in eodem habemus, 'Petre', inquit 'sequere me'. Sed Cristus huiusmodi regimen coram Pilato abnegavit: 'Regnum inquit' meum non est de hoc mundo; si ex hoc mundo esset regnum meum, ministri mei utique decertarent ut non traderer Iudeis; nunc autem regnum meum non est hinc'. Quod non sic intelligendum est ac si Cristus, qui Deus est, non sit dominus regni huius; cum Psalmista dicat 'quoniam ipsius est mare, et ipse fecit illud, et aridam fundaverunt manus eius'; sed quia, ut exemplar Ecclesie, regni huius curam non habebat ... Ex quo colligitur quod virtus auctorizandi regnum hoc sit contra naturam Ecclesie.

(*Monarchia* 3.14.3–6 and 9)[50]

---

50 'Now the form of the Church is simply the life of Christ, meaning by this both his words and his deeds; for his life was the idea and exemplar for the church militant, for its pastors especially, and above all for the supreme pastor, to whom it falls to feed the lambs and the sheep. Whence in the Gospel of John, handing on as he does this same form, he says: "I have given you an example, that you should do as I have done to you"; and to Peter in particular, after bestowing upon him the office of pastor, he said as we read in the same Gospel, "Peter, follow me". But in the presence of Pilate Christ renounced this kind of worldly power, saying: "My kingdom is not of this world; if my kingdom were of this world, then would my servants fight, that I should not be delivered to the Jews; but my kingdom comes not from hence"—which should not be taken to mean that Christ, who is God, is not Lord of this kingdom, for as the Psalmist says "the sea is his, and he made it: and his hands formed the dry land", but that, as a model for the Church, he had no concern for it ... from which we gather that the power of conferring temporal authority is at odds with the nature of the Church.' For a Dantean Christology, Paolo di Somma, 'Il mistero di Cristo nelle opere di Dante', in *Saggistica* (Naples: Laurenziana, 1995), 39–100; Antonio D'Elia, *La cristologia dantesca logos-veritas-caritas: Il codice poetico-teologico del pellegrino* (Cosenza: Pellegrini, 2012); Emmanuele Rotundo, *Umanesimo cristologico: Riflessioni a partire da una lettura teologica della 'Divina Commedia' di Dante Alighieri* (Rome: Aracne, 2016). For an ecclesiology, Raoul Manselli, 'Dante e l'*ecclesia spiritualis*', in *Dante e Roma. Atti del Convegno di studi, Roma 8–10 aprile*, ed. Casa di Dante sotto gli auspici del Comune di Roma (Florence: Le Monnier, 1965), 115–35; Paolo Acquaviva and Jennifer Petrie (eds.), *Dante and the Church* (Dublin: Four Courts Press, 2007); Paola Nasti, 'Of This World and the Other: "Caritas"—Ecclesiology in Dante's *Paradiso*', *The Italianist* 27.2 (2007), 206–32; Paola Nasti, 'Caritas and Ecclesiology in Dante's Heaven of the Sun', in *Dante's Commedia: Theology as Poetry*, ed. Vittorio Montemaggi and Matthew Treherne (Notre Dame, IN: University of Notre Dame Press, 2010), 210–44; Paola Nasti, 'Dante and Ecclesiology', in *Reviewing*

With what amounts, then, to a seeing off of the hierocratic case in point both of substance and of method, both of the leading idea and of the strategies devised for its recommendation, Dante proceeds to the *sed contra* or counterproposal phase of the argument—a phase turning in the way we have seen upon a separating out of the priestly and the princely by way of a now strict periodization of human activity, of a thoroughgoing distinction between the kind of happiness awaiting man here and now and the kind awaiting him hereafter. True, Dante himself comes eventually to reflect upon the deep substance of what now he is about to say, but for the moment it is entirely a question of otherness, of marking the difference. First, then, comes the psychosomatic moment of the argument, the notion that man, sharing as he does both in the corruptibility of the flesh and in the incorruptibility of the spirit, has not one but two proper ends ('duo ultima'), the one temporal and the other eternal:

> Et cum omnis natura ad ultimum quendam finem ordinetur, consequitur ut hominis duplex finis existat: ut, sicut inter omnia entia solus incorruptibilitatem et corruptibilitatem participat, sic solus inter omnia entia in duo ultima ordinetur, quorum alterum sit finis eius prout corruptibilis est, alterum vero prout incorruptibilis.
>
> (*Monarchia* 3.15.6)[51]

Straightaway, however, a relatively unpromising distinction between the *soma* and the *psyche* as a way of going about it shades off into something at once more refined and, upon reflection, more fraught, namely into an account of man's knowing himself by way of two kinds of properly human happiness: in the kind open to accomplishment here and now on the basis of the moral virtues and overseen in its orderly implementation by the emperor in respect of his power to compel

---

Dante's Theology, vol. 2, ed. Claire E. Honess and Matthew Treherne (Bern: Peter Lang, 2013), 43–88; Alberto Forni, 'Aristotele e l'"ecclesia spiritualis": La nuova cittadinanza "di quella Roma onde Cristo è romano"', in *Il mondo errante. Atti del Convegno internazionale di Studio, Bertinoro, 13–16 settembre 2010*, ed. Marco Veglia et al. (Spoleto: Fondazione Centro italiano di studi sull'alto Medioevo, 2013), 313–58.

51 'And since every nature is ordered towards its own ultimate goal, it follows that man's is a twofold goal; for just as he alone of all beings shares in both incorruptibility and corruptibility, so he alone of all beings is ordered to two ultimate ends, the one in respect of his nature as corruptible and the other in respect of his nature as incorruptible.' Christian Trottmann, 'Guido Vernani critique des "duo ultima" de Dante: Théories de la béatitude et conceptions du pouvoir politiques', in *Les philosophies morales et politiques au Moyen Age. Actes du IXème Congrès International de Philosophie Médiévale, Ottawa, du 17 au 22 Août 1992*, ed. Carlos B. Bazán et al. (New York: Legas, 1995), 1147–67; Patrick M. Gardner, 'Thomas on the "duo ultima hominis"', *The Thomist* 75.3 (2011), 415–59; José Blanco Jiménez, 'Los "duo ultima" entro Tomás y Dante', in *"Gratia non tollit naturam sed perfecit eam". Actas del Segundo Congreso Internacional de Filosofia Tomista*, ed. Carlos A. Casanova et al. (Santiago: RIL editores, 2016), 441–47.

and by the philosopher in respect of his power to persuade; and in the kind open to accomplishment hereafter on the basis of the theological virtues and overseen in its orderly anticipation by the pope as shepherd to the sheep. With this, Dante thinks, everything falls into place: two species of well-being, two species of happiness, two species of jurisdiction and two species of authority, the reduction of the one to the other at any point along the way making only for man's present and perpetual destitution. First, then—but in a now drastically revised form—we have once again the 'two ends' moment of the argument, an essay if ever there was one in otherness as the way of self-interpretation:

> Duos igitur fines providentia illa inenarrabilis homini proposuit intenden-
> dos: beatitudinem scilicet huius vite, que in operatione proprie virtutis
> consistit et per terrestrem paradisum figuratur; et beatitudinem vite ec-
> terne, que consistit in fruitione divini aspectus ad quam propria virtus
> ascendere non potest, nisi lumine divino adiuta, que per paradisum cele-
> stem intelligi datur. Ad has quidem beatitudines, velut ad diversas con-
> clusiones, per diversa media venire oportet. Nam ad primam per phylo-
> sophica documenta venimus, dummodo illa sequamur secundum virtutes
> morales et intellectuales operando; ad secundam vero per documenta
> spiritualia que humanam rationem transcendunt, dummodo illa sequa-
> mur secundum virtutes theologicas operando, fidem spem scilicet et
> karitatem.
>
> (*Monarchia* 3.15.7–8)[52]

with, hard on the heels of its now more sophisticated statement, the need as Dante sees it for two guides in Christendom, the one to lead man to his mortal happiness on the basis of a now well-nigh complete repertoire of philosophical wisdom, and the other to lead him to his immortal happiness on the basis of everything God in his goodness has chosen to make known to us. True, the aforesaid qualifications with respect to the nature and extent of imperial power still obtain, the emperor for his part functioning as but a keeper of the peace, but that, for the moment, is not what matters, what matters being the twofoldness of it all—the twofold character of man's proper end and the twofold character of the authority set over him,

---

52 'Ineffable providence has thus set before us two goals: happiness in this life, which consists in the exercise of our own proper powers and is figured in the earthly paradise, and happiness in the eternal life, which consists in the enjoyment of the divine countenance itself, something to which our own powers cannot raise us other than with the help of divine light and which is typified by the heavenly paradise. Now just as one reaches different conclusions by different means, so also with these two kinds of happiness, for we arrive at the first by way of philosophical teaching and a faithful implementation of the moral and intellectual virtues, whereas we arrive at the second by way of the kind of spiritual teaching which transcends human reason, implementing now the theological virtues of faith, hope and charity.'

anything less than this, Dante thinks, delivering him to his otherwise unbridled bestiality:

Has igitur conclusiones et media, licet ostensa sint nobis hec ab humana ratione que per phylosophos tota nobis innotuit, hec a Spiritu Sancto qui per prophetas et agiographos, qui per coecternum sibi Dei filium Iesum Cristum et per eius discipulos supernaturalem veritatem ac nobis necessariam revelavit, humana cupiditas postergaret nisi homines, tanquam equi, sua bestialitate vagantes 'in camo et freno' compescerentur in via. Propter quod opus fuit homini duplici directivo secundum duplicem finem: scilicet summo Pontifice, qui secundum revelata humanum genus perduceret ad vitam ecternam, et Imperatore, qui secundum phylosophica documenta genus humanum ad temporalem felicitatem dirigeret. Et cum ad hunc portum vel nulli vel pauci, et hii cum difficultate nimia, pervenire possint, nisi sedatis fluctibus blande cupiditatis genus humanum liberum in pacis tranquillitate quiescat, hoc est illud signum ad quod maxime debet intendere curator orbis, qui dicitur romanus Princeps, ut scilicet in areola ista mortalium libere cum pace vivatur.

(*Monarchia* 3.15.9–11)[53]

But now, just as the sun is setting over a nothing if not forceful utterance, comes a moment of reflection, a no less carefully conceived caveat turning upon the notion that, in the degree to which the happiness of this life is in some sense ordered to that of the next, then the emperor must after all bend the knee to the pope, this and this alone being the way of his more gracious operation in the world:

Que quidem veritas ultime questionis non sic stricte recipienda est, ut romanus Princeps in aliquo romano Pontifici non subiaceat, cum mortalis ista felicitas quodammodo ad inmortalem felicitatem ordinetur. Illa igitur

53 'These ends and the means to their accomplishment have been shown to us on the one hand by human reason as unfolded in its totality by the philosophers, and on the other by the Holy Spirit, who through the prophets and sacred writers, through Jesus Christ as the son of God and coeternal with him, and through his disciples has revealed to us the supernatural truth necessary to our salvation. Yet human greed would cast aside these aids if like horses stampeding to satisfy their bestiality, were they not held to the right way "by bit and bridle", which is why man has need of two guides to lead him on to his twofold goal—the supreme Pontiff, that is to say, to lead him to eternal life in accordance with revelation, and the emperor to guide him to temporal happiness in accordance with the teachings of philosophy. And since none or at any rate few, and then only with great difficulty, would reach this harbour unless the waves of alluring cupidity were calmed and the human race set free to rest in the tranquillity of peace, this is the goal which the protector of the world, to wit the Roman Prince, must strive with all his might to bring about—to ensure the peace and freedom whereby men may pass safely through the testing time of this life.'

reverentia Cesar utatur ad Petrum qua primogenitus illius debet uti ad patrem; ut luce paterne gratie illustratus virtuosius orbem terre irradiet, cui
ab Illo solo prefectus est, qui est omnium spiritualium et temporalium
gubernator.

(Monarchia 3.15.17–18)[54]

A moment of reflection indeed, and one that calls for a pause on the part of
the reader too, for politically or as regards Dante's commitment to the separation
of papal and imperial power both in principle and in practice nothing has changed,
any overstepping of the mark hereabouts tending straightaway to scandalize his
spirit. But that, where the *Monarchia* is concerned, is not all, for pausing as we
must over the philosophical as distinct from the publicistic aspect of the text then
what we have here is further testimony to the tension everywhere at work in
Dante's heart and mind and everywhere rising up Leviathan-like to tax him in
conscience between the *other* and the *immanent* as ways of seeing and celebrating
the structure of human experience in the round. On the one hand, then, there is
the *otherness* of it all, the separating out of the here and now and the hereafter, of
reason and revelation, of nature and grace, of moral and theological virtue, all to
be sure, as far as the *Monarchia* is concerned, in the interest of resolving a high-
level issue in the area of power politics but all subsisting even so as antecedent
and by this stage inveterate structures of consciousness. On the other hand, and

54 'Yet the truth upon this last issue is not to be interpreted so narrowly as to mean that the Roman
Prince is not in some sense subject to the Roman Pontiff, since in some sense our temporal happiness
is indeed ordered to our eternal happiness. Let Caesar therefore show that reverence towards Peter
which a firstborn son should show his father, so that, illumined by the light of paternal grace, he may
the more powerfully enlighten the world, over which he has been placed by the One who alone is ruler
over all things spiritual and temporal.' Similarly at 3.4.20: 'Sic ergo dico quod regnum temporale non
recipit esse a spirituali, nec virtutem que est eius auctoritas, nec etiam operationem simpliciter; sed
bene ab eo recipit ut virtuosius operetur per lucem gratie quam in celo et in terra benedictio summi
pontificis infundit illi' (I likewise maintain that temporal government does not owe its existence to
spiritual government, nor the power all of a piece with its authority, nor even its operation as such,
though by the light of that grace which God breathes into it in heaven and which on the earth is dispensed by the supreme pontiff it certainly receives from that government the wherewithal to function
more powerfully); also, *Epistole* 5.ult. (to the princes and peoples of Italy): 'Hic est quem Petrus, Dei
vicarius, honorificare nos monet; quem Clemens, nunc Petri successor, luce Apostolice benedictionis
illuminat; ut ubi radius spiritualis non sufficit, ibi splendor minoris luminaris illustret' (This is he whom
Peter, the Vicar of God, exhorts us to honour, and whom Clement, the present successor of Peter, illumines with the light of the Apostolic benediction, that where the spiritual ray suffices not, there the
splendour of the lesser luminary may lend its light). For the sword and crozier motif, *Purgatorio* 16.106–
12: 'Soleva Roma, che 'l buon mondo feo, / due soli aver, che l'una e l'altra strada / facean vedere, e del
mondo e di Deo. / L'un l'altro ha spento; ed è giunta la spada / col pasturale, e l'un con l'altro insieme /
per viva forza mal convien che vada; / però che, giunti, l'un l'altro non teme' (Rome, which made good
the world, used to have two suns making plain the one way and the other, that of the world and that of
God. The one has quenched the other and the sword is joined to the crozier; and the one conjoined
with the other must perforce go ill, since thus conjoined the one fears not the other).

represented now by the nicely unassuming but at the same time nicely eloquent 'quodammodo' of 3.15.17, there is a sense of the mutual indwelling of these things in the living experience of the one who says 'I', at which point alterity gives way to accommodation, to a sense of the co-involvement of each and every exigency of the spirit at each and every point along the way.[55] What then are we to say of the *Monarchia*? Many things to be sure, but two above all. On the one hand this, that for all its presupposing and indeed countenancing of the publicistic tradition in which it stands, what we have in the *Monarchia* is a political theology of unique majesty, a theology unfolded in terms of government by one as the condition of man's proper emergence as man (book 1), of the substance and spectacle of Rome as co-involved from beforehand in the soteriological scheme (book 2) and of the structures of human governance as pondered in the recesses of the divine mind (book 3), none of this wanting either for passion or for piety. On the other hand, however, this, that here we have a text foundering at last upon its own premises, on a characteristic tendency in Dante to proceed by way less of continuity than of contradistinction, of the over-againstness of his cultural allegiances. Now of this Dante was himself aware, the triumph of the contemporary *Commedia* lying precisely in its bringing home of one thing to another in the name and for the sake of a consistent act of specifically human being. But just for the moment, and albeit for the most just of just causes, a looking in the other direction, a momentary passing by on the other side.

55 Bortolo Martinelli, 'Sul "Quodammodo" di *Monarchia* III.xv.17', in *Miscellanea di studi in onore di Vittore Branca*, vol. 1 (Florence: Olschki, promoted by Armando Balduino et al., 1993 [1983]), 193–214; Nicola Fosca, 'Ancora sul "quodammodo" di *Monarchia* III.xv.17', *Electronic Bulletin of the Dante Society of America*, ed. Simone Marchesi, 2015 (http://www.princeton.edu/~dante/ebdsa).

The *Questio de situ aque et terre,* the Letter to Cangrande della Scala and the *Eclogues*

Likewise subsisting in the shadow of the *Commedia* are three occasional pieces of slighter inspiration but testifying even so to the completeness of Dante's commitment both to the high-scholastic and to the romance-vernacular way of being a poet and philosopher. First, then, comes the treatise *De forma et situ aque et terre,* a text delivered orally on 20 January 1320 in the church of Sant'Elena in Verona, but conceived and encouraged by a dispute—'dispute' in the sense of a scholastic *quaestio*—witnessed at an earlier stage in Mantua. Meticulously quodlibetal as it is in Dante's handling of it, the basic question is simple enough; for if indeed the universe consists of a series of concentric spheres such that the sphere of the earth is contained by that of the water, that of the water by that of the air, and that of the air by that of the fire, all these in turn being contained by those of the planets, the firmament, the primum mobile and divine mind as all-circumscribing but uncircumscribed, then how is it that a certain point here below the earth actually stands proud of the water? How, given the perfect concentricity of it all, are we to account for the rising up of the earth in our neighbourhood, in, to be more exact, the *quarta habitabilis* or habitable part of the northern hemisphere? His opponents, Dante explains, resort typically to one or other of two things: either (*a*) to a denial of concentricity as a principle of cosmic organization, a notion, he says, nothing short of preposterous, or (*b*) to a system of humps and bumps making it possible for the earth to stand proud of the water while preserving even so the aforesaid concentricity of things—an idea, Dante says, if anything more bizarre still. What then? The answer, he goes on—this, in fact, constituting his point of arrival in the treatise—is theological rather than merely cosmological in kind, God himself seeing to it that, in order that every potentiality in the world be realized, there be some adjustment to the overall scheme such that not only the fish of the sea, the fowl of the air and every creeping thing that creepeth upon the earth but man too be properly accommodated. It is all, in other words, a question of divine intentionality, of God's making provision for every creature according to kind:

Et ideo dicendum ad hanc questionem, quod ille dispensator Deus glorio-
sus, qui dispensavit de situ polorum, de situ centri mundi, de distantia ultime circumferentie universi a centro eius, et de aliis consimilibus, hoc fecit
tanquam melius, sicut et illa. Unde cum dixit: 'Congregentur aque in locum
unum, et appareat arida', simul et virtuatum est celum ad agendum, et terra
potentiata ad patiendum.

(Questio de situ aque et terre 21.76)[1]

—lines to which, as bearing more precisely on the notion of emergence—of the
land's standing proud of the water—as the condition of every complex life-form,
we may add these from a little earlier in the treatise:

Et cum omnes forme materiales generabilium et corruptibilium, preter for-
mas elementorum, requirant materiam et subiectum mixtum et complexio-
natum, ad quod tanquam ad finem ordinata sunt elementa in quantum elementa, et mixtio esse non possit ubi miscibilia simul esse non possunt, ut de
se patet; necesse est esse partem in universo ubi omnia miscibilia, scilicet
elementa, convenire possint; hec autem esse non posset, nisi terra in aliqua
parte emergeretur, ut patet intuenti.

(Questio de situ aque et terre 18.47)[2]

---

1 'And therefore to this question we must reply that the great dispenser of all things, the glorious
God, who settled by decree the position of the poles, the whereabouts of the centre of the universe,
the distance of the far circumference of the universe from its centre, together with other things of the
kind, ordained these, even as those, for the best. Wherefore when he said "Let the waters be gathered
together in one place and let the dry land appear", the heaven was at the same time endowed with the
power to act and the earth with the power to be acted upon.' John Freccero, 'Satan's Fall and the *Quaestio
de aqua et terra*', *Italica* 38 (1961), 99–115; Francesco Mazzoni, 'Il punto sulla Quaestio de aqua et terra',
SD 39 (1962), 39–84; Giorgio Padoan, 'La *Quaestio de aqua et terra*', in *Dante nella critica di oggi*, ed.
Umberto Bosco (Florence: Le Monnier, 1965), 758–67; Klaus Ley, 'Dante als Wissenschaftler: Die
Quaestio de aqua et terra', *DDJ* 58 (1983), 41–71; Zygmunt G. Barański, 'The Mystery of Dante's *Questio
de aqua et terra*', in *"In amicizia": Essays in Honour of Giulio Lepschy*, ed. Zygmunt Barański and Lino
Pertile (Reading: University of Reading; Department of Italian Studies, 1997), 146–64; Sabrina Ferrara,
'Il progetto della *Questio de aqua et terra*: Dante "magister"', in *La parola dell'esilio: Autore e lettori nelle
opere di Dante in esilio* (Florence: Cesati, 2016), 303–10. For a contemporary cosmology and cartogra-
phy, Alessandro Ghisalberti, 'La cosmologia nel Duecento e Dante', *LC* 13 (1984), 33–48; Alessandro
Ghisalberti, 'L'ordine del cosmo tra scienza e Bibbia', in *Dante e il pensiero scolastico medievale* (Milan:
Edizioni di Sofia, 2008), 47–59; Alessandro Scafi, *Mapping Paradise: A History of Heaven on Earth*
(London: British Library, 2006); Alessandro Scafi, *Maps of Paradise* (London: British Library, 2013);
Theodore J. Cachey, 'Cosmology, Geography and Cartography', in *Dante in Context*, ed. Zygmunt G.
Barański and Lino Pertile (Cambridge: Cambridge University Press, 2015), 221–40. For the authenticity
of the *Questio*, Edward Moore, 'The Genuineness of the *Quaestio de aqua et terra*', in *Studies in Dante:
Second Series* (Oxford: Oxford University Press, 1968 [1899]), 303–57; Bruno Nardi, 'La caduta di
Lucifero e l'autenticità della *Quaestio de aqua et terra*', in *'Lecturae' e altri studi danteschi*, ed. Ruby
Abardo (Florence: Le Lettere, 1990), 227–65.

2 'And since all material forms (elemental forms apart) coming into and passing out of existence

With this, then, it remains only to stress once more, for the benefit of the serried ranks of philosophers and cosmologists likewise busy hereabouts, the ultimately providential origin of it all and thus of its both predating and transcending reason pure and simple. 'Let men therefore desist', Dante proclaims in the twilight moments of the treatise, 'let them desist from searching out things that are above them. Let them seek as far as it lies with them to draw more closely to the immortal and the divine and cease to meddle in matters that are far greater than anything they themselves might understand or speak of',[3] at which point Ulysseanism in all the impiety thereof is once again seen off. And it is precisely this combination of pique and peremptoriness that takes us to the heart of the *De situ et forma aque et terre*, for what matters about it over and above its engaging with, again, a nothing if not fashionable topic of the day is its status as an *acte de revendication* on the part of a Dante Alighieri quite as capable, he thinks, as the next man when it comes to resolving this matter satisfactorily. For the fact is that by the time of the *Questio* he had already addressed it, and this in terms of the literally earthshaking drama of Lucifer's expulsion from the high consistory of heaven, a drama occasioning (*a*) a fleeing of the dry land south of the equator (the whereabouts of Lucifer's fall) to the northern and henceforth habitable part of the globe, and (*b*) a contrary movement of the earth beneath Jerusalem to the southern hemisphere and its rising up to form Mount Purgatory:

> Da questa parte cadde giù dal cielo;
> e la terra, che pria di qua si sporse,
> per paura di lui fé del mar velo,
>   e venne a l'emisperio nostro; e forse
> per fuggir lui lasciò qui loco vòto
> quella ch'appar di qua, e sù ricorse.

> (*Inferno* 34.121–26)[4]

---

require a complex integration of matter and substance whereto, as to their end, the elements, as elements, are ordained, and since (as is obvious enough) there can be no mixture other than somewhere where those things susceptible of being mixed can indeed come together, there must needs be some place in the universe where those same things—namely the elements—may foregather. But, as appears plainly upon reflection, this might not be unless the earth is at some point emergent.'

3 *Questio* 22: 'Desinant ergo, desinant homines querere que supra eos sunt, et querant usque quo possunt, ut trahant se ad inmortalia et divina pro posse, ac maiora se relinquant.'

4 'On this side he fell down from heaven, and the earth, here hitherto prominent, for fear of him made a veil of the sea and retreated to our hemisphere; and, perhaps in order to escape from him, that which appears on this side left here an empty space and rushed upwards.' Silvio Pasquazi, 'Sulla cosmogonia di Dante (*Inferno* XXXIV e *Quaestio di aqua et terra*)', in *D'Egitto in Ierusalemme: Studi danteschi* (Rome: Bulzoni, 1985), 121–56; Saverio Bellomo, 'Lucifero e la cosmologia poetica di Dante: Lettura di *Inferno* XXXIV', *L'Alighieri (RD)* 43 (2014), 91–106.

This, clearly, is cosmology under its vatic aspect, cosmology for that very reason possessed of the power to terrify, but—again for that very reason—liable straightaway to draw upon its author and architect the scorn of the more properly leaden-footed, this in turn accounting both for the deep substance and for the surface complexion of the *Questio*, for its startling combination of the self-affirmative, the self-deprecatory and the downright vitriolic. Hence, on the threshold of the treatise, greetings in the name of the Lord, but, withal, something more splenetic:

> Universis et singulis presentes litteras inspecturis, Dantes Alagherii de Florentia inter vere phylosophantes minimus, in Eo salutem qui est principium veritatis et lumen. Manifestum sit omnibus vobis quod, existente me Mantue, questio quedam exorta est, que dilatrata multotiens ad apparentiam magis quam ad veritatem, indeterminata restabat. Unde cum in amore veritatis a pueritia mea continue sim nutritus, non sustinui questionem prefatam linquere indiscussam; sed placuit de ipsa verum ostendere, nec non argumenta facta contra dissolvere, tum veritatis amore, tum etiam odio falsitatis. Et ne livor multorum, qui absentibus viris invidiosis mendacia confingere solent, post tergum bene dicta transmutent, placuit insuper in hac cedula meis digitis exarata quod determinatum fuit a me relinquere, et formam totius disputationis calamo designare.
>
> (*Questio de situ aque et terre* prin. and 1)[5]

while all of a piece with this, but immeasurably intensified now by way of irony as but the art of saying the unsayable we have these lines from the final moments of the text:

> Determinata est hec phylosophia dominante invicto domino, domino Cane Grandi de Scala pro Imperio sacrosancto Romano, per me Dantem Alagherium, phylosophorum minimum, in inclita urbe Verona, in sacello Helene gloriose, coram universo clero Veronensi, preter quosdam qui, nimia cari-

---

5 'To all, collectively and individually, who shall inspect the document to hand, Dante Alighieri of Florence, least among the true students of philosophy, offers in the name of him who is the beginning of truth and light greeting. Be it known to you all that when I was in Mantua a certain discussion arose which, much pursued as it was on the basis, however, less of truth than of appearance, remained unresolved. Wherefore I, nurtured as I have been from childhood in a love of the truth, could not abstain from discussing the aforesaid question, but was pleased instead to make plain the fact of the matter, and, further—and as much for a love of truth as for a detesting of falsehood—to refute the arguments urged against it. And lest the envy of the many wont in the absence of those envied to foist lies upon those they hate should pervert behind my back what I had rightly said, it was my further pleasure in this document, prepared as it is by my own hand, to leave a record of my findings and trace with my own pen the course of the argument.'

tate ardentes, aliorum rogamina non admittunt, et per humilitatis virtutem Spiritus Sancti pauperes, ne aliorum excellentiam probare videantur, sermonibus eorum interesse refugiunt.

(*Questio de situ aque et terre* 24)[6]

With this, then, the *De situ*, the nicely quodlibetal *De situ*, shows its true colours; for this, in the final analysis, has less to do with the irregularity of the world over against self than with self itself, with the predicament of one who, anxious in respect no less of his public than of his private persona, has long since known himself as an outsider and, as is the way with outsiders, as an object at best of indifference and at worst of derision. Cosmology, in other words, in the *Questio*, shades off into something closer to confession, into a yet further meditation on the agony of exile, of what in truth it means to live far from home.

No less eloquent with respect to the deep substance of Dante's existence as a poet and philosopher in the romance-vernacular way of being these things—though 'eloquent' in quite different ways of being eloquent—are two further items dating from the latter part of this second decade of the century (1318 or 1319), namely the letter to Cangrande della Scala and the Latin eclogues forming part of an exchange with the Bolognese humanist Giovanni del Virgilio . Eloquent, then, in a quite particular way of being eloquent is the first of these things, the letter to Cangrande della Scala, a letter that, even setting aside the issues surrounding its authenticity, raises as many problems as it solves;[7] for this is a text

---

6 'This philosophical issue was resolved by me, Dante Alighieri, least among philosophers, under the rule of the unconquered lord—Lord Can Grande della Scala—representing the sacred Roman empire in the illustrious city of Verona, in the sanctuary of the glorious Helen, and in the presence of the clergy of that city, with the exception of those who, burning with an excess of charity, accept not the invitation of others, and who, in virtue of their humility as but poor pensioners of the Holy Spirit, absent themselves, lest they should seem to endorse the excellence of others, from the discussion.'

7 On the authenticity of the letter, Giorgio Brugnoli, *Epistole* (ed.), in *La letteratura italiana: Storia e testi*, vol. 5, part 2 (*Opere minori di Dante Alighieri*) (Milan: Ricciardi, 1979), 512–21; and Robert Hollander, *Dante's Epistle to Cangrande* (Ann Arbor: University of Michigan Press, 1993). Among those inclined to accept its authenticity either in part or in the round are Edward Moore, 'The Genuineness of the Dedicatory Epistle to Can Grande', in *Studies in Dante: Third Series (Miscellaneous Essays)* (Oxford: Clarendon Press, 1903; repr. 1968), 284–69; Francesco Mazzoni, 'L'epistola a Cangrande', *RSANL* 10 (1955), 157–98; and Giorgio Padoan, 'La mirabile visione di Dante', in *Dante e Roma. Atti del Convegno di Studi* (Florence: Le Monnier, 1965), 283–314. Variously sceptical, by contrast, Francesco D'Ovidio, 'L'epistola a Cangrande', in *Studi sulla Divina Commedia*, vol. 2 (Naples: Guida, 1931), 229–89; Luigi Pietrobono, 'L'epistola a Cangrande', *GD* 40 (1937), 1–51; Colin Hardie, 'The Epistle to Cangrande Again', *DDJ* 38 (1960), 51–74; Bruno Nardi, 'Il punto sull'Epistola a Cangrande', in *Lectura Dantis Scaligera* (Florence: Le Monnier, 1960); Bruno Nardi, *'Lecturae' e altri studi danteschi* (Florence: Le Lettere, 1990), 205–25; Peter Dronke, *Dante and Medieval Latin Traditions* (Cambridge: Cambridge University Press, 1986); Henry Ansgar Kelly, *Tragedy and Comedy from Dante to Pseudo-Dante* (Berkeley: University of California Press, 1989); Zygmunt G. Barański, '*Comedia*: Notes on Dante, the Epistle to Cangrande, and Medieval Comedy', *LD* 8 (1991), 26–55. See also, Gennaro Sasso, 'Sull'"Epistola" a Cangrande', *Cultura* 51.3 (2013), 359–445. For Cangrande himself, his person and his regime, see in

that, for all its intimacy with the poem upon which it sets out to comment (the *Commedia* in general and the *Paradiso* in particular) and for all its erudition, clarity, clear-sightedness and consistency at every point along the way, testifies to the greatness of the poem only at a remove, by way only of its—somewhere in the depths—self-conscious inadequacy to the task in hand, to the elucidation of the poetic utterance by way merely of its formalities. But with this, and indeed with what amounts in the twilight moments of the letter to a positive passing by on the other side where the originary text is concerned, we are getting ahead of ourselves, for that same erudition, clarity, clear-sightedness and consistency, not to mention the status of the letter as an expression of friendship and esteem, need first of all to be properly registered and properly honoured. Taken in the round, then, the letter falls into three parts, the first bearing on the circumstances of its coming about (sections 1–4), the second on the substance and structure of the *Commedia* as a whole (sections 5–16) and the third on the first few lines of the *Paradiso* in particular (sections 17–33). As far, then, as the first section is concerned it is a question of Dante's hymning the twofold magnificence and munificence of his host (the reality of these things far surpassing everything he has heard tell of them), of his confirming the possibility of genuine friendship between unequals and thus of defending himself from the charge of presumptuousness, and of his offering what he can by way of repaying his patron's kindness and generosity—namely the sublime canto of his *Commedia*:

> Preferens ergo amicitiam vestram quasi thesaurum carissimum, providentia diligenti et accurata solicitudine illam servare desidero. Itaque, cum in dogmatibus moralis negotii amicitiam adequari et salvari analogo doceatur, ad retribuendum pro collatis beneficiis plus quam semel analogiam sequi mihi votivum est; et propter hoc munuscula mea sepe multum conspexi et ab invicem segregavi nec non segregata percensui, digniusque gratiusque vobis inquirens. Neque ipsi preheminentie vestre congruum comperi magis quam Comedie sublimem canticam que decoratur titulo Paradisi; et illam sub presenti epistola, tanquam sub epigrammate proprio dedicatam, vobis ascribo, vobis offero, vobis denique recommendo.
>
> (*Epistole* 13.3)[8]

---

addition to Philip Wicksteed and Edmund Garratt Gardner, *Dante and Giovanni del Virgilio* (London: Constable, 1902; repr. 1971) Alice Maude Allen, *A History of Verona* (London: Methuen, 1910) and Gian Maria Varanini, *Gli Scaligeri 1277–1387* (Verona: Mondadori, 1988).

8 'Deeming, then, your friendship a most precious treasure, my only wish, looking to anything in the least harmful to it, is to maintain it intact. Since therefore that it is a cardinal principle in ethics that friendship be regulated and preserved by way of reciprocity, it is my purpose to honour that principle by way of reciprocating the bounty on more than one occasion bestowed upon me, for which reason I have often had a long and hard look at the meagre gifts I myself might offer, setting them out and scrutinizing them each in turn with a view to deciding which might be the most worthy and acceptable

The second section, by contrast, getting down as it does to the business of explication proper, sets about confirming the reader in a sense of how, technically, the *Commedia* may be said to function. First, then, there is what Dante calls the polysemousness of the text, the fact of its having about it a variety of meanings, for the purpose of explaining which he takes as the archetypal instance of specifically biblical allegorism Israel's coming up out of Egypt in the time of Moses, only then coming to the implication of this for his own poem. With respect, then, to the biblical exodus, we have on the one hand the literal meaning of the text, the narrative pure and simple, while on the other we have the various alternative or—in just for the moment the more ample and inclusive sense of the term—'allegorical' meanings conveyed by it, namely the allegorical meaning stricto sensu (where it is a question of Christ's postfiguring the Pentateuchal delivery of Israel); the moral meaning (where it is a question of the coming forth of the soul from a state of sin into a state of grace); and the anagogical meaning (where it is a question of the soul's ultimate emancipation, of its coming home at last to the bliss of the hereafter), each of these things so to speak inhering in the plain sense of the text but each of them being at the same time *other* than the plain sense (that precisely—'alien' or 'different'—being what the term 'allegory' means):

> Ad evidentiam itaque dicendorum sciendum est quod istius operis non est simplex sensus, ymo dici potest polysemos, hoc est plurium sensuum; nam primus sensus est qui habetur per litteram, alius est qui habetur per significata per litteram. Et primus dicitur litteralis, secundus vero allegoricus, sive moralis, sive anagogicus. Qui modus tractandi, ut melius pateat, potest considerari in hiis versibus: 'In exitu Israel de Egipto, domus Iacob de populo barbaro, facta est Iudea sanctificatio eius, Israel potestas eius'. Nam si ad litteram solam inspiciamus, significatur nobis exitus filiorum Israel de Egipto, tempore Moysis; si ad allegoriam, nobis significatur nostra redemptio facta per Christum; si ad moralem sensum, significatur nobis conversio anime de luctu et miseria peccati ad statum gratie; si ad anagogicum, significatur exitus anime sancte ab huius corruptionis servitute ad eterne glorie libertatem. Et quanquam isti sensus mystici variis appellentur nominibus, generaliter omnes dici possunt allegorici, cum sint a litterali sive historiali diversi. Nam allegoria dicitur ab 'alleon' grece, quod in latinum dicitur 'alienum', sive 'diversum'.
>
> (*Epistole* 13.7)[9]

---

to you. And I have found nothing more befitting your exalted station than the sublime canticle of the *Comedy* glorying in the title of *Paradise*. This, then, thus dedicated together with the present letter serving as a superscription, I inscribe, I offer, and, in fine, trust unto you.'

9 'For the sake, then, of clarifying what we have to say, it has to be understood that the meaning

As far, then, as the *Commedia* is concerned, it has, Dante explains, a twofold subject ('duplex subiectum') about which the various senses of the text—not all of them active at any one time—may be said to turn ('circa quod currant alterni sensus'). Thus, literally it is all about the state of souls after death pure and simple while allegorically it is all about man here and now as meriting by virtue of his status as a creature of free moral determination reward or punishment hereafter:

> Hiis visis, manifestum est quod duplex oportet esse subiectum, circa quod currant alterni sensus. Et ideo videndum est de subiecto huius operis, prout ad litteram accipitur; deinde de subiecto, prout allegorice sententiatur. Est ergo subiectum totius operis, litteraliter tantum accepti, status animarum post mortem simpliciter sumptus; nam de illo et circa illum totius operis versatur processus. Si vero accipiatur opus allegorice, subiectum est homo prout merendo et demerendo per arbitrii libertatem iustitie premiandi et puniendi obnoxius est.
>
> *(Epistole* 13.8)[10]

---

of this work is not of one kind only; rather, it may be described as "polysemous", as having, that is to say, several meanings; for the first meaning is that conveyed by the letter, while the next is that conveyed by what the letter signifies, the first of which we call the literal meaning, and the second the allegorical or mystical meaning. And for the better illustration of this way of conducting the argument we may take the following verses: "When Israel came out of Egypt and the house of Jacob from a barbarous people, Judah was his sanctuary and Israel his dominion." For if we consider the letter alone, what is signified is the coming out of the children of Israel from Egypt in the time of Moses; if, by contrast, the allegory, what is meant is our redemption through Christ; if, again, the moral sense, what is meant is the conversion of the soul from the sorrow and misery of sin to a state of grace; and if the anagogical, what is meant is the passing of the sanctified soul from the slavery of our present corruption to the liberty of our everlasting glory. And although these mystical meanings have various names, they may all of them in a general sense be termed allegorical, inasmuch as they are all of them different from the literal or historical meaning; for the word "allegory" is so called from the Greek "alleon", which in Latin is "alienum" or "diversum." ' John A. Scott, 'Dante's Allegory', *RP* 26 (1973), 558–91; John A. Scott, 'Dante's Allegory of the Theologians', in *The Shared Horizon*, ed. Tom O'Neill (Dublin: Irish Academic Press, 1990), 27–40; Lucia Battaglia Ricci, 'Polisemanticità e struttura nella *Commedia*', *GSLI* 152 (1975), 161–97; Manfred Lentzen, 'Zur Konzeption der Allegorie in Dantes *Convivio* und im Brief an Cangrande della Scala', in *Dante Alighieri 1985: In memoriam Hermann Gmelin*, ed. Richard Baum et al. (Tübingen: Stauffenburg Verlag, 1985), 169–90; Michelangelo Picone (ed.), *Dante e le forme dell'allegoresi* (Ravenna: Longo, 1987); Vincenzo Placella, 'Dante e l'esegesi medievale', *Sapienza: Rivista di Filosofia e Teologia* 42 (1988), 171–93. More generally, Henri de Lubac, *Exégèse médiévale: Les quatre sens de l'Écriture*, part 2, vol. 2 (Paris: Aubier, 1964), 319–25; Jon Whitman, *Allegory: The Dynamics of an Ancient and Medieval Technique* (Oxford: Clarendon Press, 1987).

10 'This being understood, it is clear that the subject about which the alternate meanings play must be twofold. This same subject, then, needs to be considered in respect first of its literal and then of its allegorical meaning. Taken, therefore, in its literal sense, the subject of the work as a whole is the state of souls after death, pure and simple, for it is on and about this that the entire argument turns. Taken allegorically, by contrast, the subject is man inasmuch as by his merits or demerits in the exercise of his free will he justly deserves reward or punishment.'

With this, then, Dante comes to the question of form in the poem, to, more exactly, the *forma tractatus* or general structure of the text and the *forma tractandi* or its discursive means, the first of these things consisting of an account (*a*) of its threefold canticle-by-canticle organization, (*b*) of the subdivision of each canticle into cantos, and (*c*) of each canto as consisting of so many rhymed lines, and the second of them of an itemizing of its various procedures, at once, Dante explains, 'poetic, fictive, descriptive, digressive, figurative, definitive, analytical, demonstrative, refutative and exemplary' in kind:

> Forma vero est duplex: forma tractatus et forma tractandi. Forma tractatus est triplex, secundum triplicem divisionem. Prima divisio est, qua totum opus dividitur in tres canticas. Secunda, qua quelibet cantica dividitur in cantus. Tertia, qua quilibet cantus dividitur in rithimos. Forma sive modus tractandi est poeticus, fictivus, descriptivus, digressivus, transumptivus, et cum hoc diffinitivus, divisivus, probativus, improbativus, et exemplorum positivus.
>
> (*Epistole* 11.9)[11]

But that is not all, for pressing on now with the more properly glossatorial aspect of the text, Dante comes (*a*) to the title and justification thereof of his poem; (*b*) to the linguistic register proper to comedy as a literary genre or species of literary undertaking; (*c*) to the object or final cause of the poem; and (*d*) to the branch of philosophy to which it may properly be said to belong. With respect, then, to the first and second of these things, namely the notion of 'comedia' in Dante's understanding of it and the linguistic tenor of the whole, we have the following passage from section 10 with its sense of comedy, over and against tragedy, as a matter of happy resolution and of style, here in the *Commedia* at least, as a matter of unstudied eloquence:

> Et est comedia genus quoddam poetice narrationis ab omnibus aliis differens. Differt ergo a tragedia in materia per hoc, quod tragedia in principio

---

11 'And the form is twofold: the form of the treatise and the form of the treatment. The form of the treatise is threefold, according to the threefold division. The first division is that whereby the whole work is divided into three cantiche; the second, whereby each cantica is divided into cantos; and the third, whereby each canto is divided into rhymed lines. The form or manner of treatment is poetic, fictive, descriptive, digressive and figurative; and further, it is definitive, analytical, probative, refutative and exemplificative.' Hiram Pflaum, 'Il "modus tractandi" della *Divina Commedia*', GD 39 (1936), 153–78; Richard P. Blackmur, 'Dante's Ten Terms for the Treatment of the Treatise', *Kenyon Review* 14 (1952), 286–300; Sergio Corsi, *Il "modus digressivus" nella Divina Commedia* (Potomac, MD: Scripta Humanistica, 1987), 9–23; Lino Pertile, '*Canto-cantica-Comedia* e l'Epistola a Cangrande', LD 9 (1991), 105–23; Lino Pertile, '*Cantica* nella tradizione medievale e in Dante', *Rivista di Storia e Letteratura* 27.3 (1992), 389–412 (and, with additions, in *La puttana e il gigante* [Ravenna: Longo, 1998], 227–45).

est admirabilis et quieta, in fine seu exitu est fetida et horribilis; et dicitur propter hoc a 'tragos' quod est hircus et 'oda' quasi 'cantus hircinus', idest fetidus ad modum hirci; ut patet per Senecam in suis tragediis. Comedia vero inchoat asperitatem alicuius rei, sed eius materia prospere terminatur, ut patet per Terentium in suis comediis . . . Et per hoc patet quod Comedia dicitur presens opus. Nam si ad materiam respiciamus, a principio horribilis et fetida est, quia Infernus, in fine prospera, desiderabilis et grata, quia Paradisus; ad modum loquendi, remissus est modus et humilis, quia locutio vulgaris in qua et muliercule comunicant.[12]

while with respect to the third and fourth of them, namely the overall point and purpose of the poem together with the genus to which it belongs, we have in sections 15 and 16 this passage with its commitment to the well-being of the reader as its final cause and thus its preeminently moral as distinct from metaphysical complexion:

Finis totius et partis esse posset et multiplex, scilicet propinquus et remotus; sed, omissa subtili investigatione, dicendum est breviter quod finis totius et partis est removere viventes in hac vita de statu miserie et perducere ad statum felicitatis. Genus vero phylosophie sub quo hic in toto et parte proceditur, est morale negotium, sive ethica; quia non ad speculandum, sed ad opus inventum est totum et pars. Nam si in aliquo loco vel passu pertractatur ad modum speculativi negotii, hoc non est gratia speculativi negotii, sed gratia operis; quia, ut ait Phylosophus in secundo Metaphysicorum, 'ad aliquid et nunc speculantur practici aliquando'.[13]

12 'Now comedy is a certain kind of poetical narration which differs from all others. It differs, then, from tragedy in its subject matter, in that tragedy at the beginning is admirable and placid, but at the end or issue is foul and horrible. And tragedy is so called from "tragos", a goat, and "oda"; as it were a "goat song", that is to say, foul like a goat, as appears from the tragedies of Seneca. Whereas comedy begins with sundry adverse conditions, but ends happily, as appears from the comedies of Terence . . . Tragedy and comedy differ likewise in their style of language; for that of tragedy is high flown and sublime, while that of comedy is unstudied and lowly.' Pio Rajna, 'Il titolo della Divina Commedia', SD 4 (1921), 27–37; Manfredi Porena, 'Il titolo della Divina Commedia', RSANL 9 (1933), 114–41; Luis Jennaro-MacLennan, '"Remissus est modus et humilis" (Epistle to Cangrande, §10)', LI 31 (1979), 406–18; Rossella D'Alfonso, '"Comico" e "Commedia": Appunti sul titolo del poema dantesco', FC 7 (1982), 3–41; Carlo Paolazzi, 'Nozione di "comedia" e tradizione retorica nella dantesca Epistola a Cangrande', SD 58 (1986), 87–186 (and in Carlo Paolazzi, Dante e la 'Commedia' nel Trecento [Milan: Vita e Pensiero, 1989], 3–110).

13 'The aim of the whole and of the part may be manifold, immediate, that is to say, or remote. But leaving aside any more detailed account of this question, it may in brief be said that the object of both the whole and the part is to remove those living in this life from a state of misery and to bring them to one of happiness. Inasmuch, then, as both in the round and in its various parts the work was conceived less for speculative than for practical purposes, the branch of philosophy to which—again both in the round and in its various parts—the work belongs is that of morality or ethics. If, therefore, in this or

More properly expository, by contrast, is that part of the letter given over to an account of the 'prologue' (*prologus*) or exordium to the *Paradiso*, the prologue or exordium consisting, Dante explains, of two parts: a 'prenuntiatio' or preliminary announcement relative to the theme generally of the canticle (sections 19–30) and a 'petitio' or invocation to the effect that Dante may now be made equal to the matter in hand (section 31). Now the 'prenuntiatio' or preliminary announcement moment of the *Paradiso*—the very first lines, in fact, thereof—runs as follows:

> La gloria di colui che tutto move
> per l'universo penetra, e risplende
> in una parte più e meno altrove.
>   Nel ciel che più de la sua luce prende
> fu' io, e vidi cose che ridire
> né sa né può chi di là sù discende;
>   perché appressando sé al suo disire,
> nostro intelletto si profonda tanto,
> che dietro la memoria non può ire.
>   Veramente quant' io del regno santo
> ne la mia mente potei far tesoro,
> sarà ora materia del mio canto.

(Paradiso 1.1–12)[14]

and is open to elucidation, Dante goes on, by way of its at once Neoperipatetic and Neoplatonic content. On the Neoperipatetic side it is a question of *existence*, of the referability of everything that *is* in the world to the existence which is God himself as the *prius* or first principle of all existence:

Ratio sic: Omne quod est, aut habet esse a se, aut ab alio; sed constat quod habere esse a se non convenit nisi uni, scilicet primo seu principio, qui Deus est, cum habere esse non arguat per se necesse esse, et per se necesse esse non competat nisi uni, scilicet primo seu principio, quod est causa omnium;

---

that section or passage it proceeds in the manner of speculative philosophy, this is not for the sake of speculation in itself but of practicality, for as the Philosopher says in the second book of the *Metaphysics*: "now and again, and in this or that respect, practical men proceed speculatively."'

14 'The glory of the One who moves all things irradiates the universe, shining forth in one part more and in another less. In that part of heaven partaking most amply of his light, there I have been, and have seen things which whoso descends from there above has neither the knowledge nor the power to relate, for, drawing near to its desire, our intellect enters so deep that memory cannot follow on. But what indeed of the sacred realm I could treasure up in my mind shall now be the matter of my song.'

ergo omnia que sunt, preter unum ipsum, habent esse ab alio. Si ergo accipiatur ultimum in universo, non quodcunque, manifestum est quod id habet
esse ab aliquo; et illud a quo habet, a se vel ab aliquo habet. Si a se, sic est
primum; si ab aliquo, et illud similiter vel a se vel ab aliquo. Et cum esset sic
procedere in infinitum in causis agentibus, ut probatur in secundo Metaphysicorum, erit devenire ad primum, qui Deus est.

(*Epistole* 13.20)[15]

while on the Neoplatonic side it is a question of *essence*, of the gradual materialization and individualization of the idea by way of the mediatory work of the
Intelligences:

Propter quod patet quod omnis essentia et virtus procedat a prima, et in-
telligentie inferiores recipiant quasi a radiante, et reddant radios superioris
ad suum inferius ad modum speculorum. Quod satis aperte tangere videtur
Dionysius de Celesti Hierarchia loquens. Et propter hoc dicitur in libro De
Causis quod 'omnis intelligentia est plena formis'. Patet ergo quomodo ratio
manifestat divinum lumen, id est divinam bonitatem, sapientiam et virtutem, resplendere ubique.

(*Epistole* 13.21)[16]

It is, however, at this point that the difficulty of the letter to Cangrande moves
into view, difficulty in the sense of the equality of commentary in any form or
degree of sophistication to the ipse dixit of the text itself, to the word as, in the
hands of the poet, uniquely empowered with respect to the matter in hand. Glancing for a moment, then, in the direction of the poem itself we have, as not least
among its gems, the magnificent 'O buono Apollo' moment of *Paradiso* 1, mag-

15 'We reason, then, thus: everything which exists has its being either from itself or from some
other thing. But it is plain that self-existence can be the attribute of one being only, namely the First
or Beginning, which is God, since to have being does not argue necessary self-existence, and necessary
self-existence appertains to one being only, namely the First or Beginning, which is the cause of all
things; therefore everything which exists, except that One itself, has its being from some other thing.
If, then, we take, not any thing whatsoever, but that thing which is the most remote in the universe, it
is manifest that this has its being from something; and that from which it derives either has its being
from itself or from something else. If from itself, then it is primal; if from something else, then that
again must either be self-existent or derive from something still further. But in this way we should go
on to infinity in the chain of effective causes, as is shown in the second book of the *Metaphysics*. So we
must come to a primal existence, which is God.' Bortolo Martinelli, '*Esse et essentia* nell'Epistola a
Cangrande', *CL* 12 (1984), 627–72.
16 'Whence it is evident that every essence and every virtue proceeds from a primal one; and that
the lower intelligences have their effect as it were from a radiating body, and, after the fashion of mirrors,
reflect the rays of the higher to the one below them. Which matter appears to be discussed clearly
enough by Dionysius in his work *On the Celestial Hierarchy*. And therefore it is stated in the book *On
Causes* that "every intelligence is full of forms".'

nificent in its intermingling of pride and piety as the basic mood of the undertaking—of pride in respect of the sublimity and of piety in respect of the grace-dependence of it all:

> O buono Appollo, a l'ultimo lavoro
> fammi del tuo valor sì fatto vaso,
> come dimandi a dar l'amato alloro.
>   Infino a qui l'un giogo di Parnaso
> assai mi fu; ma or con amendue
> m'è uopo intrar ne l'aringo rimaso.
>   Entra nel petto mio, e spira tue
> sì come quando Marsïa traesti
> de la vagina de le membra sue.
>   O divina virtù, se mi ti presti
> tanto che l'ombra del beato regno
> segnata nel mio capo io manifesti,
>   vedra'mi al piè del tuo diletto legno
> venire, e coronarmi de le foglie
> che la materia e tu mi farai degno.
>   Sì rade volte, padre, se ne coglie
> per trïunfare o cesare o poeta,
> colpa e vergogna de l'umane voglie,
>   che parturir letizia in su la lieta
> delfica deïtà dovria la fronda
> peneia, quando alcun di sé asseta.
> Poca favilla gran fiamma seconda:
> forse di retro a me con miglior voci
> si pregherà perché Cirra risponda.

(*Paradiso* 1.13–36)[17]

---

17 'O good Apollo, for this my last labour make me such a vessel of your power as you require for the gift of your beloved laurel. Thus far, one peak of Parnassus has been enough, but now, entering the arena that remains, I have need of both. Come into my breast there to breathe as when you drew Marsyas from the scabbard of his limbs. O power divine, should you grant me so much of myself that I show forth the shadow of the blessed kingdom imprinted upon my mind, you will see me come to your chosen tree there, with those leaves, to take the crown of which both theme and you yourself will make me worthy. So seldom, father—fault and shame of human willing—are men gathered for the triumph be it of Caesar or of poet that, whensoever any thirst for it, the Peneian bough cannot but beget gladness in the Delphic deity. Great flame follows a small spark. Perhaps, after me, prayer will find words still more refined such that Cyrrha may reply.'

while upon turning to Cangrande all we have is a mere *divisio textus*, a reduction of the power, passion and piety of the original to a bare-bones indication of what in the event comes next:

> Deinde cum dicit: 'O bone Apollo', etc., facit invocationem suam. Et dividitur ista pars in partes duas: in prima invocando petit; in secunda suadet Apollini petitionem factam, remunerationem quandam prenuntians; et incipit secunda pars ibi: 'O divina virtus'. Prima pars dividitur in partes duas: in prima petit divinum auxilium, in secunda tangit necessitatem sue petitionis, quod est iustificare ipsam, ibi: 'Hucusque alterum iugum Parnassi' etc.
>
> (*Epistole* 13.31)[18]

And that is not all, for hardly have we recovered from the peremptoriness of it all than procrastination and a passing nod in the direction of two, in fact, of Dante's most cherished *auctores*—to wit, John the Evangelist and Boethius of the *Consolation*—put in an appearance as his point of arrival in the letter to Cangrande : procrastination in the sense of his having to postpone the whole thing on account of more pressing business on the home front, and a passing nod in the sense of a gesture scarcely adequate to the status either of the Johannine or of the Boethian text as a condition of his own undertaking in the *Commedia*:

> Hec est sententia secunde partis prologi in generali. In speciali vero non exponam ad presens; urget enim me rei familiaris angustia, ut hec et alia utilia reipublice derelinquere oporteat. Sed spero de Magnificentia vestra ita ut alias habeatur procedendi ad utilem expositionem facultas. In parte vero executiva, que fuit divisa iuxta totum prologum, nec dividendo nec sententiando quicquam dicetur ad presens, nisi hoc, quod ubique procedetur ascendendo de celo in celum, et recitabitur de animabus beatis inventis in quolibet orbe, et quod vera illa beatitudo in sentiendo veritatis principium consistit; ut patet per Iohannem ibi: 'Hec est vita eterna, ut cognoscant te Deum verum etc.'; et per Boetium in tertio De Consolatione ibi: 'Te cernere finis'. Inde est quod ad ostendendum gloriam beatitudinis in illis animabus, ab eis tanquam videntibus omnem veritatem multa querentur que magnam habent utilitatem et delectationem. Et quia, invento principio seu

---

18 'Then when he says: "O buono Apollo", etc., he makes his invocation. And this part is divided into two sections: in the first, he invokes the deity and makes a petition while in the second he inclines Apollo to the granting of that petition by the promise of a certain recompense, the second section thus beginning: "O divina virtù". The first section again has two parts: in the first, he prays for divine aid while in the second he touches on the need for his petition, at which point he also justifies it. This part, then, begins "Infino a qui l'un giogo di Parnaso".'

primo, videlicet Deo, nichil est quod ulterius queratur, cum sit Alfa et O, idest principium et finis, ut visio Iohannis designat, in ipso Deo terminatur tractatus, qui est benedictus in secula seculorum.

(*Epistole* 13.32–33)[19]

What, then, are we to make of the letter to Cangrande ? A text more than ever solicitous in respect of a friend and patron of the poet as but one far from home? Certainly. A text more than ever refined in point of its learning, of its moving at ease amid the complexities of high-medieval exegetical and rhetorical conscious-ness? This too. A text uniquely competent in its handling of the metaphysical niceties of the case, of essence, existence and the at once classical and contempo-rary provenance of it all? Again most definitely. But more than this, and serving beyond its every technical competence to guarantee the lasting significance of this letter to Cangrande, a discourse sensitive from somewhere deep within it to the status of the original utterance as transcending absolutely the means of its rationalization, as indifferent to the intervention of even the most accredited of its commentators.

Altogether more persuasive, therefore—for it is a question now, not of eluci-dating but of celebrating the text in the consummate vernacularity thereof—is the in truth sparkling intervention represented by the Latin eclogues dating ide-ally from a little later. Dante, then, settled now in Ravenna and at last resting in the company of friends and family apt in some measure to assuage his troubled spirit, had been approached by Giovanni del Virgilio as a scholar and disciple of his namesake with a view to the possibility of his writing something good and epic—and Latin—reflecting the now changing complexion of Italian letters, a fresh singing of arms and the man in honour of, say, Henry VII of Luxembourg or Cangrande or Robert of Naples or Frederick of Austria. The time, in other

19 'This is the general meaning of the second part of the prologue; the particular meaning I shall not expound on the present occasion; for anxiety as to my domestic affairs presses so heavily upon me that I must perforce abandon this and other tasks of public utility. I trust, however, that your Magnif-icence may afford me the opportunity to continue this useful exposition at some other time. With regard to the executive part of the work, which was divided after the same manner as the prologue taken as a whole, I shall say nothing either as to its divisions or its interpretation at present; save only that the process of the narrative will be by ascent from heaven to heaven, and that an account will be given of the blessed spirits who are met with in each sphere; and that their true blessedness consists in the apprehension of Him who is the beginning of truth, as appears from what John says: "This is life eternal, to know thee the true God", etc.; and from what Boethius says in his third book *On Consolation*: "To behold thee is the end". Hence it is that, in order to reveal the glory of the blessedness of those spirits, many things which have great profit and delight will be asked of them, as of those who behold the fullness of truth. And since, once the beginning or first which is God has been reached, there is naught besides to seek out inasmuch as—as the vision of John tells us—He indeed is the Alpha and the Omega, the beginning and the end, the work ends in God himself, who is blessed forevermore, world without end.'

words, had come for him to proclaim more loudly his status as sixth among those welcoming him in the *Inferno* (Homer, Horace, Ovid, Lucan and Virgil himself) and thus freshly to garb the Castalian sisters with something more properly worthy of them:

> Pyeridum vox alma, novis qui cantibus orbem
> mulces letifluum, vitali tollere ramo
> dum cupis, evolvens triplicis confinia sortis
> indita pro meritis animarum—sontibus Orcum,
> astripetis Lethen, epyphebia regna beatis—,
> tanta quid heu semper iactabis seria vulgo,
> et nos pallentes nichil ex te vate legemus?
> Ante quidem cythara pandum delphyna movebis,
> Davus et ambigue Sphyngos problemata solvet,
> Tartareum preceps quam gens ydiota figuret
> et secreta poli vix experata Platoni:
> que tamen in triviis nunquam digesta coaxat
> comicomus nebulo, qui Flaccum pelleret orbe.
> 'Non loquor his, ymmo studio callentibus', inquis.
> Carmine sed laico: clerus vulgaria tempnit,
> et si non varient, cum sint ydiomata mille.
> Preterea nullus, quos inter es agmine sextus,
> nec quem consequeris celo, sermone forensi
> descripsit. Quare, censor liberrime vatum,
> fabor, si fandi paulum concedis habenas.
> Nec margaritas profliga prodigus apris,
> nec preme Castalias indigna veste sorores;
> at, precor, ore cie que te distinguere possint
> carmine vatisono, sorti comunis utrique.
> Et iam multa tuis lucem narratibus orant.

(*Egloge*, Giovanni del Virgilio to Dante 1, lines 1–24)[20]

---

20 'O sacred voice of the Pierides who with songs unwonted sweeten the world in its wretchedness as with life-giving branch you seek to upraise it, showing forth the regions of threefold fate as assigned to souls according to their deserts, Orcus to the impious, Lethe to those seeking the stars, the realms above to the blessed, why cast you still such weighty matter before the vulgar, while we wan students read nothing of yours as a poet? For sure you will stir the arched dolphin with your lyre and Davus solve the riddles of the arcane Sphinx ere the unlettered make any sense of Tartarus's abyss and secrets of the high heavens scarcely elicited by Plato himself. Yet these are the very themes which are croaked forth, all undigested, at street corners by this or that charlatan with a comic actor's shock of hair who for his part would dispatch Flaccus himself from the world. "Not to such speak I", you say, "but rather to those skilled in study". Indeed, but in the poetry of the people! Were there but one of them (whereas

To this, Dante replied by way of a pastoral eclogue as accomplished as it is astute in resolving an entire literary, linguistic and—as far as he himself is concerned—existential issue. First, then, there is the confection itself, Dante's pastorally encrypted account of how, having received an invitation from a certain Mopsus (Giovanni del Virgilio) to sojourn for a while in the far-off meadows of Bologna, and having explained its content to his gentle but less sophisticated companion Melibeus (according to Boccaccio, a certain Dino Perini, a colleague and fellow exile of Dante's in Ravenna), he—Tityrus in the text—must even so decline the invitation and trust to the *Paradiso* for his glorious homecoming as a poet. True, the high pastures of Bologna (Menalus in the poem) are not without their charm, for they are indeed the pastures of high culture, of the lush humanism now presaging and indeed already shaping and substantiating a new era in Italian letters:

> Pascua sunt ignota tibi que Menalus alto
> vertice declivi celator solis inumbrat,
> herbarum vario florumque inpicta colore.
> Circuit hec humilis et tectus fronde saligna
> perpetuis undis a summo margine ripas
> rorans alveolus, qui, quas mons desuper edit,
> sponte viam, qua mitis erat, se fecit aquarum.
> Mopsus in his, dum lenta boves per gramina ludunt,

---

in truth there are thousands), the learned scorn the vernacular. Besides, not one of those in whose company you are sixth, nor yet him whom you follow to the sky, wrote in the language of the marketplace. Wherefore, judge as you are of all things poetic, grant me but a moment to speak and I shall tell you what I think. Cast not freely your pearls before the swine, nor burden the Castalian sisters with garb unworthy of them, but rather, I pray you, speak in such a way as marks you out, among learned and unlearned alike, as a truly vatic spirit.' Philip H. Wicksteed and Edmund Garratt Gardner, *Dante and Giovanni del Virgilio* (London: Constable, 1902; repr. Freeport, NY: Books for Libraries Press, 1971); Giovanni Lidònnici, 'Dante e Giovanni del Virgilio', *GD* 29 (1926), 141–58; Antonio Belloni, 'Genesi e carattere della bucolica dantesca', *La Rassegna* 37–38 (1929–30), 113–22; Guido Mazzoni, 'Dante e il Polifemo bolognese', *ASI* 96.1 (1938), 1–40; Carlo Battisti, 'Le ecloghe dantesche', *SD* 33 (1955–56), 61–111; Giovanni Reggio, *Le 'Egloghe' di Dante* (Florence: Olschki, 1969); Aldo Vallone, 'Il biografismo dell'Epistola XIII e delle *Egloghe* di Dante', *RCCM* 19 (1977), 777–90; Mauda Bregoli-Russo, 'Le *Egloghe* di Dante: Un analisi', *Italica* 62 (1985), 34–40; Guy Raffa, 'Dante's Mocking Pastoral Muse', *DS* 114 (1996), 271–91; Lino Pertile, 'Le *Egloghe*, Polifemo e il *Paradiso*', *SD* 71 (2006), 285–330; Lino Pertile, 'Le *Egloghe* di Dante e l'antro di Polifemo', in *Dante the Lyric and Ethical Poet: Dante lirico e etico*, ed. Zygmunt G. Barański and Martin McLaughlin (London: Maney; Modern Humanities Research Association, 2010), 153–67 (with Claudia Villa, 'Il problema dello stile umile [e il riso di Dante]' at 138–52 and Paola Allegretti, 'Dante "Tityrus annosus" [*Egloghe*, IV.12]' at 168–208 in the same volume); Luciano Gargan, 'Dante e Giovanni del Virgilio: Le *Egloghe*', *GSLI* 187 (2010), 342–69; Saverio Bellomo, '*Egloghe*', in *Filologia e critica dantesca*, 2nd ed. (Brescia: La scuola, 2012), 167–77; Giovanni Polara, 'Note di lettura alla corrispondenza fra Giovanni del Virgilio e Dante', in *"Per beneficio e concordia di studio": Studi danteschi offerti a Enrico Malato per i suoi ottant'anni*, ed. Andrea Mazzucchi (Cittadella: Bertoncello Artigrafiche, 2015), 769–82.

contemplatur ovans hominum superumquc labores;
inde per inflatos calamos interna recludit
gaudia, sic ut dulce melos armenta sequantur,
placatique ruant campis de monte leones,
et refluant unde, frondes et Menala nutent.

(Egloge, Dante to Giovanni del Virgilio 1, lines 11–23)[21]

But, for all that, the notion of a retreat to Bologna, Tityrus insists, is as illusory as it is insane, for in Bologna the spirit of poetry as he himself understands it has, he says, long since been dead, his lot, were he to return there, being but the wretched bleating and ignorant antagonism of a new generation. Better, he says, bide his time until at last he rest once more by his own ancestral stream, there to shake free his triumphant albeit aged locks:

'O Melibee, decus vatum, quoque nomen in auras
fluxit, et insonmem vix Mopsum Musa peregit';
retuleram, cum sic dedit indignatio vocem:
'Quantos balatus colles et prata sonabunt,
si viridante coma fidibus peana ciebo!
Sed timeam saltus et rura ignara deorum.
Nonne triumphales melius pexare capillos
et patrio, redeam si quando, abscondere canos
fronde sub inserta solitum flavescere Sarno?'

(Egloge, Dante to Giovanni del Virgilio 1, lines 36–44)[22]

Even so, he goes on, the gesture was a kind one, and by way, therefore, of honouring it Tityrus will send along to the generous-spirited Mopsus ten measures

---

21 'Pastures there are unknown to you, which Mænalus's lofty peak the darkening sun o'ershadows, pastures painted with varying tint of grasses and of flowers. Around them, under the osiers, gently flows, with ripples never-ending, a streamlet which, from its brimming verges, bedews its banks, offering as it does so ready passage for the water descending softly from the mountain heights. In these pastures Mopsus, his kine sporting on the tender grass, triumphantly surveys the toils of men and gods alike, proclaiming then, by the breath-bearing reeds, his inner joy until at last the very herds follow his sweet strain, the lions hasten down appeased from the mountainside to the fields, the stream itself turns back, and Mænalus's very boughs signal their consent.'

22 'Hardly had I replied: "O Melibeus, the glory, nay the very name of poet has vanished into air, and scarcely has the Muse been sufficient to sustain our ever-alert Mopsus" when indignation thus spoke up: "To what bleatings would the hills and pastures echo were I, my locks leaf-entwined, to offer a paean on my lyre! But let me eschew with dread the groves and open places that know not the gods. Were it not better to trim my locks in triumph, and indeed to hide them, hoary now (I who erstwhile was auburn), under the leaves entwined if whenever it be I come once more to my ancestral Arno?"'

of milk from the choicest of his sheep, from a ewe not only more than ordinarily fecund but free-spirited and knowing not her equal:

'Est mecum quam noscis ovis gratissima', dixi
'ubera vix que ferre potest, tam lactis abundans;
rupe sub ingenti carptas modo ruminat herbas.
Nulli iuncta gregi nullis assuetaque caulis,
sponte venire solet, nunquam vi, poscere mulctram.
Hanc ego prestolor manibus mulgere paratis,
hac implebo decem missurus vascula Mopso'.

(*Egloge*, Dante to Giovanni del Virgilio 1, lines 58–64)[23]

All this, then, as meditated beneath the old oak, in a humble hut and over an oaten meal by way of acknowledging a courteous and civilized exchange, the niceties of it all being matched only by its clever contrivance, by its deft implementation of the bucolic way. And this, to come now to the point of it all, is what matters, for it is in the context of a by this stage deep familiarity with the bucolic way and of all this now symbolizes as regards a sea change in Italian letters, that in a moment of exquisite self-possession Dante confirms afresh his now settled allegiances, the at once vatic and vernacular substance of his own presence in the world; for his, as of the essence, is a speaking out by way of the *volgare* to those both in his own generation and in the generations to come that they might enter at last upon their proper patrimony as creatures of seeing, understanding and orderly choosing. Vernacularity, in short, triumphs as it always does in Dante over Latinity as the in-and-through-which of self-actualization, but now with a smile more than ever gracious to behold.

23 ' "I have", said I, "one sheep—the which you know—most loved, so full of milk she scarce may bear her udders. Even now under a mighty rock she chews the late-cropped grass. Associate with no flock, familiar with no pen, of her own will she ever comes, nor ever must be driven to the milking pale. Her do I think to milk with ready hands; from her, ten measures will I fill and send to Mopsus." ' Eugenio Chiarini, 'I "decem vascula" della prima egloga dantesca', in *Dante e Bologna nei tempi di Dante*, ed. Facoltà di Lettere e Filosofia dell'Università di Bologna (Bologna: Commissione per i testi di lingua, 1967), 77–88; Christine Ott, 'Brot und Milch: Die Metaphorik der geistigen Speise im *Paradiso* und in der ersten Ekloge an Giovanni del Virgilio und ihre metapoetischen Implikationem', *DDJ* 91 (2016), 95–113.

A Coruscation of Delight

E che è ridere se non una corruscazione de la dilettazione de l'anima,
cioè uno lume apparente di fuori secondo sta dentro?

Convivio 3.8.11[1]

To speak of the smile as but a showing forth of what *is* in the depths is by no means to qualify what in Dante amounts to the terrifying seriousness of it all, the 'serietà terribile' standing both at the beginning and at the end of his every undertaking and sustaining that undertaking at every point along the way. First, then, come the *rime*, busy from the outset about seeing off the levity of a Dante da Maiano in favour of the substance and psychology of loving and loving well. Then there is the *Vita nova*, where it is a question of that same love contemplated under the aspect less now of acquisition than of disposition as the in-and-through-which of new life. Then comes the *Convivio*, the magnanimous *Convivio*, where it is a question of philosophy as but the love of wisdom coeval and consubstantial with the Godhead itself as the way of properly human being and becoming, as that whereby 'the many men and women in this language of ours burdened by domestic and civic care' might know themselves in the fullness of their proper humanity. And then, as belonging to much the same moment as the *Convivio*, comes the no less precious *De vulgari eloquentia* with its sense of the *illustre* (*a*) as that whereby a certain set of people at a certain stage of their sociopolitical and cultural development know themselves in the now consummate character of their presence in the world (book 1), and (*b*) as that whereby the would-be poet in the high style confirms and lives out the substance of his own astripetal or star-seeking humanity (book 2). And then there is the *Commedia*, an essay likewise busy at the point of ultimate concern, in the coming home of the pilgrim spirit as hitherto but a wanderer in the region of unlikeness. Seriousness this, therefore, of a high order, and all the more so for its reaching out to involve every man—including those

---

1 'And what is laughter if not a coruscation of the soul's delight, a light bearing witness in its outward aspect to how it stands within?' David Edward Ruzicka, ' "Uno lume apparente di fuori secondo sta dentro": The Expressive Body in Dante's *Commedia*', *The Italianist* 34.1 (2014), 1–22.

perforce 'deeming this time ancient'—in an act of ontological rejoicing, of know-ing self in the freedom of self for its proper destiny.

But to speak thus of ontological rejoicing, of delight in (as Dante himself puts it) the butterfly-emergence of the spirit into the fullness of its proper presence in the world, is already to speak of the way in which the truth utterance is for him a smiling utterance, herein—in his ever-deepening commitment to the smile as but the outward aspect of seriousness—lying final confirmation of the seasoned sub-stance of his own humanity; so, for example, the 'sorrise parolette' moment of *Paradiso* 1 where it is a question of words, not simply as spoken but as smiled forth, as irradiated both within and without by their smiling aspect:

> S'io fui del primo dubbio disvestito
> per le sorrise parolette brevi,
> dentro ad un nuovo più fu' inretito
> e dissi: 'Già contento *requïevi*
> di grande ammirazion; ma ora ammiro
> com' io trascenda questi corpi levi'.

> (*Paradiso* 1.94–99)[2]

or the 'ella sorrise alquanto' moment of *Paradiso* 2 where it is a question of the smile as preparing the way for a fresh act of spiritual intelligence:

> Ella sorrise alquanto, e poi 'S'elli erra
> l'oppinïon', mi disse, 'd'i mortali
> dove chiave di senso non diserra,

---

2 'If I was freed from my perplexity by the words she smiled to me I was all the more caught up in a new one, and said: "Content I was for a moment and relieved in respect of a great wonder, but marvel now how I should be rising above these light substances."' Carla Casagrande, 'Ridere in *Paradiso*: Gaudio, giubilo e riso tra angeli e beati', in Francesco Mosetti Casaretto (ed.), *Il riso: Capacità di ridere e pratica del riso nelle civiltà medievali* (Alessandria: Edizioni dell'Orso, 2005), 177–93; Peter S. Hawkins, 'All Smiles: Poetry and Theology in Dante's *Commedia*', in Vittorio Montemaggi and Matthew Treherne (eds.), *Dante's 'Commedia': Theology as Poetry* (Notre Dame: University of Notre Dame Press, 2010), 2–29; Giulia Gaimari, 'Il sorriso dei beati nella *Commedia*: Un'interpretazione letterale', *LI* 66.4 (2014), 469–95; Giulia Gaimari, 'Il sorriso dei beati: La rappresentazione della gioia paradisiaca dalle visioni medievali a Dante', in *I cantieri dell'italianistica. Atti del XVIII congresso dell' ADI (Padova, 10–13 settem-bre 2014)*, ed. Guido Baldassari et al. (Rome: Adi editore, 2016) (www.italianisti.it/upload/userfiles/files/gaimari%202014.pdf). For the 'butterfly-emergence' motif, *Purgatorio* 10.121–26: 'O superbi cris-tian, miseri lassi, / che, de la vista de la mente infermi, / fidanza avete ne' retrosi passi, / non v'accorgete voi che noi siam vermi / nati a formar l'angelica farfalla, / che vola a la giustizia sanza schermi?' (O proud Christians, weary and wretched souls who, sick in point of understanding, trust only to backward steps, do you not perceive that we are worms born to come forth as angelic butterflies soaring without shield to justice?).

> certo non ti dovrien punger li strali
> d'ammirazione omai, poi dietro ai sensi
> vedi che la ragione ha corte l'ali.'

(*Paradiso* 2.52–57)[3]

or the 'sorridendo, ardea ne li occhi santi' moment of *Paradiso* 3 where it is a question of the smile as testimony to the love-intensity of it all:

> Con quelle altr' ombre pria sorrise un poco;
> da indi mi rispuose tanto lieta,
> ch'arder parea d'amor nel primo foco.

(*Paradiso* 3.67–69)[4]

or the 'sorridendo ... facendosi più mera' moment of *Paradiso* 11 where it is a question of the smile as—here as throughout—prefacing and pervading the more than ever ardent utterance:

> E io senti' dentro a quella lumera
> che pria m'avea parlato, sorridendo
> incominciar, faccendosi più mera.
>   'Così com' io del suo raggio resplendo,
> sì, riguardando ne la luce etterna,
> li tuoi pensieri onde cagioni apprendo.'

(*Paradiso* 11.16–21)[5]

—and all this by way of participation, of an ever more complete sharing in the life of the One who, perfectly self-inseated, self-understanding and self-loving as he is, knows himself by way only of the self-smiling proper to being in its pure form:

---

3 'She smiled a little and then said to me: "If mortal judgement errs where the key of sense fails to unlock, surely the shafts of wonder should not prick you henceforth, since following on from the senses reason's wings, as you can see, are short indeed."'
4 'With those other shades she first smiled a little, then answered me with the joy of one burning, it seemed, in the first fire of love.'
5 'And within that radiance that just addressed me I heard begin as it smiled and grew all the more in brightness: "Even as I reflect its beams, so, gazing into the eternal light, I perceive your thoughts and the origin thereof."'

O luce etterna che sola in te sidi,
sola t'intendi, e da te intelletta
e intendente te ami e arridi!

(*Paradiso* 33.124–26)[6]

This, then, for all the seriousness of the text, must constitute the terminus ad quem or point of arrival for any account of Dante as spokesman-in-chief for the existential point of view in the Middle Ages; for presupposing as it does the agony of existence in its moment-by-moment unfolding (for there is, in Dante, no speaking as a child, no understanding as a child and no thinking as a child), his withal is an account of the human situation in its properly speaking radiant complexion, in its forever opening out in a rapt coruscation of the spirit.

6 'O Light Eternal that solely abides in yourself, solely knows yourself, and, by yourself alone understood and understanding, loves and smiles upon yourself!'

SELECT BIBLIOGRAPHY

Given the massive and massively exponential character of Dante bibliography, I have in what follows privileged (*a*) texts available in English, (*b*) texts in Italian and, occasionally, in other languages especially important for an overall interpretation of this or that work along the way and/or for the circumstances of its coming about, and (*c*) material that I myself have found especially useful, all these things, however, offering suggestions for further reading.

1. *Texts and Translations*
    1.1. Principal Texts
    1.2. Other Editions
    1.3. Translations
2. *Preliminary and General Considerations*
    2.1. Introduction and General Interpretation
    2.2. Biography
    2.3. Dante, Florence and Italy
    2.4. Dante, Philosophy and Theology
    2.5. Rhetoric, Poetic and Style
3. *The Early Years*
    3.1. Pre-Exilic *Rime*
    3.2. *Fiore* and *Detto d'amore*
    3.3. *Vita nova*
4. *The Middle Years*
    4.1. Post-Exilic *Rime*
    4.2. *Convivio*
    4.3. *De vulgari eloquentia*
5. *The Final Years*
    5.1. *Commedia*
    5.2. *Epistole*
    5.3. *Monarchia*
    5.4. *Questio de situ aque et terre*
    5.5. Letter to Cangrande
    5.6. *Eclogues*

1. Texts and Translations

1.1. Principal Texts

Rime, ed. Gianfranco Contini, in *Dante Alighieri. Opere minori*, vol. 1, part 1, 249–552 (Milan and Naples: Riccardo Ricciardi Editore, 1984).

Fiore, ed. Gianfranco Contini, in *Dante Alighieri. Opere minori*, vol. 1, part 1, 553–798 (Milan and Naples: Riccardo Ricciardi Editore, 1984).

Detto d'amore, ed. Gianfranco Contini, in *Dante Alighieri. Opere minori*, vol. 1, part 1, 799–827 (Milan and Naples: Riccardo Ricciardi Editore, 1984).

Vita nova, ed. Gianfranco Contini, in *Dante Alighieri. Opere minori*, vol. 1, part 1, 1–247 (Milan and Naples: Riccardo Ricciardi Editore, 1984).

Convivio, ed. Cesare Vasoli and Domenico de Robertis, in *Dante Alighieri. Opere minori*, vol. 1, part 2 (Milan and Naples: Riccardo Ricciardi Editore, 1988).

De vulgari eloquentia, ed. Pier Vincenzo Mengaldo, in *Dante Alighieri. Opere minori*, vol. 2, 1–237 (Milan and Naples: Riccardo Ricciardi Editore, 1979).

Monarchia, ed. Bruno Nardi, in *Dante Alighieri. Opere minori*, vol. 2, 239–503 (Milan and Naples: Riccardo Ricciardi Editore, 1979).

Monarchia, ed. Pier Giorgio Ricci (Milan: Mondadori, 1965).

Monarchia, ed. Prue Shaw (Florence: Le Lettere. Edizione Nazionale a cura della Società Dantesca, 2009).

Epistole, ed. Arsenio Frugoni and Giorgio Brugnoli, in *Dante Alighieri. Opere minori*, vol. 2, 505–643 (Milan and Naples: Riccardo Ricciardi Editore, 1979).

Egloge, ed. Enzo Cecchini, in *Dante Alighieri. Opere minori*, vol. 2, 645–89 (Milan and Naples: Riccardo Ricciardi Editore, 1979).

Questio de aqua et terra, ed. Francesco Mazzoni, in *Dante Alighieri. Opere minori*, vol. 2, 691–880 (Milan and Naples: Riccardo Ricciardi Editore, 1979).

La Commedia secondo l'antica vulgata, ed. Giorgio Petrocchi, 4 vols. (Milan: Mondadori. Edizione Nazionale a cura della Società Dantesca Italiana, 1966–67).

1.2. Other Editions

Rime giovanili e della Vita Nuova, ed. Teodolinda Barolini with commentary by Manuele Gragnolati (Milan: BUR Rizzoli, 2009).

Il Fiore e il Detto d'Amore attribuibili a Dante Alighieri, ed. Gianfranco Contini (Milan: Mondadori, 1984).

Il Fiore (with the *Detto d'Amore*), ed. Luca Carlo Rossi (Milan: Mondadori, 1996).

Vita Nuova, ed. Jennifer Petrie and June Salmons (Dublin: Belfield Italian Library, 1994).

Vita Nova, ed. Luca Carlo Rossi, with an introduction by Guglielmo Gorni (Milan: Mondadori, 1999).

Il Convivio, ed. Giovanni Busnelli and Giuseppe Vandelli, 2 vols. (Florence: Felice Le Monnier, 1968, with an introduction by Michele Barbi and a revised bibliography by Antonio Enzo Quaglio).

Il Convivio, ed. Maria Simonelli (Bologna: Pàtron, 1966).

De vulgari eloquentia, ed. and trans. Steven Botterill (Cambridge: Cambridge University Press, 1996).

De vulgari eloquentia, ed. Aristide Marigo, 3rd edn. (Florence: Felice Le Monnier, 1968).

Monarchia, ed. and trans. Prue Shaw (Cambridge: Cambridge University Press, 1995).

Monarchia, ed. and trans. Gustavo Vinay (Florence: Sansoni, 1950).

De situ et forma aque et terre, ed. Giorgio Padoan (Florence: Felice Le Monnier, 1968).

La Divina Commedia, ed. Umberto Bosco and Giovanni Reggio, 3 vols. (Florence: Le Monnier, 1979).

La Divina Commedia, ed. Natalino Sapegno, 3 vols. (Florence: La Nuova Italia, 1968).

1.3. *Translations*

Dante's Lyric Poetry. Poems of Youth and of the Vita Nuova *(1283–1292),* ed. Teodolinda Barolini with translations by Anthony Frisardi and Richard Lansing (Toronto and Buffalo: University of Toronto Press, 2014).

Dante's Lyric Poetry, ed. Kenelm Foster and Patrick Boyde. 2 vols. (Oxford: Clarendon Press, 1967).

Rime, trans. John Gordon Nichols and Anthony Mortimer (London: One World Classics, 2009).

The Fiore and the Detto d'Amore. A Late 13th-century Italian Translation of the Roman de la rose *attributable to Dante,* trans. Santa Casciani and Christopher Kleinhenz (Notre Dame: University of Notre Dame Press, 2000).

Il Fiore (The Flower), Introduction, text, translation and commentary by John Took (Lewiston, Queenston and Lampeter: The Edwin Mellen Press, 2004).

The New Life, trans. William Anderson (Harmondsworth: Penguin Books, 1964).

Vita nuova, trans. Dino S. Cervigni and Edward Vasta (Notre Dame, Ind.: University of Notre Dame Press, 1995).

La Vita Nuova (Poems of Youth), trans. Barbara Reynolds (Harmondsworth: Penguin Books, 1969 with reprints).

Il Convivio (The Banquet), trans. Richard H. Lansing (New York and London: Garland, 1990).

The Banquet, trans. Christopher J. Ryan (Saratoga: Anma Libri, 1989).

De vulgari eloquentia, trans. Alan George Ferrers Howell (London: The Rebel Press, 1973).

De vulgari eloquentia: Dante's Book of Exile, trans. Marianne Shapiro (Lincoln and London: University of Nebraska Press, 1990).

On World Government (*De Monarchia*), trans. Herbert W. Schneider (New York: Griffon House, 2008 [1949]).

The Letters of Dante (*Dantis Alagherii Epistolae*), 2nd edn, trans. Paget Toynbee (Oxford: Clarendon Press, 1966; with a preface and bibliographical appendix by Colin Hardie).

The Divine Comedy, trans. Robin Kirkpatrick, 3 vols (London: Penguin Books, 2006; combined in one volume with a revised introduction, 2012).

The Divine Comedy, trans. Allen Mandelbaum (New York: Alfred A. Knopf, 1995).

The Divine Comedy, trans. Mark Musa, 3 vols. (Harmondsworth: Penguin Books, 1971-).

The Divine Comedy of Dante Alighieri, trans. Charles Eliot Norton, 3 vols. (Boston and New York: The Riverside Press, 1892 and reprints).

The Divine Comedy, trans. John D. Sinclair, 3 vols (New York: Oxford University Press, 1939 and reprints).

The Divine Comedy, trans. Charles S. Singleton, 6 vols. (Princeton: Princeton University Press, 1970).

2. Preliminary and General Considerations

2.1. Introduction and General Interpretation

Anderson, William, *Dante the Maker* (London: Routledge and Kegan Paul, 1980).

Ascoli, Albert Russell, *Dante and the Making of a Modern Author* (Cambridge: Cambridge University Press, 2010).

Auerbach, Erich, *Dante, Poet of the Secular World*, trans. Ralph Manheim (Chicago: University of Chicago Press, 1961).

Barolini, Teodolinda, *Dante and the Origins of Italian Literary Culture* (New York: Fordham University Press, 2006).

Bergin, Thomas Goddard, *An Approach to Dante* (London: Bodley Head, 1965).

Brandeis, Irma, *The Ladder of Vision: A Study of the Dante's 'Comedy'* (London: Chatto and Windus, 1960; repr. Garden City, NY: Doubleday, 1962).

Cachey, Theodore (ed.), *Dante Now: Current Trends in Dante Studies* (Notre Dame: University of Notre Dame Press, 1995).

Caesar, Michael (ed.), *Dante: The Critical Heritage, 1314(?)–1870* (London: Routledge, 1989).

Hainsworth, Peter, and Robey, David, *Dante: A Very Short Introduction* (Oxford: Oxford University Press, 2015).

Havely, Nick, *Dante* (Malden, MA: Blackwell, 2007).

———. *Dante's British Public: Readers and Texts from the Fourteenth Century to the Present* (Oxford: Oxford University Press, 2014).

Hawkins, Peter S., *Dante: A Brief History* (Oxford: Blackwell, 2006).

Holmes, George, *Dante* (Oxford: Clarendon Press, 1980).

Jacoff, Rachel (ed.), *The Cambridge Companion to Dante*, 2nd ed. (Cambridge: Cambridge University Press, 2007).

Kirkpatrick, Robin, *Dante: The Divine Comedy* (Cambridge: Cambridge University Press, 1987).

Limentani, Uberto (ed.), *The Mind of Dante* (Cambridge: Cambridge University Press, 1965).

Malato, Enrico, *Dante* (Rome: Salerno, 1999).

Mazzotta, Giuseppe, *Reading Dante* (New Haven: Yale University Press, 2014).

Padoan, Giorgio, *Introduzione a Dante*, 2nd ed. (Florence: Sansoni, 1981).

Parker, Deborah, *Commentary and Ideology: Dante in the Renaissance* (Durham, NC: Duke University Press, 1993).

Reynolds, Barbara, *Dante: The Poet, the Political Thinker, the Man* (London: I. B. Tauris, 2006).

Scott, John Alfred, *Understanding Dante* (Notre Dame: University of Notre Dame Press, 2004).

Shaw, Prue, *Reading Dante: From Here to Eternity* (New York: Liveright, 2014).

Took, John, *Dante: Lyric Poet and Philosopher: An Introduction to the Minor Works* (Oxford: Clarendon Press, 1990).

Vallone, Aldo, *Storia della critica dantesca dal XIV al XX secolo*, 2 vols. (Padua: Vallardi. 1981).

2.2. Biography

Barbi, Michele, *Life of Dante*, trans. and ed. Paul G. Ruggiers (Berkeley: University of California Press, 1954; originally *Vita di Dante* [Florence: Sansoni, 1933 and 1965]).

Bemrose, Stephen, *A New Life of Dante* (Exeter: University of Exeter Press, 2000; rev. ed. 2014).

Cosmo, Umbert, *Vita di Dante*, 3rd ed. (Florence: La Nuova Italia, 1965).

Fraticelli, Pietro, *Storia della vita di Dante Alighieri* (Florence: Barbèra, 1861).

Hollander, Robert, *Dante: A Life in Works* (New Haven: Yale University Press, 2001).

Mazzotta, Giuseppe, 'Life of Dante', in *The Cambridge Companion to Dante*, ed. Rachel Jacoff, 1–13 (Cambridge: Cambridge University Press, 1993).

Petrocchi, Giorgio. *Vita di Dante* (Bari: Laterza, 1983).

Piattoli, Renato. *Codice diplomatico dantesco*, 2nd ed. (Florence: L. Gonelli, 1950; with further additions in *SD* 30 [1951], 203–6; 42 [1965], 393–417; 44 [1967], 223–68; and *ASI* 127.1 [1969], 3–108).

Santagata, Marco, *Dante: The Story of His Life*, trans. Richard Dixon (Cambridge, MA: Harvard University Press (Belknap Press), 2016; from the Italian *Dante: Il romanzo della sua vita* [Milan: Mondadori, 2012]).

Toynbee, Paget, *Dante Alighieri: His Life and Works* (New York: Dover Publications, 2005; from the 4th ed. of 1910, originally 1900, with an intro. by Robert Hollander).

2.3. Dante, Italy and Florence

Catto, Jeremy, 'Florence, Tuscany, and the World of Dante', in *The World of Dante: Essays on Dante and His Times*, ed. Cecil Grayson, 1–17 (Oxford: Clarendon Press, 1980).

Dacciati, Silvia, *Popolani e magnati: Società e politica nella Firenze del Duecento* (Spoleto: Centro italiano di studi sull'alto medioevo, 2011).

Davidsohn, Robert, *Geschichte von Florenz* (Berlin: E. S. Mittler und Sohn, 1896–1927; Italian trans. Giovanni Battista Klein, *Storia di Firenze* [Florence: Sansoni, 1956–68]).

Davis, Charles T., *Dante's Italy and Other Essays* (Philadelphia: University of Philadelphia Press, 1984; includes essays on education in Dante's Florence, Brunetto Latini and Remigo de' Girolami).

———, 'The Florentine *Studia* and Dante's "Library"', in *The 'Divine Comedy' and the Encyclopedia of Arts and Sciences*, ed. Giuseppe di Scipio and Aldo Scaglione, 339–66 (Amsterdam: John Benjamins, 1988).

D'Entrèves, Alexander Passerin, 'Civitas', in *Dante: A Collection of Critical Essays*, ed. J. Freccero, 141–50 (Englewood Cliffs, NJ: Prentice-Hall, 1965).

Holmes, George, *Florence, Rome and the Origin of the Renaissance* (Oxford: Oxford University Press, 1986; especially 'Guelf Ascendancy, 1265–1277', 3–24).

Hyde, John Kenneth, *Society and Politics in Medieval Italy: The Evolution of the Civil Life, 1000–1350* (London: Macmillan, 1973).

Keen, Catherine, *Dante and the City* (Stroud: Tempus, 2003).

Lansing, Carol, *The Florentine Magnates: Lineage and Faction in a Medieval Commune* (Princeton: Princeton University Press, 1991).

Lansing, Richard (ed.), *Dante: The Critical Complex*, vol. 5, *Dante and History:*

From Florence and Rome to the Heavenly Jerusalem (New York: Routledge, 2003).

Larner, John, *Italy in the Age of Dante and Petrarch, 1216–1380* (New York: Longman, 1980).

Najemy, John Michael, 'Dante and Florence', in *The Cambridge Companion to Dante*, ed. Rachel Jacoff, 80–99 (Cambridge: Cambridge University Press, 1993).

———, *A History of Florence, 1200–1575* (Malden, MA: Blackwell, 2006).

Ottokar, Nicola, *Il comune di Firenze alla fine del Dugento*, 2nd ed. (Turin: Einaudi, 1962 [1926]).

Pampaloni, Guido, *Firenze al tempo di Dante: Documenti sull'urbanistica fiorentina* (Rome: Pubblicazioni degli archivi di Stato, 1973).

Raveggi, Sergio, *L'Italia dei guelfi e dei ghibellini* (Milan: Mondadori, 2009).

Rubinstein, Nicolai, 'The Beginnings of Political Thought in Florence', *Journal of the Warburg and Courtauld Institutes* 5 (1942), 198–227.

Salvemini, Gaetano, *Magnati e popolani in Firenze dal 1280 al 1295* (Turin: Einaudi, 1960 [1899]).

Schevill, Ferdinand, *History of Florence from the Founding of the City through the Renaissance* (New York: Harcourt Brace, 1936; repr., *Medieval and Renaissance Florence*, 2 vols. [New York: Harper & Row, 1963]).

Tabacco, Giovanni, *The Struggle for Power in Medieval Italy: Structures of Political Rule*, trans. Rosalind Brown Jensen (Cambridge: Cambridge University Press, 1989).

Waley, Daniel, *The Italian City-Republics*, 3rd rev. ed. (New York: Longman, 1988).

2.4. Dante, Philosophy and Theology

Bemrose, Stephen, *Dante's Angelic Intelligences: Their Importance in the Cosmos and in Pre-Christian Religion* (Rome: Edizioni di Storia e Letteratura, 1983).

Botterill, Steven, *Dante and the Mystical Tradition: Bernard of Clairvaux in the 'Commedia'* (Cambridge: Cambridge University Press, 1994).

Boyde, Patrick, *Dante Philomythes and Philosopher: Man in the Cosmos* (Cambridge: Cambridge University Press, 1981).

———, *Human Vices and Human Worth in Dante's 'Comedy'* (Cambridge: Cambridge University Press, 2000).

———, *Perception and Passion in Dante's 'Comedy'* (Cambridge: Cambridge University Press, 1993).

Corti, Maria, *Dante a un nuovo crocevia* (Florence: Sansoni, 1982).

Foster, Kenelm, O.P., *God's Tree: Essays on Dante and Other Matters* (London: Blackfriars, 1957).

————, 'Religion and Philosophy in Dante', in *The Mind of Dante*, ed. Uberto Limentani, 47–78 (Cambridge: Cambridge University Press, 1965).

————, *The Two Dantes and Other Studies* (London: Darton, Longman and Todd, 1977).

Gardner, Edmund, *Dante and the Mystics: A Study of the Mystical Aspects of the 'Divina Commedia' and Its Relations with Some of Its Medieval Sources* (New York: Haskell House, 1968 [1913]).

Gilson, Étienne, *Dante and Philosophy*, trans. David Moore (New York: Harper and Row, 1963; *Dante et la philosophie* [Paris: Vrin, 1939]).

————, 'Poésie et théologie dans la Divine Comédie', in *Atti del Congresso Internazionale di Studi Danteschi (20–27 April, 1965)*, vol. 1, 197–223 (Florence: Sansoni, 1965).

Honess, Claire E., and Treherne, Matthew (eds.), *Reviewing Dante's Theology*, 2 vols. (Bern: Peter Lang, 2013).

Livi, François, *Dante e la teologia: L'immaginazione poetica nella 'Divina Commedia' come interpretazione del dogma* (Rome: Casa editrice Leonardo da Vinci, 2008).

Mandonnet, Pierre, O.P., *Dante le théologien: Introduction à l'intelligence de la vie, des œuvres et de l'art de Dante Alighieri* (Paris: Desclée de Brouwer, 1935).

Masseron, Alexandre, *Dante et saint Bernard* (Paris: Albin Michel, 1953).

Mastrobuono, Antonio C., *Dante's Journey of Sanctification* (Washington, DC: Regnery Gateway, 1990).

Mazzoni, Francesco, 'San Bernardo e la visione poetica della *Divina Commedia*', in *Seminario dantesco internazionale / International Dante Seminar*, vol. 1: *Atti del primo convegno tenutosi al Chauncey Conference Centre, Princeton, 21–23 ottobre, 1994*, ed. Zygmunt G. Barański, 171–241 (Florence: Le Lettere, 1997).

Meerseman, Gilles Gérard, 'Dante come teologo', in *Atti del Congresso Internazionale di Studi Danteschi (20–27 April, 1965)*, vol. 1, 177–93 (Florence: Sansoni, 1965).

Moevs, Christian, *The Metaphysics of Dante's 'Comedy'* (Oxford: Oxford University Press, 2005).

Montemaggi, Vittorio, and Treherne, Matthew (eds.), *Dante's 'Commedia': Theology as Poetry* (Notre Dame: University of Notre Dame Press, 2010).

Nardi, Bruno, *Dante e la cultura medievale*, ed. Paolo Mazzantini (Rome: Laterza, 1983 [1942]).

————, *'Lecturae' e altri studi danteschi* (Florence: Le Lettere, 1990).

————, *Nel mondo di Dante* (Rome: Edizioni di Storia e Letteratura, 2012 [1944]).

————, *Saggi di filosofia dantesca*, 2nd ed. (Florence: La Nuova Italia, 1967).

————, *Saggi e note di critica dantesca* (Milan: Ricciardi, 1966).

O'Connell Baur, Christine, *Dante's Hermeneutics of Salvation: Passages to Freedom in the 'Divine Comedy'* (Toronto: University of Toronto Press, 2007).

Ryan, Christopher J., 'The Theology of Dante', in *The Cambridge Companion to Dante*, ed. Rachel Jacoff, 136–52 (Cambridge: Cambridge University Press, 1993).

Scott, John Alfred, 'Dante and Philosophy', *AdI* 8 (1990), 258–77.

Took, John, *Conversations with Kenelm: Essays on the Theology of the 'Commedia'* (London: Arts and Humanities Publications [Ubiquity Press], 2013).

———, *Dante's Phenomenology of Being* (Glasgow: Glasgow University Press, 2000).

———, *L'Etterno Piacer: Aesthetic Ideas in Dante* (Oxford: Clarendon Press, 1984).

Vasoli, Cesare, 'Filosofia e teologia in Dante', in *Otto saggi per Dante*, 13–40 (Florence: Le Lettere, 1995).

2.5. Rhetoric, Poetic and Style

Arbusow, Leonid, *Colores rhetorici: Eine Auswahl rhetorische Figuren und Gemeinplätze als Hilfsmittel für akadmische Übungen an mittelalterlichen Texten* (Göttingen: Vandenhoeck & Ruprecht, 1948).

Baldelli, Ignazio, 'Lingua e stile delle opere in volgare di Dante', *ED*, vol. 6, 55–112 (and, as 'Voci dell' *ED*: Lingua e stile', in *Studi danteschi*, ed. Luca Serianni and Ugo Vignuzzi, 355–486 [Spoleto: Centro italiano di studi sull'alto medioevo, 2015], with a further selection of entries in the *Enciclopedia*—entries in the area of both prosody and rhetoric—from 486 to 613).

Baldwin, Charles Sears, *Mediaeval Rhetoric and Poetic (to 1400) Interpreted from Representative Works* (New York: Macmillan, 1928; with various reprints).

Barnes, John C., and Zaccarello, Michelangelo (eds.), *Language and Style in Dante* (Dublin: Four Courts Press, 2013).

Battaglia Ricci, Lucia, *Dante e la tradizione letteraria medievale* (Pisa: Giardini, 1983).

Battaglia, Salvatore, *La coscienza letteraria del Medioevo* (Naples: Liguori, 1965).

Beltrami, Pietro G., *La metrica italiana*, 4th ed. (Bologna: Il Mulino, 2002).

Bertone, Giorgio, *Breve dizionario di metrica italiana* (Turin: Einaudi, 1999).

Boyde, Patrick, *Dante's Style in His Lyric Poetry* (Cambridge: Cambridge University Press, 1971).

Buck, August, 'Gli studi sulla poetica e sulla retorica di Dante e del suo tempo', in *Atti del Congresso Internazionale di Studi Danteschi*, vol. 1, 249–78 (Florence: Sansoni, 1965).

Cambon, Glauco, *Dante's Craft: Studies in Language and Style* (Minneapolis: University of Minnesota Press, 1969).

Corti, Maria, *Percorsi dell'invenzione: Il linguaggio poetico e Dante* (Turin: Einaudi, 1993).

Curtius, Ernst Robert, *European Literature and the Latin Middle Ages*, trans. Willard R. Trask (Princeton: Princeton University Press, 2013).

De Bruyne, Edgar. *Études d'esthétique médiévale*, 3 vols. (Bruges: De Tempel, 1946).

Del Monte, Alberto, *Retorica stilistica versificazione: Introduzione allo studio della letteratura* (Turin: Loescher, 1973).

D'Ovidio, Francesco, *Versificazione romanza, poetica e poesia medievale* (Naples: A. Guida, 1932).

Dronke, Peter, *The Medieval Poet and His World* (Rome: Edizioni di Storia e Letteratura, 1984).

Elwert, Wilhelm Theodor, *Italienische Metrik* (Munich: M. Hueber, 1968).

Fasani, Remo, *La metrica della 'Divina Commedia' e altri saggi di metrica italiana* (Ravenna: Longo, 1992).

Fubini, Mario, *Metrica e poesia: Lezioni sulle forme metriche italiane*, vol. 1: *Dal 200 al Petrarca* (Milan: Feltrinelli, 1962).

Garavelli, Bice Mortara, *Manuale di retorica* (Milan: Bompiani, 1989).

Guarnerio, Pier Enea, *Manuale di versificazione italiana*, 3rd ed. (Milan Vallardi, 1913).

Inglese, Giorgio, and Zanni, Rafaella, *Metrica e retorica nel medioevo* (Rome: Carocci, 2011).

Lausberg, Heinrich, *Handbuch der literarischen Rhetorik: Eine Grundlegung der Literaturwissenschaft* (Munich: M. Hueber, 1960).

Marti, Mario, *Realismo dantesco e altri studi* (Milan: R. Ricciardo, 1961).

McKeon, Richard, 'Rhetoric in the Middle Ages', *Spec* 17 (1942), 1–32.

Mengaldo, Pier Vincenzo, *Linguistica e retorica di Dante* (Pisa: Nistri-Lischi, 1978).

Menichetti, *Metrica italiana: Fondamenti metrici, prosodia, rima* (Padua: Antenore, 1993).

Nencioni, Giovanni, 'Dante e la retorica', in *Dante e Bologna nei tempi di Dante*, 91–112 (Bologna: Commissione per i testi di lingua, 1967).

Pazzaglia, Mario, *Il verso e l'arte della canzone nel 'De vulgari eloquentia'* (Florence: La Nuova Italia, 1967).

——, *Manuale di metrica italiana* (Florence: Sansoni, 1990).

Pernicone, Vincenzo, 'Storia e svolgimento della metrica', in *Tecnica e teoria letteraria*, ed. Mario Fubini et al., 297–349 (Milan: Marzorati, 1951).

Quadlbauer, Franz, *Die antike Theorie der 'genera dicendi' im lateinischen Mittelalter* (Vienna: Bölhaus, 1962).

Robey, David, *Sound and Structure in the 'Divine Comedy'* (Oxford: Oxford University Press, 2000).

Schiaffini, Alfredo, *Tradizione e poesia nella prosa d'arte italiana dalla latinità medievale al Boccaccio*, 2nd ed. (Rome: Edizione di Storia e Letteratura, 1943).

Segre, Cesare, *Lingua, stile e società*, 2nd ed. (Milan: Feltrinelli, 1976).

Spongano, Raffaele, *Nozioni ed esempi di metrica italiana* (Bologna: Pàtron, 1966).

Tateo, Francesco, *Retorica e poetica fra Medioevo e Rinascimento* (Bari: Adriatica Editrice, 1960).

Vincent, Eric Reginald Pearce, 'Dante's Choice of Words', *ItSt* 10 (1955), 1–18.

Wieruszowski, Helene, '*Ars Dictaminis* in the Time of Dante', *MH* 1 (1943), 95–108.

Wilkins, Ernest Hatch, *The Invention of the Sonnet and Other Studies in Italian Literature* (Rome: Edizioni di Storia e Letteratura, 1959).

3. The Early Years

3.1. Pre-Exilic Rime

Auerbach, Erich, 'La poesia giovanile di Dante', in *Studi su Dante* (Milan: Feltrinelli, 1967).

Barbi, Michele, *Studi sul Canzoniere di Dante* (Florence: Sansoni, 1915).

Barolini, Teodolinda, 'Dante and the Lyric Past', in *The Cambridge Companion to Dante*, ed. Rachel Jacoff, 14–33 (Cambridge: Cambridge University Press, 1993).

Bigi, Emilio, 'Genesi di un concetto storiografico: "Dolce stil novo"', *GSLI* 132 (1955), 333–71.

Biondolillo, Francesco, *Le rime amorose di Dante* (Messina: G. D'Anna, 1960).

Boyde, Patrick, 'Dante's Lyric Poetry', in *The Mind of Dante*, ed. Uberto Limentani, 79–112 (Cambridge: Cambridge University Press, 1965).

———, *Dante's Style in His Lyric Poetry* (Cambridge: Cambridge University Press, 1971).

De Robertis, Domenico, 'Sulla cultura giovanile di Dante', *LC* 4 (1973), 229–60.

Dronke, Peter, *Medieval Latin and the Rise of European Love-Lyric*, 2 vols., 2nd ed. (Oxford: Clarendon Press, 1968).

Favati, Guido, *Inchiesta sul Dolce stil nuovo* (Florence: Le Monnier, 1975).

Fubini, Mario, *Metrica e poesia: Lezioni sulle forme metriche italiane; I. Dal 200 al Petrarca*, rev. ed. (Milan: Feltrinelli, 1970–72).

Gorni, Guglielmo, *Dante prima della 'Commedia'* (Florence: Cadmo, 2001).

Marti, Mario, *Con Dante fra i poeti del suo tempo*, 2nd ed. (Lecce: Milella, 1971).

Moleta, Vincent, *Guinizzelli in Dante* (Rome: Edizioni di storia e di letteratura, 1980).

Montanari, Fausto, *L'esperienza poetica di Dante*, 2nd ed. (Florence: Le Monnier, 1968).

Sapegno, Natalino, 'Le rime di Dante', *Cultura* 9 (1930), 801–17.

Zonta, Giuseppe, 'La lirica di Dante', *GSLI* supplement 19–21 (1922), 45–204.

3.2. Fiore and Detto d'amore

Armour Peter, 'The *Roman de la Rose* and the *Fiore*: Aspects of a Literary Trans-plantation, *JIRS* 2 (1993), 63–81.

Barański, Zygmunt G., 'Il *Fiore* e la tradizione delle *translationes*', *RELI* 5–6 (1995), 31–41.

Barański, Zygmunt G., and Boyde, Patrick (eds.), *The 'Fiore' in Context: Dante, France, Tuscany* (Notre Dame: Notre Dame University Press, 1997).

Benedetto, Luigi Foscolo, *Il 'Roman de la rose' e la letteratura italiana* (Halle: Niemeyer, 1910).

Contini, Gianfranco, 'Fiore', *ED*, vol. 2, 895b–901a.

———, 'La questione del *Fiore*', in *Dante nella critica di oggi*, ed. Umberto Bosco, 768–73 (Florence: Le Monnier, 1965).

———, 'Un nodo della cultura medievale: La serie *Roman de la rose—Fiore—Divina Commedia*', in *Un'idea di Dante*, 245–83 (Turin: Einaudi, 1976).

Fasani, Remo, 'L'attribuzione del *Fiore*', *SPCT* 39 (1989), 5–40.

Harrison, Robert Pogue, 'The Bare Essential: The Landscape of the *Fiore*', in *Rethinking the Romance of the Rose: Text, Image, Reception*, ed. Kevin Brownlee and Sylvia Huot, 289–303 (Philadelphia: University of Pennsylvania Press, 1992).

Huot, Sylvia, *The 'Romance of the Rose' and Its Medieval Readers: Interpretation, Reception, Manuscript Transmission* (Cambridge: Cambridge University Press, 1993).

Peirone, Luigi, *'Il Detto d'amore' tra 'Il Fiore' e Dante* (Genoa: Tilgher, 1983).

———, *Tra Dante e 'Il Fiore': Lingua e parola* (Genoa: Tilgher, 1982).

Picone, Michelangelo, 'Il *Fiore*: Struttura profonda e problemi attributivi', *VR* 33 (1974), 145–56.

Richards, Earl Jeffrey, *Dante and the 'Roman de la Rose'* (Tübingen: Niemeyer, 1981).

———, 'The *Fiore* and the *Roman de la Rose*', in *Medieval Translators and Their Craft*, ed. J. Beer, 265–83 (Kalamazoo: Western Michigan University; Medieval Institute Publications, 1989).

Took, John, 'Towards an Interpretation of the *Fiore*', *Spec* 54 (1979), 500–527.

Vanossi, Luigi, *Dante e il 'Roman de la rose': Saggio sul 'Fiore'* (Florence: Olschki, 1979).

———, 'Detto d'amore', *ED*, vol. 2, 393b–95a.

———, *La teologia poetica del 'Detto d'amore'* (Florence: Olschki, 1974).

3.3. Vita nova

Branca, Vittore, 'Poetics of Renewal and Hagiographic Tradition in the *Vita nuova*', in *Lectura Dantis Newberryiana I*, ed. Paolo Cherchi and Antonio C. Mastrobuono, 123–53 (Evanston, IL: Northwestern University Press, 1988).

De Robertis, Domenico, *Il libro della Vita nuova*, 2nd ed. (Florence: Sansoni, 1970 [1961]).

Harrison, Robert Pogue, 'Approaching the *Vita nuova*', in *The Cambridge Companion to Dante*, ed. Rachel Jacoff, 34–44 (Cambridge: Cambridge University Press, 1993).

———, *The Body of Beatrice* (Baltimore: Johns Hopkins University Press, 1988).

Hollander, Robert, '*Vita nuova*: Dante's Perceptions of Beatrice', *DS* 92 (1974), 1–18.

Martinez, Ronald L., 'Mourning Beatrice: The Rhetoric of Threnody in the *Vita nova*', *MLN* 113 (1998), 1–29.

Mazzaro, Jerome, *The Figure of Dante: An Essay on the 'Vita nuova'* (Princeton: Princeton University Press, 1981).

Mazzotta, Giuseppe, 'The Language of Poetry in the *Vita nuova*', *RSI* 1.1 (1983), 3–14 (and in *Dante: The Critical Complex*, ed. Richard Lansing, vol. 1, 93–104 [New York: Routledge, 2003]).

Pazzaglia, Mario, 'La Vita Nuova fra agiografia e letteratura', *LC* 6 (1977), 187–210.

Picone, Michelangelo, '*Vita nuova' e tradizione romanza* (Padua: Liviana, 1979).

Scott, John Alfred, 'Dante's "Sweet New Style" and the *Vita nuova*', *Italica* 4 (1965), 98–107.

———, 'Religion and the *Vita nuova*', *ItSt* 20 (1965), 17–25.

Shaw, James Eustace, *Essays on the 'Vita nuova'* (Princeton: Princeton University Press, 1929).

Singleton, Charles S., *An Essay on the 'Vita nuova'* (Baltimore: Johns Hopkins University Press, 1977 [1949]).

Topsfield, Leslie Thomas, *Troubadours and Love* (Cambridge: Cambridge University Press, 1975).

Valency, Maurice, *In Praise of Love: An Introduction to the Love Poetry of the Renaissance* (New York: Octagon Books, 1958).

4. THE MIDDLE YEARS

4.1. Mature and Post-Exilic Rime

Balbiano d'Aramengo, Maria Teresa, *Tre donne intorno al cor: Saggio di psicologia dantesca* (Turin: Ricadonna, 2006).

Baldelli, Ignazio, 'Lingua e stile dalle petrose a *Tre donne*', *RLIt* 82.1 (1978), 5–17.

Battistini, Andrea, 'Lo stile della Medusa: I processi di pietrificazione in *Io son venuto al punto de la rota*', *LC* 26 (1997), 92–110.

Blasucci, Luigi, 'L'esperienza delle *petrose* e il linguaggio della *Divina Commedia*', *Belfagor* 12 (1957), 403–31.

Bowra, Maurice, 'Dante and Arnaut Daniel', *Spec* 27 (1952), 459–74.

Boyde, Patrick, 'Style and Structure in Dante's Canzone *Doglia mi reca*', *ItSt* 20 (1965), 26–41.

Comens, Bruce, 'Stages of Love, Steps to Hell: Dante's *Rime petrose*', *MLN* 101 (1985), 157–88.

Durling, Robert M., and Martinez, Ronald L., *Time and the Crystal: Studies in Dante's 'Rime' petrose* (Berkeley: University of California Press, 1990).

Foster, Kenelm, O.P., 'Dante's Canzone *Tre donne*', *ItSt* 9 (1954), 56–68.

Took, John, 'Style and Existence in Dante: An Essay in Cognitive Poetics', in *Language and Style in Dante*, ed. John C. Barnes and Michelangelo Zaccarello, 197–222 (Dublin: Four Courts Press, 2013).

Webb, Heather, 'Dante's Stone Cold Rhymes', *DS* 121 (2003), 149–68.

4.2. Convivio

Bemrose, Stephen, 'True and False Philosophy in the *Convivio* and the *Comedy*', *ItSt* 35 (1984), 12–18.

Dronke, Peter, *Dante's Second Love: The Originality and the Contexts of the 'Convivio'* (Leeds: Maney and Sons [Society for Italian Studies Occasional Papers 2, 1997]).

Gagliardi, Antonio, *La tragedia intellettuale di Dante: Il 'Convivio'* (Catanzaro: Pullano, 1994).

Gentili, Sonia, *L'uomo aristotelico alle origini della letteratura italiana* (Rome: Carocci, 2005; especially 127–65, 'Il desiderio di conoscere e il dovere di divulgare: Il *Convivio*').

Lansing, Richard, 'Dante's Intended Audience in the *Convivio*', *DS* 110 (1992), 17–24 (and in *Dante: The Critical Complex*, ed. Richard Lansing, vol. 3, 27–34 [New York: Routledge, 2003]).

Marchesi, Simone, 'La rilettura del *De officiis* e i due tempi della composizione del *Convivio*', *GSLI* 178 (2001), 84–107.

Nardi, Bruno, *Dal Convivio alla Commedia: Sei saggi danteschi* (Rome: Istituto storico italiano per il Medio Evo, 1992 [1960]).

Ricklin, Thomas, 'Théologie et philosophie du *Convivio* de Dante Alighieri', in *La servante et la consolatrice: La philosophie dans ses rapports avec la théologie au Moyen Age*, ed. Jean-Luc Solère and Zénon Kaluza, 129–50 (Paris: Vrin, 2002).

Scott, John Alfred, 'The Unfinished *Convivio* as a Pathway to the *Comedy*', in *DS* 113 (1995), 31–56 (and in *Dante: The Critical Complex*, vol. 3, ed. Richard Lansing, 1–26 [New York: Routledge, 2003]).

Trovato, Marco, 'Dante's Stand against "l'errore de l'umana bontade": Bonum, Nobility and Rational Soul in the Fourth Treatise of the *Convivio*', *DS* 108 (1990), 79–96.

Ulrich, Leo, 'The Unfinished *Convivio* and Dante's Rereading of the *Aeneid*', *Mediaeval Studies* 12 (1951), 41–64.

Vallone, Aldo, *La prosa del 'Convivio'* (Florence: Le Monnier, 1967).

Vasoli, Cesare, 'Il *Convivio* di Dante e l'enciclopedismo medievale', in *L'enciclopedismo medievale: Atti del Convegno, San Gemignano 8–10 ottobre 1992*, ed. Michelangelo Picone, 363–81 (Ravenna: Longo, 1994).

Winklehner, Brigitte, 'Die politische problematik des *Convivio*', in *DDJ* 67 (1992), 83–102.

4.3. De vulgari eloquentia

Baldwin, Charles Sears, *Medieval Rhetoric and Poetic Interpreted from Representative Works* (New York: Macmillan, 1928).

Cremona, Joseph Anthony, 'Dante's Views on Language', in *The Mind of Dante*, ed. Uberto Limentani, 138–62 (Cambridge: Cambridge University Press, 1965).

Curtius, Ernst Robert, *European Literature and the Latin Middle Ages*, trans. Willard R. Trask (Princeton: Princeton University Press, 2013; but many editions).

Devoto, Giacomo, *Profilo di storia linguistica italiana* (Florence: La Nuova Italia, 1953).

Faral Edmond, *Les arts poétiques du XIIe et di XIIIe siècle: Recherches et documents sur la technique littéraire du moyen âge* (Paris: Honoré: Champion, 1962).

Fubini, Mario, *Metrica e poesia: Lezioni sulle forme metriche italiane; I. Dal Duecento al Petrarca* (Milan: Feltrinelli, 1962).

Grayson, Cecil, 'Dante's Theory and Practice of Poetry', in *The World of Dante: Essays on Dante and His Times*, ed. Cecil Grayson, 146–63 (Oxford: Clarendon Press, 1980).

———, ' "Nobilior est vulgaris": Latin and Vernacular in Dante's Thought', in *Centenary Essays on Dante*, 54–76 (Oxford: Clarendon Press, 1965; essays by members of the Oxford Dante Society).

Mengaldo, Pier Vincenzo, *Linguistica e retorica di Dante* (Pisa: Nistri-Lischi, 1978).

Migliorini, Bruno, *Storia della lingua italiana* (Florence: Sansoni, 1960).

Murphy, James Jerome, *Rhetoric in the Middle Ages: A History of Rhetorical Theory from Saint Augustine to the Renaissance* (Berkeley: University of California Press, 1974).

Murphy, James Jerome (ed.), *Medieval Eloquence* (Berkeley: University of California Press, 1978).

Pagani, Ileana, *La teoria linguistica di Dante: 'De vulgari eloquentia'; Discussioni, scelte, proposte* (Naples: Liguori, 1982).

Paterson, Linda, *Troubadours and Eloquence* (Oxford: Clarendon Press, 1982).

Pazzaglia, Mario, *Il verso e l'arte della canzone nel 'De vulgari eloquentia'* (Florence: La Nuova Italia, 1967).

Quadlbauer, Franz, *Die antike Theorie der genera dicendi im lateinischen Mittelalter* (Vienna: H. Böhlaus, 1962).

Shapiro, Marianne, *De vulgari eloquentia: Dante's Book of Exile* (Lincoln: University of Nebraska Press, 1990; includes an English translation).

5. THE FINAL YEARS

5.1. Commedia

Armour, Peter, *Dante's Griffin and the History of the World: A Study of the Earthly Paradise ('Purgatorio' cantos xxix–xxxiii)* (Oxford: Clarendon Press, 1989).

——, *The Door of Purgatory: A Study of Multiple Symbolism in Dante's 'Purgatorio'* (Oxford: Clarendon Press, 1983).

Barolini, Teodolinda, *Dante's Poets: Textuality and Truth in the 'Comedy'* (Princeton: Princeton University Press, 1984).

——, *The Undivine Comedy: Detheologizing Dante* (Princeton: Princeton University Press, 1992).

Bergin, Thomas, *Perspectives on the 'Divine Comedy'* (New Brunswick, NJ: Rutgers University Press, 1967).

Botterill, Steven, 'Dante's Poetics of the Sacred Word', *Philosophy and Literature* 20.1 (1996), 154–62.

Brandeis, Irma, *The Ladder of Vision: A Study of Dante's 'Comedy'* (London: Chatto and Windus, 1960).

Charity, Alan Clifford, *Events and Their Afterlife: The Dialectics of Christian Typology in the Bible and Dante* (Cambridge: Cambridge University Press, 1966).

Cogan, Mark, *The Design in the Wax: The Structure of the 'Divine Comedy' and Its Meaning* (Notre Dame: University of Notre Dame Press, 1999).

Fergusson, Francis, *Dante's Drama of the Mind: A Modern Reading of 'Purgatorio'* (Princeton: Princeton University Press, 1953).

Ferrante, Joan M., *The Political Vision of the 'Divine Comedy'* (Princeton: Princeton University Press, 1984).

Fowlie, Wallace, *A Reading of Dante's 'Inferno'* (Chicago: University of Chicago Press, 1981).

Hollander, Robert, *Allegory in Dante's 'Commedia'* (Princeton: Princeton University Press, 1969).

Kirkpatrick, Robin, *Dante: The 'Divine Comedy'* (Cambridge: Cambridge University Press, 1987).

Lansing, Richard H., *From Image to Idea: A Study of Simile in Dante's 'Commedia'* (Ravenna: Longo, 1977).

Ledda, Giuseppe, *La guerra della lingua: Ineffabilità, retorica e narrativa nella 'Commedia'* (Ravenna: Longo, 2002).

Mazzeo, Joseph Anthony, *Medieval Cultural Tradition in Dante's 'Comedy'* (Ithaca: Cornell University Press, 1960).

———, *Structure and Thought in the 'Paradiso'* (Ithaca: Cornell University Press, 1958).

Mazzotta, Giuseppe, *Dante, Poet of the Desert: History and Allegory in the 'Divine Comedy'* (Princeton: Princeton University Press, 1979).

———, *Dante's Vision and the Circle of Knowledge* (Princeton: Princeton University Press, 1993).

Montanari, Fausto, *L'esperienza poetica di Dante* (Florence: Le Monnier, 1959).

Morgan, Alison, *Dante and the Medieval Other World* (Cambridge: Cambridge University Press, 1990).

Nardi, Bruno, *Dal 'Convivio' alla 'Commedia': Sei saggi danteschi* (Rome: Istituto Storico Italiano per il Medio Evo, 1992 [1960]).

Scott, John Alfred, *Dante's Political Purgatory* (Philadelphia: University of Pennsylvania Press, 1996).

Schnapp, Jeffrey T., *The Transfiguration of History at the Center of Dante's 'Paradise'* (Princeton: Princeton University Press, 1986).

Singleton, Charles S., *Dante's 'Commedia': Elements of Structure* (Baltimore: Johns Hopkins University Press, 1977; originally Cambridge, MA: Harvard University Press, 1954).

5.2. Epistole

Honess, Claire, E., *Dante Alighieri: Four Political Letters* (London: Modern Humanities Research Association, 2007).

Morghen, Raffaello, 'Le lettere politiche di Dante: Testimonianza della sua vita in esilio', in *Dante profeta: Tra la storia e l'eterno*, 89–107 (Milan: Jaca Book, 1983; with 'La lettera ai cardinali italiani' at 109–38).

Pertile, Lino, 'Dante Looks Forward and Back: Political Allegory in the Epistles', *DS* 115 (1997), 1–17.

5.3. *Monarchia*

Barbi, Michele, 'L'ideale politico religioso', 'L'Italia nell'ideale politico di Dante', and 'Impero e chiesa', in *Problemi fondamentali per un nuovo commento alla 'Divina Commedia'*, 49–68, 69–89, and 91–114 (Florence: Sansoni, 1955).

Barraclough, Geoffrey, *The Medieval Papacy* (London: Thames and Hudson, 1968).

Battaglia, Felice, *Impero, Chiesa e Stati particolari nel pensiero di Dante* (Bologna: Zanichelli, 1944).

Black, Antony, *Political Thought in Europe, 1250–1450* (Cambridge: Cambridge University Press, 1992).

Bowsky, William M., *Henry VII in Italy: The Conflict of Empire and City-State, 1310–1313* (Lincoln: University of Nebraska Press, 1960).

Capitani, Ovidio, '*Monarchia*, il pensiero politico', in *Dante nella critica d'oggi*, ed. Umberto Bosco, 722–38 (Florence: Le Monnier, 1965).

Carlyle, Robert Warrand, and James, Alexander, *A History of Medieval Political Theory in the West* (Edinburgh: Blackwood and Sons, 1903–36; various reprints).

Cassell, Anthony K., *The 'Monarchia' Controversy: An Historical Study with Accompanying Translations of Dante Alighieri's 'Monarchia', Guido Vernani's 'Refutation of the Monarchia' Composed by Dante, and Pope John XXII's Bull 'Si Fratrum'* (Washington, DC: Catholic University of America Press, 2004).

Chiavacci Leonardi, Anna Maria, 'La *Monarchia* di Dante alla luce della *Commedia*', *SM* 18 (1977), 147–83.

Costanza, Joseph F., 'The De *Monarchia* of Dante Alighieri', *Thought* 43.1 (1968), 87–126.

Davis, Charles T., 'Dante and the Empire', in *The Cambridge Companion to Dante*, ed. Rachel Jacoff, 67–79 (Cambridge: Cambridge University Press, 1993).

———, *Dante and the Idea of Rome* (Oxford: Clarendon Press, 1957).

De Lagarde, Georges, *La Naissance de l'esprit laïque au declin du moyen âge*, 5 vols. (Louvain: E. Nauwelaerts, 1956–70).

D'Entrèves, Alexander Passerin, *Dante as a Political Thinker* (Oxford: Clarendon Press, 1952).

Di Scipio, Giuseppe, 'Dante and Politics', in *The 'Divine Comedy' and the Encyclopedia of Arts and Sciences*, ed. Giuseppe di Scipio and Aldo Scaglione, 267–84 (Amsterdam: John Benjamins, 1988).

Ercole, Francesco, *Il pensiero politico di Dante*, 2 vols. (Milan: Terragni and Caligari, 1927–28).

Gierke, Otto Friedrich von, *Political Theories of the Middle Age*, trans. Frederic William Maitland (Cambridge: Cambridge University Press, 1900; repr. 1968).

Gilbert, Allan H., *Dante's Conception of Justice* (New York: AMS Press, 1971 [1925]).

Goudet, Jacques, *La politique de Dante* (Lyon: Hermès, 1981).

Herde, Peter, *Dante als Florentiner Politiker* (Wiesbaden: Steiner, 1976).

Jordan, Edouard, 'Dante et la théorie romaine de l'empire', *Nouvelle revue historique de droit français et étranger* 45 (1921), 353–96 and (series 4) 1 (1922), 191–232 and 333–90.

———, 'Le Gibelinisme de Dante: La doctrine de la monarchie universelle', in *Dante: Mélanges de critique et d'érudition françaises publiés à l'occasion du sixième centenaire du poète*, 60–91 (Paris: Union Intellectuelle Franco-Italienne, 1921).

Kelsen, Hans, *La teoria dello stato in Dante*, trans. W. Sangiorgi (Bologna: Boni, 1974).

Limentani, Uberto, 'Dante's Political Thought', in *The Mind of Dante*, ed. Uberto Limentani, 113–37 (Cambridge: Cambridge University Press, 1965).

Maccarrone, Michele, 'Papato e Impero nella *Monarchia*', *Nuove letture dantesche* 8 (1976), 259–332.

Mancusi-Ungaro, Donna, *Dante and the Empire* (New York: Peter Lang, 1987).

Matteini, Nevio, *Il più antico oppositore di Dante: Guido Vernani da Rimini; Testo critico del 'De reprobatione Monarchiae'* (Padua: CEDAM, 1958).

Mazzoni, Francesco, 'Teoresi e prassi in Dante politico', in *Dante Alighieri: Monarchia; Epistole politiche*, ix–cxi (Turin: Edizioni RAI, 1966).

Montano, Rocco, 'La *Monarchia* e il pensiero politico di Dante', in *Suggerimenti per una lettura di Dante*, 191–219 (Naples: Conte, 1956).

Morrall, John B., *Political Thought in Medieval Times*, 3rd ed. (London: Hutchinson, 1971).

Morris, Colin, *The Papal Monarchy: The Western Church from 1050 to 1250* (Oxford: Clarendon Press, 1991).

Muresu, Gabriele, *Dante politico: Individuo e instituzioni nell'autunno del Medioevo* (Turin: Paravia, 1979).

Nardi, Bruno, 'Il concetto dell'Impero nello svolgimento del pensiero dantesco', in *Saggi di filosofia dantesca*, 2nd ed., 215–75 (Florence: La Nuova Italia, 1967; with 'Tre pretese fasi del pensiero politico di Dante' at 276–310).

Piccini, Guido (Jarro), *Fra Guidonis Vernani: Tractatus De Reprobatione Monarchiae compositae a Dante Alighiero Florentino* (Florence: Bemporad, 1906).

Reade, William Henry Vincent, 'The Political Theory of Dante', in *Dante: 'De Monarchia'*, ed. Edward Moore, vi–xxxi (Oxford: Clarendon Press, 1916).

Reeves, Marjorie, 'Marsiglio of Padua and Dante Alighieri', in *Trends in Medieval Political Thought*, ed. Beryl Smalley, 86–92 (Oxford: Blackwell, 1965).

Ricci, Pier Giorgio, 'Dante e l'impero di Roma', in *Dante e Roma. Atti del Convegno di Studi; Rome, 8–9–10 aprile, 1965*, ed. Casa di Dante, 137–49 (Florence: Le Monnier, 1965).

Solari, Gioele, 'Il pensiero politico di Dante', *Rivista storica italiana* 40 (1923), 373–455.

————, *Il pensiero politico di Dante: Studi storici* (Florence: La voce, 1922).

————, 'L'idea imperiale di Dante', in *Studi su Dante*, vol. 7, ed. Comitato milanese della Società Dantesca Italiana, 1–31 (Milan: Hoepli, 1944).

Ullmann, Walter, *A History of Political Thought: The Middle Ages* (Harmondsworth: Penguin, 1970; 1965 with revisions).

Vasoli, Cesare, 'Filosofia e politica in Dante fra *Convivio* e *Monarchia*', LC 9–10 (1982), 11–37.

Vinay, Gustavo, *Interpretazione della 'Monarchia' di Dante* (Florence: Le Monnier, 1962).

5.4. Questio de situ aque et terre

Barański, Zygmunt G., 'The Mystery of Dante's *Questio de aqua et terra*', in *In Amicizia: Essays in Honour of Giulio Lepschy*, ed. Zygmunt G. Barański and Lino Pertile, 146–64 (Reading: University of Reading, 1997).

Freccero, John, 'Satan's Fall and the *Quaestio de acqua et terra*', *Italica* 38.2 (1961), 99–115.

Mazzoni, Francesco, 'Il punto sulla *Quaestio de aqua et terra*', *SD* 39 (1962), 39–84.

Moore, Edward, 'The Genuineness of the *Quaestio de aqua et terra*', in *Studies in Dante: Second Series; Miscellaneous Essays*, 303–57 (New York: Greenwood Press, 1968 [1899]).

Nardi, Bruno, *La caduta di Lucifero e l'autenticità della 'Quaestio de aque et terra'* (Turin: SEI, 1959).

Padoan, Giorgio, 'La *Quaestio de aqua et terra*', in *Dante nella critica di oggi*, ed. Umberto Bosco, 758–67 (Florence: Le Monnier, 1965).

5.5. Letter to Cangrande

Costa, Dennis, 'One Good Reception Deserves Another: The Epistle to Can Grande', *SIR* 5 (1985), 5–17.

Dronke, Peter, 'The *Epistle* to Cangrande and Latin Prose Rhythm', in *Dante and the Medieval Tradition*, 103–11 (Cambridge: Cambridge University Press, 1986).

Hollander, Robert, *Dante's Epistle to Cangrande* (Ann Arbor: University of Michigan Press, 1993).

Jennaro-MacLennan, Luis, *The Trecento Commentaries on the 'Divina Commedia' and the 'Epistle to Cangrande'* (Oxford: Clarendon Press, 1974).

Kelly, Henry Ansgar, *Tragedy and Comedy from Dante to Pseudo-Dante* (Berkeley: University of California Press, 1989).

Mazzoni, Francesco, 'Per l'Epistola a Cangrande', in *Contributi di filologia dantesca*, 7–37 (Florence: Sansoni, 1966).

Nardi, Bruno, 'Il punto sull'Epistola a Cangrande', *Lectura Dantis Scaligera* (Florence: Le Monnier, 1960; and in *'Lecturae' e altri studi danteschi*, ed. Rudy Abardo, 205–25 [Florence: Le Lettere, 1990]).

Sasso, Gennero, 'Sull *Epistola a Cangrande*', *AIISS* 25 (2010), 33–130 and *Cultura* 51.3 (2013), 359–445.

5.6. Eclogues

Barański, Zygmunt G., and McLaughlin, Martin (eds.), *Dante the Lyric and Ethical Poet: Dante lirico e etico*, 137–208 (Oxford: Legenda, 2010); with essays by Claudia Villa ('Il problema dello stile umile [e il riso di Dante]'), Lino Pertile ('Le Egloghe di Dante e l'antro di Polifemo'), and Paola Allegretti ('Dante "Tityrus annosus" ' [*Egloghe* 4.12]).

Eitel, Astrid, *Die Wiederendeckung der Bukolic: Der Dichterwettstreit zwischen Dante Alighieri und Giovanni del Virgilio* (Kiel: Solivagus, 2014).

Reggio, Giovanni, *Le egloghe di Dante* (Florence: Olschki, 1969).

Vallone, Aldo, 'Il biografismo dell'Epistola XIII e delle Ecloghe di Dante', *RCCM* 19.1–3 (1977), 777–90.

Wicksteed, Philip Henry, and Gardner, Edmund Garratt, *Dante and Giovanni del Virgilio* (London: Constable, 1902).

INDEX OF NAMES

Accardo, Salvatore: 196n28, 365n50

Aegidius Romanus: 509

Aelred of Rievaulx: 76, 77n, 153, 190n22

Ahern, John: 184n13, 457n163

Albert the Great: 36

Albonico, Simone: 339n19

Alcorn, John: 415n

Alessio, Gian Carlo: 213n, 288n

Alfie, Fabian: 206, 234n29

Alinei, Mario: 259n, 342n22, 452n156

Alisova, Tatiana: 280n48

Allan, Mowbray: 330n9, 364n47

Allavena, Oreste: 472n197

Allegretti, Paola: 539n20

Allen, Alice Maude: 528n7

Allevi, Febo: 365n49

Ambrosini, Riccardo: 60n50, 360n42

Andreotti, Giulio: 213n4

Angiolillo, Giuliana: 510n41

Antonelli, Roberto: 87, 196n28, 197n29, 299n16

Apollonio, Mario: 256n23, 332n13, 333n14, 418n111, 419n112, 423n117

Aquilecchia, Giovanni: 26n25

Arbery, Glen C.: 291n4

Ardissino, Erminia: 346n26, 452n156

Ardizzone, Maria Luisa: 100n21, 122n10, 187–88n18, 211n2, 273n41

Arduini, Beatrice: 257n25

Ariani, Marco: 457n163, 473n198

Aristotle: 41, 76n2, 153, 190, 238n3, 245n11, 254, 260n28, 270–71, 275–76, 285–86, 380, 397n87, 398n88, 402n92, 415, 416n109, 489, 499n25, 502n30, 504n32, 507n36, 514n46

Armour, Peter: 32n8, 55n45, 134n24, 332n13, 348n28, 385n72, 437n139, 449n153, 481n3

Arqués, Rossend: 296n11

Artale, Elena: 318n4

Ascoli, Albert Russell: 184, 278n45

Asperti, Stefano: 82n1, 98n19

Auerbach, Erich: 373n58

Augustine of Hippo: 41–43, 152–53, 347n27, 352n34, 400n89, 421–22, 424–26, 432, 434, 488n14, 507, 512–13

Aurigemma, Marcello: 332n13

Austin, Herbert Douglas: 472n198

Avalle, D'Arco Silvio: 428n123, 430n125, 461n173, 465n180

Averroes: 273, 274n42, 494n19, 495, 496n22

Baika, Gabriella I.: 446n151

Balbiano d'Aramengo, Maria Teresa: 58n48, 315n2

Baldassaro, Lawrence: 437n139, 543n2

Baldelli, Ignazio: 161n71, 205n38, 228n22, 288n1, 301n17, 315n2, 428n123, 430n125, 461n173, 467n186

Baldi, Agnello: 35n11, 92n12, 445–46n151

Baldwin, Charles Sears: 312

Balfour, Mark: 7n5, 338n18, 452n155

Ballarini, Marco: 368–69n54, 371n56, 451–52n155

Balogh, Joseph: 506n35

Balthasar, Hans Urs von: 451n155

Barański, Zygmunt G.: 28n2, 46n32, 122n10, 134n24, 140n34, 177n5, 220n15, 260n28, 303n20, 314n21, 319n5, 410n101, 417n110, 467–68n187, 524n1, 527n7, 539n20

Barber, Joseph A.: 133–34n

Bàrberi Squarotti, Giorgio: 188n19, 319n5, 400n89, 426n121, 430–31n126, 433n147, 445–46n151, 460n168

Barbi, Michele: 28, 48, 315n2, 430n125, 490n16

Barbieri, Aroldo: 430n125

Barblan, Giovanni: 186n15

Bardazzi, Giovanni: 331n10, 418n111

Barletti, Raffaele: 246
Barnes, John C.: 43n28, 64n56, 161n71, 232n27, 234n29, 260n28, 319n5, 410n101, 433n130, 443n147, 497n23
Barolini, Teodolinda: 64n56, 114n1, 121–22n10, 126n16, 132n23, 260n28, 330n9, 364n47, 385n72, 433n130, 467–68n187
Barthes, Roland: xxn3
Bartoli, Vittorio: 434–35n135, 483n7
Bartuschat, Johannes: 31–32n8, 54–55n45, 56n46, 213n4, 216n7, 228n22, 237–38n3, 357–58n40, 429n124
Barucci, Guglielmo: 226n21
Basile, Bruno: 20n33, 245n11, 345n25, 430n125, 437n139
Basile, Paola: 200, 245, 245n11, 345n25, 430n125, 437n139
Battaglia Ricci, Lucia: 441n145, 529–30n9
Battaglia, Salvatore: 231n26
Battesti, Isabelle: 219n14
Battestini, Andrea: 364n47
Battisti, Carlo: 538–39n20
Battistini, Andrea: 228n22, 364n47, 368–69n54
Bausi, Francesco: 317–18n4, 353n35
Bec, Pierre: 84n3, 340n20, 467–68n187
Beccaria, Gian Luigi: 464n179, 467n186
Beck, Friedrich: 472n198
Beer, Jeanette: 133–34n24
Belliotti, Raymond Angelo: 418n111
Bellomo, Saverio: 288n1, 525n4, 538–39n20
Belloni, Antonio: 538–39n20
Beltrami, Pietro G.: 305n23, 463n177, 465n179
Bemrose, Stephen: 28n2, 234n30, 260n28, 380n68, 397n87, 434–35n135
Benedetto, Luigi Foscolo: 133n24, 151n55
Benedict Pope: 62, 342n22, 364–65, 395n86, 482
Benfell, V. Stanley: 35n11
Benvenuti, Anna: 482n5
Berényl, Márk: 495n21
Berger, Harry, Jr.: 471n196
Bernard of Clairvaux: 41, 190, 341, 342n2, 371–72, 434, 456
Bernardo, Aldo S.: 243n9, 352n33, 390n79, 463n177
Bertelli, Italo: 95n16

Bertin, Emiliano: 54–55n45, 336n15, 494–95n19, 517–18n50
Bertolucci Pizzorusso, Valeria: 442n146
Bertoni, Giulio: 86n4
Bertran de Born: 82, 301n18, 325n3
Berube, Camille: 392n81
Bettarini, Rosanna: 114n1
Bezzola, Reto R.: 460–61n169
Biagi, Vincenzo: 482n5
Bianchi, Bruna: 64n56
Bianchi, Dante: 467n186
Bianchi, Luca: 270–71n38, 273n41
Biffi, Inos: 352n35, 373n58, 454n159
Bigi, Emilio: 113n39
Bigongiari, Dino: 307–8n26, 331–32n12, 331–33n14, 336n15, 338n18, 382n69, 391–92n81, 401n90, 430–31n126, 451–52n155
Billanovich, Giuseppe: 275–76n43
Billy, Dominique: 230n26
Biondo, Furio: 218n12
Biondolillo, Francesco: 95n16
Bisceglia, Antonio Alessandro: 481n3
Blackmur, Richard P.: 531n11
Blanco Jimémez, José: 518n51
Blasucci, Luigi: 228n22, 451n155
Bodei, Remo: 390n79
Boethius: 34n10, 152–53, 190, 212, 212–13n4, 248, 249n14, 255n23, 274n42, 275–76n43, 536
Boggione, Valter: 408n98
Bognini, Filippo: 187–88n18, 481n3
Boitani, Piero: 233–34n29, 360n42, 430nn125–26
Boler, John F.: 391–92n81
Bologna, Orazio Antonio: 7n5
Bolognesi, Davide: 36n11
Bonagiunta da Lucca: 90–91, 108, 112, 113n4
Bonaini, Francesco: 12
Bonaventure of Bagnoreggio: 16n16, 34–36, 353
Bondanella, Peter E.: 228n22
Borsa, Paolo: 95–96n16, 108n33, 132n23, 216n7, 226n21, 257n25
Borsellino, Nino: 348n28, 481n3
Borst, Arno: 292n6
Borzi, Italo: 331n12, 429n124, 447–48n152
Botterill, Steven: 180n9, 373n58
Boucher, Holly Wallace: 471n196

Bowra, Maurice: 230–31n26
Bowsky, William M.: 24n24, 65n57, 510n41
Boyde, Patrick: 36n13, 114n1, 133–34n24,
    140n34, 214n5, 255–56n23, 293–94n7, 318–
    19n4, 391–92n81, 408n98, 417n110, 418n111,
    422n115, 430n125, 443n147
Bozzola, Sergio: 307–8n26
Brambilla Ageno, Franca: 279–80n48,
    462n176
Branca, Vittore: 86n4
Brandeis, Irma: 173n1, 522n55
Bregoli-Russo, Mauda: 538–39n20
Brestolino, Lucia: 233–34n29
Brezzi, Paolo: 348n28
Brilli, Elisa: 54–55n45, 357–58n40, 360n42,
    472–73n198, 484n8
Brown, Eric: 331n12
Brugnoli, Giorgio: 401n90, 527n7
Brugnolo, Furio: 160n70, 219n14, 277–78n45
Brundage, James A.: 352n33
Brunetti, Giuseppina: 35n11, 155
Brunetto Latini: 31–32, 43, 46, 47, 50, 212–
    13n4, 311–12n29, 332n13
Bruni, Francesco: 92, 211n2, 243n9, 437n139
Bruni, Leonardo: 14n13, 28n2, 44, 45, 48n35,
    53, 60n51, 63
Buck, August: 300n17, 484n8, 508n38
Bufano, Antonietta: 383n17, 445–46n151
Burckhardt, Jacob: 275–76n43
Burr, David: 35n11, 354–55n36
Busnelli, Giovanni: 254n20, 361n43, 375n61

Cacciaglia, Norberto: 330n9, 363n46
Cacciaguida: 28–29, 50, 56, 58, 357–60,
    389–90, 412
Cacciari, Massimo: 430n125
Cachey, Theodore J.: 270–71n39, 524n1
Calenda, Corrado: 198n31
Camboni, Maria Clotilde: 218n12, 307–8n26,
    340n20
Campana, Augusto: 70n63
Campanelli, Maurizio: 54–55n45
Canaccini, Federico: 5–6n3, 11n11
Canettieri, Paolo: 156n65
Cangrande della Scala: xxii, 69, 242, 243n9,
    267n36, 395n86, 527, 529–30n9, 531n11,
    532n12, 534–37
Cannavò Giuseppe: 363n46

Capéran, Louis: 330n9, 363n46
Capitani, Ovidio: 16n16, 42–43n28, 479n1
Cappelletti, Leonardo: 16n16
Caputo, Rino: 339n19
Carapezza, Sandra: 338n18, 367n52
Cardellino, Lodovico: 29n4, 331n11,
    430–31n126
Carducci, Giosue: 315n2
Carletti, Gabriele: 511n42
Carpi, Umberto: 301–2n18, 315n2, 318n2,
    319n5, 422n116
Carrai, Stefano: 195n27, 228n22, 428n123
Carugati, Giuliana: 433n130
Casadei, Alberto: 174n2, 201n34
Casagrande, Carla: 233–34n29, 418n111,
    543n2
Casagrande, Gino: 374n59, 419n112, 457n163
Casciani, Santa: 35n11, 354n36
Casella, Mario: 97–98n18, 100n21, 297n12
Casini, Tommaso: 463n177
Cassata, Letterio: 133–34n24, 279n47, 417n110
Cassell, Anthony K.: 335–36n15, 438n142,
    494n19, 511n42
Castellani Pollidori, Ornella: 296
Castelnuovo, Guido: 259n27
Castets, Ferdinand: 133n24
Catellari, Alessandro: 474–75n202
Catenazzi, Flavio: 82n1
Cattani, Giovanni: 365n49
Cavalcanti, Guido: 16–17, 32–33, 43, 46, 49,
    99–100, 103–10, 121–30, 132n23, 133, 166,
    176, 187n18, 192, 193n25, 199n32, 296–97,
    318, 324
Cavedoni, Celestino: 373n58
Caverni, Raffaello: 461n170
Cecchini, Leonardo: 442n146
Cecco Angiolieri: 233
Cella, Roberta: 460–61n169
Celli, Andrea: 444n148, 452n156
Cerbo, Anna: 408n98
Chambers, Frank M.: 84n3
Chaytor, Henry John: 82n1
Cheneval, Francis: 495n19
Cherchi, Paolo: 82n1, 173n1, 437n139,
    454n159
Chersoni, Emmanuele: 306n24
Chiampi, James T.: 32–33n8, 437n139, 454n159
Chiappelli, Fredi: 233–34n29, 483n7

Chiappelli, Luigi: 324–25n2
Chiarenza, Marguerite Mills: 354n36, 390n79
Chiari, Alberto: 347n27, 365–66n50
Chiarini, Eugenio: 541n23
Chiaro Davanzati: 95
Chiavacci Leonardi, Anna Maria: 339n19, 363n46, 410n101
Ciacci, Otello: 344–45n24, 514n46
Ciccia, Carmelo: 442–43n146
Ciccuto, Marcello: 100n21, 109n34
Cicero: 31, 34n10, 41, 76, 76–77n1, 190, 212–13n4, 248, 249n14, 263n32, 264n33
Cino da Pistoia: 111, 112n38, 121–22n10, 295, 324–25n2, 514n46
Cioffi, Caron Ann: 42–43n28, 331n11
Clark, Albert Curtis: 306n24, 489n15
Classen, Albert: 442n146
Clavorella, Giuseppe: 342n22
Coda, Piero: 376n62
Coffari, Elda: 91n10
Cogan, Marc: 338n18, 438n142
Coglievina, Leonella: 243n9, 369n55, 494–95n19
Cognasso, Francesco: 65n57
Colish, Marcia L.: 243n9, 328n6, 330n9, 361n43, 392n81, 423n117
Colombo, Gherardo: 438n142
Colombo, Manuela: 164n75
Comens, Bruce: 228n22
Comollo, Adriano: 482n4
Conrieri, Davide: 369n55
Consoli, Andrea: 353n35
Conte, Silvia: 348n28
Contini, Gianfranco: xixn1, 86n4, 91n10, 92n12, 96n17, 100n21, 121–22n10, 133n24, 135n26, 151n55, 164n75, 230n26
Contrada, Deborah L.: 332n13
Copeland, Rita: 311–12n29
Copleston, S.J., Frederick C.: 267n36
Corbett, George: 329n7, 331–32n12
Corrado, Massimiliano: 291n4
Corsaro, Antonio: 161n71
Corsi, Sergio: 531n11
Corso Donati: 11, 13, 15–22, 62
Cortezo, Carlos López: 219–20n14, 401n90, 442n146
Corti, Maria: 100n, 100n21, 121–22n10, 252b, 252n, 252n18, 259n, 259n27, 270–71n39,

292n, 292n6, 324–25n2, 461n173, 461n 173, 462n174, 462n 174, 495n21
Cosmo, Umberto: 354n36
Cossutta, Fabio: 428n123
Costantini, Aldo M.: 211n2, 506n35
Cotter, James Finn: 437n139
Cottignoli, Alfredo: 418n111, 463n177
Courcelle, Pierre: 212–13n4
Cremona, Joseph: 293–94n7
Crescini, Vincenzo: 180n9
Crespo, Roberto: 311–12n29
Crouse, Robert D.: 270–71n39
Cuboni, Giovanni: 54–55n45
Cudini, Piero: 230–31n26
Cursietti, Mauro: 233–34n29
Curtius, Ernst Robert: 275–76n43, 470n190
Curto, Carlo: 242n8

D'Agostino, Alfonso: 446n
D'Alfonso, Rossella: 532n12
D'Alverny, Marie-Thérèse: 250n15, 252n18
D'Amico, Juan Carlos: 348n28
D'Andrea, Antonio: 197n29, 243n9
D'Andria, Michele: 331n10
D'Angelo, Edoardo: 213n
D'Elia, Antonio: 517n
D'Onofrio, Giulio: 262n31
D'Ovidio, Francesco: 118n5, 288n, 308n, 426n, 527n7
D'Urso, Daniele: 196n11
Dahlberg, Charles: 153n63
Dales, Richard C.: 390n79
Damon, Philip: 243n, 291n4
Daniel, Arnaut: 82, 84, 228n22, 231n26, 235n3
Dante da Maiano: 114–16, 542
Dauphiné, James: 438n142
Davidsohn, Robert: 5–6n3
Davidson, F. J. A.: 230n26
Davie, Mark: 140n
Davis, Charles T.: 26n25, 29n4, 30n7, 31–32n, 36n13, 40n21, 348n28, 354–55n36, 357–58n40, 377n63, 497n23, 507n36, 508n38, 514n46
De Bartholomaeis, Vincenzo: 86n4
De Blasi, Nicola: 242n8
De Bonfils Templer, Margherita: 173n1, 252n18, 254n20
De Lubac, Henri: 530n9

De Marco, Giuseppe: 313–14n
De Matteis, Maria Consiglia: 40n21, 42–43n28
De Monticelli, Roberta: 418n111
De Mottoni, Barbara Faes: 386n73
De Robertis, Domenico: 100n, 112n, 113n, 173n, 174n, 184n, 187n, 189n, 215n, 233–34n29, 243n, 324–25n2
De Salvio, Alfonso: 467n186
De Sanctis, Francesco: 428n, 429n124, 444n148
Decaria, Alessio: 226n
Del Lungo, Isidoro: 3n, 357–58n40, 357n
Delcorno Branca, Daniela: 442n
Dell'Aquila, Michele: 442
Della Terza, Dante: 339n19, 365–66n50
Della Torre, Arnaldo: 490n
Delle Donne, Fulvio: 254n21
Deneffe, August: 375–76n61
Di Capua, Francesco: 300n, 306n, 484n, 488n, 506n
Di Giammarino, Gabriele: 212–13n
Di Giannatale, Giovanni: 353n35
Di Giovanni, Alberto: 250n16, 382n
Di Gregorio, Francesco: 368–69n54
Di Paola Dollorenzo, Gabriella: 368–69n54
Di Pretoro, Piero A.: 460n167
Di Scipio, Giuseppe: 36n, 185–86n15, 426n, 484n
Di Somma, Paolo: 517n50
Dieckmann, Sandra: 468n189
Dillon, Emma: 467–68n187
Dino Compagni: 3n, 10, 12n, 13, 17–18, 24, 26n, 121
Diomedi, Adriana: 254n21, 262n31
Dod, Bernard G.: 270–71n39
Doglio, Maria Luisa: 331n10
Doherty, A. J.: 478n209
Dolcini, Carlo: 479n
Dominic (Saint): 353, 355, 405n
Donà, Massimo: 475
Dorigatti, Marco: 419n
Dragonetti, Roger: 292n, 300–301n17, 307–8n26
Dronke, Peter: 82n, 210n, 212–13n4, 214n5, 244n, 495n21, 527n
Duhem, Pierre: 385n
Dupré Theseider, Eugenio: 487n, 506n

Durighetto, Roberto: 154n
Durling, Robert M.: 187n, 228

Eco, Umberto: *xx–xxi*n3, 472–73n198, 474–75n202
Edwards, Robert: 96n17
Egidi, Francesco: 96n17
Eliot, Thomas Stearns: *xix, xix–xx, xxii*
Elwert, Wilhelm Theodor: 188n5, 472n197
Enright, Nancy: 482n4
Ernst, O.P., Cornelius: 455n, 455n160, 478n209
Esposito, Enzo: 233–34n29, 364n48, 377n63, 411n103
Ewert, Alfred: 288n1

Fallani, Giovanni: 36–37n13, 64n56, 370–71n56, 375n61, 452n156
Falzone, Paolo: 237–38n3, 257n25, 259n27, 260n28, 268–69n37, 409n99, 410n101
Fasani, Remo: 133–34n24, 305n23, 464–65n180
Fasolani, Diego: 411n105
Favaro, Francesco: 351–52n32
Favati, Guido: 100n21, 109n34, 113n39, 324–25n2, 367n52
Federzoni, Giovanni: 97–98n18
Fenzi, Enrico: 100n21, 132n23, 154n64, 211n2, 215–16n7, 226n21, 243n9, 315n2, 319n5, 422n116, 479n1
Fergusson, Francis: 449n153
Ferrante, Joan: 461n172
Ferrara, Sabrina: 286n56, 310n28, 524n1
Ferrari, Attilio: 245–46n11
Ferrario, Edoardo: 293–94n7
Ferrers Howell, Alan George: 3n1, 82n1
Ferrucci, Franco: 260n28
Figurelli, Fernando: 357–58n40
Filosa, Carlo: 507n36
Finazzi, Silvia: 472–73n198
Fineo, Saverio: 440–41n144
Fioravanti, Gianfranco: 36–37n13, 237–38n3, 273n41
Fioretti, Francesco: 121–22n10
Fiorilla, Maurizio: 189n7
Fleming, John V.: 153n63
Flood, David: 35n11
Föking, Marc: 434–35n135

Folena, Gianfranco: 82n1, 86n4, 161n71, 489n15

Fontanella, Francesca: 484–85n8

Fontes Baratto, Anna: 360n42, 484n8

Fordyce, Cristiana: 383n71

Formisano, Luciano: 230–31n26

Forni, Alberto: 35n11, 233–34n29, 460–61n169, 506n35, 517–18n50

Forti, Fiorenzo: 418n111, 472n198

Fosca, Nicola: 260–61n28, 340n20, 364n48, 522n55

Foster, O.P., Kenelm: 36–37n13, 114n1, 214n5, 255–56n38, 257n25, 286n56, 293–94n7, 315n2, 329n7, 361n43, 377n63, 382n69, 443n147, 455n160

Francesca da Rimini: 428n123, 442n146

Francesconi, Giampaolo: 22n21

Francis of Assisi: 35–36, 353–55, 447n152

Frank, Maria Esposito: 411n103

Frappier, Jean: 153n63

Frasca, Gabriella: 230–31n26

Fraser, Jennifer: 260n28, 380n68, 397n87

Frasso, Giuseppe: 370–71n56, 482n4

Fraticelli, Pietro: 48n36

Fratta, Aniello: 133–34n24

Freccero, John: 42–43n28, 437n139, 463n177, 524n1

Frezza, Mario: 330n9, 363n46

Friedman, Lionel J.: 153n63

Frugoni, Arsenio: 488n14

Fubini, Mario: 230n26

Fumagalli, Edoardo: 364n47, 365n49, 373n58

Gagliardi, Antonio: 92–93n12, 100n21, 262n31, 286n, 430n125, 486n10, 495n21

Gagliardi, Federico: 65n, 486n10

Gaimari, Giulia: 454n158, 543n2

Galanti, Livio: 64n

Galfrè, Claudia: 331n11, 418n111

Gallarino, Marco: 259n, 415n

Gallo, Ernest: 311n

Gambale, Giacomo: 291n4

Gardiner, Frank Cook: 200n

Gardner, Edmund Garratt: 71n, 354n, 527–28n7, 538–39n

Gardner, Patrick M.: 518n51

Gargan, Luciano: 36n13, 275–76n43, 538–39

Gaunt, Simon: 82n

Gavazzeni, Franco: 463n

Gavric, Anton: 463n

Geddes da Filicaia, Costanza: 7n

Gentili, Sonia: 35n11, 155, 237–38n3, 247, 270–71n38, 443n147

Geoffrey of Vinsauf: 311–12

George-Tvrtkovic, Rita: 40n21

Gessani, Alberto: 121–22n10, 124–25n14, 124n13, 193n, 370n

Getto, Giovanni: 368–69n54

Ghetti, Noemi: 109n, 121–22n10, 124–25n14, 195n, 215–16n7

Ghinassi, Ghino: 462n176

Ghisalberti, Alessandro: 349–50n29, 383n71, 524n1

Giacalone, Giuseppe: 331–32n12, 390n79, 452n156

Giacomino Pugliese: 85

Giacomo da Lentini: 85, 87, 89, 96–97

Giano della Bella: 12–15, 22

Gibbons, David: 472–73n198

Gigante, Claudio: 349–50n29

Gilbert, Allan H.: 402n, 467n186, 499n26

Gilson, Étienne: 36n13, 173n, 201n34, 214n5, 244n10, 267n, 270–71n39, 270n38, 373n, 493n, 495n21

Gilson, Simon A.: 36–37n13, 270–71n39

Giotto: 64

Giovanni Boccaccio: 28n2, 53, 69–70, 121, 279–80n48, 306n

Giovanni del Virgilio: 70–71, 527, 527–28n 7, 537–41

Giovanni Villani: 3n, 4n, 5–6n3, 6n4, 7n5, 9nn7–9, 10n, 11n, 12n, 14n, 14n13, 15n, 16nn15–16, 18–19n, 20n20, 23n22, 24, 26n, 27n, 28n3, 29n4, 30, 30n7, 31–32n8, 49n37, 53, 61n52, 62–63n54, 65–66n57, 121

Giovanni, Alberto di: 250n16, 382n

Girardi, Enzo Noè: 383n71

Giraut de Bornelh: 82–83, 325n3

Giunta, Claudio: 108n33, 226n21

Givone, Sergio: 439–40n143

Gmelin, Hermann: 243n, 460n168, 529–30n9

Godbarge, Clément: 31–32n

Godenzi, Giuseppe: 336n16

Gordon, N.P.J.: 16n16

Gorni, Guglielmo: 95n16, 108n33, 121–22n10,

124n14, 135n25, 156n65, 173n, 180n, 302n19,
  307–8n26, 319n, 324–25n2, 339n19, 428n,
  463n177
Gosselin, Christine: 197n
Goudet, Jacques: 358–59n41
Grabmann, Martin: 270–71n39
Graf, Arturo: 506n
Gragnolati, Manuele: 114n, 260n, 410n101,
  439–40n143
Grayson, Cecil: 20n19, 201n34, 270–71n39,
  279–80n48, 290n3, 402n, 508n38
Green, Louis: 26n, 194n
Grillo, Paolo: 5n
Grimaldi, Marco: 315n
Grossvogel, Steven: 348n
Gualdo Rosa, Lucia: 275–76n43
Gualtieri, Angelo: 212–13n4
Guardini, Romano: 171n84
Guérin, Philippe: 231–32n27
Guerri, Domenico: 293–94n7
Guglielminetti, Marziano: 196n, 452n156
Guiberteau, Philippe: 132n
Guido Cavalcanti: 16, 32, 43, 46, 49n, 99,
  100n, 109n, 121–22n10, 124–25n14, 124n13,
  187n18, 199n, 295–96
Guido da Montefeltro: 44, 445–46, 447–48n
Guido delle Colonne: 85–86, 96
Guido Guinizzelli: 91, 95–99, 108, 110–11,
  159–62, 172, 223
Guido Orlandi: 109
Guido Vernani, O.P.: 493, 494n, 508, 518n51
Guittone d'Arezzo: 90–96, 99, 108–9, 113, 117,
  161, 163n72, 461n173
Guzzardo, John J.: 181–82n11

Hagman, Edward: 35n, 377n
Hainsworth, Peter: 187n
Hardie, Colin: 201n34, 290n, 319n, 489n,
  527n7
Harrison, Robert Pogue: 140n
Havely, Nick: 35n, 354n
Hawkins, Peter S.: 42–43n28, 365–66n50,
  430–31n126, 481n3, 543n
Heidegger, Martin: 284n, 414, 415n
Heidemann, Malte: 65n
Heinimann, Siegfried: 307n26
Henry VII of Luxembourg: *xxii*, 21–26, 24n,
  65n, 479, 482, 486n10, 487n13, 537–38

Herzman, Ronald: 35n, 354n
Higgins, Anne: 385n
Hirdt, Willi: 243n, 387n75
Hollander, Robert: 28n2, 42–43n28, 71n, 82n,
  112n, 185n14, 270–71n39, 286n, 324–25n2,
  428n, 527n7
Holloway, Julia Bolton: 31–32n, 212–13n4,
  237–38n3
Holmes, George: 20n18, 35n, 64n
Holmes, Olivia: 92n
Honess, Claire E.: 19n4, 36–37n13, 42–43n28,
  58n, 65n, 270–71n39, 301n18, 313–14n,
  341n21, 357–58n40, 434–35n135, 484–85n8,
  486n10, 513n45, 517–18n50
Howard, Lloyd: 193n
Huck, Oliver: 468n189
Hurley, Michael D.: 463n
Hyde, John Kenneth: 4n

Iannucci, Amilcare A.: 132n, 275–76n43, 329n,
  361n
Iglesias Rondina, María Carla: 419n
Iliescu, Nicolae: 330n9, 364n47
Imbach, Ruedi: 291n4, 292n
Indizio, Giuseppe: 30n6
Inglese, Giorgio: 339n, 363n46, 443n147
Irmscher, Cristoph: 442n

Jacoff, Rachel: 42–43n28, 348n, 352–53n34,
  401n90, 426n, 449n, 461n172
Jacomuzzi, Angelo: 218n, 228n, 340n, 357–
  58n40, 460n168, 484n
Jacomuzzi, Vincenzo: 461n172
Jacopo Mostacci: 87
James (the Apostle): 368–69
James of Viterbo: 509
Jeanroy, Alfred: 82n
Jennaro-MacLennan, Luis: 532n12
Jensen, Frede: 86n4
Johnson, Ryan,: 431n127
Jordan, Edouard: 18–19n

Kablitz, Andreas: 36–37n13
Kaske, Robert: 331–32n12, 481n3
Kastner, Leon Emile: 230n26
Kay, Richard: 31–32n, 332n13
Kay, Sarah: 82n
Kay, Tristan: 218n12, 340n

Keen, Catherine: 8n, 58n, 313–14n, 324–25n2, 360n
Kelly, Craig: 348n
Kelly, Douglas: 311–12n29
Kempshall, Matthew S.: 40n21, 497n
Kittay, Eva Feder: 474n202
Kleinhenz, Christopher: 65n, 87n6, 100n, 112n, 324–25n2
Klinkert, Thomas: 442n
Kolsen, Adolf: 83–84n2
Kranz, Walther: 212–13n4
Kuen, Heinrich: 461n170

La Favia, Louis Marcello: 350n30
Ladner, Gerhart B.: 200n
Lambert, Malcolm D.: 354b
Lambertini, Roberto: 494n
Lampugnani, Raffaele: 484n
Landoni, Elena: 373n
Langeli, Attilio Bartoli: 483n
Langley, Ernest F.: 87n6
Lannutti, Maria Sofia: 46–461n169, 307n26
Lansing, Carol: 4n, 259n
Lansing, Richard H.: 7n, 40n21, 42–43n28, 184n, 228n, 237–38n3, 243n9, 319n, 329n7, 332n13, 437n139, 438n142, 451–52n155, 472n197, 497n
Lanza, Adriano: 330n9, 332n13, 351n32, 360n, 363n, 423n
Lanza, Antonio: 124n14, 156n65, 233–34n29, 293–94n7, 301n18, 319n, 352n33, 442n
Lanza, Franco: 338n
Laqué, Stephan: 408n
Lazzerini, Lucia: 231–32n27
Le Goff, Jacques: 449n
Leclercq, Jean: 373n
Ledda, Giuseppe: 210n, 326n4, 353n35, 360n, 365n49, 369n55, 373n, 439–40n143, 472n198, 484–85n8
Lenkeith, Nancy: 348n, 506n
Lentzen, Manfred: 243n, 529–30n9
Lenzi, Eugenio: 27n
Leo, Ulrich: 286n
Leonardo Bruni: 14n, 28n2, 44, 48n, 53, 60n51, 63
Leoncini, Letizia: 279–80n48
Leporatti, Roberto: 224n
Leuker, Tobias: 410n101

Levers, Toby: 184n
Levy, Bernard S.: 181n10
Lewis, Clive Staples: 472n197
Ley, Klaus: 254n21, 524n1
Lia, Pierluigi: 370–71n56, 374n, 400n, 457n
Libaude, Christophe: 439–40n143
Lidònnici, Giovanni: 538–39n
Lisio, Giuseppe: 279n48, 462n174
Livi, François: 340n
Livorni, Ernesto: 205n38
Livraghi, Leyla M. G.: 324–25n2, 326n4
Lizerand, Georges: 23n23
Lluch-Baixauli, Miguel: 212–13n4
Lombardi, Elena: 42–43n28, 132n, 428–29n123, 442n
Lombardo, Luca: 212–13n4
Lonergan, Bernard J. F.: 355–56n38, 455n
Longo, Nicola: 470n190
López Cortezo, Carlos: 219–20n14, 401n90, 442n
Lorinczi, Marinella: 296n10
Luzzi, Joseph: 461n172

Maccarrone, Michele: 510n
Macquarrie, John: 415n
Maffei, Domenico: 324–25n2, 514–15n46, 514n
Maffia Scariati, Irene: 140n, 228n
Maggini, Francesco: 319n
Maia, Andrea: 336n16, 408n
Maierù, Alfonso,: 391–92n81
Majuri, Vincenzo Massimo: 370–71n56
Malato, Enrico: 28n2, 121–22n10, 174n, 193n, 199n, 330n8, 331n10, 345n25, 349–50n29, 353n35, 383n71, 417n110, 428n, 430–31n126, 482n4
Maldina, Nicolò: 237–38n3
Malinar, Smiljka: 461n173
Mallette, Karla: 86n
Manescalchi, Romano,: 454n158
Manfred (of Hohenstaufen): 5–7, 337–38, 451, 451–52n155
Manni, Paola: 296n10
Manselli, Raoul: 35n, 354n, 517n
Marani, Giuseppe: 129n
Marazzi, Martino: 442n
Marazzini, Claudio: 297n12
Marcenaro, Simone: 88n
Marchesi, Concetto: 237–38n3

Marchesi, Simone: 212–13n4, 297n12, 512–13n44, 522n

Marchi, Gian Paolo: 331n10, 483n6

Marconi, Paola: 439–40n143

Marcozzi, Luca: 417n

Marenbon, John: 329n, 330n9, 495n21

Margueron, Claude: 92n

Marigo, Aristide: 306n

Marrocco, W. Th.: 307–8n26

Marshall, John Henry: 180n

Marti, Mario: 92n, 114n, 124n13, 161n

Martinelli, Bortolo: 181–82n11, 195n, 267n, 363n, 373n, 376n62, 482n4, 522n, 534n15

Martinez, Ronald L.: 113n, 228n, 229–30n24, 431n127

Marzo, Antonio: 332b13

Mascetta-Caracci, Lorenzo: 489n

Masciandaro, Franco: 385n

Masini, Andrea: 229n23

Mason, H. A.: 361n

Masseron, Alexandre: 373n

Mastrobuono, Antonio C.: 36–37n13, 173n, 368–69n54, 437n139, 454n159, 508n38

Matsuda, Takami: 449n

Matthews, William: 153n63

May, Rollo: 415n

Mazzaro, Jerome: 173n

Mazzeo, Felice: 70n

Mazzeo, Joseph Anthony: 426n

Mazzocco, Angelo: 293n7, 297n12

Mazzoleni, Marco: 462n176

Mazzoni, Francesco: 64n, 243n, 319n5, 484n8, 524n1, 527n7

Mazzoni, Guido: 538–39n

Mazzotta, Giuseppe: 35n, 173n, 332n13

McCormick, Colin A.: 333n

McInerny, Ralph M.: 478n209

McMenamin, James F.: 28n3

McNair, Philip: 377n

Medici, Mario: 462n175, 470nn192–93

Meersseman, Gilles Gerard: 451n

Meier, Franziska: 237–38n3

Mellone, O.F.M., Attilio: 345n25, 354n, 514n

Menache, Sophia: 23n23, 510n

Mengaldo, Pier Vincenzo: 196n28, 288n, 293–94n7, 306n, 443n147

Menichetti, Aldo: 91n10, 129n, 305n, 464–65n180

Mercuri, Roberto: 328n6

Mérigoux, Jean Marie: 40n21

Midkiff, Gerald R.: 382n

Miethke, Jürgen: 514–15n46

Milani, Giuliano: 54–55n45

Miles, Thomas: 431n127

Milizia, Umberto Maria: 64n

Miller, Edward G.: 391–92n81

Milonia, Stefano: 415n

Mineo, Nicolò: 197n, 201n34, 340n

Minio Paluello, Lorenzo: 40n21, 270–71n39, 402n

Mocan, Mira: 195n, 337n, 409n99

Modesto, Filippa: 237–38n3

Moevs, Christian: 345n25, 385n, 390n80

Moleta, Vincent: 92n, 97–98n18, 160n, 173n, 174n, 180n, 181–82n11, 194n, 354n

Molinari, Carla: 219–20n14

Mölk, Ulrich: 89–90n9

Mollat, Guillaume: 23n23, 487n13

Momigliano, Attilio: 357–58n40

Mongiello, Emilia: 479n

Montanari, Fausto: 226n, 319n

Montemaggi, Vittorio: 433n130, 517n, 543n

Monterosso, Raffaello: 307n26

Monti, Gennaro Maria: 324–25n2

Monticelli, Daniele: 417n, 418n

Moore, Edward: 212–13n4, 245n, 270–71n39, 339n, 524n1, 527n7

Morettini Bura, Maria Antonietta: 338n

Morghen, Raffaello: 330n9, 363n, 488n, 495n21

Moroldo, Arnaldo: 133–34n

Morris, Colin: 510n

Morvidi, Leto: 447–48n

Mossé, Claude: 23n23

Mozzillo-Howell, Elizabeth: 511n

Mulchahey, Marian Michèle: 36n13, 40n21

Münchberg, Katharina: 442n

Murari, Rocco: 212–13n4, 373n

Muresu, Gabriele: 350n30, 363n, 364n48, 409m99, 443n147, 445–46n151

Murray, Alexander: 332n13

Mussio, Thomas E.: 28n3

Nagy, József: 500n27

Najemy, John M.: 31–32n

Nardi, Bruno: 36n, 100n, 121–22n10, 244n,

Nardi, Bruno (*cont.*)
254n20, 260n, 262n31, 270–71n39, 286n, 288n, 293–94n7, 345n25, 387n75, 391–92n81, 430n125, 451–52n155, 494–95n19, 494n, 495n21, 514n46, 524n1, 527n7
Nasti, Paola: 513n45, 517n
Nencioni, Giovanni: 300–301n17
Nichols, Stephen G.: 297n12
Nicolau, Mathieu G.: 306n
Nohrnberg, James C.: 333n
Novikoff, Alex: 65n, 486n10
Nuzzi, Nicola: 91n10

O'Connell Baur, Christine: 330n9
O'H. Hahn, Thomas: 362n44
Oerter, Herbert L.: 11n
Olson, Kristina: 357–58n40
Ombres, O.P., Robert: 449n
Onesto da Bologna: 95
Orlando, Sandro: 82n
Orr, Mary Acworth: 245n
Ortony, Andrew: 474n202
Orvieto, Paolo: 233–34n29
Ossola, Carlo: 340n, 430n125
Ott, Christine: 541n
Ottokar, Nicola: 10n

Pacifico, Roberto: 425n119
Padoan, Giorgio: 329n, 361n, 430n125, 506n, 524n1, 527n7
Pagani, Ileana: 288n
Pagliaro, Antonino: 124n13, 203n, 426n
Pagliaro, Antonio: 284n55
Palgen, Rudolf: 472n198
Palmieri, Pantaleo: 365n49
Panella, O.P., Emilio: 36n13, 40n21
Panvini, Bruno: 83–84n2, 86n4, 299n16
Paolazzi, Carlo: 532n12
Paolini, Shirley J.: 42–43n28
Paolucci, Anne: 335–36n15, 358–59n41, 382n, 391–92n81, 401n90, 430–31n126
Paparelli, Gioacchino: 277n, 428n
Pappalardo, Fernando: 100n
Paradisi, Enrico: 239n
Paradisi, Gioia: 457n163
Paratore, Ettore: 444–45n149
Park, Dabney G.: 16–17n16, 514n
Parodi, Ernesto Giacomo: 467n186, 489n
Pasero, Nicolò: 109n

Pasi, Romano: 70n
Pasquazi, Silvio: 383n71, 408n, 525n4
Pasquini, Emilio: 28n3, 70n, 86n4, 151–52n55, 228n, 319n, 369n55, 418n, 472n198
Pasquini, Laura: 335–336n15
Pastore Stocchi, Manlio: 329n
Paterson, Linda: 82n
Paul (the Apostle): 190, 400n89, 425–26, 484n, 497, 497n23, 505n33, 510n
Payton, Rodney J.: 332n13
Pazzaglia, Mario: 118n5, 219n14, 307–8n26
Pecoraro, Paolo: 245–46n11
Peirone, Luigi: 133–34n, 156n65, 259n, 288n, 307n25, 329n, 364n47
Pellegrini, Silvio: 82n, 177n
Pellizzari, Achille: 92n
Pelosi, Pietro: 95–96n16, 231–32n27
Pépin, Jean: 243n
Pequigney, Joseph: 332n13
Pernicone, Vincenzo: 112n
Peron, Gianfelice: 160n
Perotti, Pier Angelo: 373n, 430–31n126, 441–42n144
Perrus, Claude: 233–34n29
Pertile, Lino: 28n2, 113n, 377n, 410n101, 430n125, 481n, 524n1, 531n, 538–39n
Peter (the Apostle): 54n45, 480n
Peter Damian: 164–65, 393–94n84
Peter of Blois: 76, 76–77n2, 153
Peterman, Larry: 402n
Petrie, Jennifer: 8n, 20n19, 35n11, 42–43n28, 161n71, 260n, 410n101, 517n
Petrocchi, Giorgio: 28n2, 45n32, 61–62n53, 185–86n15, 197n, 332n13, 339n19, 354n
Petrucci, Armando: 483n7
Pézard, André: 29n4, 332n13
Pflaum, Hiram: 53n
Phillimore, Catherine Mary: 70n
Phillips-Robins, Helena: 403n93
Piattoli, Renato: 30n6, 47n34, 52n42, 54n
Pica, Maria: 112n, 325n3
Picone, Michelangelo: 60n50, 82n, 83–84n2, 88n, 92, 112n, 133–34n, 156n65, 173n, 188n19, 200n, 229n23, 230–31n26, 243n, 270–71n39, 275–76n43, 301–2n18, 319n, 333n, 352n33, 363n, 442n, 529n530n9
Pier delle Vigne: 87–89, 332n13, 443, 444n148, 445
Pierantozzi, Decio: 91n10

Pietro di Giovanni Olivi: 34–36
Pietrobono, Luigi: 527n7
Pinto, Raffaele: 277–78n45, 326–27n5
Pipa, Arshi: 194n
Pirastu, Annalisa: 335–36n15
Pirot, François: 82n
Pirovano, Donato: 95n16, 100n, 112n, 199n,
    245–46n11, 351n32, 370n
Pispisa, Enrico: 15n
Placella, Vincenzo: 408n, 529–30n9
Poirier, Jean-Louis: 430n125
Polara, Giovanni: 212–13n4, 538–39n
Pollack, Tamara: 435–36n135
Poole, Gordon: 315n
Porena, Manfredi: 532n12
Porro, Pasquale: 76–77n2, 364n48, 383n71
Pound, Ezra: 100n
Praloran, Marco: 307–8n26, 464–65n180
Puccetti, Valter Leonardo: 119n
Pulega, Andrea: 230–31n26
Punzi, Arianna: 467n186
Purcell, William: 472–73n198

Quaglio, Antonio Enzo: 86n4, 113n,
    233–34n29
Quaglioni, Diego: 551n
Quartieri, Franco: 64n
Quilici, Brunetto: 330n9, 363n

Rabuse, Georg: 249–50n15
Raczyńska, Alicja: 275–76n43
Raffa, Guy P.: 58n, 538–39n
Raffi, Alessandro: 290n
Raimondi, Ezio: 472n198
Rajna, Pio: 306n, 532n12
Ramacciotti, Mary Dominic: 133–34n
Rati, Giancarlo: 383n71
Ratzinger, Joseph: 449n
Ravasi, Gianfranco: 368–69n54
Raveggi, Sergio: 4n
Rea, Roberto: 95n16, 161n71, 331n10, 417n,
    418n
Reade, William Henry Vincent: 508n38
Rebuffat, Enrico: 333–34n, 417n
Reeves, Marjorie: 508n38
Reggio, Giovanni: 538–39n
Remigio de' Girolami: 36n13, 40–41, 497n
Renaudet, Augustin: 275–76n43
Renna, Thomas: 23n23

Renouard, Yves: 23n23
Renucci, Paul: 275–76n43
Renzi, Lorenzo: 462n176, 470n191
Ricci, Corrado: 70n
Ricci, Pier Giorgio: 479n
Ricciardelli, Fabrizio: 54–55n
Richard of St. Victor: 432n, 433–34
Richards, Earl Jeffrey: 133–34n
Rigo, Paola: 484n
Rinaldi, Michele: 331n10
Rinaldo d'Aquino: 85–86
Ringger, Kurt: 439–40n143
Rivière, Jean: 510n
Rizzo, Gino: 361n
Robertson, Durant Waite, Jr.: 153n63
Robey, David: 464n179, 467n186
Robiglio, Andrea A.: 31–32n, 212–13n4, 215–
    16n7, 236–38n, 259n27
Rohlfs, Gerhard: 467n186
Rollo-Koster, Joelle: 23n23
Romano, Andrea: 379n66, 395n85
Roncaglia, Aurelio: 113n, 230n26
Ronconi, Alessandro: 212–13n4
Rosier-Catach, Irène: 292n
Rossi, Giuliano: 260n, 380n68, 397n, 410n101
Rossi, Luca Carlo: 133n, 330n8
Rossi, Luciano: 160n, 229n23
Rossini, Antonio: 374n
Rotundo, Emmanuele: 517n
Rubinstein, Nicolai: 259n
Ruffini, Francesco: 330n9, 363n
Rupp, Teresa Pugh: 12n
Russell, Anthony Presti: 205n38
Russell, Jeffrey Burton: 335–36n15
Russo, Florence: 65n, 423n, 486n10
Russo, Vittorio: 36n, 113n, 215n, 313–14n,
    332n13, 391–92n81, 400n
Rustico di Filippo: 95, 233
Ruzicka, David Edward: 542n
Ryan, Christopher J.: 36–37n13, 368–69n54,
    383n71, 410n
Ryan, Lawrence V.: 439–40n143
Ryden, Edmund: 478n209

Sabbatino, Pasquale: 340n, 452n156
Salerno, Franco: 428n
Salsano, Fernando: 277n, 437n139
Salvemini, Gaetano: 12n
Sanfilippo, Mario: 9n9

Sangirardi, Giuseppe: 118n5
Sanguineti, Edoardo: 96n17
Santagata, Marco: 65n, 173, 181n10, 317–18n, 360n, 484n
Santangelo, Giorgio: 331n12, 390n79
Santangelo, Salvatore: 82n, 86n4, 88n
Sarteschi, Selene: 42–43n28, 160n, 219n, 360n, 447–48n, 461n171
Sasso, Gennaro: 197n, 239n, 244n, 270–71n39, 290n, 292n, 297n12, 427n7, 447–48n, 527n7
Savarese, Gennaro: 233–34n29
Savino, Giancarlo: 21n
Sbacchi, Diego: 188n19, 344–45n24
Scafi, Alessandro: 524n1
Scariati, Irene Maffia: 140n, 228n
Schiaffini, Alfredo: 279n48, 288n, 300–301n17, 306n, 461n170
Schildgen, Brenda Deen: 362n44, 461n172
Schnapp, Jeffrey T.: 449n
Scholz, Richard: 510n
Schwertsik, Peter: 31–32n
Sciuto, Italo: 390n79, 495n21
Scott, John A.: 6n4, 7n, 173n, 243n9, 286n, 338n, 341n, 423n, 429n14, 430n125, 451–52n155, 497n, 529–30n9
Scott, Stan: 391–92n81
Scrimieri, Rosario: 224n, 301–2n18
Scrivano, Riccardo: 351n32, 482n4
Sears, Elizabeth: 387n75
Sebastio, Leonardo: 124–25n14, 133–34n
Segre, Cesare: 254n21, 279–80n48
Seitschek, Gisela: 154n, 243n
Semola, Mariangela: 439–40n143
Seriacopi, Massimo: 447–48n, 482n4
Sertillanges, Antonin Gilbert: 355–56n38
Sesini, Ugo: 305n, 307–8n26, 464–65n180
Shapiro, Marianne: 288n
Shaw, James Eustace: 100n, 173n, 249–50n15
Sheehan, David: 249–50n15, 444–45n149
Shogimen, Takashi: 497n
Silverstein, Theodore: 486n10, 506n
Silvestrini, Flavio: 511n
Simonelli, Maria Picchio: 108n33, 196n, 230–31n26, 237–38n3
Singleton, Charles S.: 173n, 196n, 243n
Skinner, Quentin: 31–32n
Sluiter, Ineke: 311–12n29

Smith, James Robinson: 28n2
Solerti, Angelo: 28n2
Somelli, Lorenzo: 307–8n26
Sorabji, Richard: 385n
Soskice, Janet Martin: 472–73n198
Sowell, Madison U.: 472n197
Spagnolo, Luigi: 310n
Speer, Andreas: 252n18
Spera, Francesco: 338n, 340n, 367n52, 445–46n151
Spitzer, Leo: 444–45n149
Spongano, Raffaele: 95n16
Squillacioti, Paolo: 352n33
Stanghellini, Menotti: 233–34n29
Starn, Randolph: 54–55n
Stefanini, Ruggiero: 233–34n29
Steinberg, Justin: 177n
Stepanova, Larissa G.: 197n12
Stephany, William A.: 426n
Stierle, Karlheinz: 360n
Stramara, Daniel F.: 375–76n61
Sturm-Maddox, Sara: 228n

Tambling, Jeremy: 420n113, 423n
Tanturli, Giuliano: 229n21
Tartaro, Achille: 26n, 65n57, 161n71, 369n55, 452–53n156
Tateo, Francesco: 189n, 344–45n24, 438n142, 470n190, 472n198
Tavoni, Mirko: 196n, 239n, 306n, 445–46n151
Taylor, Robert Longley: 464n179
Terni, Clemente: 307–8n26
Terracini, Aron Benvenuto: 291n4
Terracini, Benvenuto: 181n10, 291n4
Tesi, Riccardo: 291n5, 296n10
Teske, Roland J.: 512–13n44
Tholemy of Lucca: 509
Thomas Aquinas: 36, 267n, 274n, 355, 405n, 410n101, 449n, 478
Thompson, David: 361n, 506n, 507n36
Thorp, John: 419n
Tierney, Brian: 510n41
Tillich, Paul: xix
Todorović, Jelena: 180n, 184n, 212–13n4
Toja, Gianluigi: 84n3
Tomazzoli, Gaia: 472–73n198
Tonelli, Natascia: 195n, 211n2, 220n15, 319n

Took, John: 42–43n28, 112n, 133n, 231–32n27, 255–56n22, 326–27n5, 351n31, 362n, 454n159, 503n
Topsfield, Leslie T.: 82n
Torraca, Francesco: 97–98n18
Toscano, Tobia R.: 357–58n40
Tosti-Croce, Mauro: 24n, 65n
Toynbee, Paget Jackson: 28n2, 71n, 483n7, 489n
Traina, Maria Rita: 210n
Trottmann, Christian: 518n51
Trovato, Mario: 259n27
Turner, Denys: 267n
Turner, Ralph V.: 330n9, 363n
Tuve, Rosemond: 153n63

Ubertino da Casale: 16–17n16, 34–35, 34–36, 354–55n36
Ugolini, Francesco: 86n4
Ullmann, Walter: 510n
Ureni, Paola: 461n173
Utley, Francis L.: 153n63

Valency, Maurice: 82n
Valesio, Paolo: 464n179
Vallone, Aldo: 133–34n24, 183n, 229n23, 279–80n48, 367n52, 373n, 510n, 538–39n20
Valterza, Lorenzo: 119n, 324–25n2, 348n
Vanasco, Rocco R.: 230–31n26
Vanossi, Luigi: 133–34n, 151–52n55, 156n65
Varanini, Gian Maria: 527–28n7
Varanini, Giorgio: 64n, 329n
Varela-Portas de Orduña, Juan: 58n, 315n2, 360n, 472n197
Vasina, Augusto: 70n
Vasoli, Cesare: 36n13, 245–46n11, 259n27
Vattimo, Gianni: 283–84n54
Vazzana, Steno: 328n, 423n, 444–45n149, 472n197
Vecce, Carlo: 181–82n11
Vecchi Galli, Paola: 463n
Venturi, Luigi: 472n197
Vescovini, Graziella Federici: 245–46n11

Veselovskij, Aleksandr N.: 423n
Vilella, Eduard: 219–20n14
Villa, Claudia: 538–39n
Villa, Marianna: 451–52n155
Vinay, Gustavo: 288n, 479n, 488n
Vincent, Eric R.: 460n167
Virgil: 275–76n43, 304n, 330n9, 336–37, 364n47, 388, 399, 408, 443, 470n190, 489, 505, 538
Vitto, Cindy L.: 330n9, 361n

Watt, John A.: 510n, 513n45
Watt, Mary Alexandra: 242n
Wawrykow, Joseph P.: 455n
Wei Wei, Yeo: 360n
Weiss, Roberto: 275–76n43
Werge, Thomas: 388n77
West, Simon: 100n, 124–25n14
Whatley, Gordon: 364n47
Wheelock, James: 464n179
White, Hugh: 352
Whitman, Jon: 529–30n9
Wicksteed, Philip H.: 3n, 28n2, 36–37n13, 71n, 449n, 527–28n7, 538–39n
Wieruszowski, Helene: 31–32n, 249–50n15
Wilhelm, James J.: 84n3
Wilkins, Ernest Hatch: 87n6, 97–98n18
Wilks, Michael J.: 510n
Williams, Pamela: 351n32, 410n101
Wilson, Robert: 481n
Wlassics, Tibor: 463n177
Wolfzettel, Friedrich: 197n
Wood, Charles: 510n

Zaccarello, Michelangelo: 119n, 231–32n27, 234–35n29
Zambon, Francesco: 196n28, 370–71n56
Zampese, Cristina: 187–88n18
Zanni, Raffaella: 36n13, 298n14
Ziegler, Joseph: 260n
Zingarelli, Nicola: 460n167
Zini, Alfredo: 365n49
Zorzi, Andrea: 26n